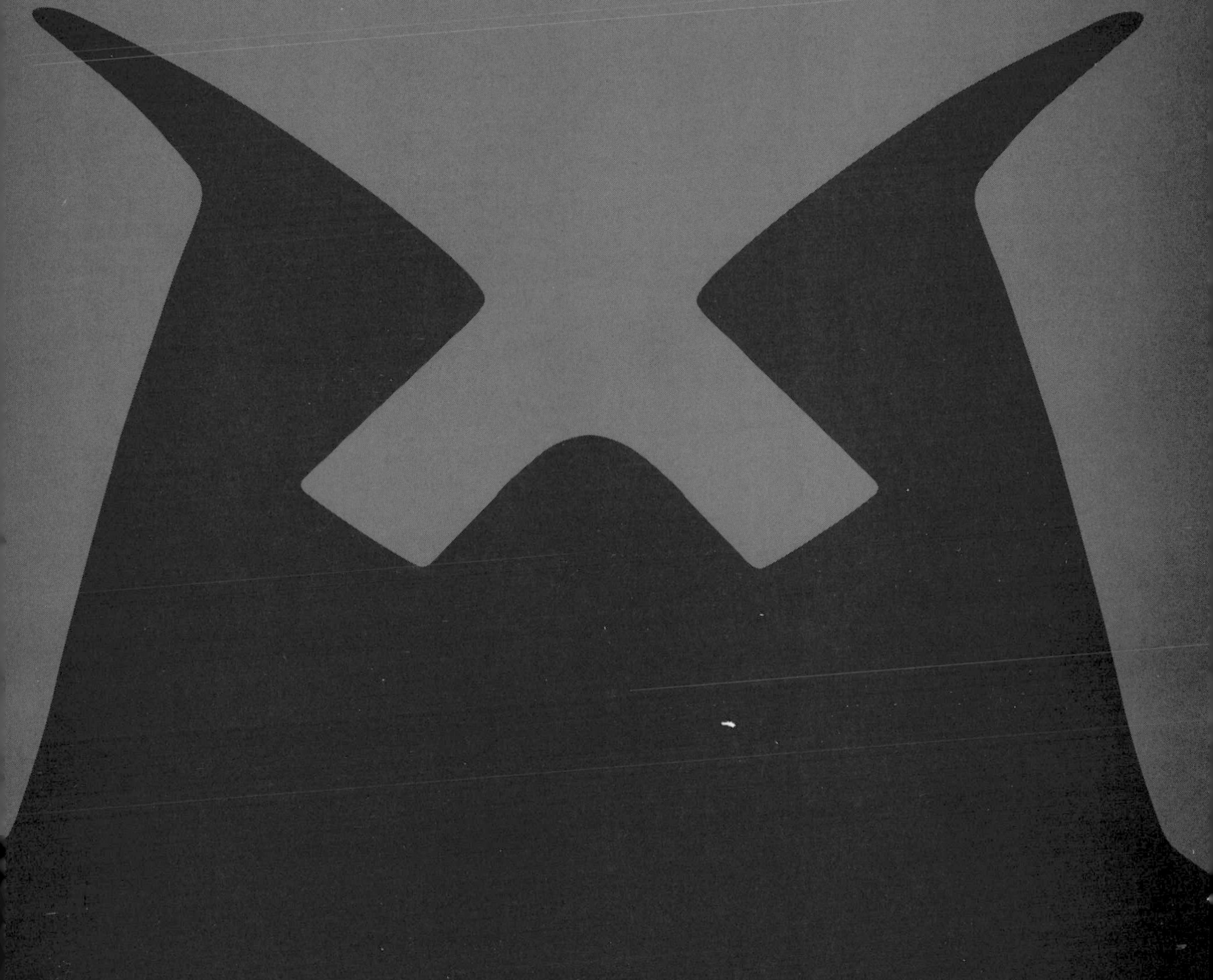

JUDGE DREDD

THE COMPLETE CASE FILES 05

JUDGE DREDD CREATED BY JOHN WAGNER AND CARLOS EZQUERRA

JUDGE DREDD
THE COMPLETE CASE FILES 05

JOHN WAGNER ★ ALAN GRANT
Writers

MICK McMAHON ★ RON SMITH ★ BRIAN BOLLAND ★ IAN GIBSON ★ STEVE DILLON
COLIN WILSON ★ BARRY MITCHELL ★ JOHN COOPER ★ CARLOS EZQUERRA
Artists

TOM FRAME ★ STEVE POTTER
Letters

CARLOS EZQUERRA
Cover Artist

Creative Director and CEO: Jason Kingsley
Chief Technical Officer: Chris Kingsley
2000 AD Editor in Chief: Matt Smith
Graphic Novels Editor: Keith Richardson
Graphic Design: Simon Parr & Luke Preece
Reprographics: Kathryn Symes
PR: Michael Molcher
Original Commissioning Editor: Steve MacManus

Published by Rebellion, Riverside House, Osney Mead, Oxford OX2 0ES, UK.
www.rebellion.co.uk

ISBN: 978-1-78108-028-3
Printed in the USA
10 9 8 7 6 5 4 3 2 1
1st Printing: June 2012

For information on other *2000 AD* graphic novels, or if you have any comments on this book, please email books@2000ADonline.com

To find out more about *2000 AD*, visit www.2000ADonline.com

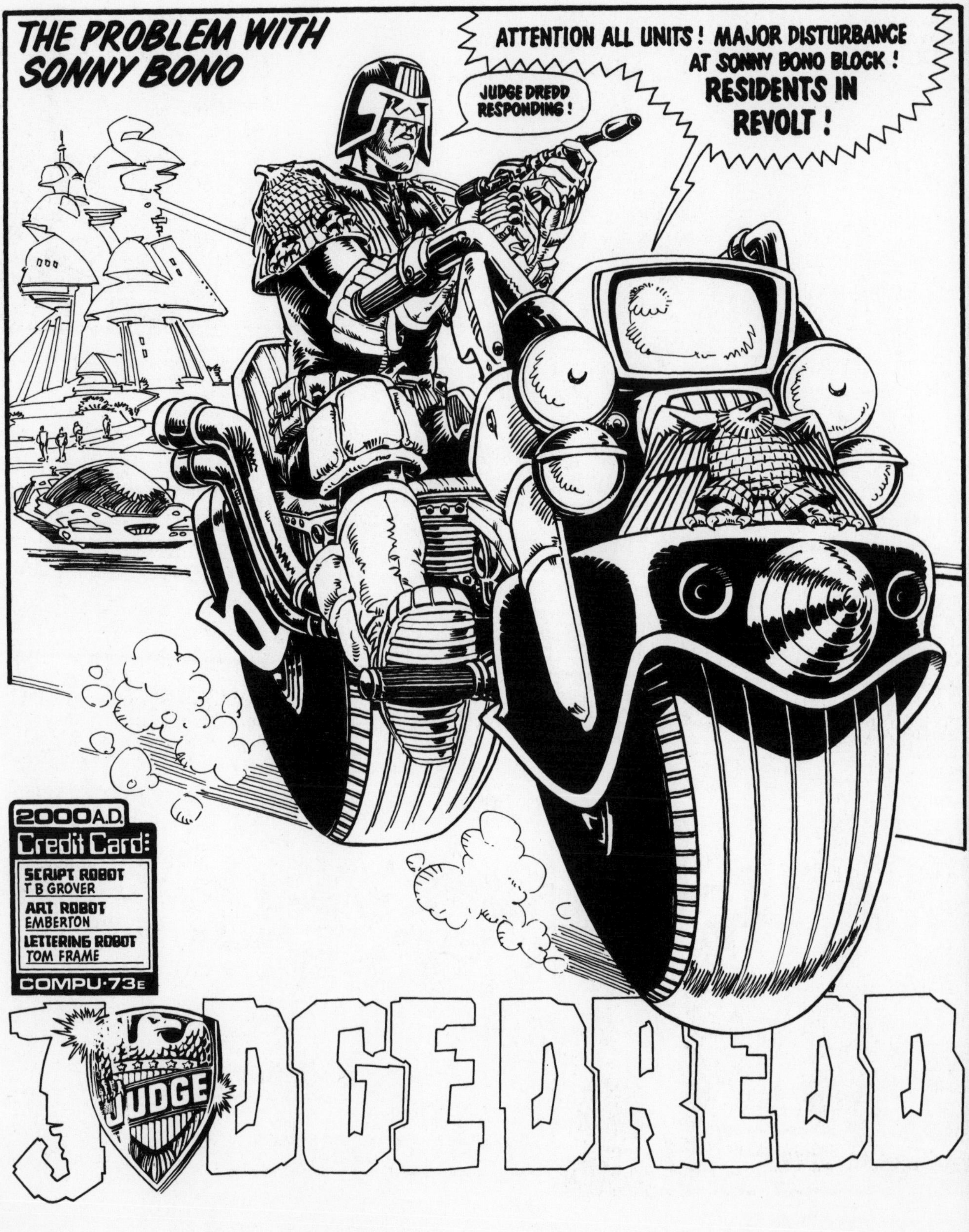

THE PROBLEM WITH SONNY BONO
ATTENTION ALL UNITS! MAJOR DISTURBANCE AT SONNY BONO BLOCK! RESIDENTS IN REVOLT!
JUDGE DREDD RESPONDING!
2000 A.D.
Credit Card:
SCRIPT ROBOT T B GROVER
ART ROBOT EMBERTON
LETTERING ROBOT TOM FRAME
COMPU·73E
JUDGE
JUDGE DREDD

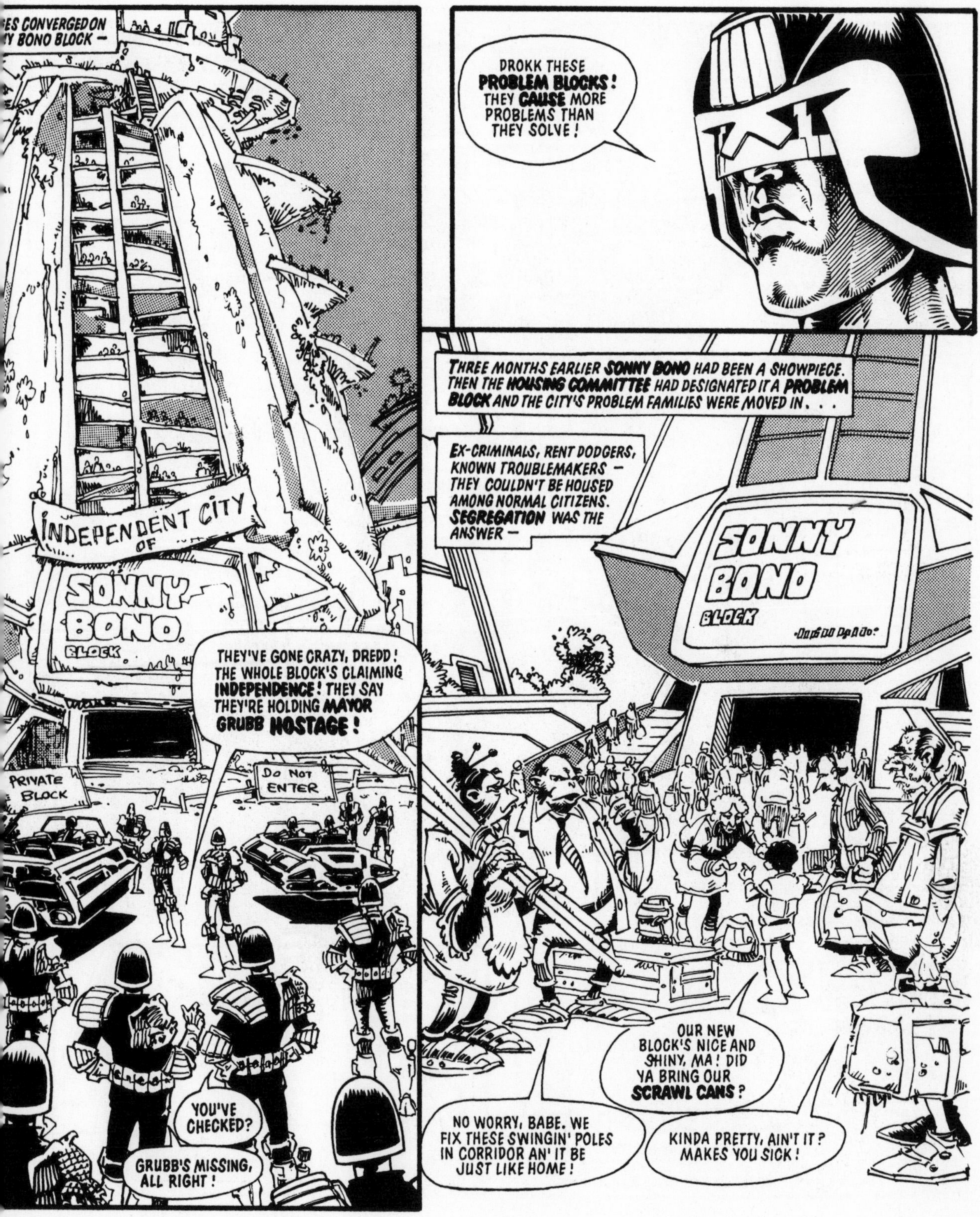

ES CONVERGED ON
Y BONO BLOCK –
INDEPENDENT CITY OF
SONNY BONO BLOCK
THEY'VE GONE CRAZY, DREDD! THE WHOLE BLOCK'S CLAIMING INDEPENDENCE! THEY SAY THEY'RE HOLDING MAYOR GRUBB HOSTAGE!
PRIVATE BLOCK
DO NOT ENTER
YOU'VE CHECKED?
GRUBB'S MISSING, ALL RIGHT!
DROKK THESE PROBLEM BLOCKS! THEY CAUSE MORE PROBLEMS THAN THEY SOLVE!
THREE MONTHS EARLIER SONNY BONO HAD BEEN A SHOWPIECE. THEN THE HOUSING COMMITTEE HAD DESIGNATED IT A PROBLEM BLOCK AND THE CITY'S PROBLEM FAMILIES WERE MOVED IN . . .
EX-CRIMINALS, RENT DODGERS, KNOWN TROUBLEMAKERS – THEY COULDN'T BE HOUSED AMONG NORMAL CITIZENS. SEGREGATION WAS THE ANSWER –
SONNY BONO BLOCK
OUR NEW BLOCK'S NICE AND SHINY, MA! DID YA BRING OUR SCRAWL CANS?
NO WORRY, BABE. WE FIX THESE SWINGIN' POLES IN CORRIDOR AN' IT BE JUST LIKE HOME!
KINDA PRETTY, AIN'T IT? MAKES YOU SICK!

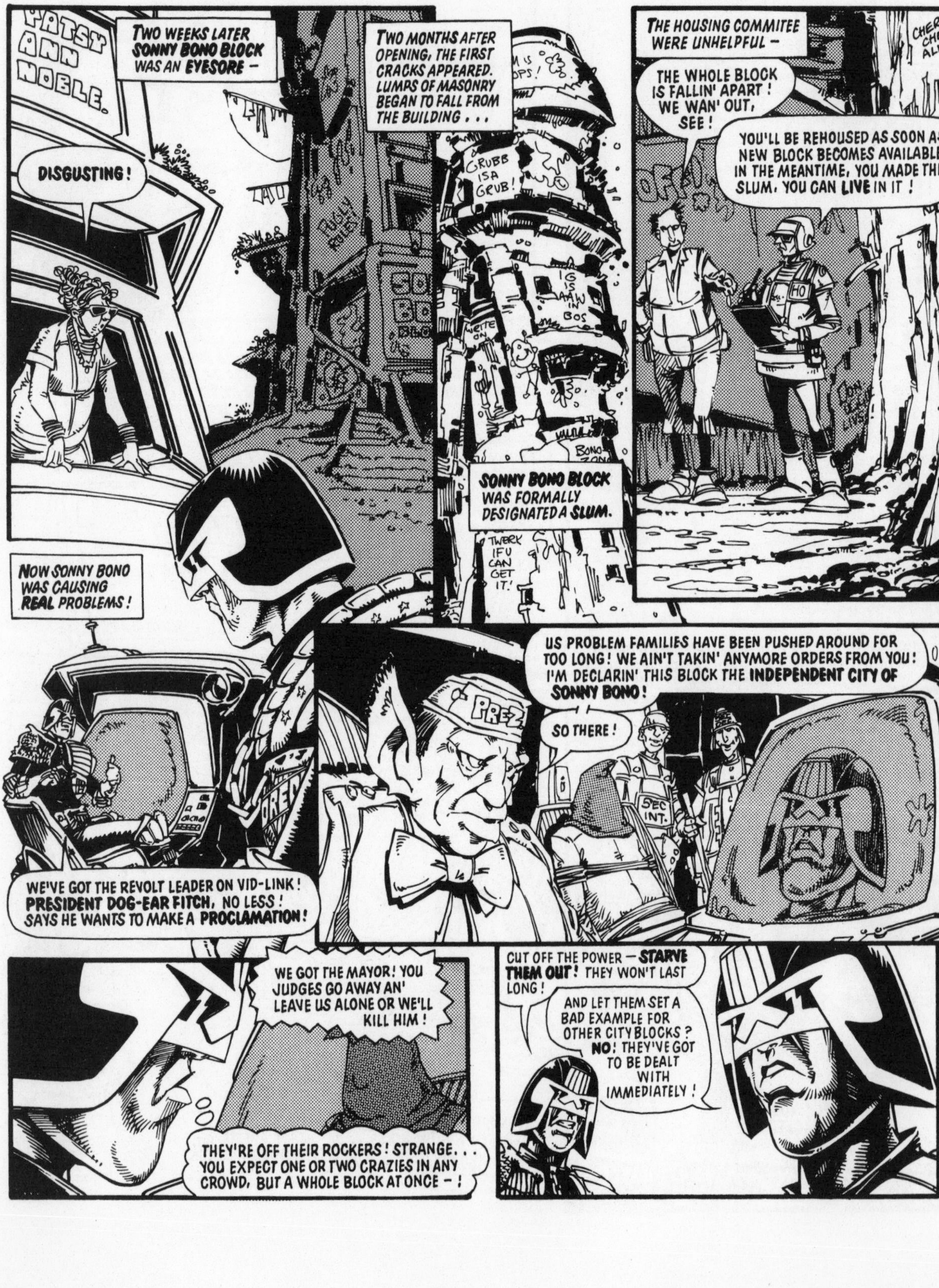
PATSY ANN NOBLE.
TWO WEEKS LATER SONNY BONO BLOCK WAS AN EYESORE –
DISGUSTING!
TWO MONTHS AFTER OPENING, THE FIRST CRACKS APPEARED. LUMPS OF MASONRY BEGAN TO FALL FROM THE BUILDING . . .
GRUBB ISA GRUB!
SONNY BONO BLOCK WAS FORMALLY DESIGNATED A SLUM.
THE HOUSING COMMITEE WERE UNHELPFUL –
CHER + CHER ALIKE.
THE WHOLE BLOCK IS FALLIN' APART! WE WAN' OUT, SEE!
YOU'LL BE REHOUSED AS SOON AS A NEW BLOCK BECOMES AVAILABLE! IN THE MEANTIME, YOU MADE THIS SLUM, YOU CAN LIVE IN IT!
NOW SONNY BONO WAS CAUSING REAL PROBLEMS!
WE'VE GOT THE REVOLT LEADER ON VID-LINK! PRESIDENT DOG-EAR FITCH, NO LESS! SAYS HE WANTS TO MAKE A PROCLAMATION!
US PROBLEM FAMILIES HAVE BEEN PUSHED AROUND FOR TOO LONG! WE AIN'T TAKIN' ANYMORE ORDERS FROM YOU! I'M DECLARIN' THIS BLOCK THE INDEPENDENT CITY OF SONNY BONO!
SO THERE!
PREZ
WE GOT THE MAYOR! YOU JUDGES GO AWAY AN' LEAVE US ALONE OR WE'LL KILL HIM!
THEY'RE OFF THEIR ROCKERS! STRANGE. . . YOU EXPECT ONE OR TWO CRAZIES IN ANY CROWD, BUT A WHOLE BLOCK AT ONCE –!
CUT OFF THE POWER — STARVE THEM OUT! THEY WON'T LAST LONG!
AND LET THEM SET A BAD EXAMPLE FOR OTHER CITY BLOCKS? NO! THEY'VE GOT TO BE DEALT WITH IMMEDIATELY!

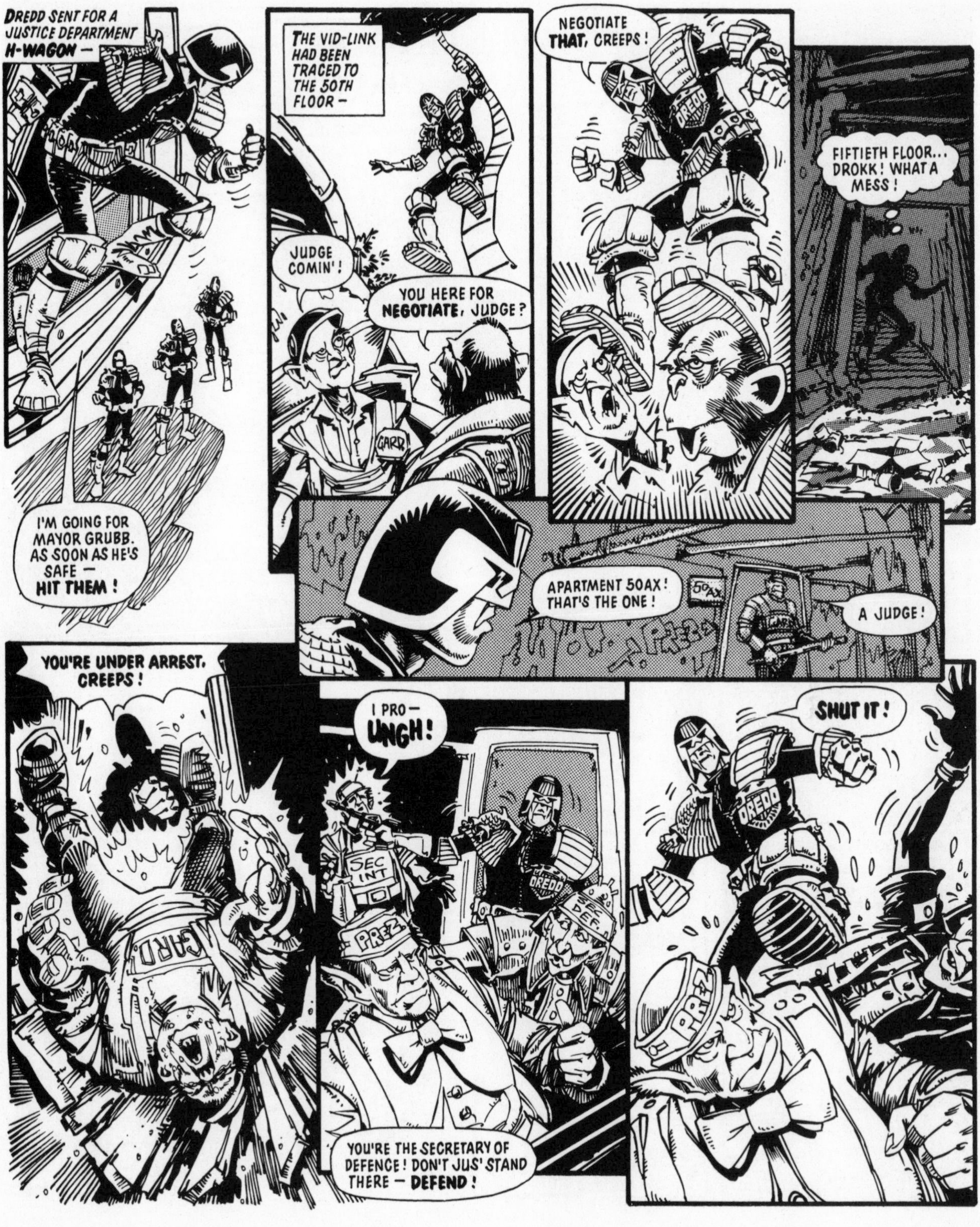

DREDD SENT FOR A JUSTICE DEPARTMENT H-WAGON –
I'M GOING FOR MAYOR GRUBB. AS SOON AS HE'S SAFE – HIT THEM!
THE VID-LINK HAD BEEN TRACED TO THE 50TH FLOOR –
JUDGE COMIN'!
YOU HERE FOR NEGOTIATE, JUDGE?
GARD
NEGOTIATE THAT, CREEPS!
DREDD
FIFTIETH FLOOR... DROKK! WHAT A MESS!
APARTMENT 50AX! THAT'S THE ONE!
50AX
A JUDGE!
YOU'RE UNDER ARREST, CREEPS!
GARD
I PRO– UNGH!
SEC INT
DREDD
PREZ
SEC DEF
YOU'RE THE SECRETARY OF DEFENCE! DON'T JUS' STAND THERE – DEFEND!
SHUT IT!
DREDD
PREZ

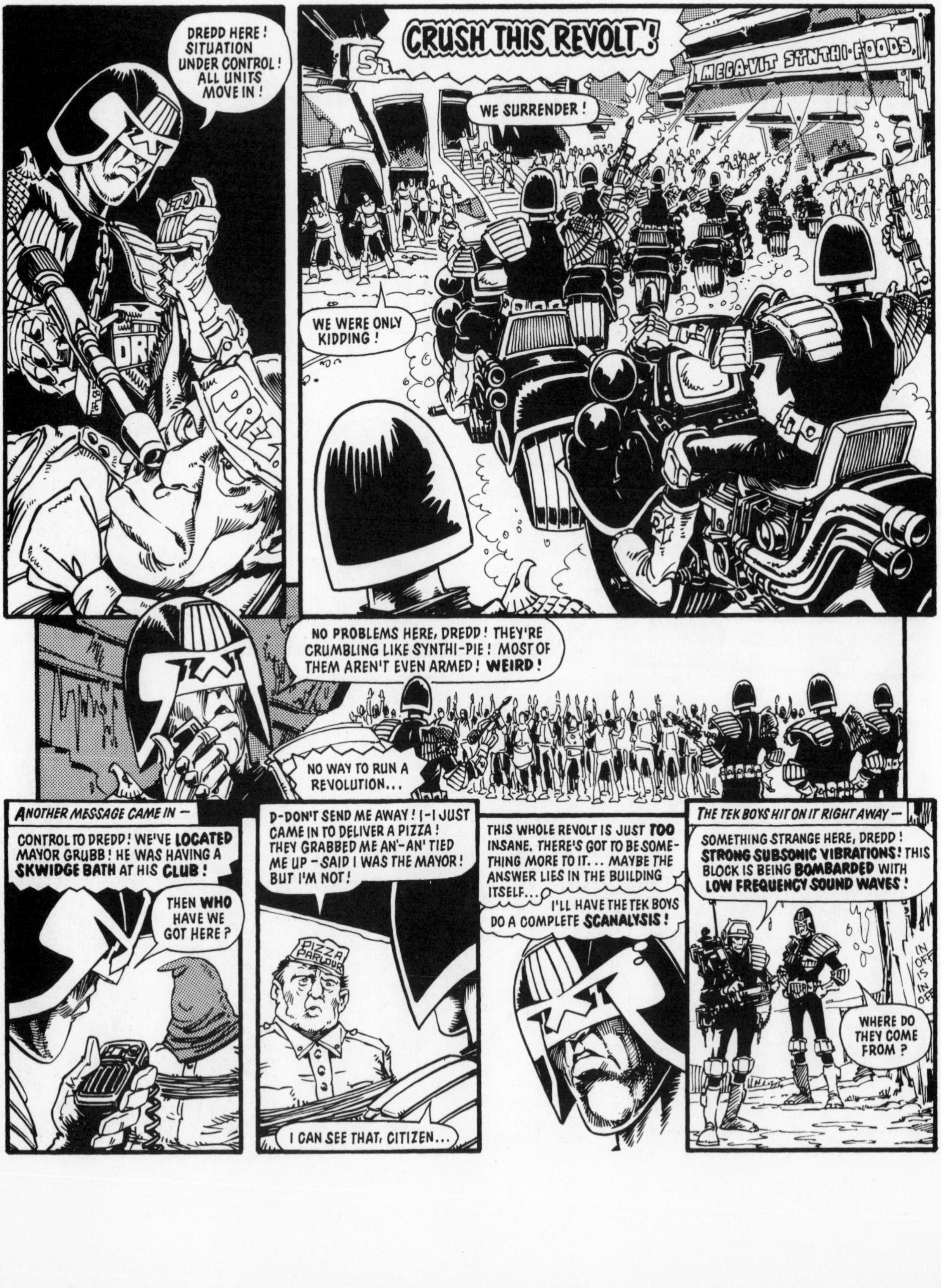
DREDD HERE! SITUATION UNDER CONTROL! ALL UNITS MOVE IN!
CRUSH THIS REVOLT!
MEGA-VIT SYNTHI-FOODS.
WE SURRENDER!
WE WERE ONLY KIDDING!
NO PROBLEMS HERE, DREDD! THEY'RE CRUMBLING LIKE SYNTHI-PIE! MOST OF THEM AREN'T EVEN ARMED! WEIRD!
NO WAY TO RUN A REVOLUTION...
ANOTHER MESSAGE CAME IN —
CONTROL TO DREDD! WE'VE LOCATED MAYOR GRUBB! HE WAS HAVING A SKWIDGE BATH AT HIS CLUB!
THEN WHO HAVE WE GOT HERE?
D-DON'T SEND ME AWAY! I-I JUST CAME IN TO DELIVER A PIZZA! THEY GRABBED ME AN'-AN' TIED ME UP - SAID I WAS THE MAYOR! BUT I'M NOT!
PIZZA PARLOUR
I CAN SEE THAT, CITIZEN...
THIS WHOLE REVOLT IS JUST TOO INSANE. THERE'S GOT TO BE SOMETHING MORE TO IT... MAYBE THE ANSWER LIES IN THE BUILDING ITSELF...
I'LL HAVE THE TEK BOYS DO A COMPLETE SCANALYSIS!
THE TEK BOYS HIT ON IT RIGHT AWAY —
SOMETHING STRANGE HERE, DREDD! STRONG SUBSONIC VIBRATIONS! THIS BLOCK IS BEING BOMBARDED WITH LOW FREQUENCY SOUND WAVES!
WHERE DO THEY COME FROM?

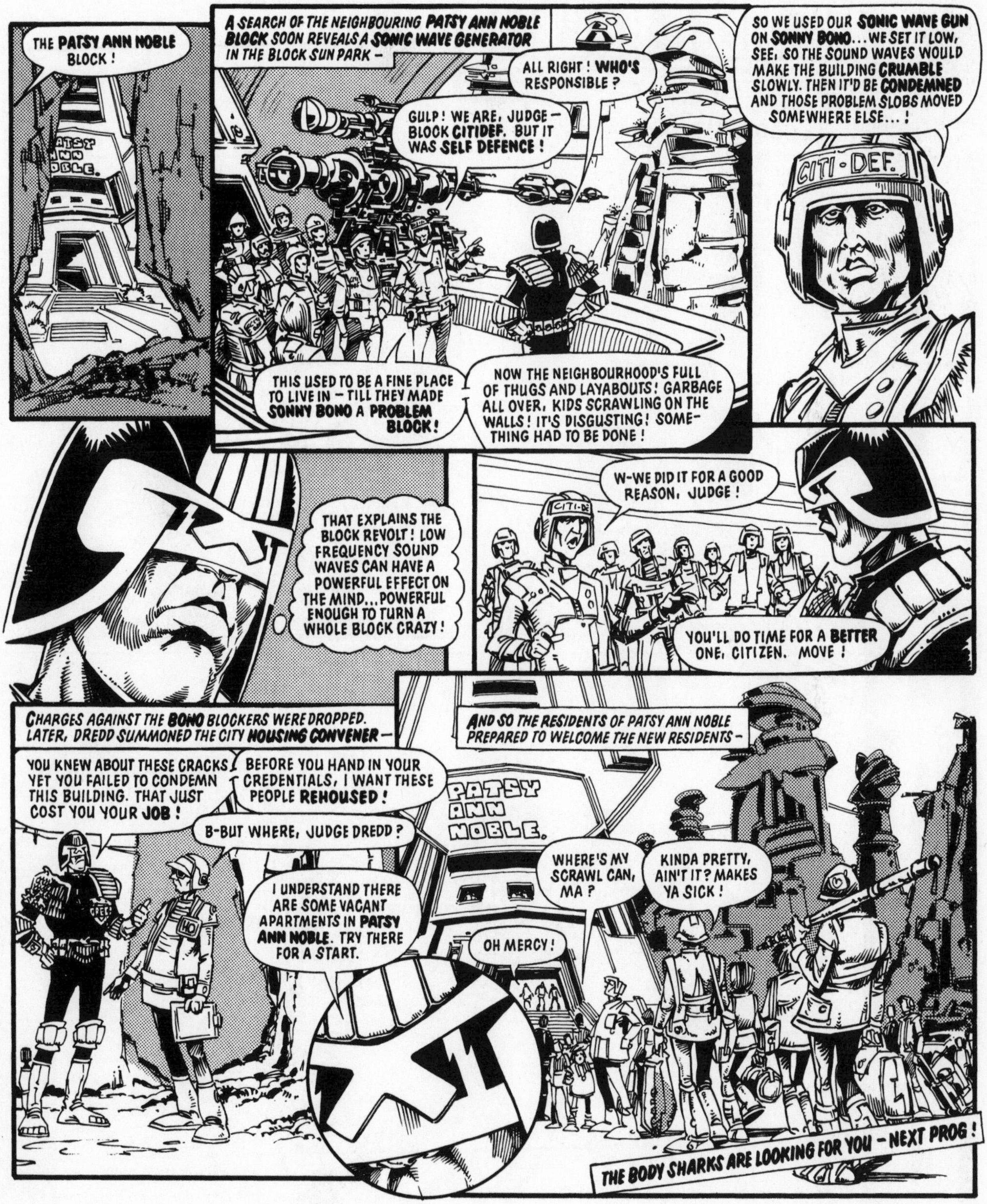

THE PATSY ANN NOBLE BLOCK!
PATSY ANN NOBLE.
A SEARCH OF THE NEIGHBOURING PATSY ANN NOBLE BLOCK SOON REVEALS A SONIC WAVE GENERATOR IN THE BLOCK SUN PARK -
ALL RIGHT! WHO'S RESPONSIBLE?
GULP! WE ARE, JUDGE - BLOCK CITIDEF. BUT IT WAS SELF DEFENCE!
THIS USED TO BE A FINE PLACE TO LIVE IN - TILL THEY MADE SONNY BONO A PROBLEM BLOCK!
NOW THE NEIGHBOURHOOD'S FULL OF THUGS AND LAYABOUTS! GARBAGE ALL OVER, KIDS SCRAWLING ON THE WALLS! IT'S DISGUSTING! SOMETHING HAD TO BE DONE!
SO WE USED OUR SONIC WAVE GUN ON SONNY BONO... WE SET IT LOW, SEE, SO THE SOUND WAVES WOULD MAKE THE BUILDING CRUMBLE SLOWLY. THEN IT'D BE CONDEMNED AND THOSE PROBLEM SLOBS MOVED SOMEWHERE ELSE...!
CITI-DEF.
THAT EXPLAINS THE BLOCK REVOLT! LOW FREQUENCY SOUND WAVES CAN HAVE A POWERFUL EFFECT ON THE MIND... POWERFUL ENOUGH TO TURN A WHOLE BLOCK CRAZY!
W-WE DID IT FOR A GOOD REASON, JUDGE!
YOU'LL DO TIME FOR A BETTER ONE, CITIZEN. MOVE!
CHARGES AGAINST THE BONO BLOCKERS WERE DROPPED. LATER, DREDD SUMMONED THE CITY HOUSING CONVENER -
YOU KNEW ABOUT THESE CRACKS YET YOU FAILED TO CONDEMN THIS BUILDING. THAT JUST COST YOU YOUR JOB!
BEFORE YOU HAND IN YOUR CREDENTIALS, I WANT THESE PEOPLE REHOUSED!
B-BUT WHERE, JUDGE DREDD?
I UNDERSTAND THERE ARE SOME VACANT APARTMENTS IN PATSY ANN NOBLE. TRY THERE FOR A START.
AND SO THE RESIDENTS OF PATSY ANN NOBLE PREPARED TO WELCOME THE NEW RESIDENTS -
PATSY ANN NOBLE.
WHERE'S MY SCRAWL CAN, MA?
KINDA PRETTY, AIN'T IT? MAKES YA SICK!
OH MERCY!
THE BODY SHARKS ARE LOOKING FOR YOU - NEXT PROG!

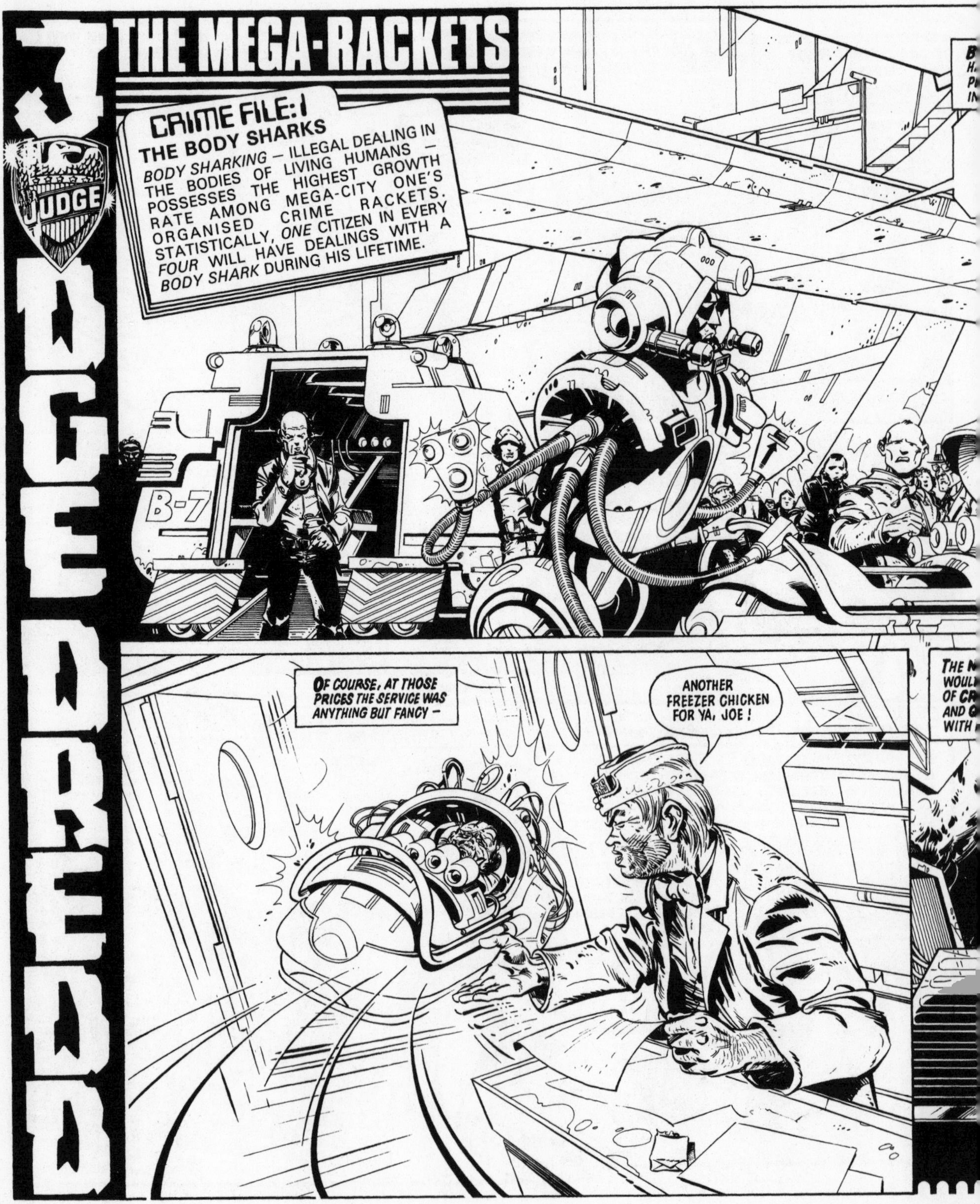
JUDGE DREDD
JUDGE
THE MEGA-RACKETS
CRIME FILE: 1
THE BODY SHARKS
BODY SHARKING — ILLEGAL DEALING IN THE BODIES OF LIVING HUMANS — POSSESSES THE HIGHEST GROWTH RATE AMONG MEGA-CITY ONE'S ORGANISED CRIME RACKETS. STATISTICALLY, ONE CITIZEN IN EVERY FOUR WILL HAVE DEALINGS WITH A BODY SHARK DURING HIS LIFETIME.
B-7
OF COURSE, AT THOSE PRICES THE SERVICE WAS ANYTHING BUT FANCY —
ANOTHER FREEZER CHICKEN FOR YA, JOE!

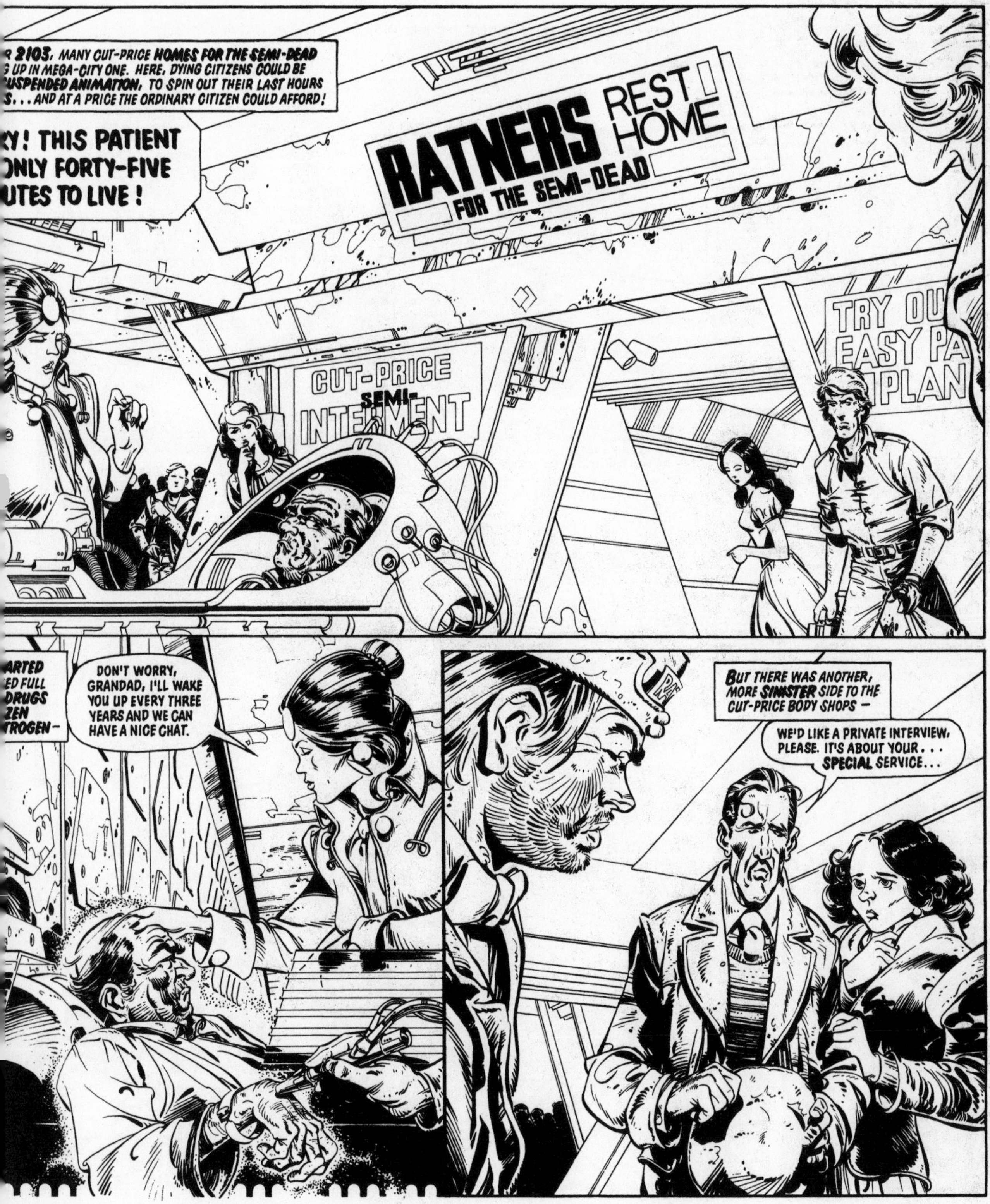
R 2103, MANY CUT-PRICE HOMES FOR THE SEMI-DEAD
G UP IN MEGA-CITY ONE. HERE, DYING CITIZENS COULD BE
SUSPENDED ANIMATION, TO SPIN OUT THEIR LAST HOURS
S... AND AT A PRICE THE ORDINARY CITIZEN COULD AFFORD!
Y! THIS PATIENT
ONLY FORTY-FIVE
UTES TO LIVE!
RATNERS REST HOME
FOR THE SEMI-DEAD
CUT-PRICE SEMI-INTERMENT
TRY OU
EASY PA
PLAN
ARTED
ED FULL
DRUGS
ZEN
TROGEN—
DON'T WORRY, GRANDAD, I'LL WAKE YOU UP EVERY THREE YEARS AND WE CAN HAVE A NICE CHAT.
BUT THERE WAS ANOTHER, MORE SINISTER SIDE TO THE CUT-PRICE BODY SHOPS —
WE'D LIKE A PRIVATE INTERVIEW, PLEASE. IT'S ABOUT YOUR... SPECIAL SERVICE...

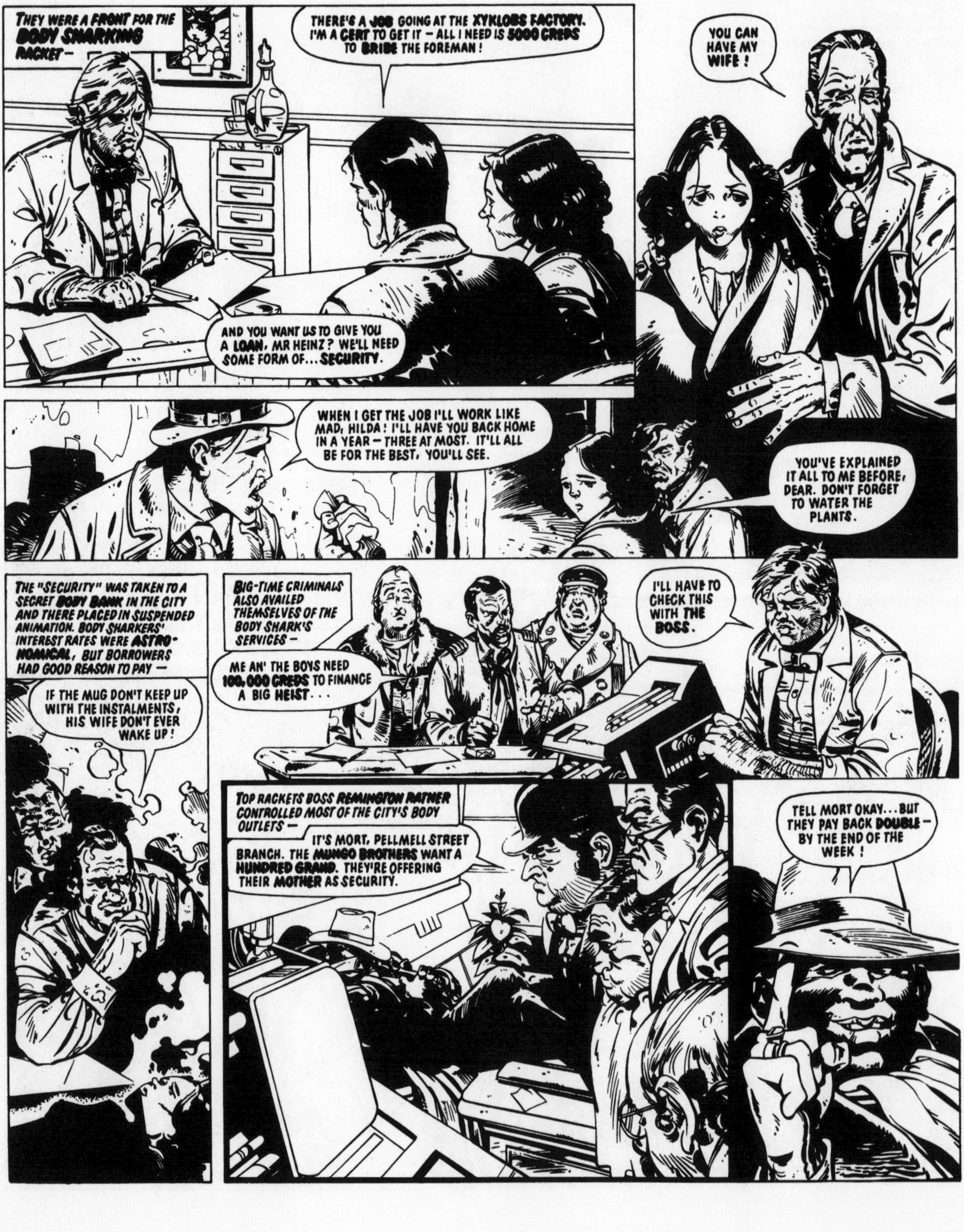
THEY WERE A FRONT FOR THE BODY SHARKING RACKET –
THERE'S A JOB GOING AT THE XYKLOBS FACTORY. I'M A CERT TO GET IT – ALL I NEED IS 5000 CREDS TO BRIBE THE FOREMAN!
AND YOU WANT US TO GIVE YOU A LOAN, MR HEINZ? WE'LL NEED SOME FORM OF... SECURITY.
YOU CAN HAVE MY WIFE!
WHEN I GET THE JOB I'LL WORK LIKE MAD, HILDA! I'LL HAVE YOU BACK HOME IN A YEAR – THREE AT MOST. IT'LL ALL BE FOR THE BEST, YOU'LL SEE.
YOU'VE EXPLAINED IT ALL TO ME BEFORE, DEAR. DON'T FORGET TO WATER THE PLANTS.
THE "SECURITY" WAS TAKEN TO A SECRET BODY BANK IN THE CITY AND THERE PLACED IN SUSPENDED ANIMATION. BODY SHARKERS' INTEREST RATES WERE ASTRONOMICAL, BUT BORROWERS HAD GOOD REASON TO PAY –
IF THE MUG DON'T KEEP UP WITH THE INSTALMENTS, HIS WIFE DON'T EVER WAKE UP!
BIG-TIME CRIMINALS ALSO AVAILED THEMSELVES OF THE BODY SHARK'S SERVICES –
ME AN' THE BOYS NEED 100,000 CREDS TO FINANCE A BIG HEIST...
I'LL HAVE TO CHECK THIS WITH THE BOSS.
TOP RACKETS BOSS REMINGTON RATNER CONTROLLED MOST OF THE CITY'S BODY OUTLETS –
IT'S MORT, PELLMELL STREET BRANCH. THE MUNGO BROTHERS WANT A HUNDRED GRAND. THEY'RE OFFERING THEIR MOTHER AS SECURITY.
TELL MORT OKAY... BUT THEY PAY BACK DOUBLE – BY THE END OF THE WEEK!

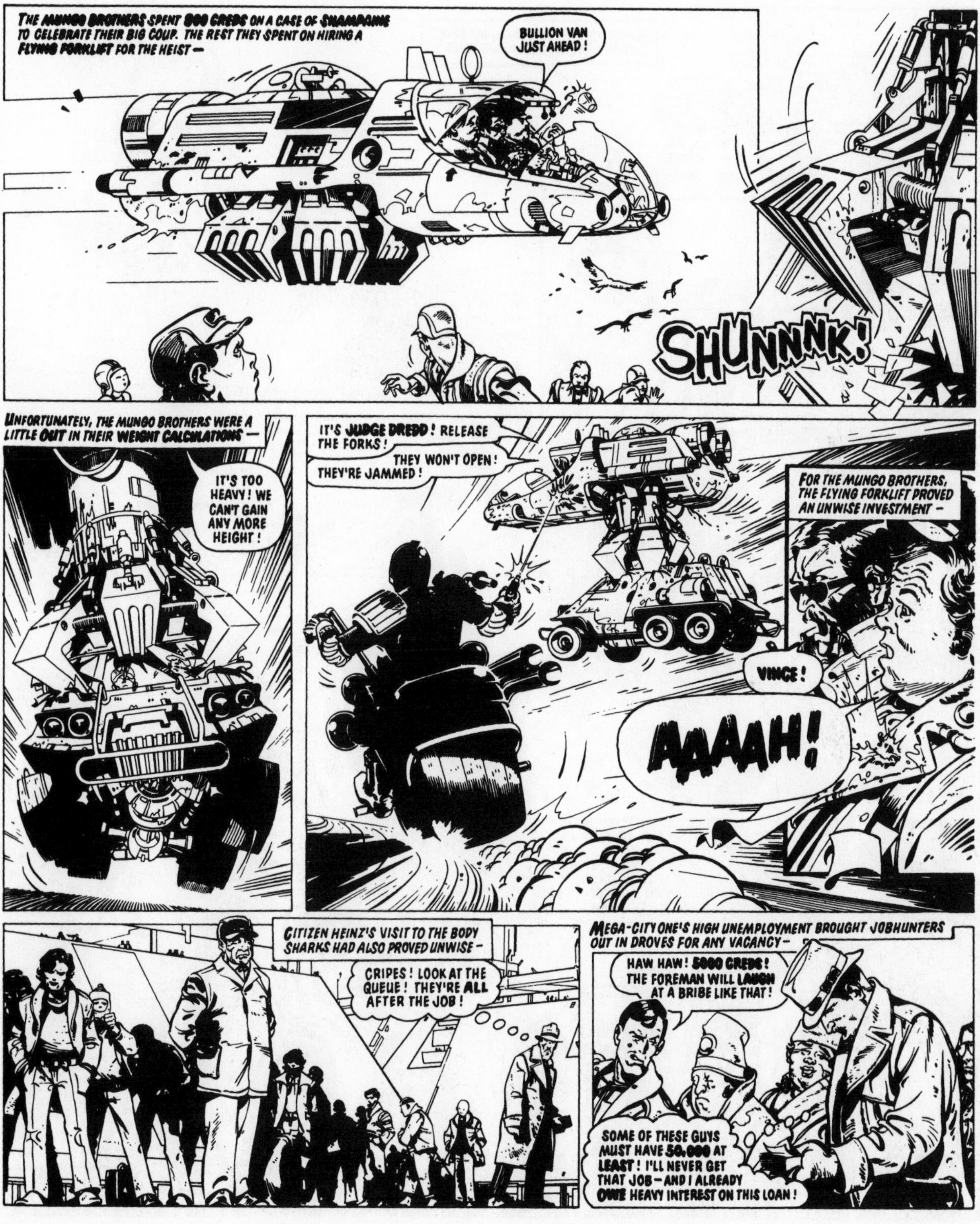
THE MUNGO BROTHERS SPENT 800 CREDS ON A CASE OF SHAMPAINE TO CELEBRATE THEIR BIG COUP. THE REST THEY SPENT ON HIRING A FLYING FORKLIFT FOR THE HEIST —
BULLION VAN JUST AHEAD!
SHUNNNK!
UNFORTUNATELY, THE MUNGO BROTHERS WERE A LITTLE OUT IN THEIR WEIGHT CALCULATIONS —
IT'S TOO HEAVY! WE CAN'T GAIN ANY MORE HEIGHT!
IT'S JUDGE DREDD! RELEASE THE FORKS!
THEY WON'T OPEN! THEY'RE JAMMED!
FOR THE MUNGO BROTHERS, THE FLYING FORKLIFT PROVED AN UNWISE INVESTMENT —
VINCE!
AAAAH!
CITIZEN HEINZ'S VISIT TO THE BODY SHARKS HAD ALSO PROVED UNWISE —
CRIPES! LOOK AT THE QUEUE! THEY'RE ALL AFTER THE JOB!
MEGA-CITY ONE'S HIGH UNEMPLOYMENT BROUGHT JOBHUNTERS OUT IN DROVES FOR ANY VACANCY —
HAW HAW! 5000 CREDS! THE FOREMAN WILL LAUGH AT A BRIBE LIKE THAT!
SOME OF THESE GUYS MUST HAVE 50,000 AT LEAST! I'LL NEVER GET THAT JOB — AND I ALREADY OWE HEAVY INTEREST ON THIS LOAN!

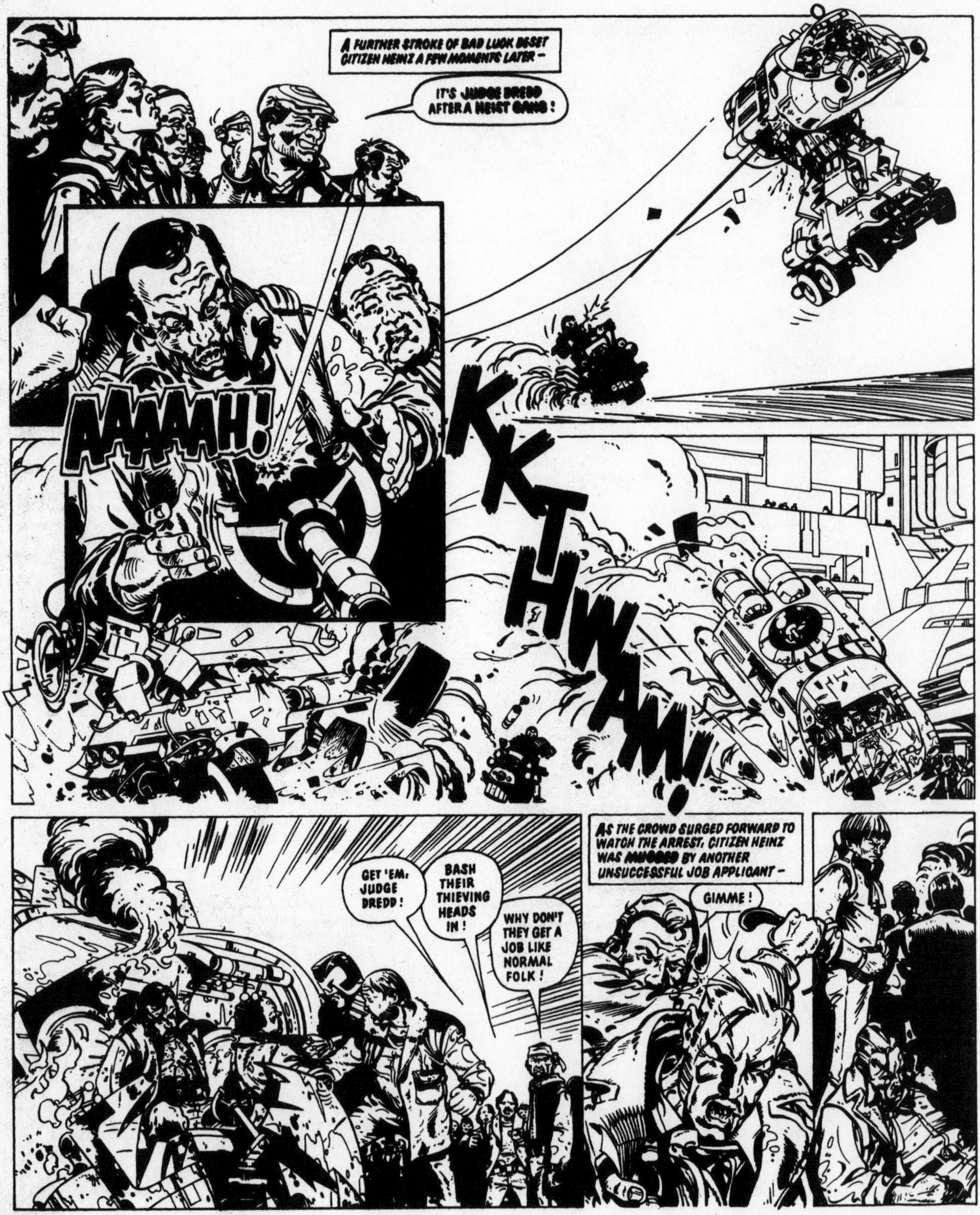
A FURTHER STROKE OF BAD LUCK BESET CITIZEN HEINZ A FEW MOMENTS LATER –
IT'S JUDGE DREDD AFTER A HEIST GANG!
AAAAAH!
KKTHWAM!
GET 'EM, JUDGE DREDD!
BASH THEIR THIEVING HEADS IN!
WHY DON'T THEY GET A JOB LIKE NORMAL FOLK!
AS THE CROWD SURGED FORWARD TO WATCH THE ARREST, CITIZEN HEINZ WAS MUGGED BY ANOTHER UNSUCCESSFUL JOB APPLICANT –
GIMME!

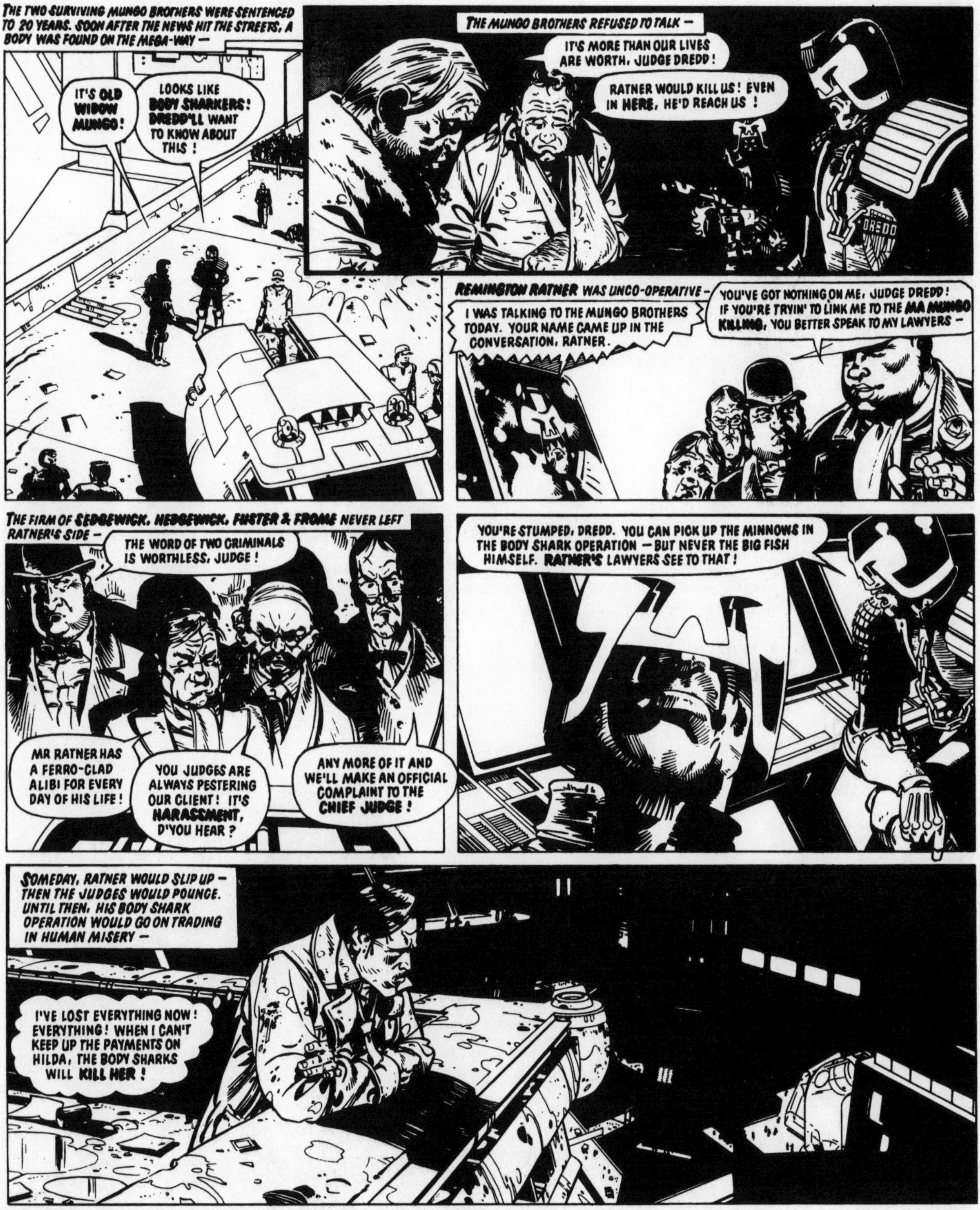
THE TWO SURVIVING MUNGO BROTHERS WERE SENTENCED TO 20 YEARS. SOON AFTER THE NEWS HIT THE STREETS, A BODY WAS FOUND ON THE MEGA-WAY –
IT'S OLD WIDOW MUNGO!
LOOKS LIKE BODY SHARKERS! DREDD'LL WANT TO KNOW ABOUT THIS!
THE MUNGO BROTHERS REFUSED TO TALK –
IT'S MORE THAN OUR LIVES ARE WORTH, JUDGE DREDD!
RATNER WOULD KILL US! EVEN IN HERE, HE'D REACH US!
REMINGTON RATNER WAS UNCO-OPERATIVE –
I WAS TALKING TO THE MUNGO BROTHERS TODAY. YOUR NAME CAME UP IN THE CONVERSATION, RATNER.
YOU'VE GOT NOTHING ON ME, JUDGE DREDD! IF YOU'RE TRYIN' TO LINK ME TO THE MA MUNGO KILLING, YOU BETTER SPEAK TO MY LAWYERS –
THE FIRM OF SEDGEWICK, HEDGEWICK, FUSTER & FROME NEVER LEFT RATNER'S SIDE –
THE WORD OF TWO CRIMINALS IS WORTHLESS, JUDGE!
MR RATNER HAS A FERRO-CLAD ALIBI FOR EVERY DAY OF HIS LIFE!
YOU JUDGES ARE ALWAYS PESTERING OUR CLIENT! IT'S HARASSMENT, D'YOU HEAR?
ANY MORE OF IT AND WE'LL MAKE AN OFFICIAL COMPLAINT TO THE CHIEF JUDGE!
YOU'RE STUMPED, DREDD. YOU CAN PICK UP THE MINNOWS IN THE BODY SHARK OPERATION – BUT NEVER THE BIG FISH HIMSELF. RATNER'S LAWYERS SEE TO THAT!
SOMEDAY, RATNER WOULD SLIP UP – THEN THE JUDGES WOULD POUNCE. UNTIL THEN, HIS BODY SHARK OPERATION WOULD GO ON TRADING IN HUMAN MISERY –
I'VE LOST EVERYTHING NOW! EVERYTHING! WHEN I CAN'T KEEP UP THE PAYMENTS ON HILDA, THE BODY SHARKS WILL KILL HER!

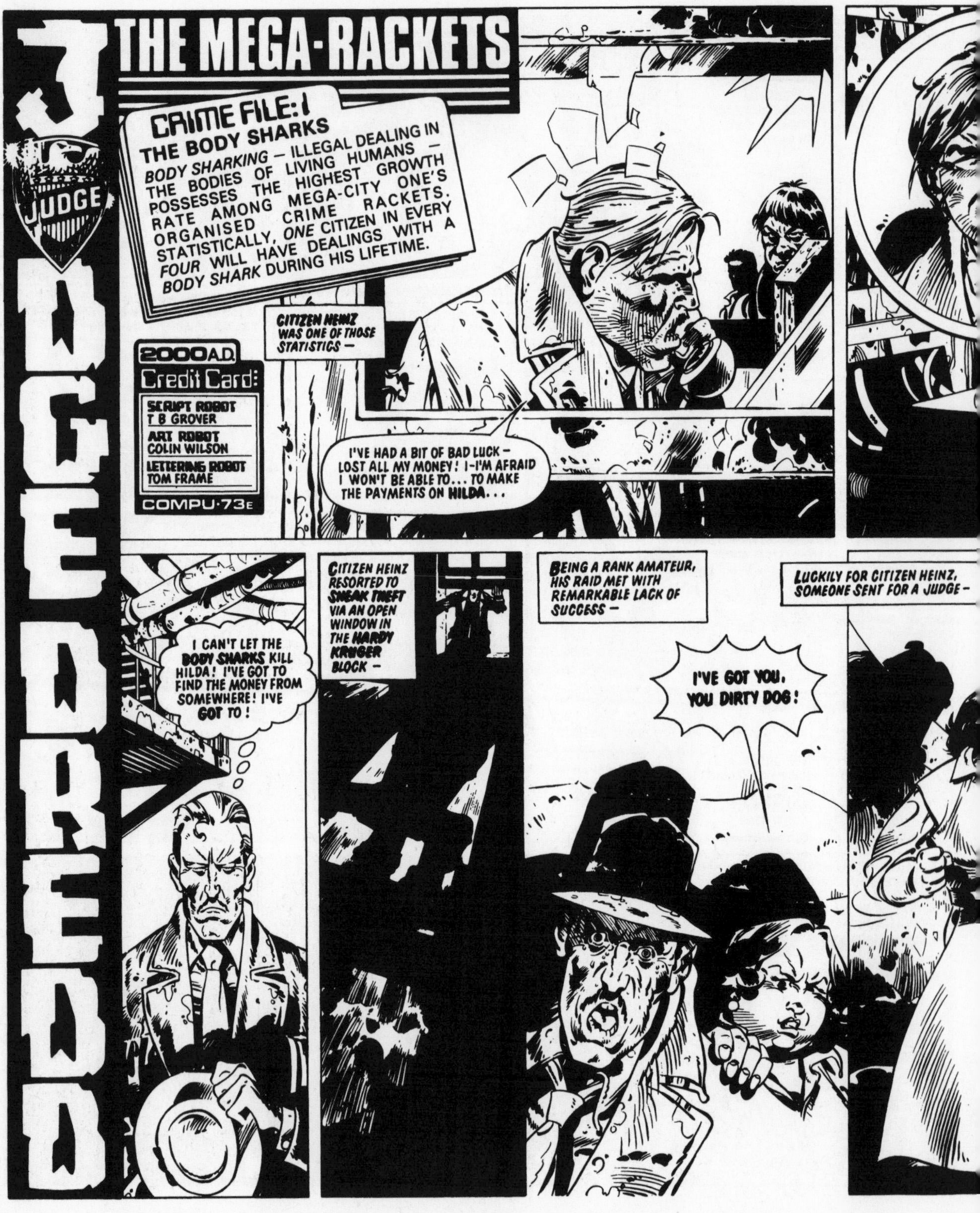
JUDGE DREDD
THE MEGA-RACKETS
CRIME FILE: I
THE BODY SHARKS
BODY SHARKING — ILLEGAL DEALING IN THE BODIES OF LIVING HUMANS — POSSESSES THE HIGHEST GROWTH RATE AMONG MEGA-CITY ONE'S ORGANISED CRIME RACKETS. STATISTICALLY, ONE CITIZEN IN EVERY FOUR WILL HAVE DEALINGS WITH A BODY SHARK DURING HIS LIFETIME.
2000 A.D. Credit Card: SCRIPT ROBOT T B GROVER ART ROBOT COLIN WILSON LETTERING ROBOT TOM FRAME COMPU·73E
CITIZEN HEINZ WAS ONE OF THOSE STATISTICS —
I'VE HAD A BIT OF BAD LUCK — LOST ALL MY MONEY! I-I'M AFRAID I WON'T BE ABLE TO... TO MAKE THE PAYMENTS ON HILDA...
I CAN'T LET THE BODY SHARKS KILL HILDA! I'VE GOT TO FIND THE MONEY FROM SOMEWHERE! I'VE GOT TO!
CITIZEN HEINZ RESORTED TO SNEAK THEFT VIA AN OPEN WINDOW IN THE HARDY KRUGER BLOCK —
BEING A RANK AMATEUR, HIS RAID MET WITH REMARKABLE LACK OF SUCCESS —
I'VE GOT YOU, YOU DIRTY DOG!
LUCKILY FOR CITIZEN HEINZ, SOMEONE SENT FOR A JUDGE —

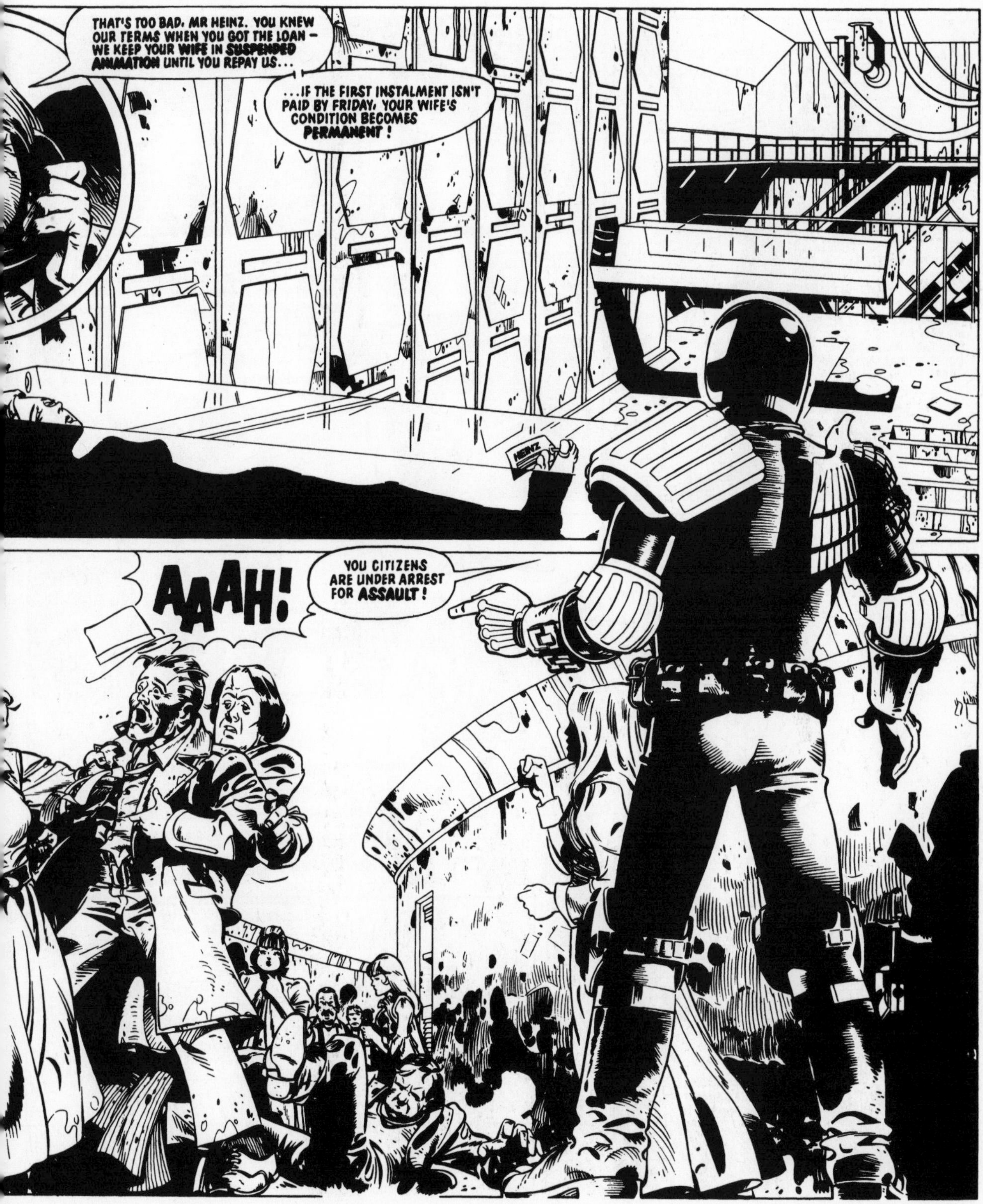
THAT'S TOO BAD, MR HEINZ. YOU KNEW OUR TERMS WHEN YOU GOT THE LOAN – WE KEEP YOUR WIFE IN SUSPENDED ANIMATION UNTIL YOU REPAY US...
...IF THE FIRST INSTALMENT ISN'T PAID BY FRIDAY, YOUR WIFE'S CONDITION BECOMES PERMANENT!
HEINZ
AAAH!
YOU CITIZENS ARE UNDER ARREST FOR ASSAULT!

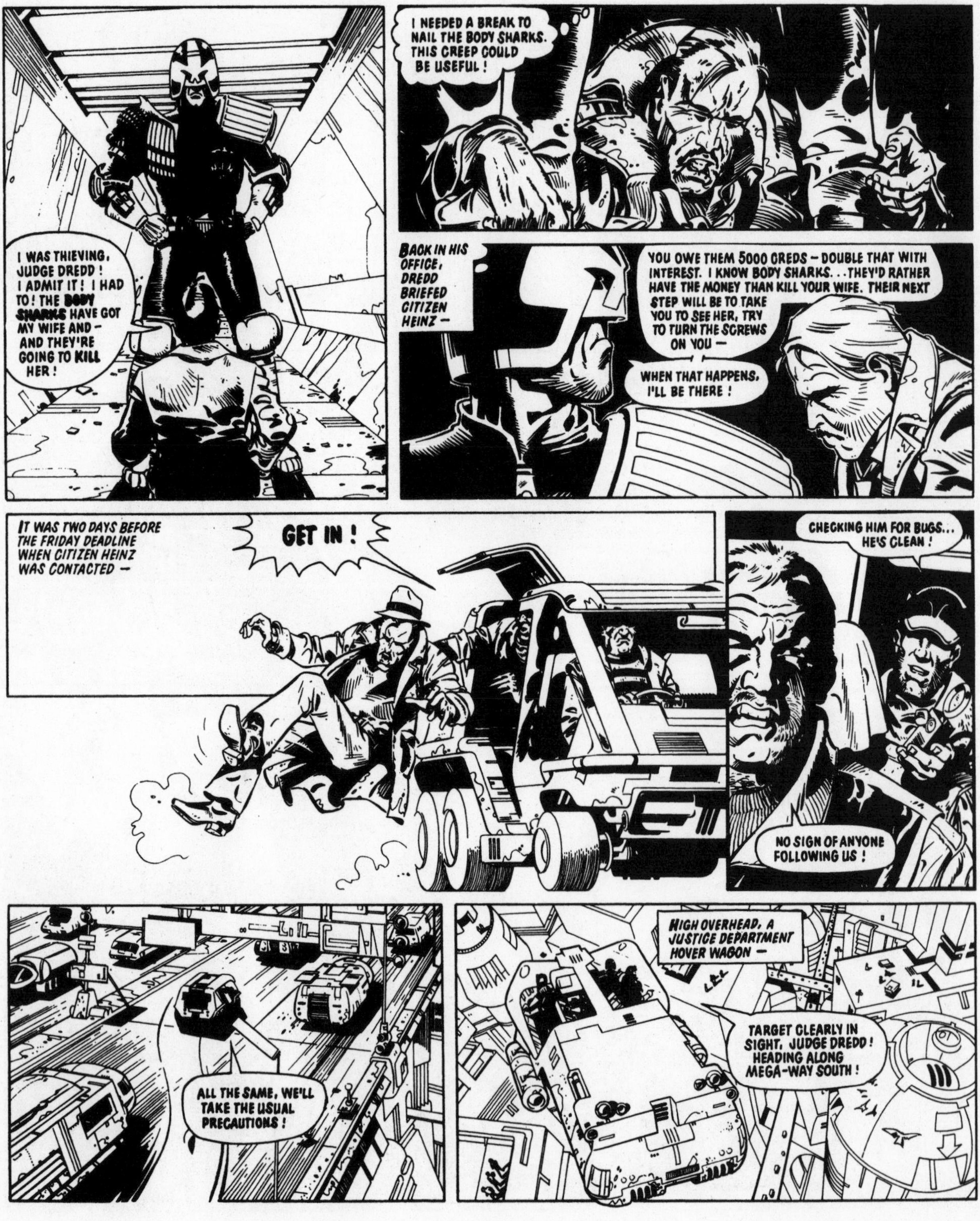
I WAS THIEVING, JUDGE DREDD! I ADMIT IT! I HAD TO! THE BODY SHARKS HAVE GOT MY WIFE AND – AND THEY'RE GOING TO KILL HER!
I NEEDED A BREAK TO NAIL THE BODY SHARKS. THIS CREEP COULD BE USEFUL!
BACK IN HIS OFFICE, DREDD BRIEFED CITIZEN HEINZ –
YOU OWE THEM 5000 CREDS – DOUBLE THAT WITH INTEREST. I KNOW BODY SHARKS... THEY'D RATHER HAVE THE MONEY THAN KILL YOUR WIFE. THEIR NEXT STEP WILL BE TO TAKE YOU TO SEE HER, TRY TO TURN THE SCREWS ON YOU –
WHEN THAT HAPPENS, I'LL BE THERE!
IT WAS TWO DAYS BEFORE THE FRIDAY DEADLINE WHEN CITIZEN HEINZ WAS CONTACTED –
GET IN!
CHECKING HIM FOR BUGS... HE'S CLEAN!
NO SIGN OF ANYONE FOLLOWING US!
ALL THE SAME, WE'LL TAKE THE USUAL PRECAUTIONS!
HIGH OVERHEAD, A JUSTICE DEPARTMENT HOVER WAGON –
TARGET CLEARLY IN SIGHT, JUDGE DREDD! HEADING ALONG MEGA-WAY SOUTH!

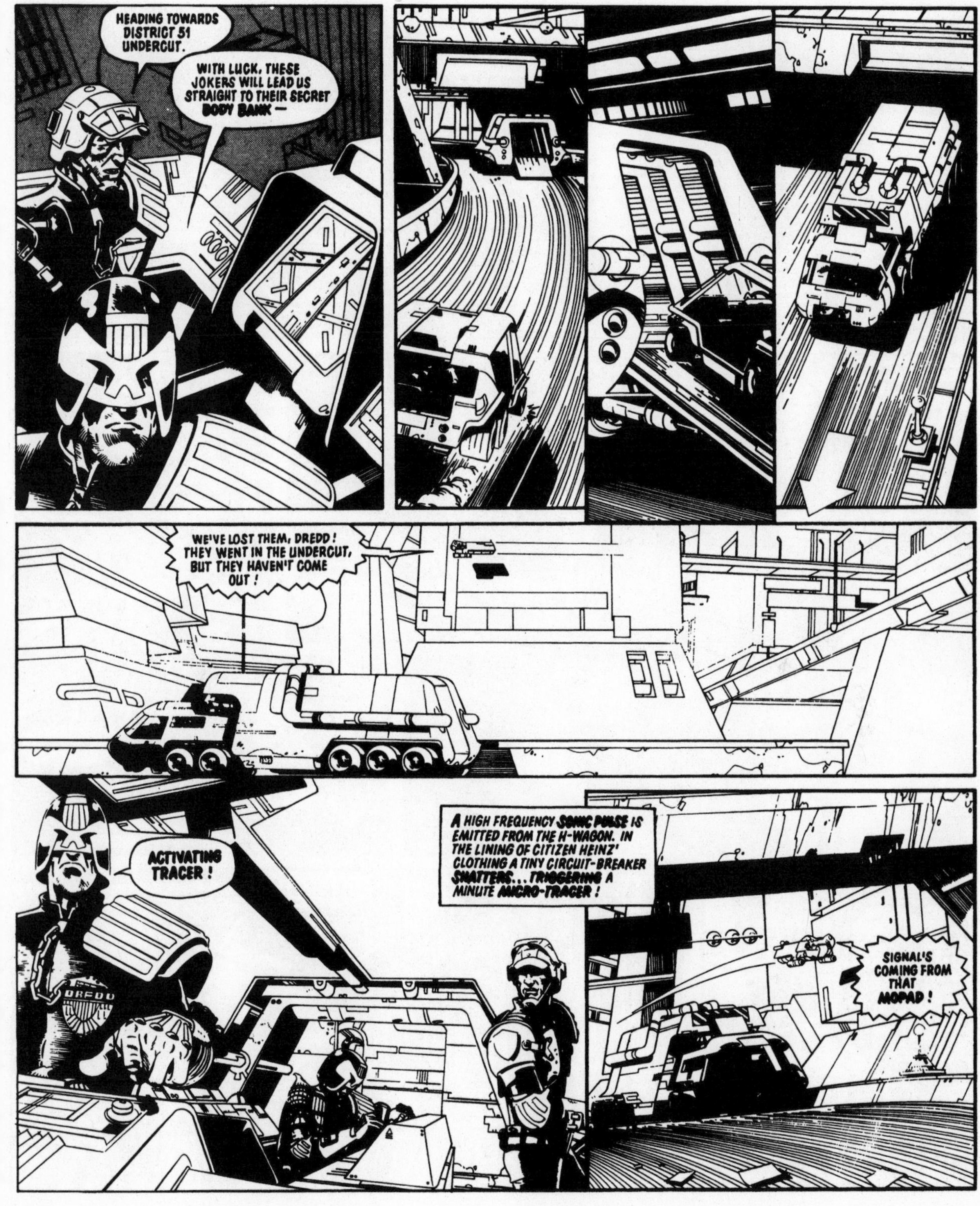
HEADING TOWARDS DISTRICT 51 UNDERCUT.
WITH LUCK, THESE JOKERS WILL LEAD US STRAIGHT TO THEIR SECRET BODY BANK —
WE'VE LOST THEM, DREDD! THEY WENT IN THE UNDERCUT, BUT THEY HAVEN'T COME OUT!
ACTIVATING TRACER!
A HIGH FREQUENCY SONIC PULSE IS EMITTED FROM THE H-WAGON. IN THE LINING OF CITIZEN HEINZ' CLOTHING A TINY CIRCUIT-BREAKER SHATTERS... TRIGGERING A MINUTE MICRO-TRACER!
SIGNAL'S COMING FROM THAT MOPAD!

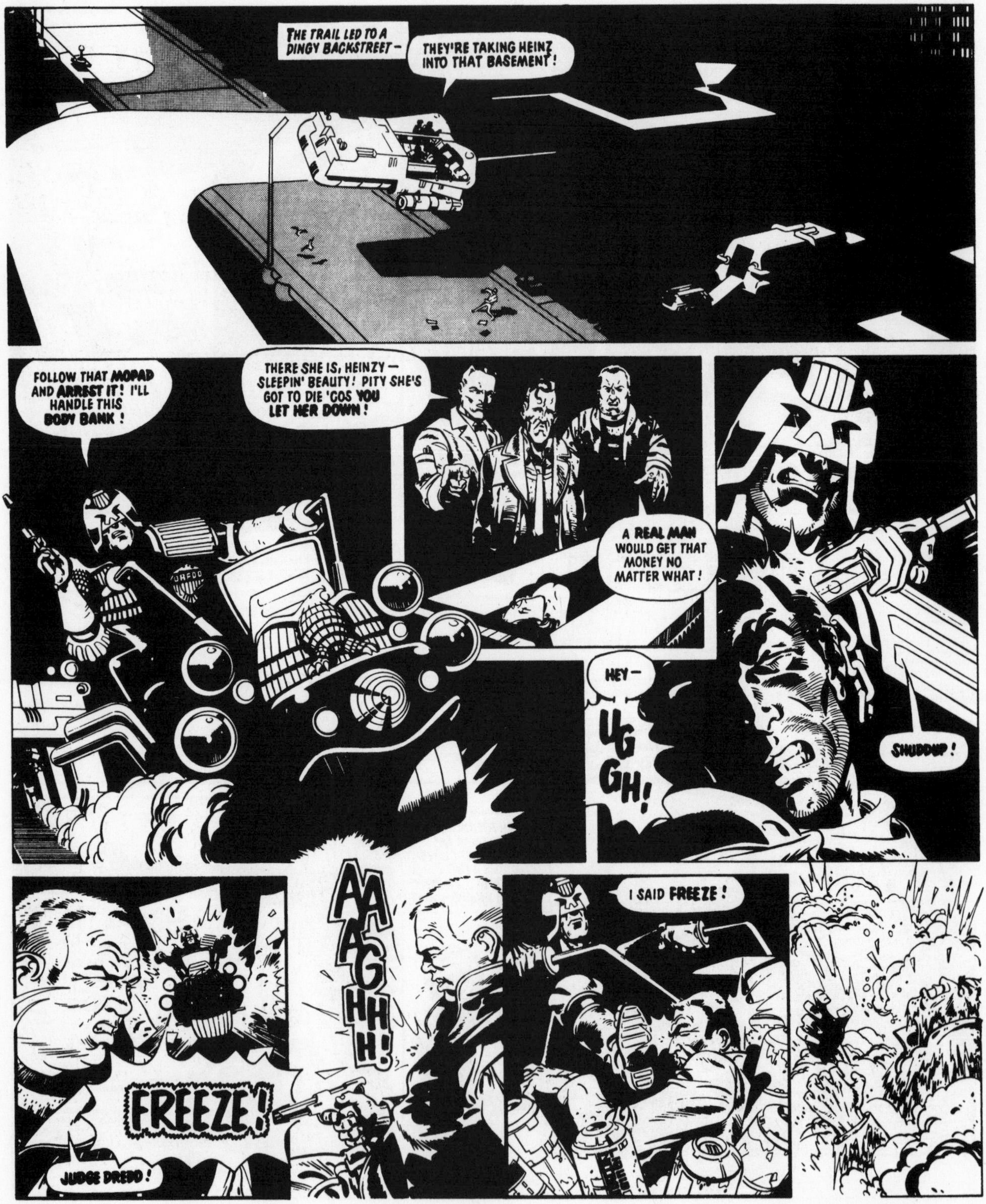
THE TRAIL LED TO A DINGY BACKSTREET –
THEY'RE TAKING HEINZ INTO THAT BASEMENT!
FOLLOW THAT MOPAD AND ARREST IT! I'LL HANDLE THIS BODY BANK!
THERE SHE IS, HEINZY — SLEEPIN' BEAUTY! PITY SHE'S GOT TO DIE 'COS YOU LET HER DOWN!
A REAL MAN WOULD GET THAT MONEY NO MATTER WHAT!
HEY –
UGGH!
SHUDDUP!
FREEZE!
JUDGE DREDD!
AAAGHHH!
I SAID FREEZE!

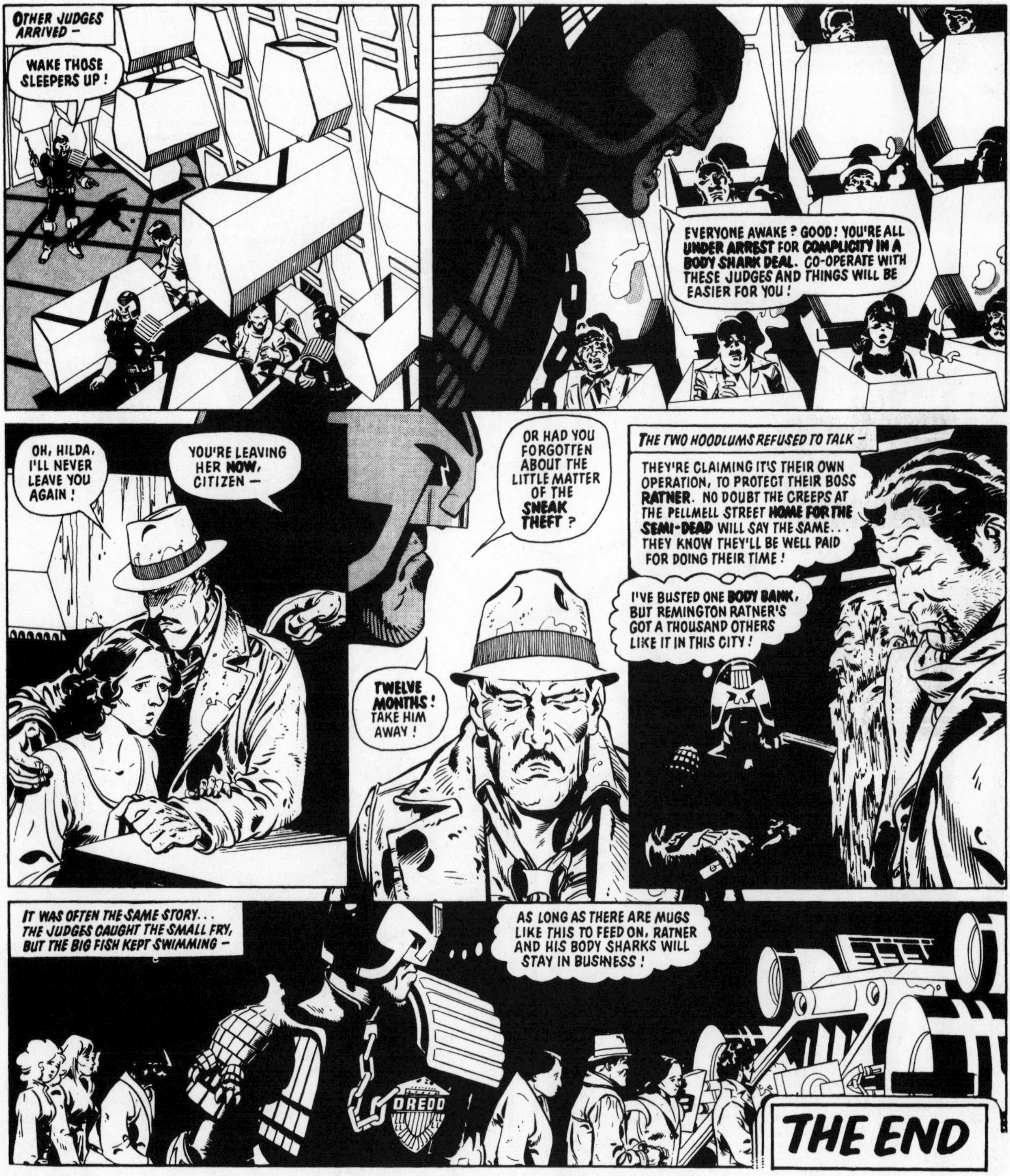
OTHER JUDGES ARRIVED –
WAKE THOSE SLEEPERS UP!
EVERYONE AWAKE? GOOD! YOU'RE ALL UNDER ARREST FOR COMPLICITY IN A BODY SHARK DEAL. CO-OPERATE WITH THESE JUDGES AND THINGS WILL BE EASIER FOR YOU!
OH, HILDA, I'LL NEVER LEAVE YOU AGAIN!
YOU'RE LEAVING HER NOW, CITIZEN –
OR HAD YOU FORGOTTEN ABOUT THE LITTLE MATTER OF THE SNEAK THEFT?
TWELVE MONTHS! TAKE HIM AWAY!
THE TWO HOODLUMS REFUSED TO TALK –
THEY'RE CLAIMING IT'S THEIR OWN OPERATION, TO PROTECT THEIR BOSS RATNER. NO DOUBT THE CREEPS AT THE PELLMELL STREET HOME FOR THE SEMI-DEAD WILL SAY THE SAME... THEY KNOW THEY'LL BE WELL PAID FOR DOING THEIR TIME!
I'VE BUSTED ONE BODY BANK, BUT REMINGTON RATNER'S GOT A THOUSAND OTHERS LIKE IT IN THIS CITY!
IT WAS OFTEN THE SAME STORY... THE JUDGES CAUGHT THE SMALL FRY, BUT THE BIG FISH KEPT SWIMMING –
... AS LONG AS THERE ARE MUGS LIKE THIS TO FEED ON, RATNER AND HIS BODY SHARKS WILL STAY IN BUSINESS!
DREDD
THE END

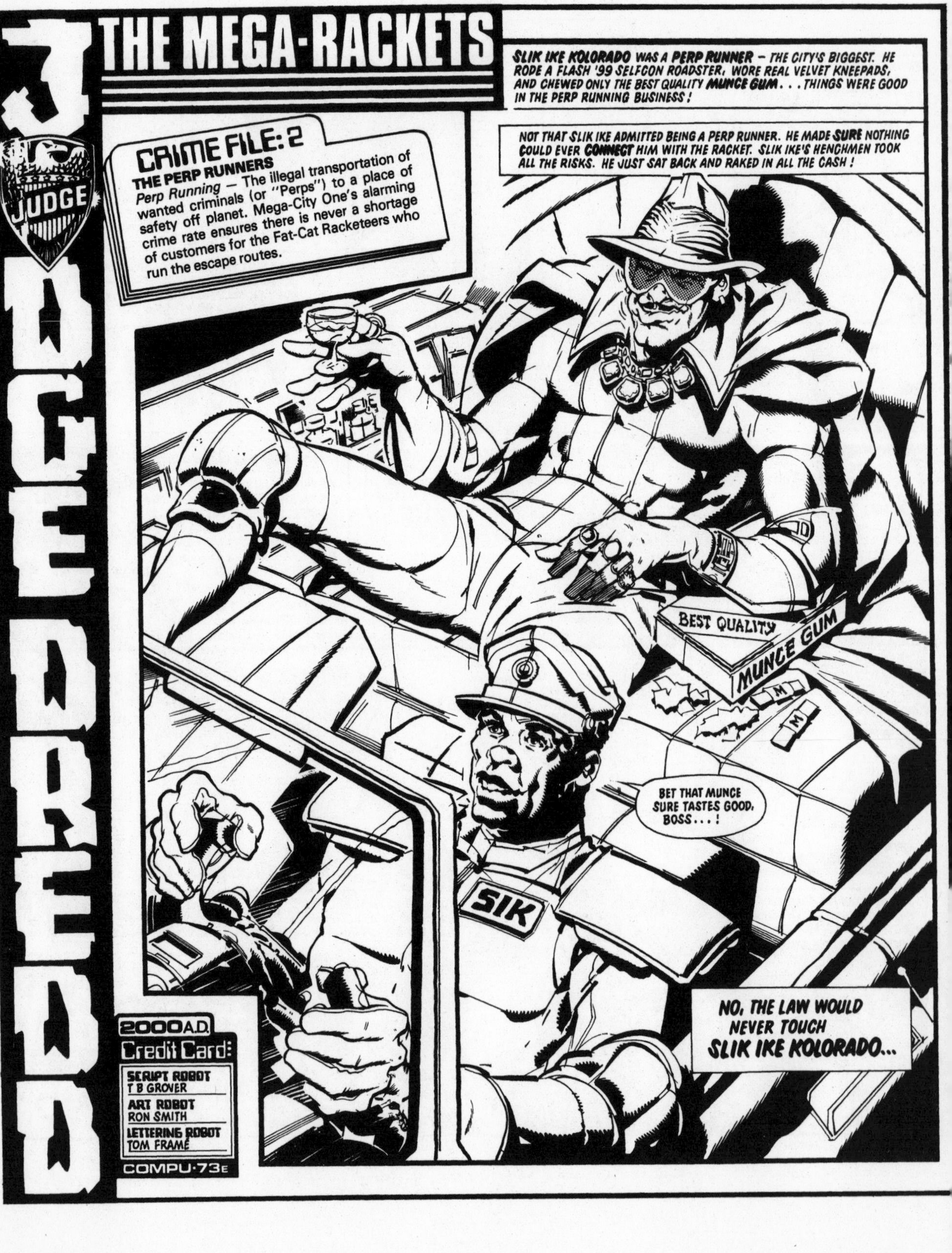
JUDGE DREDD
JUDGE
THE MEGA-RACKETS
SLIK IKE KOLORADO WAS A PERP RUNNER – THE CITY'S BIGGEST. HE RODE A FLASH '99 SELFCON ROADSTER, WORE REAL VELVET KNEEPADS, AND CHEWED ONLY THE BEST QUALITY MUNCE GUM . . . THINGS WERE GOOD IN THE PERP RUNNING BUSINESS!
CRIME FILE: 2
THE PERP RUNNERS
Perp Running – The illegal transportation of wanted criminals (or "Perps") to a place of safety off planet. Mega-City One's alarming crime rate ensures there is never a shortage of customers for the Fat-Cat Racketeers who run the escape routes.
NOT THAT SLIK IKE ADMITTED BEING A PERP RUNNER. HE MADE SURE NOTHING COULD EVER CONNECT HIM WITH THE RACKET. SLIK IKE'S HENCHMEN TOOK ALL THE RISKS. HE JUST SAT BACK AND RAKED IN ALL THE CASH!
BEST QUALITY
MUNCE GUM
BET THAT MUNCE SURE TASTES GOOD, BOSS . . . !
SIK
NO, THE LAW WOULD NEVER TOUCH SLIK IKE KOLORADO...
2000 A.D. Credit Card:
SCRIPT ROBOT T B GROVER
ART ROBOT RON SMITH
LETTERING ROBOT TOM FRAMÉ
COMPU·73E

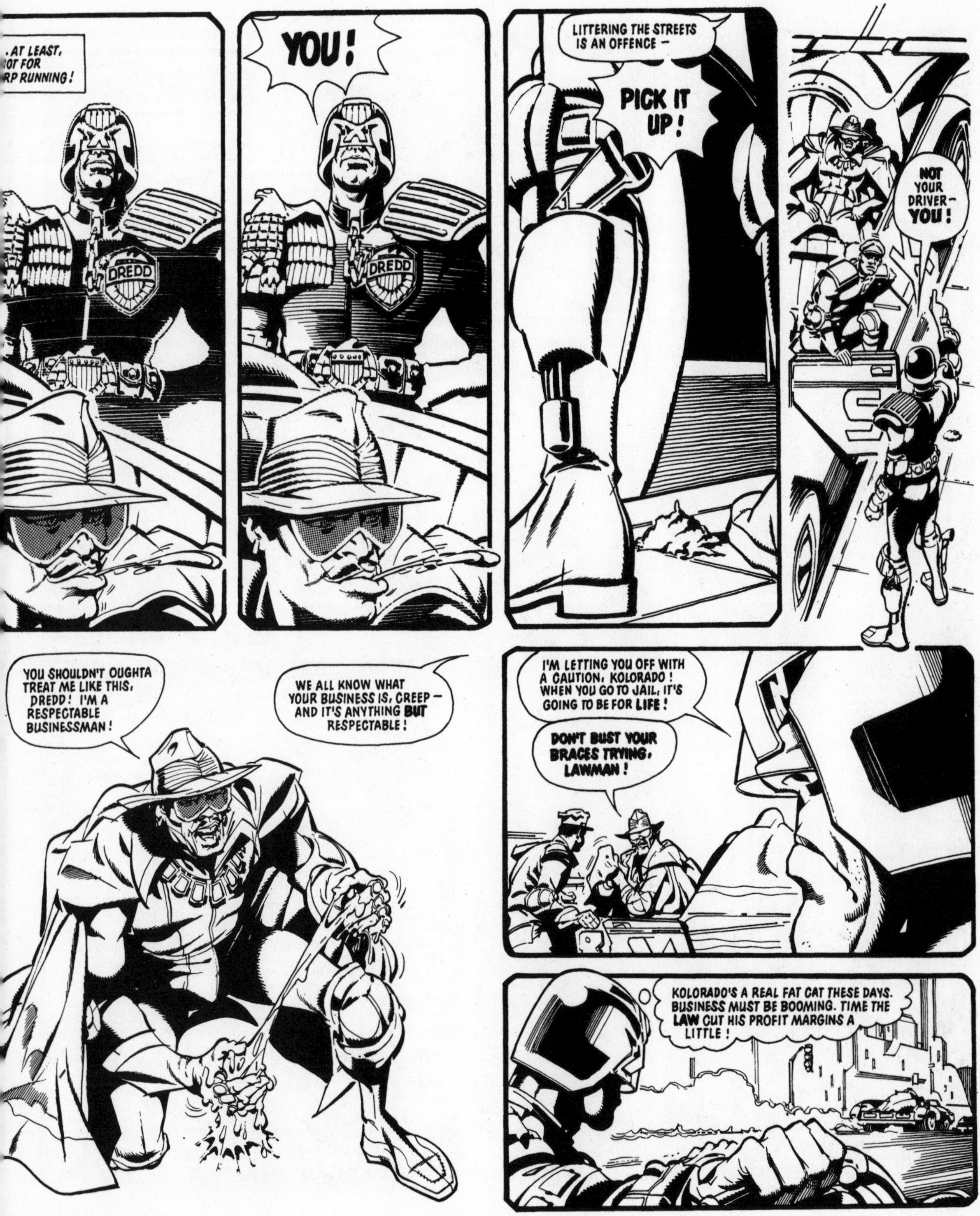

. AT LEAST, OT FOR RP RUNNING!
YOU!
LITTERING THE STREETS IS AN OFFENCE —
PICK IT UP!
NOT YOUR DRIVER— YOU!
YOU SHOULDN'T OUGHTA TREAT ME LIKE THIS, DREDD! I'M A RESPECTABLE BUSINESSMAN!
WE ALL KNOW WHAT YOUR BUSINESS IS, CREEP — AND IT'S ANYTHING BUT RESPECTABLE!
I'M LETTING YOU OFF WITH A CAUTION, KOLORADO! WHEN YOU GO TO JAIL, IT'S GOING TO BE FOR LIFE!
DON'T BUST YOUR BRACES TRYING, LAWMAN!
KOLORADO'S A REAL FAT CAT THESE DAYS. BUSINESS MUST BE BOOMING. TIME THE LAW CUT HIS PROFIT MARGINS A LITTLE!

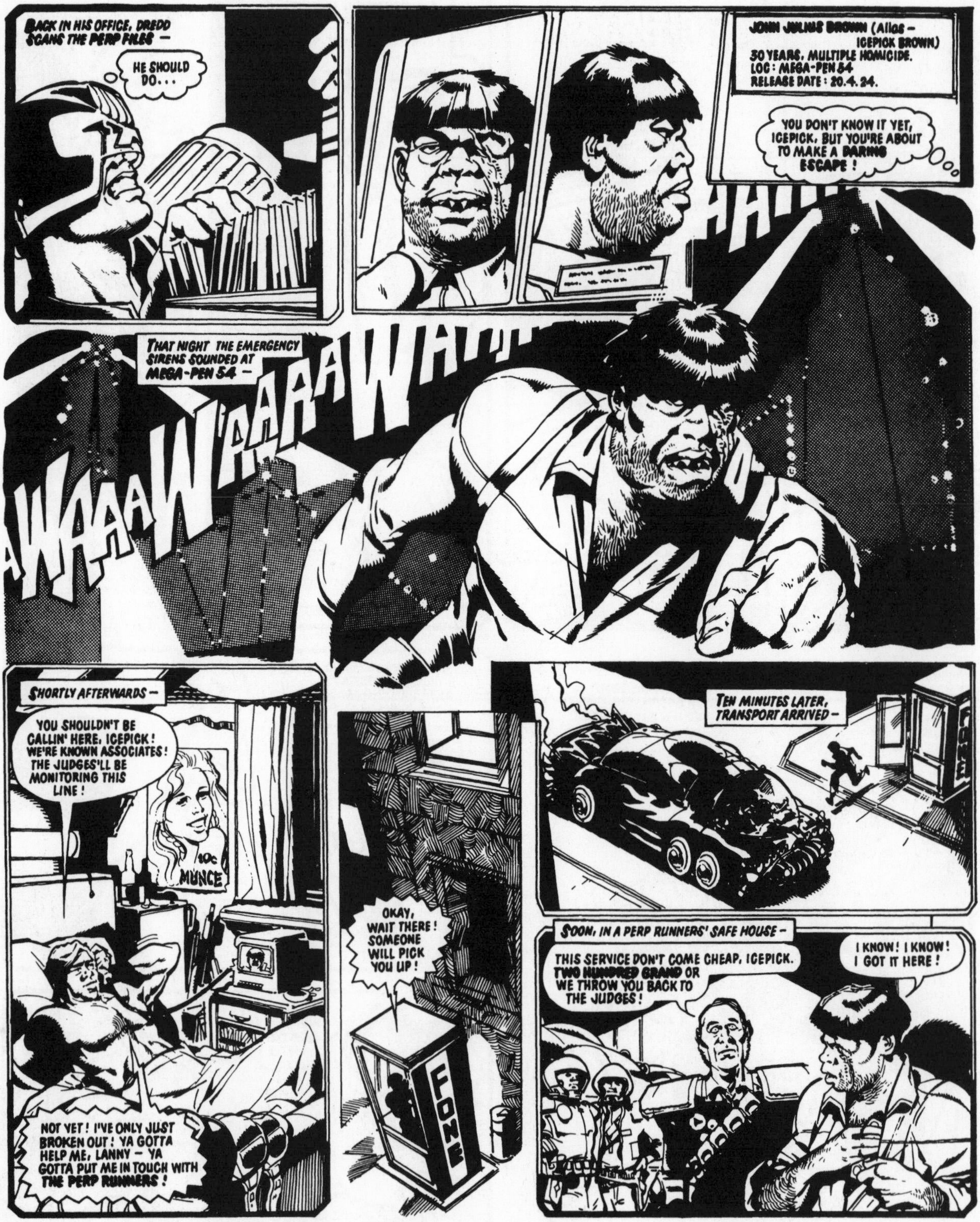
BACK IN HIS OFFICE, DREDD SCANS THE PERP FILES –
HE SHOULD DO...
JOHN JULIUS BROWN (Alias – ICEPICK BROWN)
30 YEARS, MULTIPLE HOMICIDE.
LOC : MEGA-PEN 54
RELEASE DATE : 20.4.24.
YOU DON'T KNOW IT YET, ICEPICK, BUT YOU'RE ABOUT TO MAKE A DARING ESCAPE !
THAT NIGHT THE EMERGENCY SIRENS SOUNDED AT MEGA-PEN 54 –
AWAAAWAARAAWAHHH
SHORTLY AFTERWARDS –
YOU SHOULDN'T BE CALLIN' HERE, ICEPICK! WE'RE KNOWN ASSOCIATES! THE JUDGES'LL BE MONITORING THIS LINE!
MUNCE
NOT YET! I'VE ONLY JUST BROKEN OUT! YA GOTTA HELP ME, LANNY – YA GOTTA PUT ME IN TOUCH WITH THE PERP RUNNERS!
OKAY, WAIT THERE! SOMEONE WILL PICK YOU UP!
FONE
TEN MINUTES LATER, TRANSPORT ARRIVED –
FONE
SOON, IN A PERP RUNNERS' SAFE HOUSE –
THIS SERVICE DON'T COME CHEAP, ICEPICK. TWO HUNDRED GRAND OR WE THROW YOU BACK TO THE JUDGES!
I KNOW! I KNOW! I GOT IT HERE!

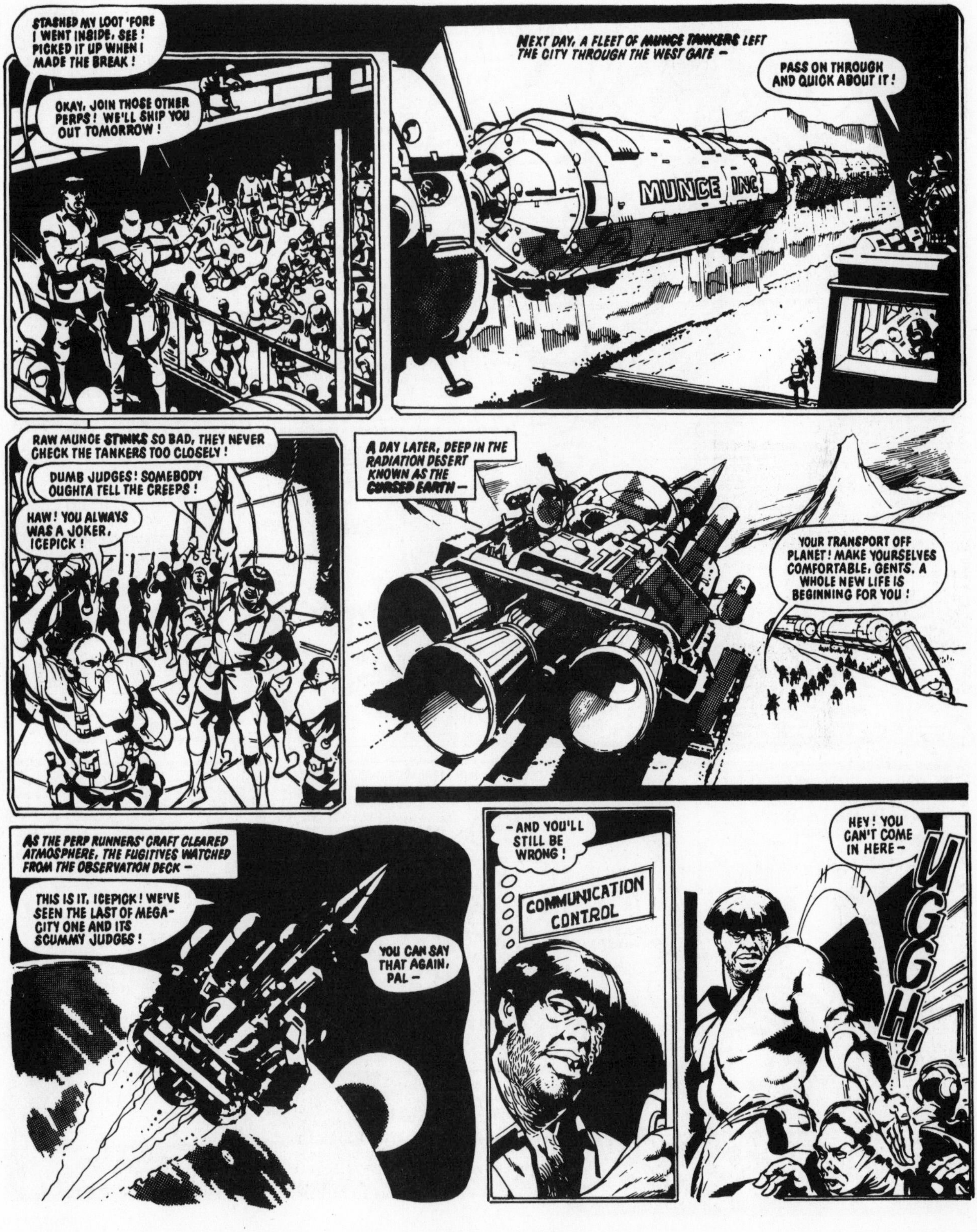

STASHED MY LOOT 'FORE I WENT INSIDE, SEE! PICKED IT UP WHEN I MADE THE BREAK!
OKAY, JOIN THOSE OTHER PERPS! WE'LL SHIP YOU OUT TOMORROW!
NEXT DAY, A FLEET OF MUNCE TANKERS LEFT THE CITY THROUGH THE WEST GATE —
PASS ON THROUGH AND QUICK ABOUT IT!
MUNCE INC
RAW MUNCE STINKS SO BAD, THEY NEVER CHECK THE TANKERS TOO CLOSELY!
DUMB JUDGES! SOMEBODY OUGHTA TELL THE CREEPS!
HAW! YOU ALWAYS WAS A JOKER, ICEPICK!
A DAY LATER, DEEP IN THE RADIATION DESERT KNOWN AS THE CURSED EARTH —
YOUR TRANSPORT OFF PLANET! MAKE YOURSELVES COMFORTABLE, GENTS. A WHOLE NEW LIFE IS BEGINNING FOR YOU!
AS THE PERP RUNNERS' CRAFT CLEARED ATMOSPHERE, THE FUGITIVES WATCHED FROM THE OBSERVATION DECK —
THIS IS IT, ICEPICK! WE'VE SEEN THE LAST OF MEGA-CITY ONE AND ITS SCUMMY JUDGES!
YOU CAN SAY THAT AGAIN, PAL —
— AND YOU'LL STILL BE WRONG!
COMMUNICATION CONTROL
HEY! YOU CAN'T COME IN HERE —
UGGH!

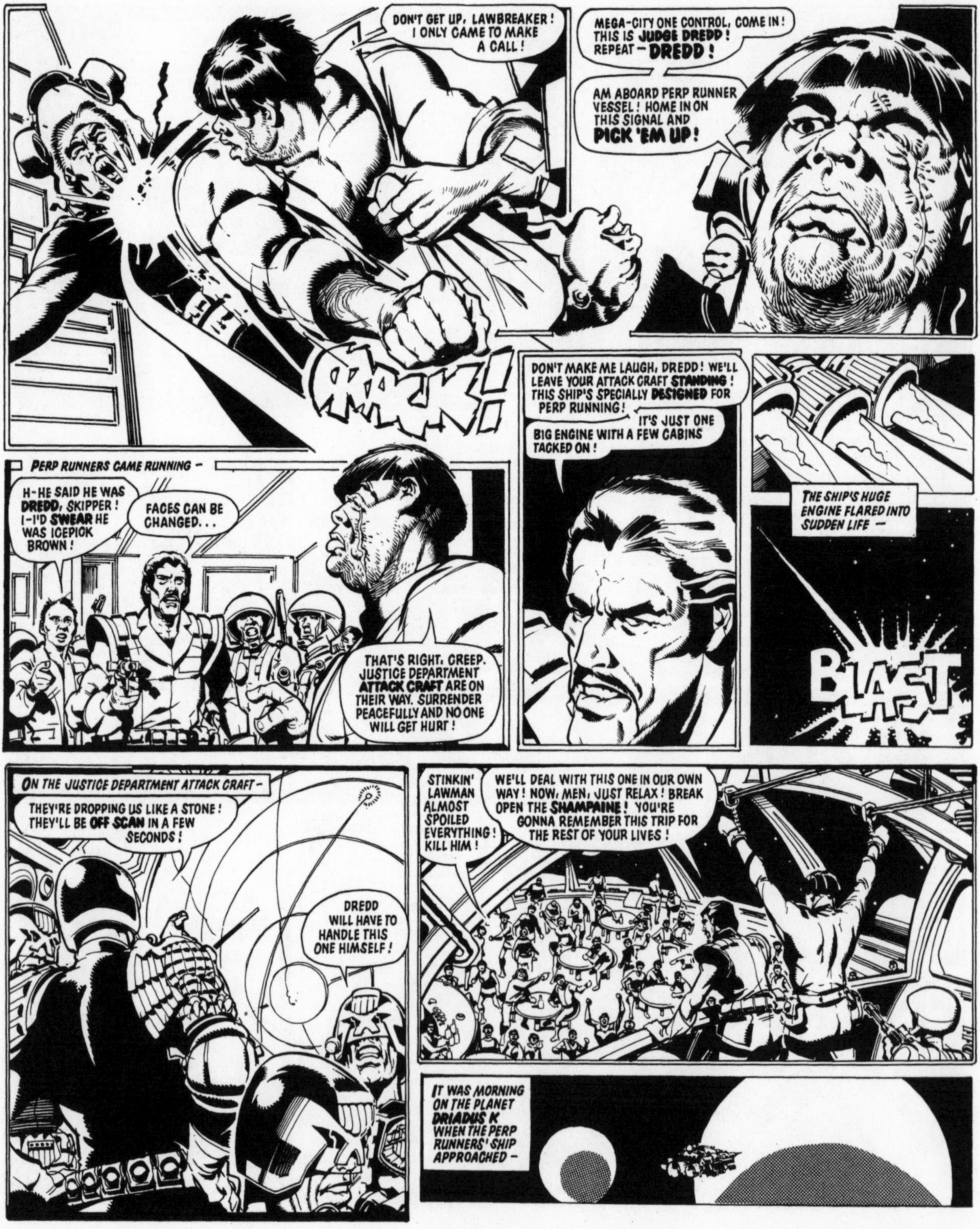
DON'T GET UP, LAWBREAKER! I ONLY CAME TO MAKE A CALL!
CRACK!
MEGA-CITY ONE CONTROL, COME IN! THIS IS JUDGE DREDD! REPEAT – DREDD!
AM ABOARD PERP RUNNER VESSEL! HOME IN ON THIS SIGNAL AND PICK 'EM UP!
PERP RUNNERS CAME RUNNING –
H-HE SAID HE WAS DREDD, SKIPPER! I-I'D SWEAR HE WAS ICEPICK BROWN!
FACES CAN BE CHANGED...
THAT'S RIGHT, CREEP. JUSTICE DEPARTMENT ATTACK CRAFT ARE ON THEIR WAY. SURRENDER PEACEFULLY AND NO ONE WILL GET HURT!
DON'T MAKE ME LAUGH, DREDD! WE'LL LEAVE YOUR ATTACK CRAFT STANDING! THIS SHIP'S SPECIALLY DESIGNED FOR PERP RUNNING!
IT'S JUST ONE BIG ENGINE WITH A FEW CABINS TACKED ON!
THE SHIP'S HUGE ENGINE FLARED INTO SUDDEN LIFE –
BLAST
ON THE JUSTICE DEPARTMENT ATTACK CRAFT –
THEY'RE DROPPING US LIKE A STONE! THEY'LL BE OFF SCAN IN A FEW SECONDS!
DREDD WILL HAVE TO HANDLE THIS ONE HIMSELF!
STINKIN' LAWMAN ALMOST SPOILED EVERYTHING! KILL HIM!
WE'LL DEAL WITH THIS ONE IN OUR OWN WAY! NOW, MEN, JUST RELAX! BREAK OPEN THE SHAMPAINE! YOU'RE GONNA REMEMBER THIS TRIP FOR THE REST OF YOUR LIVES!
IT WAS MORNING ON THE PLANET DRIADUS K WHEN THE PERP RUNNERS' SHIP APPROACHED –

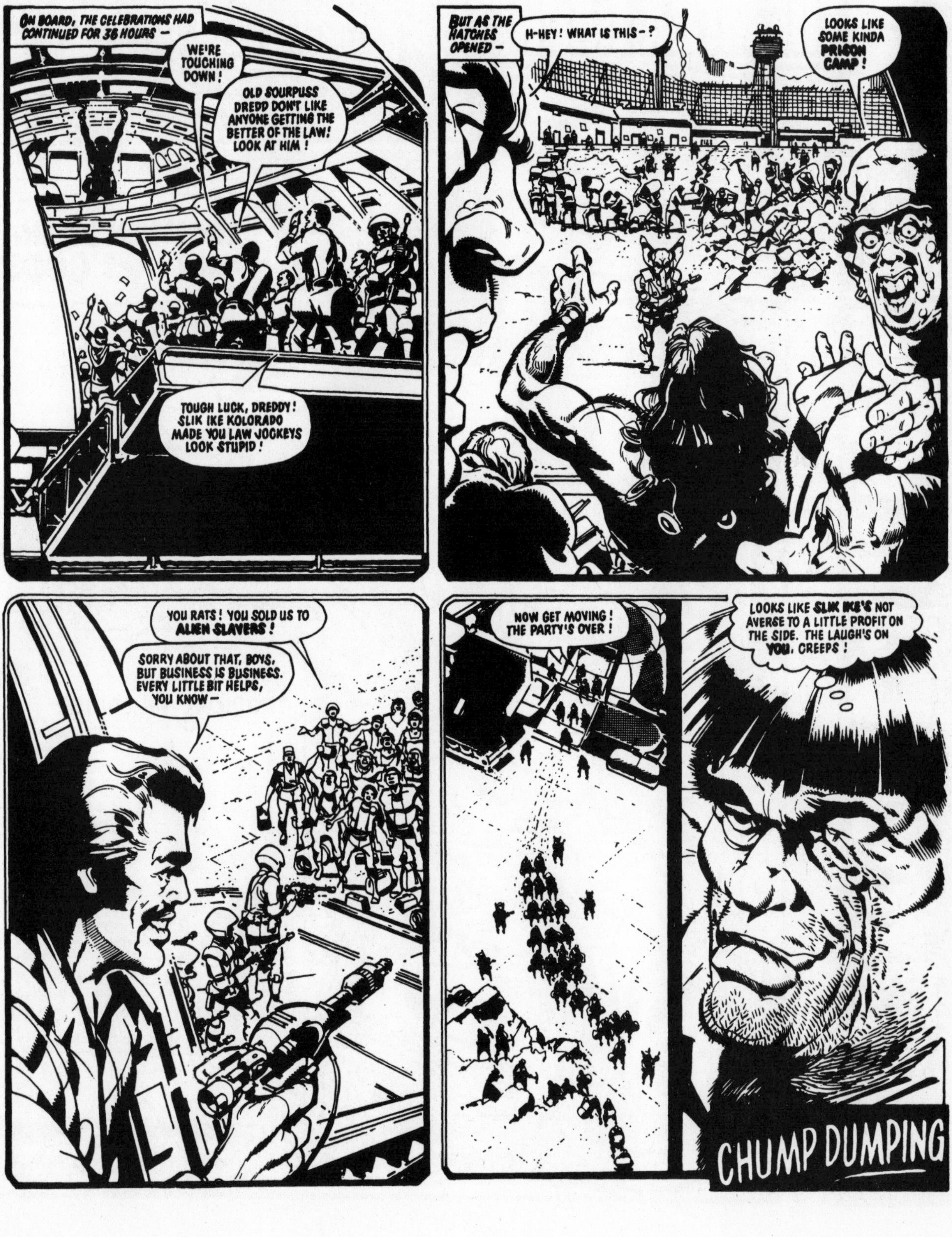
ON BOARD, THE CELEBRATIONS HAD CONTINUED FOR 36 HOURS –
WE'RE TOUCHING DOWN!
OLD SOURPUSS DREDD DON'T LIKE ANYONE GETTING THE BETTER OF THE LAW! LOOK AT HIM!
TOUGH LUCK, DREDDY! SLIK IKE KOLORADO MADE YOU LAW JOCKEYS LOOK STUPID!
BUT AS THE HATCHES OPENED –
H-HEY! WHAT IS THIS –?
LOOKS LIKE SOME KINDA PRISON CAMP!
YOU RATS! YOU SOLD US TO ALIEN SLAVERS!
SORRY ABOUT THAT, BOYS, BUT BUSINESS IS BUSINESS. EVERY LITTLE BIT HELPS, YOU KNOW –
NOW GET MOVING! THE PARTY'S OVER!
LOOKS LIKE SLIK IKE'S NOT AVERSE TO A LITTLE PROFIT ON THE SIDE. THE LAUGH'S ON YOU, CREEPS!
CHUMP DUMPING

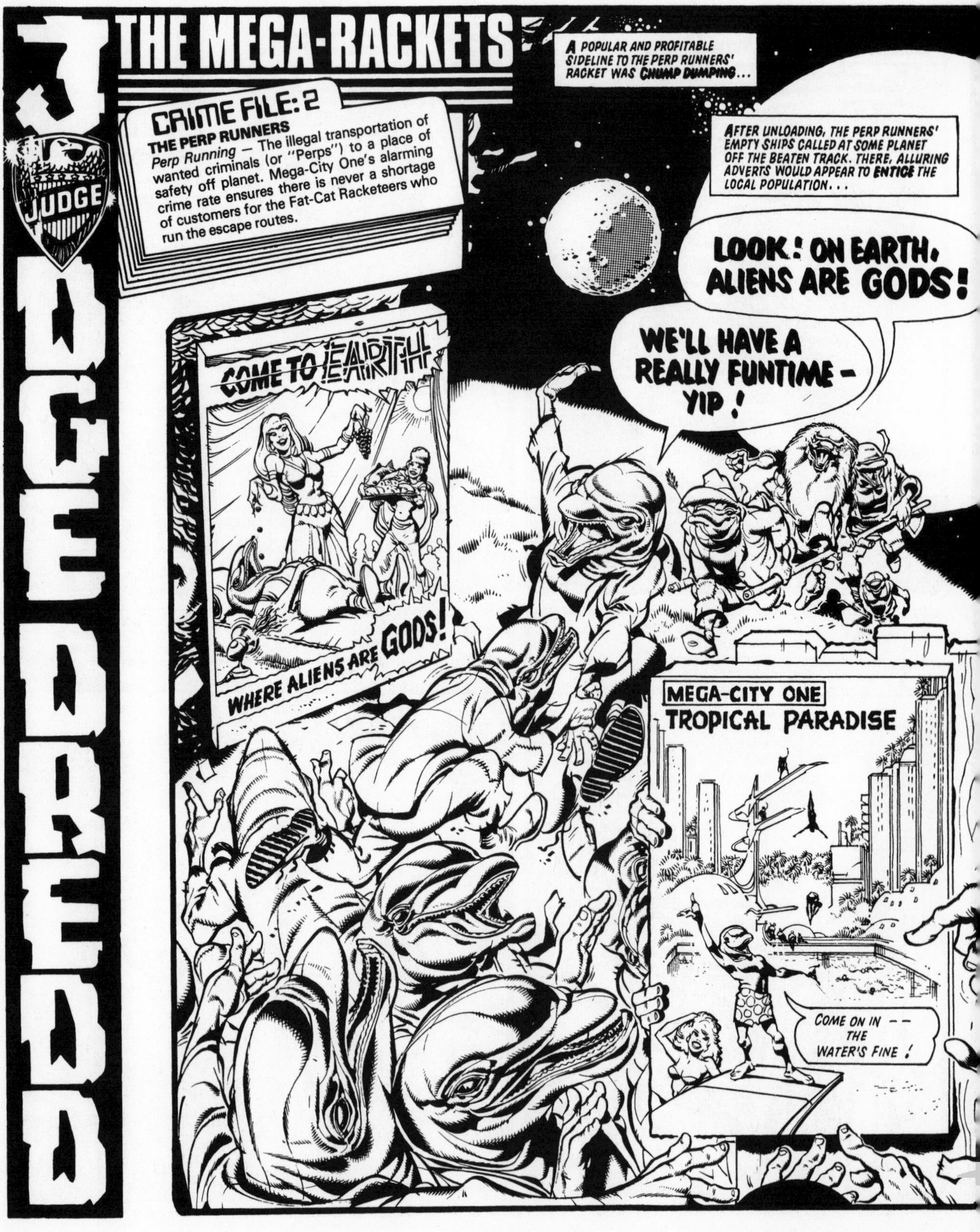
JUDGE DREDD
THE MEGA-RACKETS
A POPULAR AND PROFITABLE SIDELINE TO THE PERP RUNNERS' RACKET WAS CHUMP DUMPING...
CRIME FILE: 2
THE PERP RUNNERS
Perp Running — The illegal transportation of wanted criminals (or "Perps") to a place of safety off planet. Mega-City One's alarming crime rate ensures there is never a shortage of customers for the Fat-Cat Racketeers who run the escape routes.
AFTER UNLOADING, THE PERP RUNNERS' EMPTY SHIPS CALLED AT SOME PLANET OFF THE BEATEN TRACK. THERE, ALLURING ADVERTS WOULD APPEAR TO ENTICE THE LOCAL POPULATION...
LOOK! ON EARTH, ALIENS ARE GODS!
WE'LL HAVE A REALLY FUNTIME - YIP!
COME TO EARTH
WHERE ALIENS ARE GODS!
MEGA-CITY ONE
TROPICAL PARADISE
COME ON IN -- THE WATER'S FINE!

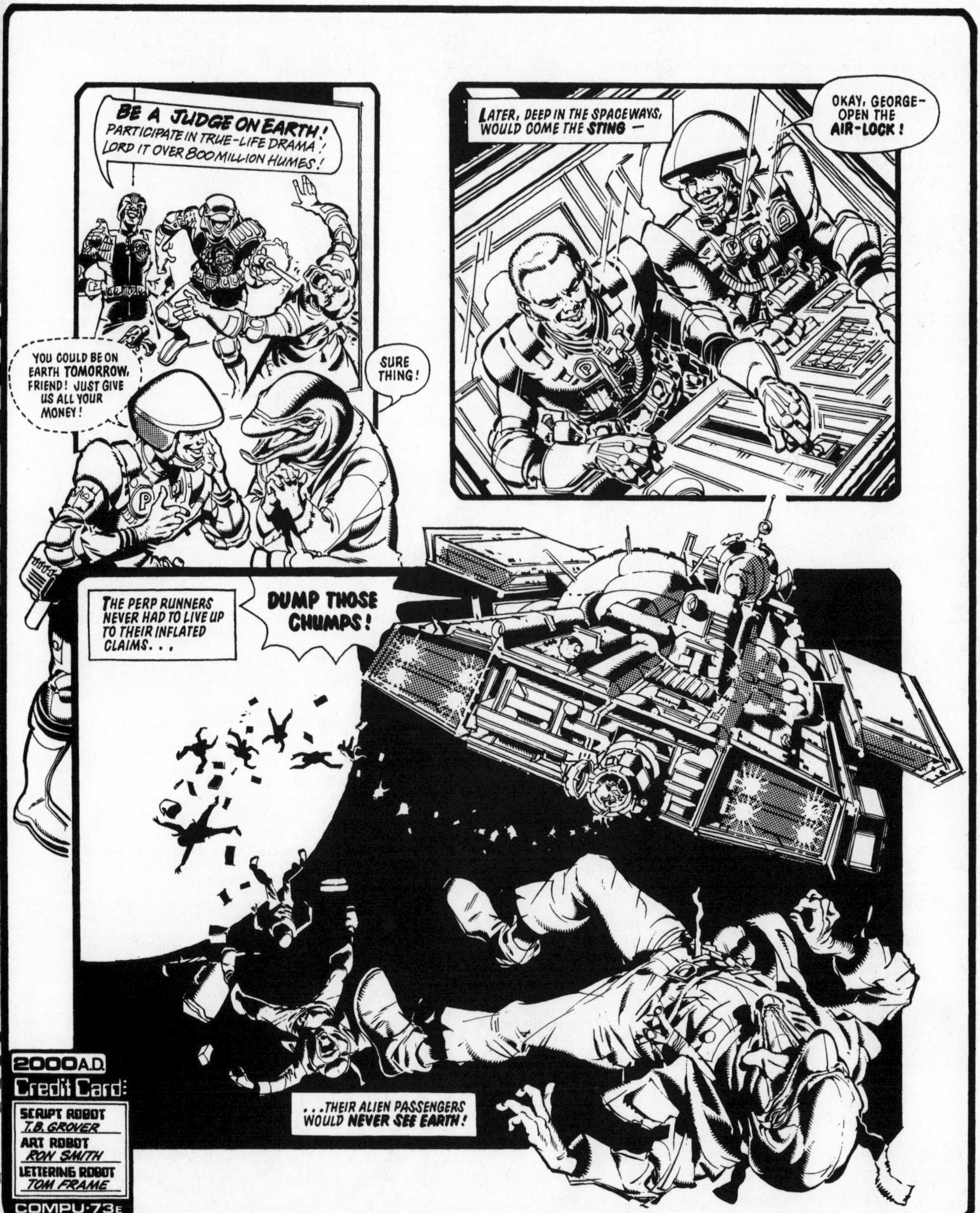
BE A JUDGE ON EARTH!
PARTICIPATE IN TRUE-LIFE DRAMA!
LORD IT OVER 800 MILLION HUMES!
YOU COULD BE ON EARTH TOMORROW, FRIEND! JUST GIVE US ALL YOUR MONEY!
SURE THING!
LATER, DEEP IN THE SPACEWAYS, WOULD COME THE STING —
OKAY, GEORGE- OPEN THE AIR-LOCK!
THE PERP RUNNERS NEVER HAD TO LIVE UP TO THEIR INFLATED CLAIMS...
DUMP THOSE CHUMPS!
...THEIR ALIEN PASSENGERS WOULD NEVER SEE EARTH!
2000 A.D.
Credit Card:
SCRIPT ROBOT T.B. GROVER
ART ROBOT RON SMITH
LETTERING ROBOT TOM FRAME
COMPU·73E

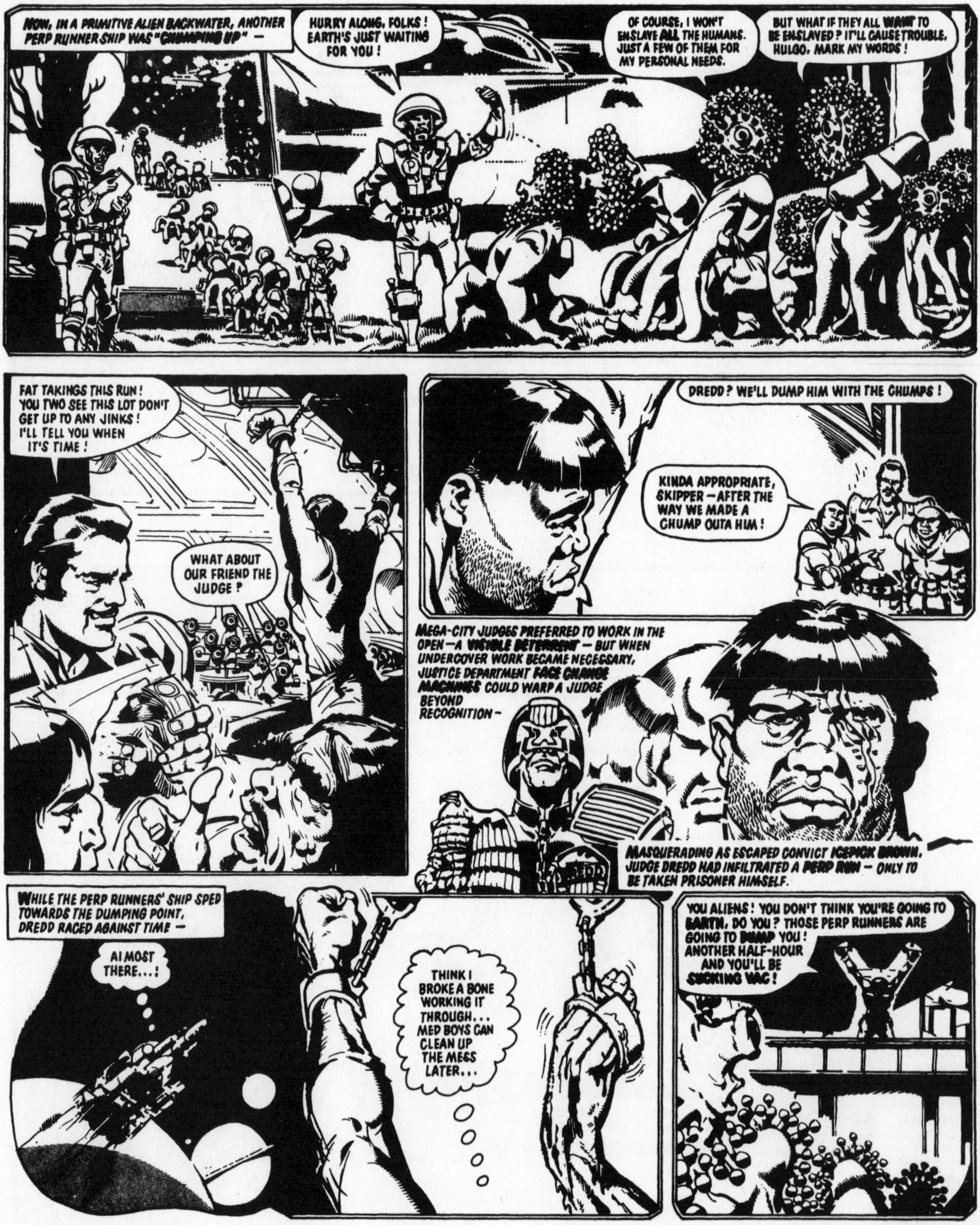
NOW, IN A PRIMITIVE ALIEN BACKWATER, ANOTHER PERP RUNNER SHIP WAS "CHUMPING UP" —
HURRY ALONG, FOLKS! EARTH'S JUST WAITING FOR YOU!
OF COURSE, I WON'T ENSLAVE ALL THE HUMANS. JUST A FEW OF THEM FOR MY PERSONAL NEEDS.
BUT WHAT IF THEY ALL WANT TO BE ENSLAVED? IT'LL CAUSE TROUBLE, HULGO, MARK MY WORDS!
FAT TAKINGS THIS RUN! YOU TWO SEE THIS LOT DON'T GET UP TO ANY JINKS! I'LL TELL YOU WHEN IT'S TIME!
WHAT ABOUT OUR FRIEND THE JUDGE?
DREDD? WE'LL DUMP HIM WITH THE CHUMPS!
KINDA APPROPRIATE, SKIPPER — AFTER THE WAY WE MADE A CHUMP OUTA HIM!
MEGA-CITY JUDGES PREFERRED TO WORK IN THE OPEN — A VISIBLE DETERRENT — BUT WHEN UNDERCOVER WORK BECAME NECESSARY, JUSTICE DEPARTMENT FACE CHANGE MACHINES COULD WARP A JUDGE BEYOND RECOGNITION —
MASQUERADING AS ESCAPED CONVICT ICEPICK BROWN, JUDGE DREDD HAD INFILTRATED A PERP RUN — ONLY TO BE TAKEN PRISONER HIMSELF.
WHILE THE PERP RUNNERS' SHIP SPED TOWARDS THE DUMPING POINT, DREDD RACED AGAINST TIME —
ALMOST THERE...!
THINK I BROKE A BONE WORKING IT THROUGH... MED BOYS CAN CLEAN UP THE MESS LATER...
YOU ALIENS! YOU DON'T THINK YOU'RE GOING TO EARTH, DO YOU? THOSE PERP RUNNERS ARE GOING TO DUMP YOU! ANOTHER HALF-HOUR AND YOU'LL BE SUCKING VAC!

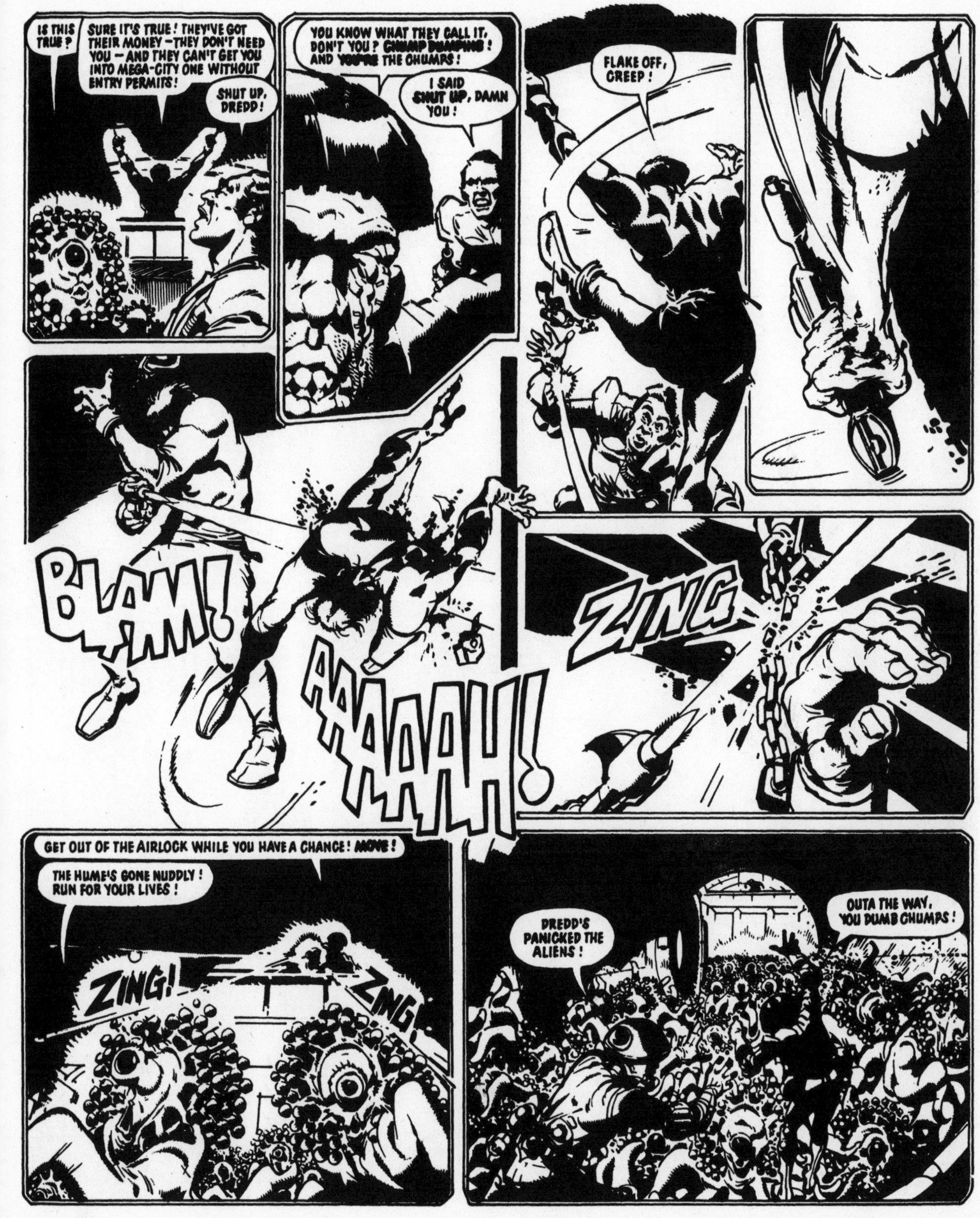

IS THIS TRUE?
SURE IT'S TRUE! THEY'VE GOT THEIR MONEY — THEY DON'T NEED YOU — AND THEY CAN'T GET YOU INTO MEGA-CITY ONE WITHOUT ENTRY PERMITS!
SHUT UP, DREDD!
YOU KNOW WHAT THEY CALL IT, DON'T YOU? CHUMP DUMPING! AND YOU'RE THE CHUMPS!
I SAID SHUT UP, DAMN YOU!
FLAKE OFF, CREEP!
BLAM!
AAAAAH!
ZING
GET OUT OF THE AIRLOCK WHILE YOU HAVE A CHANCE! MOVE!
THE HUME'S GONE NUDDLY! RUN FOR YOUR LIVES!
ZING!
ZING
DREDD'S PANICKED THE ALIENS!
OUTA THE WAY, YOU DUMB CHUMPS!

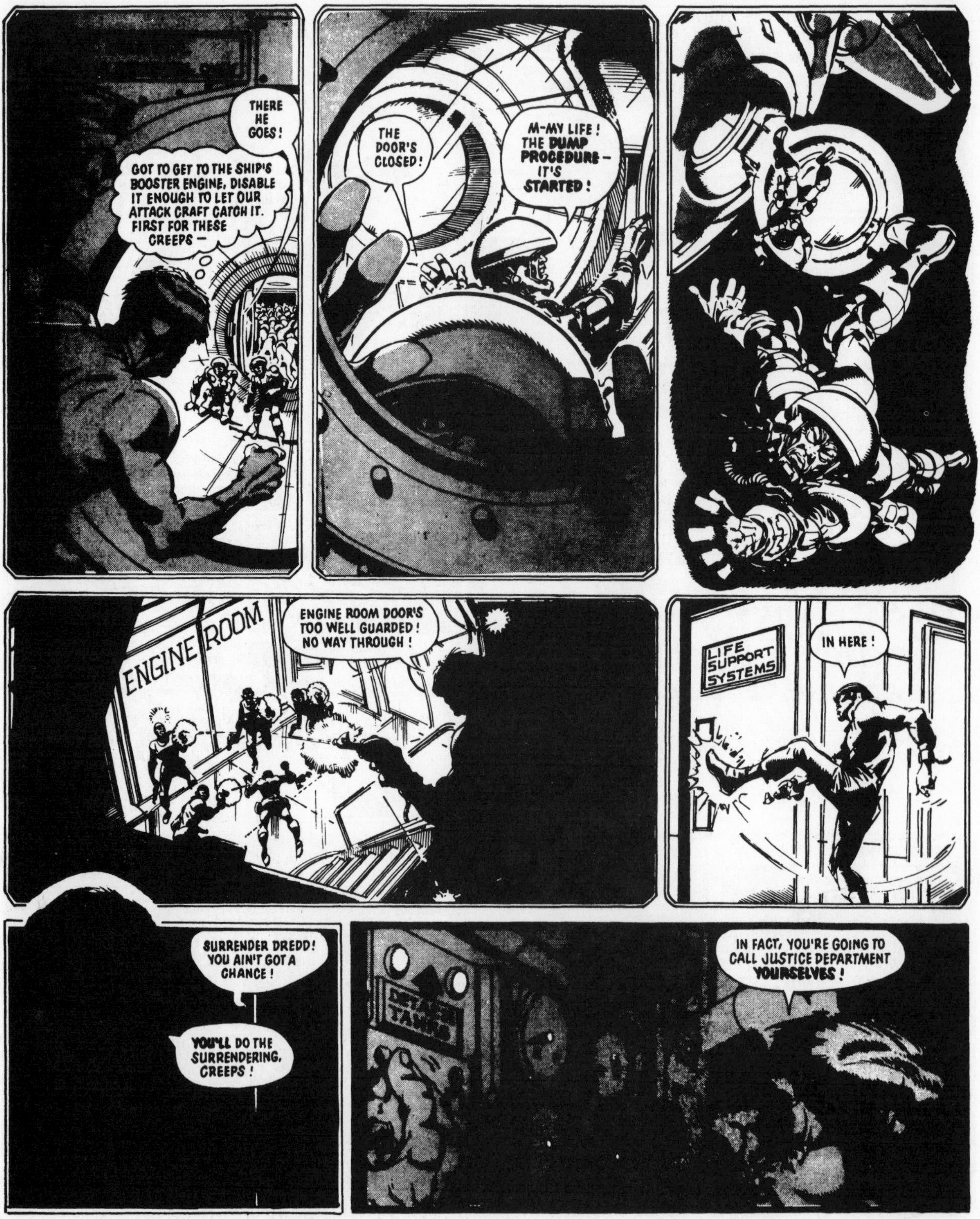
THERE HE GOES!
GOT TO GET TO THE SHIP'S BOOSTER ENGINE, DISABLE IT ENOUGH TO LET OUR ATTACK CRAFT CATCH IT. FIRST FOR THESE CREEPS –
THE DOOR'S CLOSED!
M-MY LIFE! THE DUMP PROCEDURE – IT'S STARTED!
ENGINE ROOM
ENGINE ROOM DOOR'S TOO WELL GUARDED! NO WAY THROUGH!
LIFE SUPPORT SYSTEMS
IN HERE!
SURRENDER DREDD! YOU AIN'T GOT A CHANCE!
YOU'LL DO THE SURRENDERING, CREEPS!
IN FACT, YOU'RE GOING TO CALL JUSTICE DEPARTMENT YOURSELVES!

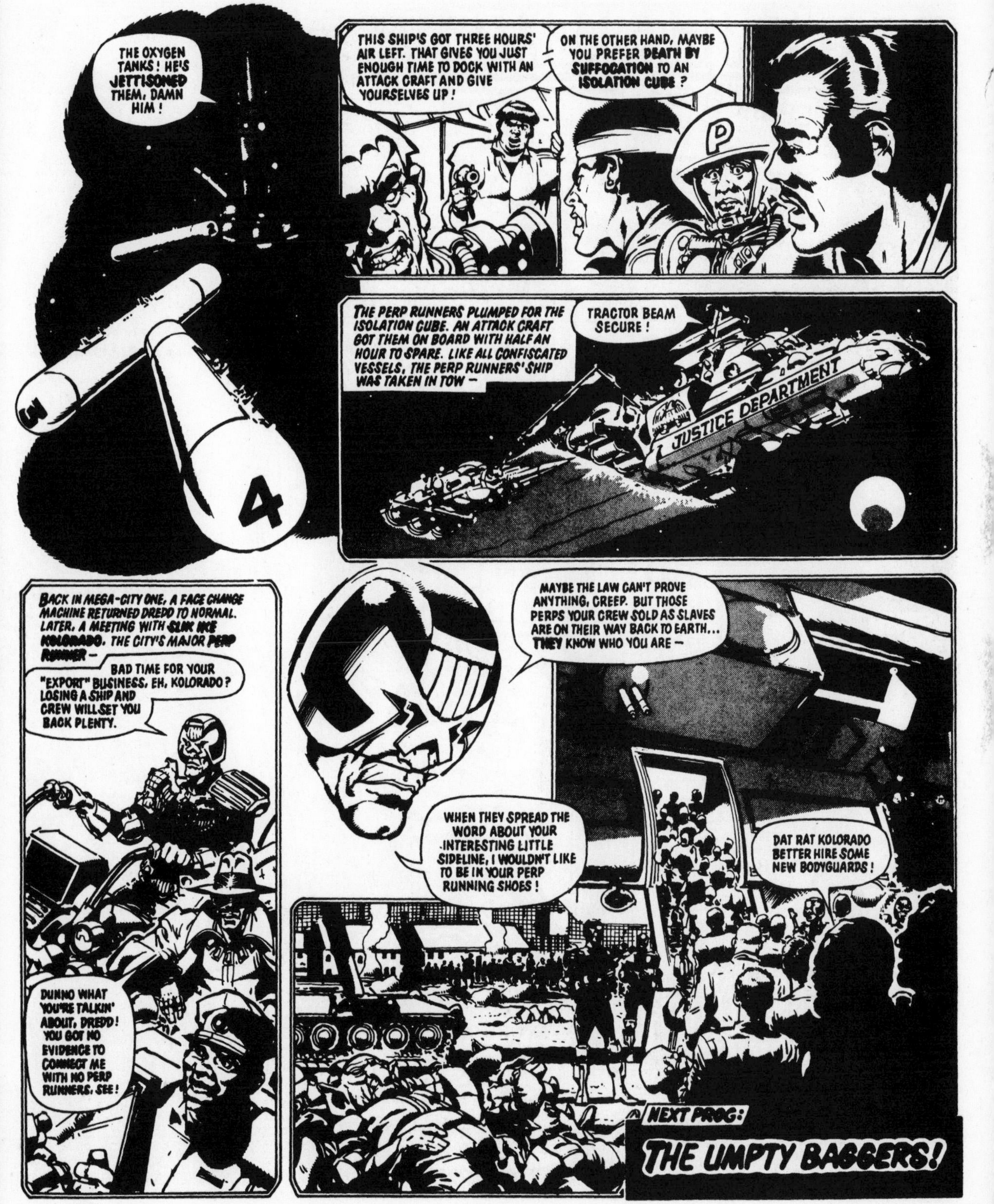
THE OXYGEN TANKS! HE'S JETTISONED THEM, DAMN HIM!
3
4
THIS SHIP'S GOT THREE HOURS' AIR LEFT. THAT GIVES YOU JUST ENOUGH TIME TO DOCK WITH AN ATTACK CRAFT AND GIVE YOURSELVES UP!
ON THE OTHER HAND, MAYBE YOU PREFER DEATH BY SUFFOCATION TO AN ISOLATION CUBE?
P
THE PERP RUNNERS PLUMPED FOR THE ISOLATION CUBE. AN ATTACK CRAFT GOT THEM ON BOARD WITH HALF AN HOUR TO SPARE. LIKE ALL CONFISCATED VESSELS, THE PERP RUNNERS' SHIP WAS TAKEN IN TOW –
TRACTOR BEAM SECURE!
JUSTICE DEPARTMENT
BACK IN MEGA-CITY ONE, A FACE CHANGE MACHINE RETURNED DREDD TO NORMAL. LATER, A MEETING WITH SLICK NICE KOLORADO, THE CITY'S MAJOR PERP RUNNER –
BAD TIME FOR YOUR "EXPORT" BUSINESS, EH, KOLORADO? LOSING A SHIP AND CREW WILL SET YOU BACK PLENTY.
DUNNO WHAT YOU'RE TALKIN' ABOUT, DREDD! YOU GOT NO EVIDENCE TO CONNECT ME WITH NO PERP RUNNERS, SEE!
MAYBE THE LAW CAN'T PROVE ANYTHING, CREEP. BUT THOSE PERPS YOUR CREW SOLD AS SLAVES ARE ON THEIR WAY BACK TO EARTH... THEY KNOW WHO YOU ARE –
WHEN THEY SPREAD THE WORD ABOUT YOUR INTERESTING LITTLE SIDELINE, I WOULDN'T LIKE TO BE IN YOUR PERP RUNNING SHOES!
DAT RAT KOLORADO BETTER HIRE SOME NEW BODYGUARDS!
NEXT PROG:
THE UMPTY BAGGERS!

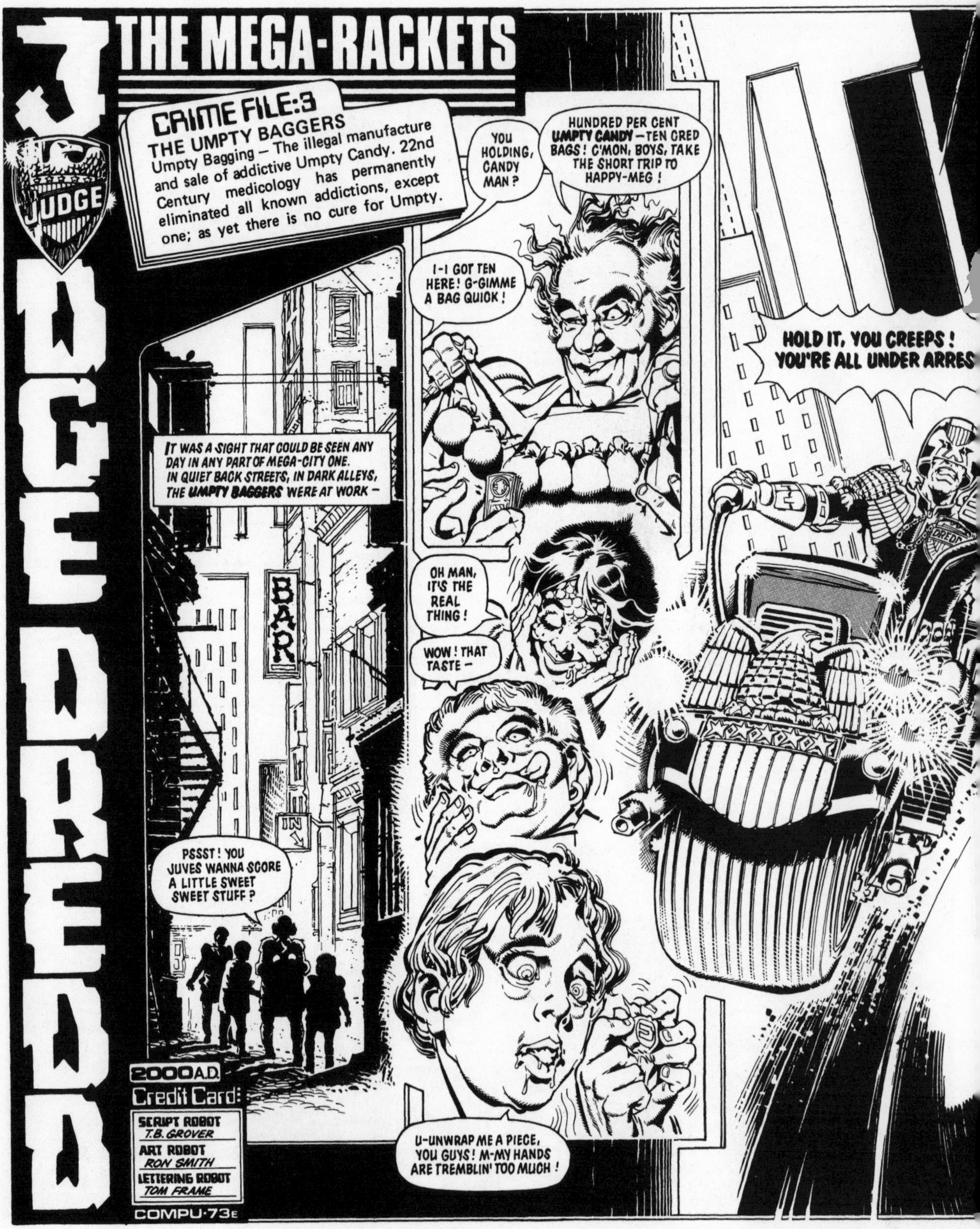
JUDGE DREDD
THE MEGA-RACKETS
CRIME FILE: 3
THE UMPTY BAGGERS
Umpty Bagging – The illegal manufacture and sale of addictive Umpty Candy. 22nd Century medicology has permanently eliminated all known addictions, except one; as yet there is no cure for Umpty.
IT WAS A SIGHT THAT COULD BE SEEN ANY DAY IN ANY PART OF MEGA-CITY ONE. IN QUIET BACK STREETS, IN DARK ALLEYS, THE UMPTY BAGGERS WERE AT WORK –
BAR
PSSST! YOU JUVES WANNA SCORE A LITTLE SWEET SWEET STUFF?
YOU HOLDING, CANDY MAN?
HUNDRED PER CENT UMPTY CANDY – TEN CRED BAGS! C'MON, BOYS, TAKE THE SHORT TRIP TO HAPPY-MEG!
I-I GOT TEN HERE! G-GIMME A BAG QUICK!
OH MAN, IT'S THE REAL THING!
WOW! THAT TASTE –
U-UNWRAP ME A PIECE, YOU GUYS! M-MY HANDS ARE TREMBLIN' TOO MUCH!
HOLD IT, YOU CREEPS! YOU'RE ALL UNDER ARRES
2000 A.D. Credit Card:
SCRIPT ROBOT T.B. GROVER
ART ROBOT RON SMITH
LETTERING ROBOT TOM FRAME
COMPU-73E

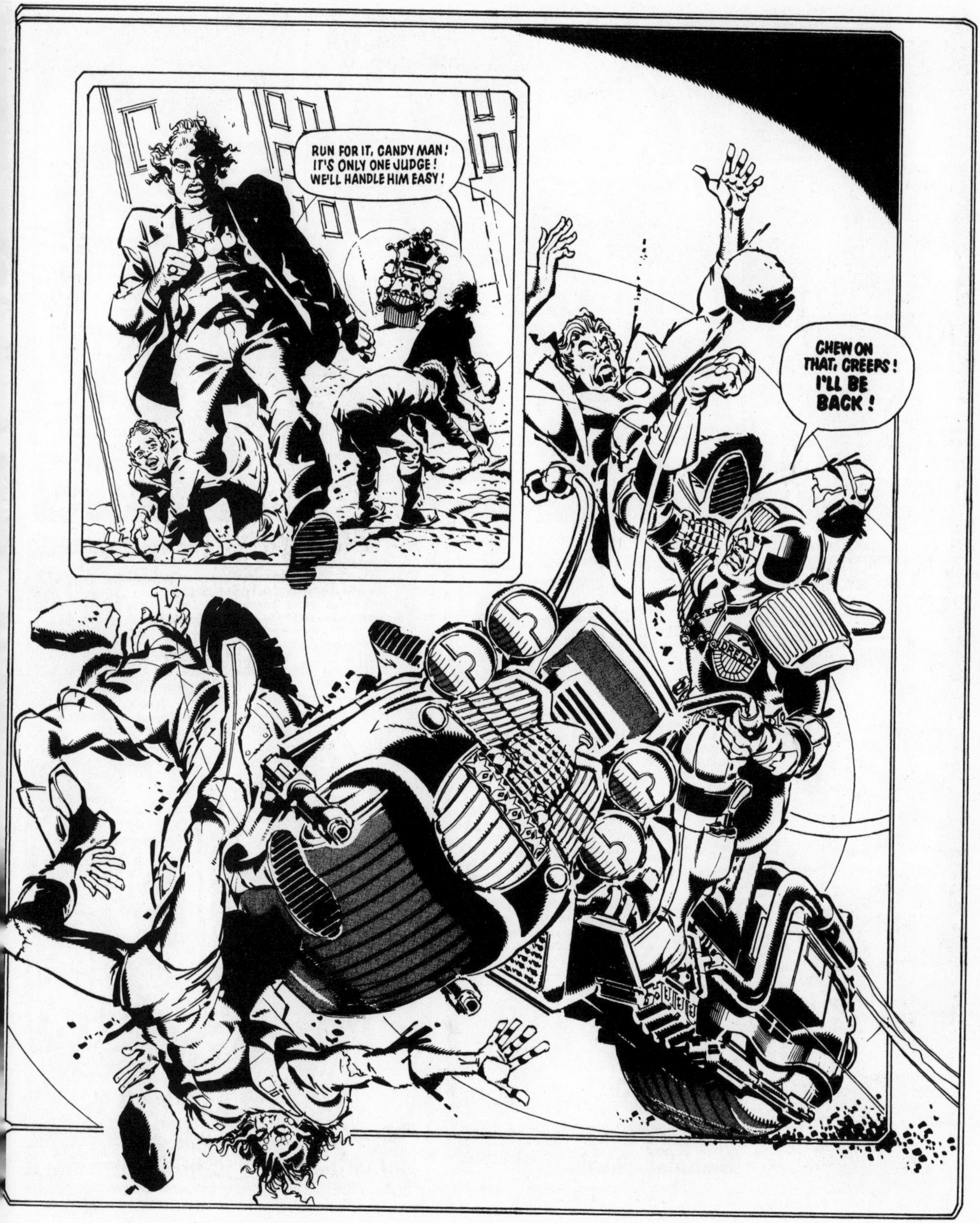
RUN FOR IT, CANDY MAN! IT'S ONLY ONE JUDGE! WE'LL HANDLE HIM EASY!
CHEW ON THAT, CREEPS! I'LL BE BACK!
DREDD

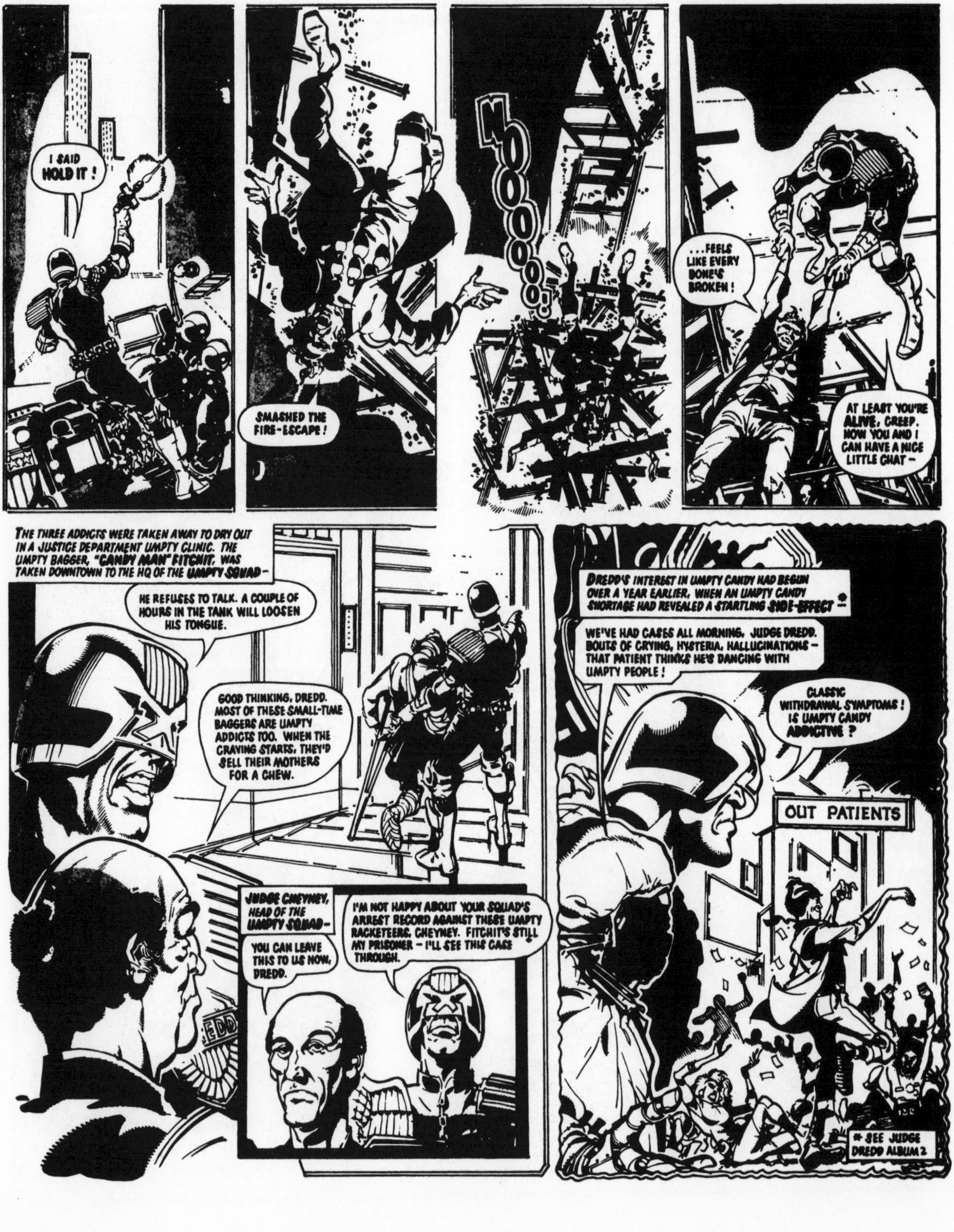
I SAID HOLD IT!
SMASHED THE FIRE-ESCAPE!
NOOOOOO!
...FEELS LIKE EVERY BONE'S BROKEN!
AT LEAST YOU'RE ALIVE, CREEP. NOW YOU AND I CAN HAVE A NICE LITTLE CHAT –
THE THREE ADDICTS WERE TAKEN AWAY TO DRY OUT IN A JUSTICE DEPARTMENT UMPTY CLINIC. THE UMPTY BAGGER, "CANDY MAN" FITCHIT, WAS TAKEN DOWNTOWN TO THE HQ OF THE UMPTY SQUAD –
HE REFUSES TO TALK. A COUPLE OF HOURS IN THE TANK WILL LOOSEN HIS TONGUE.
GOOD THINKING, DREDD. MOST OF THESE SMALL-TIME BAGGERS ARE UMPTY ADDICTS TOO. WHEN THE CRAVING STARTS, THEY'D SELL THEIR MOTHERS FOR A CHEW.
JUDGE CHEYNEY, HEAD OF THE UMPTY SQUAD –
YOU CAN LEAVE THIS TO US NOW, DREDD.
I'M NOT HAPPY ABOUT YOUR SQUAD'S ARREST RECORD AGAINST THESE UMPTY RACKETEERS, CHEYNEY. FITCHIT'S STILL MY PRISONER – I'LL SEE THIS CASE THROUGH.
DREDD'S INTEREST IN UMPTY CANDY HAD BEGUN OVER A YEAR EARLIER, WHEN AN UMPTY CANDY SHORTAGE HAD REVEALED A STARTLING SIDE-EFFECT *
WE'VE HAD CASES ALL MORNING, JUDGE DREDD. BOUTS OF CRYING, HYSTERIA, HALLUCINATIONS – THAT PATIENT THINKS HE'S DANCING WITH UMPTY PEOPLE!
CLASSIC WITHDRAWAL SYMPTOMS! IS UMPTY CANDY ADDICTIVE?
OUT PATIENTS
* SEE JUDGE DREDD ALBUM 2

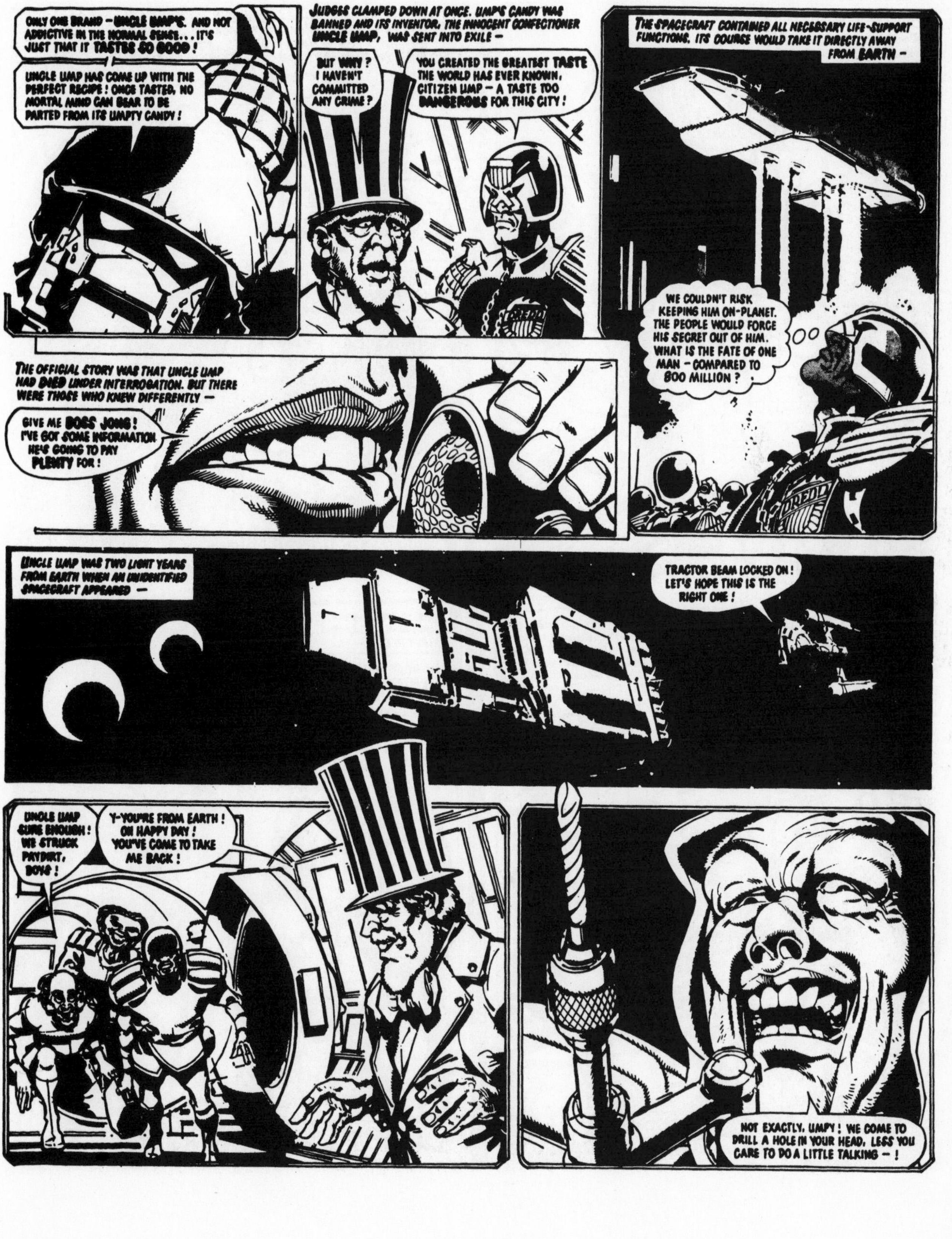

ONLY ONE BRAND — UNCLE UMP'S. AND NOT ADDICTIVE IN THE NORMAL SENSE... IT'S JUST THAT IT TASTES SO GOOD!
UNCLE UMP HAS COME UP WITH THE PERFECT RECIPE! ONCE TASTED, NO MORTAL MIND CAN BEAR TO BE PARTED FROM ITS UMPTY CANDY!
JUDGES CLAMPED DOWN AT ONCE. UMP'S CANDY WAS BANNED AND ITS INVENTOR, THE INNOCENT CONFECTIONER UNCLE UMP, WAS SENT INTO EXILE —
BUT WHY? I HAVEN'T COMMITTED ANY CRIME?
YOU CREATED THE GREATEST TASTE THE WORLD HAS EVER KNOWN, CITIZEN UMP — A TASTE TOO DANGEROUS FOR THIS CITY!
THE SPACECRAFT CONTAINED ALL NECESSARY LIFE-SUPPORT FUNCTIONS. ITS COURSE WOULD TAKE IT DIRECTLY AWAY FROM EARTH —
WE COULDN'T RISK KEEPING HIM ON-PLANET. THE PEOPLE WOULD FORCE HIS SECRET OUT OF HIM. WHAT IS THE FATE OF ONE MAN — COMPARED TO 800 MILLION?
THE OFFICIAL STORY WAS THAT UNCLE UMP HAD DIED UNDER INTERROGATION. BUT THERE WERE THOSE WHO KNEW DIFFERENTLY —
GIVE ME BOSS JONG! I'VE GOT SOME INFORMATION HE'S GOING TO PAY PLENTY FOR!
UNCLE UMP WAS TWO LIGHT YEARS FROM EARTH WHEN AN UNIDENTIFIED SPACECRAFT APPEARED —
TRACTOR BEAM LOCKED ON! LET'S HOPE THIS IS THE RIGHT ONE!
UNCLE UMP SURE ENOUGH! WE STRUCK PAYDIRT, BOYS!
Y-YOU'RE FROM EARTH! OH HAPPY DAY! YOU'VE COME TO TAKE ME BACK!
NOT EXACTLY, UMPY! WE COME TO DRILL A HOLE IN YOUR HEAD, LESS YOU CARE TO DO A LITTLE TALKING —!

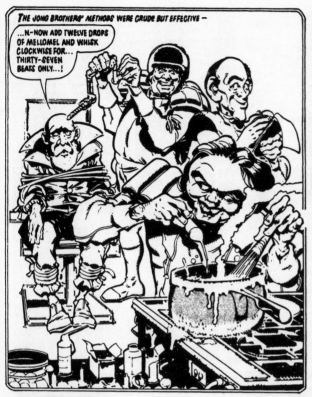

THE JONG BROTHERS' METHODS WERE CRUDE BUT EFFECTIVE —

...N-NOW ADD TWELVE DROPS OF MELLOMEL AND WHISK CLOCKWISE FOR... THIRTY-SEVEN BEATS ONLY...!

MMMM! THAT'S THE STUFF, ALL RIGHT!

YOU'VE BEEN A BIG HELP, UMPY. NOW I'M AFRAID IT'S TIME FOR YOU TO TAKE A LITTLE **SPACE WALK!**

LET'S GET BACK TO MA AND PA WITH THIS RECIPE, BOYS!

AND SO THE JONG FAMILY FOUNDED MEGA-CITY ONE'S NEWEST RACKET — UMPTY BAGGING —

EACH ONE OF US MEMORISES THE RECIPE. THEN WE **BURN** IT. THAT WAY IT ALWAYS STAYS IN THE FAMILY!

WE'LL PLAY THIS SMART — DON'T OVERLOAD THE MARKET — KEEP THE PRICE HIGH. THAT WAY, UMPTY BAGGING WILL MAKE US ALL BILLIONAIRES!

NOW, IN UMPTY SQUAD HQ, CANDY MAN FITCHIT WAS READY TO TALK —

LET ME OUTA HERE! UMPTY! **I NEED UMPTY!**

TALK FIRST — UMPTY LATER!

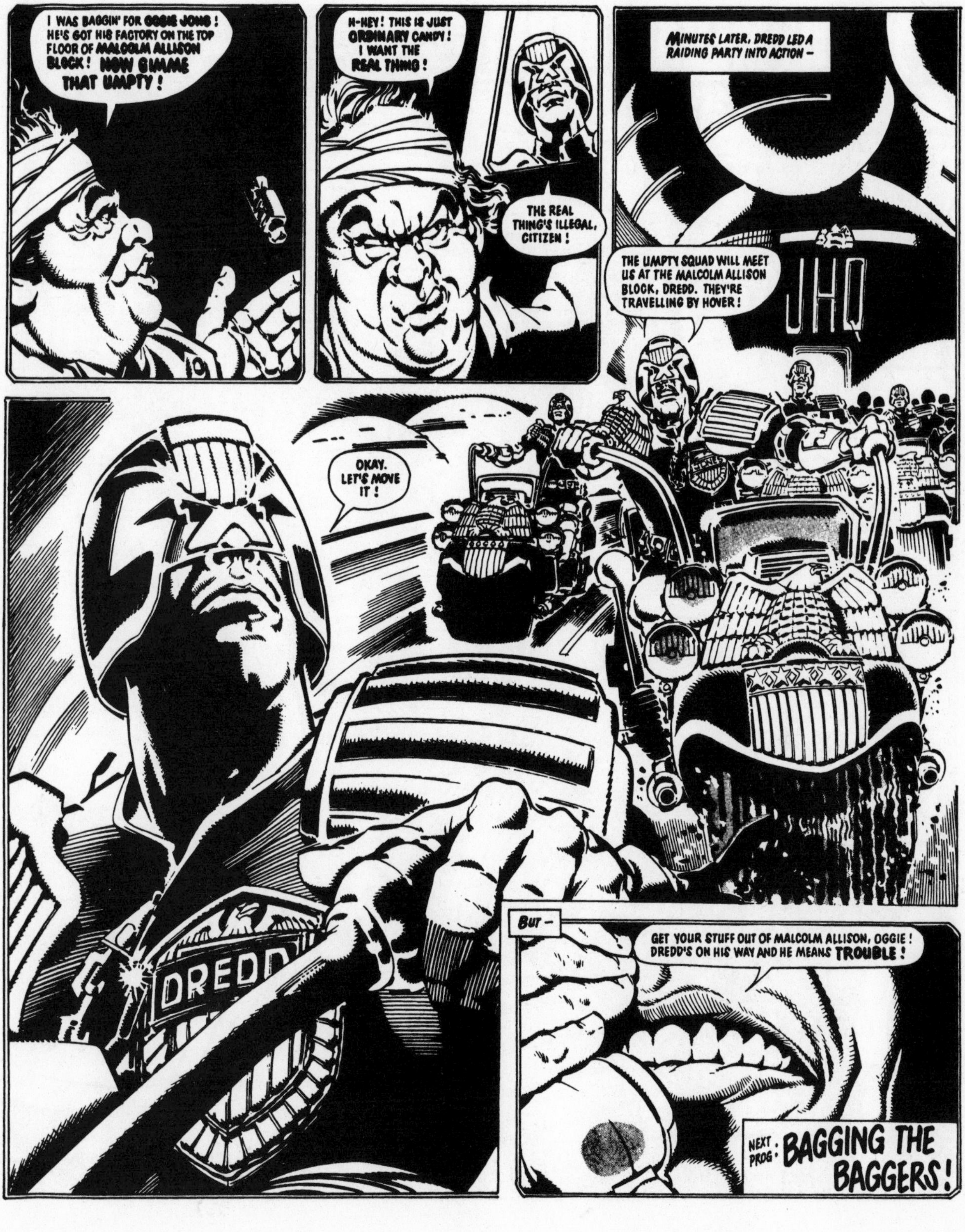
I WAS BAGGIN' FOR OGGIE JONS ! HE'S GOT HIS FACTORY ON THE TOP FLOOR OF MALCOLM ALLISON BLOCK ! NOW GIMME THAT UMPTY !
H-HEY ! THIS IS JUST ORDINARY CANDY ! I WANT THE REAL THING !
THE REAL THING'S ILLEGAL, CITIZEN !
MINUTES LATER, DREDD LED A RAIDING PARTY INTO ACTION –
JHQ
THE UMPTY SQUAD WILL MEET US AT THE MALCOLM ALLISON BLOCK, DREDD. THEY'RE TRAVELLING BY HOVER !
OKAY. LET'S MOVE IT !
DREDD
BUT –
GET YOUR STUFF OUT OF MALCOLM ALLISON, OGGIE ! DREDD'S ON HIS WAY AND HE MEANS TROUBLE !
NEXT PROG : BAGGING THE BAGGERS !

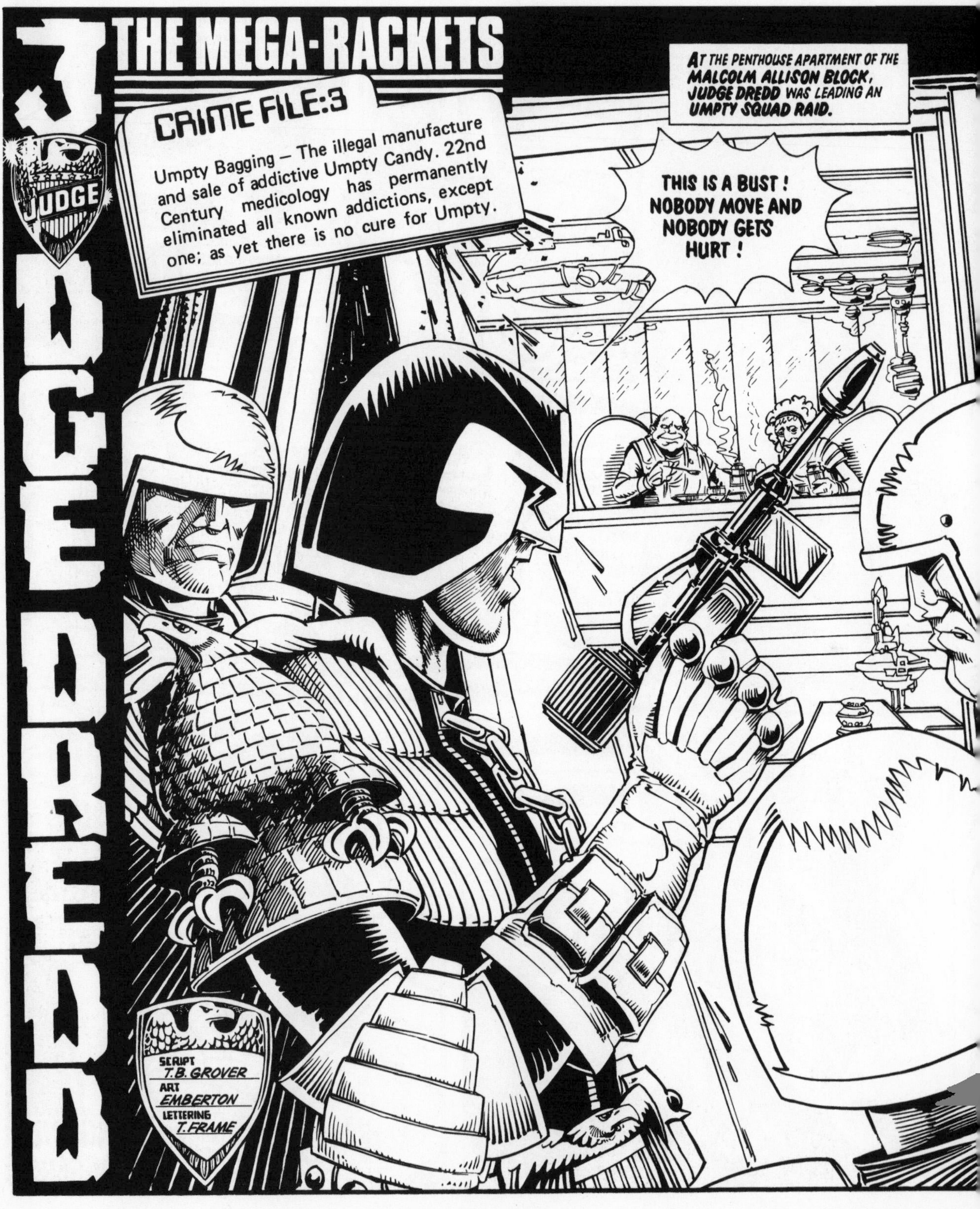
JUDGE DREDD
THE MEGA-RACKETS
CRIME FILE:3
Umpty Bagging – The illegal manufacture and sale of addictive Umpty Candy. 22nd Century medicology has permanently eliminated all known addictions, except one; as yet there is no cure for Umpty.
AT THE PENTHOUSE APARTMENT OF THE MALCOLM ALLISON BLOCK, JUDGE DREDD WAS LEADING AN UMPTY SQUAD RAID.
THIS IS A BUST! NOBODY MOVE AND NOBODY GETS HURT!
SCRIPT T.B. GROVER
ART EMBERTON
LETTERING T. FRAME

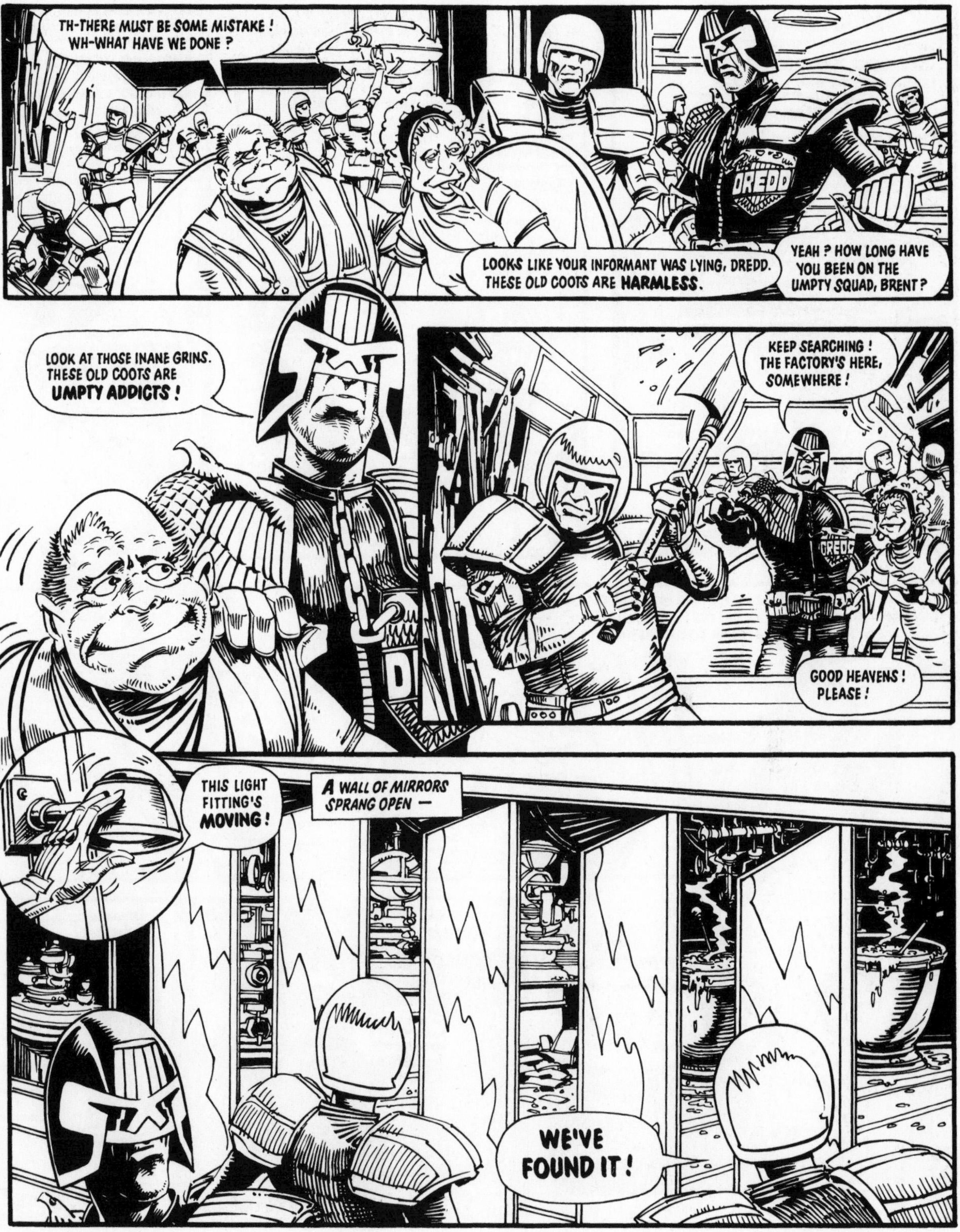
TH-THERE MUST BE SOME MISTAKE ! WH-WHAT HAVE WE DONE ?
LOOKS LIKE YOUR INFORMANT WAS LYING, DREDD. THESE OLD COOTS ARE HARMLESS.
YEAH ? HOW LONG HAVE YOU BEEN ON THE UMPTY SQUAD, BRENT ?
LOOK AT THOSE INANE GRINS. THESE OLD COOTS ARE UMPTY ADDICTS !
KEEP SEARCHING ! THE FACTORY'S HERE, SOMEWHERE !
GOOD HEAVENS ! PLEASE !
THIS LIGHT FITTING'S MOVING !
A WALL OF MIRRORS SPRANG OPEN —
WE'VE FOUND IT !

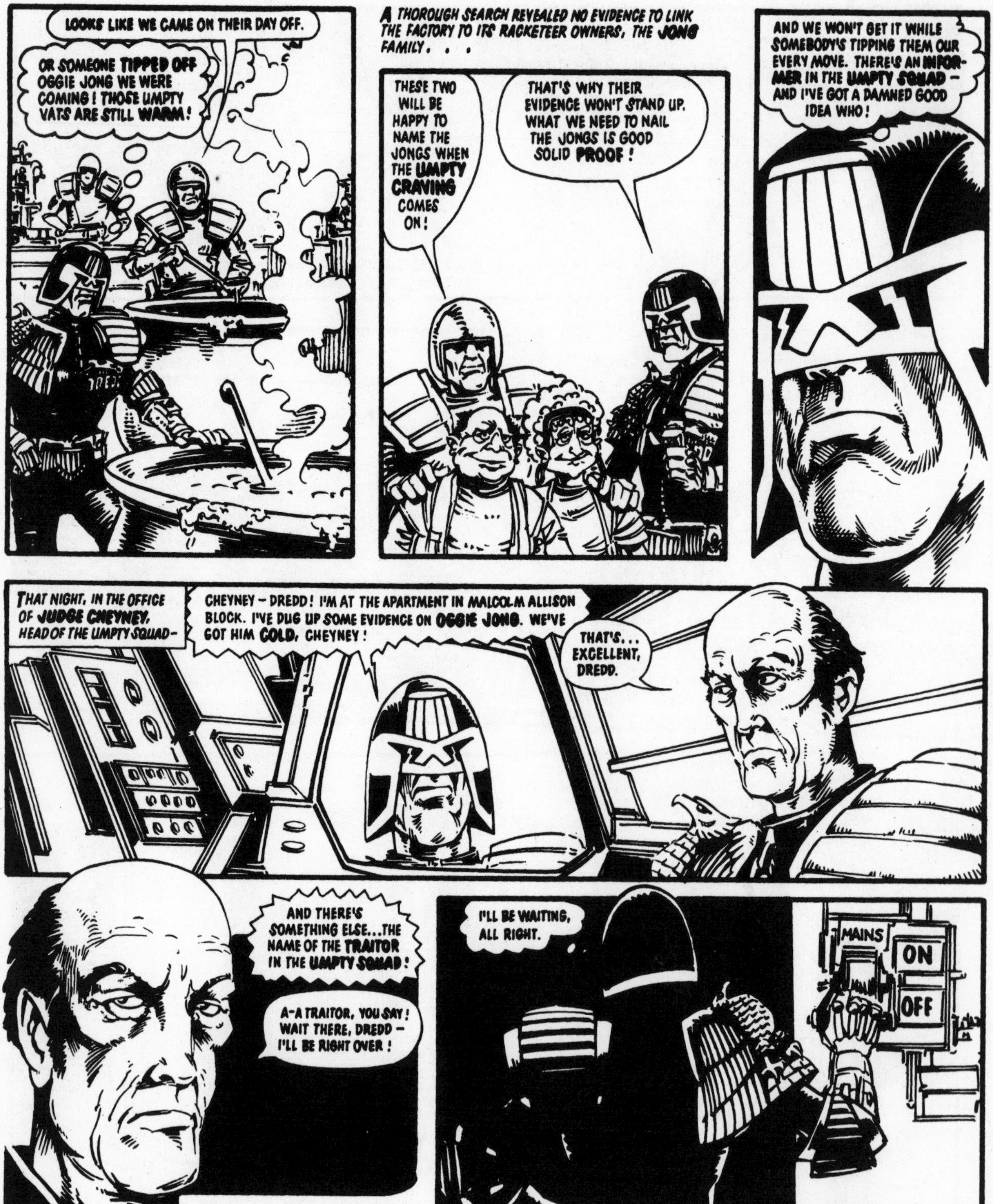
LOOKS LIKE WE CAME ON THEIR DAY OFF.
OR SOMEONE TIPPED OFF OGGIE JONG WE WERE COMING! THOSE UMPTY VATS ARE STILL WARM!
A THOROUGH SEARCH REVEALED NO EVIDENCE TO LINK THE FACTORY TO ITS RACKETEER OWNERS, THE JONG FAMILY. . .
THESE TWO WILL BE HAPPY TO NAME THE JONGS WHEN THE UMPTY CRAVING COMES ON!
THAT'S WHY THEIR EVIDENCE WON'T STAND UP. WHAT WE NEED TO NAIL THE JONGS IS GOOD SOLID PROOF!
AND WE WON'T GET IT WHILE SOMEBODY'S TIPPING THEM OUR EVERY MOVE. THERE'S AN INFORMER IN THE UMPTY SQUAD – AND I'VE GOT A DAMNED GOOD IDEA WHO!
THAT NIGHT, IN THE OFFICE OF JUDGE CHEYNEY, HEAD OF THE UMPTY SQUAD–
CHEYNEY – DREDD! I'M AT THE APARTMENT IN MALCOLM ALLISON BLOCK. I'VE DUG UP SOME EVIDENCE ON OGGIE JONG. WE'VE GOT HIM COLD, CHEYNEY!
THAT'S... EXCELLENT, DREDD.
AND THERE'S SOMETHING ELSE...THE NAME OF THE TRAITOR IN THE UMPTY SQUAD!
A-A TRAITOR, YOU SAY! WAIT THERE, DREDD – I'LL BE RIGHT OVER!
I'LL BE WAITING, ALL RIGHT.
MAINS
ON
OFF

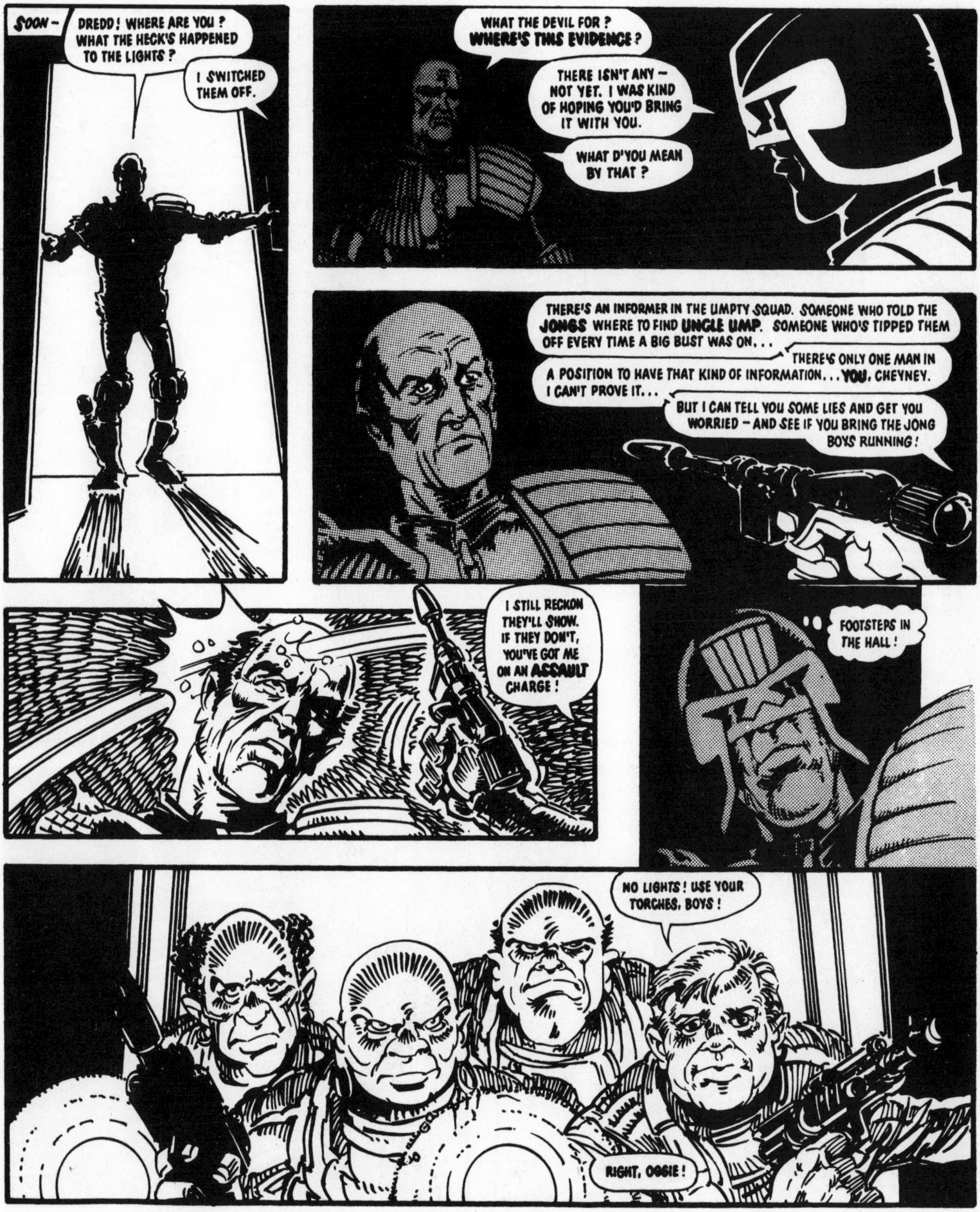
SOON –
DREDD! WHERE ARE YOU? WHAT THE HECK'S HAPPENED TO THE LIGHTS?
I SWITCHED THEM OFF.
WHAT THE DEVIL FOR? WHERE'S THIS EVIDENCE?
THERE ISN'T ANY – NOT YET. I WAS KIND OF HOPING YOU'D BRING IT WITH YOU.
WHAT D'YOU MEAN BY THAT?
THERE'S AN INFORMER IN THE UMPTY SQUAD. SOMEONE WHO TOLD THE JONGS WHERE TO FIND UNCLE UMP. SOMEONE WHO'S TIPPED THEM OFF EVERY TIME A BIG BUST WAS ON...
THERE'S ONLY ONE MAN IN A POSITION TO HAVE THAT KIND OF INFORMATION... YOU, CHEYNEY. I CAN'T PROVE IT...
BUT I CAN TELL YOU SOME LIES AND GET YOU WORRIED – AND SEE IF YOU BRING THE JONG BOYS RUNNING!
I STILL RECKON THEY'LL SHOW. IF THEY DON'T, YOU'VE GOT ME ON AN ASSAULT CHARGE!
FOOTSTEPS IN THE HALL!
NO LIGHTS! USE YOUR TORCHES, BOYS!
RIGHT, OGGIE!

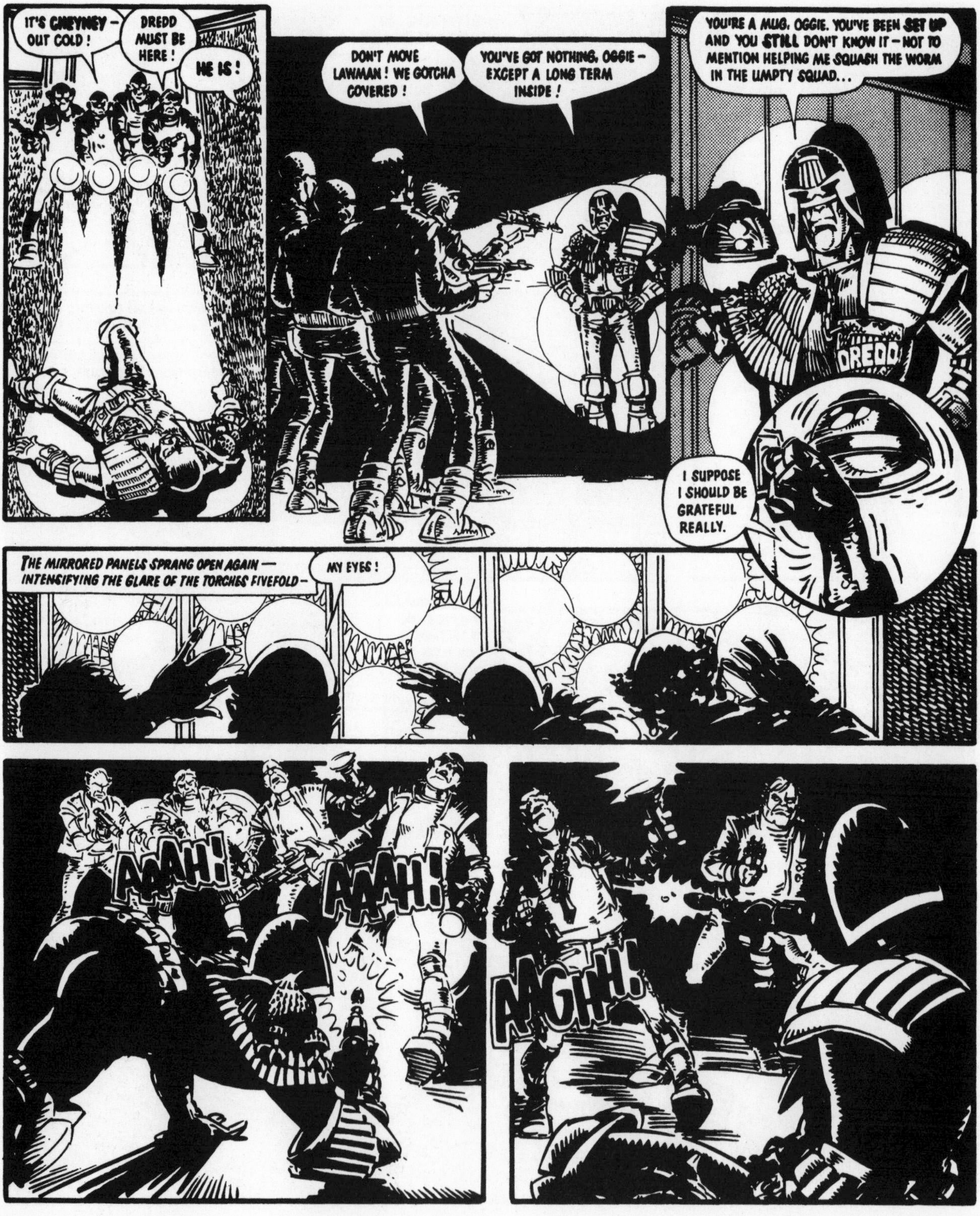

IT'S CHEYNEY — OUT COLD !
DREDD MUST BE HERE !
HE IS !
DON'T MOVE LAWMAN ! WE GOTCHA COVERED !
YOU'VE GOT NOTHING, OGGIE — EXCEPT A LONG TERM INSIDE !
YOU'RE A MUG, OGGIE. YOU'VE BEEN SET UP AND YOU STILL DON'T KNOW IT — NOT TO MENTION HELPING ME SQUASH THE WORM IN THE UMPTY SQUAD...
DREDD
I SUPPOSE I SHOULD BE GRATEFUL REALLY.
THE MIRRORED PANELS SPRANG OPEN AGAIN — INTENSIFYING THE GLARE OF THE TORCHES FIVEFOLD —
MY EYES !
AAAH!
AAAH!
AAGHH!

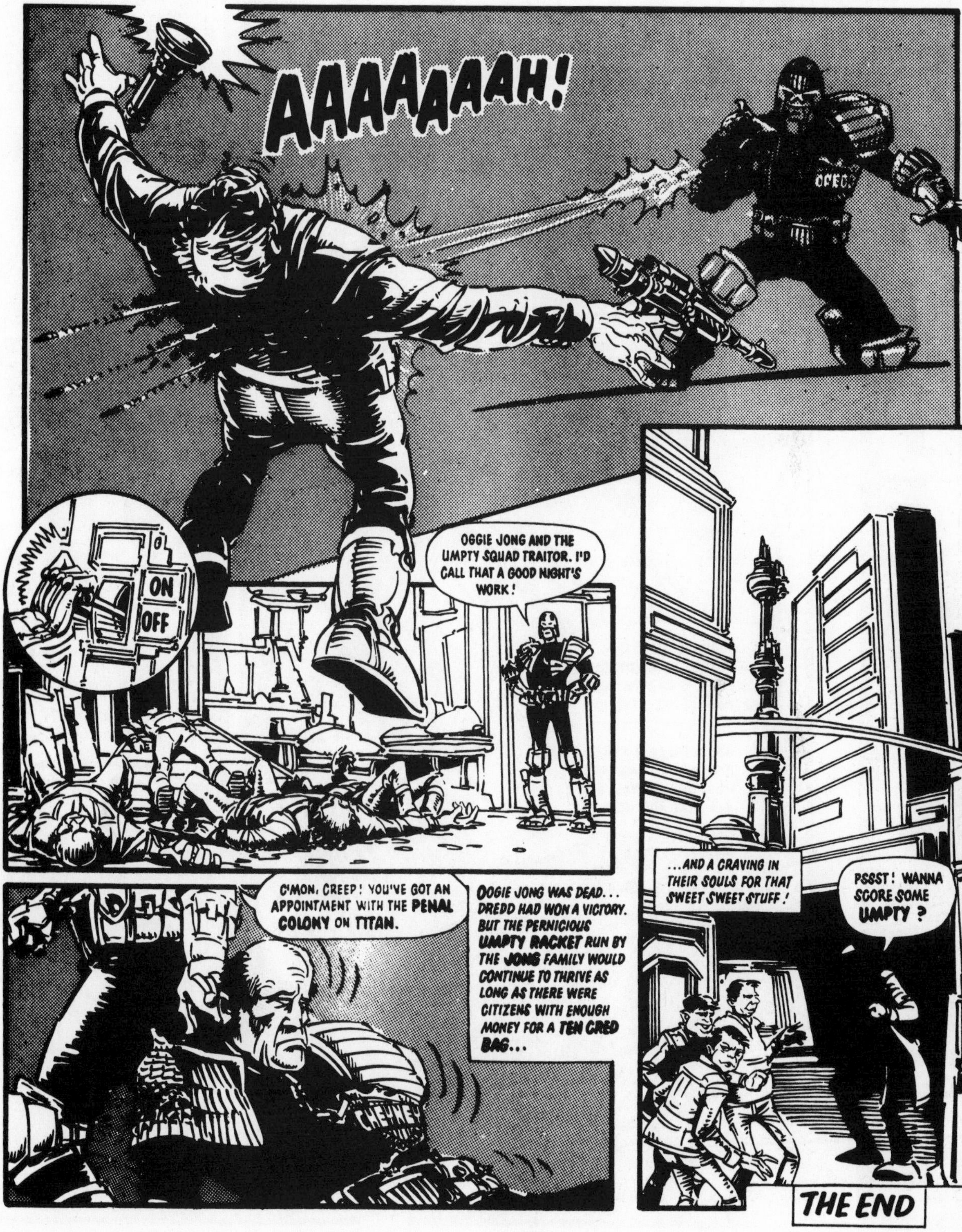
AAAAAAAH!
ON
OFF
OGGIE JONG AND THE UMPTY SQUAD TRAITOR. I'D CALL THAT A GOOD NIGHT'S WORK!
C'MON, CREEP! YOU'VE GOT AN APPOINTMENT WITH THE PENAL COLONY ON TITAN.
OOGIE JONG WAS DEAD... DREDD HAD WON A VICTORY. BUT THE PERNICIOUS UMPTY RACKET RUN BY THE JONGS FAMILY WOULD CONTINUE TO THRIVE AS LONG AS THERE WERE CITIZENS WITH ENOUGH MONEY FOR A TEN CRED BAG...
...AND A CRAVING IN THEIR SOULS FOR THAT SWEET SWEET STUFF!
PSSST! WANNA SCORE SOME UMPTY ?
THE END

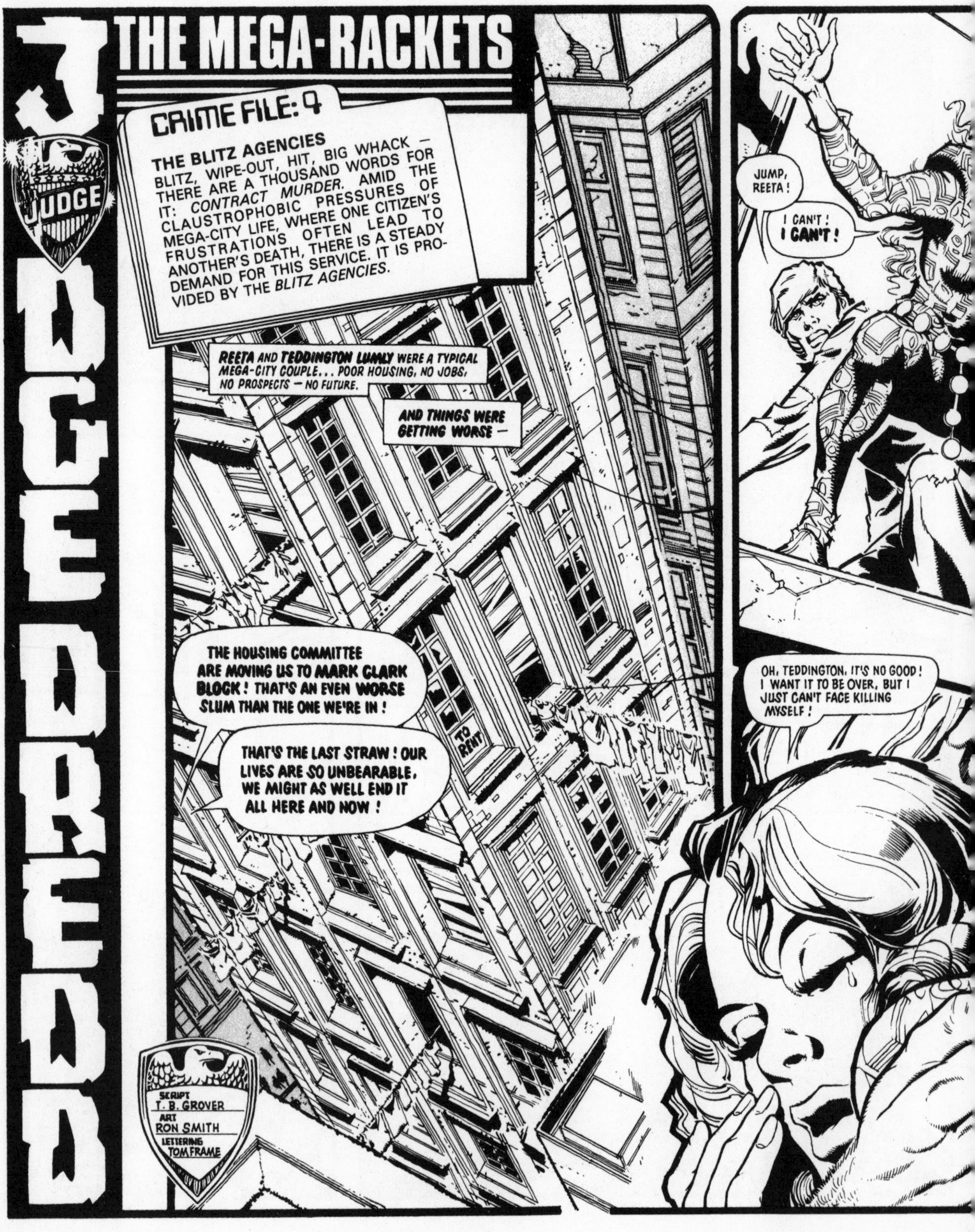
JUDGE DREDD
THE MEGA-RACKETS
CRIME FILE: 4
THE BLITZ AGENCIES
BLITZ, WIPE-OUT, HIT, BIG WHACK — THERE ARE A THOUSAND WORDS FOR IT: CONTRACT MURDER. AMID THE CLAUSTROPHOBIC PRESSURES OF MEGA-CITY LIFE, WHERE ONE CITIZEN'S FRUSTRATIONS OFTEN LEAD TO ANOTHER'S DEATH, THERE IS A STEADY DEMAND FOR THIS SERVICE. IT IS PROVIDED BY THE BLITZ AGENCIES.
REETA AND TEDDINGTON LUMLY WERE A TYPICAL MEGA-CITY COUPLE... POOR HOUSING, NO JOBS, NO PROSPECTS — NO FUTURE.
AND THINGS WERE GETTING WORSE —
THE HOUSING COMMITTEE ARE MOVING US TO MARK CLARK BLOCK! THAT'S AN EVEN WORSE SLUM THAN THE ONE WE'RE IN!
THAT'S THE LAST STRAW! OUR LIVES ARE SO UNBEARABLE, WE MIGHT AS WELL END IT ALL HERE AND NOW!
TO RENT
SCRIPT T. B. GROVER
ART RON SMITH
LETTERING TOM FRAME
JUMP, REETA!
I CAN'T! I CAN'T!
OH, TEDDINGTON, IT'S NO GOOD! I WANT IT TO BE OVER, BUT I JUST CAN'T FACE KILLING MYSELF!

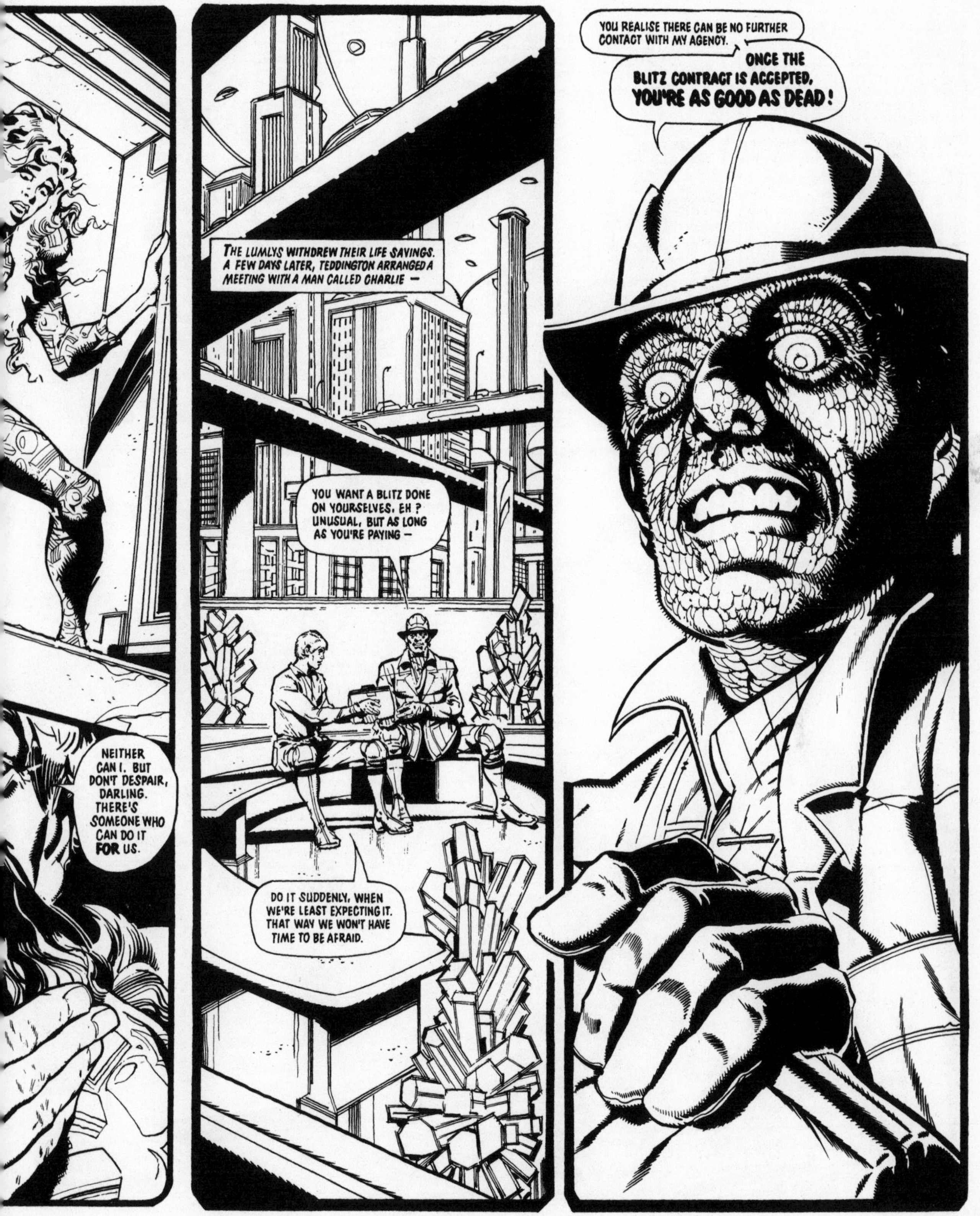
NEITHER CAN I. BUT DON'T DESPAIR, DARLING. THERE'S SOMEONE WHO CAN DO IT FOR US.
THE LUMLYS WITHDREW THEIR LIFE SAVINGS. A FEW DAYS LATER, TEDDINGTON ARRANGED A MEETING WITH A MAN CALLED CHARLIE –
YOU WANT A BLITZ DONE ON YOURSELVES, EH ? UNUSUAL, BUT AS LONG AS YOU'RE PAYING –
DO IT SUDDENLY, WHEN WE'RE LEAST EXPECTING IT. THAT WAY WE WON'T HAVE TIME TO BE AFRAID.
YOU REALISE THERE CAN BE NO FURTHER CONTACT WITH MY AGENCY.
ONCE THE BLITZ CONTRACT IS ACCEPTED, YOU'RE AS GOOD AS DEAD!

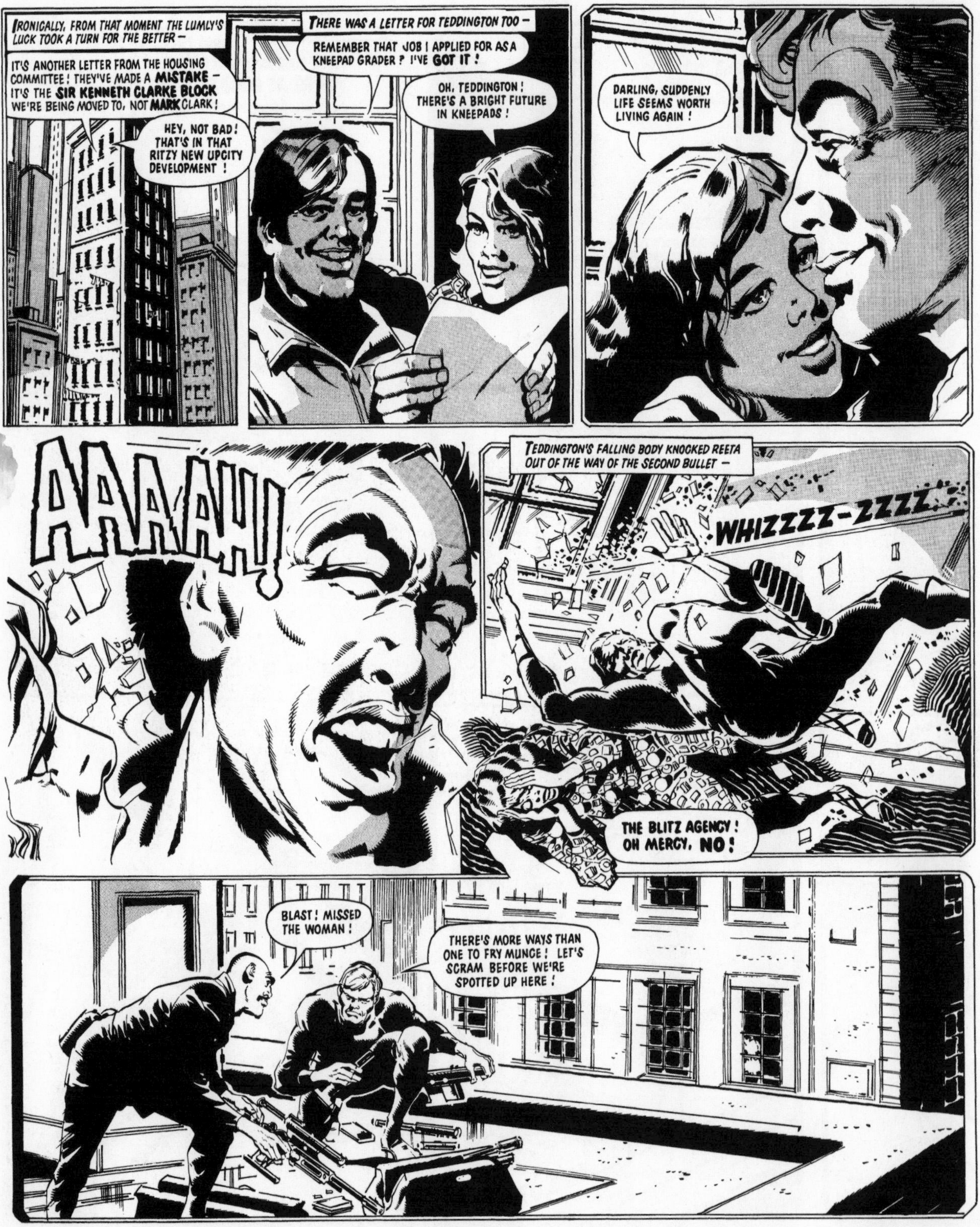
IRONICALLY, FROM THAT MOMENT THE LUMLY'S LUCK TOOK A TURN FOR THE BETTER –
IT'S ANOTHER LETTER FROM THE HOUSING COMMITTEE! THEY'VE MADE A MISTAKE – IT'S THE SIR KENNETH CLARKE BLOCK WE'RE BEING MOVED TO, NOT MARK CLARK!
HEY, NOT BAD! THAT'S IN THAT RITZY NEW UPCITY DEVELOPMENT!
THERE WAS A LETTER FOR TEDDINGTON TOO –
REMEMBER THAT JOB I APPLIED FOR AS A KNEEPAD GRADER? I'VE GOT IT!
OH, TEDDINGTON! THERE'S A BRIGHT FUTURE IN KNEEPADS!
DARLING, SUDDENLY LIFE SEEMS WORTH LIVING AGAIN!
AAAAH!
TEDDINGTON'S FALLING BODY KNOCKED REETA OUT OF THE WAY OF THE SECOND BULLET –
WHIZZZZ-ZZZZ
THE BLITZ AGENCY! OH MERCY, NO!
BLAST! MISSED THE WOMAN!
THERE'S MORE WAYS THAN ONE TO FRY MUNCE! LET'S SCRAM BEFORE WE'RE SPOTTED UP HERE!

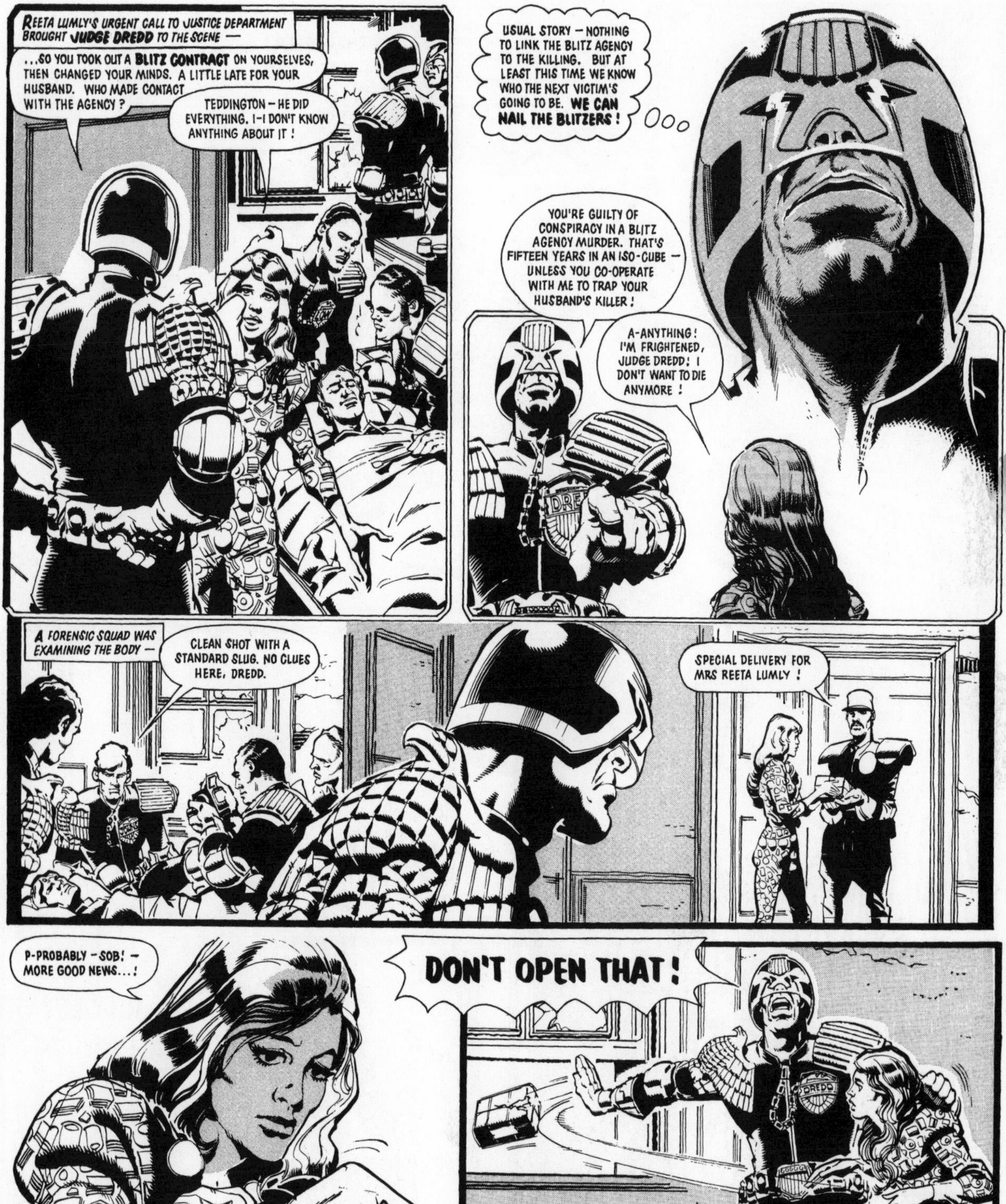

REETA LUMLY'S URGENT CALL TO JUSTICE DEPARTMENT BROUGHT JUDGE DREDD TO THE SCENE —
...SO YOU TOOK OUT A BLITZ CONTRACT ON YOURSELVES, THEN CHANGED YOUR MINDS. A LITTLE LATE FOR YOUR HUSBAND. WHO MADE CONTACT WITH THE AGENCY?
TEDDINGTON — HE DID EVERYTHING. I-I DON'T KNOW ANYTHING ABOUT IT!
USUAL STORY — NOTHING TO LINK THE BLITZ AGENCY TO THE KILLING. BUT AT LEAST THIS TIME WE KNOW WHO THE NEXT VICTIM'S GOING TO BE. WE CAN NAIL THE BLITZERS!
YOU'RE GUILTY OF CONSPIRACY IN A BLITZ AGENCY MURDER. THAT'S FIFTEEN YEARS IN AN ISO-CUBE — UNLESS YOU CO-OPERATE WITH ME TO TRAP YOUR HUSBAND'S KILLER!
A-ANYTHING! I'M FRIGHTENED, JUDGE DREDD! I DON'T WANT TO DIE ANYMORE!
A FORENSIC SQUAD WAS EXAMINING THE BODY —
CLEAN SHOT WITH A STANDARD SLUG. NO CLUES HERE, DREDD.
SPECIAL DELIVERY FOR MRS REETA LUMLY!
P-PROBABLY — SOB! — MORE GOOD NEWS...!
DON'T OPEN THAT!

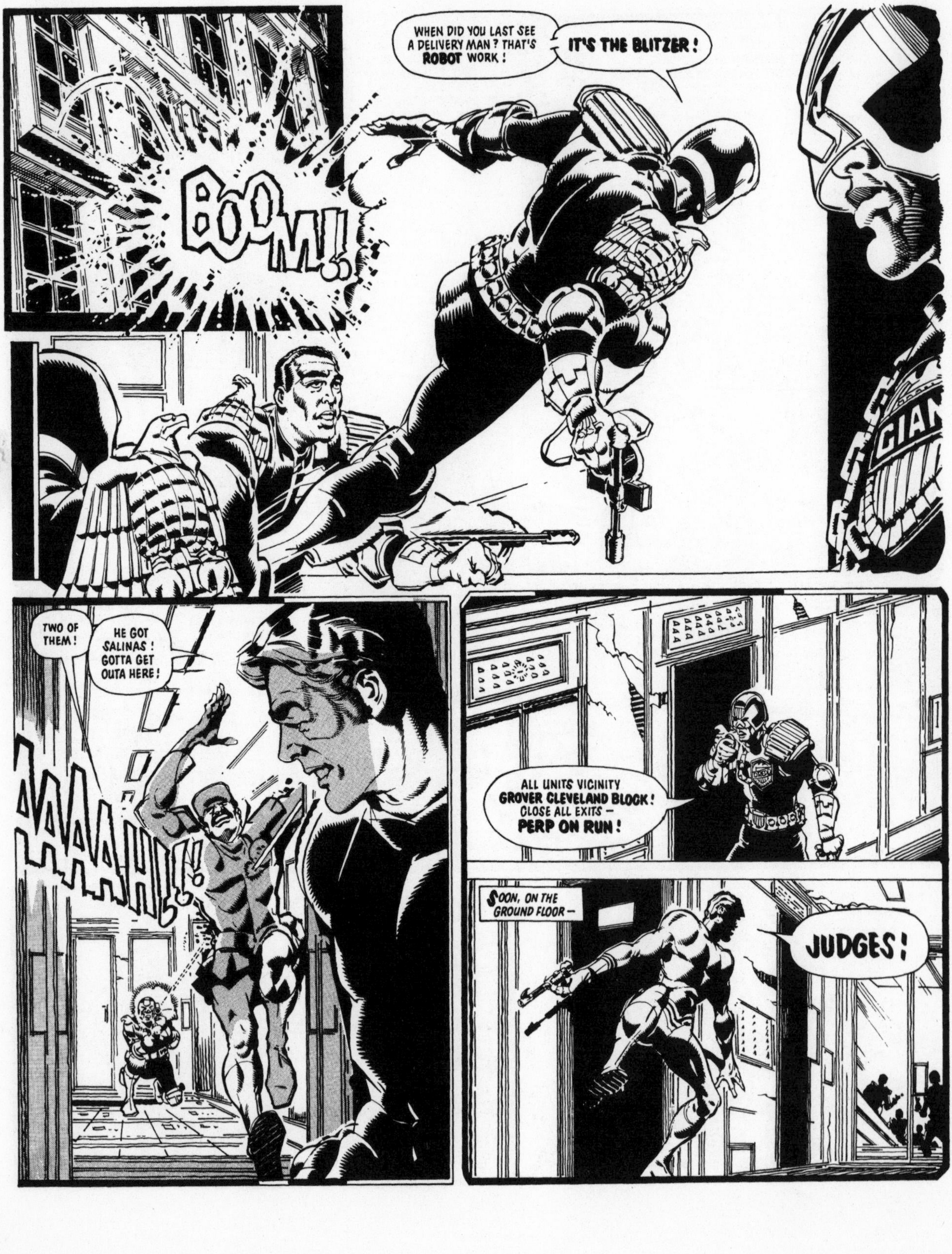
BOOM!!
WHEN DID YOU LAST SEE A DELIVERY MAN? THAT'S ROBOT WORK!
IT'S THE BLITZER!
GIANT
TWO OF THEM!
HE GOT SALINAS! GOTTA GET OUTA HERE!
AAAAAH!!
ALL UNITS VICINITY GROVER CLEVELAND BLOCK! CLOSE ALL EXITS — PERP ON RUN!
SOON, ON THE GROUND FLOOR —
JUDGES!

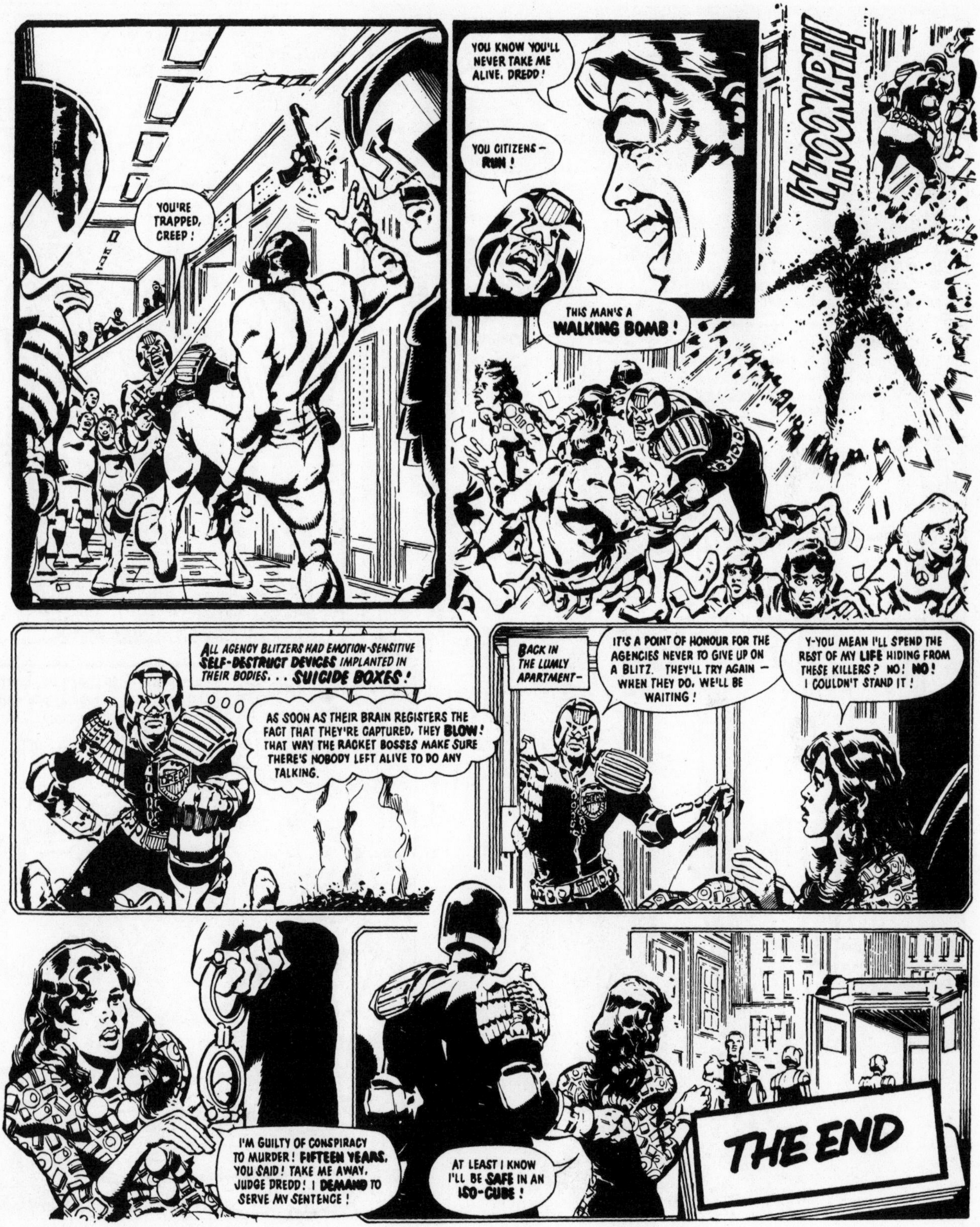
YOU'RE TRAPPED, CREEP!
YOU KNOW YOU'LL NEVER TAKE ME ALIVE, DREDD!
YOU CITIZENS — RUN!
THIS MAN'S A WALKING BOMB!
WHOOMPH!
ALL AGENCY BLITZERS HAD EMOTION-SENSITIVE SELF-DESTRUCT DEVICES IMPLANTED IN THEIR BODIES. . . SUICIDE BOXES!
AS SOON AS THEIR BRAIN REGISTERS THE FACT THAT THEY'RE CAPTURED, THEY BLOW! THAT WAY THE RACKET BOSSES MAKE SURE THERE'S NOBODY LEFT ALIVE TO DO ANY TALKING.
BACK IN THE LUMLY APARTMENT—
IT'S A POINT OF HONOUR FOR THE AGENCIES NEVER TO GIVE UP ON A BLITZ. THEY'LL TRY AGAIN — WHEN THEY DO, WE'LL BE WAITING!
Y-YOU MEAN I'LL SPEND THE REST OF MY LIFE HIDING FROM THESE KILLERS? NO! NO! I COULDN'T STAND IT!
I'M GUILTY OF CONSPIRACY TO MURDER! FIFTEEN YEARS, YOU SAID! TAKE ME AWAY, JUDGE DREDD! I DEMAND TO SERVE MY SENTENCE!
AT LEAST I KNOW I'LL BE SAFE IN AN ISO-CUBE!
THE END

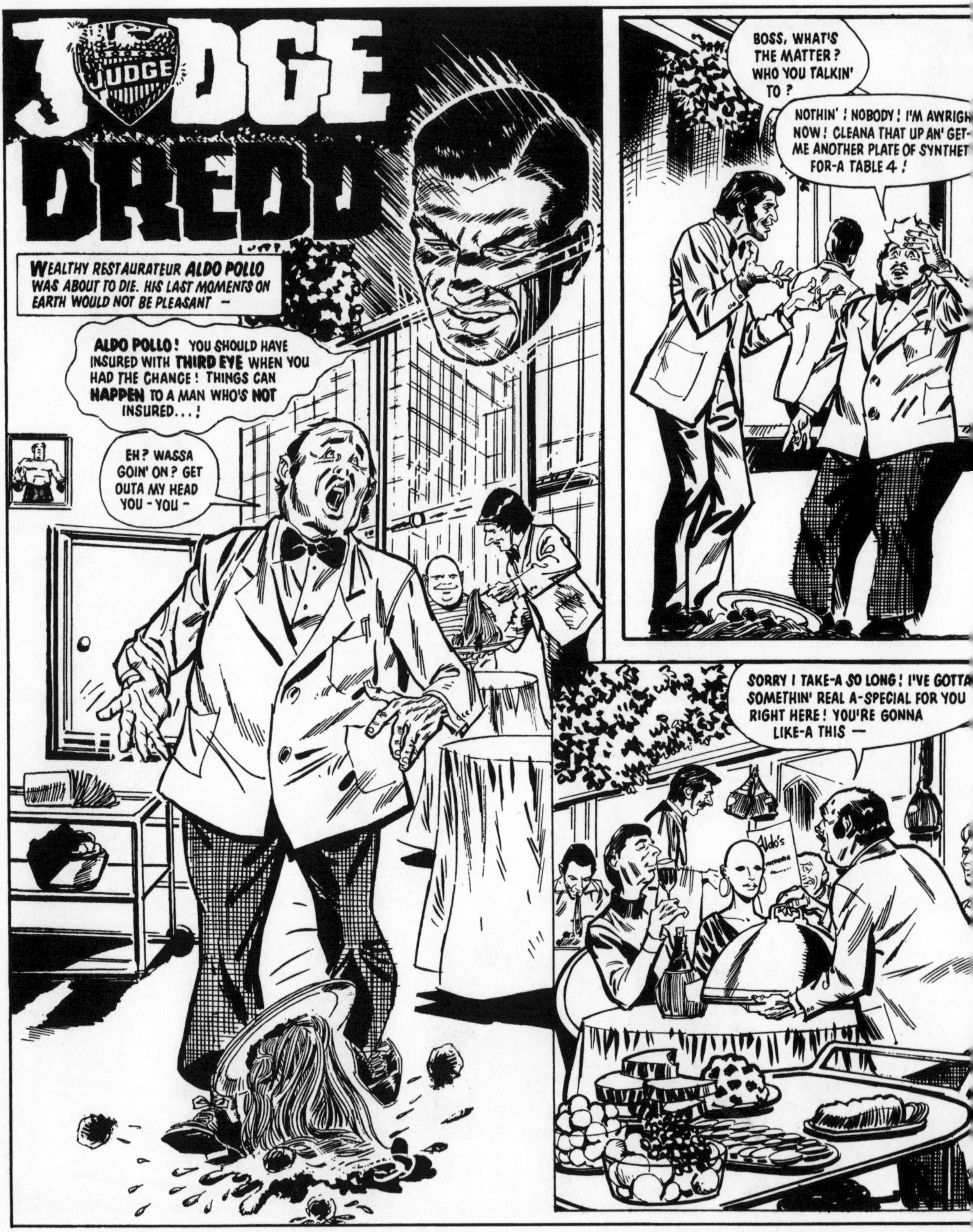
JUDGE DREDD
JUDGE
WEALTHY RESTAURATEUR ALDO POLLO WAS ABOUT TO DIE. HIS LAST MOMENTS ON EARTH WOULD NOT BE PLEASANT —
ALDO POLLO! YOU SHOULD HAVE INSURED WITH THIRD EYE WHEN YOU HAD THE CHANCE! THINGS CAN HAPPEN TO A MAN WHO'S NOT INSURED...!
EH? WASSA GOIN' ON? GET OUTA MY HEAD YOU - YOU -
BOSS, WHAT'S THE MATTER? WHO YOU TALKIN' TO?
NOTHIN'! NOBODY! I'M AWRIGH NOW! CLEANA THAT UP AN' GET-ME ANOTHER PLATE OF SYNTHET FOR-A TABLE 4!
SORRY I TAKE-A SO LONG! I'VE GOTTA SOMETHIN' REAL A-SPECIAL FOR YOU RIGHT HERE! YOU'RE GONNA LIKE-A THIS —
Aldo's

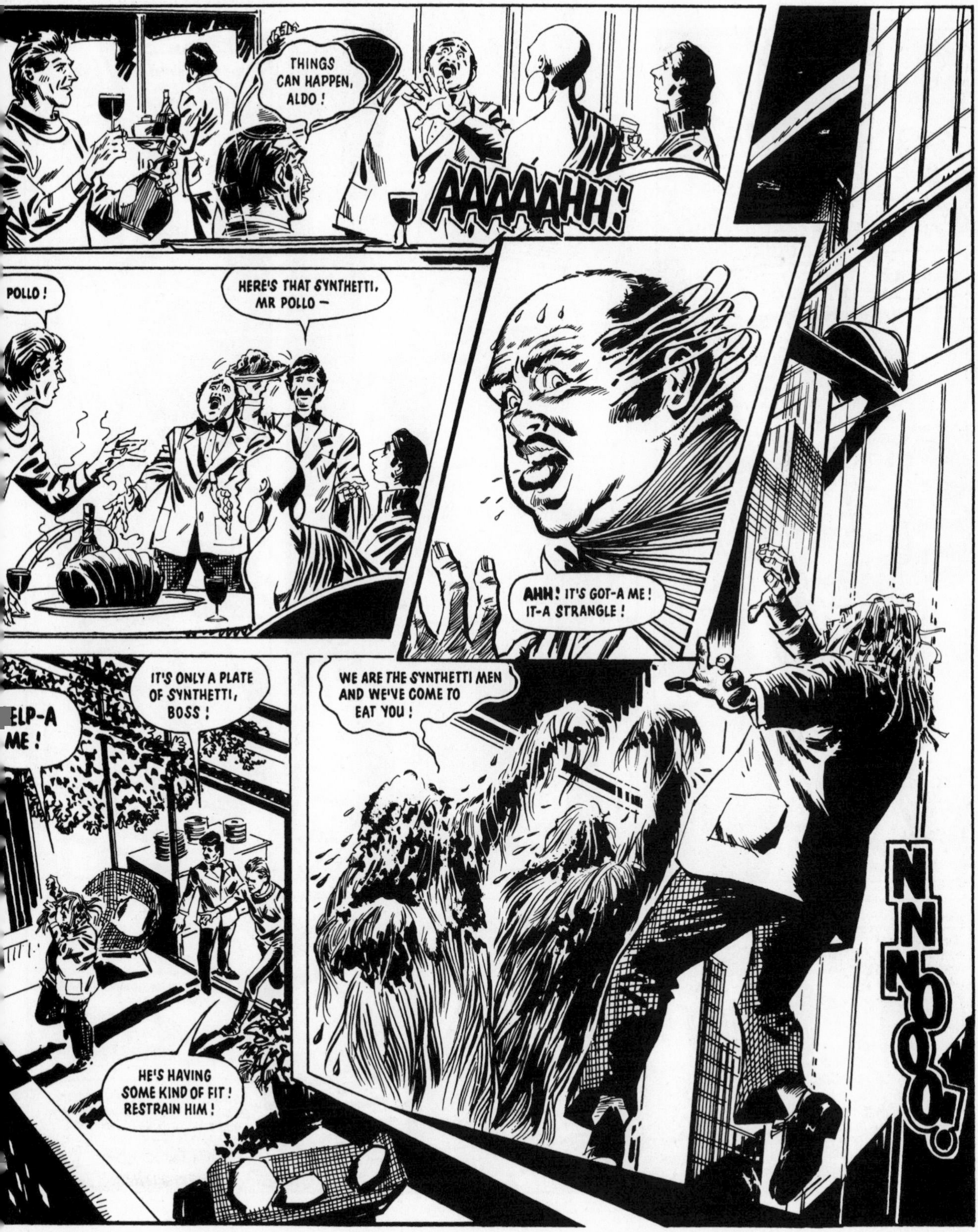

THINGS CAN HAPPEN, ALDO !
AAAAAHH !
POLLO !
HERE'S THAT SYNTHETTI, MR POLLO —
AHH ! IT'S GOT-A ME ! IT-A STRANGLE !
ELP-A ME !
IT'S ONLY A PLATE OF SYNTHETTI, BOSS !
HE'S HAVING SOME KIND OF FIT ! RESTRAIN HIM !
WE ARE THE SYNTHETTI MEN AND WE'VE COME TO EAT YOU !
NNNOOO !

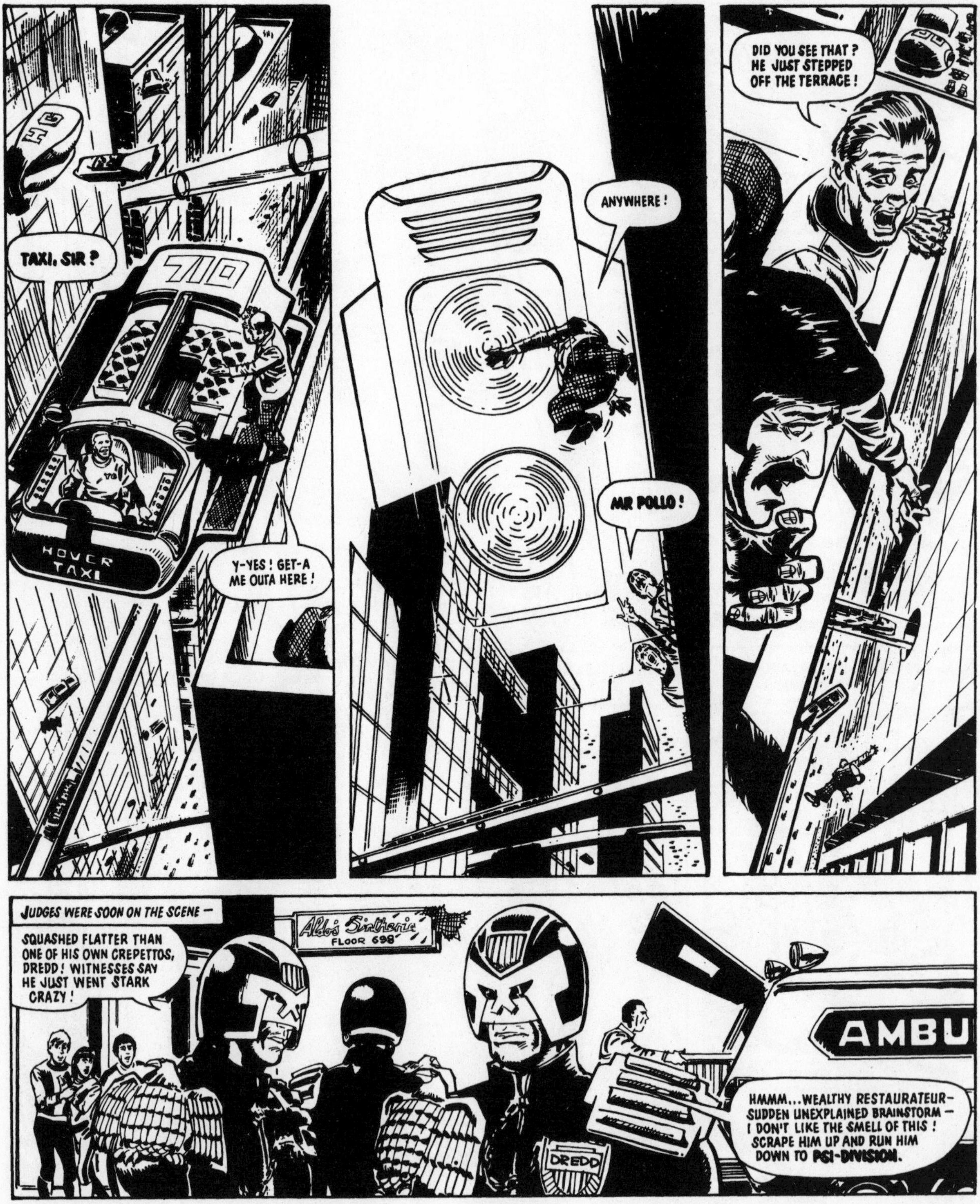
TAXI, SIR?
HOVER TAXI
Y-YES! GET-A ME OUTA HERE!
ANYWHERE!
MR POLLO!
DID YOU SEE THAT? HE JUST STEPPED OFF THE TERRACE!
JUDGES WERE SOON ON THE SCENE —
SQUASHED FLATTER THAN ONE OF HIS OWN CREPETTOS, DREDD! WITNESSES SAY HE JUST WENT STARK CRAZY!
Aldo's Sinthetic FLOOR 698
AMBU
DREDD
HMMM... WEALTHY RESTAURATEUR-SUDDEN UNEXPLAINED BRAINSTORM — I DON'T LIKE THE SMELL OF THIS! SCRAPE HIM UP AND RUN HIM DOWN TO PSI-DIVISION.

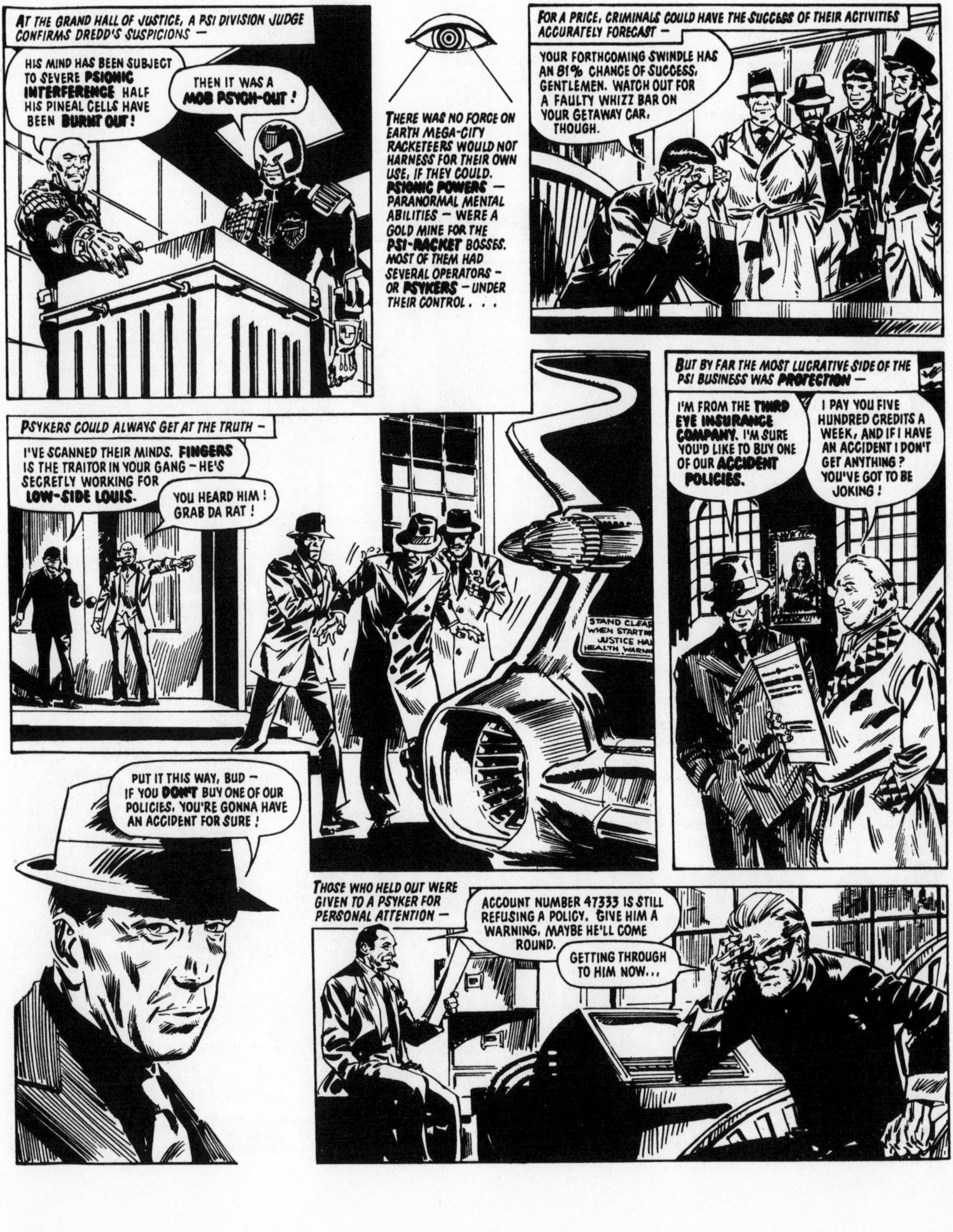
AT THE GRAND HALL OF JUSTICE, A PSI DIVISION JUDGE CONFIRMS DREDD'S SUSPICIONS —
HIS MIND HAS BEEN SUBJECT TO SEVERE PSIONIC INTERFERENCE HALF HIS PINEAL CELLS HAVE BEEN BURNT OUT!
THEN IT WAS A MOB PSYCH-OUT!
THERE WAS NO FORCE ON EARTH MEGA-CITY RACKETEERS WOULD NOT HARNESS FOR THEIR OWN USE, IF THEY COULD. PSIONIC POWERS — PARANORMAL MENTAL ABILITIES — WERE A GOLD MINE FOR THE PSI-RACKET BOSSES. MOST OF THEM HAD SEVERAL OPERATORS — OR PSYKERS — UNDER THEIR CONTROL . . .
FOR A PRICE, CRIMINALS COULD HAVE THE SUCCESS OF THEIR ACTIVITIES ACCURATELY FORECAST —
YOUR FORTHCOMING SWINDLE HAS AN 81% CHANCE OF SUCCESS, GENTLEMEN. WATCH OUT FOR A FAULTY WHIZZ BAR ON YOUR GETAWAY CAR, THOUGH.
PSYKERS COULD ALWAYS GET AT THE TRUTH —
I'VE SCANNED THEIR MINDS. FINGERS IS THE TRAITOR IN YOUR GANG — HE'S SECRETLY WORKING FOR LOW-SIDE LOUIS.
YOU HEARD HIM! GRAB DA RAT!
BUT BY FAR THE MOST LUCRATIVE SIDE OF THE PSI BUSINESS WAS PROTECTION —
I'M FROM THE THIRD EYE INSURANCE COMPANY. I'M SURE YOU'D LIKE TO BUY ONE OF OUR ACCIDENT POLICIES.
I PAY YOU FIVE HUNDRED CREDITS A WEEK, AND IF I HAVE AN ACCIDENT I DON'T GET ANYTHING? YOU'VE GOT TO BE JOKING!
PUT IT THIS WAY, BUD — IF YOU DON'T BUY ONE OF OUR POLICIES, YOU'RE GONNA HAVE AN ACCIDENT FOR SURE!
THOSE WHO HELD OUT WERE GIVEN TO A PSYKER FOR PERSONAL ATTENTION —
ACCOUNT NUMBER 47333 IS STILL REFUSING A POLICY. GIVE HIM A WARNING, MAYBE HE'LL COME ROUND.
GETTING THROUGH TO HIM NOW...

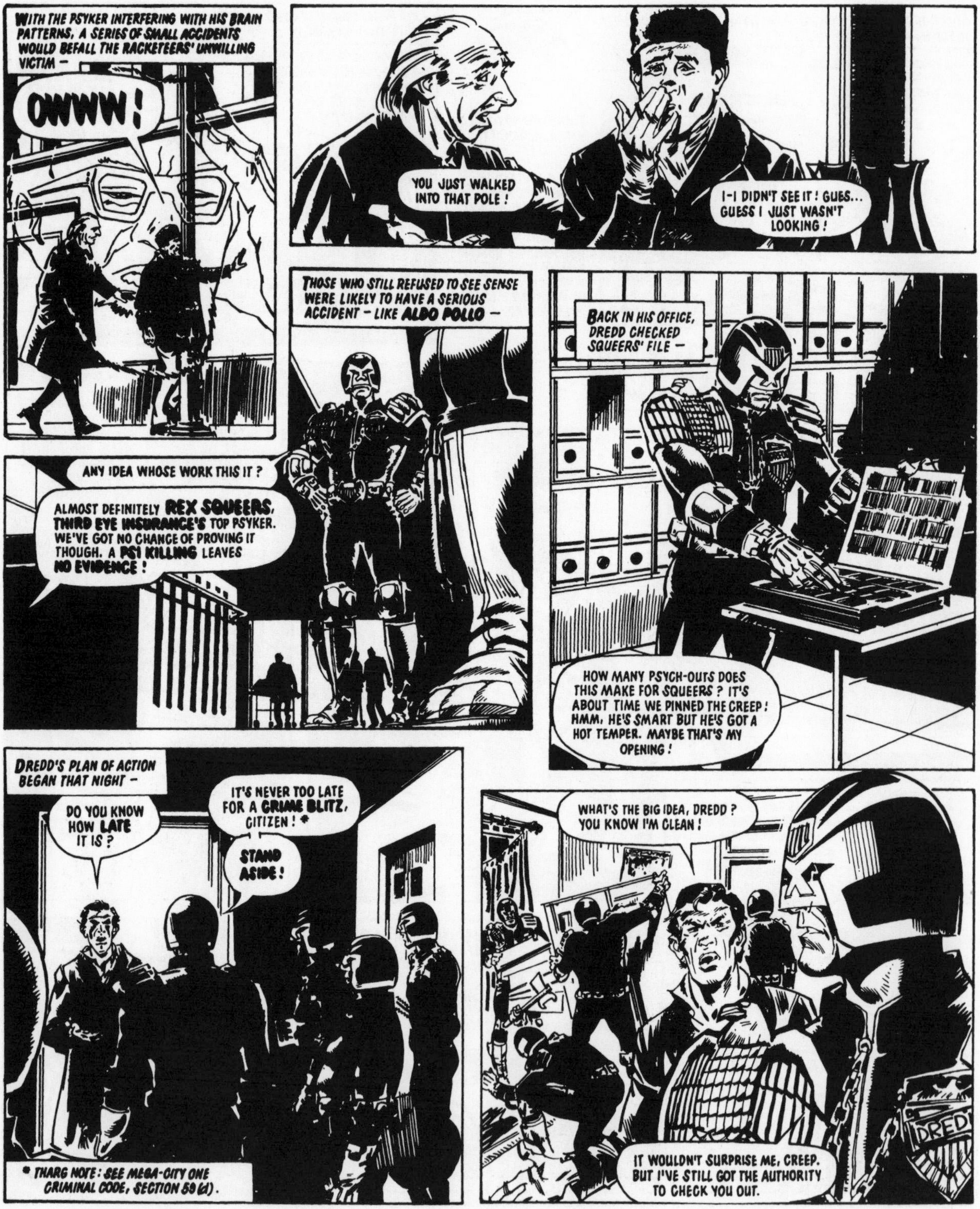

WITH THE PSYKER INTERFERING WITH HIS BRAIN PATTERNS, A SERIES OF SMALL ACCIDENTS WOULD BEFALL THE RACKETEERS' UNWILLING VICTIM –
OWWW!
YOU JUST WALKED INTO THAT POLE!
I-I DIDN'T SEE IT! GUES... GUESS I JUST WASN'T LOOKING!
THOSE WHO STILL REFUSED TO SEE SENSE WERE LIKELY TO HAVE A SERIOUS ACCIDENT – LIKE ALDO POLLO –
ANY IDEA WHOSE WORK THIS IT?
ALMOST DEFINITELY REX SQUEERS, THIRD EYE INSURANCE'S TOP PSYKER. WE'VE GOT NO CHANCE OF PROVING IT THOUGH. A PSI KILLING LEAVES NO EVIDENCE!
BACK IN HIS OFFICE, DREDD CHECKED SQUEERS' FILE –
HOW MANY PSYCH-OUTS DOES THIS MAKE FOR SQUEERS? IT'S ABOUT TIME WE PINNED THE CREEP! HMM, HE'S SMART BUT HE'S GOT A HOT TEMPER. MAYBE THAT'S MY OPENING!
DREDD'S PLAN OF ACTION BEGAN THAT NIGHT –
DO YOU KNOW HOW LATE IT IS?
IT'S NEVER TOO LATE FOR A CRIME BLITZ, CITIZEN! *
STAND ASIDE!
* THARG NOTE: SEE MEGA-CITY ONE CRIMINAL CODE, SECTION 58 (d).
WHAT'S THE BIG IDEA, DREDD? YOU KNOW I'M CLEAN!
IT WOULDN'T SURPRISE ME, CREEP. BUT I'VE STILL GOT THE AUTHORITY TO CHECK YOU OUT.

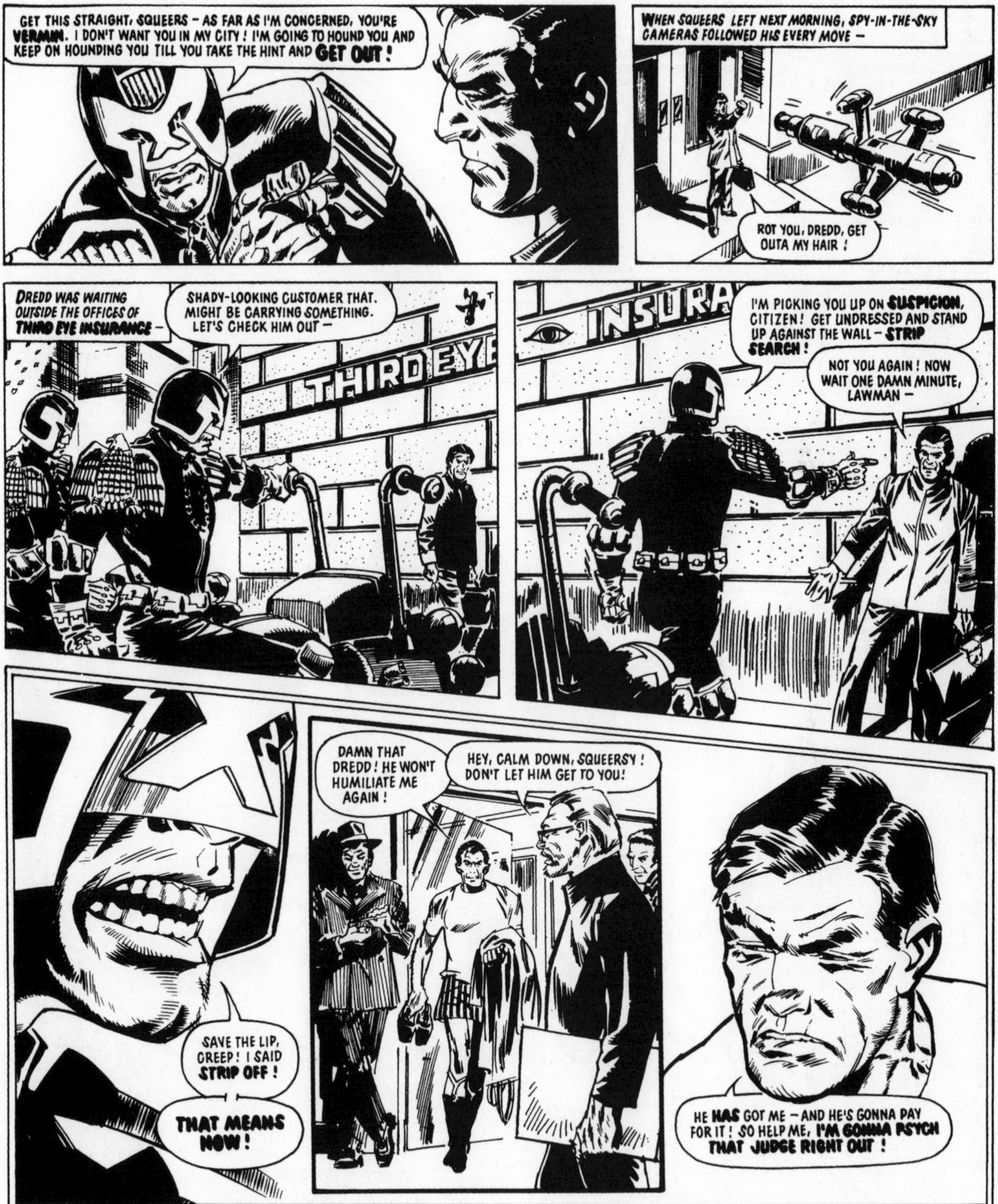

GET THIS STRAIGHT, SQUEERS – AS FAR AS I'M CONCERNED, YOU'RE VERMIN. I DON'T WANT YOU IN MY CITY! I'M GOING TO HOUND YOU AND KEEP ON HOUNDING YOU TILL YOU TAKE THE HINT AND GET OUT!
WHEN SQUEERS LEFT NEXT MORNING, SPY-IN-THE-SKY CAMERAS FOLLOWED HIS EVERY MOVE –
ROT YOU, DREDD, GET OUTA MY HAIR!
DREDD WAS WAITING OUTSIDE THE OFFICES OF THIRD EYE INSURANCE –
SHADY-LOOKING CUSTOMER THAT. MIGHT BE CARRYING SOMETHING. LET'S CHECK HIM OUT –
THIRDEYE
INSURA
I'M PICKING YOU UP ON SUSPICION, CITIZEN! GET UNDRESSED AND STAND UP AGAINST THE WALL – STRIP SEARCH!
NOT YOU AGAIN! NOW WAIT ONE DAMN MINUTE, LAWMAN –
SAVE THE LIP, CREEP! I SAID STRIP OFF!
THAT MEANS NOW!
DAMN THAT DREDD! HE WON'T HUMILIATE ME AGAIN!
HEY, CALM DOWN, SQUEERSY! DON'T LET HIM GET TO YOU!
HE HAS GOT ME – AND HE'S GONNA PAY FOR IT! SO HELP ME, I'M GONNA PSYCH THAT JUDGE RIGHT OUT!

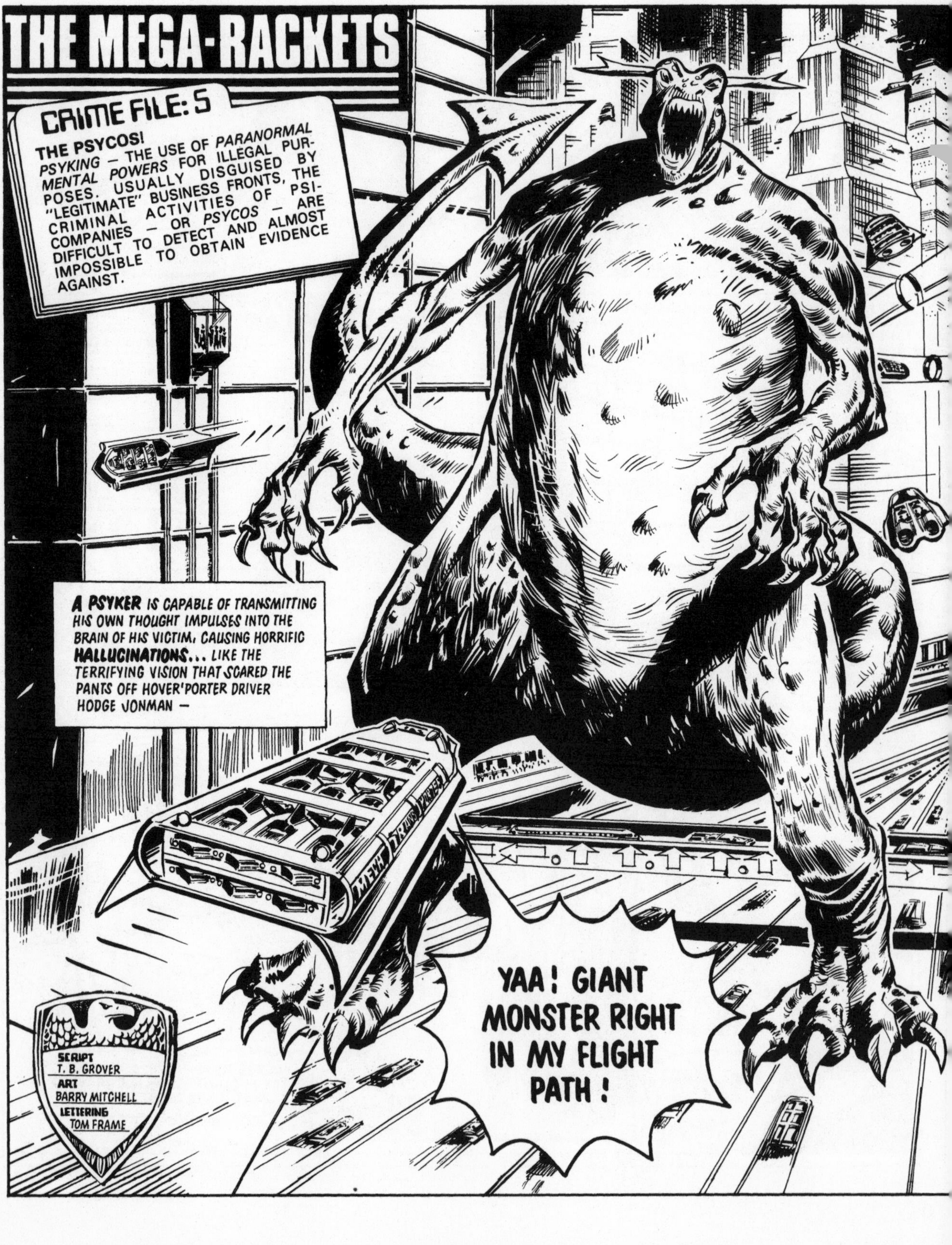

THE MEGA-RACKETS
CRIME FILE: 5
THE PSYCOS! PSYKING — THE USE OF PARANORMAL MENTAL POWERS FOR ILLEGAL PURPOSES. USUALLY DISGUISED BY "LEGITIMATE" BUSINESS FRONTS, THE CRIMINAL ACTIVITIES OF PSI-COMPANIES — OR PSYCOS — ARE DIFFICULT TO DETECT AND ALMOST IMPOSSIBLE TO OBTAIN EVIDENCE AGAINST.
A PSYKER IS CAPABLE OF TRANSMITTING HIS OWN THOUGHT IMPULSES INTO THE BRAIN OF HIS VICTIM, CAUSING HORRIFIC HALLUCINATIONS... LIKE THE TERRIFYING VISION THAT SCARED THE PANTS OFF HOVER'PORTER DRIVER HODGE JONMAN —
YAA! GIANT MONSTER RIGHT IN MY FLIGHT PATH!
SCRIPT T. B. GROVER
ART BARRY MITCHELL
LETTERING TOM FRAME

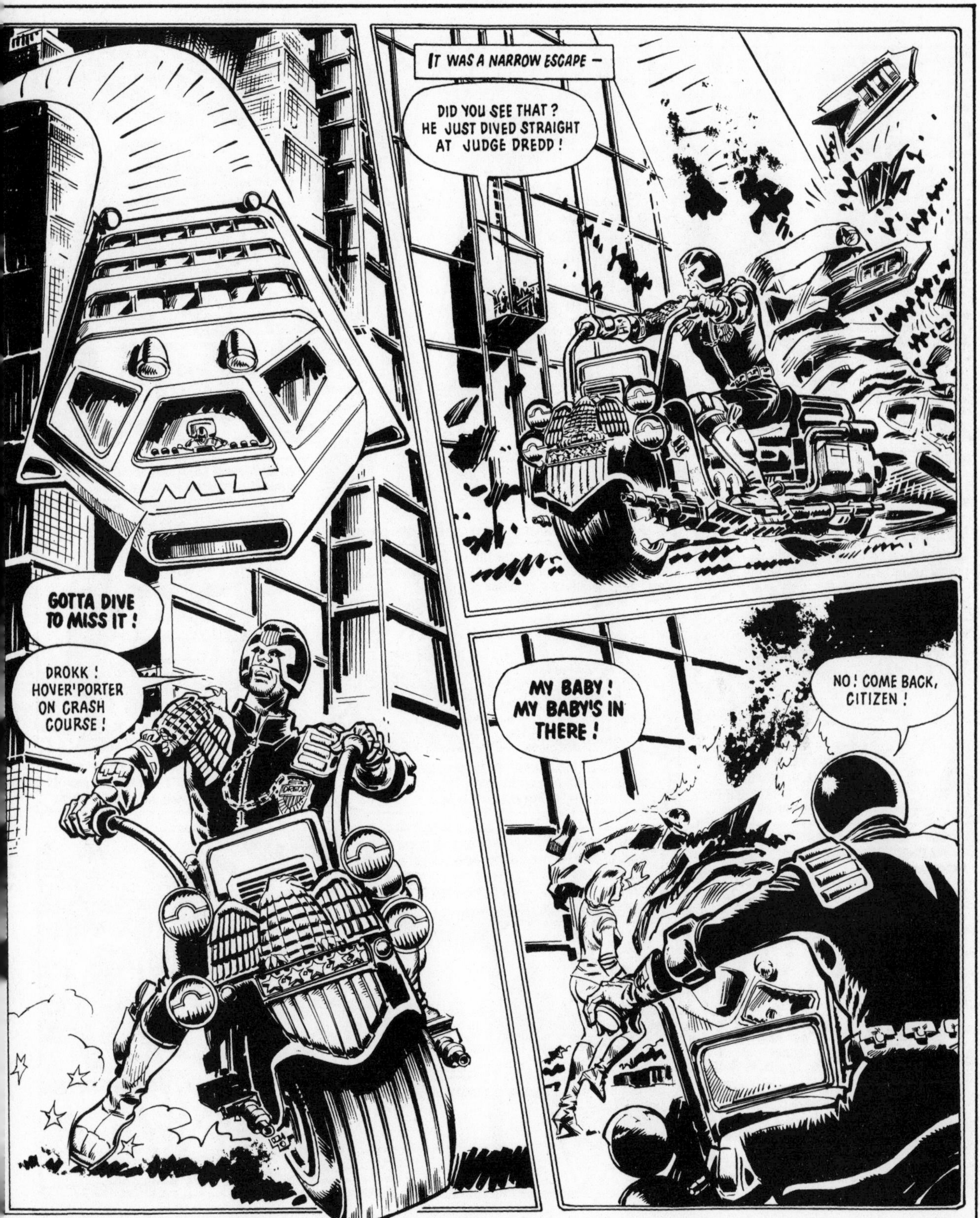
GOTTA DIVE TO MISS IT !
DROKK ! HOVER'PORTER ON CRASH COURSE !
IT WAS A NARROW ESCAPE –
DID YOU SEE THAT ? HE JUST DIVED STRAIGHT AT JUDGE DREDD !
MY BABY ! MY BABY'S IN THERE !
NO ! COME BACK, CITIZEN !

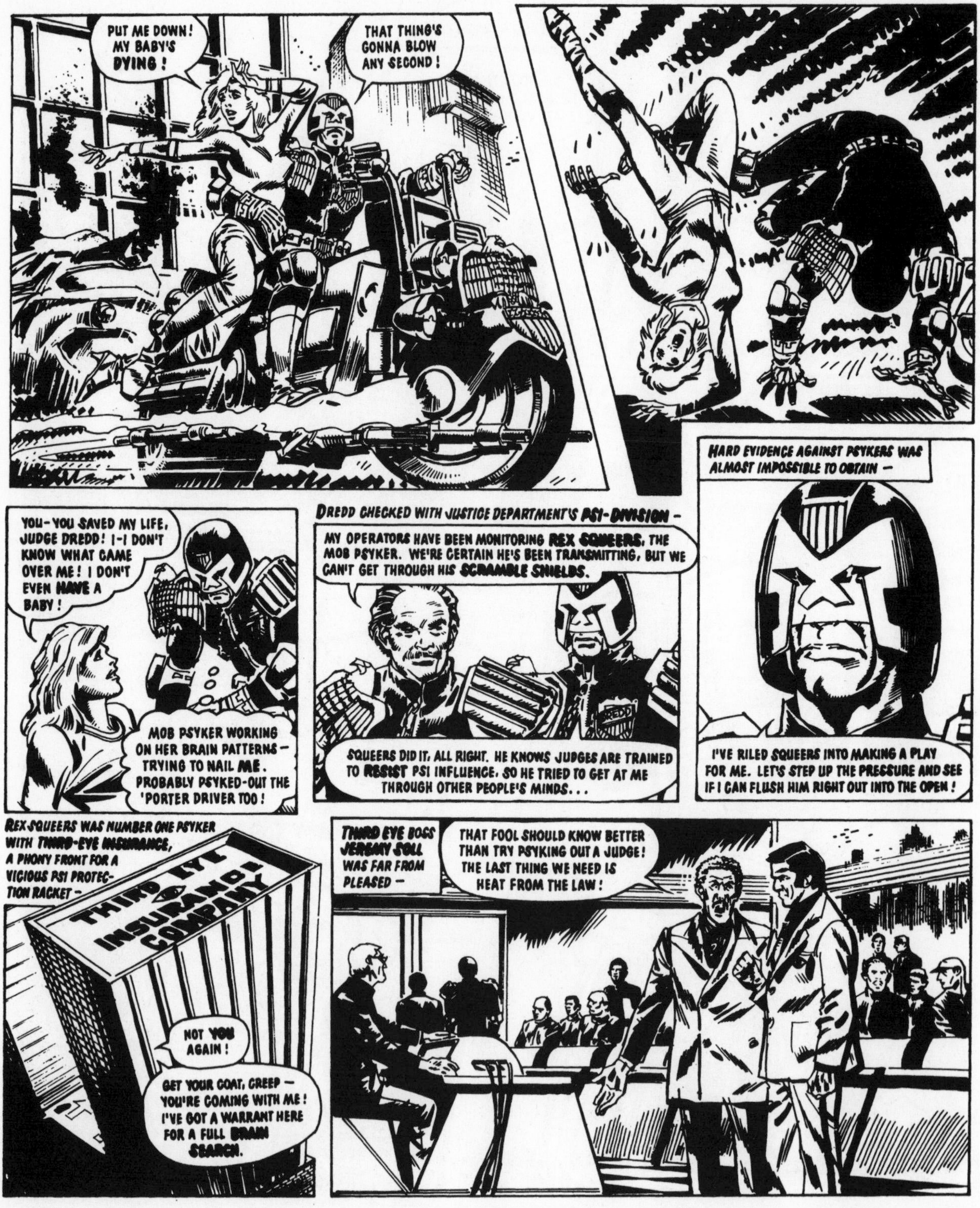
PUT ME DOWN! MY BABY'S DYING!
THAT THING'S GONNA BLOW ANY SECOND!
HARD EVIDENCE AGAINST PSYKERS WAS ALMOST IMPOSSIBLE TO OBTAIN —
I'VE RILED SQUEERS INTO MAKING A PLAY FOR ME. LET'S STEP UP THE PRESSURE AND SEE IF I CAN FLUSH HIM RIGHT OUT INTO THE OPEN!
YOU— YOU SAVED MY LIFE, JUDGE DREDD! I-I DON'T KNOW WHAT CAME OVER ME! I DON'T EVEN HAVE A BABY!
MOB PSYKER WORKING ON HER BRAIN PATTERNS— TRYING TO NAIL ME. PROBABLY PSYKED-OUT THE 'PORTER DRIVER TOO!
DREDD CHECKED WITH JUSTICE DEPARTMENT'S PSI-DIVISION —
MY OPERATORS HAVE BEEN MONITORING REX SQUEERS, THE MOB PSYKER. WE'RE CERTAIN HE'S BEEN TRANSMITTING, BUT WE CAN'T GET THROUGH HIS SCRAMBLE SHIELDS.
SQUEERS DID IT, ALL RIGHT. HE KNOWS JUDGES ARE TRAINED TO RESIST PSI INFLUENCE, SO HE TRIED TO GET AT ME THROUGH OTHER PEOPLE'S MINDS...
REX SQUEERS WAS NUMBER ONE PSYKER WITH THIRD-EYE INSURANCE, A PHONY FRONT FOR A VICIOUS PSI PROTECTION RACKET —
THIRD EYE INSURANCE COMPANY
NOT YOU AGAIN!
GET YOUR COAT, CREEP — YOU'RE COMING WITH ME! I'VE GOT A WARRANT HERE FOR A FULL BRAIN SEARCH.
THIRD EYE BOSS JEREMY SOLL WAS FAR FROM PLEASED —
THAT FOOL SHOULD KNOW BETTER THAN TRY PSYKING OUT A JUDGE! THE LAST THING WE NEED IS HEAT FROM THE LAW!

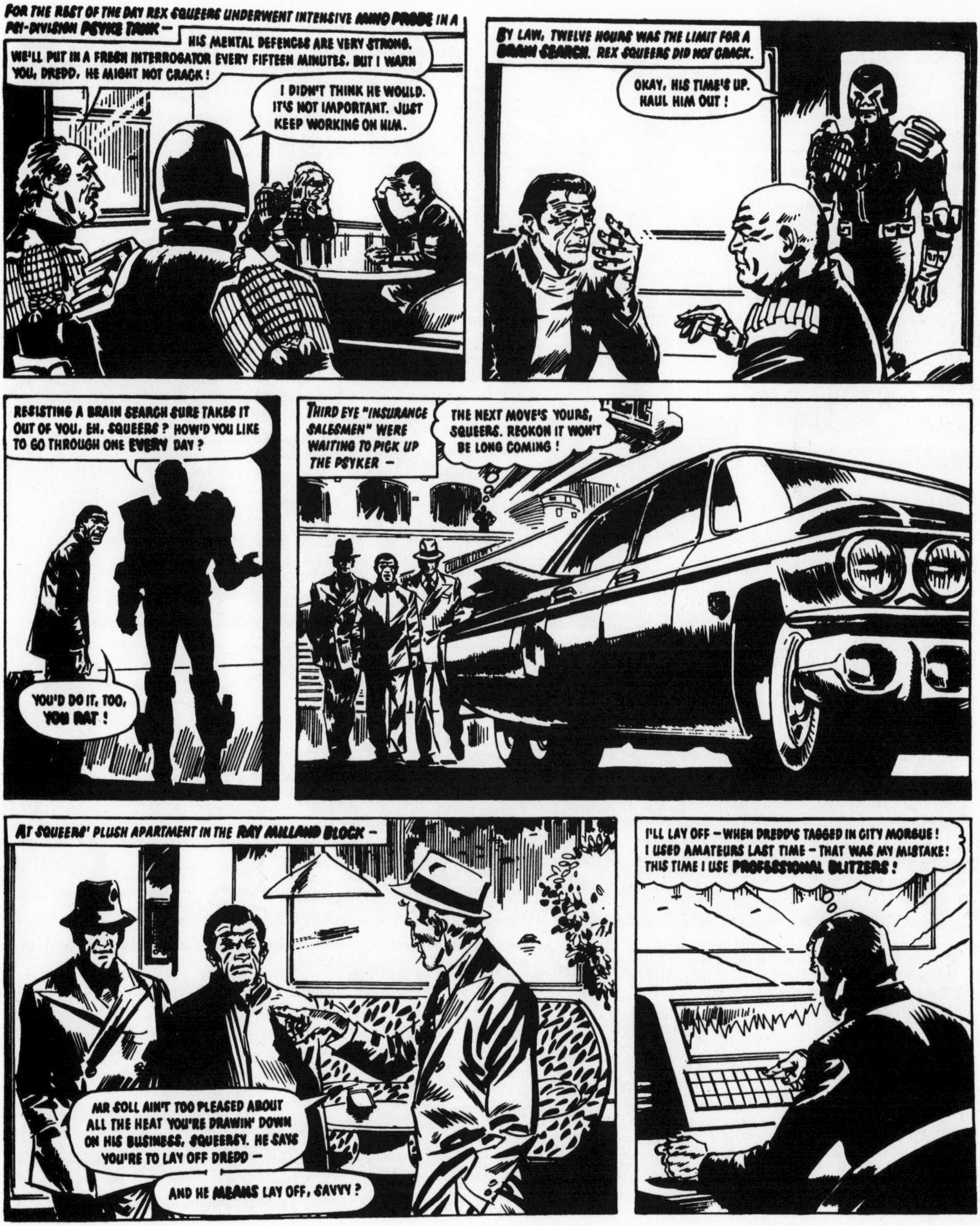

FOR THE REST OF THE DAY REX SQUEERS UNDERWENT INTENSIVE MIND PROBE IN A PSI-DIVISION PSYKE TANK —
HIS MENTAL DEFENCES ARE VERY STRONG. WE'LL PUT IN A FRESH INTERROGATOR EVERY FIFTEEN MINUTES. BUT I WARN YOU, DREDD, HE MIGHT NOT CRACK !
I DIDN'T THINK HE WOULD. IT'S NOT IMPORTANT. JUST KEEP WORKING ON HIM.
BY LAW, TWELVE HOURS WAS THE LIMIT FOR A BRAIN SEARCH. REX SQUEERS DID NOT CRACK.
OKAY, HIS TIME'S UP. HAUL HIM OUT !
RESISTING A BRAIN SEARCH SURE TAKES IT OUT OF YOU, EH, SQUEERS ? HOW'D YOU LIKE TO GO THROUGH ONE EVERY DAY ?
YOU'D DO IT, TOO, YOU RAT !
THIRD EYE "INSURANCE SALESMEN" WERE WAITING TO PICK UP THE PSYKER —
THE NEXT MOVE'S YOURS, SQUEERS. RECKON IT WON'T BE LONG COMING !
AT SQUEERS' PLUSH APARTMENT IN THE RAY MILLAND BLOCK —
MR SOLL AIN'T TOO PLEASED ABOUT ALL THE HEAT YOU'RE DRAWIN' DOWN ON HIS BUSINESS, SQUEERSY. HE SAYS YOU'RE TO LAY OFF DREDD —
AND HE MEANS LAY OFF, SAVVY ?
I'LL LAY OFF — WHEN DREDD'S TAGGED IN CITY MORGUE ! I USED AMATEURS LAST TIME — THAT WAS MY MISTAKE! THIS TIME I USE PROFESSIONAL BLITZERS !

PROTECTED BY HIS SCRAMBLE SHIELDS FROM PSI-JUDGE INTERVENTION, POWERFUL PSI-WAVES PULSED FROM SQUEERS' MIND INTO THE MINDS OF HIS CHOSEN TOOLS — THE TWO THIRD EYE SALESMEN!

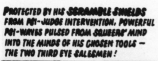

HEY! I GOT A GREAT IDEA — WHY DON'T WE GO WHACK OUT JUDGE DREDD?

SMART THINKIN', LOUIS! WHERE DO WE FIND HIM?

HE'S PATROLLING THE MEGA-DOCKS AREA, ATLANTIC GATE 3!

I KNOW — LET'S TRY THE MEGA-DOCKS!

AT THE MEGA-DOCKS —

PSI-DIVISION TO JUDGE DREDD! REX SQUEERS' SCRAMBLE SHIELDS ARE ON. HE'S UP TO SOMETHING!

I'LL BE WATCHING.

HEADLIGHTS! COULD BE THEM!

IT IS!

THE THIRD EYE MEN WERE PROFESSIONALS. BUT DREDD WAS NO AMATEUR —

AARGH!

LOUIS!

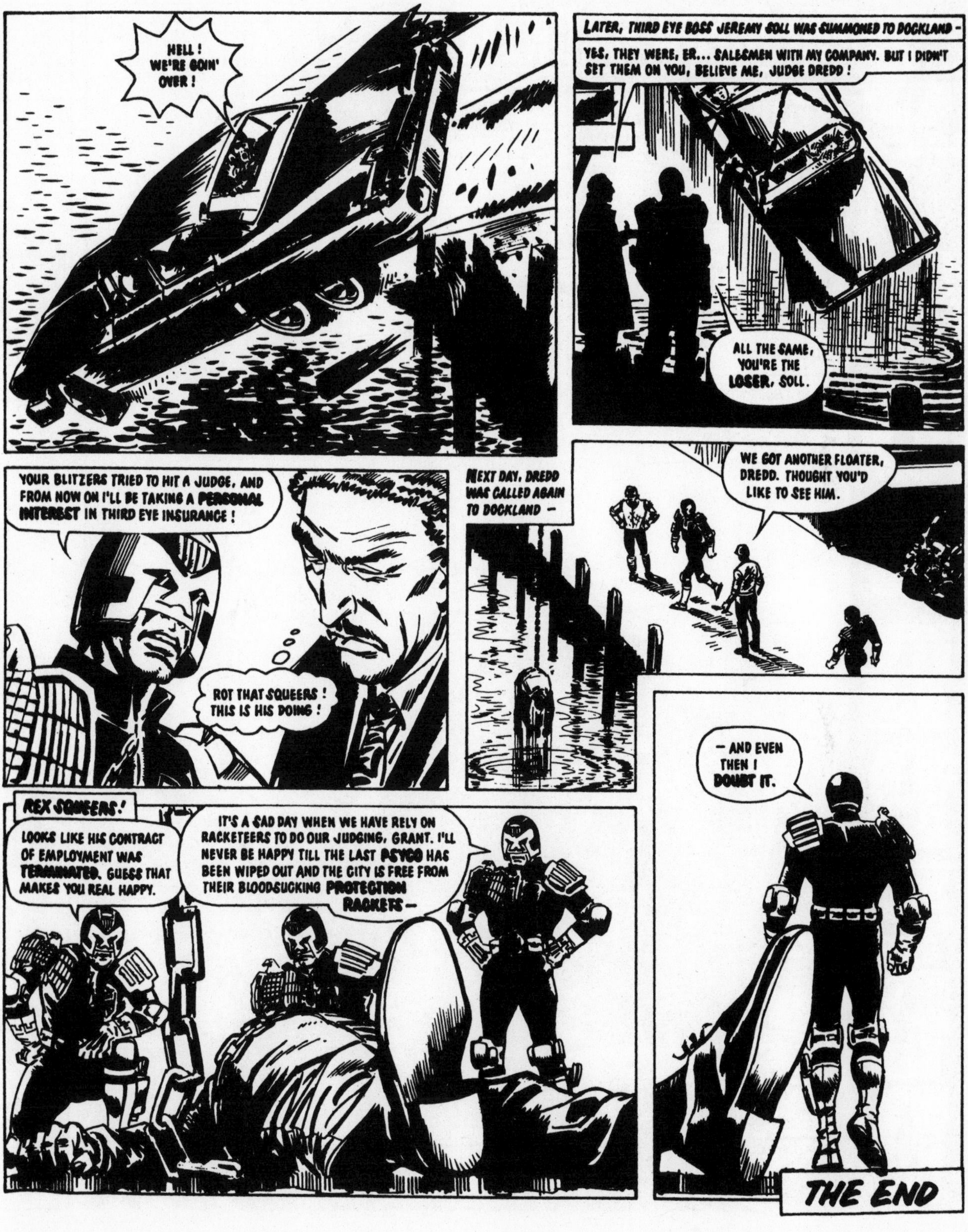

HELL ! WE'RE GOIN' OVER !
LATER, THIRD EYE BOSS JEREMY SOLL WAS SUMMONED TO DOCKLAND –
YES, THEY WERE, ER... SALESMEN WITH MY COMPANY. BUT I DIDN'T SET THEM ON YOU, BELIEVE ME, JUDGE DREDD !
ALL THE SAME, YOU'RE THE LOSER, SOLL.
YOUR BLITZERS TRIED TO HIT A JUDGE, AND FROM NOW ON I'LL BE TAKING A PERSONAL INTEREST IN THIRD EYE INSURANCE !
ROT THAT SQUEERS ! THIS IS HIS DOING !
NEXT DAY, DREDD WAS CALLED AGAIN TO DOCKLAND –
WE GOT ANOTHER FLOATER, DREDD. THOUGHT YOU'D LIKE TO SEE HIM.
REX SQUEERS!
LOOKS LIKE HIS CONTRACT OF EMPLOYMENT WAS TERMINATED. GUESS THAT MAKES YOU REAL HAPPY.
IT'S A SAD DAY WHEN WE HAVE RELY ON RACKETEERS TO DO OUR JUDGING, GRANT. I'LL NEVER BE HAPPY TILL THE LAST PSYCO HAS BEEN WIPED OUT AND THE CITY IS FREE FROM THEIR BLOODSUCKING PROTECTION RACKETS –
– AND EVEN THEN I DOUBT IT.
THE END

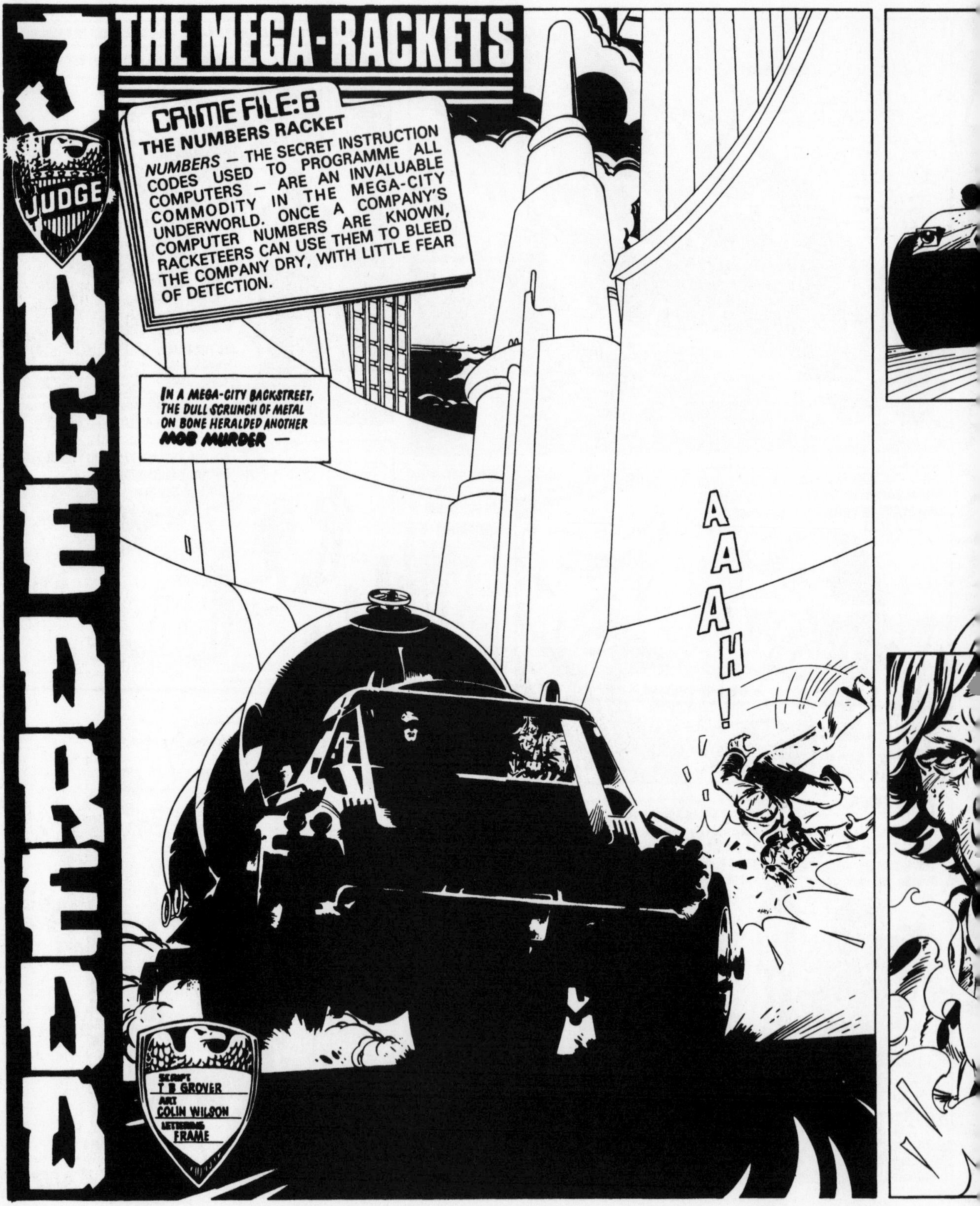
JUDGE DREDD
THE MEGA-RACKETS
CRIME FILE:6
THE NUMBERS RACKET
NUMBERS — THE SECRET INSTRUCTION CODES USED TO PROGRAMME ALL COMPUTERS — ARE AN INVALUABLE COMMODITY IN THE MEGA-CITY UNDERWORLD. ONCE A COMPANY'S COMPUTER NUMBERS ARE KNOWN, RACKETEERS CAN USE THEM TO BLEED THE COMPANY DRY, WITH LITTLE FEAR OF DETECTION.
IN A MEGA-CITY BACKSTREET, THE DULL SCRUNCH OF METAL ON BONE HERALDED ANOTHER MOB MURDER —
AAAAH!
JUDGE
SCRIPT T B GROVER
ART COLIN WILSON
LETTERING FRAME

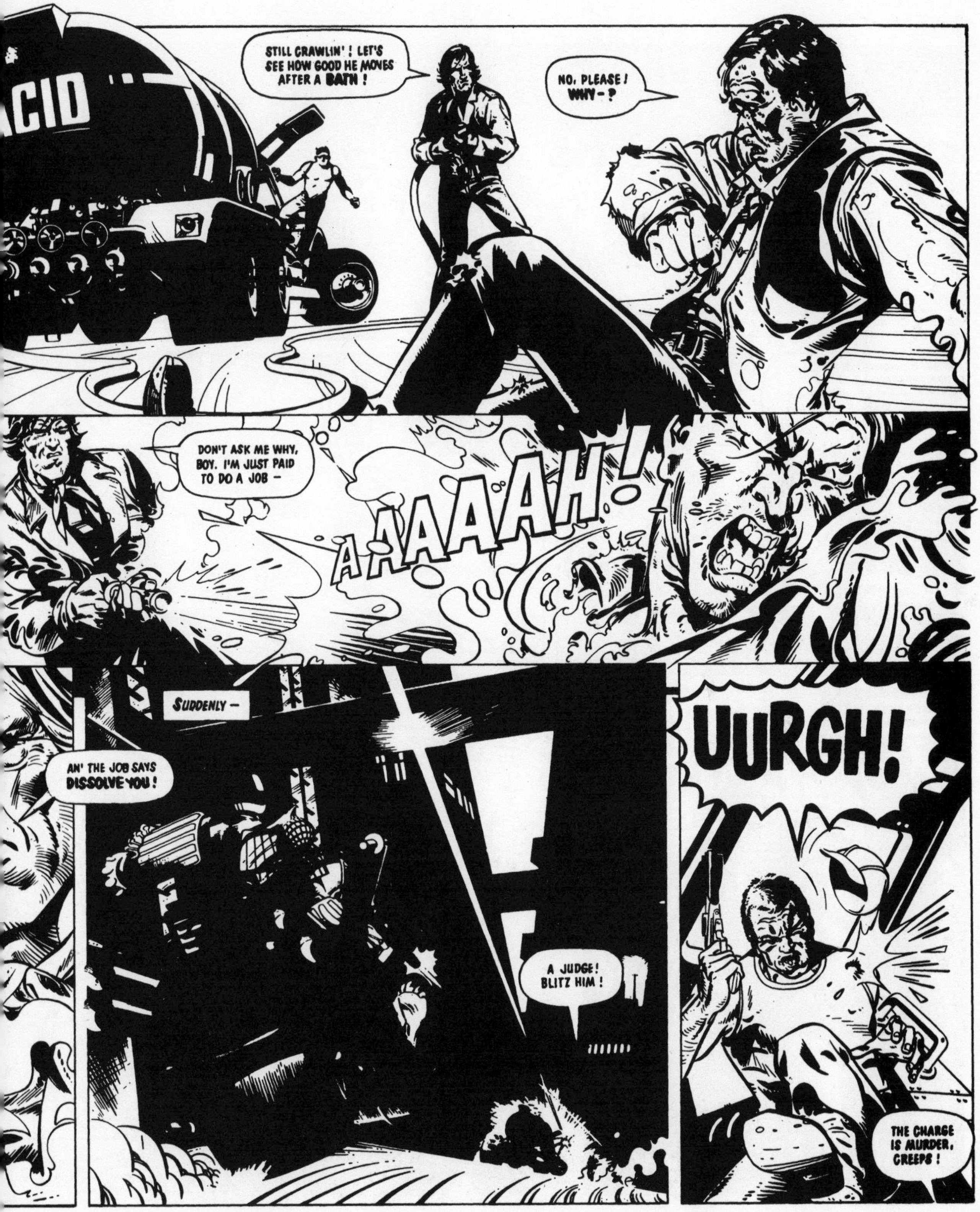
ACID
STILL CRAWLIN'! LET'S SEE HOW GOOD HE MOVES AFTER A BATH!
NO, PLEASE! WHY-?
DON'T ASK ME WHY, BOY. I'M JUST PAID TO DO A JOB -
AAAAAAH!
AN' THE JOB SAYS DISSOLVE YOU!
SUDDENLY -
A JUDGE! BLITZ HIM!
UURGH!
THE CHARGE IS MURDER, CREEPS!

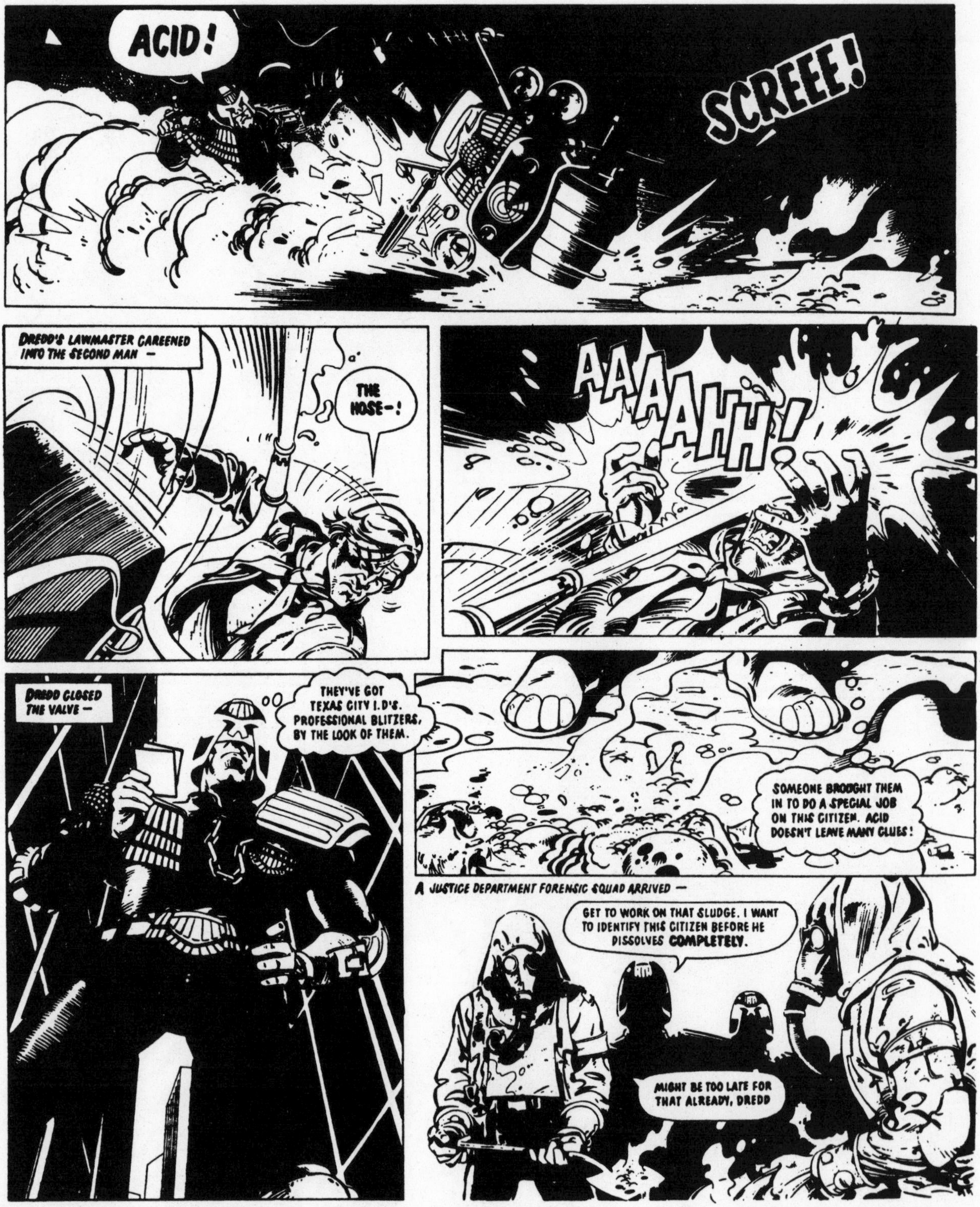
ACID!
SCREEE!
DREDD'S LAWMASTER CAREENED INTO THE SECOND MAN —
THE HOSE—!
AAAAAHH!
DREDD CLOSED THE VALVE —
THEY'VE GOT TEXAS CITY I.D'S. PROFESSIONAL BLITZERS, BY THE LOOK OF THEM.
SOMEONE BROUGHT THEM IN TO DO A SPECIAL JOB ON THIS CITIZEN. ACID DOESN'T LEAVE MANY CLUES!
A JUSTICE DEPARTMENT FORENSIC SQUAD ARRIVED —
GET TO WORK ON THAT SLUDGE. I WANT TO IDENTIFY THIS CITIZEN BEFORE HE DISSOLVES COMPLETELY.
MIGHT BE TOO LATE FOR THAT ALREADY, DREDD

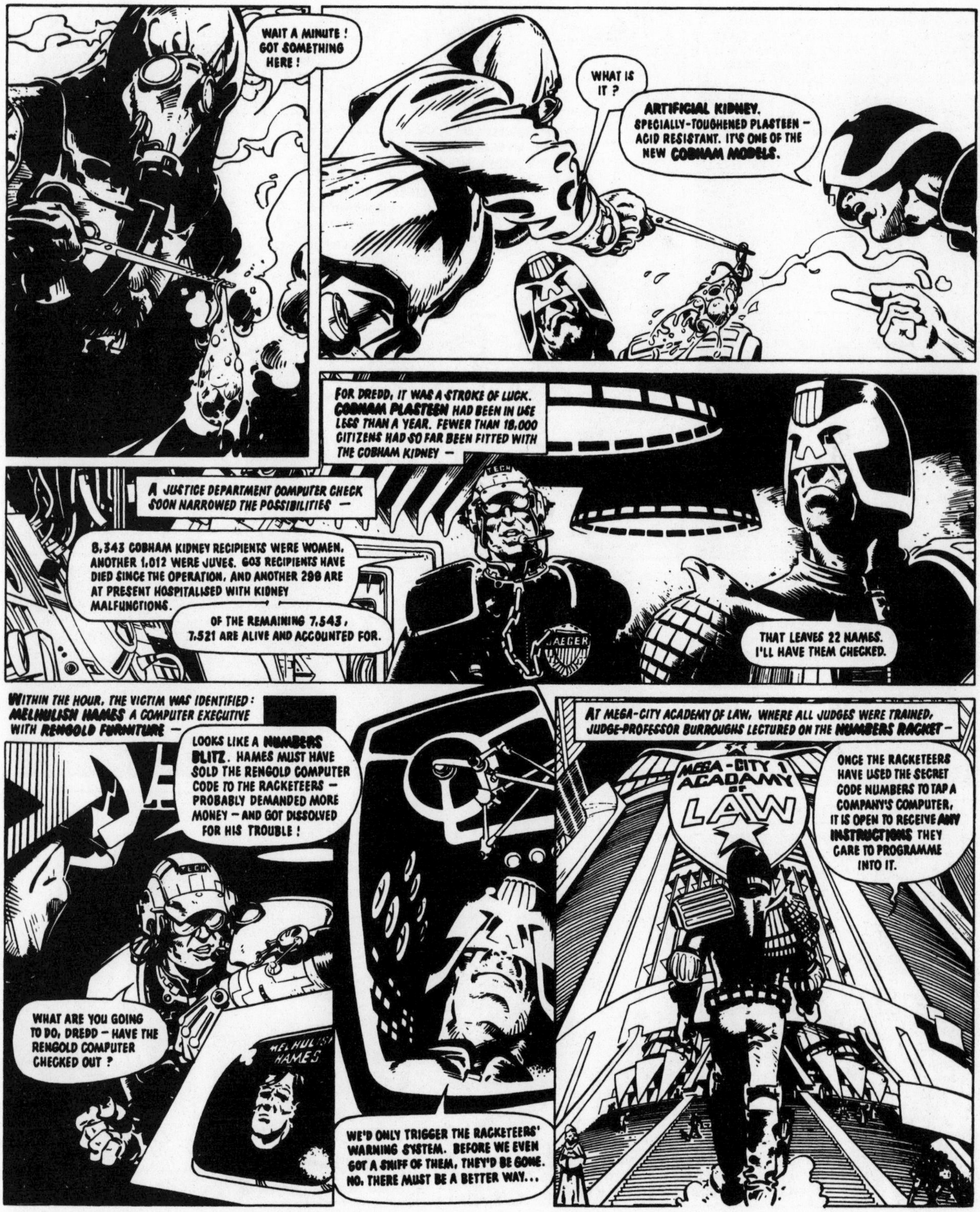
WAIT A MINUTE ! GOT SOMETHING HERE !
WHAT IS IT ?
ARTIFICIAL KIDNEY. SPECIALLY-TOUGHENED PLASTEEN – ACID RESISTANT. IT'S ONE OF THE NEW COBHAM MODELS.
FOR DREDD, IT WAS A STROKE OF LUCK. COBHAM PLASTEEN HAD BEEN IN USE LESS THAN A YEAR. FEWER THAN 18,000 CITIZENS HAD SO FAR BEEN FITTED WITH THE COBHAM KIDNEY –
A JUSTICE DEPARTMENT COMPUTER CHECK SOON NARROWED THE POSSIBILITIES –
8,343 COBHAM KIDNEY RECIPIENTS WERE WOMEN. ANOTHER 1,012 WERE JUVES. 603 RECIPIENTS HAVE DIED SINCE THE OPERATION, AND ANOTHER 299 ARE AT PRESENT HOSPITALISED WITH KIDNEY MALFUNCTIONS.
OF THE REMAINING 7,543, 7,521 ARE ALIVE AND ACCOUNTED FOR.
THAT LEAVES 22 NAMES. I'LL HAVE THEM CHECKED.
WITHIN THE HOUR, THE VICTIM WAS IDENTIFIED: MELHULISH HAMES A COMPUTER EXECUTIVE WITH RENGOLD FURNITURE –
LOOKS LIKE A NUMBERS BLITZ. HAMES MUST HAVE SOLD THE RENGOLD COMPUTER CODE TO THE RACKETEERS – PROBABLY DEMANDED MORE MONEY – AND GOT DISSOLVED FOR HIS TROUBLE !
WHAT ARE YOU GOING TO DO, DREDD – HAVE THE RENGOLD COMPUTER CHECKED OUT ?
HAMES
WE'D ONLY TRIGGER THE RACKETEERS' WARNING SYSTEM. BEFORE WE EVEN GOT A SNIFF OF THEM, THEY'D BE GONE. NO, THERE MUST BE A BETTER WAY...
AT MEGA-CITY ACADEMY OF LAW, WHERE ALL JUDGES WERE TRAINED, JUDGE-PROFESSOR BURROUGHS LECTURED ON THE NUMBERS RACKET –
MEGA-CITY 1 ACADAMY OF LAW
ONCE THE RACKETEERS HAVE USED THE SECRET CODE NUMBERS TO TAP A COMPANY'S COMPUTER, IT IS OPEN TO RECEIVE ANY INSTRUCTIONS THEY CARE TO PROGRAMME INTO IT.

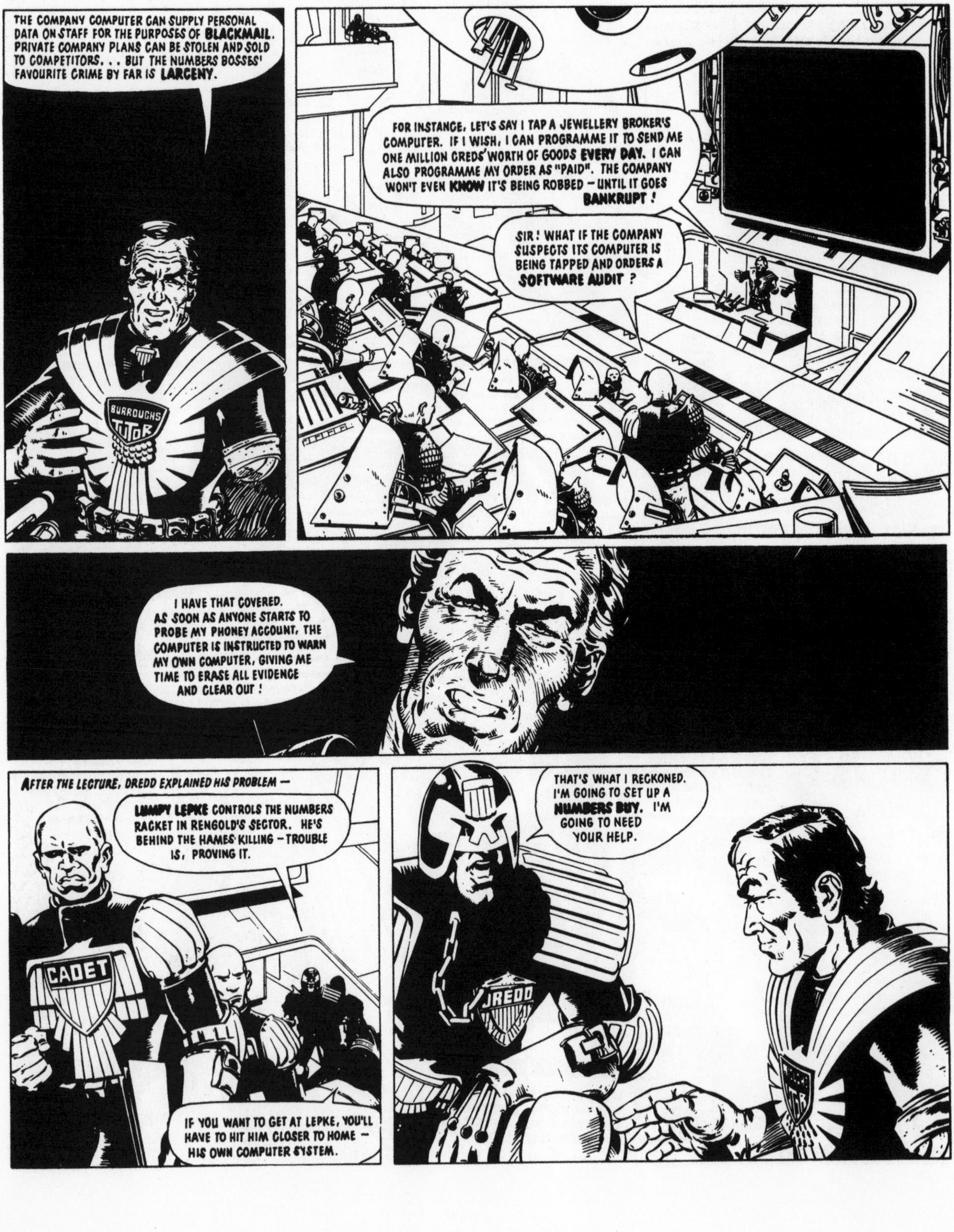
THE COMPANY COMPUTER CAN SUPPLY PERSONAL DATA ON STAFF FOR THE PURPOSES OF BLACKMAIL. PRIVATE COMPANY PLANS CAN BE STOLEN AND SOLD TO COMPETITORS... BUT THE NUMBERS BOSSES' FAVOURITE CRIME BY FAR IS LARCENY.
BURROUGHS TUTOR
FOR INSTANCE, LET'S SAY I TAP A JEWELLERY BROKER'S COMPUTER. IF I WISH, I CAN PROGRAMME IT TO SEND ME ONE MILLION CREDS' WORTH OF GOODS EVERY DAY. I CAN ALSO PROGRAMME MY ORDER AS "PAID". THE COMPANY WON'T EVEN KNOW IT'S BEING ROBBED — UNTIL IT GOES BANKRUPT!
SIR! WHAT IF THE COMPANY SUSPECTS ITS COMPUTER IS BEING TAPPED AND ORDERS A SOFTWARE AUDIT?
I HAVE THAT COVERED. AS SOON AS ANYONE STARTS TO PROBE MY PHONEY ACCOUNT, THE COMPUTER IS INSTRUCTED TO WARN MY OWN COMPUTER, GIVING ME TIME TO ERASE ALL EVIDENCE AND CLEAR OUT!
AFTER THE LECTURE, DREDD EXPLAINED HIS PROBLEM —
LUMPY LEPKE CONTROLS THE NUMBERS RACKET IN RENGOLD'S SECTOR. HE'S BEHIND THE HAMES KILLING — TROUBLE IS, PROVING IT.
CADET
IF YOU WANT TO GET AT LEPKE, YOU'LL HAVE TO HIT HIM CLOSER TO HOME — HIS OWN COMPUTER SYSTEM.
THAT'S WHAT I RECKONED. I'M GOING TO SET UP A NUMBERS BUY. I'M GOING TO NEED YOUR HELP.
DREDD

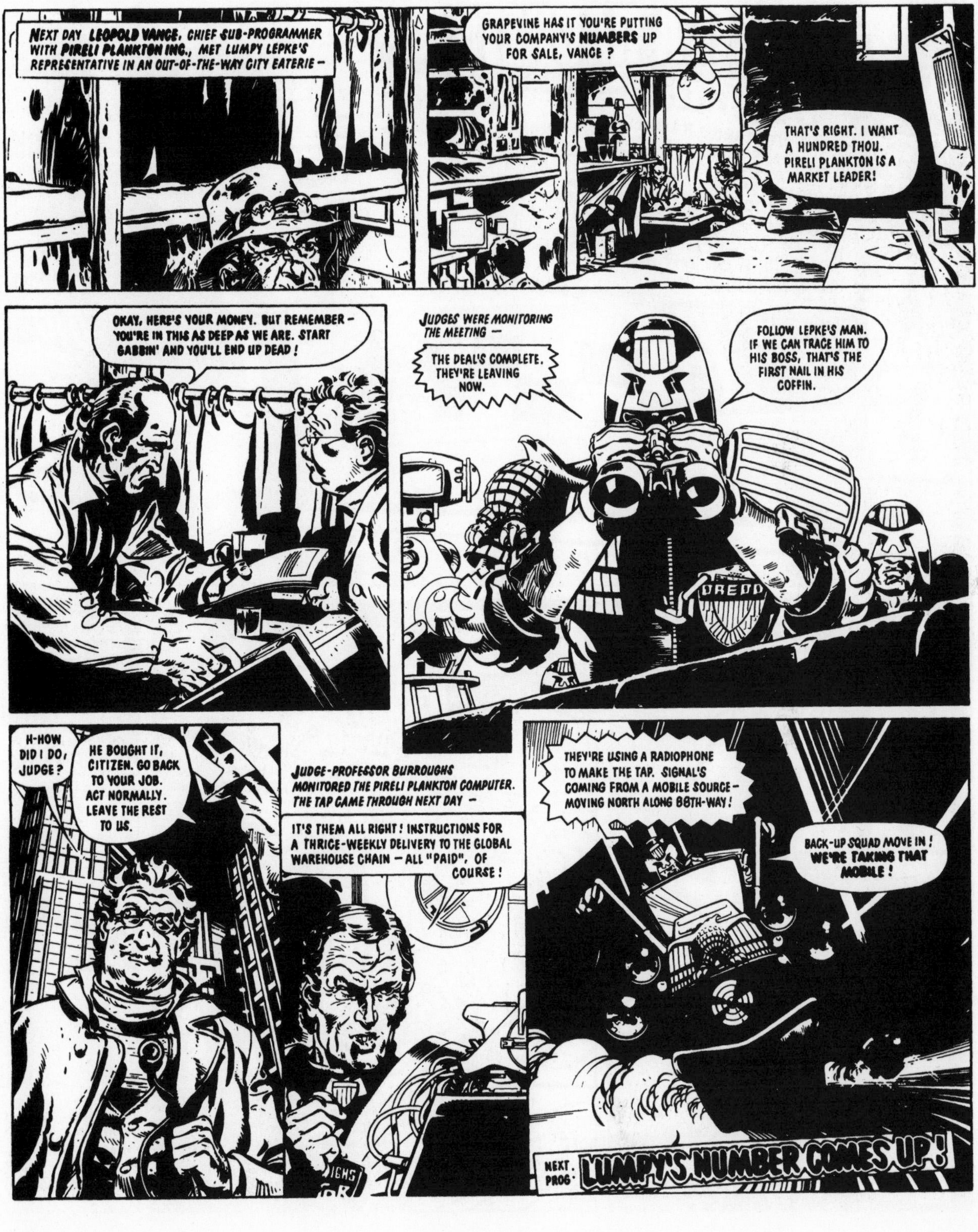
NEXT DAY LEOPOLD VANCE, CHIEF SUB-PROGRAMMER WITH PIRELI PLANKTON INC., MET LUMPY LEPKE'S REPRESENTATIVE IN AN OUT-OF-THE-WAY CITY EATERIE –
GRAPEVINE HAS IT YOU'RE PUTTING YOUR COMPANY'S NUMBERS UP FOR SALE, VANCE ?
THAT'S RIGHT. I WANT A HUNDRED THOU. PIRELI PLANKTON IS A MARKET LEADER!
OKAY, HERE'S YOUR MONEY. BUT REMEMBER – YOU'RE IN THIS AS DEEP AS WE ARE. START GABBIN' AND YOU'LL END UP DEAD !
JUDGES WERE MONITORING THE MEETING –
THE DEAL'S COMPLETE. THEY'RE LEAVING NOW.
FOLLOW LEPKE'S MAN. IF WE CAN TRACE HIM TO HIS BOSS, THAT'S THE FIRST NAIL IN HIS COFFIN.
DREDD
H-HOW DID I DO, JUDGE ?
HE BOUGHT IT, CITIZEN. GO BACK TO YOUR JOB. ACT NORMALLY. LEAVE THE REST TO US.
JUDGE-PROFESSOR BURROUGHS MONITORED THE PIRELI PLANKTON COMPUTER. THE TAP CAME THROUGH NEXT DAY –
IT'S THEM ALL RIGHT ! INSTRUCTIONS FOR A THRICE-WEEKLY DELIVERY TO THE GLOBAL WAREHOUSE CHAIN – ALL "PAID", OF COURSE !
THEY'RE USING A RADIOPHONE TO MAKE THE TAP. SIGNAL'S COMING FROM A MOBILE SOURCE – MOVING NORTH ALONG 88TH-WAY !
BACK-UP SQUAD MOVE IN ! WE'RE TAKING THAT MOBILE !
NEXT PROG: LUMPY'S NUMBER COMES UP !

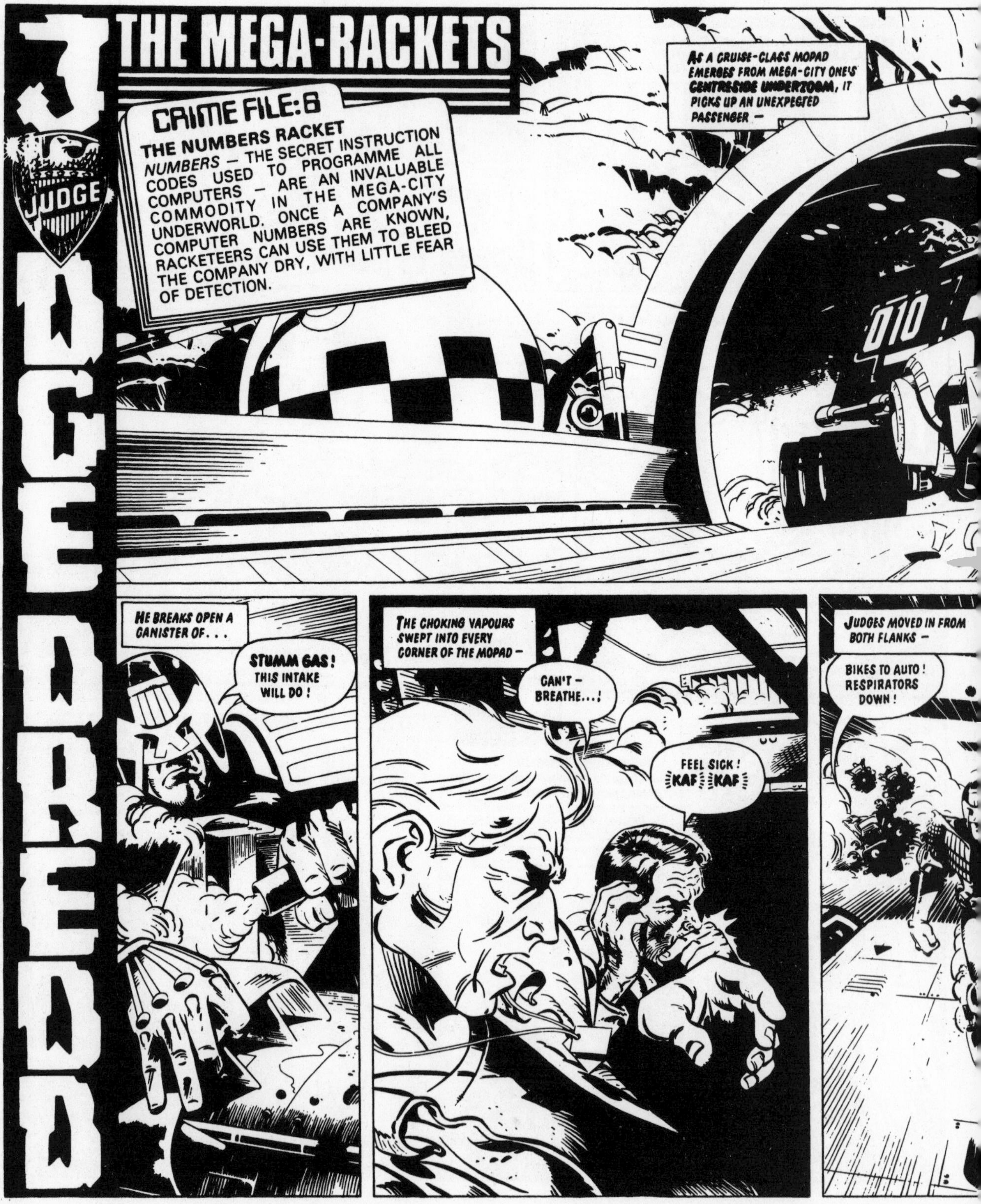
JUDGE DREDD
JUDGE
THE MEGA-RACKETS
CRIME FILE: 6
THE NUMBERS RACKET
NUMBERS — THE SECRET INSTRUCTION CODES USED TO PROGRAMME ALL COMPUTERS — ARE AN INVALUABLE COMMODITY IN THE MEGA-CITY UNDERWORLD. ONCE A COMPANY'S COMPUTER NUMBERS ARE KNOWN, RACKETEERS CAN USE THEM TO BLEED THE COMPANY DRY, WITH LITTLE FEAR OF DETECTION.
AS A CRUISE-CLASS MOPAD EMERGES FROM MEGA-CITY ONE'S CENTRESIDE UNDERZOOM, IT PICKS UP AN UNEXPECTED PASSENGER —
HE BREAKS OPEN A CANISTER OF . . .
STUMM GAS! THIS INTAKE WILL DO!
THE CHOKING VAPOURS SWEPT INTO EVERY CORNER OF THE MOPAD —
CAN'T — BREATHE . . . !
FEEL SICK! KAF! KAF!
JUDGES MOVED IN FROM BOTH FLANKS —
BIKES TO AUTO! RESPIRATORS DOWN!

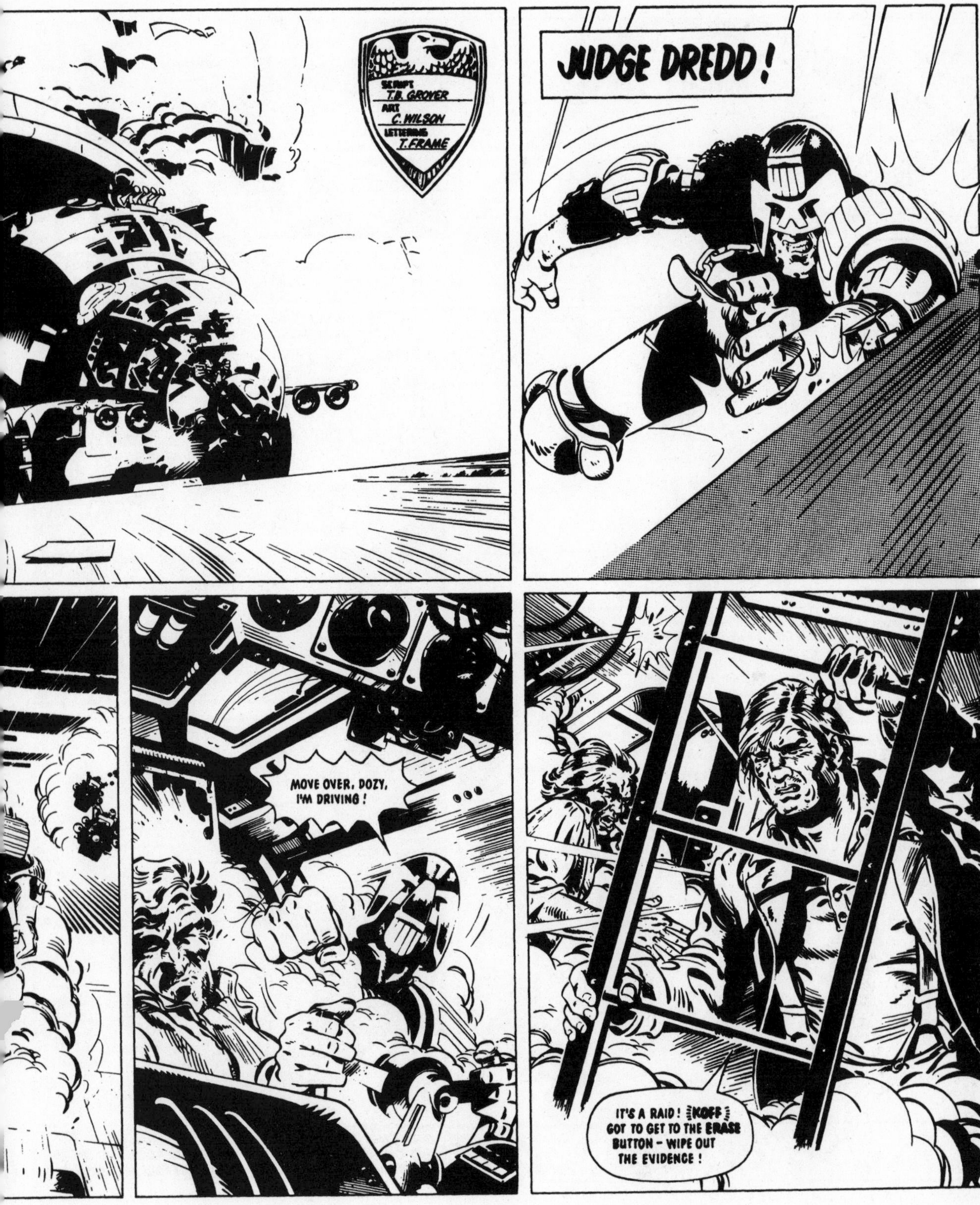
SCRIPT T.B. GROVER
ART C.WILSON
LETTERING T.FRAME
JUDGE DREDD!
MOVE OVER, DOZY, I'M DRIVING!
IT'S A RAID! KOFF GOT TO GET TO THE ERASE BUTTON – WIPE OUT THE EVIDENCE!

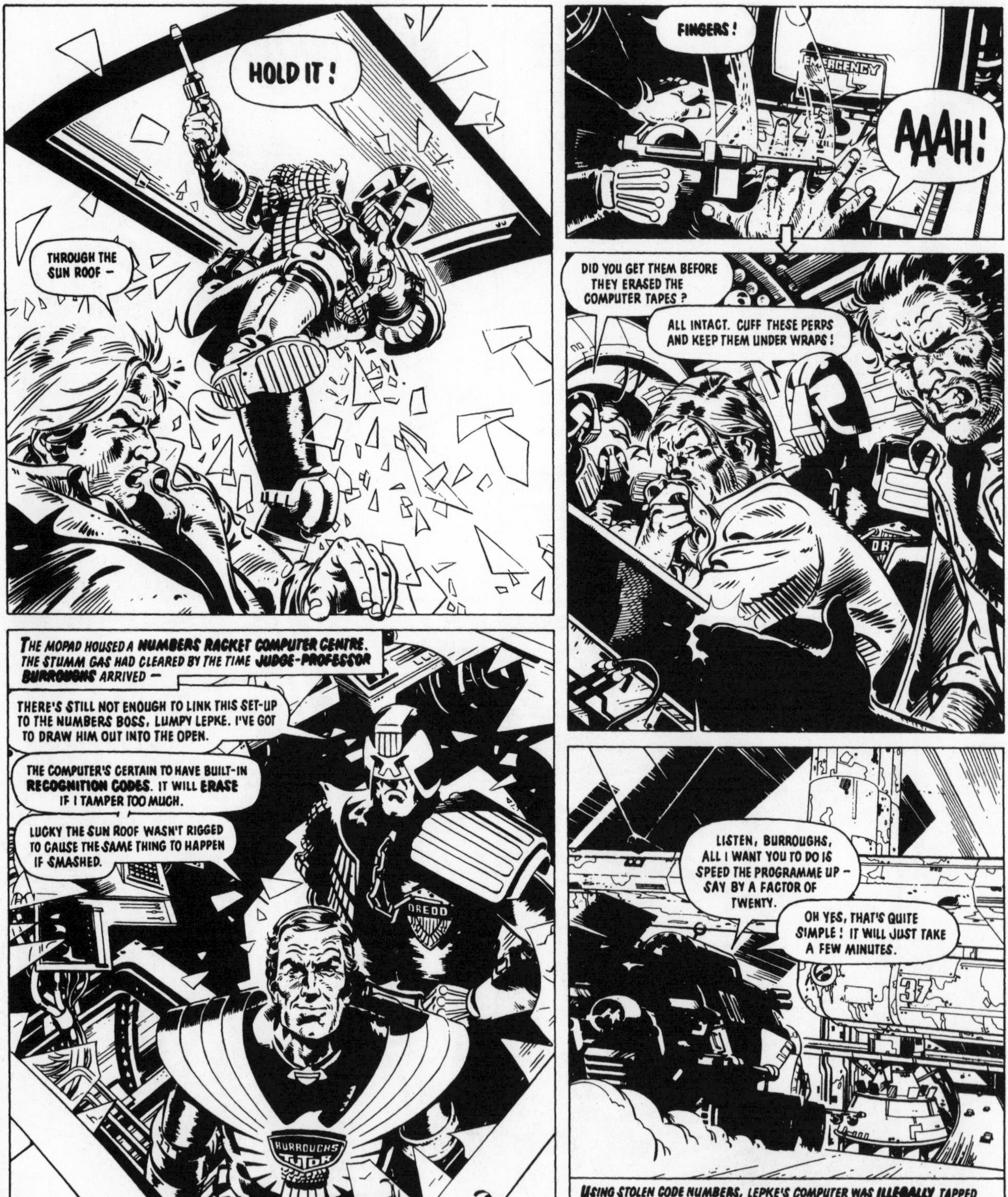

HOLD IT!
THROUGH THE SUN ROOF –
FINGERS!
AAAH!
DID YOU GET THEM BEFORE THEY ERASED THE COMPUTER TAPES?
ALL INTACT. CUFF THESE PERPS AND KEEP THEM UNDER WRAPS!
THE MOPAD HOUSED A NUMBERS RACKET COMPUTER CENTRE. THE STUMM GAS HAD CLEARED BY THE TIME JUDGE-PROFESSOR BURROUGHS ARRIVED –
THERE'S STILL NOT ENOUGH TO LINK THIS SET-UP TO THE NUMBERS BOSS, LUMPY LEPKE. I'VE GOT TO DRAW HIM OUT INTO THE OPEN.
THE COMPUTER'S CERTAIN TO HAVE BUILT-IN RECOGNITION CODES. IT WILL ERASE IF I TAMPER TOO MUCH.
LUCKY THE SUN ROOF WASN'T RIGGED TO CAUSE THE SAME THING TO HAPPEN IF SMASHED.
DREDD
BURROUGHS TUTOR
LISTEN, BURROUGHS, ALL I WANT YOU TO DO IS SPEED THE PROGRAMME UP – SAY BY A FACTOR OF TWENTY.
OH YES, THAT'S QUITE SIMPLE! IT WILL JUST TAKE A FEW MINUTES.
USING STOLEN CODE NUMBERS, LEPKE'S COMPUTER WAS ILLEGALLY TAPPED INTO COMPANY COMPUTERS IN THE CITY'S CENTRAL SECTORS, ORDERING BILLIONS OF CREDITS' WORTH OF MERCHANDISE – COMPLETELY FREE OF CHARGE!

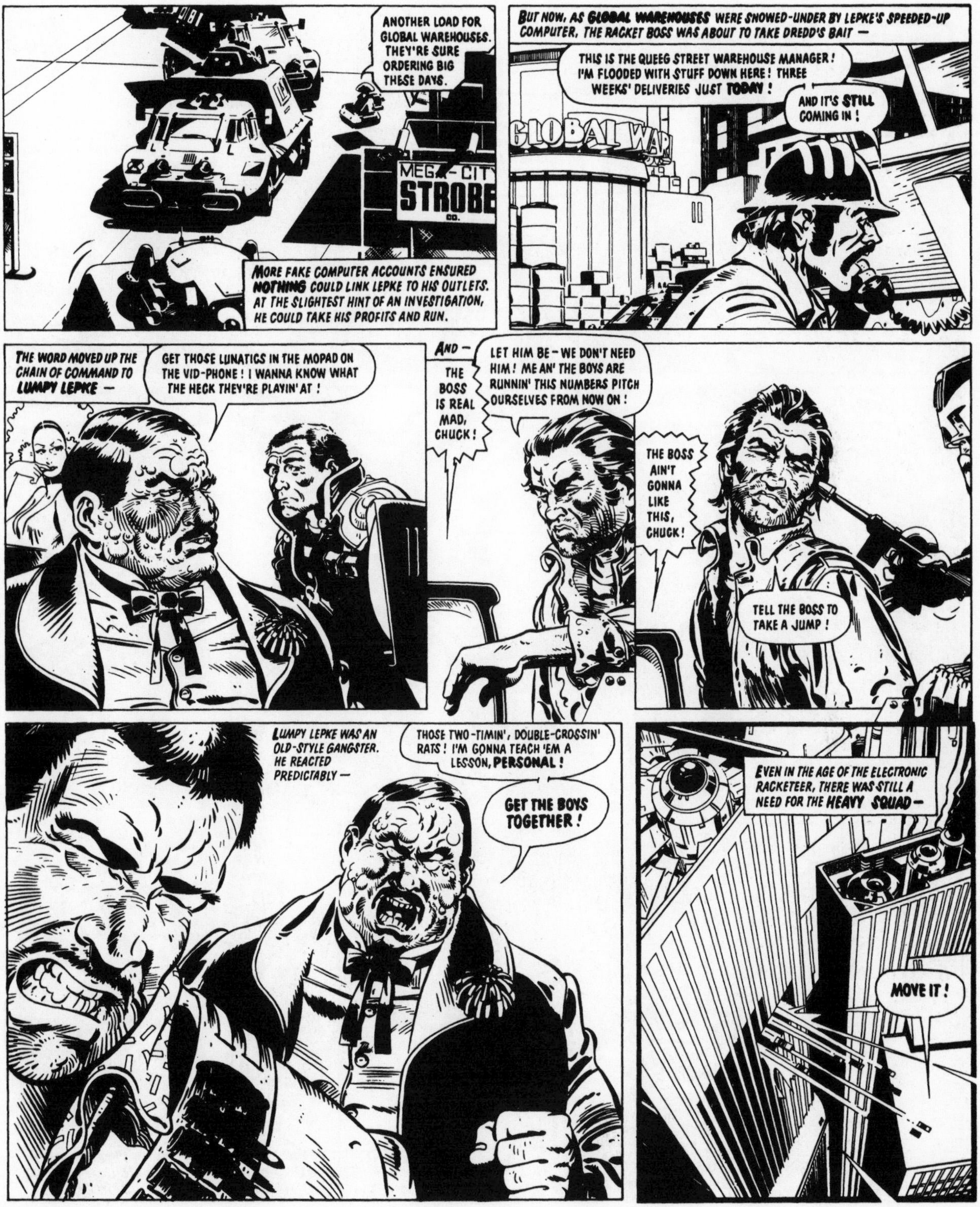
ANOTHER LOAD FOR GLOBAL WAREHOUSES. THEY'RE SURE ORDERING BIG THESE DAYS.
MEGA-CITY STROBE CO.
MORE FAKE COMPUTER ACCOUNTS ENSURED NOTHING COULD LINK LEPKE TO HIS OUTLETS. AT THE SLIGHTEST HINT OF AN INVESTIGATION, HE COULD TAKE HIS PROFITS AND RUN.
BUT NOW, AS GLOBAL WAREHOUSES WERE SNOWED-UNDER BY LEPKE'S SPEEDED-UP COMPUTER, THE RACKET BOSS WAS ABOUT TO TAKE DREDD'S BAIT —
THIS IS THE QUEEG STREET WAREHOUSE MANAGER! I'M FLOODED WITH STUFF DOWN HERE! THREE WEEKS' DELIVERIES JUST TODAY!
AND IT'S STILL COMING IN!
GLOBAL WAR
THE WORD MOVED UP THE CHAIN OF COMMAND TO LUMPY LEPKE —
GET THOSE LUNATICS IN THE MOPAD ON THE VID-PHONE! I WANNA KNOW WHAT THE HECK THEY'RE PLAYIN' AT!
AND —
THE BOSS IS REAL MAD, CHUCK!
LET HIM BE – WE DON'T NEED HIM! ME AN' THE BOYS ARE RUNNIN' THIS NUMBERS PITCH OURSELVES FROM NOW ON!
THE BOSS AIN'T GONNA LIKE THIS, CHUCK!
TELL THE BOSS TO TAKE A JUMP!
LUMPY LEPKE WAS AN OLD-STYLE GANGSTER. HE REACTED PREDICTABLY —
THOSE TWO-TIMIN', DOUBLE-CROSSIN' RATS! I'M GONNA TEACH 'EM A LESSON, PERSONAL!
GET THE BOYS TOGETHER!
EVEN IN THE AGE OF THE ELECTRONIC RACKETEER, THERE WAS STILL A NEED FOR THE HEAVY SQUAD —
MOVE IT!

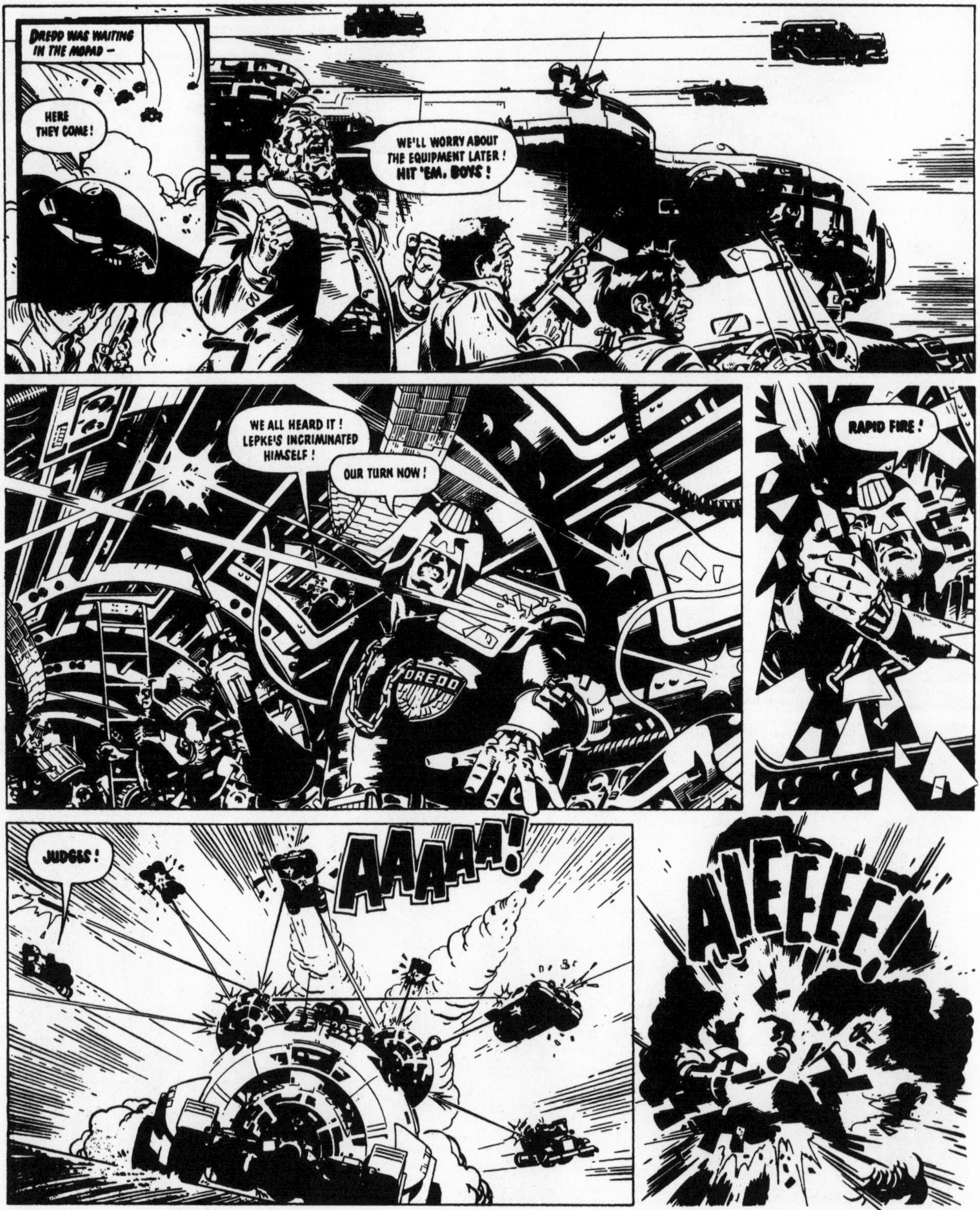
DREDD WAS WAITING IN THE MOPAD —
HERE THEY COME!
WE'LL WORRY ABOUT THE EQUIPMENT LATER! HIT 'EM, BOYS!
WE ALL HEARD IT! LEPKE'S INCRIMINATED HIMSELF!
OUR TURN NOW!
DREDD
RAPID FIRE!
JUDGES!
AAAAAA!
AIEEEE!

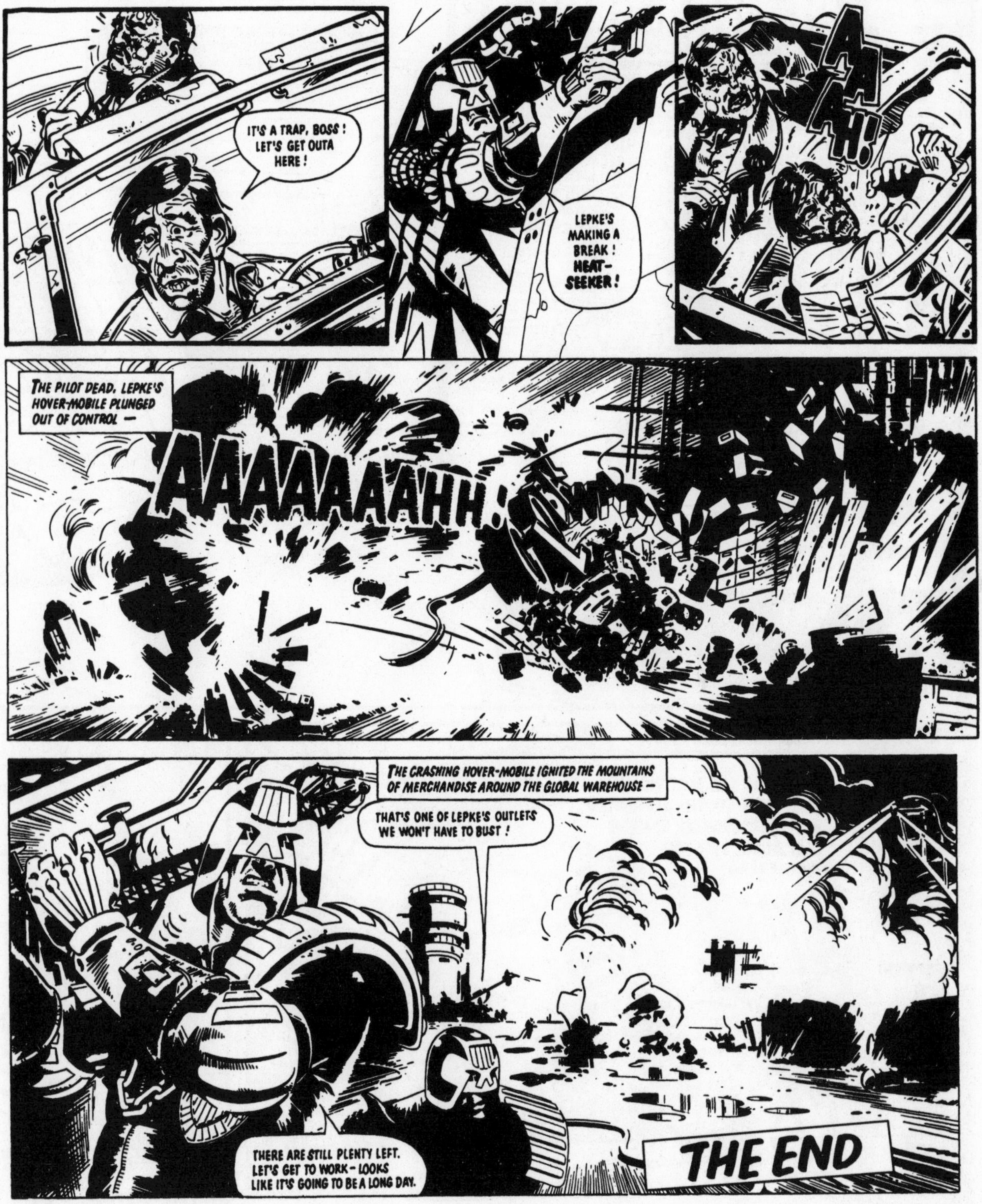

IT'S A TRAP, BOSS! LET'S GET OUTA HERE!
LEPKE'S MAKING A BREAK! HEAT-SEEKER!
AAAH!
THE PILOT DEAD, LEPKE'S HOVER-MOBILE PLUNGED OUT OF CONTROL –
AAAAAAAAHH!
THE CRASHING HOVER-MOBILE IGNITED THE MOUNTAINS OF MERCHANDISE AROUND THE GLOBAL WAREHOUSE –
THAT'S ONE OF LEPKE'S OUTLETS WE WON'T HAVE TO BUST!
THERE ARE STILL PLENTY LEFT. LET'S GET TO WORK – LOOKS LIKE IT'S GOING TO BE A LONG DAY.
THE END

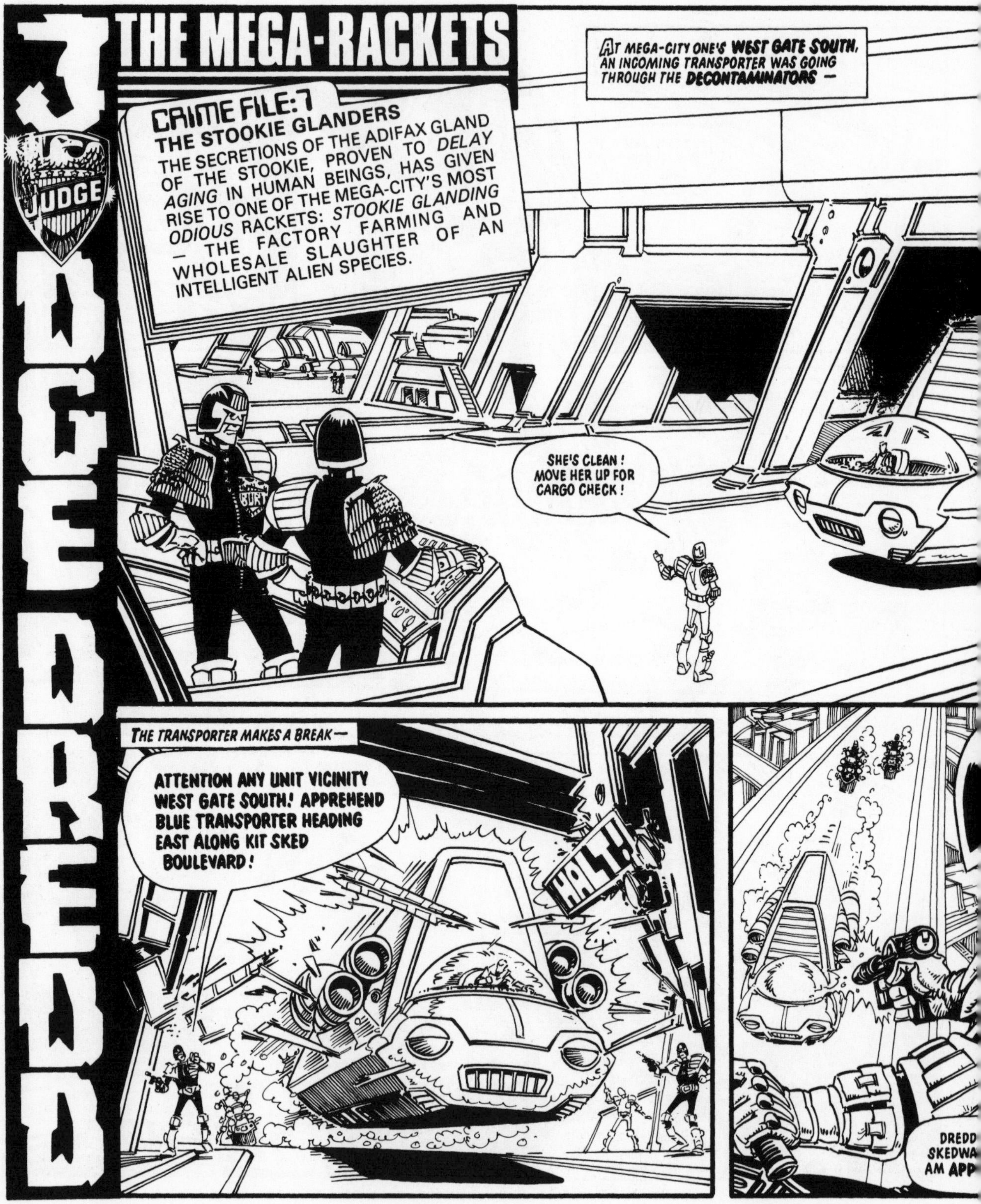
JUDGE DREDD
THE MEGA-RACKETS
AT MEGA-CITY ONE'S WEST GATE SOUTH, AN INCOMING TRANSPORTER WAS GOING THROUGH THE DECONTAMINATORS —
CRIME FILE: 7
THE STOOKIE GLANDERS
THE SECRETIONS OF THE ADIFAX GLAND OF THE STOOKIE, PROVEN TO DELAY AGING IN HUMAN BEINGS, HAS GIVEN RISE TO ONE OF THE MEGA-CITY'S MOST ODIOUS RACKETS: STOOKIE GLANDING — THE FACTORY FARMING AND WHOLESALE SLAUGHTER OF AN INTELLIGENT ALIEN SPECIES.
SHE'S CLEAN! MOVE HER UP FOR CARGO CHECK!
THE TRANSPORTER MAKES A BREAK —
ATTENTION ANY UNIT VICINITY WEST GATE SOUTH! APPREHEND BLUE TRANSPORTER HEADING EAST ALONG KIT SKED BOULEVARD!
HALT!
DREDD

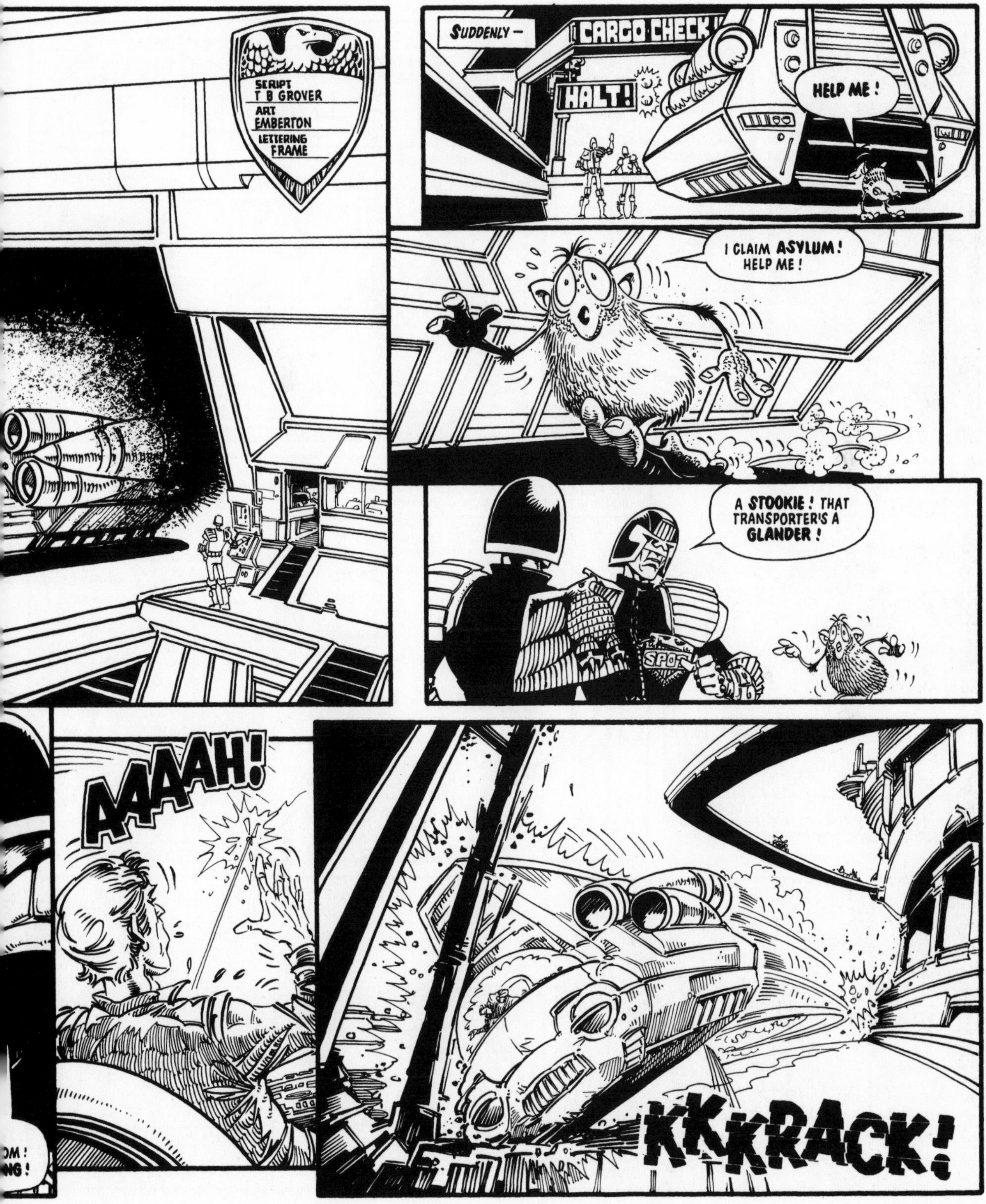
SCRIPT
T B GROVER
ART
EMBERTON
LETTERING
FRAME
SUDDENLY —
CARGO CHECK
HALT!
HELP ME!
I CLAIM ASYLUM! HELP ME!
A STOOKIE! THAT TRANSPORTER'S A GLANDER!
AAAAH!
KKKRACK!

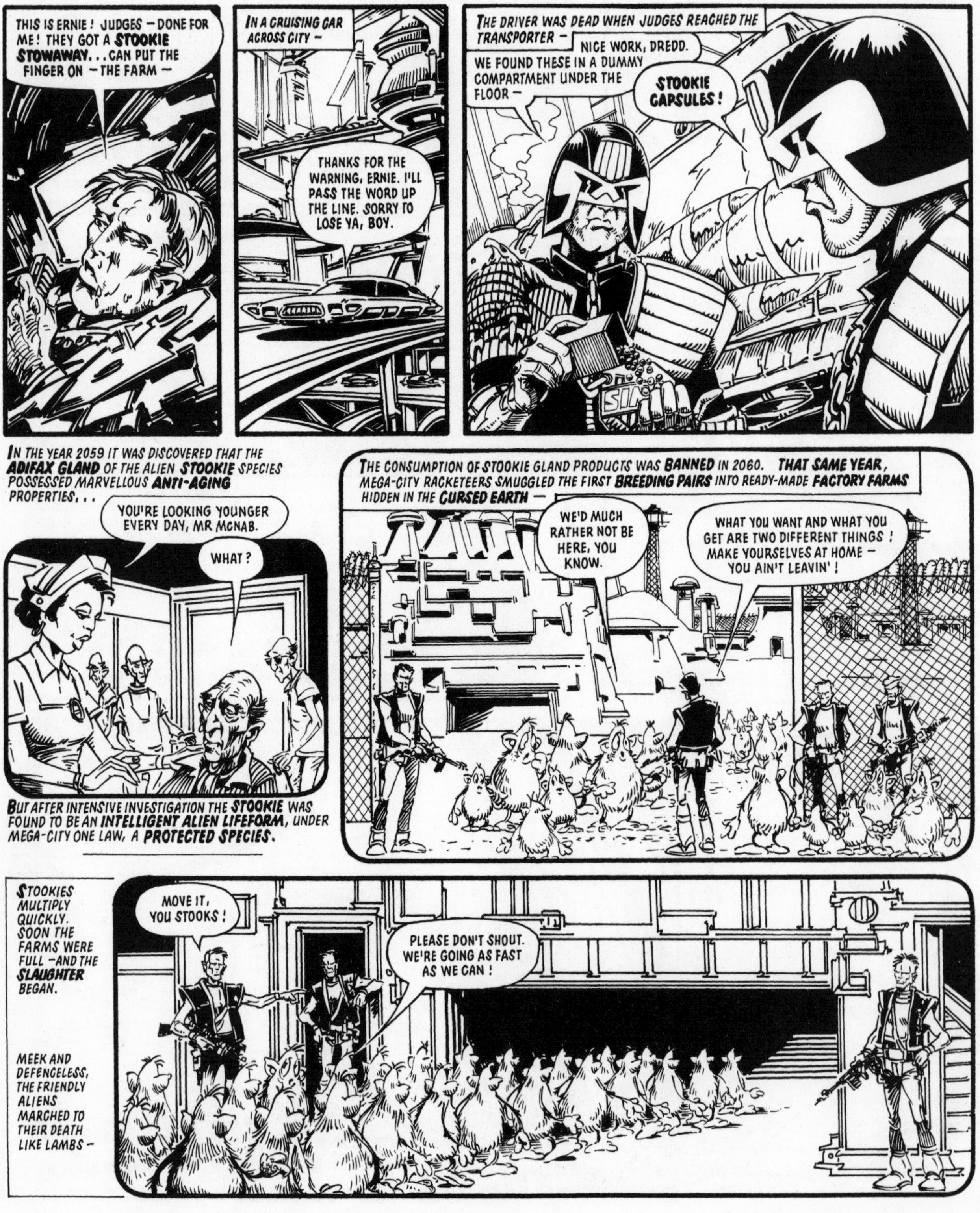
THIS IS ERNIE! JUDGES — DONE FOR ME! THEY GOT A STOOKIE STOWAWAY. . . CAN PUT THE FINGER ON — THE FARM —
IN A CRUISING CAR ACROSS CITY —
THANKS FOR THE WARNING, ERNIE. I'LL PASS THE WORD UP THE LINE. SORRY TO LOSE YA, BOY.
THE DRIVER WAS DEAD WHEN JUDGES REACHED THE TRANSPORTER —
NICE WORK, DREDD. WE FOUND THESE IN A DUMMY COMPARTMENT UNDER THE FLOOR —
STOOKIE CAPSULES!
IN THE YEAR 2059 IT WAS DISCOVERED THAT THE ADIFAX GLAND OF THE ALIEN STOOKIE SPECIES POSSESSED MARVELLOUS ANTI-AGING PROPERTIES. . .
YOU'RE LOOKING YOUNGER EVERY DAY, MR MCNAB.
WHAT?
BUT AFTER INTENSIVE INVESTIGATION THE STOOKIE WAS FOUND TO BE AN INTELLIGENT ALIEN LIFEFORM, UNDER MEGA-CITY ONE LAW, A PROTECTED SPECIES.
THE CONSUMPTION OF STOOKIE GLAND PRODUCTS WAS BANNED IN 2060. THAT SAME YEAR, MEGA-CITY RACKETEERS SMUGGLED THE FIRST BREEDING PAIRS INTO READY-MADE FACTORY FARMS HIDDEN IN THE CURSED EARTH —
WE'D MUCH RATHER NOT BE HERE, YOU KNOW.
WHAT YOU WANT AND WHAT YOU GET ARE TWO DIFFERENT THINGS! MAKE YOURSELVES AT HOME — YOU AIN'T LEAVIN'!
STOOKIES MULTIPLY QUICKLY. SOON THE FARMS WERE FULL — AND THE SLAUGHTER BEGAN.
MOVE IT, YOU STOOKS!
PLEASE DON'T SHOUT. WE'RE GOING AS FAST AS WE CAN!
MEEK AND DEFENCELESS, THE FRIENDLY ALIENS MARCHED TO THEIR DEATH LIKE LAMBS —

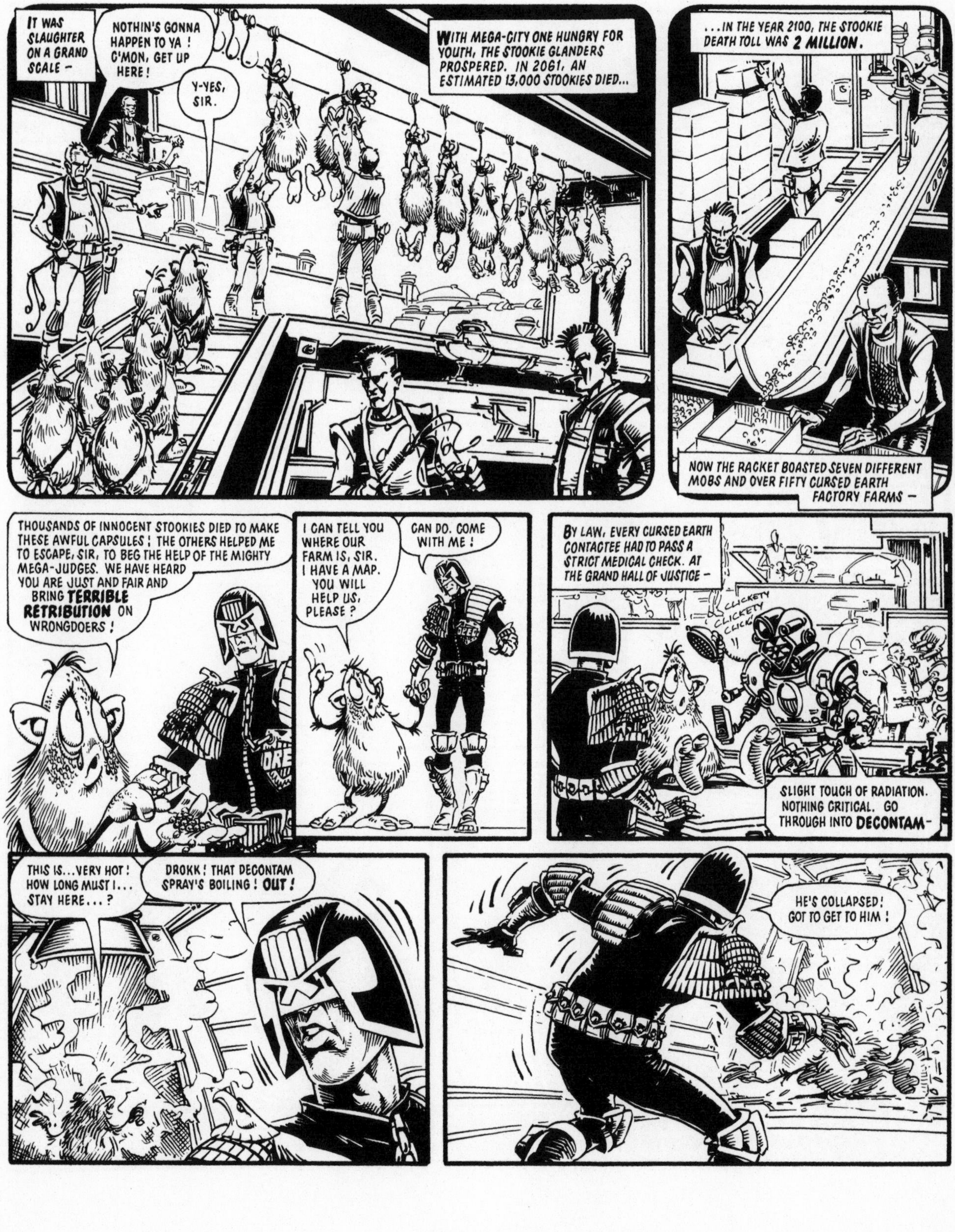
IT WAS SLAUGHTER ON A GRAND SCALE –
NOTHIN'S GONNA HAPPEN TO YA ! C'MON, GET UP HERE !
Y-YES, SIR.
WITH MEGA-CITY ONE HUNGRY FOR YOUTH, THE STOOKIE GLANDERS PROSPERED. IN 2061, AN ESTIMATED 13,000 STOOKIES DIED...
...IN THE YEAR 2100, THE STOOKIE DEATH TOLL WAS 2 MILLION.
NOW THE RACKET BOASTED SEVEN DIFFERENT MOBS AND OVER FIFTY CURSED EARTH FACTORY FARMS –
THOUSANDS OF INNOCENT STOOKIES DIED TO MAKE THESE AWFUL CAPSULES ; THE OTHERS HELPED ME TO ESCAPE, SIR, TO BEG THE HELP OF THE MIGHTY MEGA-JUDGES. WE HAVE HEARD YOU ARE JUST AND FAIR AND BRING TERRIBLE RETRIBUTION ON WRONGDOERS !
I CAN TELL YOU WHERE OUR FARM IS, SIR. I HAVE A MAP. YOU WILL HELP US, PLEASE ?
CAN DO. COME WITH ME !
BY LAW, EVERY CURSED EARTH CONTACTEE HAD TO PASS A STRICT MEDICAL CHECK. AT THE GRAND HALL OF JUSTICE –
CLICKETY CLICKETY CLICK
SLIGHT TOUCH OF RADIATION. NOTHING CRITICAL. GO THROUGH INTO DECONTAM –
THIS IS...VERY HOT ! HOW LONG MUST I... STAY HERE...?
DROKK ! THAT DECONTAM SPRAY'S BOILING ! OUT !
HE'S COLLAPSED ! GOT TO GET TO HIM !

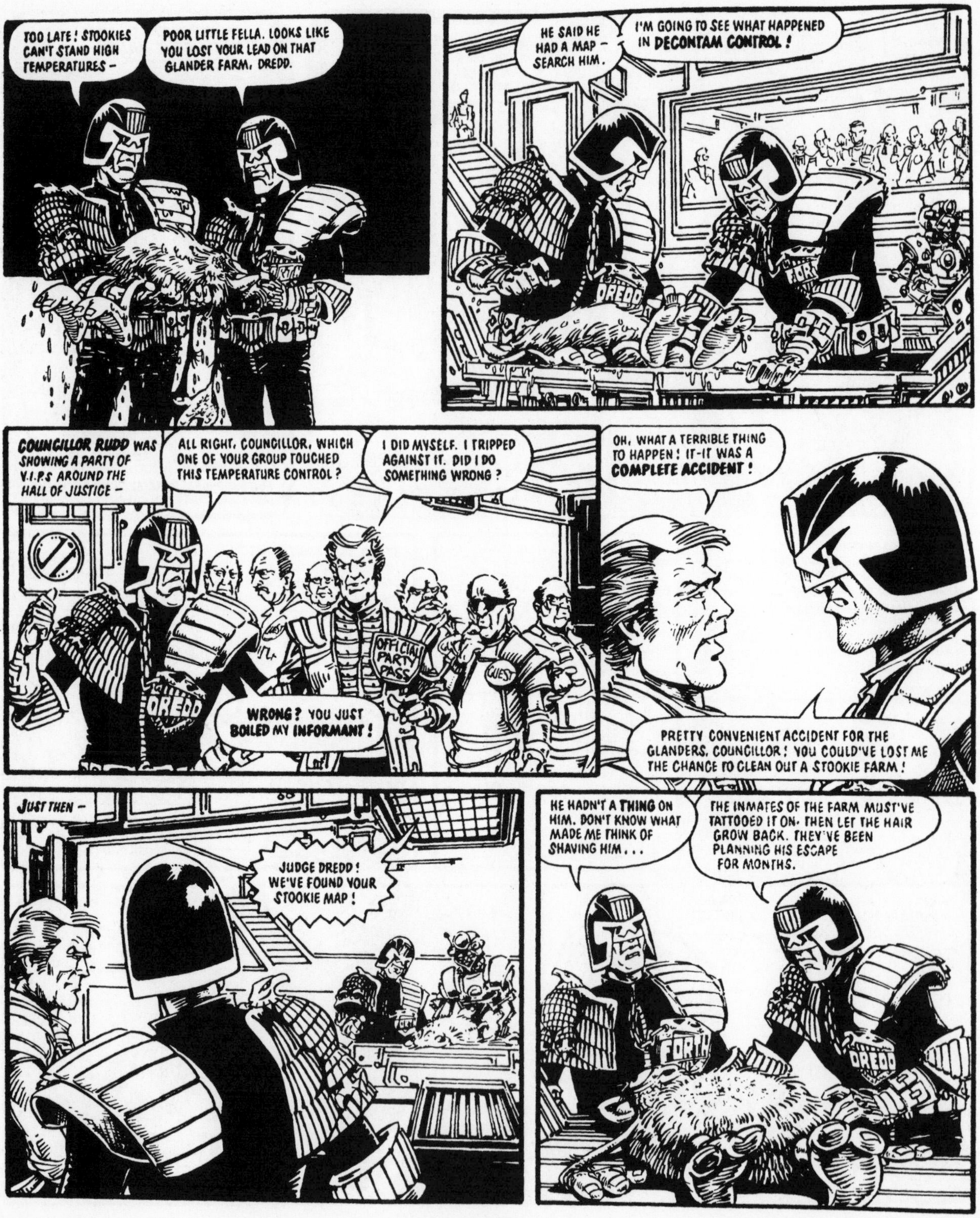
TOO LATE! STOOKIES CAN'T STAND HIGH TEMPERATURES –
POOR LITTLE FELLA. LOOKS LIKE YOU LOST YOUR LEAD ON THAT GLANDER FARM, DREDD.
HE SAID HE HAD A MAP – SEARCH HIM.
I'M GOING TO SEE WHAT HAPPENED IN DECONTAM CONTROL!
COUNCILLOR RUDD WAS SHOWING A PARTY OF V.I.P.S AROUND THE HALL OF JUSTICE –
ALL RIGHT, COUNCILLOR. WHICH ONE OF YOUR GROUP TOUCHED THIS TEMPERATURE CONTROL?
I DID MYSELF. I TRIPPED AGAINST IT. DID I DO SOMETHING WRONG?
WRONG? YOU JUST BOILED MY INFORMANT!
OH, WHAT A TERRIBLE THING TO HAPPEN! IT-IT WAS A COMPLETE ACCIDENT!
PRETTY CONVENIENT ACCIDENT FOR THE GLANDERS, COUNCILLOR! YOU COULD'VE LOST ME THE CHANCE TO CLEAN OUT A STOOKIE FARM!
JUST THEN –
JUDGE DREDD! WE'VE FOUND YOUR STOOKIE MAP!
HE HADN'T A THING ON HIM. DON'T KNOW WHAT MADE ME THINK OF SHAVING HIM...
THE INMATES OF THE FARM MUST'VE TATTOOED IT ON. THEN LET THE HAIR GROW BACK. THEY'VE BEEN PLANNING HIS ESCAPE FOR MONTHS.

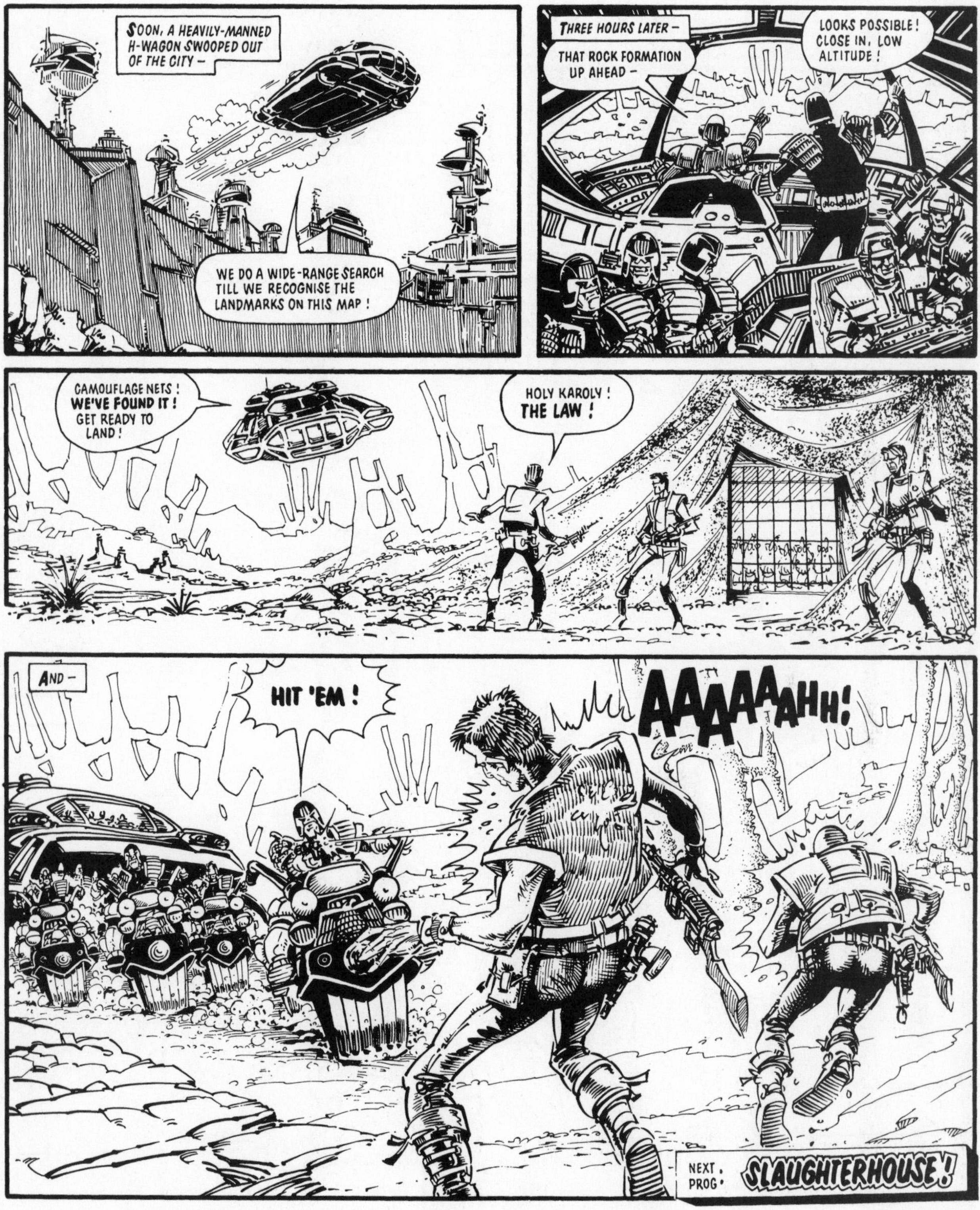
SOON, A HEAVILY-MANNED H-WAGON SWOOPED OUT OF THE CITY –
WE DO A WIDE-RANGE SEARCH TILL WE RECOGNISE THE LANDMARKS ON THIS MAP !
THREE HOURS LATER –
THAT ROCK FORMATION UP AHEAD –
LOOKS POSSIBLE ! CLOSE IN, LOW ALTITUDE !
CAMOUFLAGE NETS ! WE'VE FOUND IT ! GET READY TO LAND !
HOLY KAROLY ! THE LAW !
AND –
HIT 'EM !
AAAAAAHH!
NEXT PROG: SLAUGHTERHOUSE !

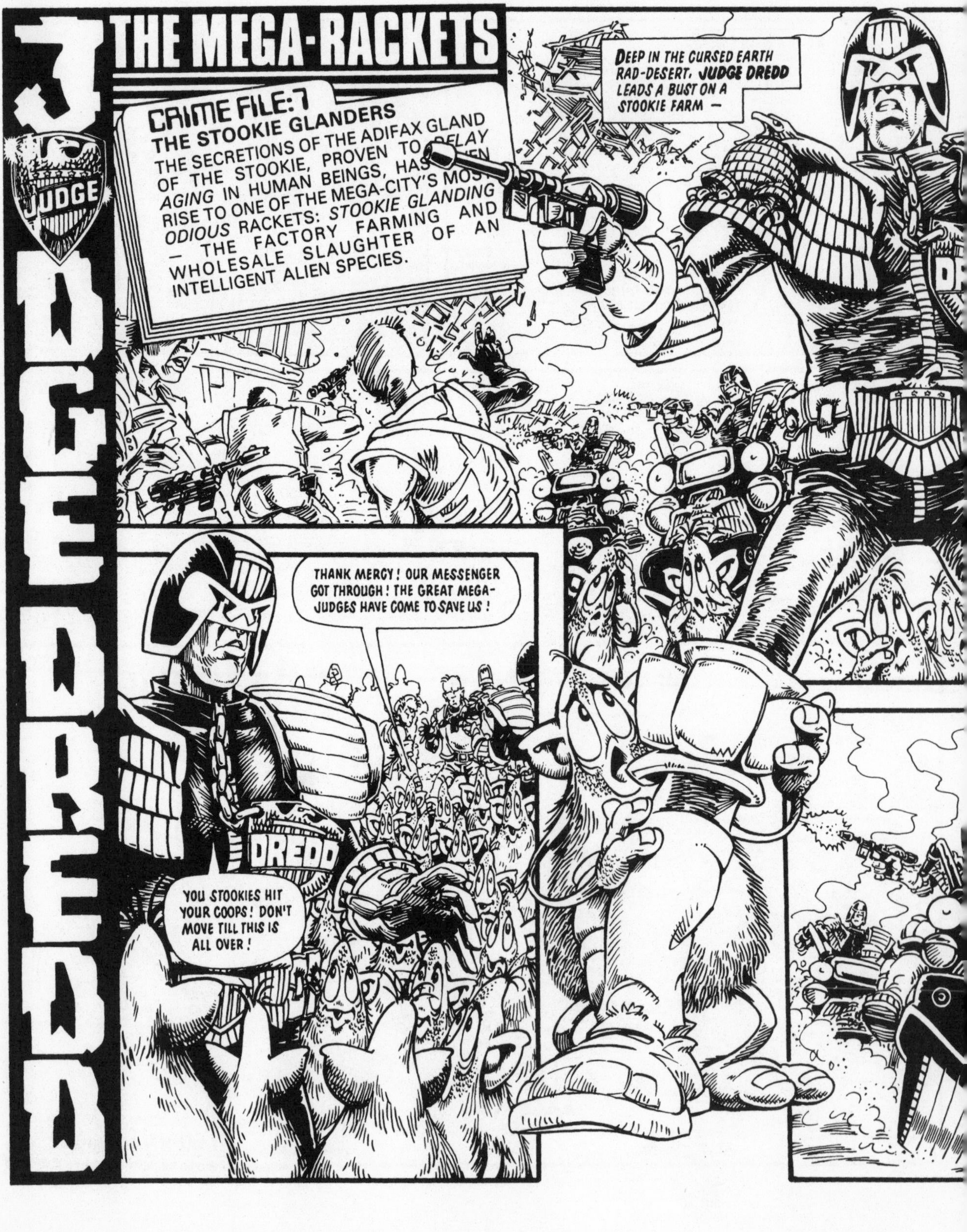
JUDGE DREDD
3
THE MEGA-RACKETS
CRIME FILE: 7
THE STOOKIE GLANDERS
THE SECRETIONS OF THE ADIFAX GLAND OF THE STOOKIE, PROVEN TO DELAY AGING IN HUMAN BEINGS, HAS GIVEN RISE TO ONE OF THE MEGA-CITY'S MOST ODIOUS RACKETS: STOOKIE GLANDING — THE FACTORY FARMING AND WHOLESALE SLAUGHTER OF AN INTELLIGENT ALIEN SPECIES.
DEEP IN THE CURSED EARTH RAD-DESERT, JUDGE DREDD LEADS A BUST ON A STOOKIE FARM —
THANK MERCY! OUR MESSENGER GOT THROUGH! THE GREAT MEGA-JUDGES HAVE COME TO SAVE US!
YOU STOOKIES HIT YOUR COOPS! DON'T MOVE TILL THIS IS ALL OVER!
DREDD

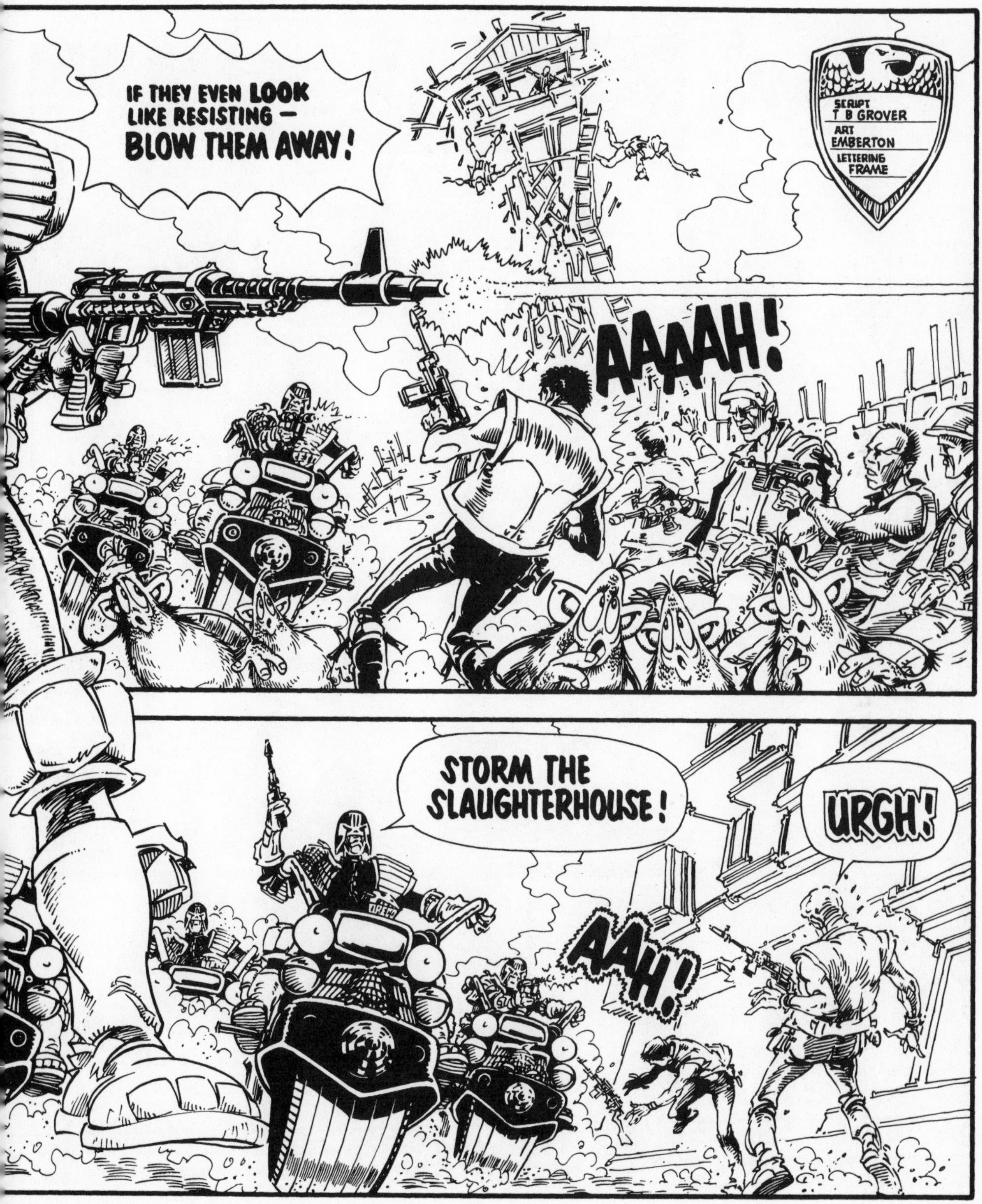
IF THEY EVEN LOOK LIKE RESISTING — BLOW THEM AWAY!
SCRIPT T B GROVER
ART EMBERTON
LETTERING FRAME
AAAAH!
STORM THE SLAUGHTERHOUSE!
URGH!
AAH!

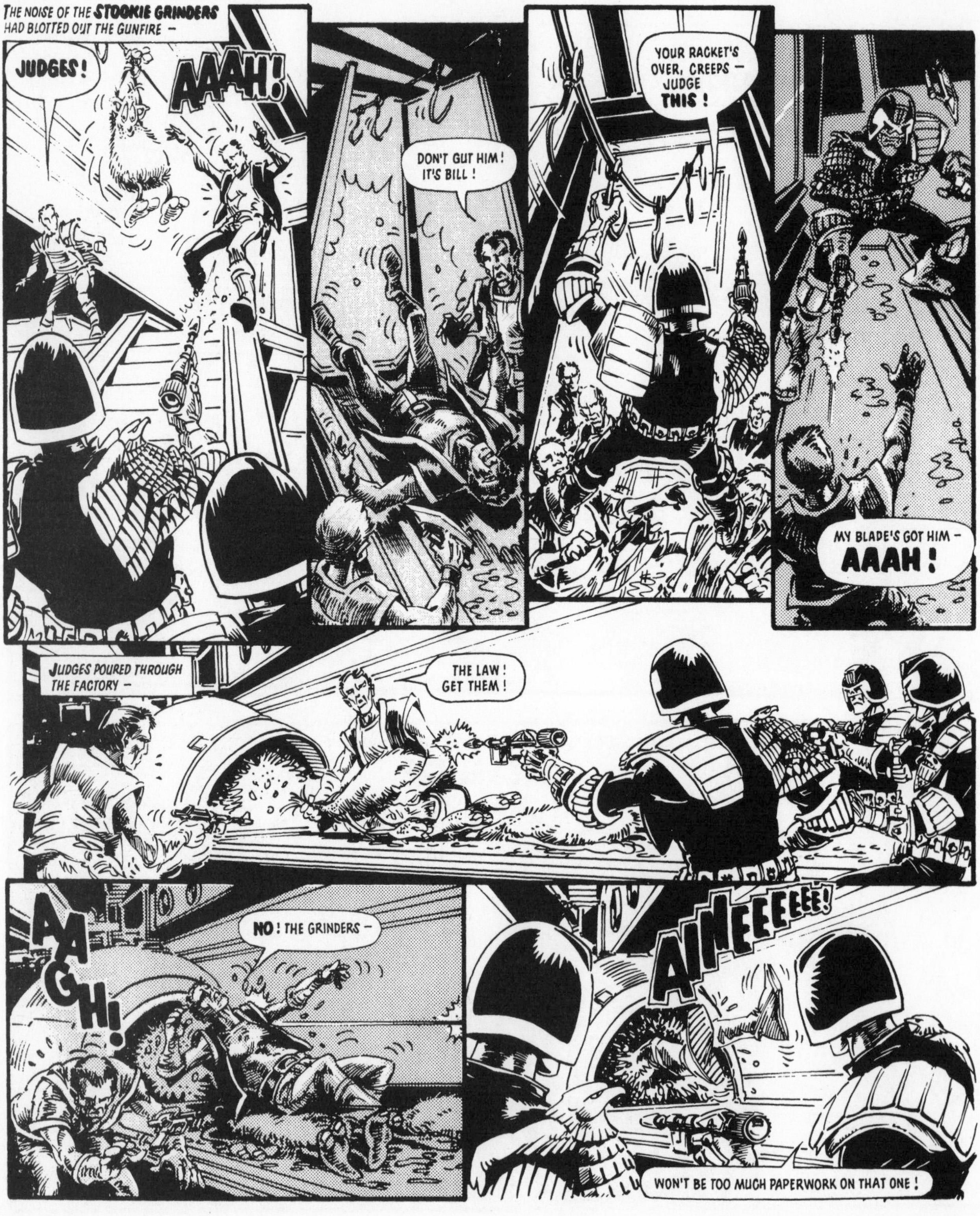
THE NOISE OF THE STOOKIE GRINDERS HAD BLOTTED OUT THE GUNFIRE –
JUDGES!
AAAH!
DON'T GUT HIM! IT'S BILL!
YOUR RACKET'S OVER, CREEPS – JUDGE THIS!
MY BLADE'S GOT HIM – AAAH!
JUDGES POURED THROUGH THE FACTORY –
THE LAW! GET THEM!
AAGHI!
NO! THE GRINDERS –
AIIEEEEEEE!
WON'T BE TOO MUCH PAPERWORK ON THAT ONE!

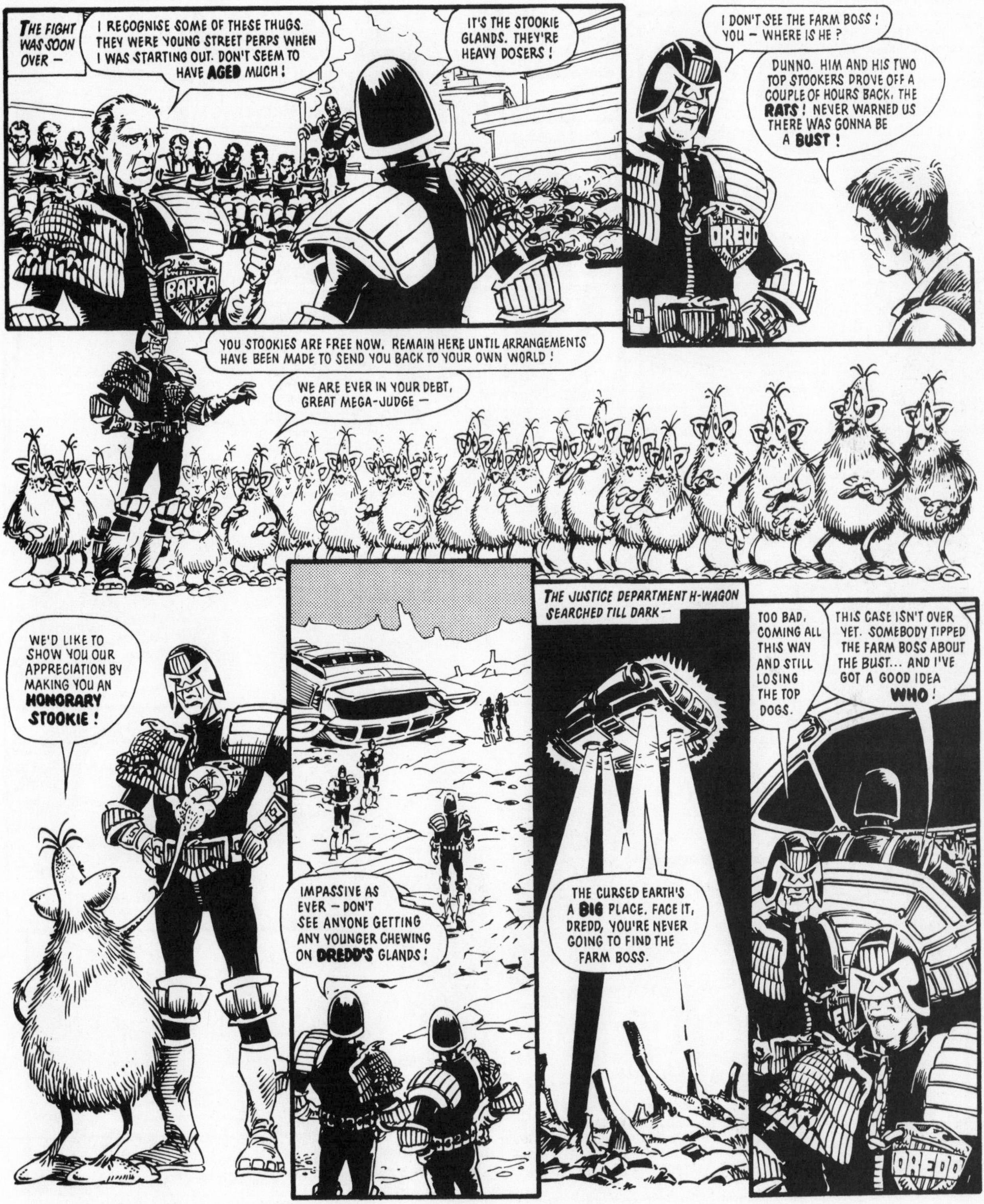
THE FIGHT WAS SOON OVER –
I RECOGNISE SOME OF THESE THUGS. THEY WERE YOUNG STREET PERPS WHEN I WAS STARTING OUT. DON'T SEEM TO HAVE AGED MUCH!
IT'S THE STOOKIE GLANDS. THEY'RE HEAVY DOSERS!
I DON'T SEE THE FARM BOSS! YOU – WHERE IS HE?
DUNNO. HIM AND HIS TWO TOP STOOKERS DROVE OFF A COUPLE OF HOURS BACK. THE RATS! NEVER WARNED US THERE WAS GONNA BE A BUST!
YOU STOOKIES ARE FREE NOW. REMAIN HERE UNTIL ARRANGEMENTS HAVE BEEN MADE TO SEND YOU BACK TO YOUR OWN WORLD!
WE ARE EVER IN YOUR DEBT, GREAT MEGA-JUDGE –
WE'D LIKE TO SHOW YOU OUR APPRECIATION BY MAKING YOU AN HONORARY STOOKIE!
IMPASSIVE AS EVER – DON'T SEE ANYONE GETTING ANY YOUNGER CHEWING ON DREDD'S GLANDS!
THE JUSTICE DEPARTMENT H-WAGON SEARCHED TILL DARK –
THE CURSED EARTH'S A BIG PLACE. FACE IT, DREDD, YOU'RE NEVER GOING TO FIND THE FARM BOSS.
TOO BAD, COMING ALL THIS WAY AND STILL LOSING THE TOP DOGS.
THIS CASE ISN'T OVER YET. SOMEBODY TIPPED THE FARM BOSS ABOUT THE BUST... AND I'VE GOT A GOOD IDEA WHO!

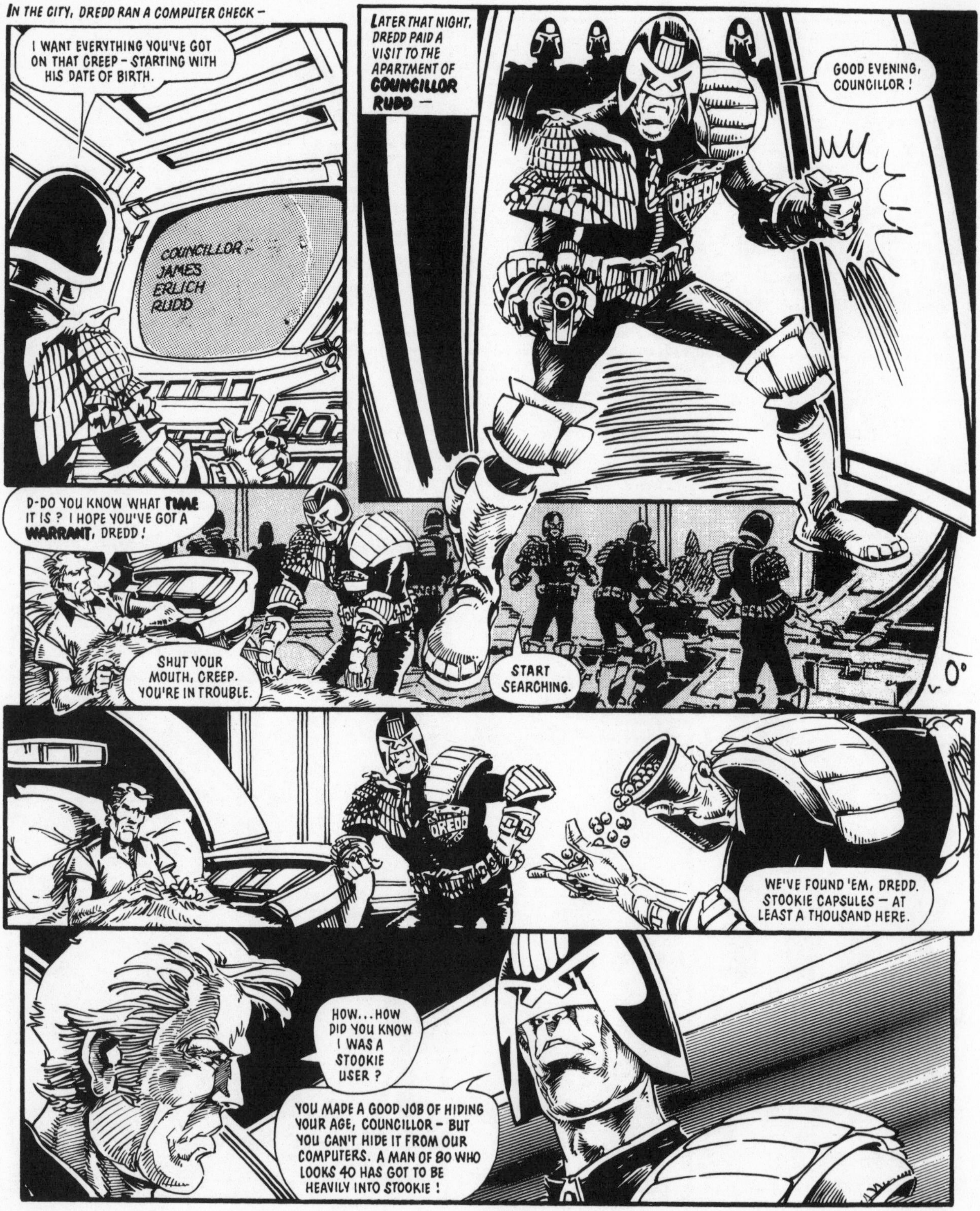

IN THE CITY, DREDD RAN A COMPUTER CHECK –
I WANT EVERYTHING YOU'VE GOT ON THAT CREEP – STARTING WITH HIS DATE OF BIRTH.
COUNCILLOR – JAMES ERLICH RUDD
LATER THAT NIGHT, DREDD PAID A VISIT TO THE APARTMENT OF COUNCILLOR RUDD –
GOOD EVENING, COUNCILLOR !
D-DO YOU KNOW WHAT TIME IT IS ? I HOPE YOU'VE GOT A WARRANT, DREDD !
SHUT YOUR MOUTH, CREEP. YOU'RE IN TROUBLE.
START SEARCHING.
WE'VE FOUND 'EM, DREDD. STOOKIE CAPSULES – AT LEAST A THOUSAND HERE.
HOW... HOW DID YOU KNOW I WAS A STOOKIE USER ?
YOU MADE A GOOD JOB OF HIDING YOUR AGE, COUNCILLOR – BUT YOU CAN'T HIDE IT FROM OUR COMPUTERS. A MAN OF 80 WHO LOOKS 40 HAS GOT TO BE HEAVILY INTO STOOKIE !

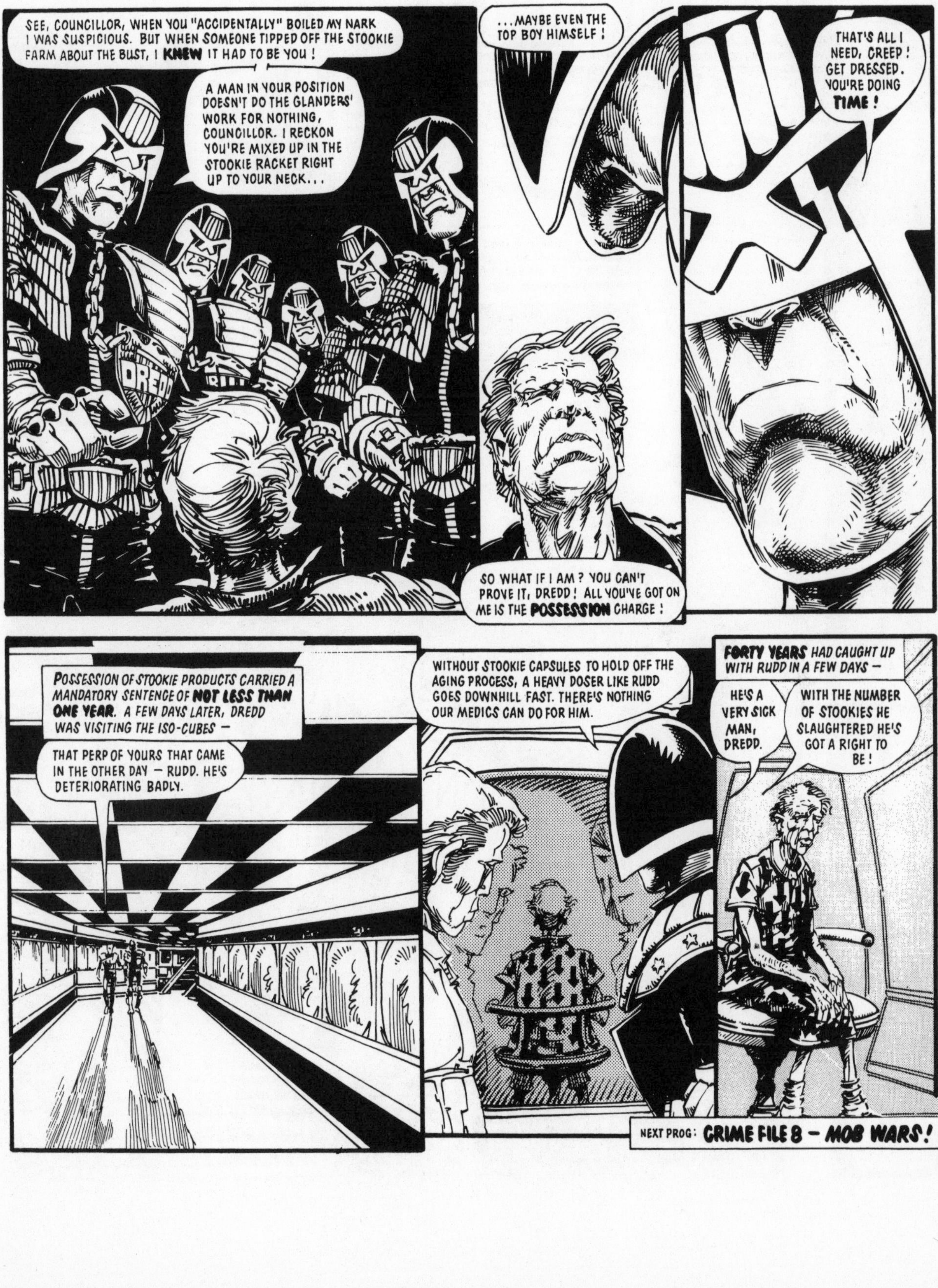
SEE, COUNCILLOR, WHEN YOU "ACCIDENTALLY" BOILED MY NARK I WAS SUSPICIOUS. BUT WHEN SOMEONE TIPPED OFF THE STOOKIE FARM ABOUT THE BUST, I KNEW IT HAD TO BE YOU!
A MAN IN YOUR POSITION DOESN'T DO THE GLANDERS' WORK FOR NOTHING, COUNCILLOR. I RECKON YOU'RE MIXED UP IN THE STOOKIE RACKET RIGHT UP TO YOUR NECK...
DREDD
...MAYBE EVEN THE TOP BOY HIMSELF!
SO WHAT IF I AM? YOU CAN'T PROVE IT, DREDD! ALL YOU'VE GOT ON ME IS THE POSSESSION CHARGE!
THAT'S ALL I NEED, CREEP! GET DRESSED. YOU'RE DOING TIME!
POSSESSION OF STOOKIE PRODUCTS CARRIED A MANDATORY SENTENCE OF NOT LESS THAN ONE YEAR. A FEW DAYS LATER, DREDD WAS VISITING THE ISO-CUBES —
THAT PERP OF YOURS THAT CAME IN THE OTHER DAY — RUDD. HE'S DETERIORATING BADLY.
WITHOUT STOOKIE CAPSULES TO HOLD OFF THE AGING PROCESS, A HEAVY DOSER LIKE RUDD GOES DOWNHILL FAST. THERE'S NOTHING OUR MEDICS CAN DO FOR HIM.
FORTY YEARS HAD CAUGHT UP WITH RUDD IN A FEW DAYS —
HE'S A VERY SICK MAN, DREDD.
WITH THE NUMBER OF STOOKIES HE SLAUGHTERED HE'S GOT A RIGHT TO BE!
NEXT PROG: CRIME FILE 8 — MOB WARS!

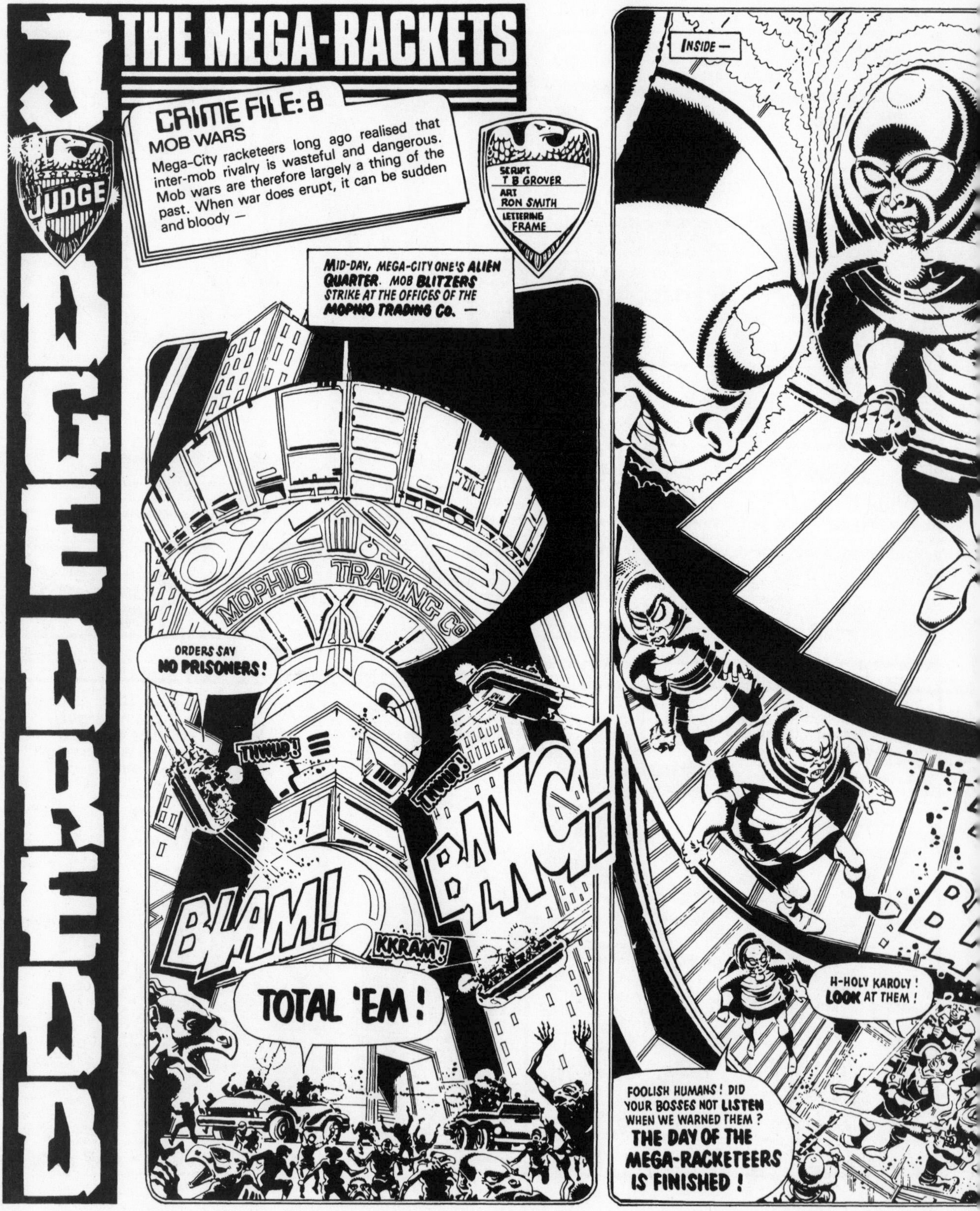
JUDGE DREDD
THE MEGA-RACKETS
CRIME FILE: 8
MOB WARS
Mega-City racketeers long ago realised that inter-mob rivalry is wasteful and dangerous. Mob wars are therefore largely a thing of the past. When war does erupt, it can be sudden and bloody —
JUDGE
SCRIPT T B GROVER
ART RON SMITH
LETTERING FRAME
MID-DAY, MEGA-CITY ONE'S ALIEN QUARTER. MOB BLITZERS STRIKE AT THE OFFICES OF THE MOPHIO TRADING Co. —
MOPHIO TRADING Co
ORDERS SAY NO PRISONERS!
THWUP!
THWUP!
BANG!
BLAM!
KKRAM!
TOTAL 'EM!
INSIDE —
H-HOLY KAROLY! LOOK AT THEM!
FOOLISH HUMANS! DID YOUR BOSSES NOT LISTEN WHEN WE WARNED THEM? THE DAY OF THE MEGA-RACKETEERS IS FINISHED!

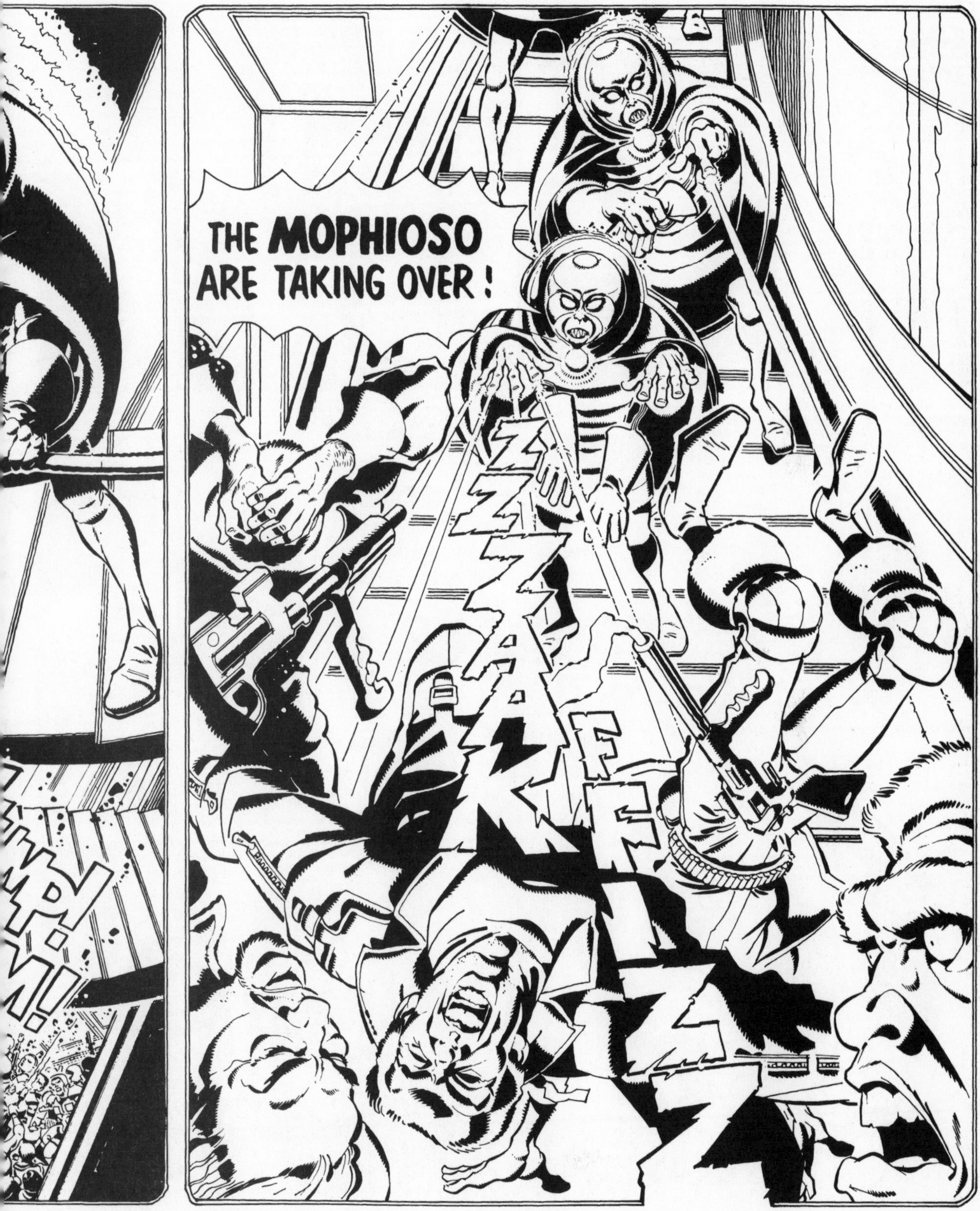
THE MOPHIOSO ARE TAKING OVER!
ZZZAAKFFIZZ

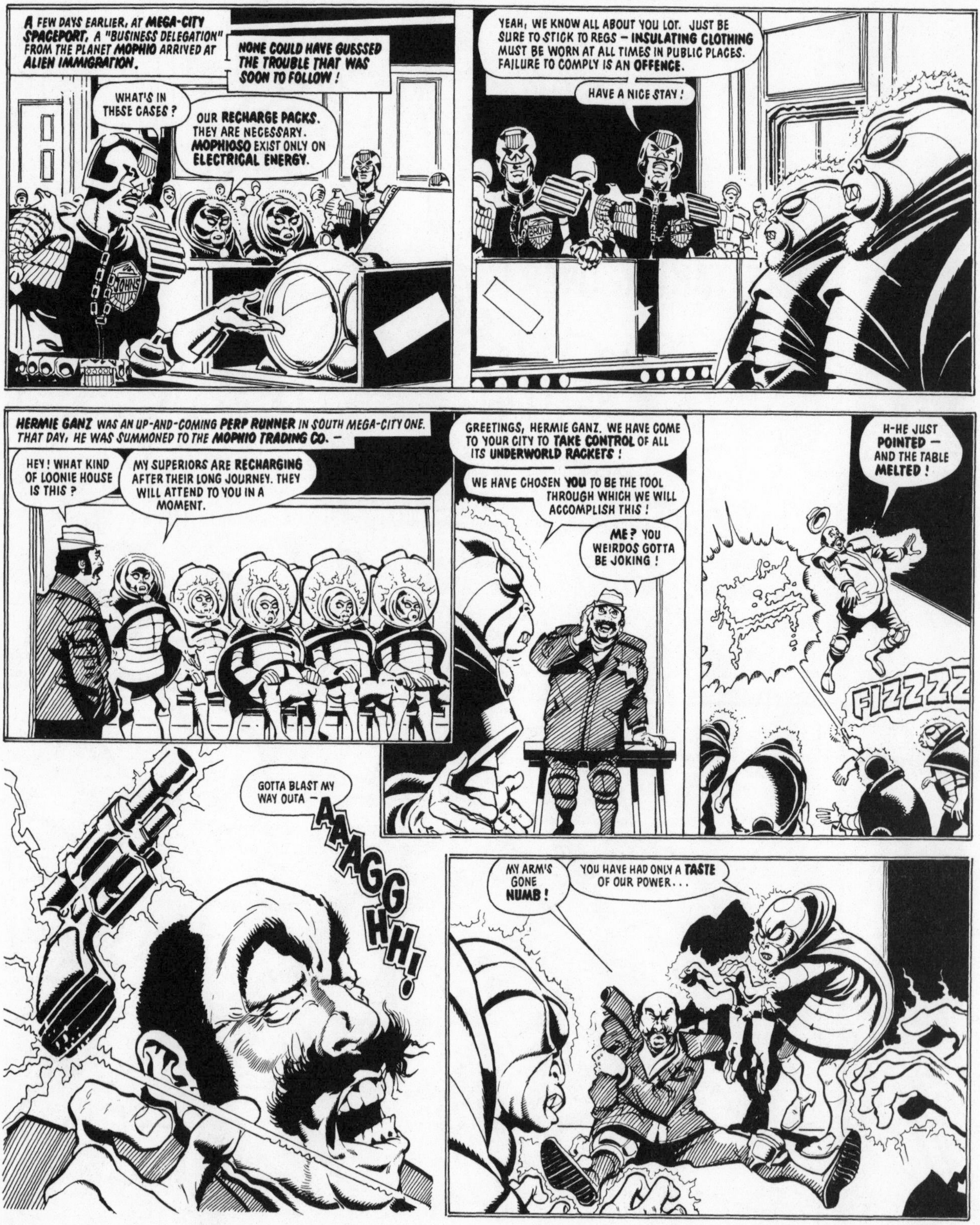
A FEW DAYS EARLIER, AT MEGA-CITY SPACEPORT, A "BUSINESS DELEGATION" FROM THE PLANET MOPHIO ARRIVED AT ALIEN IMMIGRATION.
NONE COULD HAVE GUESSED THE TROUBLE THAT WAS SOON TO FOLLOW!
WHAT'S IN THESE CASES?
OUR RECHARGE PACKS. THEY ARE NECESSARY. MOPHIOSO EXIST ONLY ON ELECTRICAL ENERGY.
YEAH, WE KNOW ALL ABOUT YOU LOT. JUST BE SURE TO STICK TO REGS – INSULATING CLOTHING MUST BE WORN AT ALL TIMES IN PUBLIC PLACES. FAILURE TO COMPLY IS AN OFFENCE.
HAVE A NICE STAY!
HERMIE GANZ WAS AN UP-AND-COMING PERP RUNNER IN SOUTH MEGA-CITY ONE. THAT DAY, HE WAS SUMMONED TO THE MOPHIO TRADING CO. –
HEY! WHAT KIND OF LOONIE HOUSE IS THIS?
MY SUPERIORS ARE RECHARGING AFTER THEIR LONG JOURNEY. THEY WILL ATTEND TO YOU IN A MOMENT.
GREETINGS, HERMIE GANZ. WE HAVE COME TO YOUR CITY TO TAKE CONTROL OF ALL ITS UNDERWORLD RACKETS!
WE HAVE CHOSEN YOU TO BE THE TOOL THROUGH WHICH WE WILL ACCOMPLISH THIS!
ME? YOU WEIRDOS GOTTA BE JOKING!
H-HE JUST POINTED – AND THE TABLE MELTED!
FIZZZZ
GOTTA BLAST MY WAY OUTA –
AAAGGHH!
MY ARM'S GONE NUMB!
YOU HAVE HAD ONLY A TASTE OF OUR POWER...

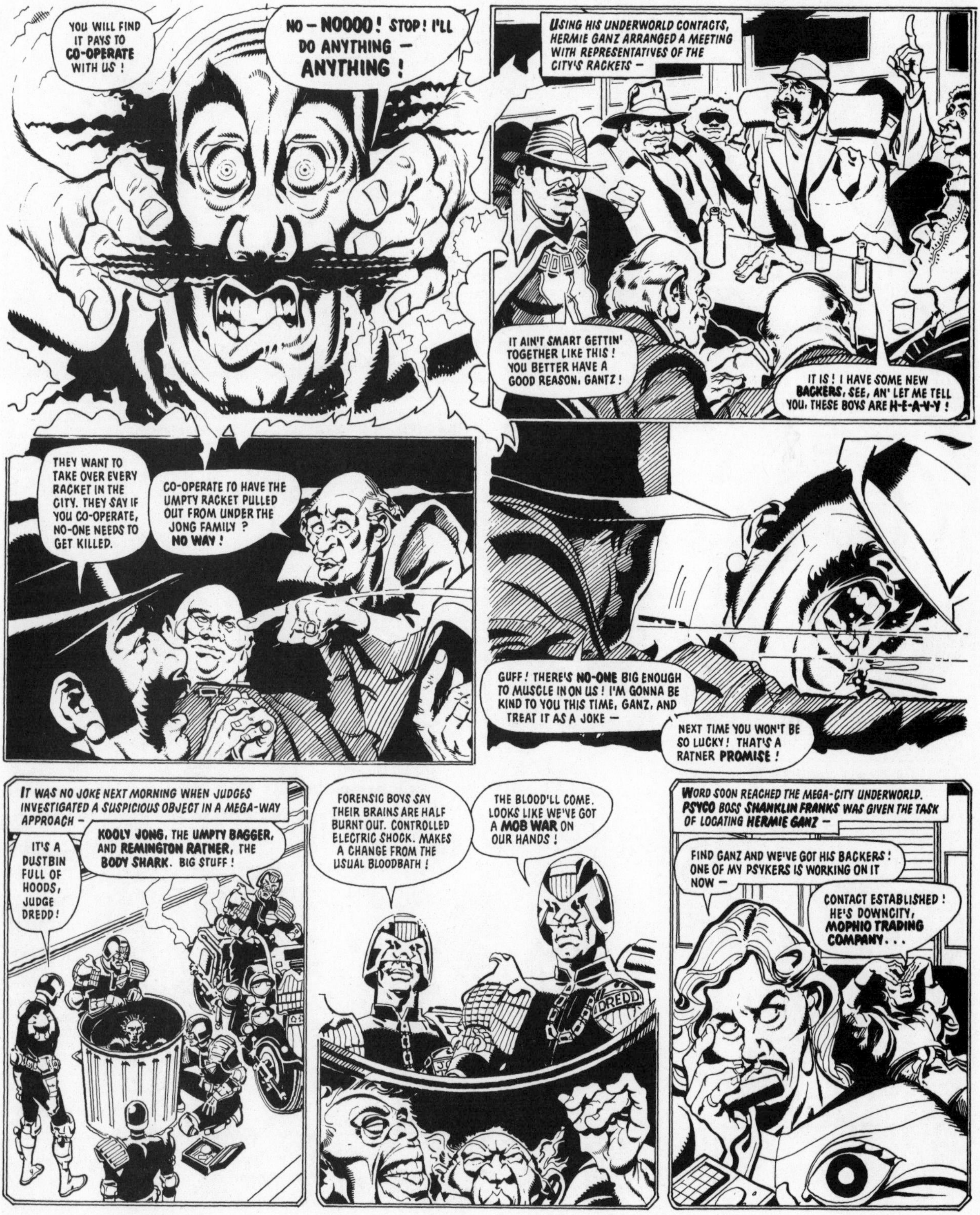

YOU WILL FIND IT PAYS TO CO-OPERATE WITH US !
NO – NOOOO ! STOP ! I'LL DO ANYTHING – ANYTHING !
USING HIS UNDERWORLD CONTACTS, HERMIE GANZ ARRANGED A MEETING WITH REPRESENTATIVES OF THE CITY'S RACKETS –
IT AIN'T SMART GETTIN' TOGETHER LIKE THIS ! YOU BETTER HAVE A GOOD REASON, GANTZ !
IT IS ! I HAVE SOME NEW BACKERS, SEE, AN' LET ME TELL YOU, THESE BOYS ARE H-E-A-V-Y !
THEY WANT TO TAKE OVER EVERY RACKET IN THE CITY. THEY SAY IF YOU CO-OPERATE, NO-ONE NEEDS TO GET KILLED.
CO-OPERATE TO HAVE THE UMPTY RACKET PULLED OUT FROM UNDER THE JONG FAMILY ? NO WAY !
GUFF ! THERE'S NO-ONE BIG ENOUGH TO MUSCLE IN ON US ! I'M GONNA BE KIND TO YOU THIS TIME, GANZ, AND TREAT IT AS A JOKE –
NEXT TIME YOU WON'T BE SO LUCKY ! THAT'S A RATNER PROMISE !
IT WAS NO JOKE NEXT MORNING WHEN JUDGES INVESTIGATED A SUSPICIOUS OBJECT IN A MEGA-WAY APPROACH –
IT'S A DUSTBIN FULL OF HOODS, JUDGE DREDD !
KOOLY JONG, THE UMPTY BAGGER, AND REMINGTON RATNER, THE BODY SHARK. BIG STUFF !
FORENSIC BOYS SAY THEIR BRAINS ARE HALF BURNT OUT. CONTROLLED ELECTRIC SHOCK. MAKES A CHANGE FROM THE USUAL BLOODBATH !
THE BLOOD'LL COME. LOOKS LIKE WE'VE GOT A MOB WAR ON OUR HANDS !
DREDD
WORD SOON REACHED THE MEGA-CITY UNDERWORLD. PSYCO BOSS SHANKLIN FRANKS WAS GIVEN THE TASK OF LOCATING HERMIE GANZ –
FIND GANZ AND WE'VE GOT HIS BACKERS ! ONE OF MY PSYKERS IS WORKING ON IT NOW –
CONTACT ESTABLISHED ! HE'S DOWNCITY, MOPHIO TRADING COMPANY . . .

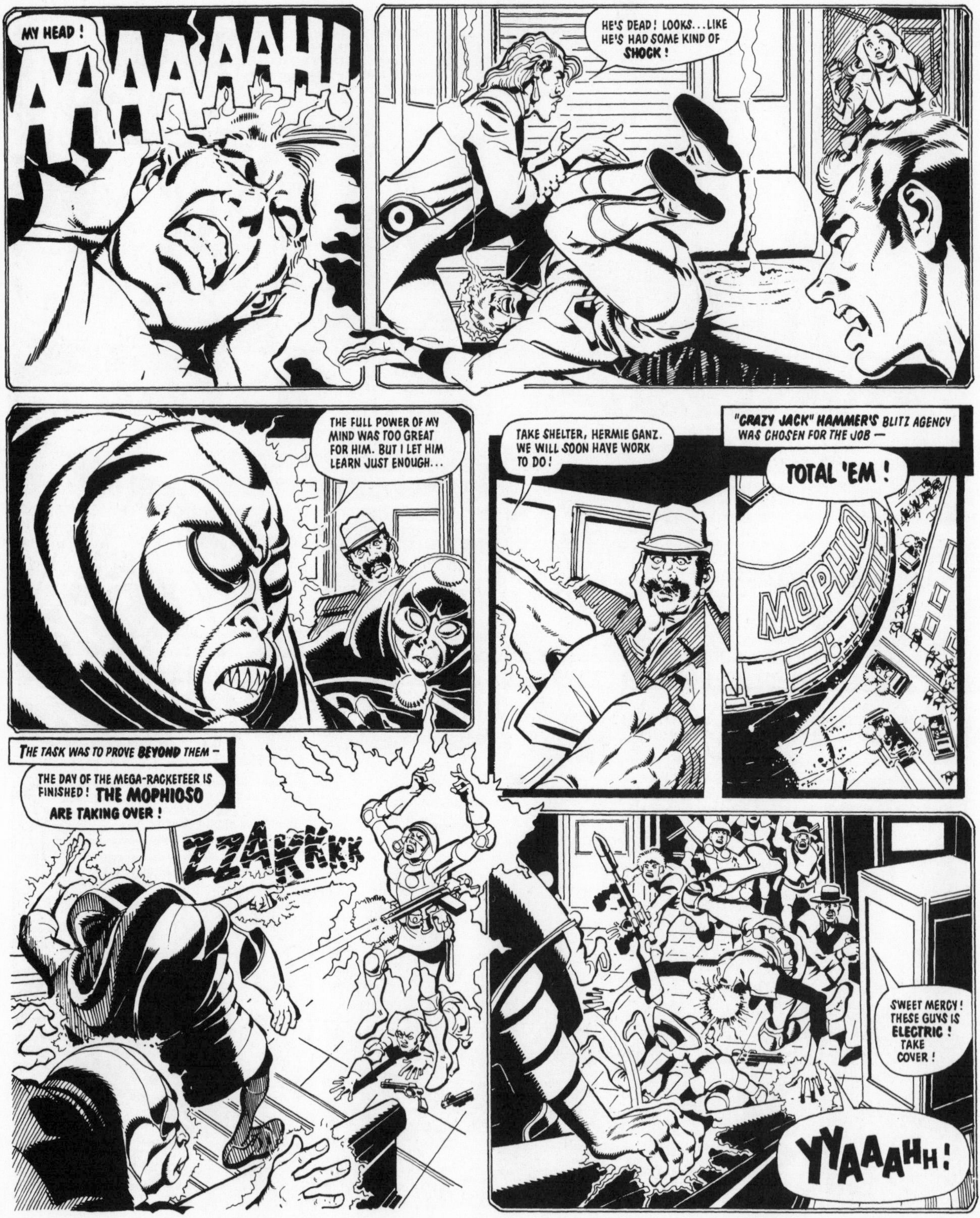
MY HEAD !
AAAAAAAH!
HE'S DEAD ! LOOKS...LIKE HE'S HAD SOME KIND OF SHOCK !
THE FULL POWER OF MY MIND WAS TOO GREAT FOR HIM. BUT I LET HIM LEARN JUST ENOUGH...
TAKE SHELTER, HERMIE GANZ. WE WILL SOON HAVE WORK TO DO !
"CRAZY JACK" HAMMER'S BLITZ AGENCY WAS CHOSEN FOR THE JOB —
TOTAL 'EM !
MOPHIO
THE TASK WAS TO PROVE BEYOND THEM —
THE DAY OF THE MEGA-RACKETEER IS FINISHED ! THE MOPHIOSO ARE TAKING OVER !
ZZAKKKK
SWEET MERCY ! THESE GUYS IS ELECTRIC ! TAKE COVER !
YYAAAHH !

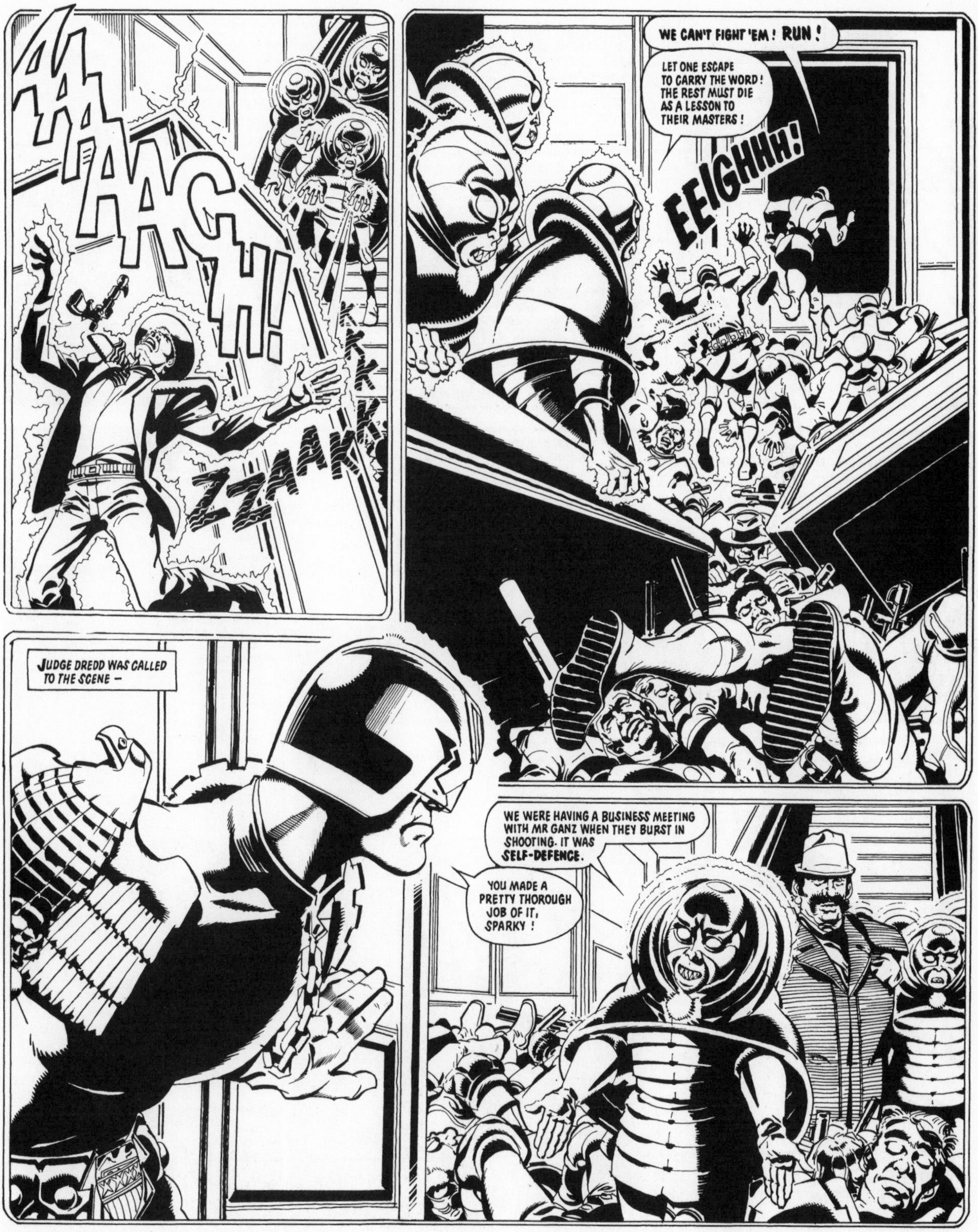
AAAACH!
KKKK
ZZAAAKK
WE CAN'T FIGHT 'EM! RUN!
LET ONE ESCAPE TO CARRY THE WORD! THE REST MUST DIE AS A LESSON TO THEIR MASTERS!
EEIGHHH!
JUDGE DREDD WAS CALLED TO THE SCENE –
WE WERE HAVING A BUSINESS MEETING WITH MR GANZ WHEN THEY BURST IN SHOOTING. IT WAS SELF-DEFENCE.
YOU MADE A PRETTY THOROUGH JOB OF IT, SPARKY!

Panel 1: WITNESSES OUTSIDE CONFIRM YOUR STORY, BUT REMEMBER – YOU'RE *VISITORS* IN THIS CITY. ANY *MORE* SELF-DEFENCE AND I'LL COME DOWN ON YOU *HARD.*

Panel 2: INTERESTING! COULD BE THESE MOPHIO CREEPS ARE THE REASON FOR THE MOB WAR. LET'S LEAVE THE POT TO SIMMER AND SEE WHAT HAPPENS...

Panel 3: LATER THAT DAY, DREDD RECEIVED A VISIT FROM CERTAIN WELL-KNOWN FACES –

THE *MOPHIOSO* ARE TRYING TO MUSCLE IN ON OUR, ER... *BUSINESSES!*

MY BOY KOOLY AND REMINGTON RATNER – THEY SHOCKED 'EM TO DEATH! YOU'VE GOT THE EVIDENCE – WHY DON'T YOU *BOOK 'EM?*

THE MANNER OF THEIR DEATH PROVES NOTHING. THERE'S A LOT OF ELECTRICITY ABOUT, JONG.

Panel 4: QUIT *STALLING!* YOU KNOW WHAT'S GOIN' ON! WE'RE CITIZENS – WE DEMAND OUR RIGHTS! WE WANT *PROTECTION* FROM THESE ALIEN THUGS!

JUDGES *PROTECTING* A *PROTECTION RACKET!* THAT'S RICH!

Panel 5: *LISTEN,* CREEPS, DON'T COME IN HERE SPOUTING YOUR RIGHTS AT *ME!* AS FAR AS I'M CONCERNED, THE ONLY THUGS ROUND HERE ARE *YOU!*

NOW BEAT IT – YOU'RE CAUSING A BAD SMELL!

Panel 6: POINT OF LAW, JUDGE DREDD. ACCORDING TO THE *ALIEN CODE* YOU CAN DEPORT THE *MOPHIOSO* ANY TIME.

Panel 7: I DON'T NEED YOU TO TELL ME THAT, COMPUTER. RIGHT NOW IT DOESN'T SUIT MY PURPOSE...

WE'VE BEEN AFTER SOME OF THESE RACKETEERS FOR YEARS. A *MOB WAR* MIGHT *JUST BE THE THING* TO DROP 'EM RIGHT IN OUR LAPS!

NEXT PROG:

SHOCK TACTICS!

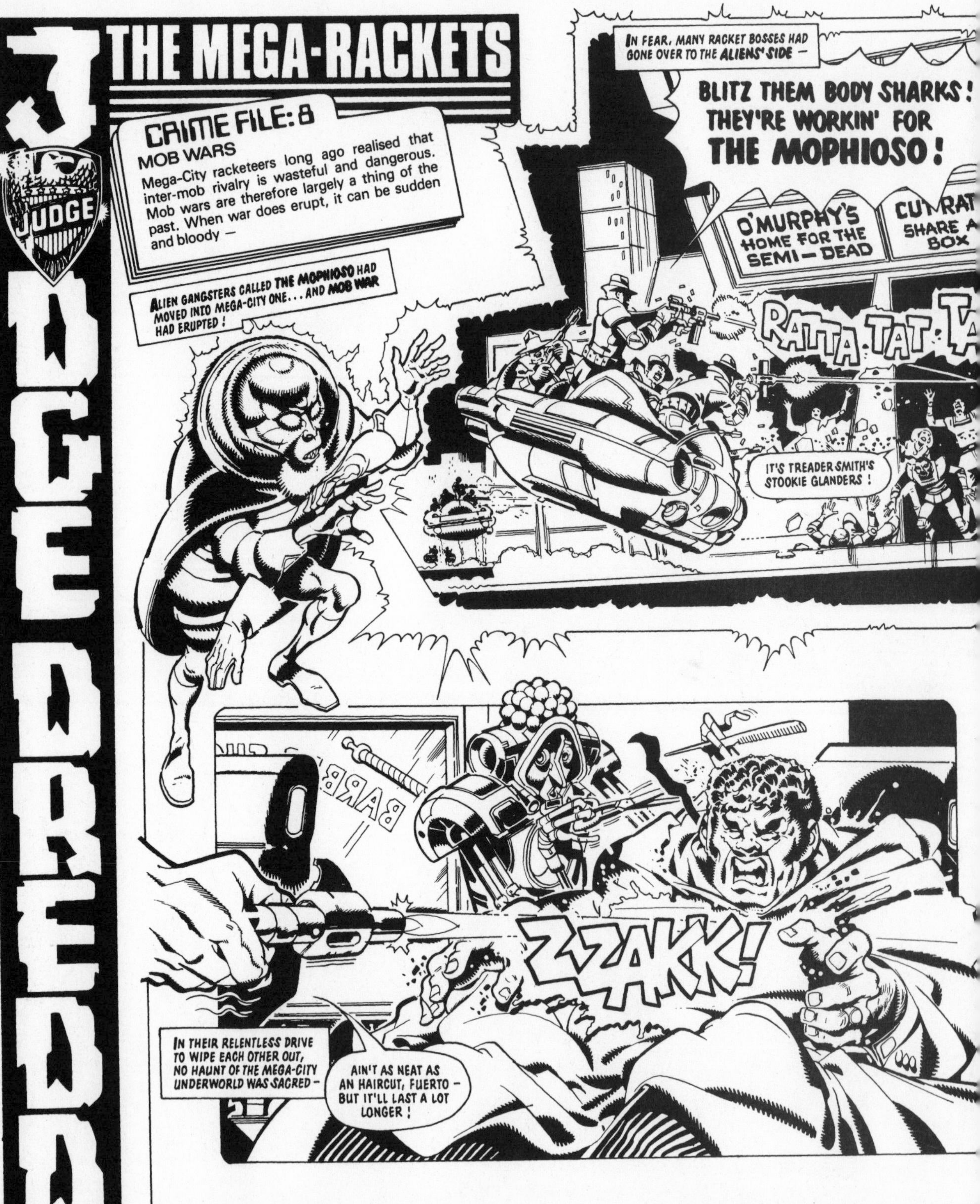
JUDGE DREDD
THE MEGA-RACKETS
CRIME FILE: 8
MOB WARS
Mega-City racketeers long ago realised that inter-mob rivalry is wasteful and dangerous. Mob wars are therefore largely a thing of the past. When war does erupt, it can be sudden and bloody —
ALIEN GANGSTERS CALLED THE MOPHIOSO HAD MOVED INTO MEGA-CITY ONE... AND MOB WAR HAD ERUPTED !
IN FEAR, MANY RACKET BOSSES HAD GONE OVER TO THE ALIENS' SIDE —
BLITZ THEM BODY SHARKS ! THEY'RE WORKIN' FOR THE MOPHIOSO !
O'MURPHY'S HOME FOR THE SEMI-DEAD
RATTA TAT TA
IT'S TREADER SMITH'S STOOKIE GLANDERS !
BARB
ZZAKK!
IN THEIR RELENTLESS DRIVE TO WIPE EACH OTHER OUT, NO HAUNT OF THE MEGA-CITY UNDERWORLD WAS SACRED —
AIN'T AS NEAT AS AN HAIRCUT, FUERTO — BUT IT'LL LAST A LOT LONGER !

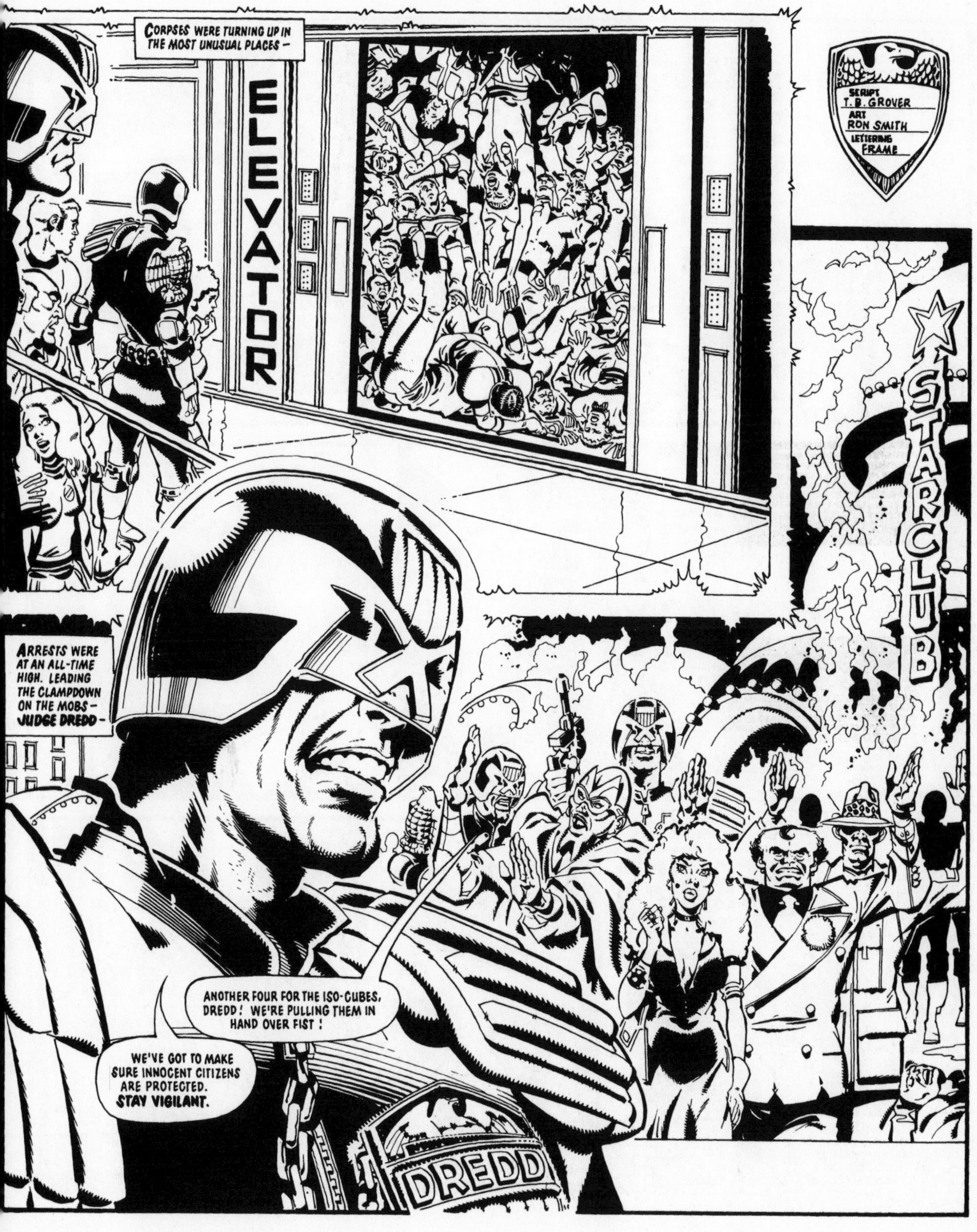
CORPSES WERE TURNING UP IN THE MOST UNUSUAL PLACES –
ELEVATOR
SCRIPT T.B. GROVER
ART RON SMITH
LETTERING FRAME
STARCLUB
ARRESTS WERE AT AN ALL-TIME HIGH. LEADING THE CLAMPDOWN ON THE MOBS – JUDGE DREDD –
ANOTHER FOUR FOR THE ISO-CUBES, DREDD! WE'RE PULLING THEM IN HAND OVER FIST!
WE'VE GOT TO MAKE SURE INNOCENT CITIZENS ARE PROTECTED. STAY VIGILANT.
DREDD

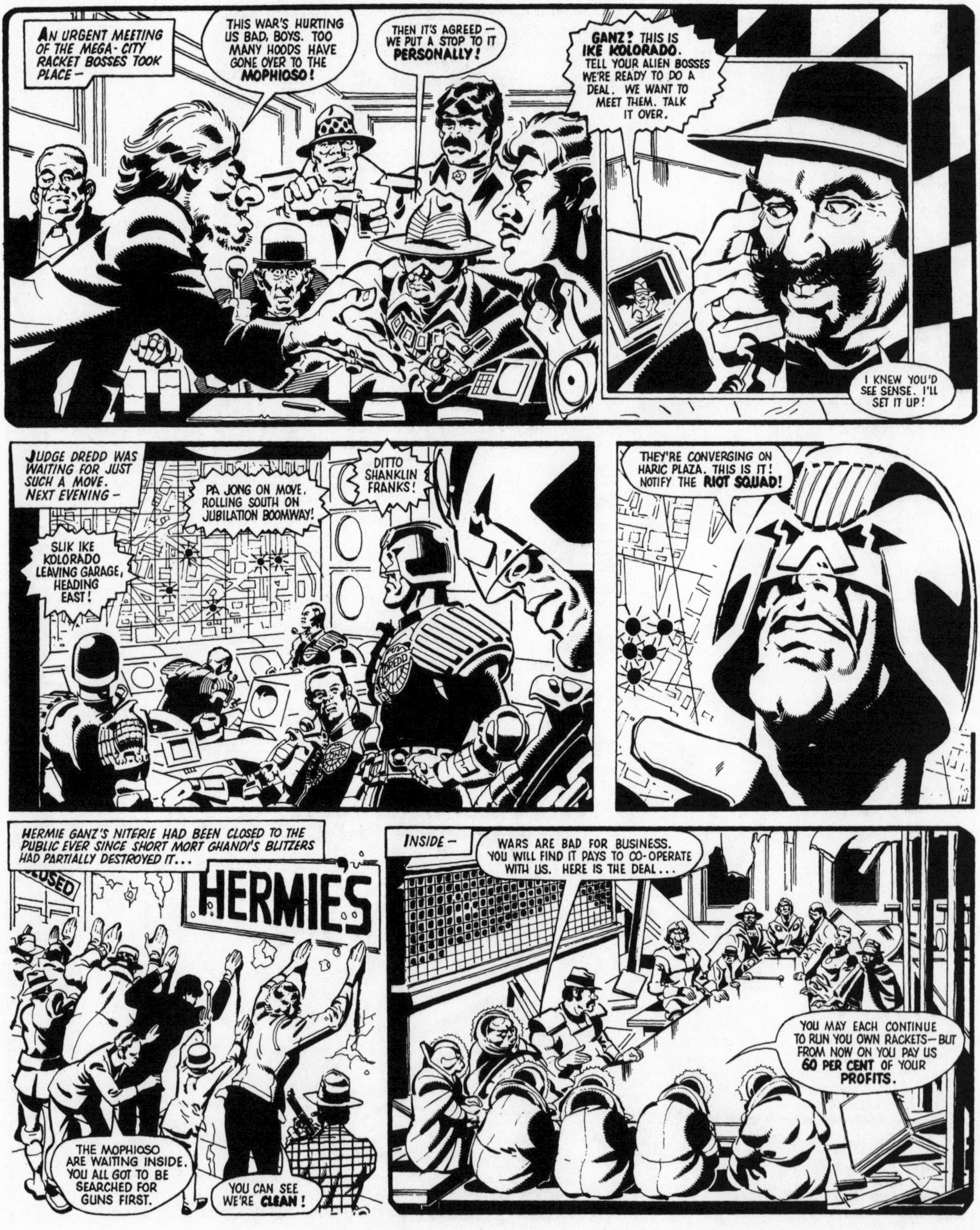

AN URGENT MEETING OF THE MEGA-CITY RACKET BOSSES TOOK PLACE –
THIS WAR'S HURTING US BAD, BOYS. TOO MANY HOODS HAVE GONE OVER TO THE **MOPHIOSO**!
THEN IT'S AGREED – WE PUT A STOP TO IT **PERSONALLY**!
GANZ? THIS IS **IKE KOLORADO**. TELL YOUR ALIEN BOSSES WE'RE READY TO DO A DEAL. WE WANT TO MEET THEM. TALK IT OVER.
I KNEW YOU'D SEE SENSE. I'LL SET IT UP!
JUDGE DREDD WAS WAITING FOR JUST SUCH A MOVE. NEXT EVENING –
PA JONG ON MOVE, ROLLING SOUTH ON JUBILATION BOOMWAY!
DITTO SHANKLIN FRANKS!
SLIK IKE KOLORADO LEAVING GARAGE, HEADING EAST!
THEY'RE CONVERGING ON HARIC PLAZA. THIS IS IT! NOTIFY THE **RIOT SQUAD**!
HERMIE GANZ'S NITERIE HAD BEEN CLOSED TO THE PUBLIC EVER SINCE SHORT MORT GHANDI'S BLITZERS HAD PARTIALLY DESTROYED IT...
HERMIE'S
THE MOPHIOSO ARE WAITING INSIDE. YOU ALL GOT TO BE SEARCHED FOR GUNS FIRST.
YOU CAN SEE WE'RE **CLEAN**!
INSIDE –
WARS ARE BAD FOR BUSINESS. YOU WILL FIND IT PAYS TO CO-OPERATE WITH US. HERE IS THE DEAL...
YOU MAY EACH CONTINUE TO RUN YOU OWN RACKETS – BUT FROM NOW ON YOU PAY US **60 PER CENT** OF YOUR **PROFITS**.

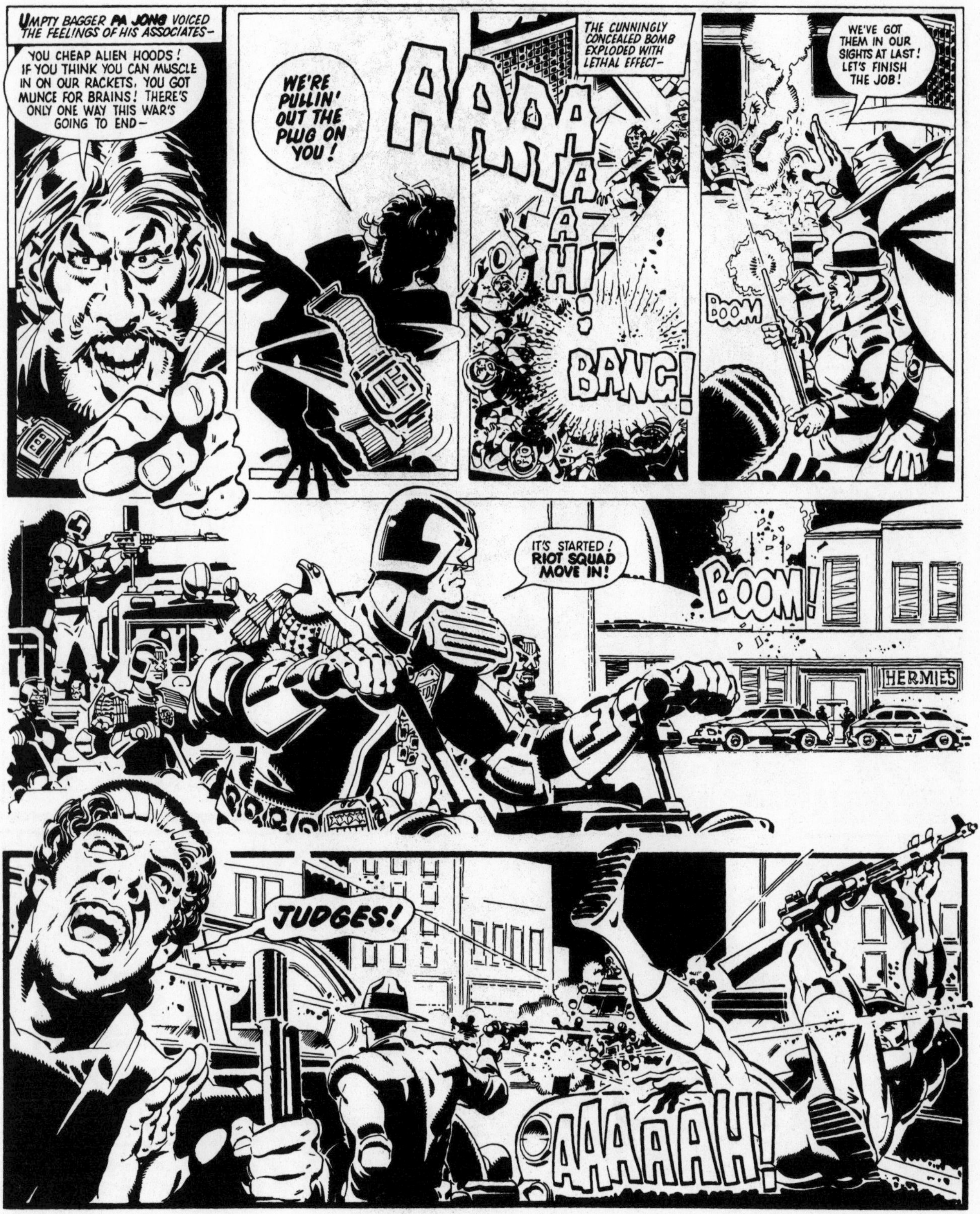
UMPTY BAGGER PA JONG VOICED THE FEELINGS OF HIS ASSOCIATES–
YOU CHEAP ALIEN HOODS! IF YOU THINK YOU CAN MUSCLE IN ON OUR RACKETS, YOU GOT MUNCE FOR BRAINS! THERE'S ONLY ONE WAY THIS WAR'S GOING TO END–
WE'RE PULLIN' OUT THE PLUG ON YOU!
THE CUNNINGLY CONCEALED BOMB EXPLODED WITH LETHAL EFFECT–
AAAAAAH!
BANG!
WE'VE GOT THEM IN OUR SIGHTS AT LAST! LET'S FINISH THE JOB!
BOOM
IT'S STARTED! RIOT SQUAD MOVE IN!
BOOM!
HERMIES
JUDGES!
AAAAAH!

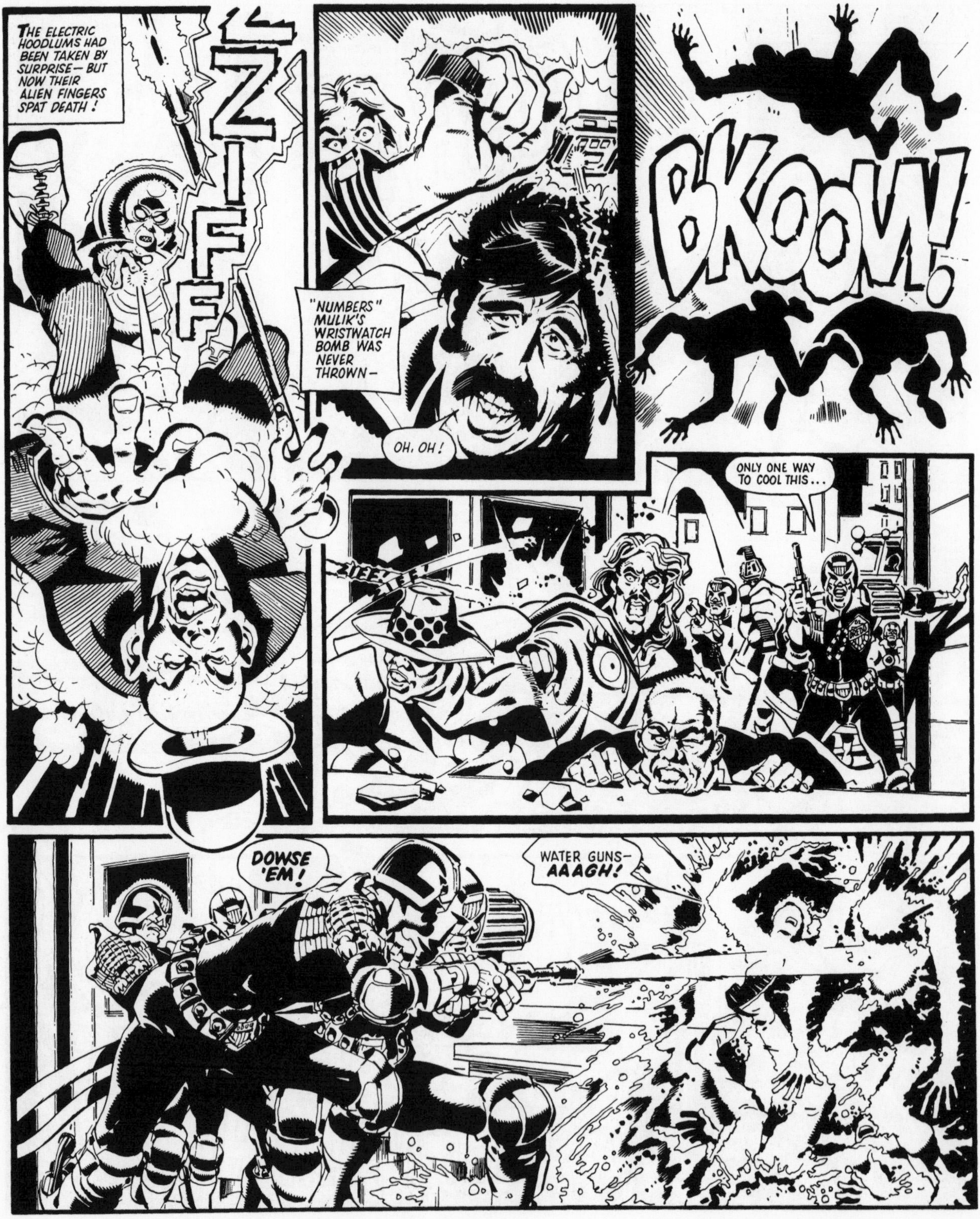
THE ELECTRIC HOODLUMS HAD BEEN TAKEN BY SURPRISE— BUT NOW THEIR ALIEN FINGERS SPAT DEATH!
ZZIFFF
"NUMBERS" MULIK'S WRISTWATCH BOMB WAS NEVER THROWN—
OH, OH!
BKOOM!
ONLY ONE WAY TO COOL THIS...
ZIFF ZIFF
DOWSE 'EM!
WATER GUNS— AAAGH!

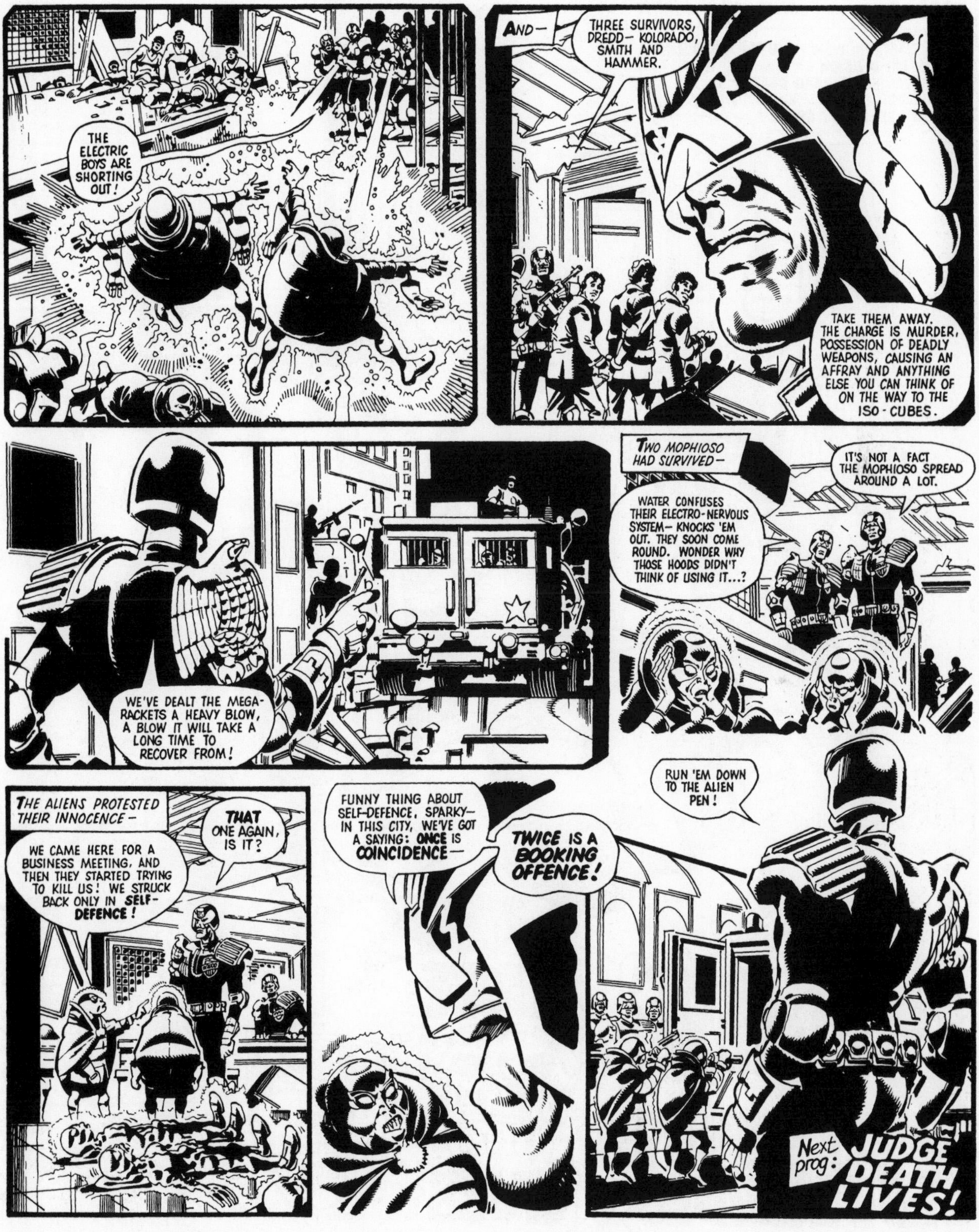
THE ELECTRIC BOYS ARE SHORTING OUT!
AND—
THREE SURVIVORS, DREDD— KOLORADO, SMITH AND HAMMER.
TAKE THEM AWAY. THE CHARGE IS MURDER, POSSESSION OF DEADLY WEAPONS, CAUSING AN AFFRAY AND ANYTHING ELSE YOU CAN THINK OF ON THE WAY TO THE ISO-CUBES.
WE'VE DEALT THE MEGA-RACKETS A HEAVY BLOW, A BLOW IT WILL TAKE A LONG TIME TO RECOVER FROM!
TWO MOPHIOSO HAD SURVIVED—
WATER CONFUSES THEIR ELECTRO-NERVOUS SYSTEM— KNOCKS 'EM OUT. THEY SOON COME ROUND. WONDER WHY THOSE HOODS DIDN'T THINK OF USING IT...?
IT'S NOT A FACT THE MOPHIOSO SPREAD AROUND A LOT.
THE ALIENS PROTESTED THEIR INNOCENCE—
WE CAME HERE FOR A BUSINESS MEETING, AND THEN THEY STARTED TRYING TO KILL US! WE STRUCK BACK ONLY IN SELF-DEFENCE!
THAT ONE AGAIN, IS IT?
FUNNY THING ABOUT SELF-DEFENCE, SPARKY— IN THIS CITY, WE'VE GOT A SAYING: ONCE IS COINCIDENCE—
TWICE IS A BOOKING OFFENCE!
RUN 'EM DOWN TO THE ALIEN PEN!
Next prog: JUDGE DEATH LIVES!

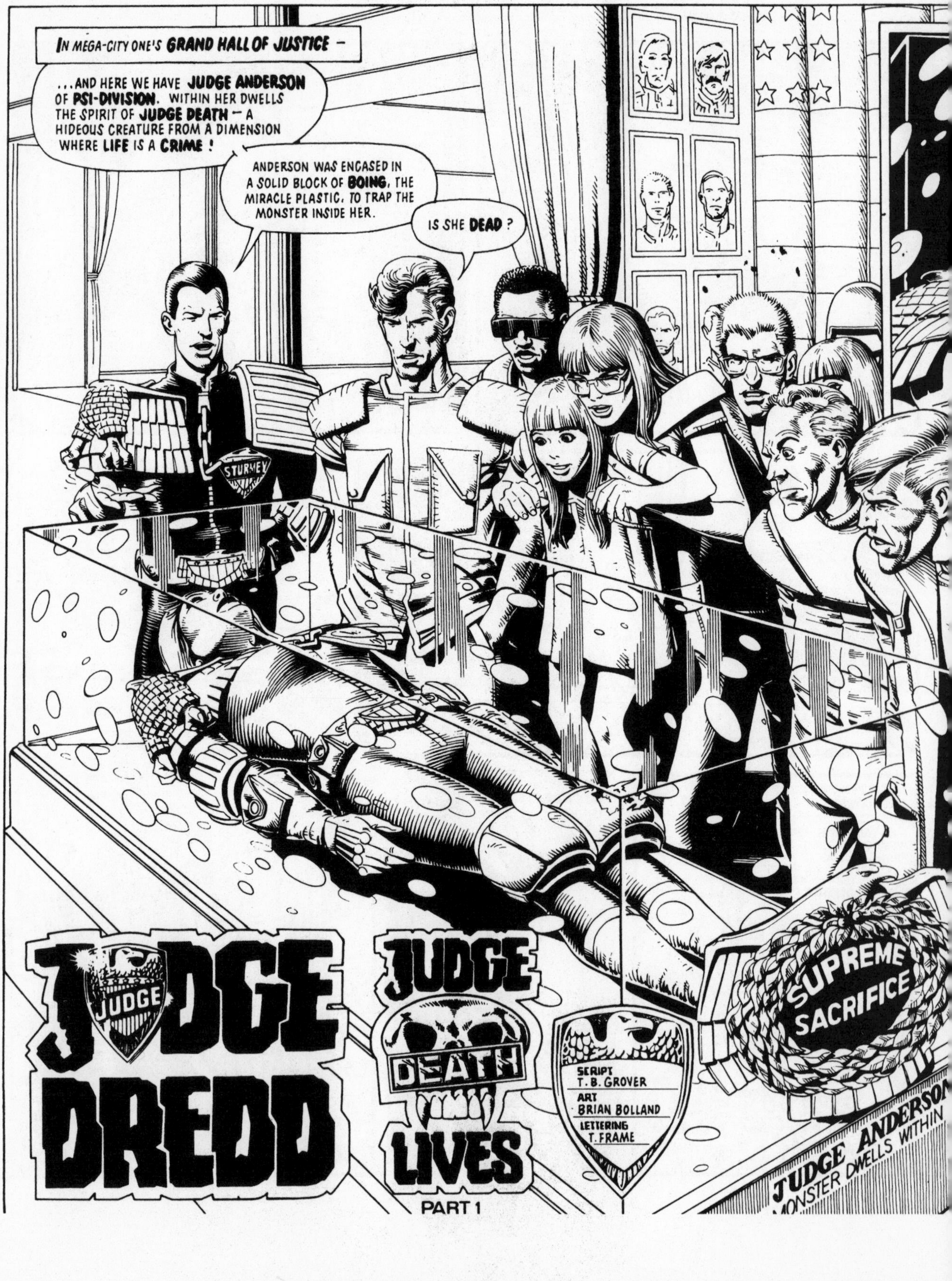
IN MEGA-CITY ONE'S GRAND HALL OF JUSTICE –
...AND HERE WE HAVE JUDGE ANDERSON OF PSI-DIVISION. WITHIN HER DWELLS THE SPIRIT OF JUDGE DEATH – A HIDEOUS CREATURE FROM A DIMENSION WHERE LIFE IS A CRIME!
ANDERSON WAS ENCASED IN A SOLID BLOCK OF BOING, THE MIRACLE PLASTIC, TO TRAP THE MONSTER INSIDE HER.
IS SHE DEAD?
STURMEY
JUDGE DREDD
JUDGE DEATH LIVES
PART 1
SCRIPT T.B. GROVER
ART BRIAN BOLLAND
LETTERING T. FRAME
SUPREME SACRIFICE
JUDGE ANDERSON
MONSTER DWELLS WITHIN

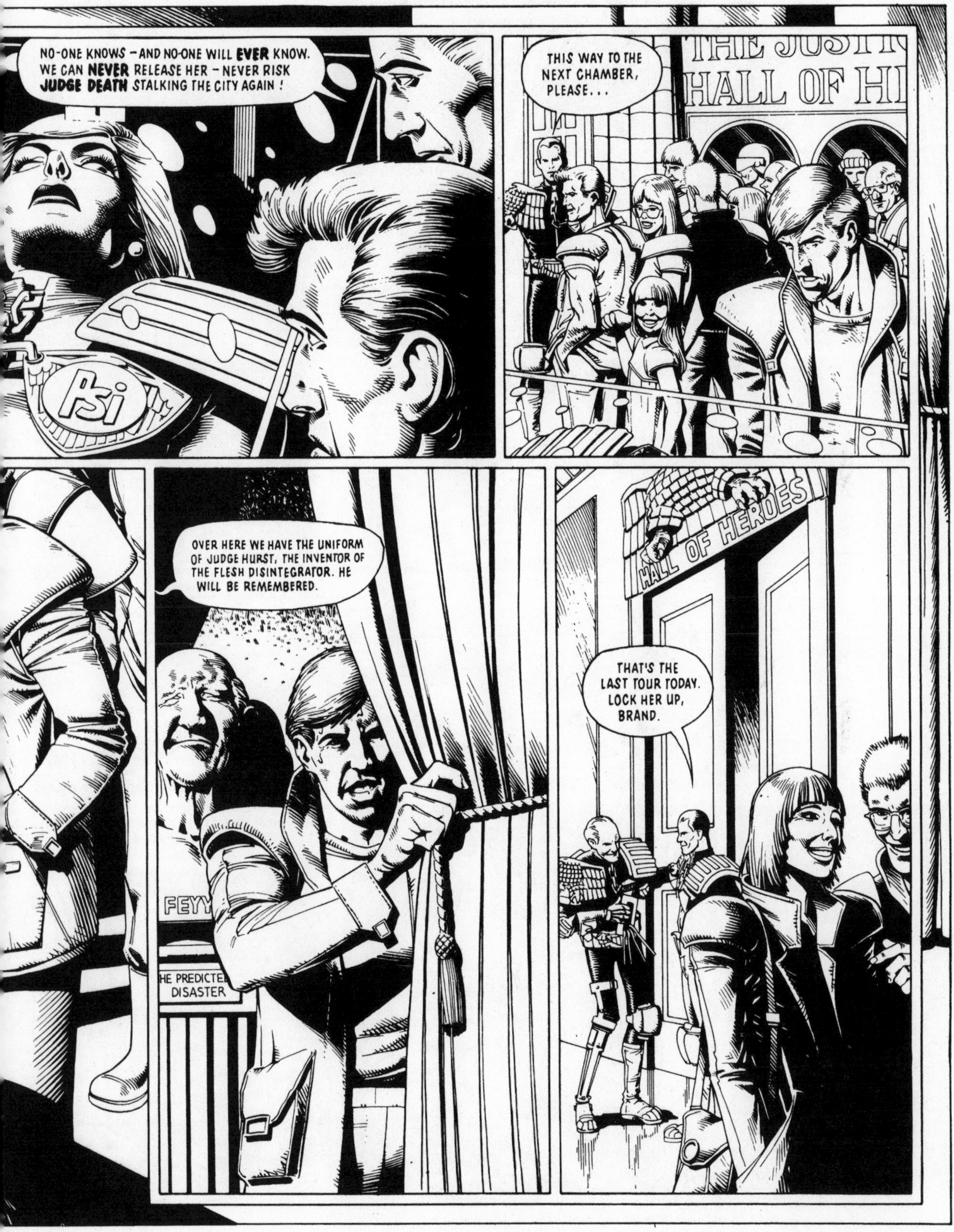
NO-ONE KNOWS – AND NO-ONE WILL EVER KNOW. WE CAN NEVER RELEASE HER – NEVER RISK JUDGE DEATH STALKING THE CITY AGAIN !
Psi
THIS WAY TO THE NEXT CHAMBER, PLEASE...
OVER HERE WE HAVE THE UNIFORM OF JUDGE HURST, THE INVENTOR OF THE FLESH DISINTEGRATOR. HE WILL BE REMEMBERED.
HALL OF HEROES
THAT'S THE LAST TOUR TODAY. LOCK HER UP, BRAND.

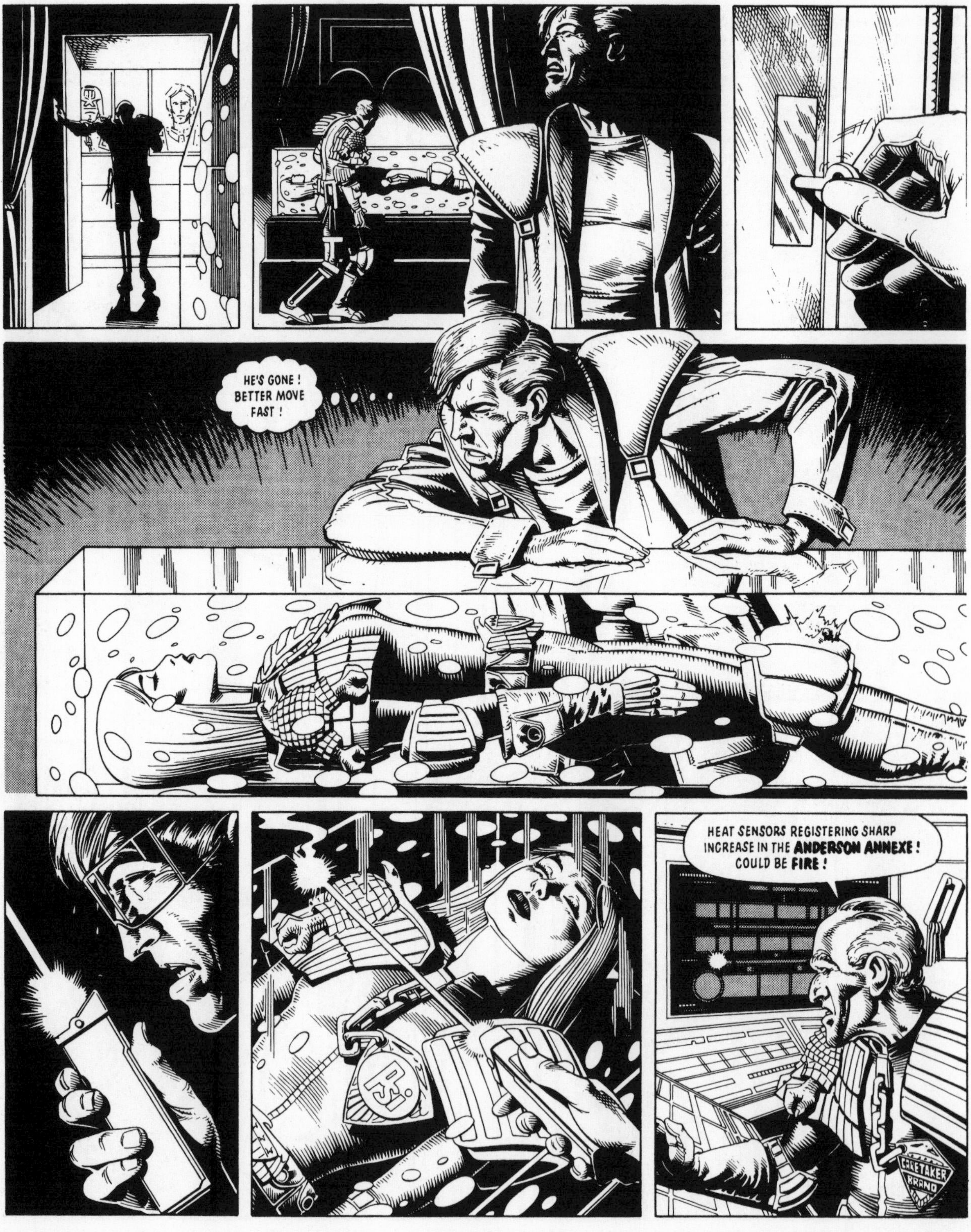
HE'S GONE ! BETTER MOVE FAST !
HEAT SENSORS REGISTERING SHARP INCREASE IN THE ANDERSON ANNEXE ! COULD BE FIRE !
CARETAKER BRAND

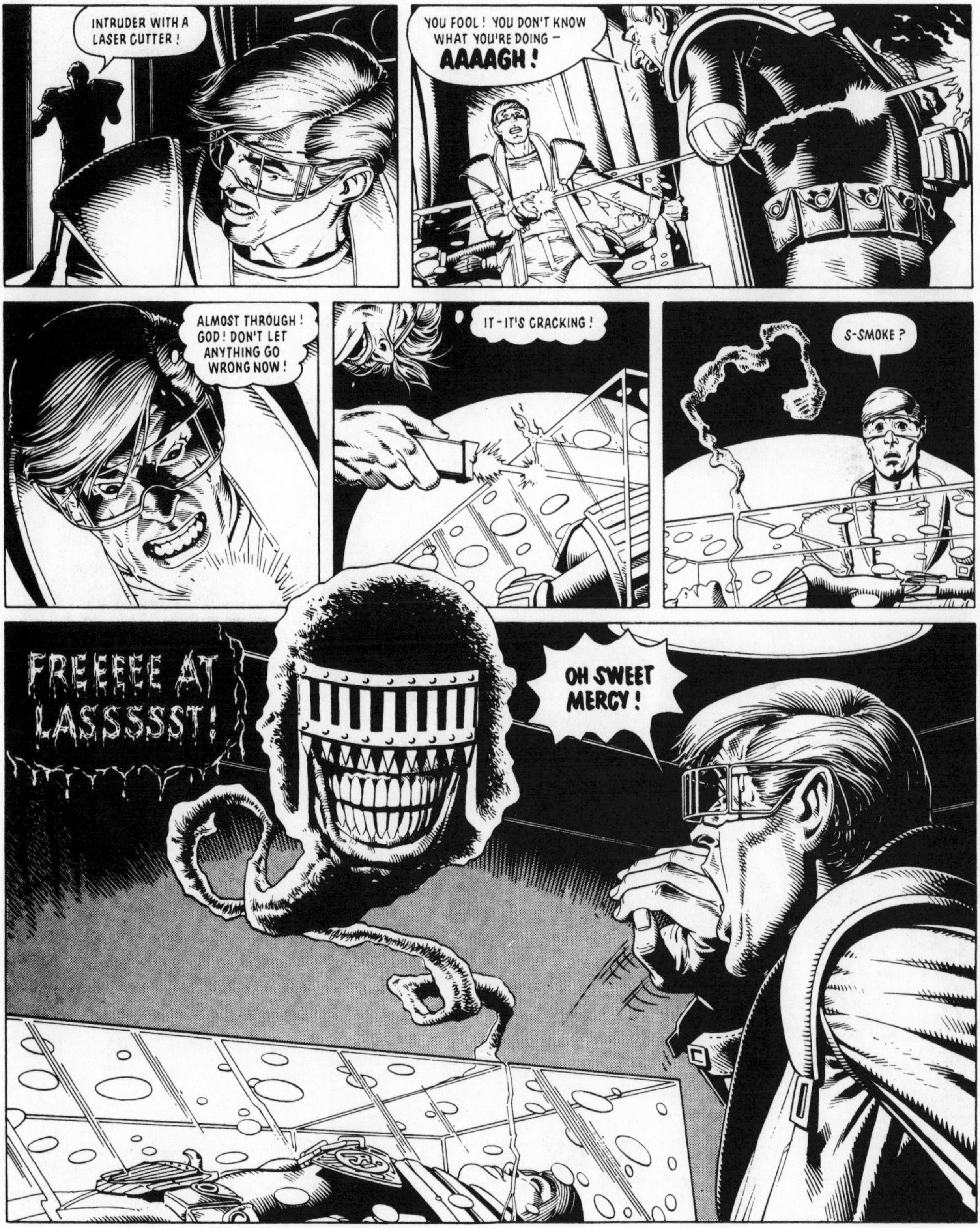
INTRUDER WITH A LASER CUTTER!
YOU FOOL! YOU DON'T KNOW WHAT YOU'RE DOING – AAAAGH!
ALMOST THROUGH! GOD! DON'T LET ANYTHING GO WRONG NOW!
IT-IT'S CRACKING!
S-SMOKE?
FREEEEE AT LASSSSST!
OH SWEET MERCY!

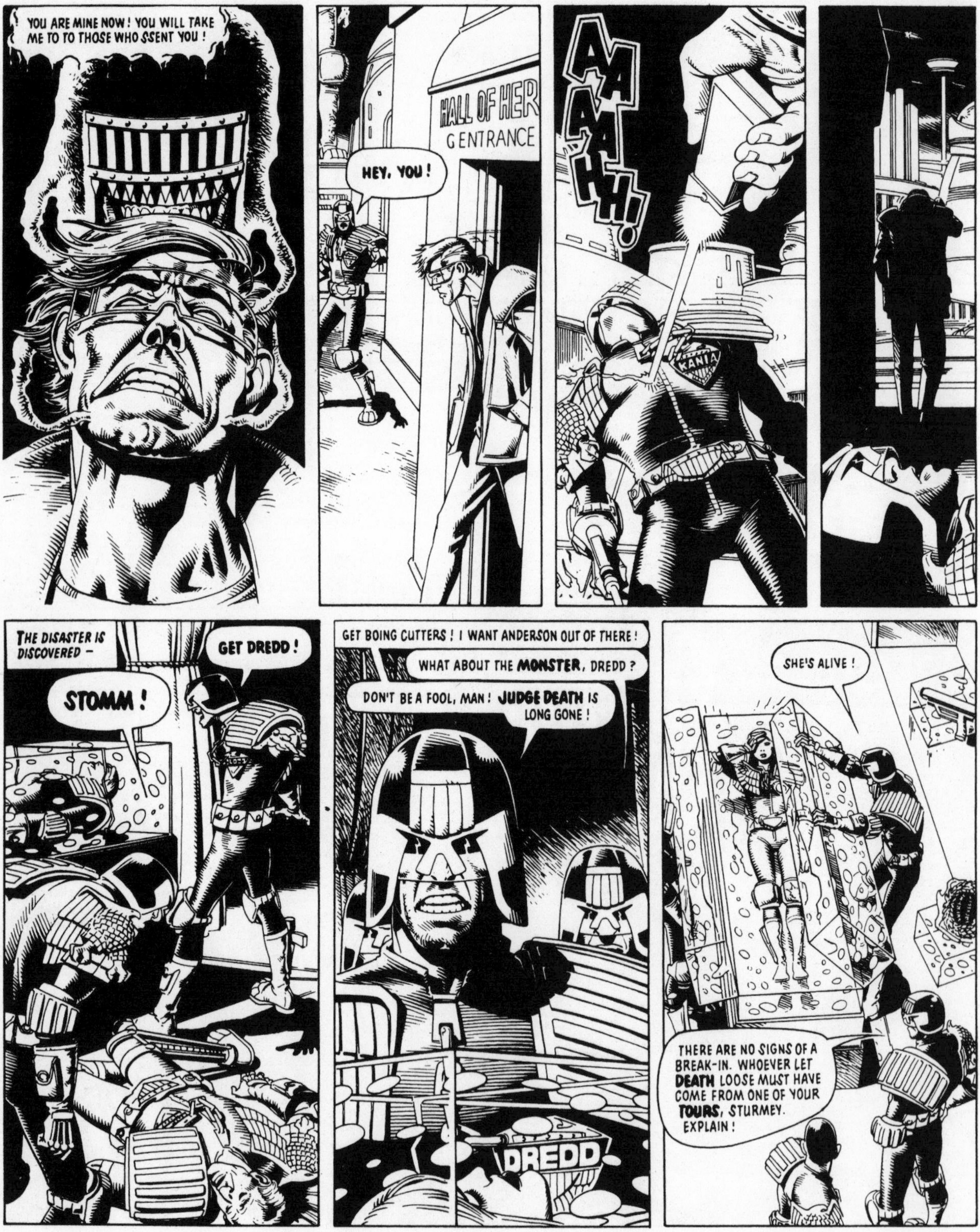
YOU ARE MINE NOW! YOU WILL TAKE ME TO TO THOSE WHO SSENT YOU!
HALL OF HER
G ENTRANCE
HEY, YOU!
AAAAHH!
KANIA
THE DISASTER IS DISCOVERED —
GET DREDD!
STOMM!
GET BOING CUTTERS! I WANT ANDERSON OUT OF THERE!
WHAT ABOUT THE MONSTER, DREDD?
DON'T BE A FOOL, MAN! JUDGE DEATH IS LONG GONE!
DREDD
SHE'S ALIVE!
THERE ARE NO SIGNS OF A BREAK-IN. WHOEVER LET DEATH LOOSE MUST HAVE COME FROM ONE OF YOUR TOURS, STURMEY. EXPLAIN!

I... MUST HAVE MISCOUNTED THE NUMBERS COMING OUT!

NOT GOOD ENOUGH, STURMEY. YOUR NEGLIGENCE MAY HAVE COST THE CITY DEAR. PLACE YOURSELF UNDER DETENTION.

FOUR THOUSAND TOURISTS VISIT THE HALL OF HEROES EACH DAY —

I WANT THEM CHECKED — EVERY ONE OF THEM. INFORM THE CHIEF JUDGE WE'VE GOT A LEVEL ONE EMERGENCY ON OUR HANDS.

WE'VE GOT TO CATCH THIS CREEP BEFORE ALL HELL BREAKS LOOSE!

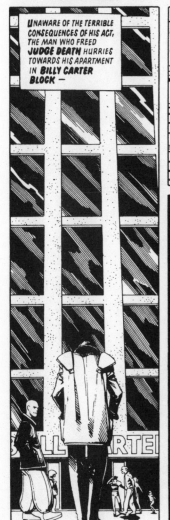

UNAWARE OF THE TERRIBLE CONSEQUENCES OF HIS ACT, THE MAN WHO FREED JUDGE DEATH HURRIES TOWARDS HIS APARTMENT IN BILLY CARTER BLOCK —

APT 1027B

J-JANINE!

YOU PROMISED! YOU PROMISED YOU W-WOULDN'T KILL HER IF I HELPED YOU!

WE LIED!

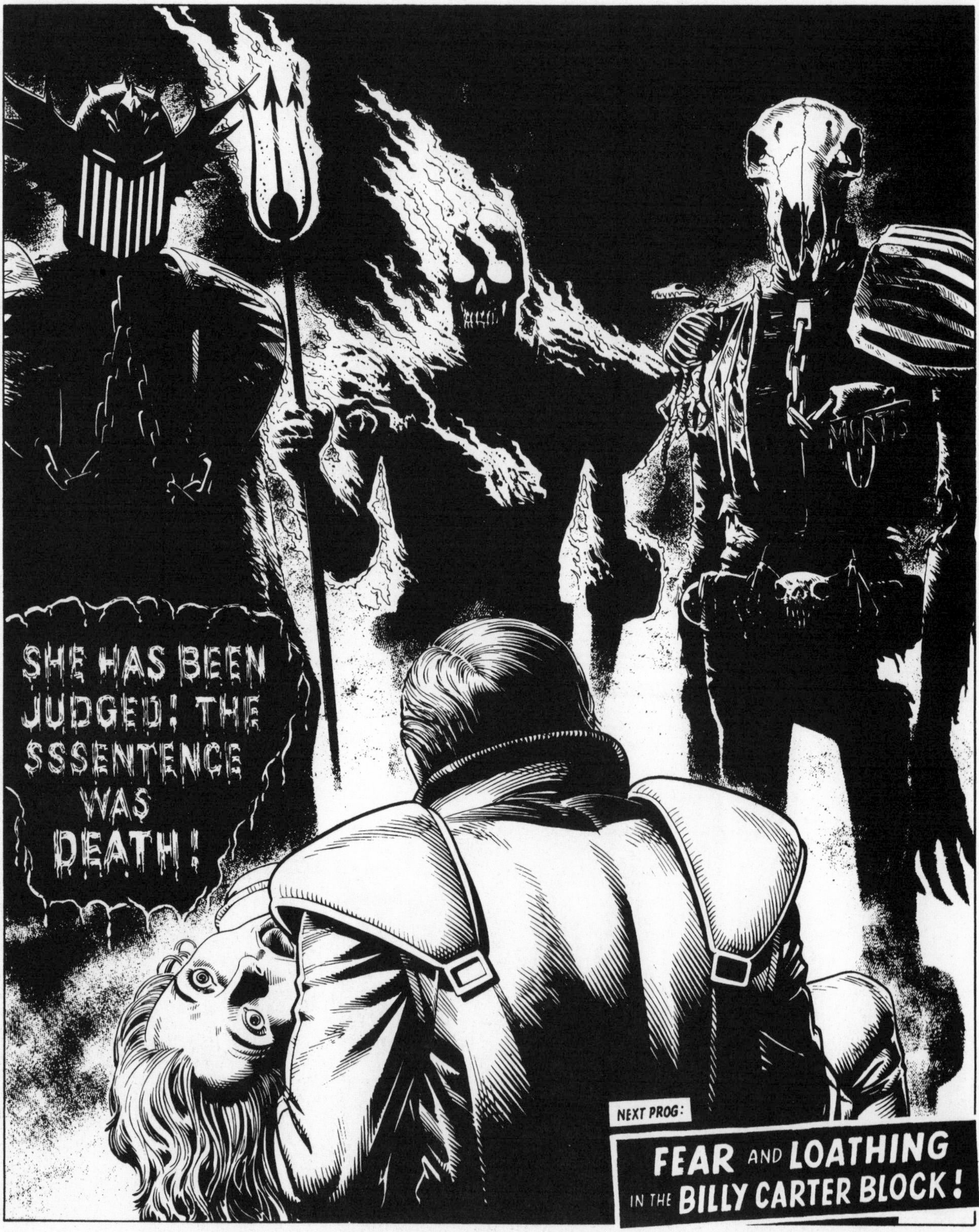
SHE HAS BEEN JUDGED! THE SSSENTENCE WAS DEATH!
NEXT PROG:
FEAR AND LOATHING IN THE BILLY CARTER BLOCK!

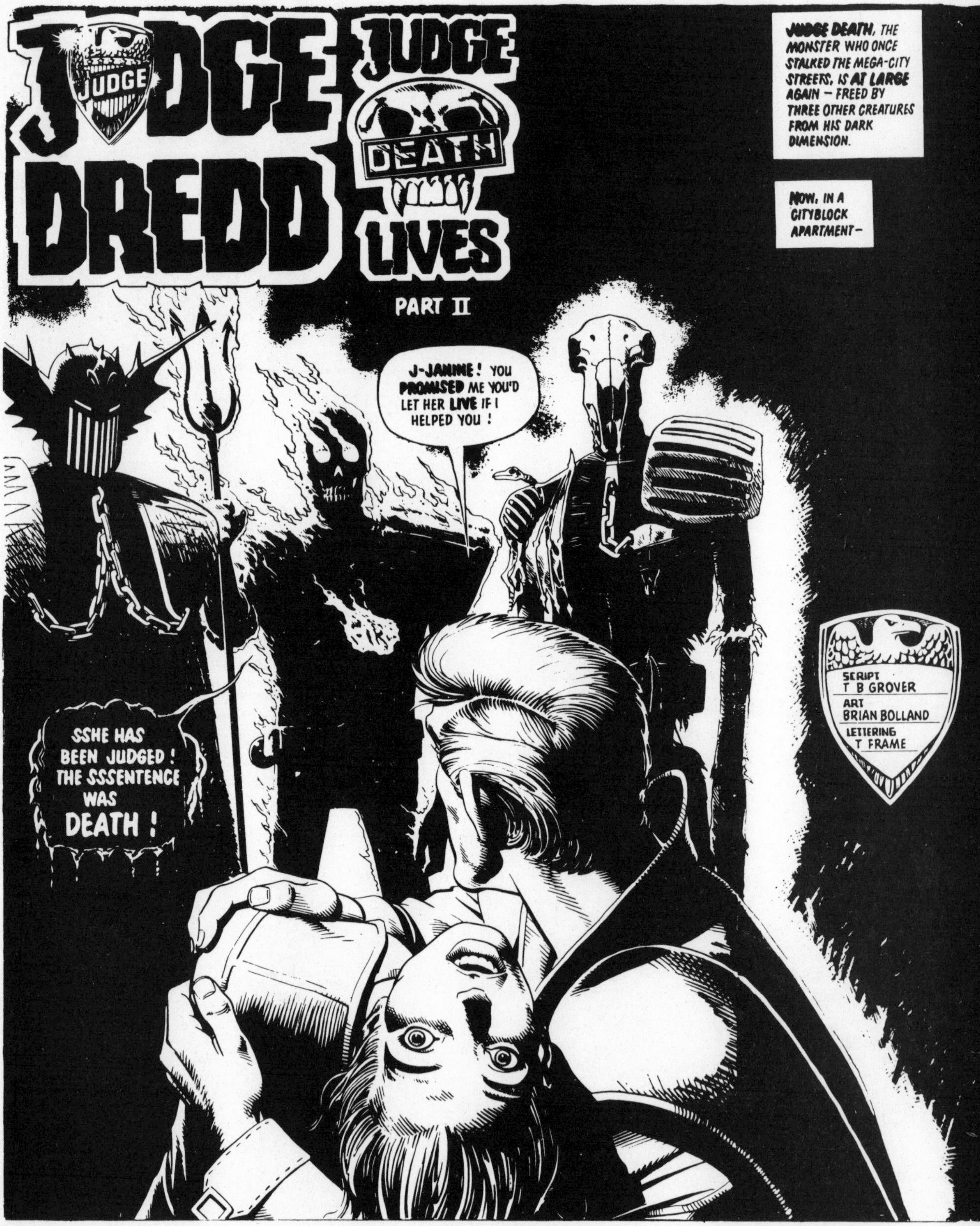
JUDGE DREDD
JUDGE DEATH LIVES
PART II
JUDGE DEATH, THE MONSTER WHO ONCE STALKED THE MEGA-CITY STREETS, IS AT LARGE AGAIN — FREED BY THREE OTHER CREATURES FROM HIS DARK DIMENSION.
NOW, IN A CITYBLOCK APARTMENT—
J-JANINE! YOU PROMISED ME YOU'D LET HER LIVE IF I HELPED YOU!
SSHE HAS BEEN JUDGED! THE SSSENTENCE WAS DEATH!
SCRIPT T B GROVER
ART BRIAN BOLLAND
LETTERING T FRAME

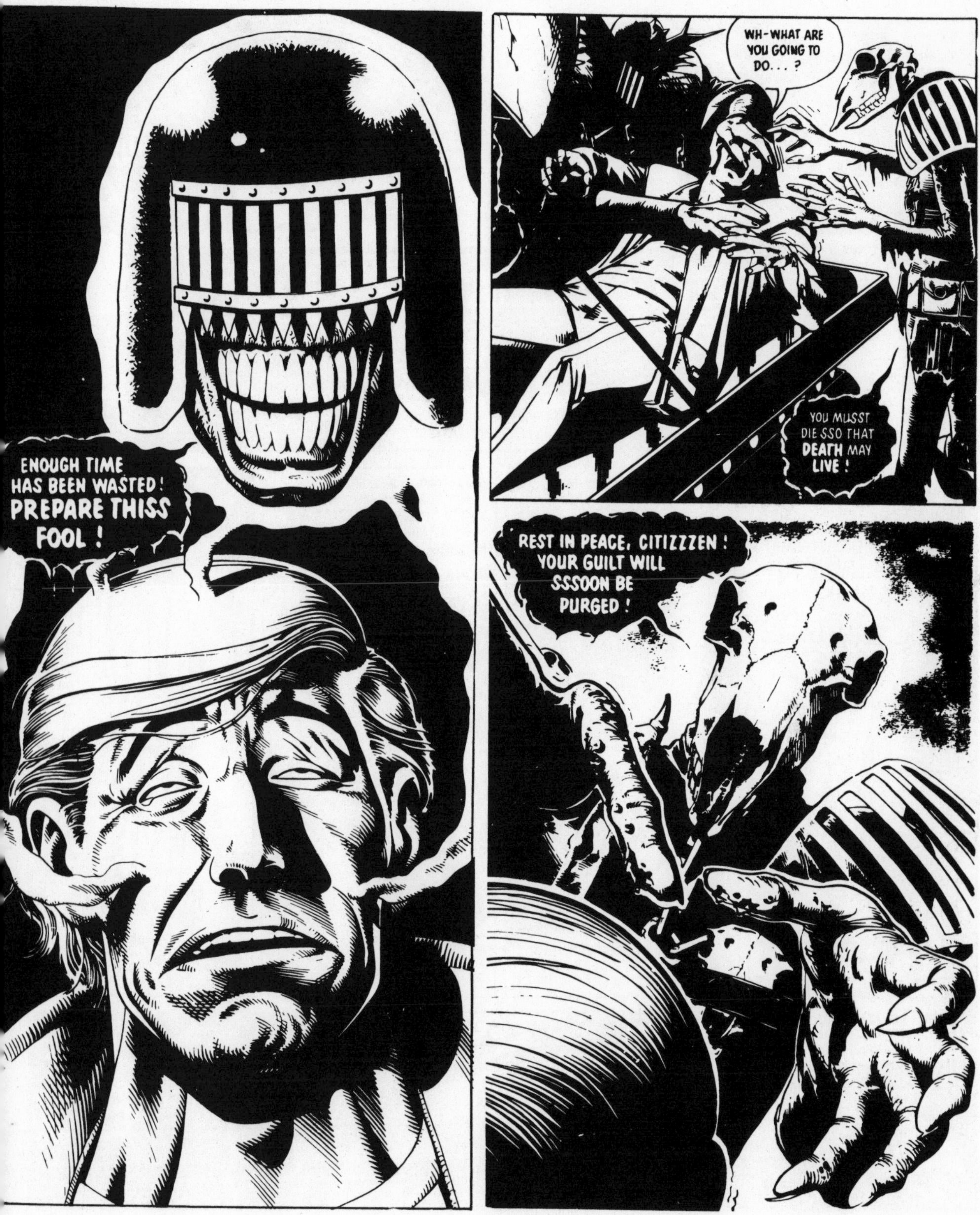

ENOUGH TIME HAS BEEN WASTED! PREPARE THISS FOOL!
WH-WHAT ARE YOU GOING TO DO...?
YOU MUSST DIE SSO THAT DEATH MAY LIVE!
REST IN PEACE, CITIZZZEN! YOUR GUILT WILL SSSOON BE PURGED!

THE FOETID TOUCH OF *JUDGE MORTIS* BRINGS... *DECAY!*

THE BODY ISS RIPE! LET THE DEAD FLUIDS FLOW OVER IT!

OUTSIDE THE GRAND HALL OF JUSTICE —

JUDGE DREDD, YOU'RE HEADING THE SEARCH! JUST WHAT *HARM* CAN THIS MONSTER DO?

ACCORDING TO THE WARPED LOGIC OF HIS DIMENSION, ALL CRIME IS COMMITTED BY THE LIVING — THEREFORE LIFE *ITSELF* IS A CRIME.

AS LONG AS JUDGE DEATH IS AT LARGE, NO CITIZEN IS SAFE!

BUT YOU SAY HE'S IN SOME KIND OF... SPIRIT FORM?

HE CAN CREATE ANOTHER BODY. HE WILL TRY TO. THAT'S ENOUGH QUESTIONS!

ATTENTION, JUDGE DREDD! SOMETHING INTERESTING HERE! ONE OF THE HALL OF HEROES TOURISTS IS REGISTERED AS HAVING *STRONG TELEPATHIC POTENTIAL* — POSSIBLY A *CARRIER* FOR *JUDGE DEATH!*

NAME OF MITSON. APARTMENT 1027b, BILLY CARTER BLOCK.

ON MY WAY!

IN THE BILLY CARTER BLOCK, THE HORRIFYING TRANSFORMATION WAS NEARING COMPLETION —

ENTER, DEATH! FILL THISS SOULLESS CARCASS!

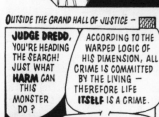

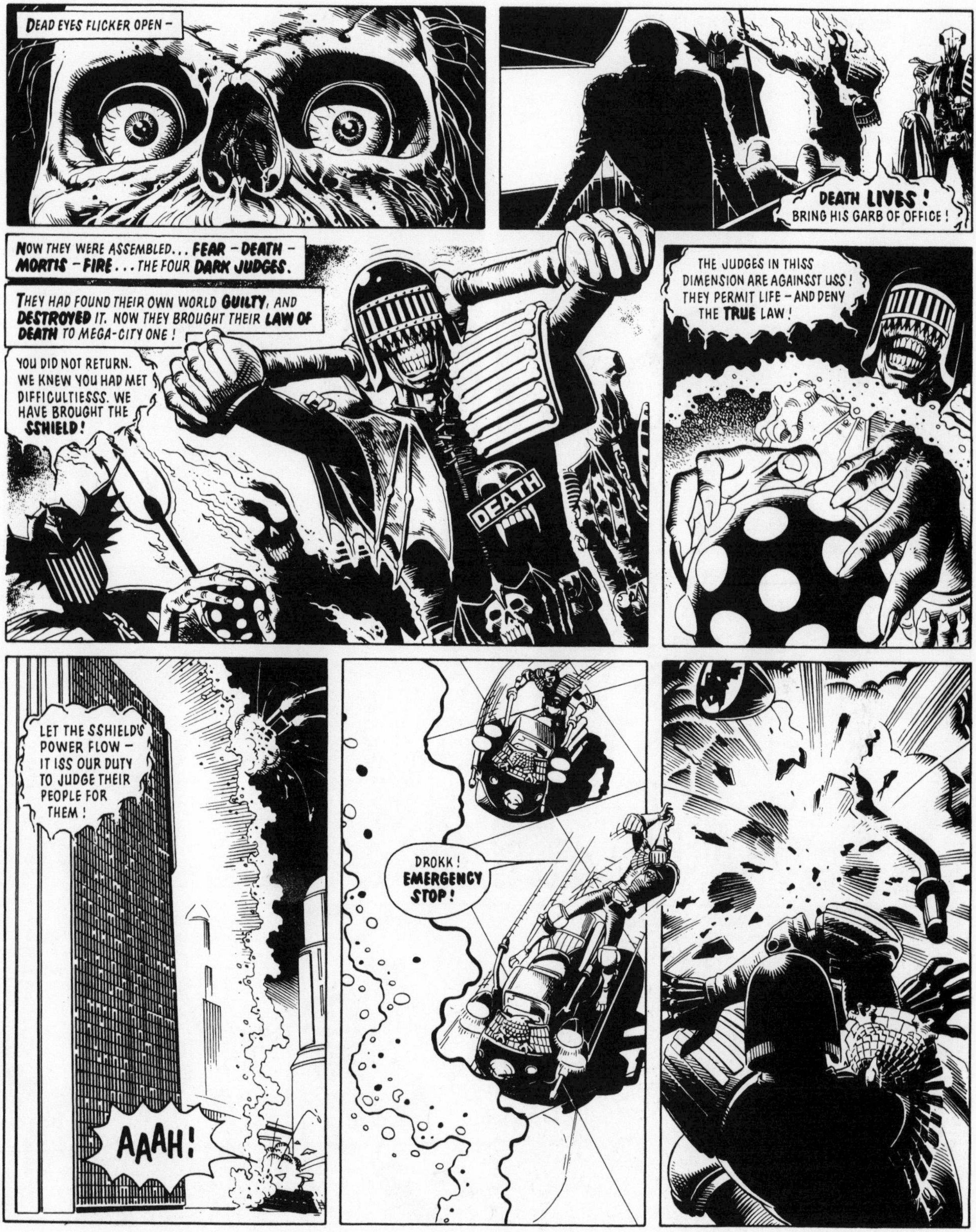
DEAD EYES FLICKER OPEN –
DEATH LIVES! BRING HIS GARB OF OFFICE!
NOW THEY WERE ASSEMBLED... FEAR – DEATH – MORTIS – FIRE... THE FOUR DARK JUDGES.
THEY HAD FOUND THEIR OWN WORLD GUILTY, AND DESTROYED IT. NOW THEY BROUGHT THEIR LAW OF DEATH TO MEGA-CITY ONE!
YOU DID NOT RETURN. WE KNEW YOU HAD MET DIFFICULTIESSS. WE HAVE BROUGHT THE SSHIELD!
DEATH
THE JUDGES IN THISS DIMENSION ARE AGAINSST USS! THEY PERMIT LIFE – AND DENY THE TRUE LAW!
LET THE SSHIELD'S POWER FLOW – IT ISS OUR DUTY TO JUDGE THEIR PEOPLE FOR THEM!
AAAH!
DROKK! EMERGENCY STOP!

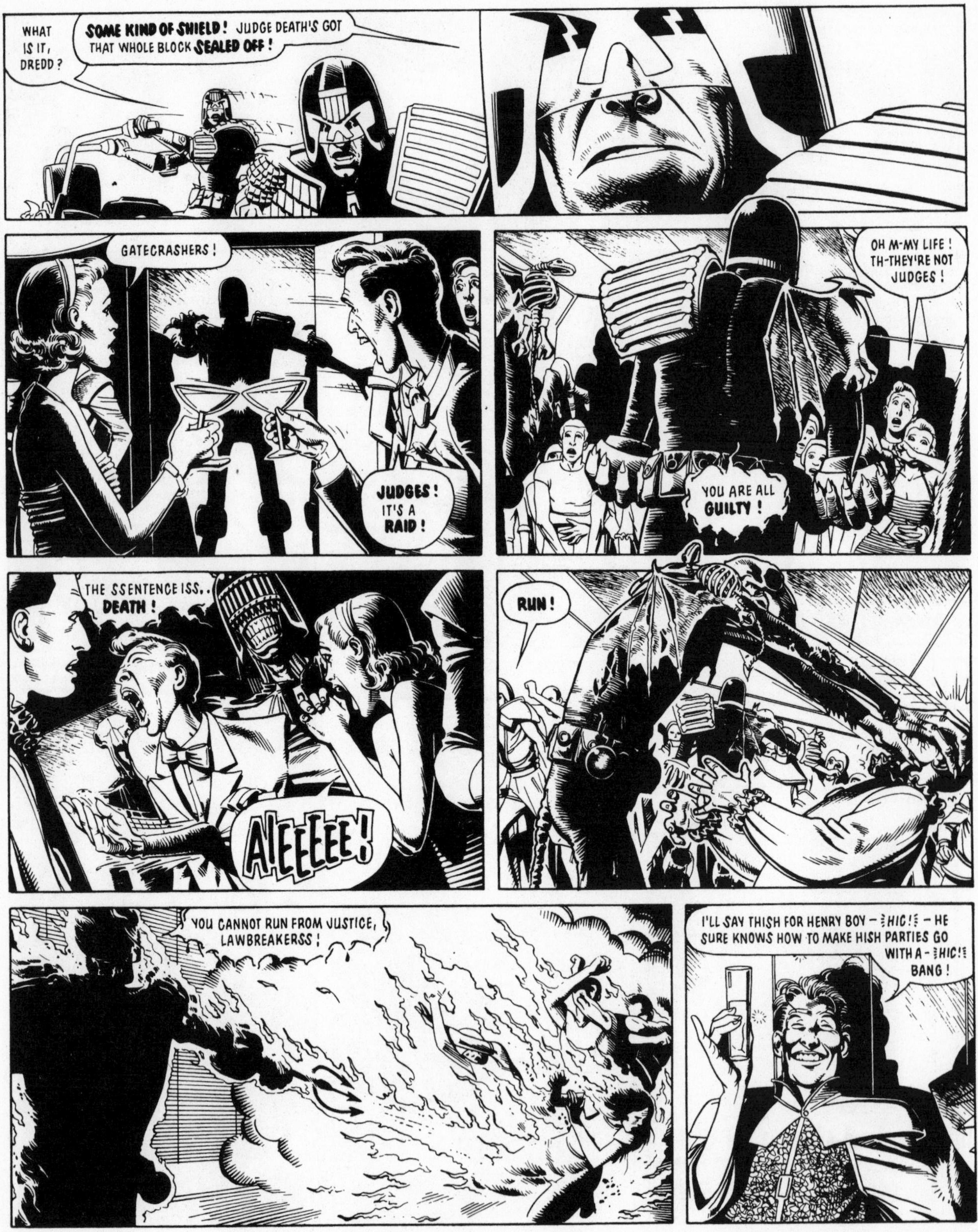
WHAT IS IT, DREDD?
SOME KIND OF SHIELD! JUDGE DEATH'S GOT THAT WHOLE BLOCK SEALED OFF!
GATECRASHERS!
JUDGES! IT'S A RAID!
OH M-MY LIFE! TH-THEY'RE NOT JUDGES!
YOU ARE ALL GUILTY!
THE SSENTENCE ISS.. DEATH!
AIEEEEE!
RUN!
YOU CANNOT RUN FROM JUSTICE, LAWBREAKERSS!
I'LL SAY THISH FOR HENRY BOY — HIC! — HE SURE KNOWS HOW TO MAKE HISH PARTIES GO WITH A — HIC! BANG!

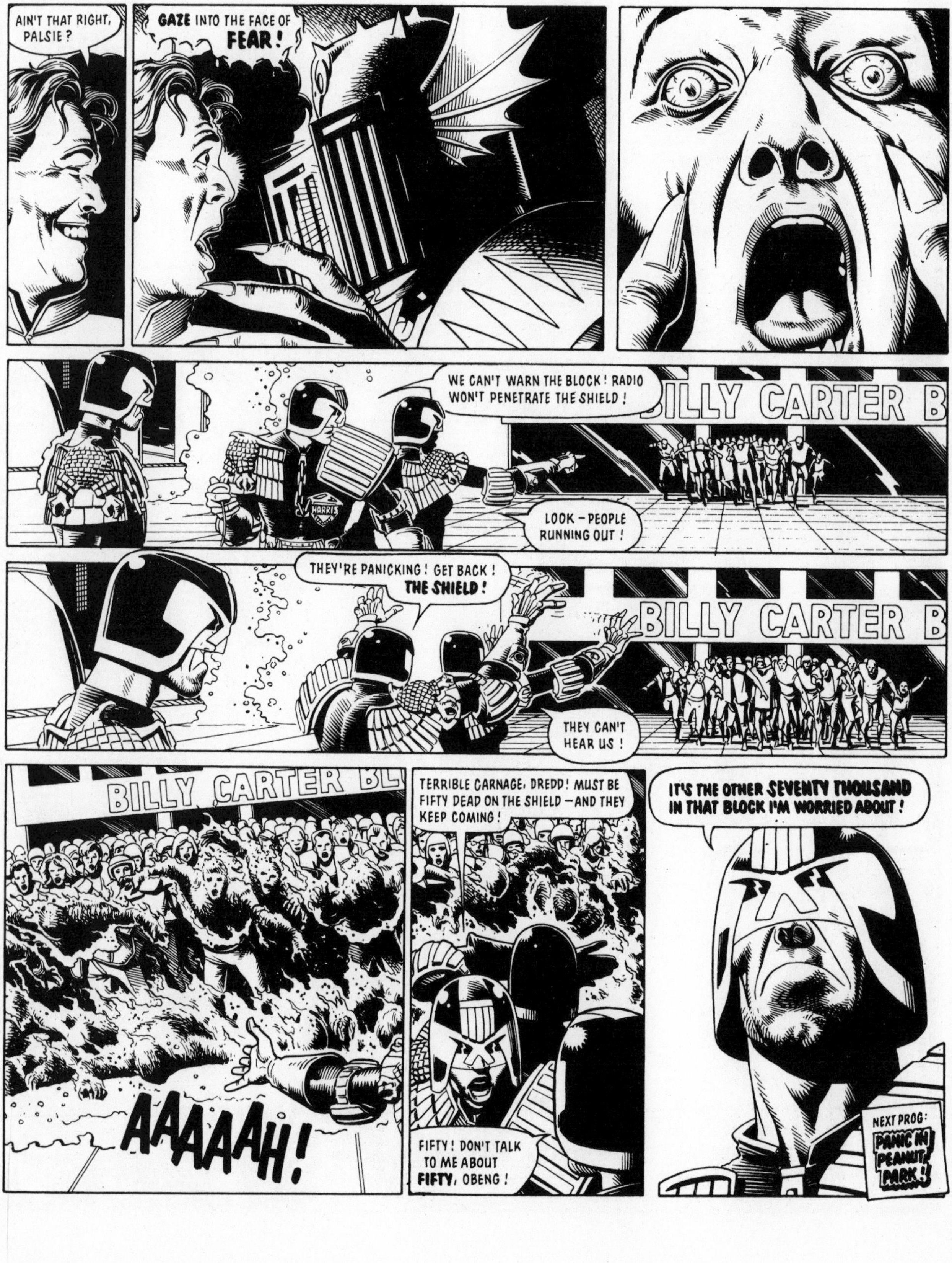
AIN'T THAT RIGHT, PALSIE?
GAZE INTO THE FACE OF FEAR!
WE CAN'T WARN THE BLOCK! RADIO WON'T PENETRATE THE SHIELD!
BILLY CARTER B
HARRIS
LOOK – PEOPLE RUNNING OUT!
THEY'RE PANICKING! GET BACK! THE SHIELD!
BILLY CARTER B
THEY CAN'T HEAR US!
BILLY CARTER BL
AAAAAH!
TERRIBLE CARNAGE, DREDD! MUST BE FIFTY DEAD ON THE SHIELD – AND THEY KEEP COMING!
FIFTY! DON'T TALK TO ME ABOUT FIFTY, OBENG!
IT'S THE OTHER SEVENTY THOUSAND IN THAT BLOCK I'M WORRIED ABOUT!
NEXT PROG: PANIC IN PEANUT PARK!

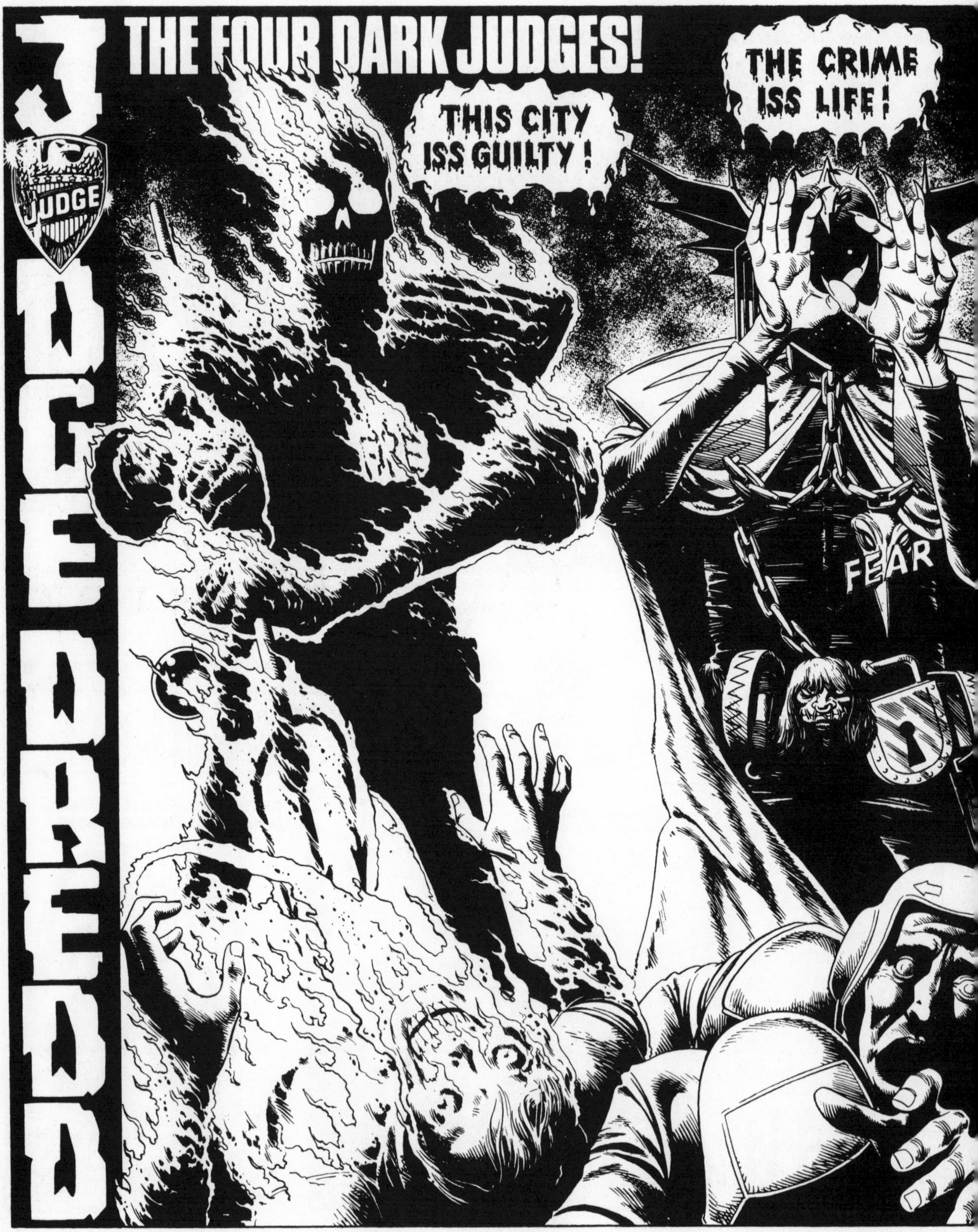
JUDGE DREDD
THE FOUR DARK JUDGES!
JUDGE
THIS CITY ISS GUILTY!
THE CRIME ISS LIFE!
FEAR

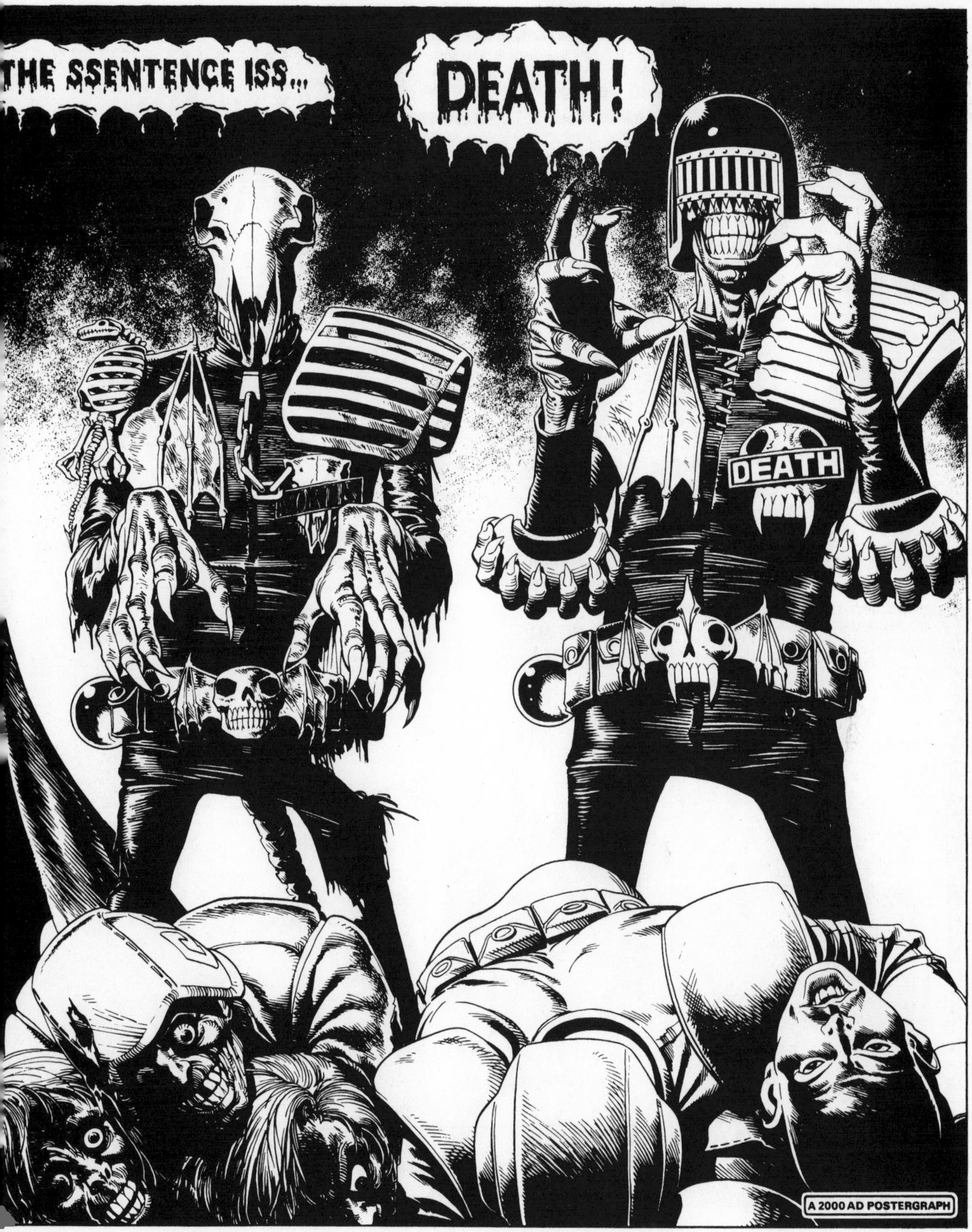
THE SSENTENCE ISS...
DEATH!
DEATH
A 2000 AD POSTERGRAPH

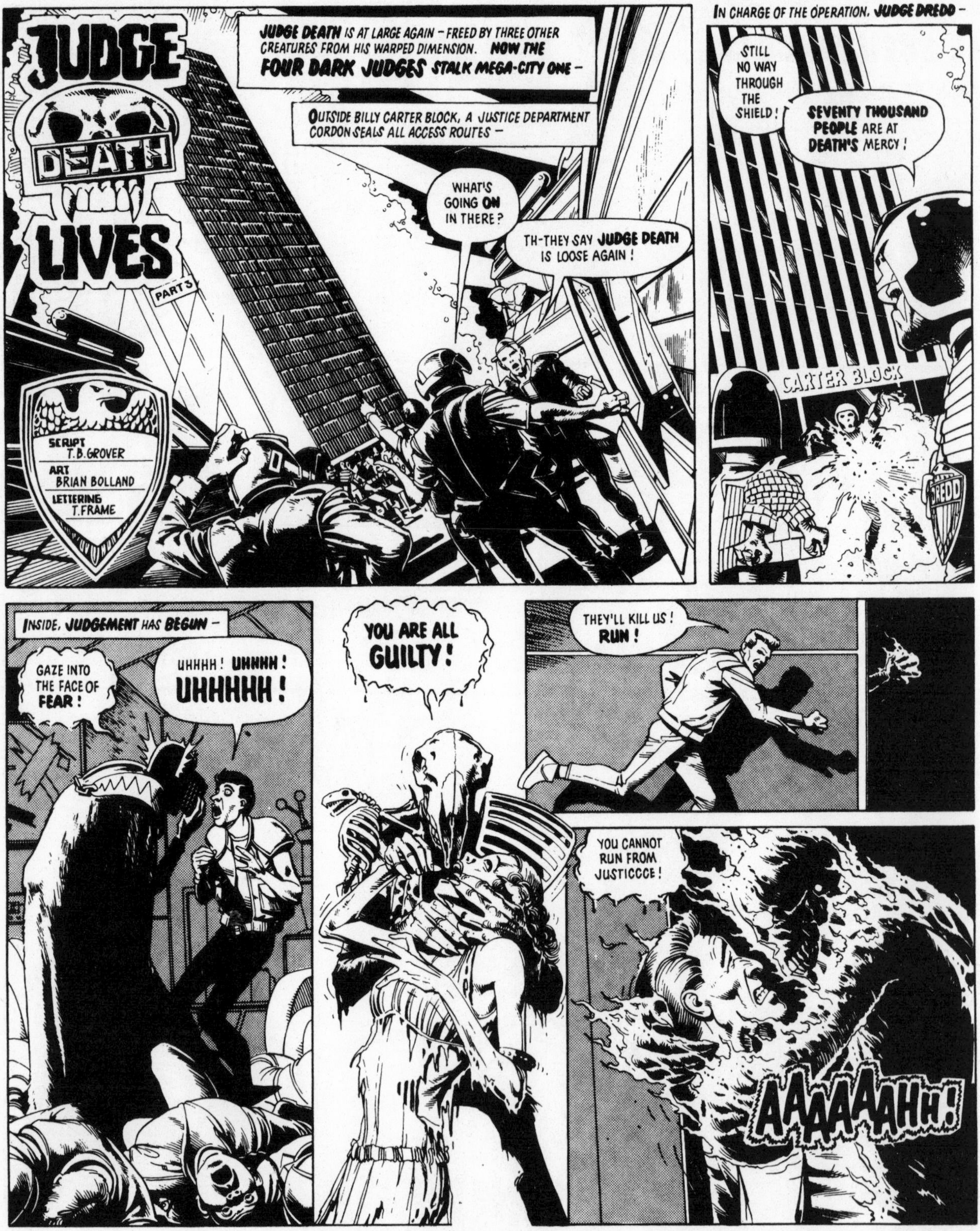

JUDGE DEATH LIVES
PART 3
SCRIPT T.B.GROVER
ART BRIAN BOLLAND
LETTERING T.FRAME
JUDGE DEATH IS AT LARGE AGAIN – FREED BY THREE OTHER CREATURES FROM HIS WARPED DIMENSION. NOW THE FOUR DARK JUDGES STALK MEGA-CITY ONE –
OUTSIDE BILLY CARTER BLOCK, A JUSTICE DEPARTMENT CORDON SEALS ALL ACCESS ROUTES –
WHAT'S GOING ON IN THERE?
TH-THEY SAY JUDGE DEATH IS LOOSE AGAIN!
IN CHARGE OF THE OPERATION, JUDGE DREDD –
STILL NO WAY THROUGH THE SHIELD!
SEVENTY THOUSAND PEOPLE ARE AT DEATH'S MERCY!
CARTER BLOCK
DREDD
INSIDE, JUDGEMENT HAS BEGUN –
GAZE INTO THE FACE OF FEAR!
UHHHH! UHHHH! UHHHHH!
YOU ARE ALL GUILTY!
THEY'LL KILL US! RUN!
YOU CANNOT RUN FROM JUSTICCCE!
AAAAAAHH!

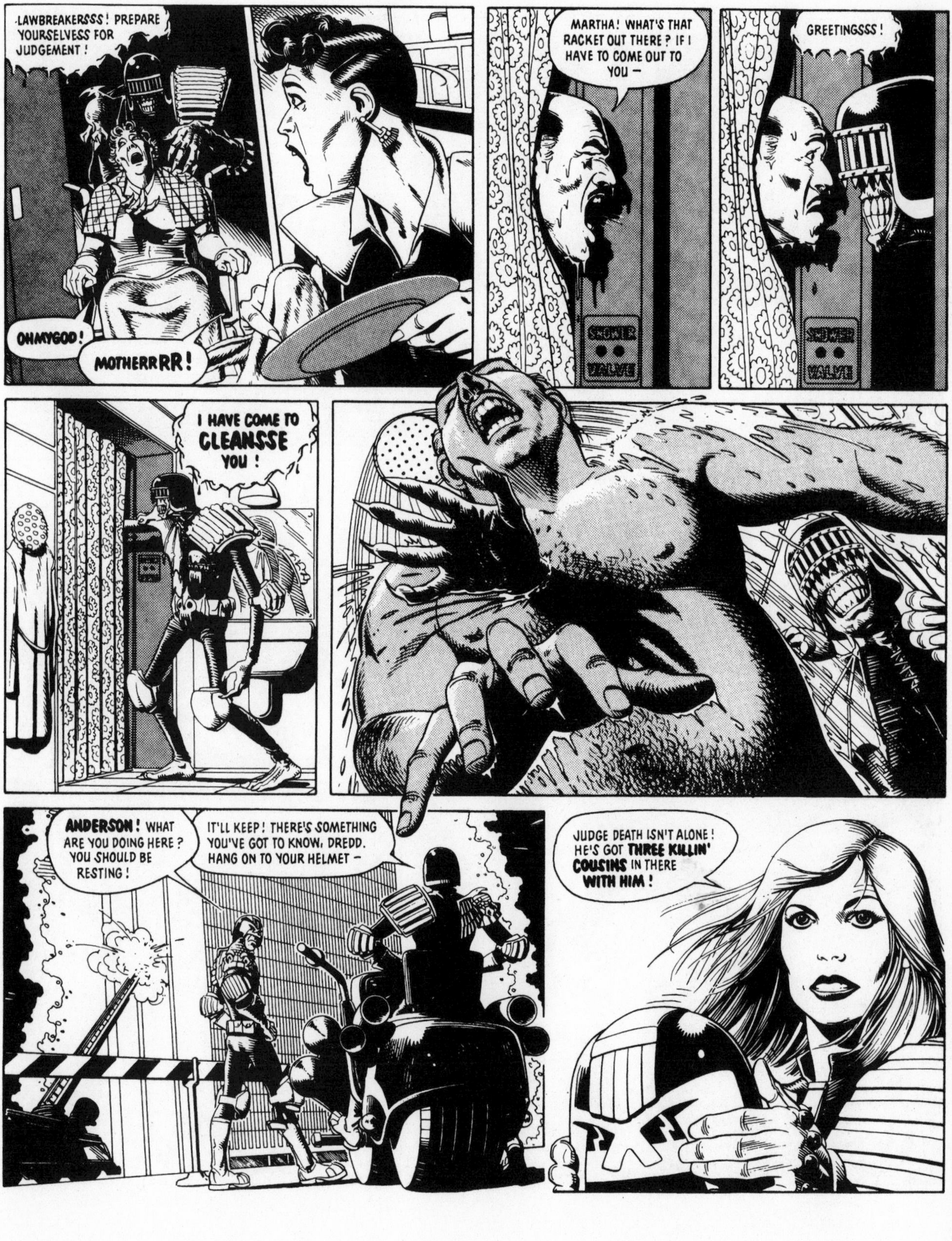

LAWBREAKERSSS! PREPARE YOURSELVESS FOR JUDGEMENT!
OHMYGOD!
MOTHERRRRR!
MARTHA! WHAT'S THAT RACKET OUT THERE? IF I HAVE TO COME OUT TO YOU —
SHOWER VALVE
GREETINGSSS!
I HAVE COME TO CLEANSSE YOU!
ANDERSON! WHAT ARE YOU DOING HERE? YOU SHOULD BE RESTING!
IT'LL KEEP! THERE'S SOMETHING YOU'VE GOT TO KNOW, DREDD. HANG ON TO YOUR HELMET —
JUDGE DEATH ISN'T ALONE! HE'S GOT THREE KILLIN' COUSINS IN THERE WITH HIM!

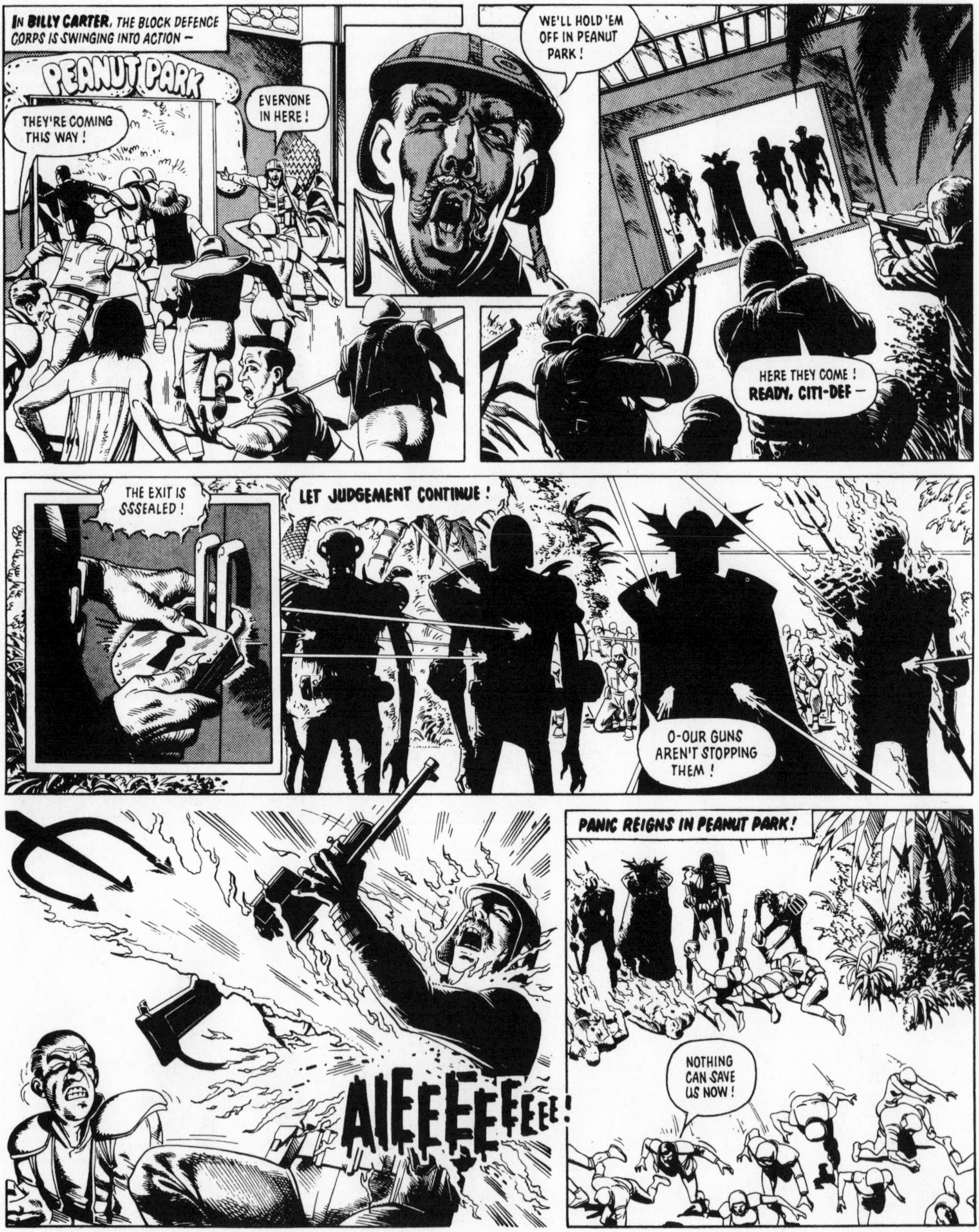
IN BILLY CARTER, THE BLOCK DEFENCE CORPS IS SWINGING INTO ACTION –
PEANUT PARK
THEY'RE COMING THIS WAY!
EVERYONE IN HERE!
WE'LL HOLD 'EM OFF IN PEANUT PARK!
HERE THEY COME! READY, CITI-DEF –
THE EXIT IS SSSEALED!
LET JUDGEMENT CONTINUE!
O-OUR GUNS AREN'T STOPPING THEM!
AIEEEEEEEE!
PANIC REIGNS IN PEANUT PARK!
NOTHING CAN SAVE US NOW!

THE MANHOLE'S NO GOOD, DREDD! THEIR SHIELD GOES RIGHT UNDER THE WHOLE BLOCK!

I CAN GET YOU THROUGH IT, DREDD!

ANDERSON OF PSI-DIVISION — JUDGES SPECIALLY TRAINED FOR THEIR ABNORMAL PSYCHIC POWER —

THAT'S A PSI-SHIELD! THEY'RE USING SOME KIND OF PSYCHIC WAVE GENERATOR! THE ONLY WAY THROUGH IS TO DEFLECT THE WAVES!

AND YOU RECKON YOU CAN DO IT?

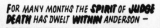

FOR MANY MONTHS THE SPIRIT OF JUDGE DEATH HAS DWELT WITHIN ANDERSON —

YOU DON'T HAVE A RAT LIKE DEATH CAMPING OUT IN YOUR BRAIN WITHOUT PICKING UP A FEW TRICKS! I KNOW I CAN DO IT! COME ON!

HOLD TIGHT — WE'RE GOING THROUGH!

THEN EVERY OUNCE OF ANDERSON'S MENTAL POWER IS FOCUSSED AGAINST THE PSI-SHIELD —

GOT TO... FORCE... IT... OPEN!

WE'RE THROUGH! GOOD WORK, ANDERSON!

AND IN PEANUT PARK —

ANDERSSON!

NEXT PROG: FACE TO FACE WITH FEAR!

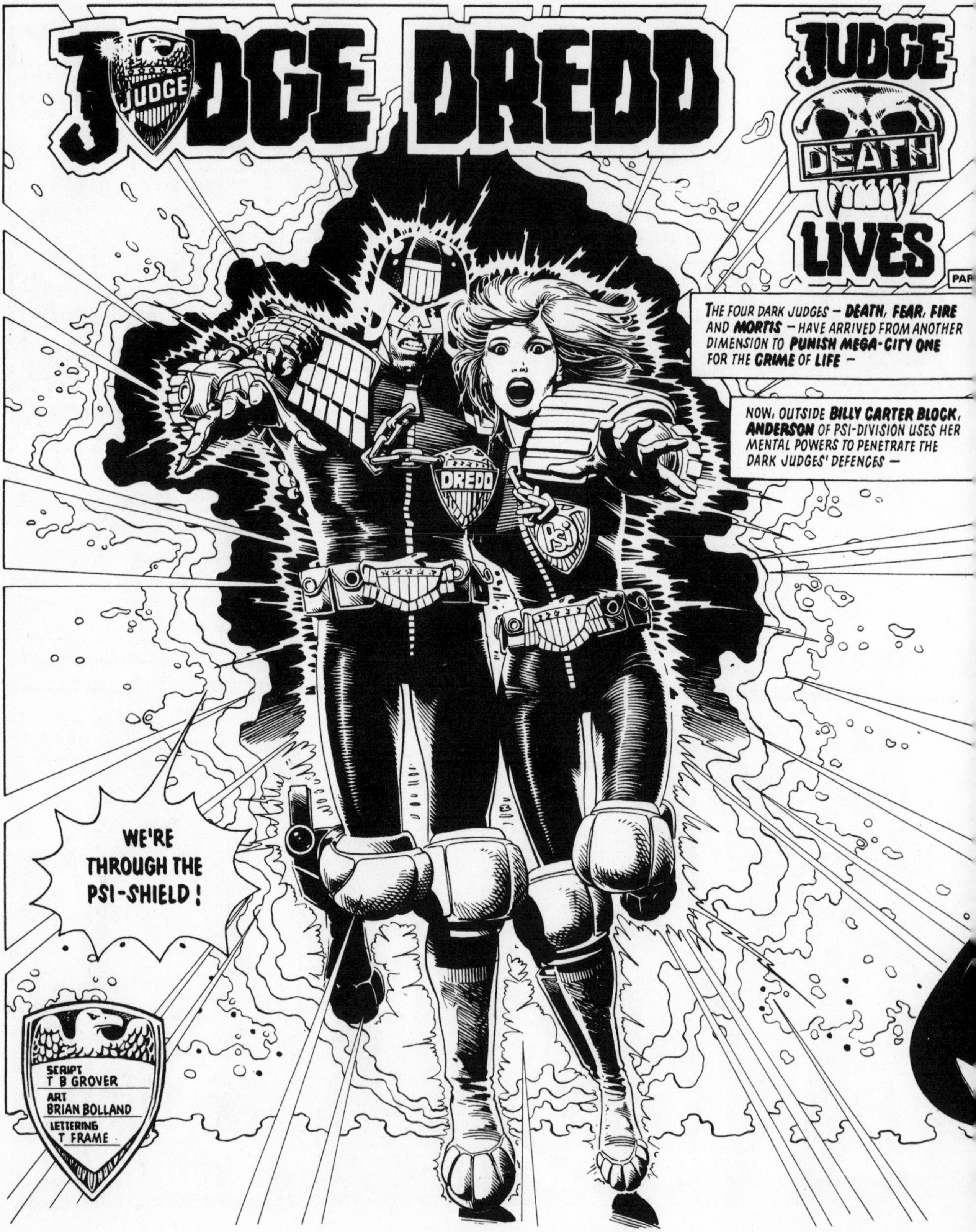
JUDGE DREDD
JUDGE
JUDGE DEATH LIVES
THE FOUR DARK JUDGES – DEATH, FEAR, FIRE AND MORTIS – HAVE ARRIVED FROM ANOTHER DIMENSION TO PUNISH MEGA-CITY ONE FOR THE CRIME OF LIFE –
NOW, OUTSIDE BILLY CARTER BLOCK, ANDERSON OF PSI-DIVISION USES HER MENTAL POWERS TO PENETRATE THE DARK JUDGES' DEFENCES –
WE'RE THROUGH THE PSI-SHIELD!
DREDD
PSI
SCRIPT T B GROVER
ART BRIAN BOLLAND
LETTERING T FRAME

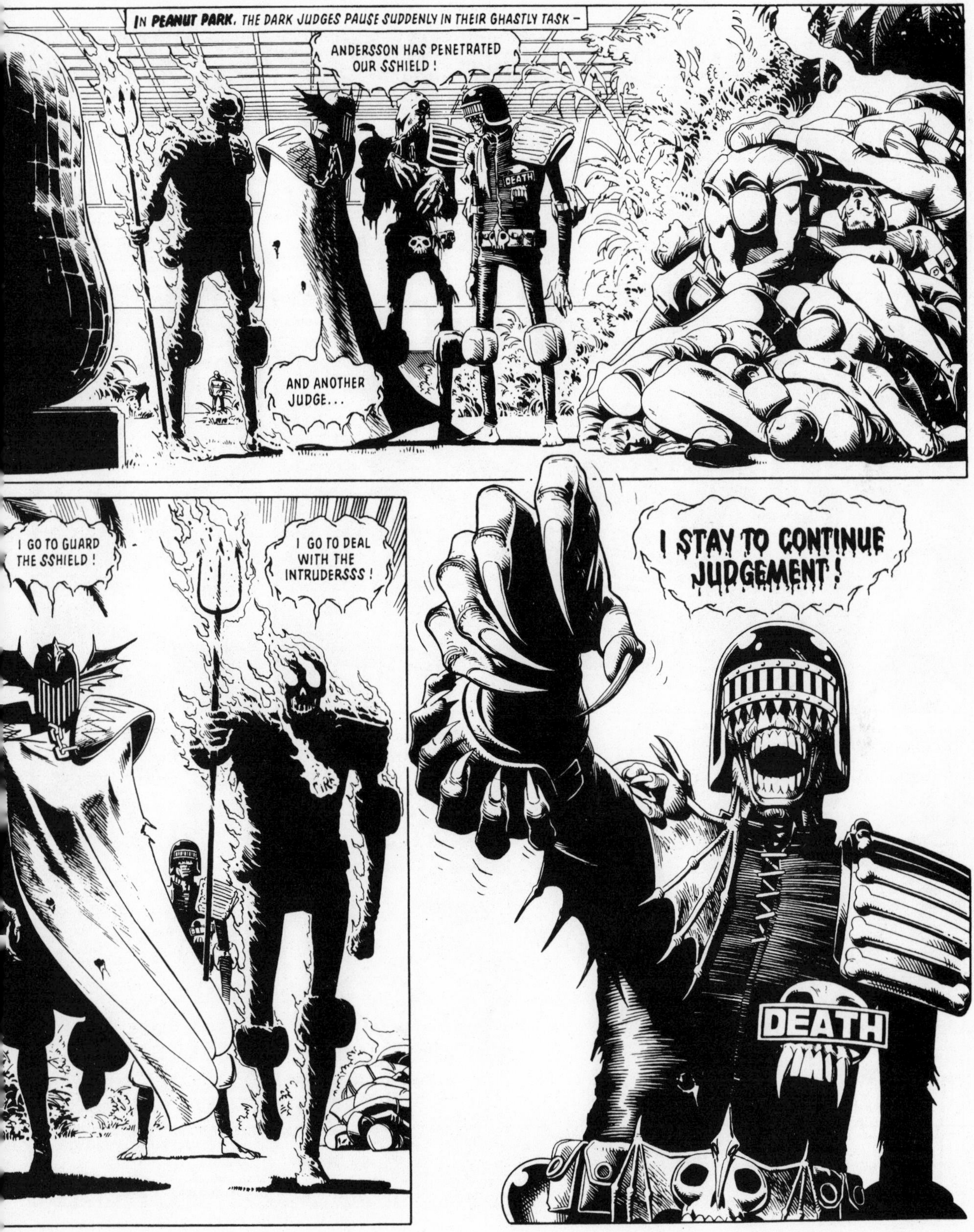
IN PEANUT PARK, THE DARK JUDGES PAUSE SUDDENLY IN THEIR GHASTLY TASK –
ANDERSSON HAS PENETRATED OUR SSHIELD!
AND ANOTHER JUDGE...
I GO TO GUARD THE SSHIELD!
I GO TO DEAL WITH THE INTRUDERSSS!
I STAY TO CONTINUE JUDGEMENT!
DEATH
DEATH

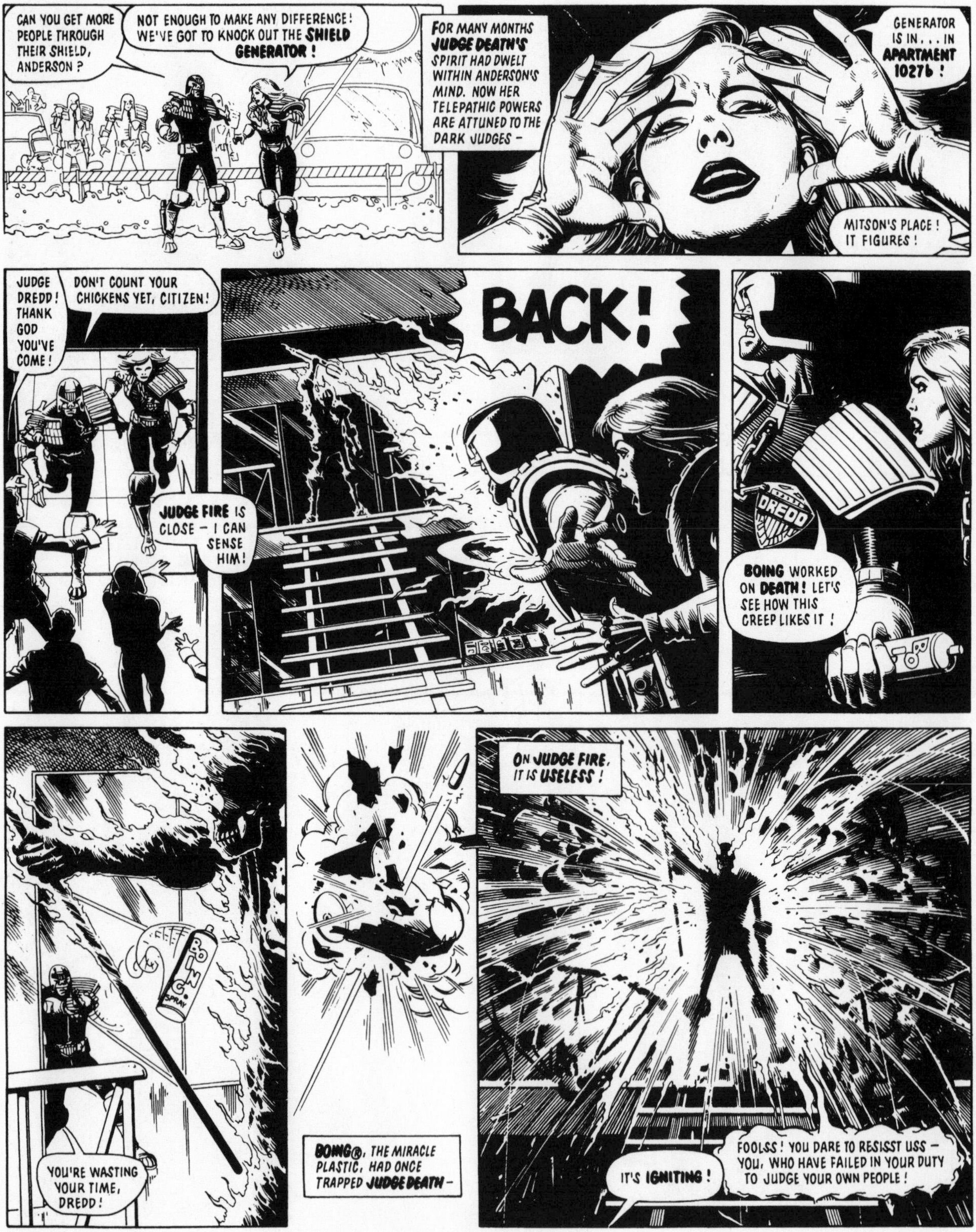
CAN YOU GET MORE PEOPLE THROUGH THEIR SHIELD, ANDERSON ?
NOT ENOUGH TO MAKE ANY DIFFERENCE! WE'VE GOT TO KNOCK OUT THE SHIELD GENERATOR !
FOR MANY MONTHS JUDGE DEATH'S SPIRIT HAD DWELT WITHIN ANDERSON'S MIND. NOW HER TELEPATHIC POWERS ARE ATTUNED TO THE DARK JUDGES –
GENERATOR IS IN. . . IN APARTMENT 1027b !
MITSON'S PLACE ! IT FIGURES !
JUDGE DREDD! THANK GOD YOU'VE COME !
DON'T COUNT YOUR CHICKENS YET, CITIZEN!
JUDGE FIRE IS CLOSE – I CAN SENSE HIM!
BACK!
BOING WORKED ON DEATH! LET'S SEE HOW THIS CREEP LIKES IT !
YOU'RE WASTING YOUR TIME, DREDD !
BOING®, THE MIRACLE PLASTIC, HAD ONCE TRAPPED JUDGE DEATH –
ON JUDGE FIRE, IT IS USELESS !
IT'S IGNITING !
FOOLSS ! YOU DARE TO RESISST USS – YOU, WHO HAVE FAILED IN YOUR DUTY TO JUDGE YOUR OWN PEOPLE !

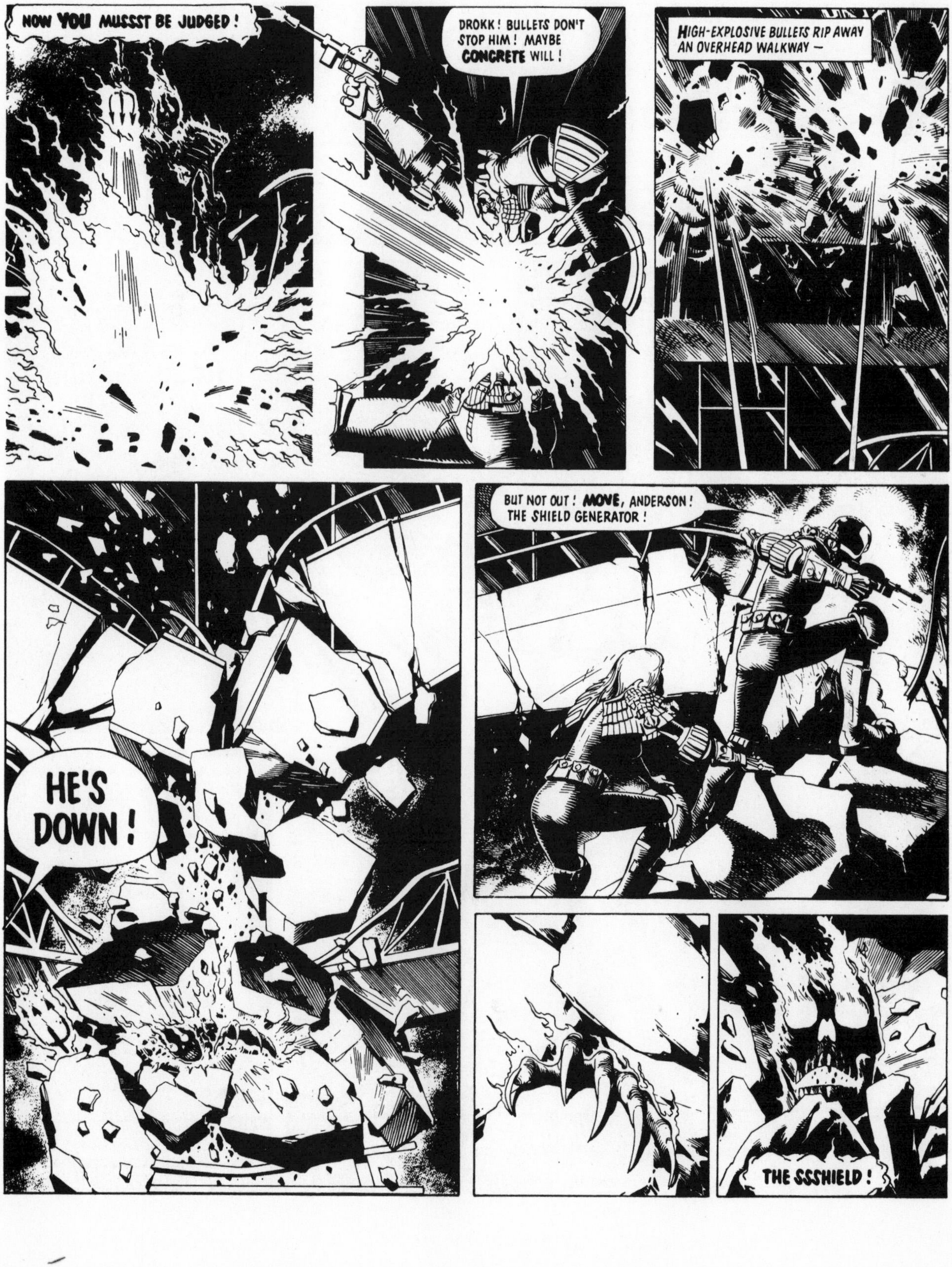
NOW YOU MUSSST BE JUDGED!
DROKK! BULLETS DON'T STOP HIM! MAYBE CONCRETE WILL!
HIGH-EXPLOSIVE BULLETS RIP AWAY AN OVERHEAD WALKWAY —
HE'S DOWN!
BUT NOT OUT! MOVE, ANDERSON! THE SHIELD GENERATOR!
THE SSSHIELD!

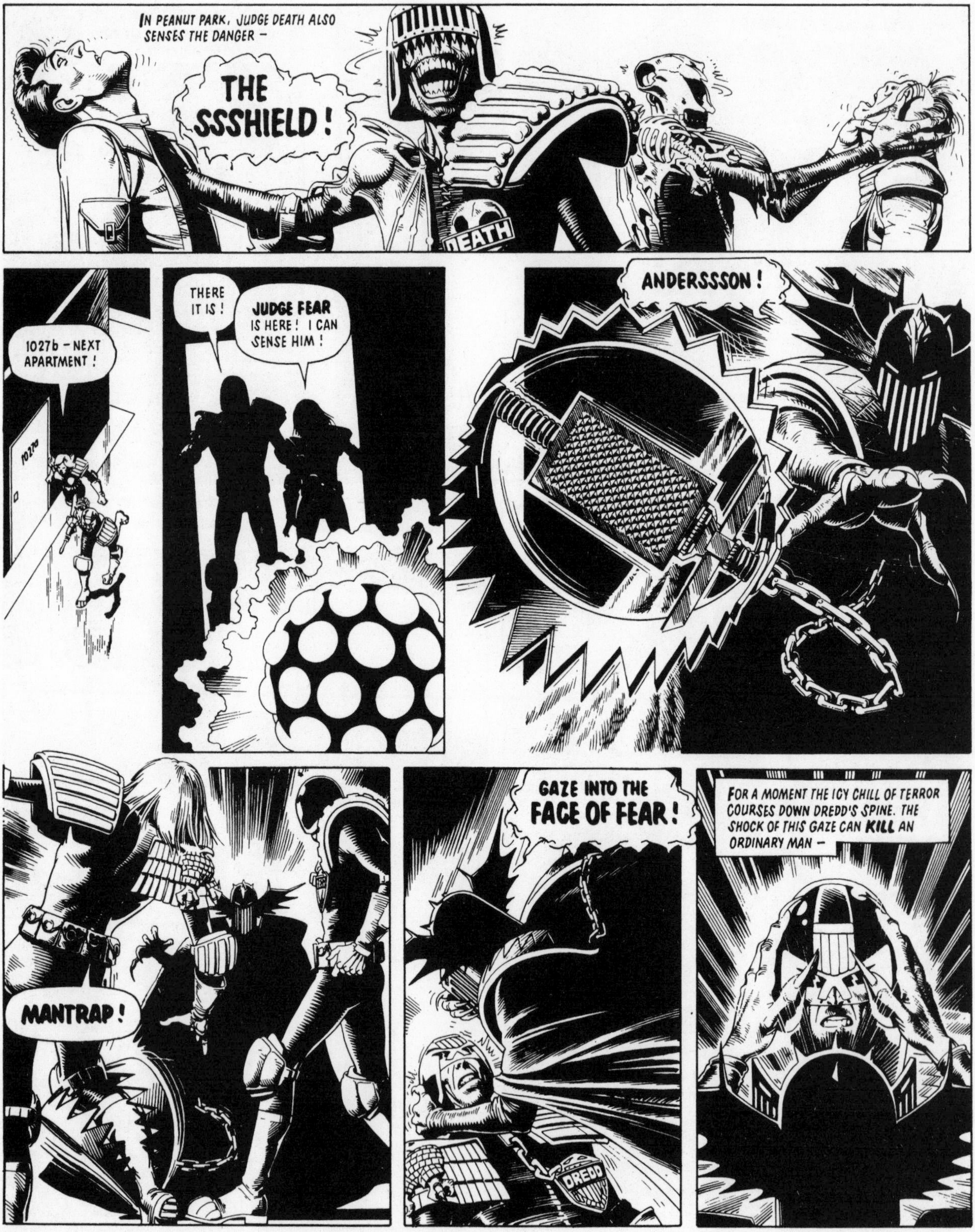

IN PEANUT PARK, JUDGE DEATH ALSO SENSES THE DANGER –
THE SSSHIELD!
DEATH
1027b – NEXT APARTMENT!
THERE IT IS!
JUDGE FEAR IS HERE! I CAN SENSE HIM!
ANDERSSSON!
MANTRAP!
GAZE INTO THE FACE OF FEAR!
FOR A MOMENT THE ICY CHILL OF TERROR COURSES DOWN DREDD'S SPINE. THE SHOCK OF THIS GAZE CAN KILL AN ORDINARY MAN –
DREDD

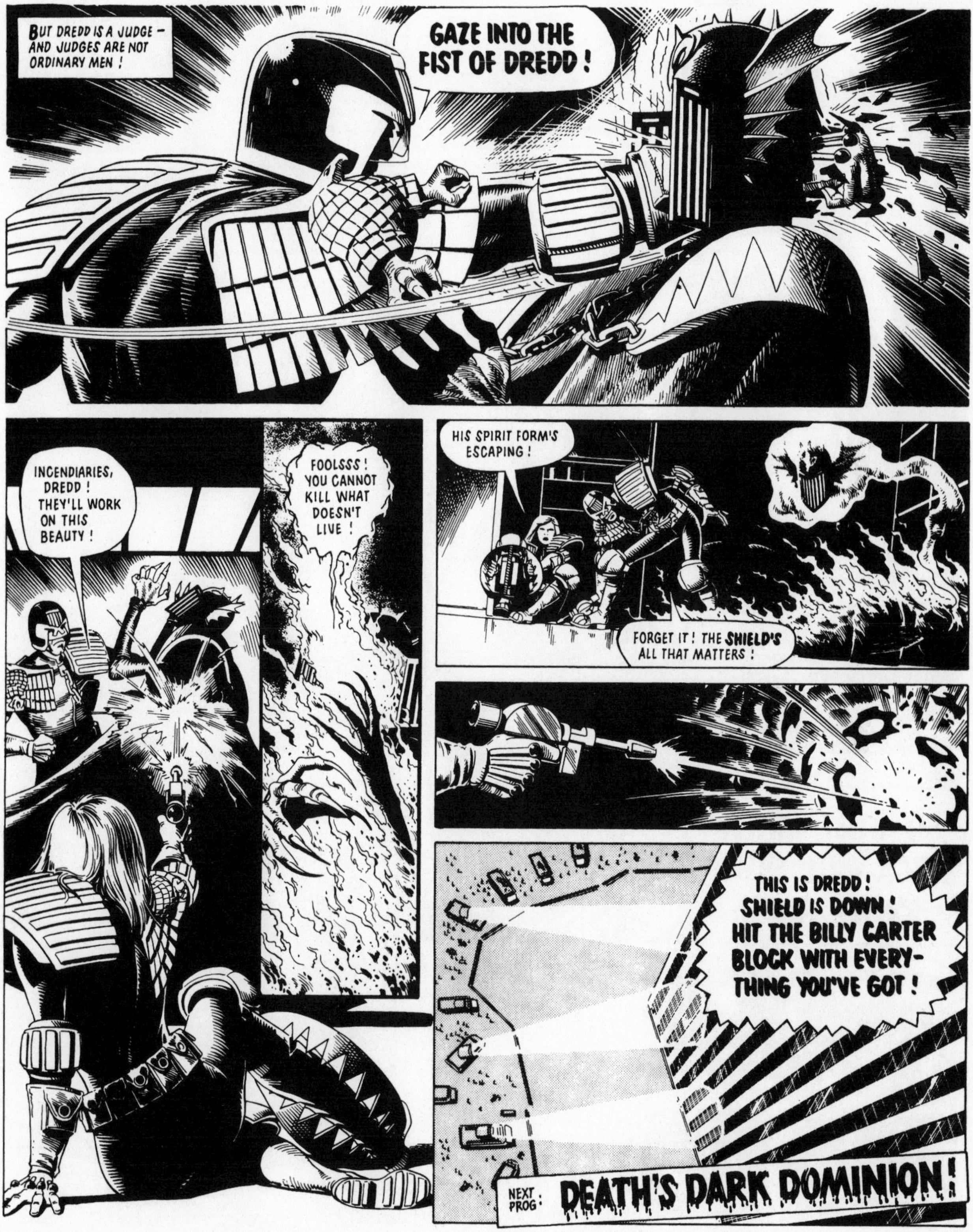
BUT DREDD IS A JUDGE – AND JUDGES ARE NOT ORDINARY MEN !
GAZE INTO THE FIST OF DREDD !
INCENDIARIES, DREDD ! THEY'LL WORK ON THIS BEAUTY !
FOOLSSS ! YOU CANNOT KILL WHAT DOESN'T LIVE !
HIS SPIRIT FORM'S ESCAPING !
FORGET IT ! THE SHIELD'S ALL THAT MATTERS !
THIS IS DREDD ! SHIELD IS DOWN ! HIT THE BILLY CARTER BLOCK WITH EVERY-THING YOU'VE GOT !
NEXT PROG: DEATH'S DARK DOMINION!

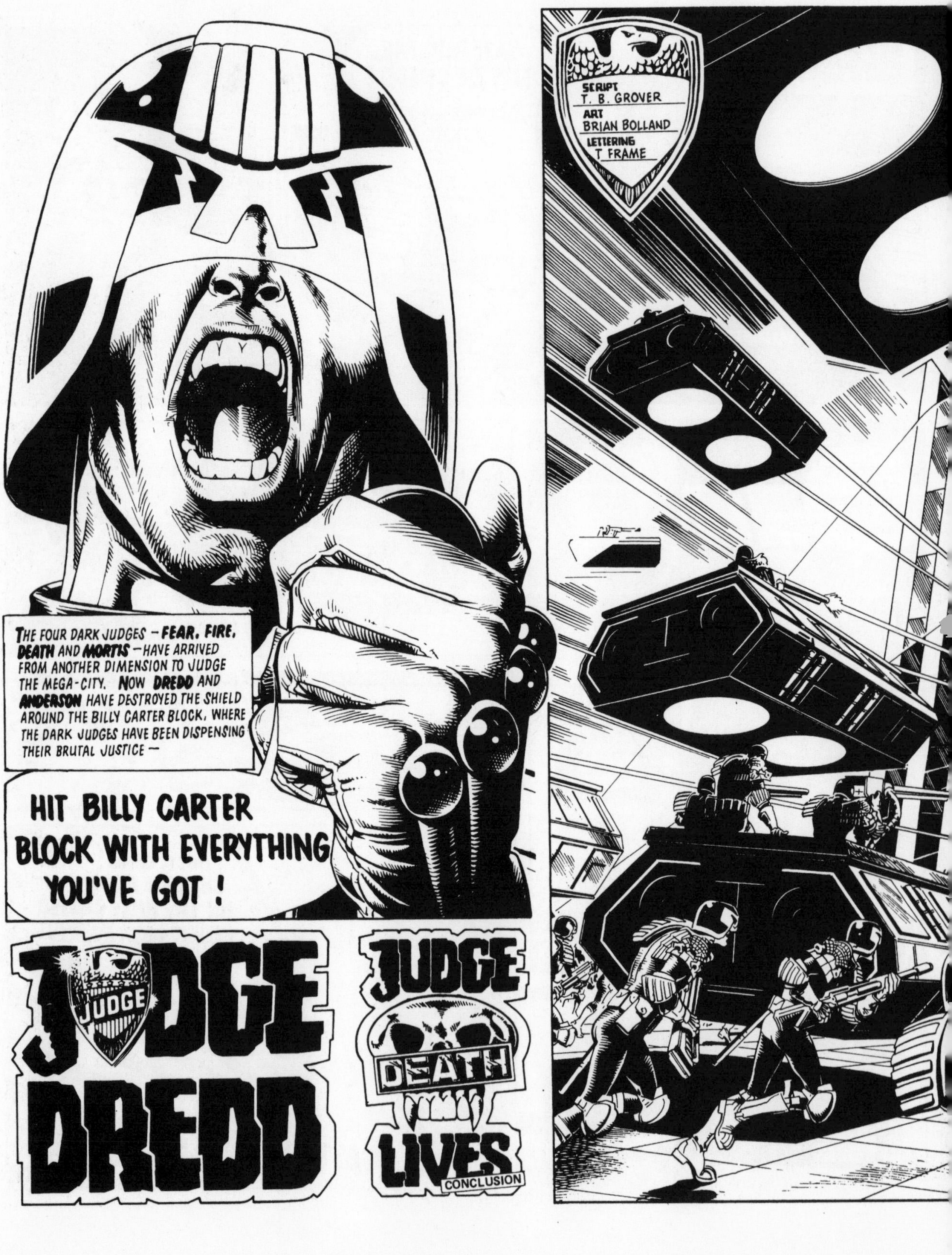

SCRIPT T. B. GROVER
ART BRIAN BOLLAND
LETTERING T FRAME
THE FOUR DARK JUDGES – FEAR, FIRE, DEATH AND MORTIS – HAVE ARRIVED FROM ANOTHER DIMENSION TO JUDGE THE MEGA-CITY. NOW DREDD AND ANDERSON HAVE DESTROYED THE SHIELD AROUND THE BILLY CARTER BLOCK, WHERE THE DARK JUDGES HAVE BEEN DISPENSING THEIR BRUTAL JUSTICE –
HIT BILLY CARTER BLOCK WITH EVERYTHING YOU'VE GOT!
JUDGE DREDD
JUDGE DEATH LIVES
CONCLUSION

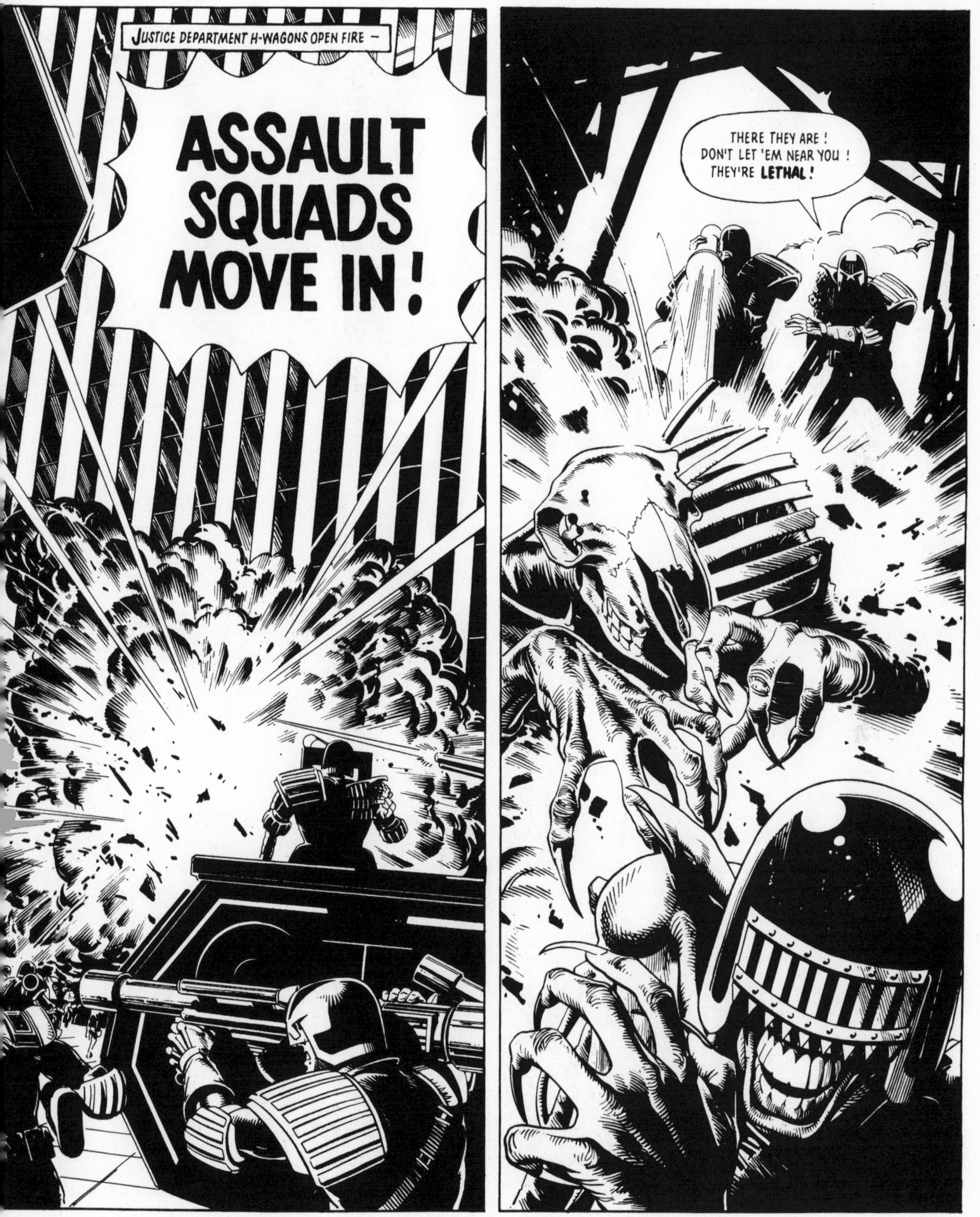
JUSTICE DEPARTMENT H-WAGONS OPEN FIRE –
ASSAULT SQUADS MOVE IN!
THERE THEY ARE! DON'T LET 'EM NEAR YOU! THEY'RE LETHAL!

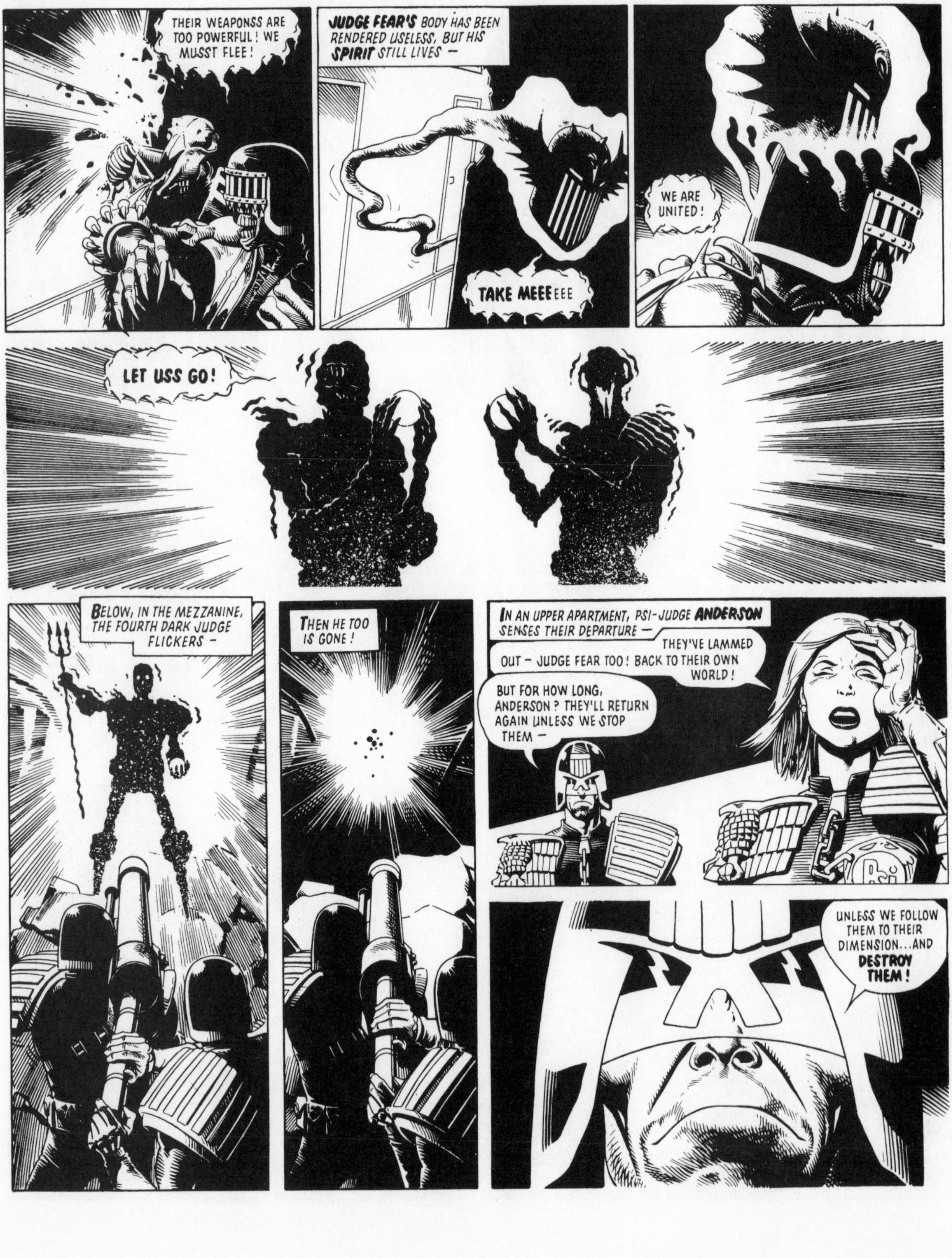
THEIR WEAPONSS ARE TOO POWERFUL! WE MUSST FLEE!
JUDGE FEAR'S BODY HAS BEEN RENDERED USELESS, BUT HIS SPIRIT STILL LIVES —
TAKE MEEEEEE
WE ARE UNITED!
LET USS GO!
BELOW, IN THE MEZZANINE, THE FOURTH DARK JUDGE FLICKERS —
THEN HE TOO IS GONE!
IN AN UPPER APARTMENT, PSI-JUDGE ANDERSON SENSES THEIR DEPARTURE —
THEY'VE LAMMED OUT — JUDGE FEAR TOO! BACK TO THEIR OWN WORLD!
BUT FOR HOW LONG, ANDERSON? THEY'LL RETURN AGAIN UNLESS WE STOP THEM —
UNLESS WE FOLLOW THEM TO THEIR DIMENSION... AND DESTROY THEM!

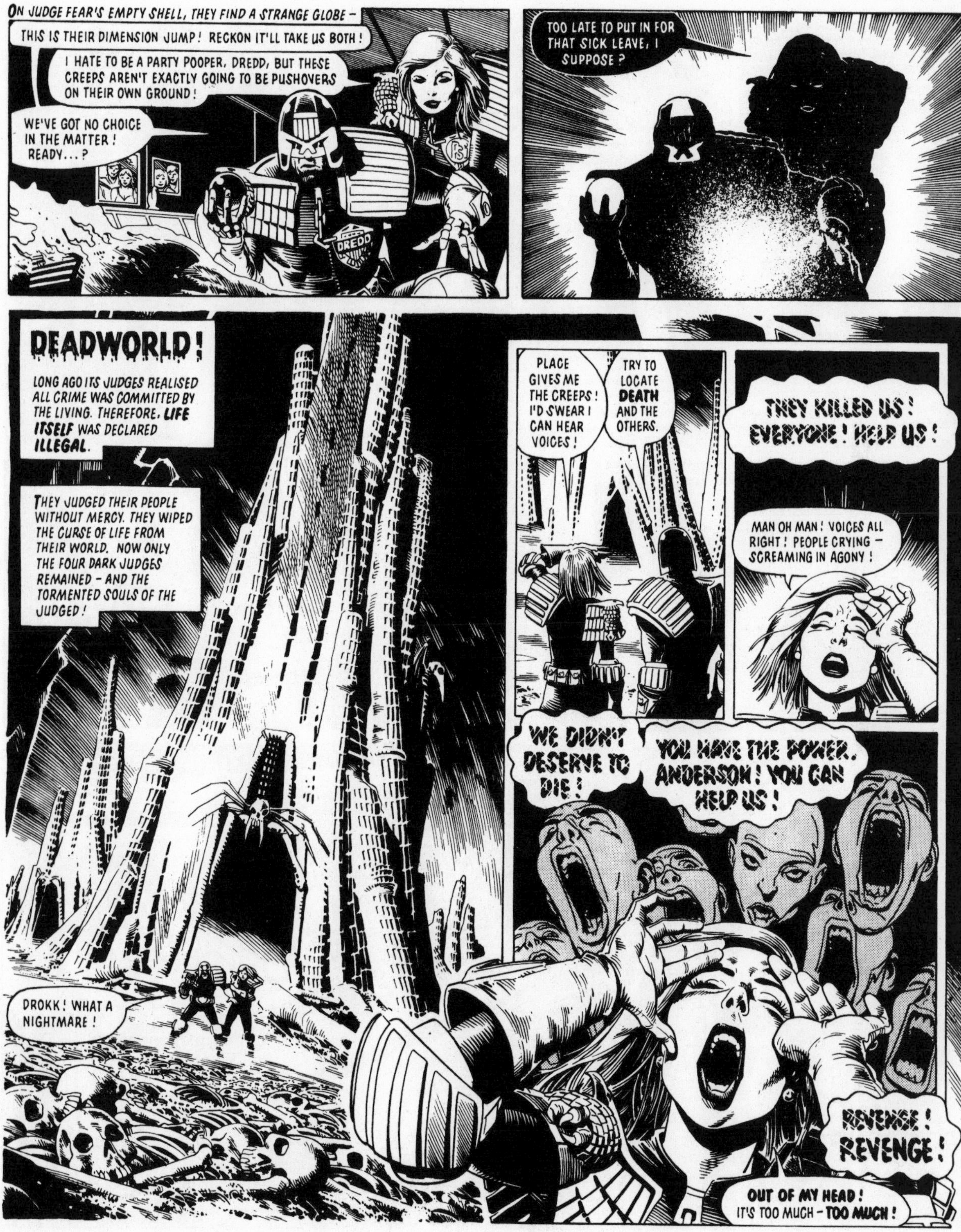

ON JUDGE FEAR'S EMPTY SHELL, THEY FIND A STRANGE GLOBE -
THIS IS THEIR DIMENSION JUMP! RECKON IT'LL TAKE US BOTH!
I HATE TO BE A PARTY POOPER, DREDD, BUT THESE CREEPS AREN'T EXACTLY GOING TO BE PUSHOVERS ON THEIR OWN GROUND!
WE'VE GOT NO CHOICE IN THE MATTER! READY...?
DREDD
TOO LATE TO PUT IN FOR THAT SICK LEAVE, I SUPPOSE?
DEADWORLD!
LONG AGO ITS JUDGES REALISED ALL CRIME WAS COMMITTED BY THE LIVING. THEREFORE, LIFE ITSELF WAS DECLARED ILLEGAL.
THEY JUDGED THEIR PEOPLE WITHOUT MERCY. THEY WIPED THE CURSE OF LIFE FROM THEIR WORLD. NOW ONLY THE FOUR DARK JUDGES REMAINED - AND THE TORMENTED SOULS OF THE JUDGED!
DROKK! WHAT A NIGHTMARE!
PLACE GIVES ME THE CREEPS! I'D SWEAR I CAN HEAR VOICES!
TRY TO LOCATE DEATH AND THE OTHERS.
THEY KILLED US! EVERYONE! HELP US!
MAN OH MAN! VOICES ALL RIGHT! PEOPLE CRYING - SCREAMING IN AGONY!
WE DIDN'T DESERVE TO DIE!
YOU HAVE THE POWER, ANDERSON! YOU CAN HELP US!
REVENGE! REVENGE!
OUT OF MY HEAD! IT'S TOO MUCH - TOO MUCH!

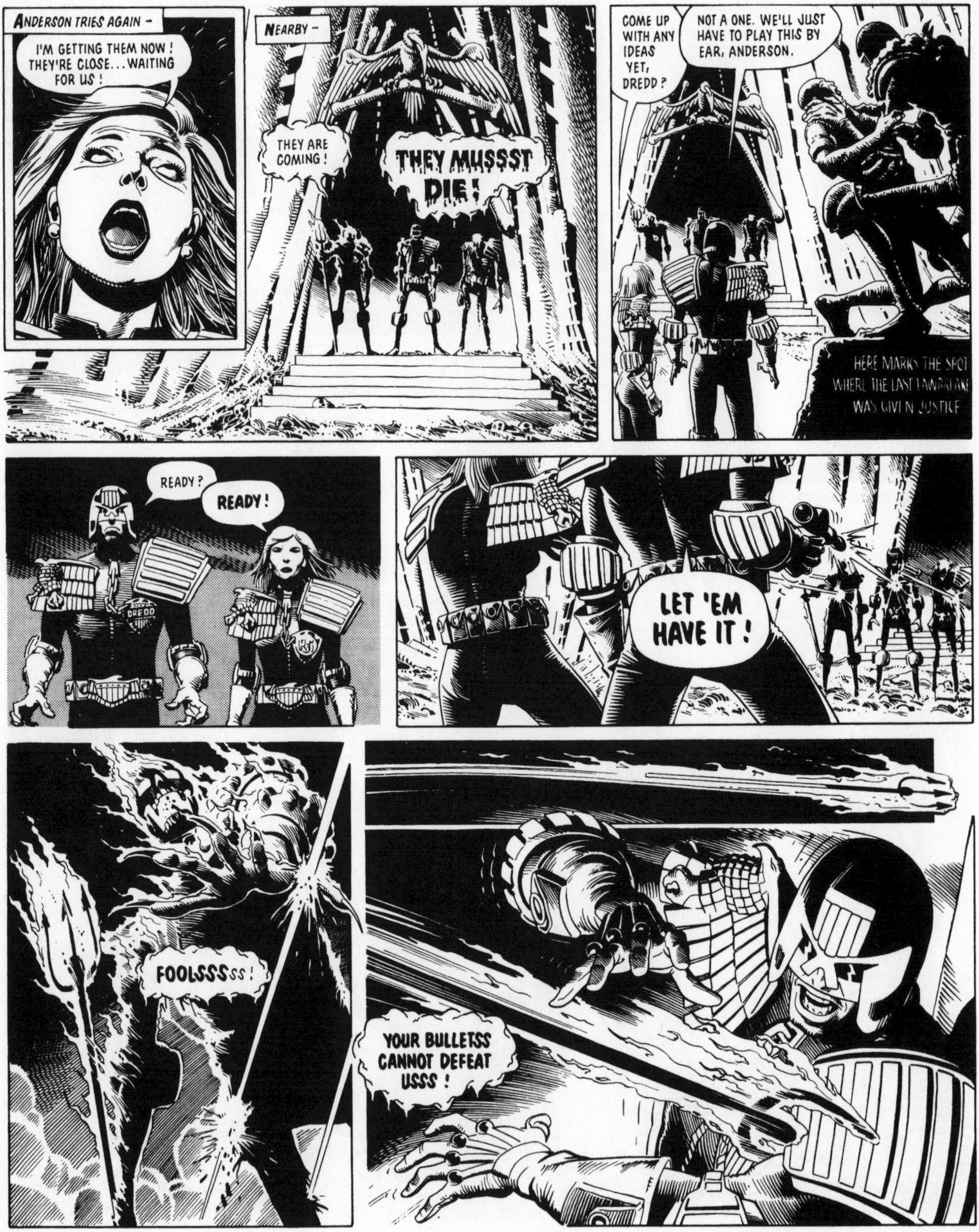
ANDERSON TRIES AGAIN –
I'M GETTING THEM NOW ! THEY'RE CLOSE... WAITING FOR US !
NEARBY –
THEY ARE COMING !
THEY MUSSST DIE !
COME UP WITH ANY IDEAS YET, DREDD ?
NOT A ONE. WE'LL JUST HAVE TO PLAY THIS BY EAR, ANDERSON.
HERE MARKS THE SPOT
WHERE THE LAST LAWBREAKER
WAS GIVEN JUSTICE
READY ?
READY !
DREDD
LET 'EM HAVE IT !
FOOLSSSss !
YOUR BULLETSS CANNOT DEFEAT USSS !

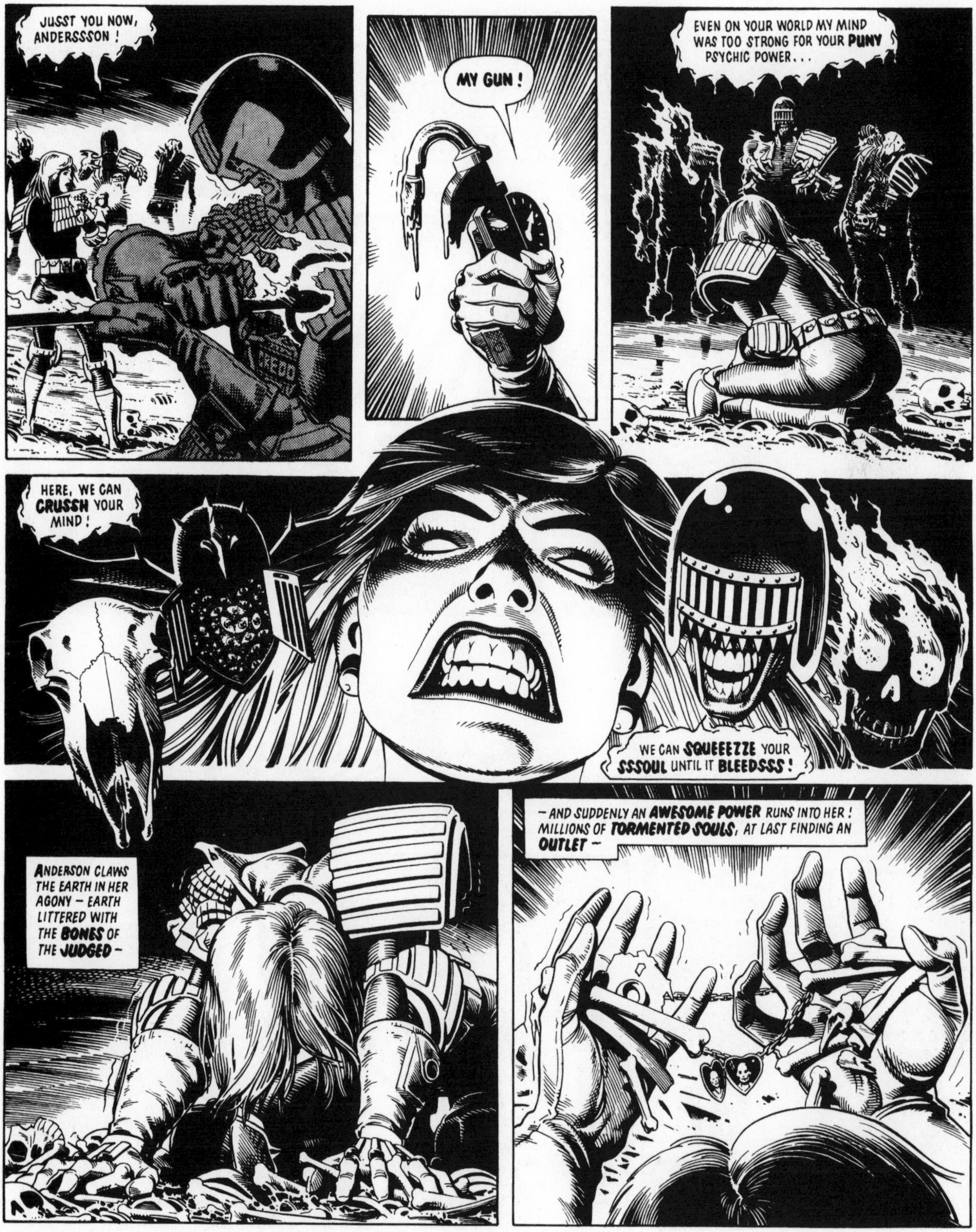
JUSST YOU NOW, ANDERSSSON!
MY GUN!
EVEN ON YOUR WORLD MY MIND WAS TOO STRONG FOR YOUR PUNY PSYCHIC POWER...
HERE, WE CAN CRUSSH YOUR MIND!
WE CAN SQUEEEZZE YOUR SSSOUL UNTIL IT BLEEDSSS!
ANDERSON CLAWS THE EARTH IN HER AGONY – EARTH LITTERED WITH THE BONES OF THE JUDGED –
– AND SUDDENLY AN AWESOME POWER RUNS INTO HER! MILLIONS OF TORMENTED SOULS, AT LAST FINDING AN OUTLET –

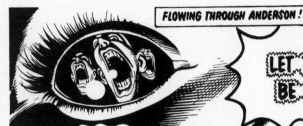

FLOWING THROUGH ANDERSON!

LET THE JUDGES BE JUDGED!

YOU ARE GUILTY!

THE SENTENCE IS DEATH!

DEATH!

DRAAAWWAAK

AS THE SPIRITS OF THE FOUR DARK JUDGES ARE EXTINGUISHED, THE DEAD CARCASSES THAT HOUSE THEM — *CRUMBLE!*

IT'S OVER, DREDD! THEY'LL NEVER TROUBLE US AGAIN!

THEY'RE STILL TROUBLING ME! GIVE ME A HAND WITH THIS PITCHFORK, ANDERSON!

AFTER THIS, I THINK I'LL PUT IN FOR THAT SICK LEAVE!

AFTER THIS, I MAY JUST JOIN YOU, ANDERSON!

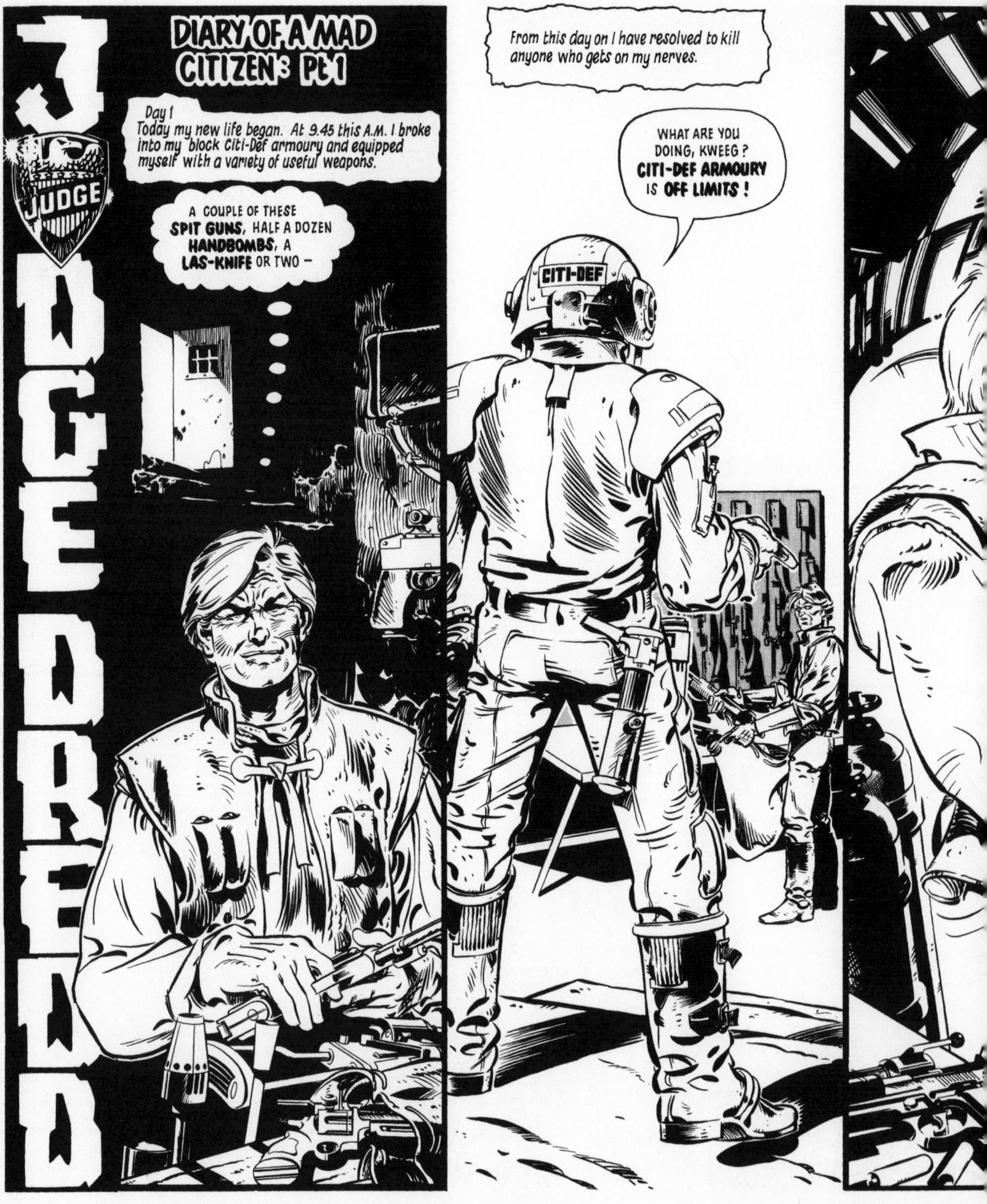
JUDGE DREDD
JUDGE
DIARY OF A MAD CITIZEN: Pt 1
Day 1
Today my new life began. At 9.45 this A.M. I broke into my block Citi-Def armoury and equipped myself with a variety of useful weapons.
A COUPLE OF THESE SPIT GUNS, HALF A DOZEN HANDBOMBS, A LAS-KNIFE OR TWO –
From this day on I have resolved to kill anyone who gets on my nerves.
WHAT ARE YOU DOING, KWEEG? CITI-DEF ARMOURY IS OFF LIMITS!
CITI-DEF

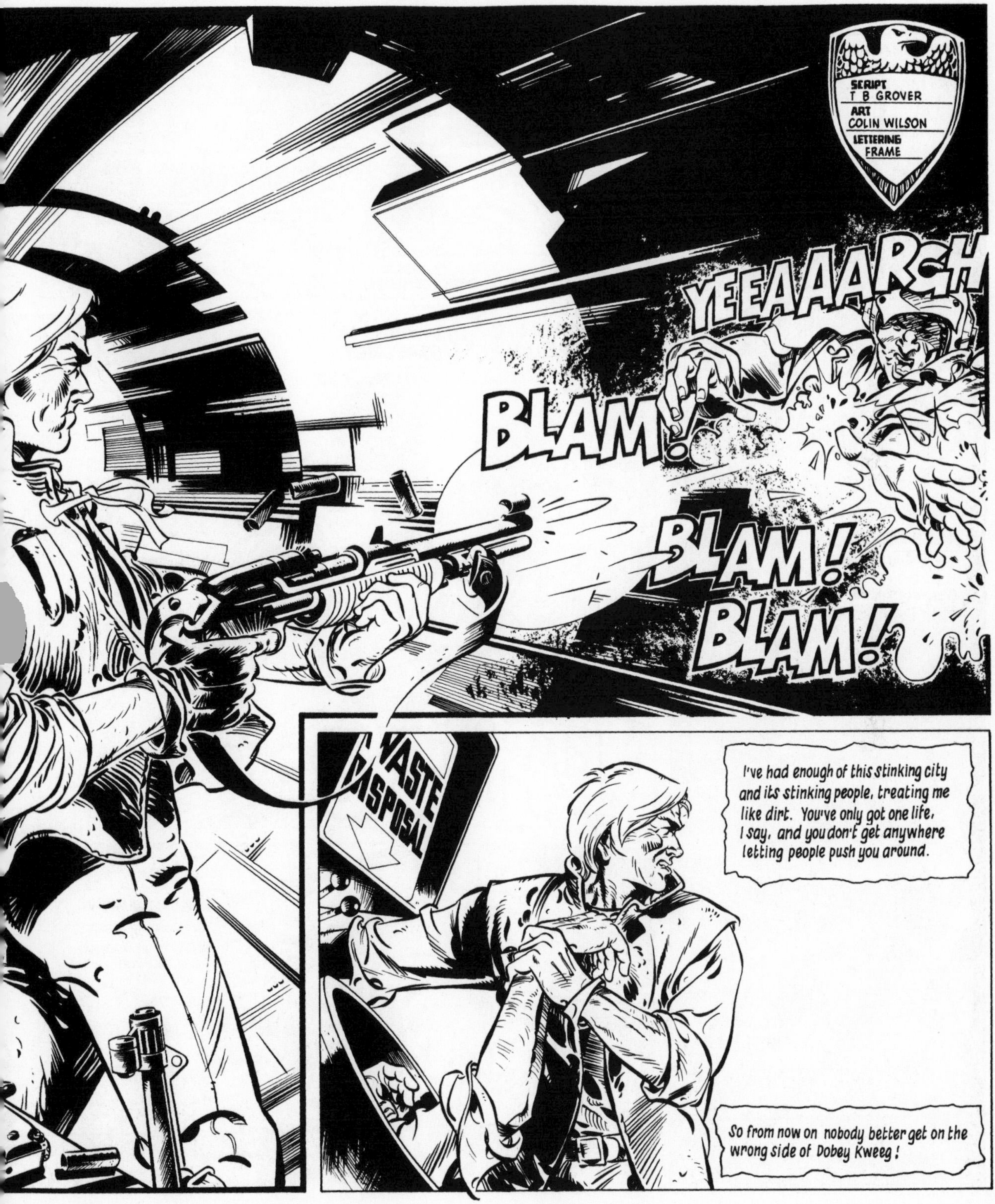
SCRIPT
T B GROVER
ART
COLIN WILSON
LETTERING
FRAME
YEEAAARGH
BLAM!
BLAM!
BLAM!
WASTE DISPOSAL
I've had enough of this stinking city and its stinking people, treating me like dirt. You've only got one life, I say, and you don't get anywhere letting people push you around.
So from now on nobody better get on the wrong side of Dobey Kweeg!

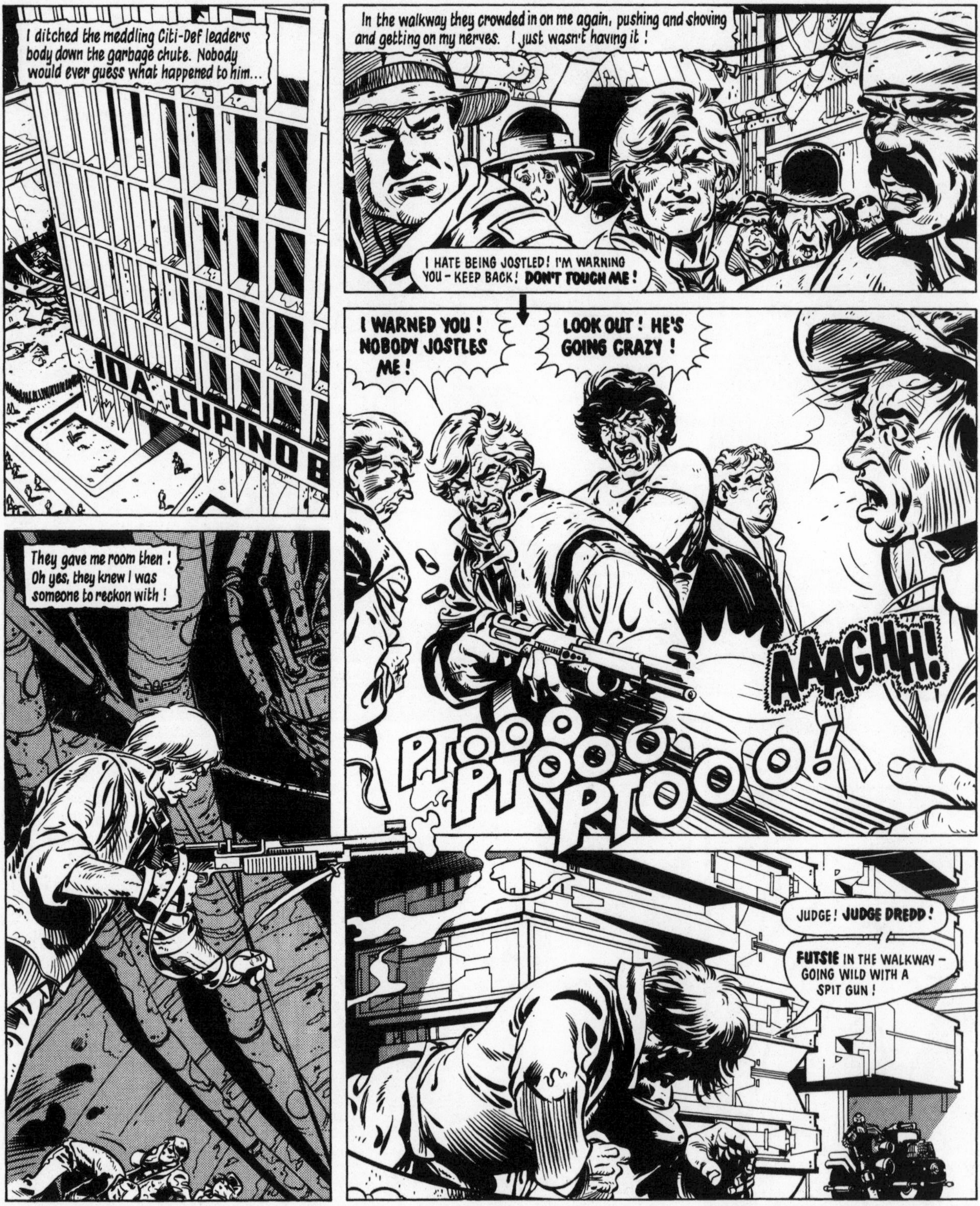
I ditched the meddling Citi-Def leader's body down the garbage chute. Nobody would ever guess what happened to him...
IDA LUPINO B
In the walkway they crowded in on me again, pushing and shoving and getting on my nerves. I just wasn't having it !
I HATE BEING JOSTLED! I'M WARNING YOU - KEEP BACK! DON'T TOUCH ME !
I WARNED YOU ! NOBODY JOSTLES ME !
LOOK OUT ! HE'S GOING CRAZY !
AAAGHH!
PTOOOO PTOOOO PTOOOO!
They gave me room then ! Oh yes, they knew I was someone to reckon with !
JUDGE ! JUDGE DREDD !
FUTSIE IN THE WALKWAY - GOING WILD WITH A SPIT GUN !

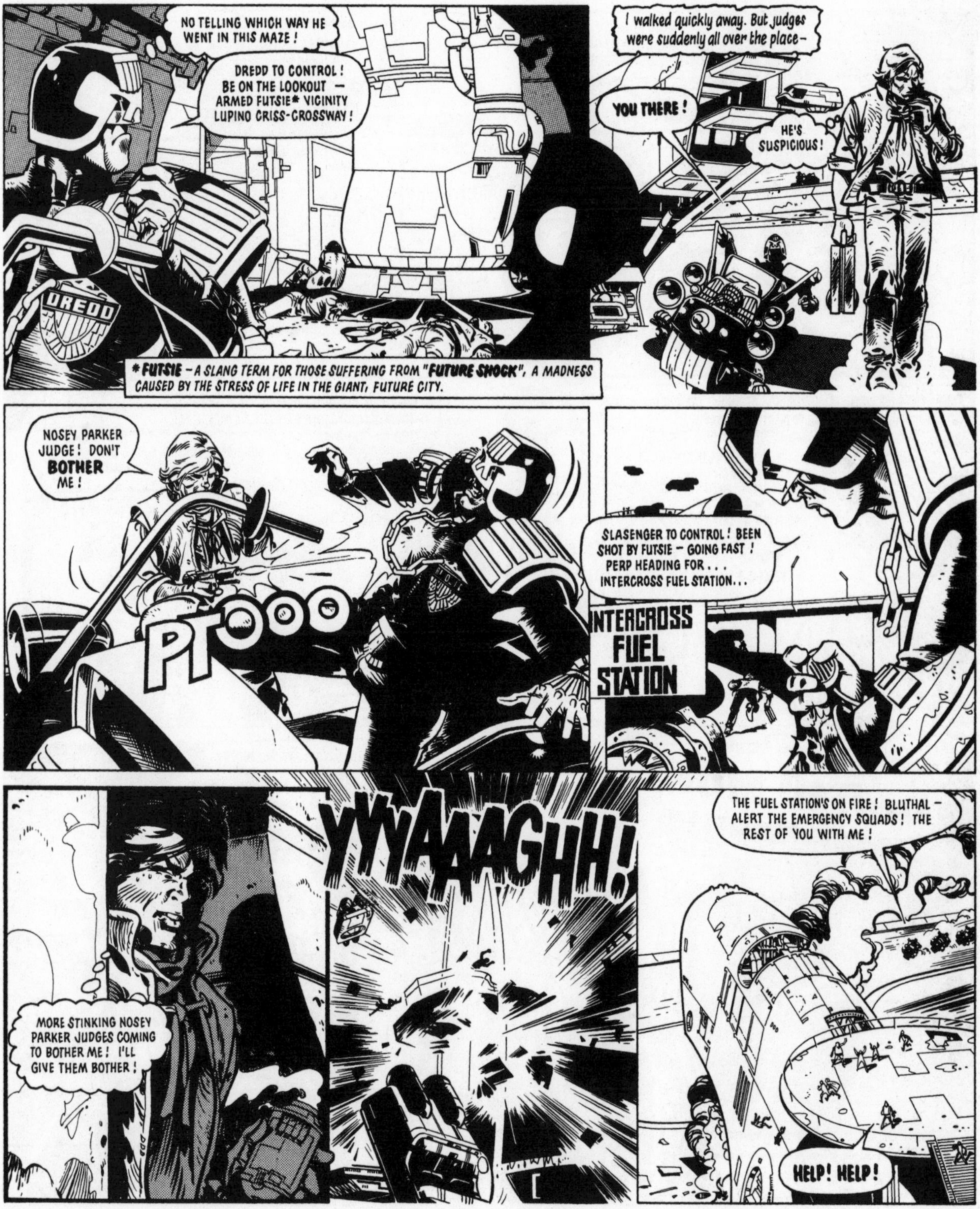
NO TELLING WHICH WAY HE WENT IN THIS MAZE !
DREDD TO CONTROL ! BE ON THE LOOKOUT — ARMED FUTSIE* VICINITY LUPINO CRISS-CROSSWAY !
DREDD
* FUTSIE – A SLANG TERM FOR THOSE SUFFERING FROM "FUTURE SHOCK", A MADNESS CAUSED BY THE STRESS OF LIFE IN THE GIANT, FUTURE CITY.
I walked quickly away. But judges were suddenly all over the place–
YOU THERE !
HE'S SUSPICIOUS !
NOSEY PARKER JUDGE ! DON'T BOTHER ME !
PTOOOO
SLASENGER TO CONTROL ! BEEN SHOT BY FUTSIE – GOING FAST ! PERP HEADING FOR . . . INTERCROSS FUEL STATION . . .
INTERCROSS FUEL STATION
MORE STINKING NOSEY PARKER JUDGES COMING TO BOTHER ME ! I'LL GIVE THEM BOTHER !
YYYAAAGHH !
THE FUEL STATION'S ON FIRE ! BLUTHAL – ALERT THE EMERGENCY SQUADS ! THE REST OF YOU WITH ME !
HELP ! HELP !

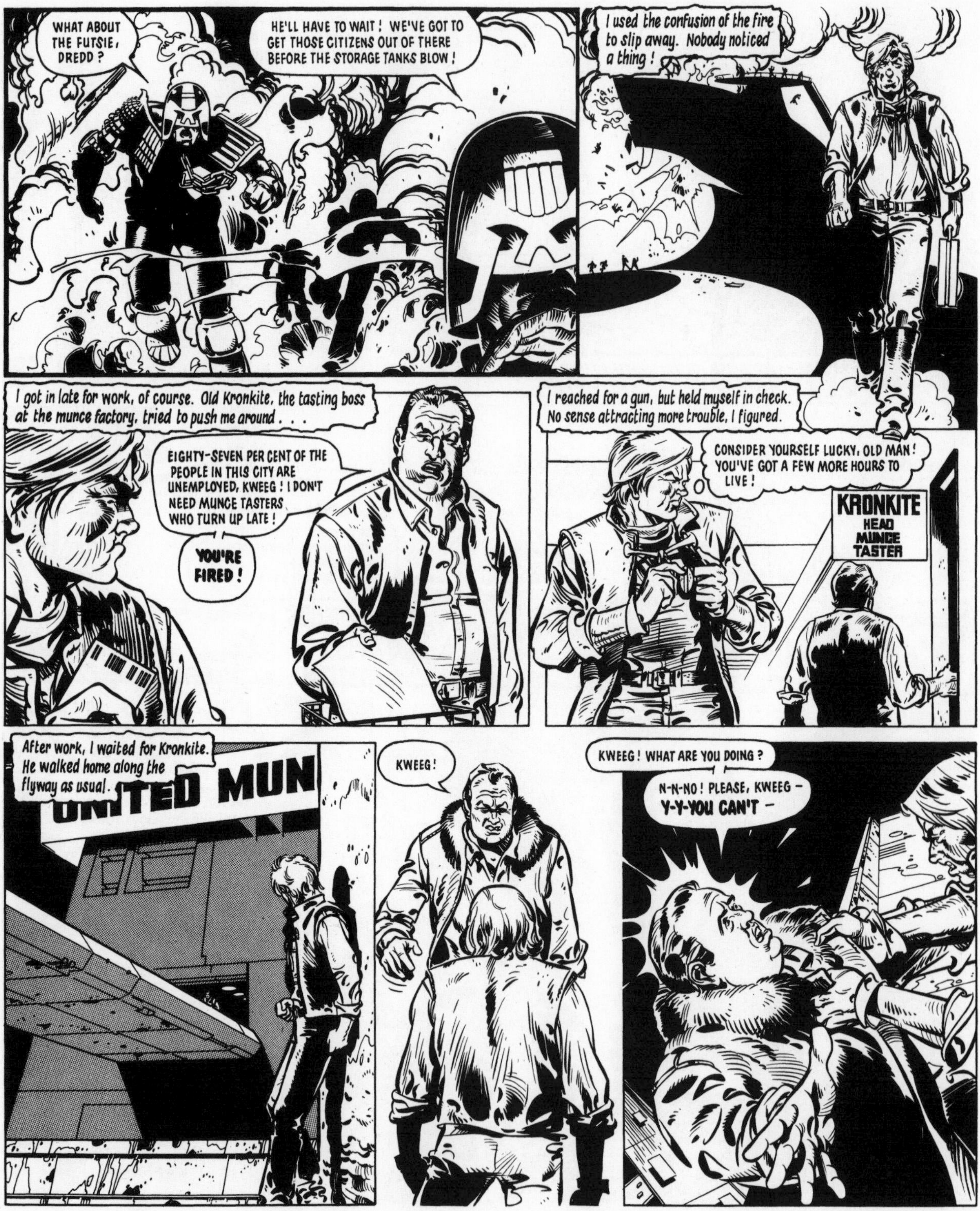
WHAT ABOUT THE FUTSIE, DREDD ?
HE'LL HAVE TO WAIT ! WE'VE GOT TO GET THOSE CITIZENS OUT OF THERE BEFORE THE STORAGE TANKS BLOW !
I used the confusion of the fire to slip away. Nobody noticed a thing !
I got in late for work, of course. Old Kronkite, the tasting boss at the munce factory, tried to push me around . . .
EIGHTY-SEVEN PER CENT OF THE PEOPLE IN THIS CITY ARE UNEMPLOYED, KWEEG ! I DON'T NEED MUNCE TASTERS WHO TURN UP LATE !
YOU'RE FIRED !
I reached for a gun, but held myself in check. No sense attracting more trouble, I figured.
CONSIDER YOURSELF LUCKY, OLD MAN ! YOU'VE GOT A FEW MORE HOURS TO LIVE !
KRONKITE
HEAD
MUNCE
TASTER
After work, I waited for Kronkite. He walked home along the flyway as usual.
UNITED MUN
KWEEG !
KWEEG ! WHAT ARE YOU DOING ?
N-N-NO ! PLEASE, KWEEG –
Y-Y-YOU CAN'T –

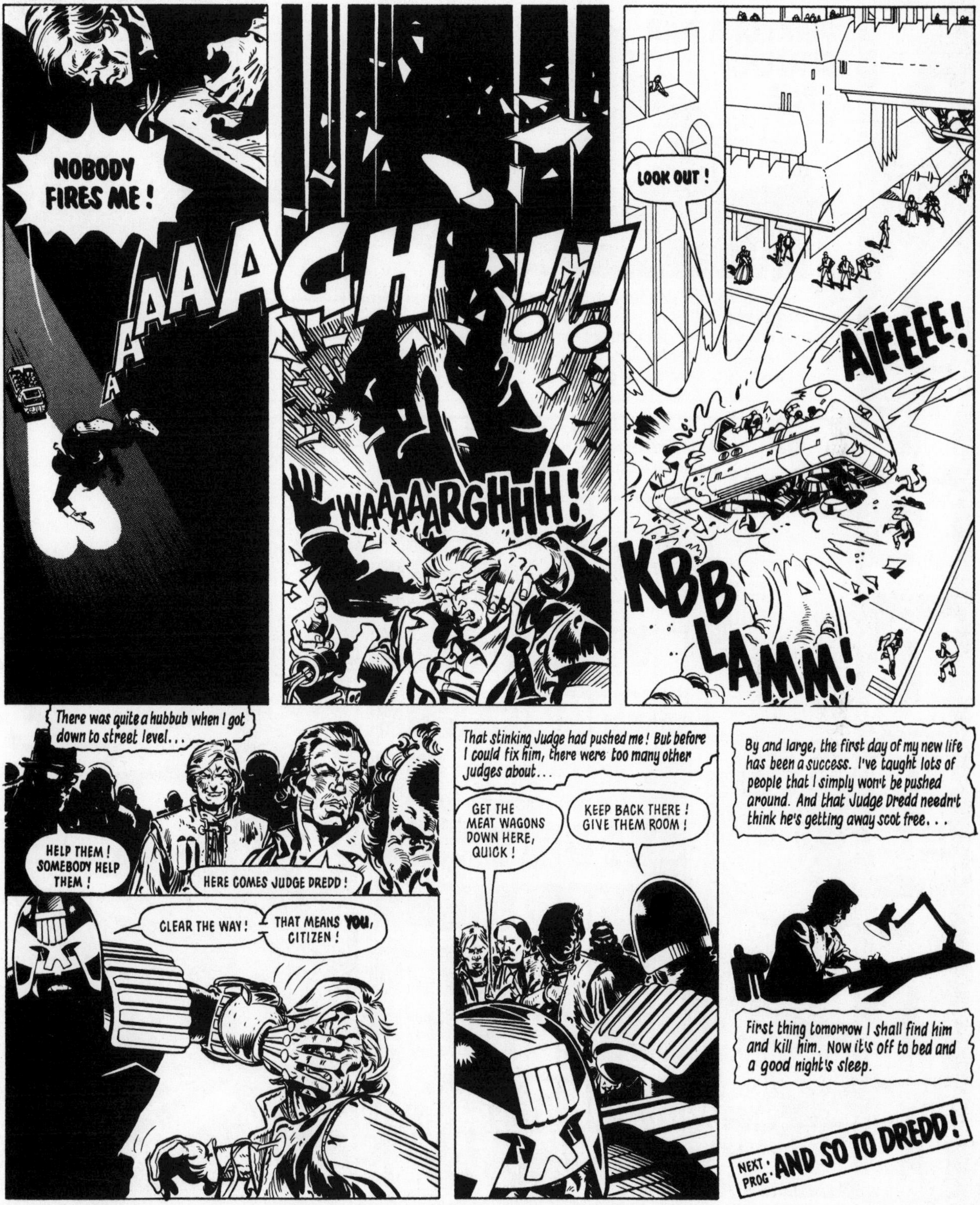
NOBODY FIRES ME !
AAAAAGH ! ! !
WAAAAARGHHH !
LOOK OUT !
AIEEEE!
KBB LAMM!
There was quite a hubbub when I got down to street level...
HELP THEM ! SOMEBODY HELP THEM !
HERE COMES JUDGE DREDD !
CLEAR THE WAY !
THAT MEANS YOU, CITIZEN !
That stinking Judge had pushed me ! But before I could fix him, there were too many other judges about...
GET THE MEAT WAGONS DOWN HERE, QUICK !
KEEP BACK THERE ! GIVE THEM ROOM !
By and large, the first day of my new life has been a success. I've taught lots of people that I simply won't be pushed around. And that Judge Dredd needn't think he's getting away scot free...
First thing tomorrow I shall find him and kill him. Now it's off to bed and a good night's sleep.
NEXT PROG : AND SO TO DREDD !

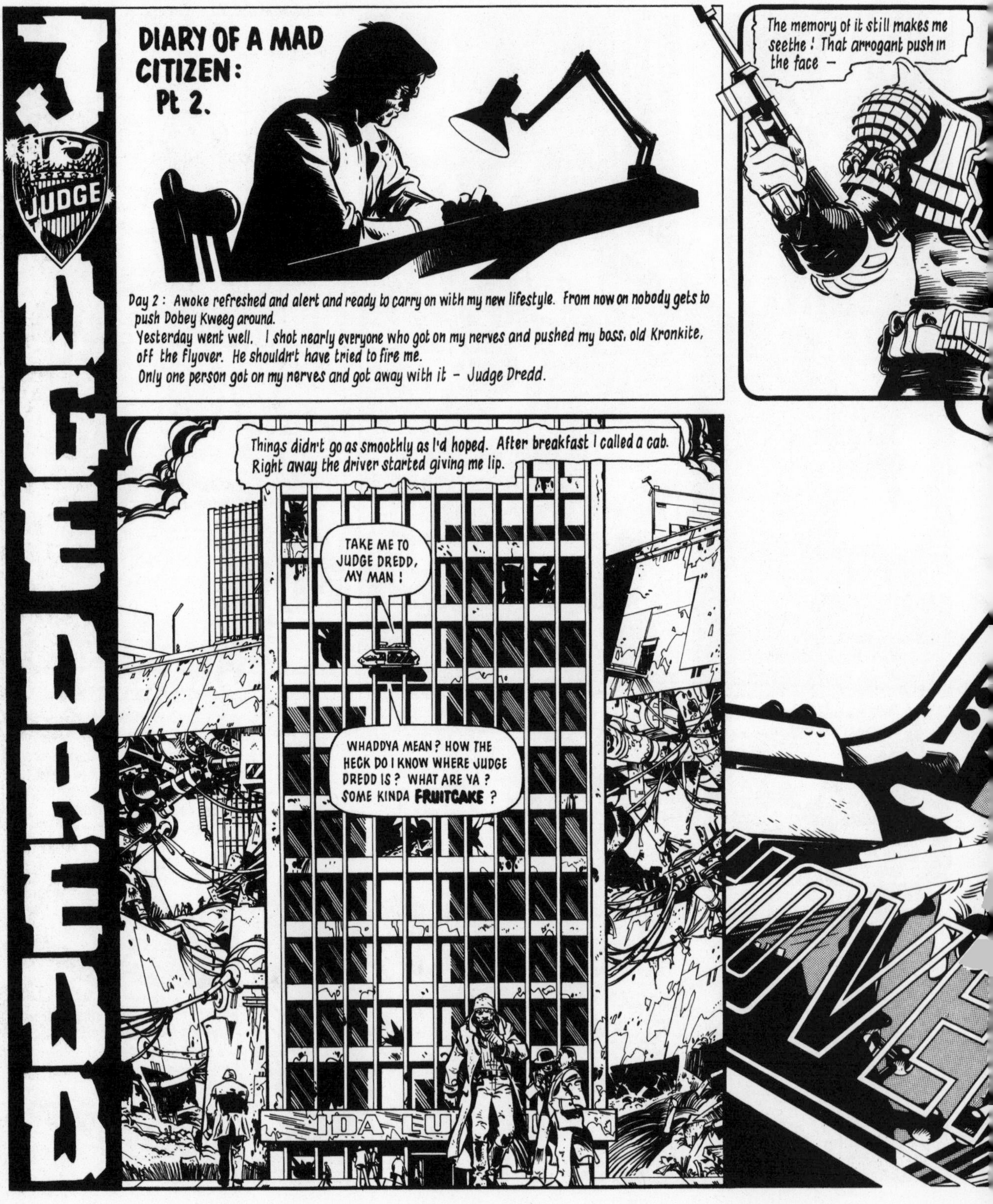
JUDGE DREDD
JUDGE
DIARY OF A MAD CITIZEN: Pt 2.
Day 2 : Awoke refreshed and alert and ready to carry on with my new lifestyle. From now on nobody gets to push Dobey Kweeg around.
Yesterday went well. I shot nearly everyone who got on my nerves and pushed my boss, old Kronkite, off the flyover. He shouldn't have tried to fire me.
Only one person got on my nerves and got away with it – Judge Dredd.
The memory of it still makes me seethe ! That arrogant push in the face –
Things didn't go as smoothly as I'd hoped. After breakfast I called a cab. Right away the driver started giving me lip.
TAKE ME TO JUDGE DREDD, MY MAN !
WHADDYA MEAN ? HOW THE HECK DO I KNOW WHERE JUDGE DREDD IS ? WHAT ARE YA ? SOME KINDA FRUITCAKE ?

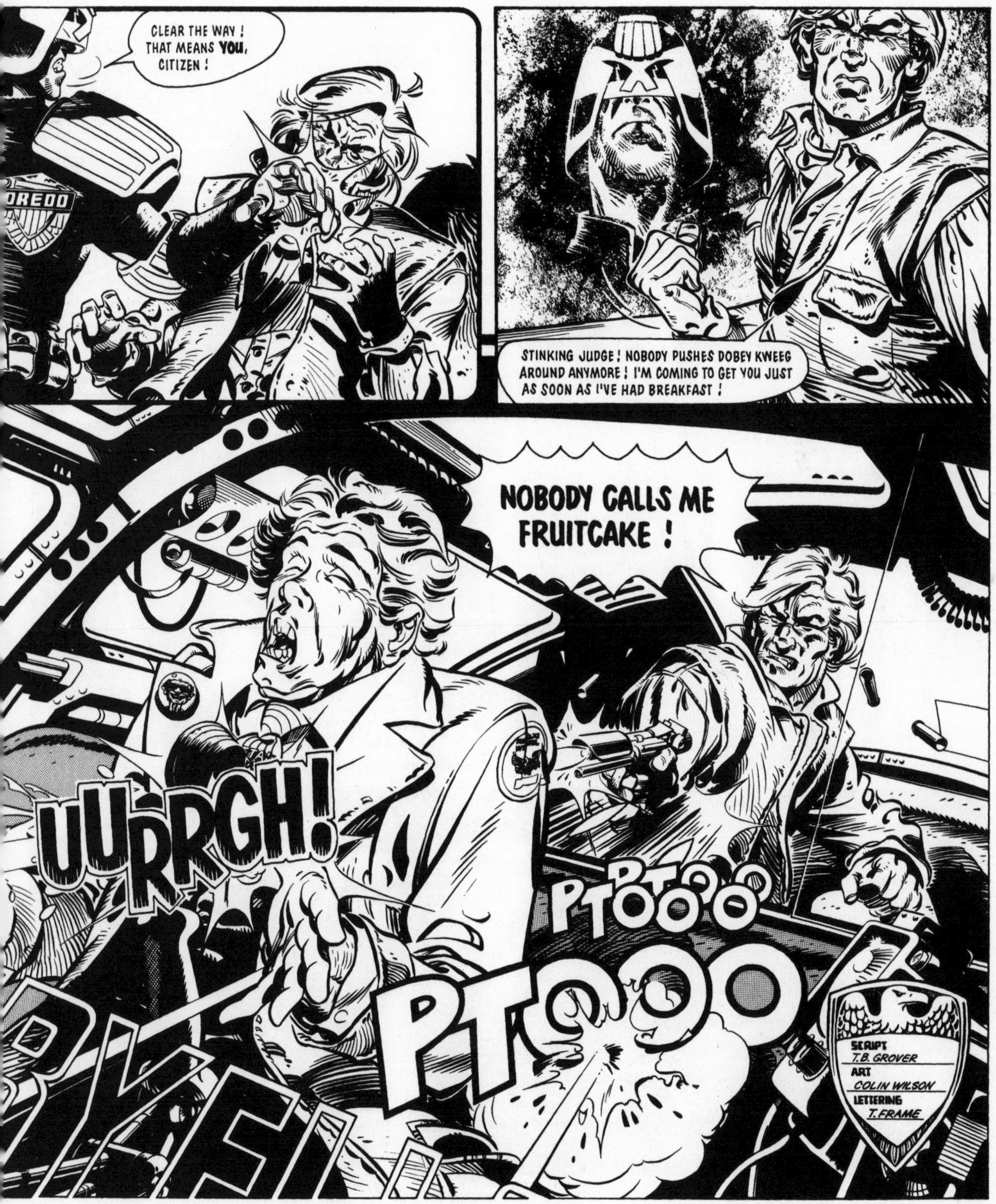
CLEAR THE WAY! THAT MEANS YOU, CITIZEN!
DREDD
STINKING JUDGE! NOBODY PUSHES DOBEY KWEEG AROUND ANYMORE! I'M COMING TO GET YOU JUST AS SOON AS I'VE HAD BREAKFAST!
NOBODY CALLS ME FRUITCAKE!
UURRGH!
PTOOO
PTOOOO
PTOOO
SCRIPT T.B. GROVER
ART COLIN WILSON
LETTERING T. FRAME

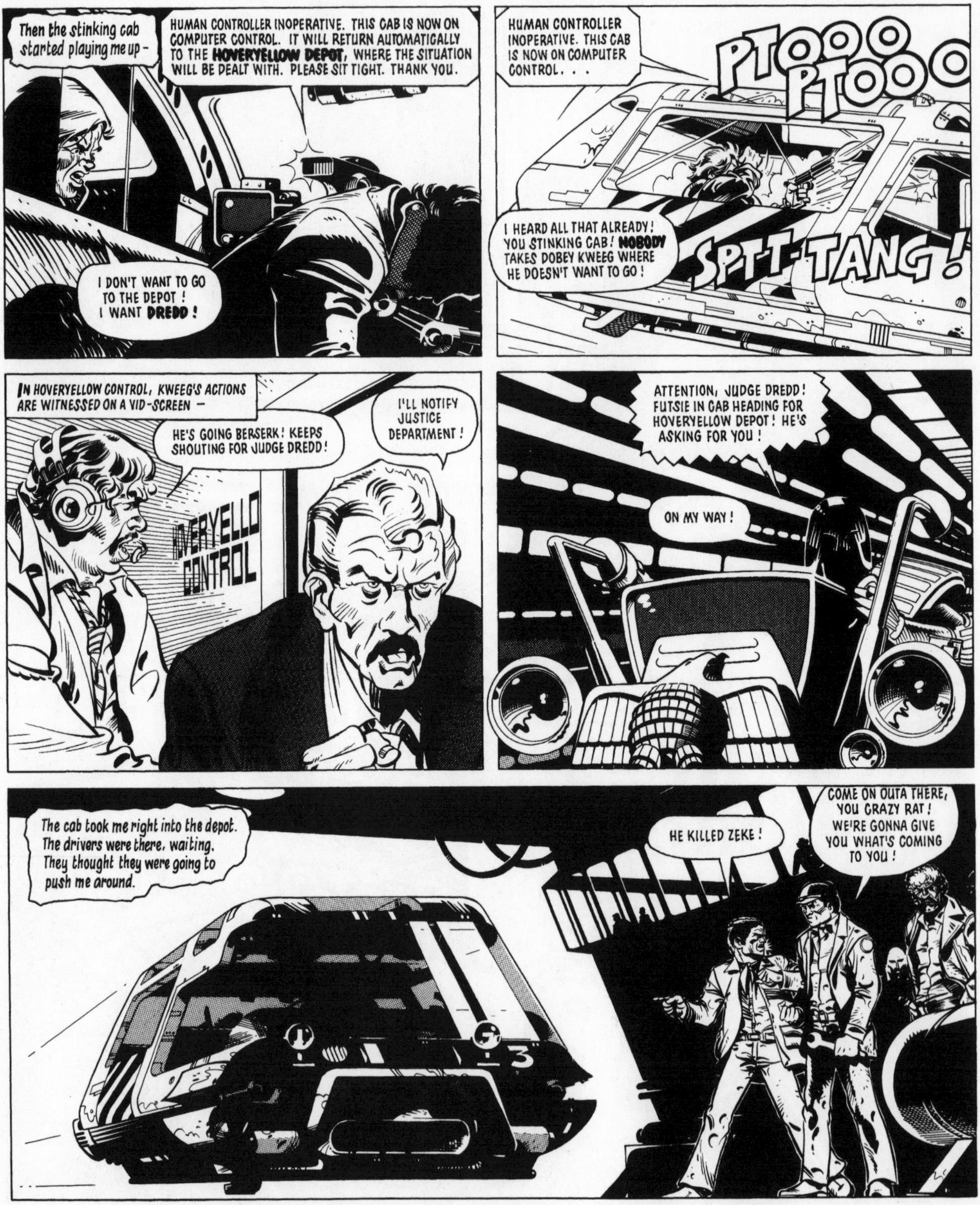

Then the stinking cab started playing me up -
HUMAN CONTROLLER INOPERATIVE. THIS CAB IS NOW ON COMPUTER CONTROL. IT WILL RETURN AUTOMATICALLY TO THE HOVERYELLOW DEPOT, WHERE THE SITUATION WILL BE DEALT WITH. PLEASE SIT TIGHT. THANK YOU.
I DON'T WANT TO GO TO THE DEPOT ! I WANT DREDD !
HUMAN CONTROLLER INOPERATIVE. THIS CAB IS NOW ON COMPUTER CONTROL. . .
PTOOO PTOOO
I HEARD ALL THAT ALREADY! YOU STINKING CAB! NOBODY TAKES DOBEY KWEEG WHERE HE DOESN'T WANT TO GO !
SPT-T-TANG !
IN HOVERYELLOW CONTROL, KWEEG'S ACTIONS ARE WITNESSED ON A VID-SCREEN —
HE'S GOING BERSERK! KEEPS SHOUTING FOR JUDGE DREDD!
I'LL NOTIFY JUSTICE DEPARTMENT !
HOVERYELLO CONTROL
ATTENTION, JUDGE DREDD! FUTSIE IN CAB HEADING FOR HOVERYELLOW DEPOT! HE'S ASKING FOR YOU !
ON MY WAY !
The cab took me right into the depot. The drivers were there, waiting. They thought they were going to push me around.
HE KILLED ZEKE !
COME ON OUTA THERE, YOU CRAZY RAT ! WE'RE GONNA GIVE YOU WHAT'S COMING TO YOU !

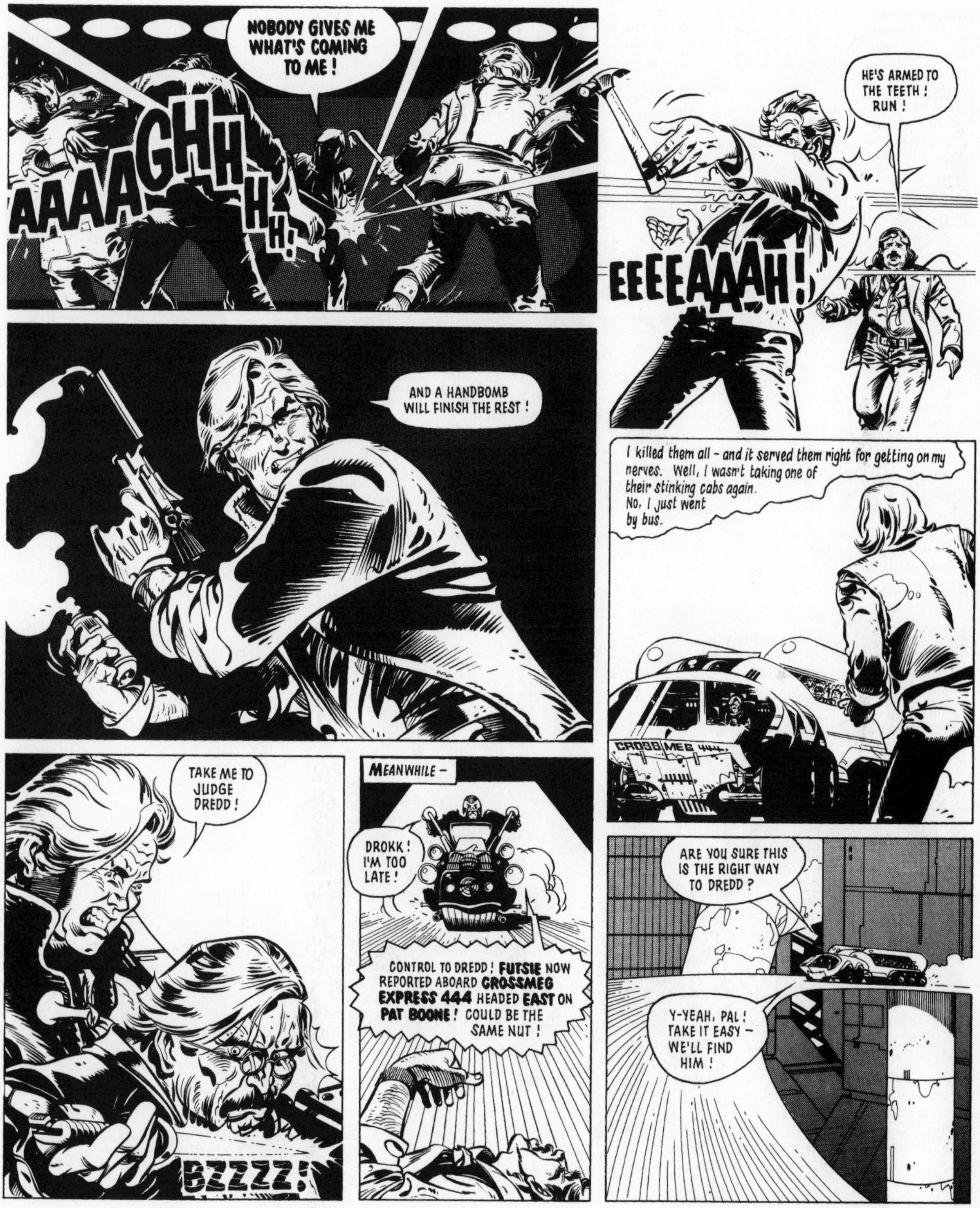
NOBODY GIVES ME WHAT'S COMING TO ME !
AAAAAGHHHHH!
HE'S ARMED TO THE TEETH ! RUN !
EEEEAAAH!
AND A HANDBOMB WILL FINISH THE REST !
I killed them all – and it served them right for getting on my nerves. Well, I wasn't taking one of their stinking cabs again. No, I just went by bus.
CROSS MEG 444
TAKE ME TO JUDGE DREDD !
BZZZZ!
MEANWHILE –
DROKK ! I'M TOO LATE !
CONTROL TO DREDD ! FUTSIE NOW REPORTED ABOARD GROSSMEG EXPRESS 444 HEADED EAST ON PAT BOONE ! COULD BE THE SAME NUT !
ARE YOU SURE THIS IS THE RIGHT WAY TO DREDD ?
Y-YEAH, PAL ! TAKE IT EASY – WE'LL FIND HIM !

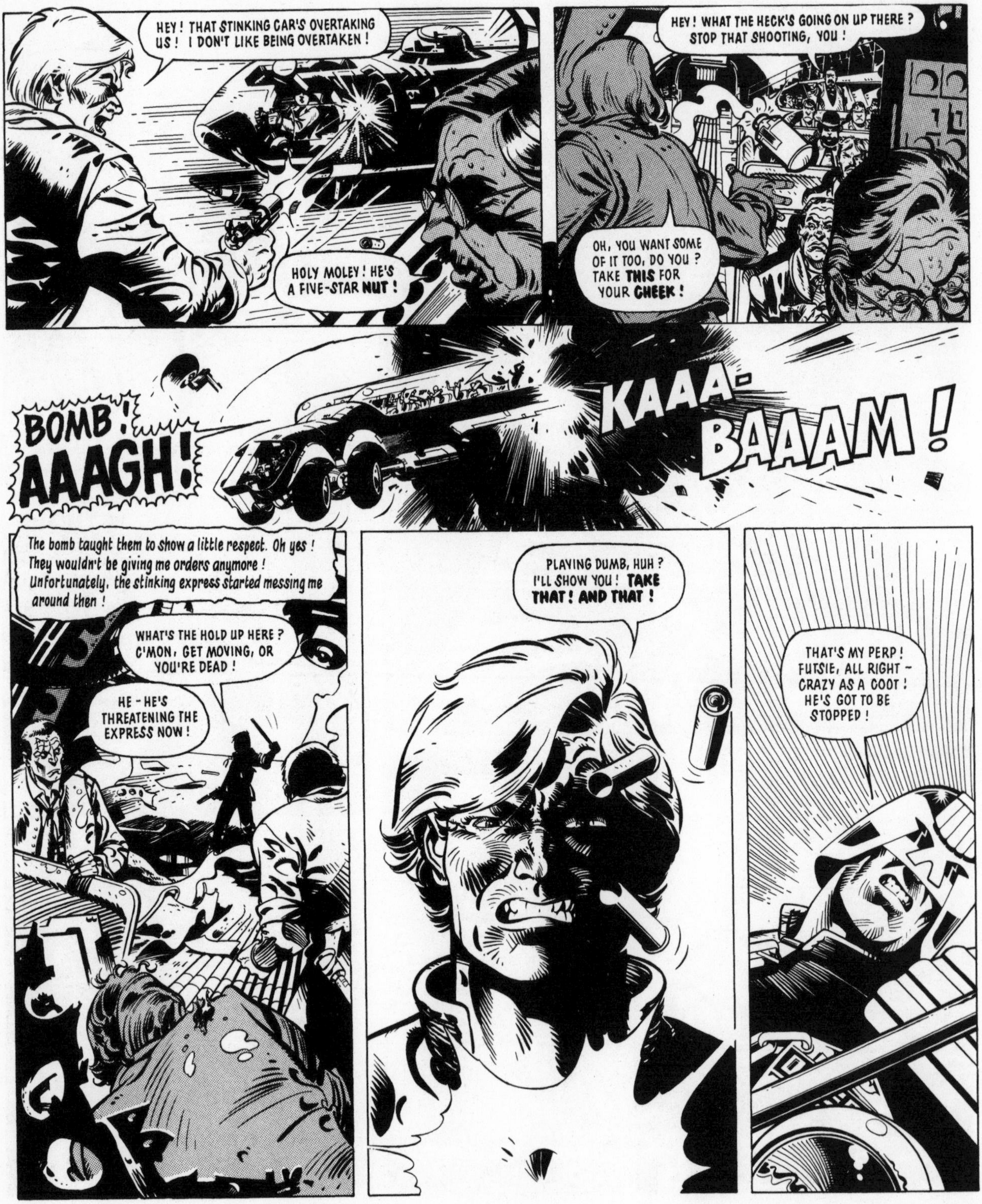
HEY! THAT STINKING CAR'S OVERTAKING US! I DON'T LIKE BEING OVERTAKEN!
HOLY MOLEY! HE'S A FIVE-STAR NUT!
HEY! WHAT THE HECK'S GOING ON UP THERE? STOP THAT SHOOTING, YOU!
OH, YOU WANT SOME OF IT TOO, DO YOU? TAKE THIS FOR YOUR CHEEK!
BOMB! AAAGH!
KAAA-BAAAM!
The bomb taught them to show a little respect. Oh yes! They wouldn't be giving me orders anymore! Unfortunately, the stinking express started messing me around then!
WHAT'S THE HOLD UP HERE? C'MON, GET MOVING, OR YOU'RE DEAD!
HE - HE'S THREATENING THE EXPRESS NOW!
PLAYING DUMB, HUH? I'LL SHOW YOU! TAKE THAT! AND THAT!
THAT'S MY PERP! FUTSIE, ALL RIGHT - CRAZY AS A COOT! HE'S GOT TO BE STOPPED!

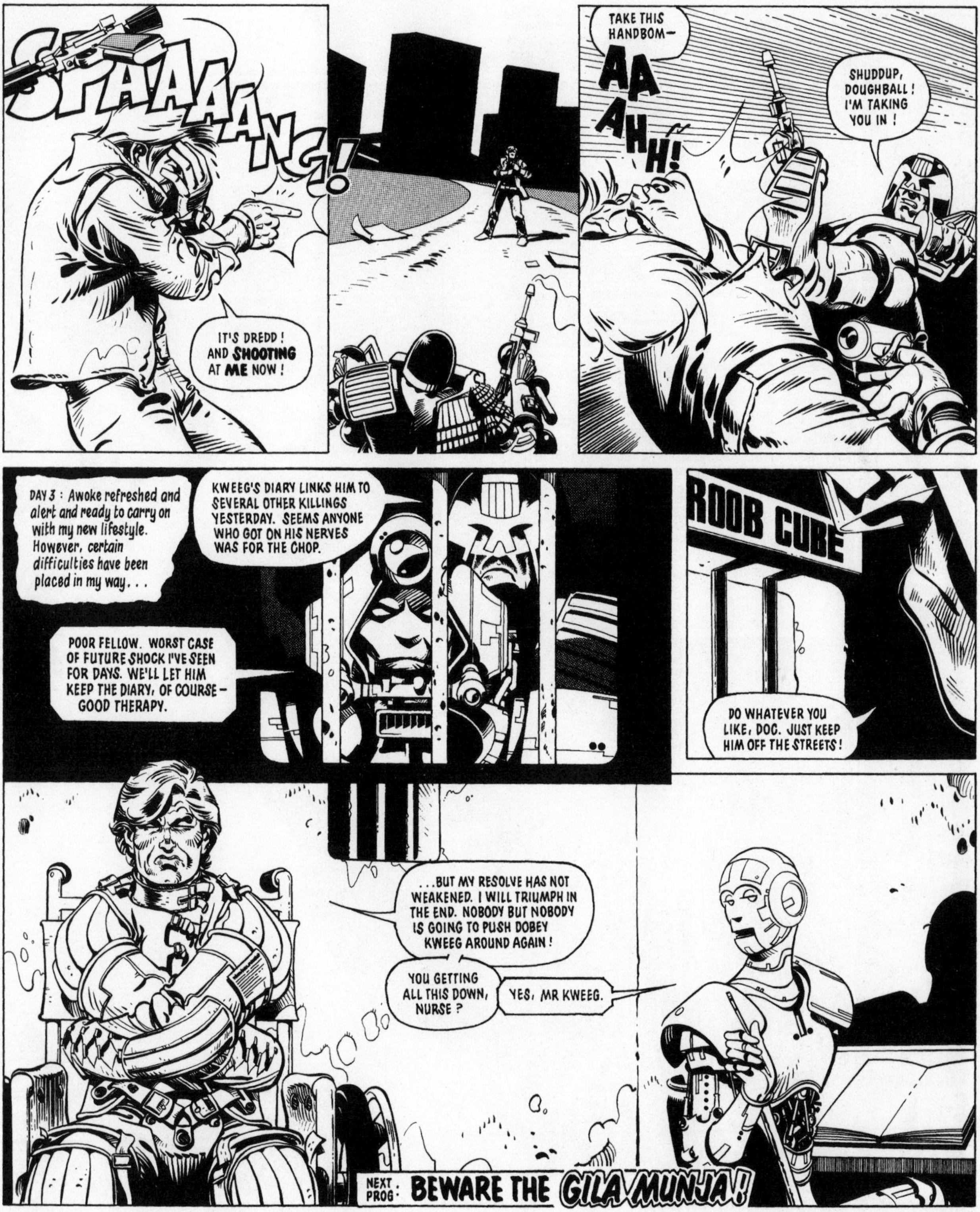
SPAAAAANG!
IT'S DREDD! AND SHOOTING AT ME NOW!
TAKE THIS HANDBOM—
AAAHH!
SHUDDUP, DOUGHBALL! I'M TAKING YOU IN!
DAY 3: Awoke refreshed and alert and ready to carry on with my new lifestyle. However, certain difficulties have been placed in my way...
KWEEG'S DIARY LINKS HIM TO SEVERAL OTHER KILLINGS YESTERDAY. SEEMS ANYONE WHO GOT ON HIS NERVES WAS FOR THE CHOP.
POOR FELLOW. WORST CASE OF FUTURE SHOCK I'VE SEEN FOR DAYS. WE'LL LET HIM KEEP THE DIARY, OF COURSE—GOOD THERAPY.
ROOB CUBE
DO WHATEVER YOU LIKE, DOC. JUST KEEP HIM OFF THE STREETS!
...BUT MY RESOLVE HAS NOT WEAKENED. I WILL TRIUMPH IN THE END. NOBODY BUT NOBODY IS GOING TO PUSH DOBEY KWEEG AROUND AGAIN!
YOU GETTING ALL THIS DOWN, NURSE?
YES, MR KWEEG.
NEXT PROG: BEWARE THE GILA MUNJA!

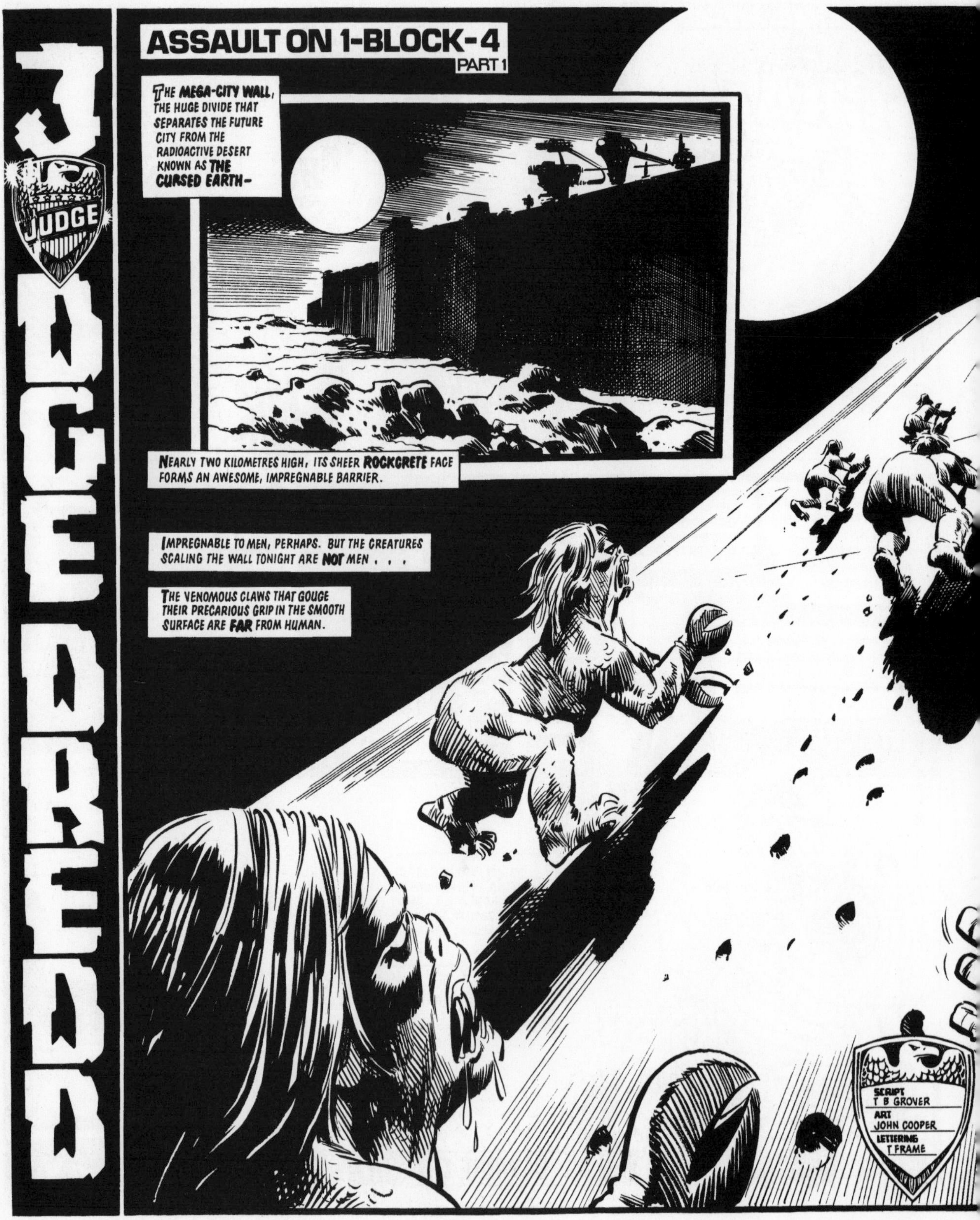

JUDGE DREDD
JUDGE
ASSAULT ON 1-BLOCK-4
PART 1
THE MEGA-CITY WALL, THE HUGE DIVIDE THAT SEPARATES THE FUTURE CITY FROM THE RADIOACTIVE DESERT KNOWN AS THE CURSED EARTH-
NEARLY TWO KILOMETRES HIGH, ITS SHEER ROCKCRETE FACE FORMS AN AWESOME, IMPREGNABLE BARRIER.
IMPREGNABLE TO MEN, PERHAPS. BUT THE CREATURES SCALING THE WALL TONIGHT ARE NOT MEN . . .
THE VENOMOUS CLAWS THAT GOUGE THEIR PRECARIOUS GRIP IN THE SMOOTH SURFACE ARE FAR FROM HUMAN.
SCRIPT
T B GROVER
ART
JOHN COOPER
LETTERING
T FRAME

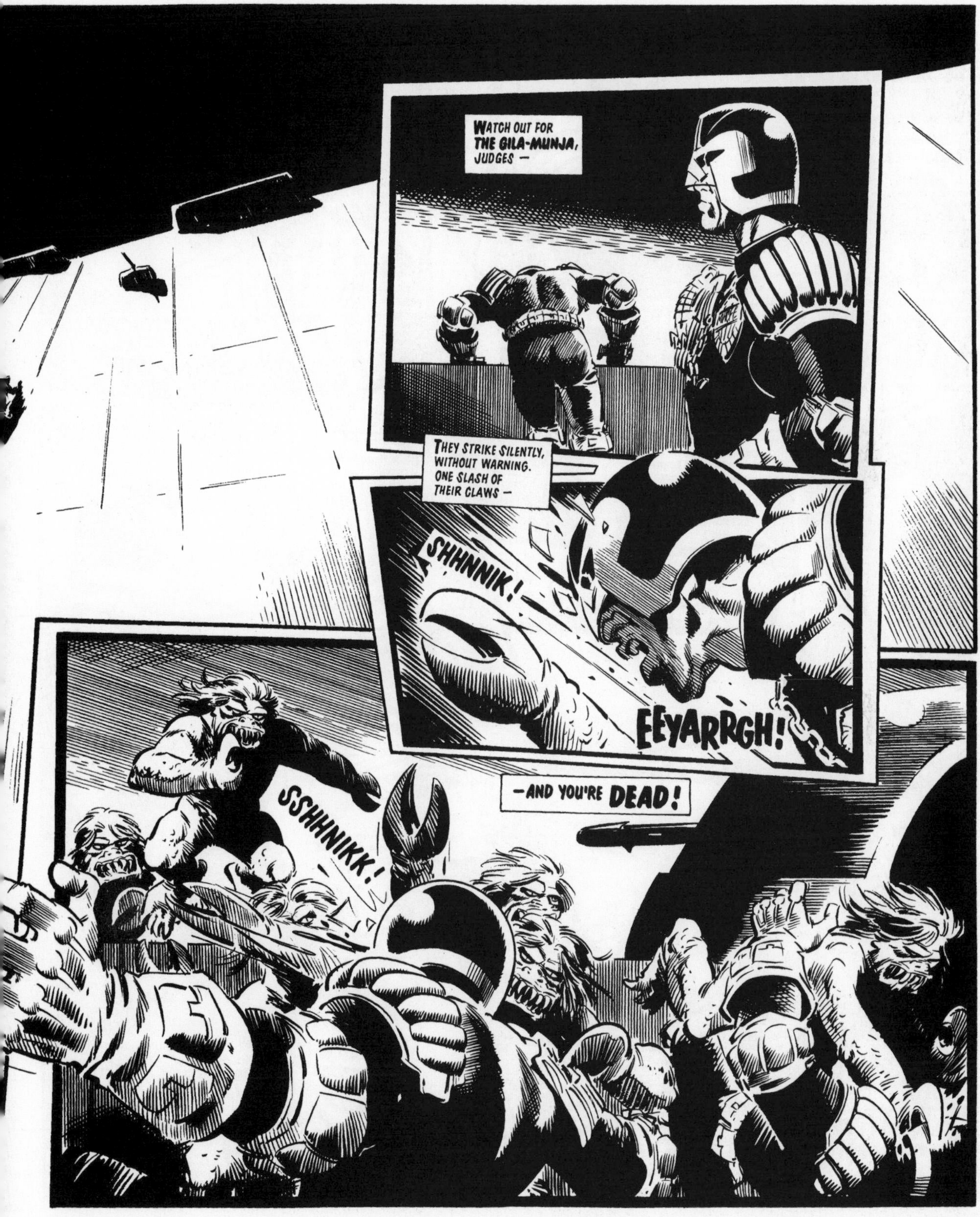
WATCH OUT FOR THE GILA-MUNJA, JUDGES —
THEY STRIKE SILENTLY, WITHOUT WARNING. ONE SLASH OF THEIR CLAWS —
SHHNNIK!
EEYARRGH!
SSHHNIKK!
—AND YOU'RE DEAD!

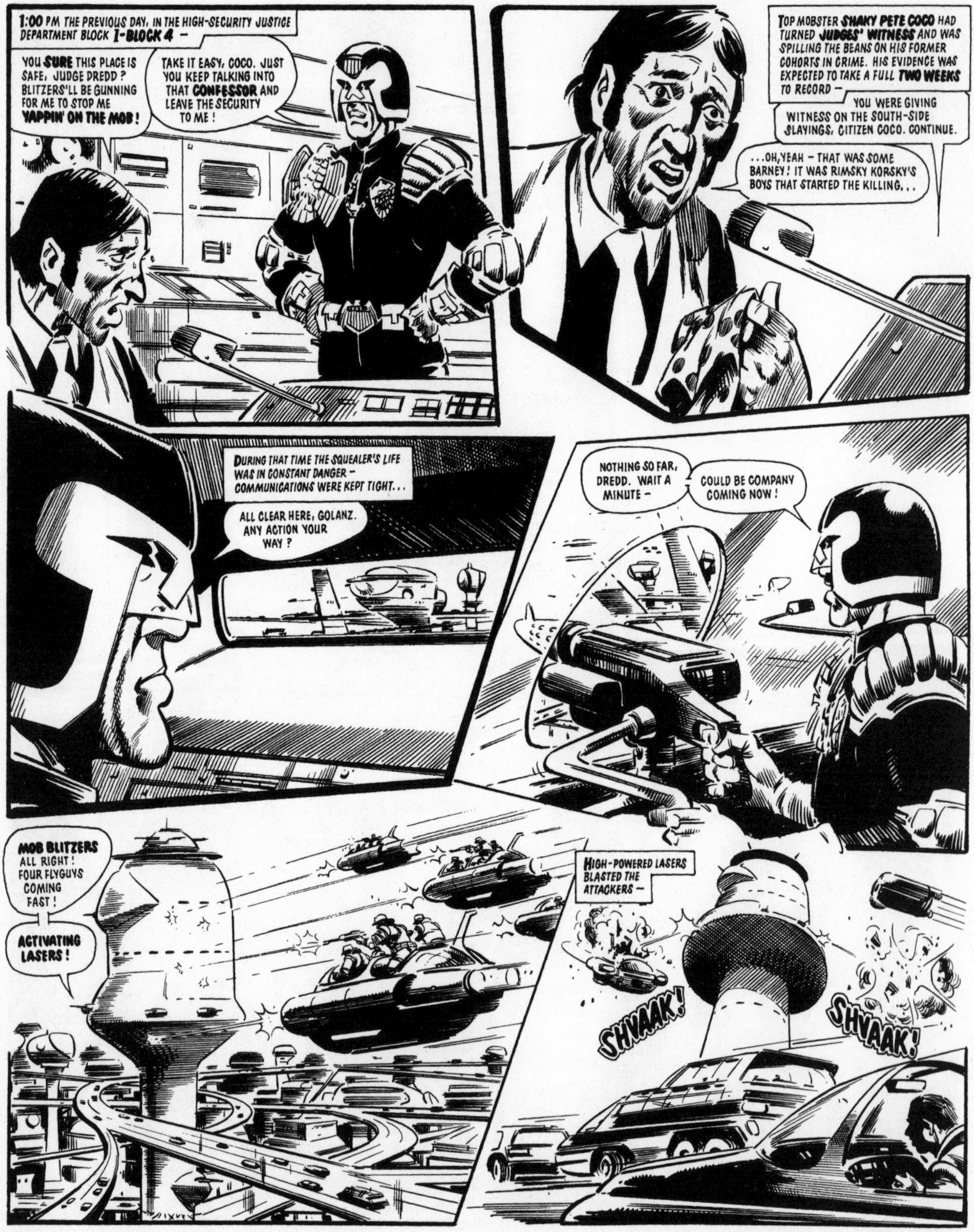

1:00 PM THE PREVIOUS DAY, IN THE HIGH-SECURITY JUSTICE DEPARTMENT BLOCK 1-BLOCK 4 –
YOU SURE THIS PLACE IS SAFE, JUDGE DREDD? BLITZERS'LL BE GUNNING FOR ME TO STOP ME YAPPIN' ON THE MOB!
TAKE IT EASY, COCO. JUST YOU KEEP TALKING INTO THAT CONFESSOR AND LEAVE THE SECURITY TO ME!
TOP MOBSTER SHAKY PETE COCO HAD TURNED JUDGES' WITNESS AND WAS SPILLING THE BEANS ON HIS FORMER COHORTS IN CRIME. HIS EVIDENCE WAS EXPECTED TO TAKE A FULL TWO WEEKS TO RECORD –
YOU WERE GIVING WITNESS ON THE SOUTH-SIDE SLAYINGS, CITIZEN COCO. CONTINUE.
...OH, YEAH – THAT WAS SOME BARNEY! IT WAS RIMSKY KORSKY'S BOYS THAT STARTED THE KILLING...
DURING THAT TIME THE SQUEALER'S LIFE WAS IN CONSTANT DANGER – COMMUNICATIONS WERE KEPT TIGHT...
ALL CLEAR HERE, GOLANZ. ANY ACTION YOUR WAY?
NOTHING SO FAR, DREDD. WAIT A MINUTE –
COULD BE COMPANY COMING NOW!
MOB BLITZERS ALL RIGHT! FOUR FLYGUYS COMING FAST!
ACTIVATING LASERS!
HIGH-POWERED LASERS BLASTED THE ATTACKERS –
SHVAAK!
SHVAAK!

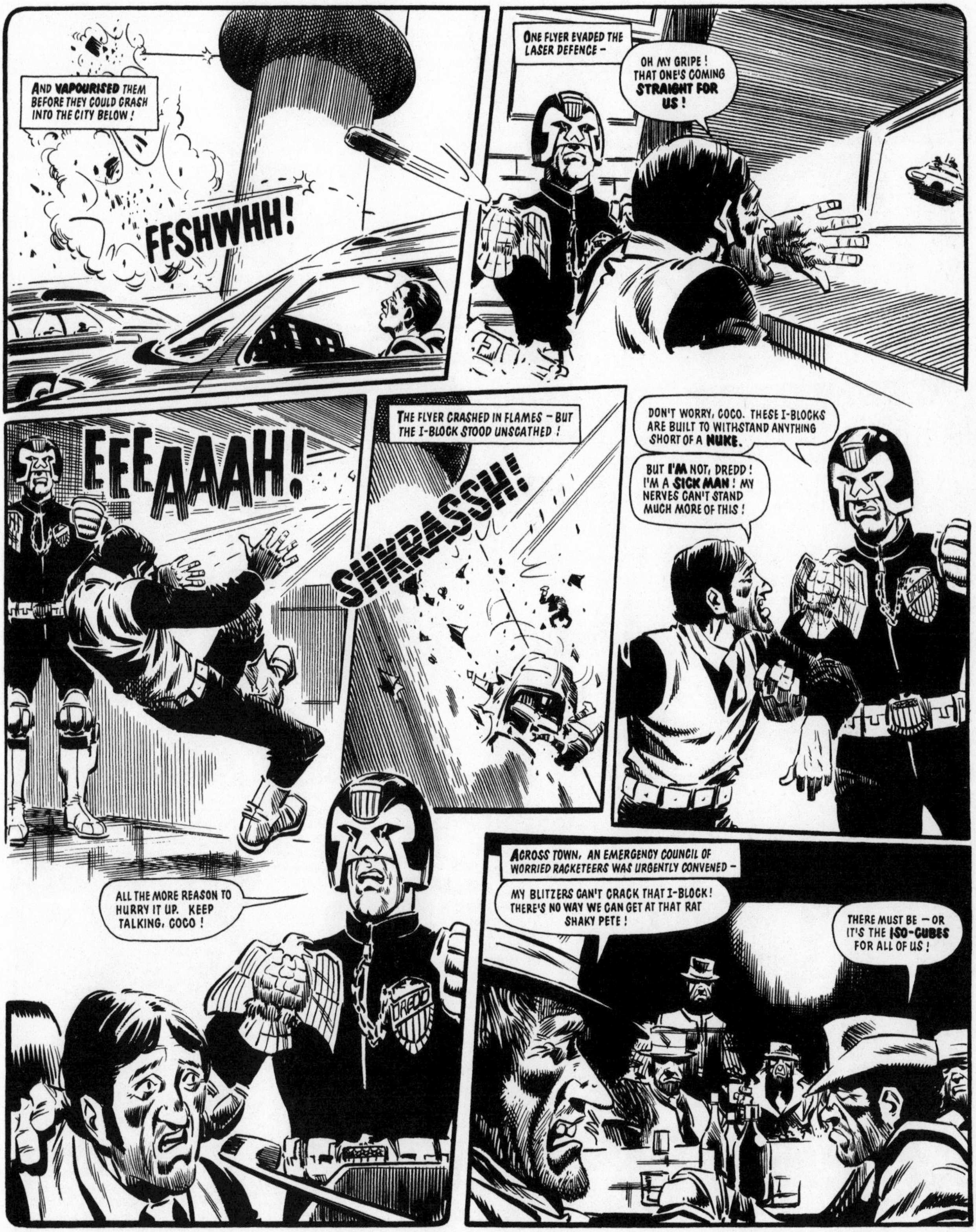
AND VAPOURISED THEM BEFORE THEY COULD CRASH INTO THE CITY BELOW!
FFSHWHH!
ONE FLYER EVADED THE LASER DEFENCE –
OH MY GRIPE! THAT ONE'S COMING STRAIGHT FOR US!
EEEAAAH!
THE FLYER CRASHED IN FLAMES – BUT THE I-BLOCK STOOD UNSCATHED!
SHKRASSH!
DON'T WORRY, COCO. THESE I-BLOCKS ARE BUILT TO WITHSTAND ANYTHING SHORT OF A NUKE.
BUT I'M NOT, DREDD! I'M A SICK MAN! MY NERVES CAN'T STAND MUCH MORE OF THIS!
ALL THE MORE REASON TO HURRY IT UP. KEEP TALKING, COCO!
ACROSS TOWN, AN EMERGENCY COUNCIL OF WORRIED RACKETEERS WAS URGENTLY CONVENED –
MY BLITZERS CAN'T CRACK THAT I-BLOCK! THERE'S NO WAY WE CAN GET AT THAT RAT SHAKY PETE!
THERE MUST BE – OR IT'S THE ISO-CUBES FOR ALL OF US!

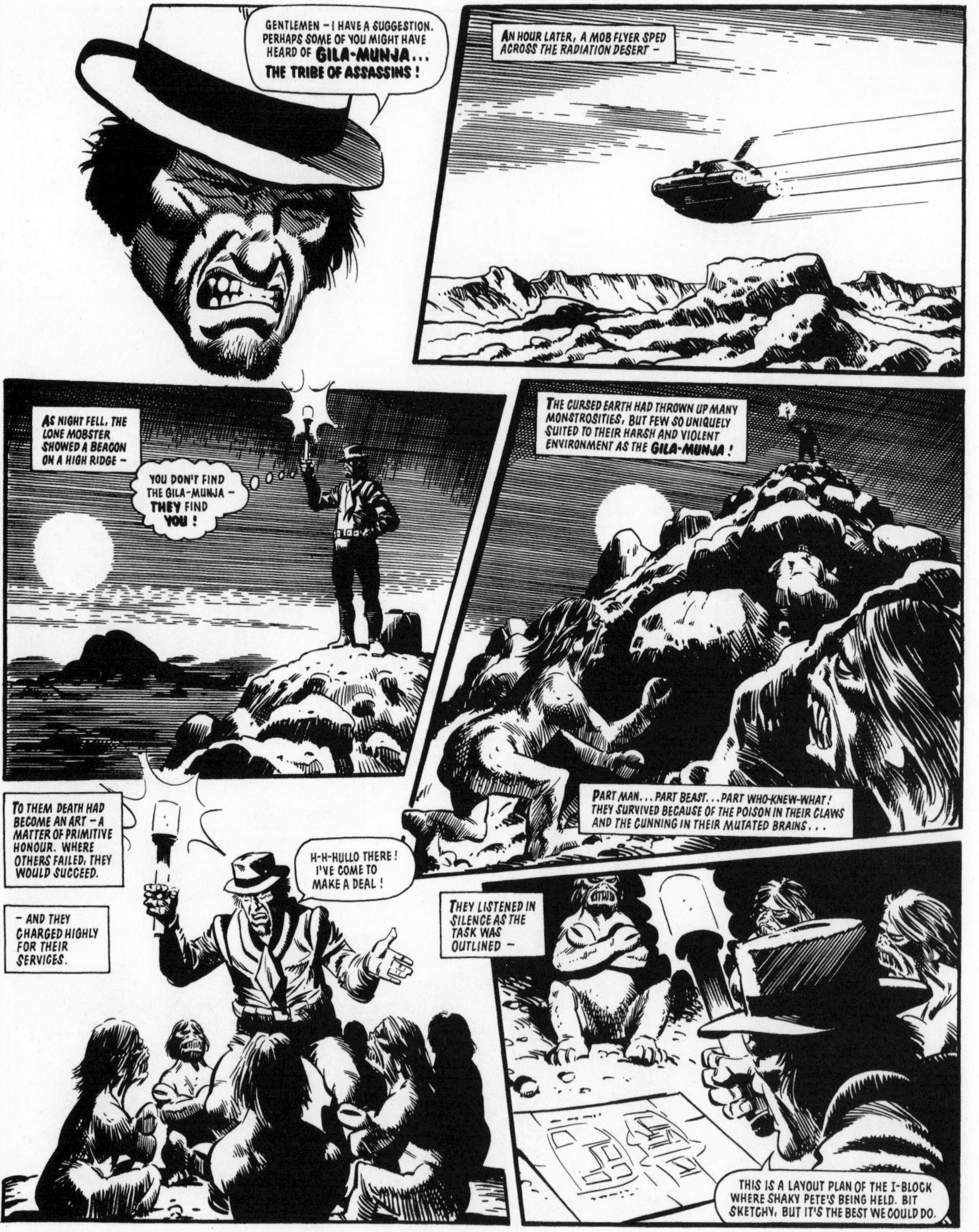

GENTLEMEN – I HAVE A SUGGESTION. PERHAPS SOME OF YOU MIGHT HAVE HEARD OF GILA-MUNJA... THE TRIBE OF ASSASSINS!
AN HOUR LATER, A MOB FLYER SPED ACROSS THE RADIATION DESERT –
AS NIGHT FELL, THE LONE MOBSTER SHOWED A BEACON ON A HIGH RIDGE –
YOU DON'T FIND THE GILA-MUNJA – THEY FIND YOU!
THE CURSED EARTH HAD THROWN UP MANY MONSTROSITIES, BUT FEW SO UNIQUELY SUITED TO THEIR HARSH AND VIOLENT ENVIRONMENT AS THE GILA-MUNJA!
PART MAN... PART BEAST... PART WHO-KNEW-WHAT! THEY SURVIVED BECAUSE OF THE POISON IN THEIR CLAWS AND THE CUNNING IN THEIR MUTATED BRAINS...
TO THEM DEATH HAD BECOME AN ART – A MATTER OF PRIMITIVE HONOUR. WHERE OTHERS FAILED, THEY WOULD SUCCEED.
H-H-HULLO THERE! I'VE COME TO MAKE A DEAL!
– AND THEY CHARGED HIGHLY FOR THEIR SERVICES.
THEY LISTENED IN SILENCE AS THE TASK WAS OUTLINED –
THIS IS A LAYOUT PLAN OF THE I-BLOCK WHERE SHAKY PETE'S BEING HELD. BIT SKETCHY, BUT IT'S THE BEST WE COULD DO.

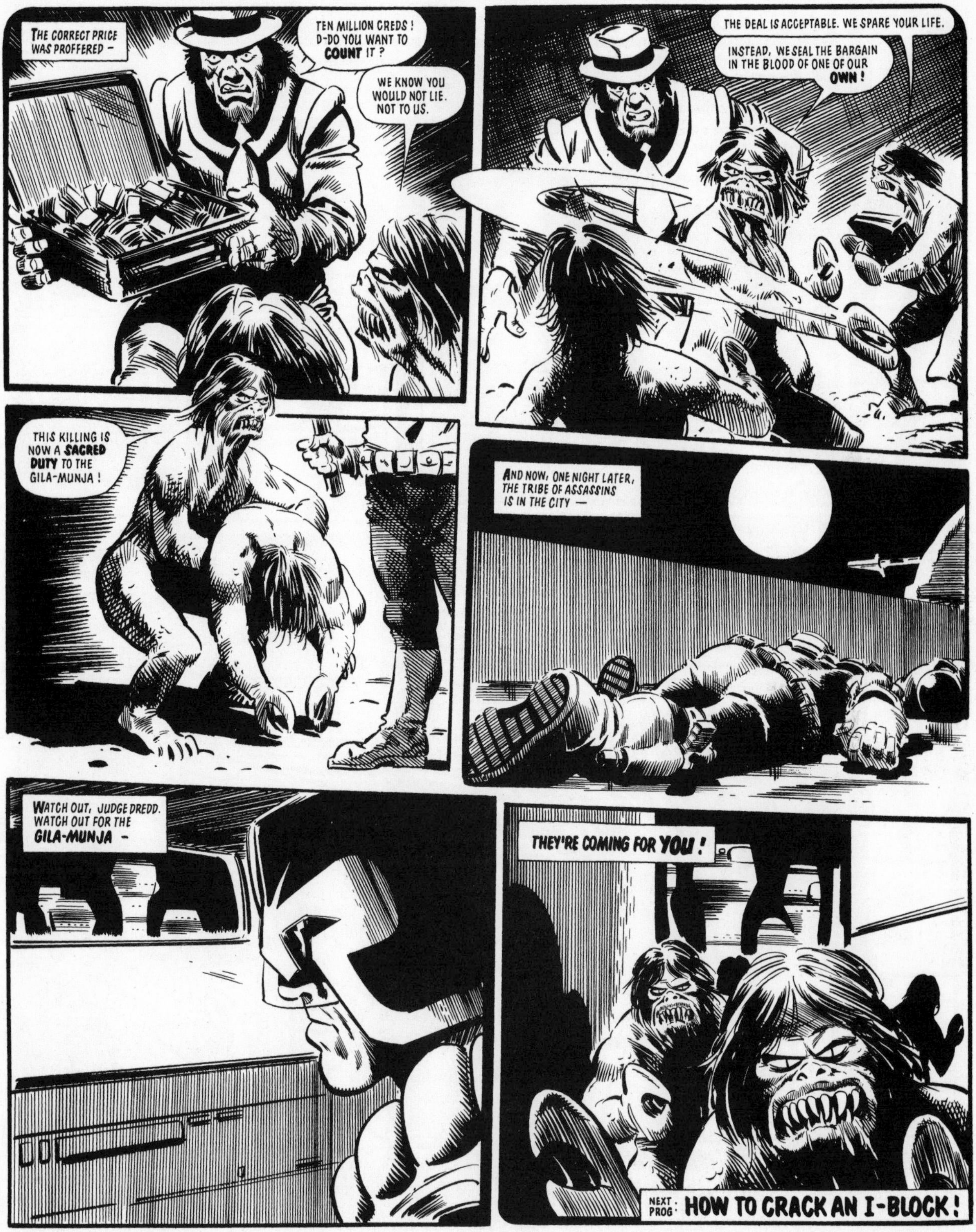

THE CORRECT PRICE WAS PROFFERED —
TEN MILLION CREDS! D-DO YOU WANT TO COUNT IT?
WE KNOW YOU WOULD NOT LIE. NOT TO US.
THE DEAL IS ACCEPTABLE. WE SPARE YOUR LIFE.
INSTEAD, WE SEAL THE BARGAIN IN THE BLOOD OF ONE OF OUR OWN!
THIS KILLING IS NOW A SACRED DUTY TO THE GILA-MUNJA!
AND NOW, ONE NIGHT LATER, THE TRIBE OF ASSASSINS IS IN THE CITY —
WATCH OUT, JUDGE DREDD. WATCH OUT FOR THE GILA-MUNJA —
THEY'RE COMING FOR YOU!
NEXT PROG: HOW TO CRACK AN I-BLOCK!

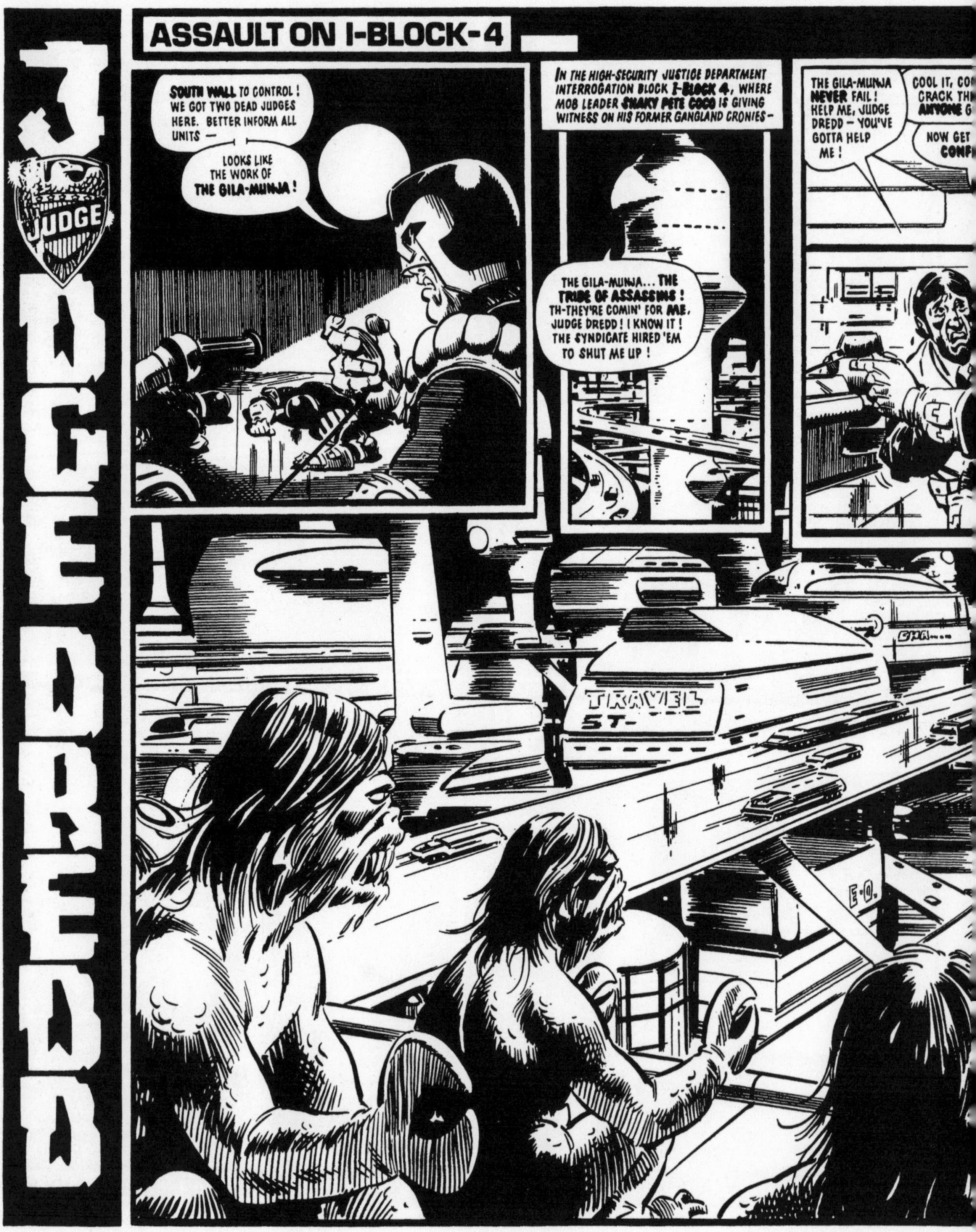
JUDGE DREDD
JUDGE
ASSAULT ON I-BLOCK-4
SOUTH WALL TO CONTROL! WE GOT TWO DEAD JUDGES HERE. BETTER INFORM ALL UNITS —
LOOKS LIKE THE WORK OF THE GILA-MUNJA!
IN THE HIGH-SECURITY JUSTICE DEPARTMENT INTERROGATION BLOCK I-BLOCK 4, WHERE MOB LEADER SHAKY PETE COCO IS GIVING WITNESS ON HIS FORMER GANGLAND CRONIES —
THE GILA-MUNJA... THE TRIBE OF ASSASSINS! TH-THEY'RE COMIN' FOR ME, JUDGE DREDD! I KNOW IT! THE SYNDICATE HIRED 'EM TO SHUT ME UP!
THE GILA-MUNJA NEVER FAIL! HELP ME, JUDGE DREDD — YOU'VE GOTTA HELP ME!
TRAVEL
ST-
E.O.

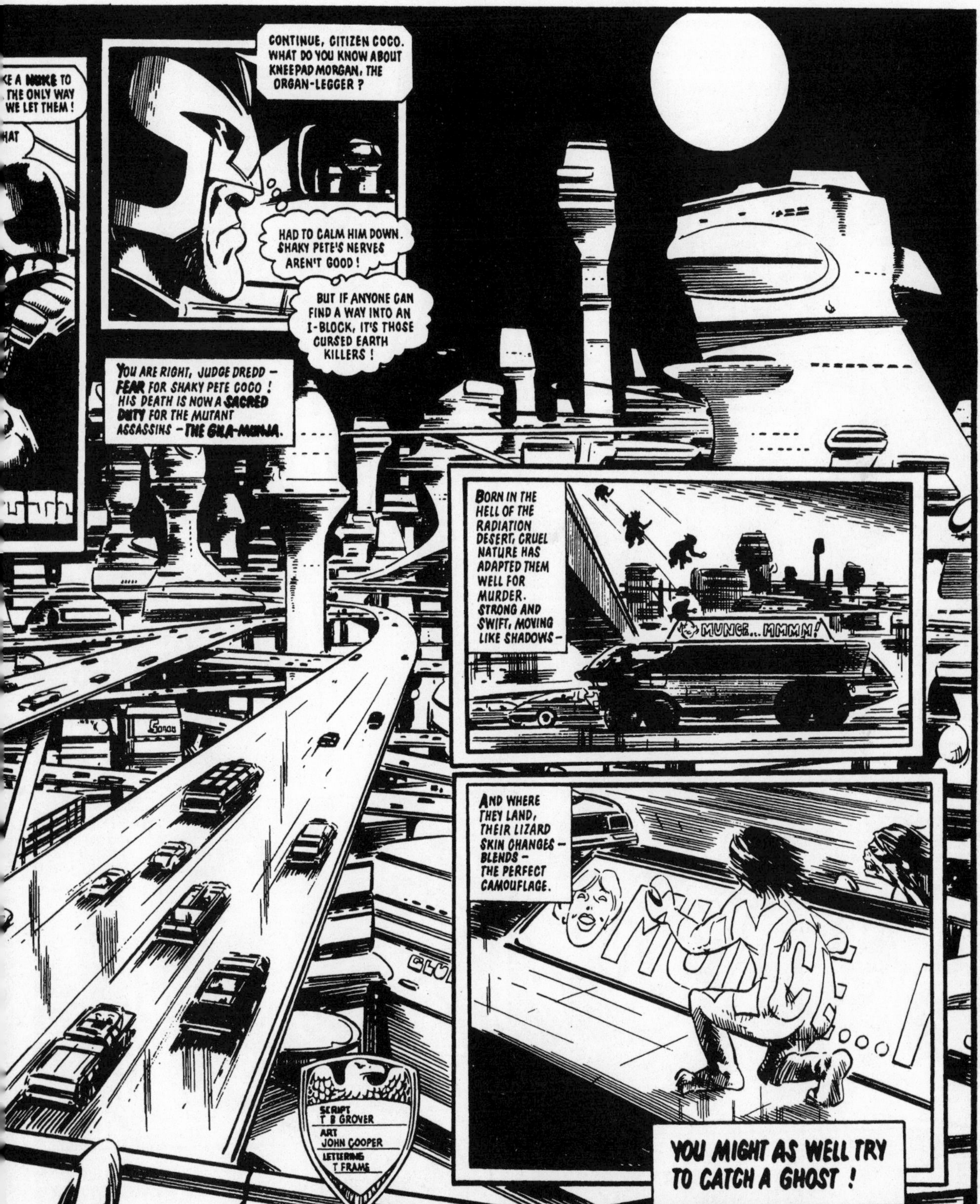

KE A MUNCE TO
THE ONLY WAY
WE LET THEM !
CONTINUE, CITIZEN COCO. WHAT DO YOU KNOW ABOUT KNEEPAD MORGAN, THE ORGAN-LEGGER ?
HAD TO CALM HIM DOWN. SHAKY PETE'S NERVES AREN'T GOOD !
BUT IF ANYONE CAN FIND A WAY INTO AN I-BLOCK, IT'S THOSE CURSED EARTH KILLERS !
YOU ARE RIGHT, JUDGE DREDD – FEAR FOR SHAKY PETE COCO ! HIS DEATH IS NOW A SACRED DUTY FOR THE MUTANT ASSASSINS – THE GILA-MUNJA.
BORN IN THE HELL OF THE RADIATION DESERT, CRUEL NATURE HAS ADAPTED THEM WELL FOR MURDER. STRONG AND SWIFT, MOVING LIKE SHADOWS –
MUNCE... MMMM!
AND WHERE THEY LAND, THEIR LIZARD SKIN CHANGES – BLENDS – THE PERFECT CAMOUFLAGE.
YOU MIGHT AS WELL TRY TO CATCH A GHOST !
SCRIPT T B GROVER
ART JOHN COOPER
LETTERING T FRAME

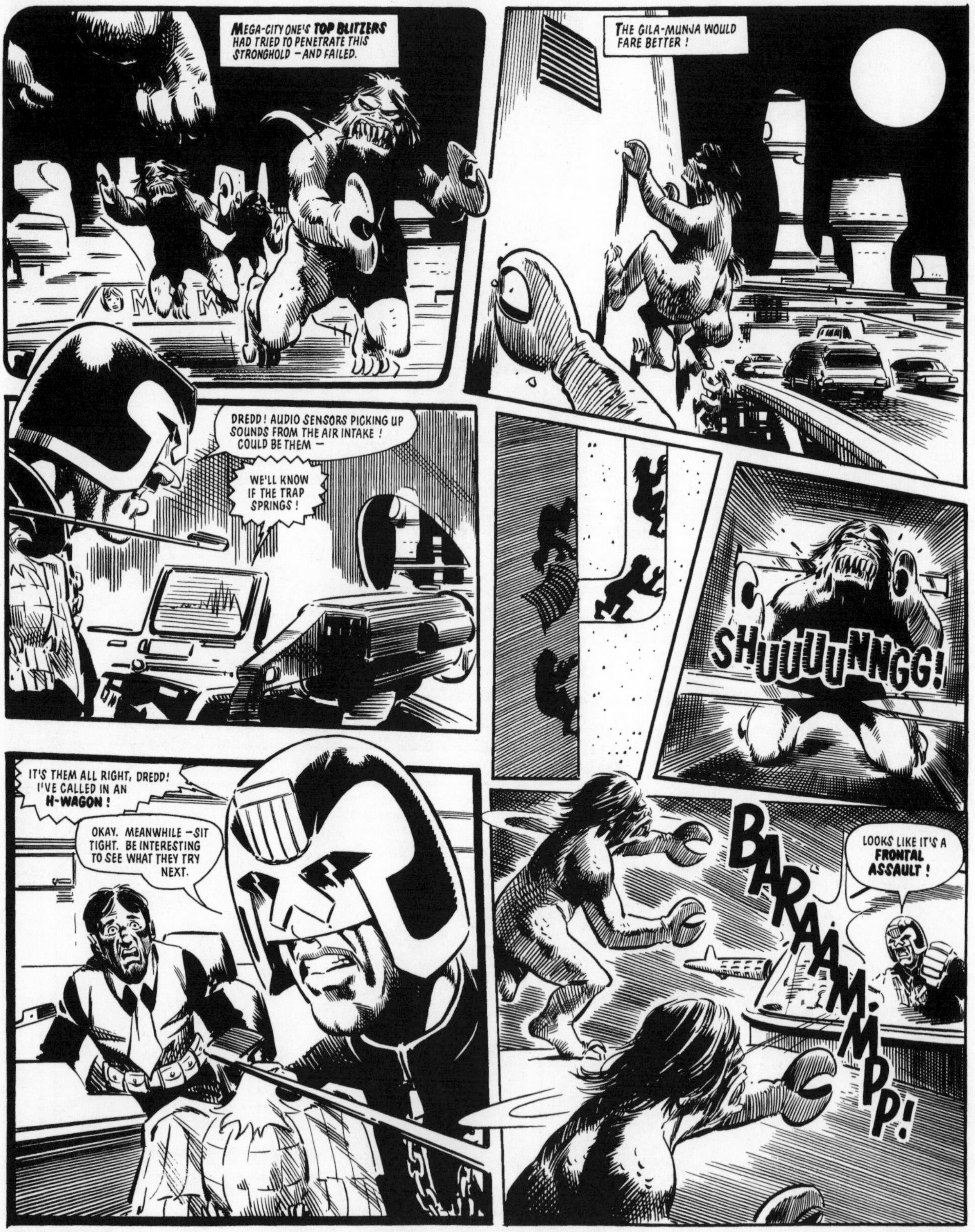

MEGA-CITY ONE'S TOP BLITZERS HAD TRIED TO PENETRATE THIS STRONGHOLD — AND FAILED.
THE GILA-MUNJA WOULD FARE BETTER !
DREDD! AUDIO SENSORS PICKING UP SOUNDS FROM THE AIR INTAKE ! COULD BE THEM —
WE'LL KNOW IF THE TRAP SPRINGS !
SHUUUUUNNGG!
IT'S THEM ALL RIGHT, DREDD! I'VE CALLED IN AN H-WAGON !
OKAY. MEANWHILE — SIT TIGHT. BE INTERESTING TO SEE WHAT THEY TRY NEXT.
BARAAAMMPP!
LOOKS LIKE IT'S A FRONTAL ASSAULT !

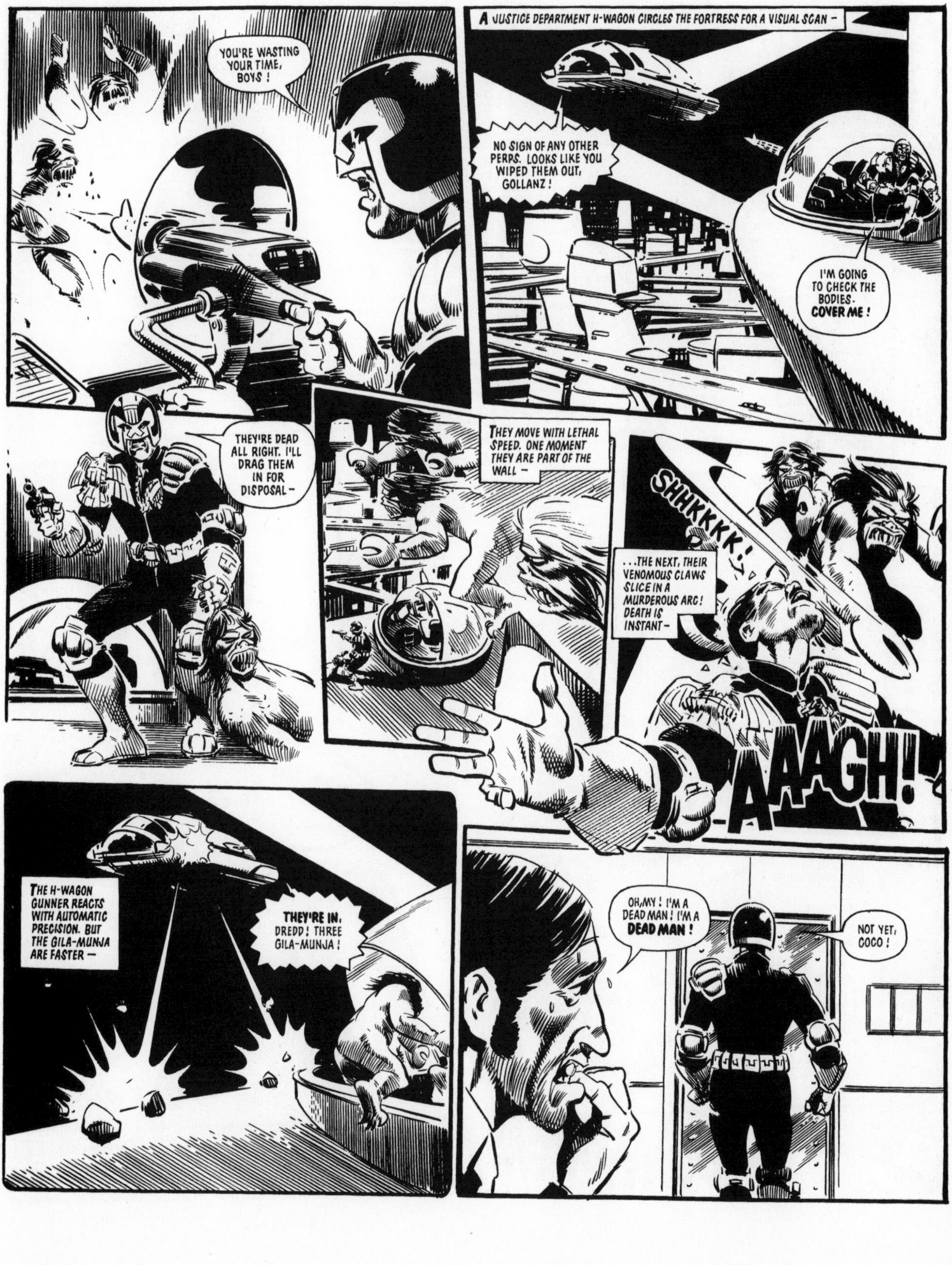
YOU'RE WASTING YOUR TIME, BOYS !
A JUSTICE DEPARTMENT H-WAGON CIRCLES THE FORTRESS FOR A VISUAL SCAN –
NO SIGN OF ANY OTHER PERPS. LOOKS LIKE YOU WIPED THEM OUT, GOLLANZ !
I'M GOING TO CHECK THE BODIES- COVER ME !
THEY'RE DEAD ALL RIGHT. I'LL DRAG THEM IN FOR DISPOSAL–
THEY MOVE WITH LETHAL SPEED. ONE MOMENT THEY ARE PART OF THE WALL –
SHHKKKK !
...THE NEXT, THEIR VENOMOUS CLAWS SLICE IN A MURDEROUS ARC ! DEATH IS INSTANT–
AAAGH !
THE H-WAGON GUNNER REACTS WITH AUTOMATIC PRECISION. BUT THE GILA-MUNJA ARE FASTER –
THEY'RE IN, DREDD ! THREE GILA-MUNJA !
OH, MY ! I'M A DEAD MAN ! I'M A DEAD MAN !
NOT YET, COCO !

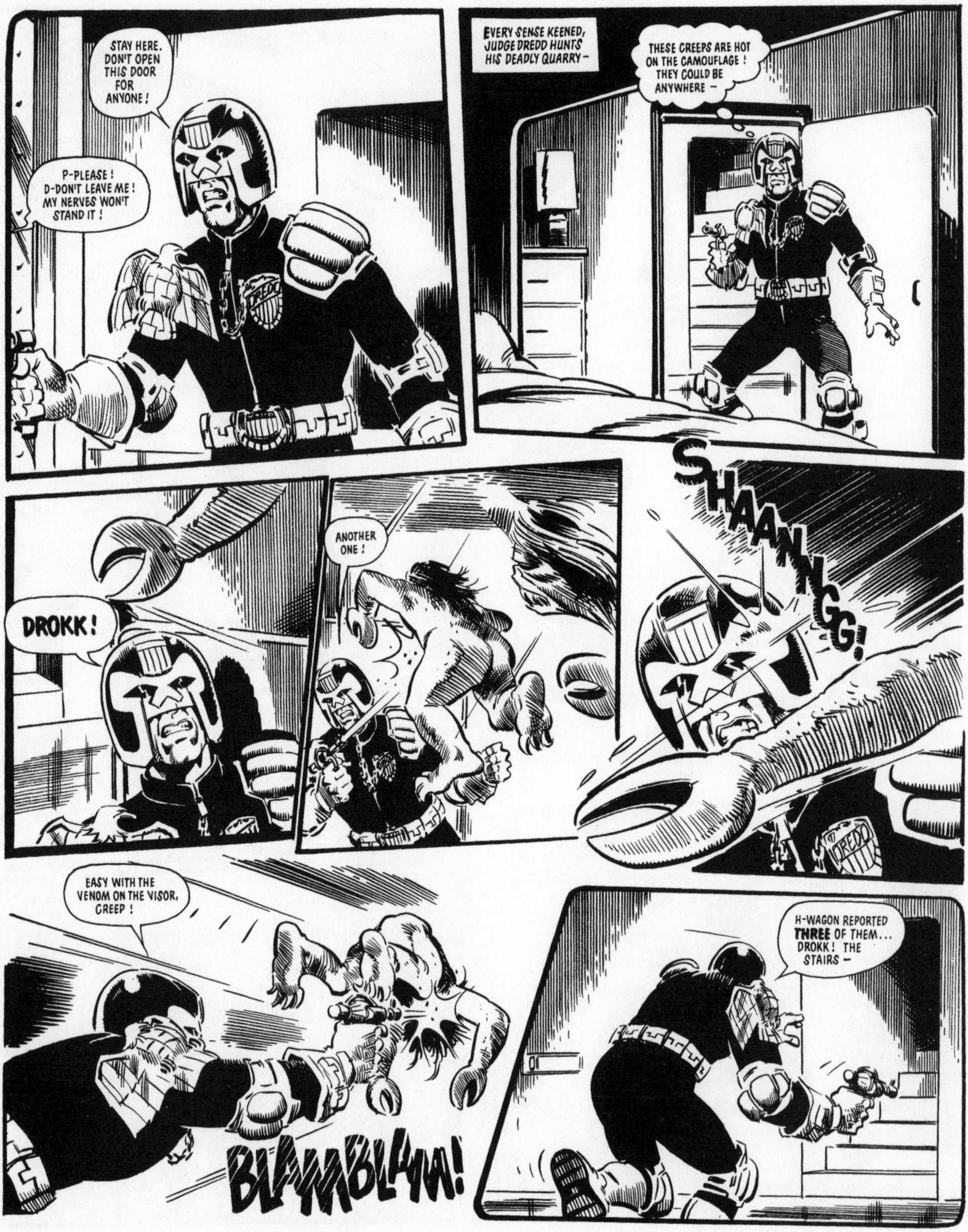
STAY HERE. DON'T OPEN THIS DOOR FOR ANYONE!
P-PLEASE! D-DON'T LEAVE ME! MY NERVES WON'T STAND IT!
EVERY SENSE KEENED, JUDGE DREDD HUNTS HIS DEADLY QUARRY –
THESE CREEPS ARE HOT ON THE CAMOUFLAGE! THEY COULD BE ANYWHERE –
DROKK!
ANOTHER ONE!
SHAANNGG!
EASY WITH THE VENOM ON THE VISOR, CREEP!
BLAMBLAM!
H-WAGON REPORTED THREE OF THEM... DROKK! THE STAIRS –

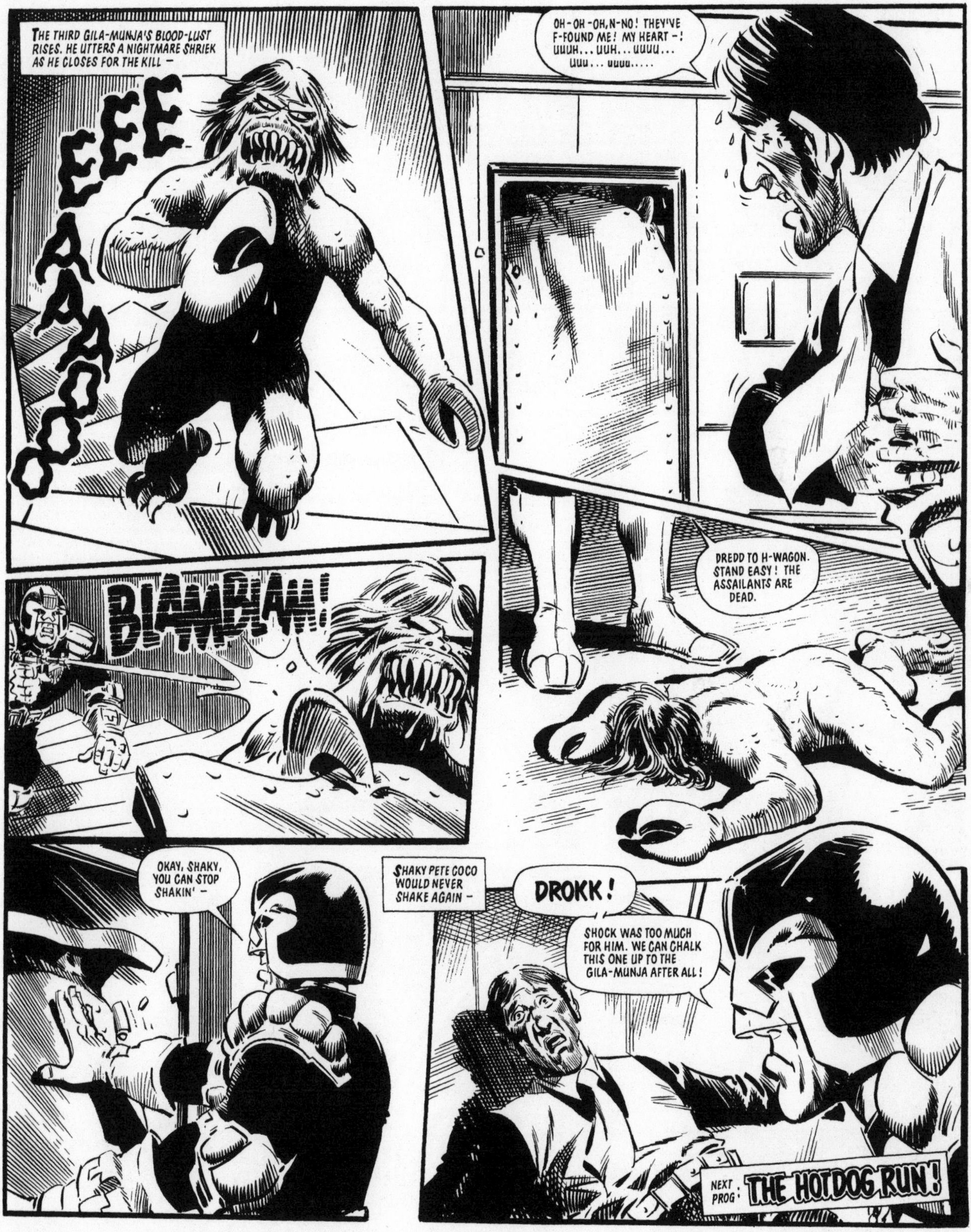
THE THIRD GILA-MUNJA'S BLOOD-LUST RISES. HE UTTERS A NIGHTMARE SHRIEK AS HE CLOSES FOR THE KILL –
EEEAAAOOOO
OH-OH-OH, N-NO! THEY'VE F-FOUND ME! MY HEART –! UUUH... UUH... UUUU... UUU... UUUU.....
BLAMBLAM!
DREDD TO H-WAGON. STAND EASY! THE ASSAILANTS ARE DEAD.
OKAY, SHAKY, YOU CAN STOP SHAKIN' –
SHAKY PETE COCO WOULD NEVER SHAKE AGAIN –
DROKK!
SHOCK WAS TOO MUCH FOR HIM. WE CAN CHALK THIS ONE UP TO THE GILA-MUNJA AFTER ALL!
NEXT PROG: THE HOTDOG RUN!

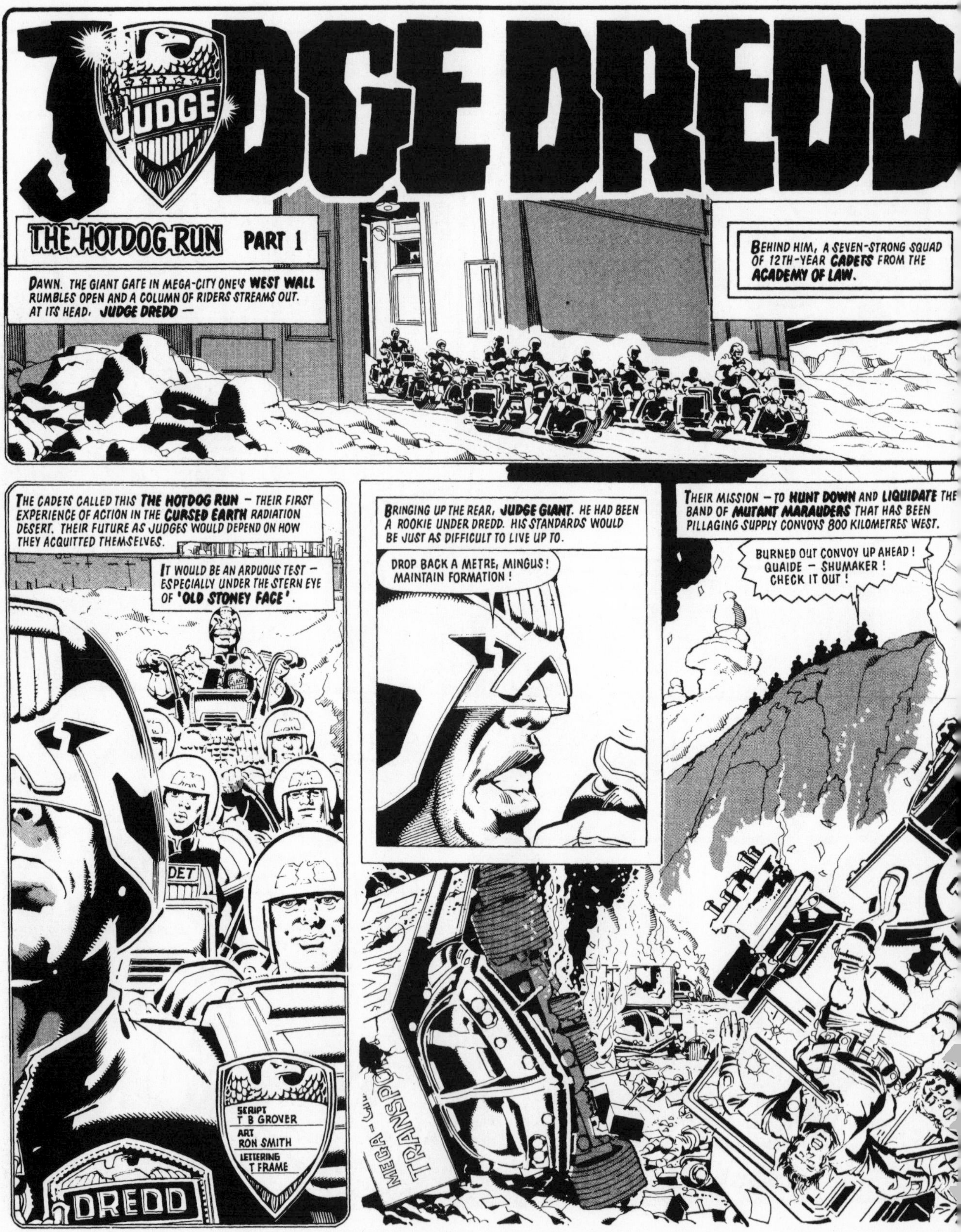
JUDGE DREDD
JUDGE
THE HOTDOG RUN PART 1
DAWN. THE GIANT GATE IN MEGA-CITY ONE'S WEST WALL RUMBLES OPEN AND A COLUMN OF RIDERS STREAMS OUT. AT ITS HEAD, JUDGE DREDD —
BEHIND HIM, A SEVEN-STRONG SQUAD OF 12TH-YEAR CADETS FROM THE ACADEMY OF LAW.
THE CADETS CALLED THIS THE HOTDOG RUN — THEIR FIRST EXPERIENCE OF ACTION IN THE CURSED EARTH RADIATION DESERT. THEIR FUTURE AS JUDGES WOULD DEPEND ON HOW THEY ACQUITTED THEMSELVES.
IT WOULD BE AN ARDUOUS TEST — ESPECIALLY UNDER THE STERN EYE OF 'OLD STONEY FACE'.
SCRIPT T B GROVER
ART RON SMITH
LETTERING T FRAME
DREDD
BRINGING UP THE REAR, JUDGE GIANT. HE HAD BEEN A ROOKIE UNDER DREDD. HIS STANDARDS WOULD BE JUST AS DIFFICULT TO LIVE UP TO.
DROP BACK A METRE, MINGUS! MAINTAIN FORMATION!
THEIR MISSION — TO HUNT DOWN AND LIQUIDATE THE BAND OF MUTANT MARAUDERS THAT HAS BEEN PILLAGING SUPPLY CONVOYS 800 KILOMETRES WEST.
BURNED OUT CONVOY UP AHEAD! QUAIDE — SHUMAKER! CHECK IT OUT!
MEGA-
TRANSPO

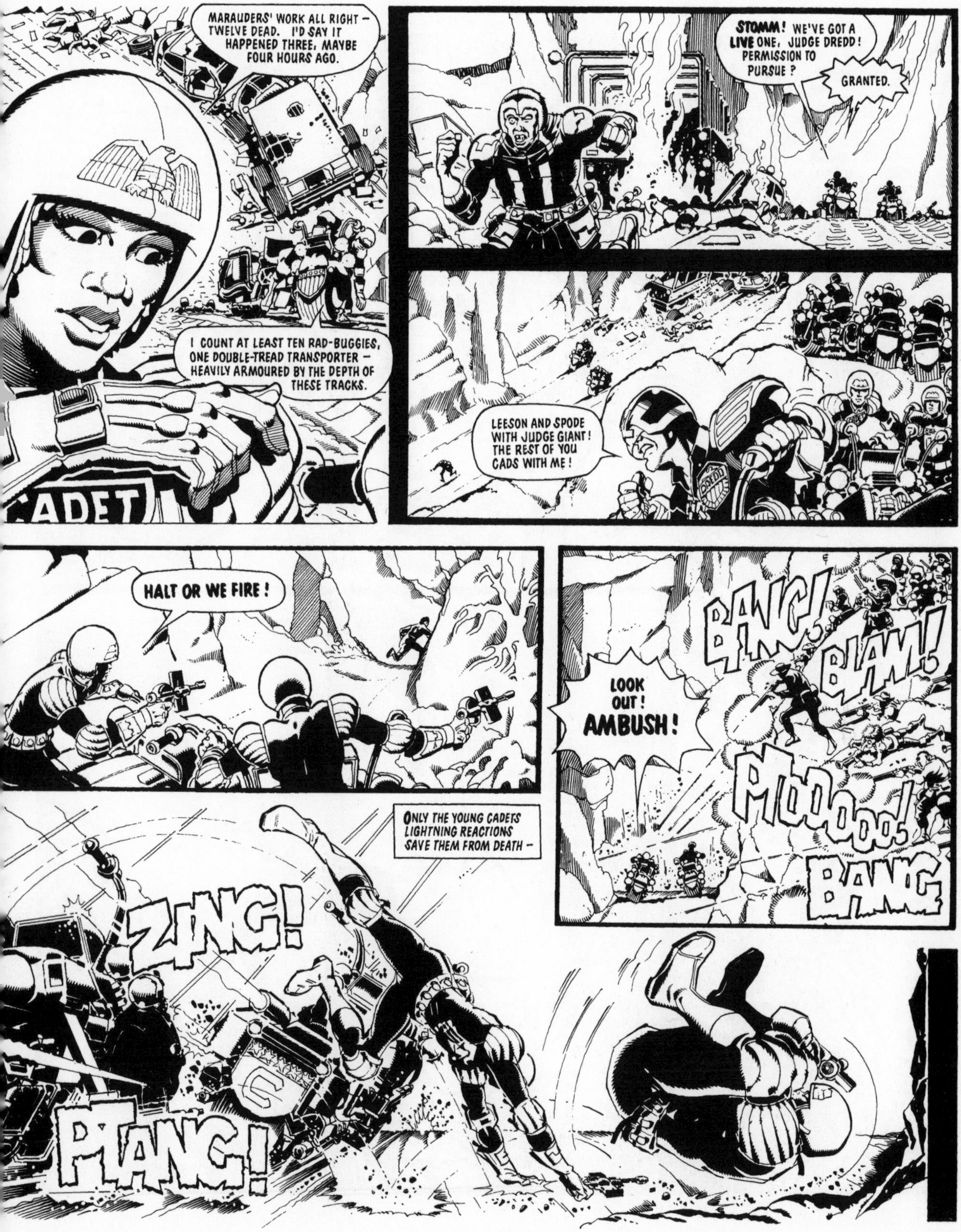

MARAUDERS' WORK ALL RIGHT — TWELVE DEAD. I'D SAY IT HAPPENED THREE, MAYBE FOUR HOURS AGO.
I COUNT AT LEAST TEN RAD-BUGGIES, ONE DOUBLE-TREAD TRANSPORTER — HEAVILY ARMOURED BY THE DEPTH OF THESE TRACKS.
CADET
STOMM! WE'VE GOT A LIVE ONE, JUDGE DREDD! PERMISSION TO PURSUE?
GRANTED.
LEESON AND SPODE WITH JUDGE GIANT! THE REST OF YOU CADS WITH ME!
HALT OR WE FIRE!
LOOK OUT! AMBUSH!
BANG!
BLAM!
PTOOOOOO!
BANG
ONLY THE YOUNG CADETS LIGHTNING REACTIONS SAVE THEM FROM DEATH —
ZING!
PTANG!

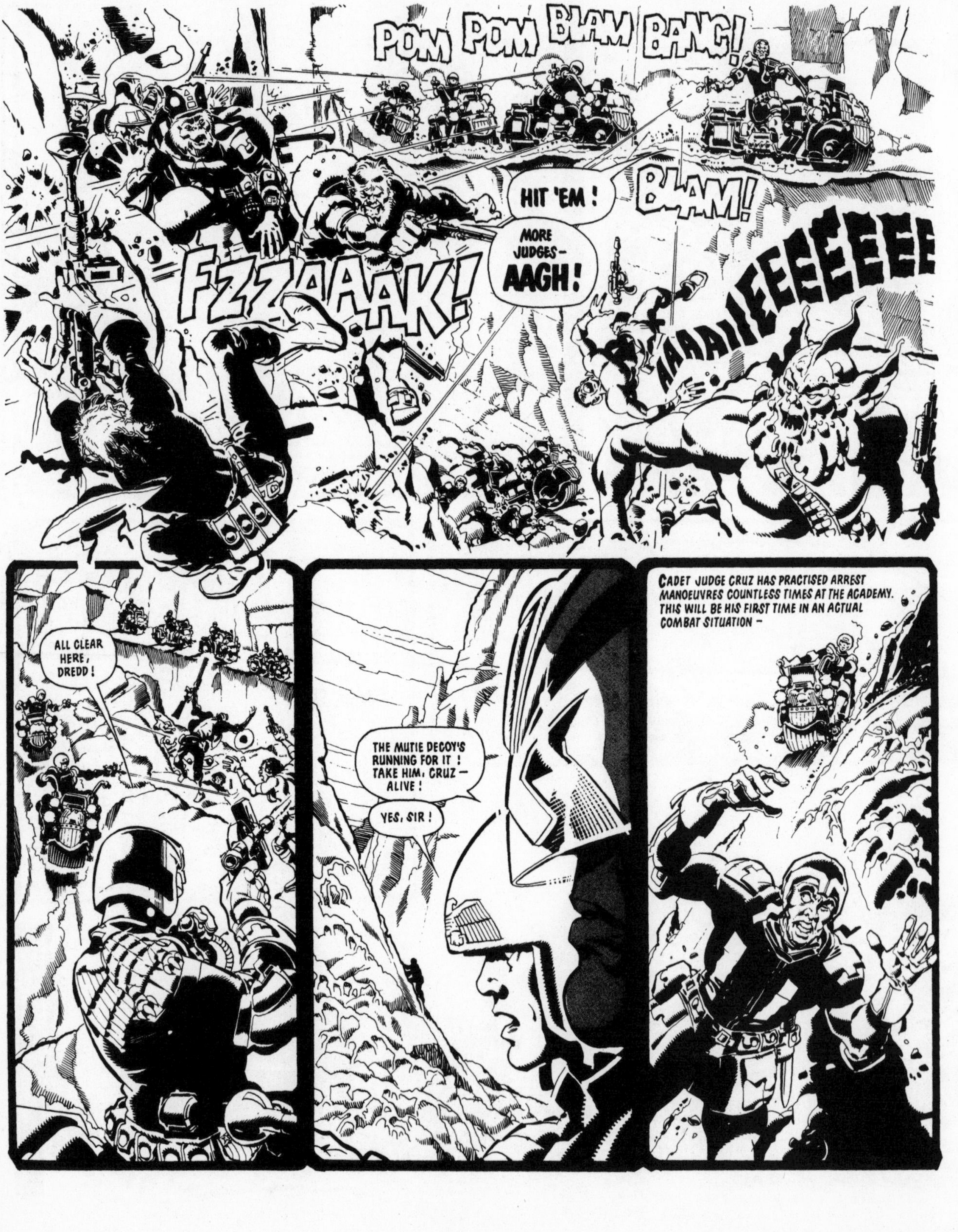
POM POM BLAM BANG!
HIT 'EM!
BLAM!
MORE JUDGES— AAGH!
FZZAAAK!
AAAAIIEEEEEEEE
ALL CLEAR HERE, DREDD!
THE MUTIE DECOY'S RUNNING FOR IT! TAKE HIM, CRUZ— ALIVE!
YES, SIR!
CADET JUDGE CRUZ HAS PRACTISED ARREST MANOEUVRES COUNTLESS TIMES AT THE ACADEMY. THIS WILL BE HIS FIRST TIME IN AN ACTUAL COMBAT SITUATION—

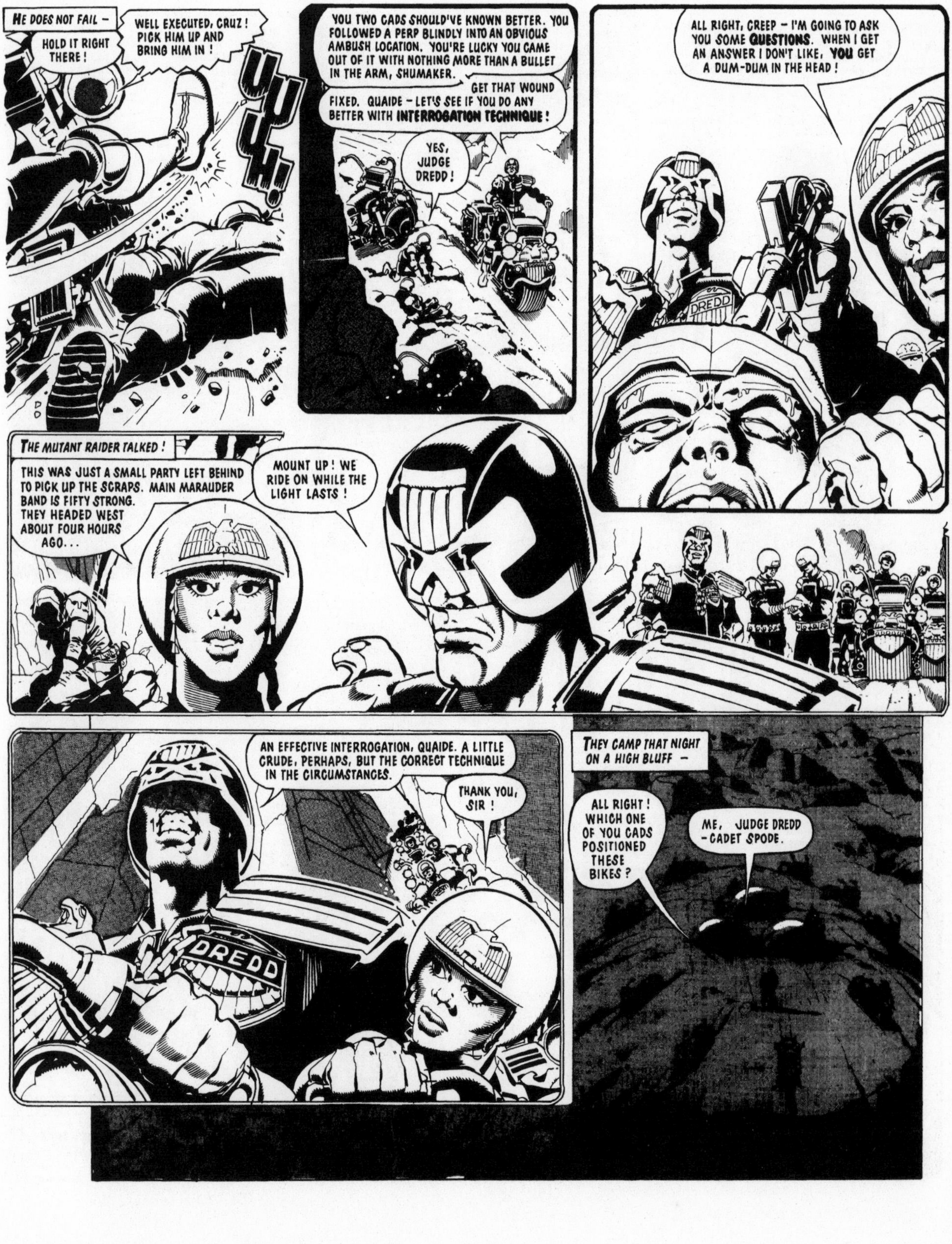
HE DOES NOT FAIL –
HOLD IT RIGHT THERE !
WELL EXECUTED, CRUZ ! PICK HIM UP AND BRING HIM IN !
UUUH !
YOU TWO CADS SHOULD'VE KNOWN BETTER. YOU FOLLOWED A PERP BLINDLY INTO AN OBVIOUS AMBUSH LOCATION. YOU'RE LUCKY YOU CAME OUT OF IT WITH NOTHING MORE THAN A BULLET IN THE ARM, SHUMAKER.
GET THAT WOUND FIXED. QUAIDE – LET'S SEE IF YOU DO ANY BETTER WITH INTERROGATION TECHNIQUE !
YES, JUDGE DREDD !
ALL RIGHT, CREEP – I'M GOING TO ASK YOU SOME QUESTIONS. WHEN I GET AN ANSWER I DON'T LIKE, YOU GET A DUM-DUM IN THE HEAD !
DREDD
THE MUTANT RAIDER TALKED !
THIS WAS JUST A SMALL PARTY LEFT BEHIND TO PICK UP THE SCRAPS. MAIN MARAUDER BAND IS FIFTY STRONG. THEY HEADED WEST ABOUT FOUR HOURS AGO...
MOUNT UP ! WE RIDE ON WHILE THE LIGHT LASTS !
AN EFFECTIVE INTERROGATION, QUAIDE. A LITTLE CRUDE, PERHAPS, BUT THE CORRECT TECHNIQUE IN THE CIRCUMSTANCES.
THANK YOU, SIR !
DREDD
THEY CAMP THAT NIGHT ON A HIGH BLUFF –
ALL RIGHT ! WHICH ONE OF YOU CADS POSITIONED THESE BIKES ?
ME, JUDGE DREDD – CADET SPODE.

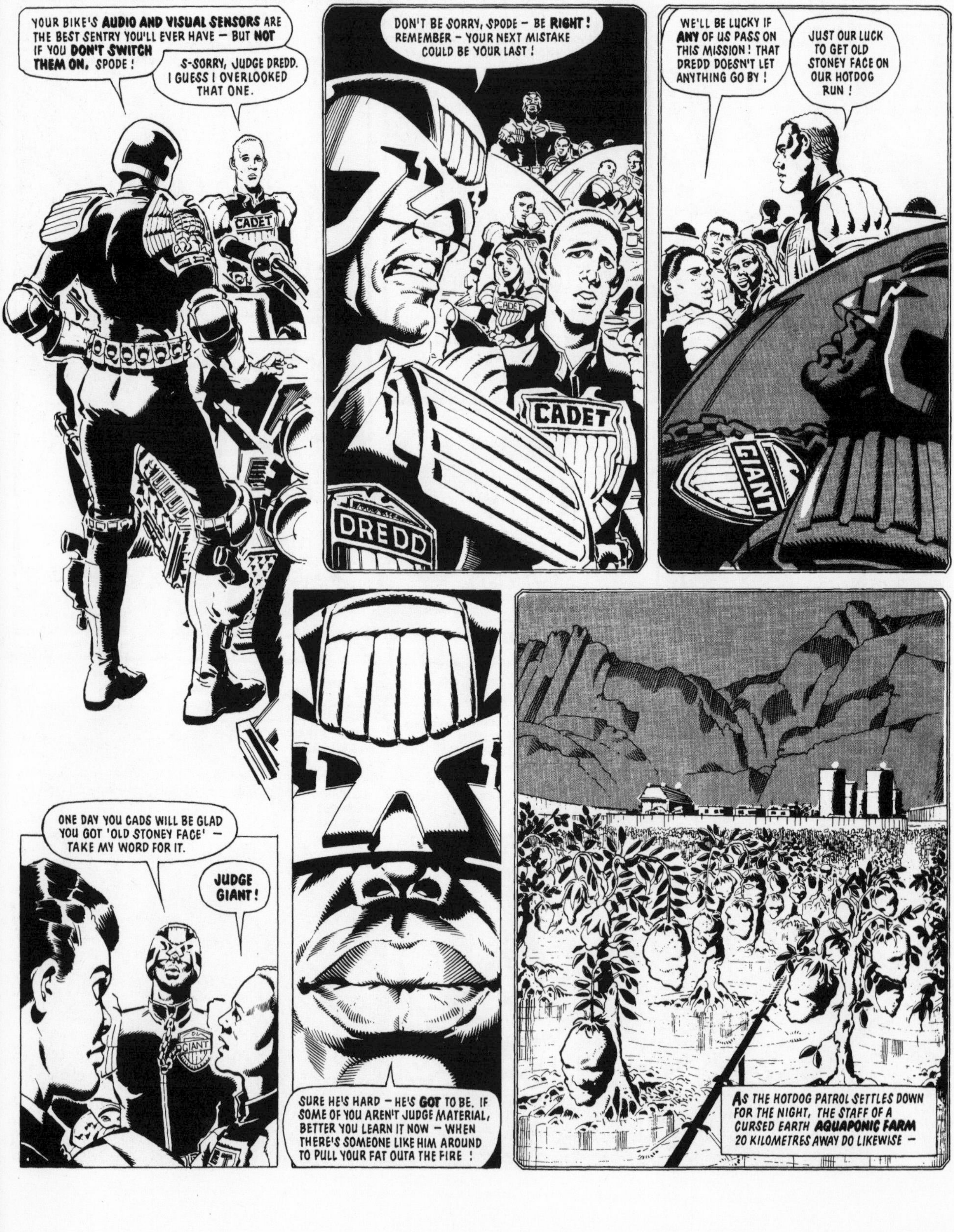

YOUR BIKE'S **AUDIO AND VISUAL SENSORS** ARE THE BEST SENTRY YOU'LL EVER HAVE — BUT **NOT** IF YOU **DON'T SWITCH THEM ON**, SPODE!
S-SORRY, JUDGE DREDD. I GUESS I OVERLOOKED THAT ONE.
DON'T BE SORRY, SPODE — BE **RIGHT**! REMEMBER — YOUR NEXT MISTAKE COULD BE YOUR LAST!
DREDD
CADET
WE'LL BE LUCKY IF **ANY** OF US PASS ON THIS MISSION! THAT DREDD DOESN'T LET ANYTHING GO BY!
JUST OUR LUCK TO GET OLD STONEY FACE ON OUR HOTDOG RUN!
GIANT
ONE DAY YOU CADS WILL BE GLAD YOU GOT 'OLD STONEY FACE' — TAKE MY WORD FOR IT.
JUDGE GIANT!
SURE HE'S HARD — HE'S **GOT** TO BE. IF SOME OF YOU AREN'T JUDGE MATERIAL, BETTER YOU LEARN IT NOW — WHEN THERE'S SOMEONE LIKE HIM AROUND TO PULL YOUR FAT OUTA THE FIRE!
AS THE HOTDOG PATROL SETTLES DOWN FOR THE NIGHT, THE STAFF OF A CURSED EARTH **AQUAPONIC FARM** 20 KILOMETRES AWAY DO LIKEWISE —

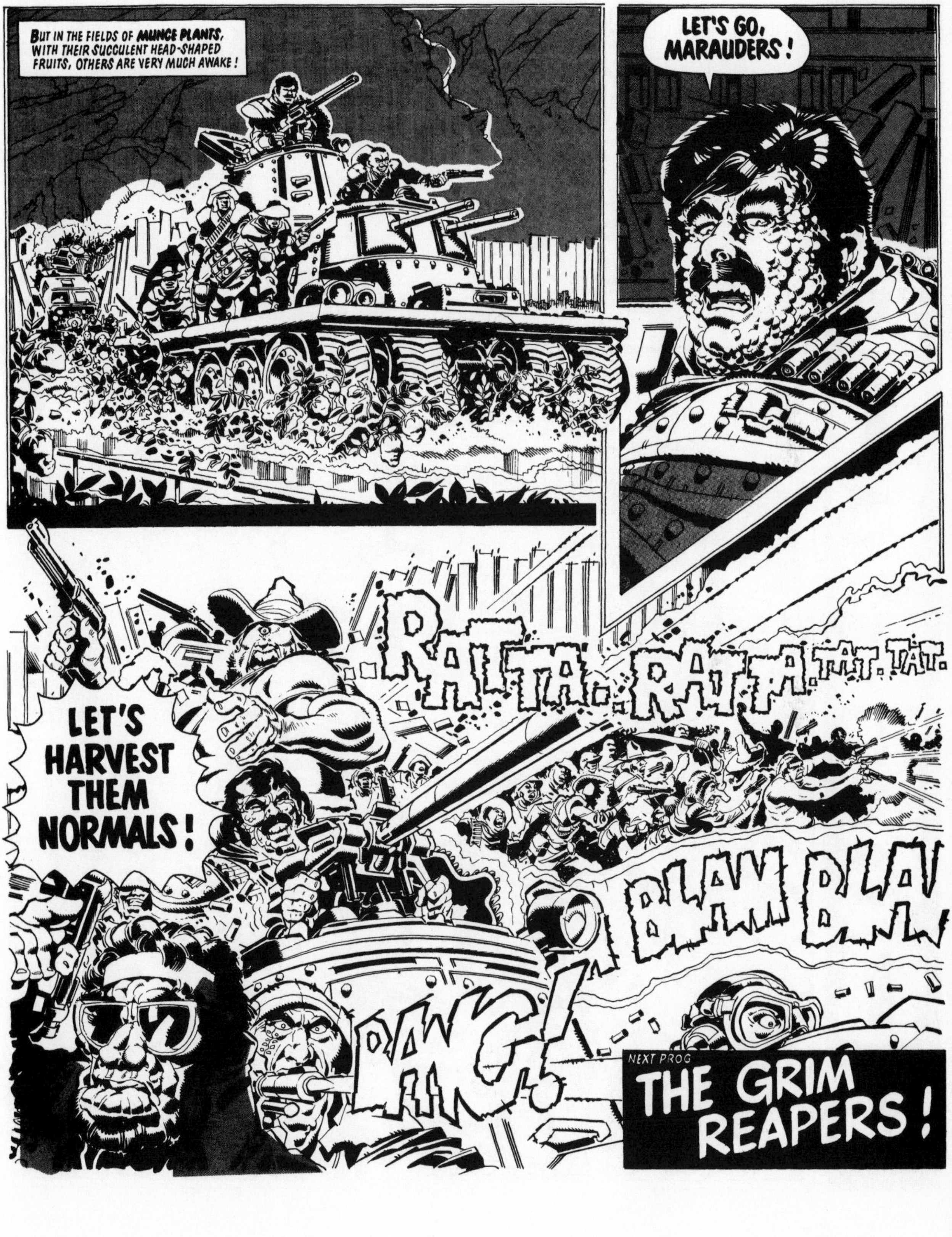
BUT IN THE FIELDS OF MUNCE PLANTS, WITH THEIR SUCCULENT HEAD-SHAPED FRUITS, OTHERS ARE VERY MUCH AWAKE!
LET'S GO, MARAUDERS!
LET'S HARVEST THEM NORMALS!
RAT-TA.. RAT-TA.. TAT. TAT.
BLAM BLAM
BANG!
NEXT PROG
THE GRIM REAPERS!

THE HOTDOG RUN PART III

SCRIPT T B GROVER
ART RON SMITH
LETTERING T FRAME

MIDNIGHT. RUTHLESS **MUTANT MARAUDERS** PLOUGH THROUGH THE MUNCE FIELDS SURROUNDING A **CURSED EARTH** AQUAPONICS FARM —

HIT 'EM MARAUDERS! LET'S HARVEST THEM NORMALS!

PT-OOOOO

BLAM·BLAM!!

FFWHUMP

REAP 'EM, BOYS! REAP 'EM!

IT'S SCABBY HAYES AND HIS MUTANT MARAUDERS! WE'RE DEAD MEN — AAAGGH!

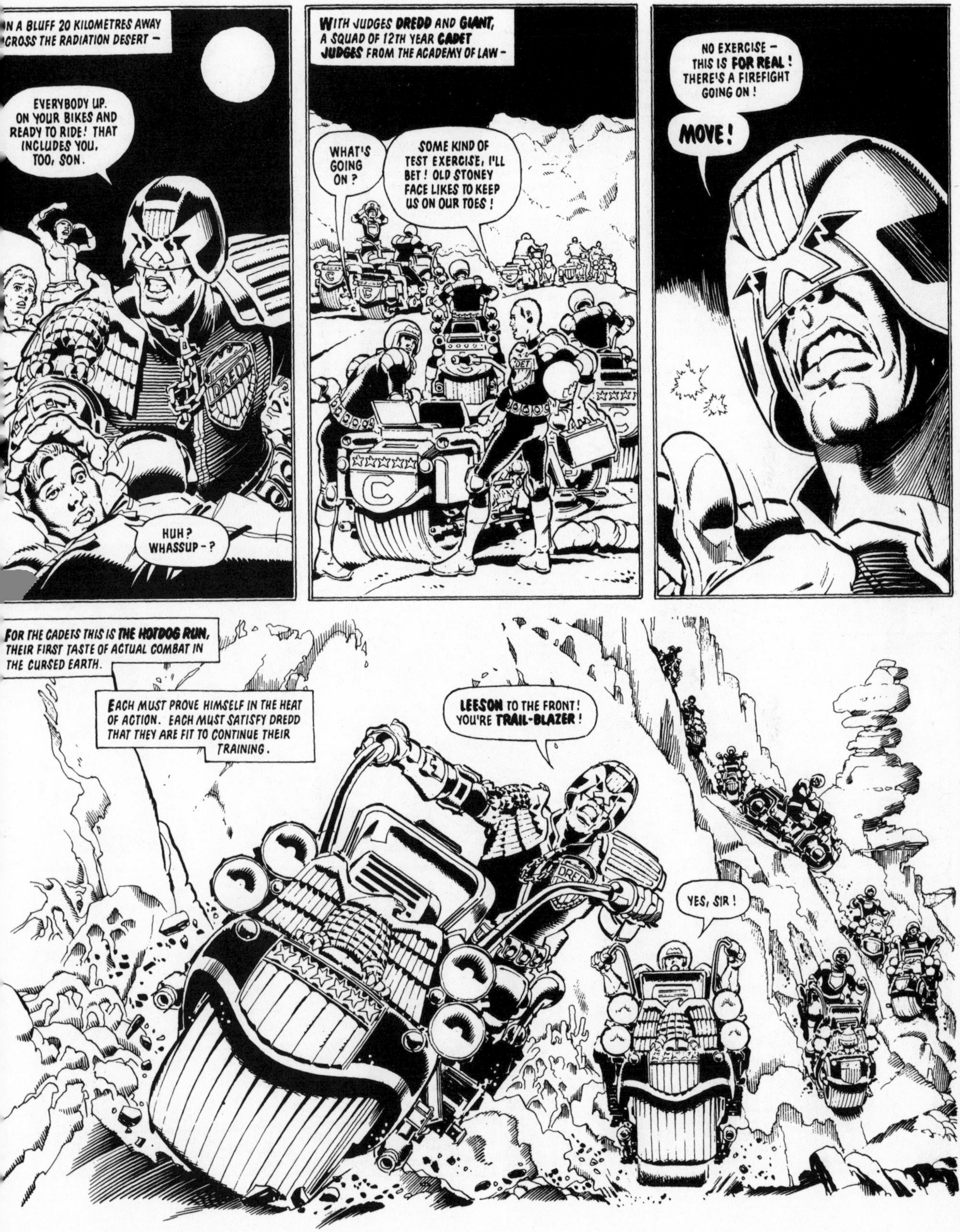
N A BLUFF 20 KILOMETRES AWAY
CROSS THE RADIATION DESERT –
EVERYBODY UP. ON YOUR BIKES AND READY TO RIDE! THAT INCLUDES YOU, TOO, SON.
HUH? WHASSUP –?
WITH JUDGES DREDD AND GIANT, A SQUAD OF 12TH YEAR CADET JUDGES FROM THE ACADEMY OF LAW –
WHAT'S GOING ON?
SOME KIND OF TEST EXERCISE, I'LL BET! OLD STONEY FACE LIKES TO KEEP US ON OUR TOES!
NO EXERCISE – THIS IS FOR REAL! THERE'S A FIREFIGHT GOING ON!
MOVE!
FOR THE CADETS THIS IS THE HOTDOG RUN, THEIR FIRST TASTE OF ACTUAL COMBAT IN THE CURSED EARTH.
EACH MUST PROVE HIMSELF IN THE HEAT OF ACTION. EACH MUST SATISFY DREDD THAT THEY ARE FIT TO CONTINUE THEIR TRAINING.
LEESON TO THE FRONT! YOU'RE TRAIL-BLAZER!
YES, SIR!

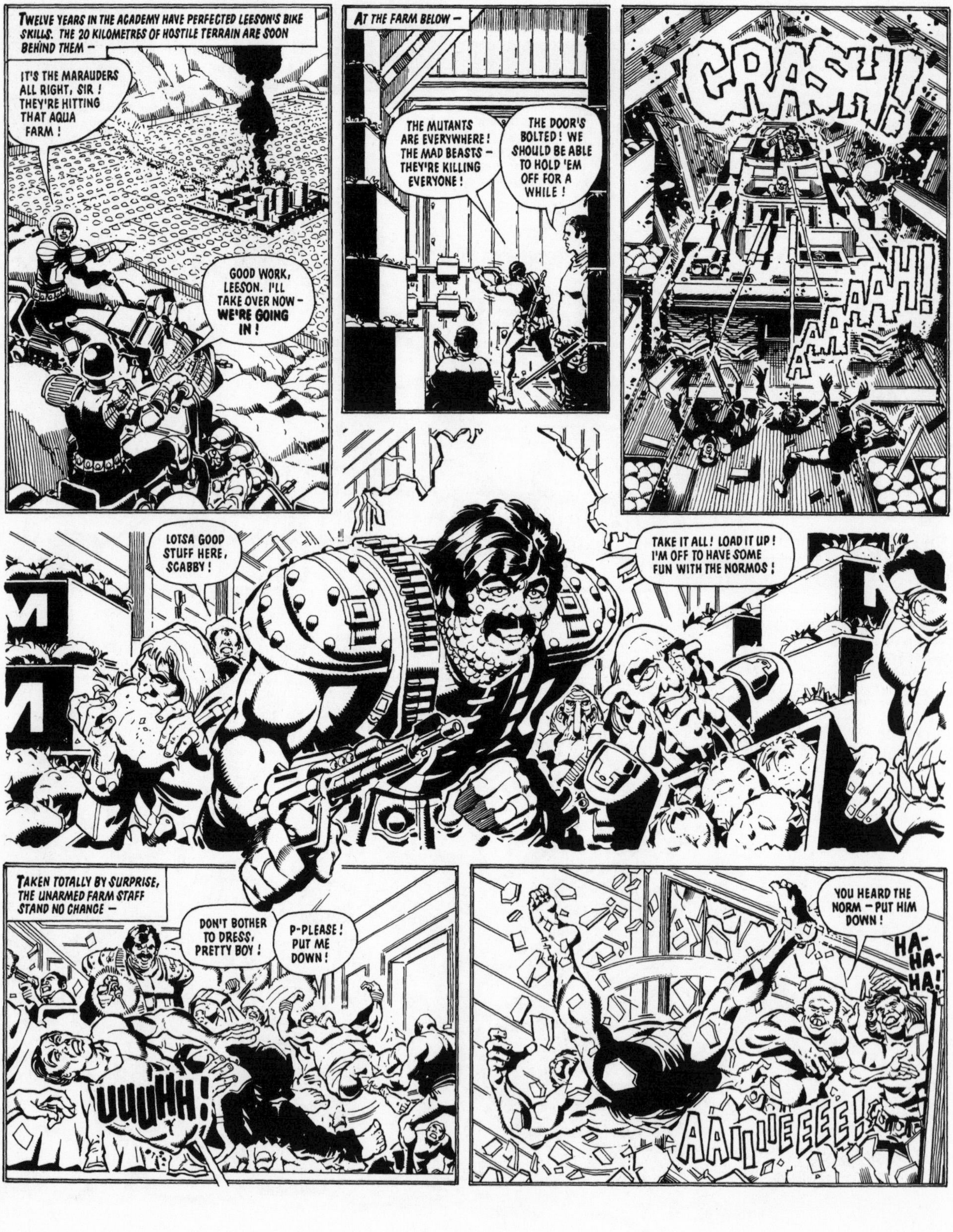
TWELVE YEARS IN THE ACADEMY HAVE PERFECTED LEESON'S BIKE SKILLS. THE 20 KILOMETRES OF HOSTILE TERRAIN ARE SOON BEHIND THEM –
IT'S THE MARAUDERS ALL RIGHT, SIR! THEY'RE HITTING THAT AQUA FARM!
GOOD WORK, LEESON. I'LL TAKE OVER NOW – WE'RE GOING IN!
AT THE FARM BELOW –
THE MUTANTS ARE EVERYWHERE! THE MAD BEASTS – THEY'RE KILLING EVERYONE!
THE DOOR'S BOLTED! WE SHOULD BE ABLE TO HOLD 'EM OFF FOR A WHILE!
CRASH!
AAAAH!
LOTSA GOOD STUFF HERE, SCABBY!
TAKE IT ALL! LOAD IT UP! I'M OFF TO HAVE SOME FUN WITH THE NORMOS!
TAKEN TOTALLY BY SURPRISE, THE UNARMED FARM STAFF STAND NO CHANCE –
DON'T BOTHER TO DRESS, PRETTY BOY!
P-PLEASE! PUT ME DOWN!
UUUHH!
YOU HEARD THE NORM – PUT HIM DOWN!
HA-HA-HA!
AAIIIEEEE!

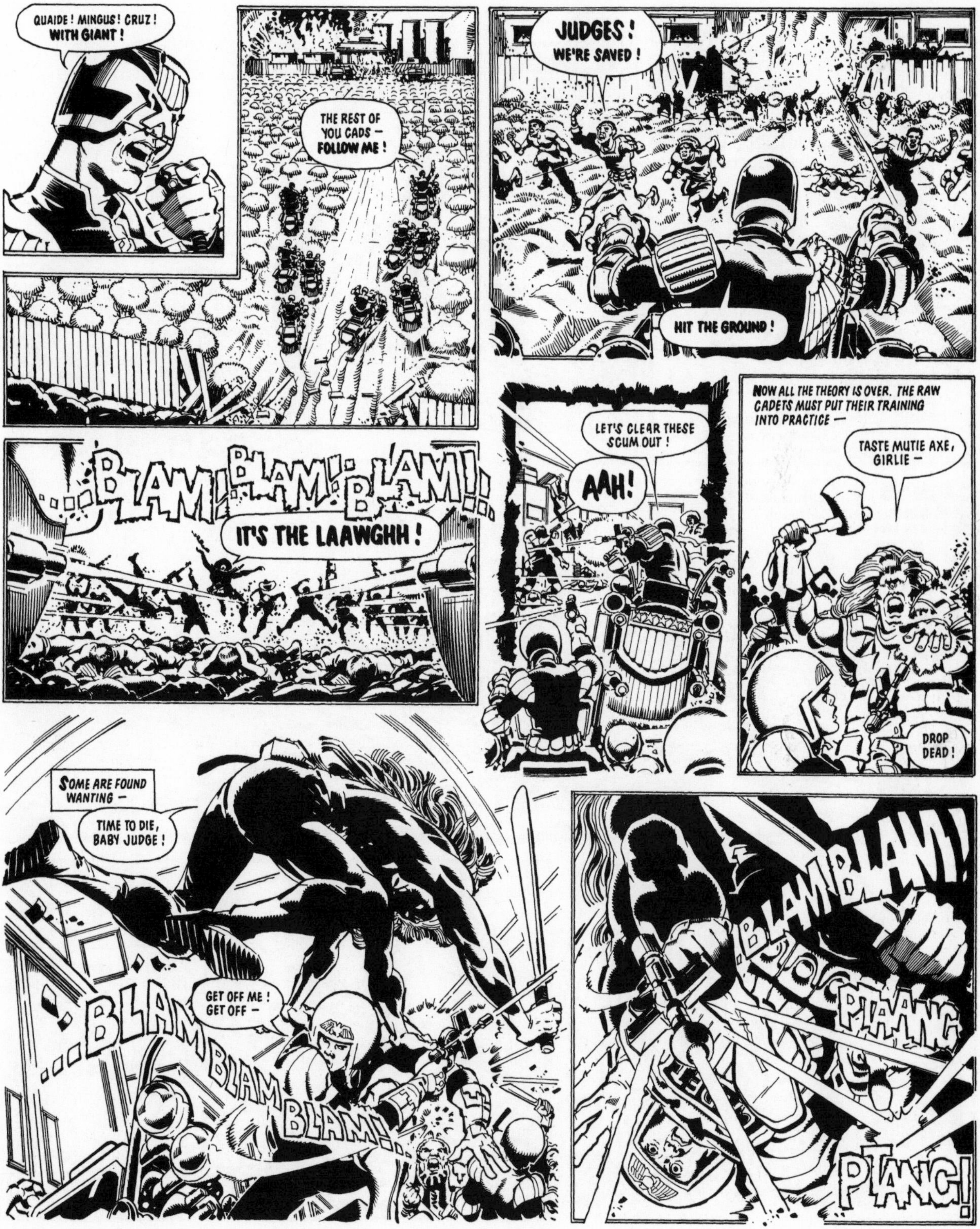
QUAIDE! MINGUS! CRUZ! WITH GIANT!
THE REST OF YOU CADS — FOLLOW ME!
JUDGES! WE'RE SAVED!
HIT THE GROUND!
...BLAM! BLAM! BLAM!!
IT'S THE LAAWGHH!
LET'S CLEAR THESE SCUM OUT!
AAH!
NOW ALL THE THEORY IS OVER. THE RAW CADETS MUST PUT THEIR TRAINING INTO PRACTICE —
TASTE MUTIE AXE, GIRLIE —
DROP DEAD!
SOME ARE FOUND WANTING —
TIME TO DIE, BABY JUDGE!
GET OFF ME! GET OFF —
...BLAM BLAM BLAM!...
BLAM BLAM!
PTAANG
PTANG!

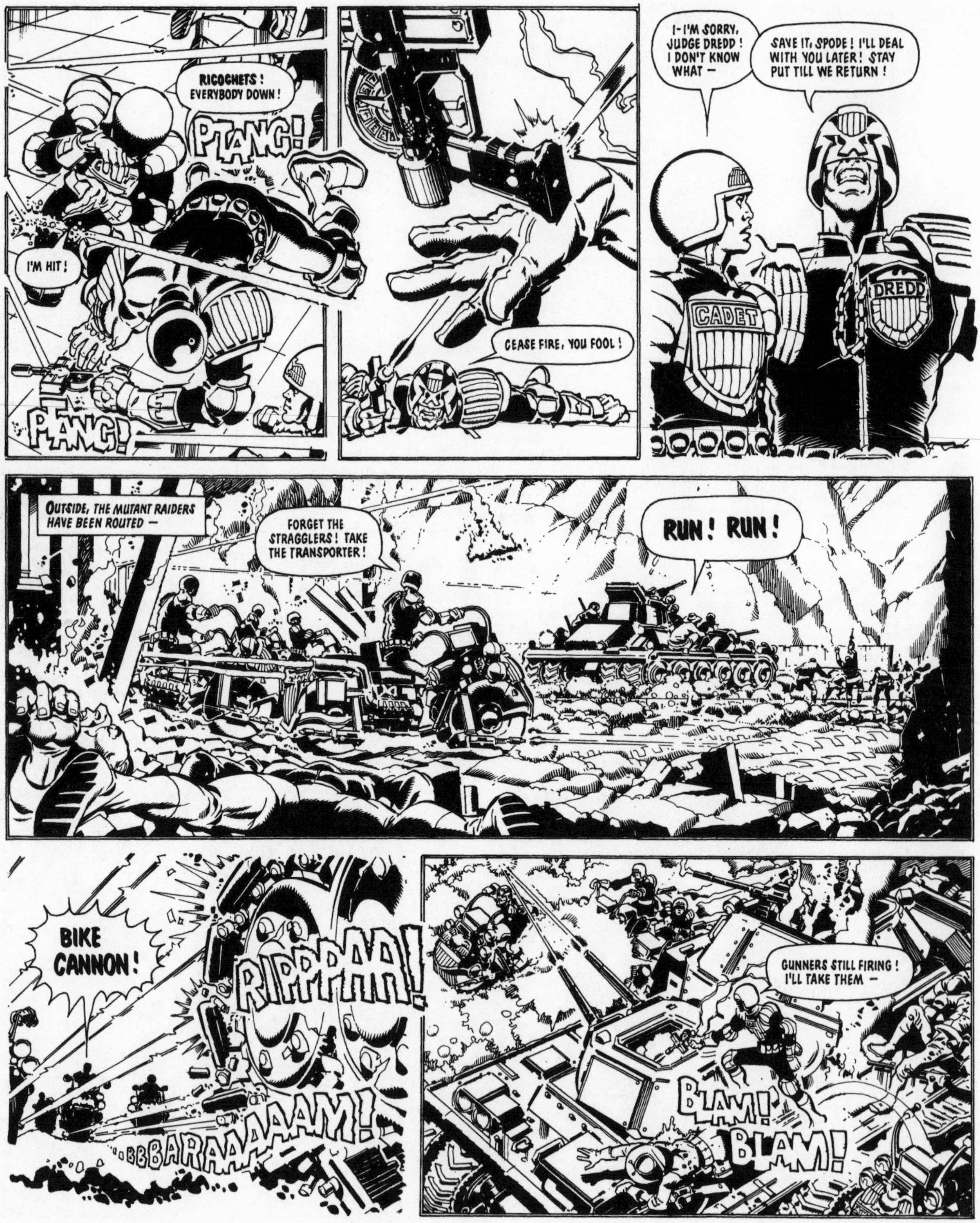
RICOCHETS ! EVERYBODY DOWN !
PTANG!
I'M HIT !
PTANG!
CEASE FIRE, YOU FOOL !
I-I'M SORRY, JUDGE DREDD ! I DON'T KNOW WHAT –
SAVE IT, SPODE ! I'LL DEAL WITH YOU LATER ! STAY PUT TILL WE RETURN !
CADET
DREDD
OUTSIDE, THE MUTANT RAIDERS HAVE BEEN ROUTED –
FORGET THE STRAGGLERS ! TAKE THE TRANSPORTER !
RUN ! RUN !
BIKE CANNON !
RIPPPAA!
BBBARAAAAAAM!
GUNNERS STILL FIRING ! I'LL TAKE THEM –
BLAM!
BLAM!

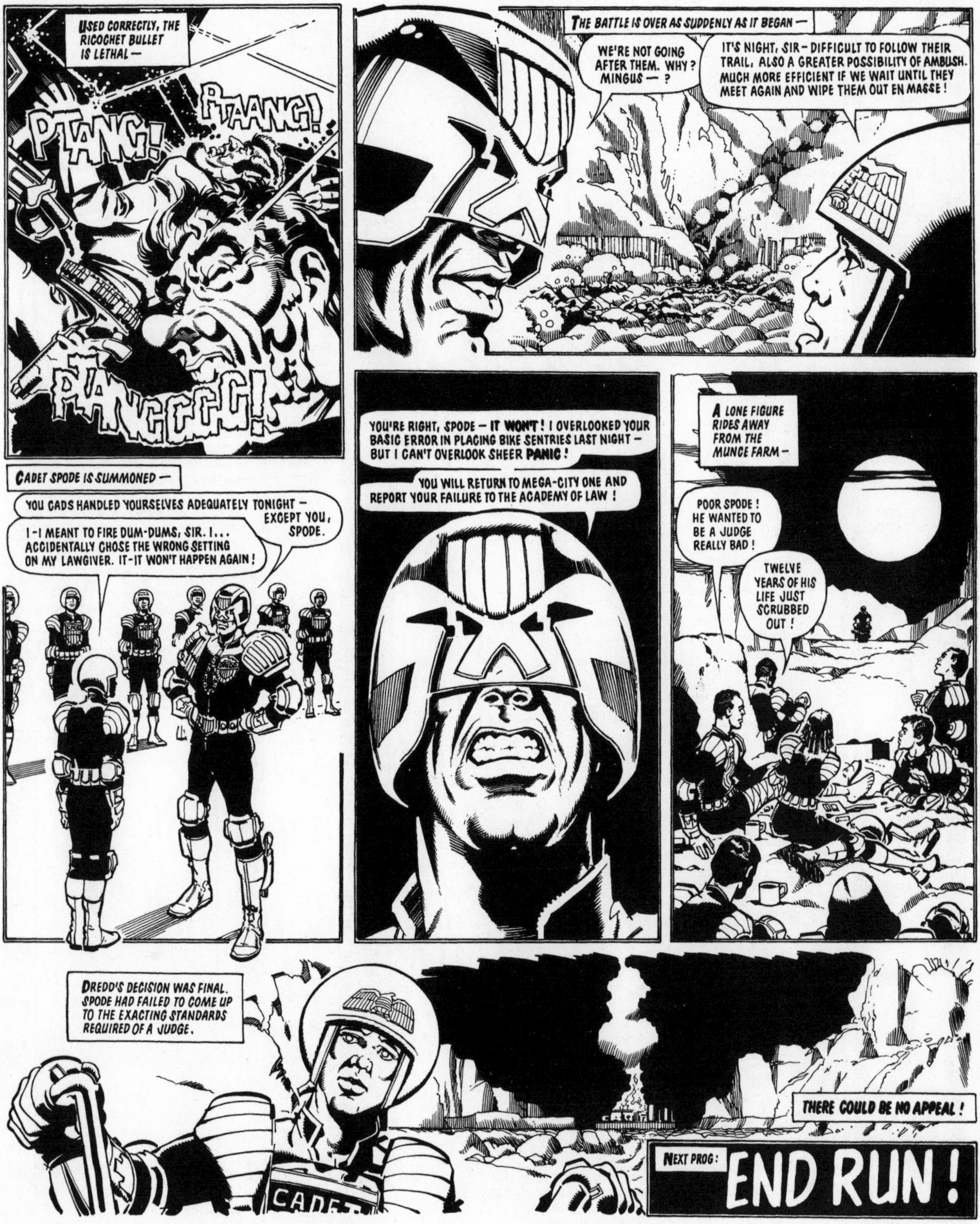

USED CORRECTLY, THE RICOCHET BULLET IS LETHAL —
PTANG!
PTAANG!
PTANGGGG!
THE BATTLE IS OVER AS SUDDENLY AS IT BEGAN —
WE'RE NOT GOING AFTER THEM. WHY? MINGUS — ?
IT'S NIGHT, SIR — DIFFICULT TO FOLLOW THEIR TRAIL, ALSO A GREATER POSSIBILITY OF AMBUSH. MUCH MORE EFFICIENT IF WE WAIT UNTIL THEY MEET AGAIN AND WIPE THEM OUT EN MASSE!
CADET SPODE IS SUMMONED —
YOU CADS HANDLED YOURSELVES ADEQUATELY TONIGHT — EXCEPT YOU, SPODE.
I-I MEANT TO FIRE DUM-DUMS, SIR. I... ACCIDENTALLY CHOSE THE WRONG SETTING ON MY LAWGIVER. IT-IT WON'T HAPPEN AGAIN!
YOU'RE RIGHT, SPODE — IT WON'T! I OVERLOOKED YOUR BASIC ERROR IN PLACING BIKE SENTRIES LAST NIGHT — BUT I CAN'T OVERLOOK SHEER PANIC!
YOU WILL RETURN TO MEGA-CITY ONE AND REPORT YOUR FAILURE TO THE ACADEMY OF LAW!
A LONE FIGURE RIDES AWAY FROM THE MUNCE FARM —
POOR SPODE! HE WANTED TO BE A JUDGE REALLY BAD!
TWELVE YEARS OF HIS LIFE JUST SCRUBBED OUT!
DREDD'S DECISION WAS FINAL. SPODE HAD FAILED TO COME UP TO THE EXACTING STANDARDS REQUIRED OF A JUDGE.
THERE COULD BE NO APPEAL!
CADET
NEXT PROG: END RUN!

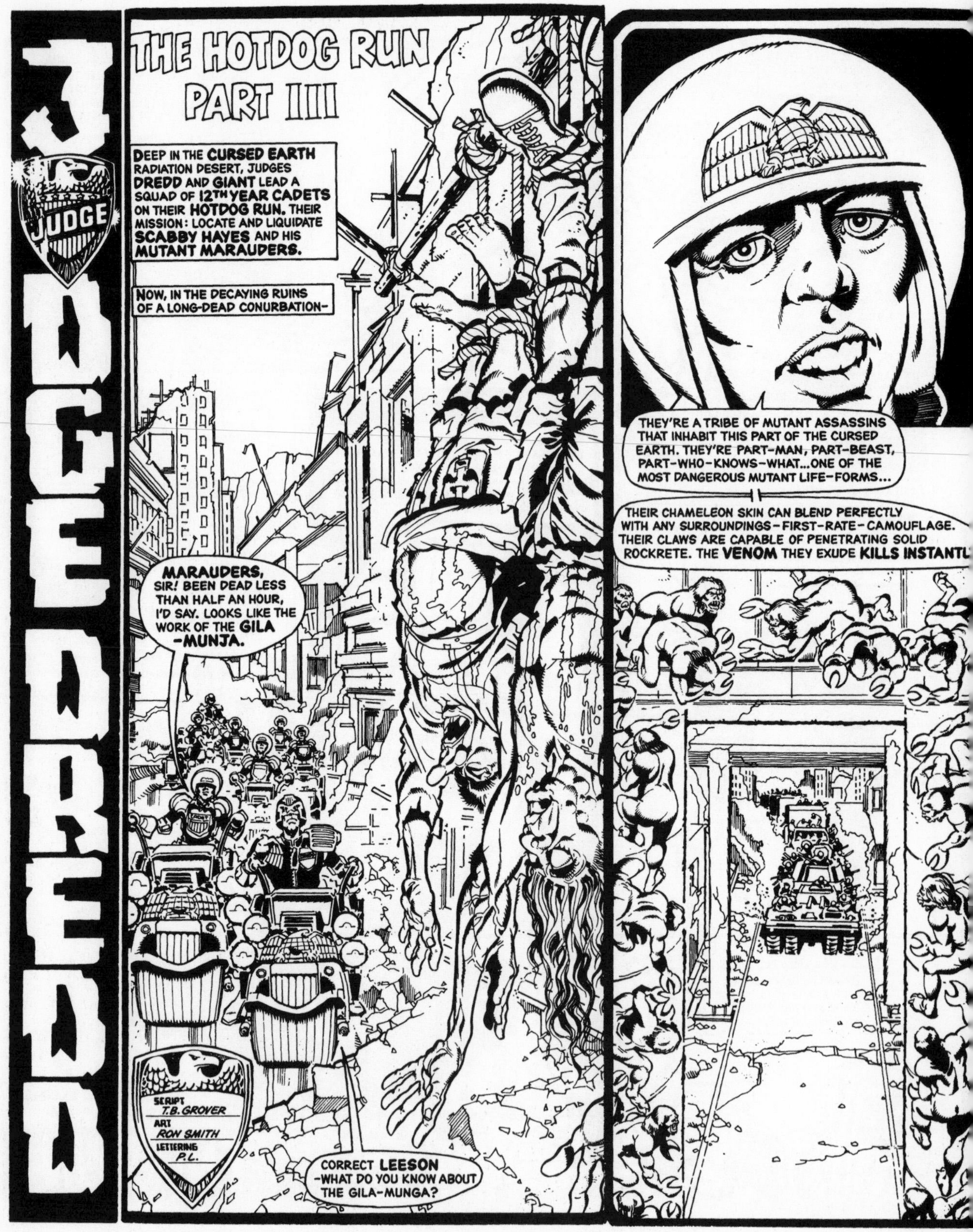
JUDGE DREDD
THE HOTDOG RUN
PART IIII
DEEP IN THE CURSED EARTH RADIATION DESERT, JUDGES DREDD AND GIANT LEAD A SQUAD OF 12TH YEAR CADETS ON THEIR HOTDOG RUN. THEIR MISSION: LOCATE AND LIQUIDATE SCABBY HAYES AND HIS MUTANT MARAUDERS.
NOW, IN THE DECAYING RUINS OF A LONG-DEAD CONURBATION-
MARAUDERS, SIR! BEEN DEAD LESS THAN HALF AN HOUR, I'D SAY. LOOKS LIKE THE WORK OF THE GILA-MUNJA.
SCRIPT T.B. GROVER
ART RON SMITH
LETTERING P.L.
CORRECT LEESON -WHAT DO YOU KNOW ABOUT THE GILA-MUNGA?
THEY'RE A TRIBE OF MUTANT ASSASSINS THAT INHABIT THIS PART OF THE CURSED EARTH. THEY'RE PART-MAN, PART-BEAST, PART-WHO-KNOWS-WHAT...ONE OF THE MOST DANGEROUS MUTANT LIFE-FORMS...
THEIR CHAMELEON SKIN CAN BLEND PERFECTLY WITH ANY SURROUNDINGS-FIRST-RATE-CAMOUFLAGE. THEIR CLAWS ARE CAPABLE OF PENETRATING SOLID ROCKRETE. THE VENOM THEY EXUDE KILLS INSTANTL

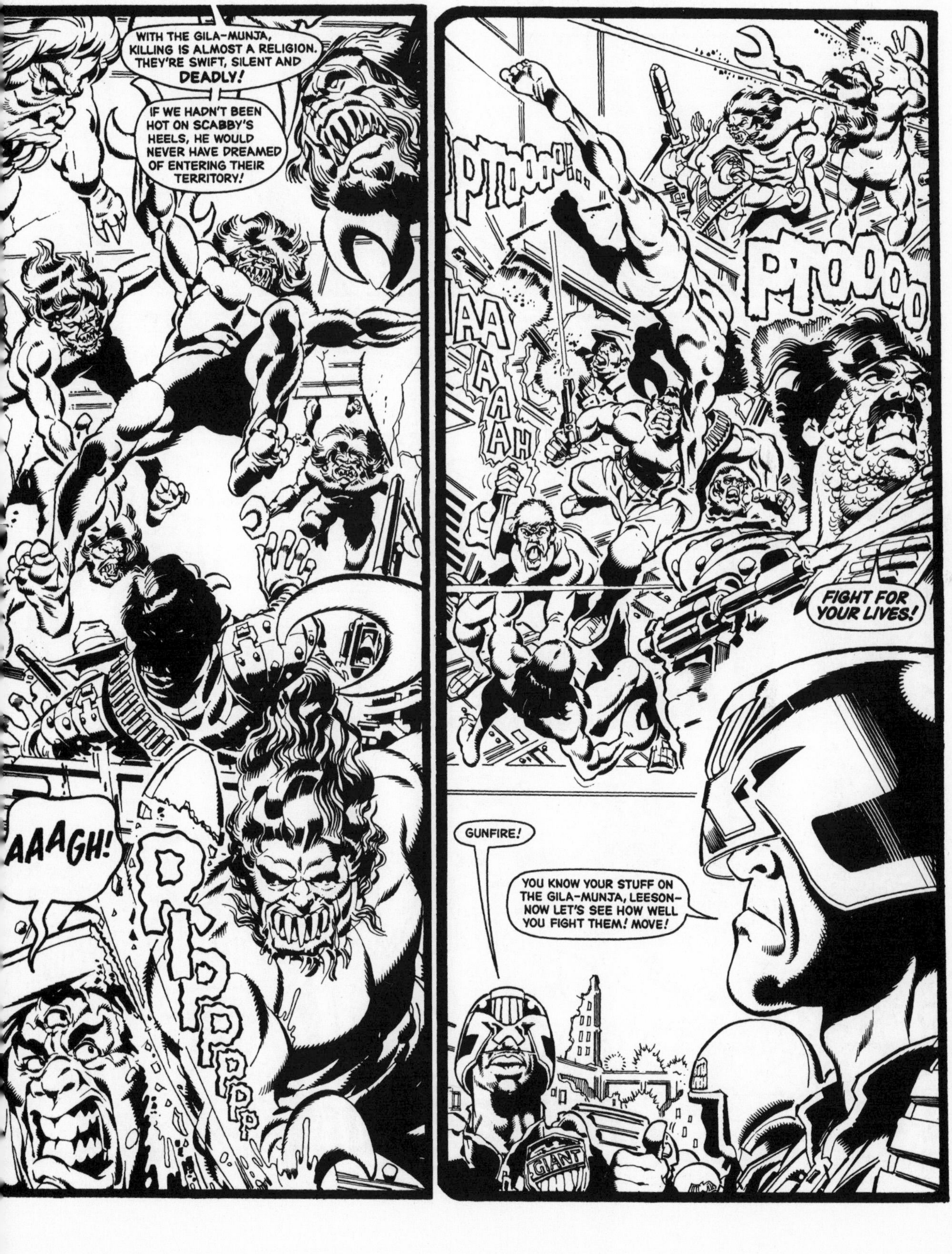
WITH THE GILA-MUNJA, KILLING IS ALMOST A RELIGION. THEY'RE SWIFT, SILENT AND DEADLY!
IF WE HADN'T BEEN HOT ON SCABBY'S HEELS, HE WOULD NEVER HAVE DREAMED OF ENTERING THEIR TERRITORY!
AAAGH!
PTOOOP!...
FIGHT FOR YOUR LIVES!
GUNFIRE!
YOU KNOW YOUR STUFF ON THE GILA-MUNJA, LEESON-NOW LET'S SEE HOW WELL YOU FIGHT THEM! MOVE!
GIANT

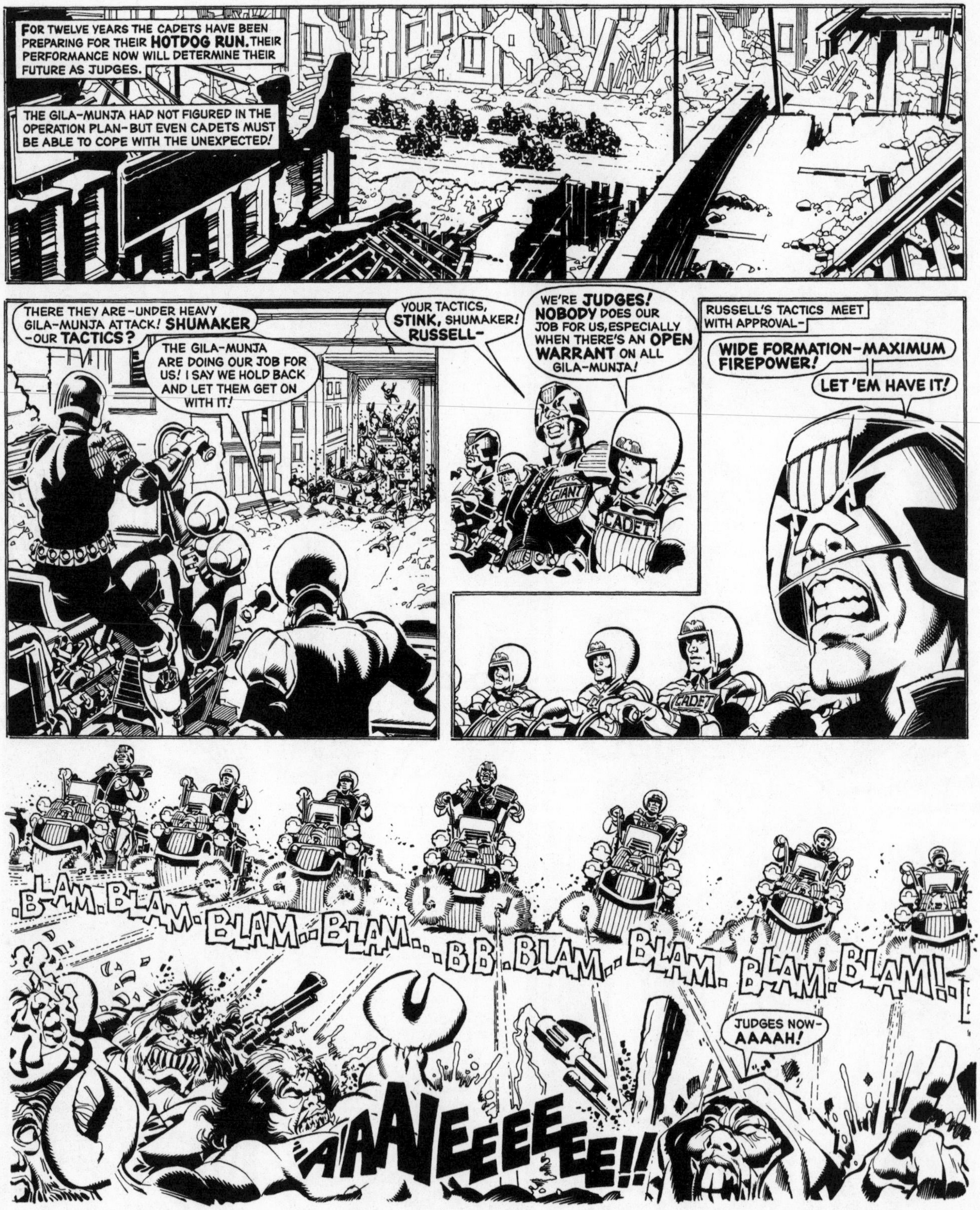
FOR TWELVE YEARS THE CADETS HAVE BEEN PREPARING FOR THEIR HOTDOG RUN. THEIR PERFORMANCE NOW WILL DETERMINE THEIR FUTURE AS JUDGES.
THE GILA-MUNJA HAD NOT FIGURED IN THE OPERATION PLAN- BUT EVEN CADETS MUST BE ABLE TO COPE WITH THE UNEXPECTED!
THERE THEY ARE-UNDER HEAVY GILA-MUNJA ATTACK! SHUMAKER -OUR TACTICS?
THE GILA-MUNJA ARE DOING OUR JOB FOR US! I SAY WE HOLD BACK AND LET THEM GET ON WITH IT!
YOUR TACTICS, STINK, SHUMAKER! RUSSELL-
WE'RE JUDGES! NOBODY DOES OUR JOB FOR US, ESPECIALLY WHEN THERE'S AN OPEN WARRANT ON ALL GILA-MUNJA!
GIANT
CADET
RUSSELL'S TACTICS MEET WITH APPROVAL-
WIDE FORMATION-MAXIMUM FIREPOWER!
LET 'EM HAVE IT!
CADET
B-LAM. BLAM. BLAM.. BLAM... B B. BLAM.. BLAM. BLAM. BLAM!
JUDGES NOW- AAAAH!
AAAIEEEEEEE!!

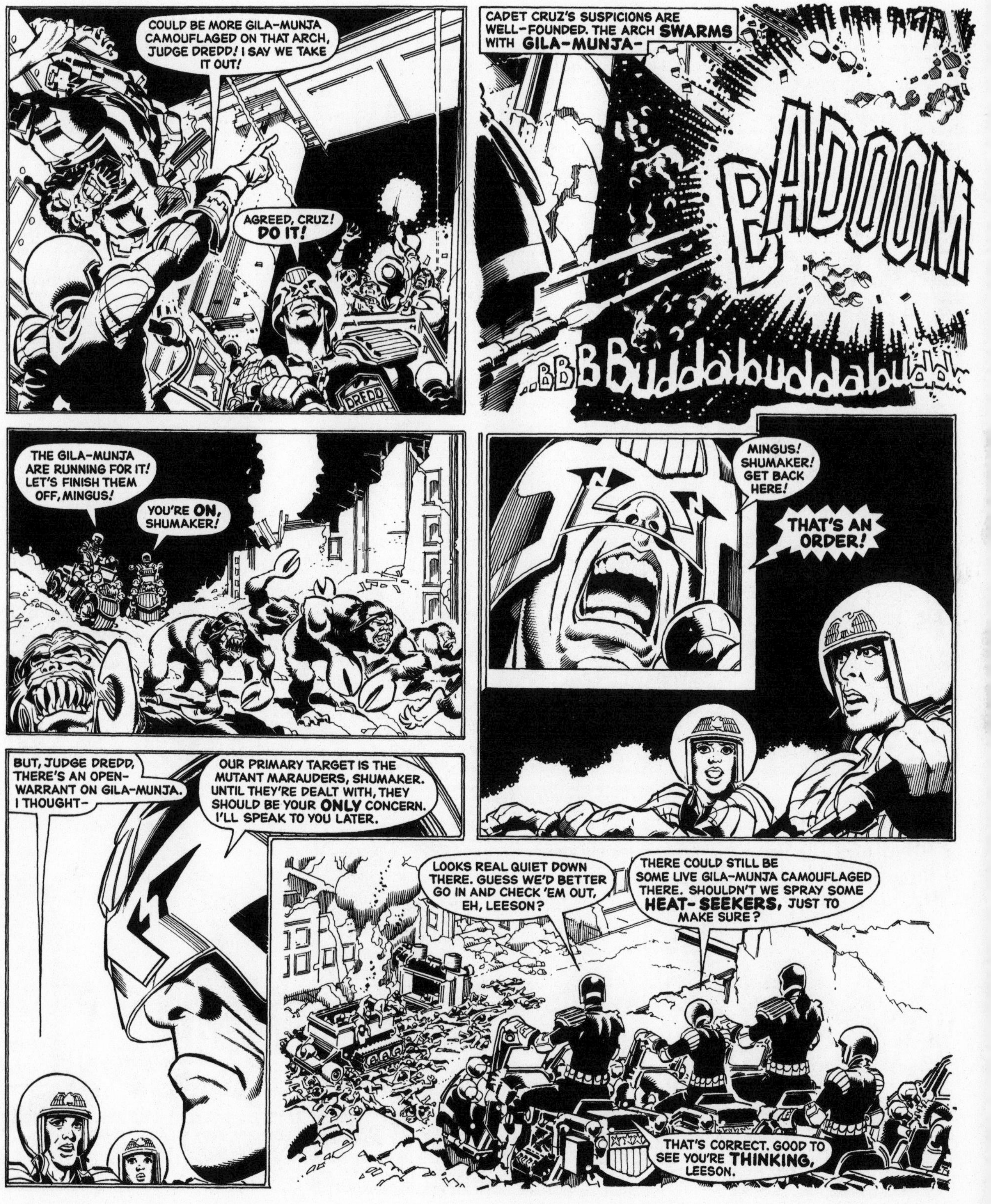

COULD BE MORE GILA-MUNJA CAMOUFLAGED ON THAT ARCH, JUDGE DREDD! I SAY WE TAKE IT OUT!
AGREED, CRUZ! **DO IT!**
DREDD
CADET CRUZ'S SUSPICIONS ARE WELL-FOUNDED. THE ARCH **SWARMS** WITH **GILA-MUNJA**-
BADOOM
..BBB Buddabuddabudd
THE GILA-MUNJA ARE RUNNING FOR IT! LET'S FINISH THEM OFF, MINGUS!
YOU'RE **ON**, SHUMAKER!
MINGUS! SHUMAKER! GET BACK HERE!
THAT'S AN ORDER!
BUT, JUDGE DREDD, THERE'S AN OPEN-WARRANT ON GILA-MUNJA. I THOUGHT-
OUR PRIMARY TARGET IS THE MUTANT MARAUDERS, SHUMAKER. UNTIL THEY'RE DEALT WITH, THEY SHOULD BE YOUR **ONLY** CONCERN. I'LL SPEAK TO YOU LATER.
LOOKS REAL QUIET DOWN THERE. GUESS WE'D BETTER GO IN AND CHECK 'EM OUT, EH, LEESON?
THERE COULD STILL BE SOME LIVE GILA-MUNJA CAMOUFLAGED THERE. SHOULDN'T WE SPRAY SOME **HEAT-SEEKERS**, JUST TO MAKE SURE?
THAT'S CORRECT. GOOD TO SEE YOU'RE **THINKING**, LEESON.

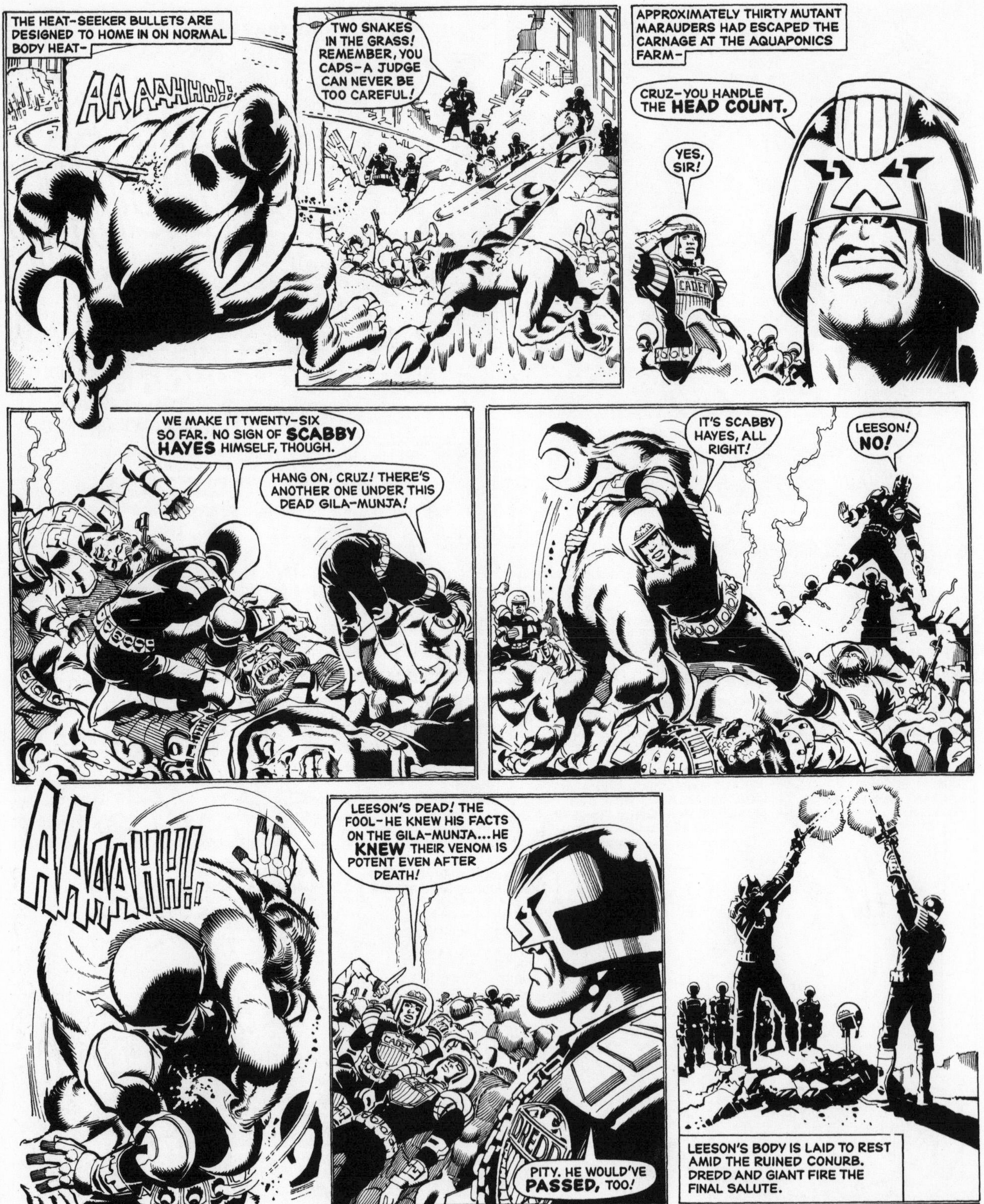
THE HEAT-SEEKER BULLETS ARE DESIGNED TO HOME IN ON NORMAL BODY HEAT-
AAAAHHH!!
TWO SNAKES IN THE GRASS! REMEMBER, YOU CADS—A JUDGE CAN NEVER BE TOO CAREFUL!
APPROXIMATELY THIRTY MUTANT MARAUDERS HAD ESCAPED THE CARNAGE AT THE AQUAPONICS FARM-
CRUZ—YOU HANDLE THE HEAD COUNT.
YES, SIR!
WE MAKE IT TWENTY-SIX SO FAR. NO SIGN OF SCABBY HAYES HIMSELF, THOUGH.
HANG ON, CRUZ! THERE'S ANOTHER ONE UNDER THIS DEAD GILA-MUNJA!
IT'S SCABBY HAYES, ALL RIGHT!
LEESON! NO!
AAAAHH!!
LEESON'S DEAD! THE FOOL—HE KNEW HIS FACTS ON THE GILA-MUNJA... HE KNEW THEIR VENOM IS POTENT EVEN AFTER DEATH!
PITY. HE WOULD'VE PASSED, TOO!
LEESON'S BODY IS LAID TO REST AMID THE RUINED CONURB. DREDD AND GIANT FIRE THE FINAL SALUTE.

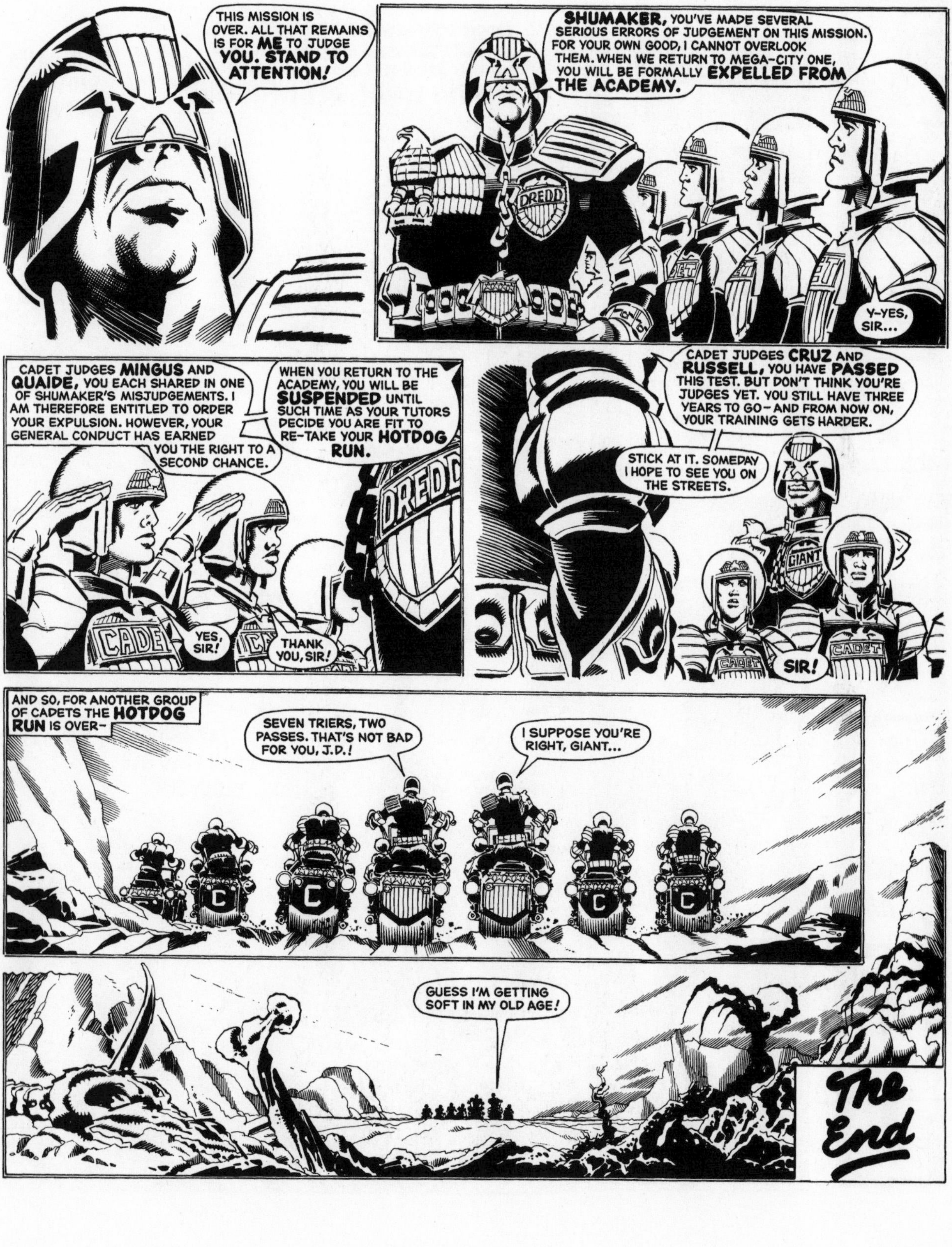

THIS MISSION IS OVER. ALL THAT REMAINS IS FOR ME TO JUDGE YOU. STAND TO ATTENTION!
SHUMAKER, YOU'VE MADE SEVERAL SERIOUS ERRORS OF JUDGEMENT ON THIS MISSION. FOR YOUR OWN GOOD, I CANNOT OVERLOOK THEM. WHEN WE RETURN TO MEGA-CITY ONE, YOU WILL BE FORMALLY EXPELLED FROM THE ACADEMY.
DREDD
Y-YES, SIR...
CADET JUDGES MINGUS AND QUAIDE, YOU EACH SHARED IN ONE OF SHUMAKER'S MISJUDGEMENTS. I AM THEREFORE ENTITLED TO ORDER YOUR EXPULSION. HOWEVER, YOUR GENERAL CONDUCT HAS EARNED YOU THE RIGHT TO A SECOND CHANCE.
WHEN YOU RETURN TO THE ACADEMY, YOU WILL BE SUSPENDED UNTIL SUCH TIME AS YOUR TUTORS DECIDE YOU ARE FIT TO RE-TAKE YOUR HOTDOG RUN.
DREDD
YES, SIR!
THANK YOU, SIR!
CADET JUDGES CRUZ AND RUSSELL, YOU HAVE PASSED THIS TEST. BUT DON'T THINK YOU'RE JUDGES YET. YOU STILL HAVE THREE YEARS TO GO—AND FROM NOW ON, YOUR TRAINING GETS HARDER.
STICK AT IT. SOMEDAY I HOPE TO SEE YOU ON THE STREETS.
GIANT
SIR!
AND SO, FOR ANOTHER GROUP OF CADETS THE HOTDOG RUN IS OVER—
SEVEN TRIERS, TWO PASSES. THAT'S NOT BAD FOR YOU, J.D.!
I SUPPOSE YOU'RE RIGHT, GIANT...
GUESS I'M GETTING SOFT IN MY OLD AGE!
The End

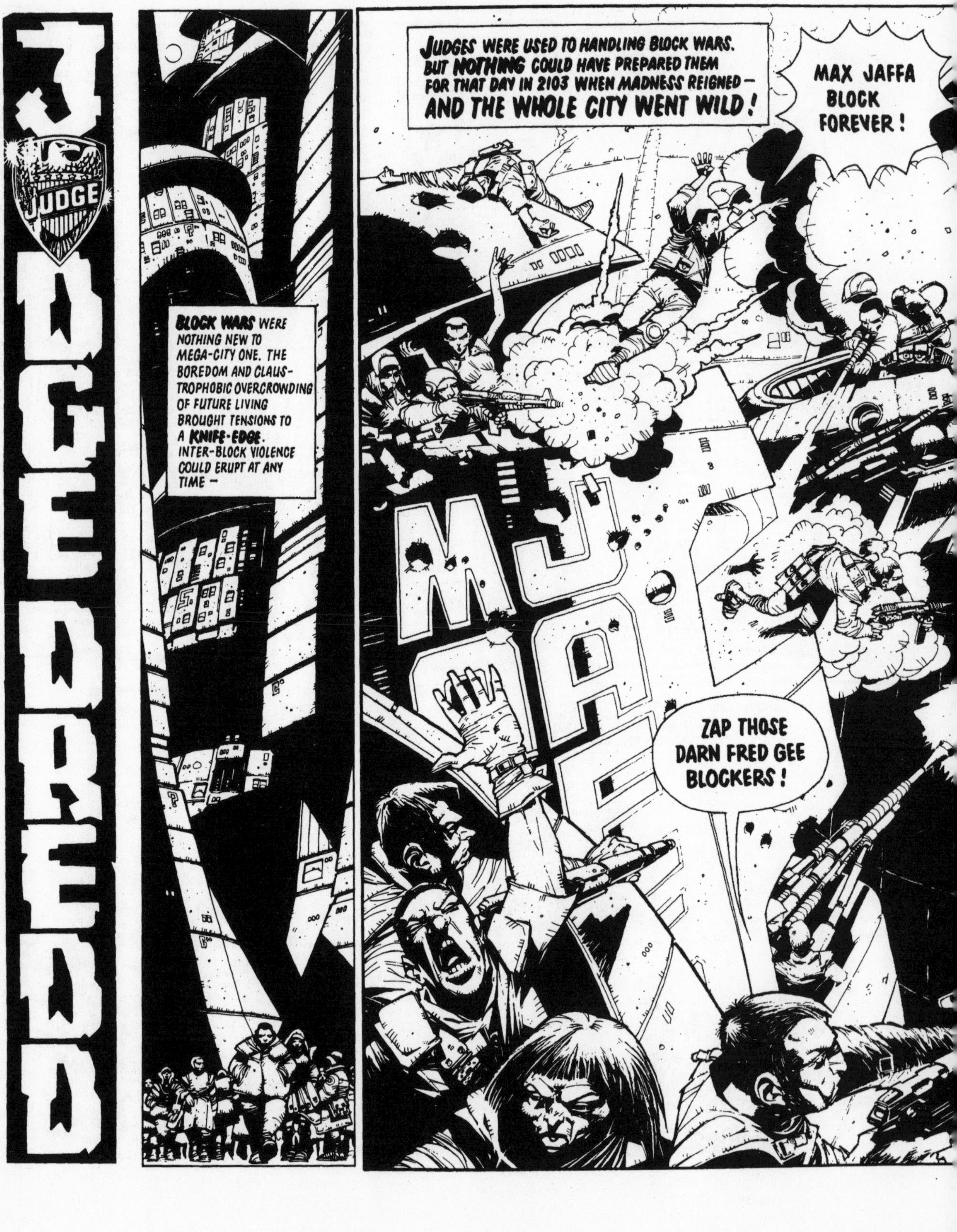
JUDGE DREDD
BLOCK WARS WERE NOTHING NEW TO MEGA-CITY ONE. THE BOREDOM AND CLAUS-TROPHOBIC OVERCROWDING OF FUTURE LIVING BROUGHT TENSIONS TO A KNIFE-EDGE. INTER-BLOCK VIOLENCE COULD ERUPT AT ANY TIME –
JUDGES WERE USED TO HANDLING BLOCK WARS. BUT NOTHING COULD HAVE PREPARED THEM FOR THAT DAY IN 2103 WHEN MADNESS REIGNED – AND THE WHOLE CITY WENT WILD!
MAX JAFFA BLOCK FOREVER!
ZAP THOSE DARN FRED GEE BLOCKERS!

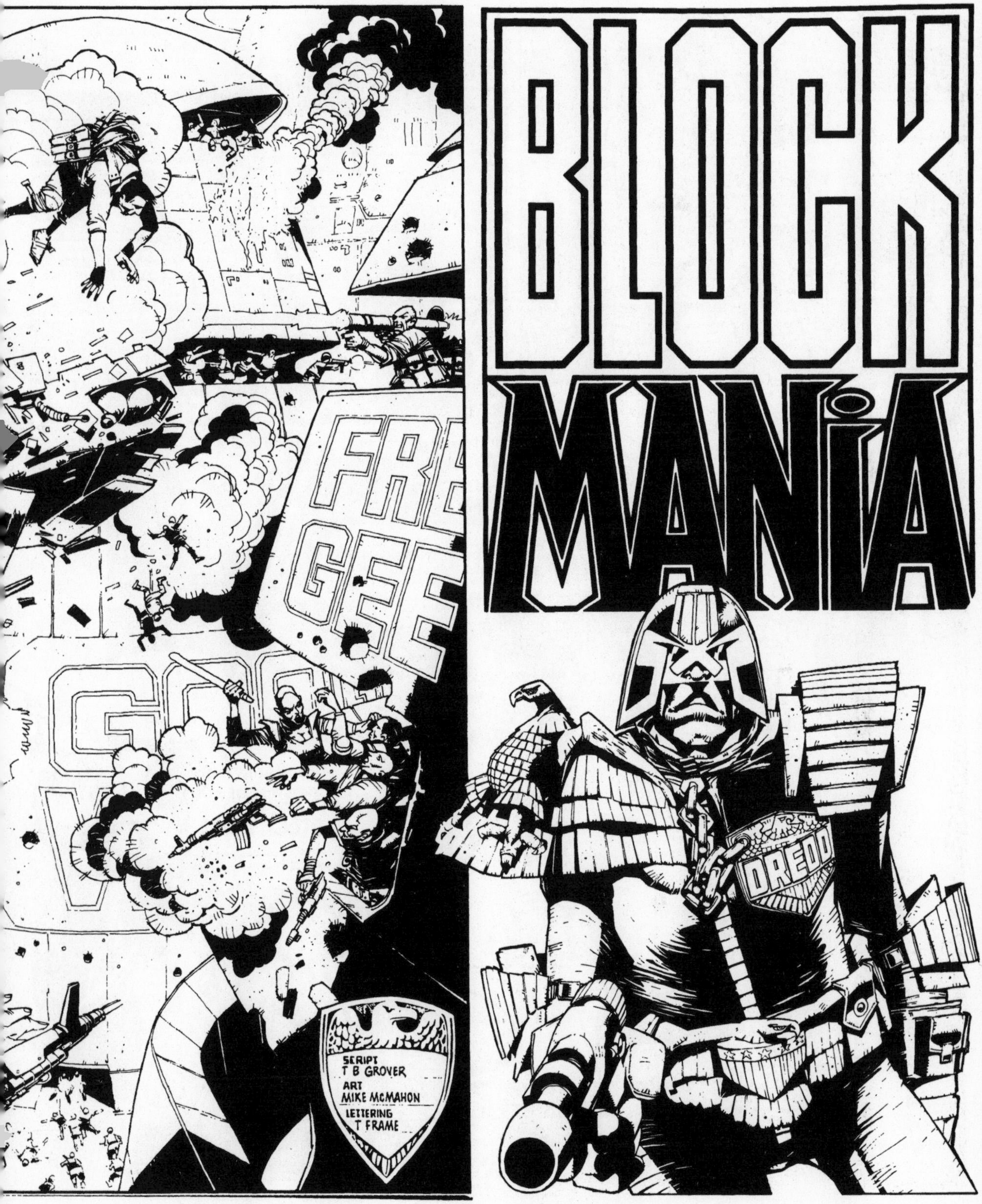
BLOCK MANIA
SCRIPT T B GROVER
ART MIKE McMAHON
LETTERING T FRAME
DREDD

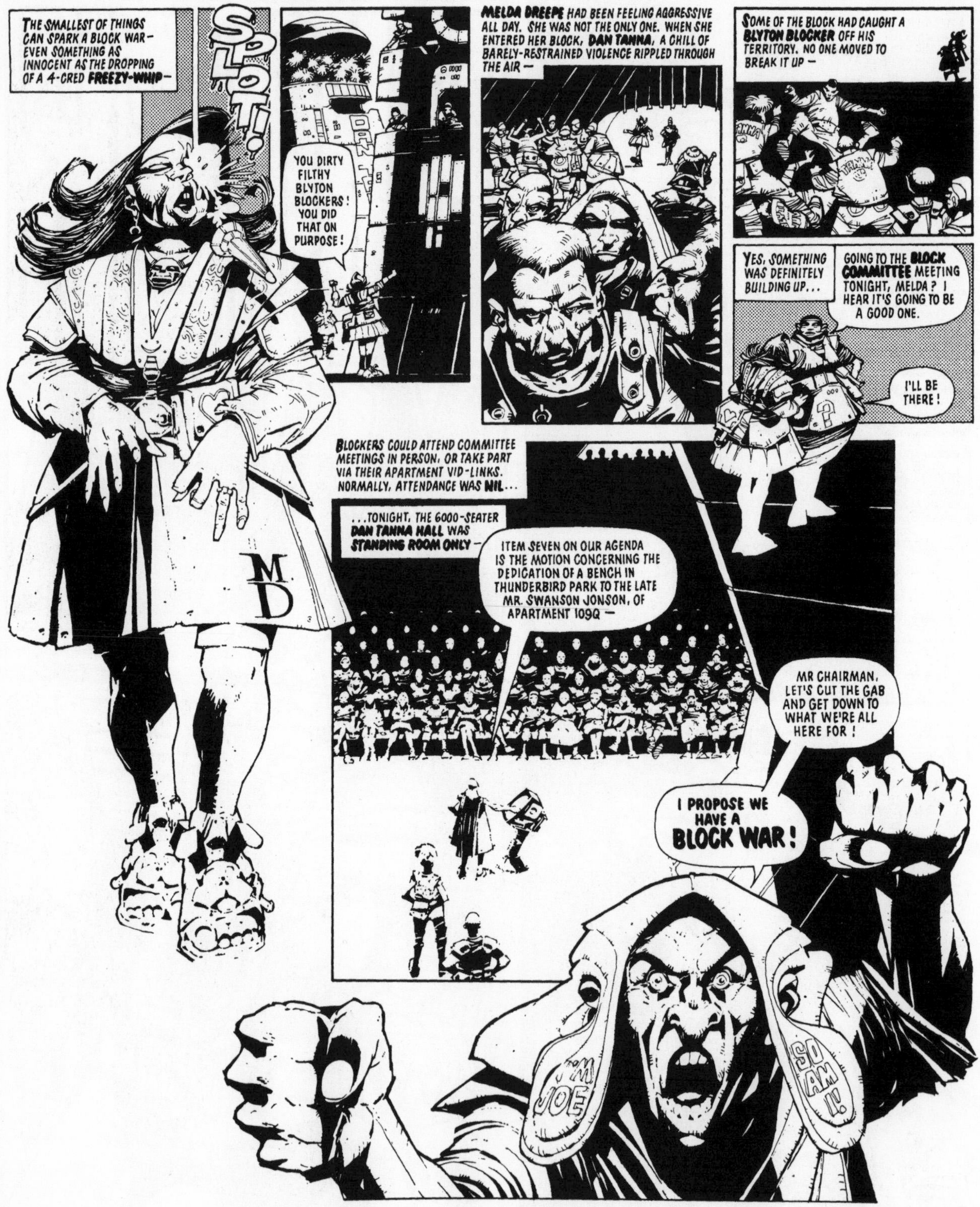

THE SMALLEST OF THINGS CAN SPARK A BLOCK WAR - EVEN SOMETHING AS INNOCENT AS THE DROPPING OF A 4-CRED FREEZY-WHIP -
SPLOT!
YOU DIRTY FILTHY BLYTON BLOCKERS! YOU DID THAT ON PURPOSE!
MELDA DREEPE HAD BEEN FEELING AGGRESSIVE ALL DAY. SHE WAS NOT THE ONLY ONE. WHEN SHE ENTERED HER BLOCK, DAN TANNA, A CHILL OF BARELY-RESTRAINED VIOLENCE RIPPLED THROUGH THE AIR -
SOME OF THE BLOCK HAD CAUGHT A BLYTON BLOCKER OFF HIS TERRITORY. NO ONE MOVED TO BREAK IT UP -
YES, SOMETHING WAS DEFINITELY BUILDING UP...
GOING TO THE BLOCK COMMITTEE MEETING TONIGHT, MELDA? I HEAR IT'S GOING TO BE A GOOD ONE.
I'LL BE THERE!
BLOCKERS COULD ATTEND COMMITTEE MEETINGS IN PERSON, OR TAKE PART VIA THEIR APARTMENT VID-LINKS. NORMALLY, ATTENDANCE WAS NIL...
...TONIGHT, THE 6000-SEATER DAN TANNA HALL WAS STANDING ROOM ONLY -
ITEM SEVEN ON OUR AGENDA IS THE MOTION CONCERNING THE DEDICATION OF A BENCH IN THUNDERBIRD PARK TO THE LATE MR. SWANSON JONSON, OF APARTMENT 109Q -
MR CHAIRMAN, LET'S CUT THE GAB AND GET DOWN TO WHAT WE'RE ALL HERE FOR!
I PROPOSE WE HAVE A BLOCK WAR!
I'M JOE
SO AM I!

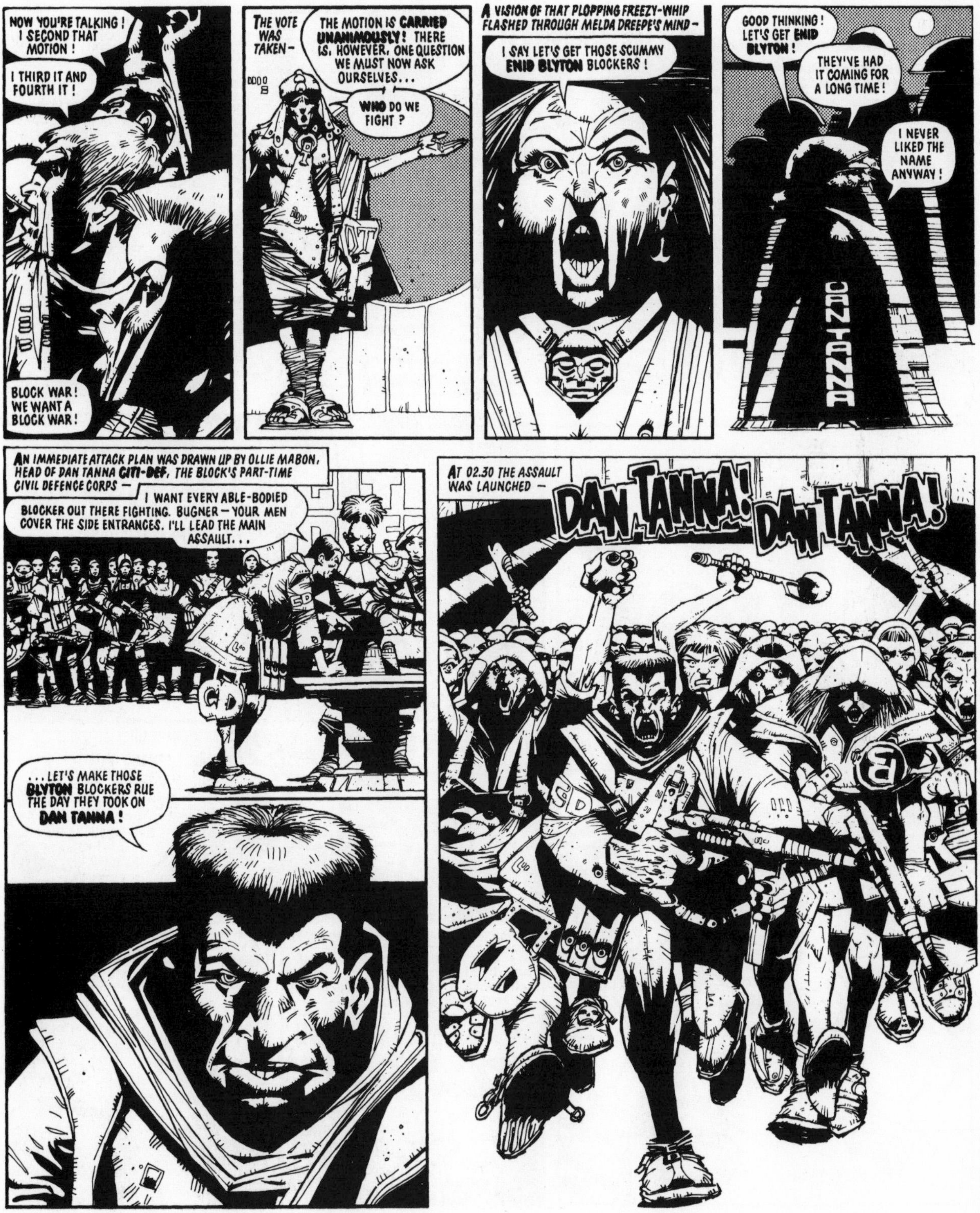
NOW YOU'RE TALKING! I SECOND THAT MOTION!
I THIRD IT AND FOURTH IT!
BLOCK WAR! WE WANT A BLOCK WAR!
THE VOTE WAS TAKEN—
THE MOTION IS CARRIED UNANIMOUSLY! THERE IS, HOWEVER, ONE QUESTION WE MUST NOW ASK OURSELVES...
WHO DO WE FIGHT?
A VISION OF THAT PLOPPING FREEZY-WHIP FLASHED THROUGH MELDA DREEPE'S MIND—
I SAY LET'S GET THOSE SCUMMY ENID BLYTON BLOCKERS!
GOOD THINKING! LET'S GET ENID BLYTON!
THEY'VE HAD IT COMING FOR A LONG TIME!
I NEVER LIKED THE NAME ANYWAY!
DAN TANNA
AN IMMEDIATE ATTACK PLAN WAS DRAWN UP BY OLLIE MABON, HEAD OF DAN TANNA CITI-DEF, THE BLOCK'S PART-TIME CIVIL DEFENCE CORPS—
I WANT EVERY ABLE-BODIED BLOCKER OUT THERE FIGHTING. BUGNER — YOUR MEN COVER THE SIDE ENTRANCES. I'LL LEAD THE MAIN ASSAULT...
...LET'S MAKE THOSE BLYTON BLOCKERS RUE THE DAY THEY TOOK ON DAN TANNA!
AT 02.30 THE ASSAULT WAS LAUNCHED—
DAN TANNA! DAN TANNA!

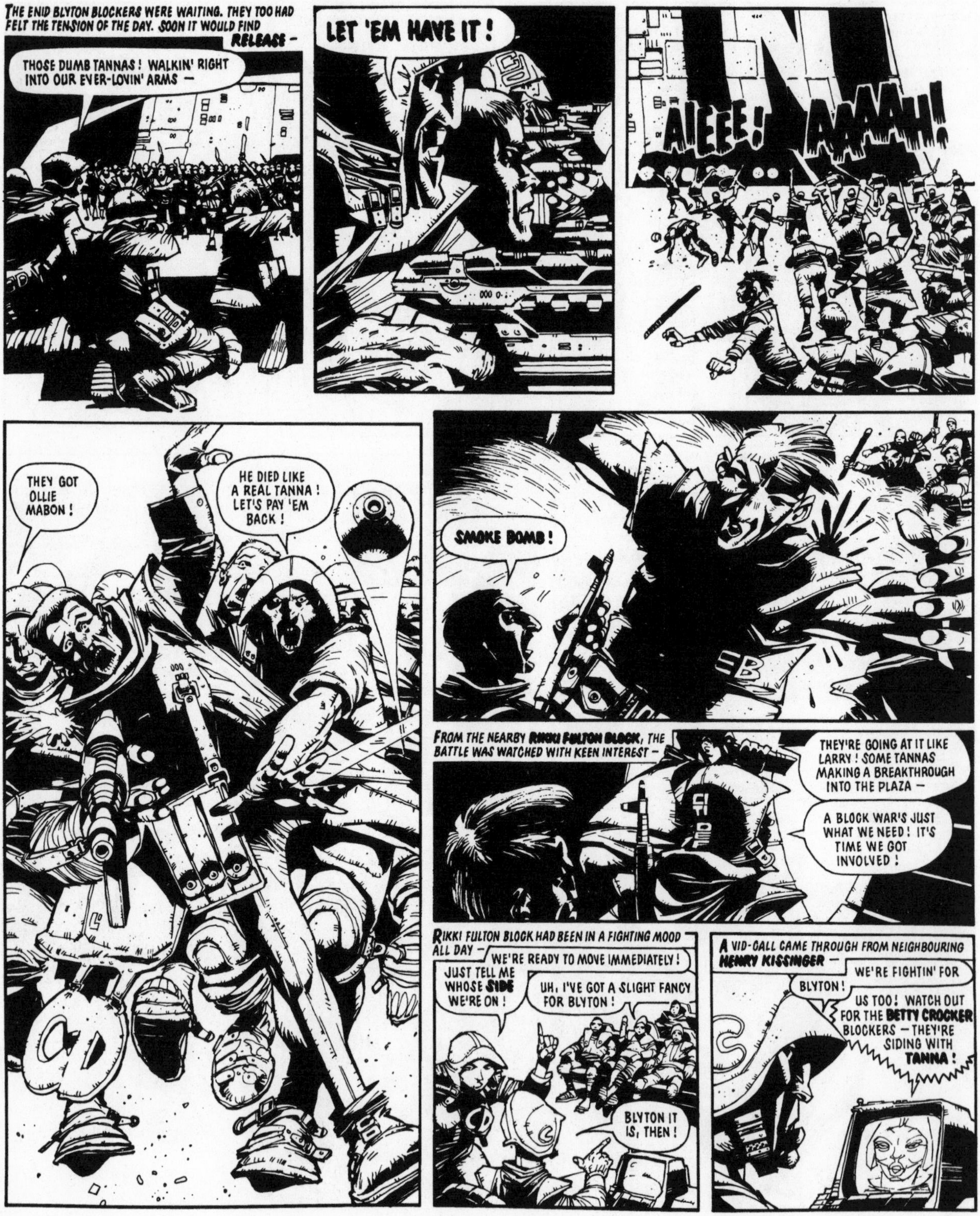
THE ENID BLYTON BLOCKERS WERE WAITING. THEY TOO HAD FELT THE TENSION OF THE DAY. SOON IT WOULD FIND RELEASE –
THOSE DUMB TANNAS! WALKIN' RIGHT INTO OUR EVER-LOVIN' ARMS –
LET 'EM HAVE IT!
AIEEE!
AAAAH!
THEY GOT OLLIE MABON!
HE DIED LIKE A REAL TANNA! LET'S PAY 'EM BACK!
SMOKE BOMB!
FROM THE NEARBY RIKKI FULTON BLOCK, THE BATTLE WAS WATCHED WITH KEEN INTEREST –
THEY'RE GOING AT IT LIKE LARRY! SOME TANNAS MAKING A BREAKTHROUGH INTO THE PLAZA –
A BLOCK WAR'S JUST WHAT WE NEED! IT'S TIME WE GOT INVOLVED!
RIKKI FULTON BLOCK HAD BEEN IN A FIGHTING MOOD ALL DAY –
WE'RE READY TO MOVE IMMEDIATELY! JUST TELL ME WHOSE SIDE WE'RE ON!
UH, I'VE GOT A SLIGHT FANCY FOR BLYTON!
BLYTON IT IS, THEN!
A VID-CALL CAME THROUGH FROM NEIGHBOURING HENRY KISSINGER –
WE'RE FIGHTIN' FOR BLYTON!
US TOO! WATCH OUT FOR THE BETTY CROCKER BLOCKERS – THEY'RE SIDING WITH TANNA!

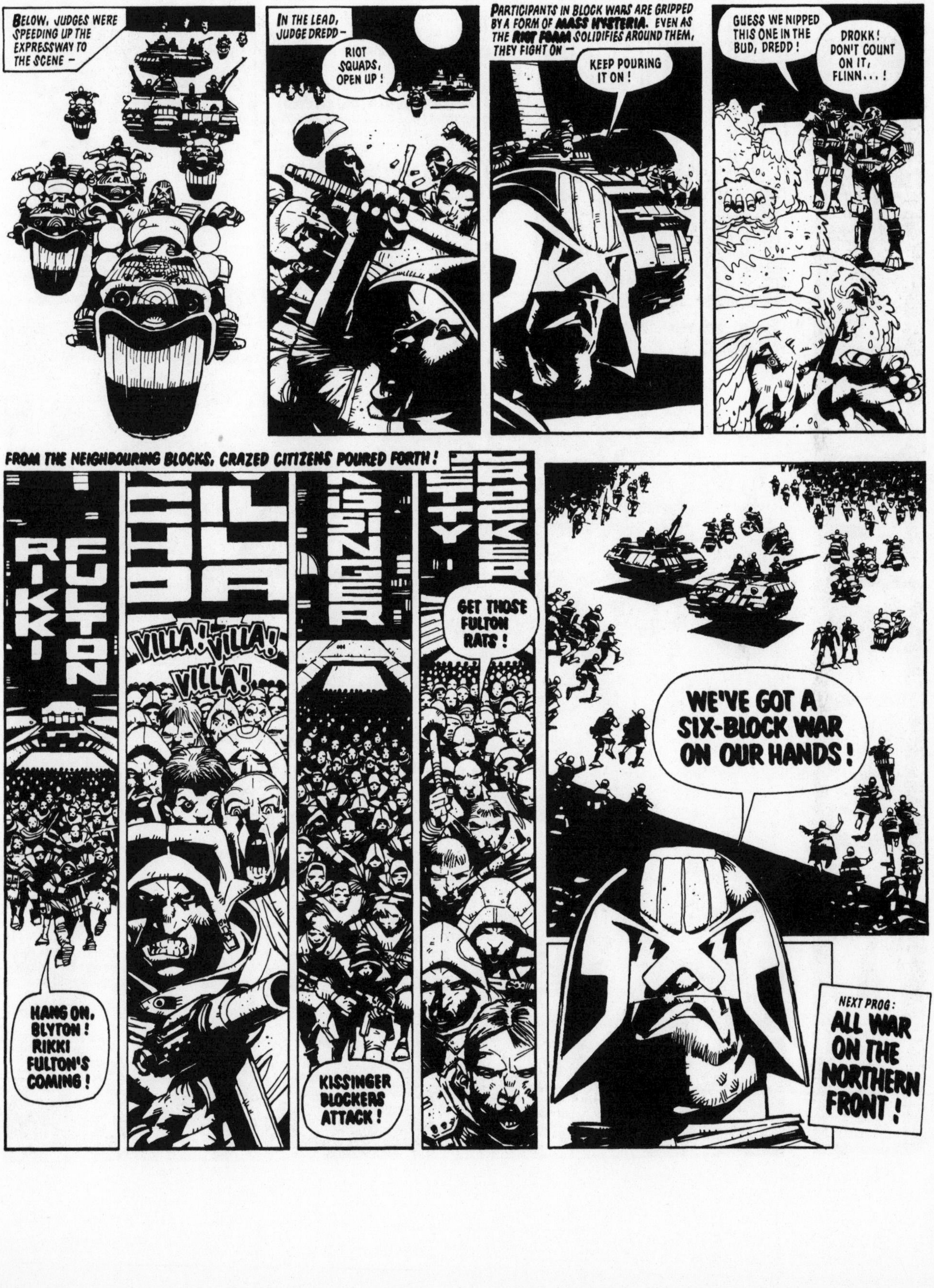
BELOW, JUDGES WERE SPEEDING UP THE EXPRESSWAY TO THE SCENE –
IN THE LEAD, JUDGE DREDD –
RIOT SQUADS, OPEN UP!
PARTICIPANTS IN BLOCK WARS ARE GRIPPED BY A FORM OF MASS HYSTERIA. EVEN AS THE RIOT FOAM SOLIDIFIES AROUND THEM, THEY FIGHT ON –
KEEP POURING IT ON!
GUESS WE NIPPED THIS ONE IN THE BUD, DREDD!
DROKK! DON'T COUNT ON IT, FLINN...!
FROM THE NEIGHBOURING BLOCKS, CRAZED CITIZENS POURED FORTH!
RIKKI FULTON
HANG ON, BLYTON! RIKKI FULTON'S COMING!
VILLA! VILLA! VILLA!
KISSINGER
KISSINGER BLOCKERS ATTACK!
GET THOSE FULTON RATS!
WE'VE GOT A SIX-BLOCK WAR ON OUR HANDS!
NEXT PROG: ALL WAR ON THE NORTHERN FRONT!

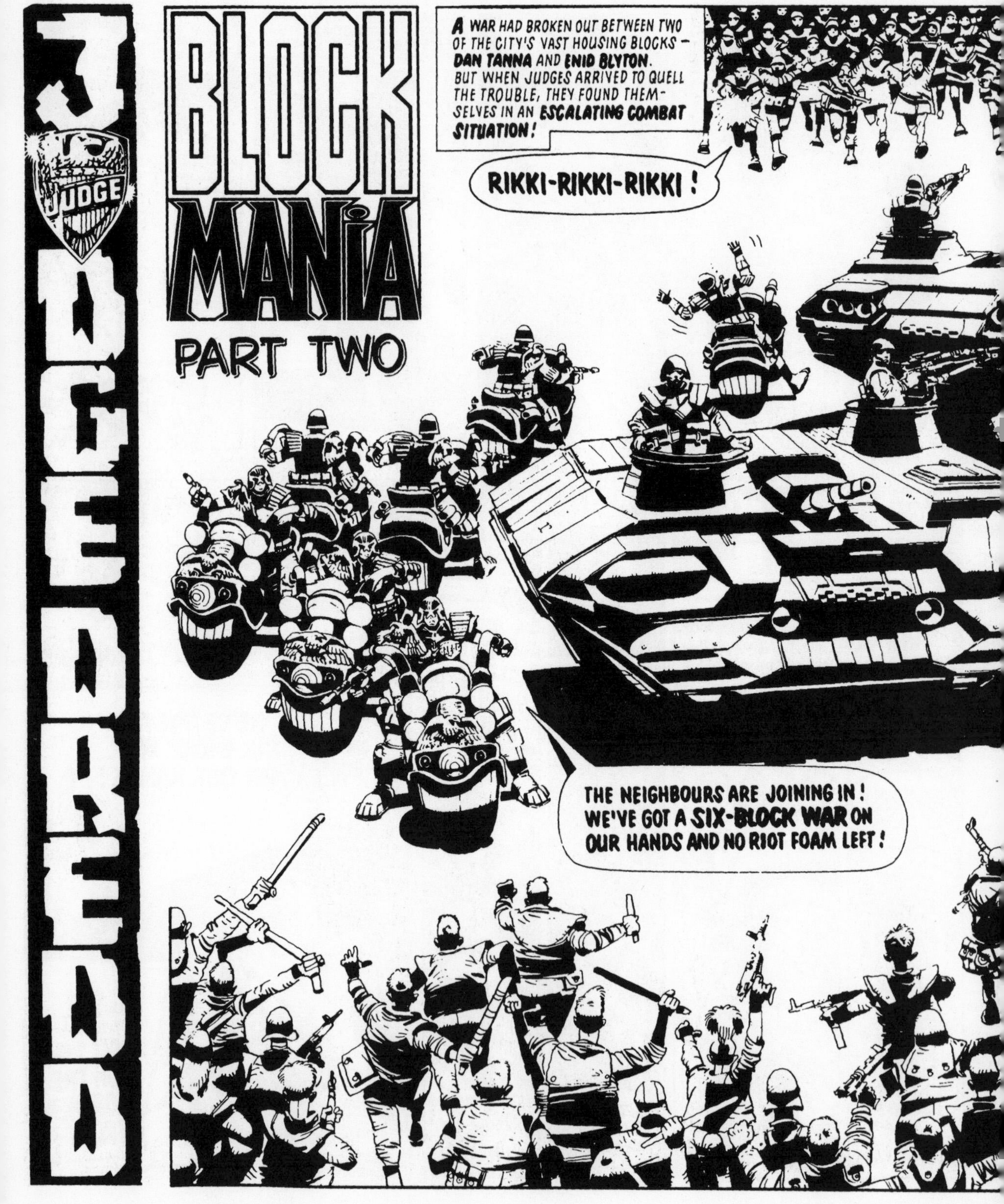
JUDGE DREDD
BLOCK MANIA
PART TWO
A WAR HAD BROKEN OUT BETWEEN TWO OF THE CITY'S VAST HOUSING BLOCKS — DAN TANNA AND ENID BLYTON. BUT WHEN JUDGES ARRIVED TO QUELL THE TROUBLE, THEY FOUND THEMSELVES IN AN ESCALATING COMBAT SITUATION!
RIKKI-RIKKI-RIKKI!
THE NEIGHBOURS ARE JOINING IN! WE'VE GOT A SIX-BLOCK WAR ON OUR HANDS AND NO RIOT FOAM LEFT!

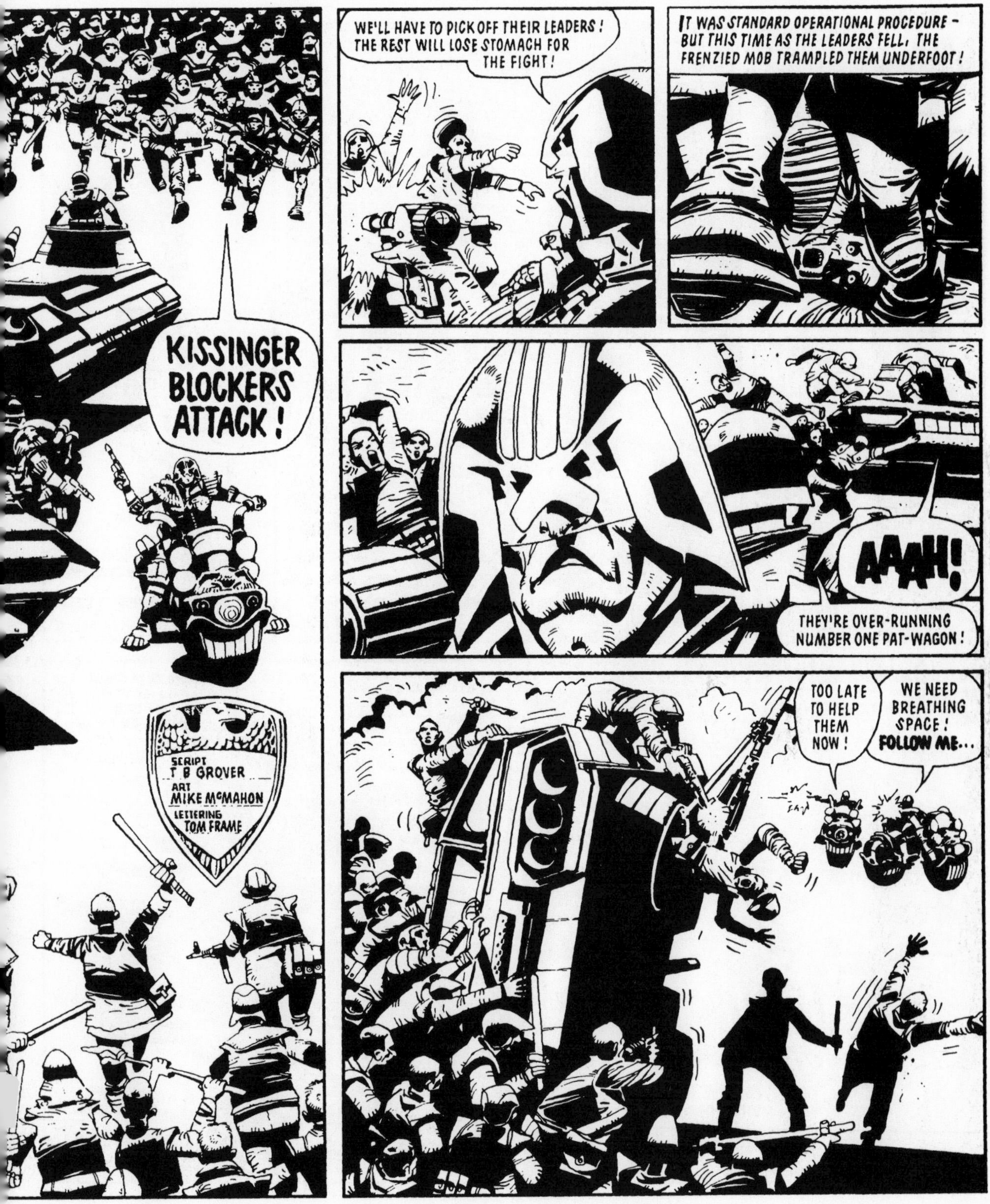
KISSINGER BLOCKERS ATTACK !
SCRIPT T B GROVER
ART MIKE McMAHON
LETTERING TOM FRAME
WE'LL HAVE TO PICK OFF THEIR LEADERS ! THE REST WILL LOSE STOMACH FOR THE FIGHT !
IT WAS STANDARD OPERATIONAL PROCEDURE - BUT THIS TIME AS THE LEADERS FELL, THE FRENZIED MOB TRAMPLED THEM UNDERFOOT !
AAAH !
THEY'RE OVER-RUNNING NUMBER ONE PAT-WAGON !
TOO LATE TO HELP THEM NOW !
WE NEED BREATHING SPACE ! FOLLOW ME...

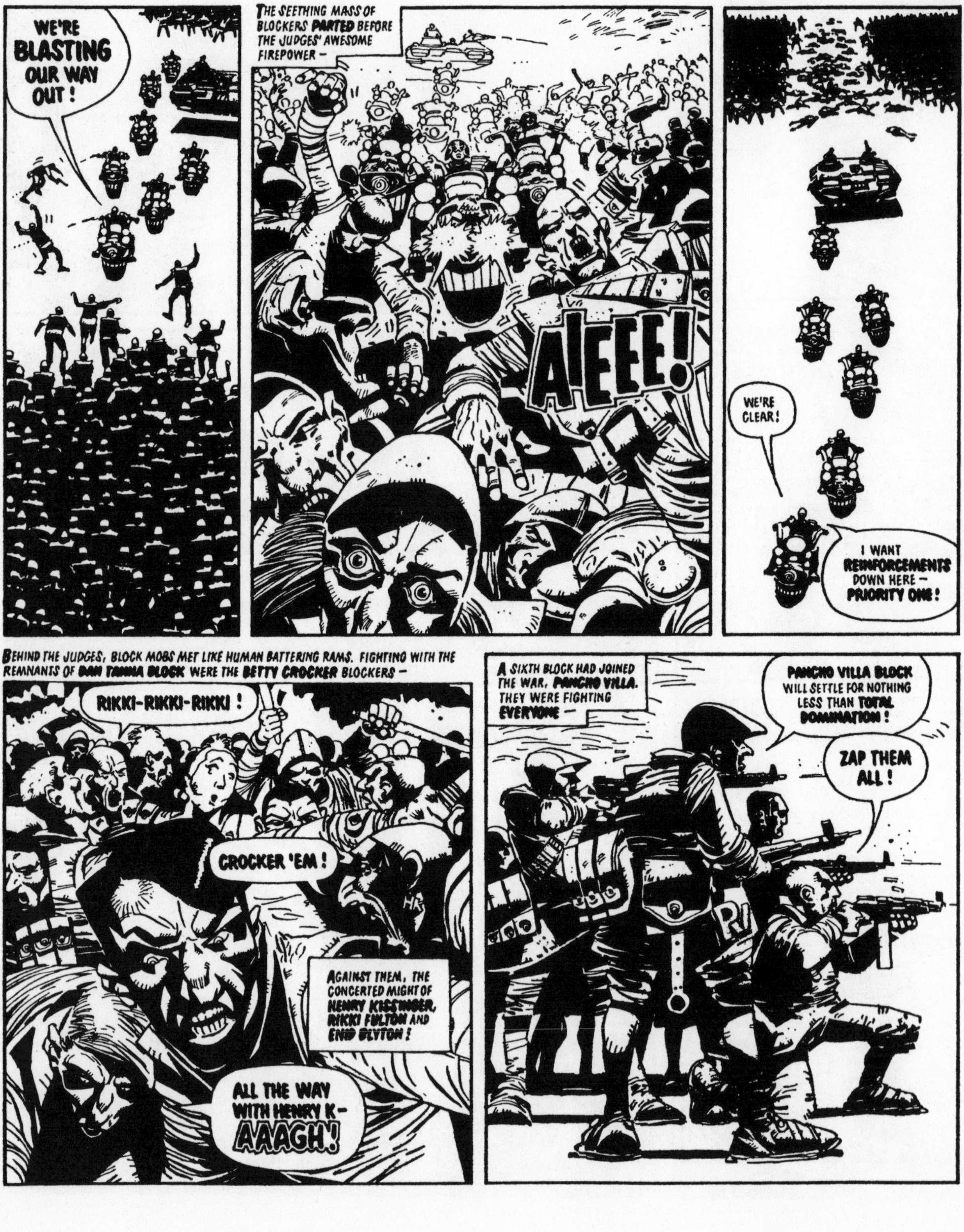

WE'RE BLASTING OUR WAY OUT!
THE SEETHING MASS OF BLOCKERS PARTED BEFORE THE JUDGES' AWESOME FIREPOWER –
AIEEE!
WE'RE CLEAR!
I WANT REINFORCEMENTS DOWN HERE – PRIORITY ONE!
BEHIND THE JUDGES, BLOCK MOBS MET LIKE HUMAN BATTERING RAMS. FIGHTING WITH THE REMNANTS OF DAN TANNA BLOCK WERE THE BETTY CROCKER BLOCKERS –
RIKKI-RIKKI-RIKKI!
CROCKER 'EM!
AGAINST THEM, THE CONCERTED MIGHT OF HENRY KISSINGER, RIKKI FULTON AND ENID BLYTON!
ALL THE WAY WITH HENRY K– AAAGH!
A SIXTH BLOCK HAD JOINED THE WAR, PANCHO VILLA. THEY WERE FIGHTING EVERYONE –
PANCHO VILLA BLOCK WILL SETTLE FOR NOTHING LESS THAN TOTAL DOMINATION!
ZAP THEM ALL!

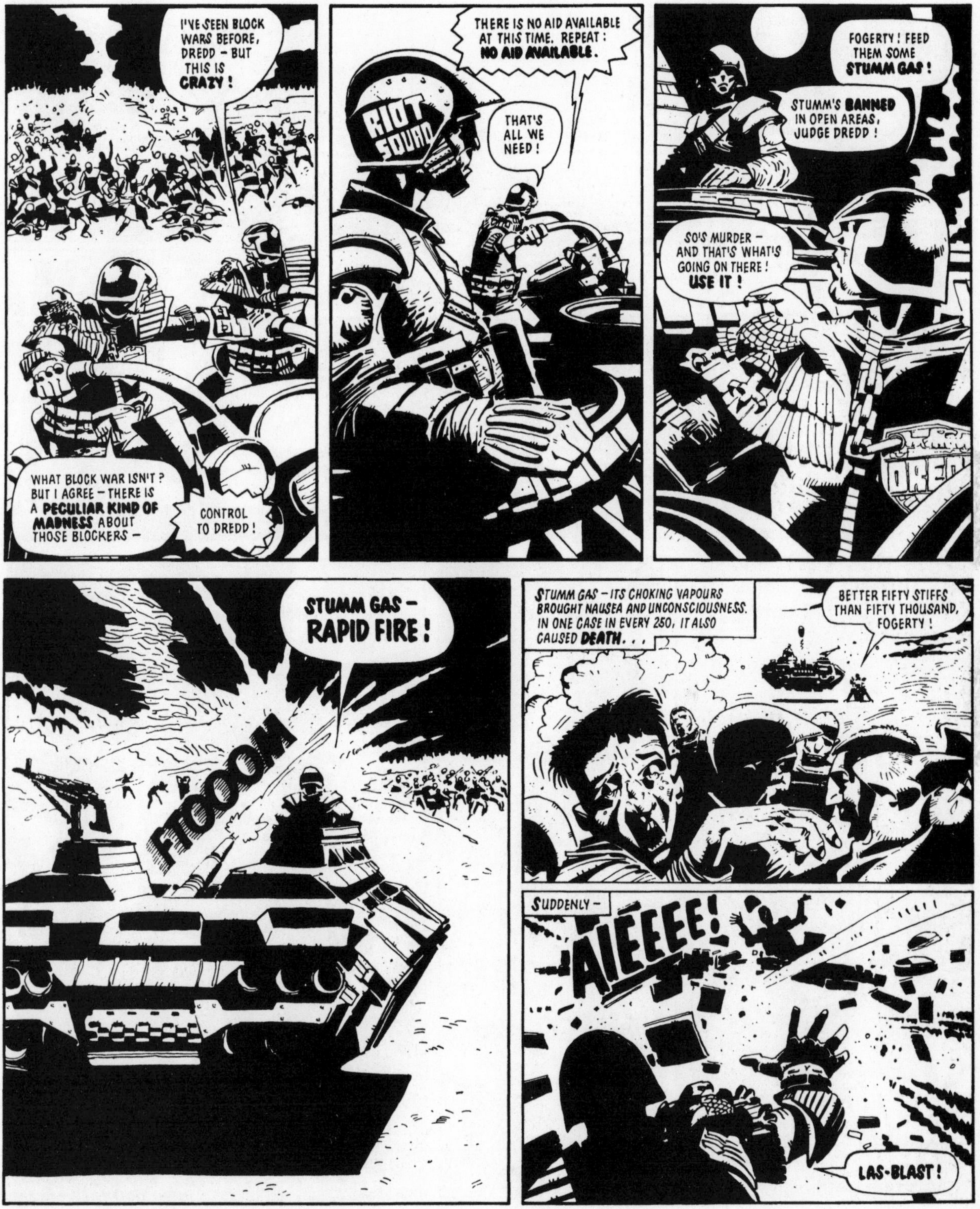
I'VE SEEN BLOCK WARS BEFORE, DREDD – BUT THIS IS **CRAZY** !
WHAT BLOCK WAR ISN'T ? BUT I AGREE – THERE IS A **PECULIAR KIND OF MADNESS** ABOUT THOSE BLOCKERS –
CONTROL TO DREDD !
THERE IS NO AID AVAILABLE AT THIS TIME. REPEAT : **NO AID AVAILABLE**.
RIOT SQUAD
THAT'S ALL WE NEED !
FOGERTY ! FEED THEM SOME **STUMM GAS** !
STUMM'S **BANNED** IN OPEN AREAS, JUDGE DREDD !
SO'S MURDER – AND THAT'S WHAT'S GOING ON THERE ! **USE IT** !
STUMM GAS – **RAPID FIRE** !
FTOOOM
STUMM GAS – ITS CHOKING VAPOURS BROUGHT NAUSEA AND UNCONSCIOUSNESS. IN ONE CASE IN EVERY 250, IT ALSO CAUSED **DEATH**. . .
BETTER FIFTY STIFFS THAN FIFTY THOUSAND, FOGERTY !
SUDDENLY –
AIEEEEE !
LAS-BLAST !

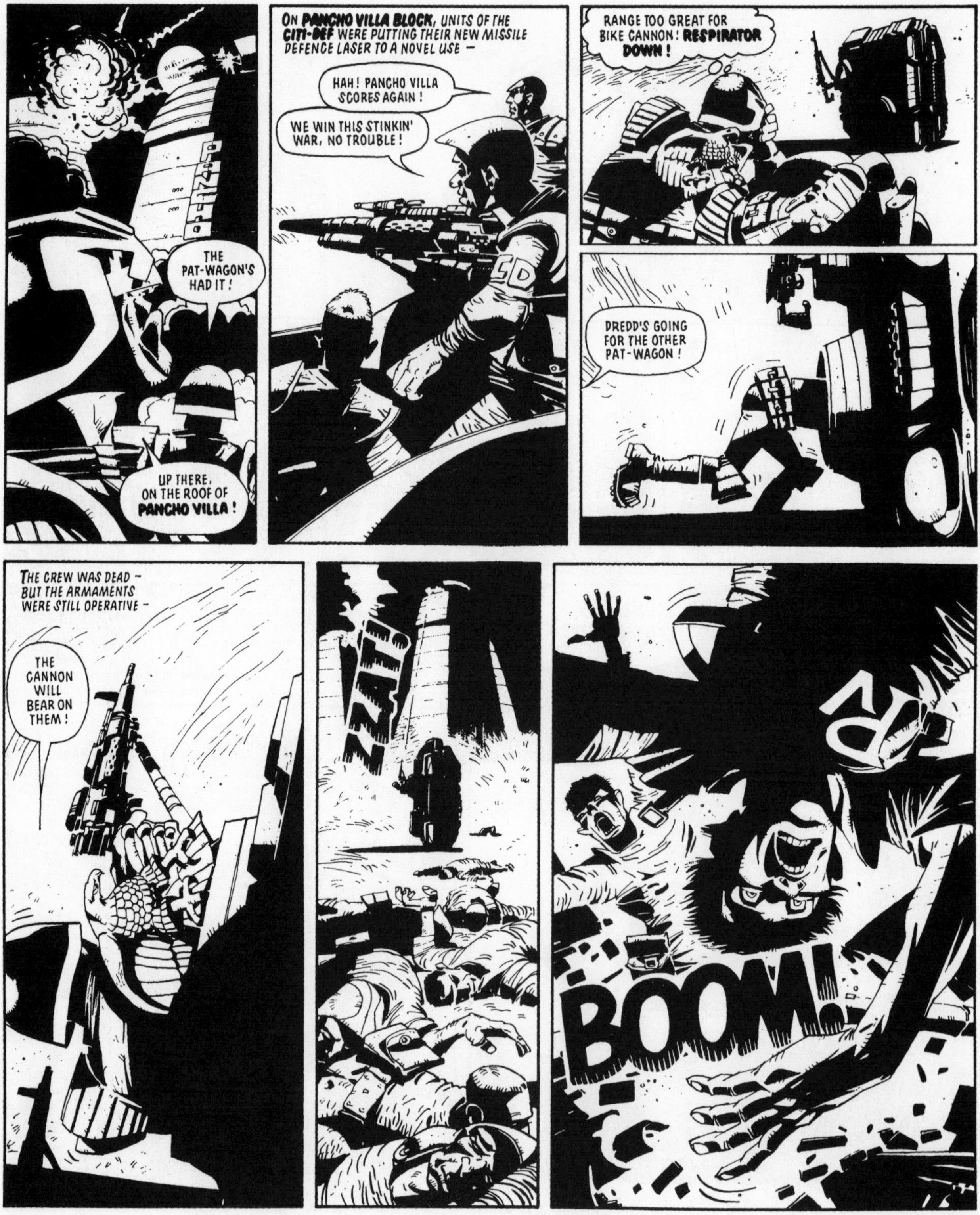

THE PAT-WAGON'S HAD IT!
UP THERE, ON THE ROOF OF PANCHO VILLA!
ON PANCHO VILLA BLOCK, UNITS OF THE CITI-DEF WERE PUTTING THEIR NEW MISSILE DEFENCE LASER TO A NOVEL USE –
HAH! PANCHO VILLA SCORES AGAIN!
WE WIN THIS STINKIN' WAR, NO TROUBLE!
RANGE TOO GREAT FOR BIKE CANNON: RESPIRATOR DOWN!
DREDD'S GOING FOR THE OTHER PAT-WAGON!
THE CREW WAS DEAD – BUT THE ARMAMENTS WERE STILL OPERATIVE –
THE CANNON WILL BEAR ON THEM!
ZZATT!
BOOM!

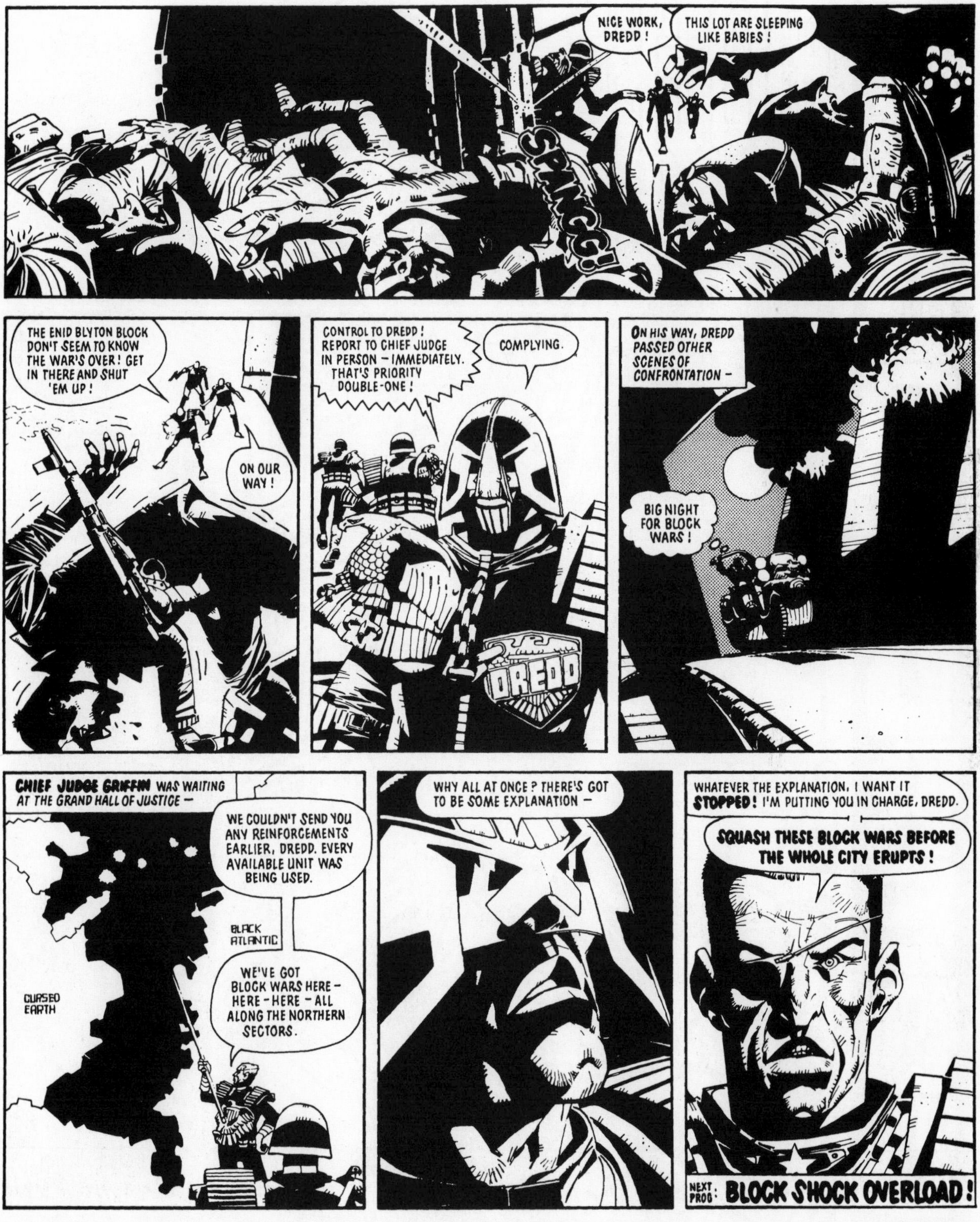
NICE WORK, DREDD!
THIS LOT ARE SLEEPING LIKE BABIES!
SPANGG!
THE ENID BLYTON BLOCK DON'T SEEM TO KNOW THE WAR'S OVER! GET IN THERE AND SHUT 'EM UP!
ON OUR WAY!
CONTROL TO DREDD! REPORT TO CHIEF JUDGE IN PERSON — IMMEDIATELY. THAT'S PRIORITY DOUBLE-ONE!
COMPLYING.
DREDD
ON HIS WAY, DREDD PASSED OTHER SCENES OF CONFRONTATION —
BIG NIGHT FOR BLOCK WARS!
CHIEF JUDGE GRIFFIN WAS WAITING AT THE GRAND HALL OF JUSTICE —
WE COULDN'T SEND YOU ANY REINFORCEMENTS EARLIER, DREDD. EVERY AVAILABLE UNIT WAS BEING USED.
BLACK ATLANTIC
CURSED EARTH
WE'VE GOT BLOCK WARS HERE — HERE — HERE — ALL ALONG THE NORTHERN SECTORS.
WHY ALL AT ONCE? THERE'S GOT TO BE SOME EXPLANATION —
WHATEVER THE EXPLANATION, I WANT IT STOPPED! I'M PUTTING YOU IN CHARGE, DREDD.
SQUASH THESE BLOCK WARS BEFORE THE WHOLE CITY ERUPTS!
NEXT PROG: BLOCK SHOCK OVERLOAD!

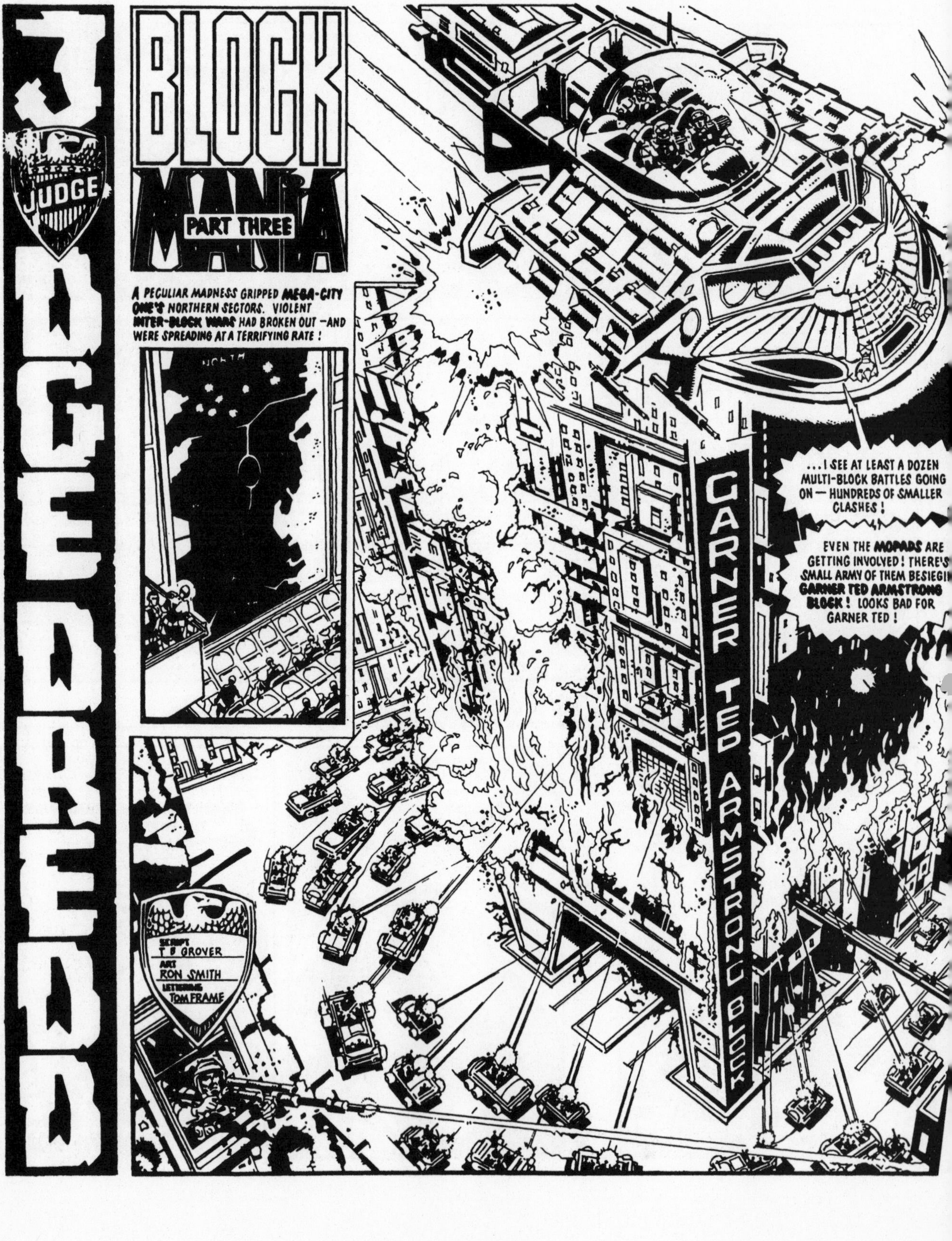
JUDGE DREDD
JUDGE
BLOCK MANIA
PART THREE
A PECULIAR MADNESS GRIPPED MEGA-CITY ONE'S NORTHERN SECTORS. VIOLENT INTER-BLOCK WARS HAD BROKEN OUT —AND WERE SPREADING AT A TERRIFYING RATE !
...I SEE AT LEAST A DOZEN MULTI-BLOCK BATTLES GOING ON — HUNDREDS OF SMALLER CLASHES !
EVEN THE MOPADS ARE GETTING INVOLVED ! THERE'S SMALL ARMY OF THEM BESIEGI GARNER TED ARMSTRONG BLOCK ! LOOKS BAD FOR GARNER TED !
GARNER TED ARMSTRONG BLOCK
SCRIPT
T B GROVER
ART
RON SMITH
LETTERING
TOM FRAME

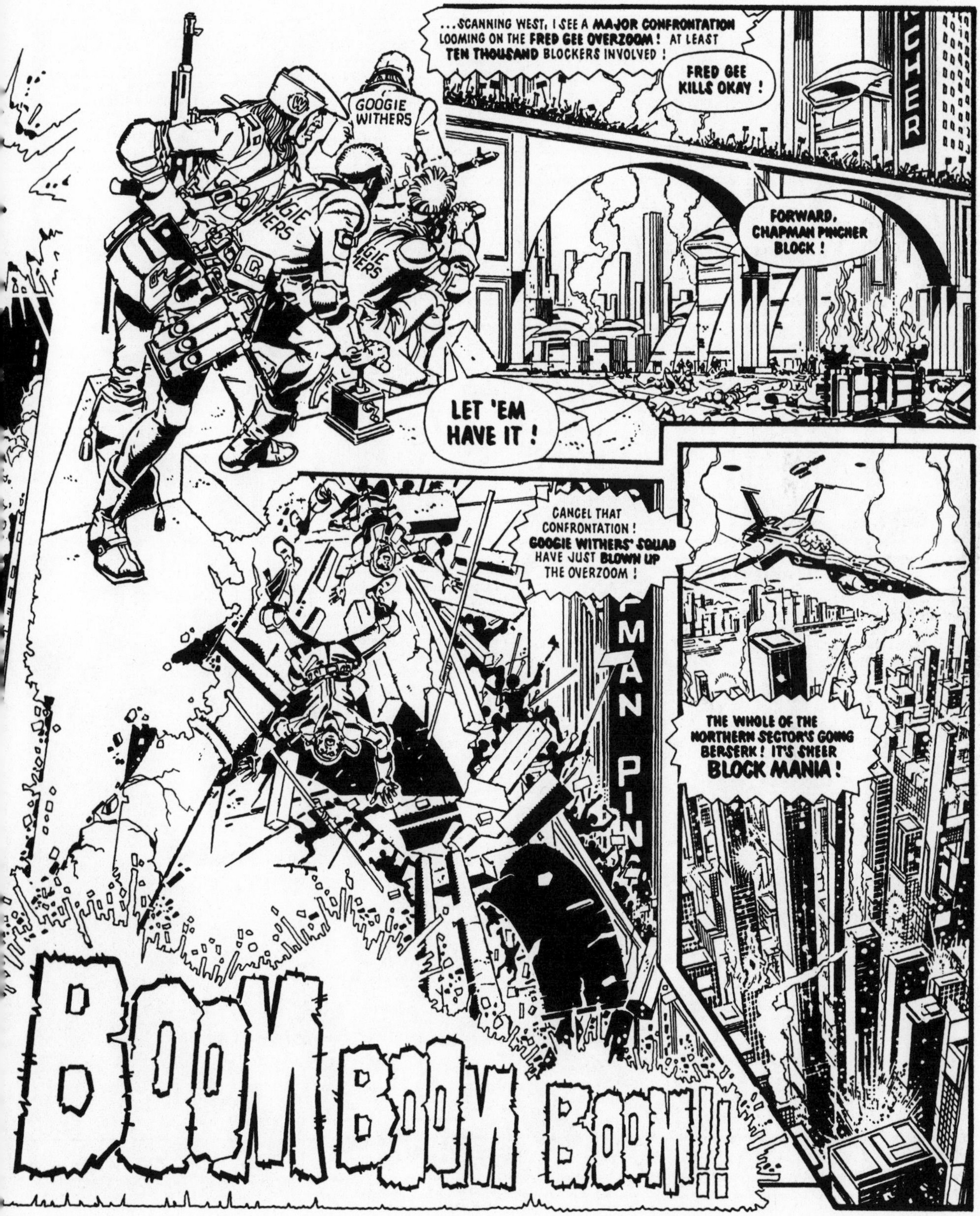
...SCANNING WEST, I SEE A MAJOR CONFRONTATION LOOMING ON THE FRED GEE OVERZOOM! AT LEAST TEN THOUSAND BLOCKERS INVOLVED!
FRED GEE KILLS OKAY!
GOOGIE WITHERS
FORWARD, CHAPMAN PINCHER BLOCK!
LET 'EM HAVE IT!
CANCEL THAT CONFRONTATION! GOOGIE WITHERS' SQUAD HAVE JUST BLOWN UP THE OVERZOOM!
THE WHOLE OF THE NORTHERN SECTOR'S GOING BERSERK! IT'S SHEER BLOCK MANIA!
BOOM BOOM BOOM!!

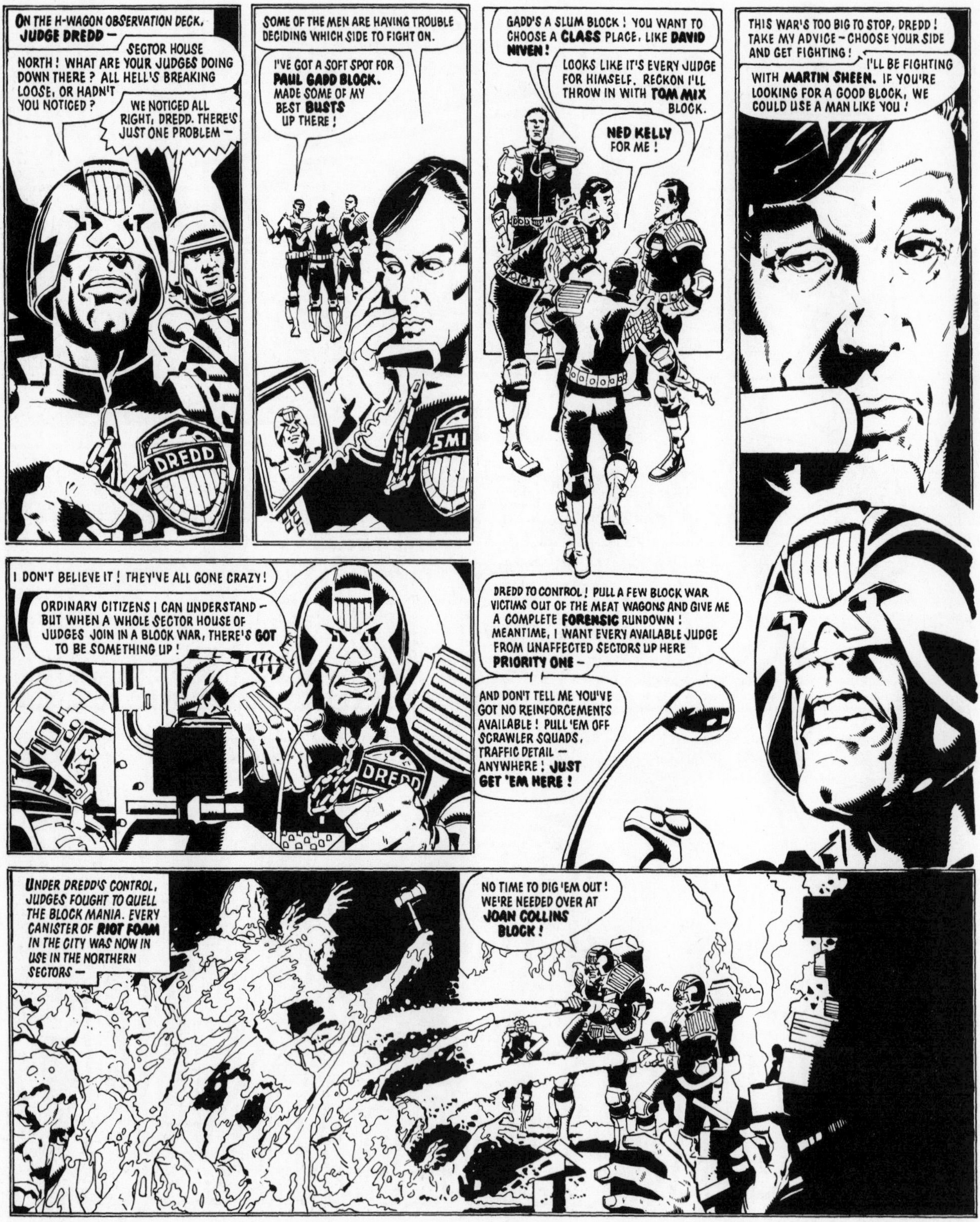
ON THE H-WAGON OBSERVATION DECK, JUDGE DREDD –
SECTOR HOUSE NORTH! WHAT ARE YOUR JUDGES DOING DOWN THERE? ALL HELL'S BREAKING LOOSE, OR HADN'T YOU NOTICED?
WE NOTICED ALL RIGHT, DREDD. THERE'S JUST ONE PROBLEM –
SOME OF THE MEN ARE HAVING TROUBLE DECIDING WHICH SIDE TO FIGHT ON.
I'VE GOT A SOFT SPOT FOR PAUL GADD BLOCK. MADE SOME OF MY BEST BUSTS UP THERE!
GADD'S A SLUM BLOCK! YOU WANT TO CHOOSE A CLASS PLACE, LIKE DAVID NIVEN!
LOOKS LIKE IT'S EVERY JUDGE FOR HIMSELF. RECKON I'LL THROW IN WITH TOM MIX BLOCK.
NED KELLY FOR ME!
THIS WAR'S TOO BIG TO STOP, DREDD! TAKE MY ADVICE – CHOOSE YOUR SIDE AND GET FIGHTING!
I'LL BE FIGHTING WITH MARTIN SHEEN. IF YOU'RE LOOKING FOR A GOOD BLOCK, WE COULD USE A MAN LIKE YOU!
I DON'T BELIEVE IT! THEY'VE ALL GONE CRAZY!
ORDINARY CITIZENS I CAN UNDERSTAND – BUT WHEN A WHOLE SECTOR HOUSE OF JUDGES JOIN IN A BLOCK WAR, THERE'S GOT TO BE SOMETHING UP!
DREDD
DREDD TO CONTROL! PULL A FEW BLOCK WAR VICTIMS OUT OF THE MEAT WAGONS AND GIVE ME A COMPLETE FORENSIC RUNDOWN! MEANTIME, I WANT EVERY AVAILABLE JUDGE FROM UNAFFECTED SECTORS UP HERE PRIORITY ONE –
AND DON'T TELL ME YOU'VE GOT NO REINFORCEMENTS AVAILABLE! PULL 'EM OFF SCRAWLER SQUADS, TRAFFIC DETAIL – ANYWHERE! JUST GET 'EM HERE!
UNDER DREDD'S CONTROL, JUDGES FOUGHT TO QUELL THE BLOCK MANIA. EVERY CANISTER OF RIOT FOAM IN THE CITY WAS NOW IN USE IN THE NORTHERN SECTORS –
NO TIME TO DIG 'EM OUT! WE'RE NEEDED OVER AT JOAN COLLINS BLOCK!

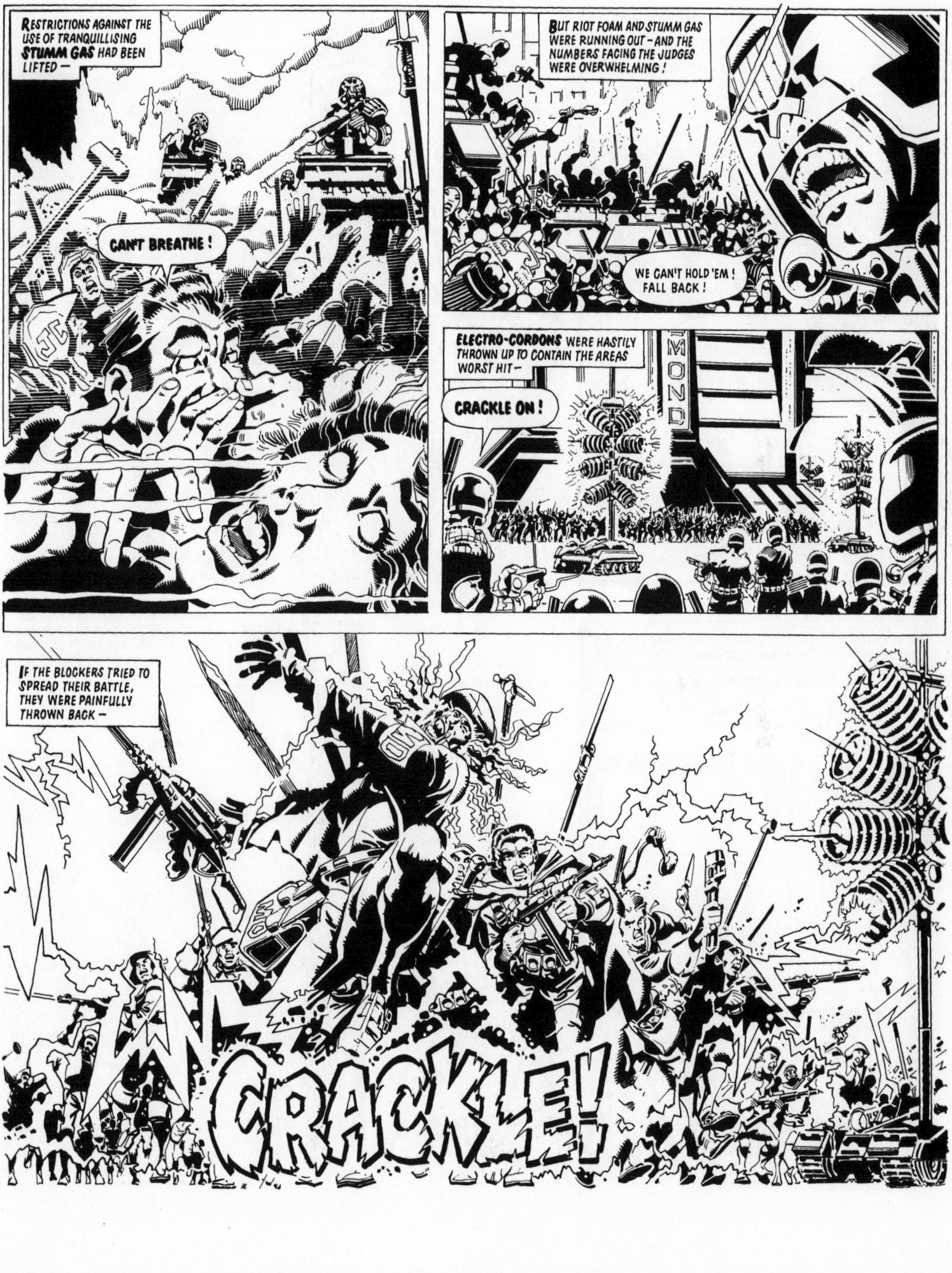
RESTRICTIONS AGAINST THE USE OF TRANQUILLISING STUMM GAS HAD BEEN LIFTED —
CAN'T BREATHE!
BUT RIOT FOAM AND STUMM GAS WERE RUNNING OUT — AND THE NUMBERS FACING THE JUDGES WERE OVERWHELMING!
WE CAN'T HOLD 'EM! FALL BACK!
ELECTRO-CORDONS WERE HASTILY THROWN UP TO CONTAIN THE AREAS WORST HIT —
CRACKLE ON!
IF THE BLOCKERS TRIED TO SPREAD THEIR BATTLE, THEY WERE PAINFULLY THROWN BACK —
CRACKLE!

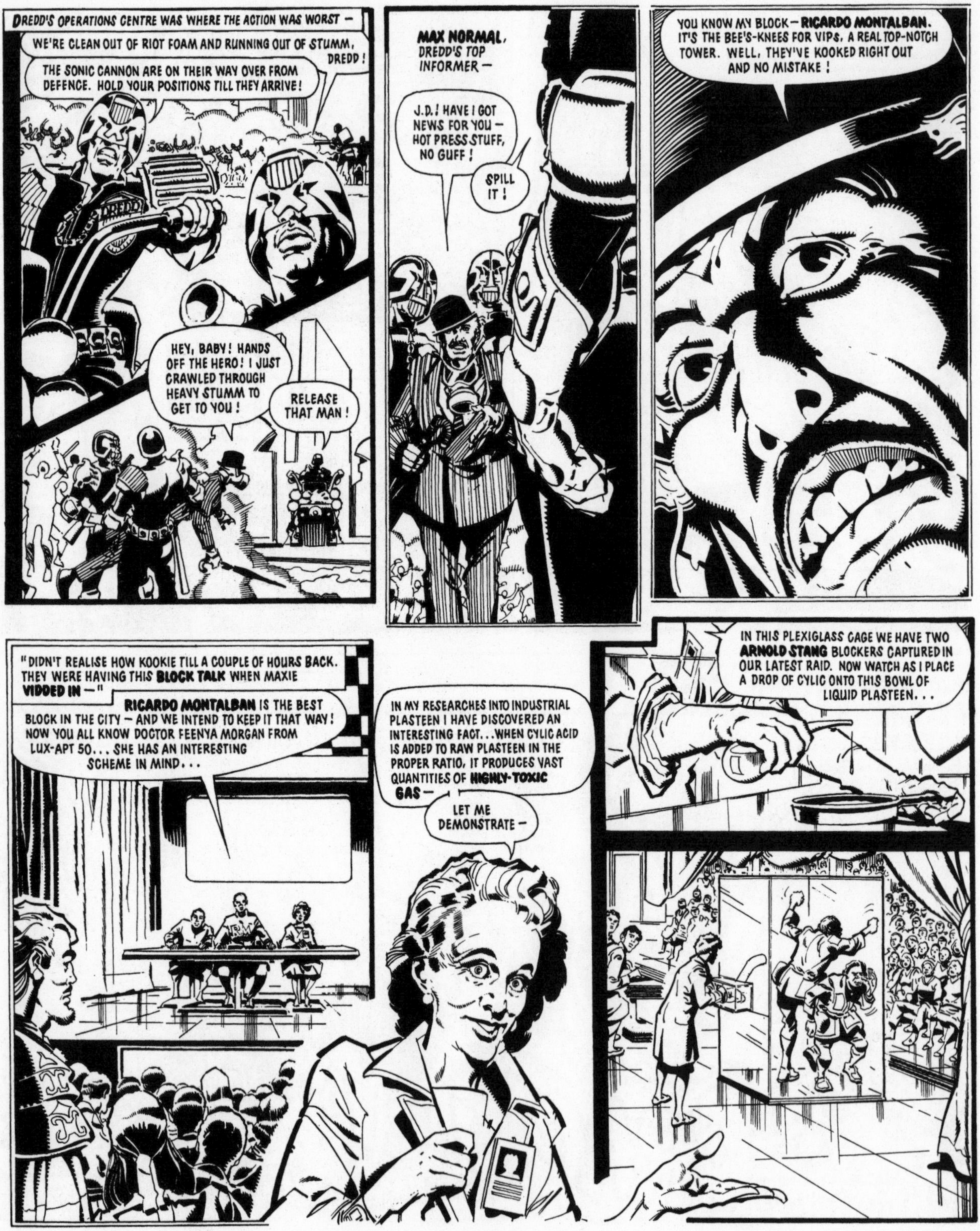

DREDD'S OPERATIONS CENTRE WAS WHERE THE ACTION WAS WORST –
WE'RE CLEAN OUT OF RIOT FOAM AND RUNNING OUT OF STUMM, DREDD!
THE SONIC CANNON ARE ON THEIR WAY OVER FROM DEFENCE. HOLD YOUR POSITIONS TILL THEY ARRIVE!
HEY, BABY! HANDS OFF THE HERO! I JUST CRAWLED THROUGH HEAVY STUMM TO GET TO YOU!
RELEASE THAT MAN!
MAX NORMAL, DREDD'S TOP INFORMER –
J.D.! HAVE I GOT NEWS FOR YOU – HOT PRESS STUFF, NO GUFF!
SPILL IT!
YOU KNOW MY BLOCK – RICARDO MONTALBAN. IT'S THE BEE'S-KNEES FOR VIPS, A REAL TOP-NOTCH TOWER. WELL, THEY'VE KOOKED RIGHT OUT AND NO MISTAKE!
"DIDN'T REALISE HOW KOOKIE TILL A COUPLE OF HOURS BACK. THEY WERE HAVING THIS BLOCK TALK WHEN MAXIE VIDDED IN –"
RICARDO MONTALBAN IS THE BEST BLOCK IN THE CITY – AND WE INTEND TO KEEP IT THAT WAY! NOW YOU ALL KNOW DOCTOR FEENYA MORGAN FROM LUX-APT 50... SHE HAS AN INTERESTING SCHEME IN MIND...
IN MY RESEARCHES INTO INDUSTRIAL PLASTEEN I HAVE DISCOVERED AN INTERESTING FACT... WHEN CYLIC ACID IS ADDED TO RAW PLASTEEN IN THE PROPER RATIO, IT PRODUCES VAST QUANTITIES OF HIGHLY-TOXIC GAS –
LET ME DEMONSTRATE –
IN THIS PLEXIGLASS CAGE WE HAVE TWO ARNOLD STANG BLOCKERS CAPTURED IN OUR LATEST RAID. NOW WATCH AS I PLACE A DROP OF CYLIC ONTO THIS BOWL OF LIQUID PLASTEEN...

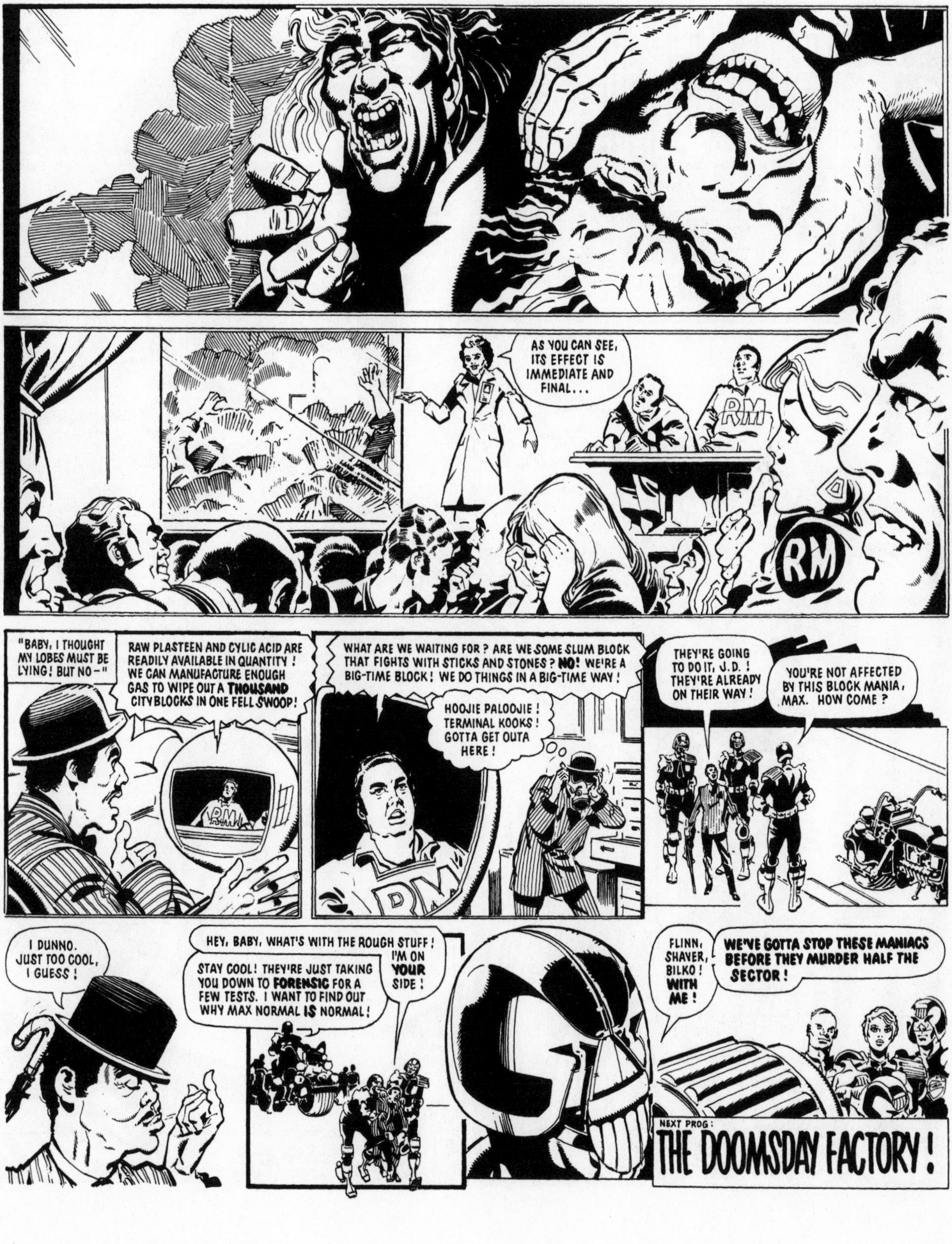
AS YOU CAN SEE, ITS EFFECT IS IMMEDIATE AND FINAL...
"BABY, I THOUGHT MY LOBES MUST BE LYING! BUT NO–"
RAW PLASTEEN AND CYLIC ACID ARE READILY AVAILABLE IN QUANTITY! WE CAN MANUFACTURE ENOUGH GAS TO WIPE OUT A THOUSAND CITY BLOCKS IN ONE FELL SWOOP!
WHAT ARE WE WAITING FOR? ARE WE SOME SLUM BLOCK THAT FIGHTS WITH STICKS AND STONES? NO! WE'RE A BIG-TIME BLOCK! WE DO THINGS IN A BIG-TIME WAY!
HOOJIE PALOOJIE! TERMINAL KOOKS! GOTTA GET OUTA HERE!
THEY'RE GOING TO DO IT, J.D.! THEY'RE ALREADY ON THEIR WAY!
YOU'RE NOT AFFECTED BY THIS BLOCK MANIA, MAX. HOW COME?
I DUNNO. JUST TOO COOL, I GUESS!
HEY, BABY, WHAT'S WITH THE ROUGH STUFF! I'M ON YOUR SIDE!
STAY COOL! THEY'RE JUST TAKING YOU DOWN TO FORENSIC FOR A FEW TESTS. I WANT TO FIND OUT WHY MAX NORMAL IS NORMAL!
FLINN, SHAVER, BILKO! WITH ME!
WE'VE GOTTA STOP THESE MANIACS BEFORE THEY MURDER HALF THE SECTOR!
NEXT PROG:
THE DOOMSDAY FACTORY!

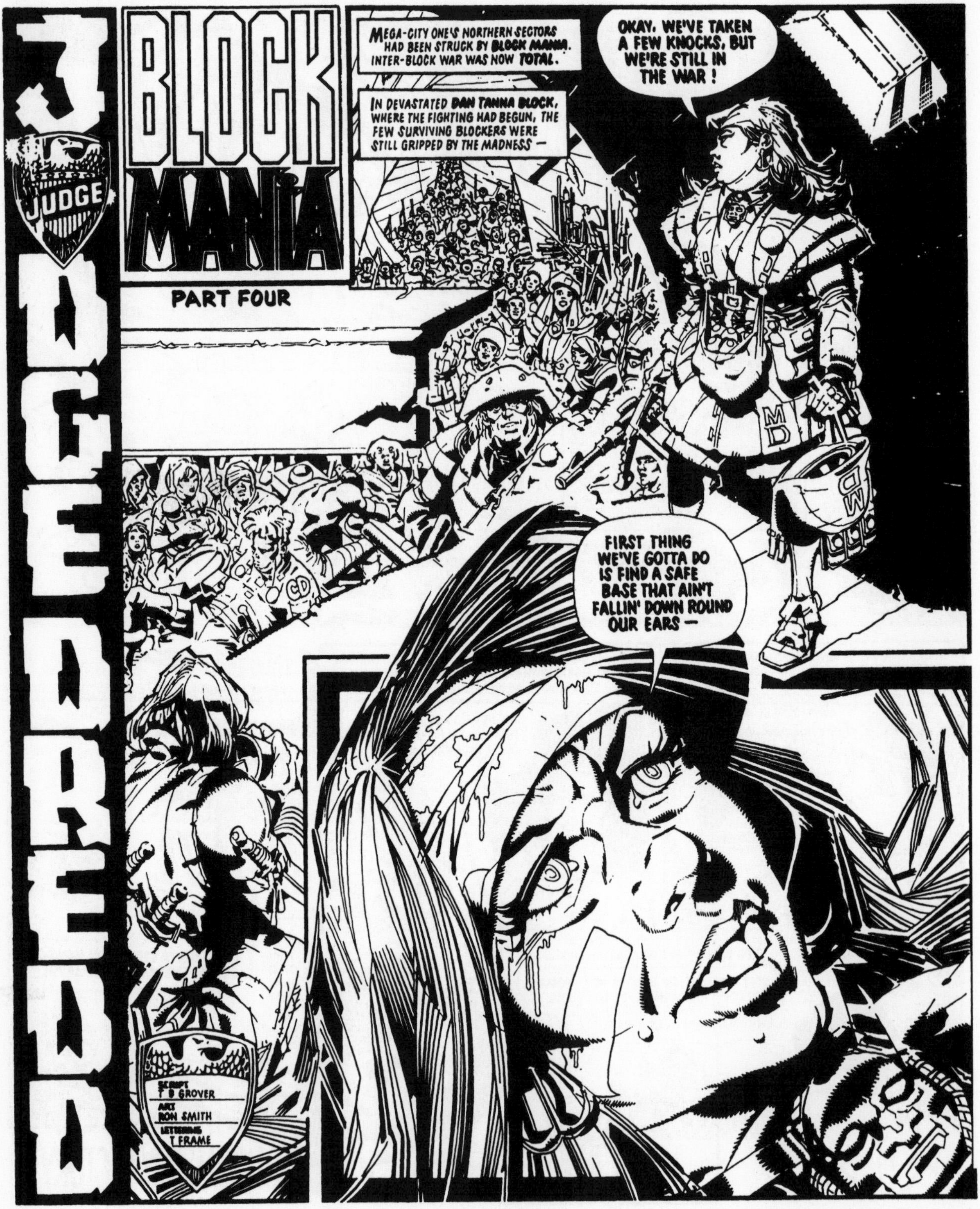
JUDGE DREDD
BLOCK MANIA
PART FOUR
MEGA-CITY ONE'S NORTHERN SECTORS HAD BEEN STRUCK BY BLOCK MANIA. INTER-BLOCK WAR WAS NOW TOTAL.
IN DEVASTATED DAN TANNA BLOCK, WHERE THE FIGHTING HAD BEGUN, THE FEW SURVIVING BLOCKERS WERE STILL GRIPPED BY THE MADNESS —
OKAY, WE'VE TAKEN A FEW KNOCKS, BUT WE'RE STILL IN THE WAR !
FIRST THING WE'VE GOTTA DO IS FIND A SAFE BASE THAT AIN'T FALLIN' DOWN ROUND OUR EARS —
SCRIPT T B GROVER
ART RON SMITH
LETTERING T FRAME

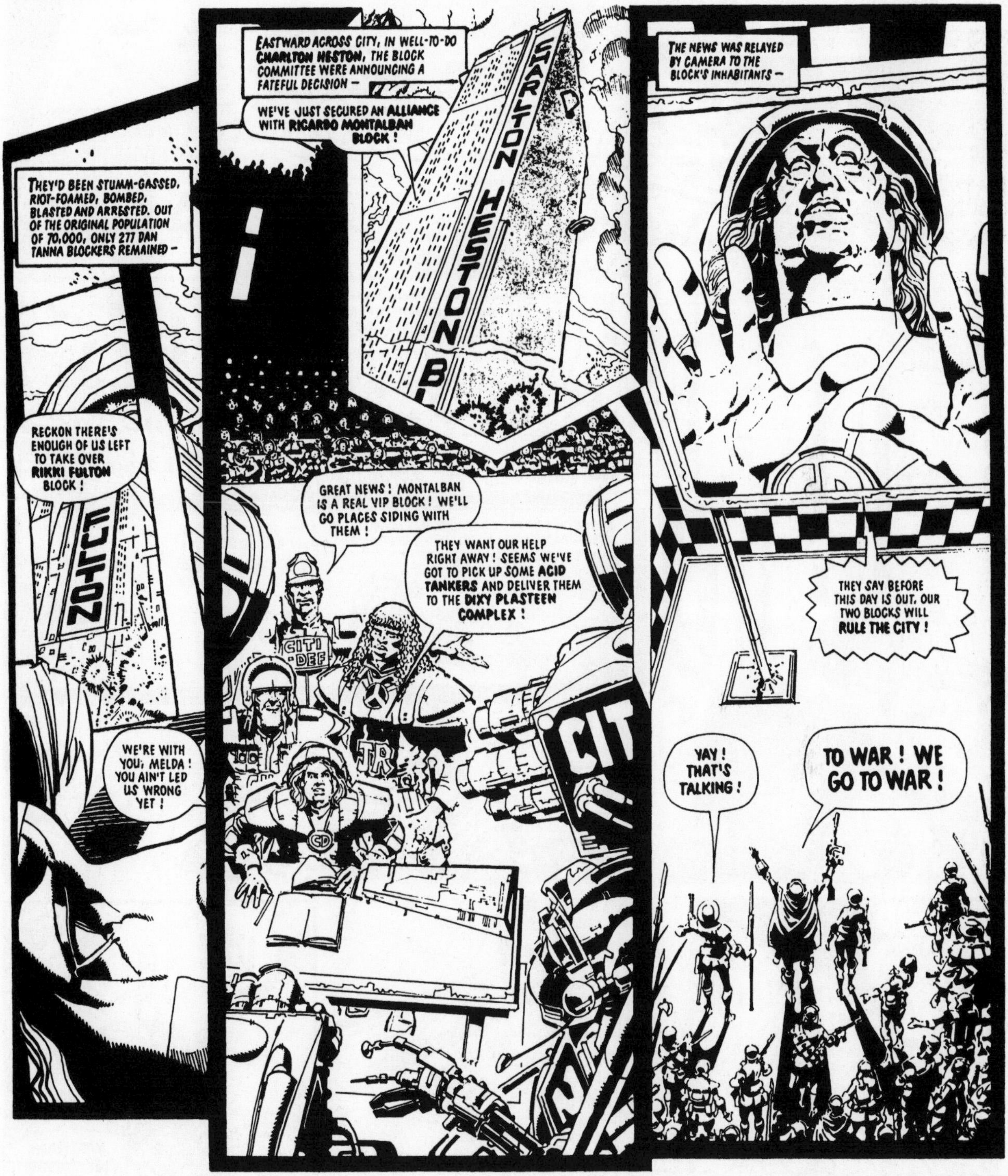

THEY'D BEEN STUMM-GASSED, RIOT-FOAMED, BOMBED, BLASTED AND ARRESTED. OUT OF THE ORIGINAL POPULATION OF 70,000, ONLY 277 DAN TANNA BLOCKERS REMAINED –
RECKON THERE'S ENOUGH OF US LEFT TO TAKE OVER RIKKI FULTON BLOCK !
FULTON
WE'RE WITH YOU, MELDA ! YOU AIN'T LED US WRONG YET !
EASTWARD ACROSS CITY, IN WELL-TO-DO CHARLTON HESTON, THE BLOCK COMMITTEE WERE ANNOUNCING A FATEFUL DECISION –
WE'VE JUST SECURED AN ALLIANCE WITH RICARDO MONTALBAN BLOCK !
CHARLTON HESTON BL
GREAT NEWS ! MONTALBAN IS A REAL VIP BLOCK ! WE'LL GO PLACES SIDING WITH THEM !
THEY WANT OUR HELP RIGHT AWAY ! SEEMS WE'VE GOT TO PICK UP SOME ACID TANKERS AND DELIVER THEM TO THE DIXY PLASTEEN COMPLEX !
CITI DEF
CIT
THE NEWS WAS RELAYED BY CAMERA TO THE BLOCK'S INHABITANTS –
THEY SAY BEFORE THIS DAY IS OUT, OUR TWO BLOCKS WILL RULE THE CITY !
YAY ! THAT'S TALKING !
TO WAR ! WE GO TO WAR !

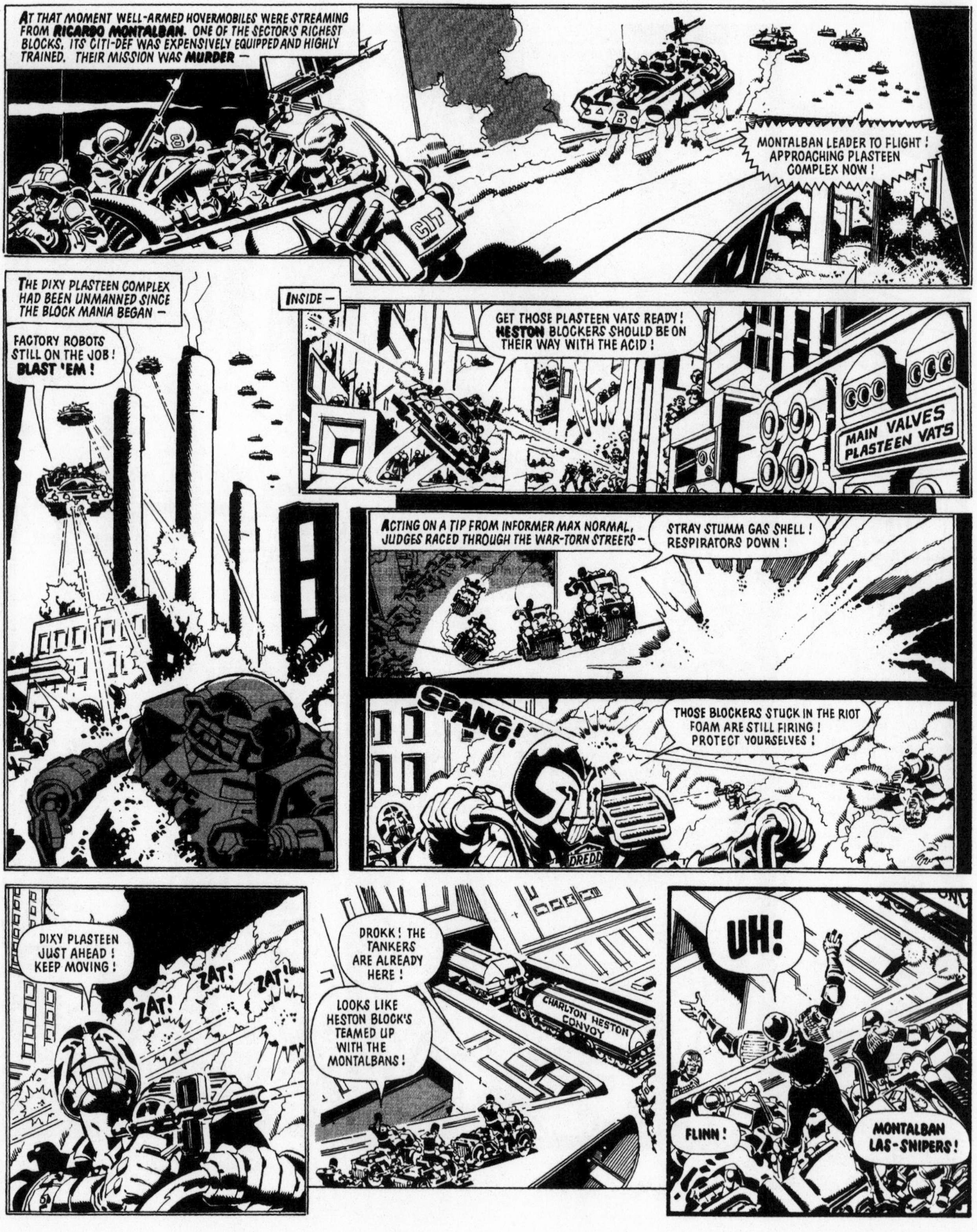
AT THAT MOMENT WELL-ARMED HOVERMOBILES WERE STREAMING FROM RICARDO MONTALBAN. ONE OF THE SECTOR'S RICHEST BLOCKS, ITS CITI-DEF WAS EXPENSIVELY EQUIPPED AND HIGHLY TRAINED. THEIR MISSION WAS MURDER —
MONTALBAN LEADER TO FLIGHT! APPROACHING PLASTEEN COMPLEX NOW!
THE DIXY PLASTEEN COMPLEX HAD BEEN UNMANNED SINCE THE BLOCK MANIA BEGAN —
FACTORY ROBOTS STILL ON THE JOB! BLAST 'EM!
INSIDE —
GET THOSE PLASTEEN VATS READY! HESTON BLOCKERS SHOULD BE ON THEIR WAY WITH THE ACID!
MAIN VALVES PLASTEEN VATS
ACTING ON A TIP FROM INFORMER MAX NORMAL, JUDGES RACED THROUGH THE WAR-TORN STREETS —
STRAY STUMM GAS SHELL! RESPIRATORS DOWN!
SPANG!
THOSE BLOCKERS STUCK IN THE RIOT FOAM ARE STILL FIRING! PROTECT YOURSELVES!
DREDD
DIXY PLASTEEN JUST AHEAD! KEEP MOVING!
ZAT! ZAT! ZAT!
DROKK! THE TANKERS ARE ALREADY HERE!
LOOKS LIKE HESTON BLOCK'S TEAMED UP WITH THE MONTALBANS!
CHARLTON HESTON CONVOY
UH!
FLINN!
MONTALBAN LAS-SNIPERS!

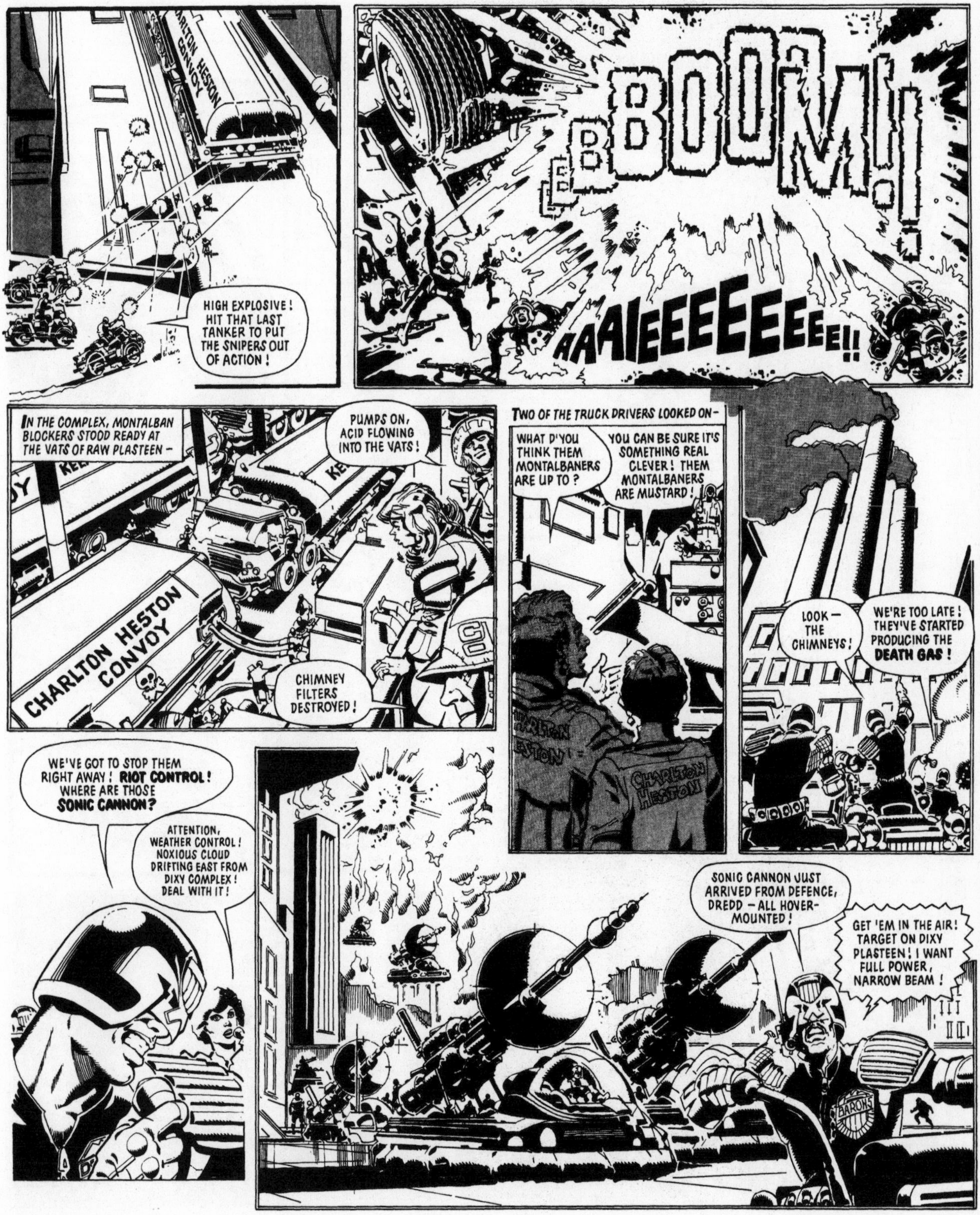
CHARLTON HESTON CONVOY
HIGH EXPLOSIVE! HIT THAT LAST TANKER TO PUT THE SNIPERS OUT OF ACTION!
BBBOOM!!
AAAIEEEEEEEEE!!
IN THE COMPLEX, MONTALBAN BLOCKERS STOOD READY AT THE VATS OF RAW PLASTEEN –
PUMPS ON, ACID FLOWING INTO THE VATS!
CHARLTON HESTON CONVOY
CHIMNEY FILTERS DESTROYED!
TWO OF THE TRUCK DRIVERS LOOKED ON –
WHAT D'YOU THINK THEM MONTALBANERS ARE UP TO?
YOU CAN BE SURE IT'S SOMETHING REAL CLEVER! THEM MONTALBANERS ARE MUSTARD!
CHARLTON HESTON
LOOK – THE CHIMNEYS!
WE'RE TOO LATE! THEY'VE STARTED PRODUCING THE DEATH GAS!
WE'VE GOT TO STOP THEM RIGHT AWAY! RIOT CONTROL! WHERE ARE THOSE SONIC CANNON?
ATTENTION, WEATHER CONTROL! NOXIOUS CLOUD DRIFTING EAST FROM DIXY COMPLEX! DEAL WITH IT!
SONIC CANNON JUST ARRIVED FROM DEFENCE, DREDD – ALL HOVER-MOUNTED!
GET 'EM IN THE AIR! TARGET ON DIXY PLASTEEN! I WANT FULL POWER, NARROW BEAM!
BAROKS

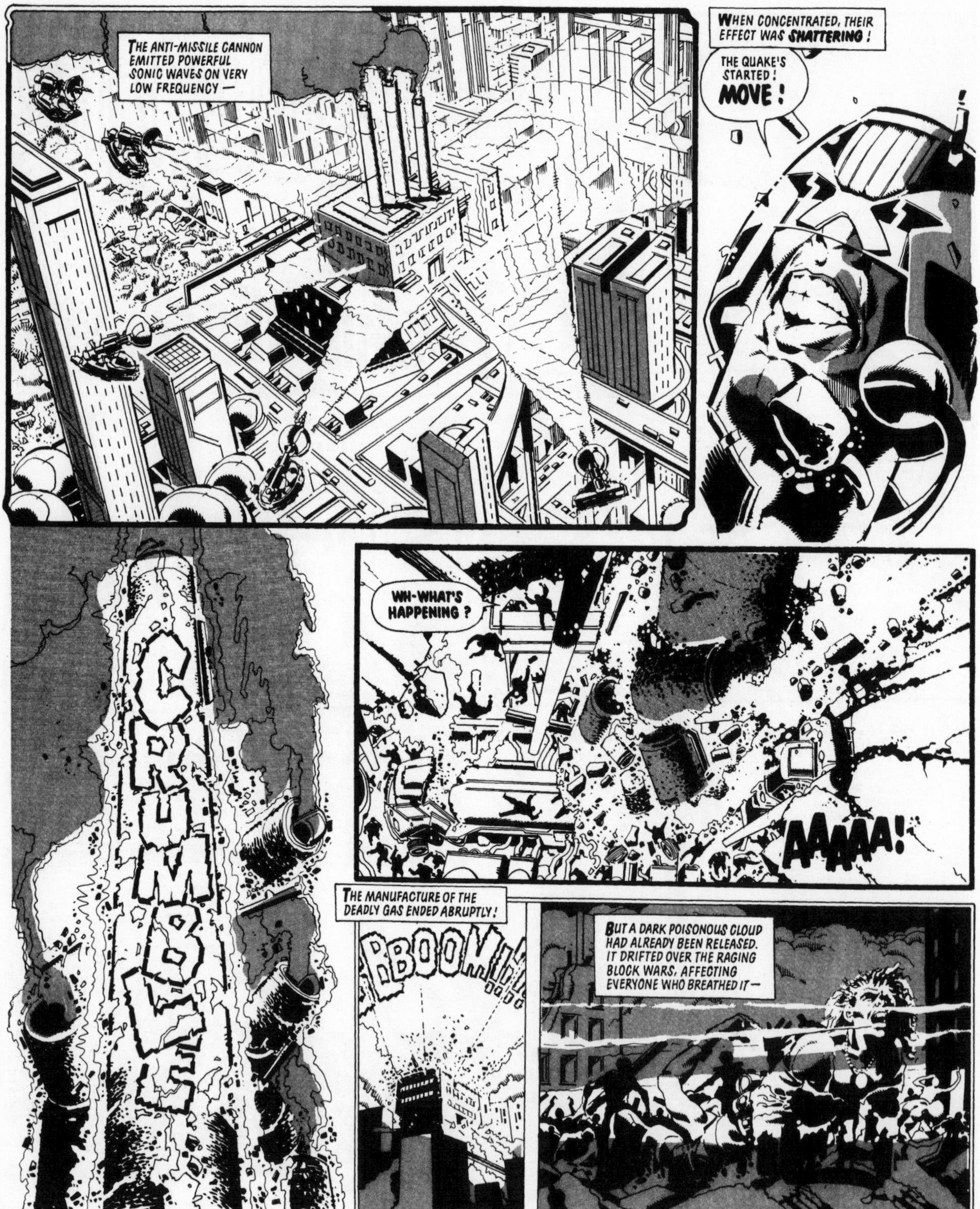
THE ANTI-MISSILE CANNON EMITTED POWERFUL SONIC WAVES ON VERY LOW FREQUENCY —
WHEN CONCENTRATED, THEIR EFFECT WAS SHATTERING !
THE QUAKE'S STARTED ! MOVE !
CRUMBLE
WH-WHAT'S HAPPENING ?
AAAAA!
THE MANUFACTURE OF THE DEADLY GAS ENDED ABRUPTLY !
BBOOM!!!
BUT A DARK POISONOUS CLOUD HAD ALREADY BEEN RELEASED. IT DRIFTED OVER THE RAGING BLOCK WARS, AFFECTING EVERYONE WHO BREATHED IT —

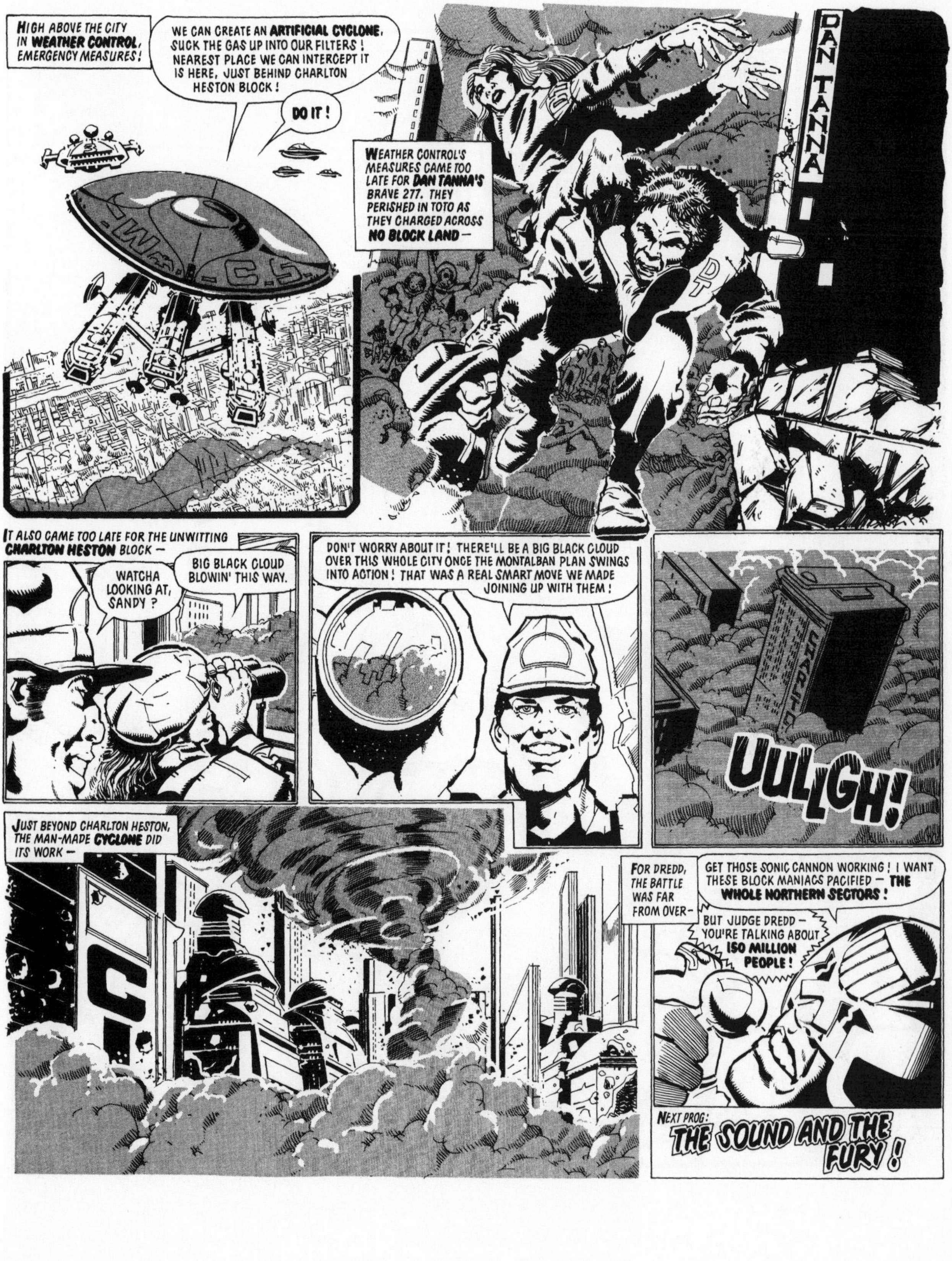
HIGH ABOVE THE CITY IN WEATHER CONTROL, EMERGENCY MEASURES!
WE CAN CREATE AN ARTIFICIAL CYCLONE, SUCK THE GAS UP INTO OUR FILTERS! NEAREST PLACE WE CAN INTERCEPT IT IS HERE, JUST BEHIND CHARLTON HESTON BLOCK!
DO IT!
DAN TANNA
WEATHER CONTROL'S MEASURES CAME TOO LATE FOR DAN TANNA'S BRAVE 277. THEY PERISHED IN TOTO AS THEY CHARGED ACROSS NO BLOCK LAND –
IT ALSO CAME TOO LATE FOR THE UNWITTING CHARLTON HESTON BLOCK –
WATCHA LOOKING AT, SANDY?
BIG BLACK CLOUD BLOWIN' THIS WAY.
DON'T WORRY ABOUT IT! THERE'LL BE A BIG BLACK CLOUD OVER THIS WHOLE CITY ONCE THE MONTALBAN PLAN SWINGS INTO ACTION! THAT WAS A REAL SMART MOVE WE MADE JOINING UP WITH THEM!
UULLGH!
JUST BEYOND CHARLTON HESTON, THE MAN-MADE CYCLONE DID ITS WORK –
FOR DREDD, THE BATTLE WAS FAR FROM OVER –
GET THOSE SONIC CANNON WORKING! I WANT THESE BLOCK MANIACS PACIFIED – THE WHOLE NORTHERN SECTORS!
BUT JUDGE DREDD – YOU'RE TALKING ABOUT 150 MILLION PEOPLE!
NEXT PROG: THE SOUND AND THE FURY!

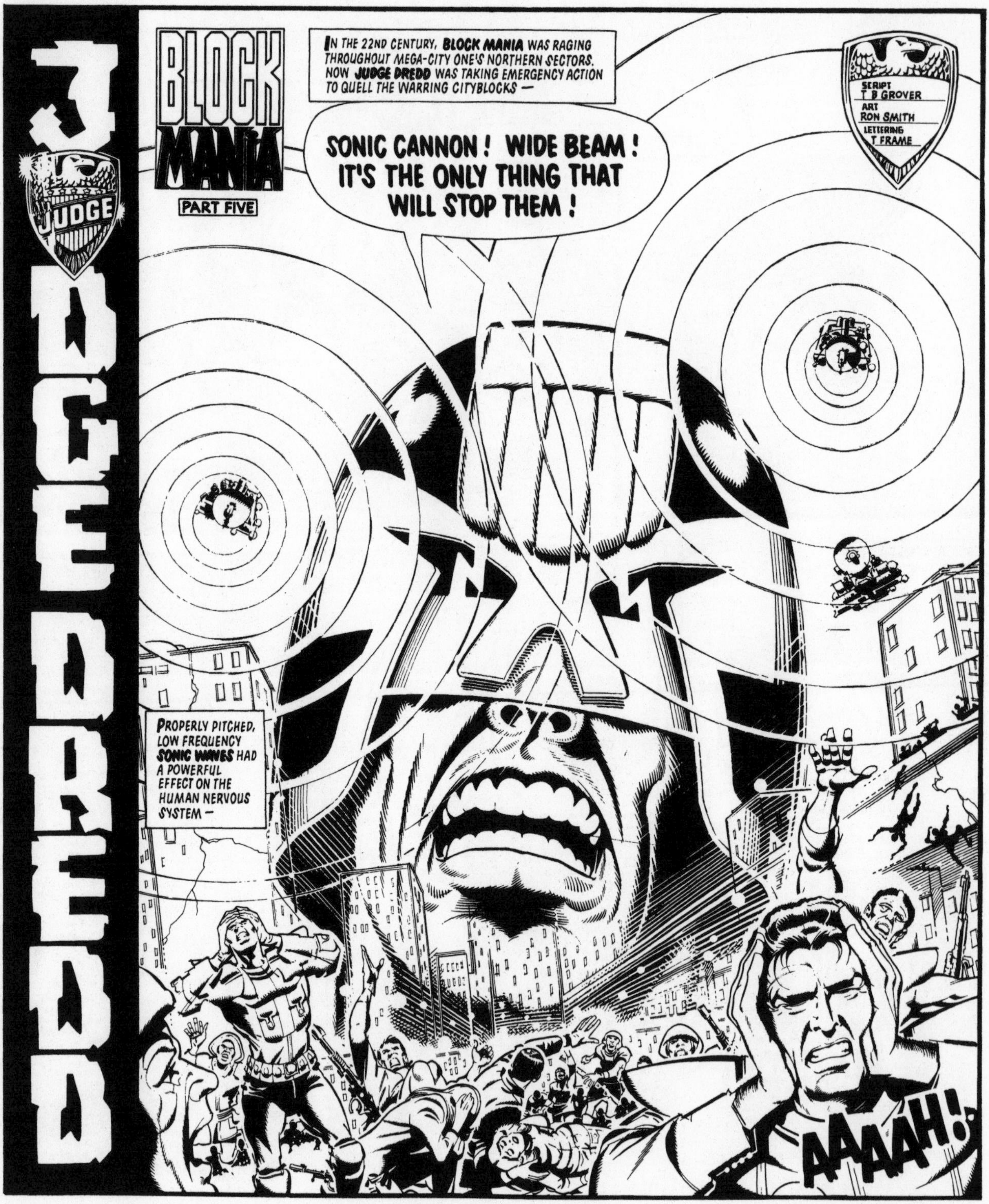
JUDGE DREDD
JUDGE
BLOCK MANIA
PART FIVE
IN THE 22ND CENTURY, BLOCK MANIA WAS RAGING THROUGHOUT MEGA-CITY ONE'S NORTHERN SECTORS. NOW JUDGE DREDD WAS TAKING EMERGENCY ACTION TO QUELL THE WARRING CITYBLOCKS —
SCRIPT T B GROVER
ART RON SMITH
LETTERING T FRAME
SONIC CANNON! WIDE BEAM! IT'S THE ONLY THING THAT WILL STOP THEM!
PROPERLY PITCHED, LOW FREQUENCY SONIC WAVES HAD A POWERFUL EFFECT ON THE HUMAN NERVOUS SYSTEM —
AAAAH!

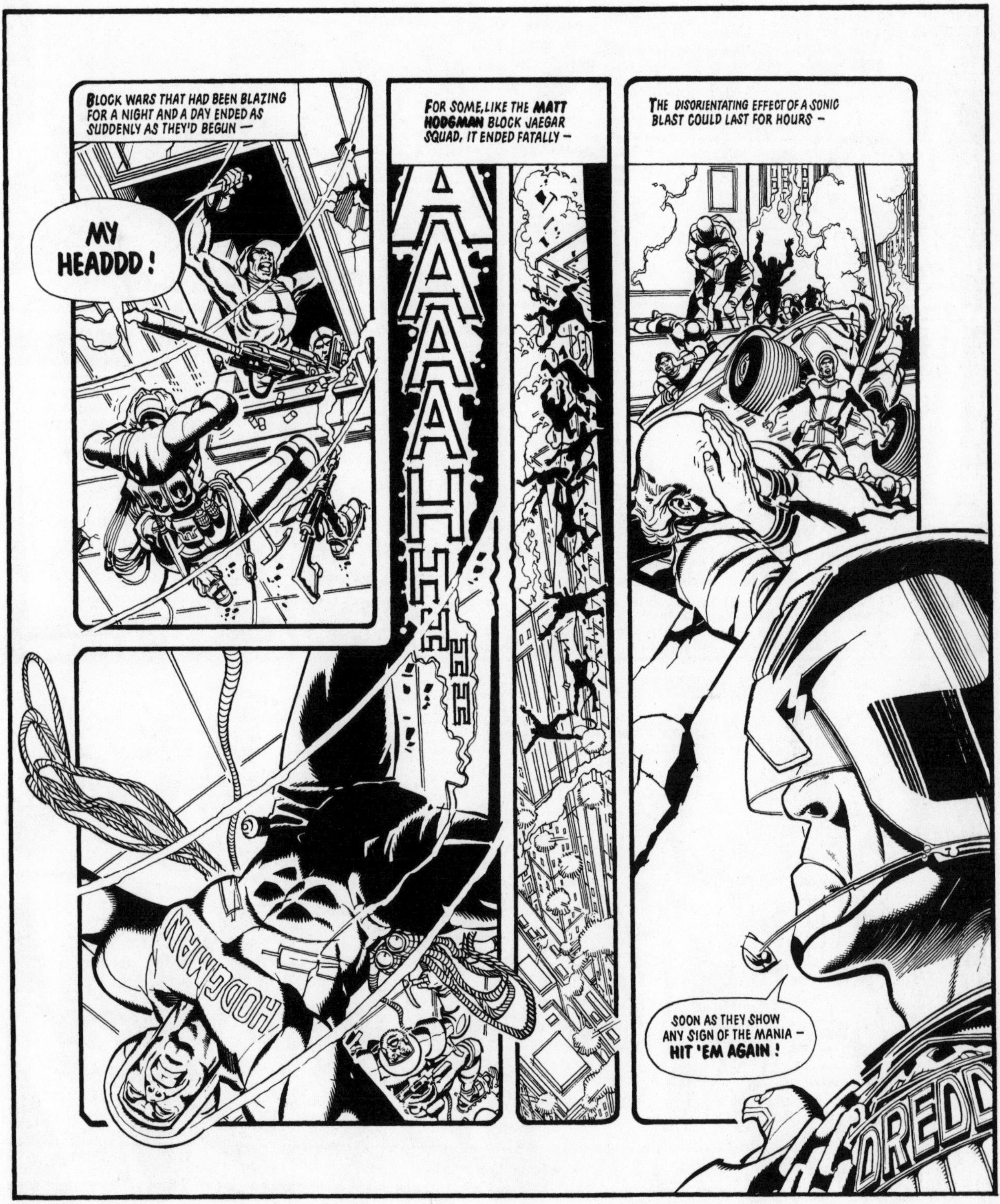
BLOCK WARS THAT HAD BEEN BLAZING FOR A NIGHT AND A DAY ENDED AS SUDDENLY AS THEY'D BEGUN —
MY HEADDD!
FOR SOME, LIKE THE MATT HODGMAN BLOCK JAEGAR SQUAD, IT ENDED FATALLY —
AAAAAHHHHH
HODGMAN
THE DISORIENTATING EFFECT OF A SONIC BLAST COULD LAST FOR HOURS —
SOON AS THEY SHOW ANY SIGN OF THE MANIA — HIT 'EM AGAIN!
DREDD

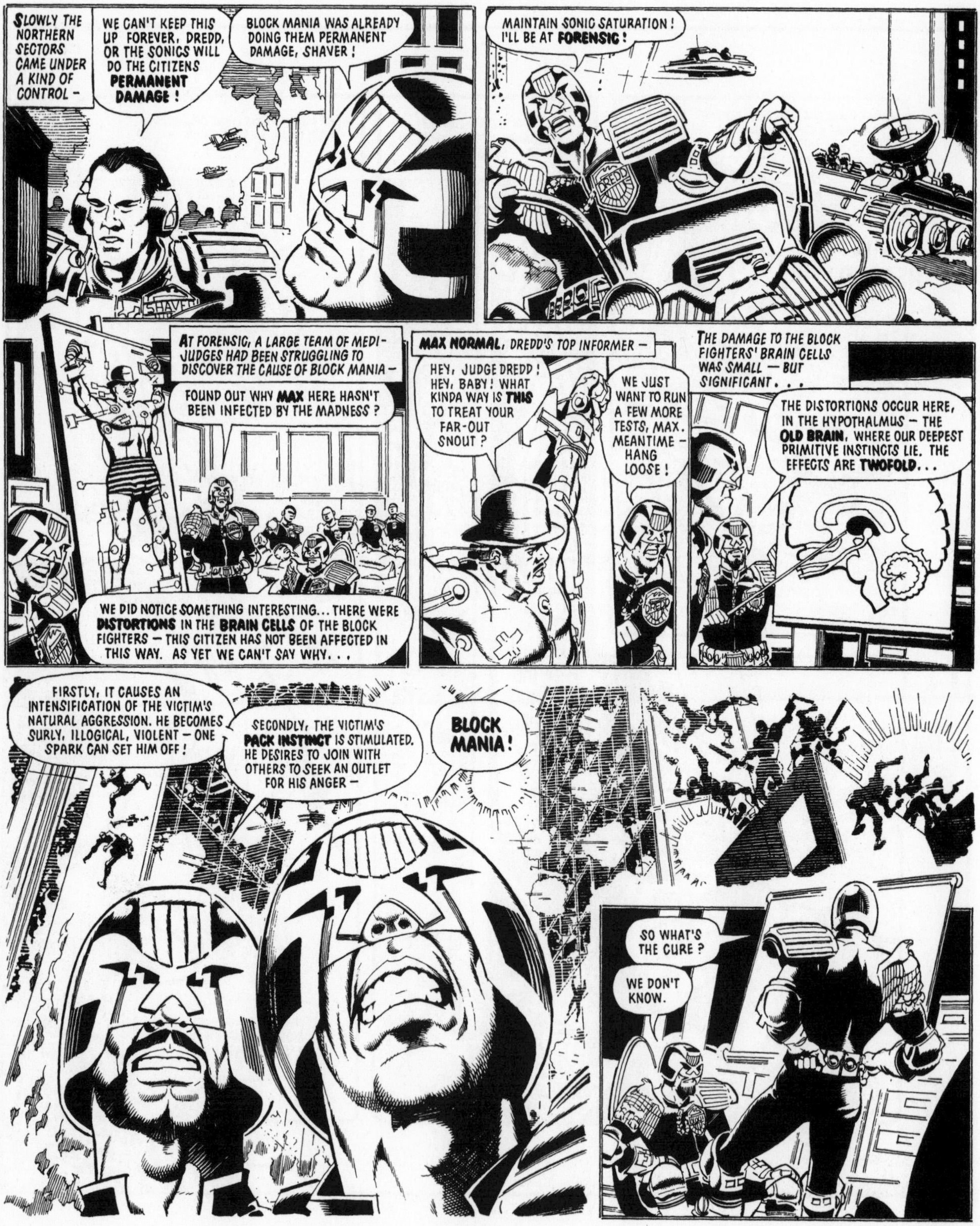
SLOWLY THE NORTHERN SECTORS CAME UNDER A KIND OF CONTROL –
WE CAN'T KEEP THIS UP FOREVER, DREDD, OR THE SONICS WILL DO THE CITIZENS PERMANENT DAMAGE!
BLOCK MANIA WAS ALREADY DOING THEM PERMANENT DAMAGE, SHAVER!
SHAVER
MAINTAIN SONIC SATURATION! I'LL BE AT FORENSIC!
DREDD
AT FORENSIC, A LARGE TEAM OF MEDI-JUDGES HAD BEEN STRUGGLING TO DISCOVER THE CAUSE OF BLOCK MANIA –
FOUND OUT WHY MAX HERE HASN'T BEEN INFECTED BY THE MADNESS?
WE DID NOTICE SOMETHING INTERESTING... THERE WERE DISTORTIONS IN THE BRAIN CELLS OF THE BLOCK FIGHTERS – THIS CITIZEN HAS NOT BEEN AFFECTED IN THIS WAY. AS YET WE CAN'T SAY WHY...
MAX NORMAL, DREDD'S TOP INFORMER –
HEY, JUDGE DREDD! HEY, BABY! WHAT KINDA WAY IS THIS TO TREAT YOUR FAR-OUT SNOUT?
WE JUST WANT TO RUN A FEW MORE TESTS, MAX. MEANTIME – HANG LOOSE!
THE DAMAGE TO THE BLOCK FIGHTERS' BRAIN CELLS WAS SMALL – BUT SIGNIFICANT...
THE DISTORTIONS OCCUR HERE, IN THE HYPOTHALMUS – THE OLD BRAIN, WHERE OUR DEEPEST PRIMITIVE INSTINCTS LIE. THE EFFECTS ARE TWOFOLD...
FIRSTLY, IT CAUSES AN INTENSIFICATION OF THE VICTIM'S NATURAL AGGRESSION. HE BECOMES SURLY, ILLOGICAL, VIOLENT – ONE SPARK CAN SET HIM OFF!
SECONDLY, THE VICTIM'S PACK INSTINCT IS STIMULATED. HE DESIRES TO JOIN WITH OTHERS TO SEEK AN OUTLET FOR HIS ANGER –
BLOCK MANIA!
SO WHAT'S THE CURE?
WE DON'T KNOW.

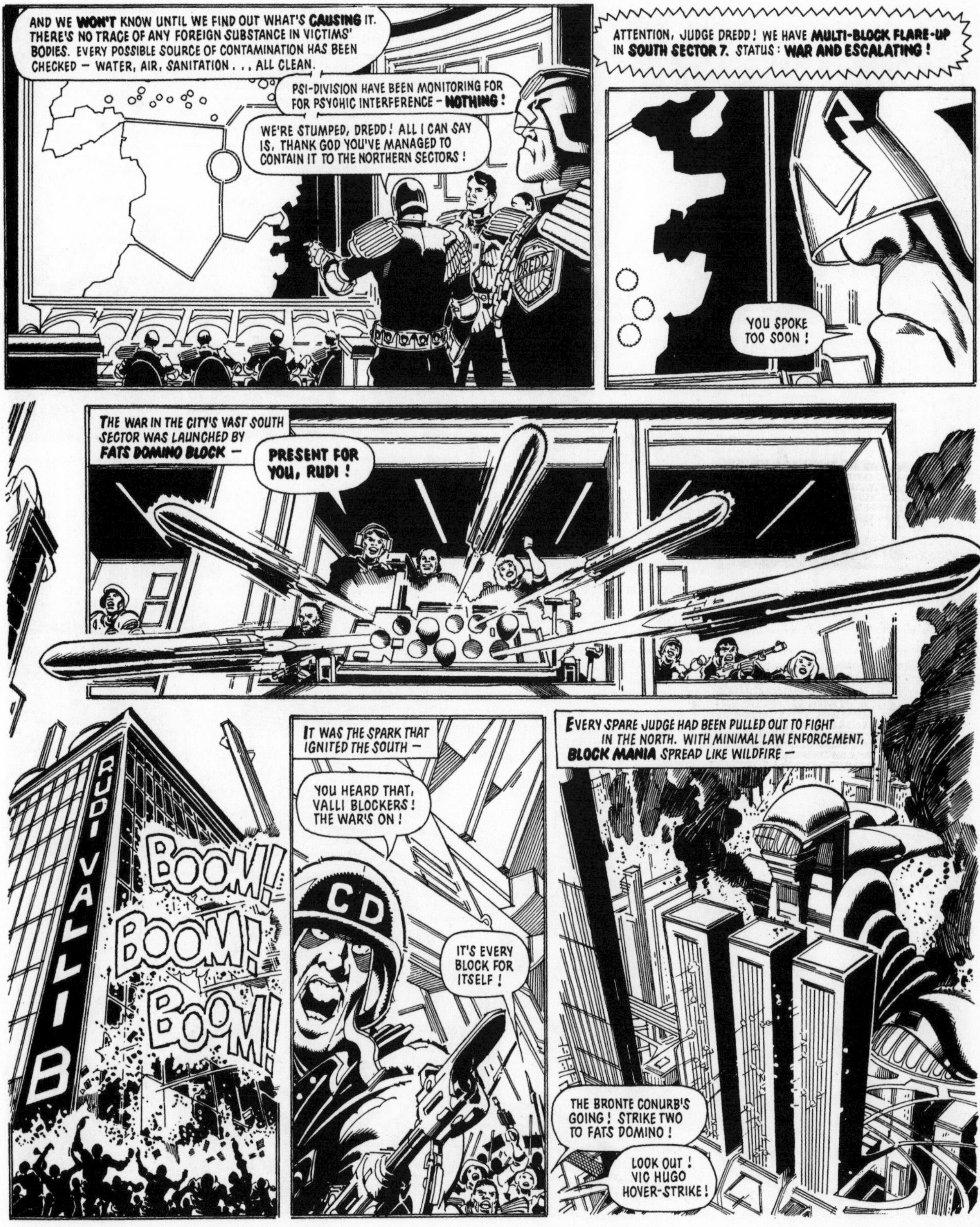
AND WE WON'T KNOW UNTIL WE FIND OUT WHAT'S CAUSING IT. THERE'S NO TRACE OF ANY FOREIGN SUBSTANCE IN VICTIMS' BODIES. EVERY POSSIBLE SOURCE OF CONTAMINATION HAS BEEN CHECKED – WATER, AIR, SANITATION . . . ALL CLEAN.
PSI-DIVISION HAVE BEEN MONITORING FOR FOR PSYCHIC INTERFERENCE – NOTHING!
WE'RE STUMPED, DREDD! ALL I CAN SAY IS, THANK GOD YOU'VE MANAGED TO CONTAIN IT TO THE NORTHERN SECTORS!
DREDD
ATTENTION, JUDGE DREDD! WE HAVE MULTI-BLOCK FLARE-UP IN SOUTH SECTOR 7. STATUS: WAR AND ESCALATING!
YOU SPOKE TOO SOON!
THE WAR IN THE CITY'S VAST SOUTH SECTOR WAS LAUNCHED BY FATS DOMINO BLOCK –
PRESENT FOR YOU, RUDI!
RUDI VALLI B
BOOM! BOOM! BOOM!
IT WAS THE SPARK THAT IGNITED THE SOUTH –
YOU HEARD THAT, VALLI BLOCKERS! THE WAR'S ON!
CD
IT'S EVERY BLOCK FOR ITSELF!
EVERY SPARE JUDGE HAD BEEN PULLED OUT TO FIGHT IN THE NORTH. WITH MINIMAL LAW ENFORCEMENT, BLOCK MANIA SPREAD LIKE WILDFIRE –
THE BRONTE CONURB'S GOING! STRIKE TWO TO FATS DOMINO!
LOOK OUT! VIC HUGO HOVER-STRIKE!

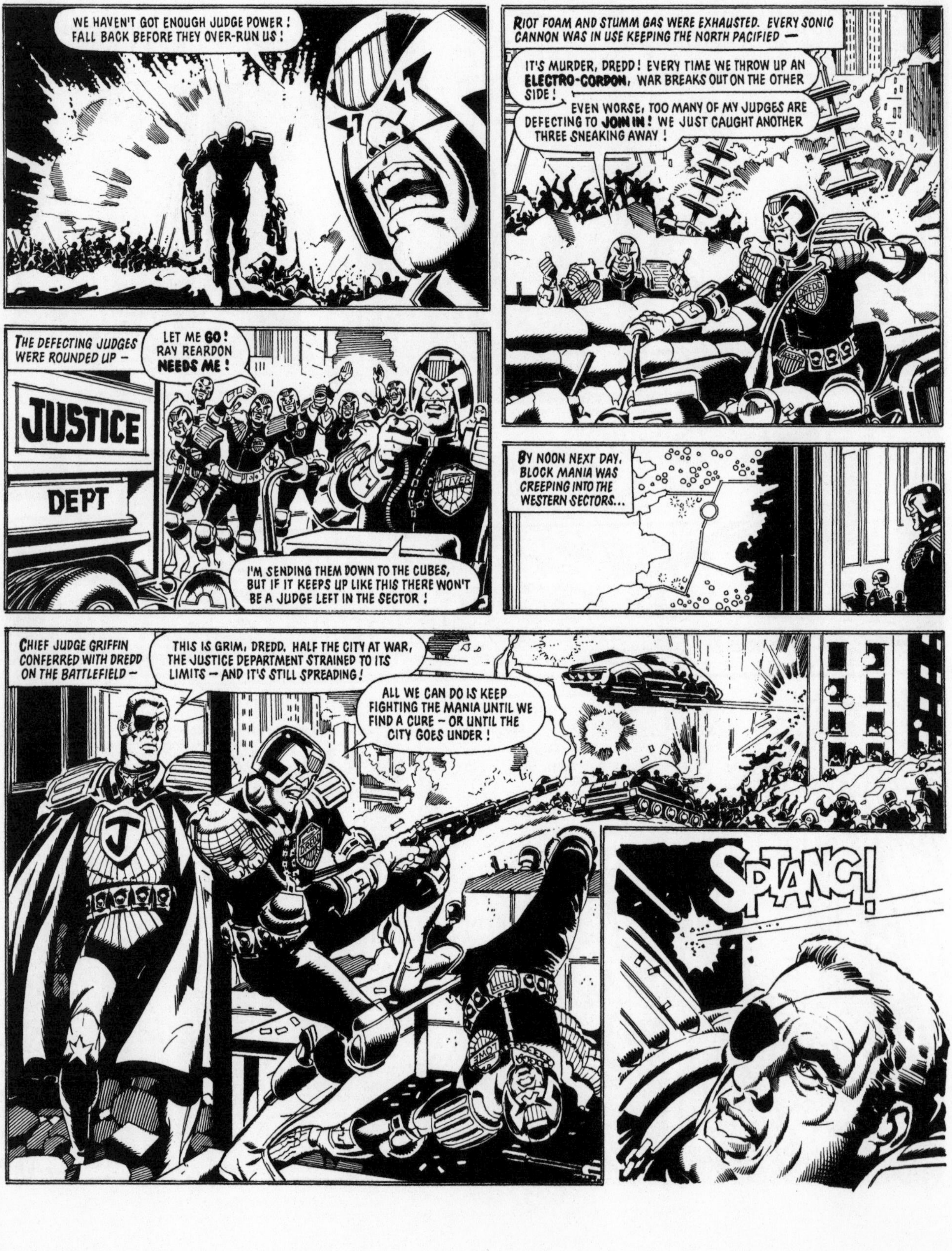
WE HAVEN'T GOT ENOUGH JUDGE POWER! FALL BACK BEFORE THEY OVER-RUN US!
RIOT FOAM AND STUMM GAS WERE EXHAUSTED. EVERY SONIC CANNON WAS IN USE KEEPING THE NORTH PACIFIED —
IT'S MURDER, DREDD! EVERY TIME WE THROW UP AN ELECTRO-CORDON, WAR BREAKS OUT ON THE OTHER SIDE!
EVEN WORSE, TOO MANY OF MY JUDGES ARE DEFECTING TO JOIN IN! WE JUST CAUGHT ANOTHER THREE SNEAKING AWAY!
THE DEFECTING JUDGES WERE ROUNDED UP —
LET ME GO! RAY REARDON NEEDS ME!
JUSTICE
DEPT
I'M SENDING THEM DOWN TO THE CUBES, BUT IF IT KEEPS UP LIKE THIS THERE WON'T BE A JUDGE LEFT IN THE SECTOR!
BY NOON NEXT DAY, BLOCK MANIA WAS CREEPING INTO THE WESTERN SECTORS...
CHIEF JUDGE GRIFFIN CONFERRED WITH DREDD ON THE BATTLEFIELD —
THIS IS GRIM, DREDD. HALF THE CITY AT WAR, THE JUSTICE DEPARTMENT STRAINED TO ITS LIMITS — AND IT'S STILL SPREADING!
ALL WE CAN DO IS KEEP FIGHTING THE MANIA UNTIL WE FIND A CURE — OR UNTIL THE CITY GOES UNDER!
SPTANG!

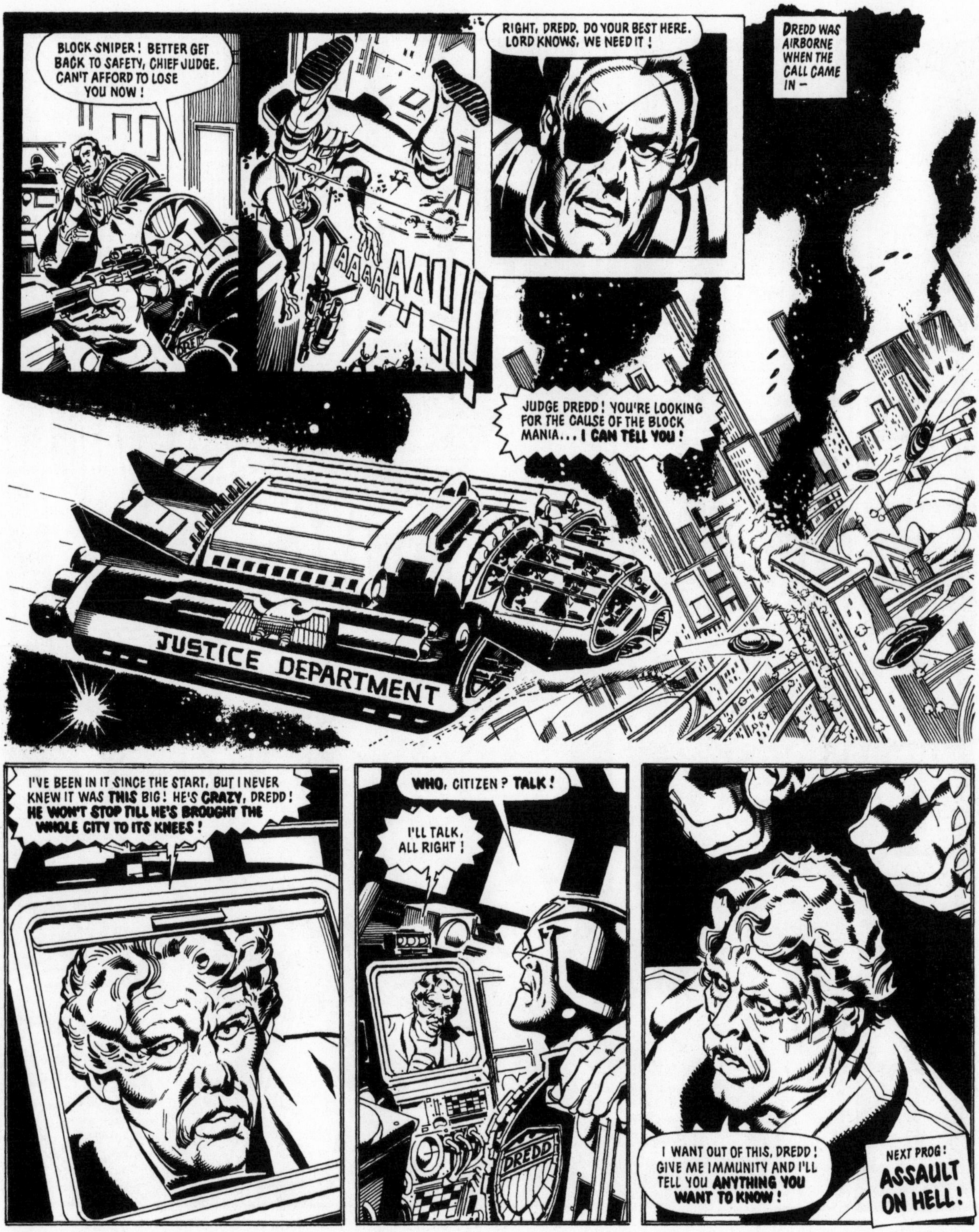
BLOCK SNIPER! BETTER GET BACK TO SAFETY, CHIEF JUDGE. CAN'T AFFORD TO LOSE YOU NOW!
AAAAAAAH!
RIGHT, DREDD. DO YOUR BEST HERE. LORD KNOWS, WE NEED IT!
DREDD WAS AIRBORNE WHEN THE CALL CAME IN –
JUDGE DREDD! YOU'RE LOOKING FOR THE CAUSE OF THE BLOCK MANIA... I CAN TELL YOU!
JUSTICE DEPARTMENT
I'VE BEEN IN IT SINCE THE START, BUT I NEVER KNEW IT WAS THIS BIG! HE'S CRAZY, DREDD! HE WON'T STOP TILL HE'S BROUGHT THE WHOLE CITY TO ITS KNEES!
WHO, CITIZEN? TALK!
I'LL TALK, ALL RIGHT!
DREDD
I WANT OUT OF THIS, DREDD! GIVE ME IMMUNITY AND I'LL TELL YOU ANYTHING YOU WANT TO KNOW!
NEXT PROG: ASSAULT ON HELL!

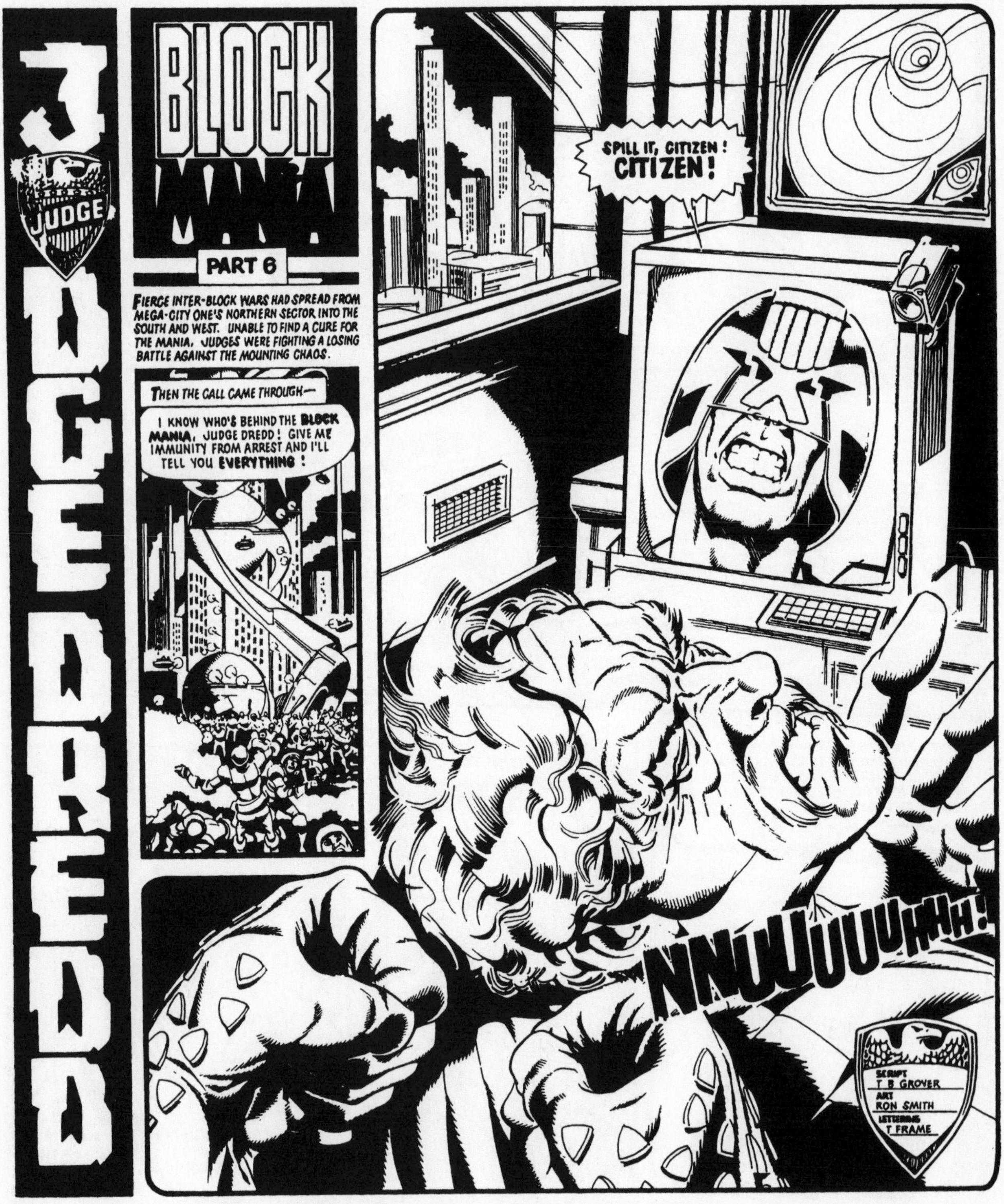
JUDGE DREDD
JUDGE
BLOCK MANIA
PART 6
FIERCE INTER-BLOCK WARS HAD SPREAD FROM MEGA-CITY ONE'S NORTHERN SECTOR INTO THE SOUTH AND WEST. UNABLE TO FIND A CURE FOR THE MANIA, JUDGES WERE FIGHTING A LOSING BATTLE AGAINST THE MOUNTING CHAOS.
THEN THE CALL CAME THROUGH—
I KNOW WHO'S BEHIND THE BLOCK MANIA, JUDGE DREDD! GIVE ME IMMUNITY FROM ARREST AND I'LL TELL YOU EVERYTHING!
SPILL IT, CITIZEN! CITIZEN!
NNUUUUUUHHH!
SCRIPT T B GROVER
ART RON SMITH
LETTERING T FRAME

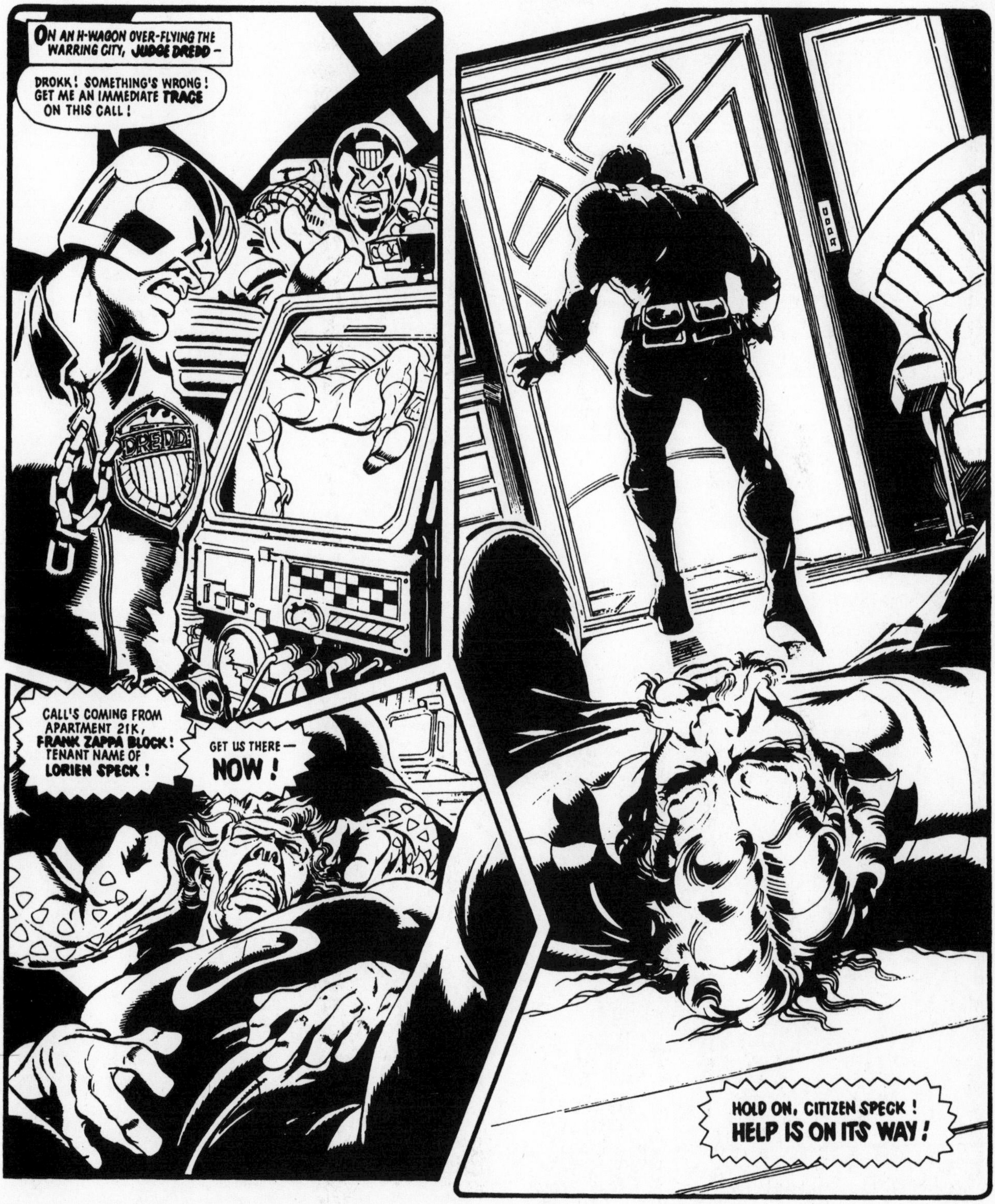

ON AN H-WAGON OVER-FLYING THE WARRING CITY, JUDGE DREDD –
DROKK! SOMETHING'S WRONG! GET ME AN IMMEDIATE TRACE ON THIS CALL!
DREDD
CALL'S COMING FROM APARTMENT 21K, FRANK ZAPPA BLOCK! TENANT NAME OF LORIEN SPECK!
GET US THERE – NOW!
HOLD ON, CITIZEN SPECK! HELP IS ON ITS WAY!

Panel 1 (caption): AS DREDD'S CRAFT RACED SOUTHWARD—

SPECK'S BEEN LIVING IN *FRANK ZAPPA* FOR NINETEEN YEARS. UNEMPLOYED EXECUTIVE, AGE 54. NO PREVIOUS CONVICTIONS.

HE IMPLIED THE *BLOCK MANIA* IS MAN-*MADE*. IT'S OUR FIRST REAL LEAD.

Panel 2: LET'S HOPE HE'S ALIVE TO TELL US MORE!

Panel 3 (caption): LORIEN SPECK'S BLOCK, *FRANK ZAPPA*, LAY IN THE CENTRE OF THE BITTEREST FIGHTING. FOR A DAY AND A HALF A *FIFTY-BLOCK WAR* HAD BEEN RAGING.

NOW, NO BLOCK KNEW WHOSE SIDE THEY WERE ON—AND NO BLOCK CARED!

ALL GUNS FIRE AT WILL!

Panel 4: AIEEE!

AAAH! IT'S THE JED CLAMPETT BIG GUNS!

Panel 5 (caption): IT WAS A WELL-AIMED SHOT FROM *CLAMPETT BLOCK'S* CRACK *AERIAL DEFENCE BATTERY* THAT HIT DREDD'S H-WAGON—

COMMAND DECK'S HIT!

Panel 6 (caption): NEXT MOMENT IT WAS PLUNGING CITYWARD—

GRIPPED BY THE MANIA, THE FRENZIED BLOCKERS BARELY PAUSED TO LOOK UP!

LOOK!

SHUDDUP! KEEP FIGHTING! *DOD CUSTER* BLOCKERS STAND FIRM!

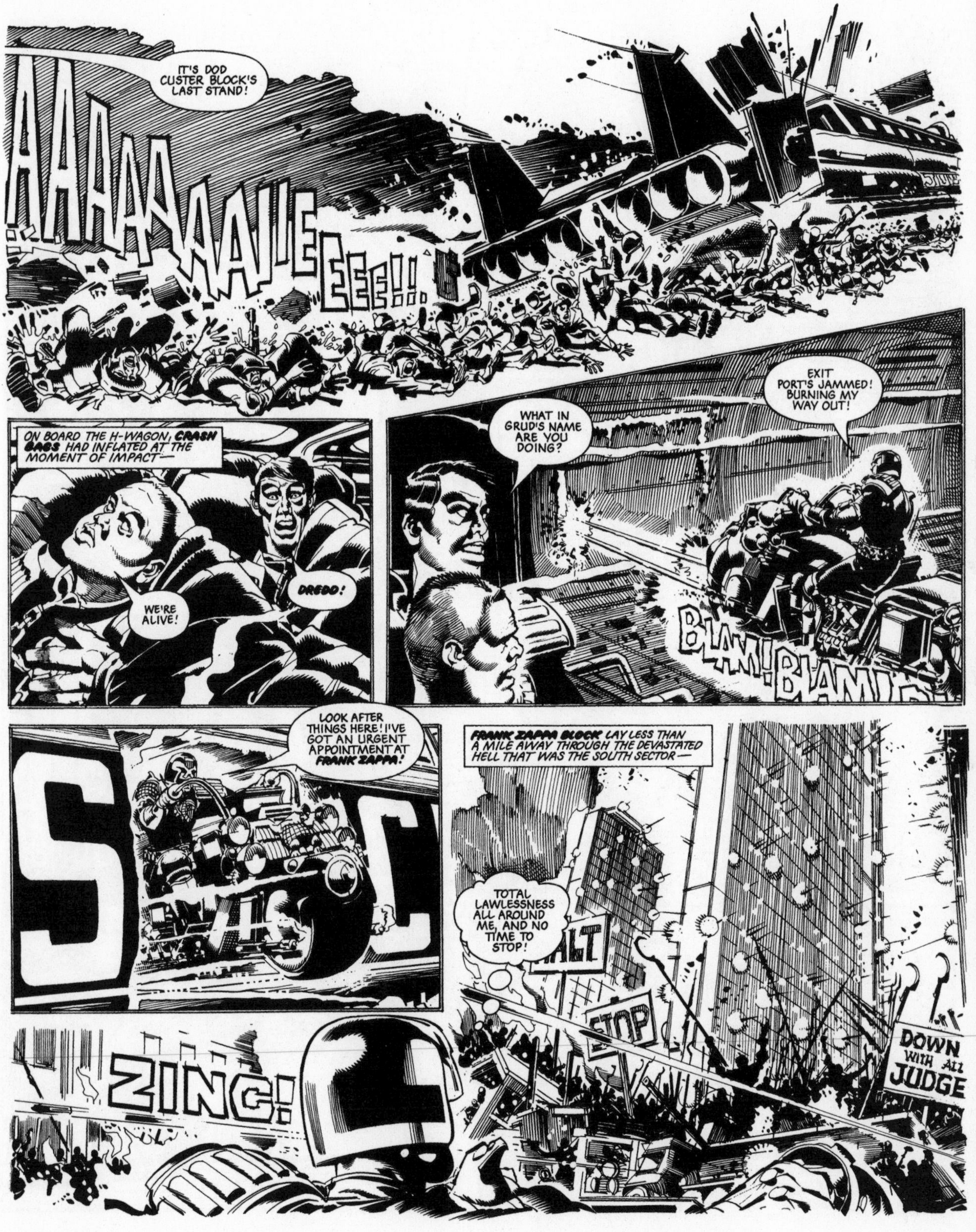
IT'S DOD CUSTER BLOCK'S LAST STAND!
AAAAAAAIIEEEE!!!
ON BOARD THE H-WAGON, CRASH BAGS HAD INFLATED AT THE MOMENT OF IMPACT—
WE'RE ALIVE!
DREDD!
WHAT IN GRUD'S NAME ARE YOU DOING?
EXIT PORT'S JAMMED! BURNING MY WAY OUT!
BLAM! BLAM!
LOOK AFTER THINGS HERE! I'VE GOT AN URGENT APPOINTMENT AT FRANK ZAPPA!
FRANK ZAPPA BLOCK LAY LESS THAN A MILE AWAY THROUGH THE DEVASTATED HELL THAT WAS THE SOUTH SECTOR—
TOTAL LAWLESSNESS ALL AROUND ME, AND NO TIME TO STOP!
STOP
DOWN WITH ALL JUDGE
ZING!

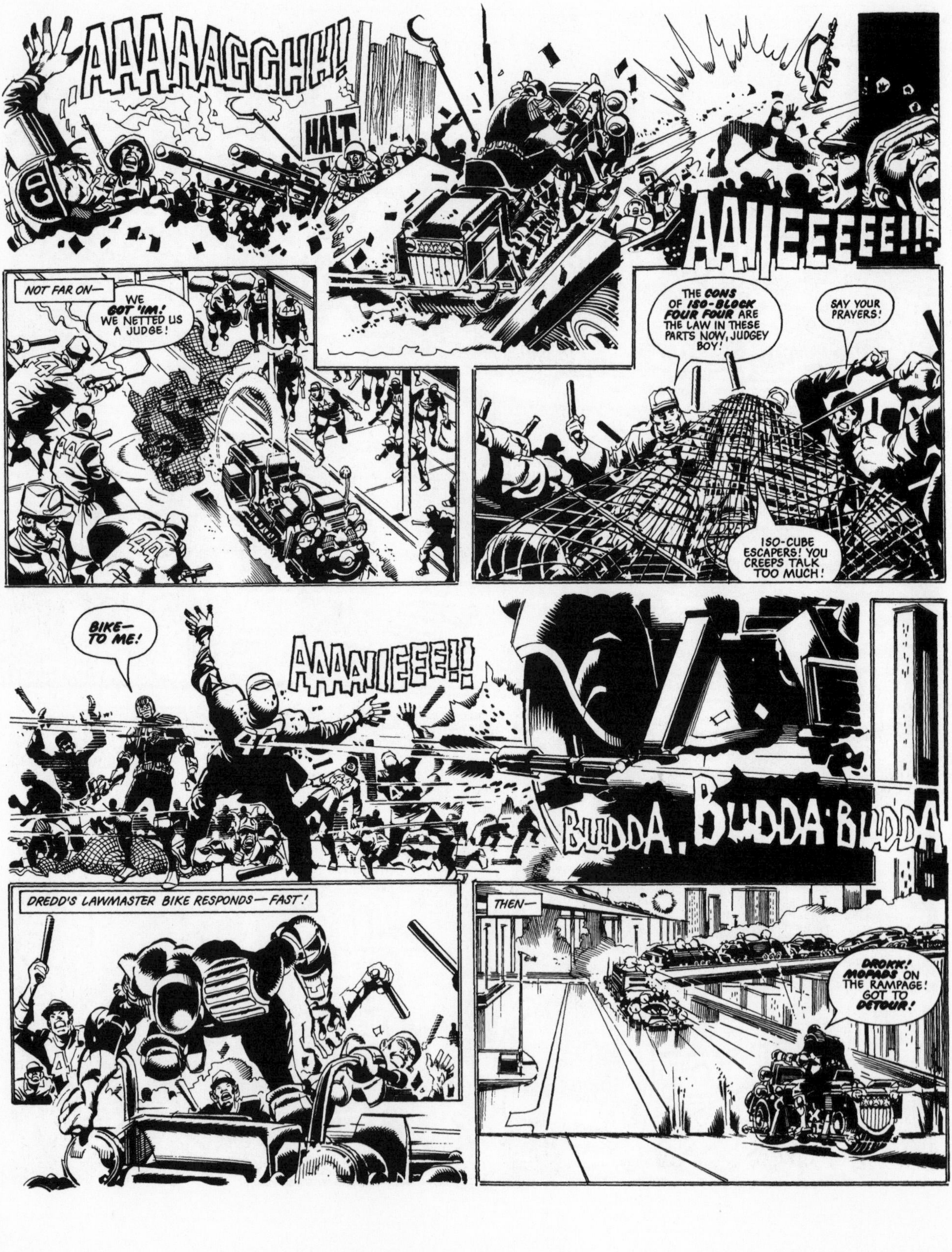

AAAAACGHH!
HALT
AAIIEEEEE!!
NOT FAR ON—
WE GOT 'IM! WE NETTED US A JUDGE!
THE CONS OF ISO-BLOCK FOUR FOUR ARE THE LAW IN THESE PARTS NOW, JUDGEY BOY!
SAY YOUR PRAYERS!
ISO-CUBE ESCAPERS! YOU CREEPS TALK TOO MUCH!
BIKE— TO ME!
AAAAIIEEE!!
BUDDA. BUDDA·BUDDA
DREDD'S LAWMASTER BIKE RESPONDS—FAST!
THEN—
DROKK! MOPADS ON THE RAMPAGE! GOT TO DETOUR!

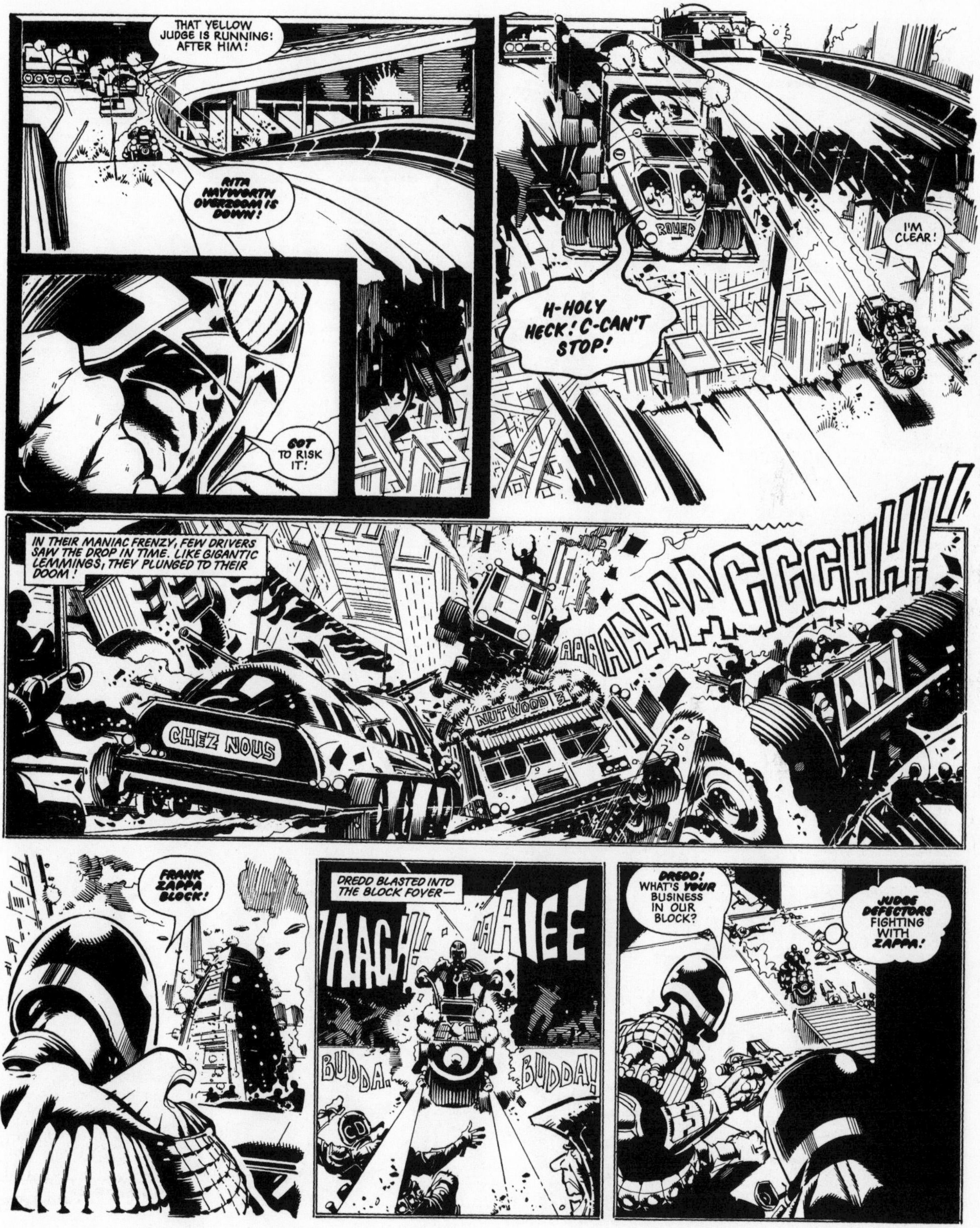

THAT YELLOW JUDGE IS RUNNING! AFTER HIM!
RITA HAYWORTH OVERZOOM IS DOWN!
GOT TO RISK IT!
ROVER
H-HOLY HECK! C-CAN'T STOP!
I'M CLEAR!
IN THEIR MANIAC FRENZY, FEW DRIVERS SAW THE DROP IN TIME. LIKE GIGANTIC LEMMINGS, THEY PLUNGED TO THEIR DOOM!
AAAAAAAAAGGGCHH!
CHEZ NOUS
NUTWOOD 3
FRANK ZAPPA BLOCK!
DREDD BLASTED INTO THE BLOCK FOYER—
AAAGH!
AAIEE
BUDDA.
BUDDA!
DREDD! WHAT'S YOUR BUSINESS IN OUR BLOCK?
JUDGE DEFECTORS FIGHTING WITH ZAPPA!

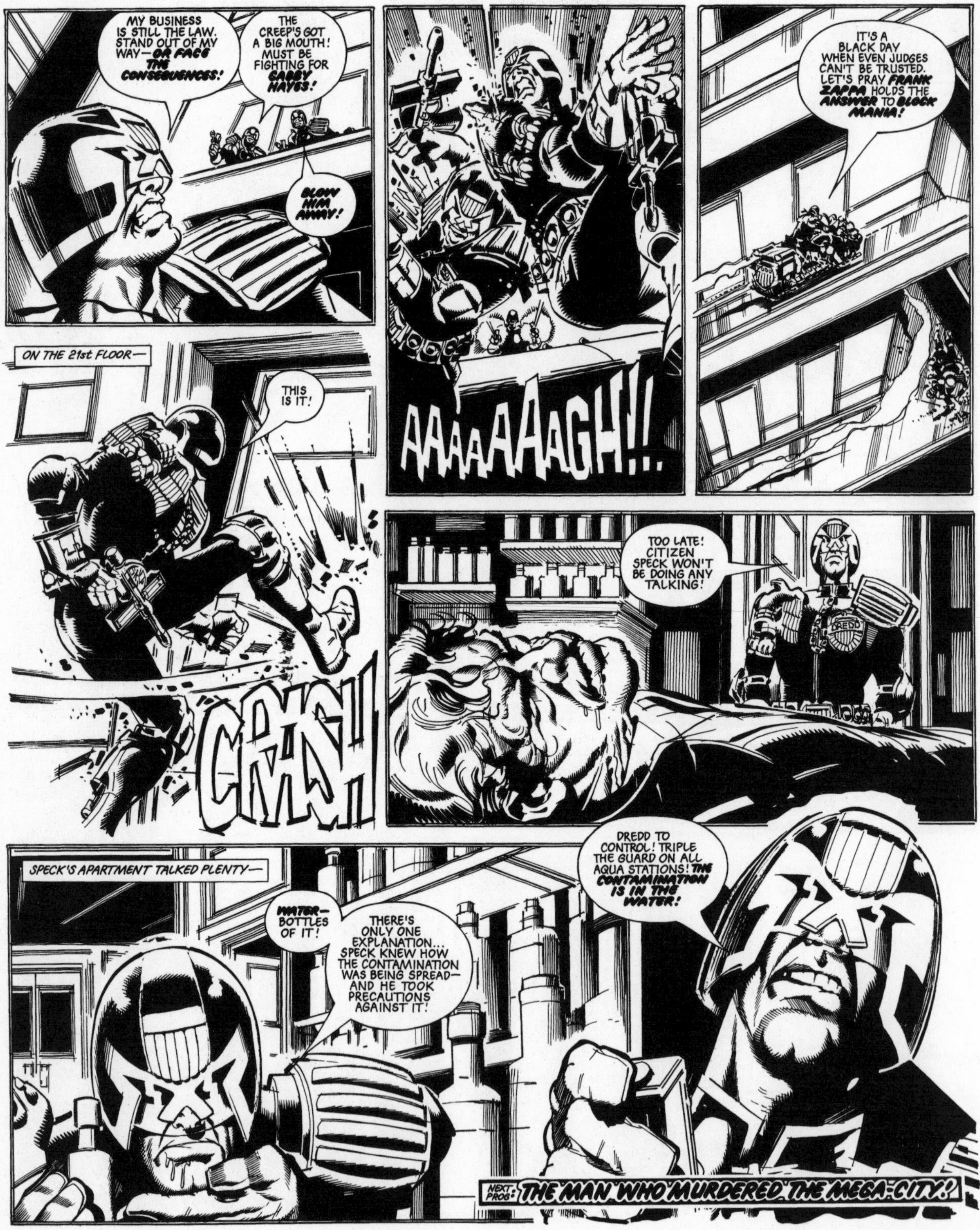

MY BUSINESS IS STILL THE LAW. STAND OUT OF MY WAY—OR FACE THE CONSEQUENCES!
THE CREEP'S GOT A BIG MOUTH! MUST BE FIGHTING FOR CABBY HAYES!
BLOW HIM AWAY!
AAAAAAAGH!!!
IT'S A BLACK DAY WHEN EVEN JUDGES CAN'T BE TRUSTED. LET'S PRAY FRANK ZAPPA HOLDS THE ANSWER TO BLOCK MANIA!
ON THE 21st FLOOR—
THIS IS IT!
CRASH!
TOO LATE! CITIZEN SPECK WON'T BE DOING ANY TALKING!
DREDD
SPECK'S APARTMENT TALKED PLENTY—
WATER—BOTTLES OF IT!
THERE'S ONLY ONE EXPLANATION... SPECK KNEW HOW THE CONTAMINATION WAS BEING SPREAD—AND HE TOOK PRECAUTIONS AGAINST IT!
DREDD TO CONTROL! TRIPLE THE GUARD ON ALL AQUA STATIONS! THE CONTAMINATION IS IN THE WATER!
NEXT PROG: THE MAN WHO MURDERED THE MEGA-CITY!

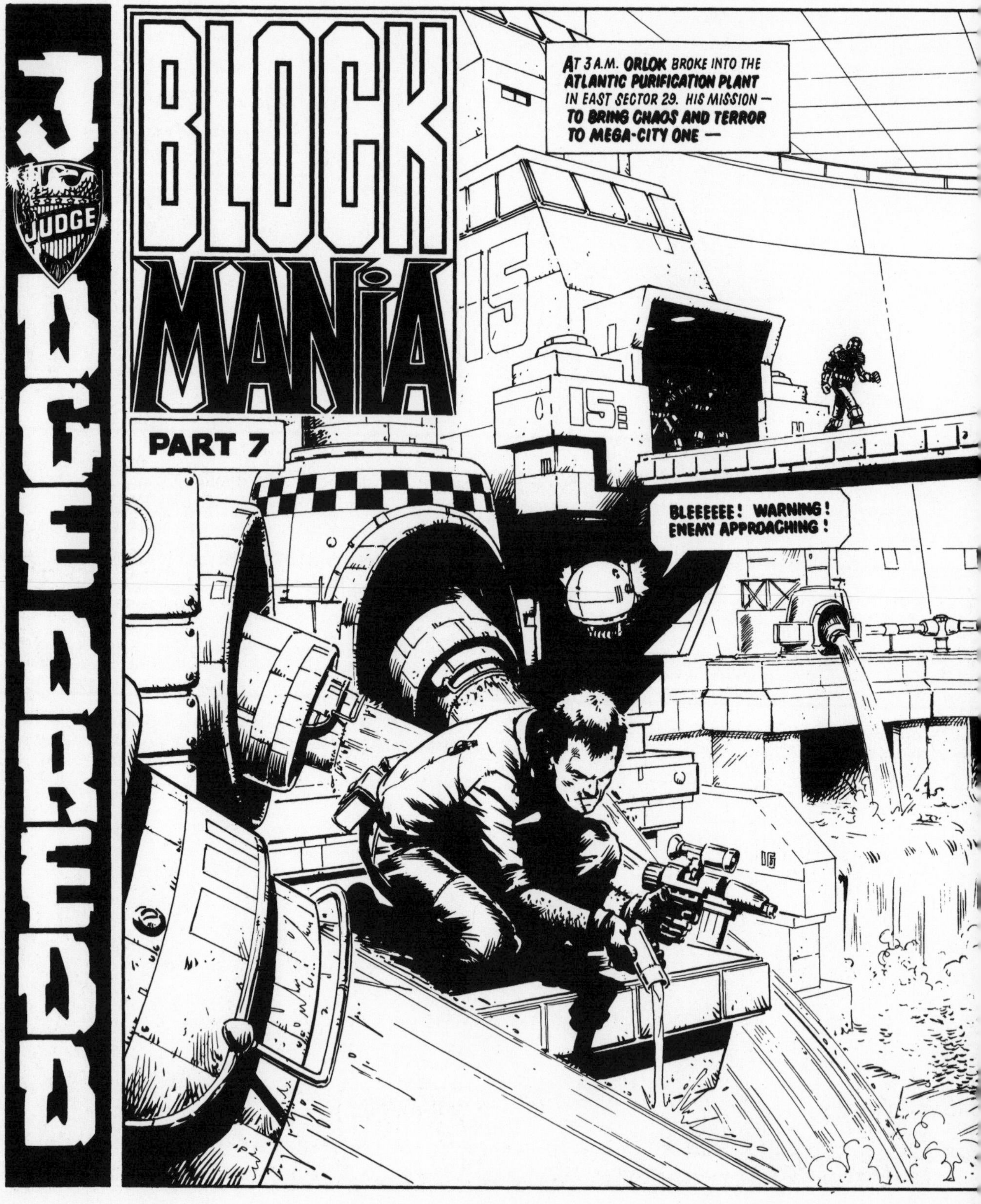
JUDGE DREDD
BLOCK MANIA
PART 7
AT 3 A.M. ORLOK BROKE INTO THE ATLANTIC PURIFICATION PLANT IN EAST SECTOR 29. HIS MISSION — TO BRING CHAOS AND TERROR TO MEGA-CITY ONE —
BLEEEEEE! WARNING! ENEMY APPROACHING!

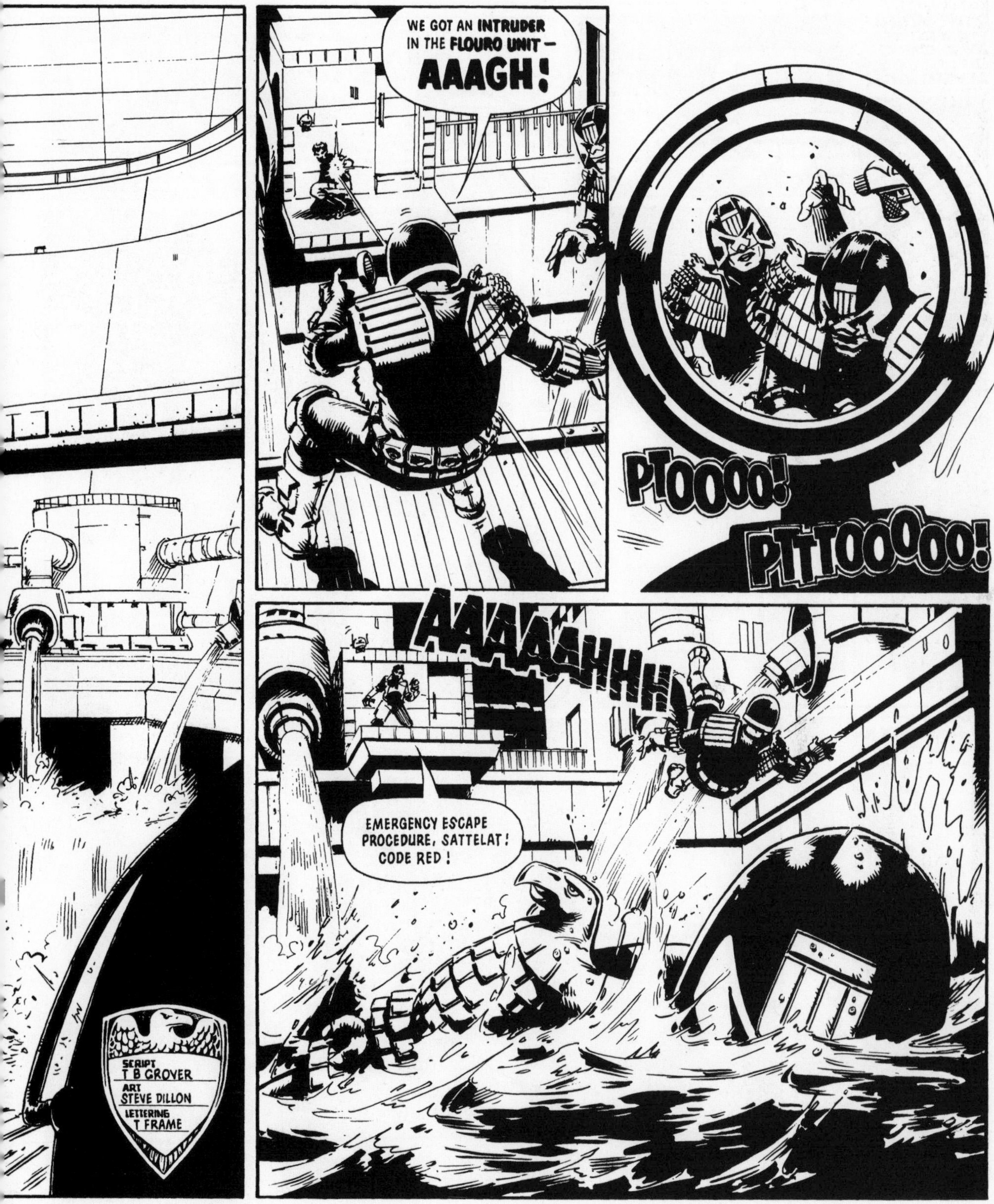
WE GOT AN INTRUDER IN THE FLOURO UNIT — AAAGH!
PTOOOO!
PTTTOOOOOO!
AAAAAHHHH
EMERGENCY ESCAPE PROCEDURE, SATTELAT! CODE RED!
SCRIPT T B GROVER
ART STEVE DILLON
LETTERING T FRAME

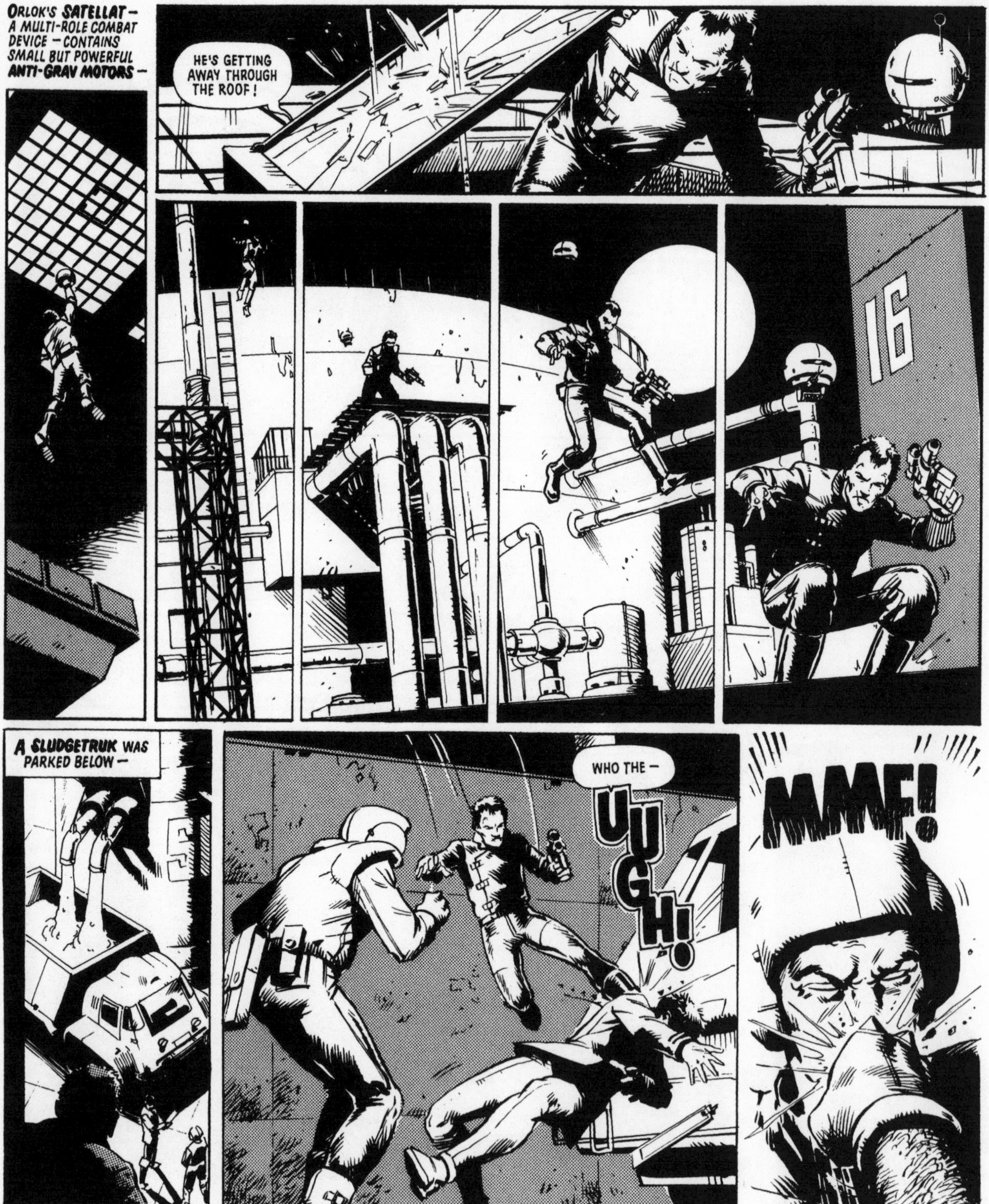
ORLOK'S SATELLAT – A MULTI-ROLE COMBAT DEVICE – CONTAINS SMALL BUT POWERFUL ANTI-GRAV MOTORS –
HE'S GETTING AWAY THROUGH THE ROOF !
16
A SLUDGETRUK WAS PARKED BELOW –
WHO THE –
UUGH!
MMMF!

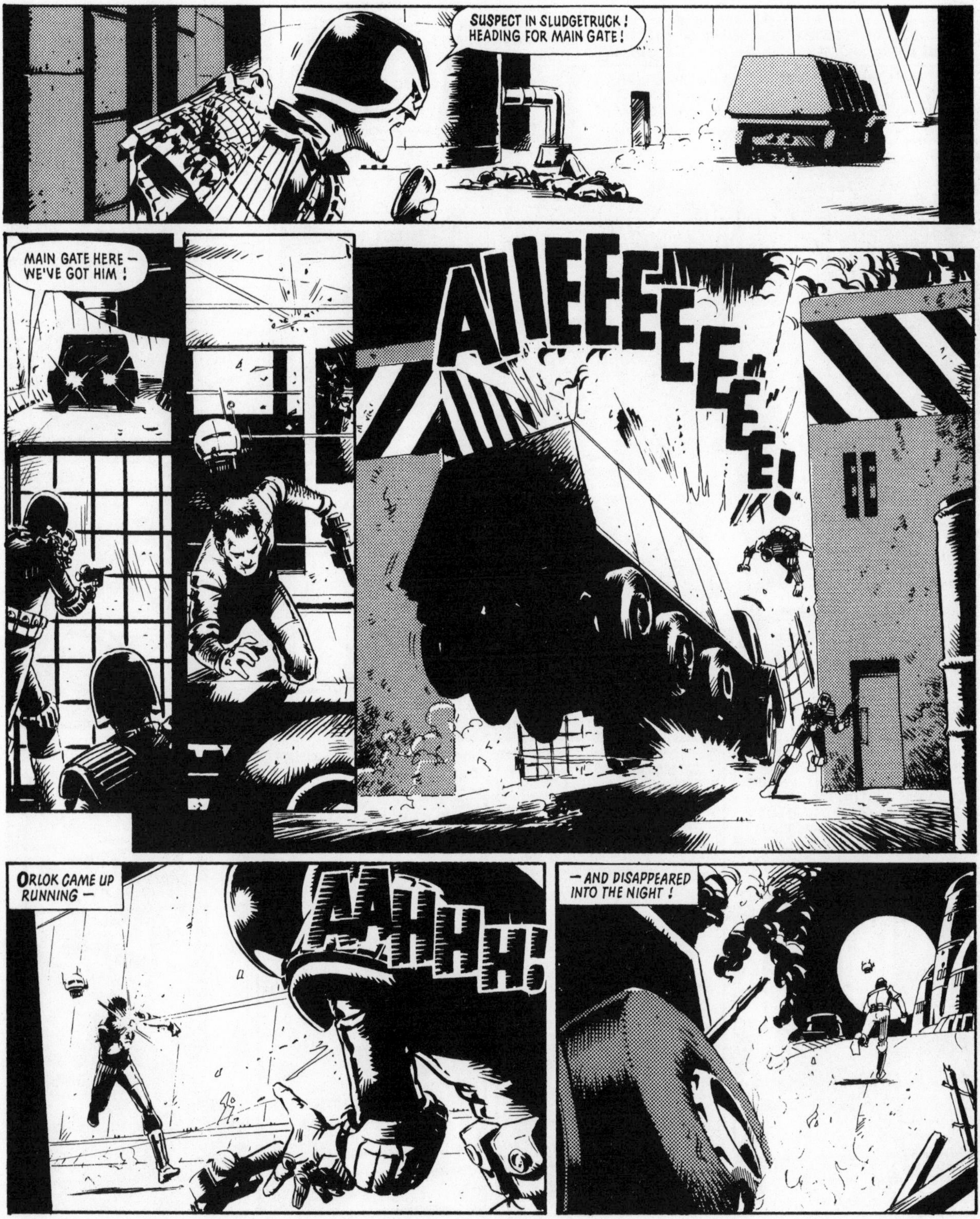
SUSPECT IN SLUDGETRUCK ! HEADING FOR MAIN GATE !
MAIN GATE HERE — WE'VE GOT HIM !
AIIEEEEEEEEE!
ORLOK CAME UP RUNNING —
AAHHHH!
— AND DISAPPEARED INTO THE NIGHT !

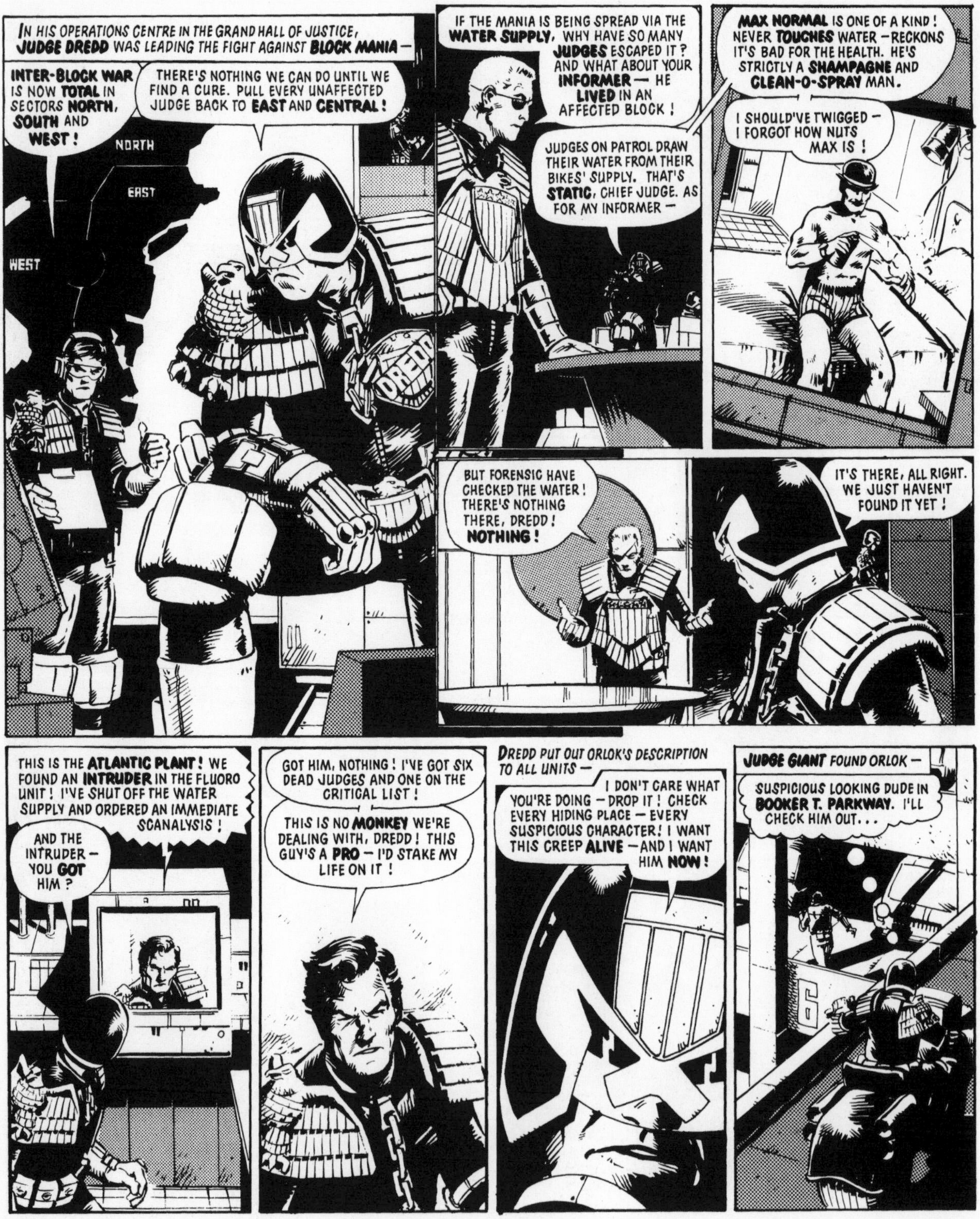
IN HIS OPERATIONS CENTRE IN THE GRAND HALL OF JUSTICE, JUDGE DREDD WAS LEADING THE FIGHT AGAINST BLOCK MANIA —
INTER-BLOCK WAR IS NOW TOTAL IN SECTORS NORTH, SOUTH AND WEST!
THERE'S NOTHING WE CAN DO UNTIL WE FIND A CURE. PULL EVERY UNAFFECTED JUDGE BACK TO EAST AND CENTRAL!
NORTH
EAST
WEST
DREDD
IF THE MANIA IS BEING SPREAD VIA THE WATER SUPPLY, WHY HAVE SO MANY JUDGES ESCAPED IT? AND WHAT ABOUT YOUR INFORMER — HE LIVED IN AN AFFECTED BLOCK!
JUDGES ON PATROL DRAW THEIR WATER FROM THEIR BIKES' SUPPLY. THAT'S STATIC, CHIEF JUDGE. AS FOR MY INFORMER —
MAX NORMAL IS ONE OF A KIND! NEVER TOUCHES WATER — RECKONS IT'S BAD FOR THE HEALTH. HE'S STRICTLY A SHAMPAGNE AND CLEAN-O-SPRAY MAN.
I SHOULD'VE TWIGGED — I FORGOT HOW NUTS MAX IS!
BUT FORENSIC HAVE CHECKED THE WATER! THERE'S NOTHING THERE, DREDD! NOTHING!
IT'S THERE, ALL RIGHT. WE JUST HAVEN'T FOUND IT YET!
THIS IS THE ATLANTIC PLANT! WE FOUND AN INTRUDER IN THE FLUORO UNIT! I'VE SHUT OFF THE WATER SUPPLY AND ORDERED AN IMMEDIATE SCANALYSIS!
AND THE INTRUDER — YOU GOT HIM?
GOT HIM, NOTHING! I'VE GOT SIX DEAD JUDGES AND ONE ON THE CRITICAL LIST!
THIS IS NO MONKEY WE'RE DEALING WITH, DREDD! THIS GUY'S A PRO — I'D STAKE MY LIFE ON IT!
DREDD PUT OUT ORLOK'S DESCRIPTION TO ALL UNITS —
I DON'T CARE WHAT YOU'RE DOING — DROP IT! CHECK EVERY HIDING PLACE — EVERY SUSPICIOUS CHARACTER! I WANT THIS CREEP ALIVE — AND I WANT HIM NOW!
JUDGE GIANT FOUND ORLOK —
SUSPICIOUS LOOKING DUDE IN BOOKER T. PARKWAY. I'LL CHECK HIM OUT...
6

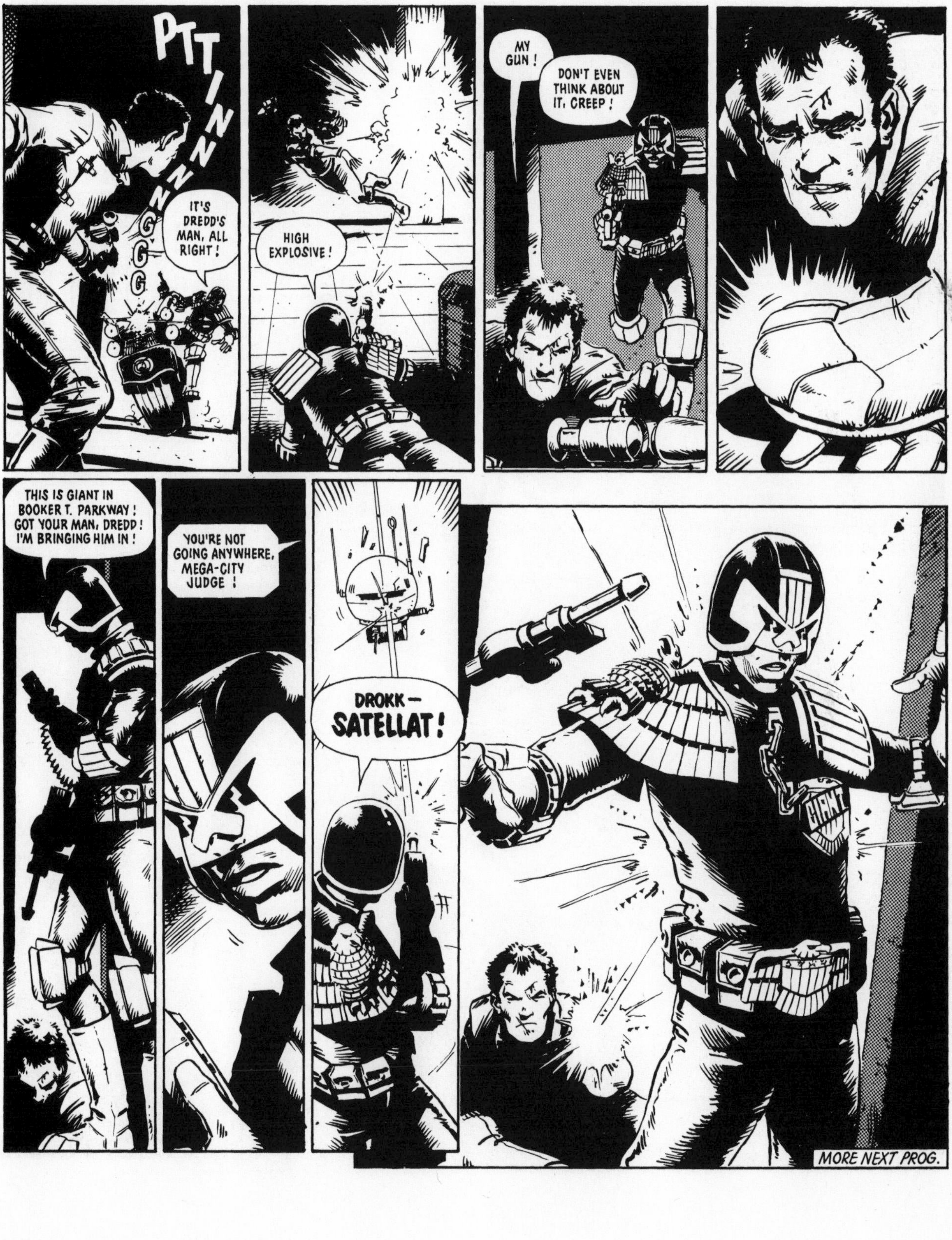
PTTINNNNGGG
IT'S DREDD'S MAN, ALL RIGHT!
HIGH EXPLOSIVE!
MY GUN!
DON'T EVEN THINK ABOUT IT, CREEP!
THIS IS GIANT IN BOOKER T. PARKWAY! GOT YOUR MAN, DREDD! I'M BRINGING HIM IN!
YOU'RE NOT GOING ANYWHERE, MEGA-CITY JUDGE!
DROKK — SATELLAT!
MORE NEXT PROG.

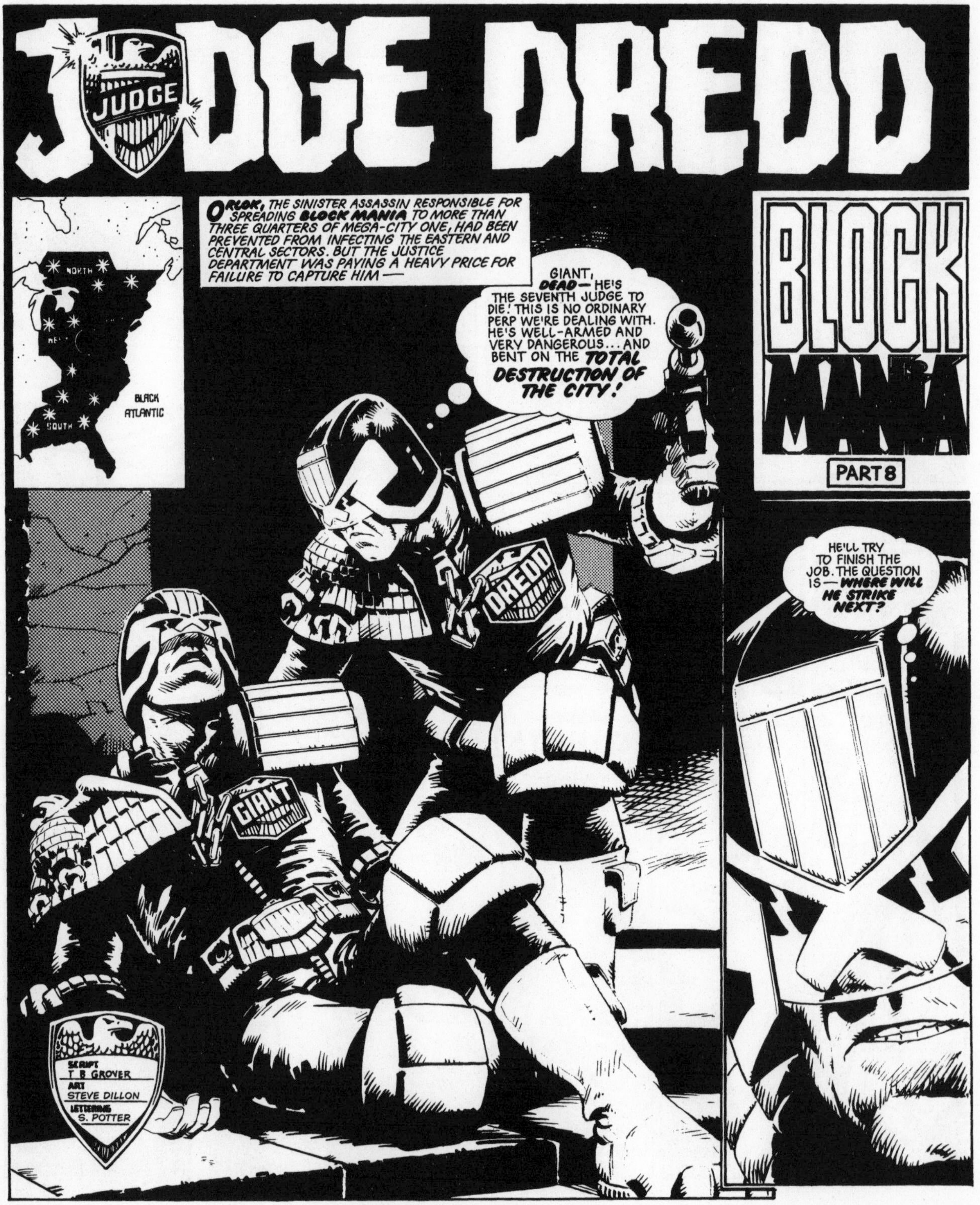
JUDGE DREDD
JUDGE
ORLOK, THE SINISTER ASSASSIN RESPONSIBLE FOR SPREADING BLOCK MANIA TO MORE THAN THREE QUARTERS OF MEGA-CITY ONE, HAD BEEN PREVENTED FROM INFECTING THE EASTERN AND CENTRAL SECTORS. BUT THE JUSTICE DEPARTMENT WAS PAYING A HEAVY PRICE FOR FAILURE TO CAPTURE HIM—
BLOCK MANIA
PART 8
NORTH
SOUTH
BLACK ATLANTIC
GIANT, DEAD— HE'S THE SEVENTH JUDGE TO DIE! THIS IS NO ORDINARY PERP WE'RE DEALING WITH. HE'S WELL-ARMED AND VERY DANGEROUS... AND BENT ON THE TOTAL DESTRUCTION OF THE CITY!
DREDD
GIANT
HE'LL TRY TO FINISH THE JOB. THE QUESTION IS— WHERE WILL HE STRIKE NEXT?
SCRIPT T B GROVER
ART STEVE DILLON
LETTERING S. POTTER

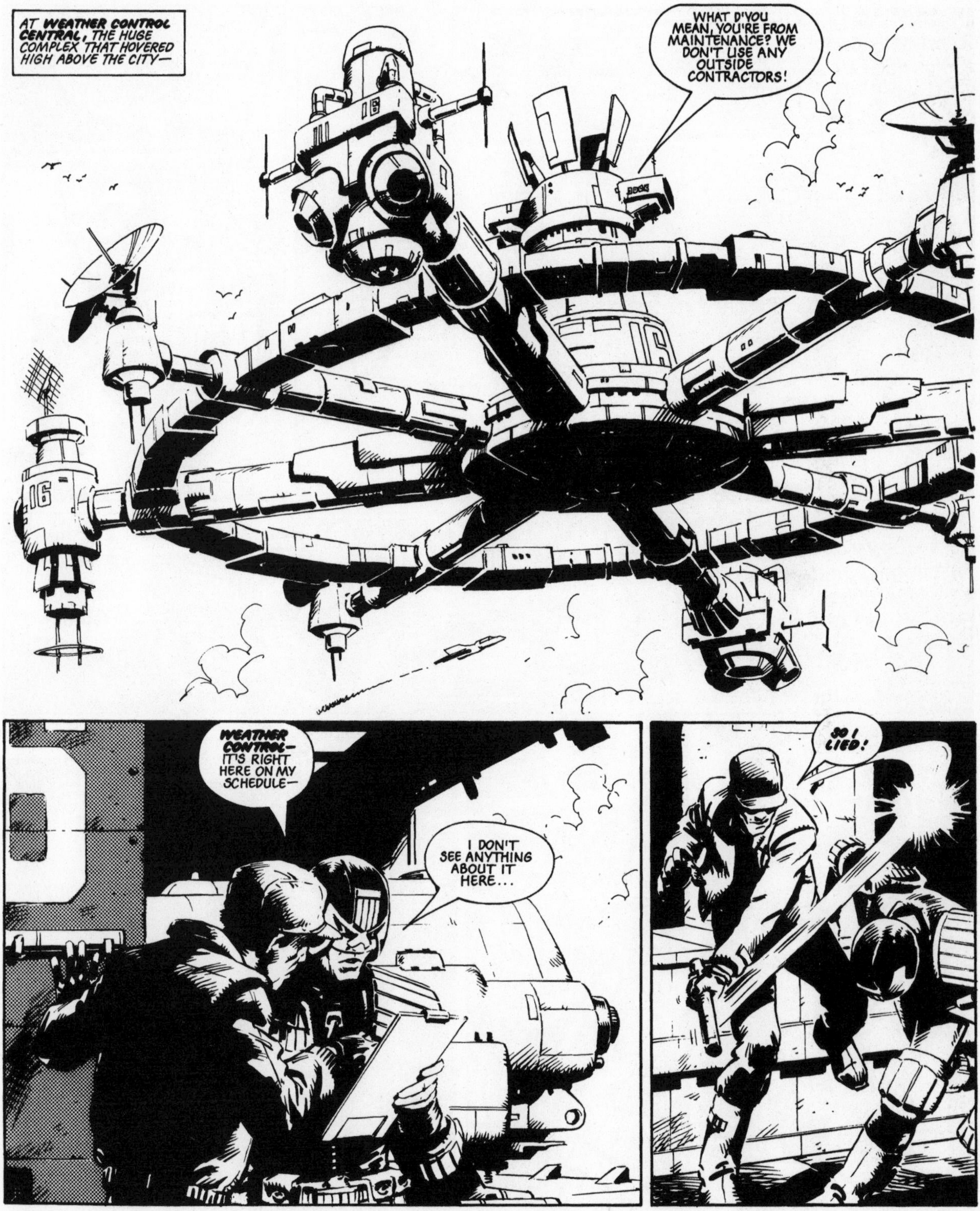

AT WEATHER CONTROL CENTRAL, THE HUGE COMPLEX THAT HOVERED HIGH ABOVE THE CITY—
WHAT D'YOU MEAN, YOU'RE FROM MAINTENANCE? WE DON'T USE ANY OUTSIDE CONTRACTORS!
WEATHER CONTROL— IT'S RIGHT HERE ON MY SCHEDULE—
I DON'T SEE ANYTHING ABOUT IT HERE...
SO I LIED!

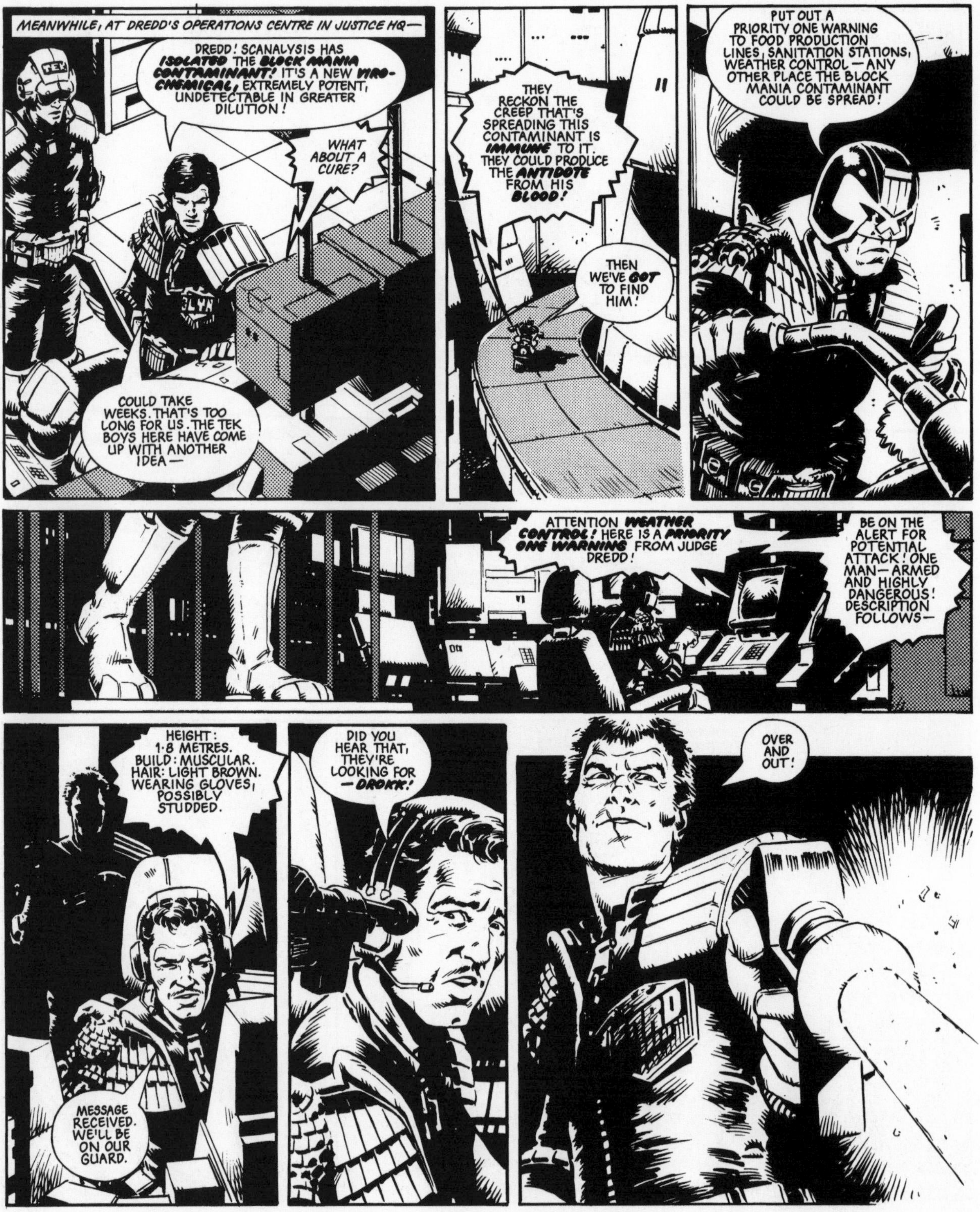
MEANWHILE, AT DREDD'S OPERATIONS CENTRE IN JUSTICE HQ—
DREDD! SCANALYSIS HAS ISOLATED THE BLOCK MANIA CONTAMINANT! IT'S A NEW VIRO-CHEMICAL, EXTREMELY POTENT, UNDETECTABLE IN GREATER DILUTION!
WHAT ABOUT A CURE?
COULD TAKE WEEKS. THAT'S TOO LONG FOR US. THE TEK BOYS HERE HAVE COME UP WITH ANOTHER IDEA—
THEY RECKON THE CREEP THAT'S SPREADING THIS CONTAMINANT IS IMMUNE TO IT. THEY COULD PRODUCE THE ANTIDOTE FROM HIS BLOOD!
THEN WE'VE GOT TO FIND HIM!
PUT OUT A PRIORITY ONE WARNING TO FOOD PRODUCTION LINES, SANITATION STATIONS, WEATHER CONTROL — ANY OTHER PLACE THE BLOCK MANIA CONTAMINANT COULD BE SPREAD!
ATTENTION WEATHER CONTROL! HERE IS A PRIORITY ONE WARNING FROM JUDGE DREDD!
BE ON THE ALERT FOR POTENTIAL ATTACK! ONE MAN— ARMED AND HIGHLY DANGEROUS! DESCRIPTION FOLLOWS—
HEIGHT: 1·8 METRES. BUILD: MUSCULAR. HAIR: LIGHT BROWN. WEARING GLOVES, POSSIBLY STUDDED.
MESSAGE RECEIVED. WE'LL BE ON OUR GUARD.
DID YOU HEAR THAT, THEY'RE LOOKING FOR —DROKK!
OVER AND OUT!

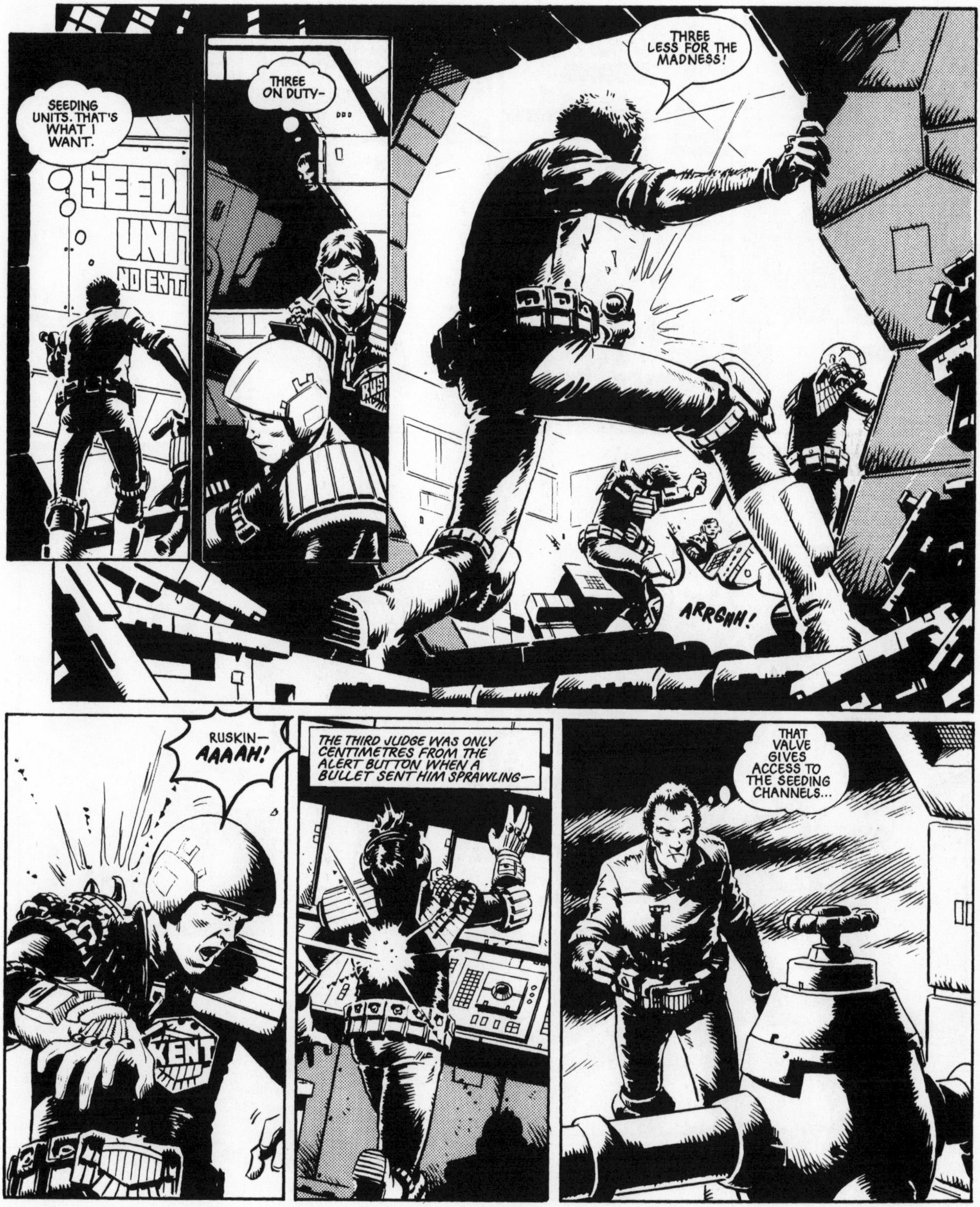

SEEDING UNITS. THAT'S WHAT I WANT.
SEEDI
UNIT
NO ENTI
THREE ON DUTY-
THREE LESS FOR THE MADNESS!
ARRGHH!
RUSKIN- AAAAH!
KENT
THE THIRD JUDGE WAS ONLY CENTIMETRES FROM THE ALERT BUTTON WHEN A BULLET SENT HIM SPRAWLING—
THAT VALVE GIVES ACCESS TO THE SEEDING CHANNELS...

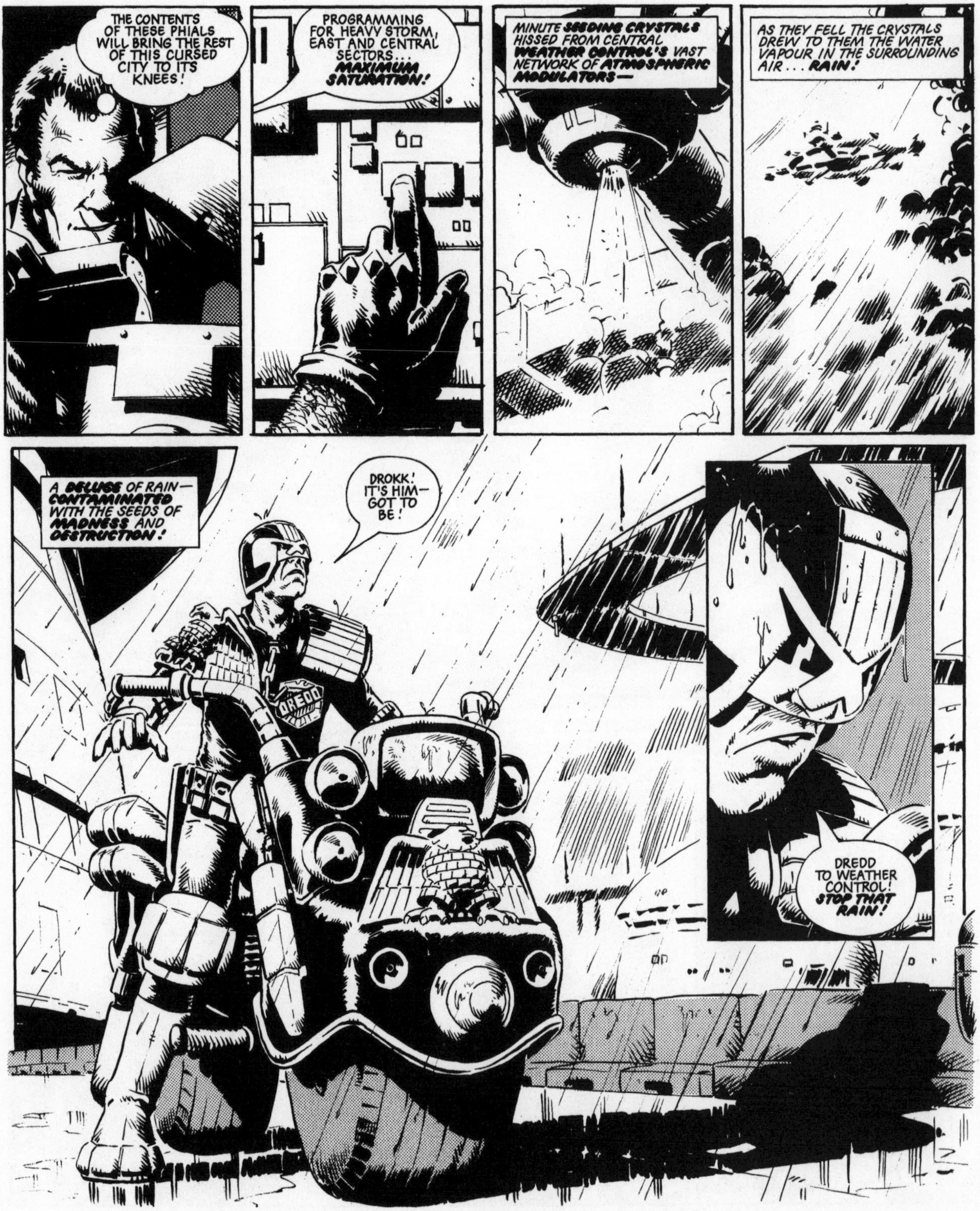
THE CONTENTS OF THESE PHIALS WILL BRING THE REST OF THIS CURSED CITY TO ITS KNEES!
PROGRAMMING FOR HEAVY STORM, EAST AND CENTRAL SECTORS... MAXIMUM SATURATION!
MINUTE SEEDING CRYSTALS HISSED FROM CENTRAL WEATHER CONTROL'S VAST NETWORK OF ATMOSPHERIC MODULATORS—
AS THEY FELL THE CRYSTALS DREW TO THEM THE WATER VAPOUR IN THE SURROUNDING AIR... RAIN!
A DELUGE OF RAIN—CONTAMINATED WITH THE SEEDS OF MADNESS AND DESTRUCTION!
DROKK! IT'S HIM—GOT TO BE!
DREDD
DREDD TO WEATHER CONTROL! STOP THAT RAIN!

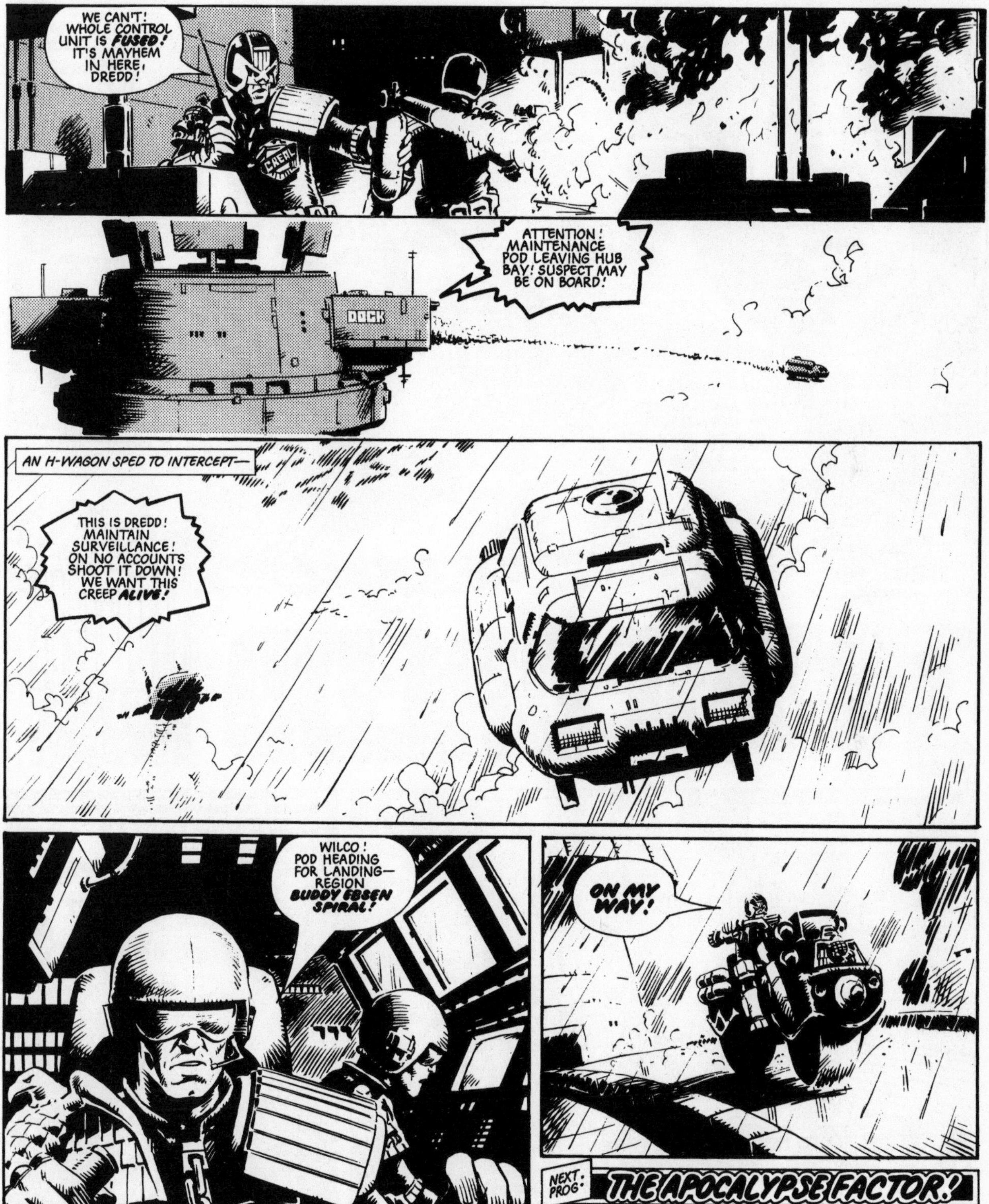
WE CAN'T! WHOLE CONTROL UNIT IS FUSED! IT'S MAYHEM IN HERE, DREDD!
ATTENTION! MAINTENANCE POD LEAVING HUB BAY! SUSPECT MAY BE ON BOARD!
DOCK
AN H-WAGON SPED TO INTERCEPT—
THIS IS DREDD! MAINTAIN SURVEILLANCE! ON NO ACCOUNTS SHOOT IT DOWN! WE WANT THIS CREEP ALIVE!
WILCO! POD HEADING FOR LANDING-REGION BUDDY EBSEN SPIRAL!
ON MY WAY!
NEXT PROG: THE APOCALYPSE FACTOR!

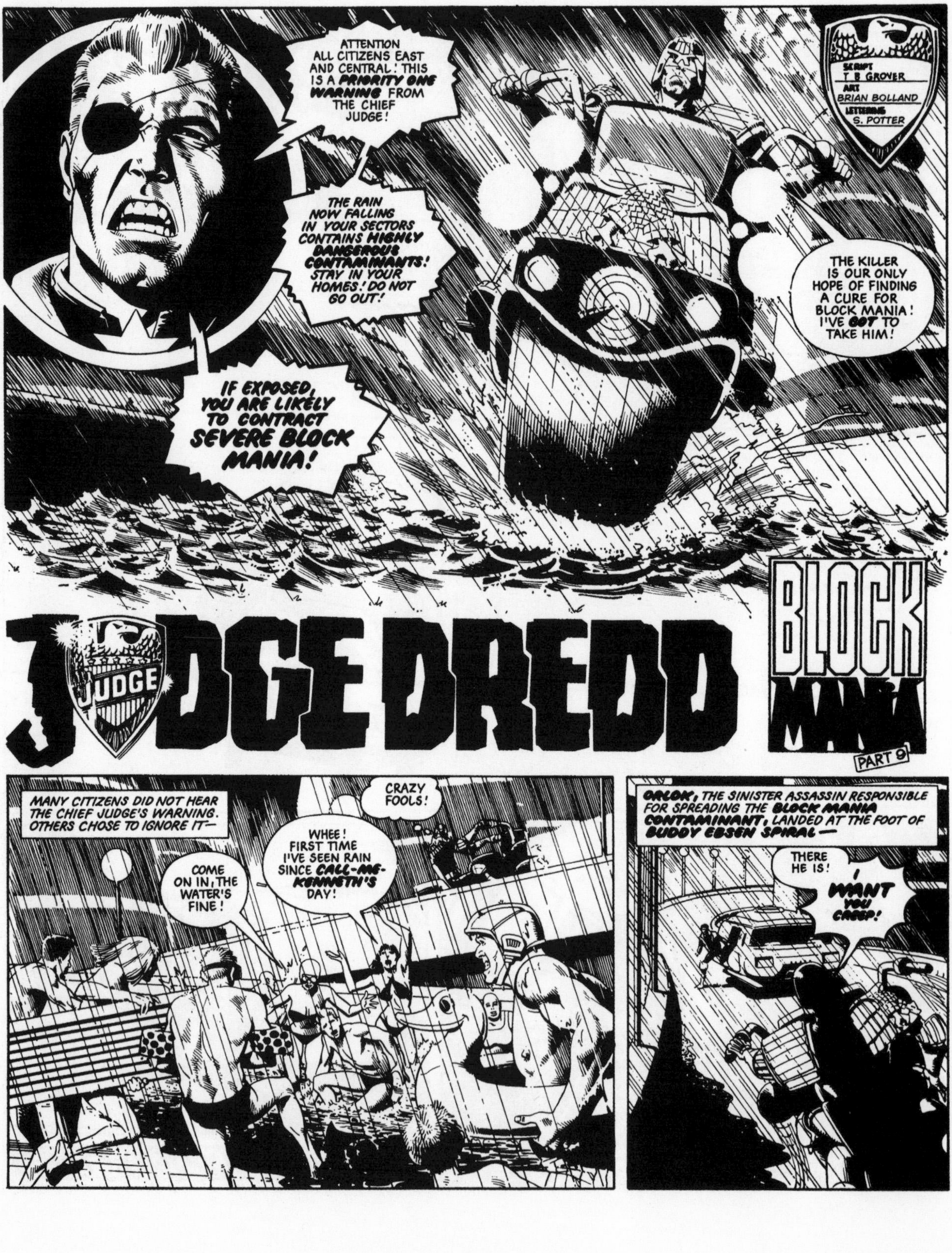
SCRIPT T B GROVER
ART BRIAN BOLLAND
LETTERING S. POTTER
ATTENTION ALL CITIZENS EAST AND CENTRAL: THIS IS A PRIORITY ONE WARNING FROM THE CHIEF JUDGE!
THE RAIN NOW FALLING IN YOUR SECTORS CONTAINS HIGHLY DANGEROUS CONTAMINANTS! STAY IN YOUR HOMES! DO NOT GO OUT!
IF EXPOSED, YOU ARE LIKELY TO CONTRACT SEVERE BLOCK MANIA!
THE KILLER IS OUR ONLY HOPE OF FINDING A CURE FOR BLOCK MANIA! I'VE GOT TO TAKE HIM!
JUDGE DREDD
BLOCK MANIA
PART 9
MANY CITIZENS DID NOT HEAR THE CHIEF JUDGE'S WARNING. OTHERS CHOSE TO IGNORE IT—
CRAZY FOOLS!
WHEE! FIRST TIME I'VE SEEN RAIN SINCE CALL-ME-KENNETH'S DAY!
COME ON IN, THE WATER'S FINE!
ORLOK, THE SINISTER ASSASSIN RESPONSIBLE FOR SPREADING THE BLOCK MANIA CONTAMINANT, LANDED AT THE FOOT OF BUDDY EBSEN SPIRAL—
THERE HE IS!
I WANT YOU CREEP!

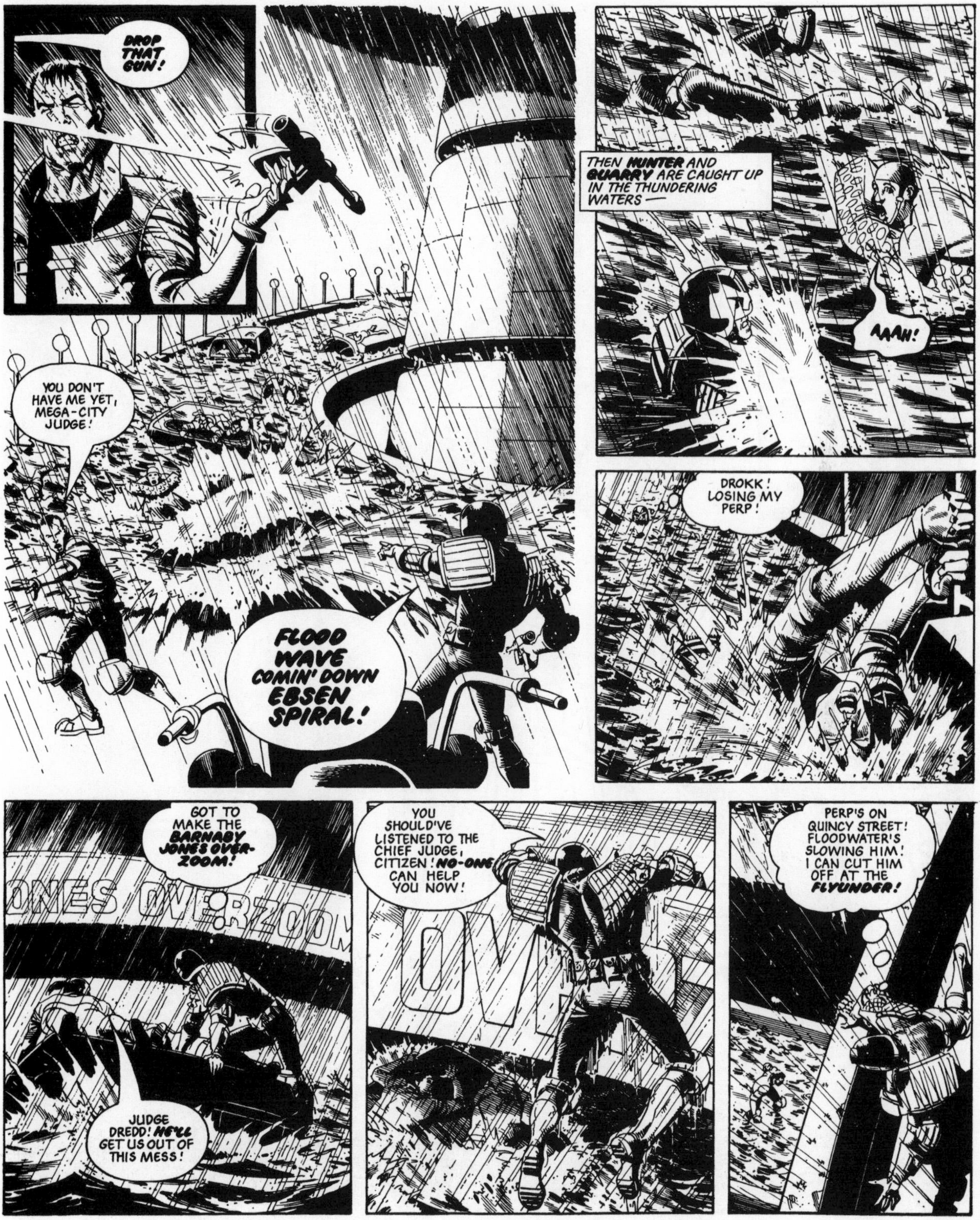
DROP THAT GUN!
YOU DON'T HAVE ME YET, MEGA-CITY JUDGE!
FLOOD WAVE COMIN' DOWN EBSEN SPIRAL!
THEN HUNTER AND QUARRY ARE CAUGHT UP IN THE THUNDERING WATERS—
AAAH!
DROKK! LOSING MY PERP!
GOT TO MAKE THE BARNABY JONES OVER-ZOOM!
ONES OVERZOOM
JUDGE DREDD! HE'LL GET US OUT OF THIS MESS!
YOU SHOULD'VE LISTENED TO THE CHIEF JUDGE, CITIZEN! NO-ONE CAN HELP YOU NOW!
OVE
PERP'S ON QUINCY STREET! FLOODWATER'S SLOWING HIM! I CAN CUT HIM OFF AT THE FLYUNDER!

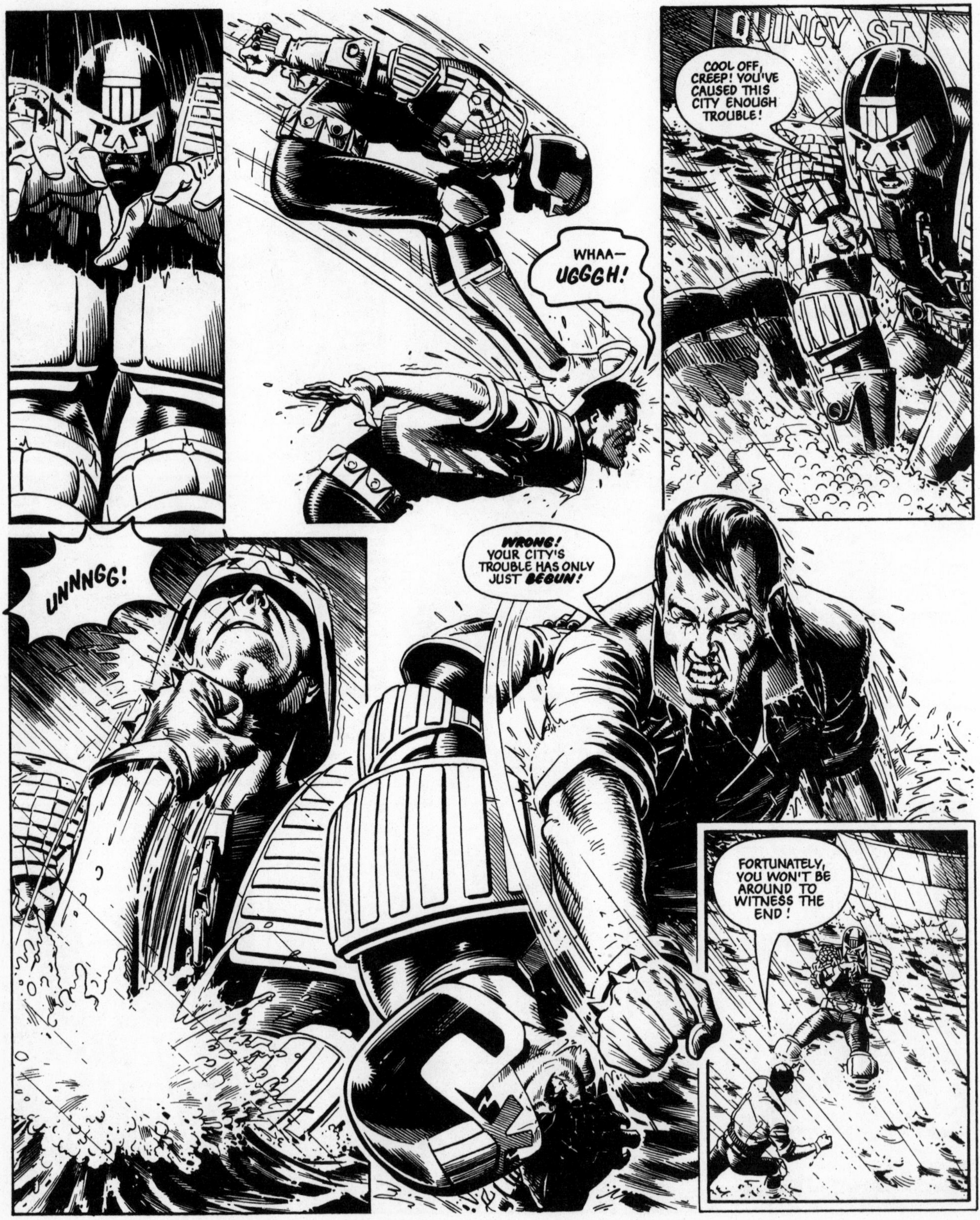
QUINCY ST
WHAA- UGGGH!
COOL OFF, CREEP! YOU'VE CAUSED THIS CITY ENOUGH TROUBLE!
UNNNGG!
WRONG! YOUR CITY'S TROUBLE HAS ONLY JUST BEGUN!
FORTUNATELY, YOU WON'T BE AROUND TO WITNESS THE END!

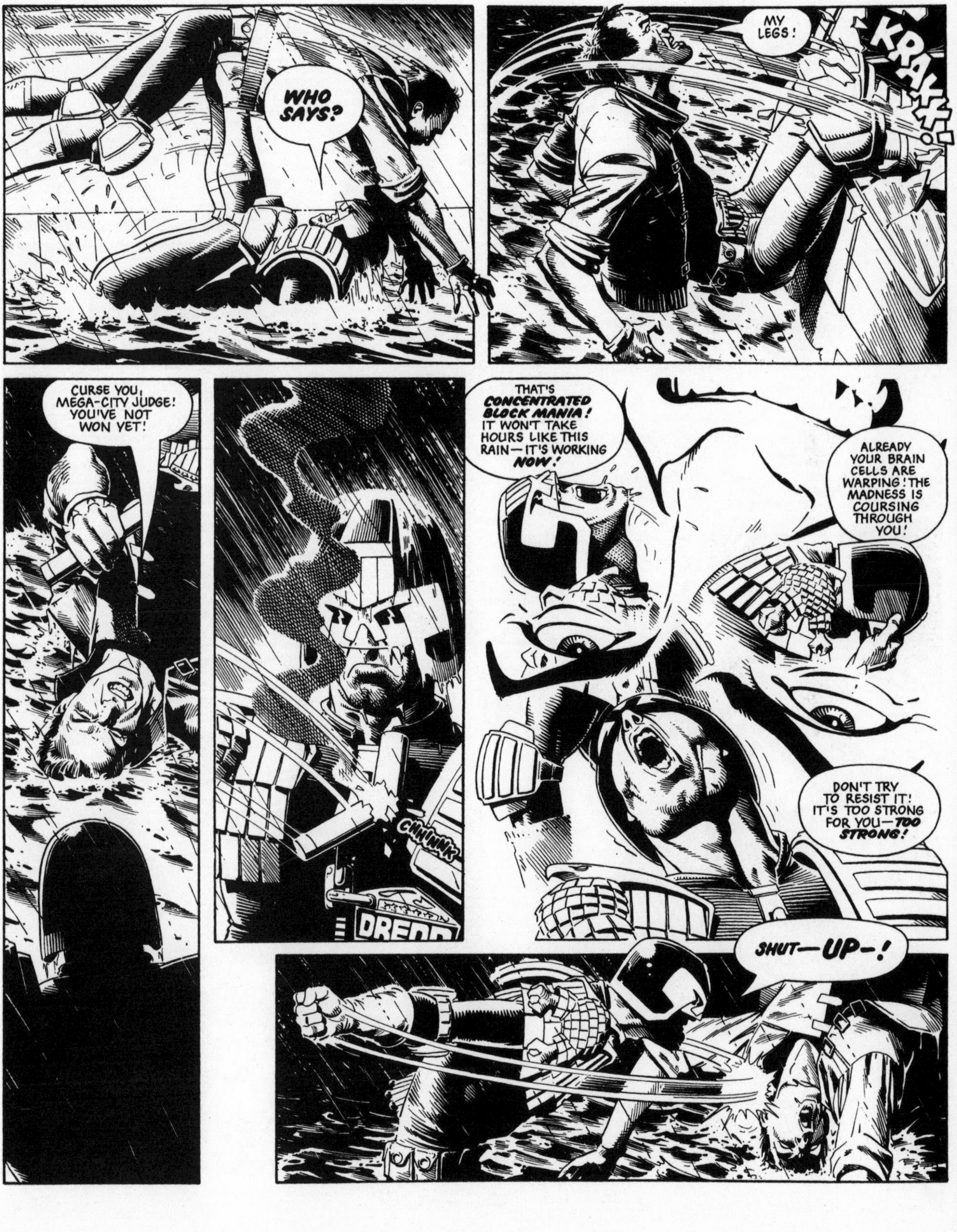
WHO SAYS?
MY LEGS!
KRAKK!
CURSE YOU, MEGA-CITY JUDGE! YOU'VE NOT WON YET!
CHNINNK
DREDD
THAT'S CONCENTRATED BLOCK MANIA! IT WON'T TAKE HOURS LIKE THIS RAIN—IT'S WORKING NOW!
ALREADY YOUR BRAIN CELLS ARE WARPING! THE MADNESS IS COURSING THROUGH YOU!
DON'T TRY TO RESIST IT! IT'S TOO STRONG FOR YOU—TOO STRONG!
SHUT—UP—!

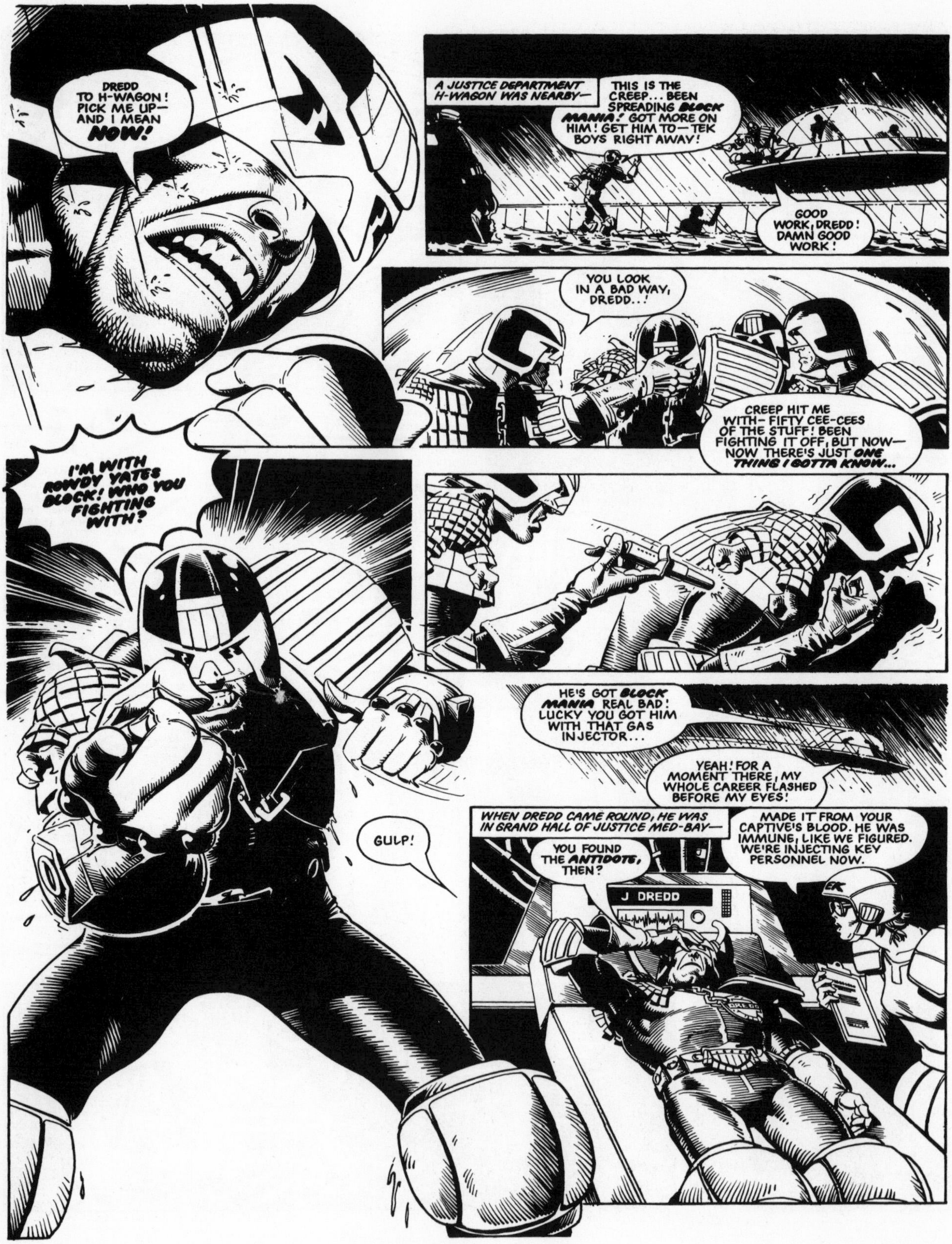

DREDD TO H-WAGON! PICK ME UP— AND I MEAN NOW!
A JUSTICE DEPARTMENT H-WAGON WAS NEARBY—
THIS IS THE CREEP... BEEN SPREADING BLOCK MANIA! GOT MORE ON HIM! GET HIM TO— TEK BOYS RIGHT AWAY!
GOOD WORK, DREDD! DAMN GOOD WORK!
YOU LOOK IN A BAD WAY, DREDD..!
CREEP HIT ME WITH— FIFTY CEE-CEES OF THE STUFF! BEEN FIGHTING IT OFF, BUT NOW— NOW THERE'S JUST ONE THING I GOTTA KNOW...
I'M WITH ROWDY YATES BLOCK! WHO YOU FIGHTING WITH?
GULP!
HE'S GOT BLOCK MANIA REAL BAD! LUCKY YOU GOT HIM WITH THAT GAS INJECTOR...
YEAH! FOR A MOMENT THERE, MY WHOLE CAREER FLASHED BEFORE MY EYES!
WHEN DREDD CAME ROUND, HE WAS IN GRAND HALL OF JUSTICE MED-BAY—
YOU FOUND THE ANTIDOTE, THEN?
MADE IT FROM YOUR CAPTIVE'S BLOOD. HE WAS IMMUNE, LIKE WE FIGURED. WE'RE INJECTING KEY PERSONNEL NOW.
J DREDD

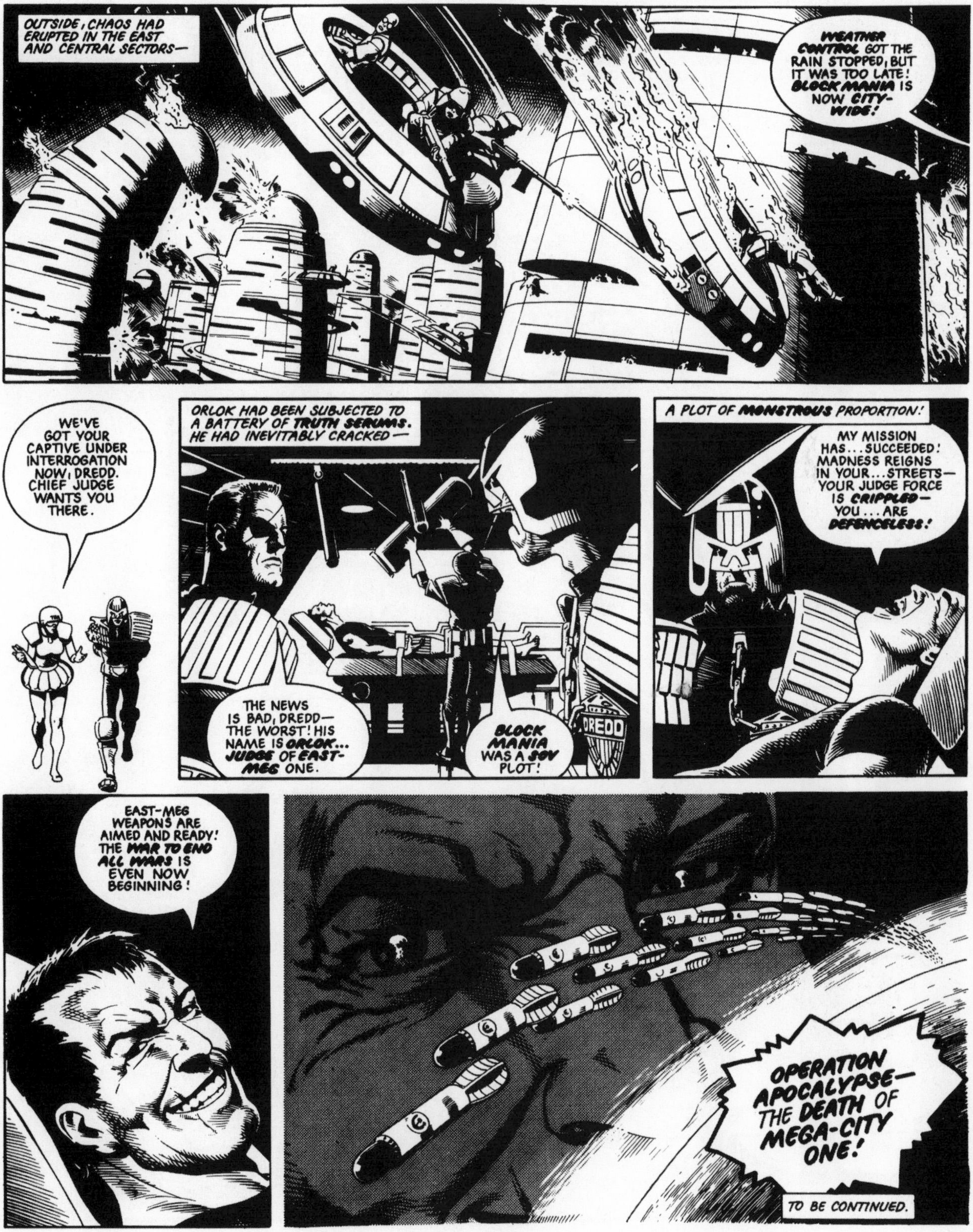
OUTSIDE, CHAOS HAD ERUPTED IN THE EAST AND CENTRAL SECTORS—
WEATHER CONTROL GOT THE RAIN STOPPED, BUT IT WAS TOO LATE! BLOCK MANIA IS NOW CITY-WIDE!
WE'VE GOT YOUR CAPTIVE UNDER INTERROGATION NOW, DREDD. CHIEF JUDGE WANTS YOU THERE.
ORLOK HAD BEEN SUBJECTED TO A BATTERY OF TRUTH SERUMS. HE HAD INEVITABLY CRACKED—
THE NEWS IS BAD, DREDD— THE WORST! HIS NAME IS ORLOK... JUDGE OF EAST-MEG ONE.
BLOCK MANIA WAS A SOV PLOT!
DREDD
A PLOT OF MONSTROUS PROPORTION!
MY MISSION HAS... SUCCEEDED! MADNESS REIGNS IN YOUR... STREETS— YOUR JUDGE FORCE IS CRIPPLED— YOU... ARE DEFENCELESS!
EAST-MEG WEAPONS ARE AIMED AND READY! THE WAR TO END ALL WARS IS EVEN NOW BEGINNING!
OPERATION APOCALYPSE— THE DEATH OF MEGA-CITY ONE!
TO BE CONTINUED.

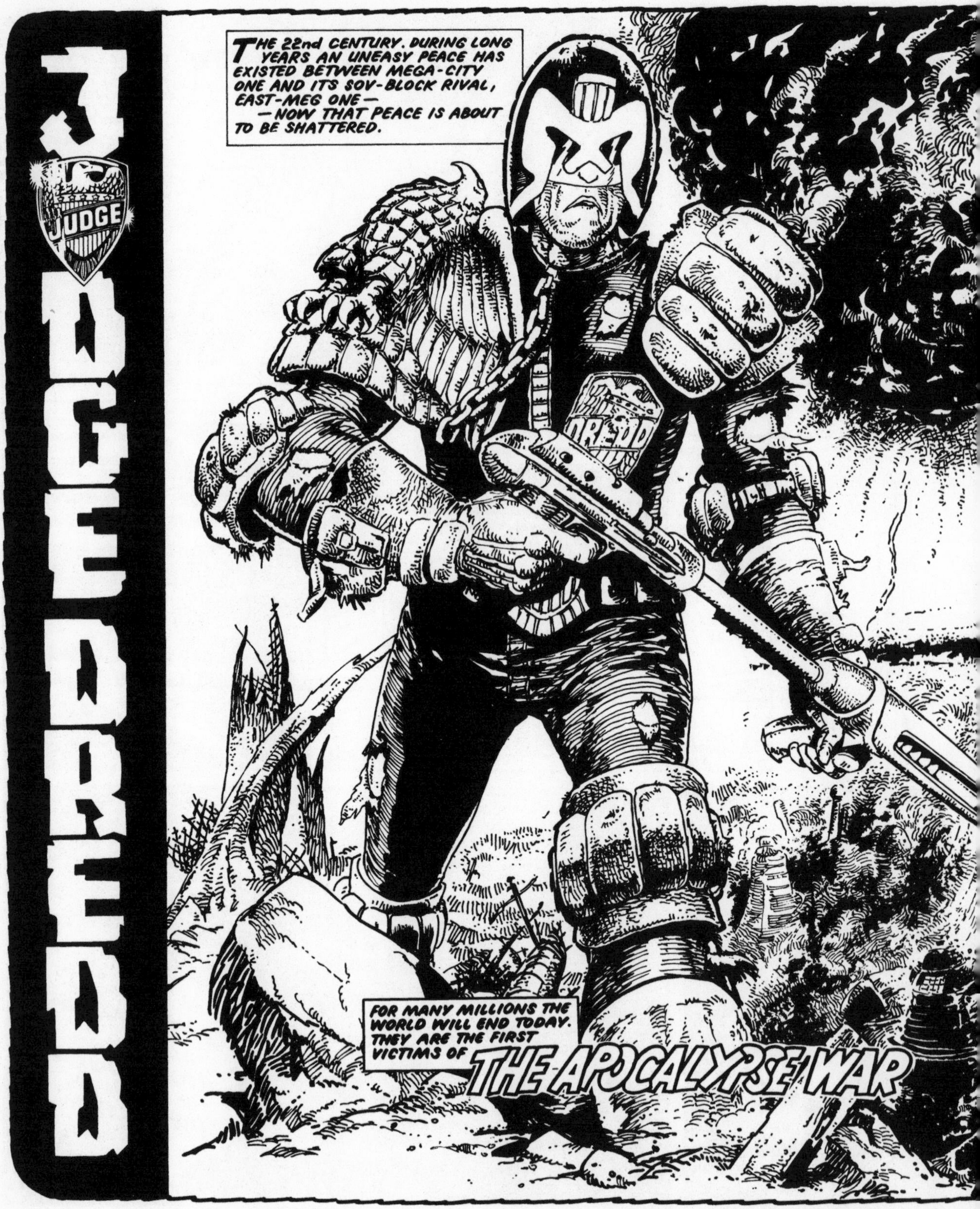
JUDGE DREDD
JUDGE
THE 22nd CENTURY. DURING LONG YEARS AN UNEASY PEACE HAS EXISTED BETWEEN MEGA-CITY ONE AND ITS SOV-BLOCK RIVAL, EAST-MEG ONE— —NOW THAT PEACE IS ABOUT TO BE SHATTERED.
DREDD
FOR MANY MILLIONS THE WORLD WILL END TODAY. THEY ARE THE FIRST VICTIMS OF
THE APOCALYPSE WAR

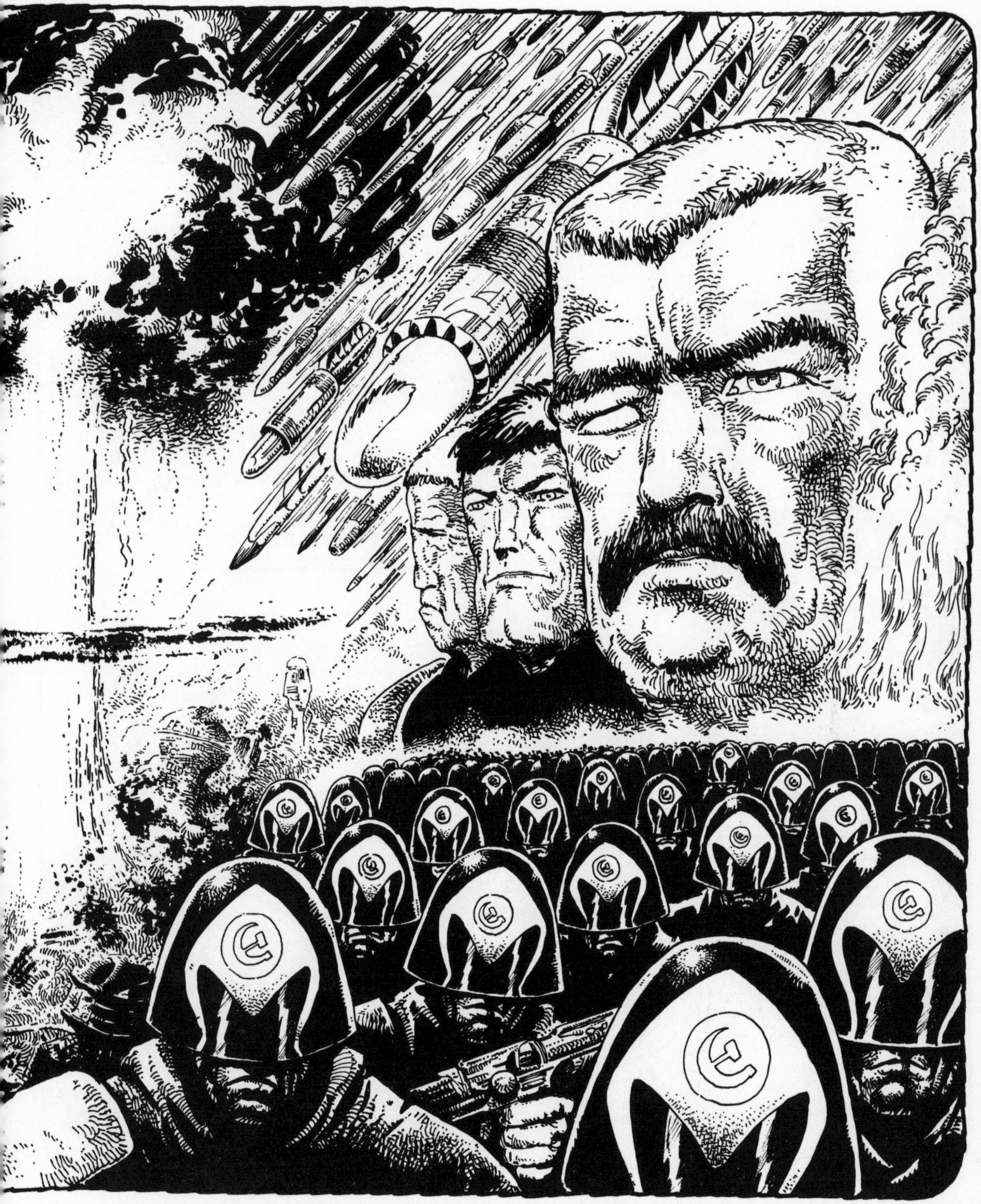

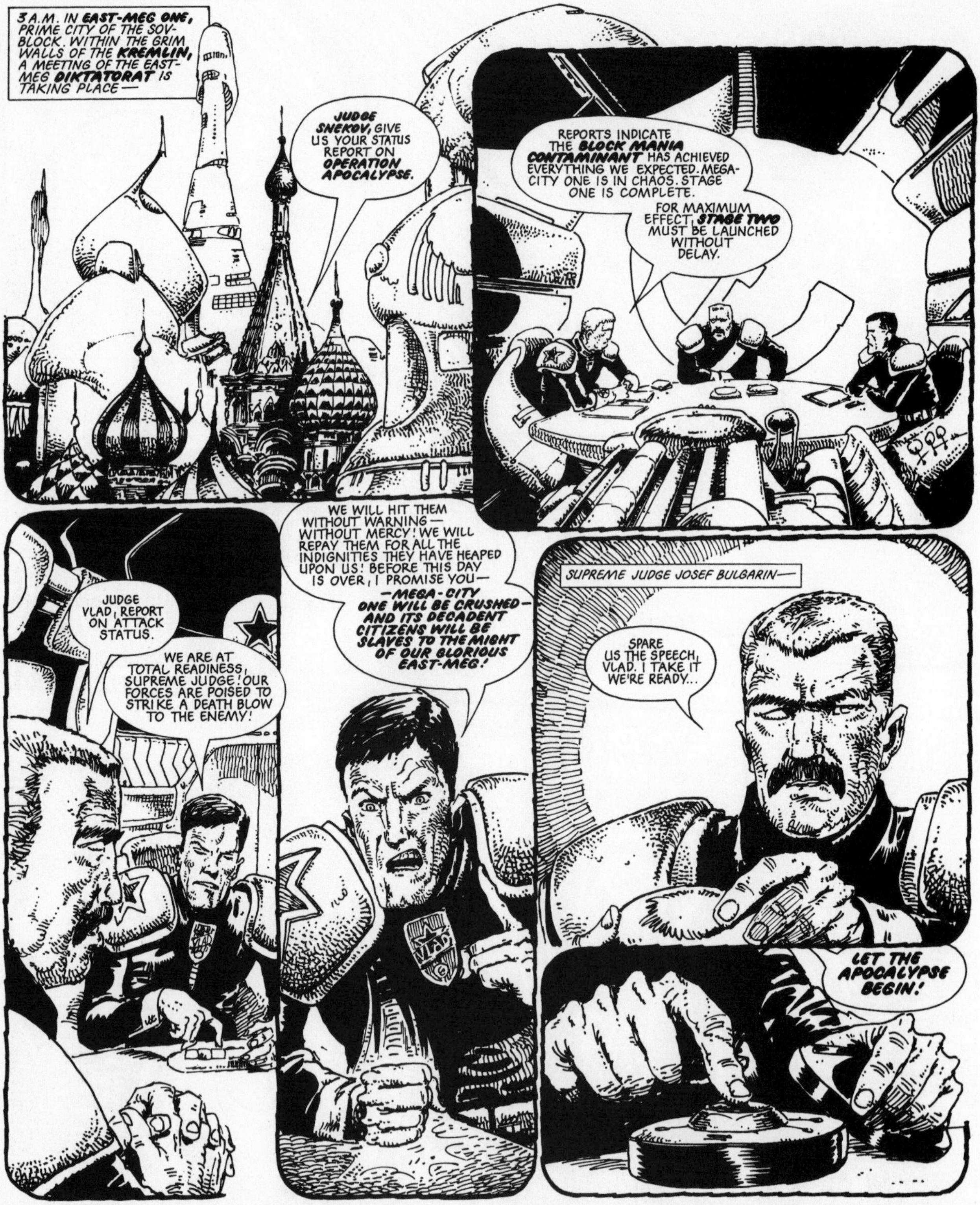
3 A.M. IN EAST-MEG ONE, PRIME CITY OF THE SOV-BLOCK. WITHIN THE GRIM WALLS OF THE KREMLIN, A MEETING OF THE EAST-MEG DIKTATORAT IS TAKING PLACE—
JUDGE SNEKOV, GIVE US YOUR STATUS REPORT ON OPERATION APOCALYPSE.
REPORTS INDICATE THE BLOCK MANIA CONTAMINANT HAS ACHIEVED EVERYTHING WE EXPECTED. MEGA-CITY ONE IS IN CHAOS. STAGE ONE IS COMPLETE.
FOR MAXIMUM EFFECT, STAGE TWO MUST BE LAUNCHED WITHOUT DELAY.
JUDGE VLAD, REPORT ON ATTACK STATUS.
WE ARE AT TOTAL READINESS, SUPREME JUDGE! OUR FORCES ARE POISED TO STRIKE A DEATH BLOW TO THE ENEMY!
WE WILL HIT THEM WITHOUT WARNING — WITHOUT MERCY! WE WILL REPAY THEM FOR ALL THE INDIGNITIES THEY HAVE HEAPED UPON US! BEFORE THIS DAY IS OVER, I PROMISE YOU—
—MEGA-CITY ONE WILL BE CRUSHED— AND ITS DECADENT CITIZENS WILL BE SLAVES TO THE MIGHT OF OUR GLORIOUS EAST-MEG!
SUPREME JUDGE JOSEF BULGARIN—
SPARE US THE SPEECH, VLAD. I TAKE IT WE'RE READY...
LET THE APOCALYPSE BEGIN!

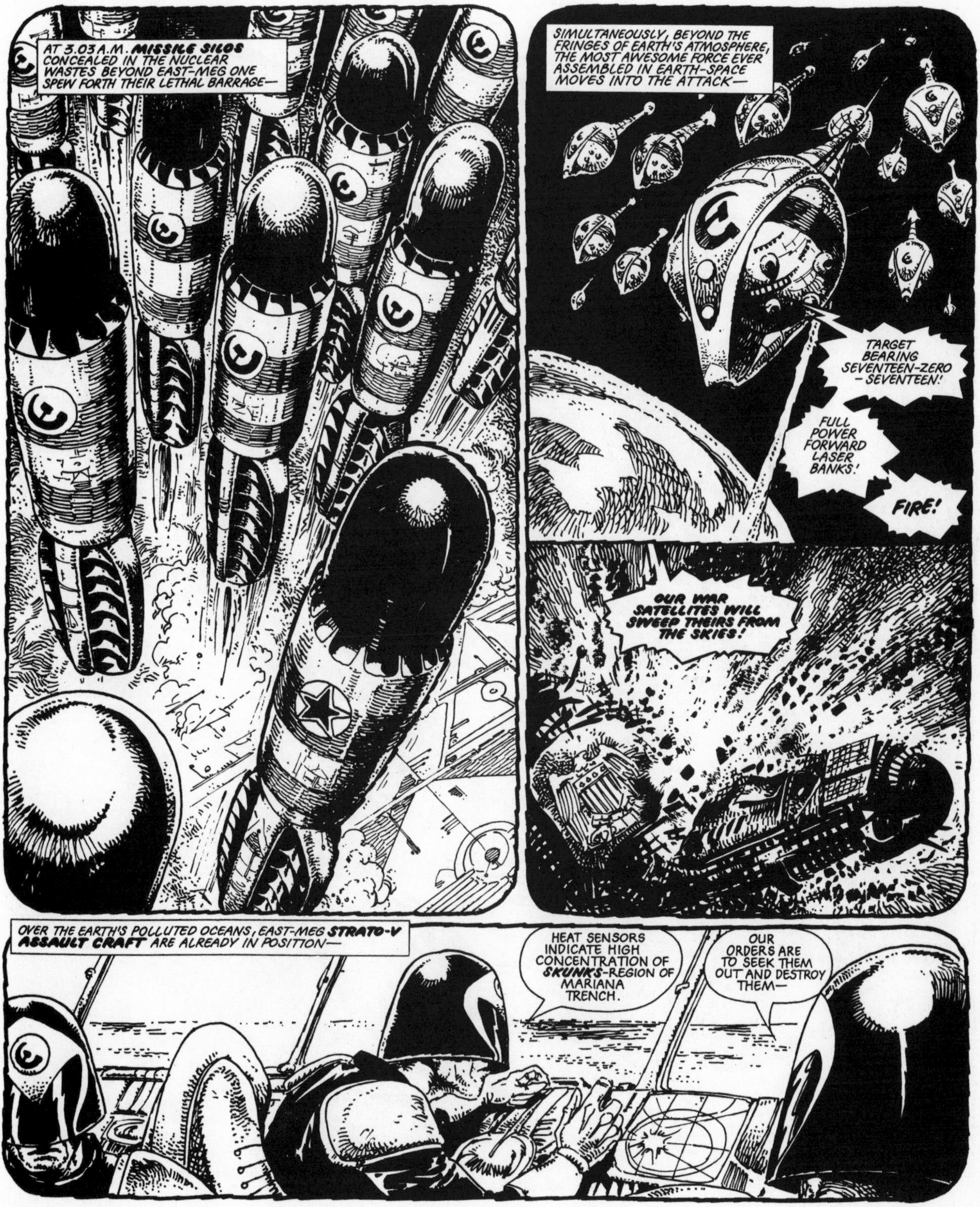
AT 3.03 A.M. MISSILE SILOS CONCEALED IN THE NUCLEAR WASTES BEYOND EAST-MEG ONE SPEW FORTH THEIR LETHAL BARRAGE—
SIMULTANEOUSLY, BEYOND THE FRINGES OF EARTH'S ATMOSPHERE, THE MOST AWESOME FORCE EVER ASSEMBLED IN EARTH-SPACE MOVES INTO THE ATTACK—
TARGET BEARING SEVENTEEN-ZERO -SEVENTEEN!
FULL POWER FORWARD LASER BANKS!
FIRE!
OUR WAR SATELLITES WILL SWEEP THEIRS FROM THE SKIES!
OVER THE EARTH'S POLLUTED OCEANS, EAST-MEG STRATO-V ASSAULT CRAFT ARE ALREADY IN POSITION—
HEAT SENSORS INDICATE HIGH CONCENTRATION OF SKUNKS-REGION OF MARIANA TRENCH.
OUR ORDERS ARE TO SEEK THEM OUT AND DESTROY THEM—

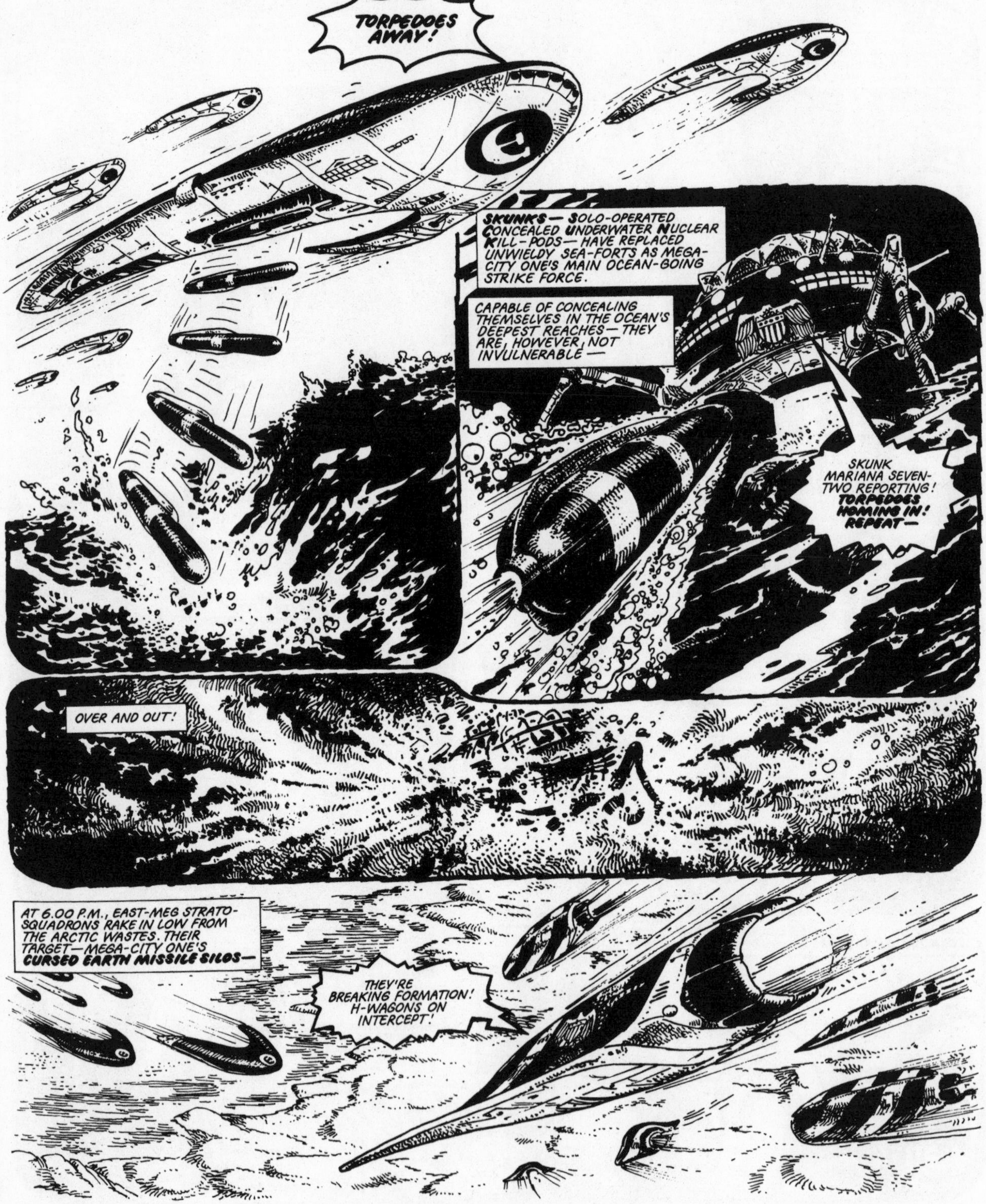

TORPEDOES AWAY!
SKUNKS— SOLO-OPERATED CONCEALED UNDERWATER NUCLEAR KILL-PODS— HAVE REPLACED UNWIELDY SEA-FORTS AS MEGA-CITY ONE'S MAIN OCEAN-GOING STRIKE FORCE.
CAPABLE OF CONCEALING THEMSELVES IN THE OCEAN'S DEEPEST REACHES— THEY ARE, HOWEVER, NOT INVULNERABLE—
SKUNK MARIANA SEVEN-TWO REPORTING! TORPEDOES HOMING IN! REPEAT—
OVER AND OUT!
AT 6.00 P.M., EAST-MEG STRATO-SQUADRONS RAKE IN LOW FROM THE ARCTIC WASTES. THEIR TARGET—MEGA-CITY ONE'S CURSED EARTH MISSILE SILOS—
THEY'RE BREAKING FORMATION! H-WAGONS ON INTERCEPT!

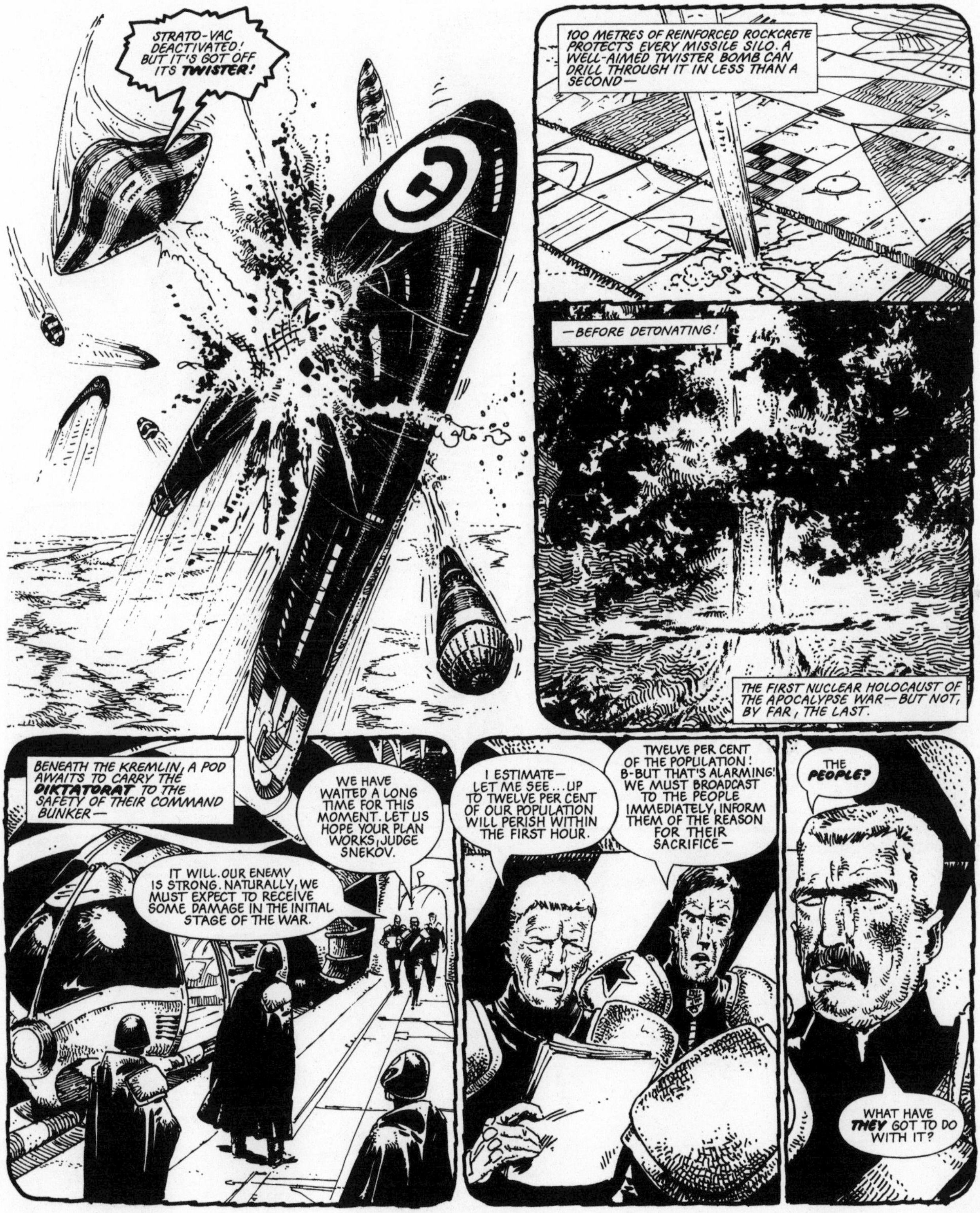

STRATO-VAC DEACTIVATED! BUT IT'S GOT OFF ITS TWISTER!
100 METRES OF REINFORCED ROCKCRETE PROTECTS EVERY MISSILE SILO. A WELL-AIMED TWISTER BOMB CAN DRILL THROUGH IT IN LESS THAN A SECOND—
—BEFORE DETONATING!
THE FIRST NUCLEAR HOLOCAUST OF THE APOCALYPSE WAR—BUT NOT, BY FAR, THE LAST.
BENEATH THE KREMLIN, A POD AWAITS TO CARRY THE DIKTATORAT TO THE SAFETY OF THEIR COMMAND BUNKER—
WE HAVE WAITED A LONG TIME FOR THIS MOMENT. LET US HOPE YOUR PLAN WORKS, JUDGE SNEKOV.
IT WILL. OUR ENEMY IS STRONG. NATURALLY, WE MUST EXPECT TO RECEIVE SOME DAMAGE IN THE INITIAL STAGE OF THE WAR.
I ESTIMATE— LET ME SEE... UP TO TWELVE PER CENT OF OUR POPULATION WILL PERISH WITHIN THE FIRST HOUR.
TWELVE PER CENT OF THE POPULATION! B-BUT THAT'S ALARMING! WE MUST BROADCAST TO THE PEOPLE IMMEDIATELY, INFORM THEM OF THE REASON FOR THEIR SACRIFICE—
THE PEOPLE?
WHAT HAVE THEY GOT TO DO WITH IT?

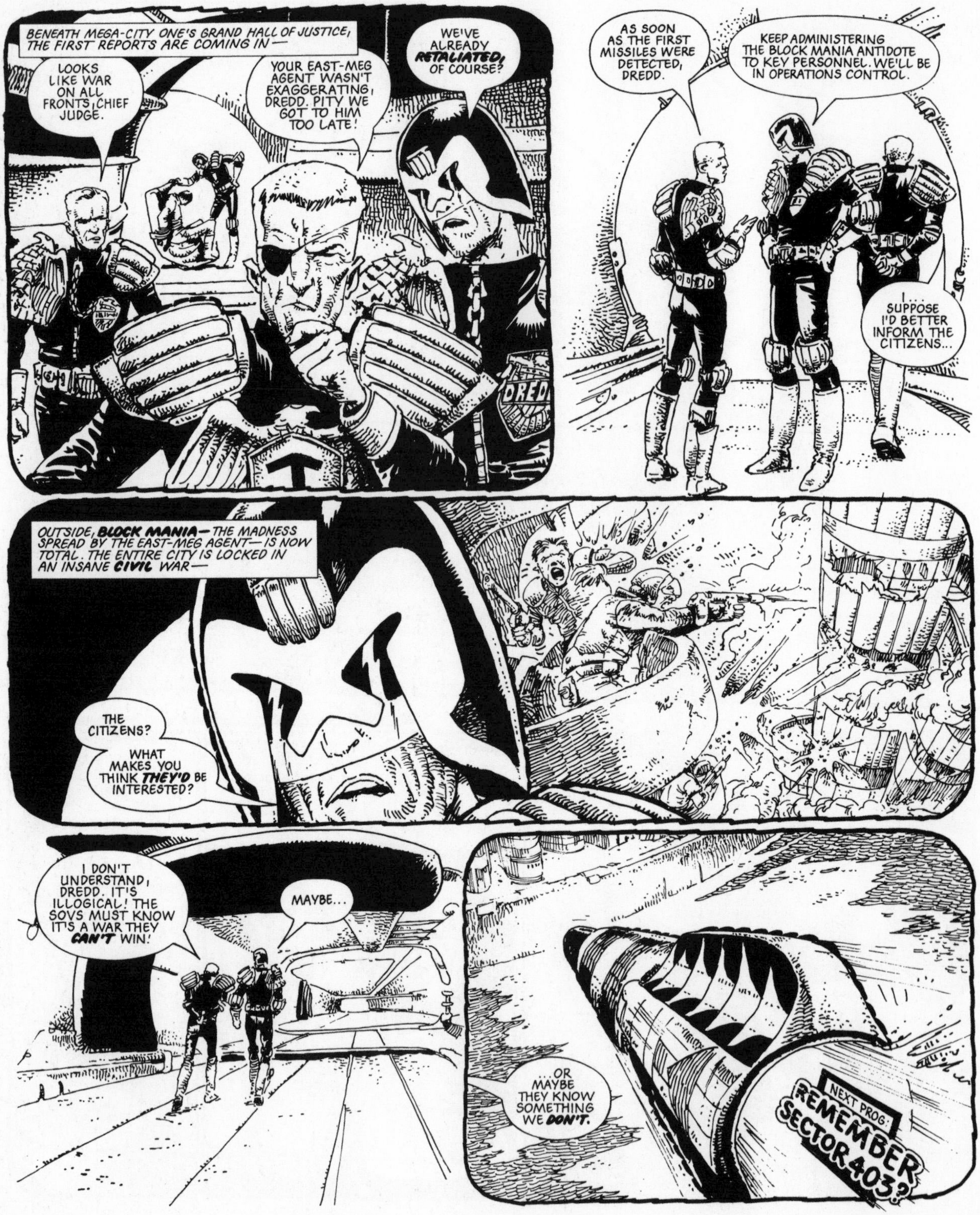
BENEATH MEGA-CITY ONE'S GRAND HALL OF JUSTICE, THE FIRST REPORTS ARE COMING IN—
LOOKS LIKE WAR ON ALL FRONTS, CHIEF JUDGE.
YOUR EAST-MEG AGENT WASN'T EXAGGERATING, DREDD. PITY WE GOT TO HIM TOO LATE!
WE'VE ALREADY RETALIATED, OF COURSE?
AS SOON AS THE FIRST MISSILES WERE DETECTED, DREDD.
KEEP ADMINISTERING THE BLOCK MANIA ANTIDOTE TO KEY PERSONNEL. WE'LL BE IN OPERATIONS CONTROL.
I... SUPPOSE I'D BETTER INFORM THE CITIZENS...
OUTSIDE, BLOCK MANIA— THE MADNESS SPREAD BY THE EAST-MEG AGENT— IS NOW TOTAL. THE ENTIRE CITY IS LOCKED IN AN INSANE CIVIL WAR—
THE CITIZENS?
WHAT MAKES YOU THINK THEY'D BE INTERESTED?
I DON'T UNDERSTAND, DREDD. IT'S ILLOGICAL! THE SOVS MUST KNOW IT'S A WAR THEY CAN'T WIN!
MAYBE...
...OR MAYBE THEY KNOW SOMETHING WE DON'T.
NEXT PROG:
REMEMBER SECTOR 403?

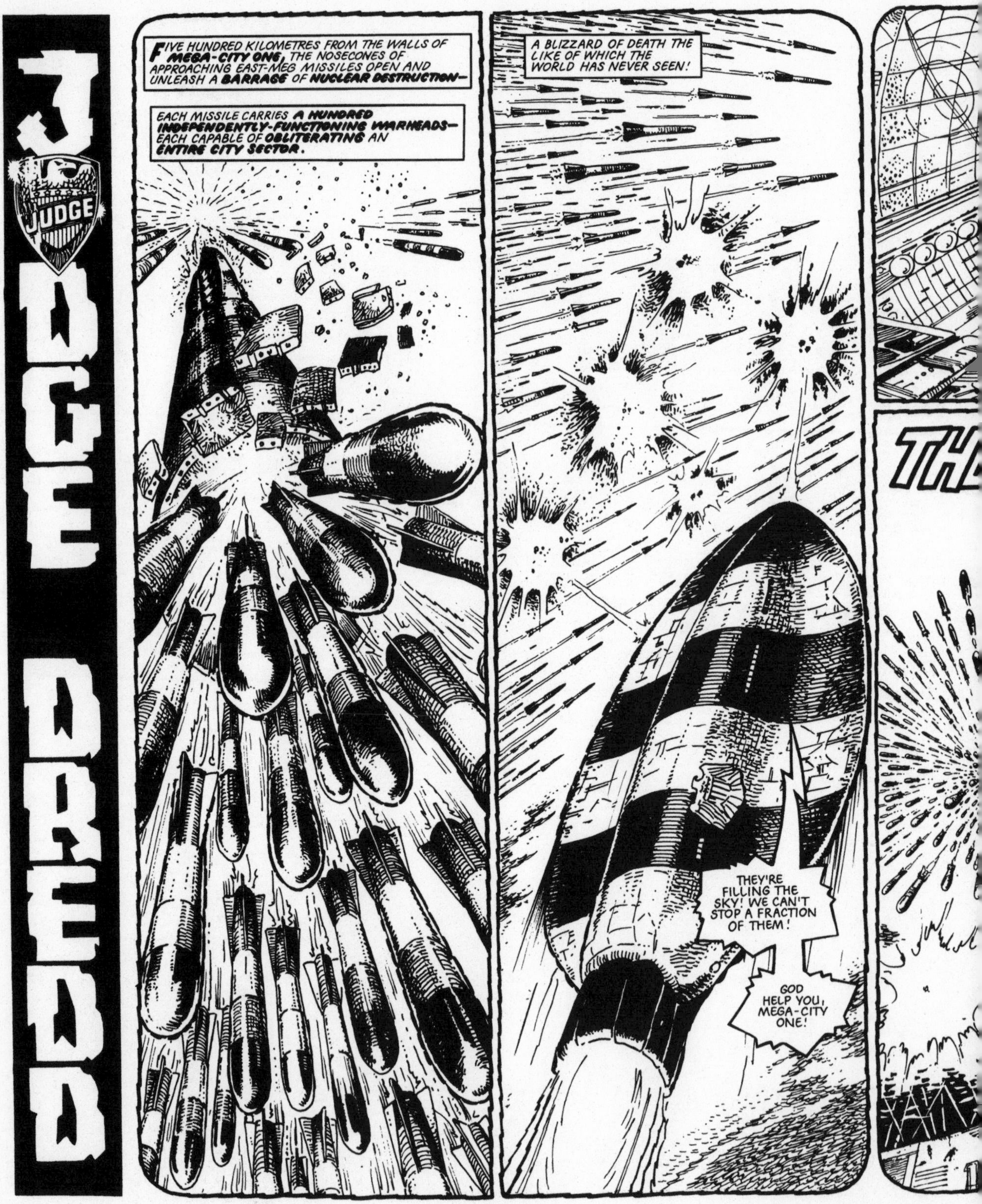
JUDGE DREDD
JUDGE
FIVE HUNDRED KILOMETRES FROM THE WALLS OF MEGA-CITY ONE, THE NOSECONES OF APPROACHING EAST-MEG MISSILES OPEN AND UNLEASH A BARRAGE OF NUCLEAR DESTRUCTION—
EACH MISSILE CARRIES A HUNDRED INDEPENDENTLY-FUNCTIONING WARHEADS— EACH CAPABLE OF OBLITERATING AN ENTIRE CITY SECTOR.
A BLIZZARD OF DEATH THE LIKE OF WHICH THE WORLD HAS NEVER SEEN!
THEY'RE FILLING THE SKY! WE CAN'T STOP A FRACTION OF THEM!
GOD HELP YOU, MEGA-CITY ONE!

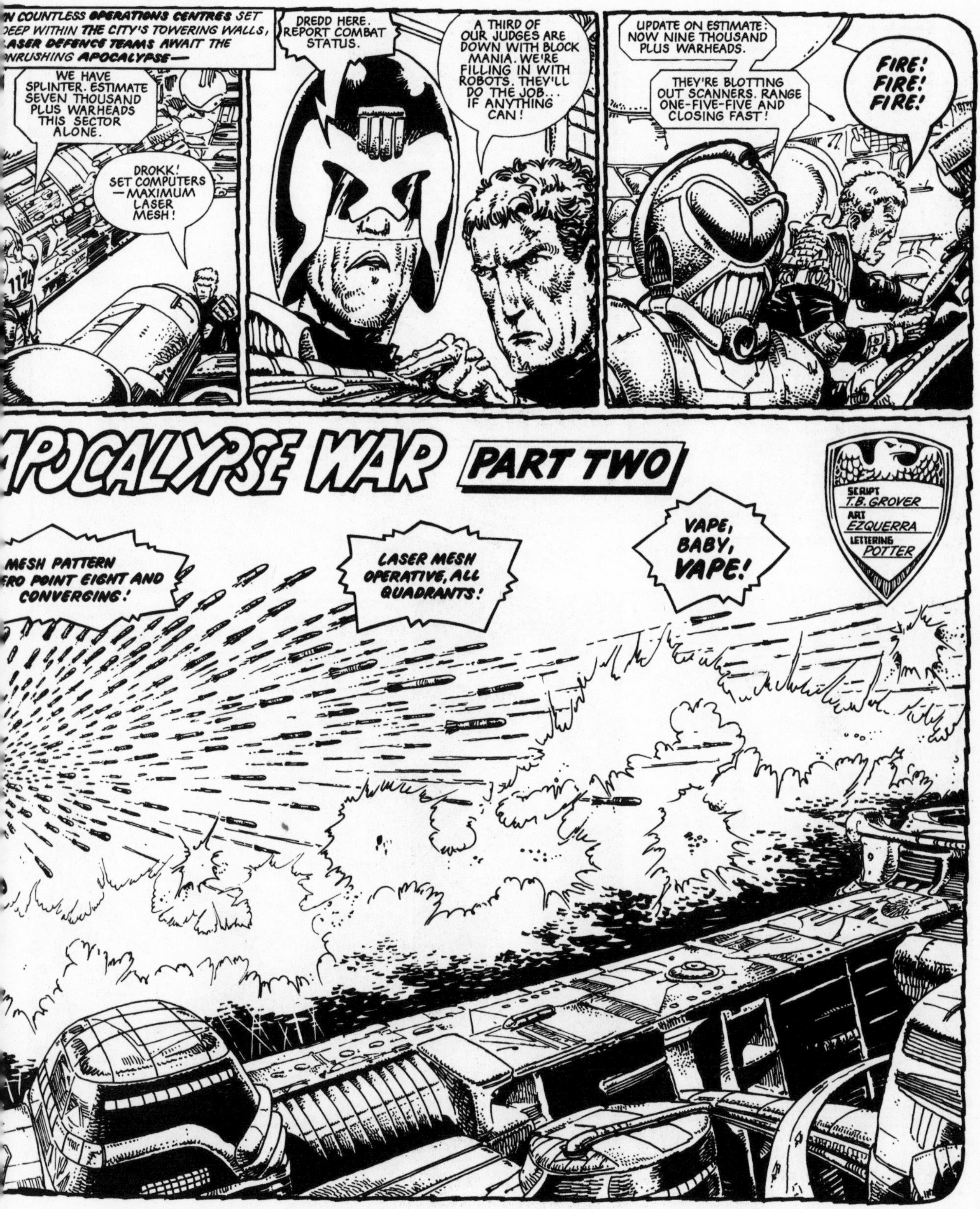
N COUNTLESS OPERATIONS CENTRES SET DEEP WITHIN THE CITY'S TOWERING WALLS, LASER DEFENCE TEAMS AWAIT THE NRUSHING APOCALYPSE—
WE HAVE SPLINTER. ESTIMATE SEVEN THOUSAND PLUS WARHEADS THIS SECTOR ALONE.
DROKK! SET COMPUTERS —MAXIMUM LASER MESH!
DREDD HERE. REPORT COMBAT STATUS.
A THIRD OF OUR JUDGES ARE DOWN WITH BLOCK MANIA. WE'RE FILLING IN WITH ROBOTS. THEY'LL DO THE JOB.. IF ANYTHING CAN!
UPDATE ON ESTIMATE: NOW NINE THOUSAND PLUS WARHEADS.
THEY'RE BLOTTING OUT SCANNERS. RANGE ONE-FIVE-FIVE AND CLOSING FAST!
FIRE! FIRE! FIRE!
POCALYPSE WAR
PART TWO
SCRIPT T.B. GROVER
ART EZQUERRA
LETTERING POTTER
MESH PATTERN ERO POINT EIGHT AND CONVERGING!
LASER MESH OPERATIVE, ALL QUADRANTS!
VAPE, BABY, VAPE!

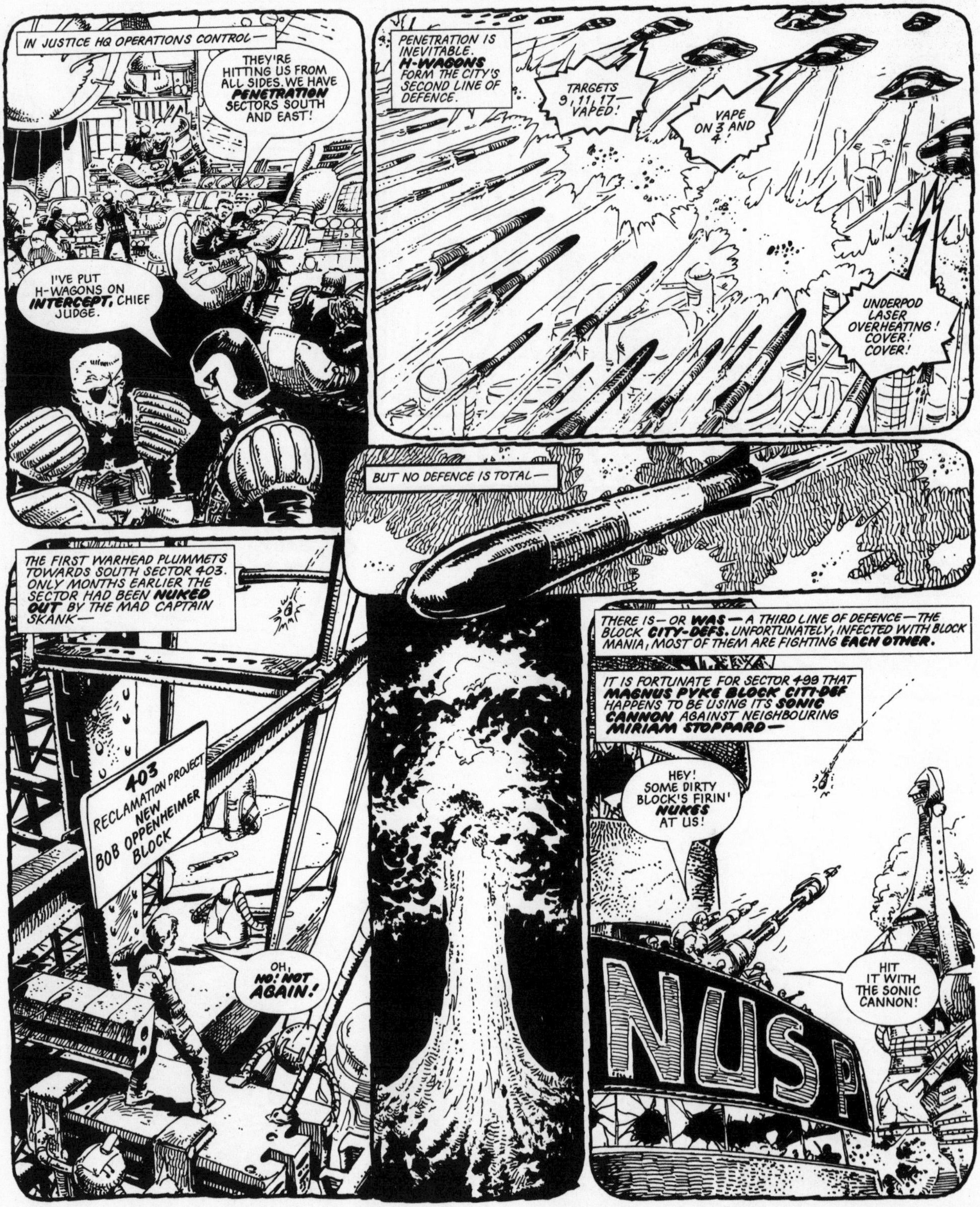

IN JUSTICE HQ OPERATIONS CONTROL—
THEY'RE HITTING US FROM ALL SIDES. WE HAVE PENETRATION SECTORS SOUTH AND EAST!
I'VE PUT H-WAGONS ON INTERCEPT, CHIEF JUDGE.
PENETRATION IS INEVITABLE. H-WAGONS FORM THE CITY'S SECOND LINE OF DEFENCE.
TARGETS 9, 11, 17— VAPED!
VAPE ON 3 AND 4.
UNDERPOD LASER OVERHEATING! COVER! COVER!
BUT NO DEFENCE IS TOTAL—
THE FIRST WARHEAD PLUMMETS TOWARDS SOUTH SECTOR 403. ONLY MONTHS EARLIER THE SECTOR HAD BEEN NUKED OUT BY THE MAD CAPTAIN SKANK—
403 RECLAMATION PROJECT NEW BOB OPPENHEIMER BLOCK
OH, NO! NOT AGAIN!
THERE IS—OR WAS—A THIRD LINE OF DEFENCE—THE BLOCK CITY-DEFS. UNFORTUNATELY, INFECTED WITH BLOCK MANIA, MOST OF THEM ARE FIGHTING EACH OTHER.
IT IS FORTUNATE FOR SECTOR 499 THAT MAGNUS PYKE BLOCK CITI-DEF HAPPENS TO BE USING ITS SONIC CANNON AGAINST NEIGHBOURING MIRIAM STOPPARD—
HEY! SOME DIRTY BLOCK'S FIRIN' NUKES AT US!
HIT IT WITH THE SONIC CANNON!
NUS P

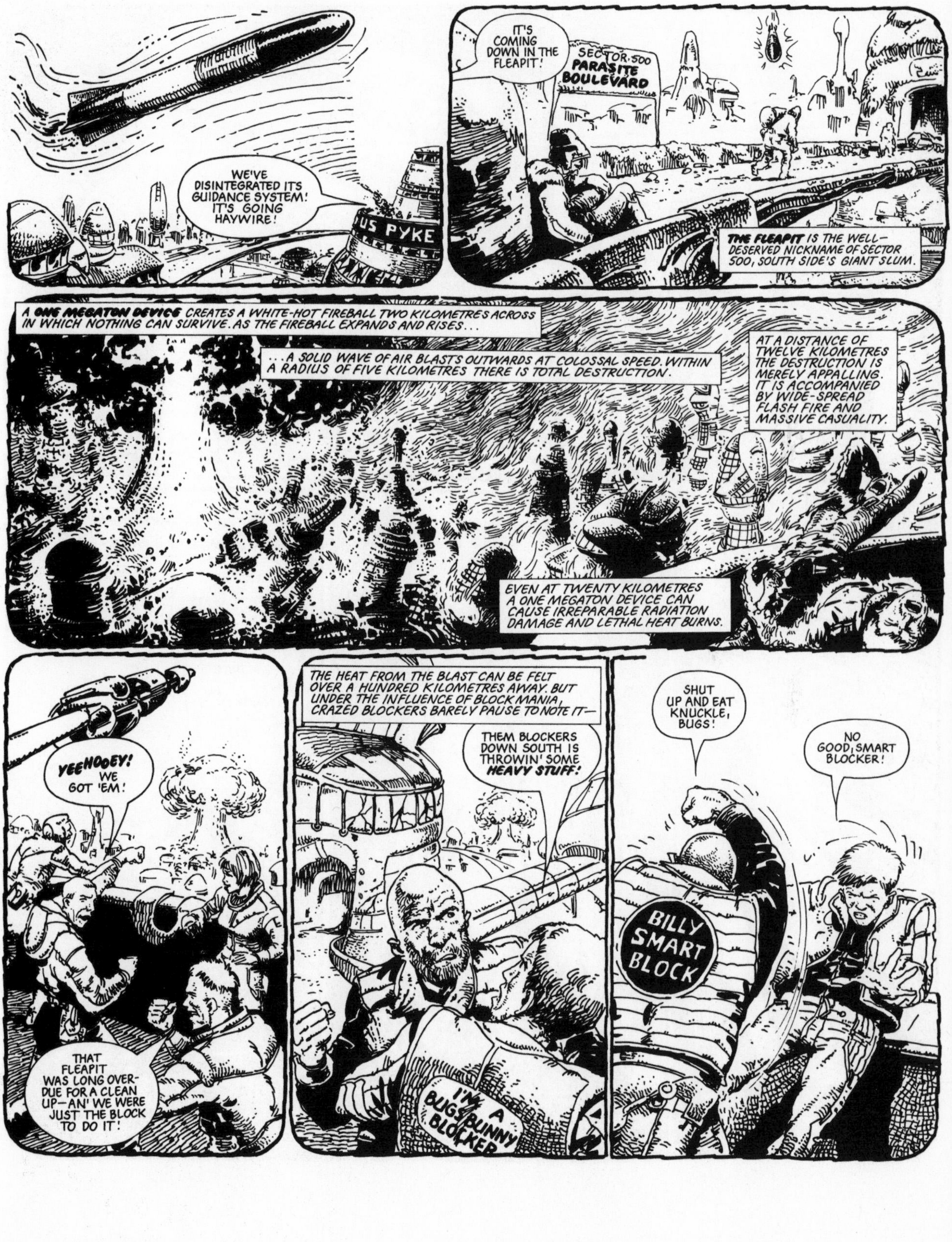

WE'VE DISINTEGRATED ITS GUIDANCE SYSTEM! IT'S GOING HAYWIRE!
US PYKE
IT'S COMING DOWN IN THE FLEAPIT!
SECTOR 500 PARASITE BOULEVARD
THE FLEAPIT IS THE WELL-DESERVED NICKNAME OF SECTOR 500, SOUTH SIDE'S GIANT SLUM.
A ONE MEGATON DEVICE CREATES A WHITE-HOT FIREBALL TWO KILOMETRES ACROSS IN WHICH NOTHING CAN SURVIVE. AS THE FIREBALL EXPANDS AND RISES...
...A SOLID WAVE OF AIR BLASTS OUTWARDS AT COLOSSAL SPEED. WITHIN A RADIUS OF FIVE KILOMETRES THERE IS TOTAL DESTRUCTION.
AT A DISTANCE OF TWELVE KILOMETRES THE DESTRUCTION IS MERELY APPALLING. IT IS ACCOMPANIED BY WIDE-SPREAD FLASH FIRE AND MASSIVE CASUALITY.
EVEN AT TWENTY KILOMETRES A ONE MEGATON DEVICE CAN CAUSE IRREPARABLE RADIATION DAMAGE AND LETHAL HEAT BURNS.
YEEHOOEY! WE GOT 'EM!
THAT FLEAPIT WAS LONG OVERDUE FOR A CLEAN UP—AN' WE WERE JUST THE BLOCK TO DO IT!
THE HEAT FROM THE BLAST CAN BE FELT OVER A HUNDRED KILOMETRES AWAY. BUT UNDER THE INFLUENCE OF BLOCK MANIA, CRAZED BLOCKERS BARELY PAUSE TO NOTE IT—
THEM BLOCKERS DOWN SOUTH IS THROWIN' SOME HEAVY STUFF!
I'M A BUGS BUNNY BLOCKER
SHUT UP AND EAT KNUCKLE, BUGS!
NO GOOD, SMART BLOCKER!
BILLY SMART BLOCK

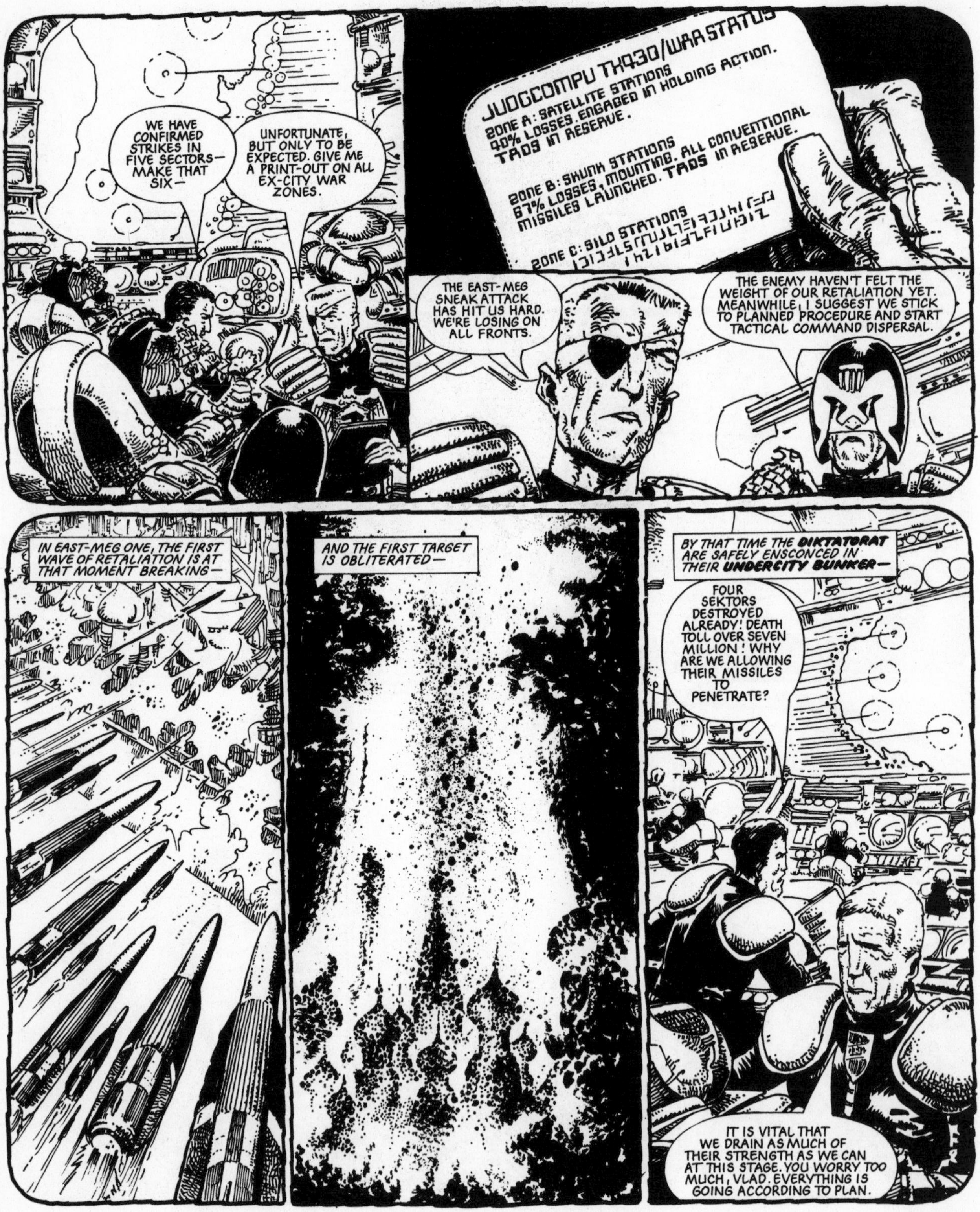

WE HAVE CONFIRMED STRIKES IN FIVE SECTORS— MAKE THAT SIX—
UNFORTUNATE, BUT ONLY TO BE EXPECTED. GIVE ME A PRINT-OUT ON ALL EX-CITY WAR ZONES.
JUDGCOMPU TX430/WAR STATUS
ZONE A: SATELLITE STATIONS 40% LOSSES. ENGAGED IN HOLDING ACTION. TADS IN RESERVE.
ZONE B: SHUNK STATIONS 67% LOSSES, MOUNTING. ALL CONVENTIONAL MISSILES LAUNCHED. TADS IN RESERVE.
ZONE C: SILO STATIONS
THE EAST-MEG SNEAK ATTACK HAS HIT US HARD. WE'RE LOSING ON ALL FRONTS.
THE ENEMY HAVEN'T FELT THE WEIGHT OF OUR RETALIATION YET. MEANWHILE, I SUGGEST WE STICK TO PLANNED PROCEDURE AND START TACTICAL COMMAND DISPERSAL.
IN EAST-MEG ONE, THE FIRST WAVE OF RETALIATION IS AT THAT MOMENT BREAKING—
AND THE FIRST TARGET IS OBLITERATED—
BY THAT TIME THE DIKTATORAT ARE SAFELY ENSCONCED IN THEIR UNDERCITY BUNKER—
FOUR SEKTORS DESTROYED ALREADY! DEATH TOLL OVER SEVEN MILLION! WHY ARE WE ALLOWING THEIR MISSILES TO PENETRATE?
IT IS VITAL THAT WE DRAIN AS MUCH OF THEIR STRENGTH AS WE CAN AT THIS STAGE. YOU WORRY TOO MUCH, VLAD. EVERYTHING IS GOING ACCORDING TO PLAN.

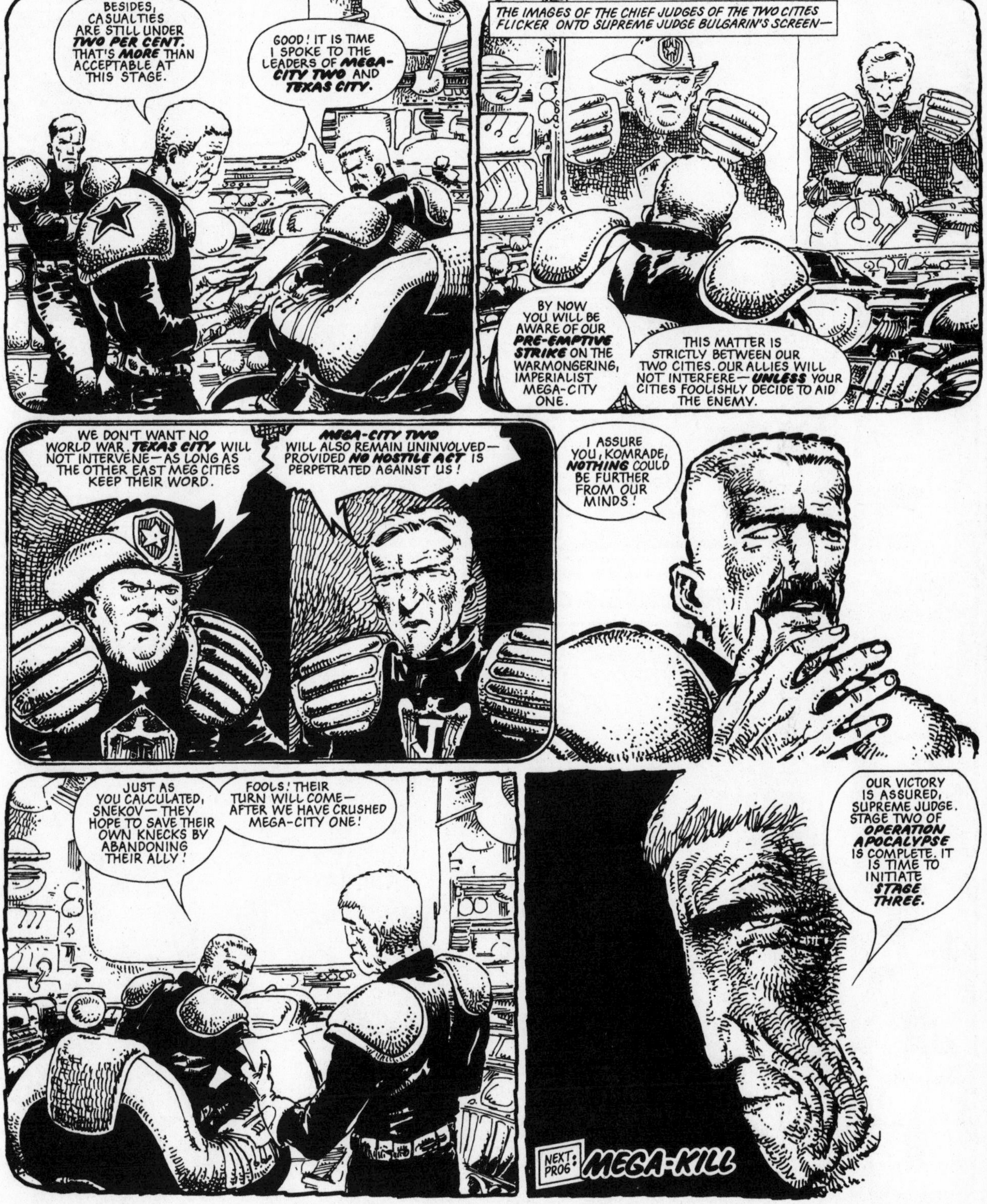
BESIDES, CASUALTIES ARE STILL UNDER TWO PER CENT. THAT'S MORE THAN ACCEPTABLE AT THIS STAGE.
GOOD! IT IS TIME I SPOKE TO THE LEADERS OF MEGA-CITY TWO AND TEXAS CITY.
THE IMAGES OF THE CHIEF JUDGES OF THE TWO CITIES FLICKER ONTO SUPREME JUDGE BULGARIN'S SCREEN—
BY NOW YOU WILL BE AWARE OF OUR PRE-EMPTIVE STRIKE ON THE WARMONGERING, IMPERIALIST MEGA-CITY ONE.
THIS MATTER IS STRICTLY BETWEEN OUR TWO CITIES. OUR ALLIES WILL NOT INTERFERE—UNLESS YOUR CITIES FOOLISHLY DECIDE TO AID THE ENEMY.
WE DON'T WANT NO WORLD WAR. TEXAS CITY WILL NOT INTERVENE—AS LONG AS THE OTHER EAST MEG CITIES KEEP THEIR WORD.
MEGA-CITY TWO WILL ALSO REMAIN UNINVOLVED—PROVIDED NO HOSTILE ACT IS PERPETRATED AGAINST US!
I ASSURE YOU, KOMRADE, NOTHING COULD BE FURTHER FROM OUR MINDS!
JUST AS YOU CALCULATED, SNEKOV—THEY HOPE TO SAVE THEIR OWN KNECKS BY ABANDONING THEIR ALLY!
FOOLS! THEIR TURN WILL COME—AFTER WE HAVE CRUSHED MEGA-CITY ONE!
OUR VICTORY IS ASSURED, SUPREME JUDGE. STAGE TWO OF OPERATION APOCALYPSE IS COMPLETE. IT IS TIME TO INITIATE STAGE THREE.
NEXT PROG: MEGA-KILL

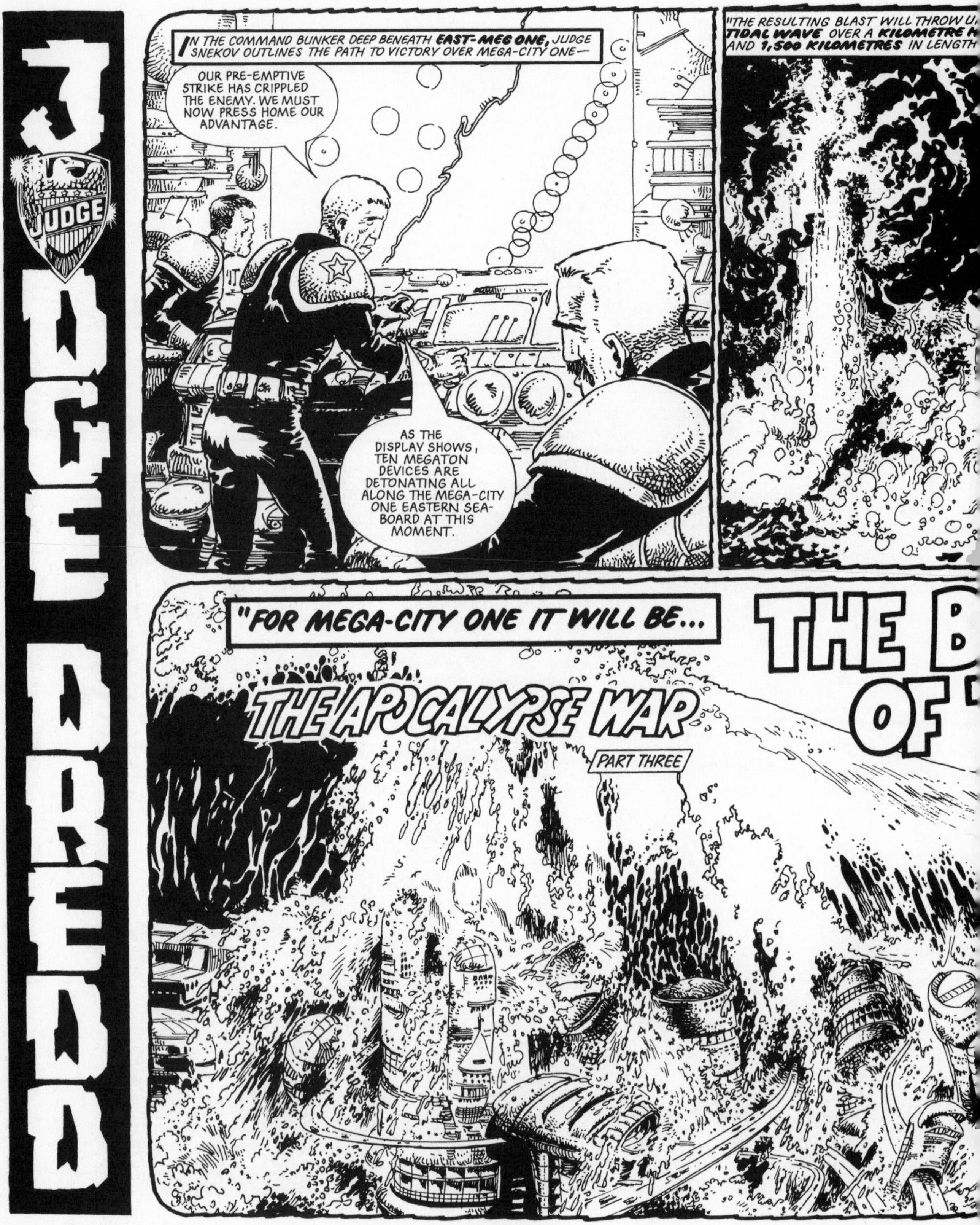
JUDGE DREDD
JUDGE
IN THE COMMAND BUNKER DEEP BENEATH EAST-MEG ONE, JUDGE SNEKOV OUTLINES THE PATH TO VICTORY OVER MEGA-CITY ONE—
OUR PRE-EMPTIVE STRIKE HAS CRIPPLED THE ENEMY. WE MUST NOW PRESS HOME OUR ADVANTAGE.
AS THE DISPLAY SHOWS, TEN MEGATON DEVICES ARE DETONATING ALL ALONG THE MEGA-CITY ONE EASTERN SEA-BOARD AT THIS MOMENT.
"THE RESULTING BLAST WILL THROW U
TIDAL WAVE OVER A KILOMETRE H
AND 1,500 KILOMETRES IN LENGTH
"FOR MEGA-CITY ONE IT WILL BE...
THE B
OF
THE APOCALYPSE WAR
PART THREE

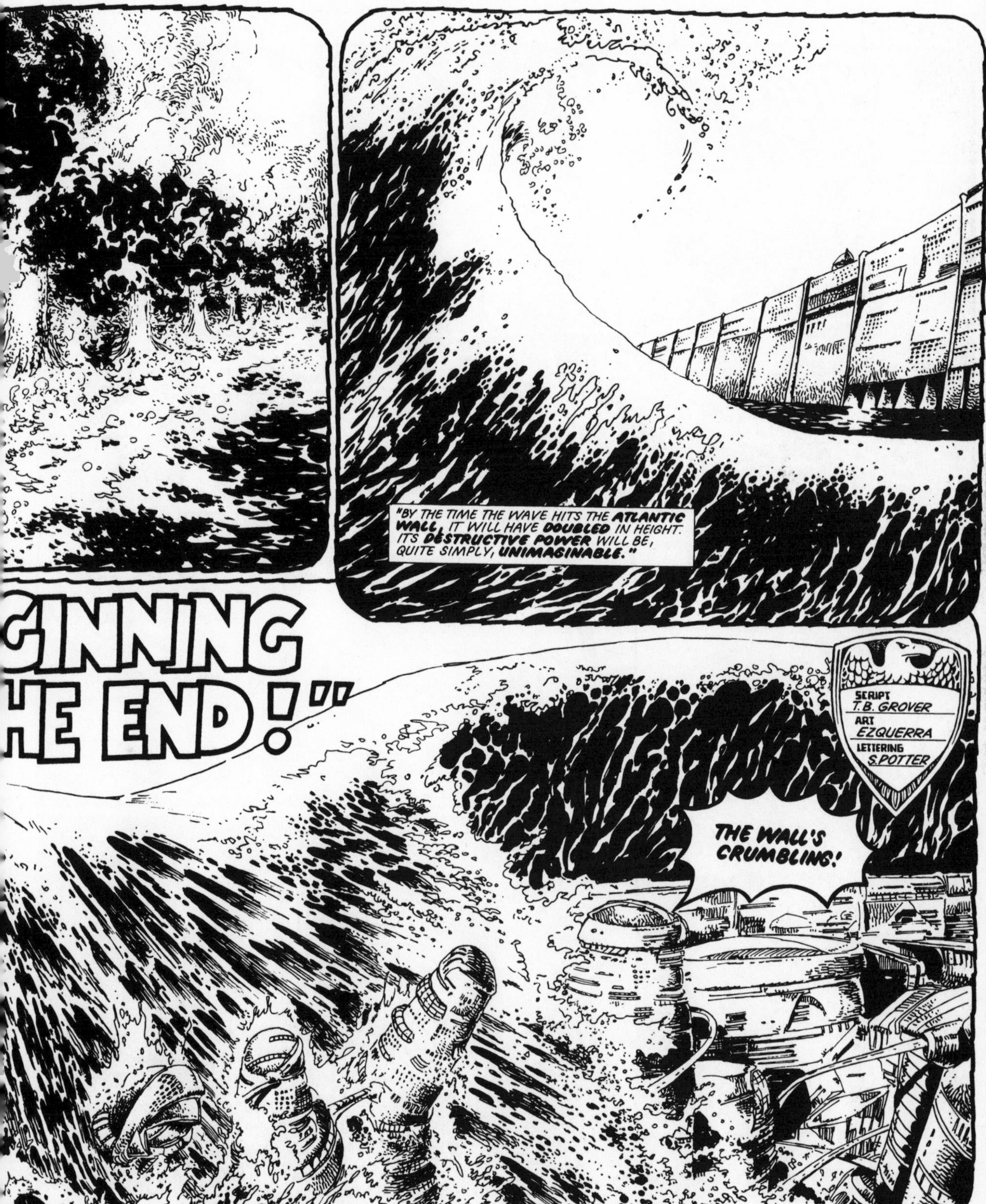
"BY THE TIME THE WAVE HITS THE ATLANTIC WALL, IT WILL HAVE DOUBLED IN HEIGHT. ITS DESTRUCTIVE POWER WILL BE, QUITE SIMPLY, UNIMAGINABLE."
GINNING
HE END!"
SCRIPT T.B. GROVER
ART EZQUERRA
LETTERING S.POTTER
THE WALL'S CRUMBLING!

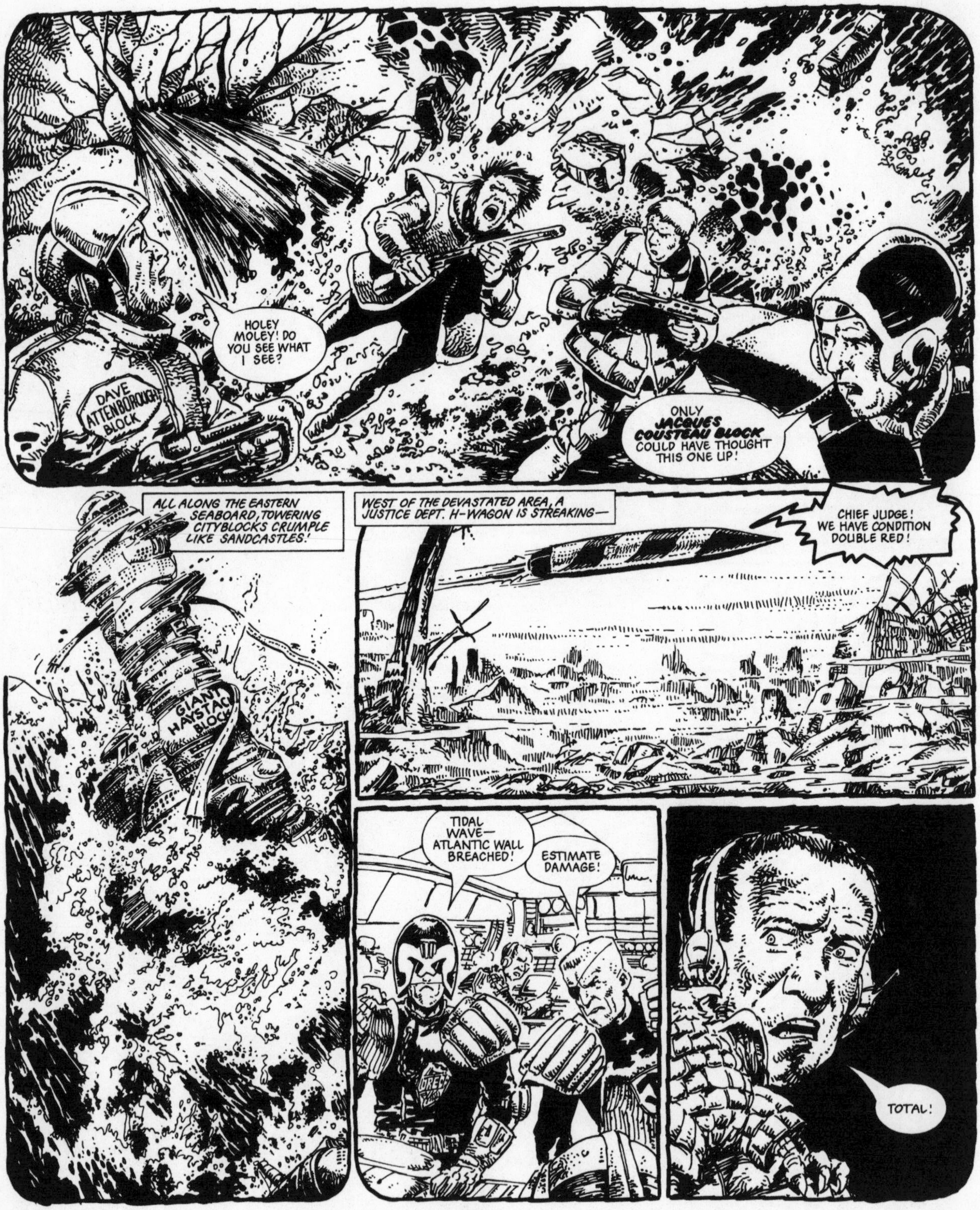
HOLEY MOLEY! DO YOU SEE WHAT I SEE?
DAVE ATTENBOROUGH BLOCK
ONLY JACQUES COUSTEAU BLOCK COULD HAVE THOUGHT THIS ONE UP!
ALL ALONG THE EASTERN SEABOARD, TOWERING CITYBLOCKS CRUMPLE LIKE SANDCASTLES!
GIANT HAYSTACK BLOCK
WEST OF THE DEVASTATED AREA, A JUSTICE DEPT. H-WAGON IS STREAKING—
CHIEF JUDGE! WE HAVE CONDITION DOUBLE RED!
TIDAL WAVE— ATLANTIC WALL BREACHED!
ESTIMATE DAMAGE!
TOTAL!

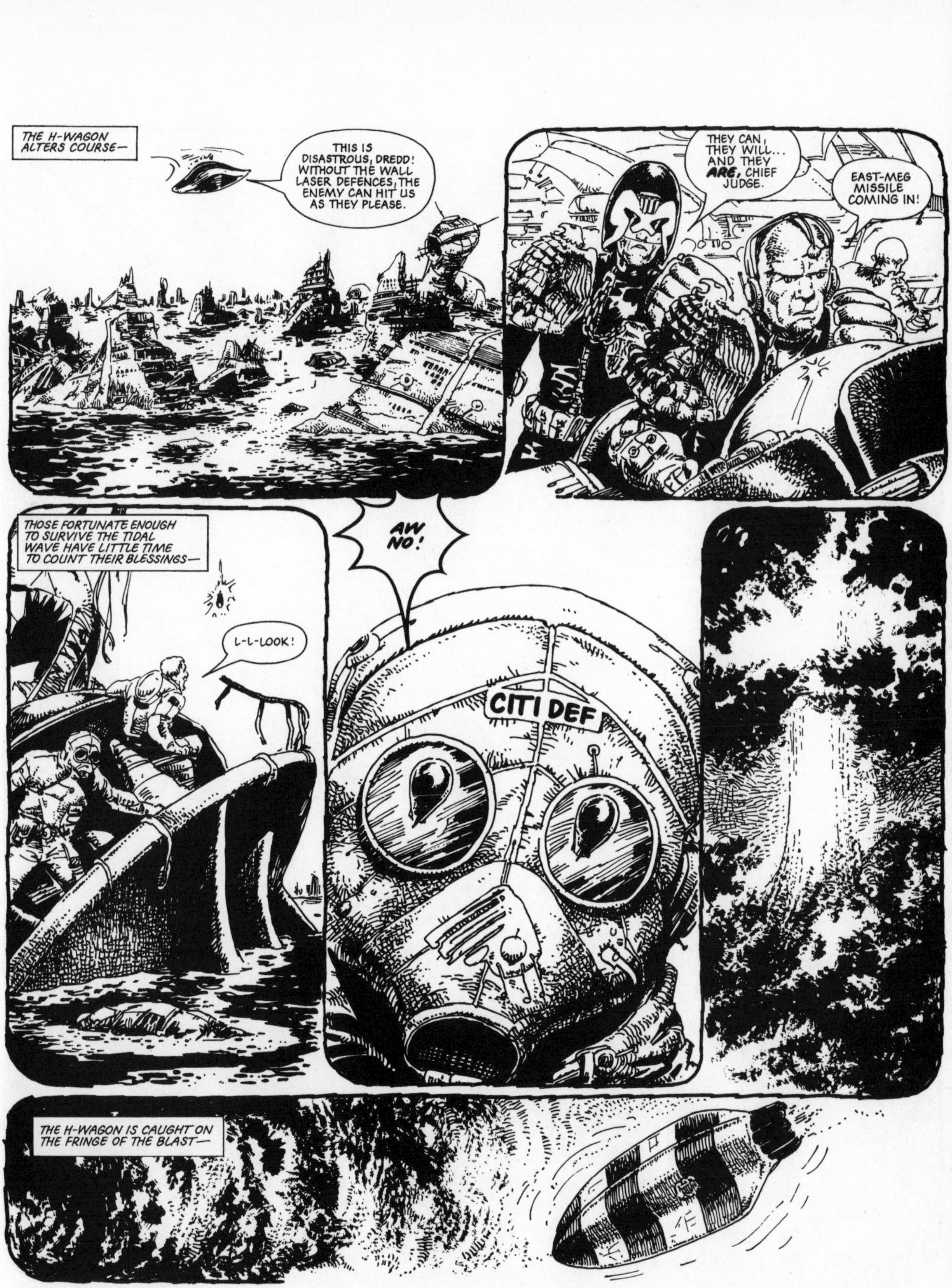

THE H-WAGON ALTERS COURSE—
THIS IS DISASTROUS, DREDD! WITHOUT THE WALL LASER DEFENCES, THE ENEMY CAN HIT US AS THEY PLEASE.
THEY CAN, THEY WILL... AND THEY **ARE**, CHIEF JUDGE.
EAST-MEG MISSILE COMING IN!
THOSE FORTUNATE ENOUGH TO SURVIVE THE TIDAL WAVE HAVE LITTLE TIME TO COUNT THEIR BLESSINGS—
L-L-LOOK!
AW NO!
CITI DEF
THE H-WAGON IS CAUGHT ON THE FRINGE OF THE BLAST—

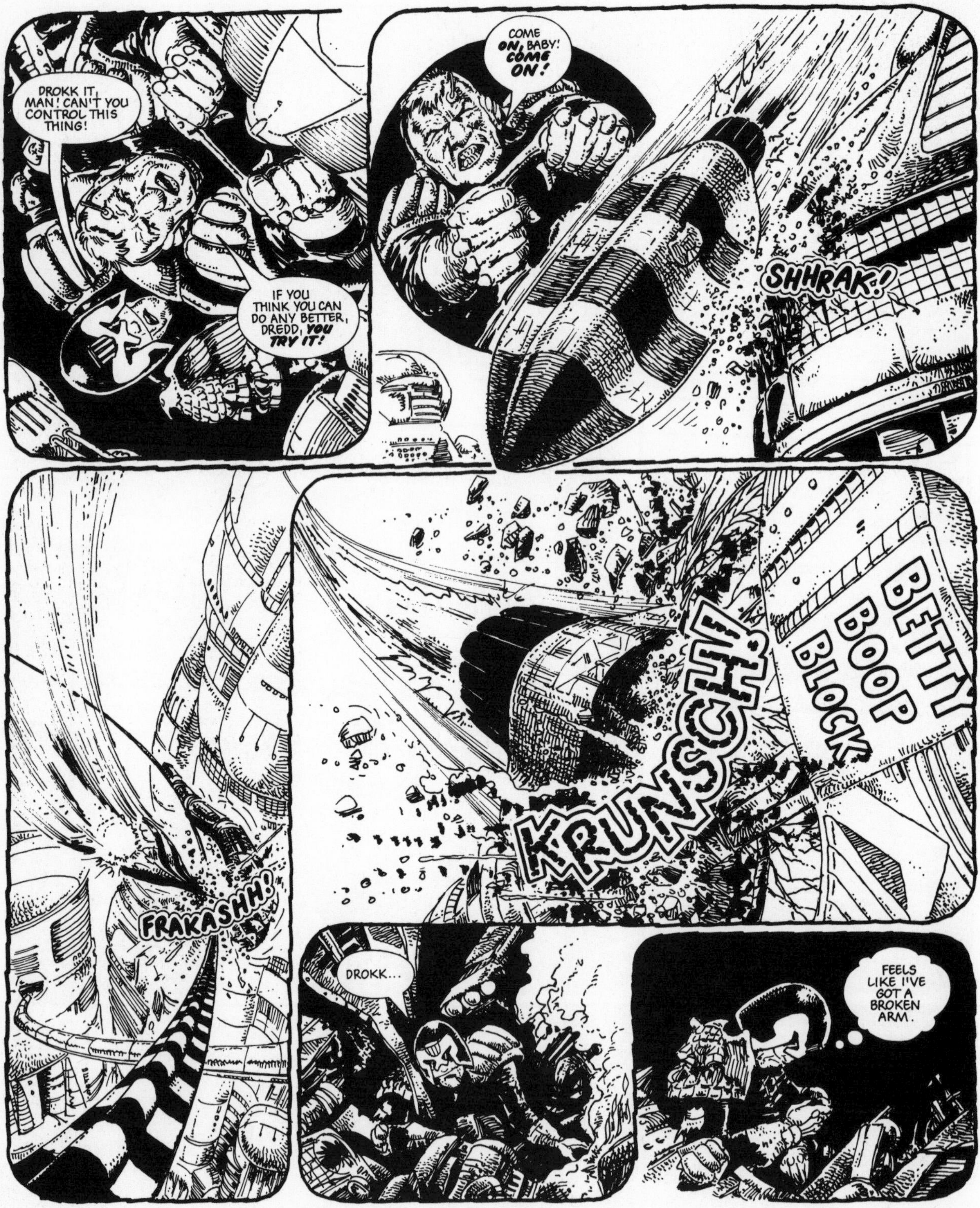
DROKK IT, MAN! CAN'T YOU CONTROL THIS THING!
IF YOU THINK YOU CAN DO ANY BETTER, DREDD, YOU TRY IT!
COME ON, BABY! COME ON!
SHHRAK!
FRAKASHH!
BETTY BOOP BLOCK
KRUNSCH!
DROKK...
FEELS LIKE I'VE GOT A BROKEN ARM.

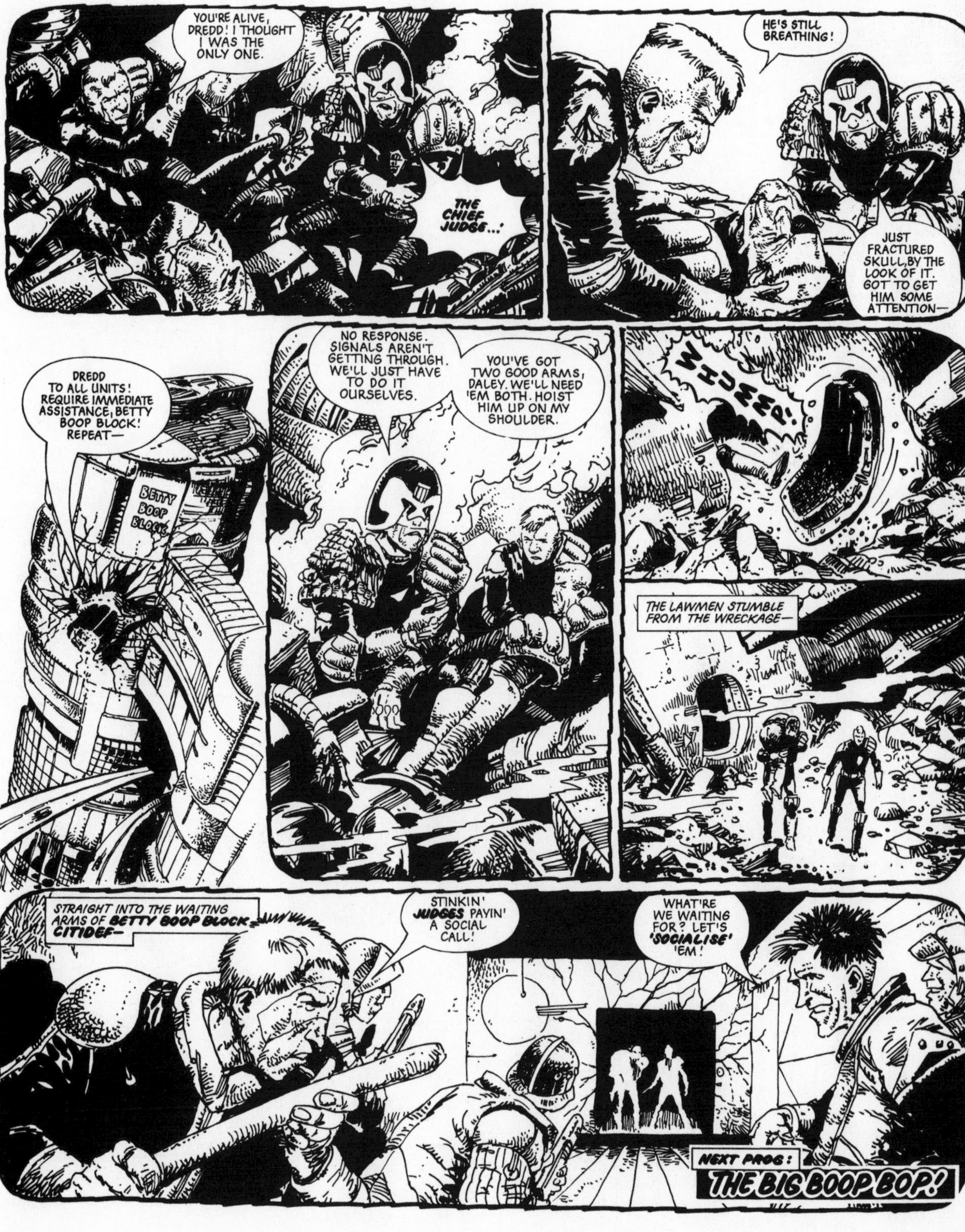

YOU'RE ALIVE, DREDD! I THOUGHT I WAS THE ONLY ONE.
THE CHIEF JUDGE...!
HE'S STILL BREATHING!
JUST FRACTURED SKULL, BY THE LOOK OF IT. GOT TO GET HIM SOME ATTENTION—
DREDD TO ALL UNITS! REQUIRE IMMEDIATE ASSISTANCE, BETTY BOOP BLOCK! REPEAT—
BETTY BOOP BLOCK
NO RESPONSE. SIGNALS AREN'T GETTING THROUGH. WE'LL JUST HAVE TO DO IT OURSELVES.
YOU'VE GOT TWO GOOD ARMS, DALEY. WE'LL NEED 'EM BOTH. HOIST HIM UP ON MY SHOULDER.
WHUMP!
THE LAWMEN STUMBLE FROM THE WRECKAGE—
STRAIGHT INTO THE WAITING ARMS OF BETTY BOOP BLOCK CITIDEF—
STINKIN' JUDGES PAYIN' A SOCIAL CALL!
WHAT'RE WE WAITING FOR? LET'S 'SOCIALISE' 'EM!
NEXT PROG:
THE BIG BOOP BOP!

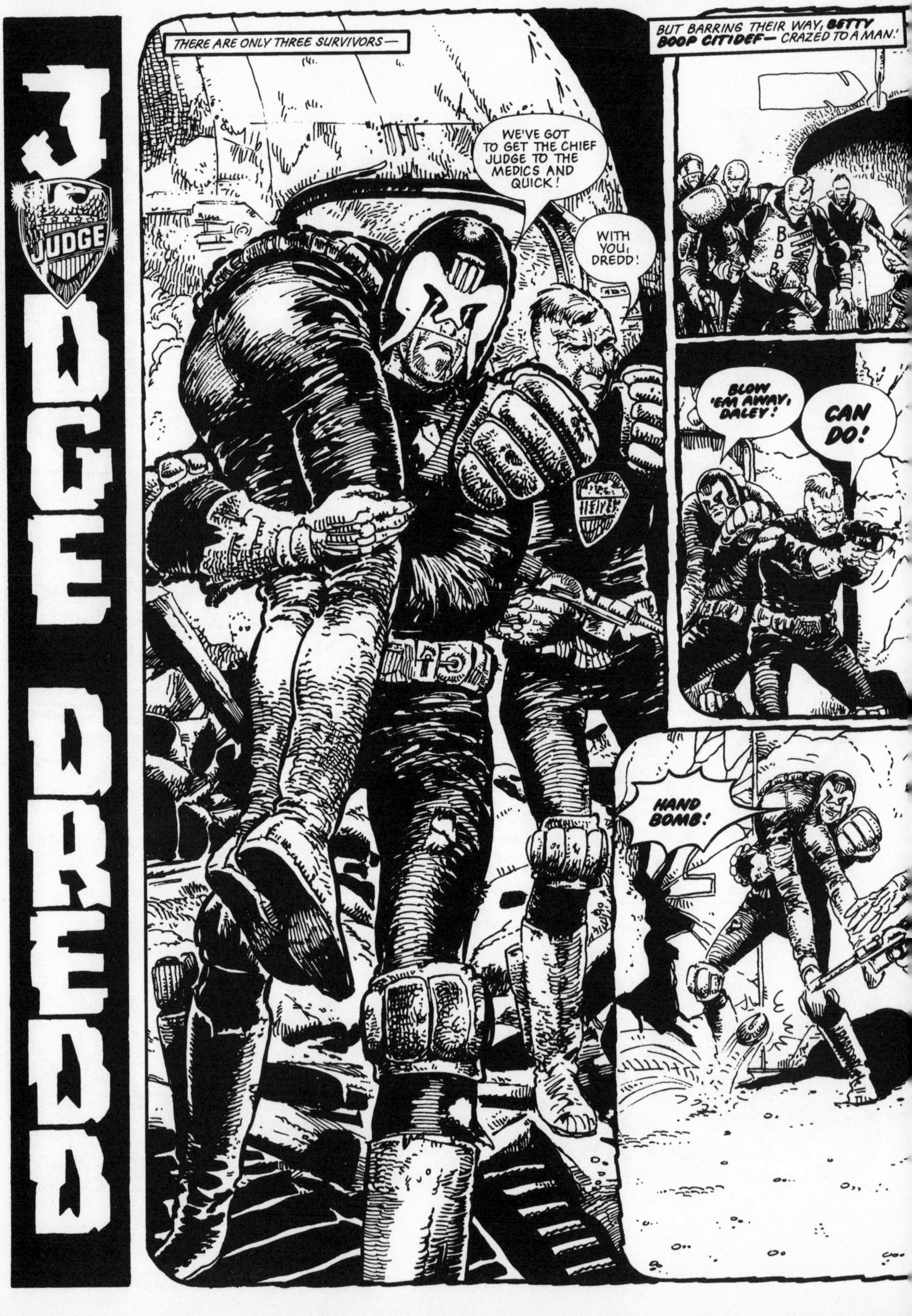
JUDGE DREDD
JUDGE
THERE ARE ONLY THREE SURVIVORS—
WE'VE GOT TO GET THE CHIEF JUDGE TO THE MEDICS AND QUICK!
WITH YOU, DREDD!
BUT BARRING THEIR WAY, BETTY BOOP CITIDEF— CRAZED TO A MAN!
BLOW 'EM AWAY, DALEY!
CAN DO!
HAND BOMB!

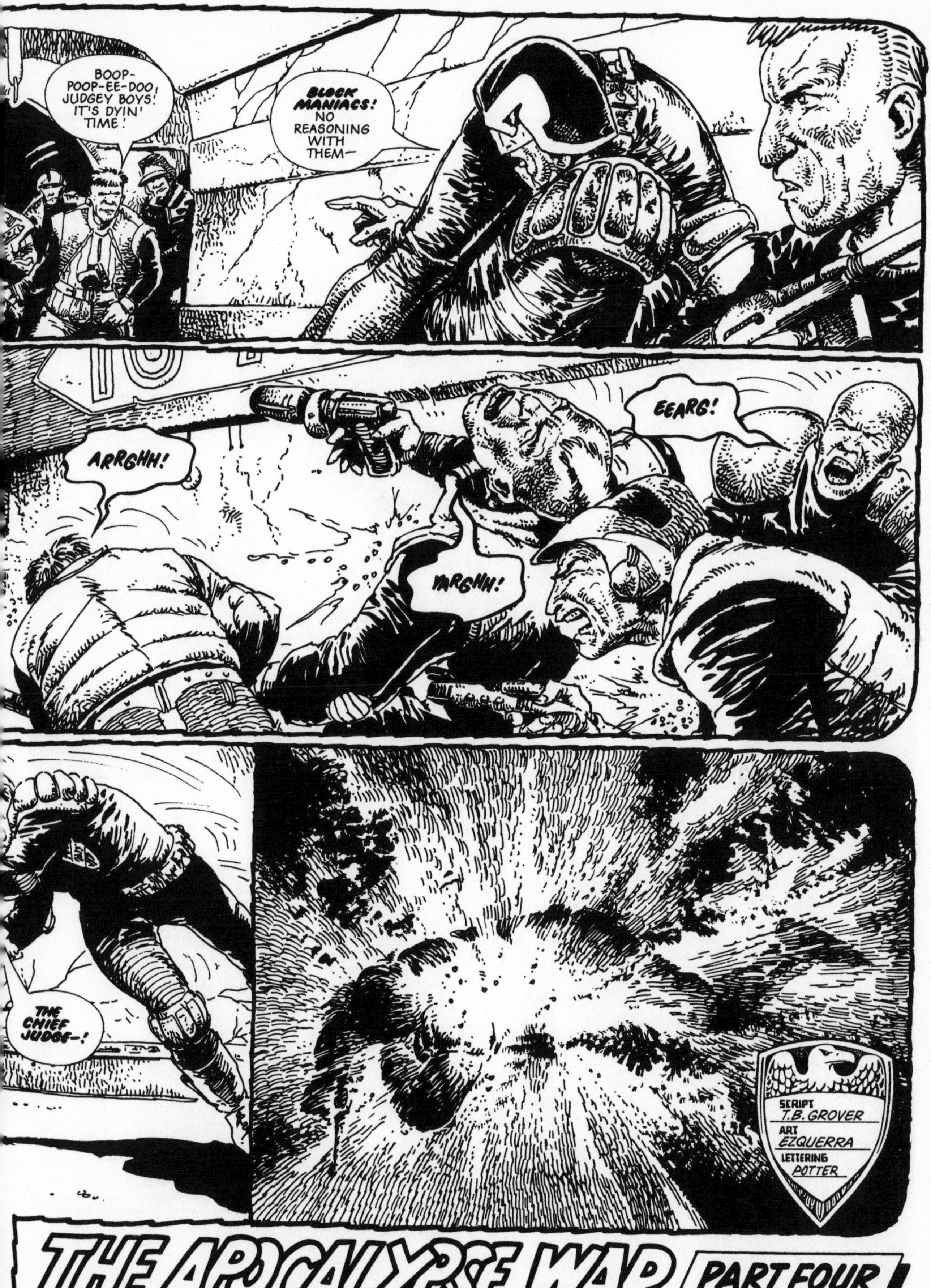

BOOP-POOP-EE-DOO! JUDGEY BOYS! IT'S DYIN' TIME!
BLOCK MANIACS! NO REASONING WITH THEM—
ARRGHH!
YARGHH!
EEARG!
THE CHIEF JUDGE—!
SCRIPT T.B. GROVER
ART EZQUERRA
LETTERING POTTER
THE APOCALYPSE WAR
PART FOUR

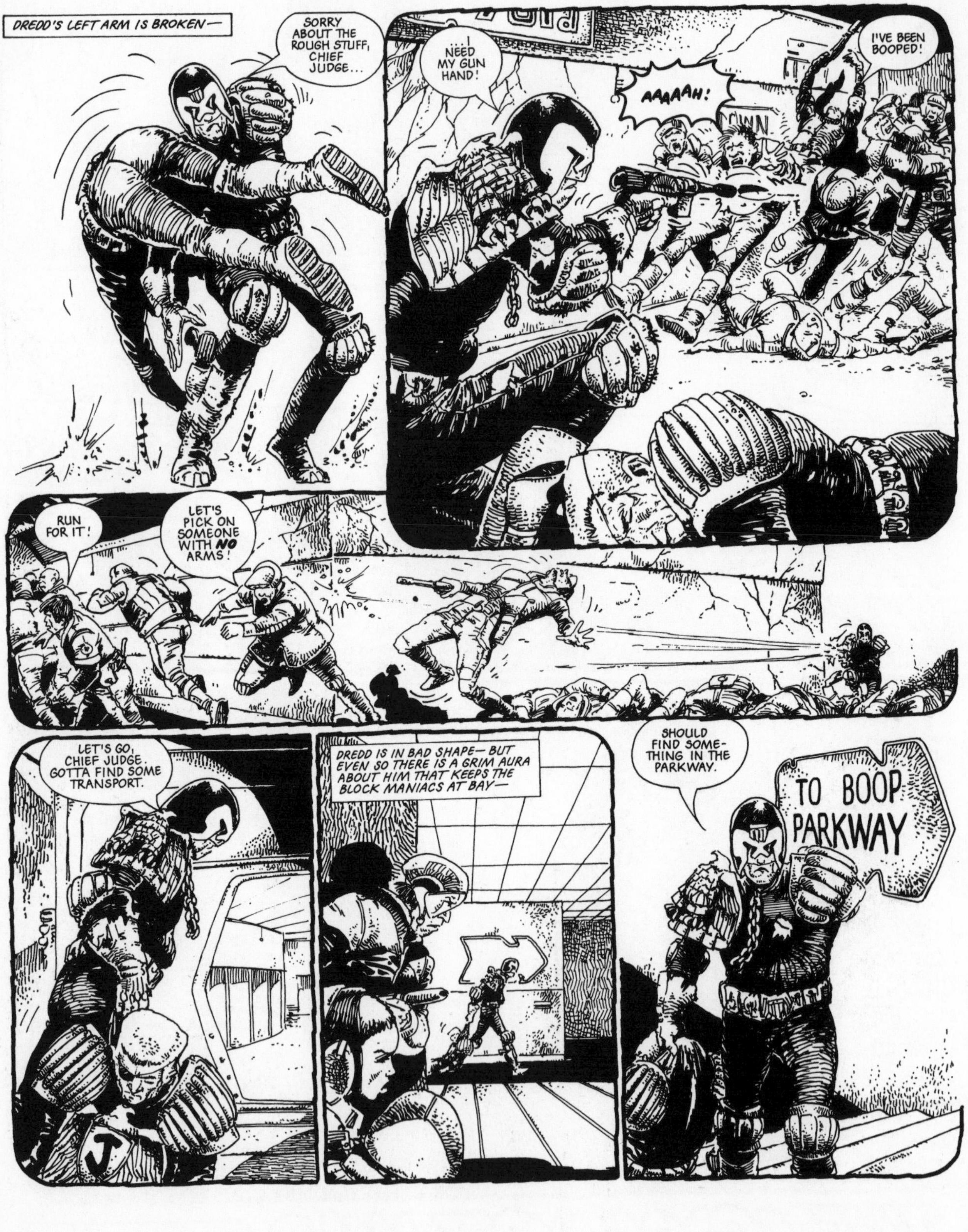
DREDD'S LEFT ARM IS BROKEN—
SORRY ABOUT THE ROUGH STUFF, CHIEF JUDGE...
...I NEED MY GUN HAND!
AAAAAH!
I'VE BEEN BOOPED!
RUN FOR IT!
LET'S PICK ON SOMEONE WITH NO ARMS!
LET'S GO, CHIEF JUDGE. GOTTA FIND SOME TRANSPORT.
DREDD IS IN BAD SHAPE— BUT EVEN SO THERE IS A GRIM AURA ABOUT HIM THAT KEEPS THE BLOCK MANIACS AT BAY—
SHOULD FIND SOMETHING IN THE PARKWAY.
TO BOOP PARKWAY

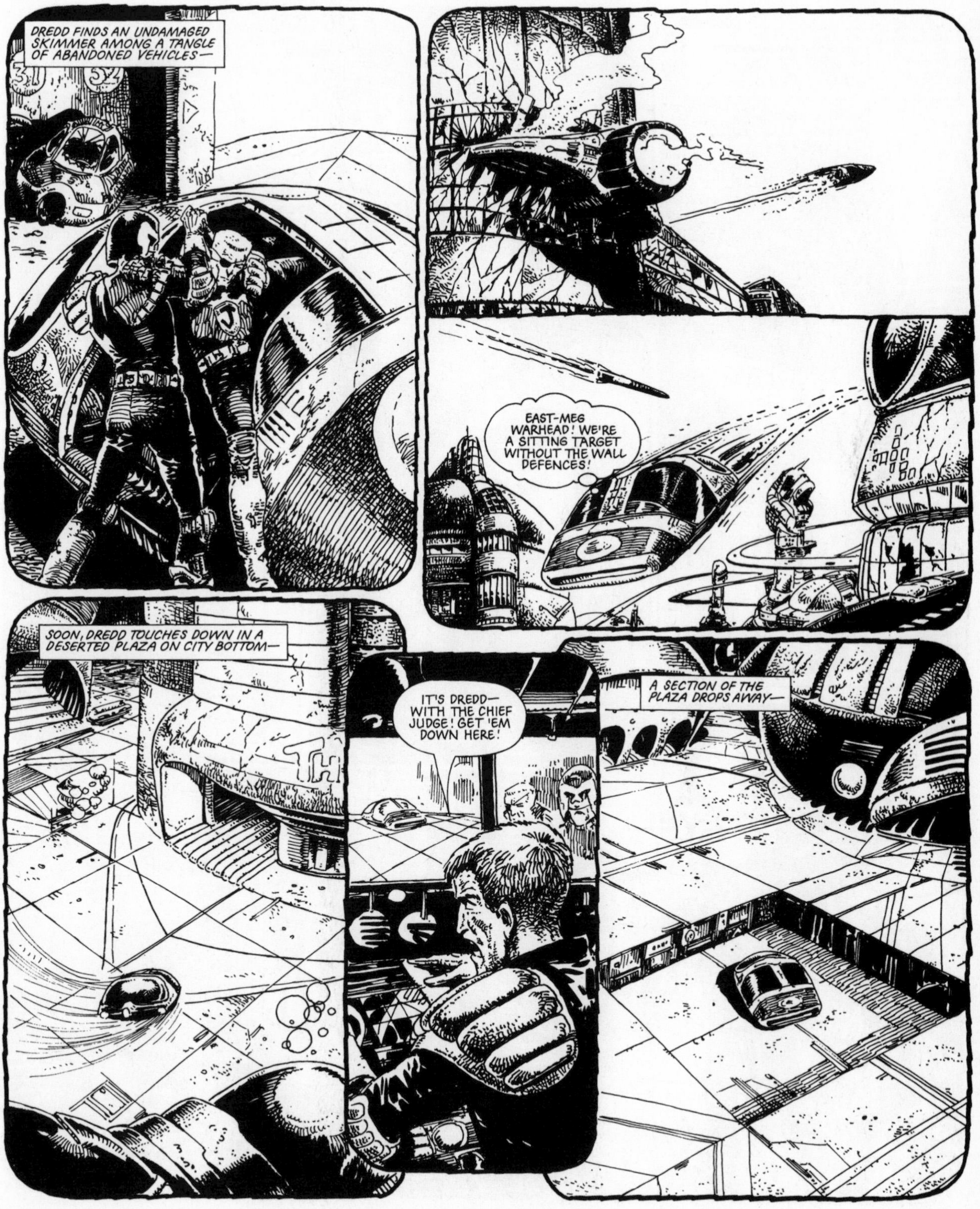
DREDD FINDS AN UNDAMAGED SKIMMER AMONG A TANGLE OF ABANDONED VEHICLES—
EAST-MEG WARHEAD! WE'RE A SITTING TARGET WITHOUT THE WALL DEFENCES!
SOON, DREDD TOUCHES DOWN IN A DESERTED PLAZA ON CITY BOTTOM—
IT'S DREDD—WITH THE CHIEF JUDGE! GET 'EM DOWN HERE!
A SECTION OF THE PLAZA DROPS AWAY—

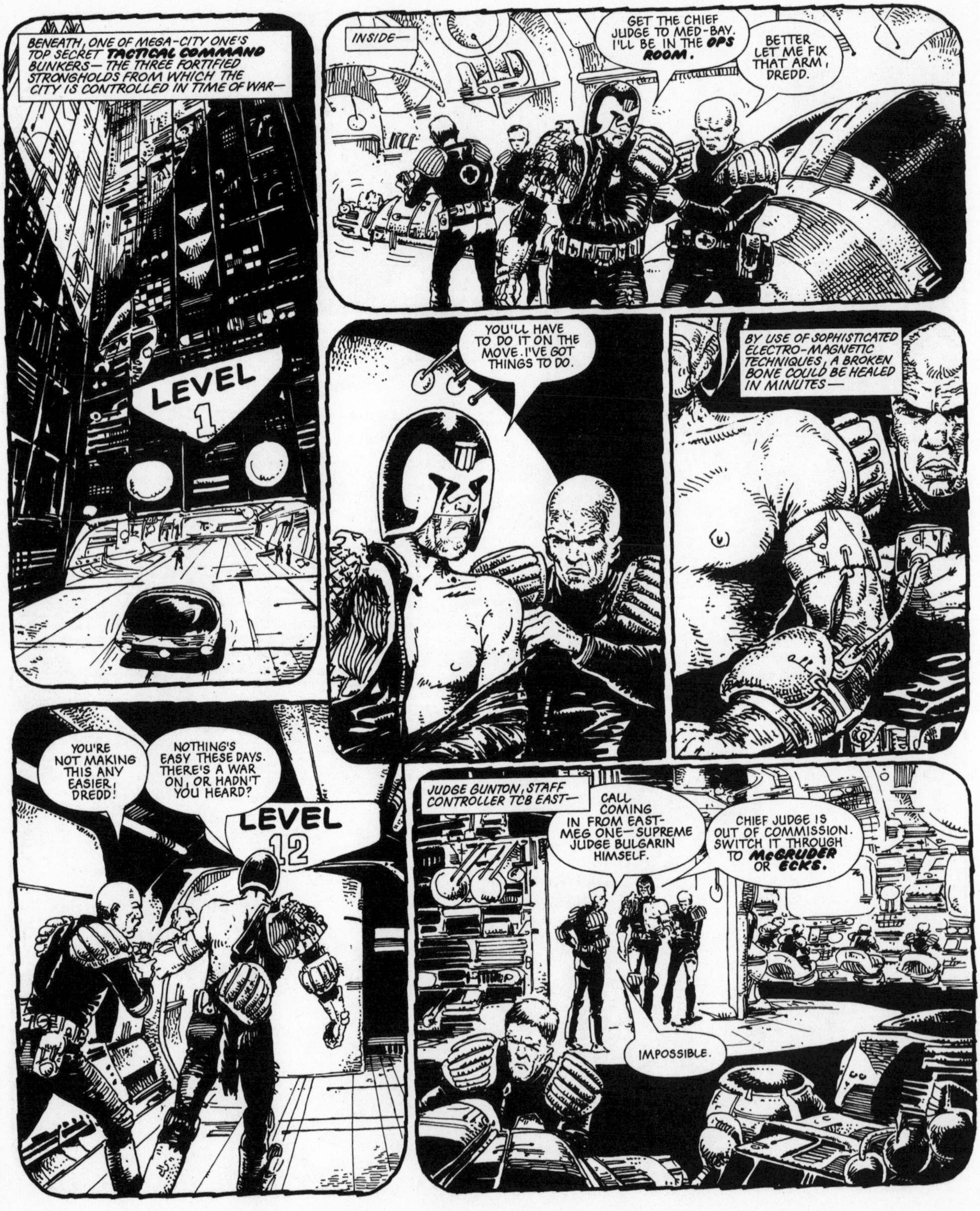

BENEATH, ONE OF MEGA-CITY ONE'S TOP SECRET TACTICAL COMMAND BUNKERS— THE THREE FORTIFIED STRONGHOLDS FROM WHICH THE CITY IS CONTROLLED IN TIME OF WAR—
LEVEL 1
INSIDE—
GET THE CHIEF JUDGE TO MED-BAY. I'LL BE IN THE OPS ROOM.
BETTER LET ME FIX THAT ARM, DREDD.
YOU'LL HAVE TO DO IT ON THE MOVE. I'VE GOT THINGS TO DO.
BY USE OF SOPHISTICATED ELECTRO-MAGNETIC TECHNIQUES, A BROKEN BONE COULD BE HEALED IN MINUTES—
YOU'RE NOT MAKING THIS ANY EASIER, DREDD!
NOTHING'S EASY THESE DAYS. THERE'S A WAR ON, OR HADN'T YOU HEARD?
LEVEL 12
JUDGE GUNTON, STAFF CONTROLLER TCB EAST—
CALL COMING IN FROM EAST-MEG ONE— SUPREME JUDGE BULGARIN HIMSELF.
CHIEF JUDGE IS OUT OF COMMISSION. SWITCH IT THROUGH TO McGRUDER OR ECKS.
IMPOSSIBLE.

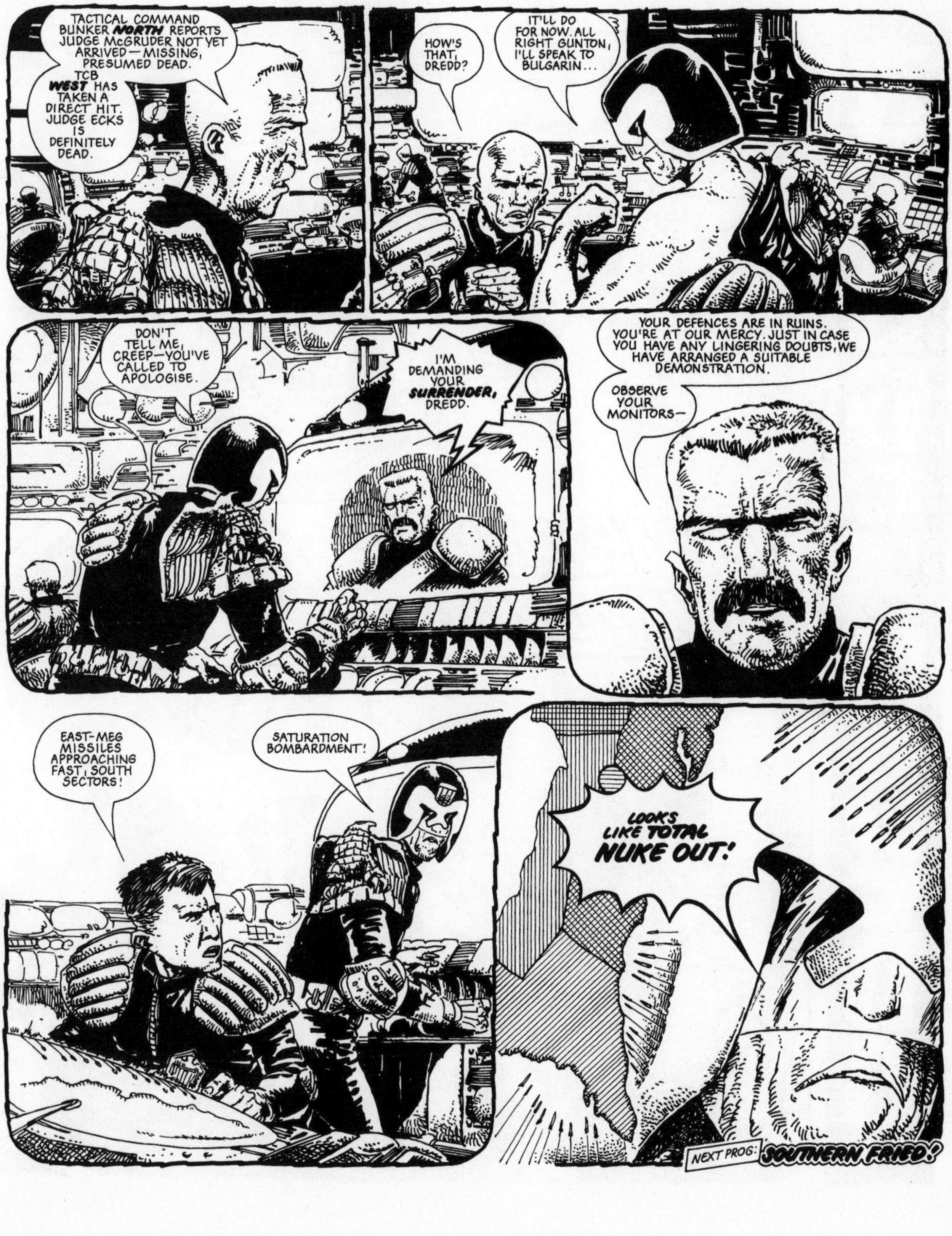
TACTICAL COMMAND BUNKER NORTH REPORTS JUDGE McGRUDER NOT YET ARRIVED—MISSING, PRESUMED DEAD.
TCB WEST HAS TAKEN A DIRECT HIT. JUDGE ECKS IS DEFINITELY DEAD.
HOW'S THAT, DREDD?
IT'LL DO FOR NOW. ALL RIGHT GUNTON, I'LL SPEAK TO BULGARIN...
DON'T TELL ME, CREEP—YOU'VE CALLED TO APOLOGISE.
I'M DEMANDING YOUR SURRENDER, DREDD.
YOUR DEFENCES ARE IN RUINS. YOU'RE AT OUR MERCY. JUST IN CASE YOU HAVE ANY LINGERING DOUBTS, WE HAVE ARRANGED A SUITABLE DEMONSTRATION.
OBSERVE YOUR MONITORS—
EAST-MEG MISSILES APPROACHING FAST, SOUTH SECTORS!
SATURATION BOMBARDMENT!
LOOKS LIKE TOTAL NUKE OUT!
NEXT PROG: SOUTHERN FRIED!

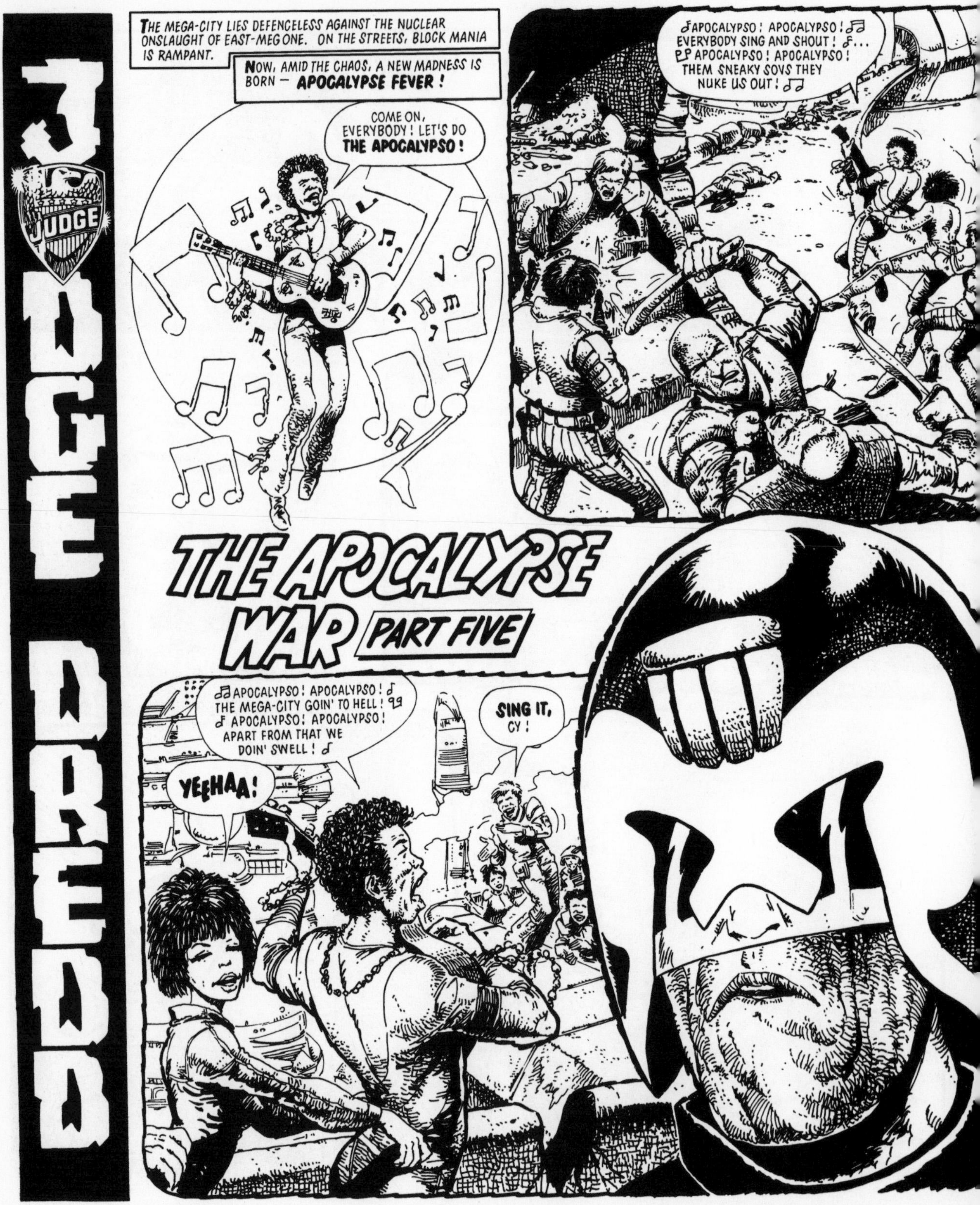
JUDGE DREDD
JUDGE
THE MEGA-CITY LIES DEFENCELESS AGAINST THE NUCLEAR ONSLAUGHT OF EAST-MEG ONE. ON THE STREETS, BLOCK MANIA IS RAMPANT.
NOW, AMID THE CHAOS, A NEW MADNESS IS BORN — APOCALYPSE FEVER!
COME ON, EVERYBODY! LET'S DO THE APOCALYPSO!
APOCALYPSO! APOCALYPSO! EVERYBODY SING AND SHOUT! ... APOCALYPSO! APOCALYPSO! THEM SNEAKY SOVS THEY NUKE US OUT!
THE APOCALYPSE WAR PART FIVE
APOCALYPSO! APOCALYPSO! THE MEGA-CITY GOIN' TO HELL! APOCALYPSO! APOCALYPSO! APART FROM THAT WE DOIN' SWELL!
SING IT, CY!
YEEHAA!

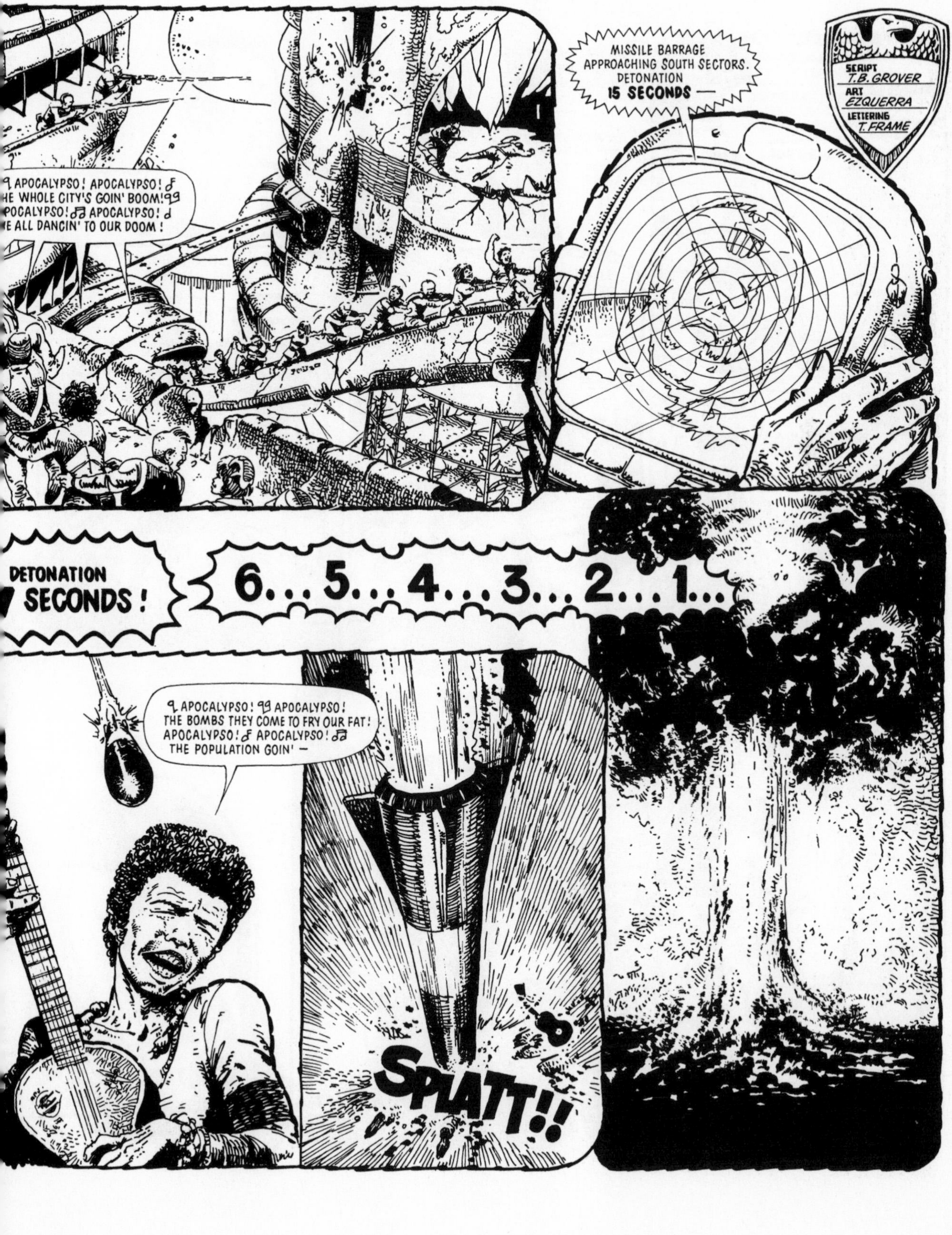

SCRIPT T.B. GROVER
ART EZQUERRA
LETTERING T. FRAME
APOCALYPSO! APOCALYPSO! HE WHOLE CITY'S GOIN' BOOM! POCALYPSO! APOCALYPSO! E ALL DANCIN' TO OUR DOOM!
MISSILE BARRAGE APPROACHING SOUTH SECTORS. DETONATION 15 SECONDS —
DETONATION 7 SECONDS!
6... 5... 4... 3... 2... 1...
APOCALYPSO! APOCALYPSO! THE BOMBS THEY COME TO FRY OUR FAT! APOCALYPSO! APOCALYPSO! THE POPULATION GOIN' —
SPLATT!!

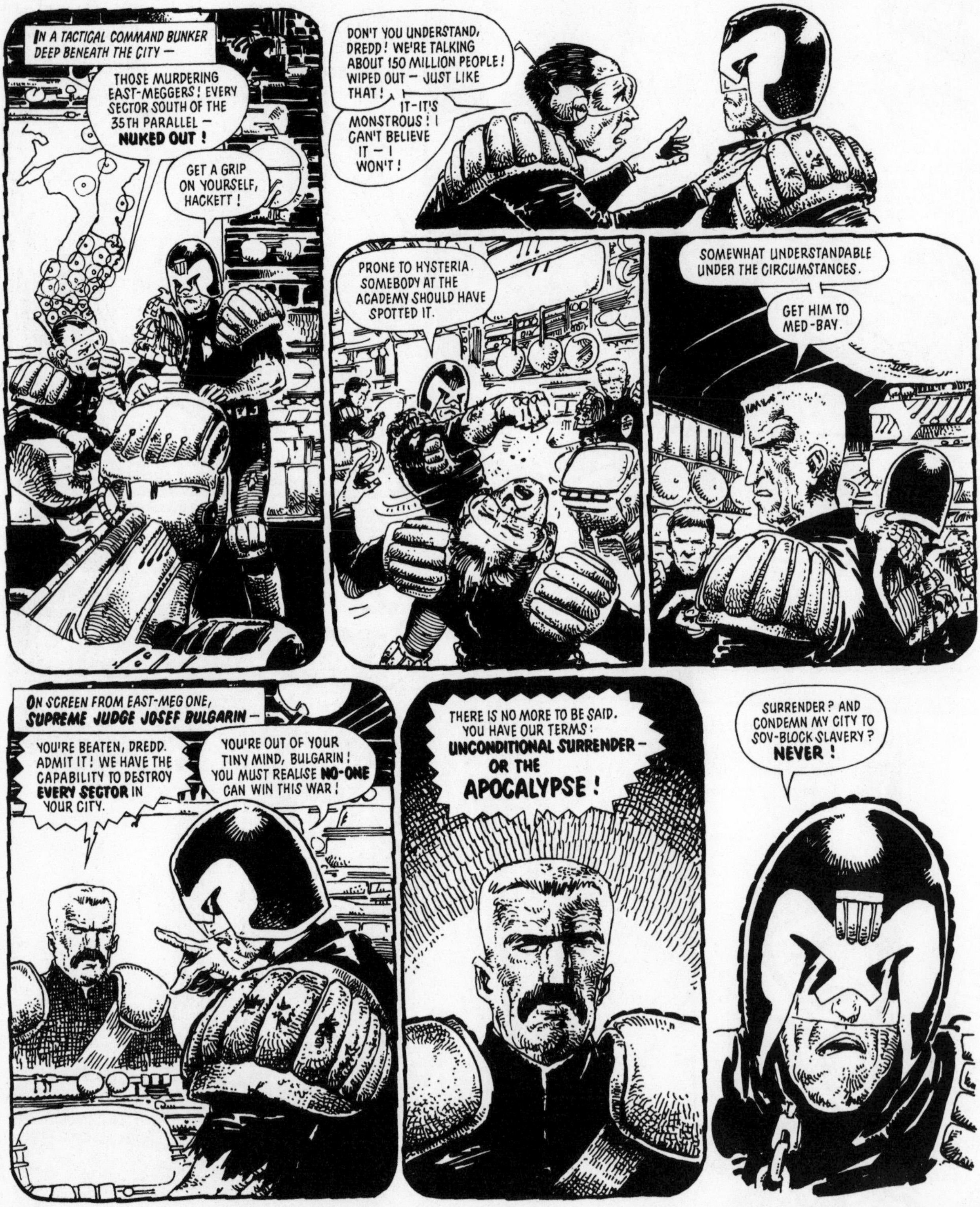
IN A TACTICAL COMMAND BUNKER DEEP BENEATH THE CITY —
THOSE MURDERING EAST-MEGGERS! EVERY SECTOR SOUTH OF THE 35TH PARALLEL — NUKED OUT!
GET A GRIP ON YOURSELF, HACKETT!
DON'T YOU UNDERSTAND, DREDD! WE'RE TALKING ABOUT 150 MILLION PEOPLE! WIPED OUT — JUST LIKE THAT!
IT-IT'S MONSTROUS! I CAN'T BELIEVE IT — I WON'T!
PRONE TO HYSTERIA. SOMEBODY AT THE ACADEMY SHOULD HAVE SPOTTED IT.
SOMEWHAT UNDERSTANDABLE UNDER THE CIRCUMSTANCES.
GET HIM TO MED-BAY.
ON SCREEN FROM EAST-MEG ONE, SUPREME JUDGE JOSEF BULGARIN —
YOU'RE BEATEN, DREDD. ADMIT IT! WE HAVE THE CAPABILITY TO DESTROY EVERY SECTOR IN YOUR CITY.
YOU'RE OUT OF YOUR TINY MIND, BULGARIN! YOU MUST REALISE NO-ONE CAN WIN THIS WAR!
THERE IS NO MORE TO BE SAID. YOU HAVE OUR TERMS: UNCONDITIONAL SURRENDER — OR THE APOCALYPSE!
SURRENDER? AND CONDEMN MY CITY TO SOV-BLOCK SLAVERY? NEVER!

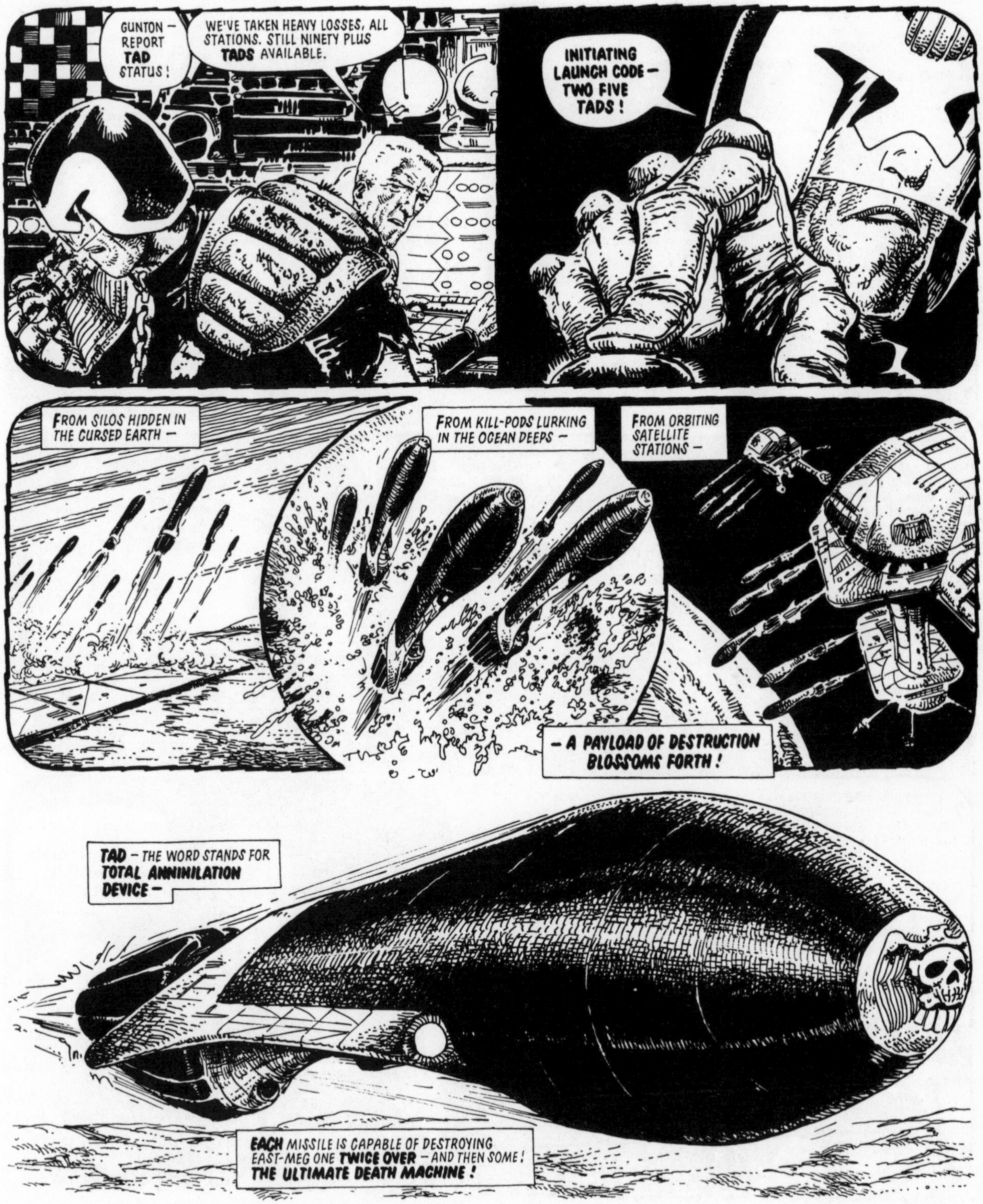
GUNTON — REPORT TAD STATUS!
WE'VE TAKEN HEAVY LOSSES, ALL STATIONS. STILL NINETY PLUS TADS AVAILABLE.
INITIATING LAUNCH CODE — TWO FIVE TADS!
FROM SILOS HIDDEN IN THE CURSED EARTH —
FROM KILL-PODS LURKING IN THE OCEAN DEEPS —
FROM ORBITING SATELLITE STATIONS —
— A PAYLOAD OF DESTRUCTION BLOSSOMS FORTH!
TAD — THE WORD STANDS FOR TOTAL ANNIHILATION DEVICE —
EACH MISSILE IS CAPABLE OF DESTROYING EAST-MEG ONE TWICE OVER — AND THEN SOME! THE ULTIMATE DEATH MACHINE!

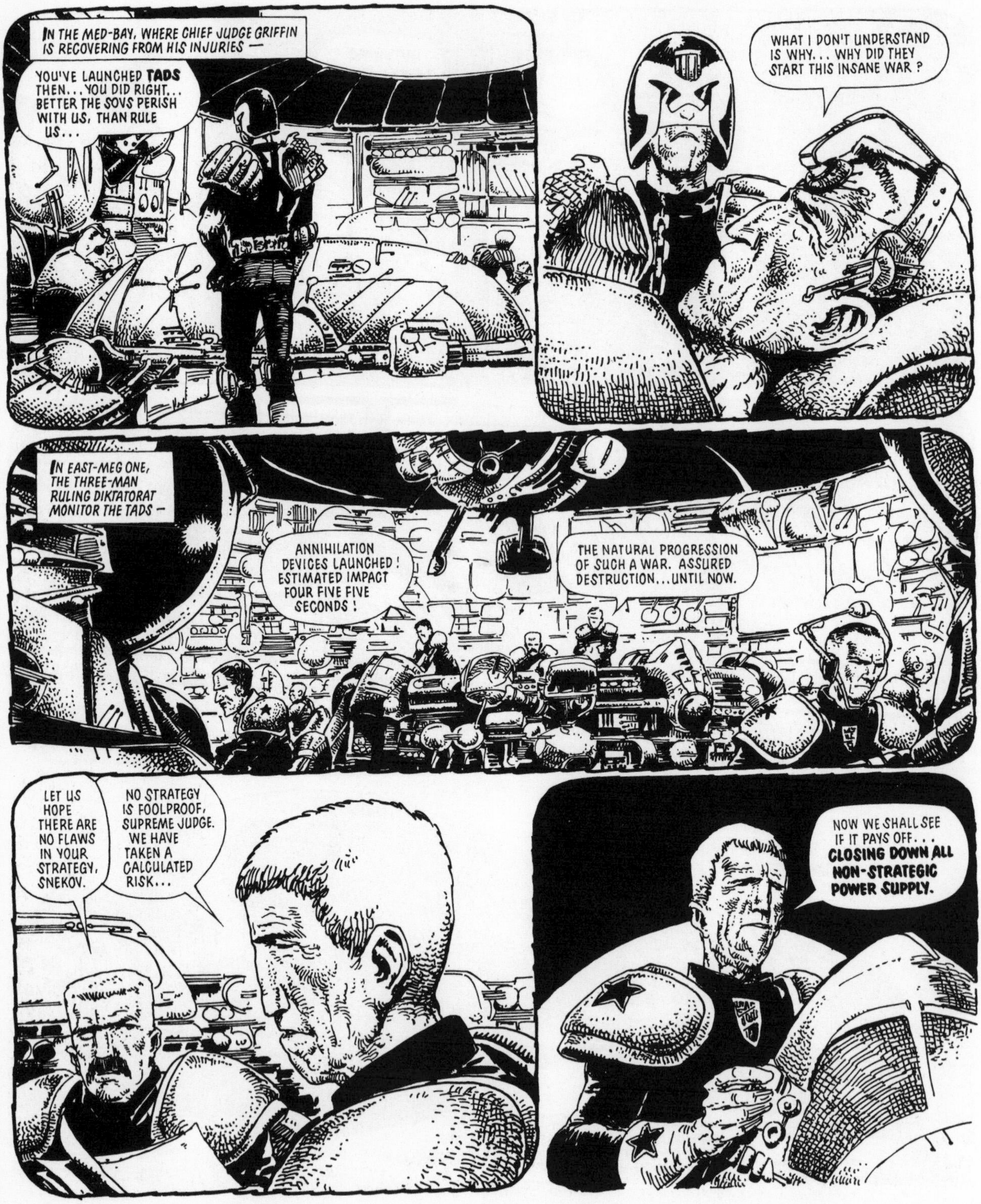

IN THE MED-BAY, WHERE CHIEF JUDGE GRIFFIN IS RECOVERING FROM HIS INJURIES —
YOU'VE LAUNCHED TADS THEN... YOU DID RIGHT... BETTER THE SOVS PERISH WITH US, THAN RULE US...
WHAT I DON'T UNDERSTAND IS WHY... WHY DID THEY START THIS INSANE WAR ?
IN EAST-MEG ONE, THE THREE-MAN RULING DIKTATORAT MONITOR THE TADS —
ANNIHILATION DEVICES LAUNCHED ! ESTIMATED IMPACT FOUR FIVE FIVE SECONDS !
THE NATURAL PROGRESSION OF SUCH A WAR. ASSURED DESTRUCTION...UNTIL NOW.
LET US HOPE THERE ARE NO FLAWS IN YOUR STRATEGY, SNEKOV.
NO STRATEGY IS FOOLPROOF, SUPREME JUDGE. WE HAVE TAKEN A CALCULATED RISK...
NOW WE SHALL SEE IF IT PAYS OFF... CLOSING DOWN ALL NON-STRATEGIC POWER SUPPLY.

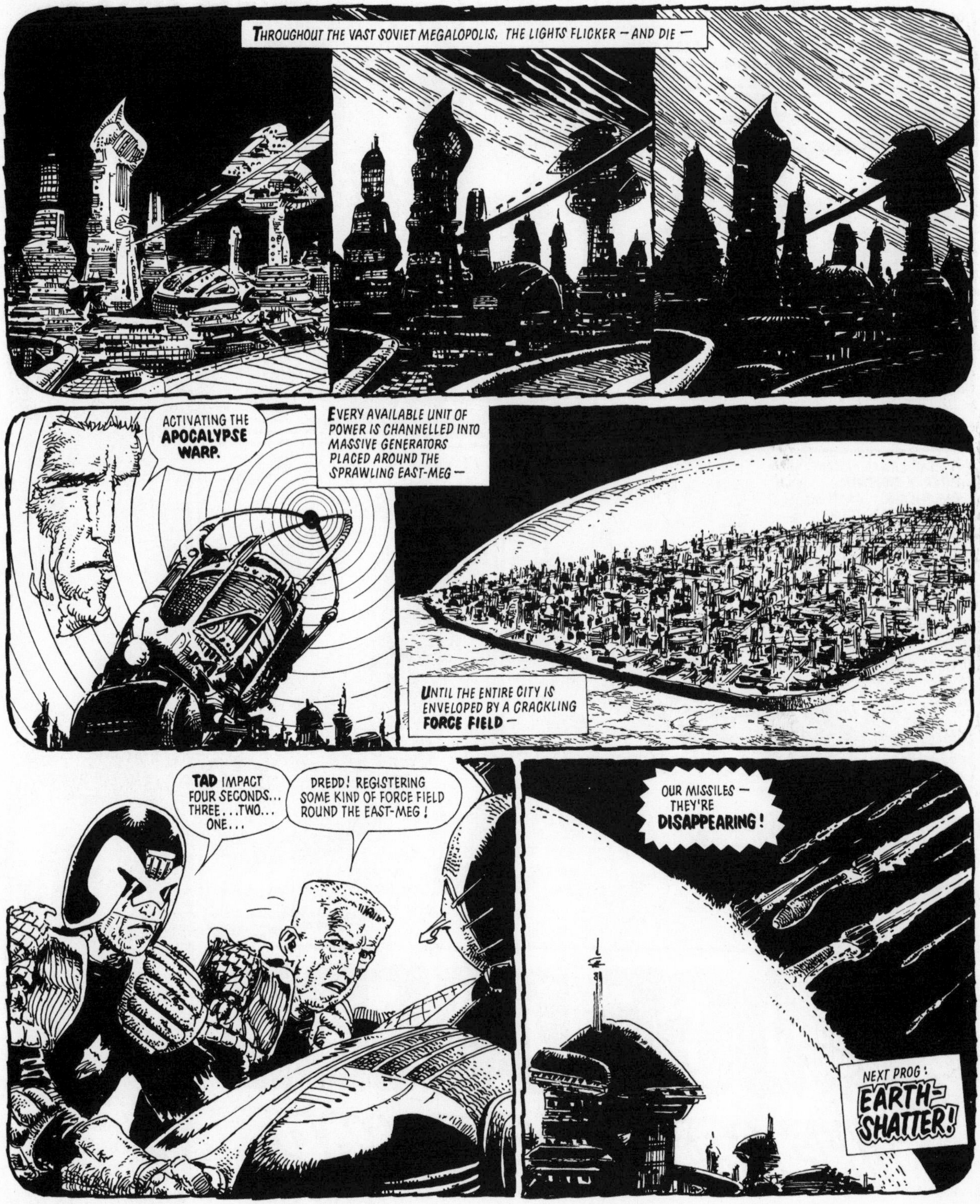
THROUGHOUT THE VAST SOVIET MEGALOPOLIS, THE LIGHTS FLICKER — AND DIE —
ACTIVATING THE APOCALYPSE WARP.
EVERY AVAILABLE UNIT OF POWER IS CHANNELLED INTO MASSIVE GENERATORS PLACED AROUND THE SPRAWLING EAST-MEG —
UNTIL THE ENTIRE CITY IS ENVELOPED BY A CRACKLING FORCE FIELD —
TAD IMPACT FOUR SECONDS... THREE...TWO... ONE...
DREDD! REGISTERING SOME KIND OF FORCE FIELD ROUND THE EAST-MEG!
OUR MISSILES — THEY'RE DISAPPEARING!
NEXT PROG: EARTH-SHATTER!

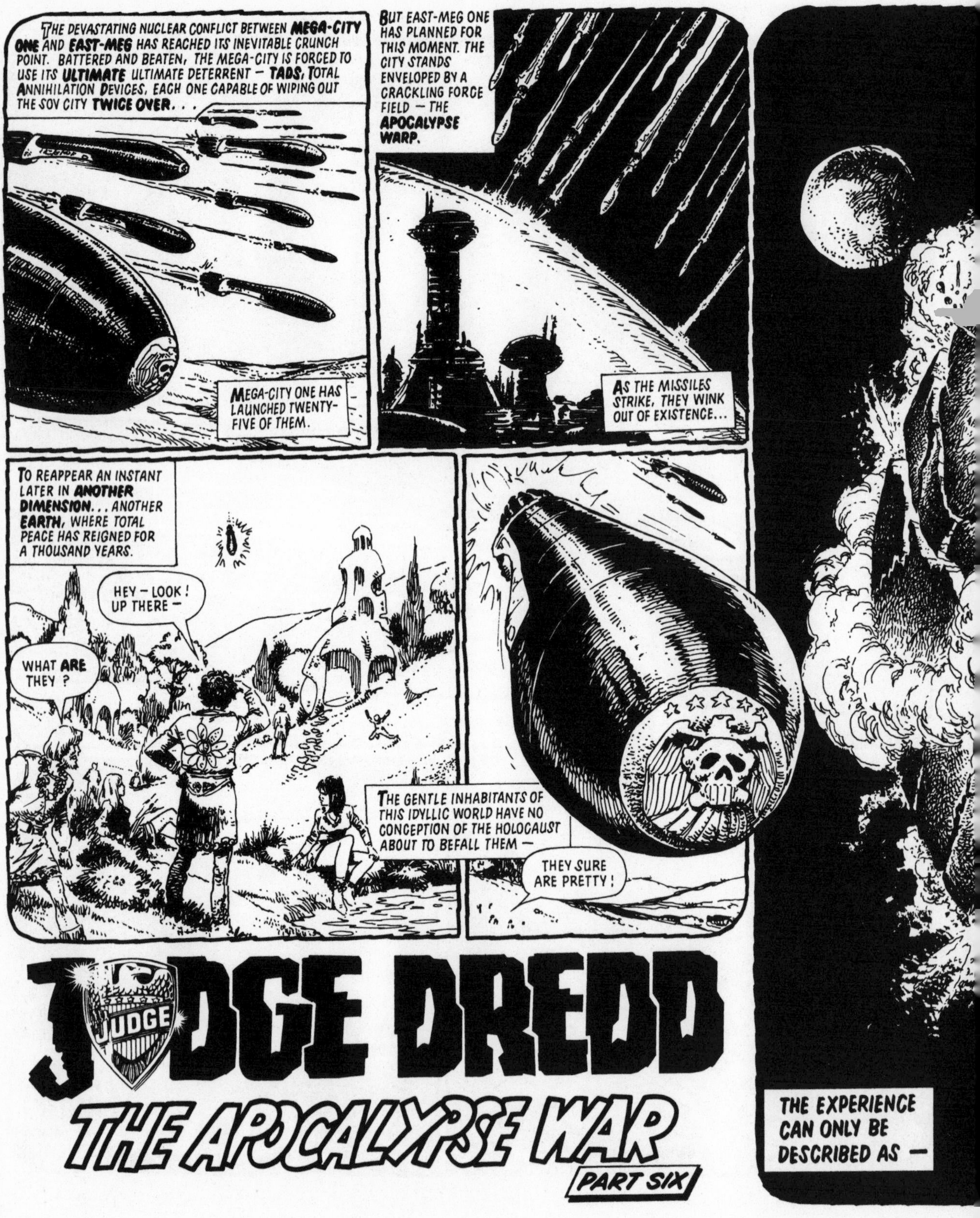

THE DEVASTATING NUCLEAR CONFLICT BETWEEN MEGA-CITY ONE AND EAST-MEG HAS REACHED ITS INEVITABLE CRUNCH POINT. BATTERED AND BEATEN, THE MEGA-CITY IS FORCED TO USE ITS ULTIMATE ULTIMATE DETERRENT — TADS, TOTAL ANNIHILATION DEVICES, EACH ONE CAPABLE OF WIPING OUT THE SOV CITY TWICE OVER. . .
MEGA-CITY ONE HAS LAUNCHED TWENTY-FIVE OF THEM.
BUT EAST-MEG ONE HAS PLANNED FOR THIS MOMENT. THE CITY STANDS ENVELOPED BY A CRACKLING FORCE FIELD — THE APOCALYPSE WARP.
AS THE MISSILES STRIKE, THEY WINK OUT OF EXISTENCE...
TO REAPPEAR AN INSTANT LATER IN ANOTHER DIMENSION. . . ANOTHER EARTH, WHERE TOTAL PEACE HAS REIGNED FOR A THOUSAND YEARS.
HEY — LOOK! UP THERE —
WHAT ARE THEY ?
THE GENTLE INHABITANTS OF THIS IDYLLIC WORLD HAVE NO CONCEPTION OF THE HOLOCAUST ABOUT TO BEFALL THEM —
THEY SURE ARE PRETTY!
JUDGE
JUDGE DREDD
THE APOCALYPSE WAR
PART SIX
THE EXPERIENCE CAN ONLY BE DESCRIBED AS —

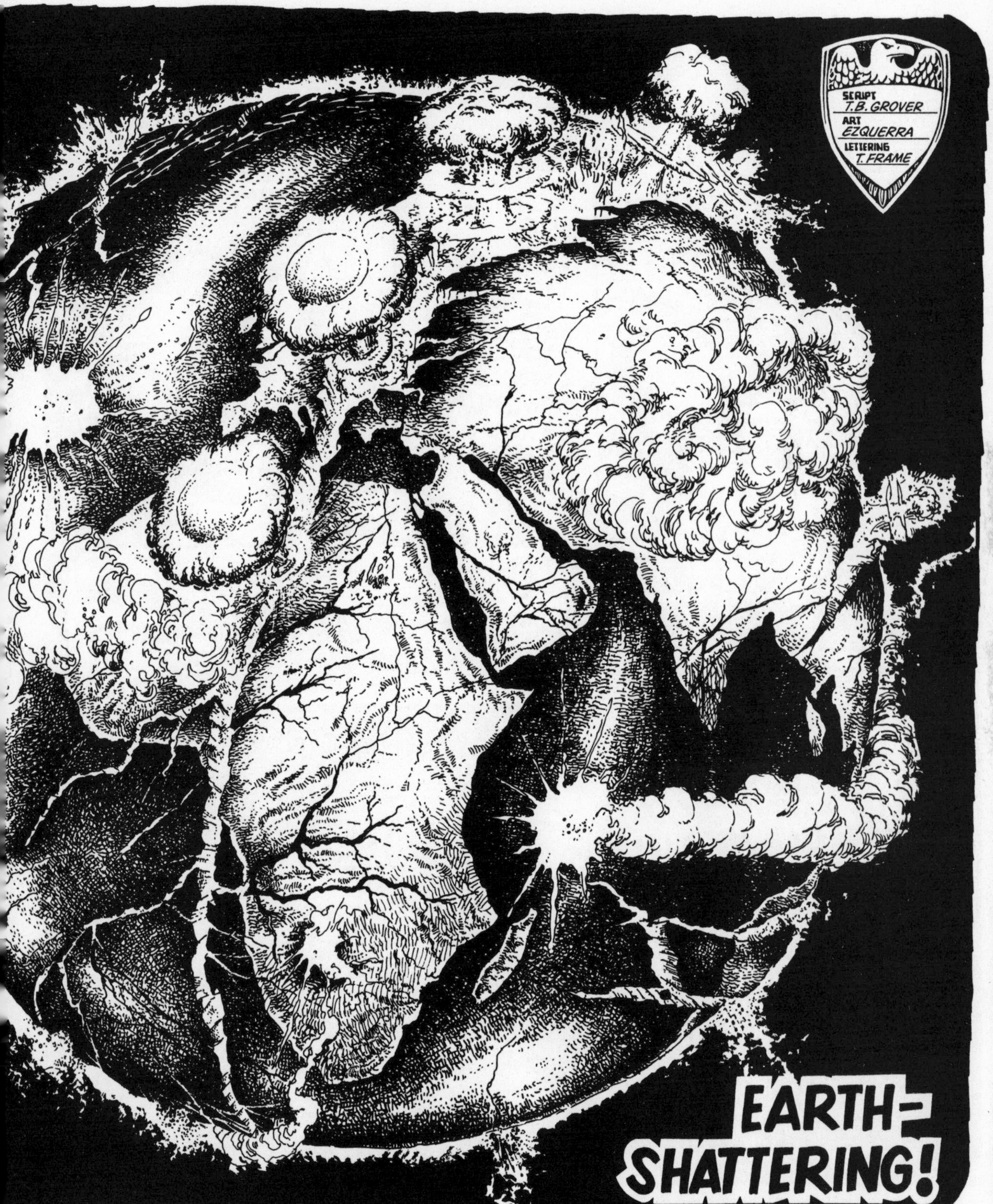

SCRIPT T.B. GROVER
ART EZQUERRA
LETTERING T. FRAME
EARTH-SHATTERING!

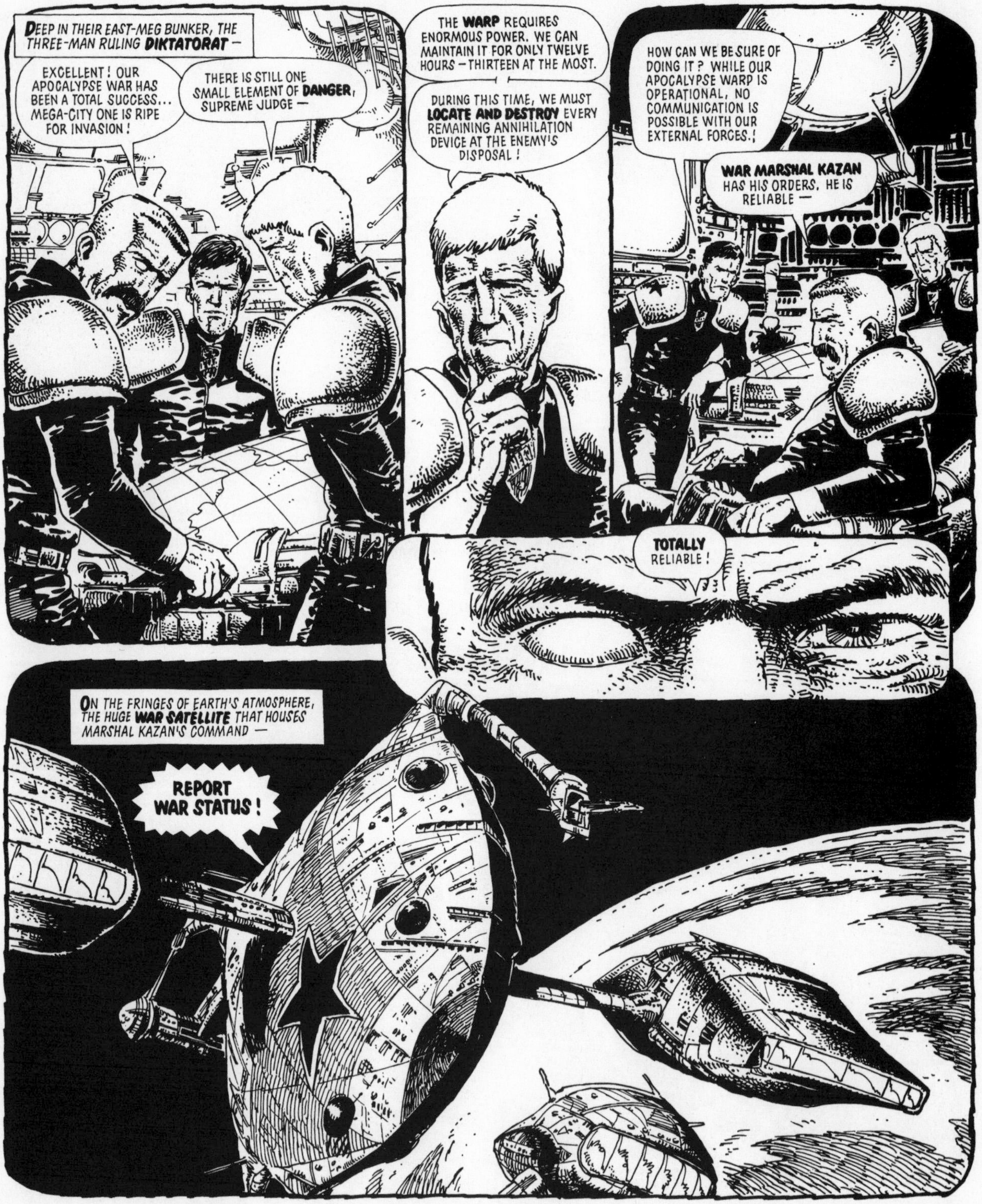
DEEP IN THEIR EAST-MEG BUNKER, THE THREE-MAN RULING DIKTATORAT —
EXCELLENT! OUR APOCALYPSE WAR HAS BEEN A TOTAL SUCCESS... MEGA-CITY ONE IS RIPE FOR INVASION!
THERE IS STILL ONE SMALL ELEMENT OF DANGER, SUPREME JUDGE —
THE WARP REQUIRES ENORMOUS POWER. WE CAN MAINTAIN IT FOR ONLY TWELVE HOURS — THIRTEEN AT THE MOST.
DURING THIS TIME, WE MUST LOCATE AND DESTROY EVERY REMAINING ANNIHILATION DEVICE AT THE ENEMY'S DISPOSAL!
HOW CAN WE BE SURE OF DOING IT? WHILE OUR APOCALYPSE WARP IS OPERATIONAL, NO COMMUNICATION IS POSSIBLE WITH OUR EXTERNAL FORCES!
WAR MARSHAL KAZAN HAS HIS ORDERS. HE IS RELIABLE —
TOTALLY RELIABLE!
ON THE FRINGES OF EARTH'S ATMOSPHERE, THE HUGE WAR SATELLITE THAT HOUSES MARSHAL KAZAN'S COMMAND —
REPORT WAR STATUS!

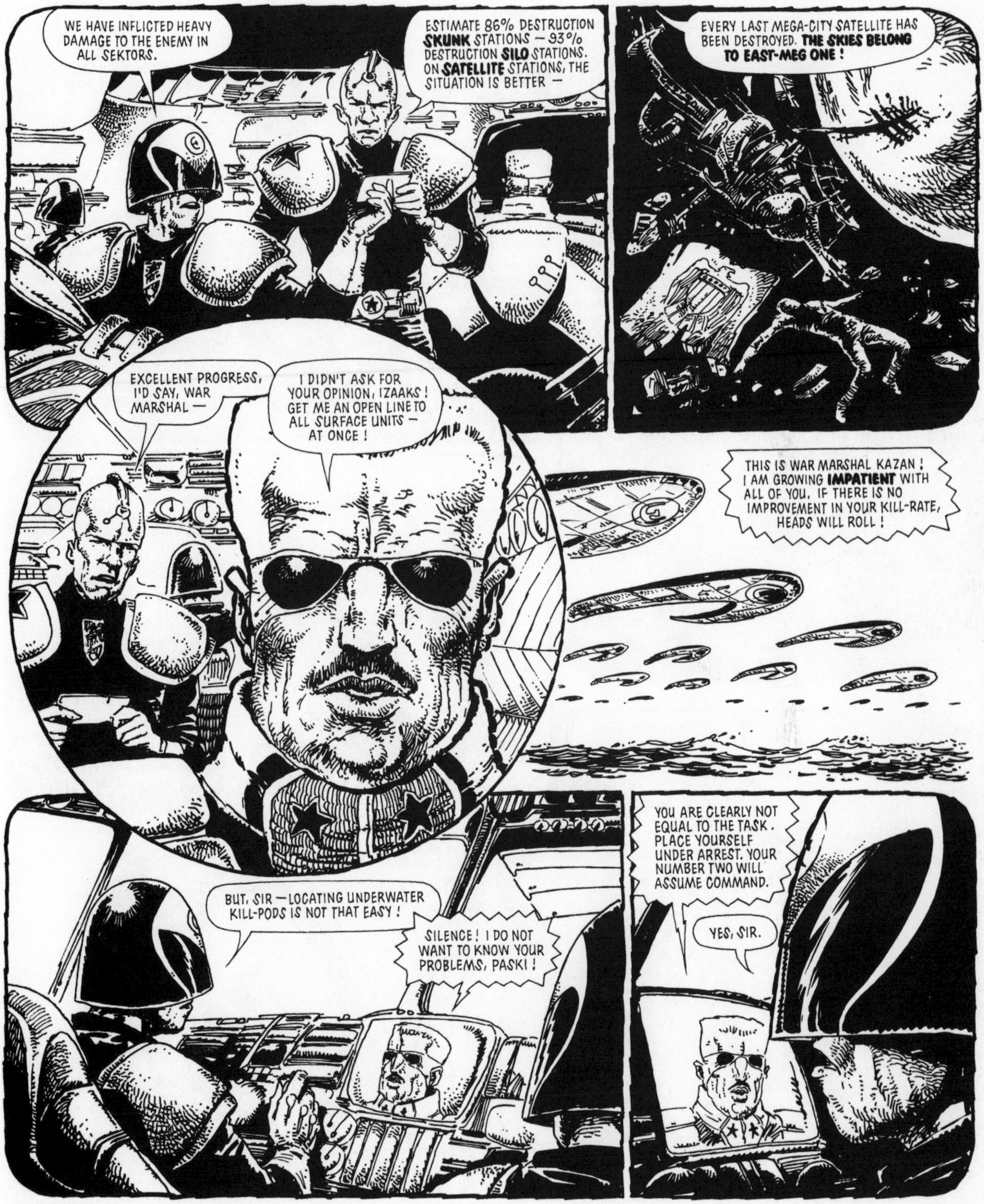
WE HAVE INFLICTED HEAVY DAMAGE TO THE ENEMY IN ALL SEKTORS.
ESTIMATE 86% DESTRUCTION SKUNK STATIONS — 93% DESTRUCTION SILO STATIONS. ON SATELLITE STATIONS, THE SITUATION IS BETTER —
EVERY LAST MEGA-CITY SATELLITE HAS BEEN DESTROYED. THE SKIES BELONG TO EAST-MEG ONE!
EXCELLENT PROGRESS, I'D SAY, WAR MARSHAL —
I DIDN'T ASK FOR YOUR OPINION, IZAAKS! GET ME AN OPEN LINE TO ALL SURFACE UNITS — AT ONCE!
THIS IS WAR MARSHAL KAZAN! I AM GROWING IMPATIENT WITH ALL OF YOU. IF THERE IS NO IMPROVEMENT IN YOUR KILL-RATE, HEADS WILL ROLL!
BUT, SIR — LOCATING UNDERWATER KILL-PODS IS NOT THAT EASY!
SILENCE! I DO NOT WANT TO KNOW YOUR PROBLEMS, PASKI!
YOU ARE CLEARLY NOT EQUAL TO THE TASK. PLACE YOURSELF UNDER ARREST. YOUR NUMBER TWO WILL ASSUME COMMAND.
YES, SIR.

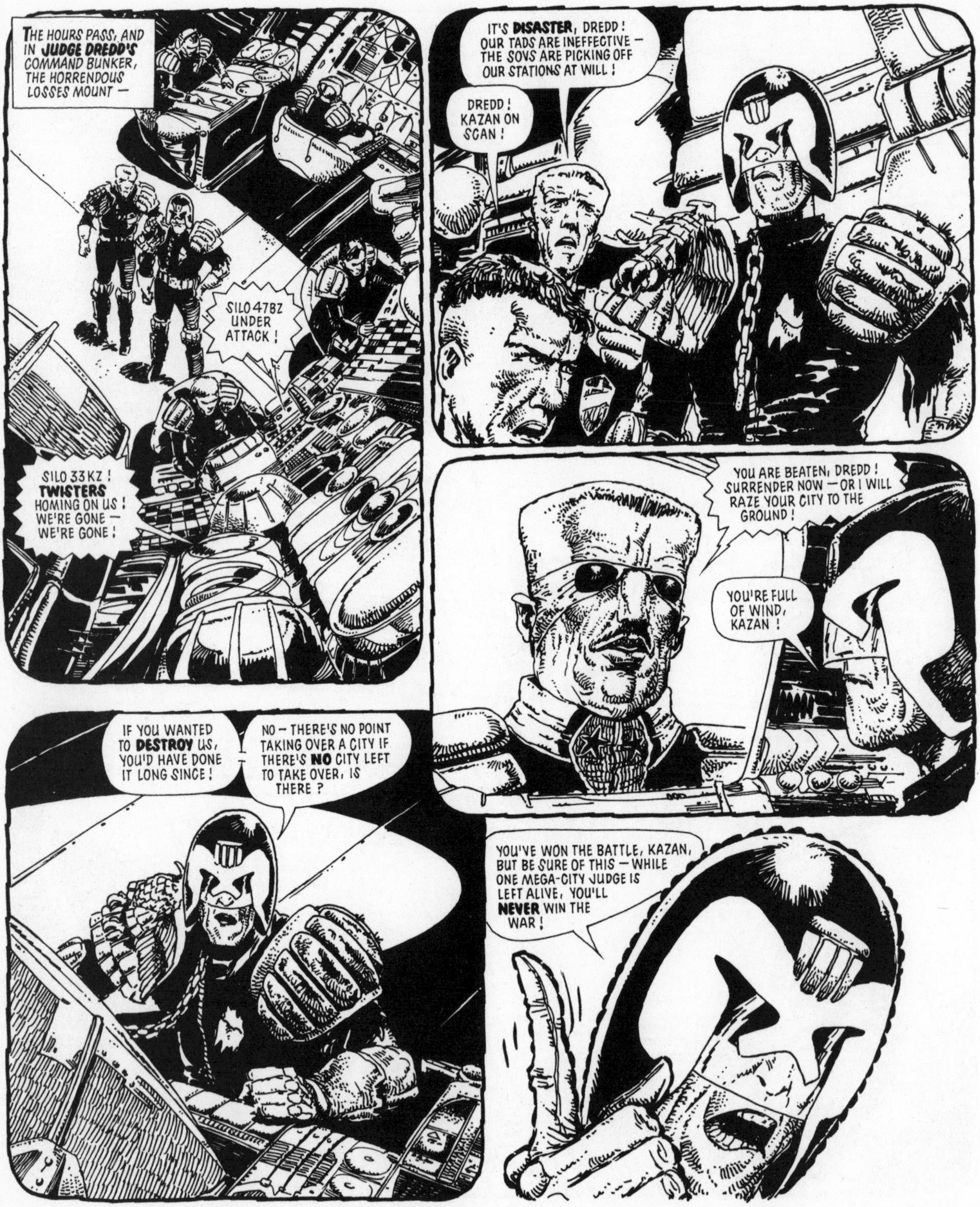
THE HOURS PASS, AND IN JUDGE DREDD'S COMMAND BUNKER, THE HORRENDOUS LOSSES MOUNT —
SILO 47BZ UNDER ATTACK!
SILO 33KZ! TWISTERS HOMING ON US! WE'RE GONE — WE'RE GONE!
IT'S DISASTER, DREDD! OUR TADS ARE INEFFECTIVE — THE SOVS ARE PICKING OFF OUR STATIONS AT WILL!
DREDD! KAZAN ON SCAN!
YOU ARE BEATEN, DREDD! SURRENDER NOW — OR I WILL RAZE YOUR CITY TO THE GROUND!
YOU'RE FULL OF WIND, KAZAN!
IF YOU WANTED TO DESTROY US, YOU'D HAVE DONE IT LONG SINCE! —
NO — THERE'S NO POINT TAKING OVER A CITY IF THERE'S NO CITY LEFT TO TAKE OVER, IS THERE?
YOU'VE WON THE BATTLE, KAZAN, BUT BE SURE OF THIS — WHILE ONE MEGA-CITY JUDGE IS LEFT ALIVE, YOU'LL NEVER WIN THE WAR!

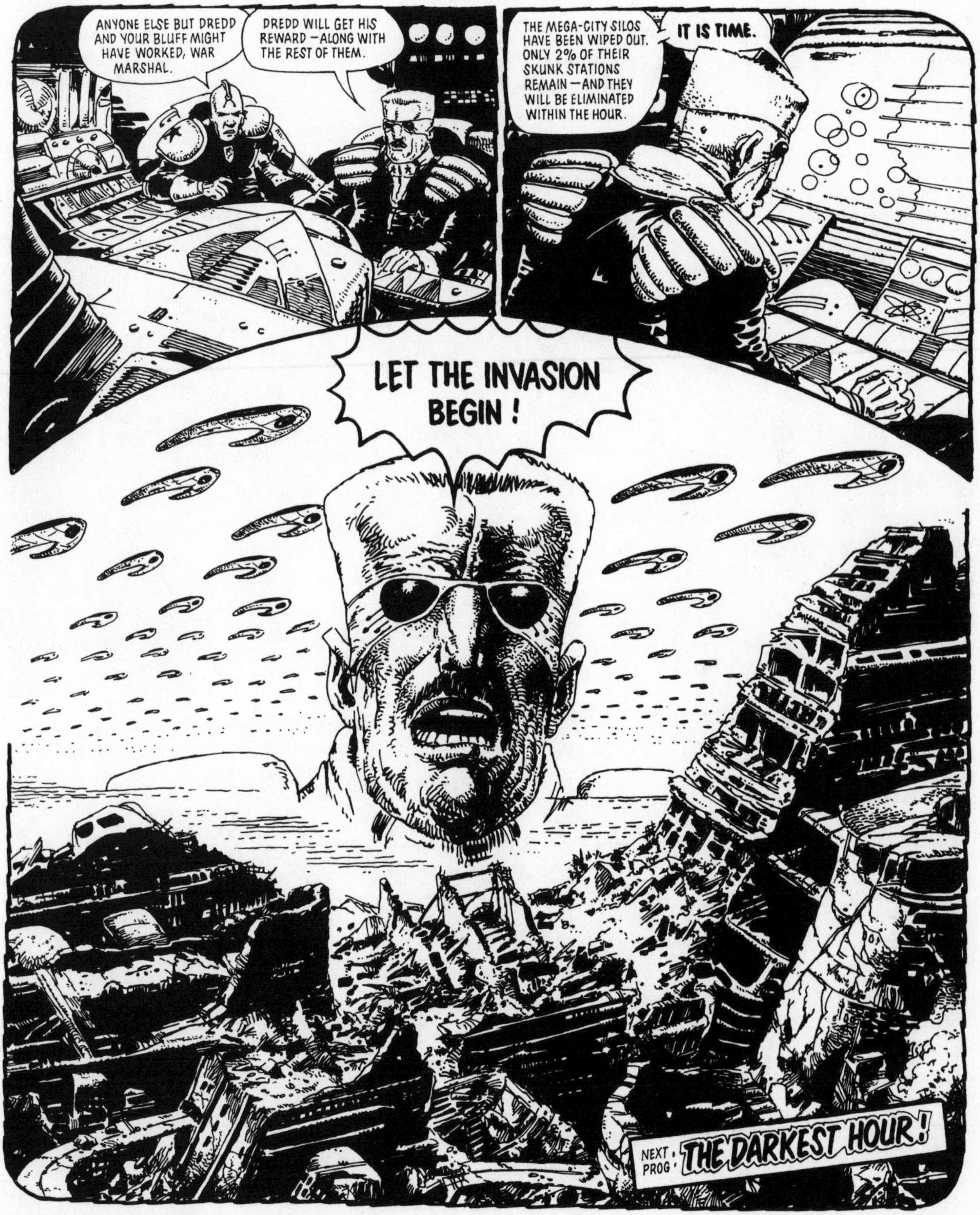

ANYONE ELSE BUT DREDD AND YOUR BLUFF MIGHT HAVE WORKED, WAR MARSHAL.
DREDD WILL GET HIS REWARD — ALONG WITH THE REST OF THEM.
THE MEGA-CITY SILOS HAVE BEEN WIPED OUT. ONLY 2% OF THEIR SKUNK STATIONS REMAIN — AND THEY WILL BE ELIMINATED WITHIN THE HOUR.
IT IS TIME.
LET THE INVASION BEGIN!
NEXT PROG: THE DARKEST HOUR!

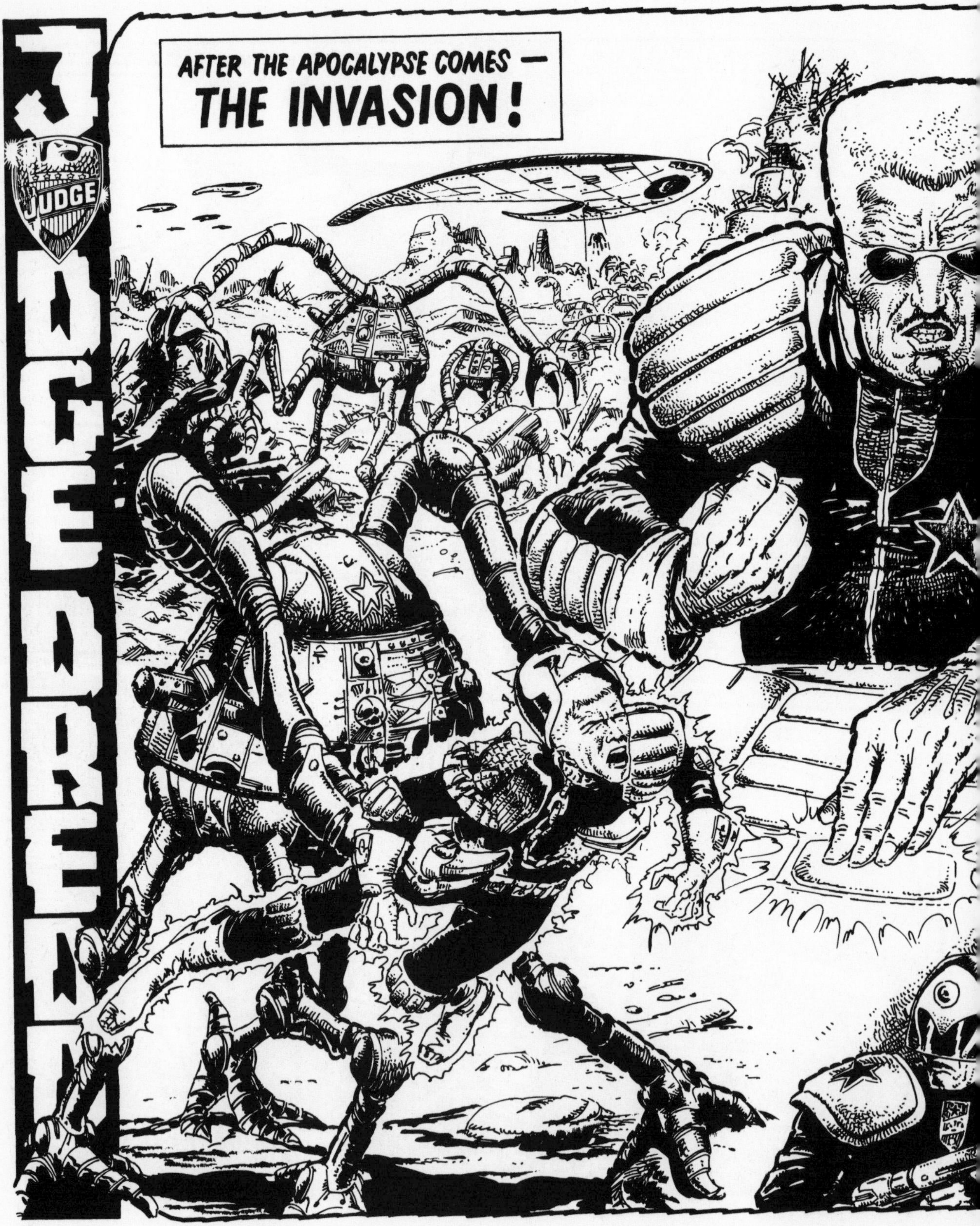
JUDGE DREDD
JUDGE
AFTER THE APOCALYPSE COMES —
THE INVASION!

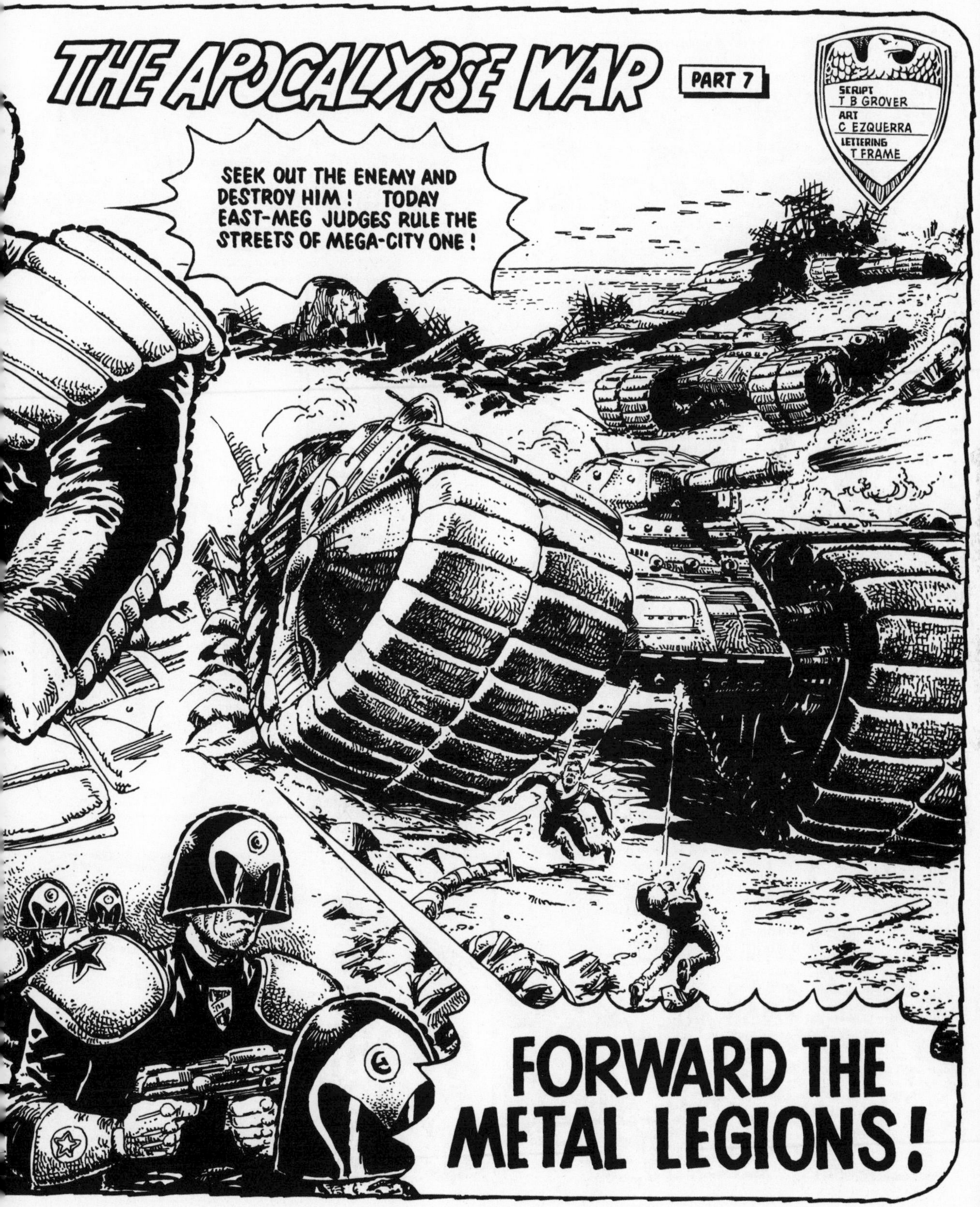
THE APOCALYPSE WAR
PART 7
SCRIPT T B GROVER
ART C EZQUERRA
LETTERING T FRAME
SEEK OUT THE ENEMY AND DESTROY HIM ! TODAY EAST-MEG JUDGES RULE THE STREETS OF MEGA-CITY ONE !
FORWARD THE METAL LEGIONS !

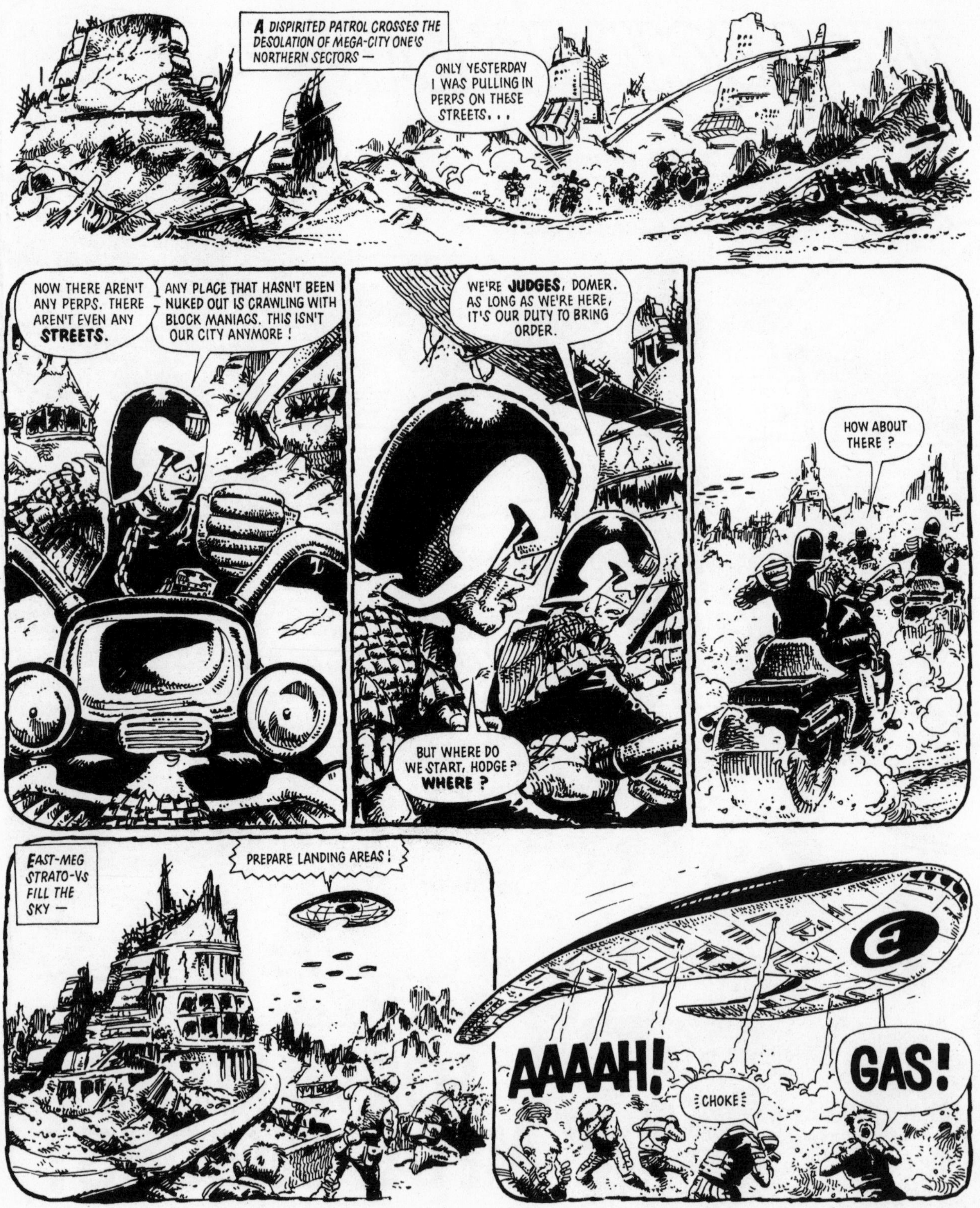
A DISPIRITED PATROL CROSSES THE DESOLATION OF MEGA-CITY ONE'S NORTHERN SECTORS —
ONLY YESTERDAY I WAS PULLING IN PERPS ON THESE STREETS . . .
NOW THERE AREN'T ANY PERPS. THERE AREN'T EVEN ANY STREETS.
ANY PLACE THAT HASN'T BEEN NUKED OUT IS CRAWLING WITH BLOCK MANIACS. THIS ISN'T OUR CITY ANYMORE !
WE'RE JUDGES, DOMER. AS LONG AS WE'RE HERE, IT'S OUR DUTY TO BRING ORDER.
BUT WHERE DO WE START, HODGE ? WHERE ?
HOW ABOUT THERE ?
EAST-MEG STRATO-VS FILL THE SKY —
PREPARE LANDING AREAS !
AAAAH!
CHOKE
GAS!

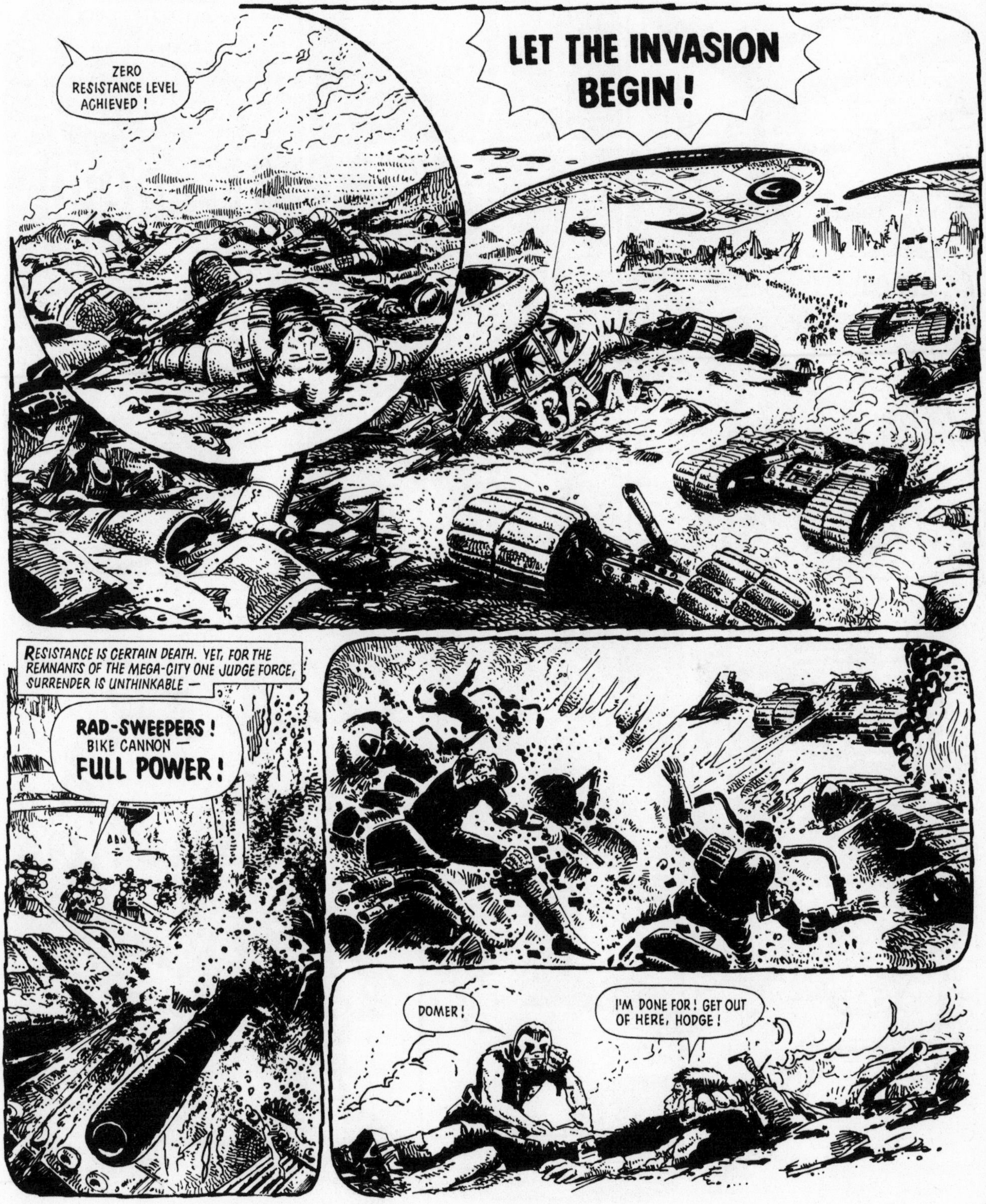
ZERO RESISTANCE LEVEL ACHIEVED !
LET THE INVASION BEGIN !
RESISTANCE IS CERTAIN DEATH. YET, FOR THE REMNANTS OF THE MEGA-CITY ONE JUDGE FORCE, SURRENDER IS UNTHINKABLE —
RAD-SWEEPERS ! BIKE CANNON — FULL POWER !
DOMER !
I'M DONE FOR ! GET OUT OF HERE, HODGE !

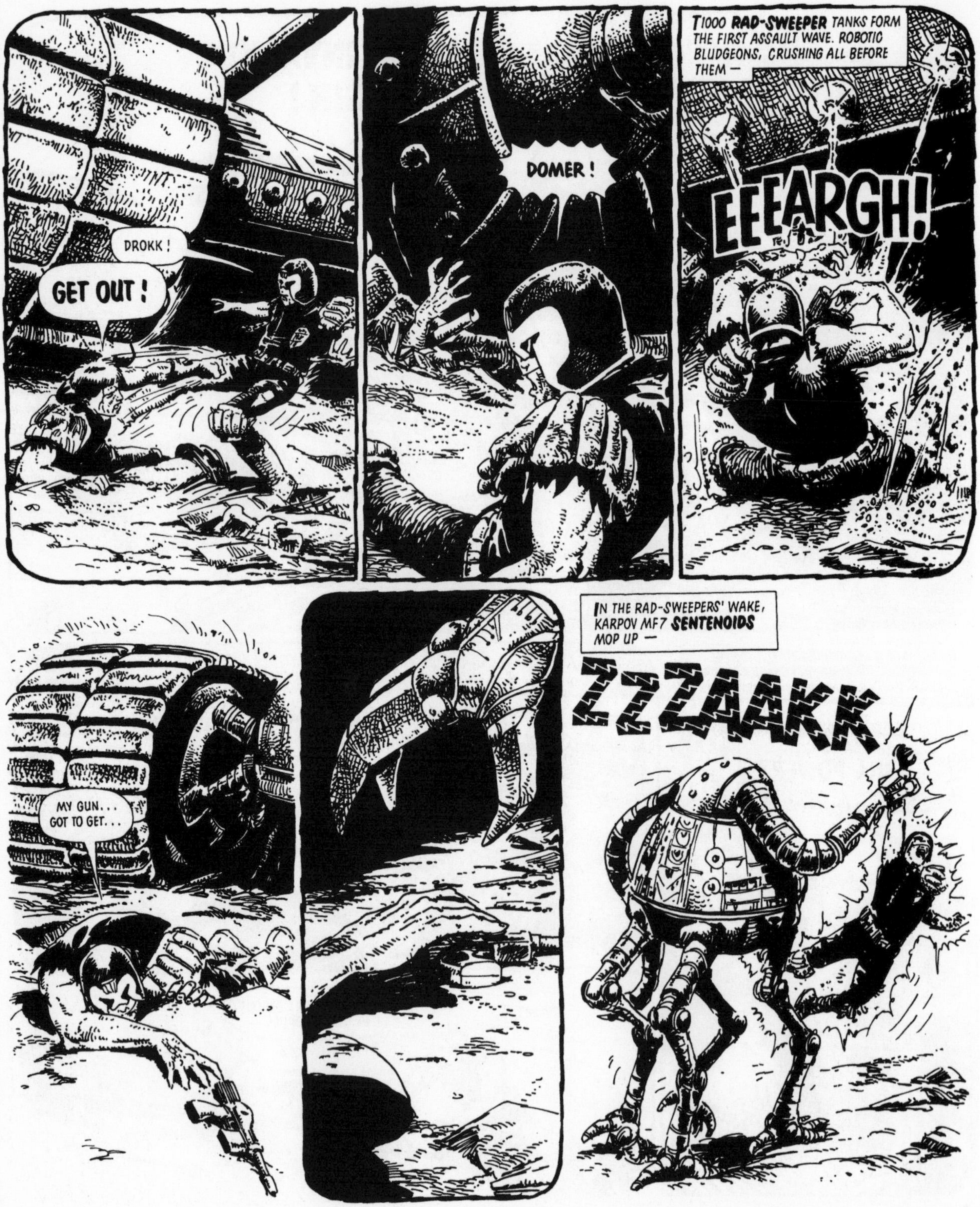

GET OUT!
DROKK!
DOMER!
T1000 RAD-SWEEPER TANKS FORM THE FIRST ASSAULT WAVE. ROBOTIC BLUDGEONS, CRUSHING ALL BEFORE THEM —
EEEARGH!
MY GUN... GOT TO GET...
IN THE RAD-SWEEPERS' WAKE, KARPOV MF7 SENTENOIDS MOP UP —
ZZZAAKK

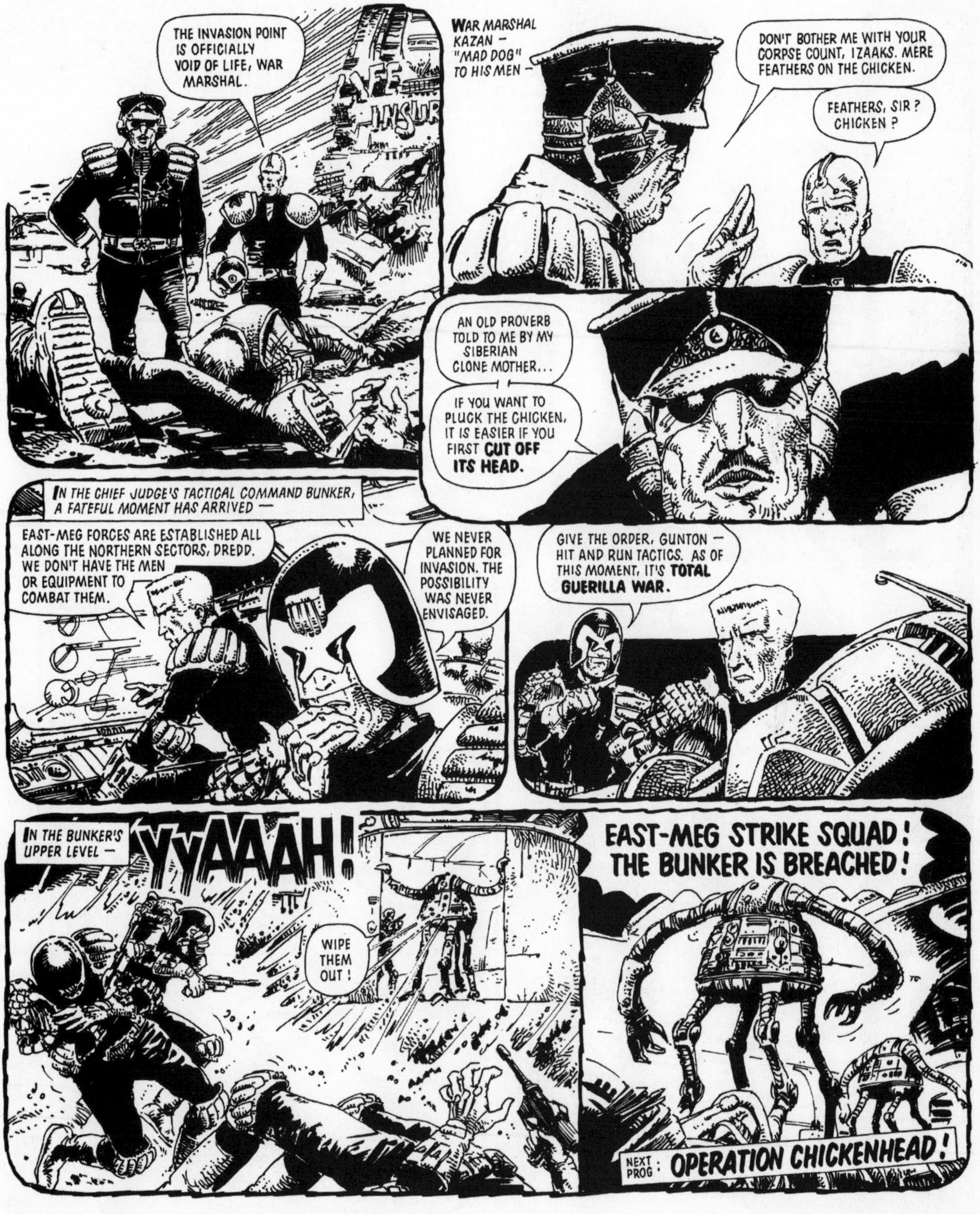
THE INVASION POINT IS OFFICIALLY VOID OF LIFE, WAR MARSHAL.
WAR MARSHAL KAZAN - "MAD DOG" TO HIS MEN -
DON'T BOTHER ME WITH YOUR CORPSE COUNT, IZAAKS. MERE FEATHERS ON THE CHICKEN.
FEATHERS, SIR? CHICKEN?
AN OLD PROVERB TOLD TO ME BY MY SIBERIAN CLONE MOTHER...
IF YOU WANT TO PLUCK THE CHICKEN, IT IS EASIER IF YOU FIRST CUT OFF ITS HEAD.
IN THE CHIEF JUDGE'S TACTICAL COMMAND BUNKER, A FATEFUL MOMENT HAS ARRIVED -
EAST-MEG FORCES ARE ESTABLISHED ALL ALONG THE NORTHERN SECTORS, DREDD. WE DON'T HAVE THE MEN OR EQUIPMENT TO COMBAT THEM.
WE NEVER PLANNED FOR INVASION. THE POSSIBILITY WAS NEVER ENVISAGED.
GIVE THE ORDER, GUNTON - HIT AND RUN TACTICS. AS OF THIS MOMENT, IT'S TOTAL GUERILLA WAR.
IN THE BUNKER'S UPPER LEVEL -
YYAAAH!
WIPE THEM OUT!
EAST-MEG STRIKE SQUAD! THE BUNKER IS BREACHED!
NEXT PROG: OPERATION CHICKENHEAD!

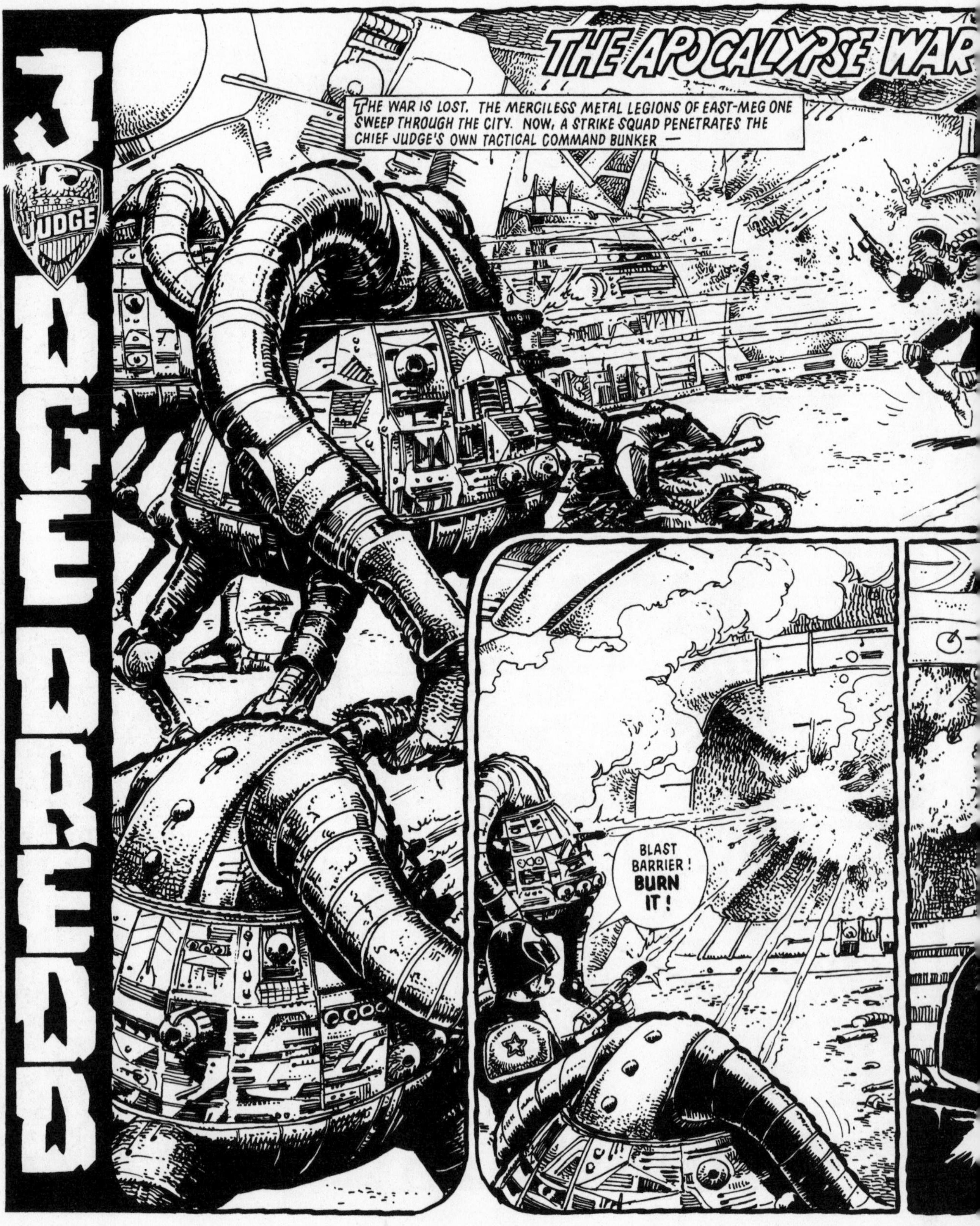
JUDGE DREDD
JUDGE
THE APOCALYPSE WAR
THE WAR IS LOST. THE MERCILESS METAL LEGIONS OF EAST-MEG ONE SWEEP THROUGH THE CITY. NOW, A STRIKE SQUAD PENETRATES THE CHIEF JUDGE'S OWN TACTICAL COMMAND BUNKER —
BLAST BARRIER! BURN IT!

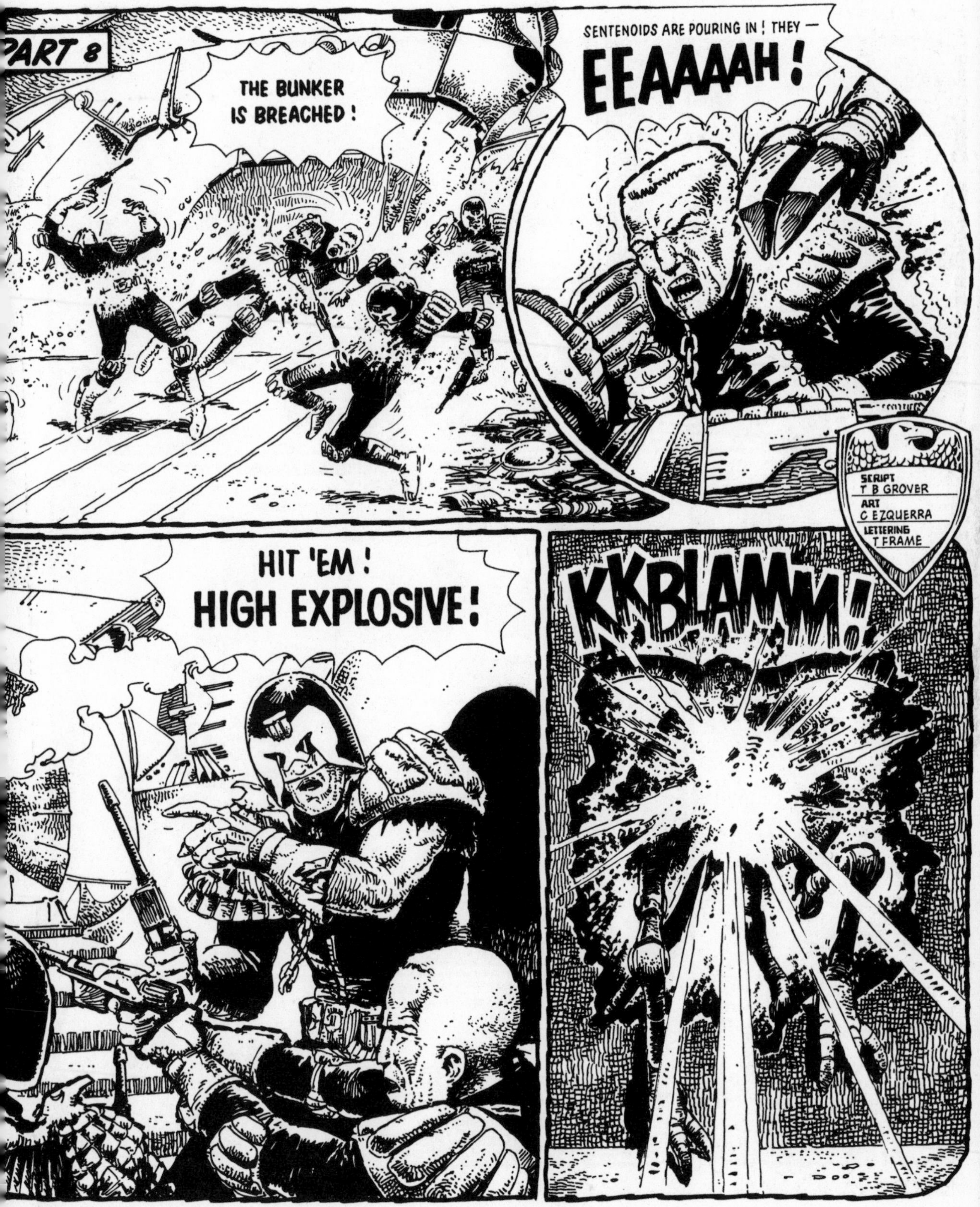
PART 8
THE BUNKER IS BREACHED!
SENTENOIDS ARE POURING IN! THEY —
EEAAAAH!
SCRIPT T B GROVER
ART C EZQUERRA
LETTERING T FRAME
HIT 'EM! HIGH EXPLOSIVE!
KKBLAMMM!

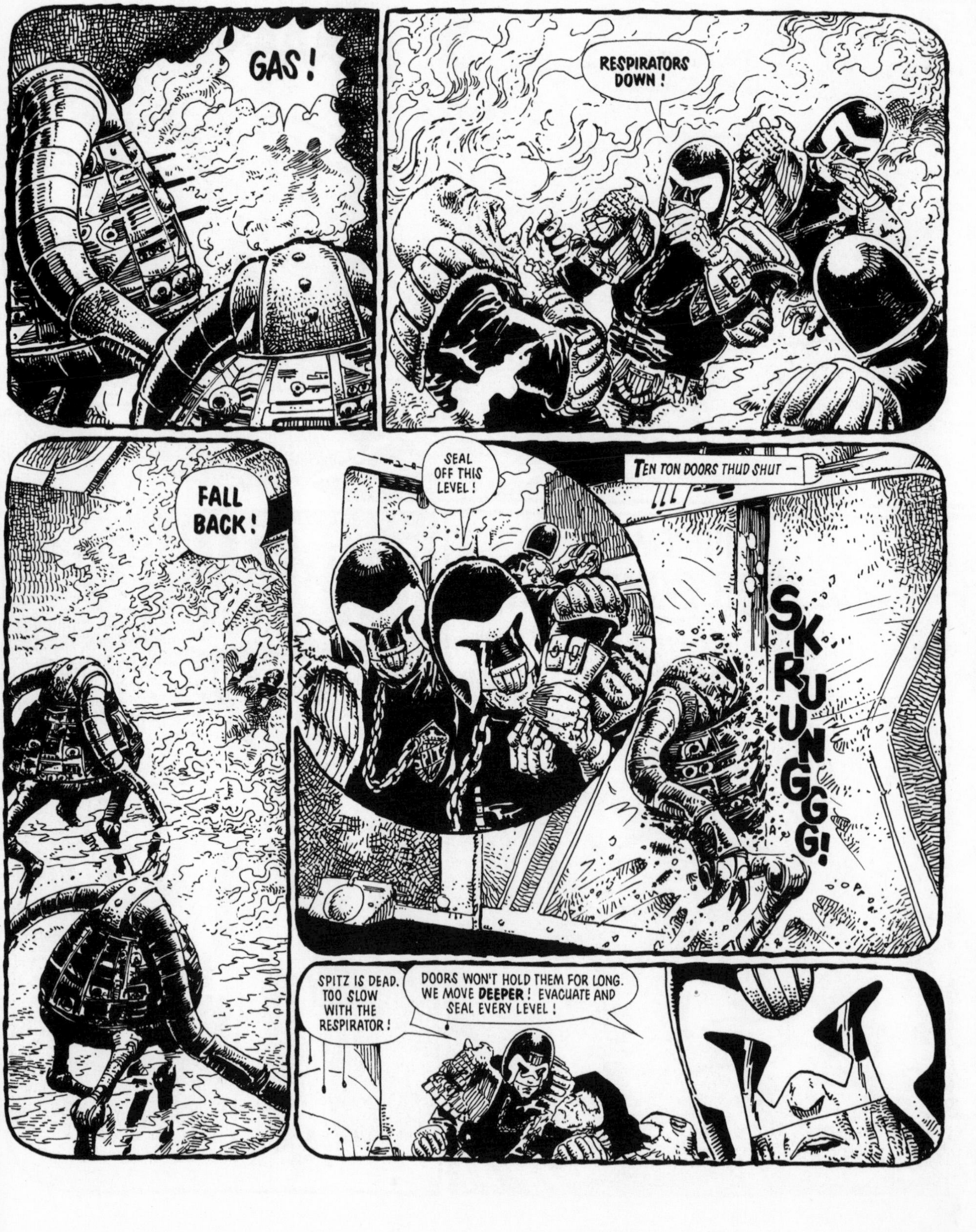
GAS!
RESPIRATORS DOWN!
FALL BACK!
SEAL OFF THIS LEVEL!
TEN TON DOORS THUD SHUT —
SKRUNGG!
SPITZ IS DEAD. TOO SLOW WITH THE RESPIRATOR!
DOORS WON'T HOLD THEM FOR LONG. WE MOVE DEEPER! EVACUATE AND SEAL EVERY LEVEL!

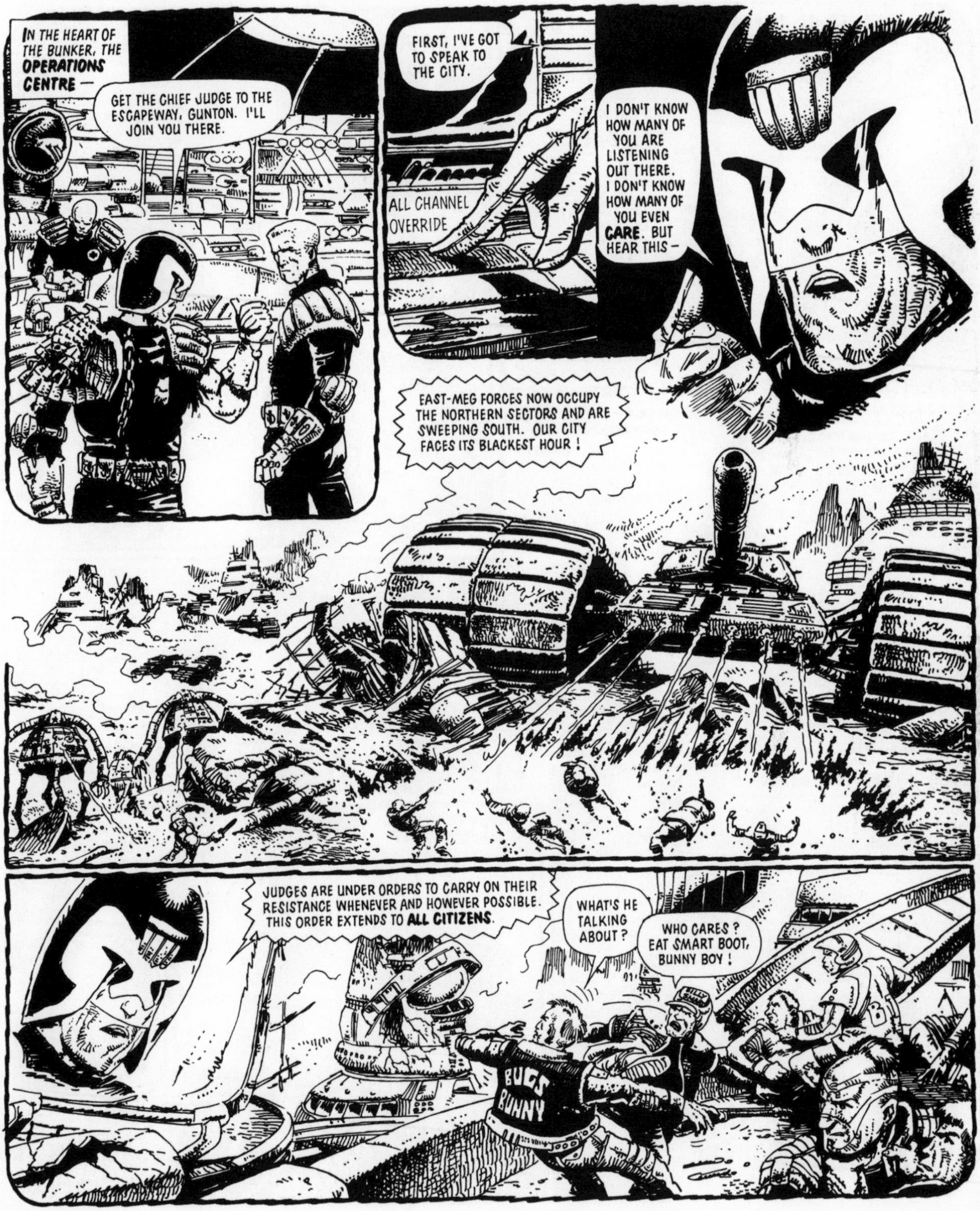
IN THE HEART OF THE BUNKER, THE **OPERATIONS CENTRE** —
GET THE CHIEF JUDGE TO THE ESCAPEWAY, GUNTON. I'LL JOIN YOU THERE.
FIRST, I'VE GOT TO SPEAK TO THE CITY.
ALL CHANNEL OVERRIDE
I DON'T KNOW HOW MANY OF YOU ARE LISTENING OUT THERE. I DON'T KNOW HOW MANY OF YOU EVEN **CARE**. BUT HEAR THIS —
EAST-MEG FORCES NOW OCCUPY THE NORTHERN SECTORS AND ARE SWEEPING SOUTH. OUR CITY FACES ITS BLACKEST HOUR !
JUDGES ARE UNDER ORDERS TO CARRY ON THEIR RESISTANCE WHENEVER AND HOWEVER POSSIBLE. THIS ORDER EXTENDS TO **ALL CITIZENS**.
WHAT'S HE TALKING ABOUT ?
WHO CARES ? EAT SMART BOOT, BUNNY BOY !
BUGS BUNNY

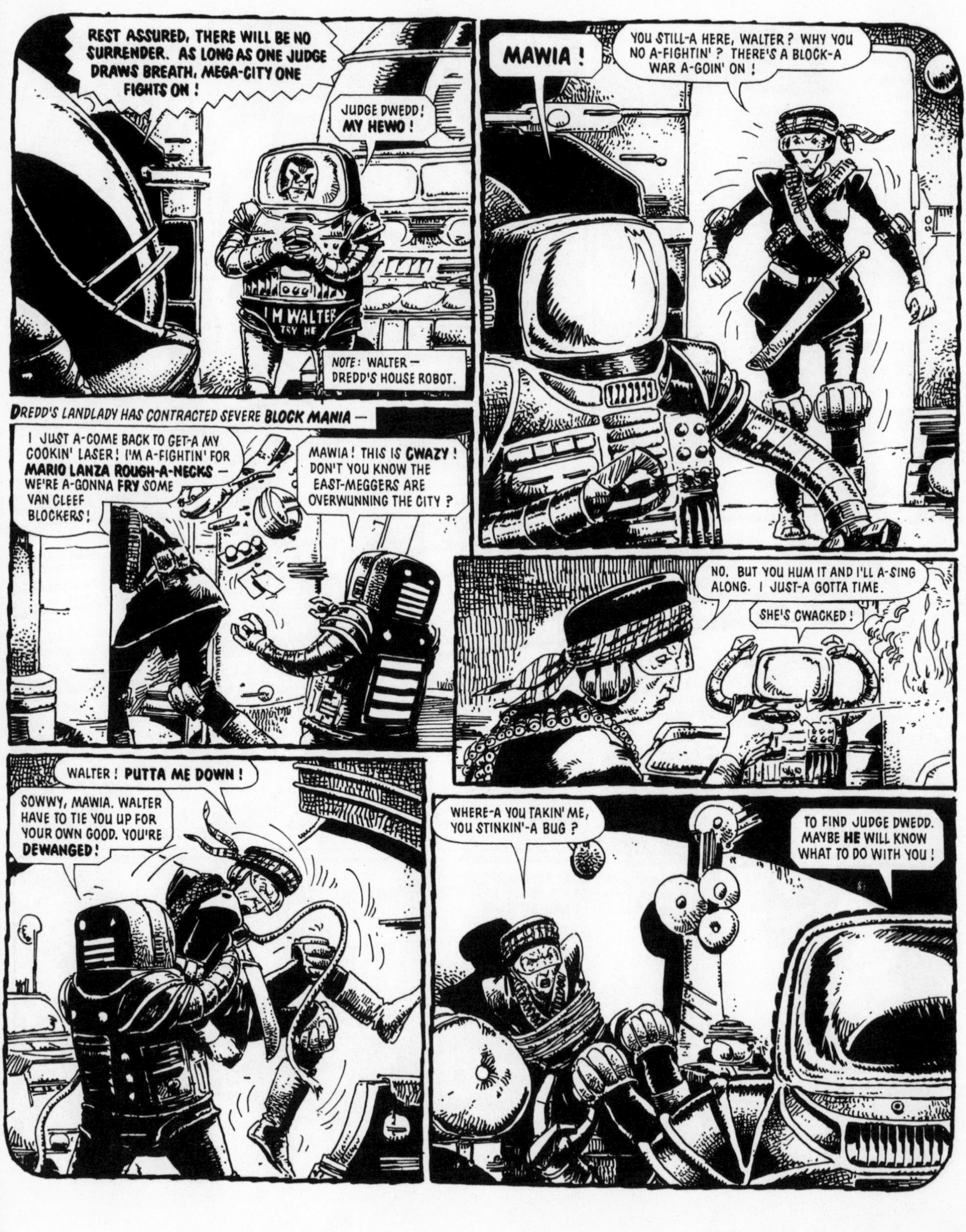
REST ASSURED, THERE WILL BE NO SURRENDER. AS LONG AS ONE JUDGE DRAWS BREATH, MEGA-CITY ONE FIGHTS ON!
JUDGE DWEDD! MY HEWO!
I'M WALTER TRY ME
NOTE: WALTER — DREDD'S HOUSE ROBOT.
MAWIA!
YOU STILL-A HERE, WALTER? WHY YOU NO A-FIGHTIN'? THERE'S A BLOCK-A WAR A-GOIN' ON!
DREDD'S LANDLADY HAS CONTRACTED SEVERE BLOCK MANIA —
I JUST A-COME BACK TO GET-A MY COOKIN' LASER! I'M A-FIGHTIN' FOR MARIO LANZA ROUGH-A-NECKS — WE'RE A-GONNA FRY SOME VAN CLEEF BLOCKERS!
MAWIA! THIS IS CWAZY! DON'T YOU KNOW THE EAST-MEGGERS ARE OVERWUNNING THE CITY?
NO. BUT YOU HUM IT AND I'LL A-SING ALONG. I JUST-A GOTTA TIME.
SHE'S CWACKED!
WALTER! PUTTA ME DOWN!
SOWWY, MAWIA. WALTER HAVE TO TIE YOU UP FOR YOUR OWN GOOD. YOU'RE DEWANGED!
WHERE-A YOU TAKIN' ME, YOU STINKIN'-A BUG?
TO FIND JUDGE DWEDD. MAYBE HE WILL KNOW WHAT TO DO WITH YOU!

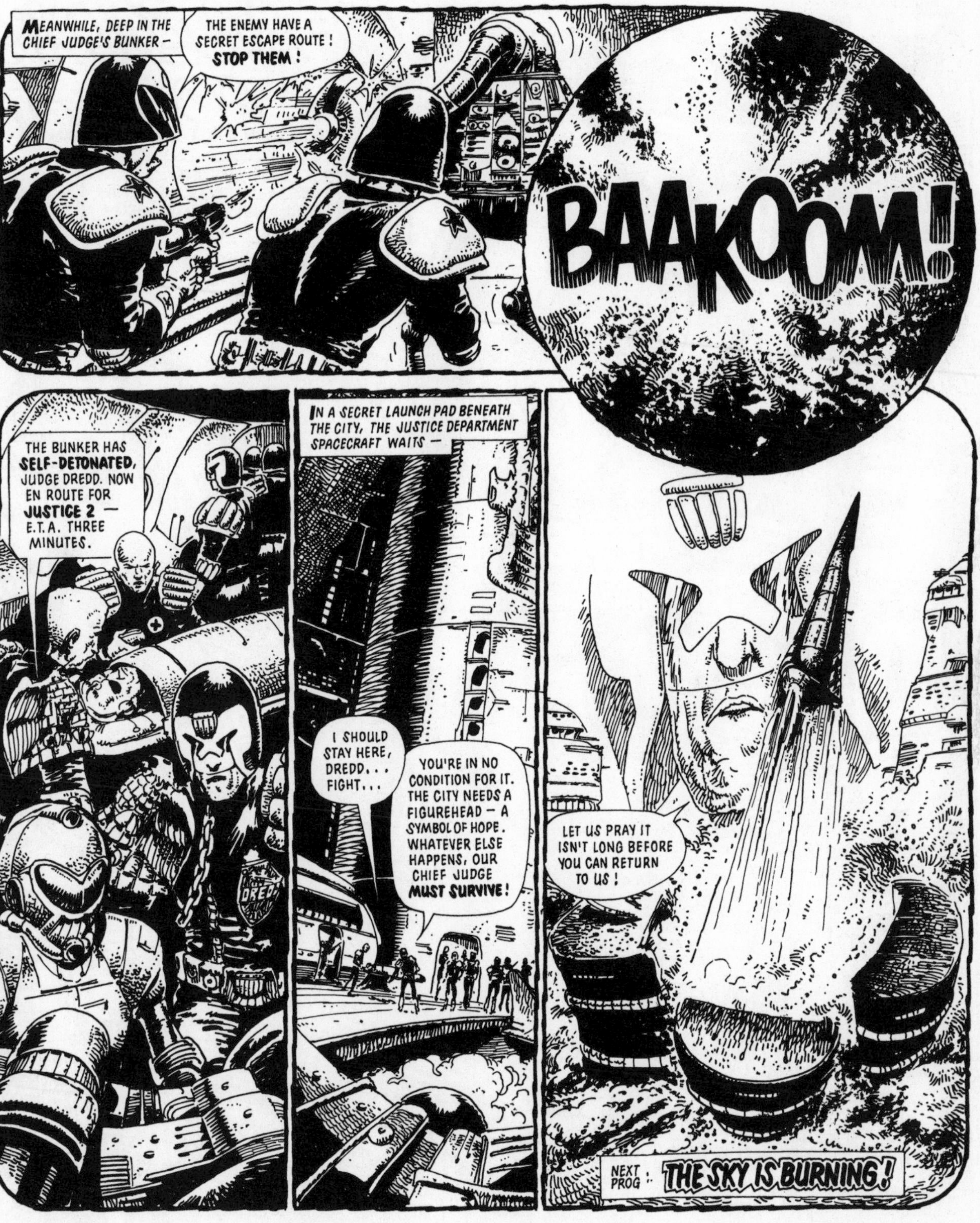

MEANWHILE, DEEP IN THE CHIEF JUDGE'S BUNKER –
THE ENEMY HAVE A SECRET ESCAPE ROUTE! STOP THEM!
BAAKOOM!
THE BUNKER HAS SELF-DETONATED, JUDGE DREDD. NOW EN ROUTE FOR JUSTICE 2 — E.T.A. THREE MINUTES.
IN A SECRET LAUNCH PAD BENEATH THE CITY, THE JUSTICE DEPARTMENT SPACECRAFT WAITS —
I SHOULD STAY HERE, DREDD... FIGHT...
YOU'RE IN NO CONDITION FOR IT. THE CITY NEEDS A FIGUREHEAD — A SYMBOL OF HOPE. WHATEVER ELSE HAPPENS, OUR CHIEF JUDGE MUST SURVIVE!
LET US PRAY IT ISN'T LONG BEFORE YOU CAN RETURN TO US!
NEXT PROG: THE SKY IS BURNING!

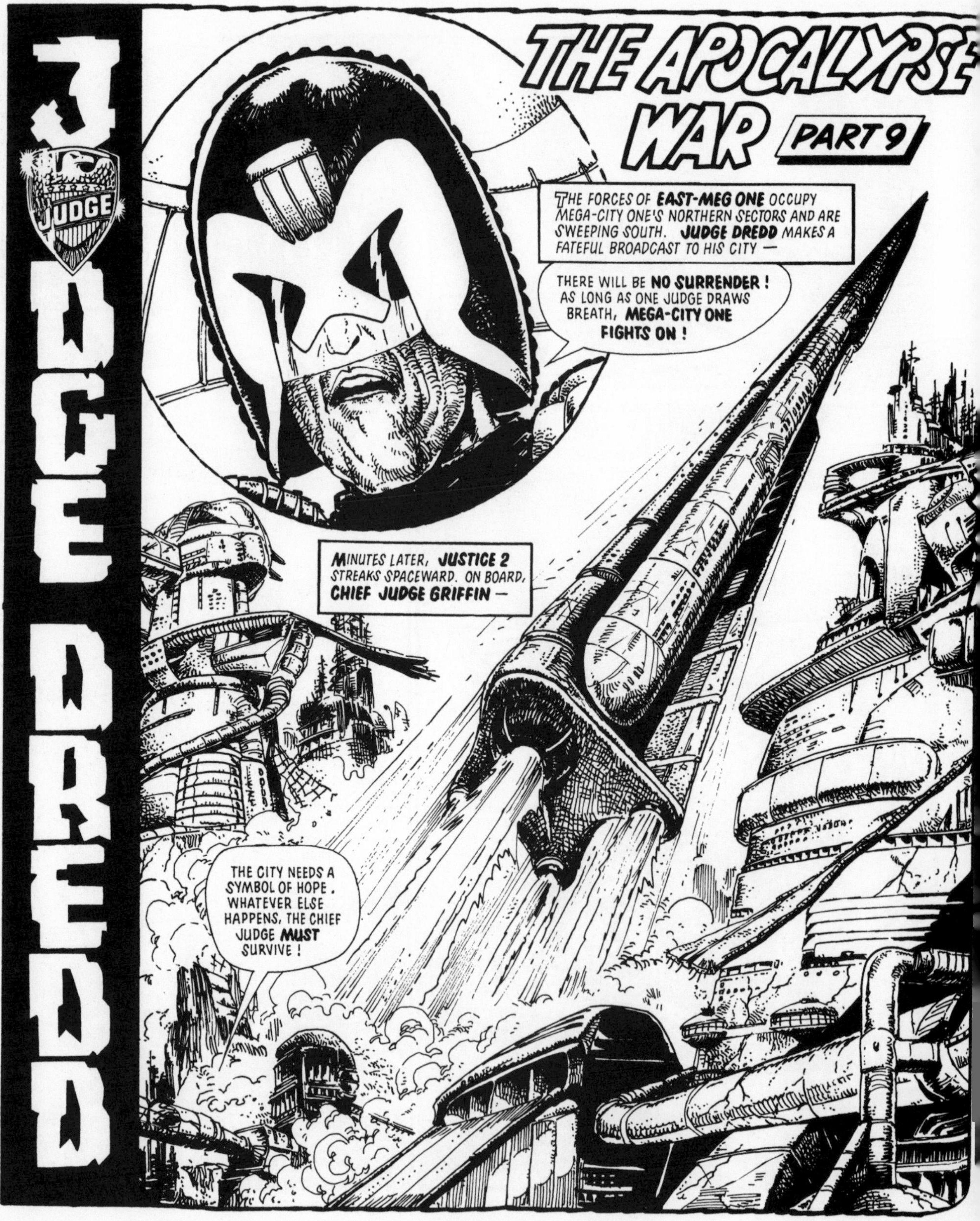
JUDGE DREDD
JUDGE
THE APOCALYPSE WAR PART 9
THE FORCES OF EAST-MEG ONE OCCUPY MEGA-CITY ONE'S NORTHERN SECTORS AND ARE SWEEPING SOUTH. JUDGE DREDD MAKES A FATEFUL BROADCAST TO HIS CITY —
THERE WILL BE NO SURRENDER! AS LONG AS ONE JUDGE DRAWS BREATH, MEGA-CITY ONE FIGHTS ON!
MINUTES LATER, JUSTICE 2 STREAKS SPACEWARD. ON BOARD, CHIEF JUDGE GRIFFIN —
THE CITY NEEDS A SYMBOL OF HOPE. WHATEVER ELSE HAPPENS, THE CHIEF JUDGE MUST SURVIVE!

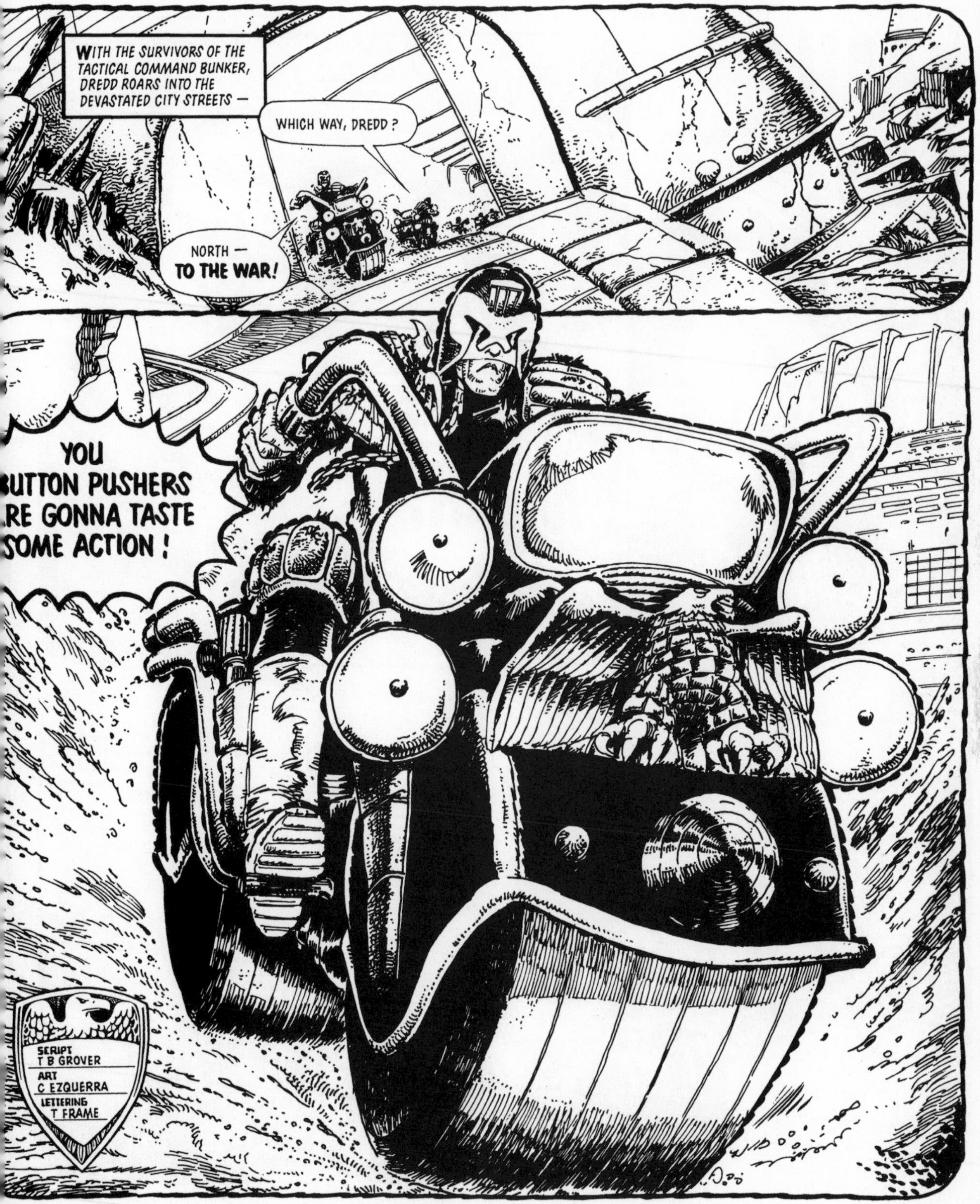
WITH THE SURVIVORS OF THE TACTICAL COMMAND BUNKER, DREDD ROARS INTO THE DEVASTATED CITY STREETS —
WHICH WAY, DREDD ?
NORTH — TO THE WAR!
YOU
UTTON PUSHERS
RE GONNA TASTE
SOME ACTION !
SCRIPT T B GROVER
ART C EZQUERRA
LETTERING T FRAME

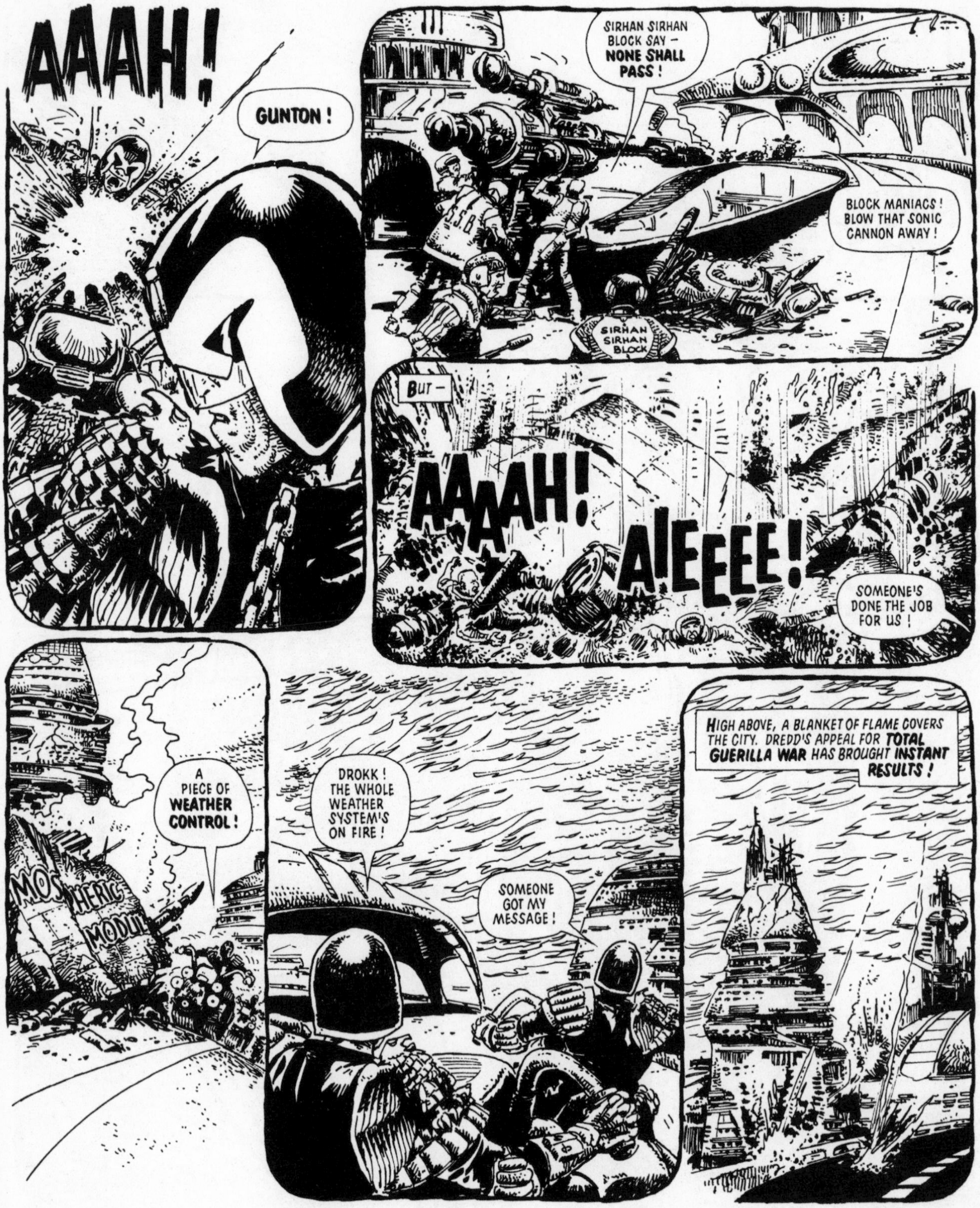
AAAH!
GUNTON!
SIRHAN SIRHAN BLOCK SAY — NONE SHALL PASS!
BLOCK MANIACS! BLOW THAT SONIC CANNON AWAY!
SIRHAN SIRHAN BLOCK
BUT —
AAAAH!
AIEEEE!
SOMEONE'S DONE THE JOB FOR US!
A PIECE OF WEATHER CONTROL!
DROKK! THE WHOLE WEATHER SYSTEM'S ON FIRE!
SOMEONE GOT MY MESSAGE!
HIGH ABOVE, A BLANKET OF FLAME COVERS THE CITY. DREDD'S APPEAL FOR TOTAL GUERILLA WAR HAS BROUGHT INSTANT RESULTS!

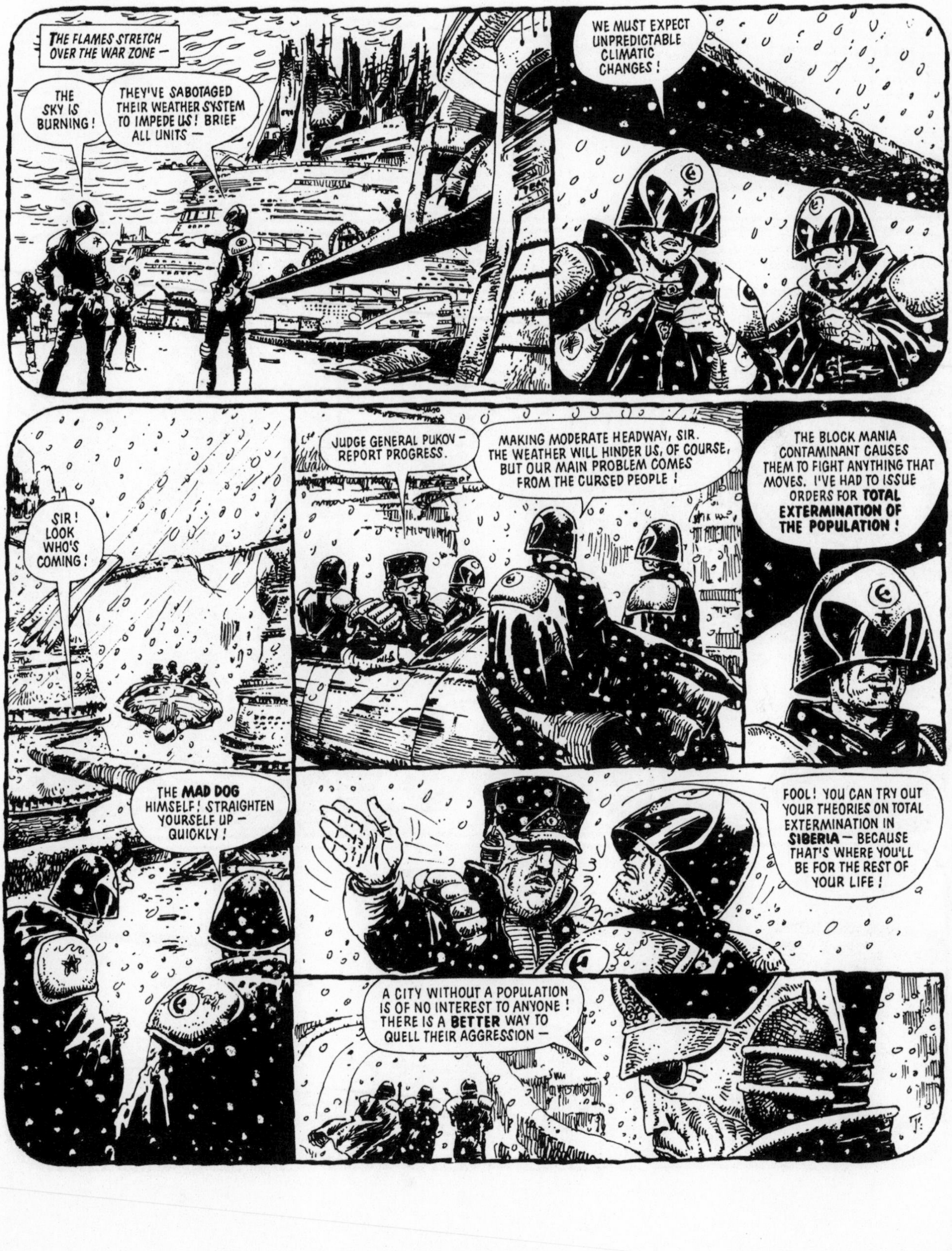
THE FLAMES STRETCH OVER THE WAR ZONE –
THE SKY IS BURNING!
THEY'VE SABOTAGED THEIR WEATHER SYSTEM TO IMPEDE US! BRIEF ALL UNITS –
WE MUST EXPECT UNPREDICTABLE CLIMATIC CHANGES!
SIR! LOOK WHO'S COMING!
THE MAD DOG HIMSELF! STRAIGHTEN YOURSELF UP – QUICKLY!
JUDGE GENERAL PUKOV – REPORT PROGRESS.
MAKING MODERATE HEADWAY, SIR. THE WEATHER WILL HINDER US, OF COURSE, BUT OUR MAIN PROBLEM COMES FROM THE CURSED PEOPLE!
THE BLOCK MANIA CONTAMINANT CAUSES THEM TO FIGHT ANYTHING THAT MOVES. I'VE HAD TO ISSUE ORDERS FOR TOTAL EXTERMINATION OF THE POPULATION!
FOOL! YOU CAN TRY OUT YOUR THEORIES ON TOTAL EXTERMINATION IN SIBERIA – BECAUSE THAT'S WHERE YOU'LL BE FOR THE REST OF YOUR LIFE!
A CITY WITHOUT A POPULATION IS OF NO INTEREST TO ANYONE! THERE IS A BETTER WAY TO QUELL THEIR AGGRESSION –

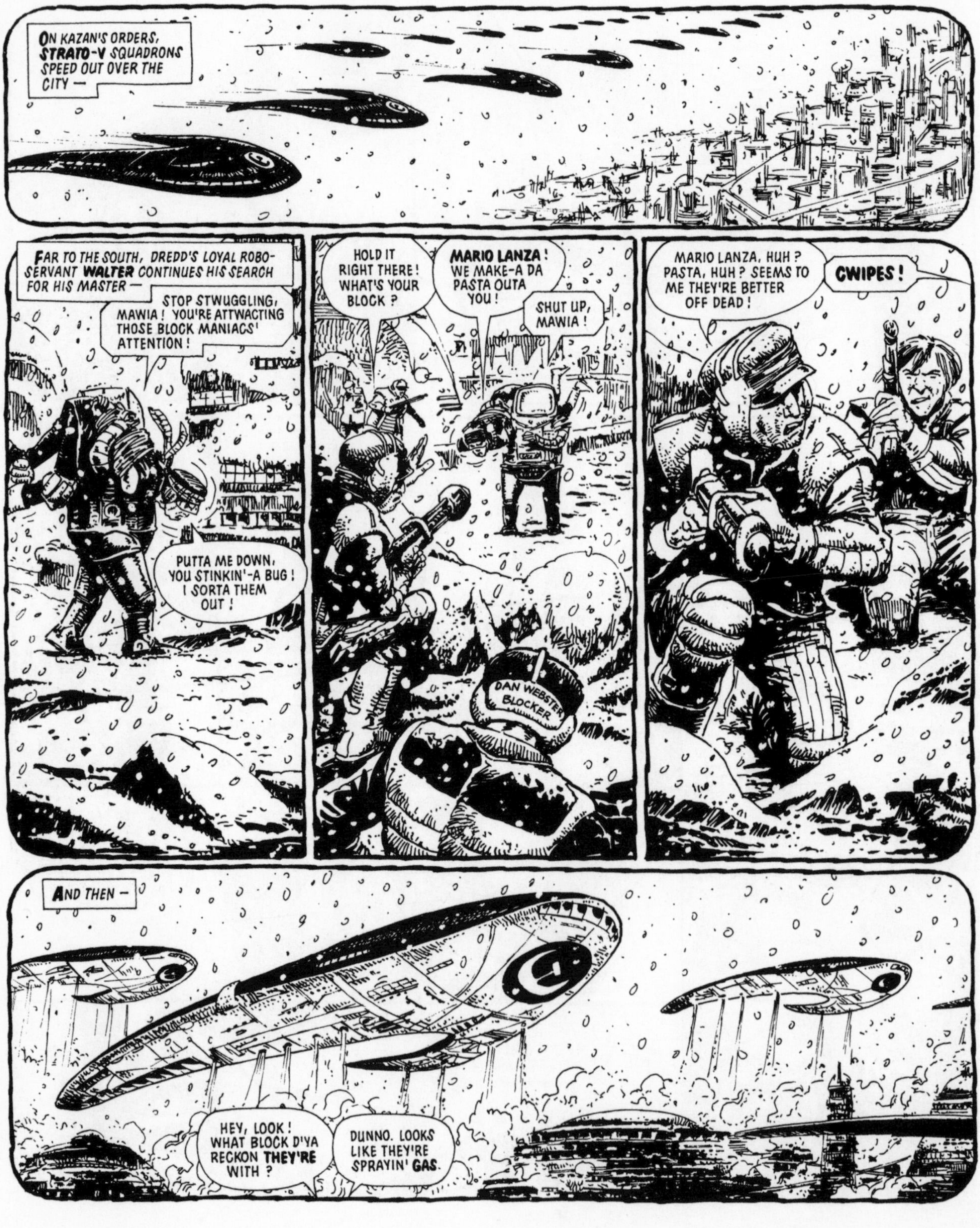

ON KAZAN'S ORDERS, STRATO-V SQUADRONS SPEED OUT OVER THE CITY —
FAR TO THE SOUTH, DREDD'S LOYAL ROBO-SERVANT WALTER CONTINUES HIS SEARCH FOR HIS MASTER —
STOP STWUGGLING, MAWIA! YOU'RE ATTWACTING THOSE BLOCK MANIACS' ATTENTION!
PUTTA ME DOWN, YOU STINKIN'-A BUG! I SORTA THEM OUT!
HOLD IT RIGHT THERE! WHAT'S YOUR BLOCK?
MARIO LANZA! WE MAKE-A DA PASTA OUTA YOU!
SHUT UP, MAWIA!
DAN WEBSTER BLOCKER
MARIO LANZA, HUH? PASTA, HUH? SEEMS TO ME THEY'RE BETTER OFF DEAD!
CWIPES!
AND THEN —
HEY, LOOK! WHAT BLOCK D'YA RECKON THEY'RE WITH?
DUNNO. LOOKS LIKE THEY'RE SPRAYIN' GAS.

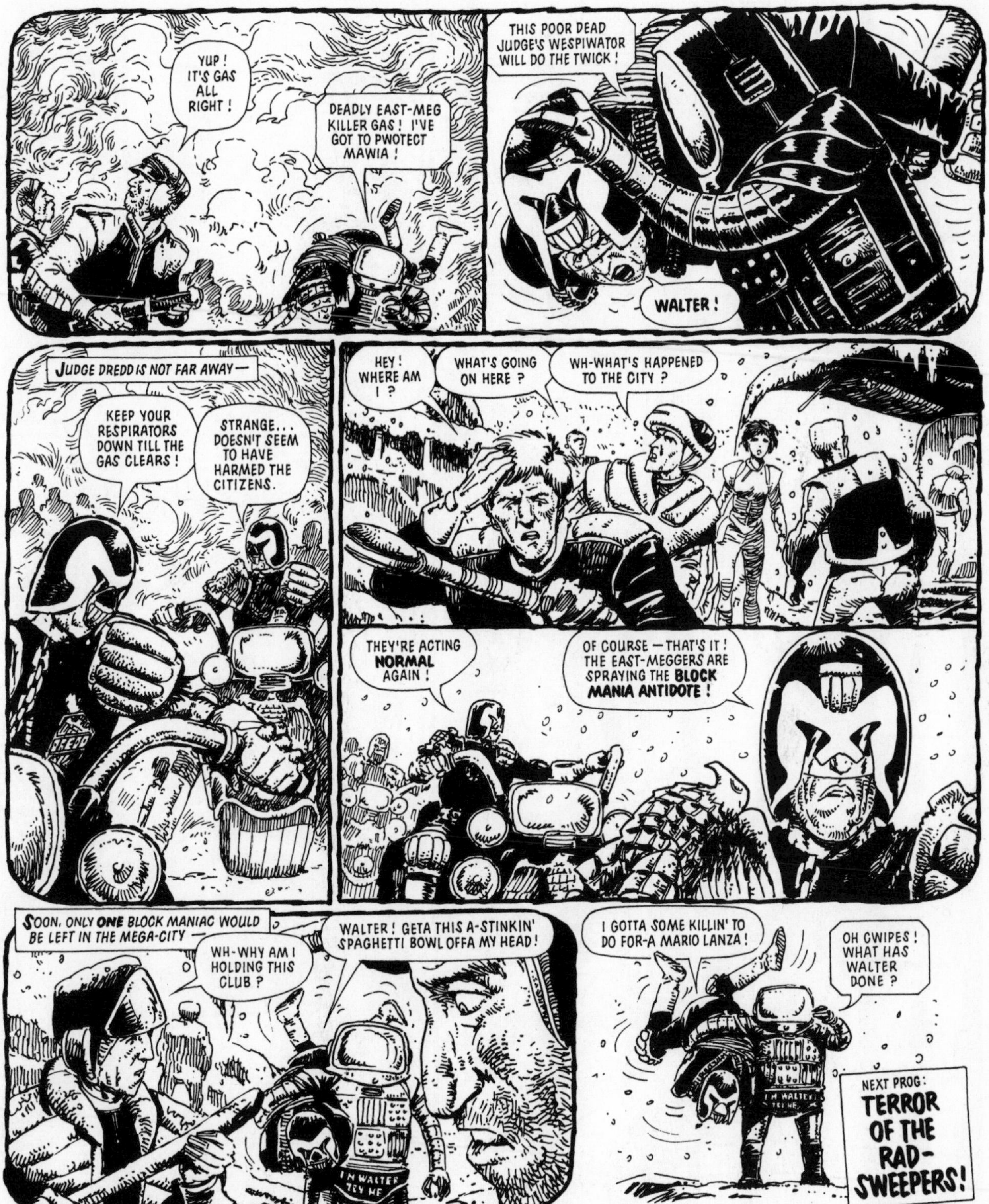
YUP ! IT'S GAS ALL RIGHT !
DEADLY EAST-MEG KILLER GAS ! I'VE GOT TO PWOTECT MAWIA !
THIS POOR DEAD JUDGE'S WESPIWATOR WILL DO THE TWICK !
WALTER !
JUDGE DREDD IS NOT FAR AWAY —
KEEP YOUR RESPIRATORS DOWN TILL THE GAS CLEARS !
STRANGE... DOESN'T SEEM TO HAVE HARMED THE CITIZENS.
HEY ! WHERE AM I ?
WHAT'S GOING ON HERE ?
WH-WHAT'S HAPPENED TO THE CITY ?
THEY'RE ACTING NORMAL AGAIN !
OF COURSE — THAT'S IT ! THE EAST-MEGGERS ARE SPRAYING THE BLOCK MANIA ANTIDOTE !
SOON, ONLY ONE BLOCK MANIAC WOULD BE LEFT IN THE MEGA-CITY —
WH-WHY AM I HOLDING THIS CLUB ?
WALTER ! GETA THIS A-STINKIN' SPAGHETTI BOWL OFFA MY HEAD !
I GOTTA SOME KILLIN' TO DO FOR-A MARIO LANZA !
OH CWIPES ! WHAT HAS WALTER DONE ?
NEXT PROG:
TERROR OF THE RAD-SWEEPERS!

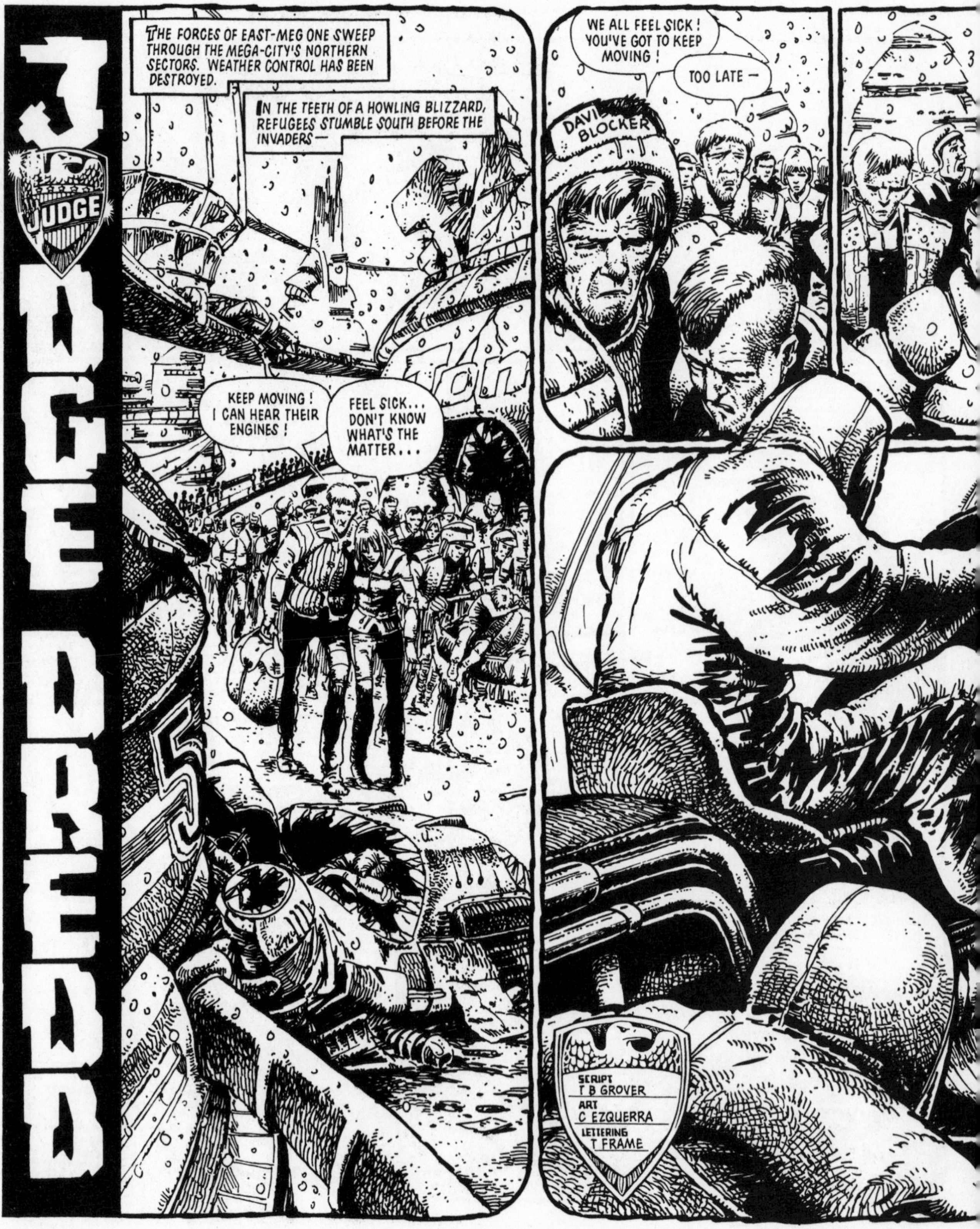
JUDGE DREDD
JUDGE
THE FORCES OF EAST-MEG ONE SWEEP THROUGH THE MEGA-CITY'S NORTHERN SECTORS. WEATHER CONTROL HAS BEEN DESTROYED.
IN THE TEETH OF A HOWLING BLIZZARD, REFUGEES STUMBLE SOUTH BEFORE THE INVADERS—
KEEP MOVING! I CAN HEAR THEIR ENGINES!
FEEL SICK... DON'T KNOW WHAT'S THE MATTER...
WE ALL FEEL SICK! YOU'VE GOT TO KEEP MOVING!
TOO LATE—
DAVI
BLOCKER
SCRIPT T B GROVER
ART C EZQUERRA
LETTERING T FRAME

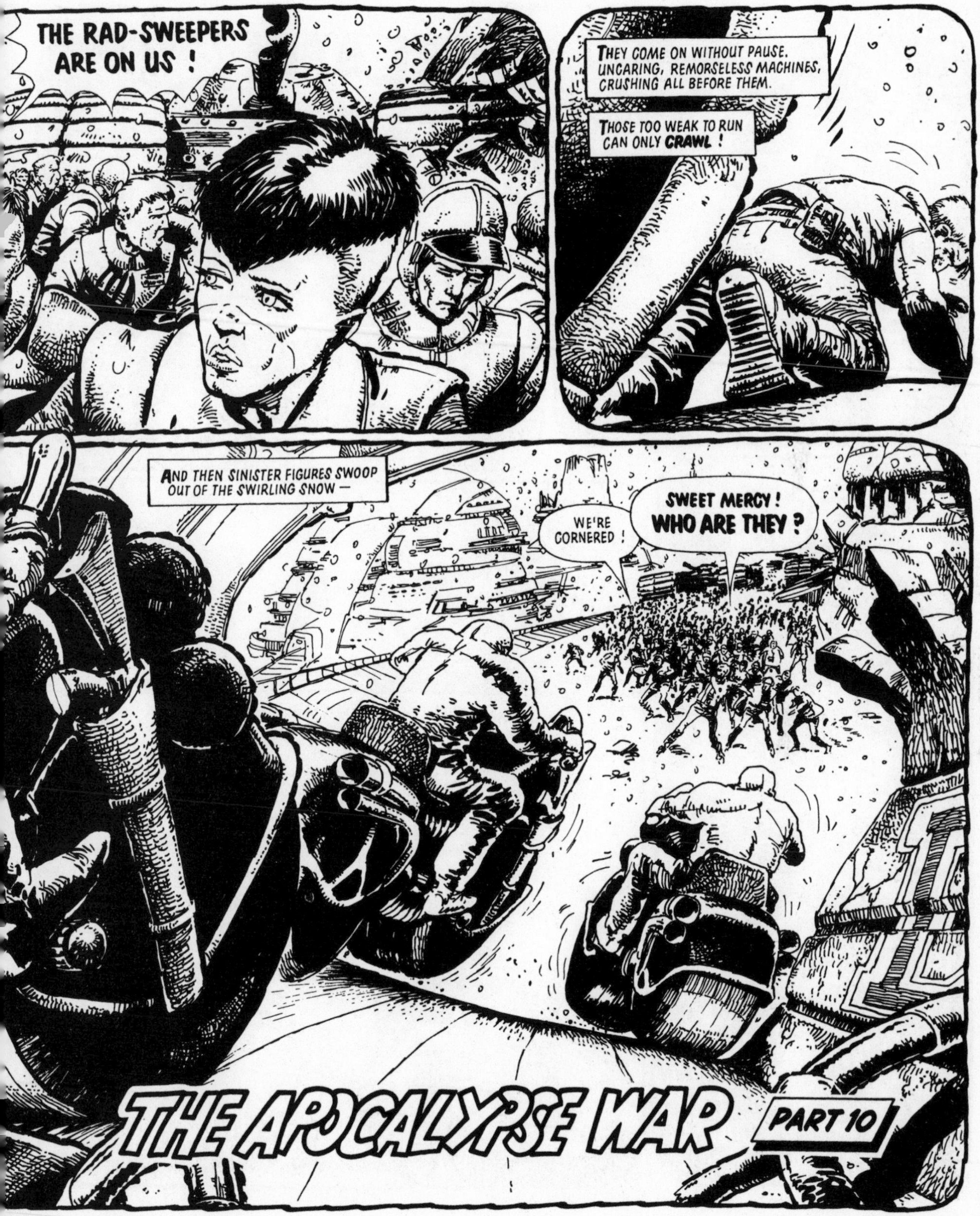
THE RAD-SWEEPERS ARE ON US !
THEY COME ON WITHOUT PAUSE. UNCARING, REMORSELESS MACHINES, CRUSHING ALL BEFORE THEM.
THOSE TOO WEAK TO RUN CAN ONLY CRAWL !
AND THEN SINISTER FIGURES SWOOP OUT OF THE SWIRLING SNOW —
WE'RE CORNERED !
SWEET MERCY ! WHO ARE THEY ?
THE APOCALYPSE WAR
PART 10

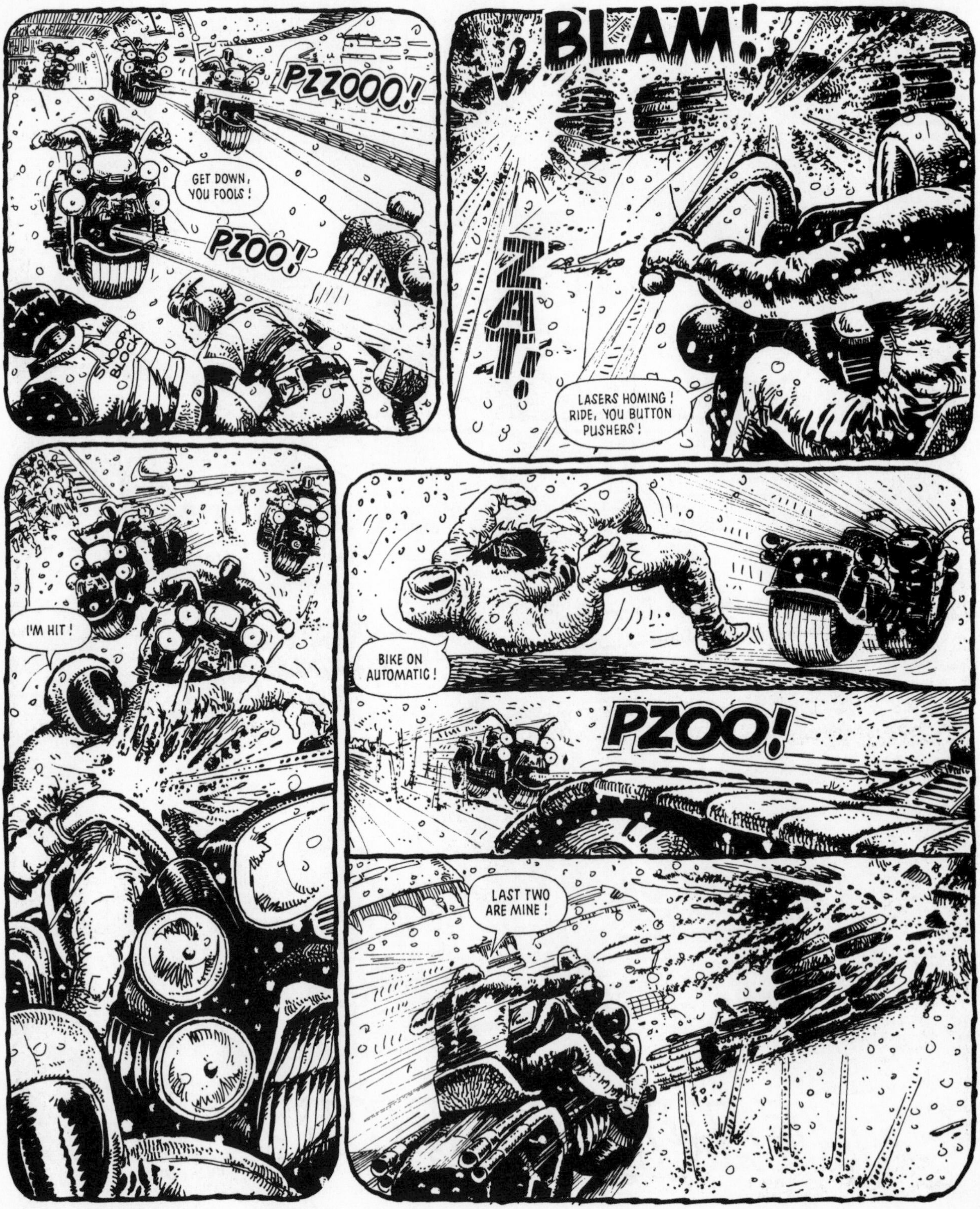
PZZOOO!
GET DOWN, YOU FOOLS!
PZOO!
BLAM!
ZAT!
LASERS HOMING! RIDE, YOU BUTTON PUSHERS!
I'M HIT!
BIKE ON AUTOMATIC!
PZOO!
LAST TWO ARE MINE!

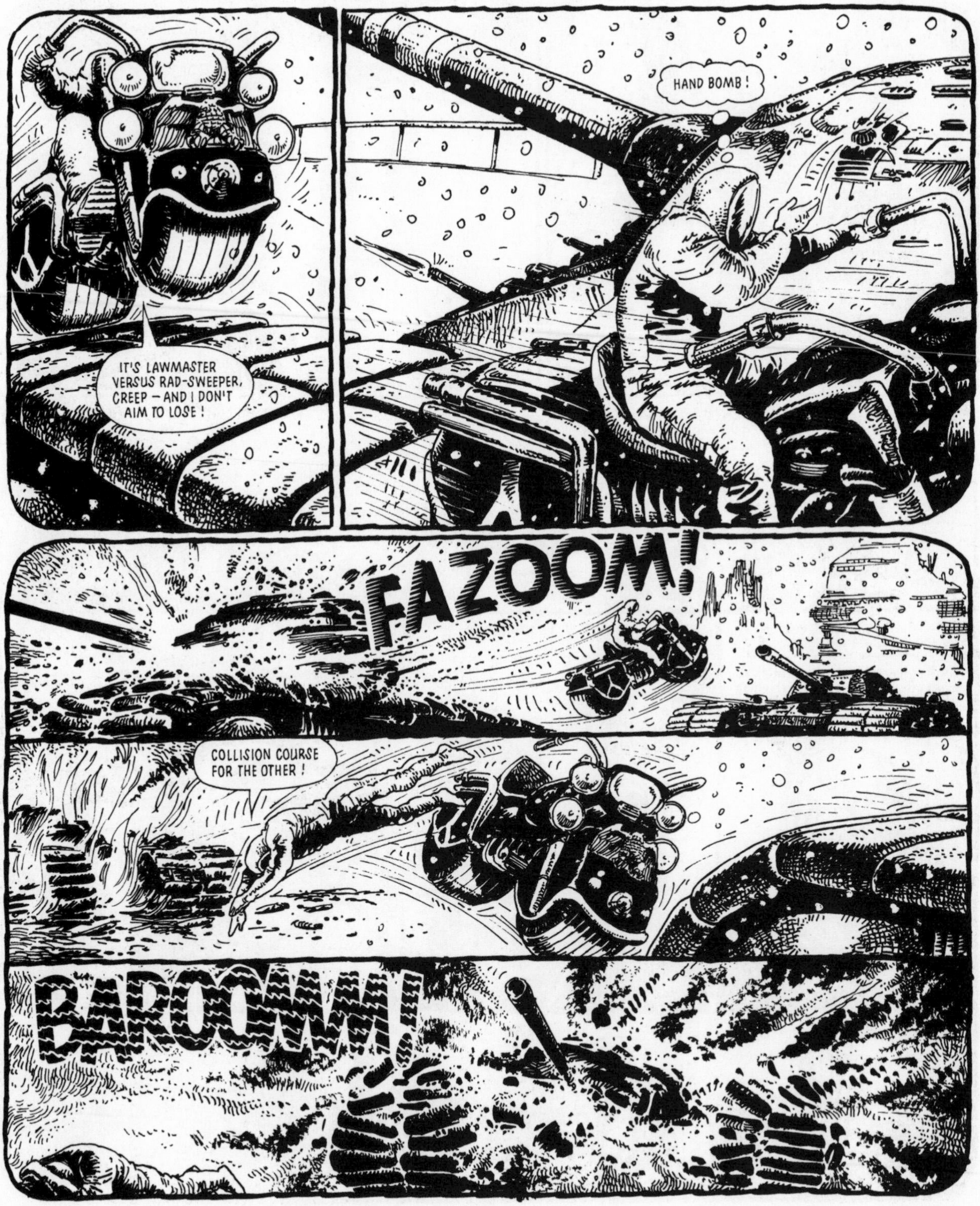
IT'S LAWMASTER VERSUS RAD-SWEEPER, CREEP — AND I DON'T AIM TO LOSE !
HAND BOMB !
FAZOOM!
COLLISION COURSE FOR THE OTHER !
BAROOMM!

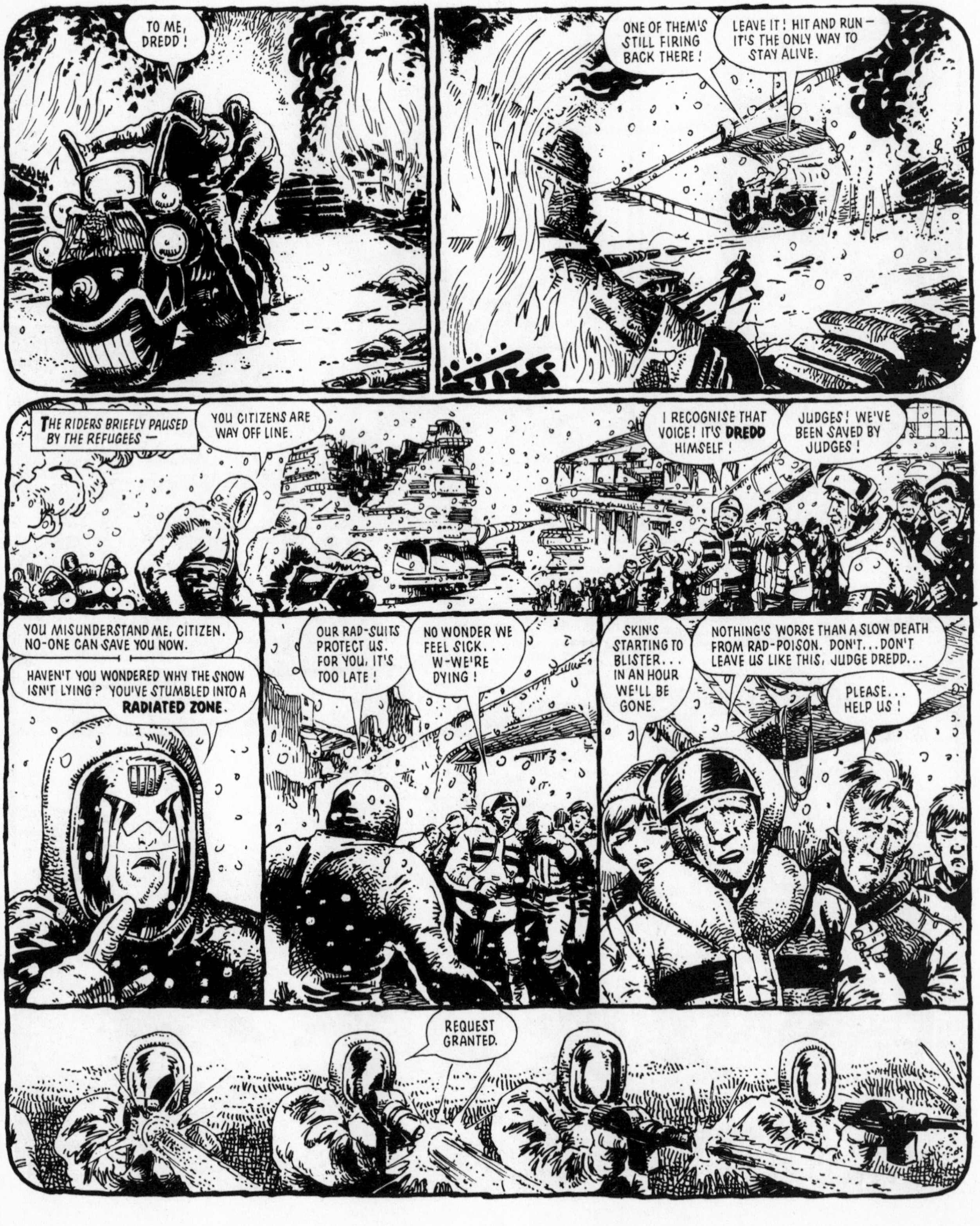
TO ME, DREDD!
ONE OF THEM'S STILL FIRING BACK THERE!
LEAVE IT! HIT AND RUN – IT'S THE ONLY WAY TO STAY ALIVE.
THE RIDERS BRIEFLY PAUSED BY THE REFUGEES –
YOU CITIZENS ARE WAY OFF LINE.
I RECOGNISE THAT VOICE! IT'S DREDD HIMSELF!
JUDGES! WE'VE BEEN SAVED BY JUDGES!
YOU MISUNDERSTAND ME, CITIZEN. NO-ONE CAN SAVE YOU NOW.
HAVEN'T YOU WONDERED WHY THE SNOW ISN'T LYING? YOU'VE STUMBLED INTO A RADIATED ZONE.
OUR RAD-SUITS PROTECT US. FOR YOU, IT'S TOO LATE!
NO WONDER WE FEEL SICK... W-WE'RE DYING!
SKIN'S STARTING TO BLISTER... IN AN HOUR WE'LL BE GONE.
NOTHING'S WORSE THAN A SLOW DEATH FROM RAD-POISON. DON'T... DON'T LEAVE US LIKE THIS, JUDGE DREDD...
PLEASE... HELP US!
REQUEST GRANTED.

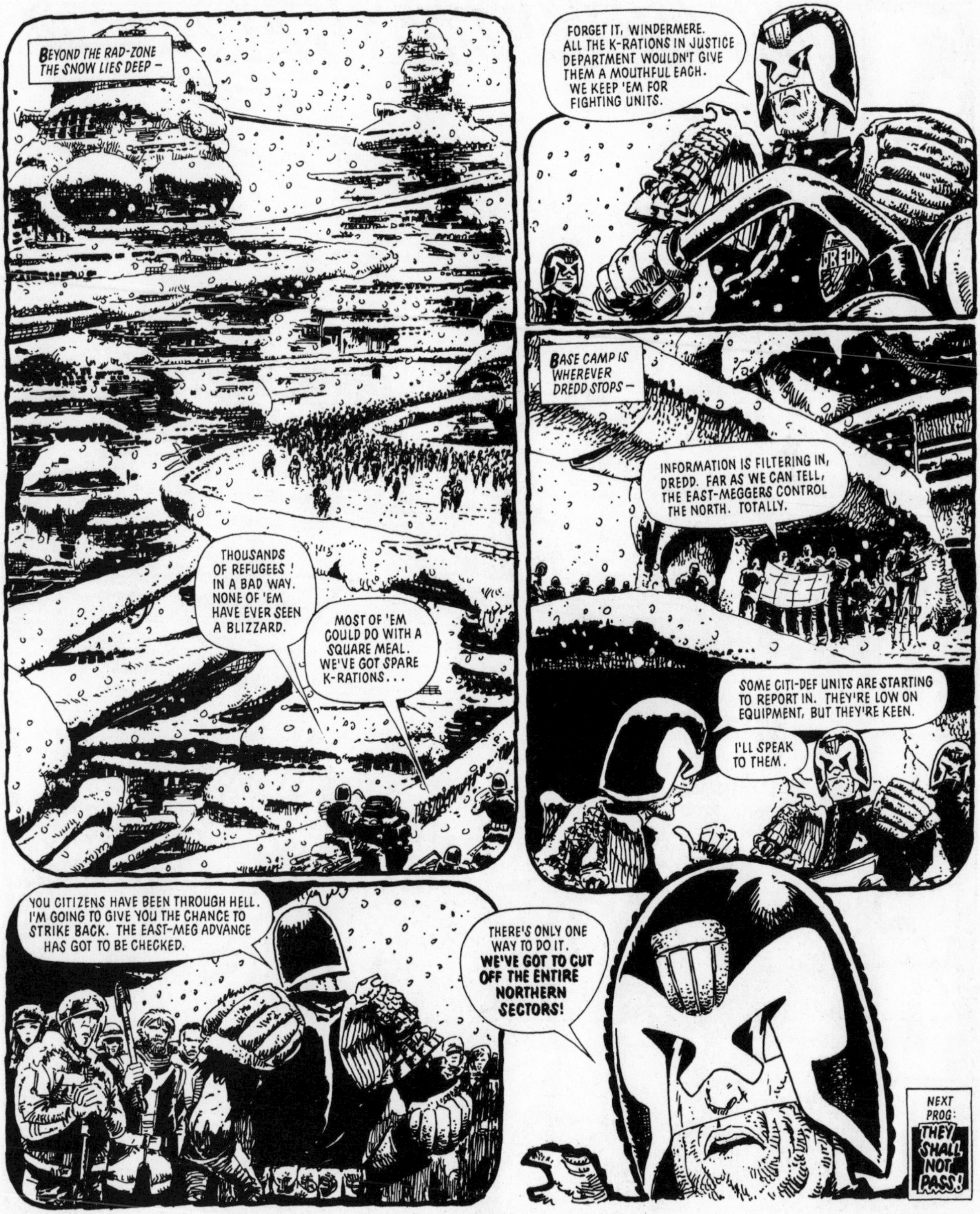
BEYOND THE RAD-ZONE THE SNOW LIES DEEP –
THOUSANDS OF REFUGEES! IN A BAD WAY. NONE OF 'EM HAVE EVER SEEN A BLIZZARD.
MOST OF 'EM COULD DO WITH A SQUARE MEAL. WE'VE GOT SPARE K-RATIONS...
FORGET IT, WINDERMERE. ALL THE K-RATIONS IN JUSTICE DEPARTMENT WOULDN'T GIVE THEM A MOUTHFUL EACH. WE KEEP 'EM FOR FIGHTING UNITS.
BASE CAMP IS WHEREVER DREDD STOPS –
INFORMATION IS FILTERING IN, DREDD. FAR AS WE CAN TELL, THE EAST-MEGGERS CONTROL THE NORTH. TOTALLY.
SOME CITI-DEF UNITS ARE STARTING TO REPORT IN. THEY'RE LOW ON EQUIPMENT, BUT THEY'RE KEEN.
I'LL SPEAK TO THEM.
YOU CITIZENS HAVE BEEN THROUGH HELL. I'M GOING TO GIVE YOU THE CHANCE TO STRIKE BACK. THE EAST-MEG ADVANCE HAS GOT TO BE CHECKED.
THERE'S ONLY ONE WAY TO DO IT. WE'VE GOT TO CUT OFF THE ENTIRE NORTHERN SECTORS!
NEXT PROG: THEY SHALL NOT PASS!

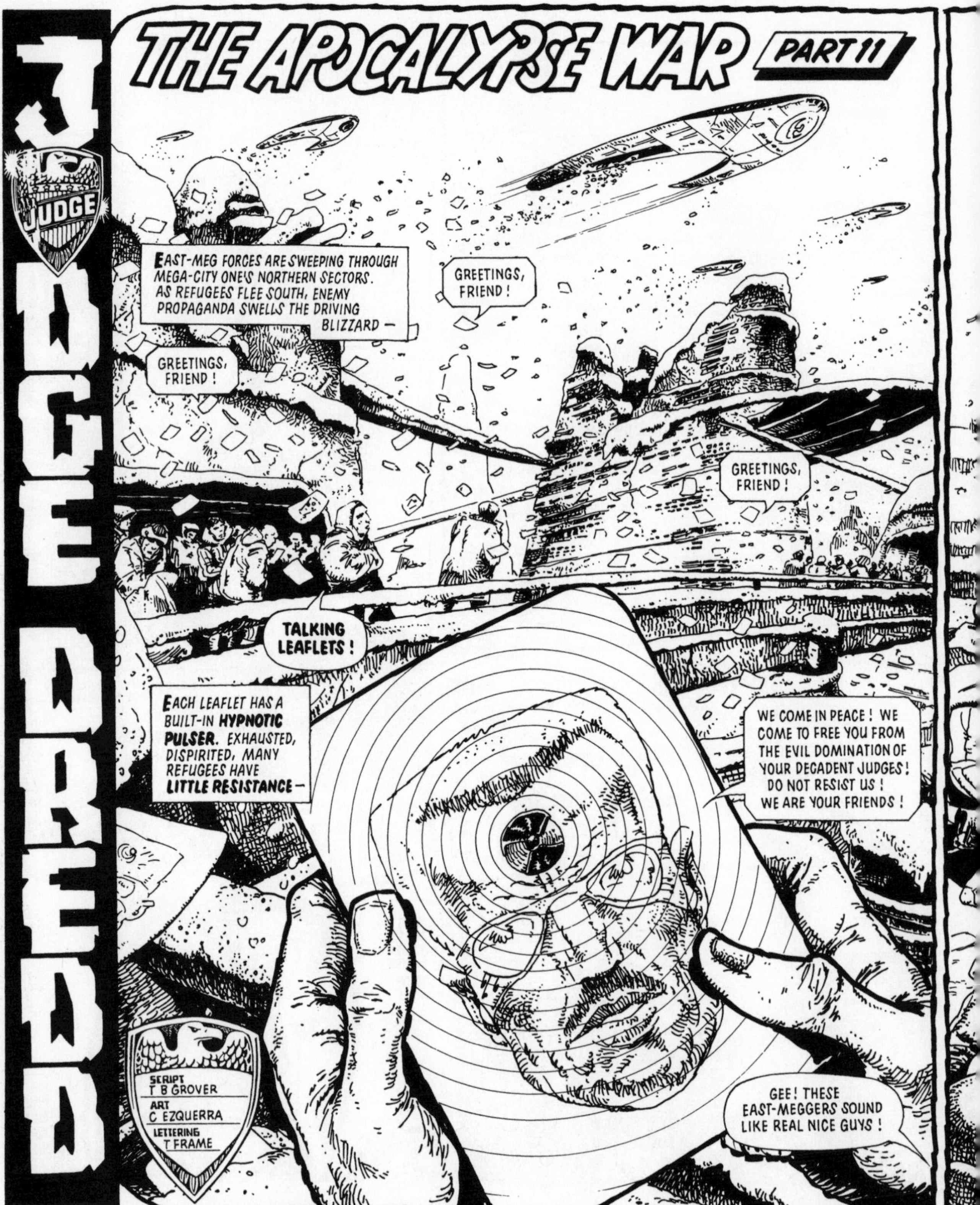
JUDGE DREDD
JUDGE
THE APOCALYPSE WAR
PART 11
EAST-MEG FORCES ARE SWEEPING THROUGH MEGA-CITY ONE'S NORTHERN SECTORS. AS REFUGEES FLEE SOUTH, ENEMY PROPAGANDA SWELLS THE DRIVING BLIZZARD –
GREETINGS, FRIEND!
GREETINGS, FRIEND!
GREETINGS, FRIEND!
TALKING LEAFLETS!
EACH LEAFLET HAS A BUILT-IN HYPNOTIC PULSER. EXHAUSTED, DISPIRITED, MANY REFUGEES HAVE LITTLE RESISTANCE –
WE COME IN PEACE! WE COME TO FREE YOU FROM THE EVIL DOMINATION OF YOUR DECADENT JUDGES! DO NOT RESIST US! WE ARE YOUR FRIENDS!
GEE! THESE EAST-MEGGERS SOUND LIKE REAL NICE GUYS!
SCRIPT T B GROVER
ART C EZQUERRA
LETTERING T FRAME

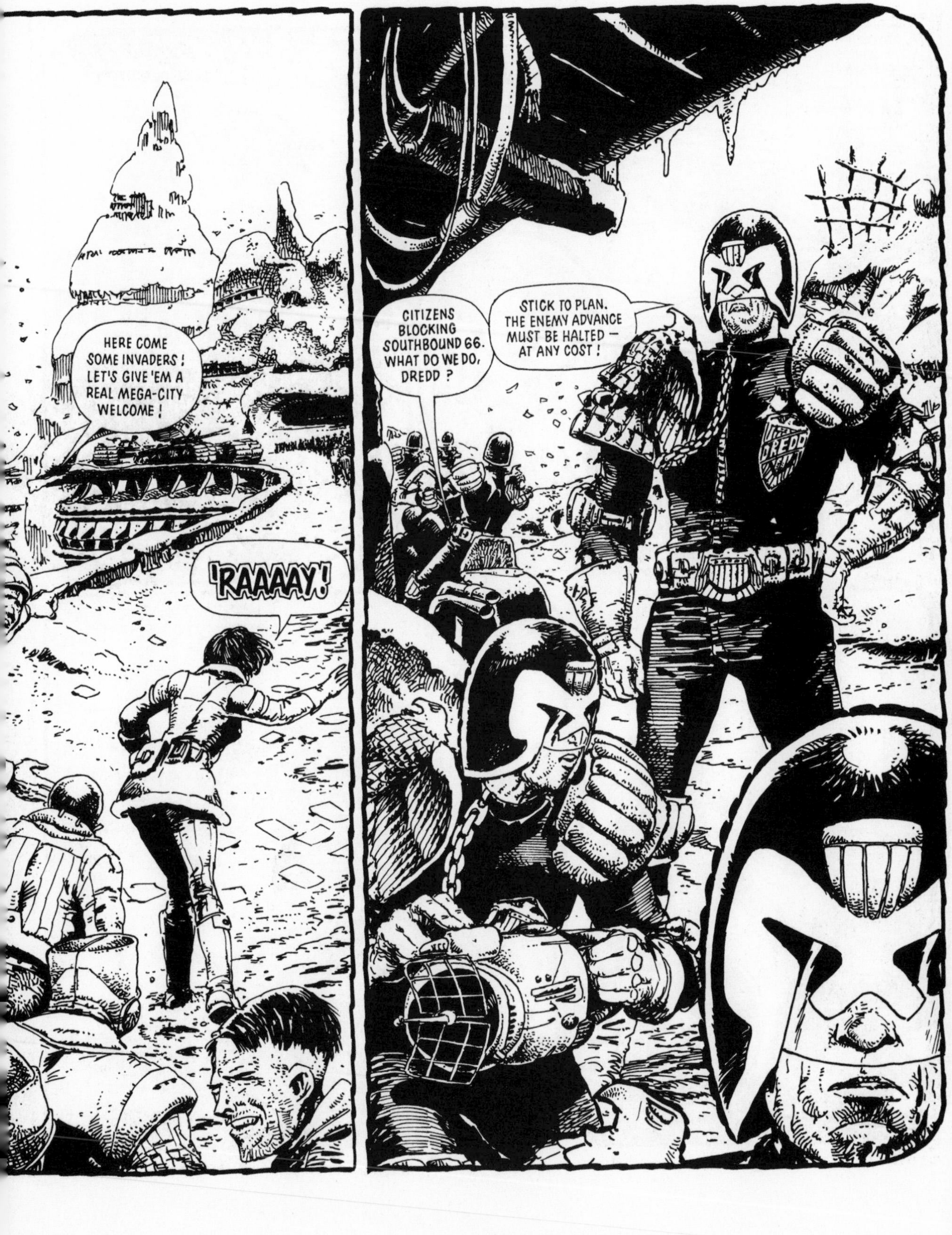
HERE COME SOME INVADERS! LET'S GIVE 'EM A REAL MEGA-CITY WELCOME!
'RAAAAY!
CITIZENS BLOCKING SOUTHBOUND 66. WHAT DO WE DO, DREDD?
STICK TO PLAN. THE ENEMY ADVANCE MUST BE HALTED — AT ANY COST!
DREDD

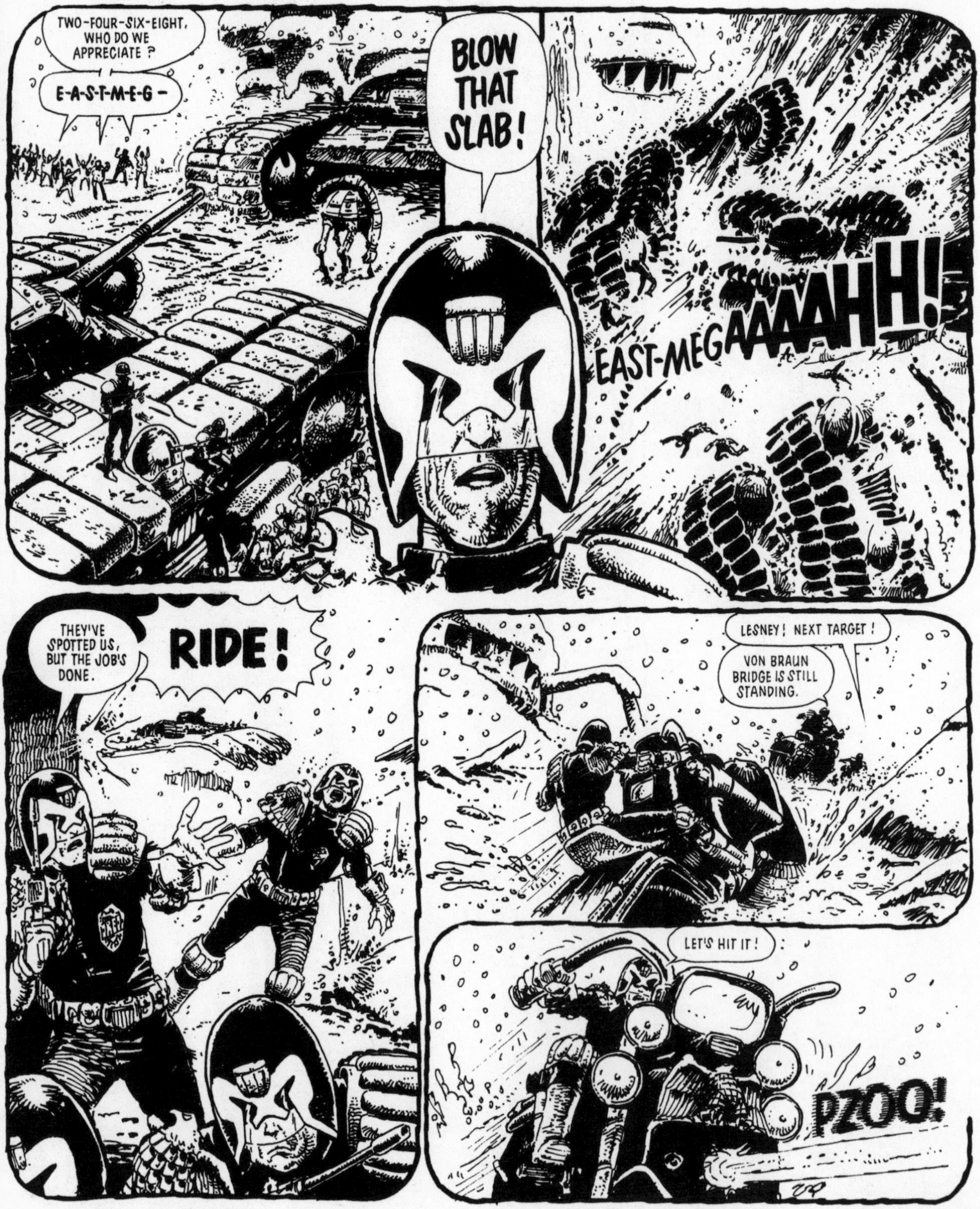
TWO-FOUR-SIX-EIGHT, WHO DO WE APPRECIATE ?
E-A-S-T-M-E-G -
BLOW THAT SLAB !
EAST-MEGAAAAAHH!
THEY'VE SPOTTED US, BUT THE JOB'S DONE.
RIDE !
LESNEY ! NEXT TARGET !
VON BRAUN BRIDGE IS STILL STANDING.
LET'S HIT IT !
PZOO!

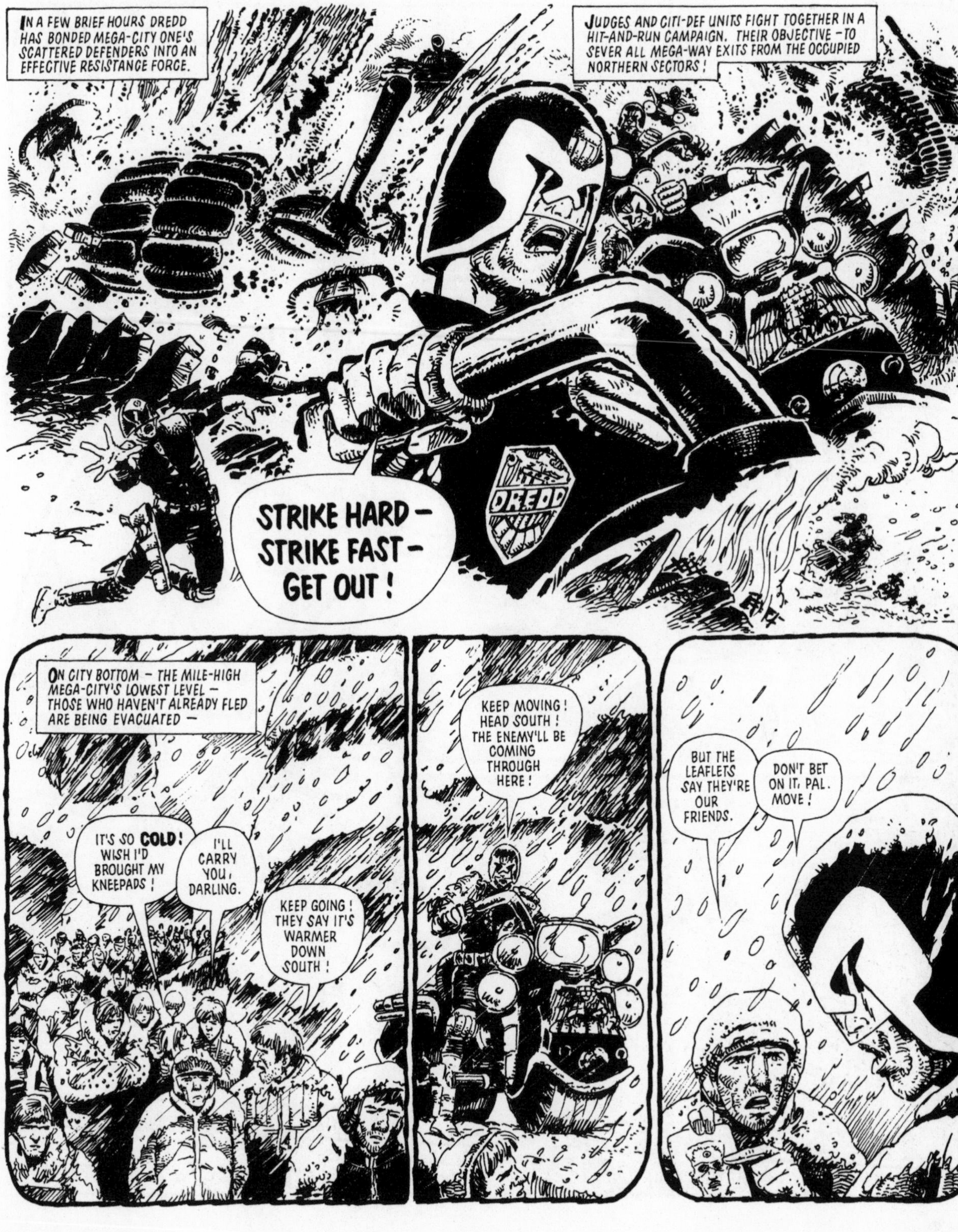
IN A FEW BRIEF HOURS DREDD HAS BONDED MEGA-CITY ONE'S SCATTERED DEFENDERS INTO AN EFFECTIVE RESISTANCE FORCE.
JUDGES AND CITI-DEF UNITS FIGHT TOGETHER IN A HIT-AND-RUN CAMPAIGN. THEIR OBJECTIVE - TO SEVER ALL MEGA-WAY EXITS FROM THE OCCUPIED NORTHERN SECTORS!
STRIKE HARD - STRIKE FAST - GET OUT!
DREDD
ON CITY BOTTOM - THE MILE-HIGH MEGA-CITY'S LOWEST LEVEL - THOSE WHO HAVEN'T ALREADY FLED ARE BEING EVACUATED -
IT'S SO COLD! WISH I'D BROUGHT MY KNEEPADS!
I'LL CARRY YOU, DARLING.
KEEP GOING! THEY SAY IT'S WARMER DOWN SOUTH!
KEEP MOVING! HEAD SOUTH! THE ENEMY'LL BE COMING THROUGH HERE!
BUT THE LEAFLETS SAY THEY'RE OUR FRIENDS.
DON'T BET ON IT, PAL. MOVE!

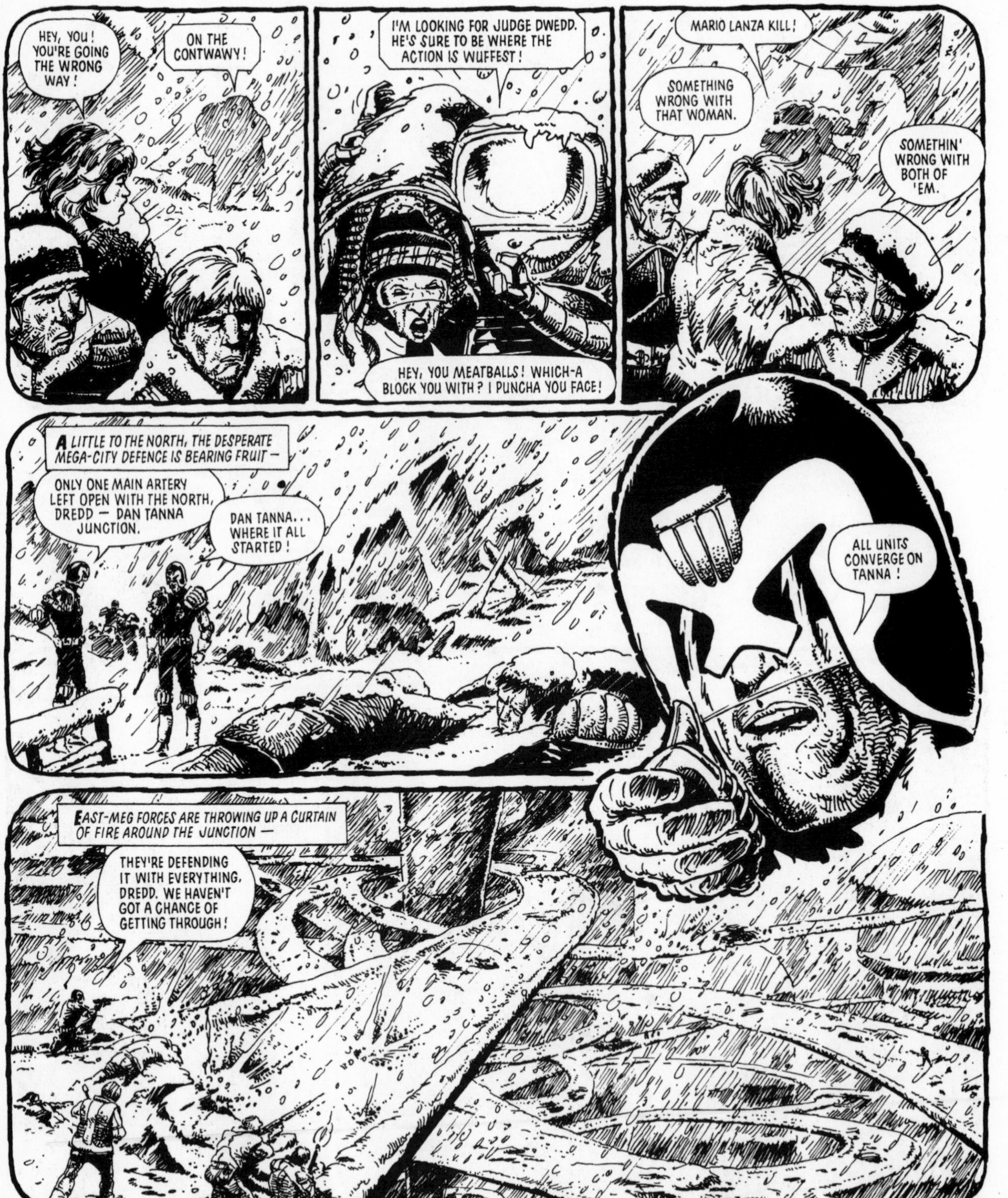
HEY, YOU! YOU'RE GOING THE WRONG WAY!
ON THE CONTWAWY!
I'M LOOKING FOR JUDGE DWEDD. HE'S SURE TO BE WHERE THE ACTION IS WUFFEST!
HEY, YOU MEATBALLS! WHICH-A BLOCK YOU WITH? I PUNCHA YOU FACE!
MARIO LANZA KILL!
SOMETHING WRONG WITH THAT WOMAN.
SOMETHIN' WRONG WITH BOTH OF 'EM.
A LITTLE TO THE NORTH, THE DESPERATE MEGA-CITY DEFENCE IS BEARING FRUIT—
ONLY ONE MAIN ARTERY LEFT OPEN WITH THE NORTH, DREDD — DAN TANNA JUNCTION.
DAN TANNA... WHERE IT ALL STARTED!
ALL UNITS CONVERGE ON TANNA!
EAST-MEG FORCES ARE THROWING UP A CURTAIN OF FIRE AROUND THE JUNCTION —
THEY'RE DEFENDING IT WITH EVERYTHING, DREDD. WE HAVEN'T GOT A CHANCE OF GETTING THROUGH!

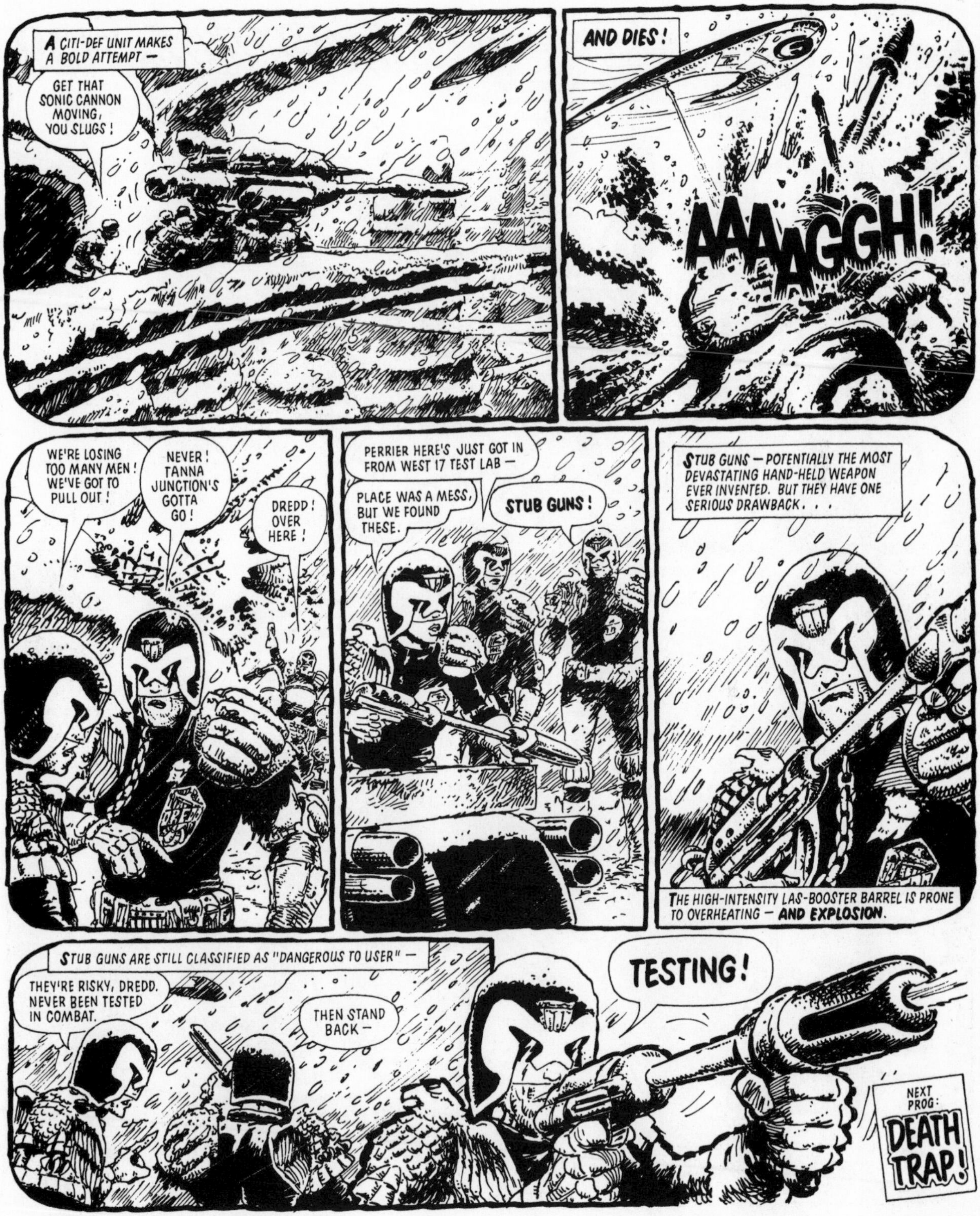
A CITI-DEF UNIT MAKES A BOLD ATTEMPT —
GET THAT SONIC CANNON MOVING, YOU SLUGS!
AND DIES!
AAAAGGH!
WE'RE LOSING TOO MANY MEN! WE'VE GOT TO PULL OUT!
NEVER! TANNA JUNCTION'S GOTTA GO!
DREDD! OVER HERE!
PERRIER HERE'S JUST GOT IN FROM WEST 17 TEST LAB —
PLACE WAS A MESS, BUT WE FOUND THESE.
STUB GUNS!
STUB GUNS — POTENTIALLY THE MOST DEVASTATING HAND-HELD WEAPON EVER INVENTED. BUT THEY HAVE ONE SERIOUS DRAWBACK...
THE HIGH-INTENSITY LAS-BOOSTER BARREL IS PRONE TO OVERHEATING — AND EXPLOSION.
STUB GUNS ARE STILL CLASSIFIED AS "DANGEROUS TO USER" —
THEY'RE RISKY, DREDD. NEVER BEEN TESTED IN COMBAT.
THEN STAND BACK —
TESTING!
NEXT PROG: DEATH TRAP!

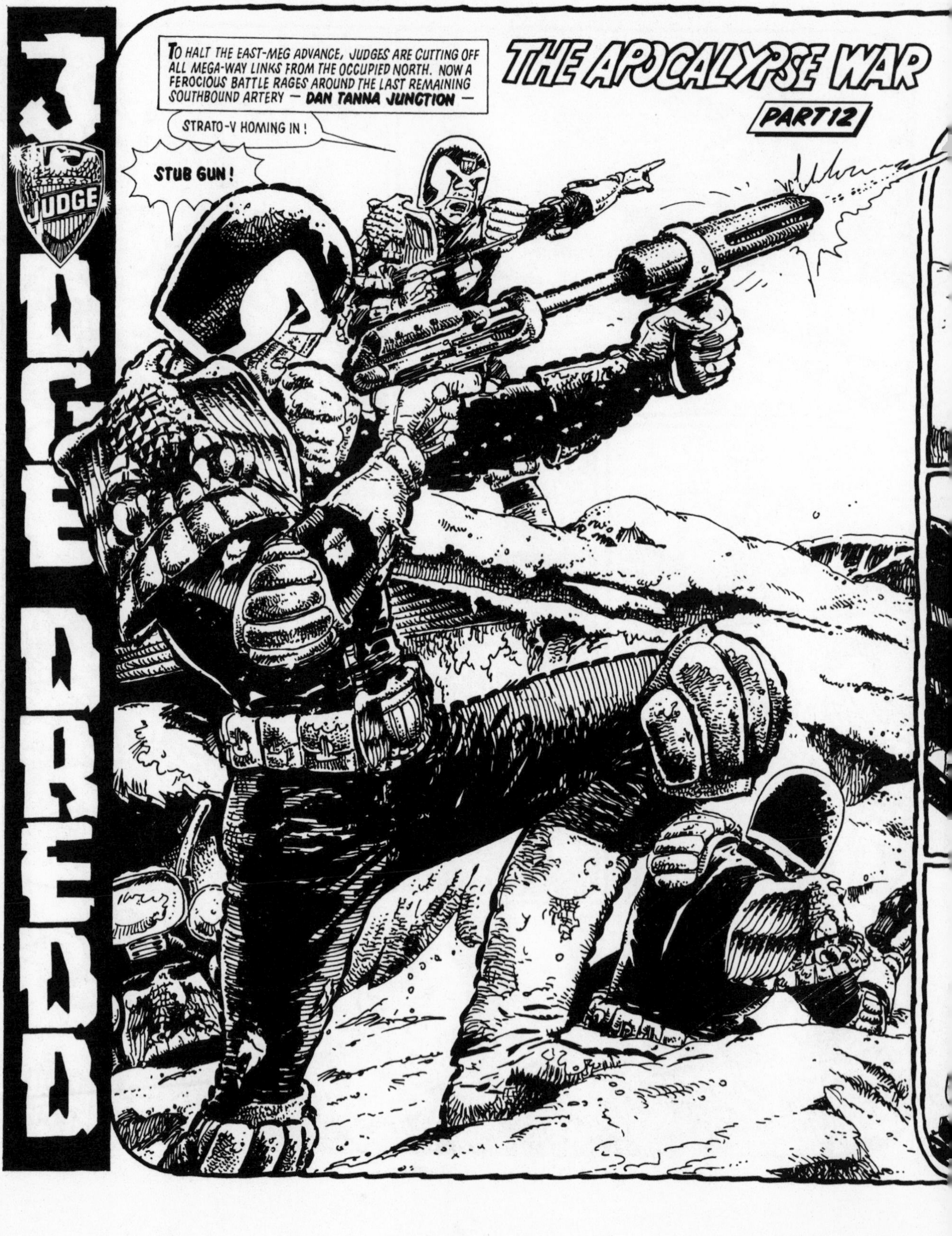
JUDGE DREDD
JUDGE
THE APOCALYPSE WAR
PART 12
TO HALT THE EAST-MEG ADVANCE, JUDGES ARE CUTTING OFF ALL MEGA-WAY LINKS FROM THE OCCUPIED NORTH. NOW A FEROCIOUS BATTLE RAGES AROUND THE LAST REMAINING SOUTHBOUND ARTERY — DAN TANNA JUNCTION —
STRATO-V HOMING IN!
STUB GUN!

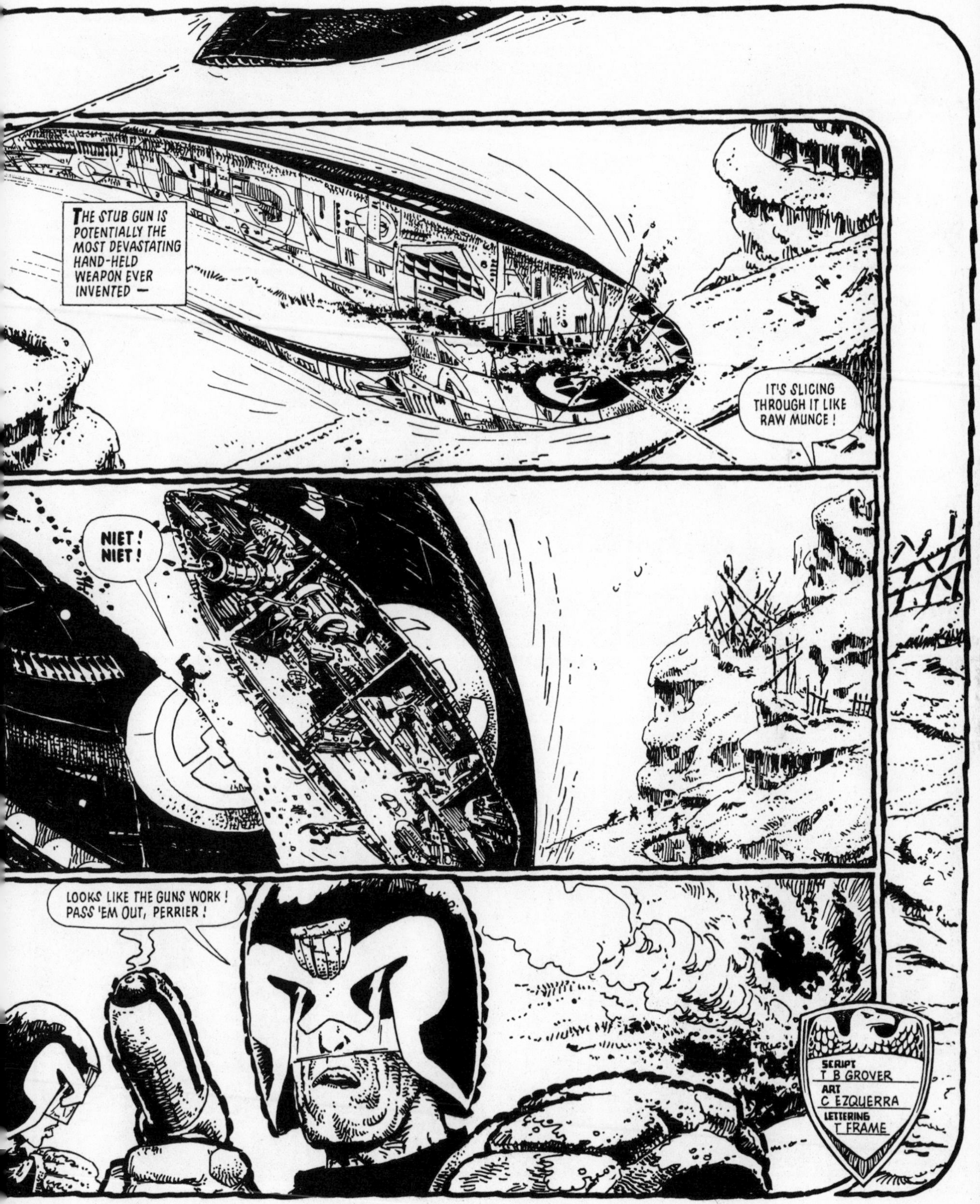
THE STUB GUN IS POTENTIALLY THE MOST DEVASTATING HAND-HELD WEAPON EVER INVENTED —
IT'S SLICING THROUGH IT LIKE RAW MUNCE !
NIET ! NIET !
LOOKS LIKE THE GUNS WORK ! PASS 'EM OUT, PERRIER !
SCRIPT T B GROVER
ART C EZQUERRA
LETTERING T FRAME

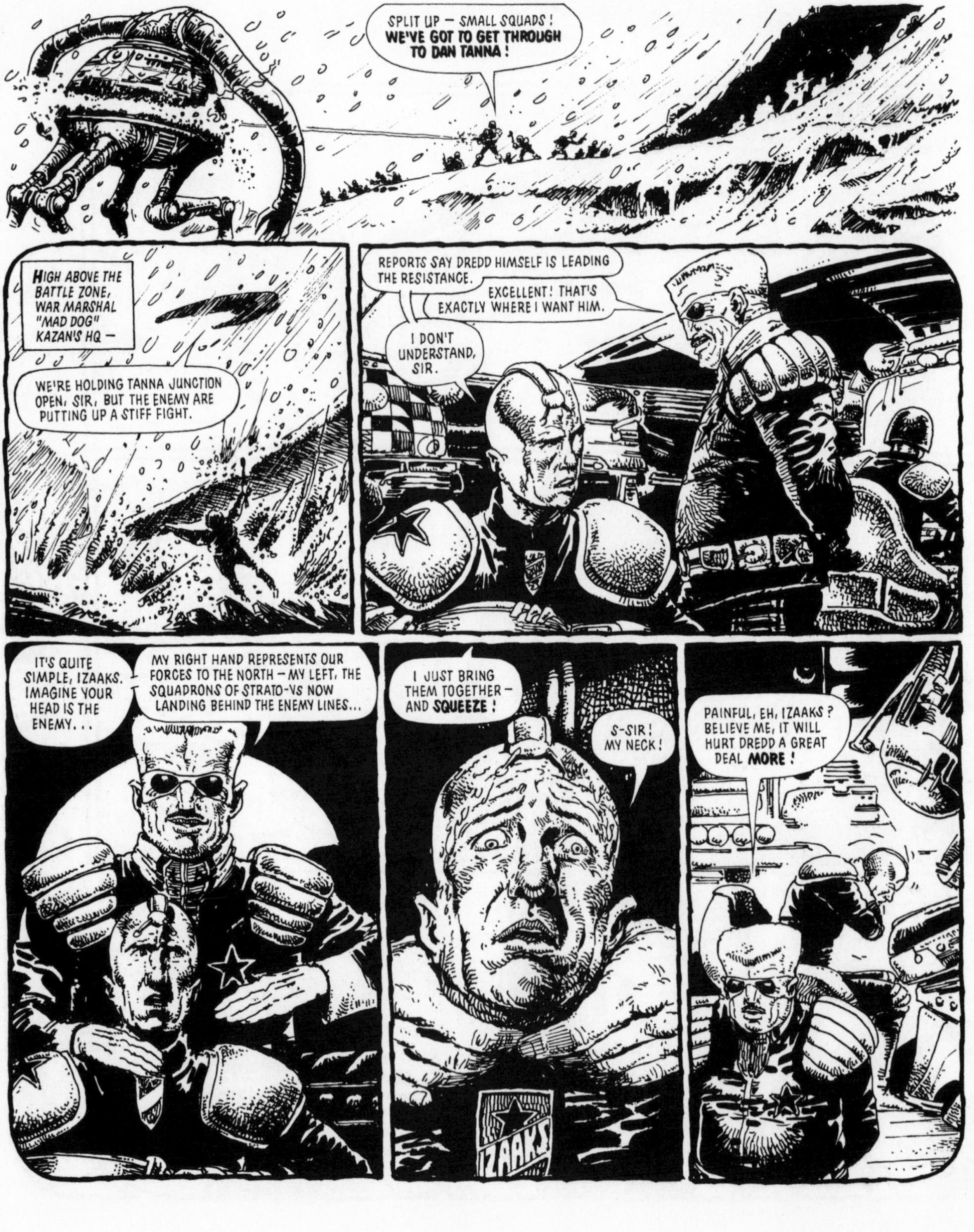

SPLIT UP — SMALL SQUADS! WE'VE GOT TO GET THROUGH TO DAN TANNA!
HIGH ABOVE THE BATTLE ZONE, WAR MARSHAL "MAD DOG" KAZAN'S HQ —
WE'RE HOLDING TANNA JUNCTION OPEN, SIR, BUT THE ENEMY ARE PUTTING UP A STIFF FIGHT.
REPORTS SAY DREDD HIMSELF IS LEADING THE RESISTANCE.
EXCELLENT! THAT'S EXACTLY WHERE I WANT HIM.
I DON'T UNDERSTAND, SIR.
IT'S QUITE SIMPLE, IZAAKS. IMAGINE YOUR HEAD IS THE ENEMY...
MY RIGHT HAND REPRESENTS OUR FORCES TO THE NORTH — MY LEFT, THE SQUADRONS OF STRATO-VS NOW LANDING BEHIND THE ENEMY LINES...
I JUST BRING THEM TOGETHER — AND SQUEEZE!
S-SIR! MY NECK!
IZAAKS
PAINFUL, EH, IZAAKS? BELIEVE ME, IT WILL HURT DREDD A GREAT DEAL MORE!

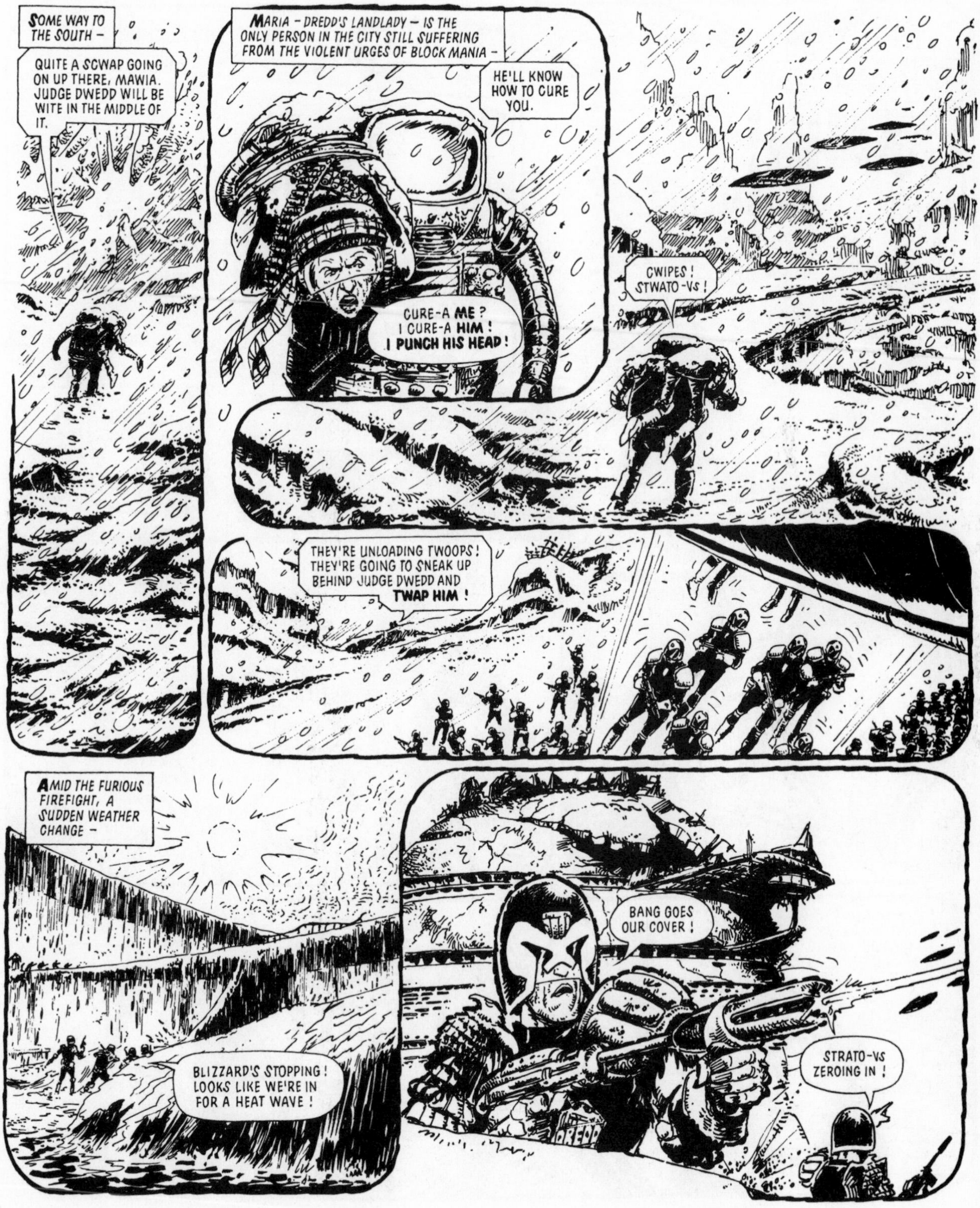
SOME WAY TO THE SOUTH –
QUITE A SCWAP GOING ON UP THERE, MAWIA. JUDGE DWEDD WILL BE WITE IN THE MIDDLE OF IT.
MARIA – DREDD'S LANDLADY – IS THE ONLY PERSON IN THE CITY STILL SUFFERING FROM THE VIOLENT URGES OF BLOCK MANIA –
HE'LL KNOW HOW TO CURE YOU.
CURE-A ME? I CURE-A HIM! I PUNCH HIS HEAD!
CWIPES! STWATO-VS!
THEY'RE UNLOADING TWOOPS! THEY'RE GOING TO SNEAK UP BEHIND JUDGE DWEDD AND TWAP HIM!
AMID THE FURIOUS FIREFIGHT, A SUDDEN WEATHER CHANGE –
BLIZZARD'S STOPPING! LOOKS LIKE WE'RE IN FOR A HEAT WAVE!
BANG GOES OUR COVER!
STRATO-VS ZEROING IN!

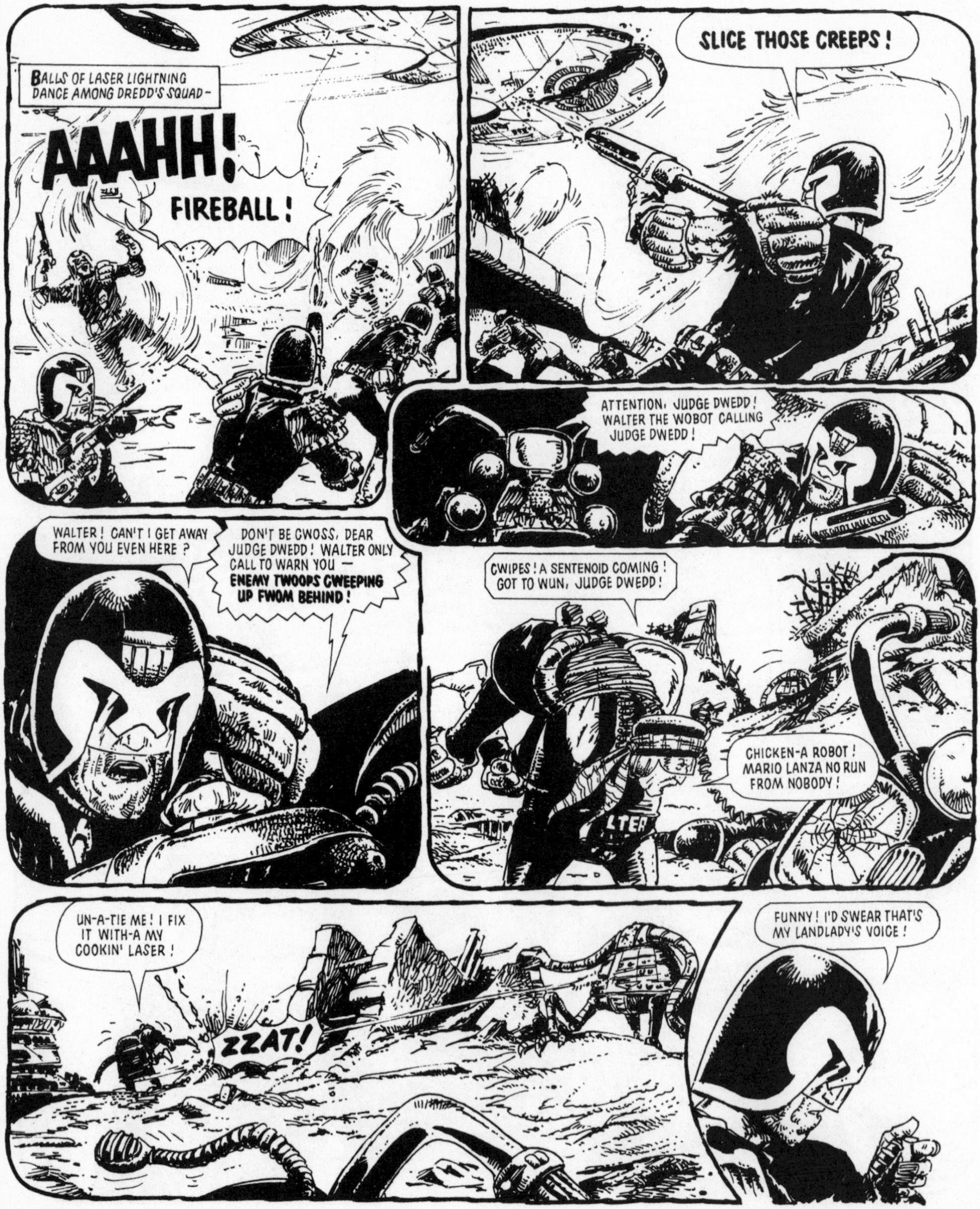
BALLS OF LASER LIGHTNING DANCE AMONG DREDD'S SQUAD –
AAAHH!
FIREBALL!
SLICE THOSE CREEPS!
ATTENTION, JUDGE DWEDD! WALTER THE WOBOT CALLING JUDGE DWEDD!
WALTER! CAN'T I GET AWAY FROM YOU EVEN HERE?
DON'T BE GWOSS, DEAR JUDGE DWEDD! WALTER ONLY CALL TO WARN YOU – ENEMY TWOOPS GWEEPING UP FWOM BEHIND!
CWIPES! A SENTENOID COMING! GOT TO WUN, JUDGE DWEDD!
CHICKEN-A ROBOT! MARIO LANZA NO RUN FROM NOBODY!
UN-A-TIE ME! I FIX IT WITH-A MY COOKIN' LASER!
ZZAT!
FUNNY! I'D SWEAR THAT'S MY LANDLADY'S VOICE!

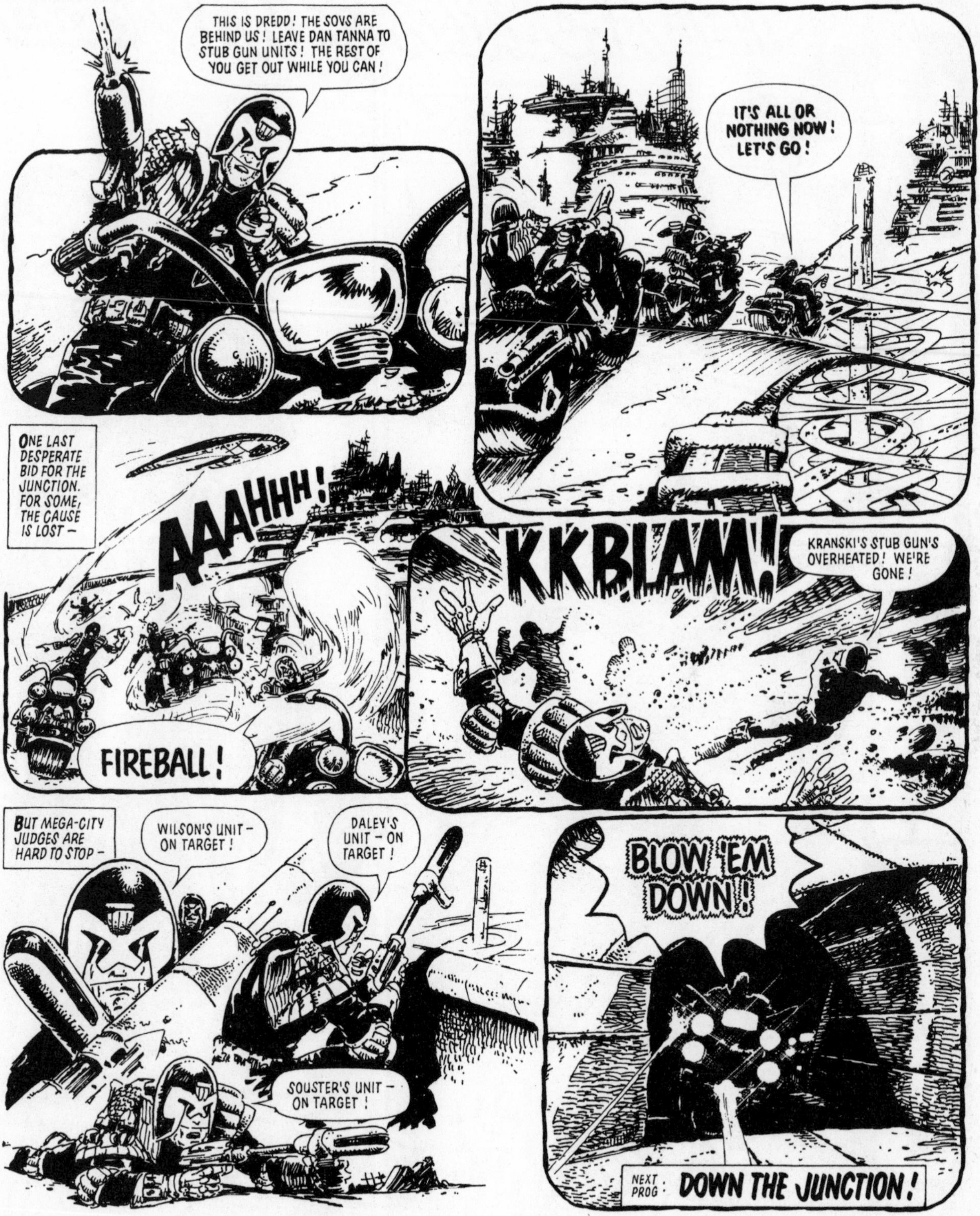

THIS IS DREDD! THE SOVS ARE BEHIND US! LEAVE DAN TANNA TO STUB GUN UNITS! THE REST OF YOU GET OUT WHILE YOU CAN!
IT'S ALL OR NOTHING NOW! LET'S GO!
ONE LAST DESPERATE BID FOR THE JUNCTION. FOR SOME, THE CAUSE IS LOST –
AAAHHH!
FIREBALL!
KKBLAM!
KRANSKI'S STUB GUN'S OVERHEATED! WE'RE GONE!
BUT MEGA-CITY JUDGES ARE HARD TO STOP –
WILSON'S UNIT – ON TARGET!
DALEY'S UNIT – ON TARGET!
SOUSTER'S UNIT – ON TARGET!
BLOW 'EM DOWN!
NEXT PROG: DOWN THE JUNCTION!

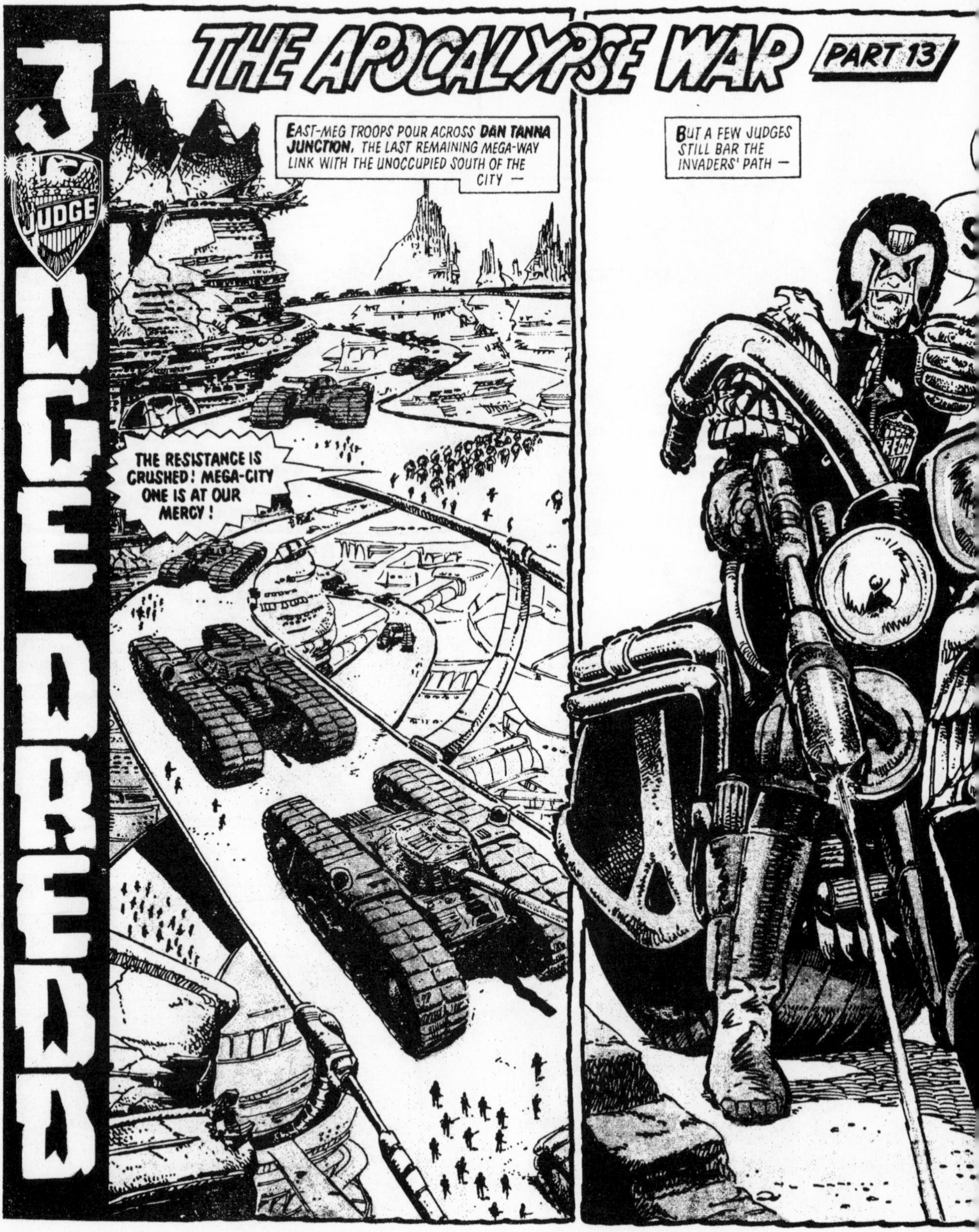
JUDGE DREDD
THE APOCALYPSE WAR
PART 13
EAST-MEG TROOPS POUR ACROSS DAN TANNA JUNCTION, THE LAST REMAINING MEGA-WAY LINK WITH THE UNOCCUPIED SOUTH OF THE CITY —
THE RESISTANCE IS CRUSHED! MEGA-CITY ONE IS AT OUR MERCY!
BUT A FEW JUDGES STILL BAR THE INVADERS' PATH —

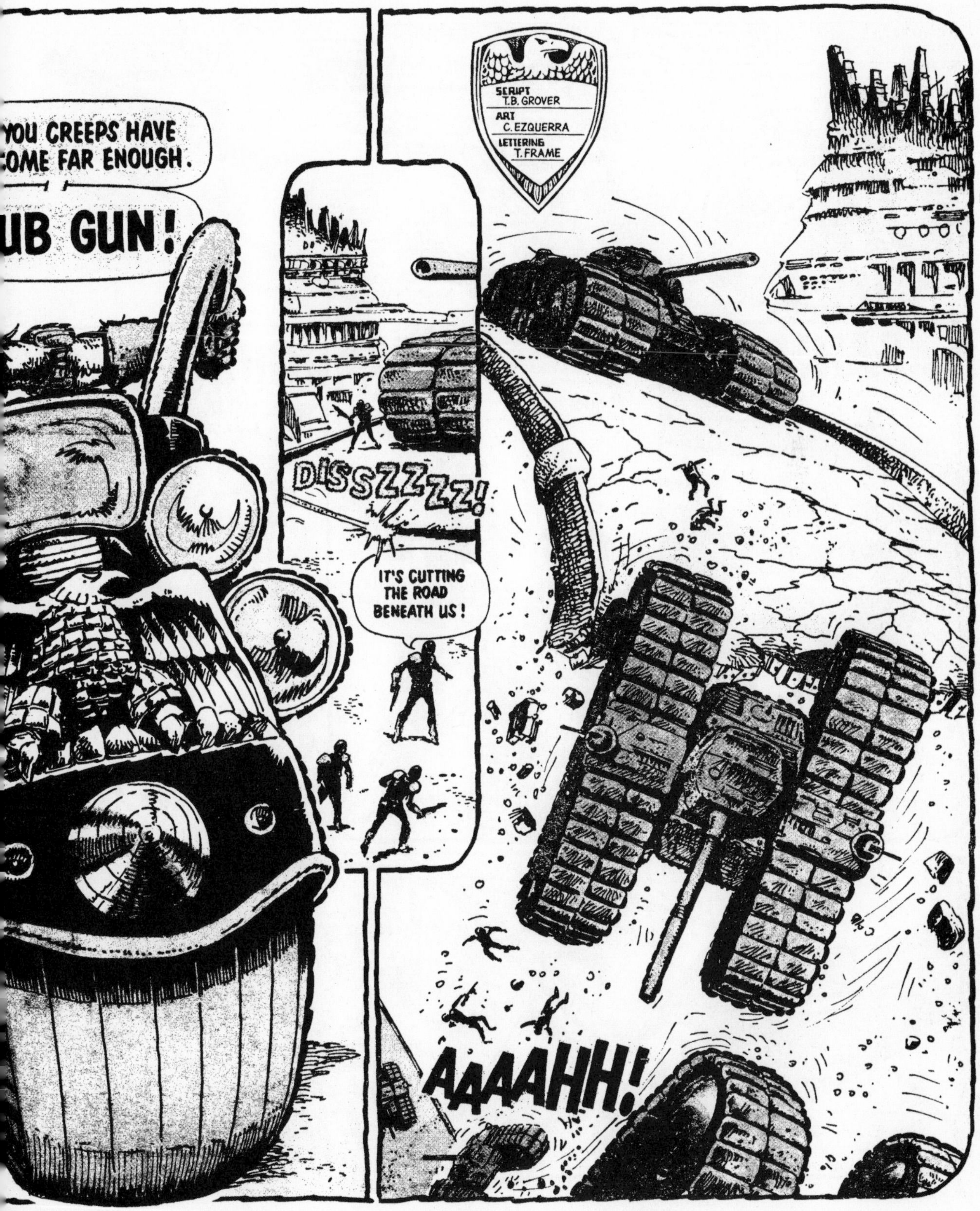
YOU CREEPS HAVE
COME FAR ENOUGH.
UB GUN!
SCRIPT T.B. GROVER
ART C. EZQUERRA
LETTERING T. FRAME
DISSZZZZZ!
IT'S CUTTING THE ROAD BENEATH US!
AAAAHH!

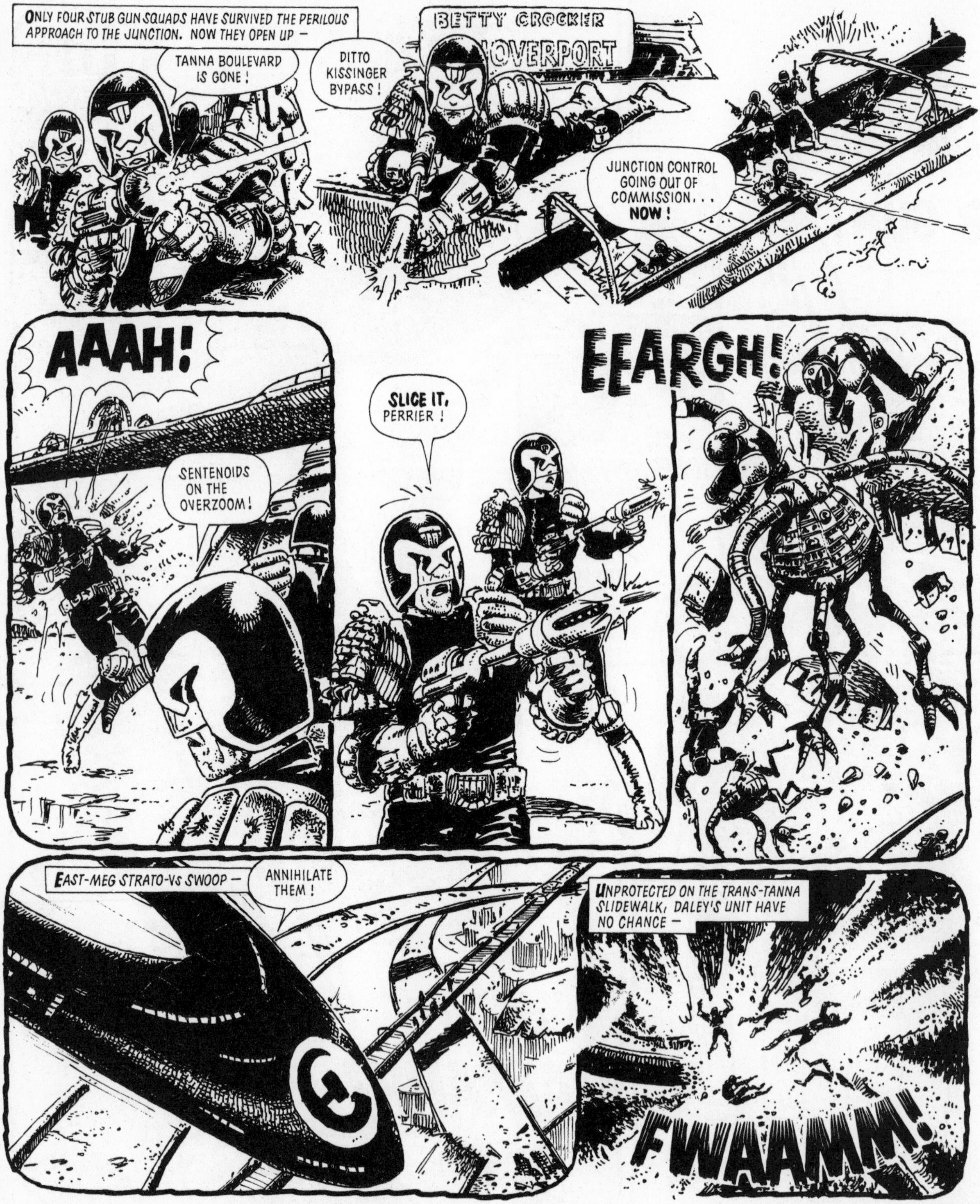
ONLY FOUR STUB GUN SQUADS HAVE SURVIVED THE PERILOUS APPROACH TO THE JUNCTION. NOW THEY OPEN UP –
TANNA BOULEVARD IS GONE!
BETTY CROCKER
HOVERPORT
DITTO KISSINGER BYPASS!
JUNCTION CONTROL GOING OUT OF COMMISSION... NOW!
AAAH!
SENTENOIDS ON THE OVERZOOM!
SLICE IT, PERRIER!
EEARGH!
EAST-MEG STRATO-Vs SWOOP –
ANNIHILATE THEM!
UNPROTECTED ON THE TRANS-TANNA SLIDEWALK, DALEY'S UNIT HAVE NO CHANCE –
FWAAMM!

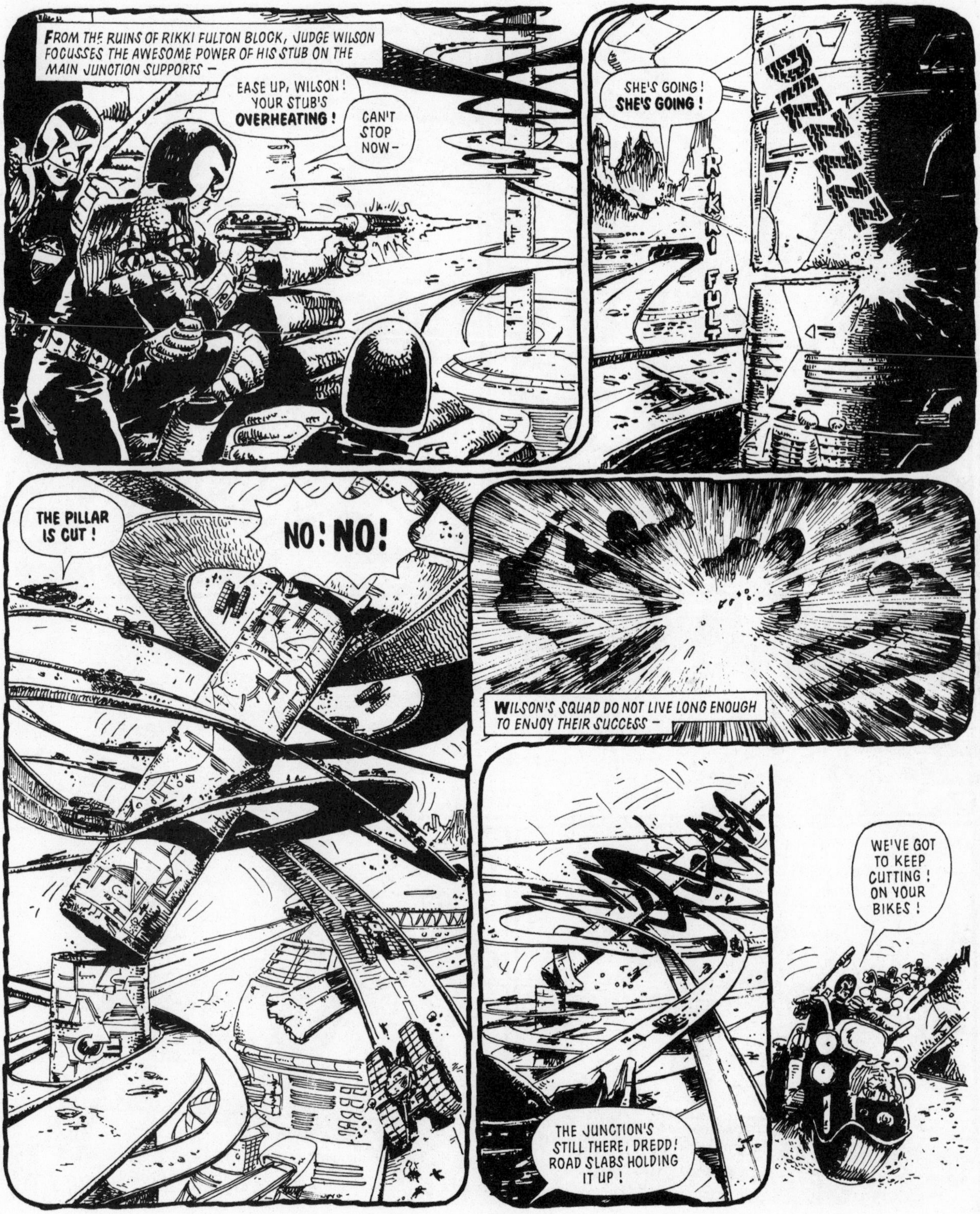
FROM THE RUINS OF RIKKI FULTON BLOCK, JUDGE WILSON FOCUSSES THE AWESOME POWER OF HIS STUB ON THE MAIN JUNCTION SUPPORTS –
EASE UP, WILSON! YOUR STUB'S OVERHEATING!
CAN'T STOP NOW–
SHE'S GOING! SHE'S GOING!
RIKKI FULT
THE PILLAR IS CUT!
NO! NO!
WILSON'S SQUAD DO NOT LIVE LONG ENOUGH TO ENJOY THEIR SUCCESS –
THE JUNCTION'S STILL THERE, DREDD! ROAD SLABS HOLDING IT UP!
WE'VE GOT TO KEEP CUTTING! ON YOUR BIKES!

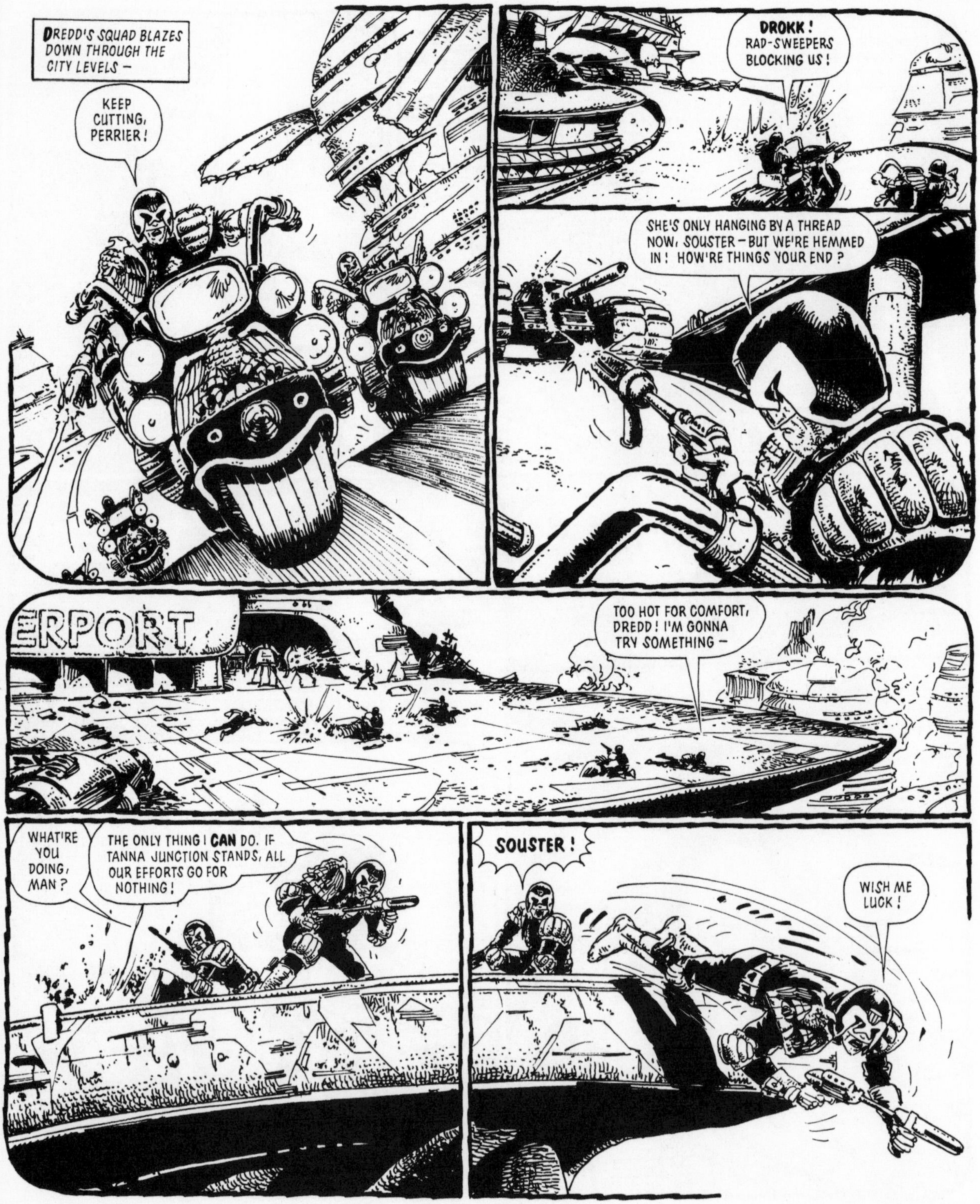
DREDD'S SQUAD BLAZES DOWN THROUGH THE CITY LEVELS –
KEEP CUTTING, PERRIER!
DROKK! RAD-SWEEPERS BLOCKING US!
SHE'S ONLY HANGING BY A THREAD NOW, SOUSTER – BUT WE'RE HEMMED IN! HOW'RE THINGS YOUR END?
ERPORT
TOO HOT FOR COMFORT, DREDD! I'M GONNA TRY SOMETHING –
WHAT'RE YOU DOING, MAN?
THE ONLY THING I CAN DO. IF TANNA JUNCTION STANDS, ALL OUR EFFORTS GO FOR NOTHING!
SOUSTER!
WISH ME LUCK!

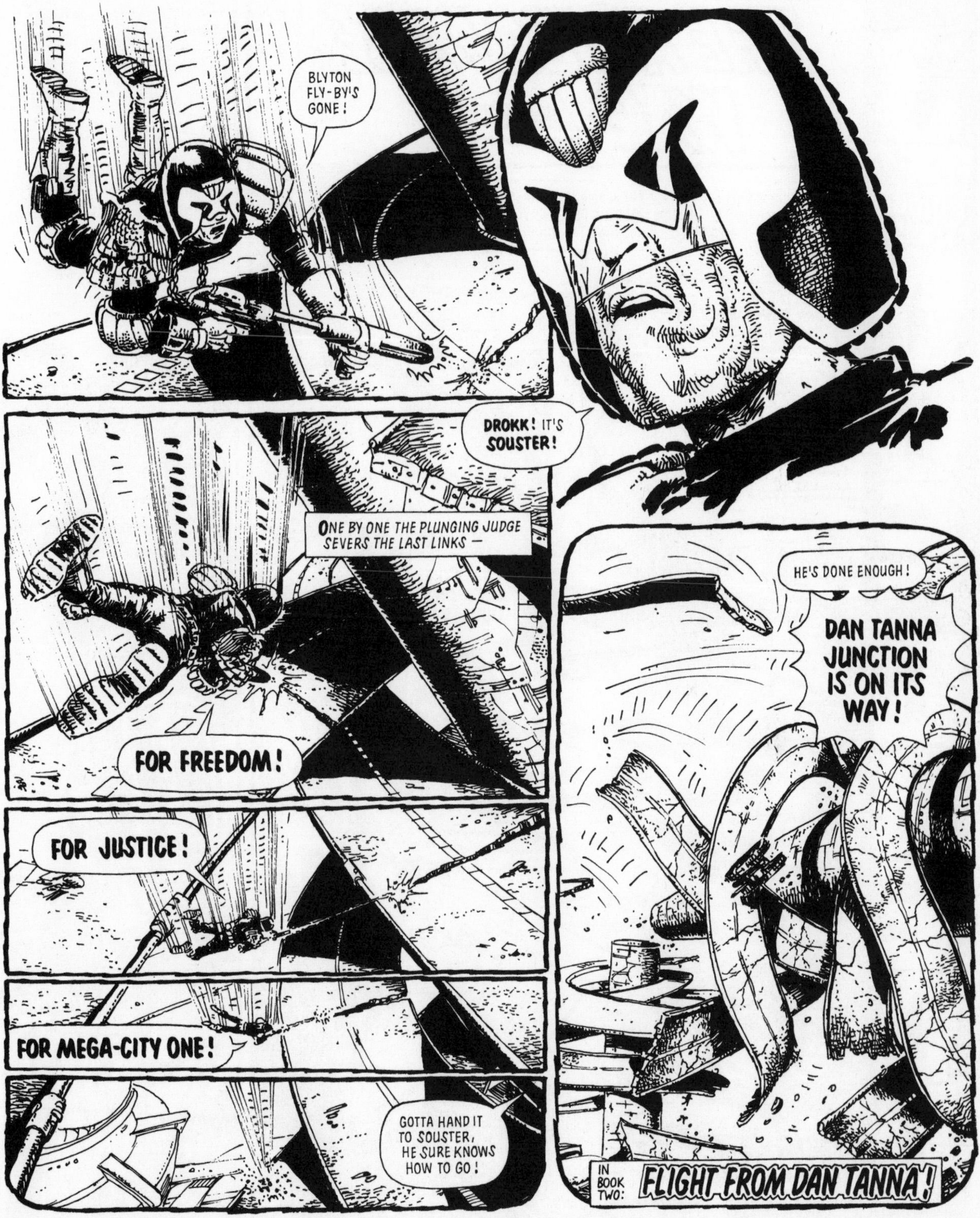
BLYTON FLY-BY'S GONE!
DROKK! IT'S SOUSTER!
ONE BY ONE THE PLUNGING JUDGE SEVERS THE LAST LINKS —
FOR FREEDOM!
FOR JUSTICE!
FOR MEGA-CITY ONE!
GOTTA HAND IT TO SOUSTER, HE SURE KNOWS HOW TO GO!
HE'S DONE ENOUGH!
DAN TANNA JUNCTION IS ON ITS WAY!
IN BOOK TWO: FLIGHT FROM DAN TANNA!

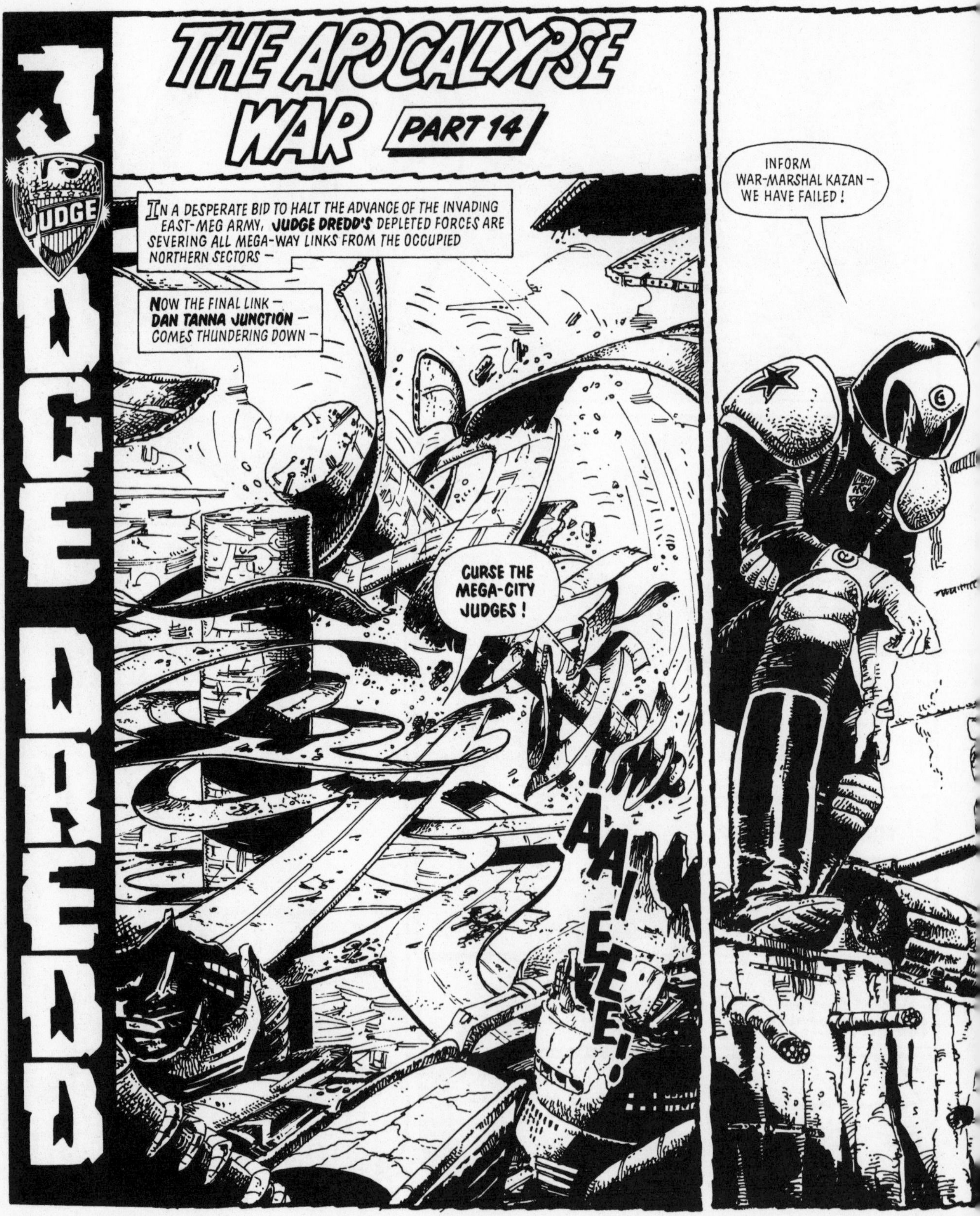
JUDGE DREDD
THE APOCALYPSE WAR
PART 14
IN A DESPERATE BID TO HALT THE ADVANCE OF THE INVADING EAST-MEG ARMY, JUDGE DREDD'S DEPLETED FORCES ARE SEVERING ALL MEGA-WAY LINKS FROM THE OCCUPIED NORTHERN SECTORS –
NOW THE FINAL LINK – DAN TANNA JUNCTION – COMES THUNDERING DOWN –
CURSE THE MEGA-CITY JUDGES!
AAIEEE!
INFORM WAR-MARSHAL KAZAN – WE HAVE FAILED!

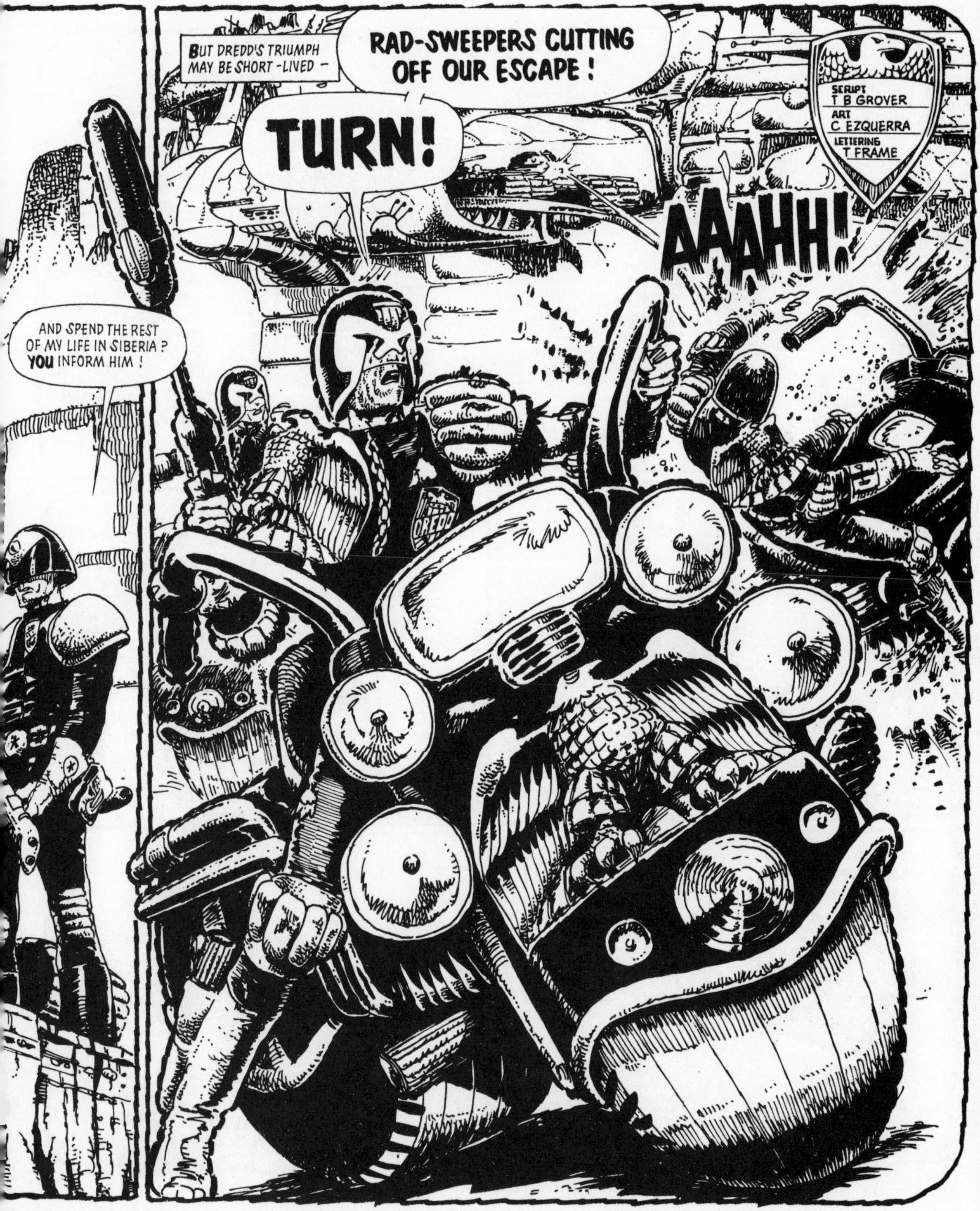

AND SPEND THE REST OF MY LIFE IN SIBERIA ? YOU INFORM HIM !
BUT DREDD'S TRIUMPH MAY BE SHORT -LIVED -
RAD-SWEEPERS CUTTING OFF OUR ESCAPE !
TURN!
SCRIPT T B GROVER
ART C. EZQUERRA
LETTERING T FRAME
AAAHH!

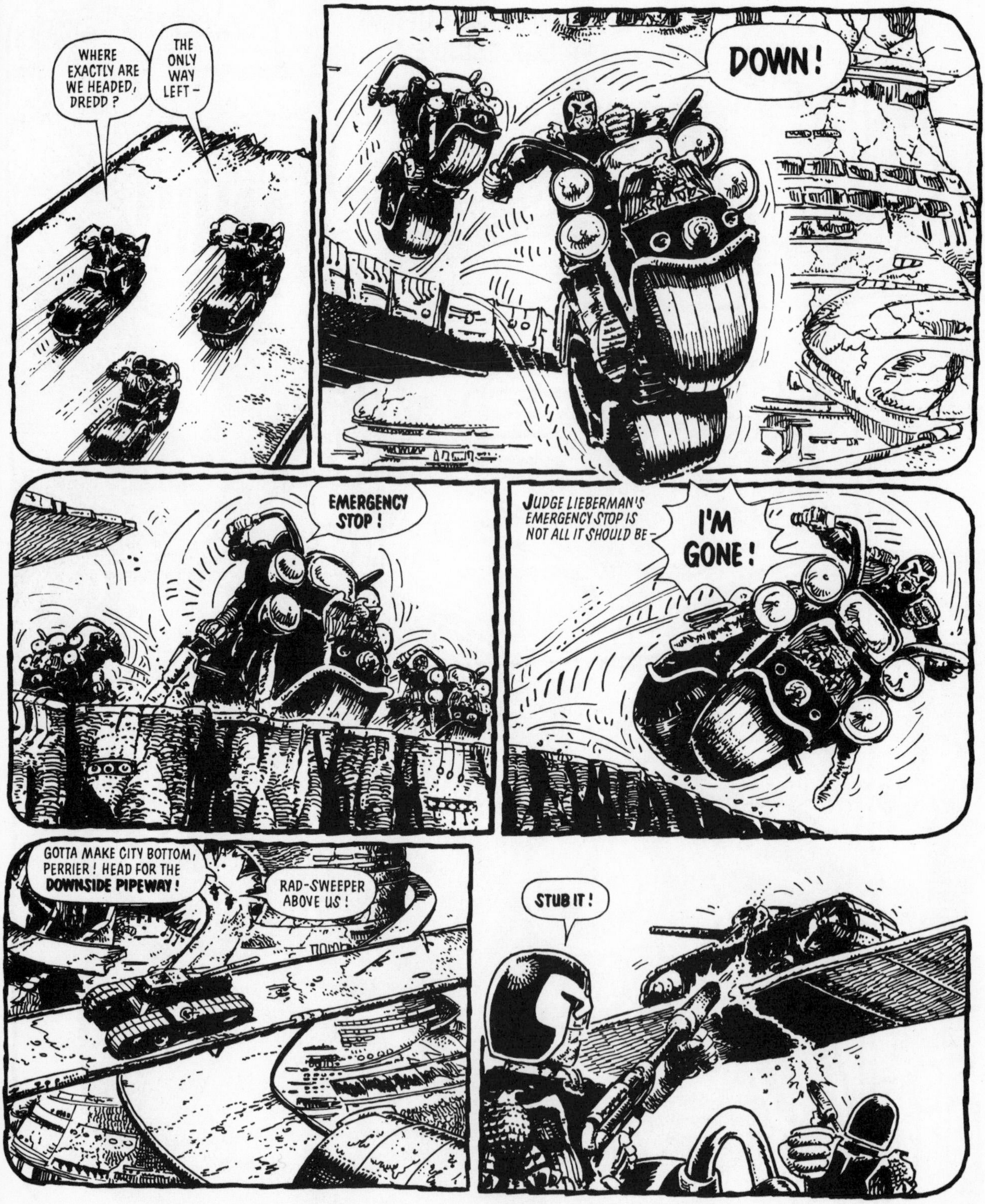
WHERE EXACTLY ARE WE HEADED, DREDD?
THE ONLY WAY LEFT—
DOWN!
EMERGENCY STOP!
JUDGE LIEBERMAN'S EMERGENCY STOP IS NOT ALL IT SHOULD BE—
I'M GONE!
GOTTA MAKE CITY BOTTOM, PERRIER! HEAD FOR THE DOWNSIDE PIPEWAY!
RAD-SWEEPER ABOVE US!
STUB IT!

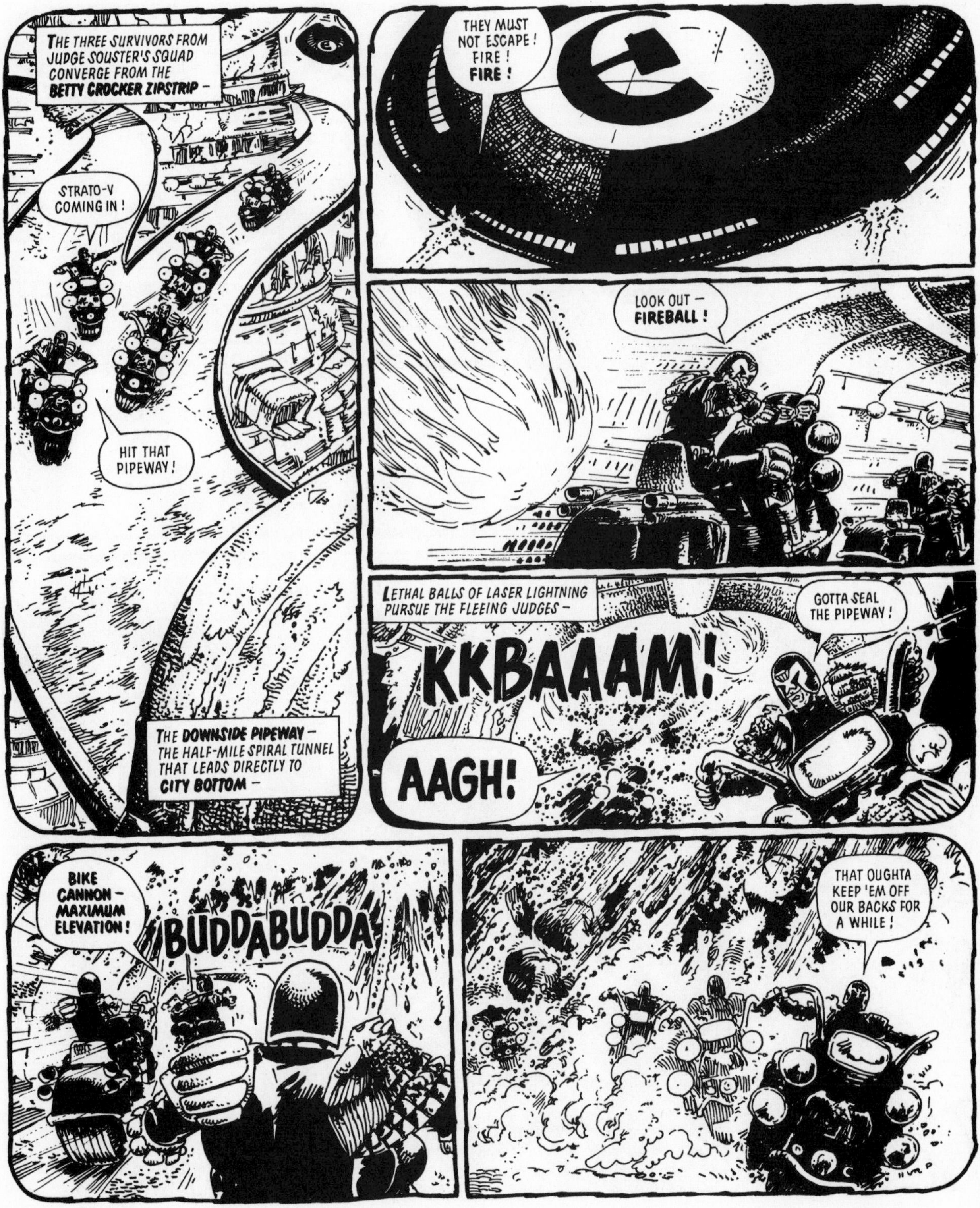
THE THREE SURVIVORS FROM JUDGE SOUSTER'S SQUAD CONVERGE FROM THE BETTY CROCKER ZIPSTRIP –
STRATO-V COMING IN !
HIT THAT PIPEWAY !
THE DOWNSIDE PIPEWAY – THE HALF-MILE SPIRAL TUNNEL THAT LEADS DIRECTLY TO CITY BOTTOM –
THEY MUST NOT ESCAPE ! FIRE ! FIRE !
LOOK OUT – FIREBALL !
LETHAL BALLS OF LASER LIGHTNING PURSUE THE FLEEING JUDGES –
GOTTA SEAL THE PIPEWAY !
KKBAAAM!
AAGH!
BIKE CANNON – MAXIMUM ELEVATION !
BUDDABUDDA
THAT OUGHTA KEEP 'EM OFF OUR BACKS FOR A WHILE !

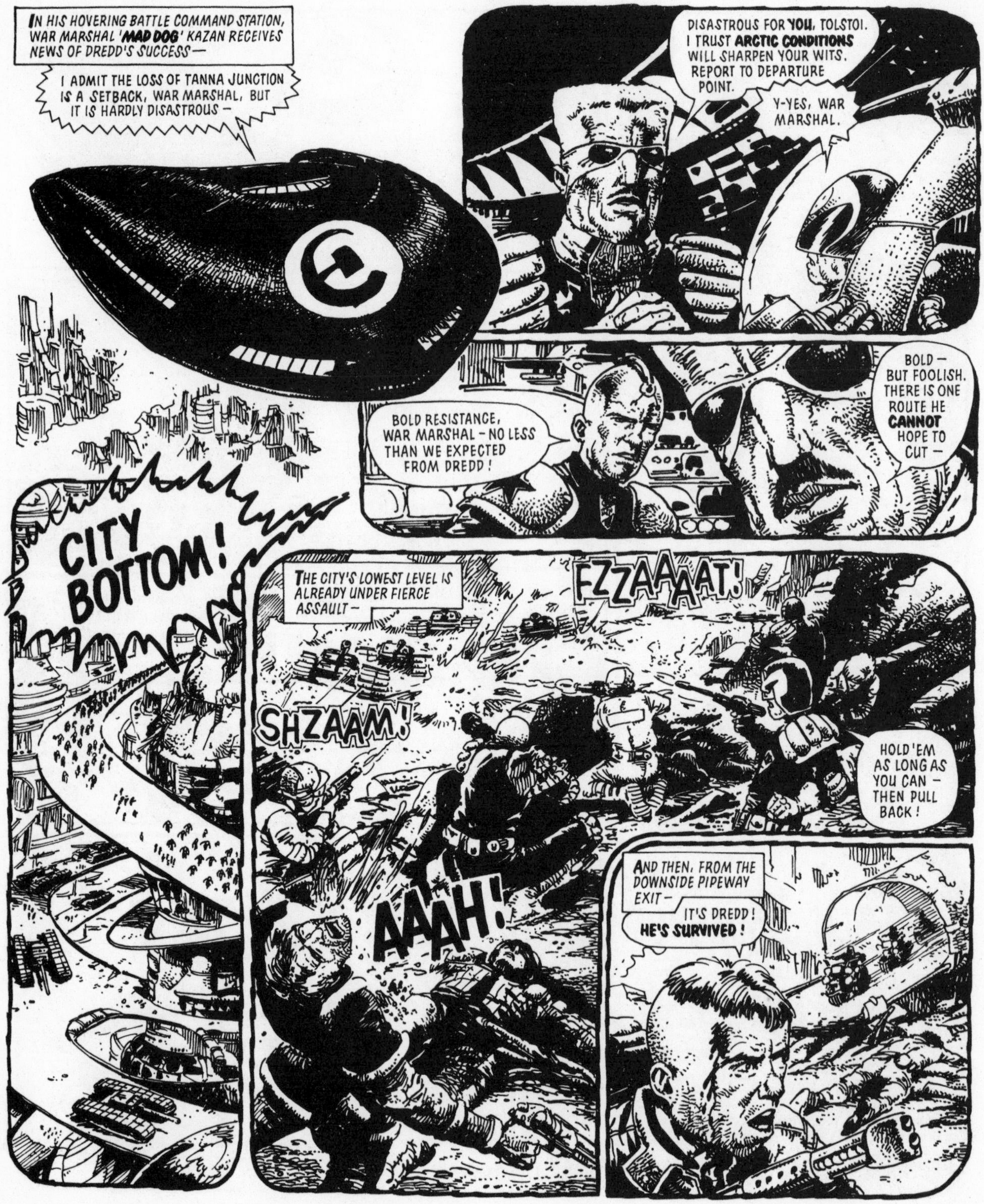
IN HIS HOVERING BATTLE COMMAND STATION, WAR MARSHAL 'MAD DOG' KAZAN RECEIVES NEWS OF DREDD'S SUCCESS—
I ADMIT THE LOSS OF TANNA JUNCTION IS A SETBACK, WAR MARSHAL, BUT IT IS HARDLY DISASTROUS—
DISASTROUS FOR YOU, TOLSTOI. I TRUST ARCTIC CONDITIONS WILL SHARPEN YOUR WITS. REPORT TO DEPARTURE POINT.
Y-YES, WAR MARSHAL.
BOLD RESISTANCE, WAR MARSHAL—NO LESS THAN WE EXPECTED FROM DREDD!
BOLD—BUT FOOLISH. THERE IS ONE ROUTE HE CANNOT HOPE TO CUT—
CITY BOTTOM!
THE CITY'S LOWEST LEVEL IS ALREADY UNDER FIERCE ASSAULT—
FZZAAAAT!
SHZAAM!
HOLD 'EM AS LONG AS YOU CAN—THEN PULL BACK!
AAAH!
AND THEN, FROM THE DOWNSIDE PIPEWAY EXIT—
IT'S DREDD! HE'S SURVIVED!

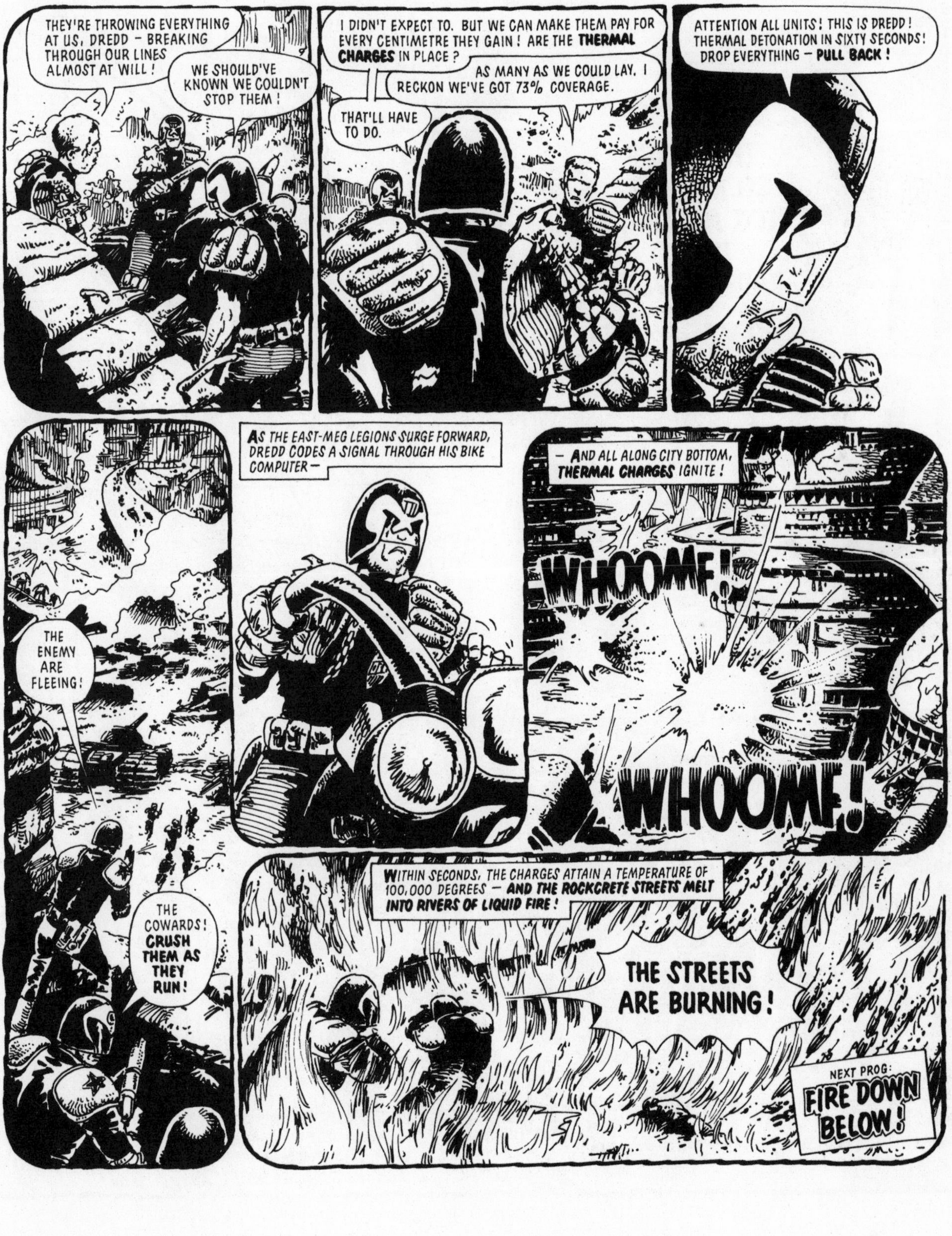

THEY'RE THROWING EVERYTHING AT US, DREDD – BREAKING THROUGH OUR LINES ALMOST AT WILL!
WE SHOULD'VE KNOWN WE COULDN'T STOP THEM!
I DIDN'T EXPECT TO. BUT WE CAN MAKE THEM PAY FOR EVERY CENTIMETRE THEY GAIN! ARE THE THERMAL CHARGES IN PLACE?
AS MANY AS WE COULD LAY. I RECKON WE'VE GOT 73% COVERAGE.
THAT'LL HAVE TO DO.
ATTENTION ALL UNITS! THIS IS DREDD! THERMAL DETONATION IN SIXTY SECONDS! DROP EVERYTHING – PULL BACK!
THE ENEMY ARE FLEEING!
THE COWARDS! CRUSH THEM AS THEY RUN!
AS THE EAST-MEG LEGIONS SURGE FORWARD, DREDD CODES A SIGNAL THROUGH HIS BIKE COMPUTER –
– AND ALL ALONG CITY BOTTOM, THERMAL CHARGES IGNITE!
WHOOMF!
WHOOMF!
WITHIN SECONDS, THE CHARGES ATTAIN A TEMPERATURE OF 100,000 DEGREES – AND THE ROCKCRETE STREETS MELT INTO RIVERS OF LIQUID FIRE!
THE STREETS ARE BURNING!
NEXT PROG:
FIRE DOWN BELOW!

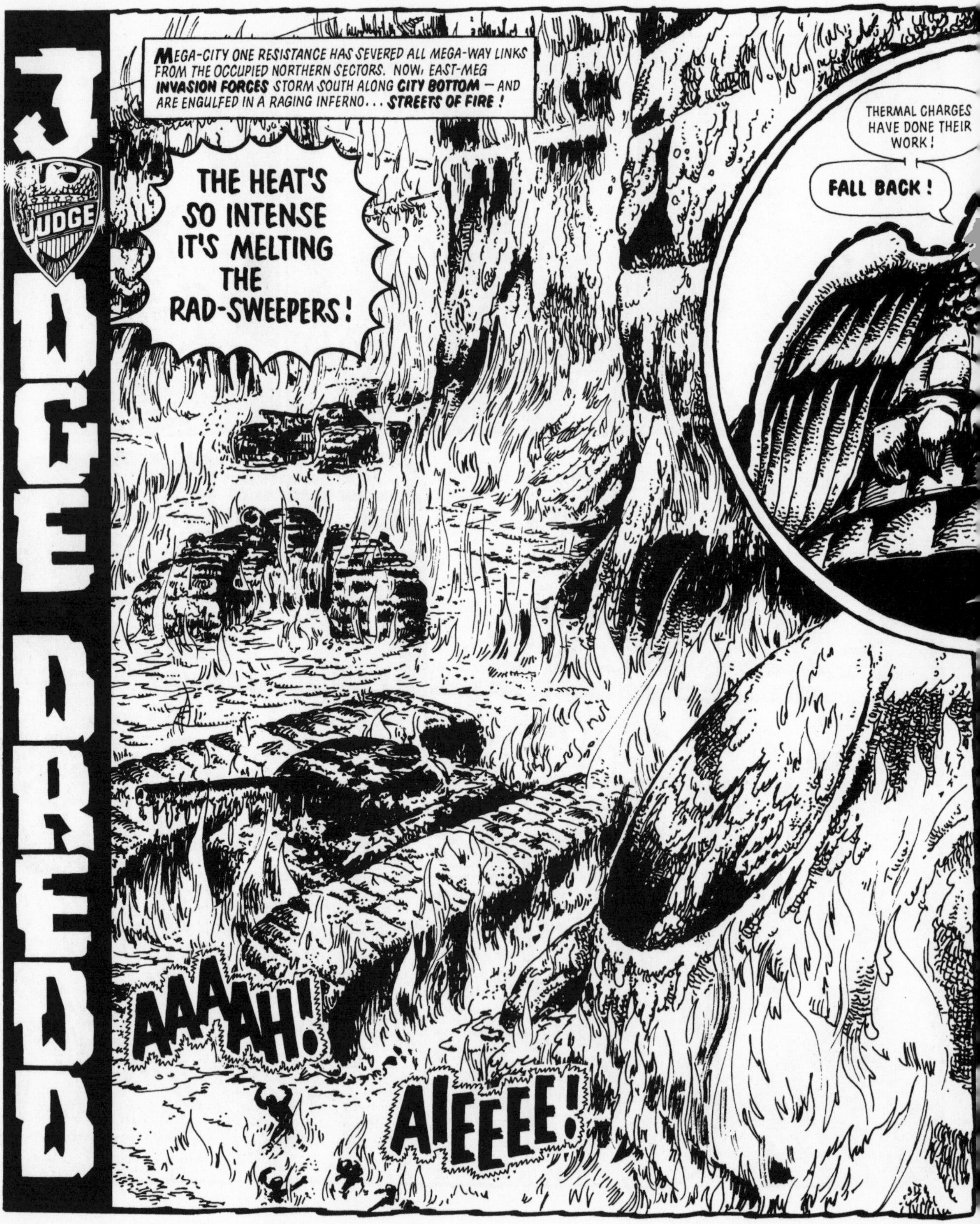
JUDGE DREDD
JUDGE
MEGA-CITY ONE RESISTANCE HAS SEVERED ALL MEGA-WAY LINKS FROM THE OCCUPIED NORTHERN SECTORS. NOW, EAST-MEG INVASION FORCES STORM SOUTH ALONG CITY BOTTOM — AND ARE ENGULFED IN A RAGING INFERNO... STREETS OF FIRE!
THE HEAT'S SO INTENSE IT'S MELTING THE RAD-SWEEPERS!
THERMAL CHARGES HAVE DONE THEIR WORK!
FALL BACK!
AAAAH!
AIEEEE!

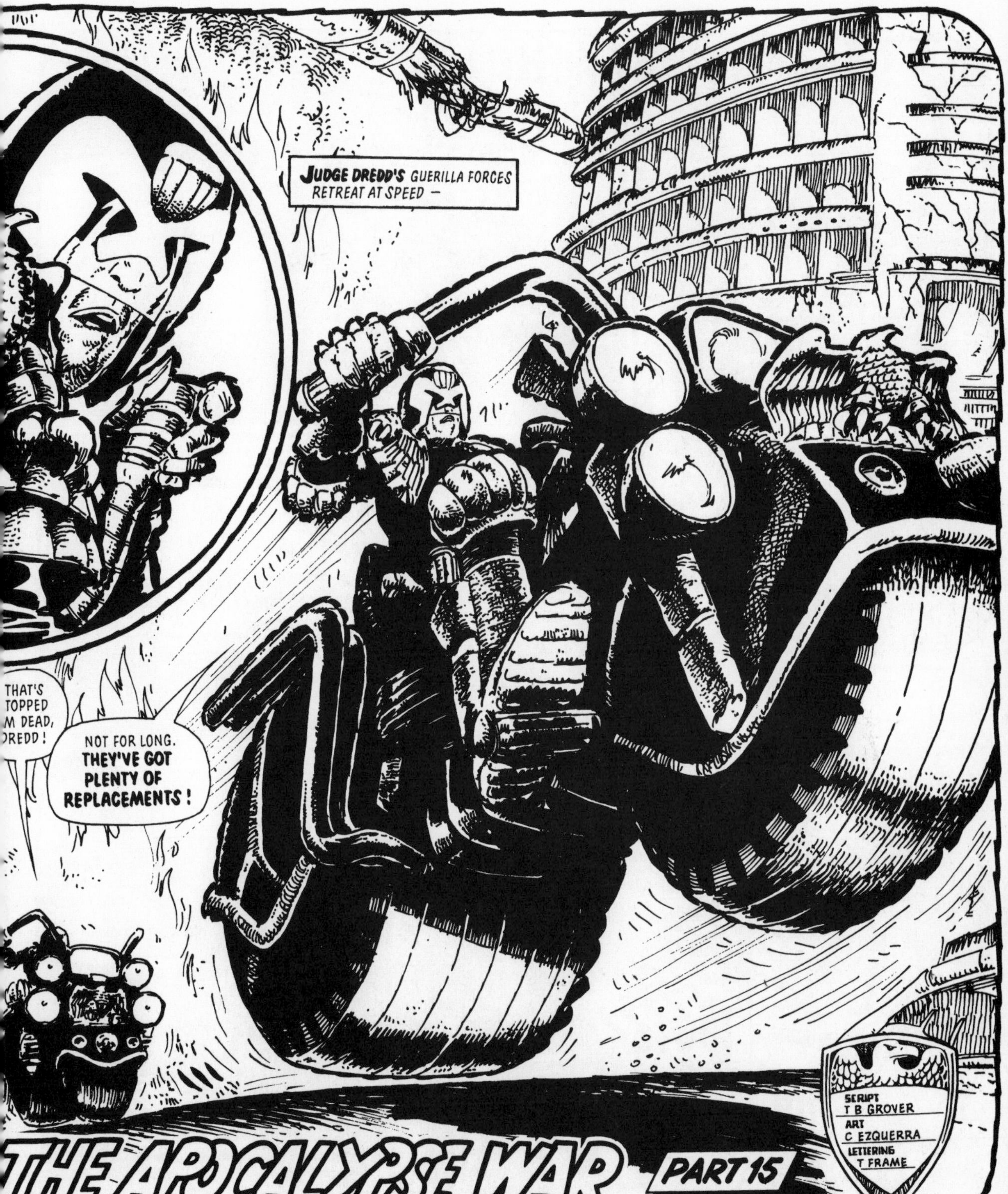
JUDGE DREDD'S GUERILLA FORCES RETREAT AT SPEED –
THAT'S TOPPED M DEAD, REDD!
NOT FOR LONG. THEY'VE GOT PLENTY OF REPLACEMENTS!
THE APOCALYPSE WAR PART 15
SCRIPT T B GROVER
ART C EZQUERRA
LETTERING T FRAME

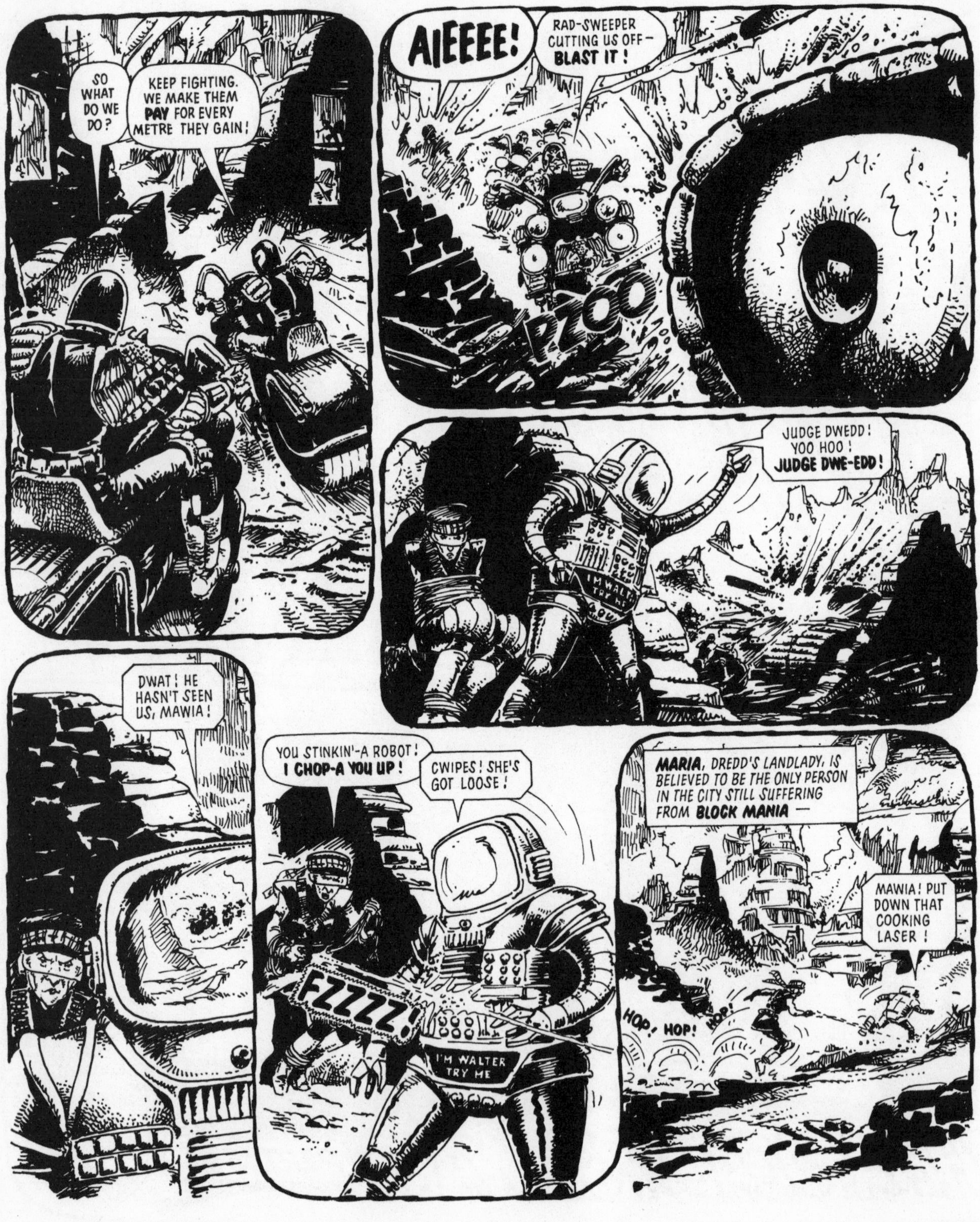

SO WHAT DO WE DO?
KEEP FIGHTING. WE MAKE THEM PAY FOR EVERY METRE THEY GAIN!
AIEEEE!
RAD-SWEEPER CUTTING US OFF- BLAST IT!
PZOO
JUDGE DWEDD! YOO HOO! JUDGE DWE-EDD!
DWAT! HE HASN'T SEEN US, MAWIA!
YOU STINKIN'-A ROBOT! I CHOP-A YOU UP!
CWIPES! SHE'S GOT LOOSE!
FZZZZ!
I'M WALTER TRY ME
MARIA, DREDD'S LANDLADY, IS BELIEVED TO BE THE ONLY PERSON IN THE CITY STILL SUFFERING FROM BLOCK MANIA —
MAWIA! PUT DOWN THAT COOKING LASER!
HOP, HOP! HOP!

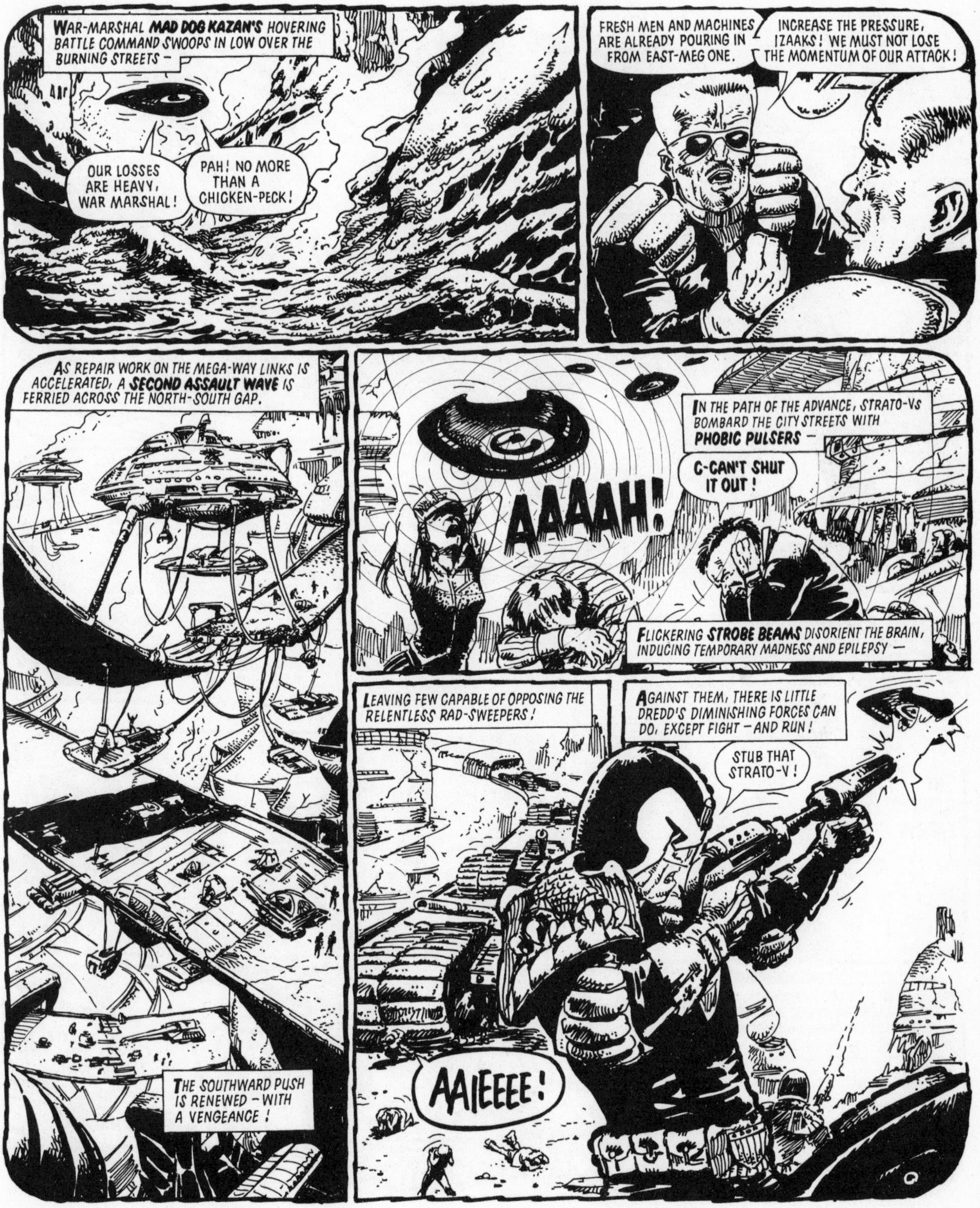

WAR-MARSHAL MAD DOG KAZAN'S HOVERING BATTLE COMMAND SWOOPS IN LOW OVER THE BURNING STREETS –
OUR LOSSES ARE HEAVY, WAR MARSHAL!
PAH! NO MORE THAN A CHICKEN-PECK!
FRESH MEN AND MACHINES ARE ALREADY POURING IN FROM EAST-MEG ONE.
INCREASE THE PRESSURE, IZAAKS! WE MUST NOT LOSE THE MOMENTUM OF OUR ATTACK!
AS REPAIR WORK ON THE MEGA-WAY LINKS IS ACCELERATED, A SECOND ASSAULT WAVE IS FERRIED ACROSS THE NORTH-SOUTH GAP.
THE SOUTHWARD PUSH IS RENEWED – WITH A VENGEANCE!
IN THE PATH OF THE ADVANCE, STRATO-VS BOMBARD THE CITY STREETS WITH PHOBIC PULSERS –
C-CAN'T SHUT IT OUT!
AAAAH!
FLICKERING STROBE BEAMS DISORIENT THE BRAIN, INDUCING TEMPORARY MADNESS AND EPILEPSY –
LEAVING FEW CAPABLE OF OPPOSING THE RELENTLESS RAD-SWEEPERS!
AGAINST THEM, THERE IS LITTLE DREDD'S DIMINISHING FORCES CAN DO, EXCEPT FIGHT – AND RUN!
STUB THAT STRATO-V!
AAIEEEE!

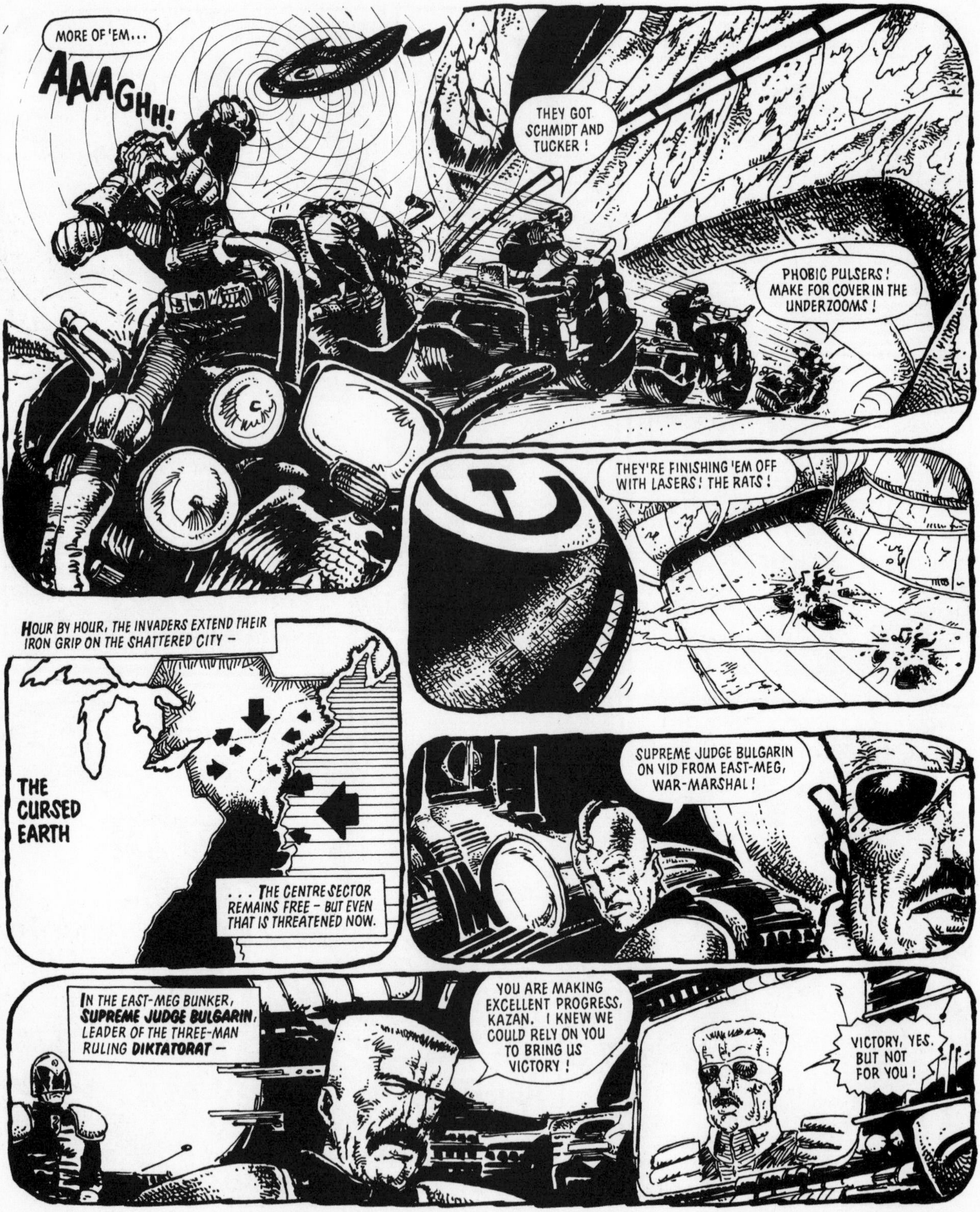

MORE OF 'EM...
AAAGHH!
THEY GOT SCHMIDT AND TUCKER !
PHOBIC PULSERS ! MAKE FOR COVER IN THE UNDERZOOMS !
THEY'RE FINISHING 'EM OFF WITH LASERS ! THE RATS !
HOUR BY HOUR, THE INVADERS EXTEND THEIR IRON GRIP ON THE SHATTERED CITY –
THE CURSED EARTH
. . . THE CENTRE SECTOR REMAINS FREE – BUT EVEN THAT IS THREATENED NOW.
SUPREME JUDGE BULGARIN ON VID FROM EAST-MEG, WAR-MARSHAL !
IN THE EAST-MEG BUNKER, **SUPREME JUDGE BULGARIN**, LEADER OF THE THREE-MAN RULING **DIKTATORAT** –
YOU ARE MAKING EXCELLENT PROGRESS, KAZAN. I KNEW WE COULD RELY ON YOU TO BRING US VICTORY !
VICTORY, YES. BUT NOT FOR YOU !

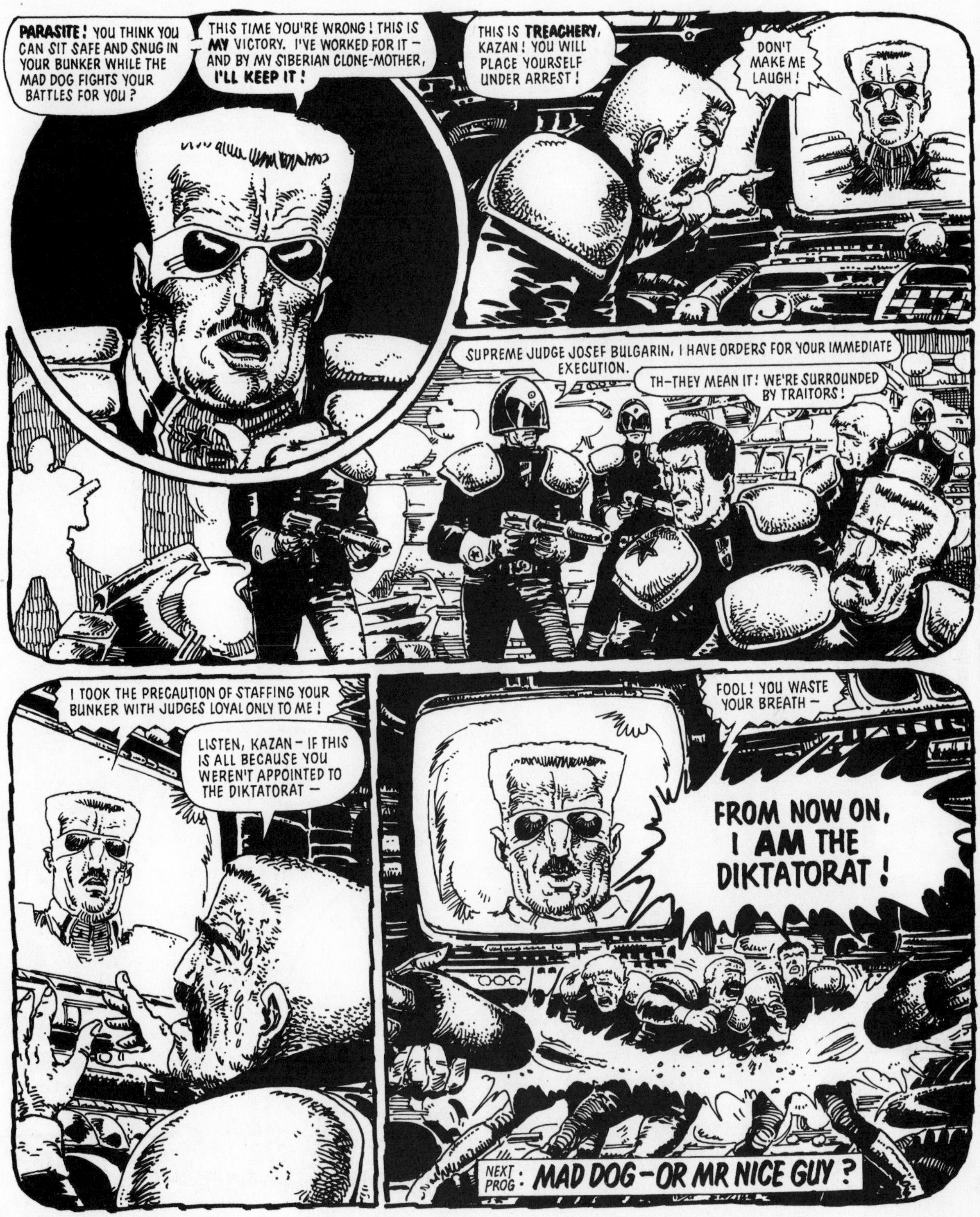
PARASITE! YOU THINK YOU CAN SIT SAFE AND SNUG IN YOUR BUNKER WHILE THE MAD DOG FIGHTS YOUR BATTLES FOR YOU?
THIS TIME YOU'RE WRONG! THIS IS MY VICTORY. I'VE WORKED FOR IT — AND BY MY SIBERIAN CLONE-MOTHER, I'LL KEEP IT!
THIS IS TREACHERY, KAZAN! YOU WILL PLACE YOURSELF UNDER ARREST!
DON'T MAKE ME LAUGH!
SUPREME JUDGE JOSEF BULGARIN, I HAVE ORDERS FOR YOUR IMMEDIATE EXECUTION.
TH-THEY MEAN IT! WE'RE SURROUNDED BY TRAITORS!
I TOOK THE PRECAUTION OF STAFFING YOUR BUNKER WITH JUDGES LOYAL ONLY TO ME!
LISTEN, KAZAN - IF THIS IS ALL BECAUSE YOU WEREN'T APPOINTED TO THE DIKTATORAT —
FOOL! YOU WASTE YOUR BREATH —
FROM NOW ON, I AM THE DIKTATORAT!
NEXT PROG: MAD DOG-OR MR NICE GUY?

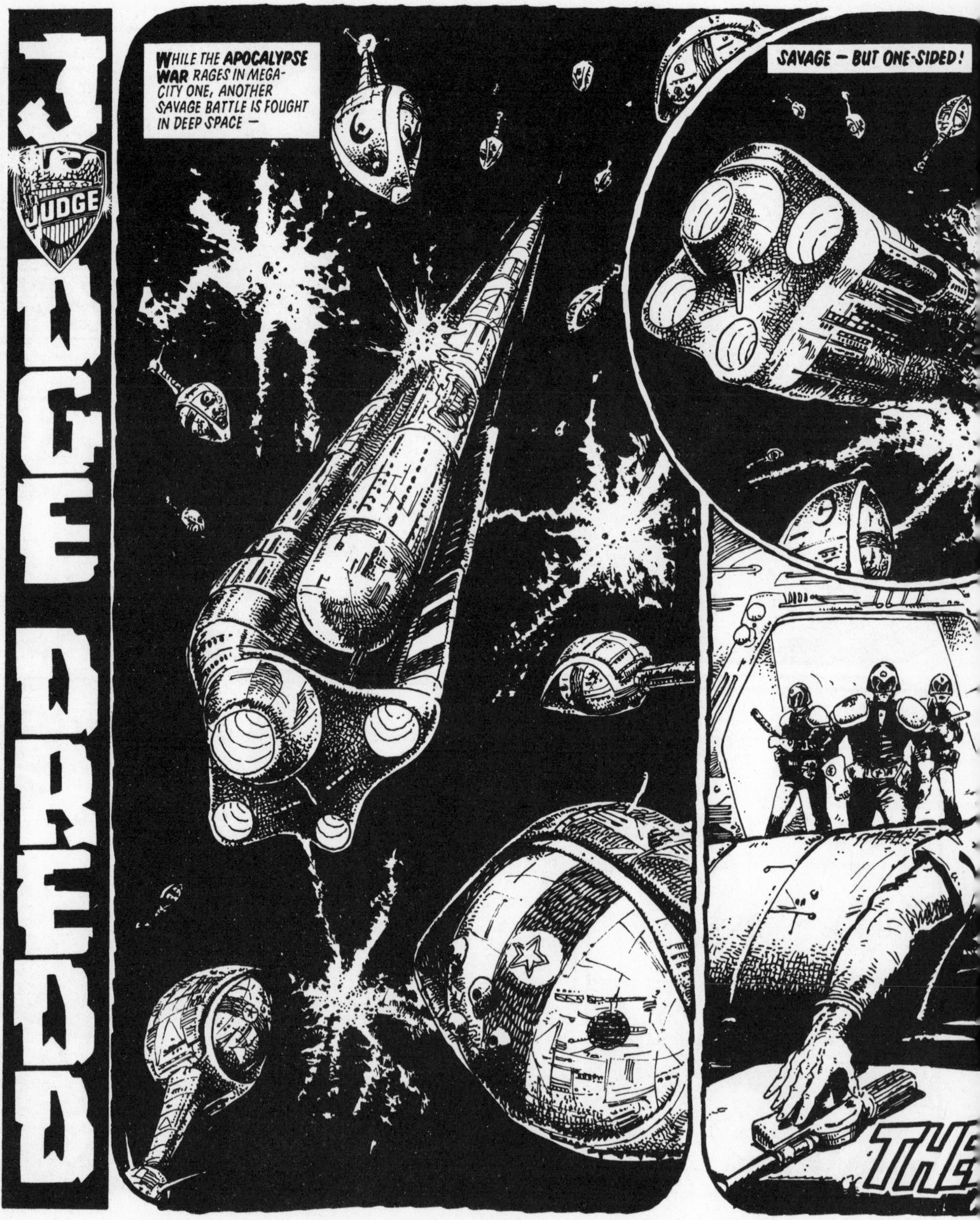

JUDGE DREDD
JUDGE
WHILE THE APOCALYPSE WAR RAGES IN MEGA-CITY ONE, ANOTHER SAVAGE BATTLE IS FOUGHT IN DEEP SPACE —
SAVAGE — BUT ONE-SIDED!

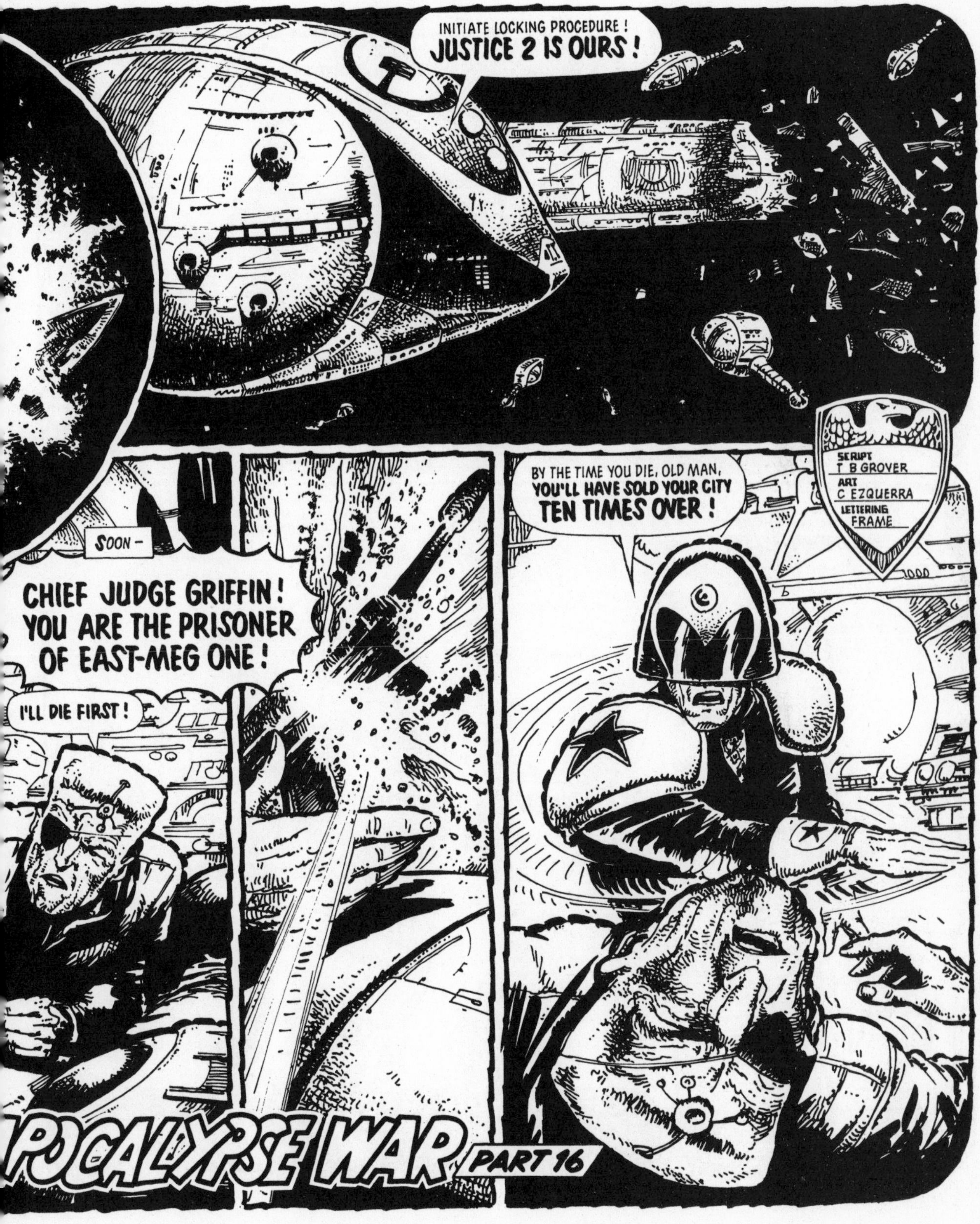
INITIATE LOCKING PROCEDURE !
JUSTICE 2 IS OURS !
SOON -
CHIEF JUDGE GRIFFIN! YOU ARE THE PRISONER OF EAST-MEG ONE!
I'LL DIE FIRST!
SCRIPT T B GROVER
ART C EZQUERRA
LETTERING FRAME
BY THE TIME YOU DIE, OLD MAN, YOU'LL HAVE SOLD YOUR CITY TEN TIMES OVER!
POCALYPSE WAR PART 16

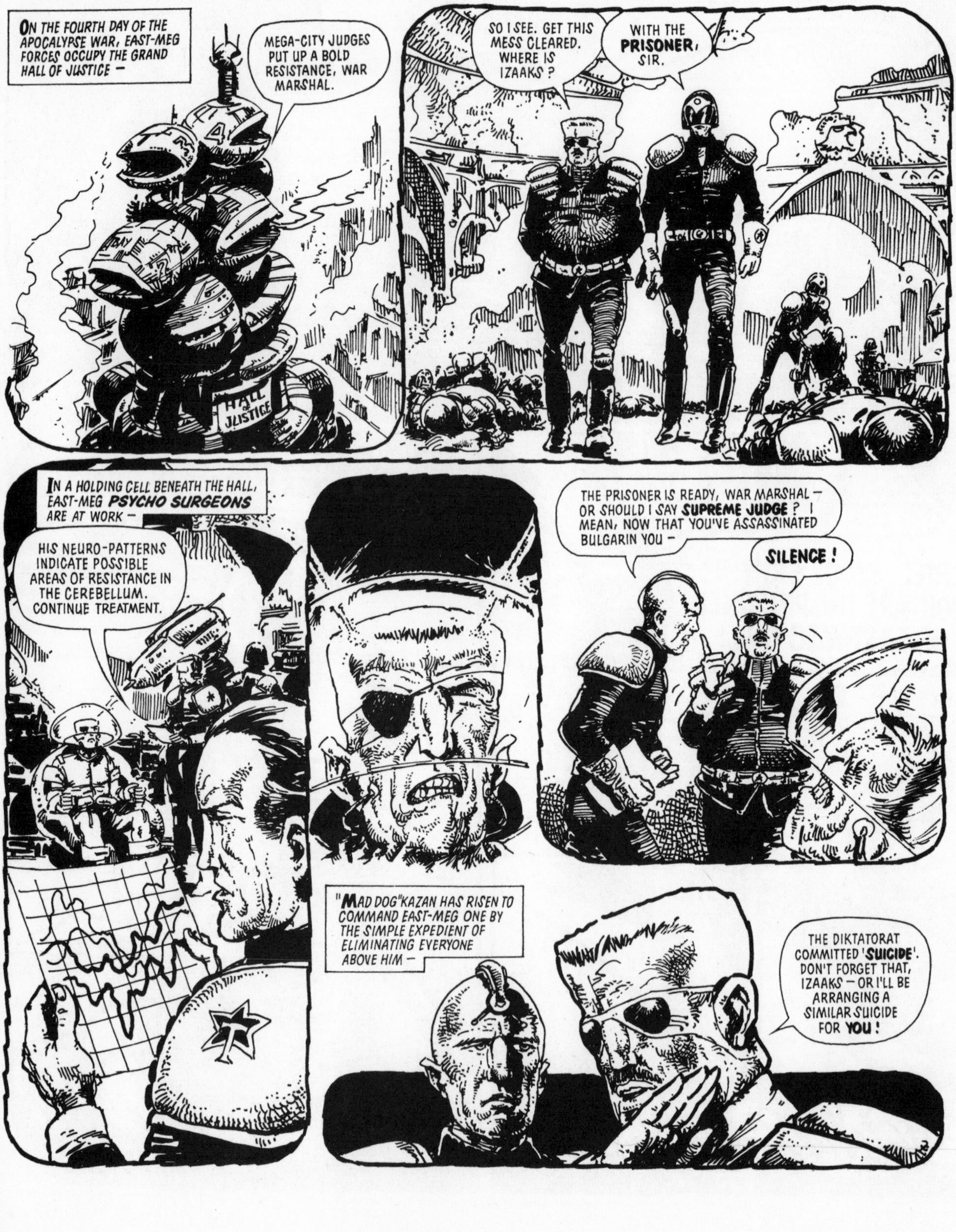

ON THE FOURTH DAY OF THE APOCALYPSE WAR, EAST-MEG FORCES OCCUPY THE GRAND HALL OF JUSTICE –
MEGA-CITY JUDGES PUT UP A BOLD RESISTANCE, WAR MARSHAL.
HALL OF JUSTICE
SO I SEE. GET THIS MESS CLEARED. WHERE IS IZAAKS ?
WITH THE PRISONER, SIR.
IN A HOLDING CELL BENEATH THE HALL, EAST-MEG PSYCHO SURGEONS ARE AT WORK –
HIS NEURO-PATTERNS INDICATE POSSIBLE AREAS OF RESISTANCE IN THE CEREBELLUM. CONTINUE TREATMENT.
THE PRISONER IS READY, WAR MARSHAL – OR SHOULD I SAY SUPREME JUDGE ? I MEAN, NOW THAT YOU'VE ASSASSINATED BULGARIN YOU –
SILENCE !
"MAD DOG" KAZAN HAS RISEN TO COMMAND EAST-MEG ONE BY THE SIMPLE EXPEDIENT OF ELIMINATING EVERYONE ABOVE HIM –
THE DIKTATORAT COMMITTED 'SUICIDE'. DON'T FORGET THAT, IZAAKS – OR I'LL BE ARRANGING A SIMILAR SUICIDE FOR YOU !

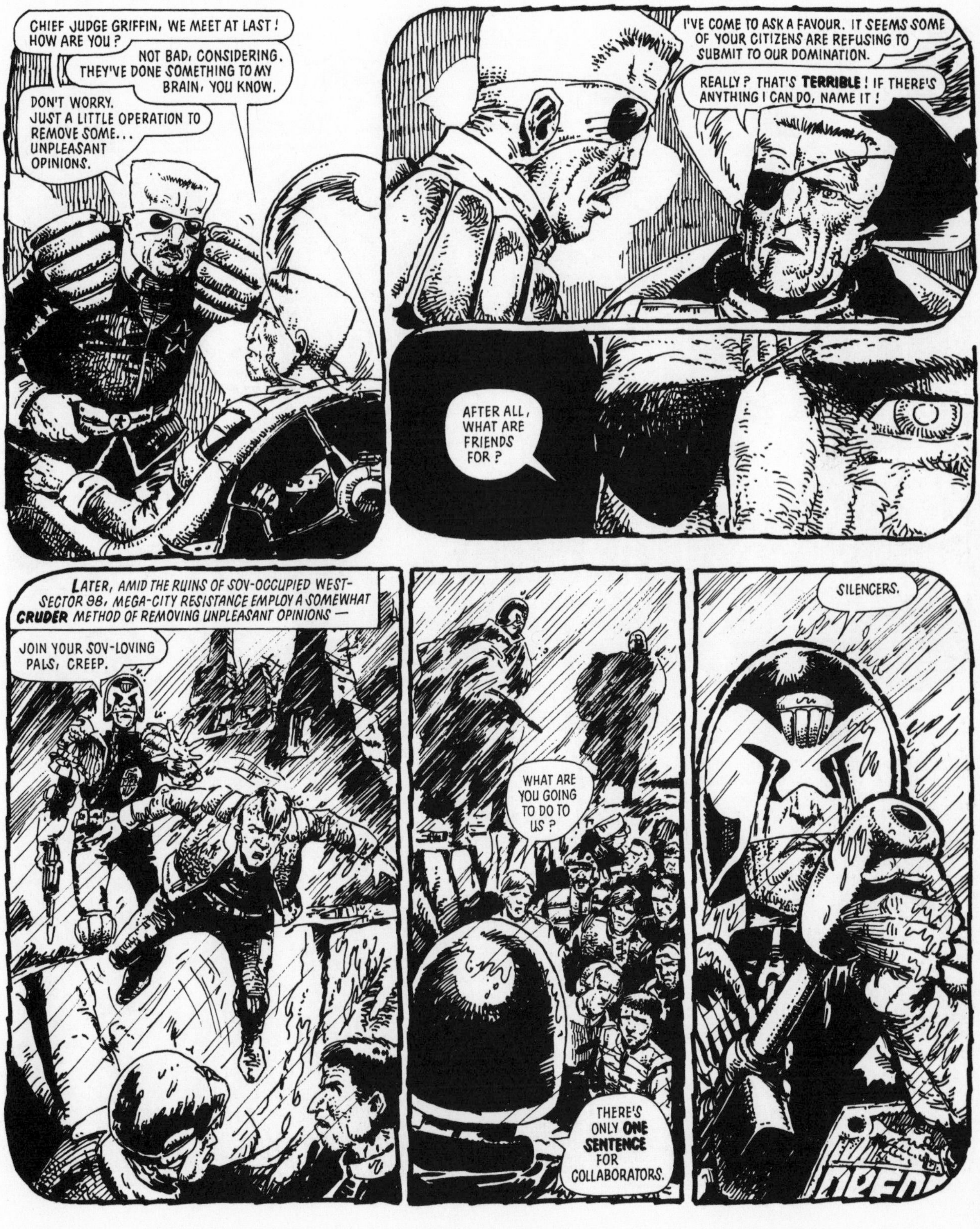
CHIEF JUDGE GRIFFIN, WE MEET AT LAST! HOW ARE YOU?
NOT BAD, CONSIDERING. THEY'VE DONE SOMETHING TO MY BRAIN, YOU KNOW.
DON'T WORRY. JUST A LITTLE OPERATION TO REMOVE SOME... UNPLEASANT OPINIONS.
I'VE COME TO ASK A FAVOUR. IT SEEMS SOME OF YOUR CITIZENS ARE REFUSING TO SUBMIT TO OUR DOMINATION.
REALLY? THAT'S TERRIBLE! IF THERE'S ANYTHING I CAN DO, NAME IT!
AFTER ALL, WHAT ARE FRIENDS FOR?
LATER, AMID THE RUINS OF SOV-OCCUPIED WEST-SECTOR 98, MEGA-CITY RESISTANCE EMPLOY A SOMEWHAT CRUDER METHOD OF REMOVING UNPLEASANT OPINIONS —
JOIN YOUR SOV-LOVING PALS, CREEP.
WHAT ARE YOU GOING TO DO TO US?
THERE'S ONLY ONE SENTENCE FOR COLLABORATORS.
SILENCERS.

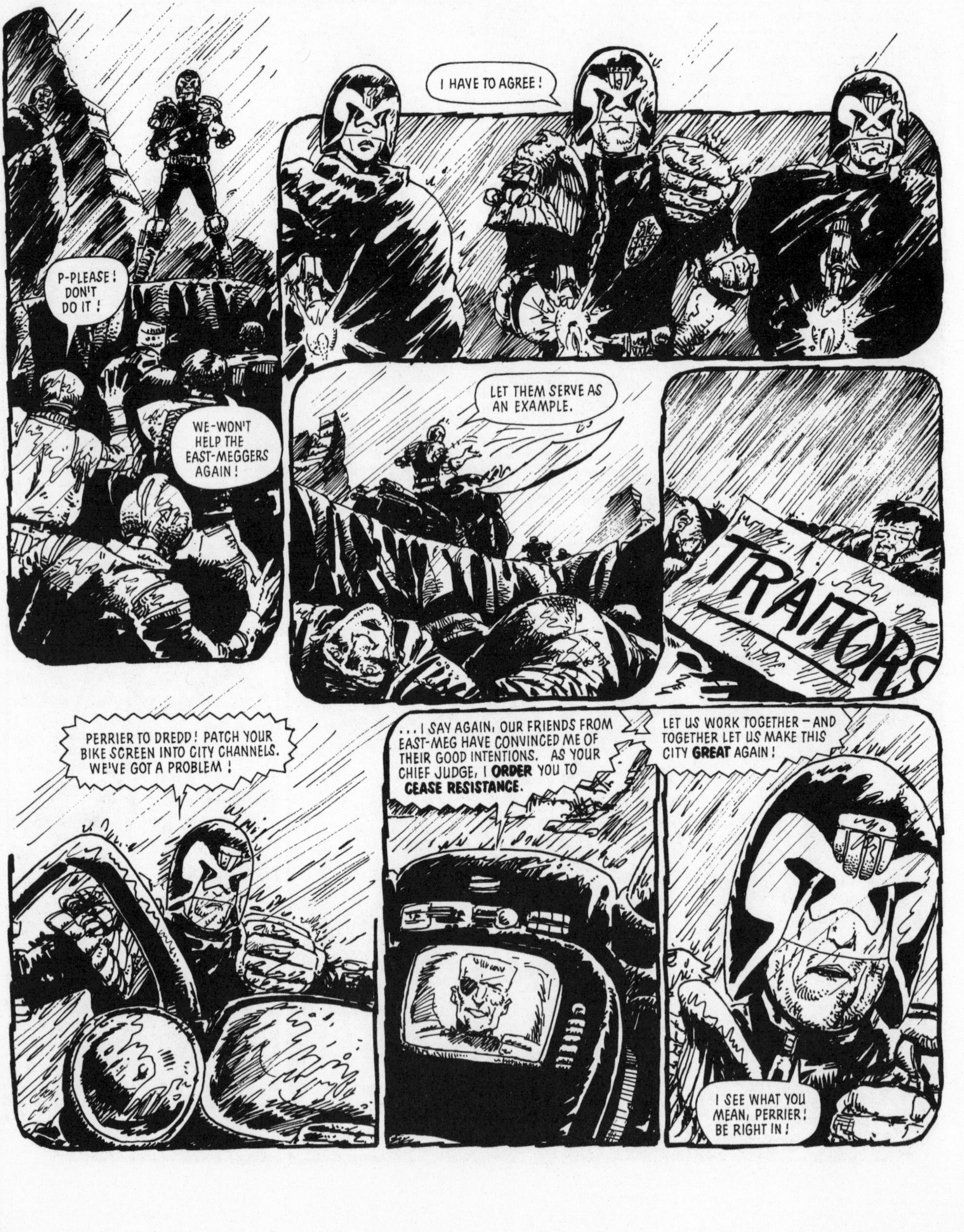
P-PLEASE! DON'T DO IT!
WE-WON'T HELP THE EAST-MEGGERS AGAIN!
I HAVE TO AGREE!
LET THEM SERVE AS AN EXAMPLE.
TRAITORS
PERRIER TO DREDD! PATCH YOUR BIKE SCREEN INTO CITY CHANNELS. WE'VE GOT A PROBLEM!
...I SAY AGAIN, OUR FRIENDS FROM EAST-MEG HAVE CONVINCED ME OF THEIR GOOD INTENTIONS. AS YOUR CHIEF JUDGE, I **ORDER** YOU TO **CEASE RESISTANCE**.
LET US WORK TOGETHER — AND TOGETHER LET US MAKE THIS CITY **GREAT** AGAIN!
I SEE WHAT YOU MEAN, PERRIER! BE RIGHT IN!

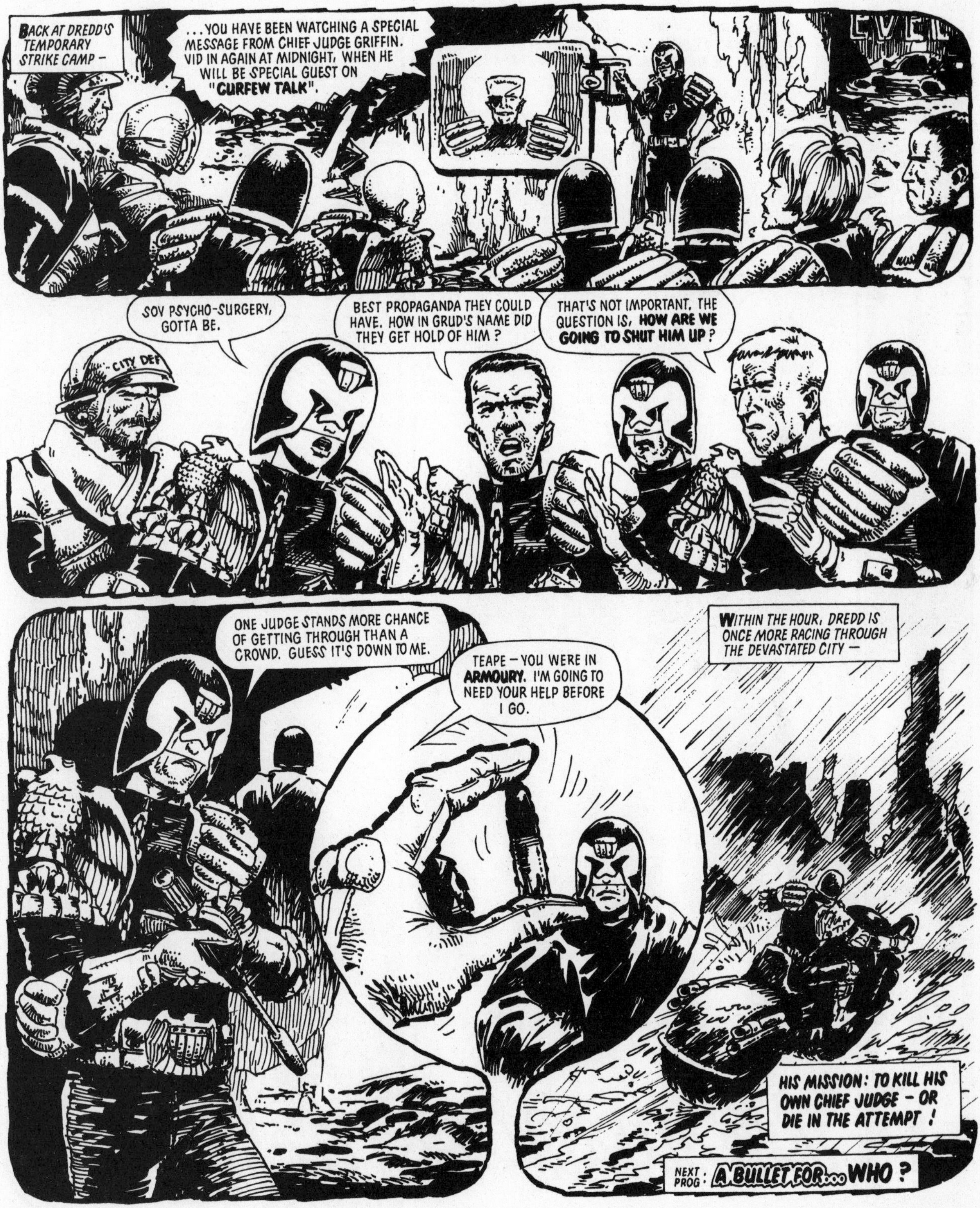
BACK AT DREDD'S TEMPORARY STRIKE CAMP –
...YOU HAVE BEEN WATCHING A SPECIAL MESSAGE FROM CHIEF JUDGE GRIFFIN. VID IN AGAIN AT MIDNIGHT, WHEN HE WILL BE SPECIAL GUEST ON "CURFEW TALK".
SOV PSYCHO-SURGERY, GOTTA BE.
BEST PROPAGANDA THEY COULD HAVE. HOW IN GRUD'S NAME DID THEY GET HOLD OF HIM?
THAT'S NOT IMPORTANT. THE QUESTION IS, HOW ARE WE GOING TO SHUT HIM UP?
CITY DEF
ONE JUDGE STANDS MORE CHANCE OF GETTING THROUGH THAN A CROWD. GUESS IT'S DOWN TO ME.
TEAPE – YOU WERE IN ARMOURY. I'M GOING TO NEED YOUR HELP BEFORE I GO.
WITHIN THE HOUR, DREDD IS ONCE MORE RACING THROUGH THE DEVASTATED CITY –
HIS MISSION: TO KILL HIS OWN CHIEF JUDGE – OR DIE IN THE ATTEMPT!
NEXT PROG: A BULLET FOR... WHO?

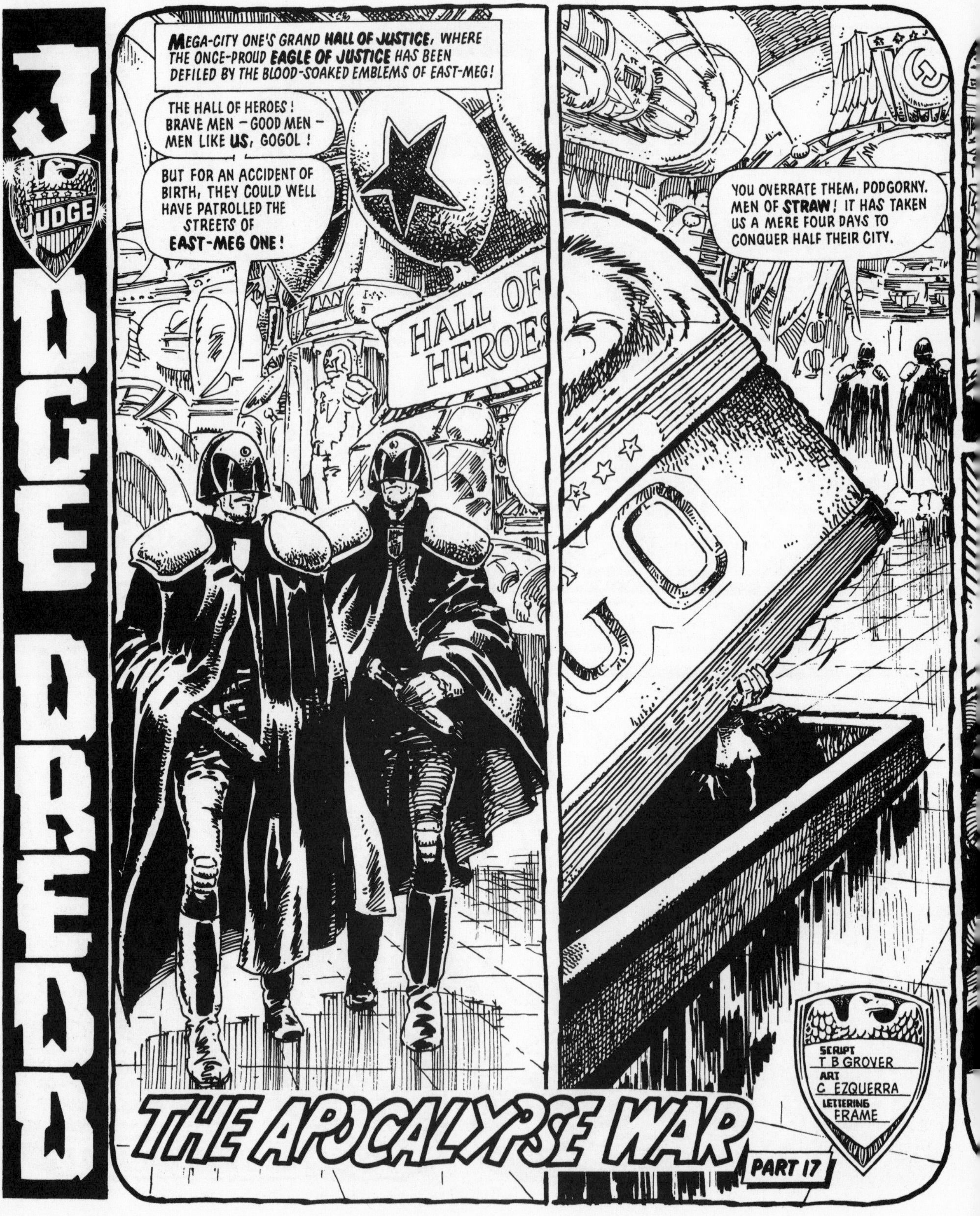
JUDGE DREDD
MEGA-CITY ONE'S GRAND HALL OF JUSTICE, WHERE THE ONCE-PROUD EAGLE OF JUSTICE HAS BEEN DEFILED BY THE BLOOD-SOAKED EMBLEMS OF EAST-MEG!
THE HALL OF HEROES! BRAVE MEN — GOOD MEN — MEN LIKE US, GOGOL!
BUT FOR AN ACCIDENT OF BIRTH, THEY COULD WELL HAVE PATROLLED THE STREETS OF EAST-MEG ONE!
HALL OF HEROES
YOU OVERRATE THEM, PODGORNY. MEN OF STRAW! IT HAS TAKEN US A MERE FOUR DAYS TO CONQUER HALF THEIR CITY.
THE APOCALYPSE WAR
PART 17
SCRIPT T B GROVER
ART C EZQUERRA
LETTERING FRAME

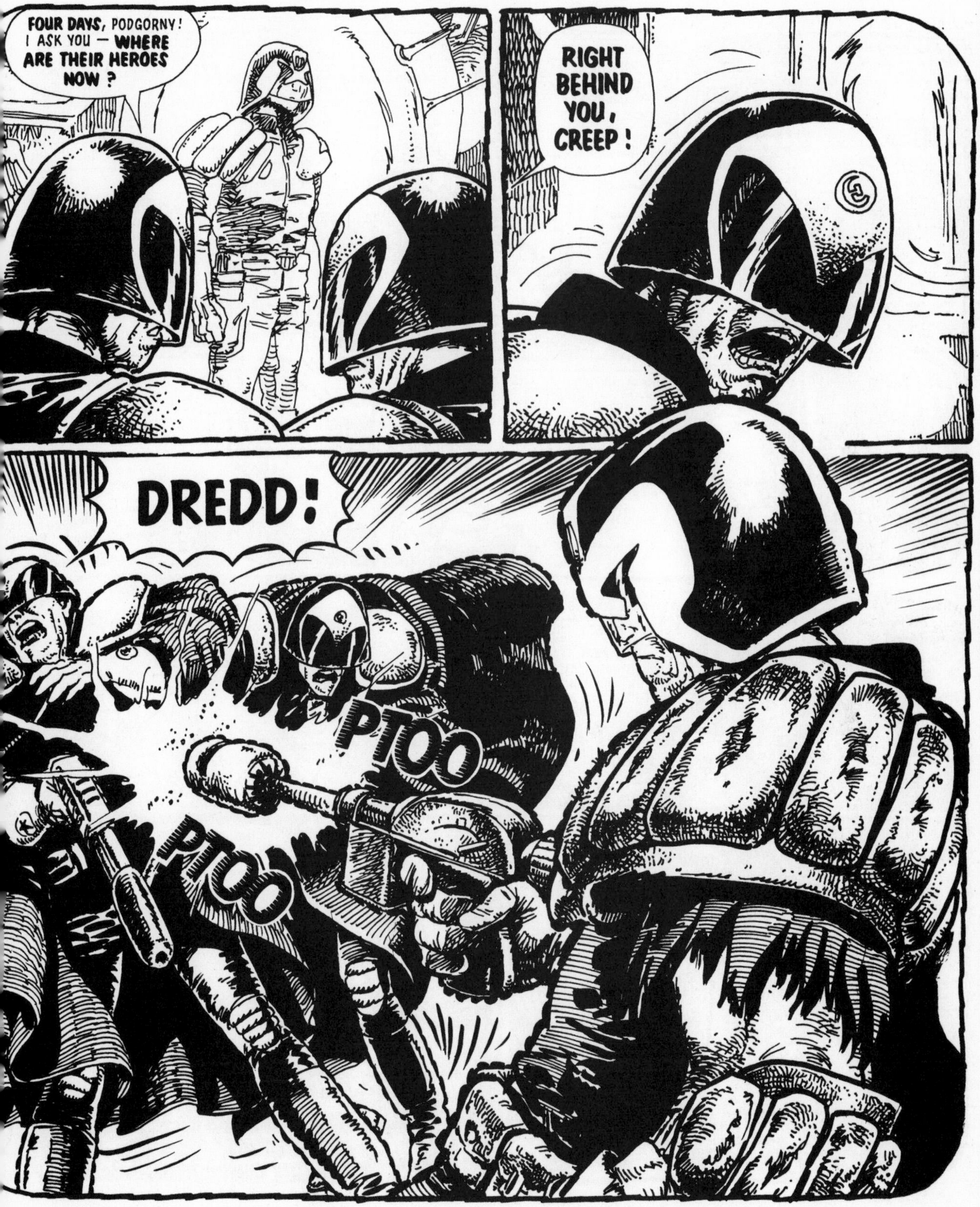
FOUR DAYS, PODGORNY! I ASK YOU — WHERE ARE THEIR HEROES NOW ?
RIGHT BEHIND YOU, CREEP !
DREDD!
PTOO
PTOO

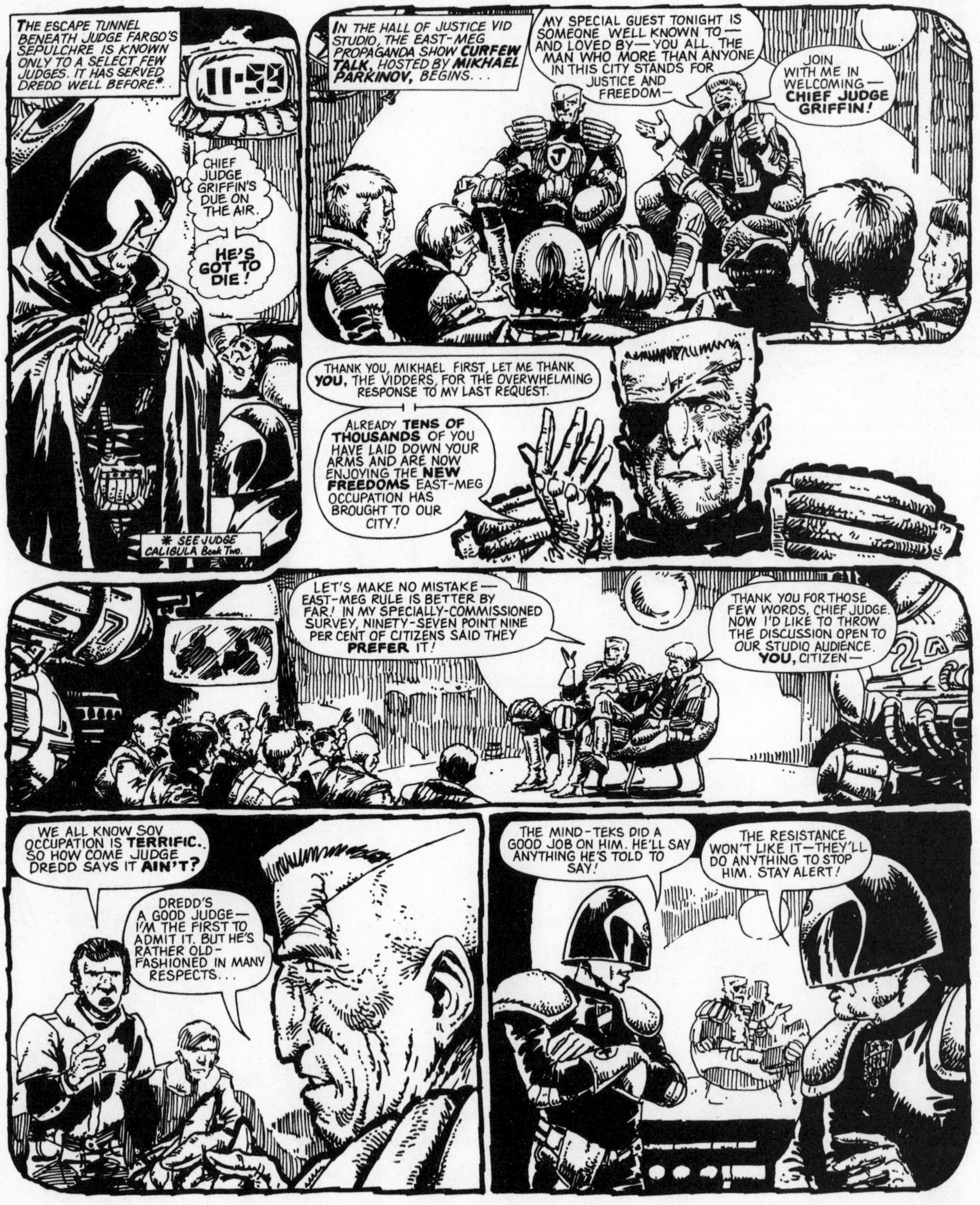

THE ESCAPE TUNNEL BENEATH JUDGE FARGO'S SEPULCHRE IS KNOWN ONLY TO A SELECT FEW JUDGES. IT HAS SERVED DREDD WELL BEFORE.*
11:59
CHIEF JUDGE GRIFFIN'S DUE ON THE AIR.
HE'S GOT TO DIE!
* SEE JUDGE CALIGULA Book Two.
IN THE HALL OF JUSTICE VID STUDIO, THE EAST-MEG PROPAGANDA SHOW CURFEW TALK, HOSTED BY MIKHAEL PARKINOV, BEGINS...
MY SPECIAL GUEST TONIGHT IS SOMEONE WELL KNOWN TO— AND LOVED BY— YOU ALL. THE MAN WHO MORE THAN ANYONE IN THIS CITY STANDS FOR JUSTICE AND FREEDOM—
JOIN WITH ME IN WELCOMING— CHIEF JUDGE GRIFFIN!
THANK YOU, MIKHAEL FIRST, LET ME THANK YOU, THE VIDDERS, FOR THE OVERWHELMING RESPONSE TO MY LAST REQUEST.
ALREADY TENS OF THOUSANDS OF YOU HAVE LAID DOWN YOUR ARMS AND ARE NOW ENJOYING THE NEW FREEDOMS EAST-MEG OCCUPATION HAS BROUGHT TO OUR CITY!
LET'S MAKE NO MISTAKE— EAST-MEG RULE IS BETTER BY FAR! IN MY SPECIALLY-COMMISSIONED SURVEY, NINETY-SEVEN POINT NINE PER CENT OF CITIZENS SAID THEY PREFER IT!
THANK YOU FOR THOSE FEW WORDS, CHIEF JUDGE. NOW I'D LIKE TO THROW THE DISCUSSION OPEN TO OUR STUDIO AUDIENCE. YOU, CITIZEN—
WE ALL KNOW SOV OCCUPATION IS TERRIFIC. SO HOW COME JUDGE DREDD SAYS IT AIN'T?
DREDD'S A GOOD JUDGE— I'M THE FIRST TO ADMIT IT. BUT HE'S RATHER OLD-FASHIONED IN MANY RESPECTS...
THE MIND-TEKS DID A GOOD JOB ON HIM. HE'LL SAY ANYTHING HE'S TOLD TO SAY!
THE RESISTANCE WON'T LIKE IT—THEY'LL DO ANYTHING TO STOP HIM. STAY ALERT!

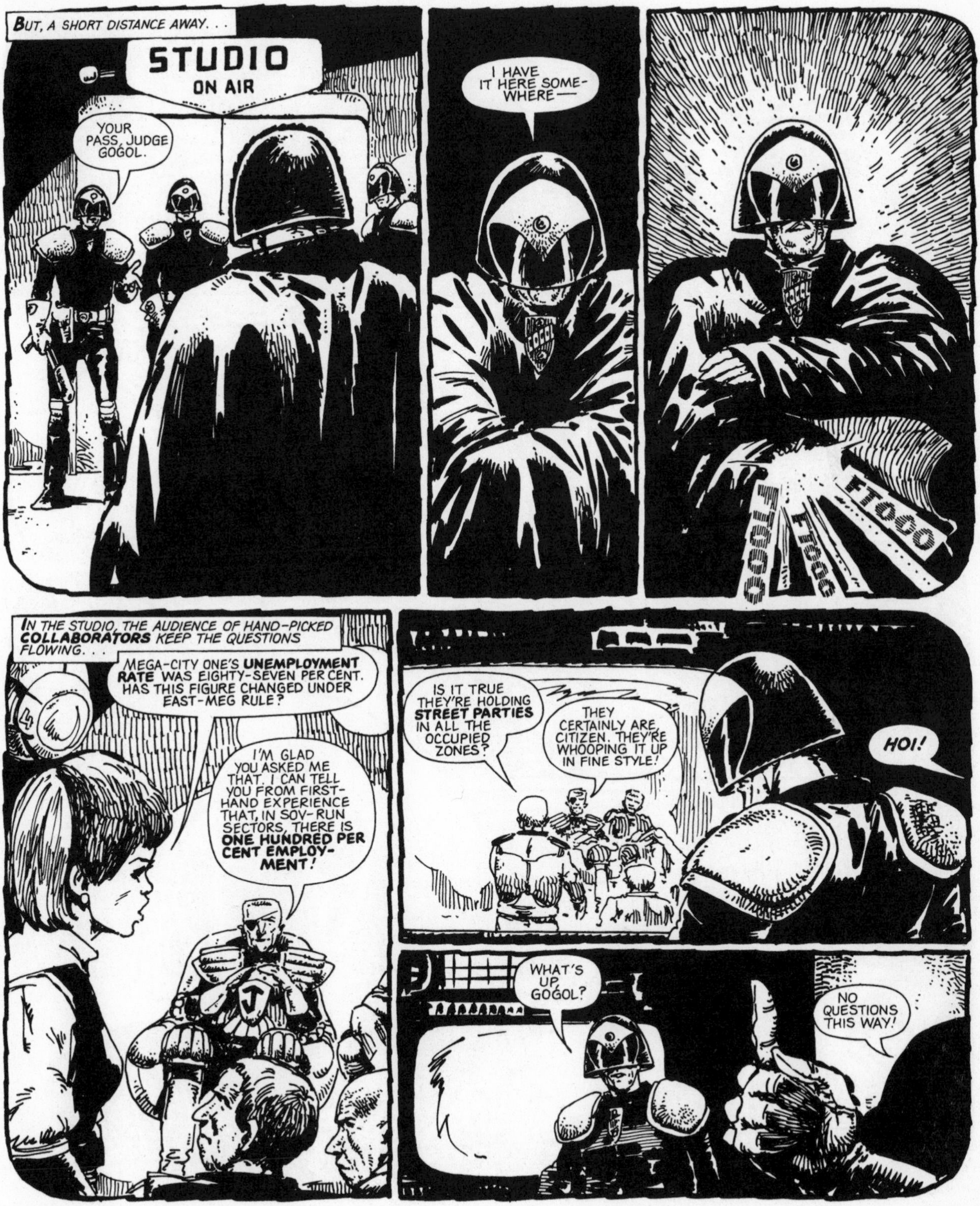
BUT, A SHORT DISTANCE AWAY. . .
STUDIO
ON AIR
YOUR PASS, JUDGE GOGOL.
I HAVE IT HERE SOME-WHERE—
FT000
FT000
FT000
IN THE STUDIO, THE AUDIENCE OF HAND-PICKED COLLABORATORS KEEP THE QUESTIONS FLOWING. . .
MEGA-CITY ONE'S UNEMPLOYMENT RATE WAS EIGHTY-SEVEN PER CENT. HAS THIS FIGURE CHANGED UNDER EAST-MEG RULE?
I'M GLAD YOU ASKED ME THAT. I CAN TELL YOU FROM FIRST-HAND EXPERIENCE THAT, IN SOV-RUN SECTORS, THERE IS ONE HUNDRED PER CENT EMPLOY-MENT!
IS IT TRUE THEY'RE HOLDING STREET PARTIES IN ALL THE OCCUPIED ZONES?
THEY CERTAINLY ARE, CITIZEN. THEY'RE WHOOPING IT UP IN FINE STYLE!
HOI!
WHAT'S UP, GOGOL?
NO QUESTIONS THIS WAY!

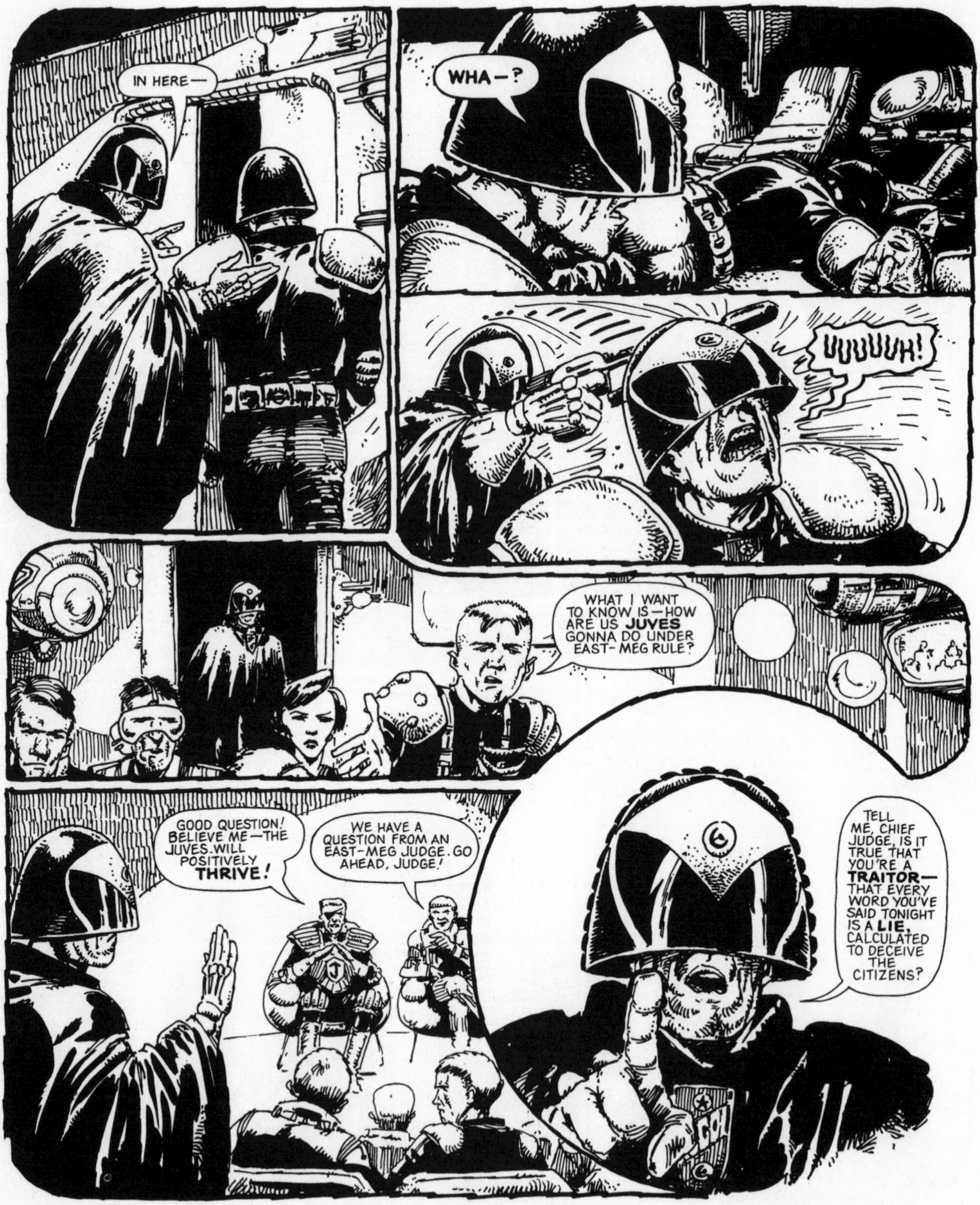
IN HERE—
WHA—?
UUUUUH!
WHAT I WANT TO KNOW IS—HOW ARE US JUVES GONNA DO UNDER EAST-MEG RULE?
GOOD QUESTION! BELIEVE ME—THE JUVES WILL POSITIVELY THRIVE!
WE HAVE A QUESTION FROM AN EAST-MEG JUDGE. GO AHEAD, JUDGE!
TELL ME, CHIEF JUDGE, IS IT TRUE THAT YOU'RE A TRAITOR—THAT EVERY WORD YOU'VE SAID TONIGHT IS A LIE, CALCULATED TO DECEIVE THE CITIZENS?

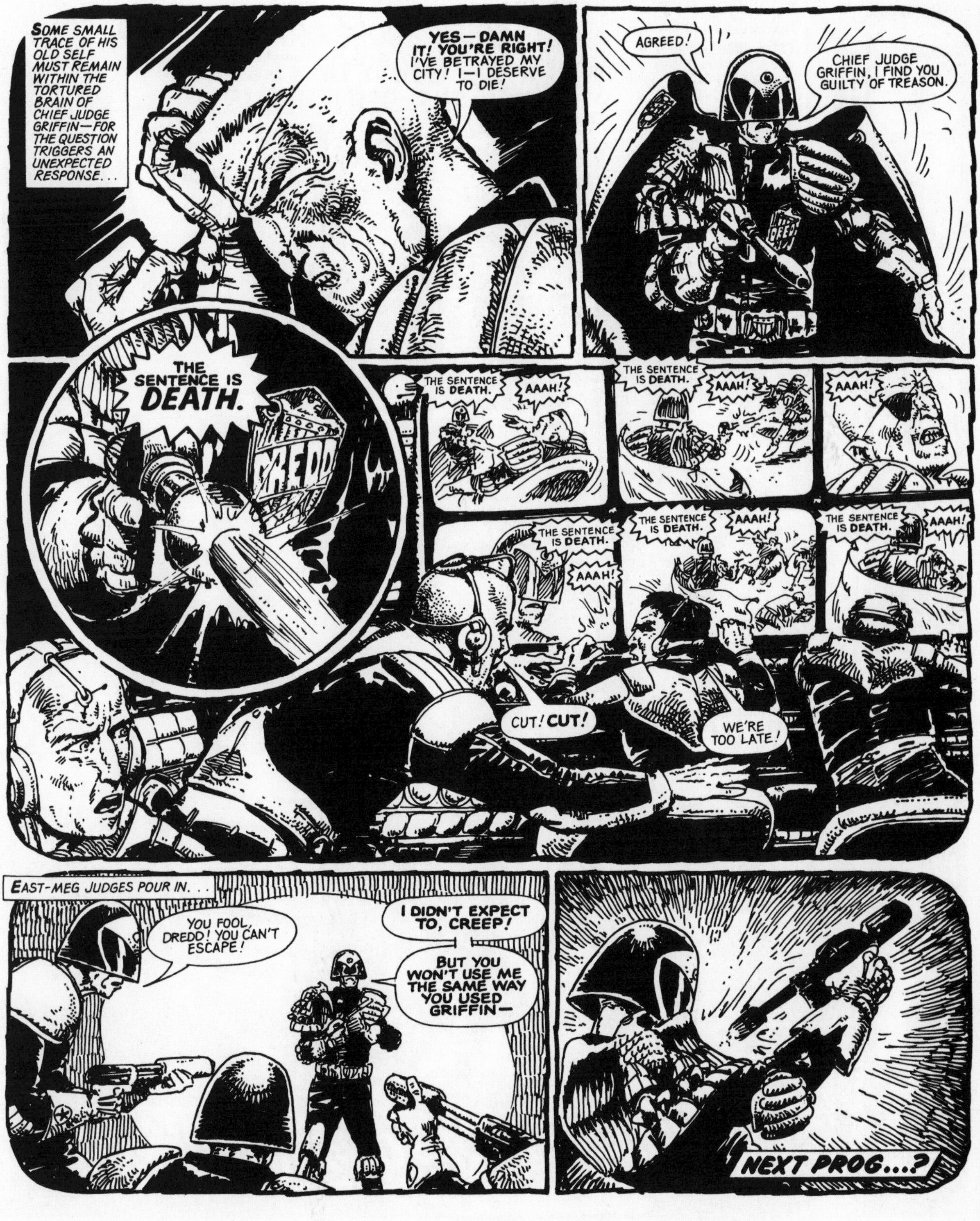
SOME SMALL TRACE OF HIS OLD SELF MUST REMAIN WITHIN THE TORTURED BRAIN OF CHIEF JUDGE GRIFFIN—FOR THE QUESTION TRIGGERS AN UNEXPECTED RESPONSE...
YES—DAMN IT! YOU'RE RIGHT! I'VE BETRAYED MY CITY! I—I DESERVE TO DIE!
AGREED!
CHIEF JUDGE GRIFFIN, I FIND YOU GUILTY OF TREASON.
THE SENTENCE IS DEATH.
DREDD
THE SENTENCE IS DEATH.
AAAH!
THE SENTENCE IS DEATH.
AAAH!
AAAH!
THE SENTENCE IS DEATH.
AAAH!
THE SENTENCE IS DEATH.
AAAH!
THE SENTENCE IS DEATH.
AAAH!
CUT! CUT!
WE'RE TOO LATE!
EAST-MEG JUDGES POUR IN...
YOU FOOL, DREDD! YOU CAN'T ESCAPE!
I DIDN'T EXPECT TO, CREEP!
BUT YOU WON'T USE ME THE SAME WAY YOU USED GRIFFIN—
NEXT PROG...?

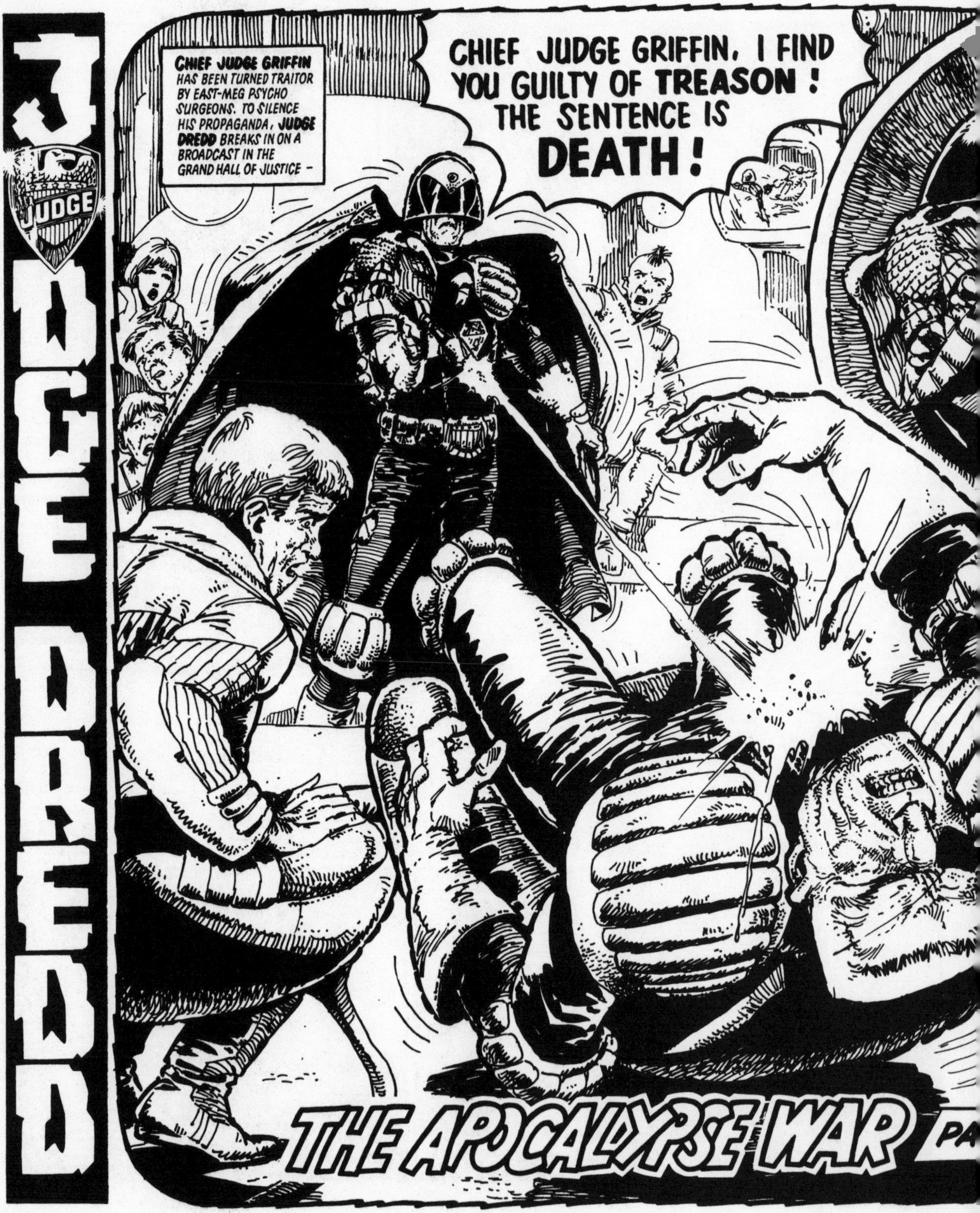
JUDGE DREDD
JUDGE
CHIEF JUDGE GRIFFIN HAS BEEN TURNED TRAITOR BY EAST-MEG PSYCHO SURGEONS. TO SILENCE HIS PROPAGANDA, JUDGE DREDD BREAKS IN ON A BROADCAST IN THE GRAND HALL OF JUSTICE -
CHIEF JUDGE GRIFFIN, I FIND YOU GUILTY OF TREASON! THE SENTENCE IS DEATH!
THE APOCALYPSE WAR

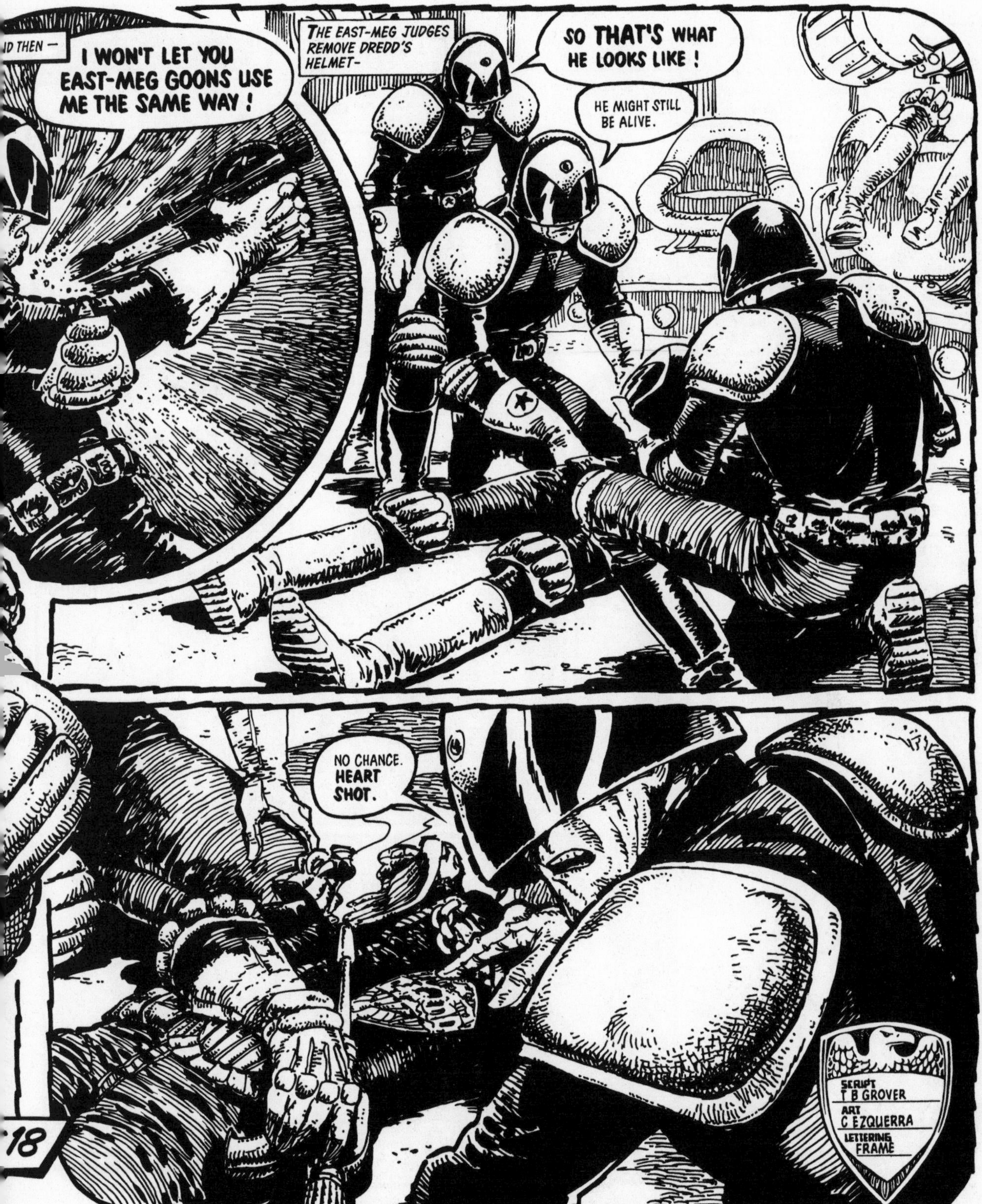

ND THEN —
I WON'T LET YOU EAST-MEG GOONS USE ME THE SAME WAY !
THE EAST-MEG JUDGES REMOVE DREDD'S HELMET-
SO THAT'S WHAT HE LOOKS LIKE !
HE MIGHT STILL BE ALIVE.
NO CHANCE. HEART SHOT.
SCRIPT T B GROVER
ART C EZQUERRA
LETTERING FRAME

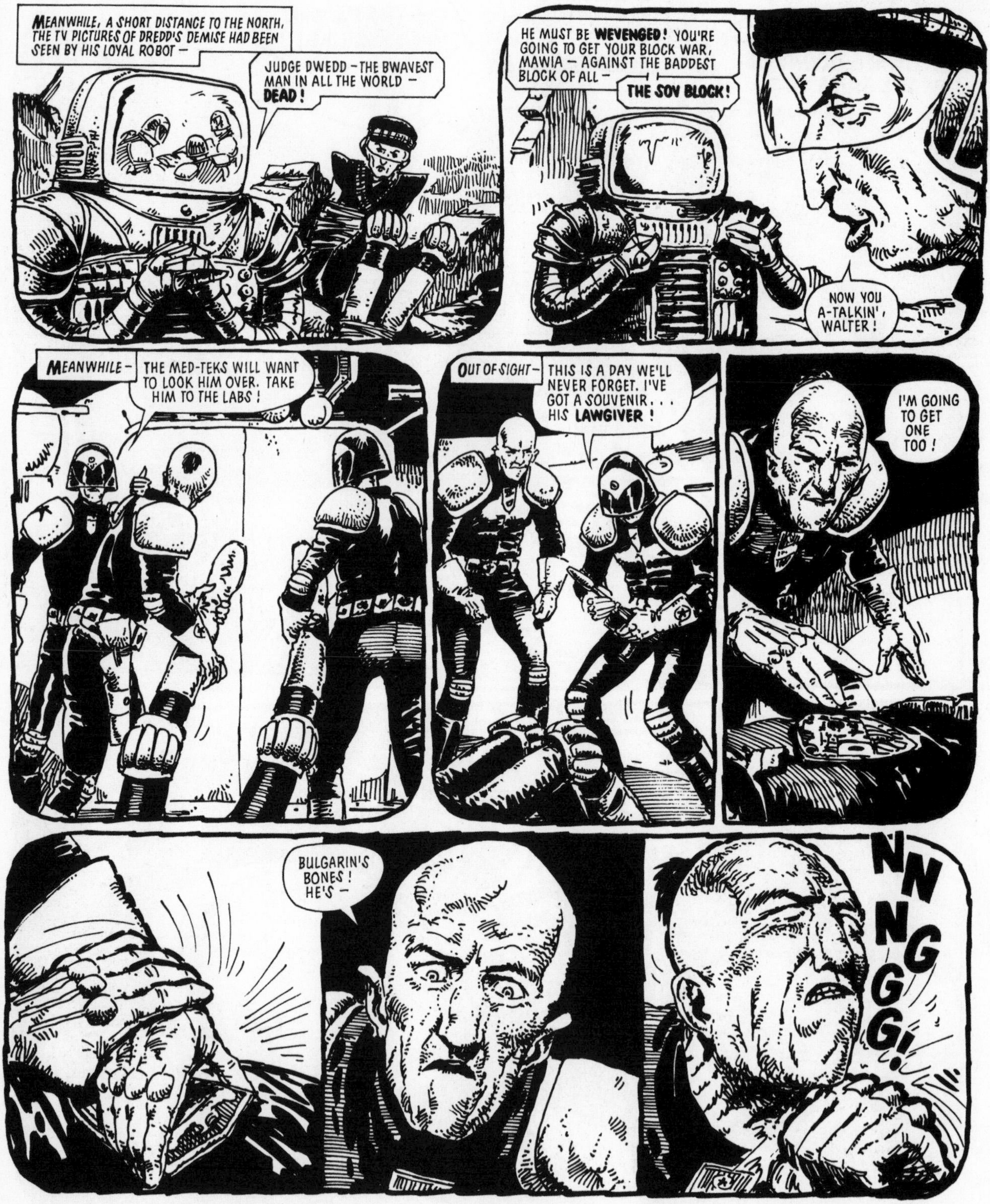
MEANWHILE, A SHORT DISTANCE TO THE NORTH, THE TV PICTURES OF DREDD'S DEMISE HAD BEEN SEEN BY HIS LOYAL ROBOT —
JUDGE DWEDD — THE BWAVEST MAN IN ALL THE WORLD — DEAD!
HE MUST BE WEVENGED! YOU'RE GOING TO GET YOUR BLOCK WAR, MAWIA — AGAINST THE BADDEST BLOCK OF ALL —
THE SOV BLOCK!
NOW YOU A-TALKIN', WALTER!
MEANWHILE —
THE MED-TEKS WILL WANT TO LOOK HIM OVER. TAKE HIM TO THE LABS!
OUT OF SIGHT —
THIS IS A DAY WE'LL NEVER FORGET. I'VE GOT A SOUVENIR . . . HIS LAWGIVER!
I'M GOING TO GET ONE TOO!
BULGARIN'S BONES! HE'S —
NNNGGG!

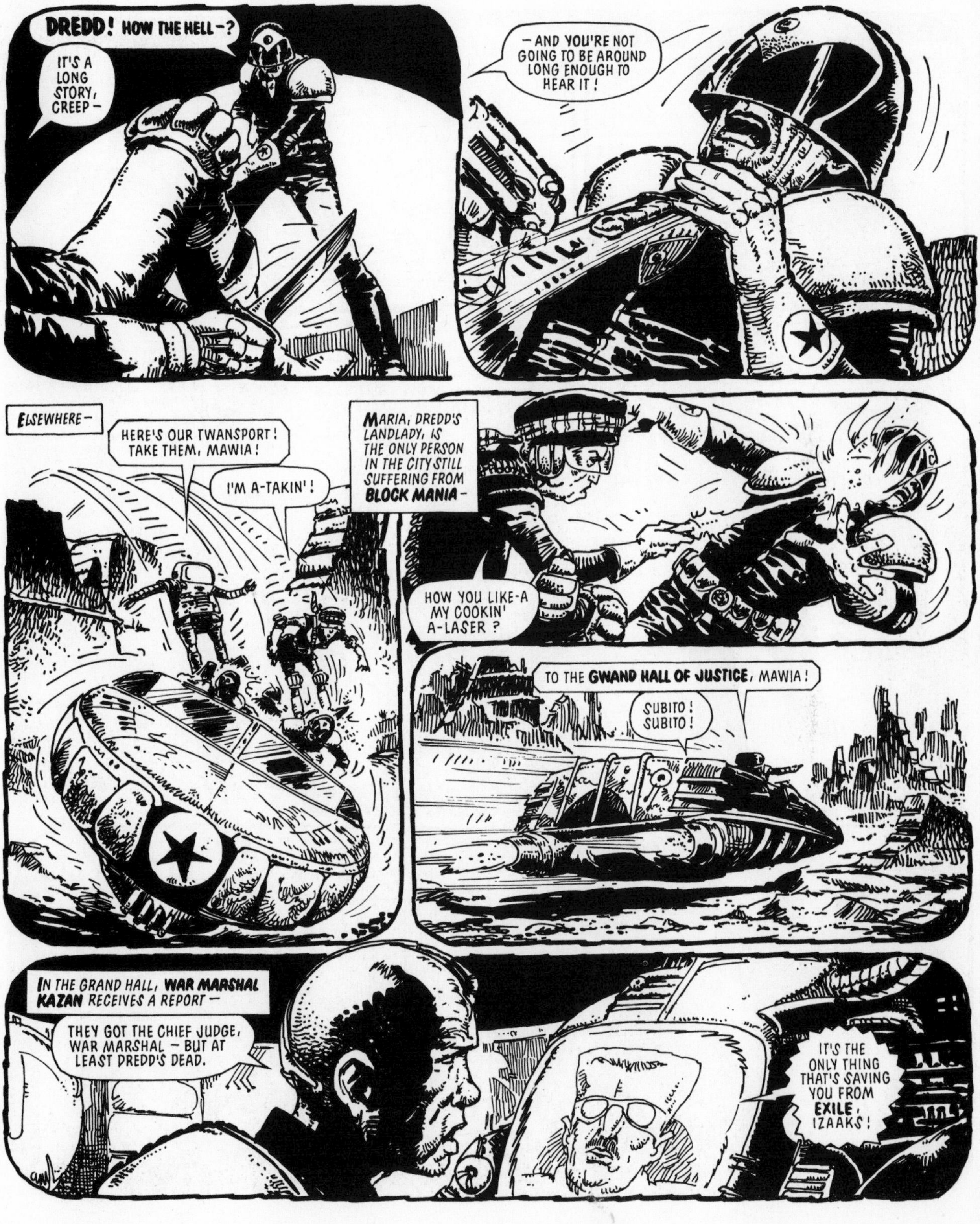
DREDD! HOW THE HELL-?
IT'S A LONG STORY, CREEP-
- AND YOU'RE NOT GOING TO BE AROUND LONG ENOUGH TO HEAR IT!
ELSEWHERE-
HERE'S OUR TWANSPORT! TAKE THEM, MAWIA!
I'M A-TAKIN'!
MARIA, DREDD'S LANDLADY, IS THE ONLY PERSON IN THE CITY STILL SUFFERING FROM BLOCK MANIA-
HOW YOU LIKE-A MY COOKIN' A-LASER?
TO THE GWAND HALL OF JUSTICE, MAWIA!
SUBITO! SUBITO!
IN THE GRAND HALL, WAR MARSHAL KAZAN RECEIVES A REPORT-
THEY GOT THE CHIEF JUDGE, WAR MARSHAL - BUT AT LEAST DREDD'S DEAD.
IT'S THE ONLY THING THAT'S SAVING YOU FROM EXILE, IZAAKS!

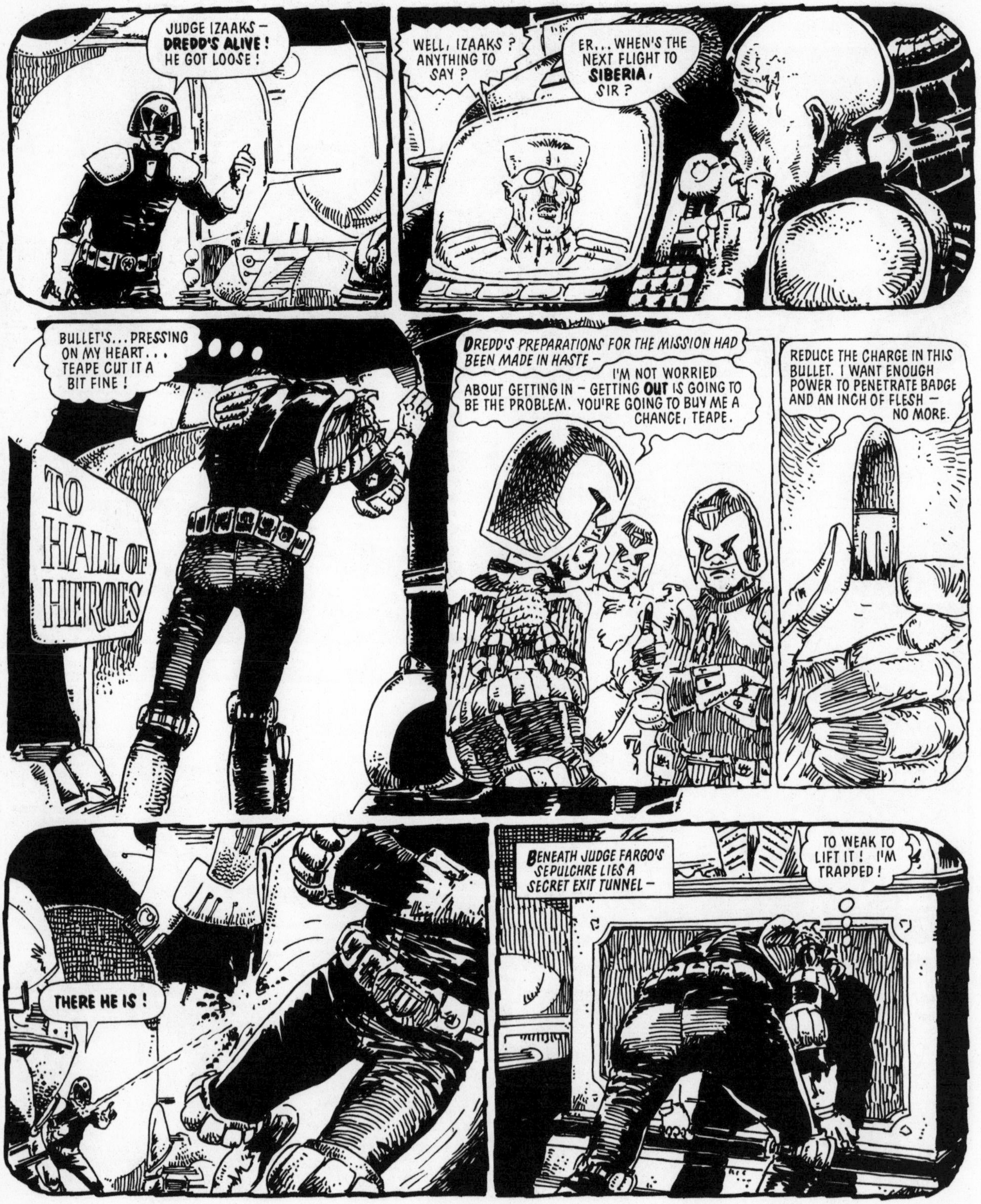
JUDGE IZAAKS — DREDD'S ALIVE! HE GOT LOOSE!
WELL, IZAAKS? ANYTHING TO SAY?
ER... WHEN'S THE NEXT FLIGHT TO SIBERIA, SIR?
BULLET'S... PRESSING ON MY HEART... TEAPE CUT IT A BIT FINE!
TO HALL OF HEROES
DREDD'S PREPARATIONS FOR THE MISSION HAD BEEN MADE IN HASTE —
I'M NOT WORRIED ABOUT GETTING IN — GETTING OUT IS GOING TO BE THE PROBLEM. YOU'RE GOING TO BUY ME A CHANCE, TEAPE.
REDUCE THE CHARGE IN THIS BULLET. I WANT ENOUGH POWER TO PENETRATE BADGE AND AN INCH OF FLESH — NO MORE.
THERE HE IS!
BENEATH JUDGE FARGO'S SEPULCHRE LIES A SECRET EXIT TUNNEL —
TO WEAK TO LIFT IT! I'M TRAPPED!

THIS IS THE ENTWANCE TO THE SECWET TUNNEL. JUDGE DWEDD USED IT BEFORE, WHEN CAL THE TYWANT WAS CHIEF JUDGE.

SKIP-A THE GUIDED TOUR, WALTER. LET'S A-GET TO THIS FIGHT!

DEAD EAST-MEG JUDGES — AND JUDGE DWEDD'S HELMET!

SOUNDS LIKE A-DA FIGHTIN' UP THERE! THEM NO-GOOD SOVS! THEY START-A WITHOUT US!

ABOVE, DREDD SELLS HIS LIFE DEARLY —

AAAH!

PTTOWW!

PTTOWW!

HE'S SWITCHED TO RICOCHET BULLETS!

ONLY INCENDIARIES LEFT! SO BE IT!

PTTOO!

ANTI-FLAME SYSTEM MUST BE DAMAGED! THE WHOLE PLACE IS GOING UP!

FALL BACK!

LOOKS LIKE... THIS IS IT...

FAR GO

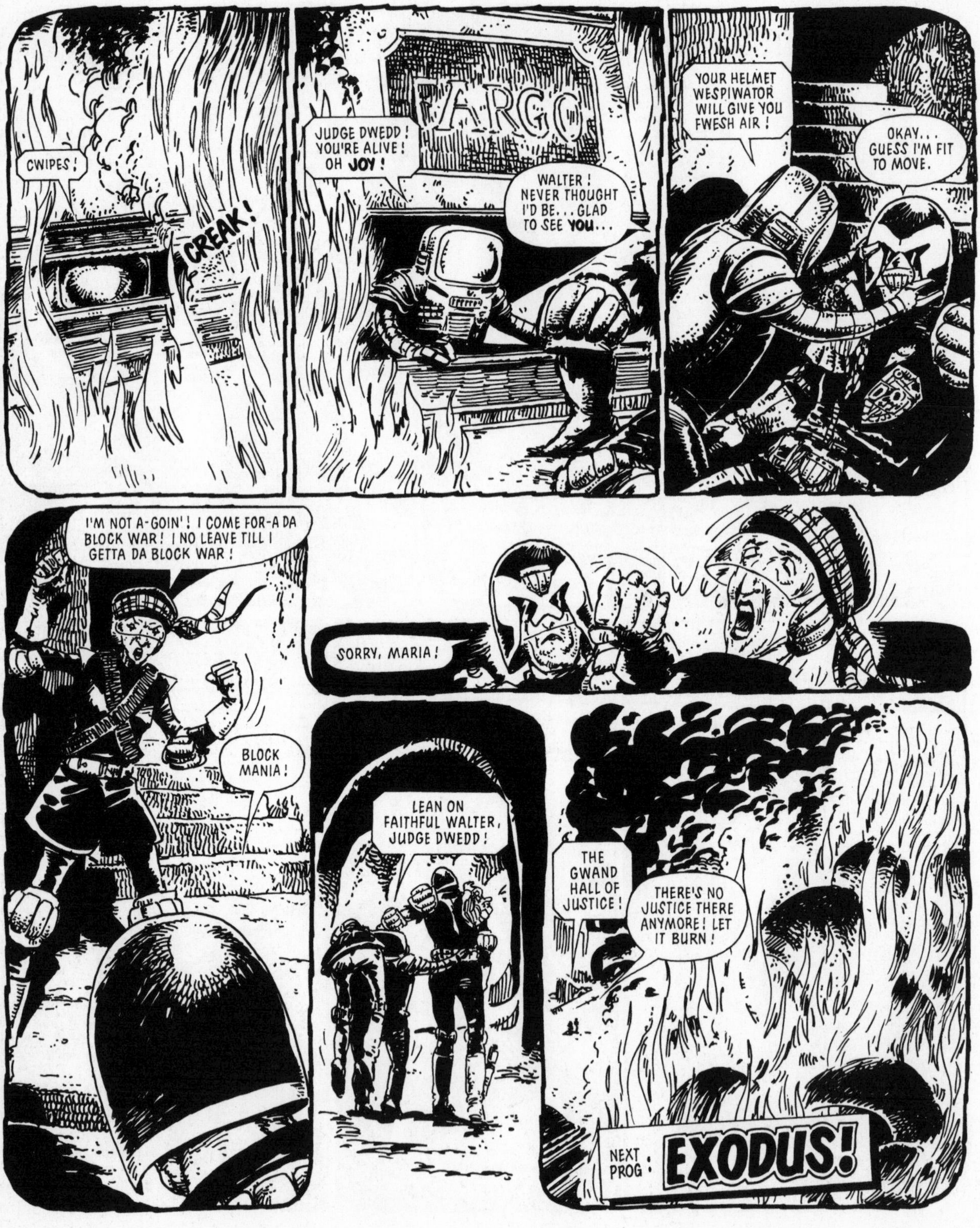

CWIPES!
CREAK!
FARGO
JUDGE DWEDD! YOU'RE ALIVE! OH JOY!
WALTER! NEVER THOUGHT I'D BE... GLAD TO SEE YOU...
YOUR HELMET WESPIWATOR WILL GIVE YOU FWESH AIR!
OKAY... GUESS I'M FIT TO MOVE.
I'M NOT A-GOIN'! I COME FOR-A DA BLOCK WAR! I NO LEAVE TILL I GETTA DA BLOCK WAR!
BLOCK MANIA!
SORRY, MARIA!
LEAN ON FAITHFUL WALTER, JUDGE DWEDD!
THE GWAND HALL OF JUSTICE!
THERE'S NO JUSTICE THERE ANYMORE! LET IT BURN!
NEXT PROG: EXODUS!

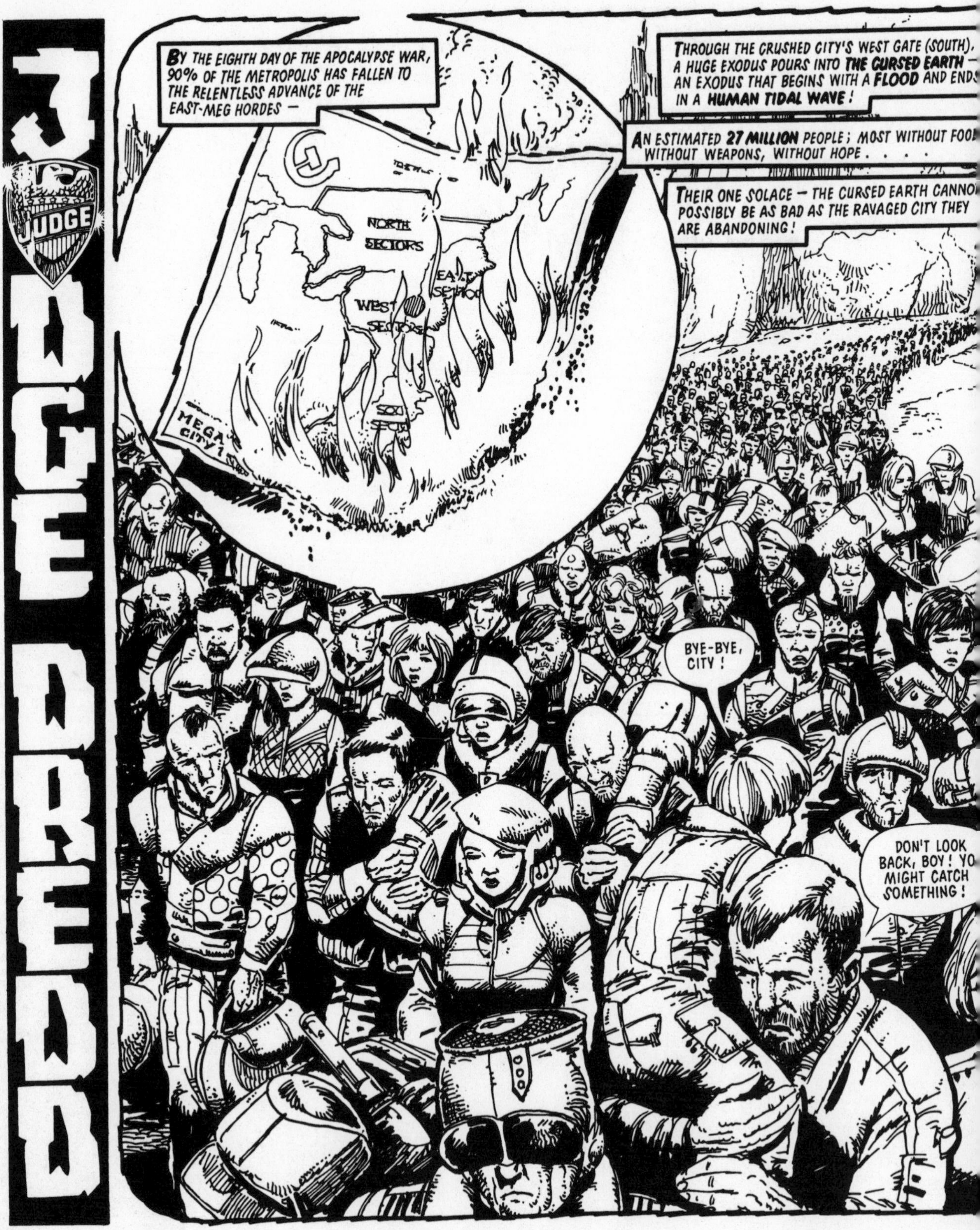
JUDGE DREDD
JUDGE
BY THE EIGHTH DAY OF THE APOCALYPSE WAR, 90% OF THE METROPOLIS HAS FALLEN TO THE RELENTLESS ADVANCE OF THE EAST-MEG HORDES –
NORTH SECTORS
WEST
MEGA CITY 1
THROUGH THE CRUSHED CITY'S WEST GATE (SOUTH), A HUGE EXODUS POURS INTO THE CURSED EARTH – AN EXODUS THAT BEGINS WITH A FLOOD AND ENDS IN A HUMAN TIDAL WAVE!
AN ESTIMATED 27 MILLION PEOPLE; MOST WITHOUT FOO WITHOUT WEAPONS, WITHOUT HOPE . . . .
THEIR ONE SOLACE – THE CURSED EARTH CANNO POSSIBLY BE AS BAD AS THE RAVAGED CITY THEY ARE ABANDONING!
BYE-BYE, CITY!
DON'T LOOK BACK, BOY! YO MIGHT CATCH SOMETHING!

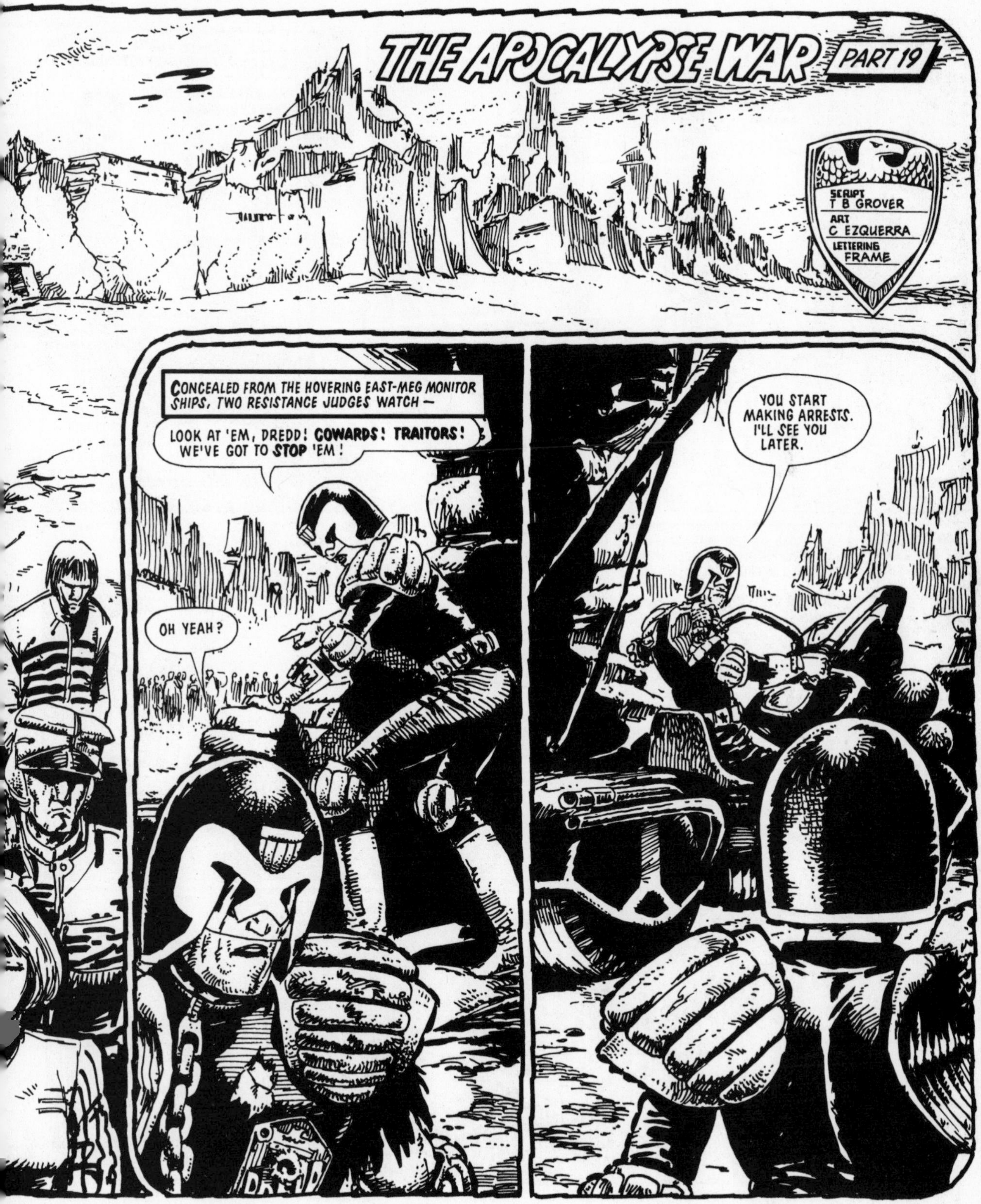
THE APOCALYPSE WAR
PART 19
SCRIPT T B GROVER
ART C EZQUERRA
LETTERING FRAME
CONCEALED FROM THE HOVERING EAST-MEG MONITOR SHIPS, TWO RESISTANCE JUDGES WATCH —
LOOK AT 'EM, DREDD! COWARDS! TRAITORS! WE'VE GOT TO STOP 'EM!
OH YEAH?
YOU START MAKING ARRESTS. I'LL SEE YOU LATER.

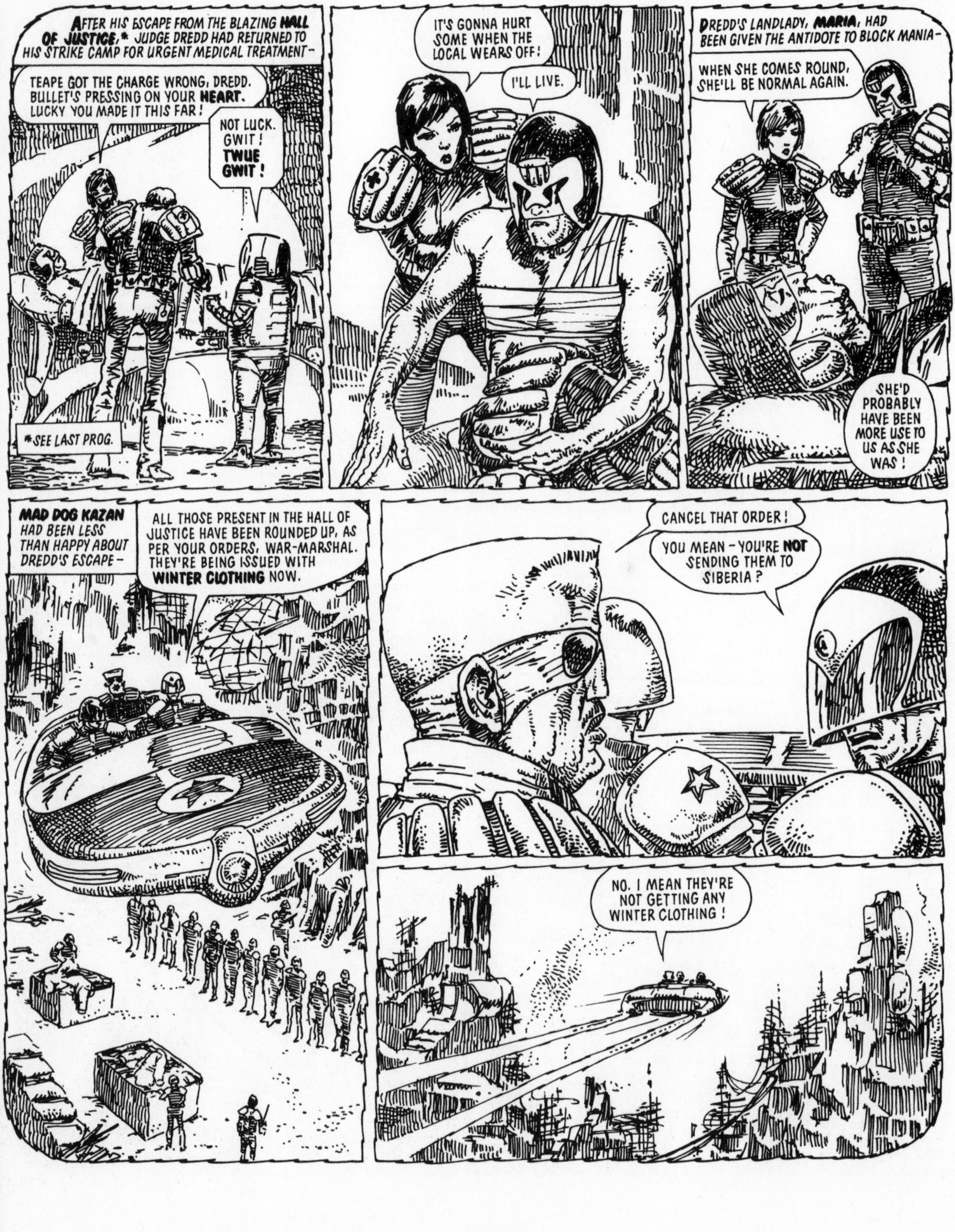
AFTER HIS ESCAPE FROM THE BLAZING HALL OF JUSTICE,* JUDGE DREDD HAD RETURNED TO HIS STRIKE CAMP FOR URGENT MEDICAL TREATMENT –
TEAPE GOT THE CHARGE WRONG, DREDD. BULLET'S PRESSING ON YOUR HEART. LUCKY YOU MADE IT THIS FAR!
NOT LUCK. GWIT! TWUE GWIT!
*SEE LAST PROG.
IT'S GONNA HURT SOME WHEN THE LOCAL WEARS OFF!
I'LL LIVE.
DREDD'S LANDLADY, MARIA, HAD BEEN GIVEN THE ANTIDOTE TO BLOCK MANIA –
WHEN SHE COMES ROUND, SHE'LL BE NORMAL AGAIN.
SHE'D PROBABLY HAVE BEEN MORE USE TO US AS SHE WAS!
MAD DOG KAZAN HAD BEEN LESS THAN HAPPY ABOUT DREDD'S ESCAPE –
ALL THOSE PRESENT IN THE HALL OF JUSTICE HAVE BEEN ROUNDED UP, AS PER YOUR ORDERS, WAR-MARSHAL. THEY'RE BEING ISSUED WITH WINTER CLOTHING NOW.
CANCEL THAT ORDER!
YOU MEAN – YOU'RE NOT SENDING THEM TO SIBERIA?
NO. I MEAN THEY'RE NOT GETTING ANY WINTER CLOTHING!

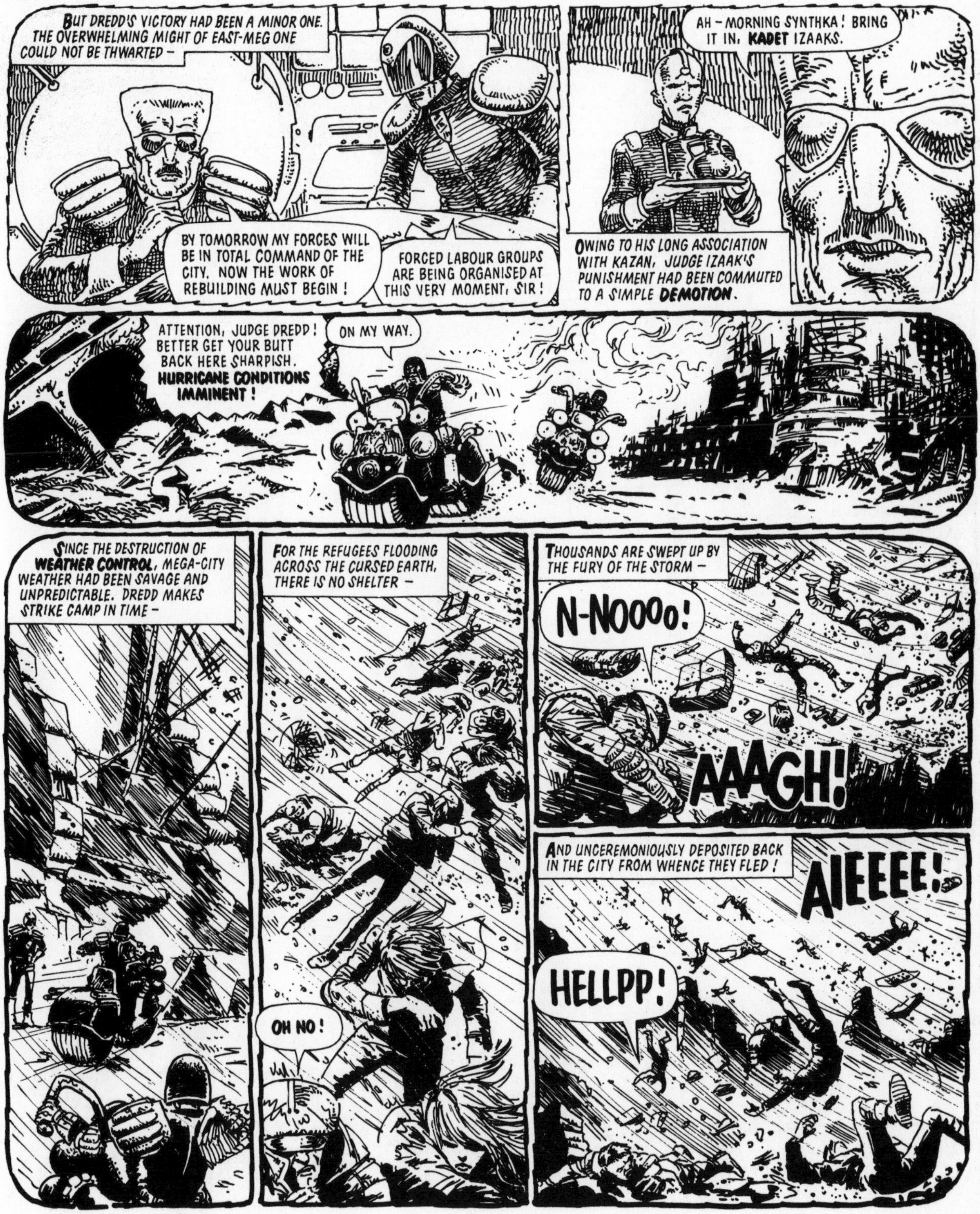
BUT DREDD'S VICTORY HAD BEEN A MINOR ONE. THE OVERWHELMING MIGHT OF EAST-MEG ONE COULD NOT BE THWARTED –
BY TOMORROW MY FORCES WILL BE IN TOTAL COMMAND OF THE CITY. NOW THE WORK OF REBUILDING MUST BEGIN!
FORCED LABOUR GROUPS ARE BEING ORGANISED AT THIS VERY MOMENT, SIR!
AH – MORNING SYNTHKA! BRING IT IN, KADET IZAAKS.
OWING TO HIS LONG ASSOCIATION WITH KAZAN, JUDGE IZAAK'S PUNISHMENT HAD BEEN COMMUTED TO A SIMPLE DEMOTION.
ATTENTION, JUDGE DREDD! BETTER GET YOUR BUTT BACK HERE SHARPISH. HURRICANE CONDITIONS IMMINENT!
ON MY WAY.
SINCE THE DESTRUCTION OF WEATHER CONTROL, MEGA-CITY WEATHER HAD BEEN SAVAGE AND UNPREDICTABLE. DREDD MAKES STRIKE CAMP IN TIME –
FOR THE REFUGEES FLOODING ACROSS THE CURSED EARTH, THERE IS NO SHELTER –
OH NO!
THOUSANDS ARE SWEPT UP BY THE FURY OF THE STORM –
N-NOOOo!
AAAGH!
AND UNCEREMONIOUSLY DEPOSITED BACK IN THE CITY FROM WHENCE THEY FLED!
AIEEEE!
HELLPP!

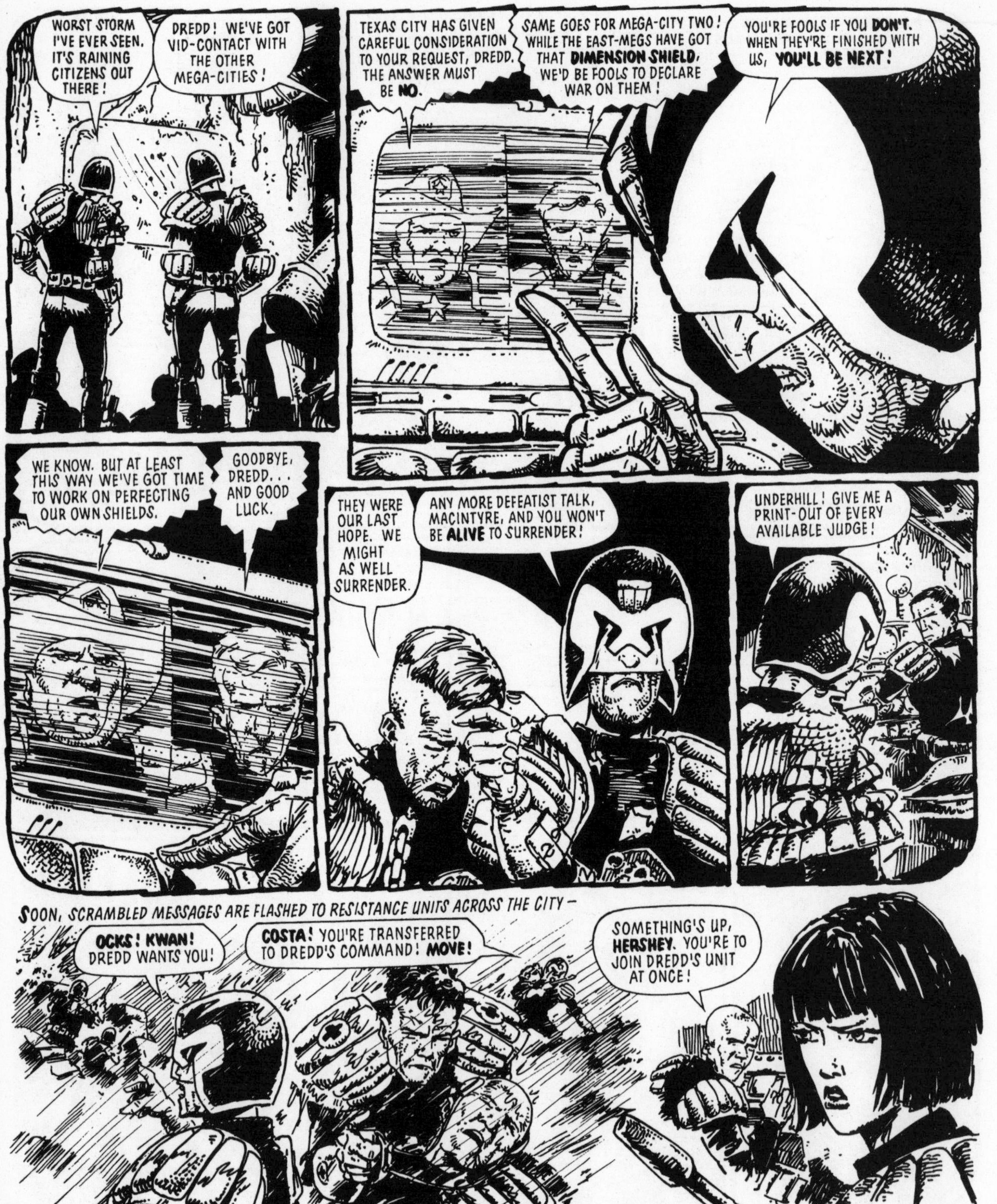
WORST STORM I'VE EVER SEEN. IT'S RAINING CITIZENS OUT THERE!
DREDD! WE'VE GOT VID-CONTACT WITH THE OTHER MEGA-CITIES!
TEXAS CITY HAS GIVEN CAREFUL CONSIDERATION TO YOUR REQUEST, DREDD. THE ANSWER MUST BE NO.
SAME GOES FOR MEGA-CITY TWO! WHILE THE EAST-MEGS HAVE GOT THAT DIMENSION SHIELD, WE'D BE FOOLS TO DECLARE WAR ON THEM!
YOU'RE FOOLS IF YOU DON'T. WHEN THEY'RE FINISHED WITH US, YOU'LL BE NEXT!
WE KNOW. BUT AT LEAST THIS WAY WE'VE GOT TIME TO WORK ON PERFECTING OUR OWN SHIELDS.
GOODBYE, DREDD... AND GOOD LUCK.
THEY WERE OUR LAST HOPE. WE MIGHT AS WELL SURRENDER.
ANY MORE DEFEATIST TALK, MACINTYRE, AND YOU WON'T BE ALIVE TO SURRENDER!
UNDERHILL! GIVE ME A PRINT-OUT OF EVERY AVAILABLE JUDGE!
SOON, SCRAMBLED MESSAGES ARE FLASHED TO RESISTANCE UNITS ACROSS THE CITY –
OCKS! KWAN! DREDD WANTS YOU!
COSTA! YOU'RE TRANSFERRED TO DREDD'S COMMAND! MOVE!
SOMETHING'S UP, HERSHEY. YOU'RE TO JOIN DREDD'S UNIT AT ONCE!

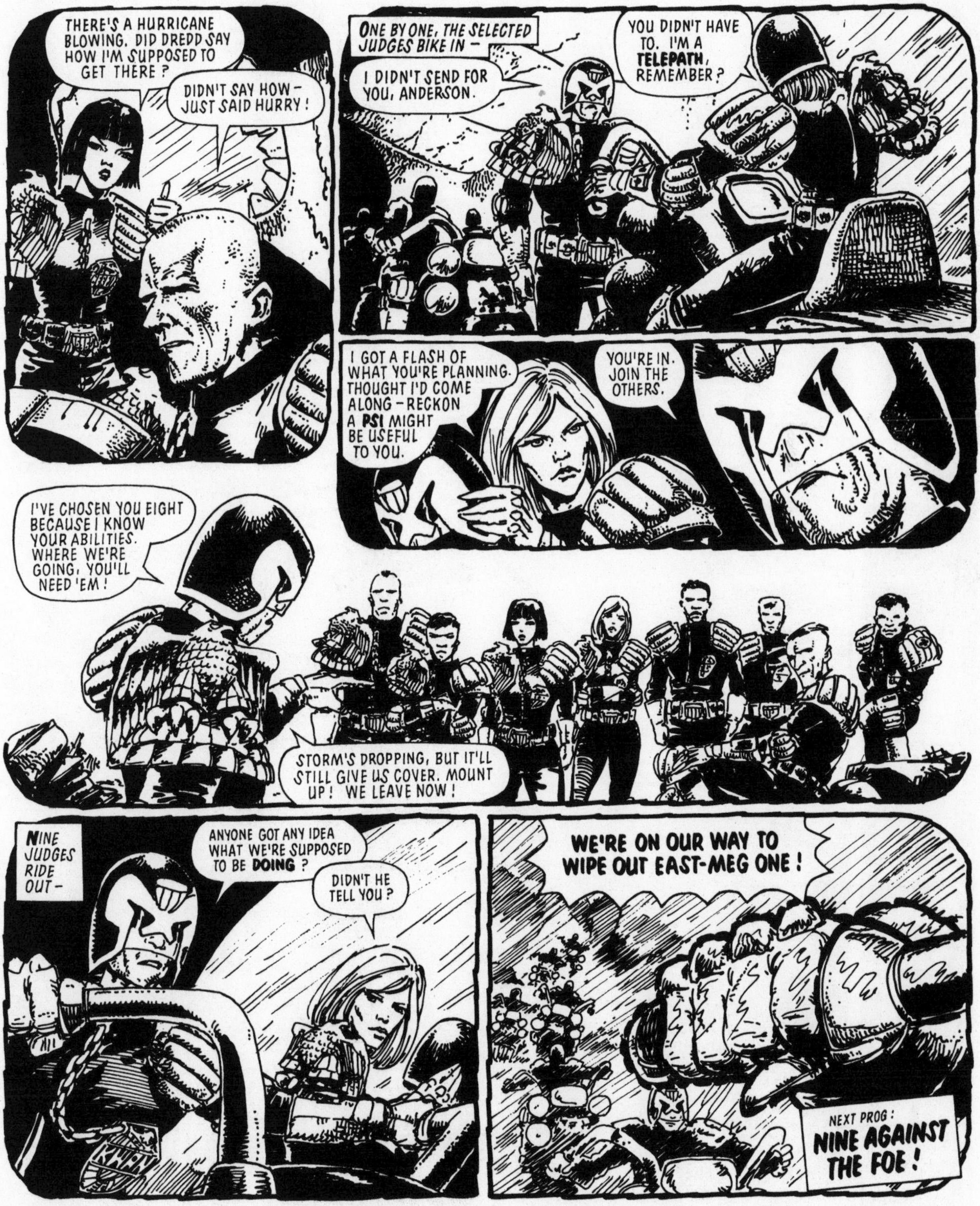
THERE'S A HURRICANE BLOWING. DID DREDD SAY HOW I'M SUPPOSED TO GET THERE ?
DIDN'T SAY HOW – JUST SAID HURRY !
ONE BY ONE, THE SELECTED JUDGES BIKE IN –
I DIDN'T SEND FOR YOU, ANDERSON.
YOU DIDN'T HAVE TO. I'M A TELEPATH, REMEMBER ?
I GOT A FLASH OF WHAT YOU'RE PLANNING. THOUGHT I'D COME ALONG – RECKON A PSI MIGHT BE USEFUL TO YOU.
YOU'RE IN. JOIN THE OTHERS.
I'VE CHOSEN YOU EIGHT BECAUSE I KNOW YOUR ABILITIES. WHERE WE'RE GOING, YOU'LL NEED 'EM !
STORM'S DROPPING, BUT IT'LL STILL GIVE US COVER. MOUNT UP ! WE LEAVE NOW !
NINE JUDGES RIDE OUT –
ANYONE GOT ANY IDEA WHAT WE'RE SUPPOSED TO BE DOING ?
DIDN'T HE TELL YOU ?
WE'RE ON OUR WAY TO WIPE OUT EAST-MEG ONE !
NEXT PROG : NINE AGAINST THE FOE !

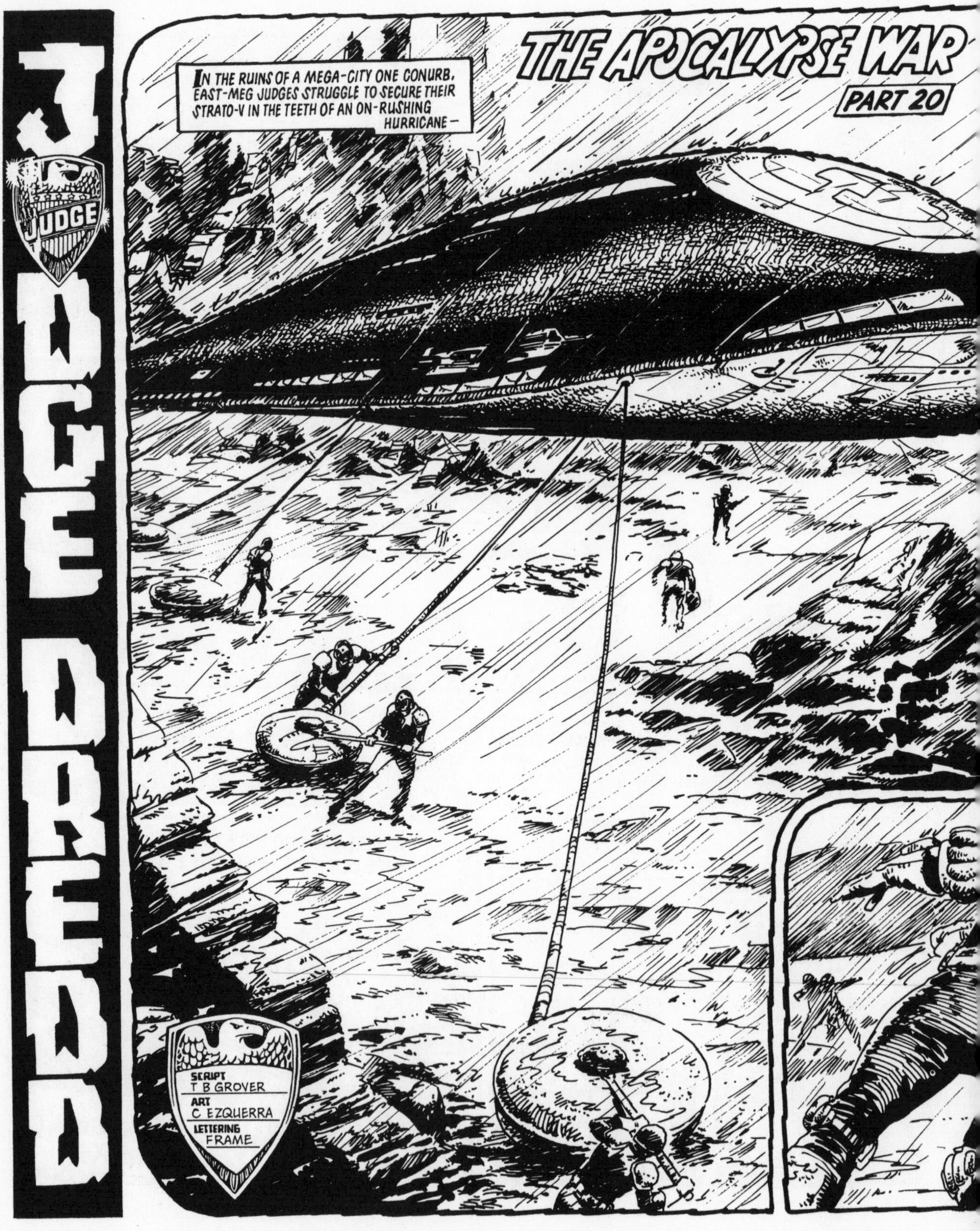
JUDGE DREDD
JUDGE
THE APOCALYPSE WAR
PART 20
IN THE RUINS OF A MEGA-CITY ONE CONURB, EAST-MEG JUDGES STRUGGLE TO SECURE THEIR STRATO-V IN THE TEETH OF AN ON-RUSHING HURRICANE —
SCRIPT
T B GROVER
ART
C EZQUERRA
LETTERING
FRAME

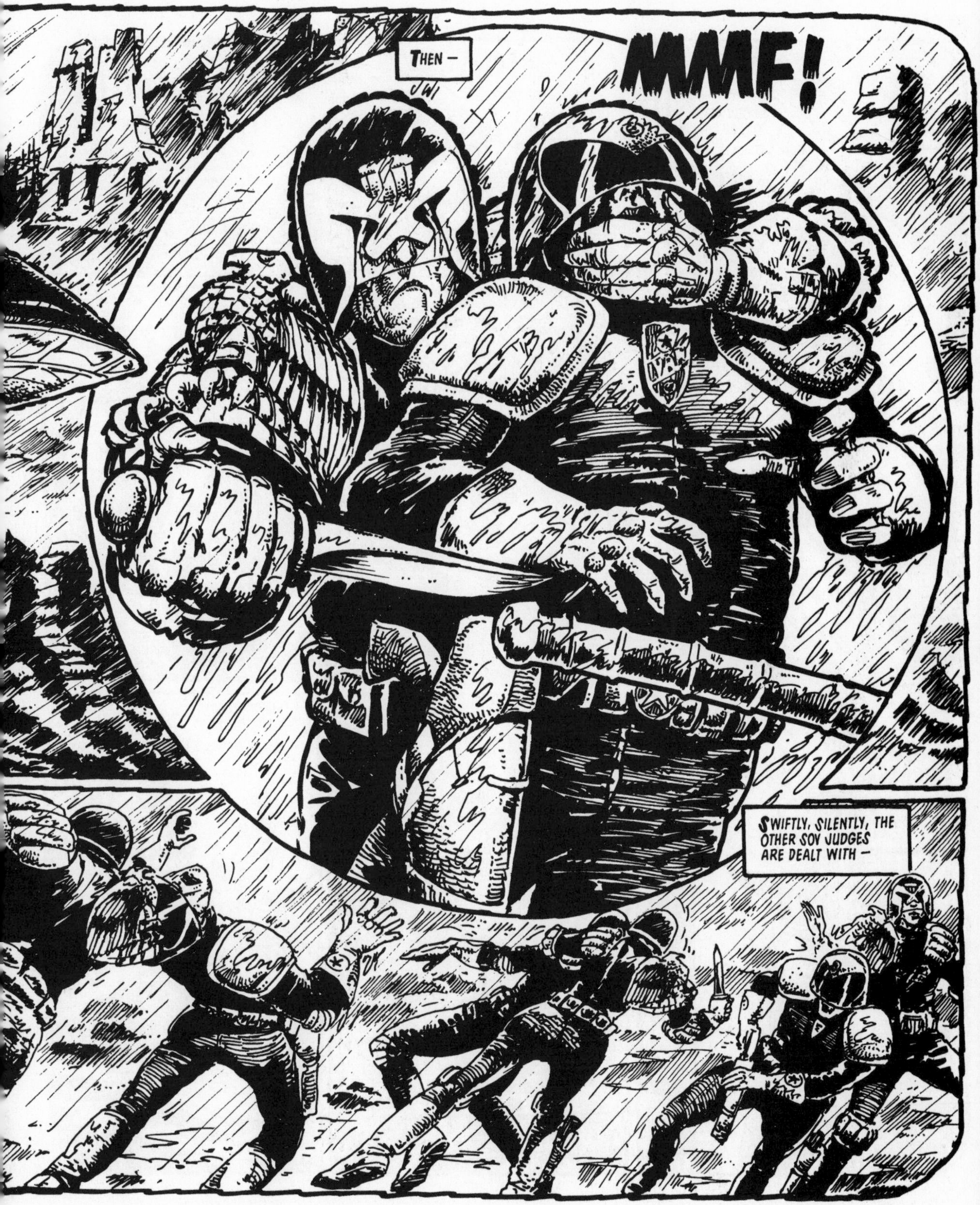
THEN –
MMF!
SWIFTLY, SILENTLY, THE OTHER SOV JUDGES ARE DEALT WITH –

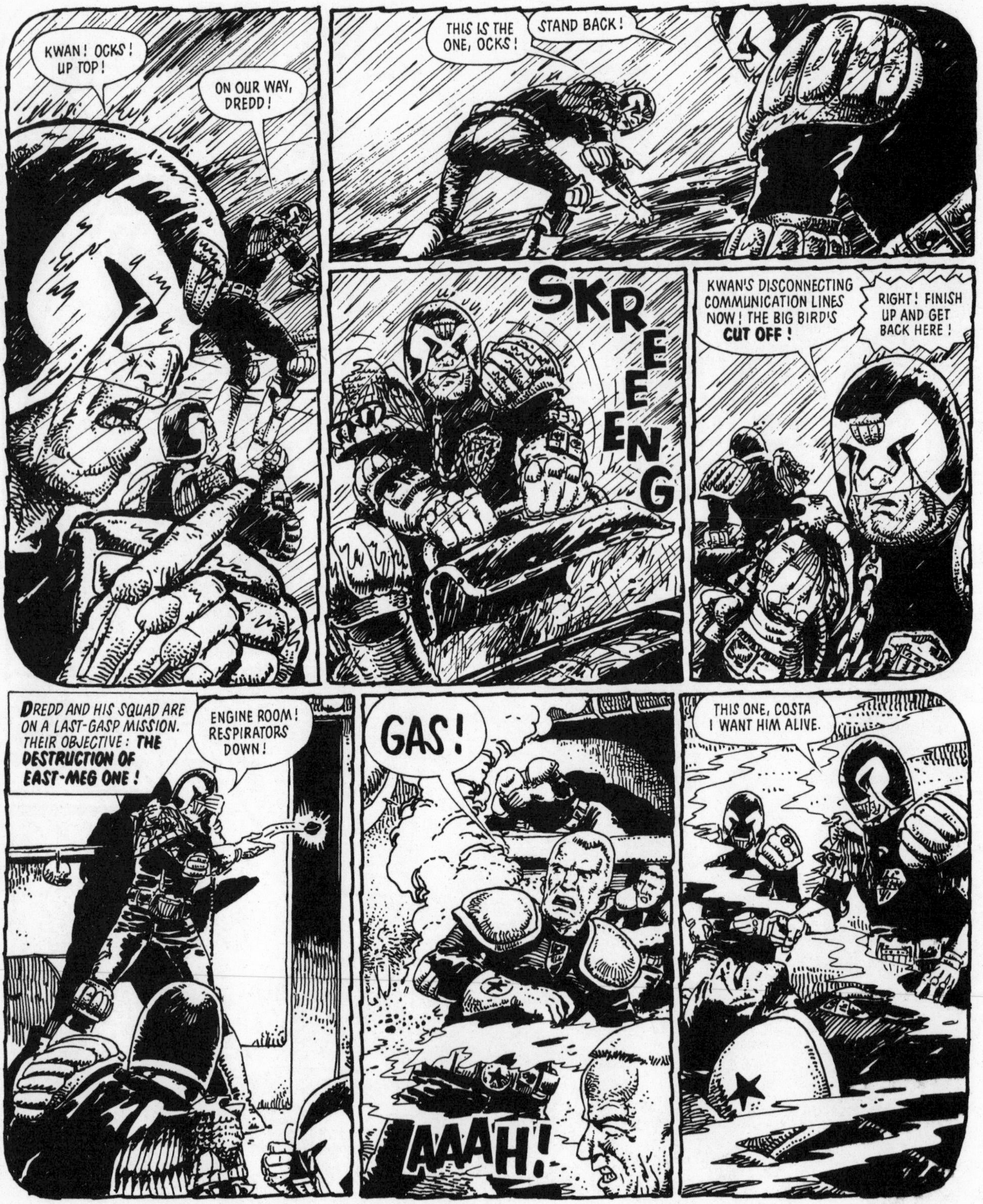
KWAN! OCKS! UP TOP!
ON OUR WAY, DREDD!
THIS IS THE ONE, OCKS!
STAND BACK!
SKREEENG
KWAN'S DISCONNECTING COMMUNICATION LINES NOW! THE BIG BIRD'S CUT OFF!
RIGHT! FINISH UP AND GET BACK HERE!
DREDD AND HIS SQUAD ARE ON A LAST-GASP MISSION. THEIR OBJECTIVE: THE DESTRUCTION OF EAST-MEG ONE!
ENGINE ROOM! RESPIRATORS DOWN!
GAS!
AAAH!
THIS ONE, COSTA I WANT HIM ALIVE.

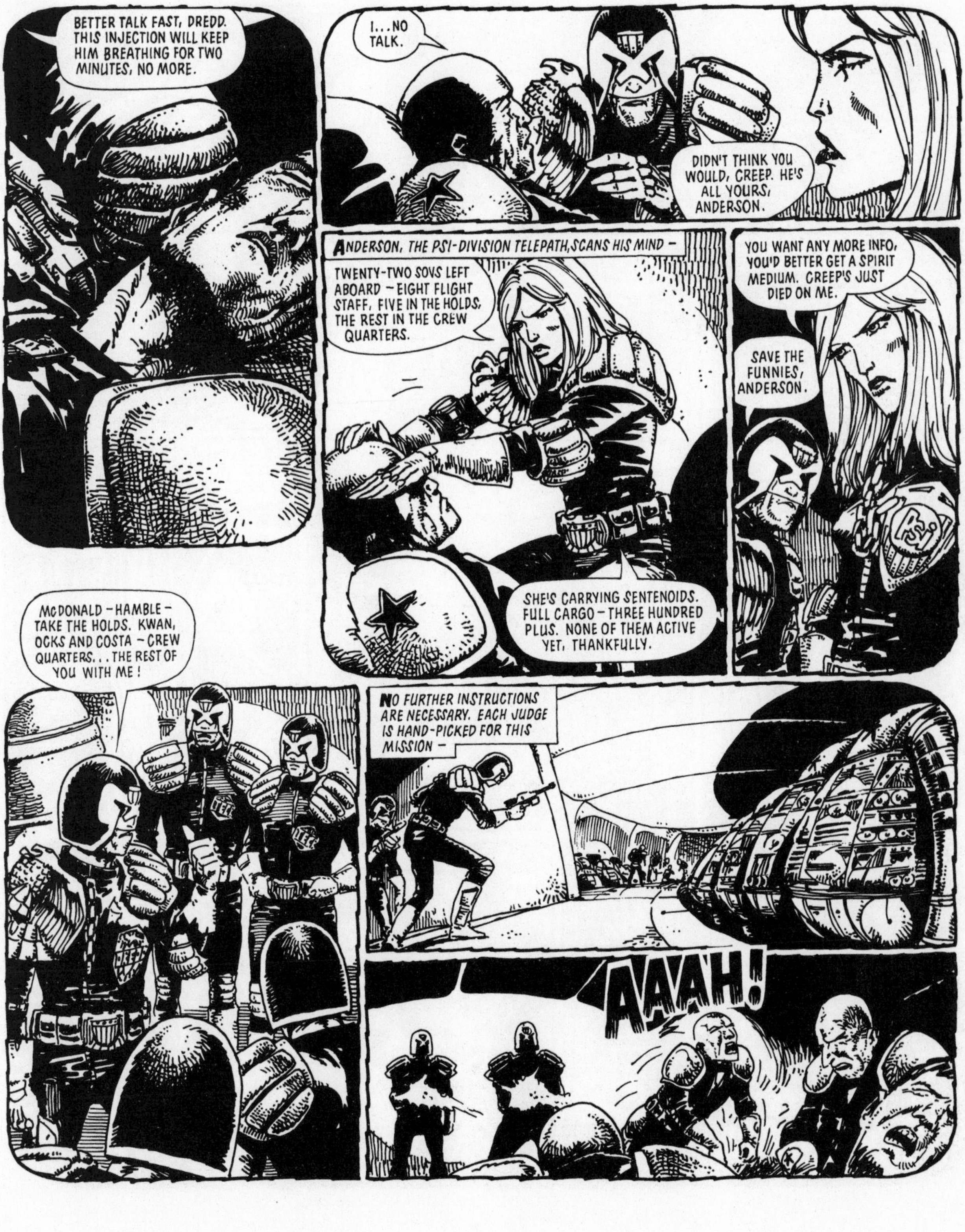
BETTER TALK FAST, DREDD. THIS INJECTION WILL KEEP HIM BREATHING FOR TWO MINUTES, NO MORE.
I...NO TALK.
DIDN'T THINK YOU WOULD, CREEP. HE'S ALL YOURS, ANDERSON.
ANDERSON, THE PSI-DIVISION TELEPATH, SCANS HIS MIND –
TWENTY-TWO SOVS LEFT ABOARD – EIGHT FLIGHT STAFF, FIVE IN THE HOLDS, THE REST IN THE CREW QUARTERS.
SHE'S CARRYING SENTENOIDS. FULL CARGO – THREE HUNDRED PLUS. NONE OF THEM ACTIVE YET, THANKFULLY.
YOU WANT ANY MORE INFO, YOU'D BETTER GET A SPIRIT MEDIUM. CREEP'S JUST DIED ON ME.
SAVE THE FUNNIES, ANDERSON.
McDONALD – HAMBLE – TAKE THE HOLDS. KWAN, OCKS AND COSTA – CREW QUARTERS... THE REST OF YOU WITH ME!
NO FURTHER INSTRUCTIONS ARE NECESSARY. EACH JUDGE IS HAND-PICKED FOR THIS MISSION –
AAAH!

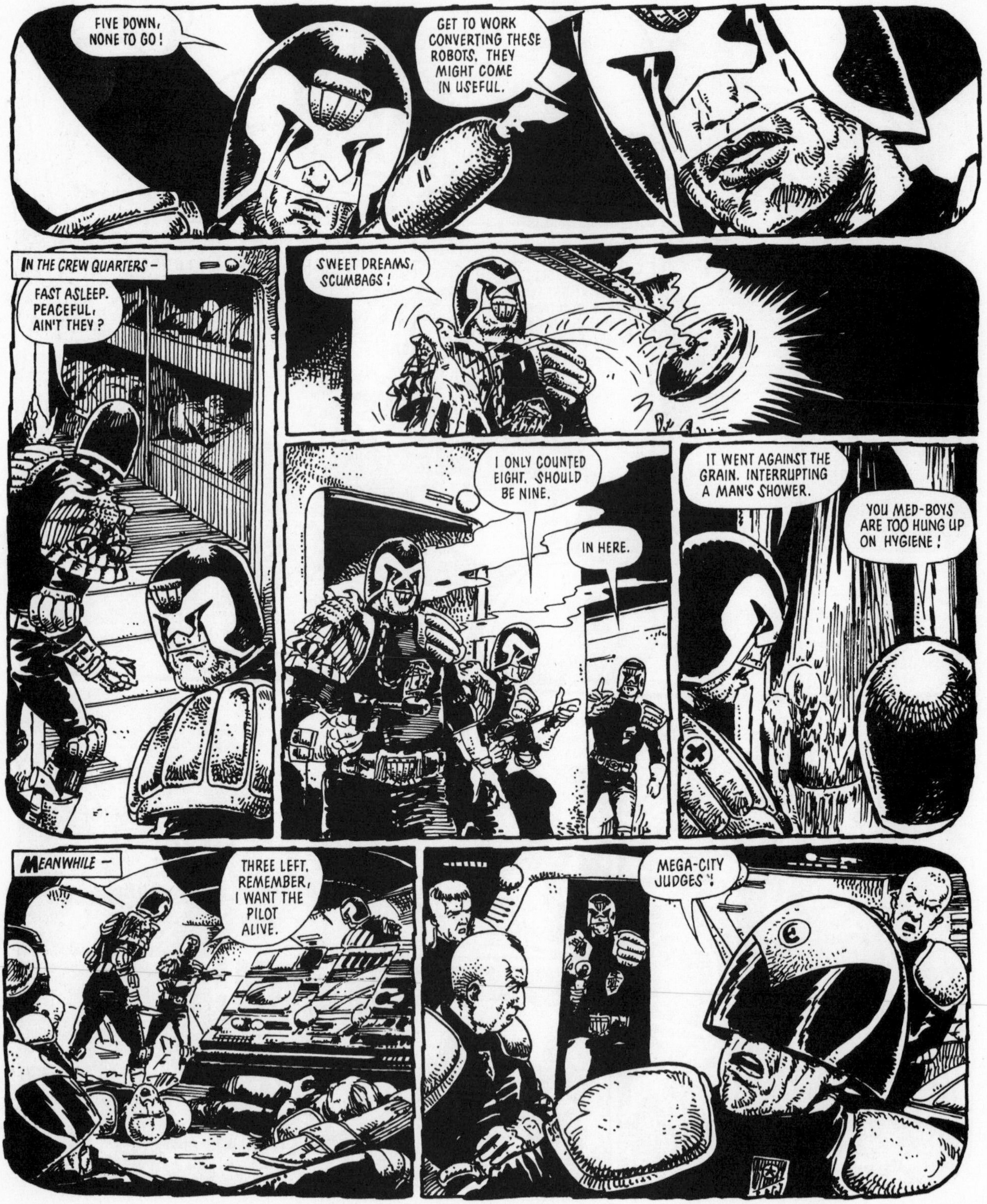
FIVE DOWN, NONE TO GO!
GET TO WORK CONVERTING THESE ROBOTS. THEY MIGHT COME IN USEFUL.
IN THE CREW QUARTERS –
FAST ASLEEP. PEACEFUL, AIN'T THEY?
SWEET DREAMS, SCUMBAGS!
I ONLY COUNTED EIGHT. SHOULD BE NINE.
IN HERE.
IT WENT AGAINST THE GRAIN. INTERRUPTING A MAN'S SHOWER.
YOU MED-BOYS ARE TOO HUNG UP ON HYGIENE!
MEANWHILE –
THREE LEFT. REMEMBER, I WANT THE PILOT ALIVE.
MEGA-CITY JUDGES!

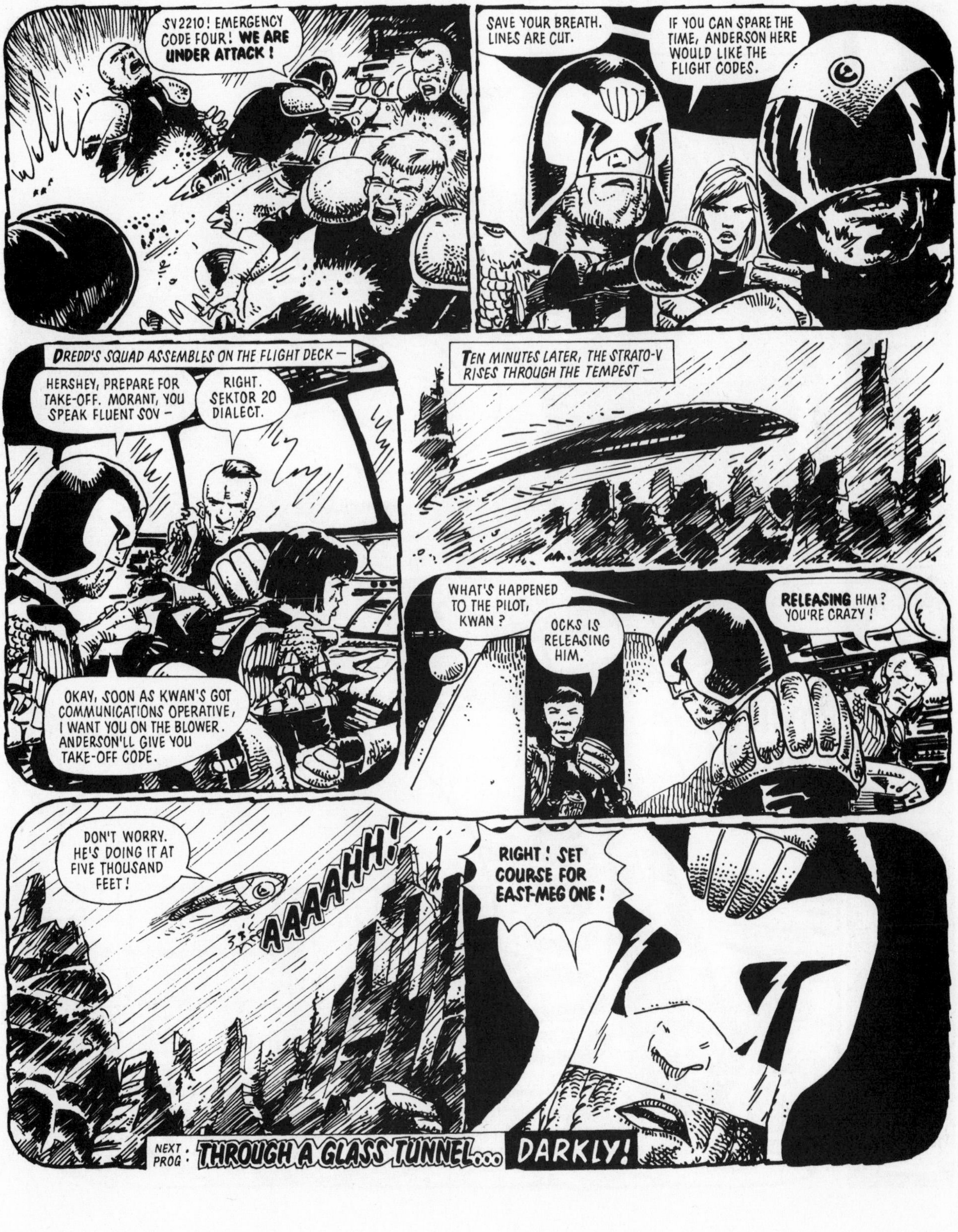
SV2210! EMERGENCY CODE FOUR! WE ARE UNDER ATTACK!
SAVE YOUR BREATH. LINES ARE CUT.
IF YOU CAN SPARE THE TIME, ANDERSON HERE WOULD LIKE THE FLIGHT CODES.
DREDD'S SQUAD ASSEMBLES ON THE FLIGHT DECK –
HERSHEY, PREPARE FOR TAKE-OFF. MORANT, YOU SPEAK FLUENT SOV –
RIGHT. SEKTOR 20 DIALECT.
OKAY, SOON AS KWAN'S GOT COMMUNICATIONS OPERATIVE, I WANT YOU ON THE BLOWER. ANDERSON'LL GIVE YOU TAKE-OFF CODE.
TEN MINUTES LATER, THE STRATO-V RISES THROUGH THE TEMPEST –
WHAT'S HAPPENED TO THE PILOT, KWAN?
OCKS IS RELEASING HIM.
RELEASING HIM? YOU'RE CRAZY!
DON'T WORRY. HE'S DOING IT AT FIVE THOUSAND FEET!
AAAAAHH!
RIGHT! SET COURSE FOR EAST-MEG ONE!
NEXT PROG: THROUGH A GLASS TUNNEL... DARKLY!

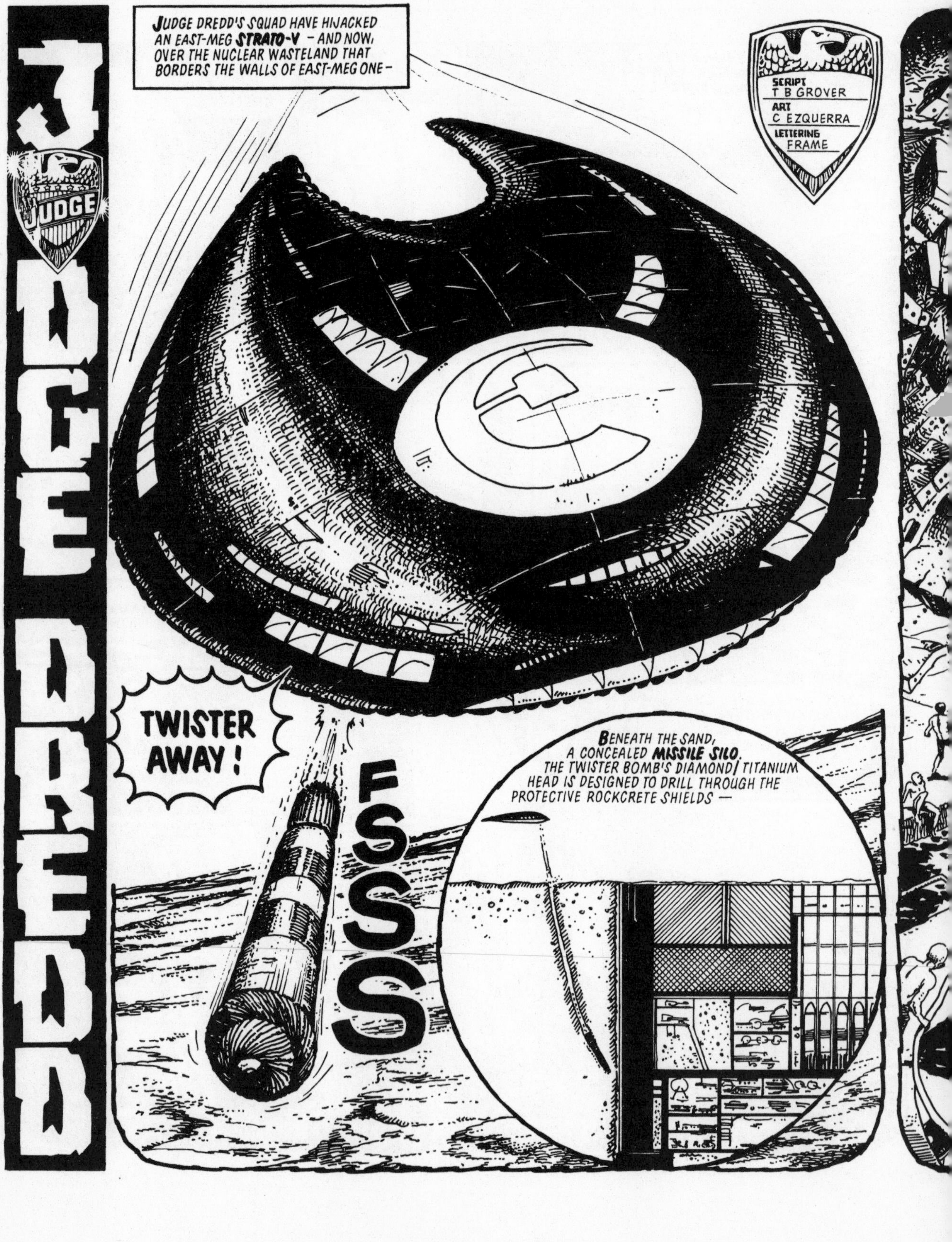
JUDGE DREDD
JUDGE DREDD'S SQUAD HAVE HIJACKED AN EAST-MEG STRATO-V – AND NOW, OVER THE NUCLEAR WASTELAND THAT BORDERS THE WALLS OF EAST-MEG ONE –
SCRIPT T B GROVER
ART C EZQUERRA
LETTERING FRAME
TWISTER AWAY!
FSSS
BENEATH THE SAND, A CONCEALED MISSILE SILO. THE TWISTER BOMB'S DIAMOND/TITANIUM HEAD IS DESIGNED TO DRILL THROUGH THE PROTECTIVE ROCKCRETE SHIELDS –

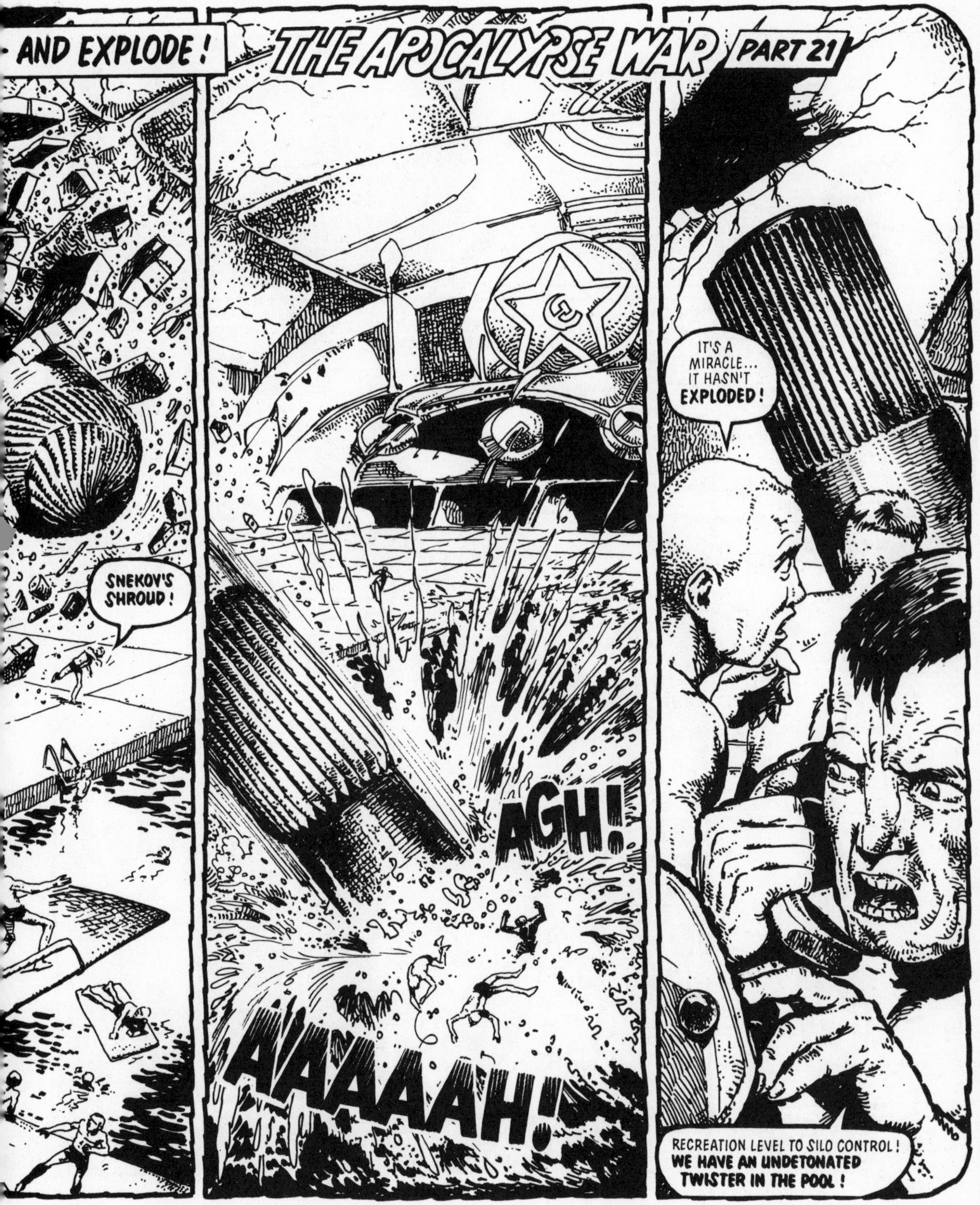

– AND EXPLODE!
THE APOCALYPSE WAR
PART 21
SNEKOV'S SHROUD!
AGH!
AAAAAH!
IT'S A MIRACLE... IT HASN'T EXPLODED!
RECREATION LEVEL TO SILO CONTROL! WE HAVE AN UNDETONATED TWISTER IN THE POOL!

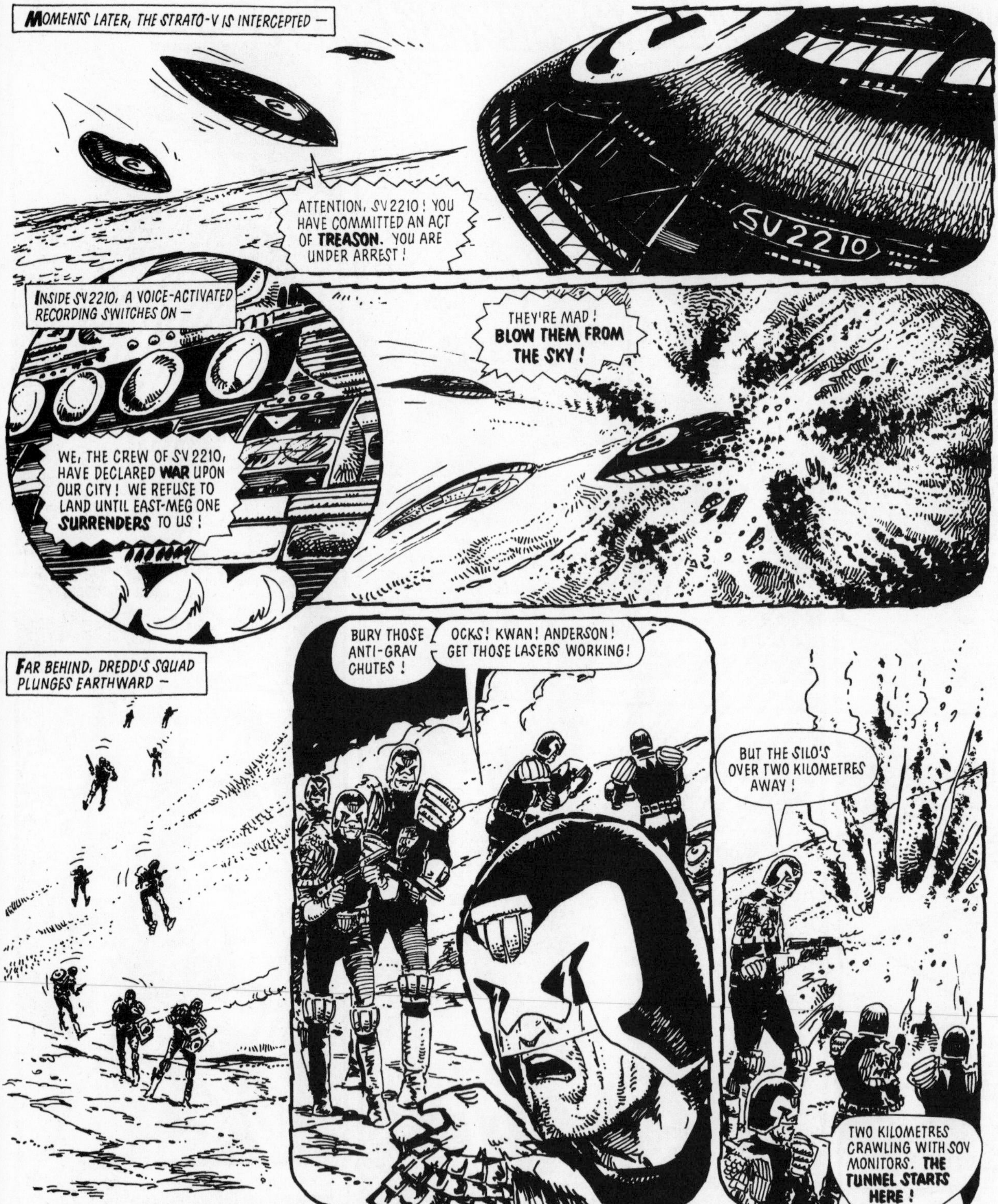
MOMENTS LATER, THE STRATO-V IS INTERCEPTED —
ATTENTION, SV 2210! YOU HAVE COMMITTED AN ACT OF TREASON. YOU ARE UNDER ARREST!
SV 2210
INSIDE SV 2210, A VOICE-ACTIVATED RECORDING SWITCHES ON —
WE, THE CREW OF SV 2210, HAVE DECLARED WAR UPON OUR CITY! WE REFUSE TO LAND UNTIL EAST-MEG ONE SURRENDERS TO US!
THEY'RE MAD! BLOW THEM FROM THE SKY!
FAR BEHIND, DREDD'S SQUAD PLUNGES EARTHWARD —
BURY THOSE ANTI-GRAV CHUTES!
OCKS! KWAN! ANDERSON! GET THOSE LASERS WORKING!
BUT THE SILO'S OVER TWO KILOMETRES AWAY!
TWO KILOMETRES CRAWLING WITH SOV MONITORS. THE TUNNEL STARTS HERE!

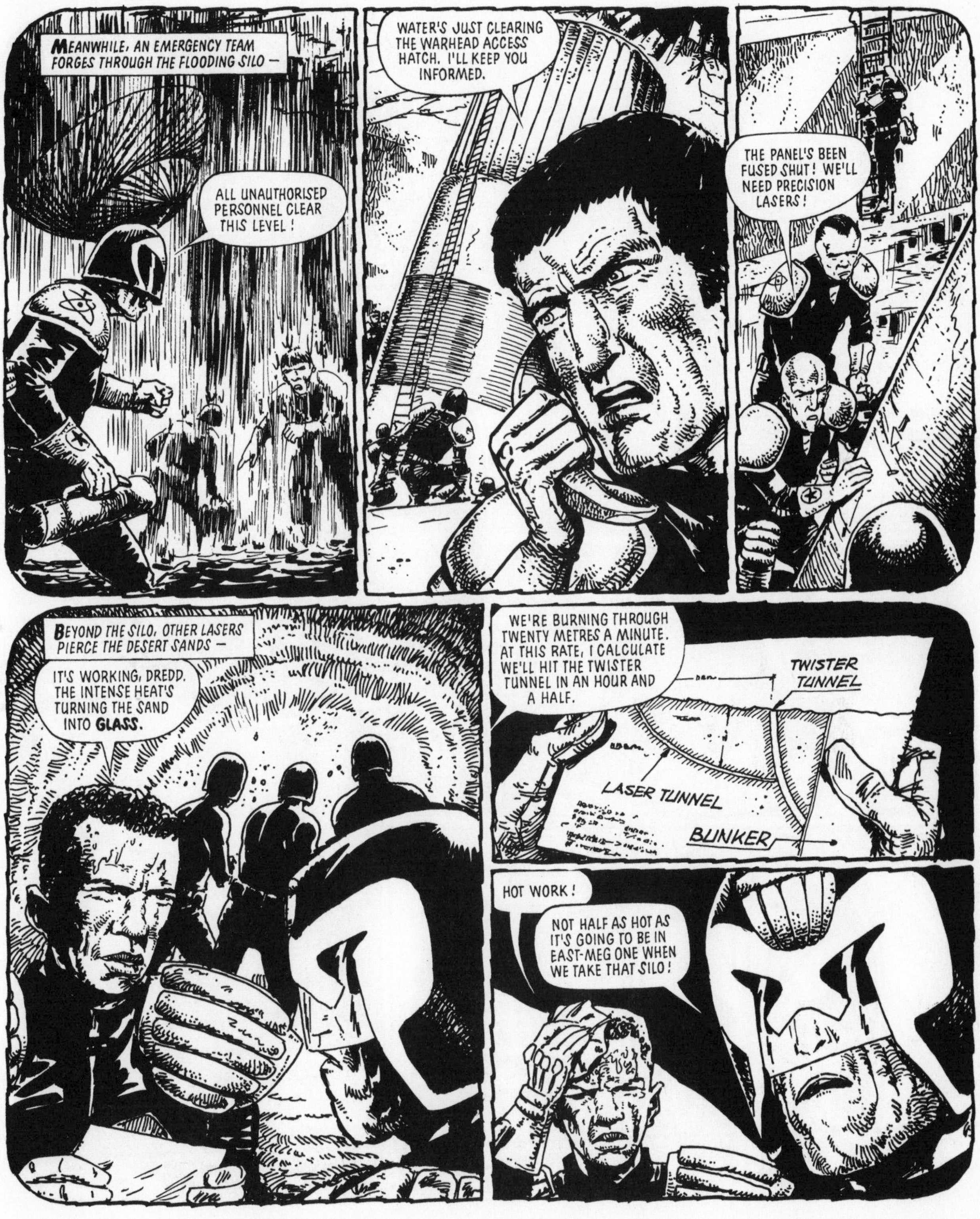
MEANWHILE, AN EMERGENCY TEAM FORGES THROUGH THE FLOODING SILO —
ALL UNAUTHORISED PERSONNEL CLEAR THIS LEVEL !
WATER'S JUST CLEARING THE WARHEAD ACCESS HATCH. I'LL KEEP YOU INFORMED.
THE PANEL'S BEEN FUSED SHUT ! WE'LL NEED PRECISION LASERS !
BEYOND THE SILO, OTHER LASERS PIERCE THE DESERT SANDS —
IT'S WORKING, DREDD. THE INTENSE HEAT'S TURNING THE SAND INTO GLASS.
WE'RE BURNING THROUGH TWENTY METRES A MINUTE. AT THIS RATE, I CALCULATE WE'LL HIT THE TWISTER TUNNEL IN AN HOUR AND A HALF.
TWISTER TUNNEL
LASER TUNNEL
BUNKER
HOT WORK !
NOT HALF AS HOT AS IT'S GOING TO BE IN EAST-MEG ONE WHEN WE TAKE THAT SILO !

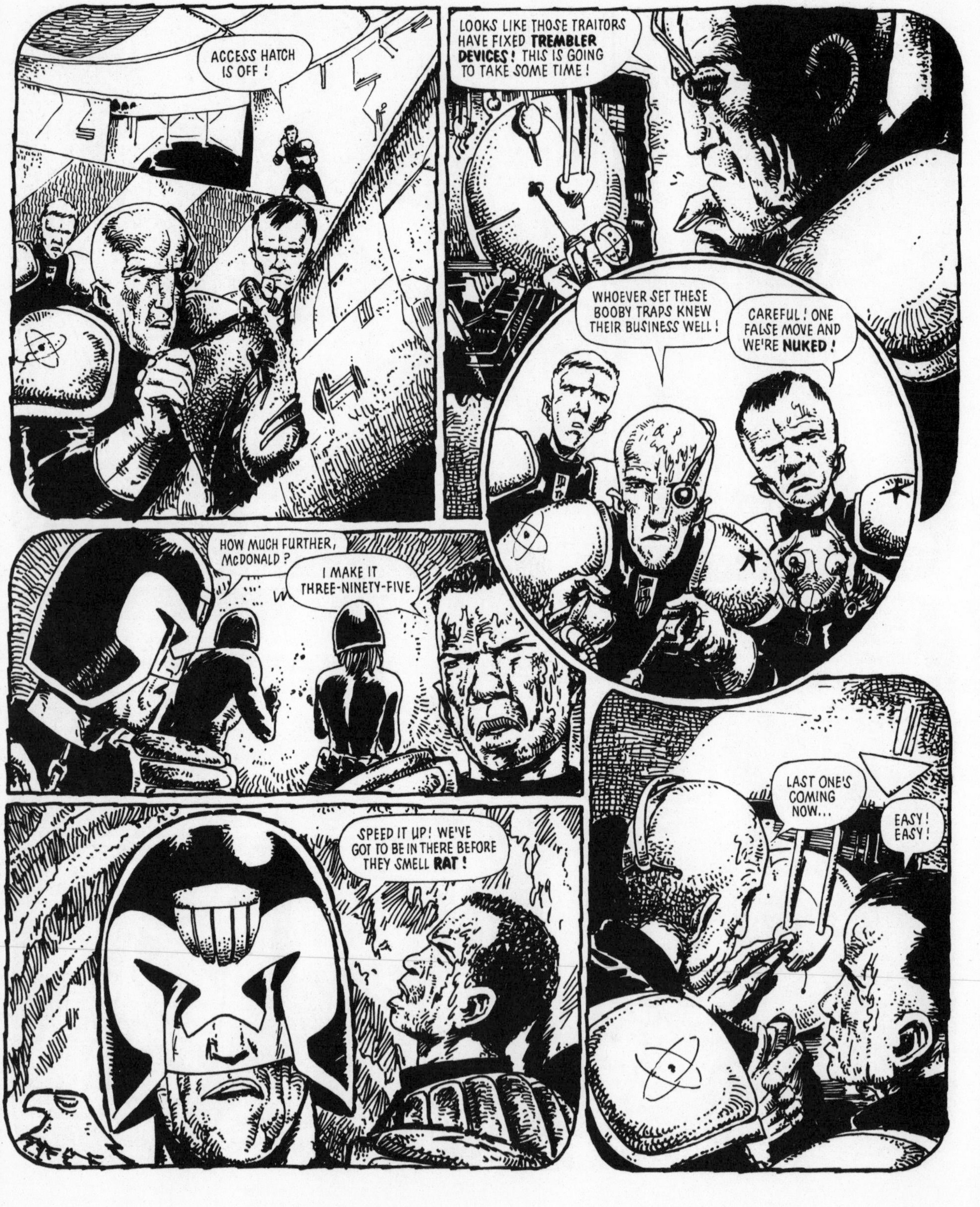
ACCESS HATCH IS OFF!
LOOKS LIKE THOSE TRAITORS HAVE FIXED **TREMBLER DEVICES!** THIS IS GOING TO TAKE SOME TIME!
WHOEVER SET THESE BOOBY TRAPS KNEW THEIR BUSINESS WELL!
CAREFUL! ONE FALSE MOVE AND WE'RE **NUKED!**
HOW MUCH FURTHER, McDONALD?
I MAKE IT THREE-NINETY-FIVE.
SPEED IT UP! WE'VE GOT TO BE IN THERE BEFORE THEY SMELL **RAT!**
LAST ONE'S COMING NOW...
EASY! EASY!

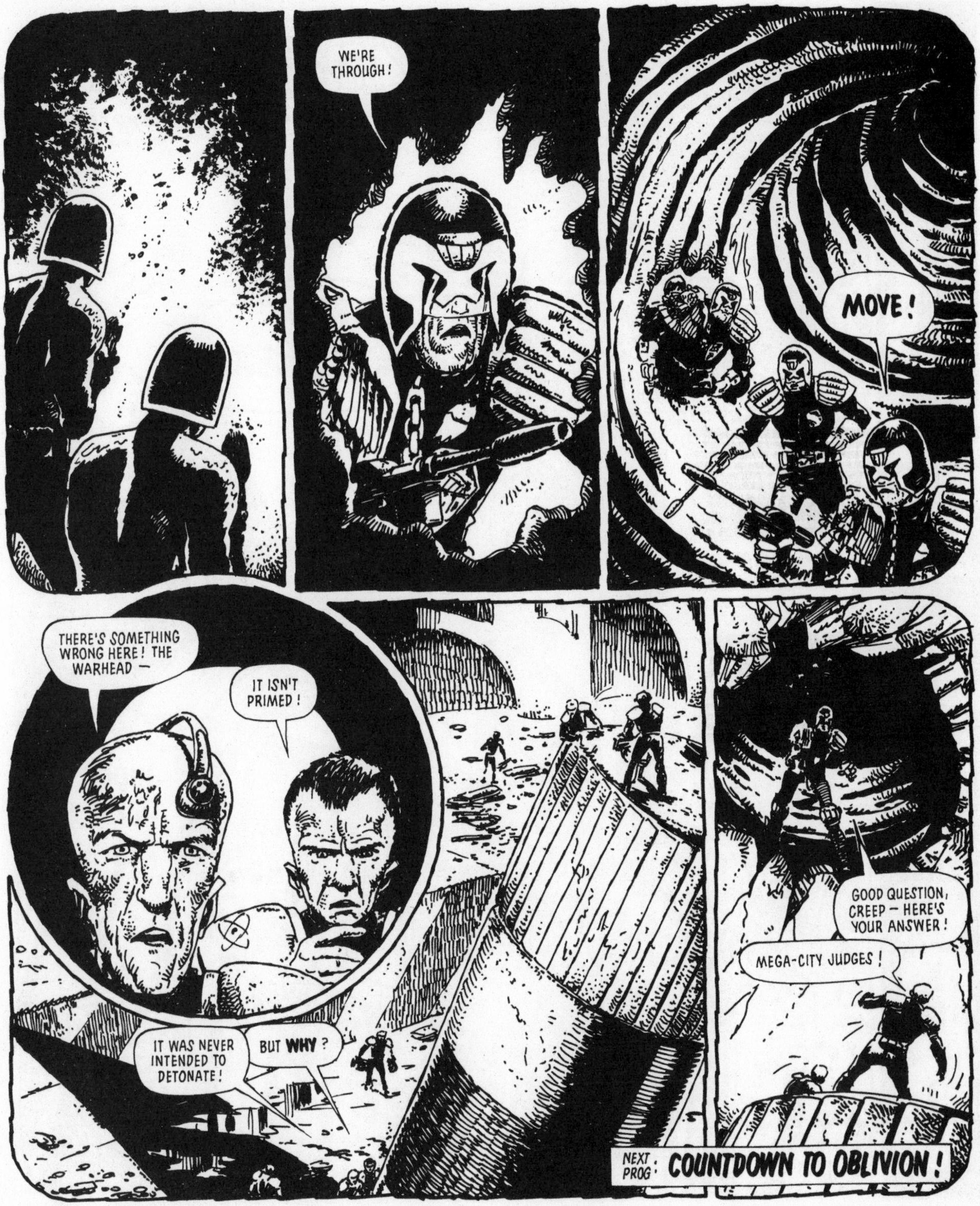
WE'RE THROUGH!
MOVE!
THERE'S SOMETHING WRONG HERE! THE WARHEAD —
IT ISN'T PRIMED!
IT WAS NEVER INTENDED TO DETONATE!
BUT WHY?
GOOD QUESTION, CREEP — HERE'S YOUR ANSWER!
MEGA-CITY JUDGES!
NEXT PROG: COUNTDOWN TO OBLIVION!

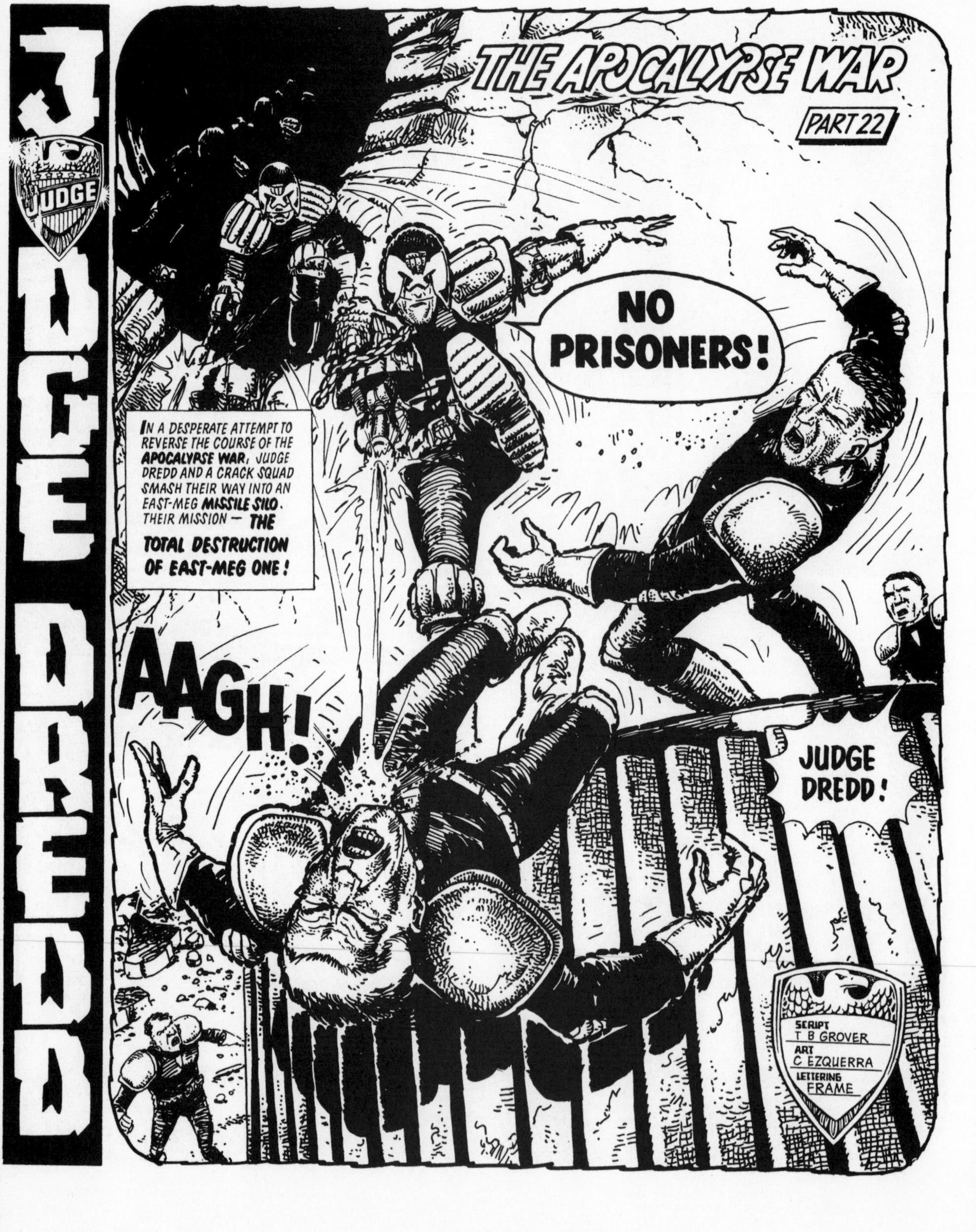
JUDGE DREDD
JUDGE
THE APOCALYPSE WAR
PART 22
IN A DESPERATE ATTEMPT TO REVERSE THE COURSE OF THE APOCALYPSE WAR, JUDGE DREDD AND A CRACK SQUAD SMASH THEIR WAY INTO AN EAST-MEG MISSILE SILO. THEIR MISSION — THE TOTAL DESTRUCTION OF EAST-MEG ONE!
NO PRISONERS!
AAGH!
JUDGE DREDD!
SCRIPT T B GROVER
ART C EZQUERRA
LETTERING FRAME

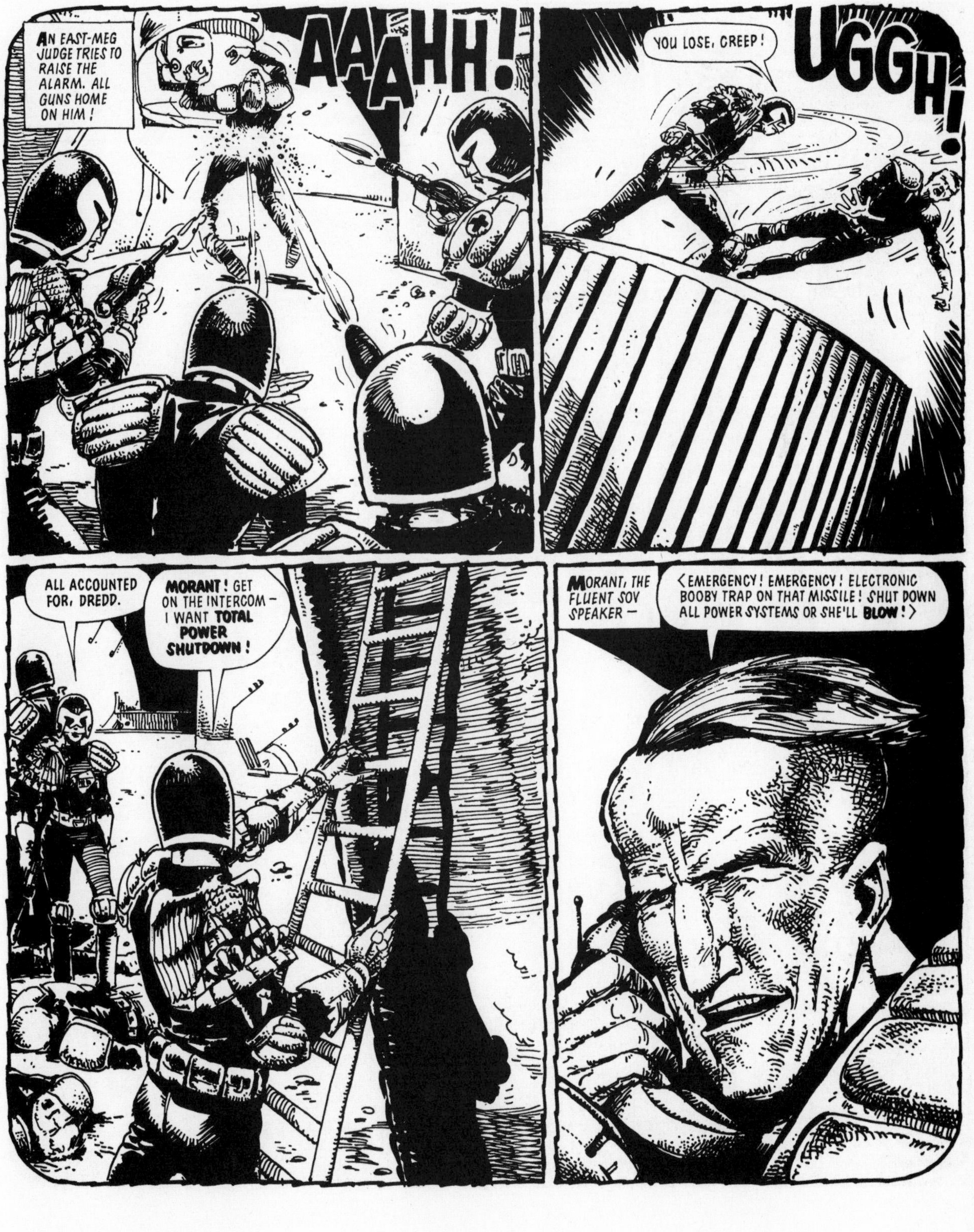

AN EAST-MEG JUDGE TRIES TO RAISE THE ALARM. ALL GUNS HOME ON HIM!
AAAAHH!
YOU LOSE, CREEP!
UGGH!
ALL ACCOUNTED FOR, DREDD.
MORANT! GET ON THE INTERCOM - I WANT TOTAL POWER SHUTDOWN!
MORANT, THE FLUENT SOV SPEAKER -
<EMERGENCY! EMERGENCY! ELECTRONIC BOOBY TRAP ON THAT MISSILE! SHUT DOWN ALL POWER SYSTEMS OR SHE'LL BLOW!>

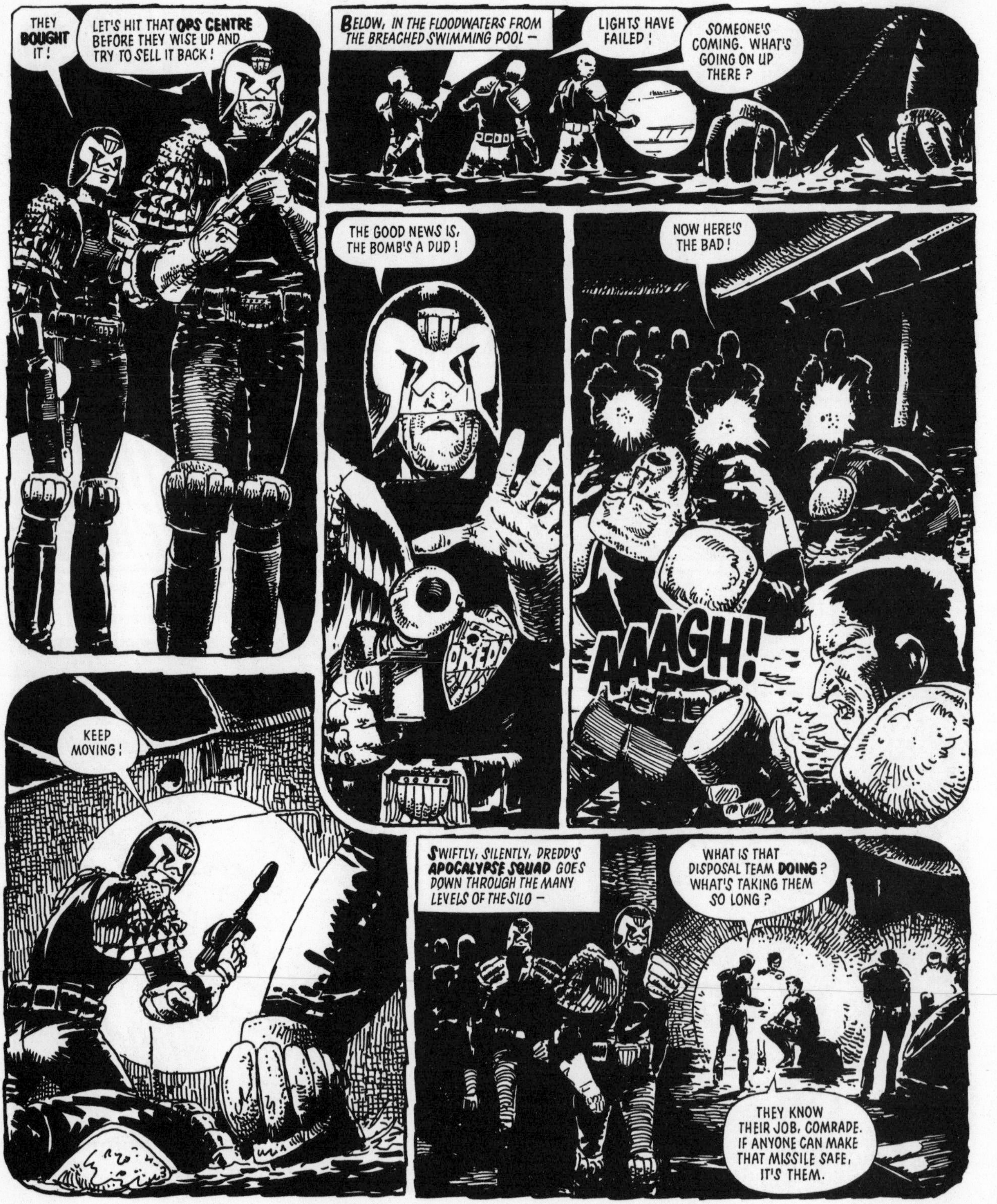
THEY BOUGHT IT!
LET'S HIT THAT OPS CENTRE BEFORE THEY WISE UP AND TRY TO SELL IT BACK!
BELOW, IN THE FLOODWATERS FROM THE BREACHED SWIMMING POOL —
LIGHTS HAVE FAILED!
SOMEONE'S COMING. WHAT'S GOING ON UP THERE?
THE GOOD NEWS IS, THE BOMB'S A DUD!
NOW HERE'S THE BAD!
AAAGH!
KEEP MOVING!
SWIFTLY, SILENTLY, DREDD'S APOCALYPSE SQUAD GOES DOWN THROUGH THE MANY LEVELS OF THE SILO —
WHAT IS THAT DISPOSAL TEAM DOING? WHAT'S TAKING THEM SO LONG?
THEY KNOW THEIR JOB, COMRADE. IF ANYONE CAN MAKE THAT MISSILE SAFE, IT'S THEM.

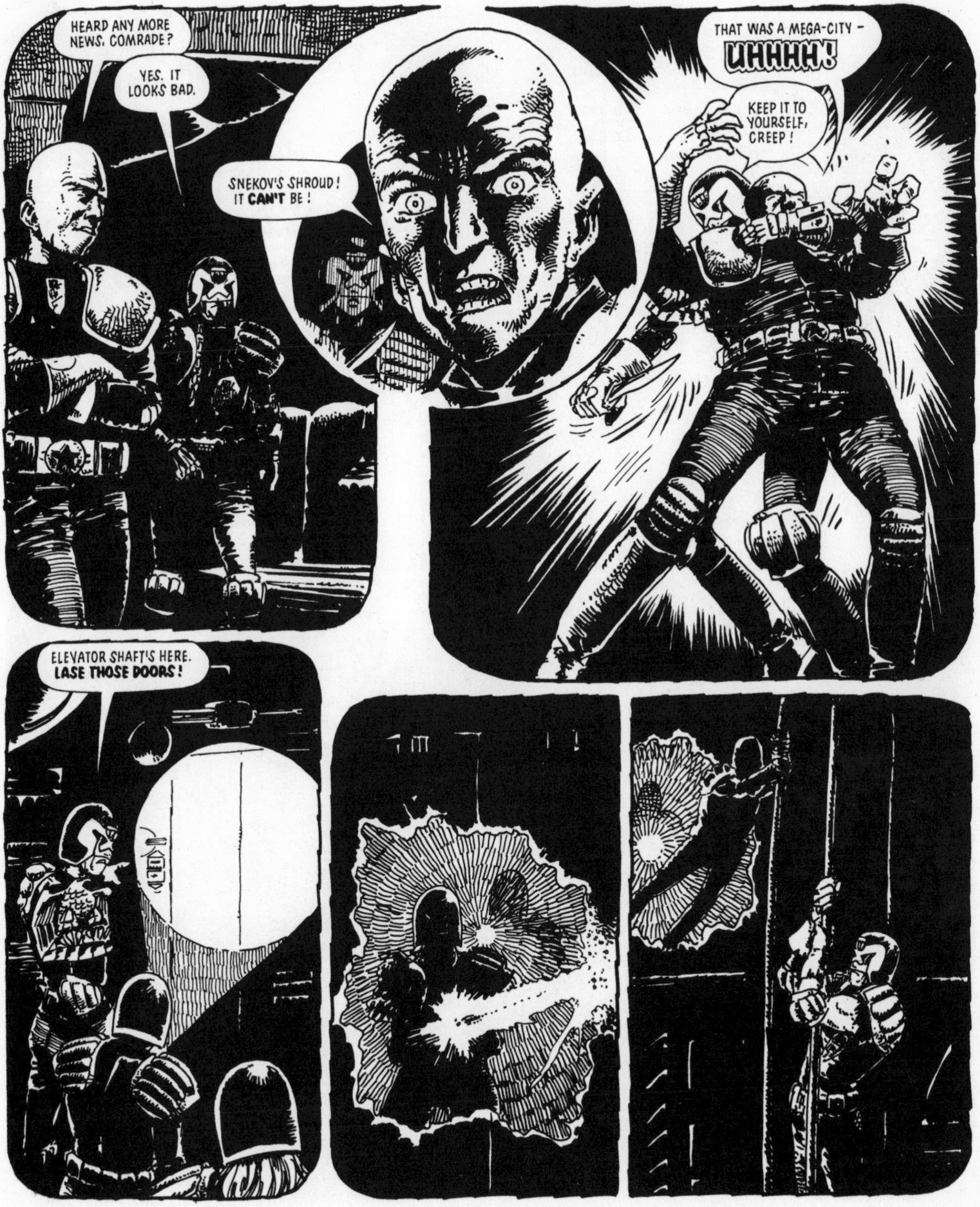
HEARD ANY MORE NEWS, COMRADE?
YES. IT LOOKS BAD.
SNEKOV'S SHROUD! IT CAN'T BE!
THAT WAS A MEGA-CITY - UHHHH!
KEEP IT TO YOURSELF, CREEP!
ELEVATOR SHAFT'S HERE. LASE THOSE DOORS!

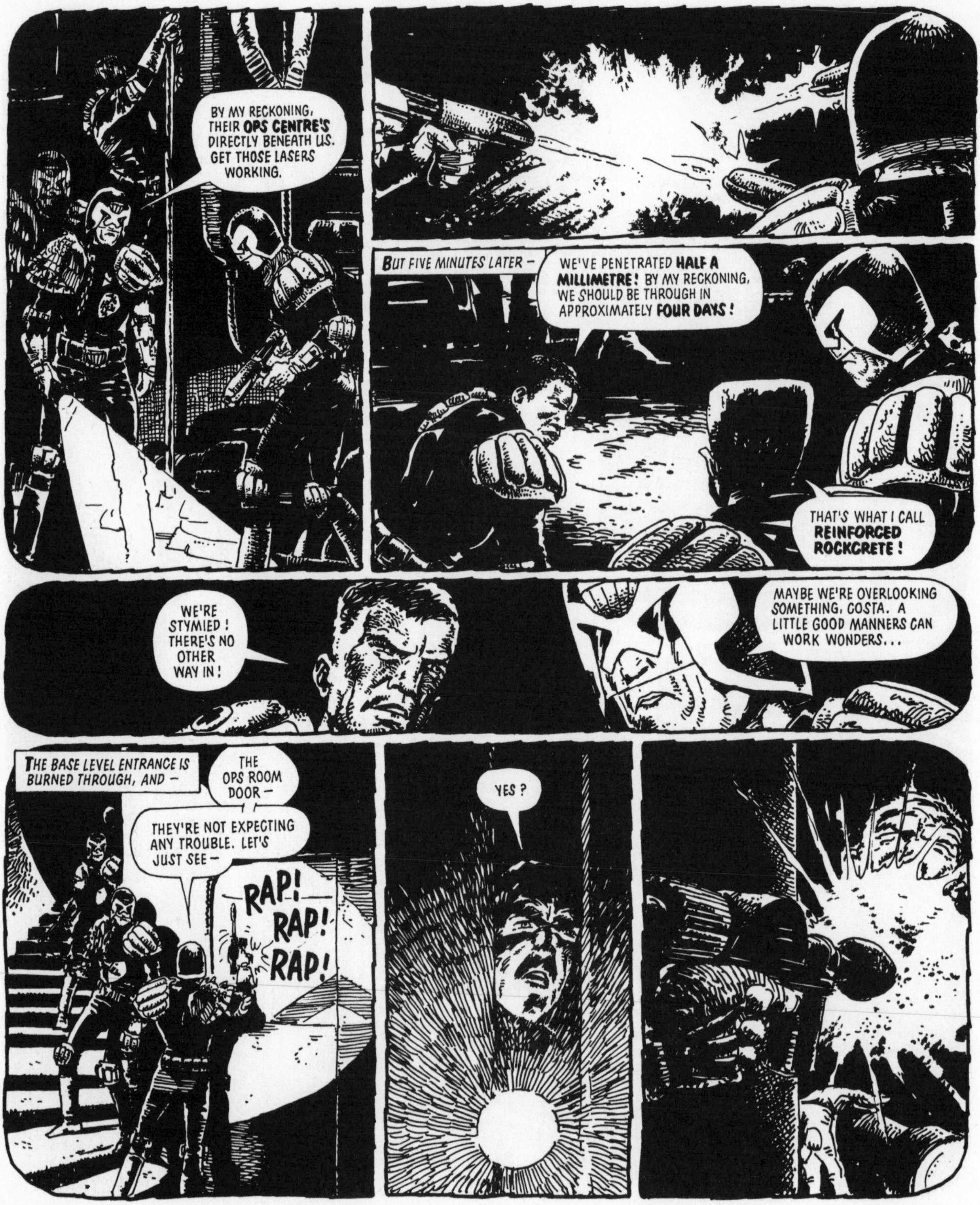
BY MY RECKONING, THEIR OPS CENTRE'S DIRECTLY BENEATH US. GET THOSE LASERS WORKING.
BUT FIVE MINUTES LATER —
WE'VE PENETRATED HALF A MILLIMETRE! BY MY RECKONING, WE SHOULD BE THROUGH IN APPROXIMATELY FOUR DAYS!
THAT'S WHAT I CALL REINFORCED ROCKCRETE!
WE'RE STYMIED! THERE'S NO OTHER WAY IN!
MAYBE WE'RE OVERLOOKING SOMETHING, COSTA. A LITTLE GOOD MANNERS CAN WORK WONDERS...
THE BASE LEVEL ENTRANCE IS BURNED THROUGH, AND —
THE OPS ROOM DOOR —
THEY'RE NOT EXPECTING ANY TROUBLE. LET'S JUST SEE —
RAP! RAP! RAP!
YES?

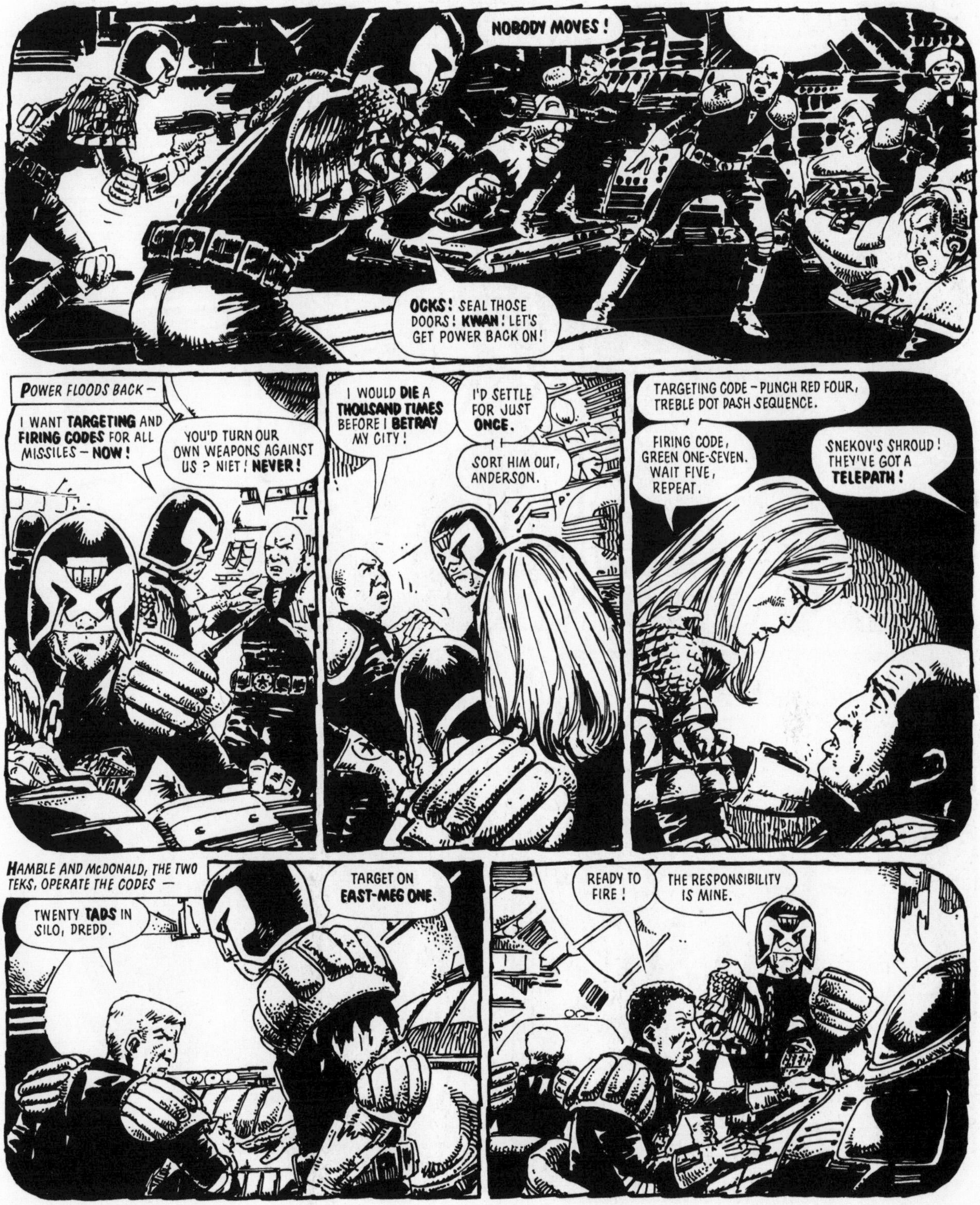
NOBODY MOVES!
OCKS! SEAL THOSE DOORS! KWAN! LET'S GET POWER BACK ON!
POWER FLOODS BACK —
I WANT TARGETING AND FIRING CODES FOR ALL MISSILES — NOW!
YOU'D TURN OUR OWN WEAPONS AGAINST US? NIET! NEVER!
I WOULD DIE A THOUSAND TIMES BEFORE I BETRAY MY CITY!
I'D SETTLE FOR JUST ONCE.
SORT HIM OUT, ANDERSON.
TARGETING CODE — PUNCH RED FOUR, TREBLE DOT DASH SEQUENCE.
FIRING CODE, GREEN ONE-SEVEN. WAIT FIVE, REPEAT.
SNEKOV'S SHROUD! THEY'VE GOT A TELEPATH!
HAMBLE AND McDONALD, THE TWO TEKS, OPERATE THE CODES —
TWENTY TADS IN SILO, DREDD.
TARGET ON EAST-MEG ONE.
READY TO FIRE!
THE RESPONSIBILITY IS MINE.

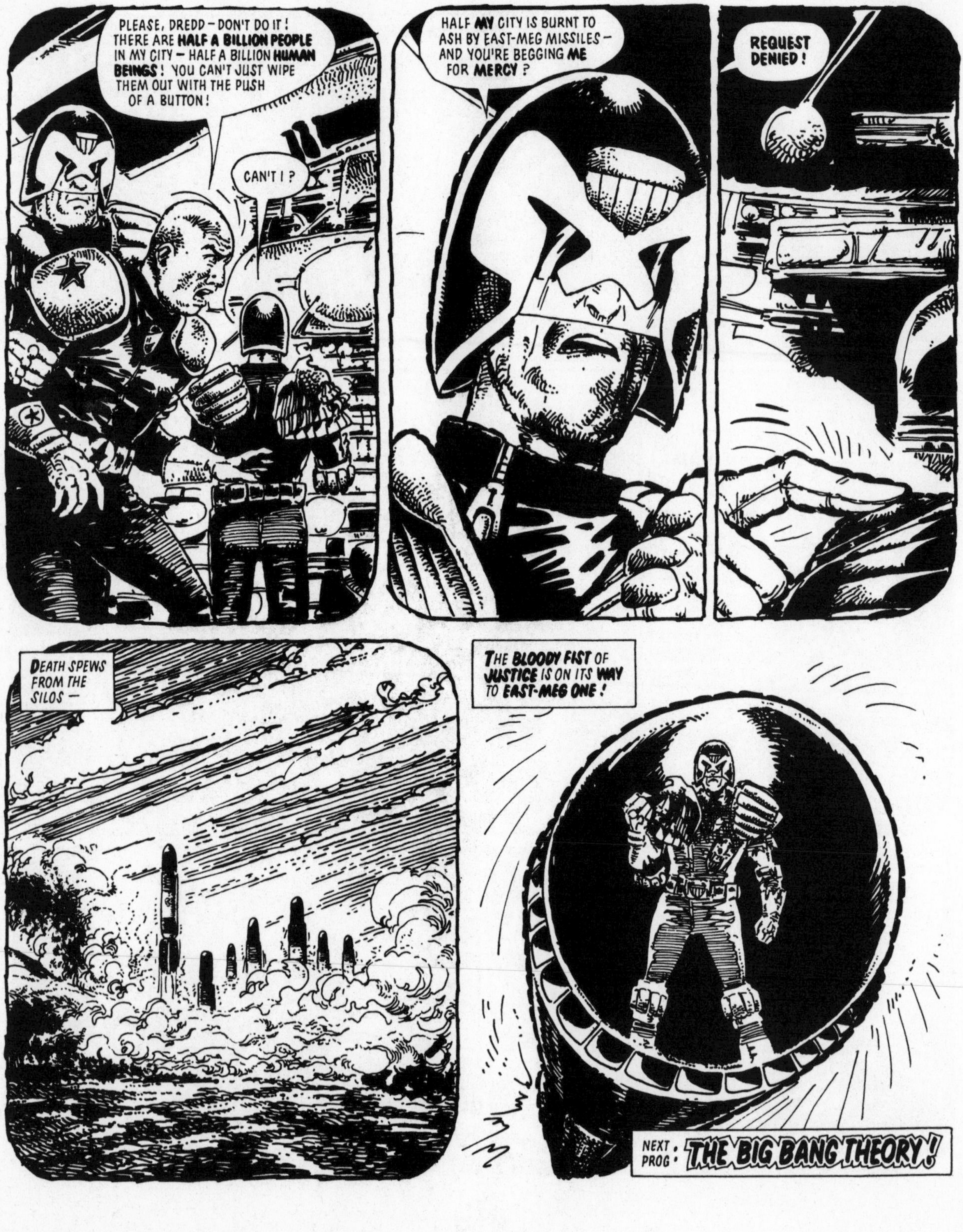
PLEASE, DREDD – DON'T DO IT! THERE ARE HALF A BILLION PEOPLE IN MY CITY – HALF A BILLION HUMAN BEINGS! YOU CAN'T JUST WIPE THEM OUT WITH THE PUSH OF A BUTTON!
CAN'T I?
HALF MY CITY IS BURNT TO ASH BY EAST-MEG MISSILES – AND YOU'RE BEGGING ME FOR MERCY?
REQUEST DENIED!
DEATH SPEWS FROM THE SILOS –
THE BLOODY FIST OF JUSTICE IS ON ITS WAY TO EAST-MEG ONE!
NEXT PROG: THE BIG BANG THEORY!

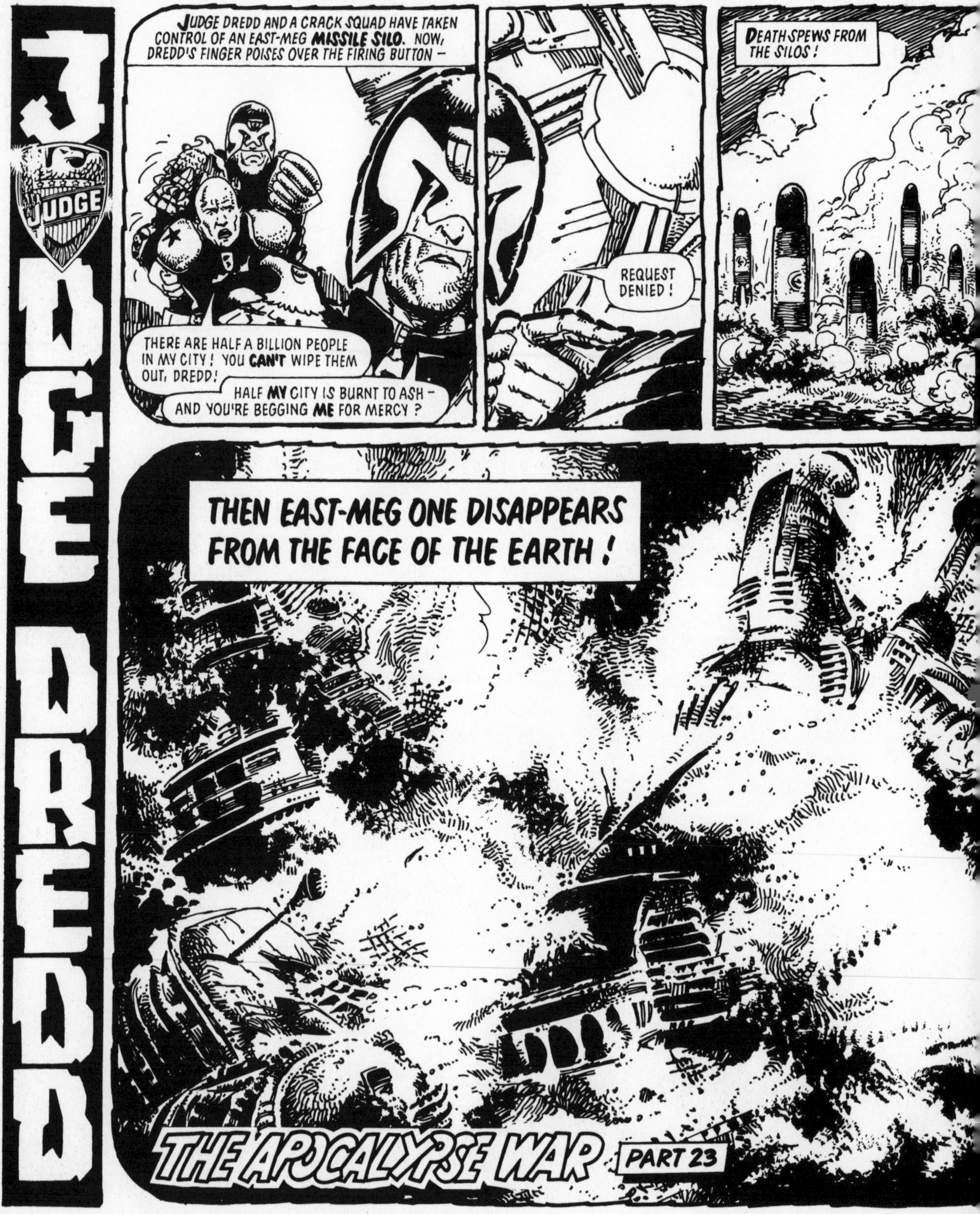
JUDGE DREDD
JUDGE
JUDGE DREDD AND A CRACK SQUAD HAVE TAKEN CONTROL OF AN EAST-MEG MISSILE SILO. NOW, DREDD'S FINGER POISES OVER THE FIRING BUTTON –
THERE ARE HALF A BILLION PEOPLE IN MY CITY! YOU CAN'T WIPE THEM OUT, DREDD!
HALF MY CITY IS BURNT TO ASH – AND YOU'RE BEGGING ME FOR MERCY?
REQUEST DENIED!
DEATH SPEWS FROM THE SILOS!
THEN EAST-MEG ONE DISAPPEARS FROM THE FACE OF THE EARTH!
THE APOCALYPSE WAR
PART 23

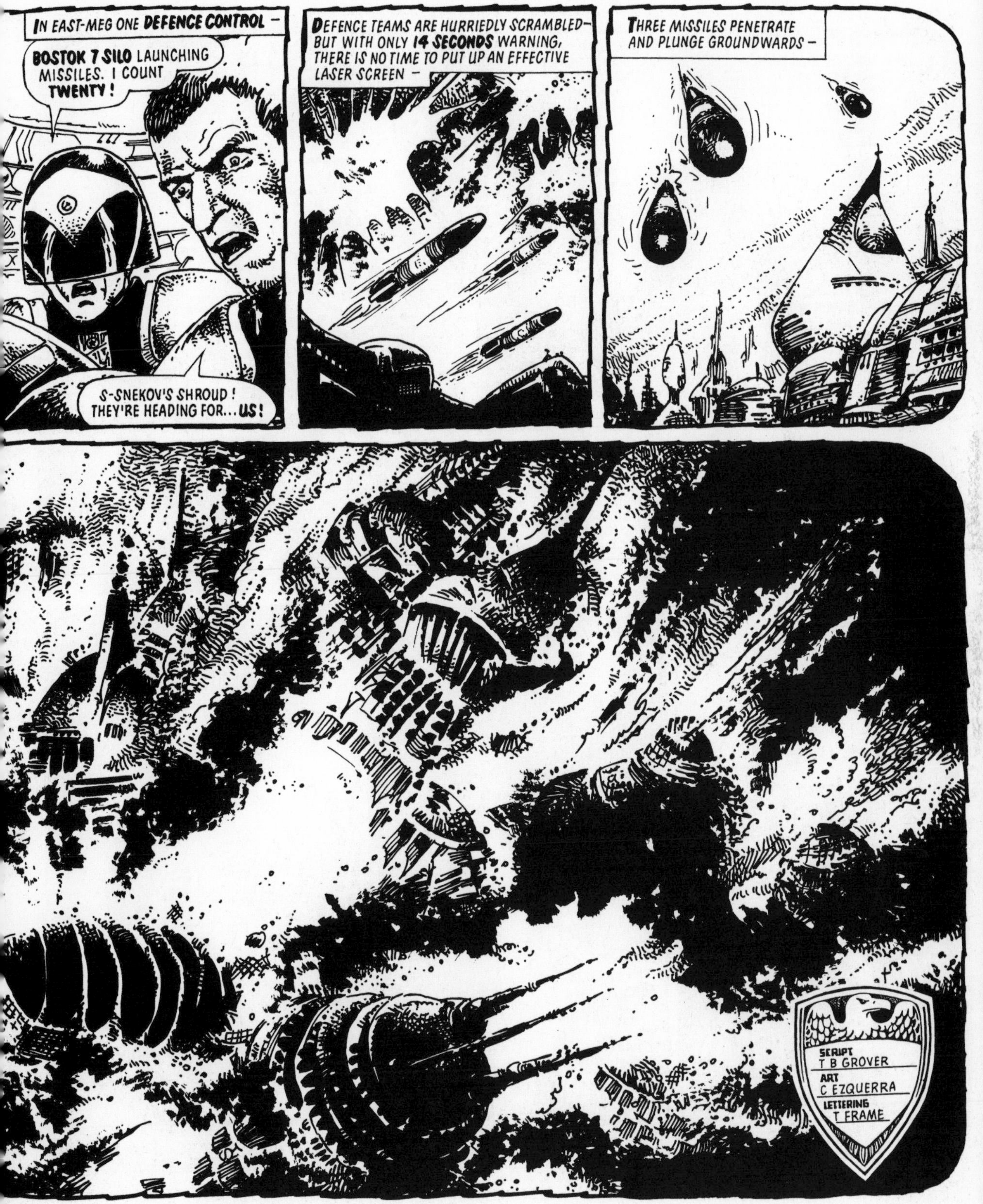

IN EAST-MEG ONE DEFENCE CONTROL –
BOSTOK 7 SILO LAUNCHING MISSILES. I COUNT TWENTY!
S-SNEKOV'S SHROUD! THEY'RE HEADING FOR... US!
DEFENCE TEAMS ARE HURRIEDLY SCRAMBLED– BUT WITH ONLY 14 SECONDS WARNING, THERE IS NO TIME TO PUT UP AN EFFECTIVE LASER SCREEN –
THREE MISSILES PENETRATE AND PLUNGE GROUNDWARDS –
SCRIPT T B GROVER
ART C EZQUERRA
LETTERING T FRAME

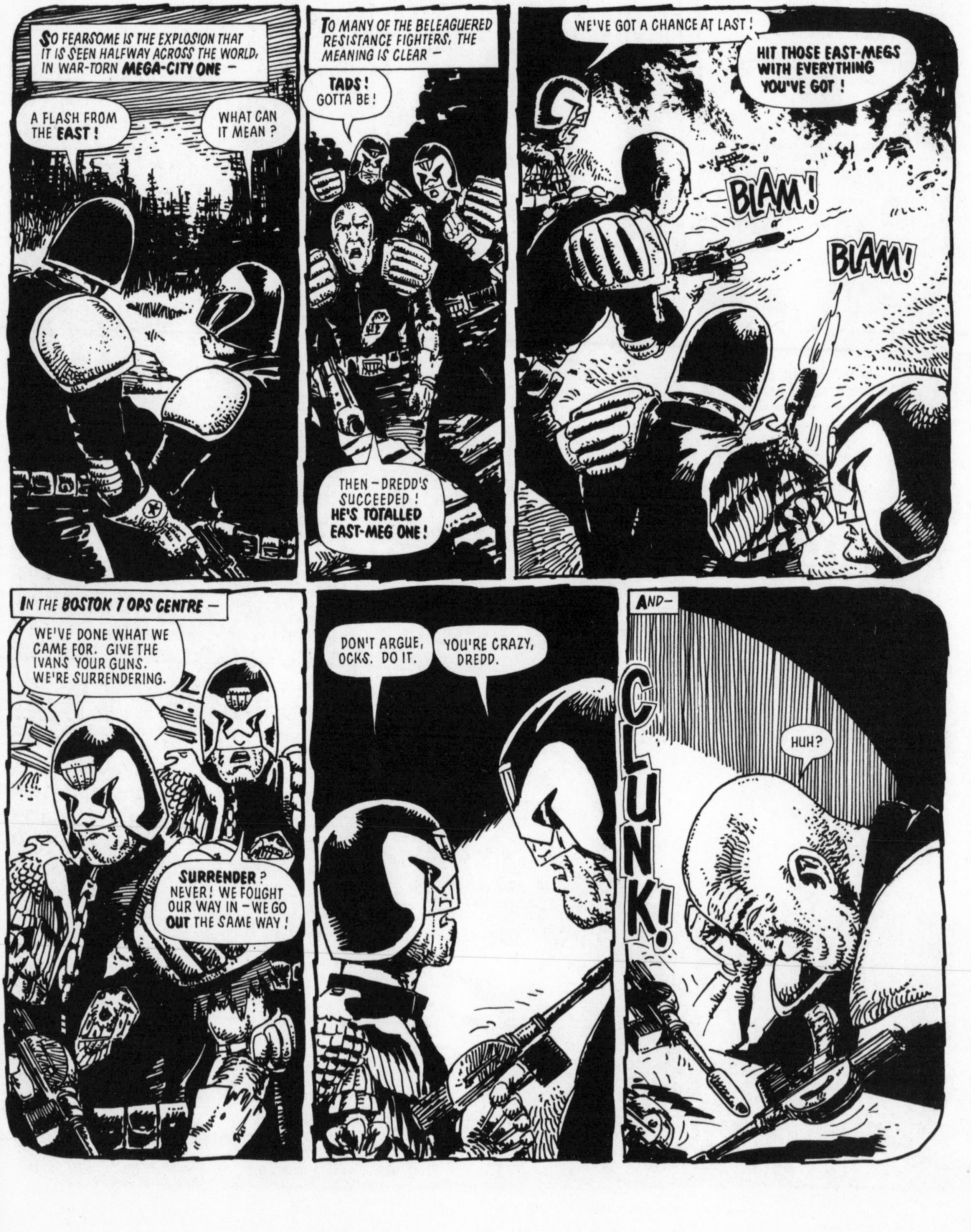
SO FEARSOME IS THE EXPLOSION THAT IT IS SEEN HALFWAY ACROSS THE WORLD, IN WAR-TORN MEGA-CITY ONE –
A FLASH FROM THE EAST!
WHAT CAN IT MEAN?
TO MANY OF THE BELEAGUERED RESISTANCE FIGHTERS, THE MEANING IS CLEAR –
TADS! GOTTA BE!
THEN – DREDD'S SUCCEEDED! HE'S TOTALLED EAST-MEG ONE!
WE'VE GOT A CHANCE AT LAST!
HIT THOSE EAST-MEGS WITH EVERYTHING YOU'VE GOT!
BLAM!
BLAM!
IN THE BOSTOK 7 OPS CENTRE –
WE'VE DONE WHAT WE CAME FOR. GIVE THE IVANS YOUR GUNS. WE'RE SURRENDERING.
SURRENDER? NEVER! WE FOUGHT OUR WAY IN – WE GO OUT THE SAME WAY!
DON'T ARGUE, OCKS. DO IT.
YOU'RE CRAZY, DREDD.
AND–
CLUNK!
HUH?

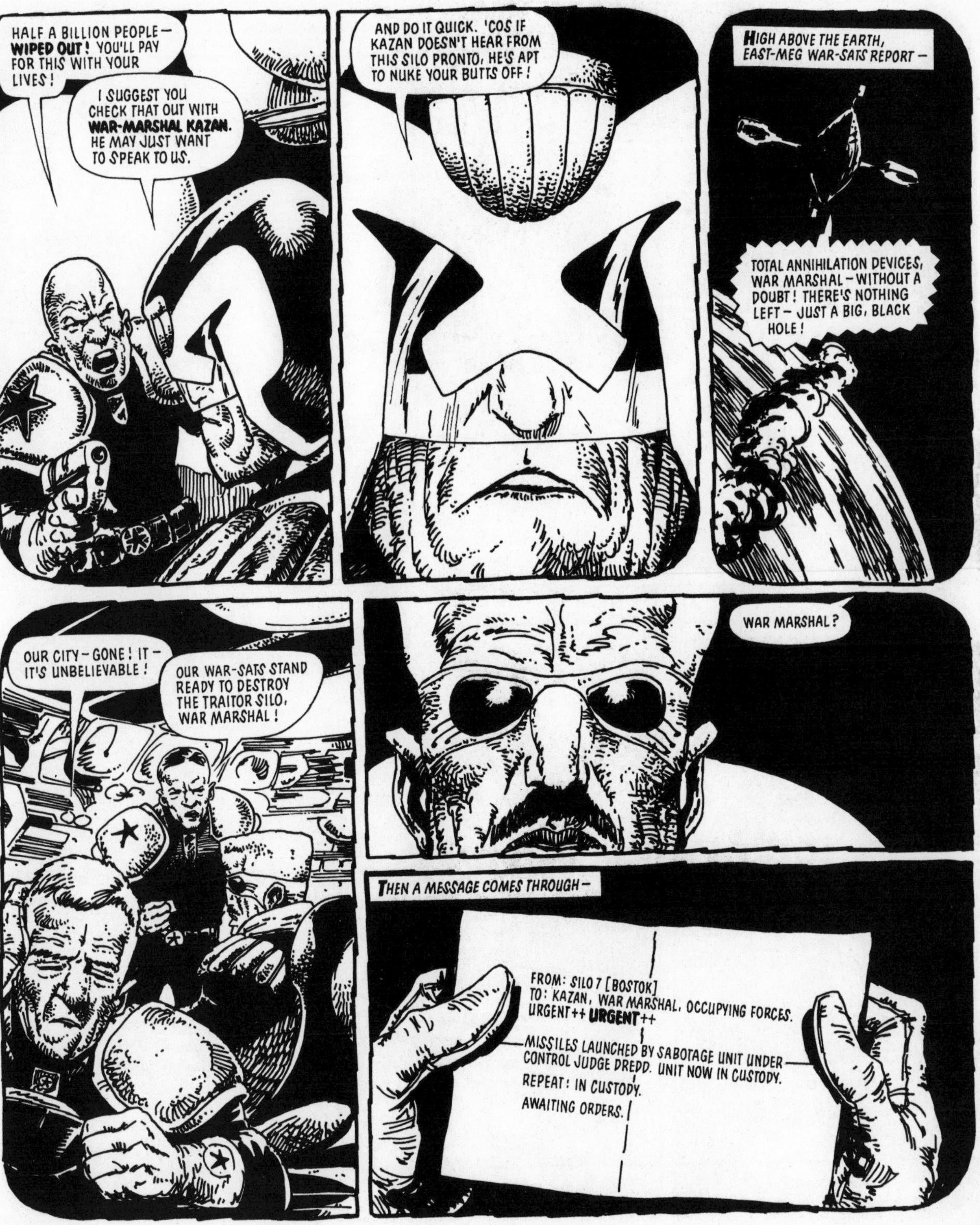
HALF A BILLION PEOPLE— WIPED OUT! YOU'LL PAY FOR THIS WITH YOUR LIVES!
I SUGGEST YOU CHECK THAT OUT WITH WAR-MARSHAL KAZAN. HE MAY JUST WANT TO SPEAK TO US.
AND DO IT QUICK. 'COS IF KAZAN DOESN'T HEAR FROM THIS SILO PRONTO, HE'S APT TO NUKE YOUR BUTTS OFF!
HIGH ABOVE THE EARTH, EAST-MEG WAR-SATS REPORT —
TOTAL ANNIHILATION DEVICES, WAR MARSHAL — WITHOUT A DOUBT! THERE'S NOTHING LEFT — JUST A BIG, BLACK HOLE!
OUR CITY — GONE! IT — IT'S UNBELIEVABLE!
OUR WAR-SATS STAND READY TO DESTROY THE TRAITOR SILO, WAR MARSHAL!
WAR MARSHAL?
THEN A MESSAGE COMES THROUGH —
FROM: SILO 7 [BOSTOK]
TO: KAZAN, WAR MARSHAL, OCCUPYING FORCES.
URGENT++ URGENT++
MISSILES LAUNCHED BY SABOTAGE UNIT UNDER CONTROL JUDGE DREDD. UNIT NOW IN CUSTODY.
REPEAT: IN CUSTODY.
AWAITING ORDERS.

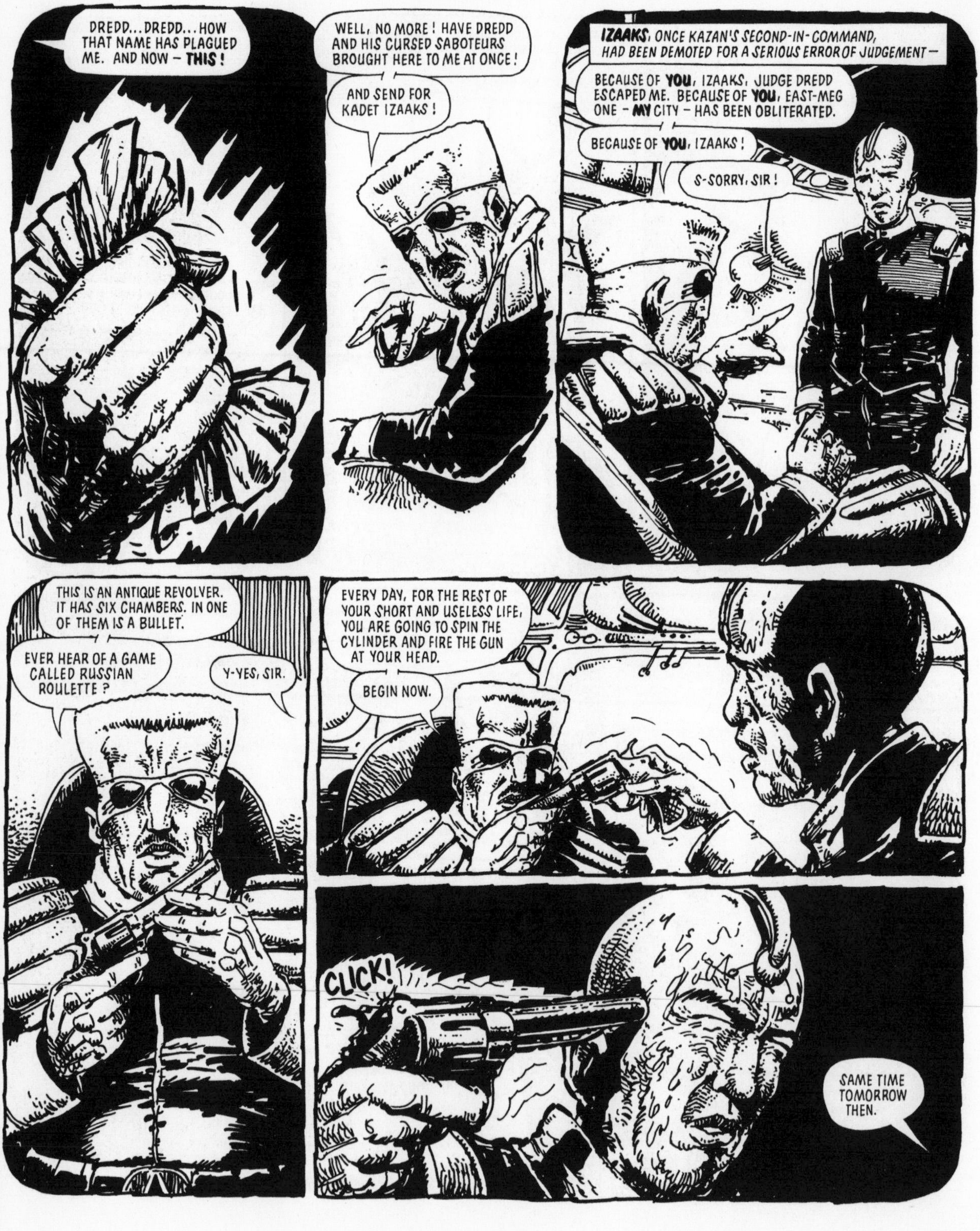
DREDD... DREDD... HOW THAT NAME HAS PLAGUED ME. AND NOW – THIS!
WELL, NO MORE! HAVE DREDD AND HIS CURSED SABOTEURS BROUGHT HERE TO ME AT ONCE!
AND SEND FOR KADET IZAAKS!
IZAAKS, ONCE KAZAN'S SECOND-IN-COMMAND, HAD BEEN DEMOTED FOR A SERIOUS ERROR OF JUDGEMENT –
BECAUSE OF YOU, IZAAKS, JUDGE DREDD ESCAPED ME. BECAUSE OF YOU, EAST-MEG ONE – MY CITY – HAS BEEN OBLITERATED.
BECAUSE OF YOU, IZAAKS!
S-SORRY, SIR!
THIS IS AN ANTIQUE REVOLVER. IT HAS SIX CHAMBERS. IN ONE OF THEM IS A BULLET.
EVER HEAR OF A GAME CALLED RUSSIAN ROULETTE?
Y-YES, SIR.
EVERY DAY, FOR THE REST OF YOUR SHORT AND USELESS LIFE, YOU ARE GOING TO SPIN THE CYLINDER AND FIRE THE GUN AT YOUR HEAD.
BEGIN NOW.
CLICK!
SAME TIME TOMORROW THEN.

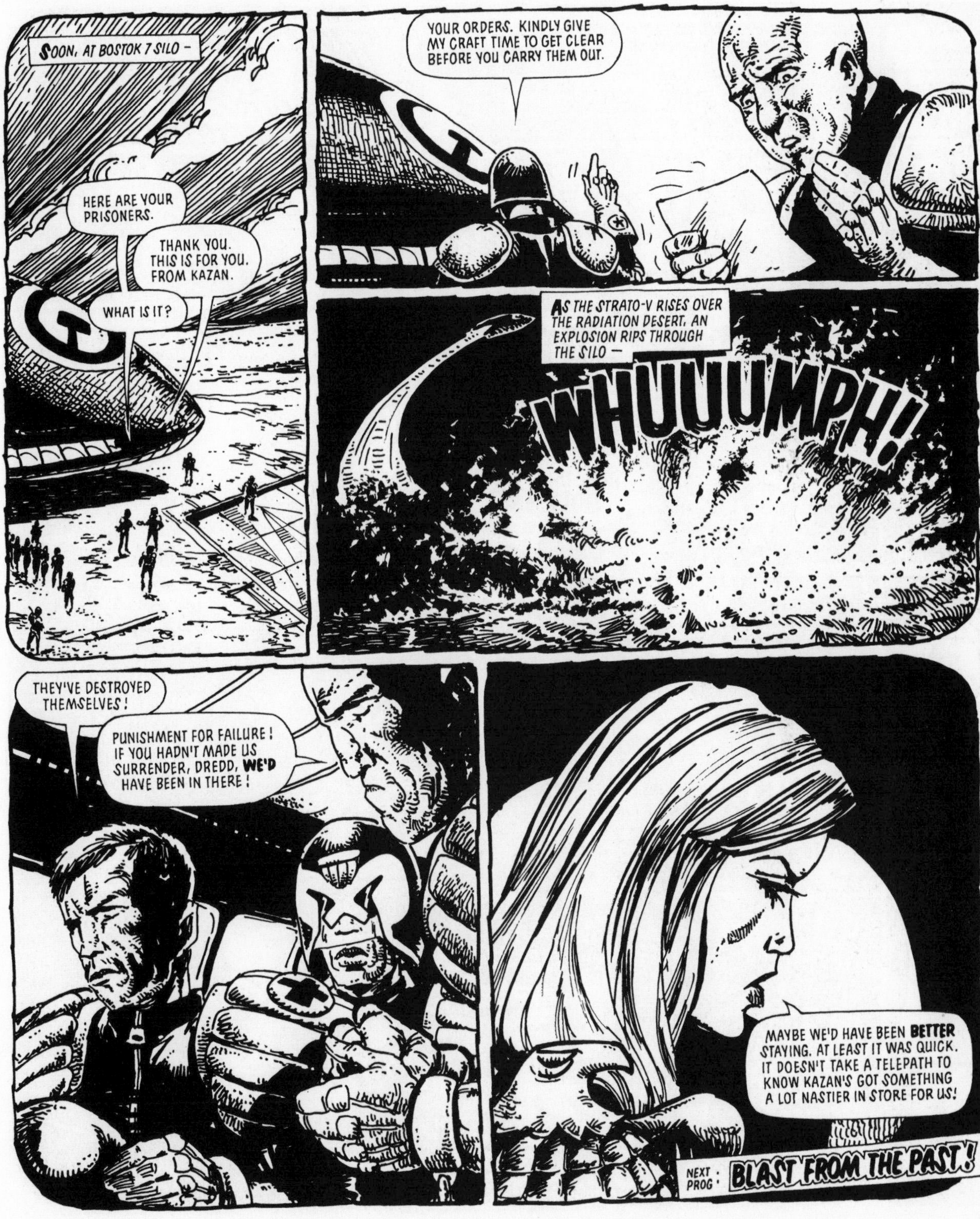
SOON, AT BOSTOK 7 SILO –
HERE ARE YOUR PRISONERS.
THANK YOU. THIS IS FOR YOU. FROM KAZAN.
WHAT IS IT?
YOUR ORDERS. KINDLY GIVE MY CRAFT TIME TO GET CLEAR BEFORE YOU CARRY THEM OUT.
AS THE STRATO-V RISES OVER THE RADIATION DESERT, AN EXPLOSION RIPS THROUGH THE SILO –
WHUUUUMPH!
THEY'VE DESTROYED THEMSELVES!
PUNISHMENT FOR FAILURE! IF YOU HADN'T MADE US SURRENDER, DREDD, WE'D HAVE BEEN IN THERE!
MAYBE WE'D HAVE BEEN BETTER STAYING. AT LEAST IT WAS QUICK. IT DOESN'T TAKE A TELEPATH TO KNOW KAZAN'S GOT SOMETHING A LOT NASTIER IN STORE FOR US!
NEXT PROG: BLAST FROM THE PAST!

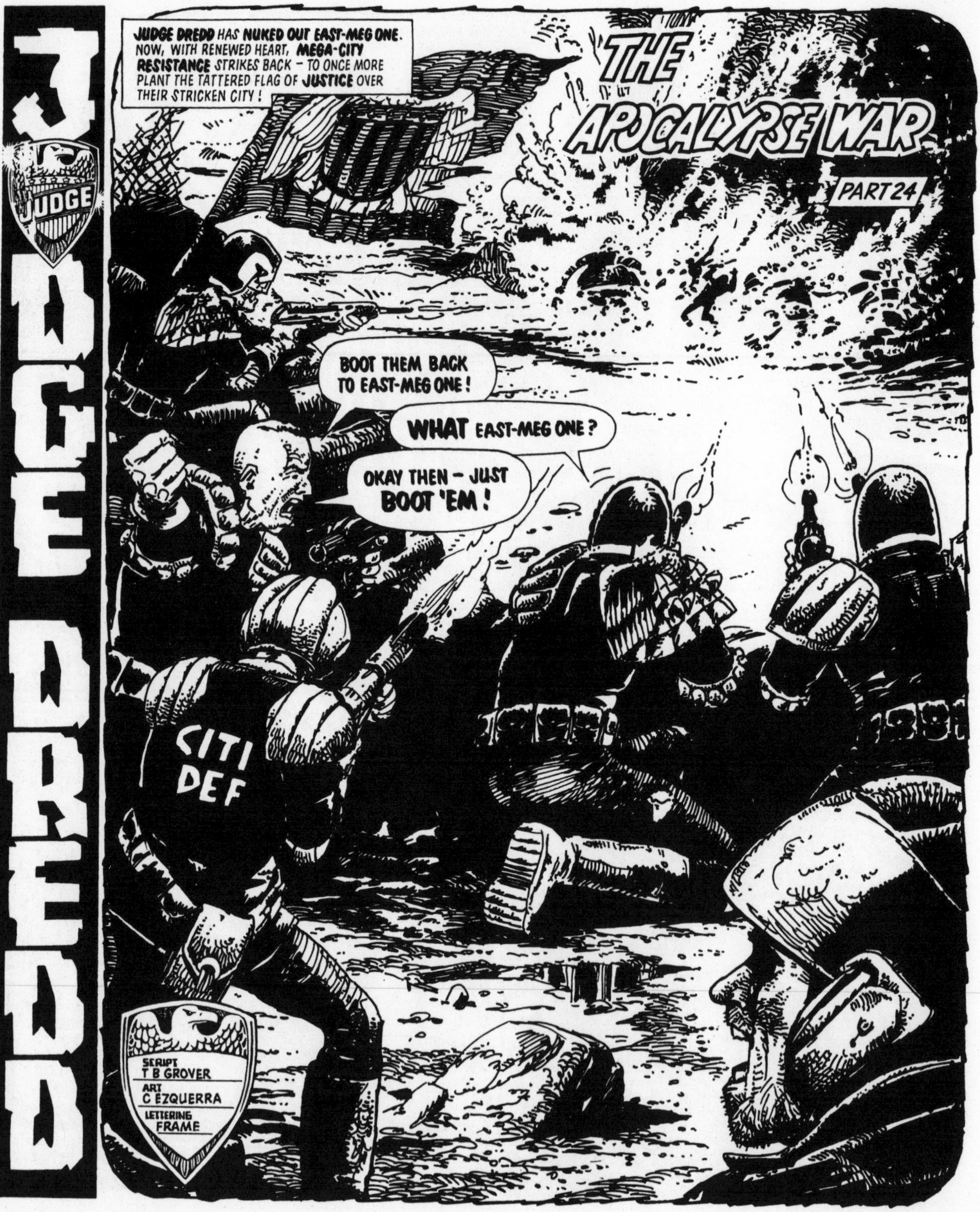
JUDGE DREDD
JUDGE DREDD HAS NUKED OUT EAST-MEG ONE. NOW, WITH RENEWED HEART, MEGA-CITY RESISTANCE STRIKES BACK – TO ONCE MORE PLANT THE TATTERED FLAG OF JUSTICE OVER THEIR STRICKEN CITY!
THE APOCALYPSE WAR
PART 24
BOOT THEM BACK TO EAST-MEG ONE!
WHAT EAST-MEG ONE?
OKAY THEN – JUST BOOT 'EM!
CITI DEF
SCRIPT T B GROVER
ART C EZQUERRA
LETTERING FRAME

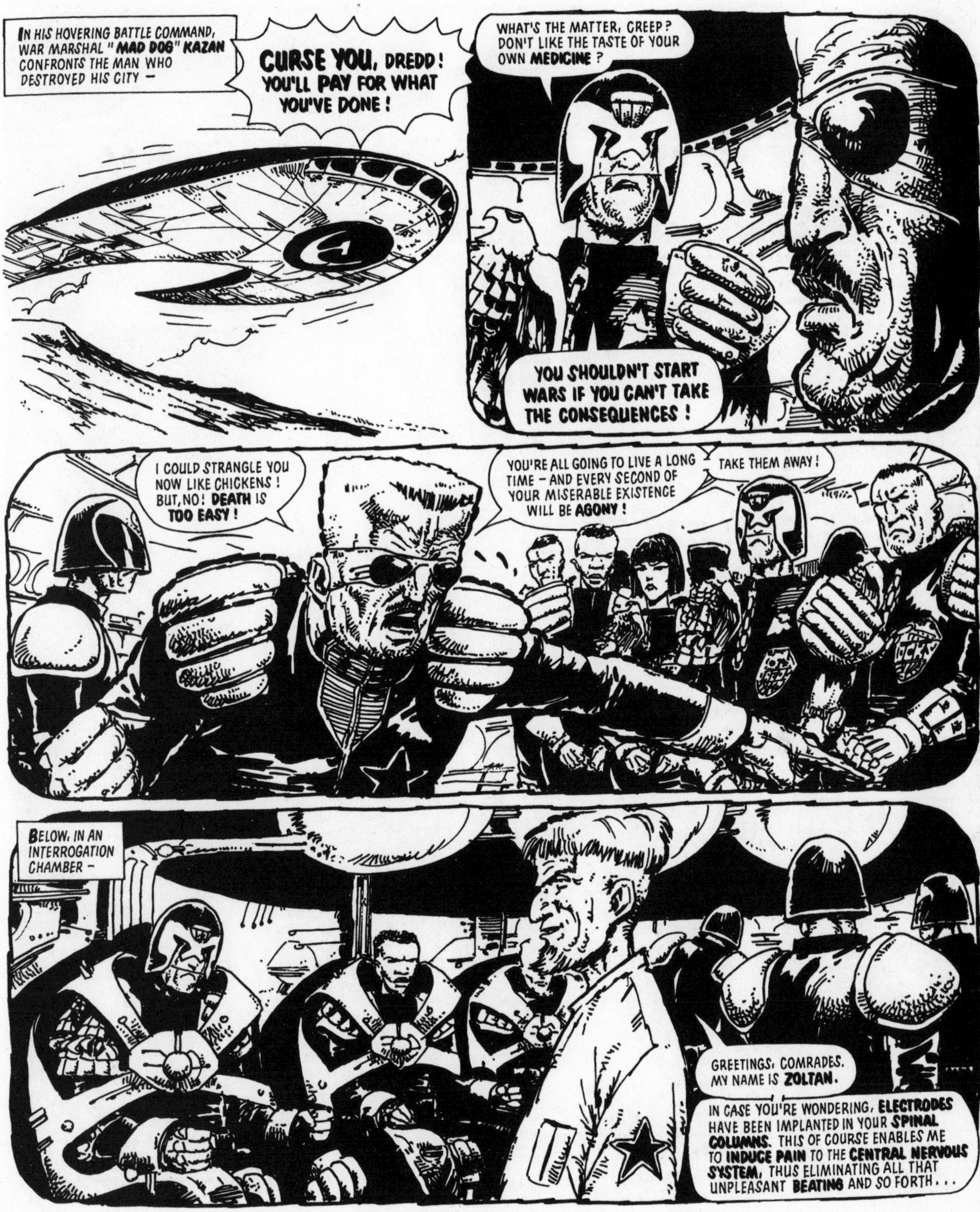
IN HIS HOVERING BATTLE COMMAND, WAR MARSHAL "MAD DOG" KAZAN CONFRONTS THE MAN WHO DESTROYED HIS CITY –
CURSE YOU, DREDD! YOU'LL PAY FOR WHAT YOU'VE DONE!
WHAT'S THE MATTER, CREEP? DON'T LIKE THE TASTE OF YOUR OWN MEDICINE?
YOU SHOULDN'T START WARS IF YOU CAN'T TAKE THE CONSEQUENCES!
I COULD STRANGLE YOU NOW LIKE CHICKENS! BUT, NO! DEATH IS TOO EASY!
YOU'RE ALL GOING TO LIVE A LONG TIME – AND EVERY SECOND OF YOUR MISERABLE EXISTENCE WILL BE AGONY!
TAKE THEM AWAY!
BELOW, IN AN INTERROGATION CHAMBER –
GREETINGS, COMRADES. MY NAME IS ZOLTAN.
IN CASE YOU'RE WONDERING, ELECTRODES HAVE BEEN IMPLANTED IN YOUR SPINAL COLUMNS. THIS OF COURSE ENABLES ME TO INDUCE PAIN TO THE CENTRAL NERVOUS SYSTEM, THUS ELIMINATING ALL THAT UNPLEASANT BEATING AND SO FORTH...

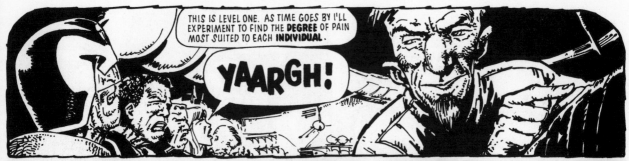

THIS IS LEVEL ONE. AS TIME GOES BY I'LL EXPERIMENT TO FIND THE **DEGREE** OF PAIN MOST SUITED TO EACH **INDIVIDUAL**.

YAARGH!

NATURALLY, MY INSTRUMENT WILL MONITOR YOU CONTINUOUSLY TO PREVENT **PREMATURE** DEATH. WITH LUCK, WE CAN KEEP YOU ALIVE FOR YOUR FULL NATURAL TERM.

IF THERE'S ANYTHING ELSE YOU'D LIKE TO KNOW, JUST **SCREAM!**

WE'RE FINISHED... BUT AT LEAST WE'VE... GIVEN THE **RESISTANCE** A CHANCE...!

*LOGICALLY, IT IS THE **SLIMMEST** OF CHANCES. THE ENEMY STRANGLEHOLD ON MEGA-CITY ONE IS BACKED UP BY OVERWHELMING MIGHT OF ARMS.*

*BUT TROOPS WHOSE **MOTHER-CITY** HAS BEEN **BLOWN** OUT OF EXISTENCE TAKE **LITTLE ACCOUNT** OF LOGIC —*

THEY'RE RUNNING! THEY'VE **LOST** THE **WILL** TO FIGHT!

SOMEBODY SHOULD TELL THAT TO THEIR RADSWEEPERS!

CITI DEF

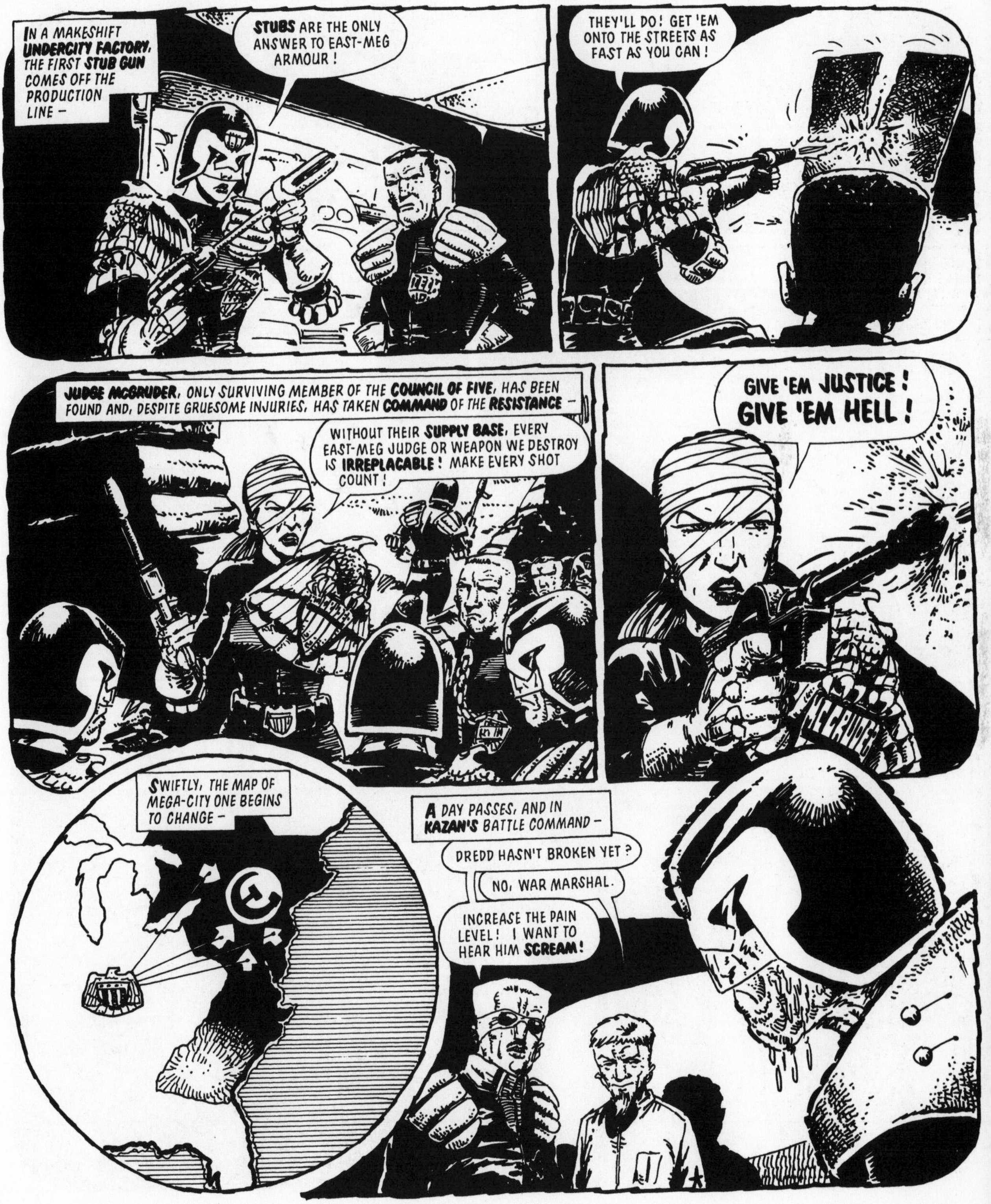

IN A MAKESHIFT UNDERCITY FACTORY, THE FIRST STUB GUN COMES OFF THE PRODUCTION LINE –
STUBS ARE THE ONLY ANSWER TO EAST-MEG ARMOUR!
THEY'LL DO! GET 'EM ONTO THE STREETS AS FAST AS YOU CAN!
JUDGE MCGRUDER, ONLY SURVIVING MEMBER OF THE COUNCIL OF FIVE, HAS BEEN FOUND AND, DESPITE GRUESOME INJURIES, HAS TAKEN COMMAND OF THE RESISTANCE –
WITHOUT THEIR SUPPLY BASE, EVERY EAST-MEG JUDGE OR WEAPON WE DESTROY IS IRREPLACABLE! MAKE EVERY SHOT COUNT!
GIVE 'EM JUSTICE! GIVE 'EM HELL!
SWIFTLY, THE MAP OF MEGA-CITY ONE BEGINS TO CHANGE –
A DAY PASSES, AND IN KAZAN'S BATTLE COMMAND –
DREDD HASN'T BROKEN YET?
NO, WAR MARSHAL.
INCREASE THE PAIN LEVEL! I WANT TO HEAR HIM SCREAM!

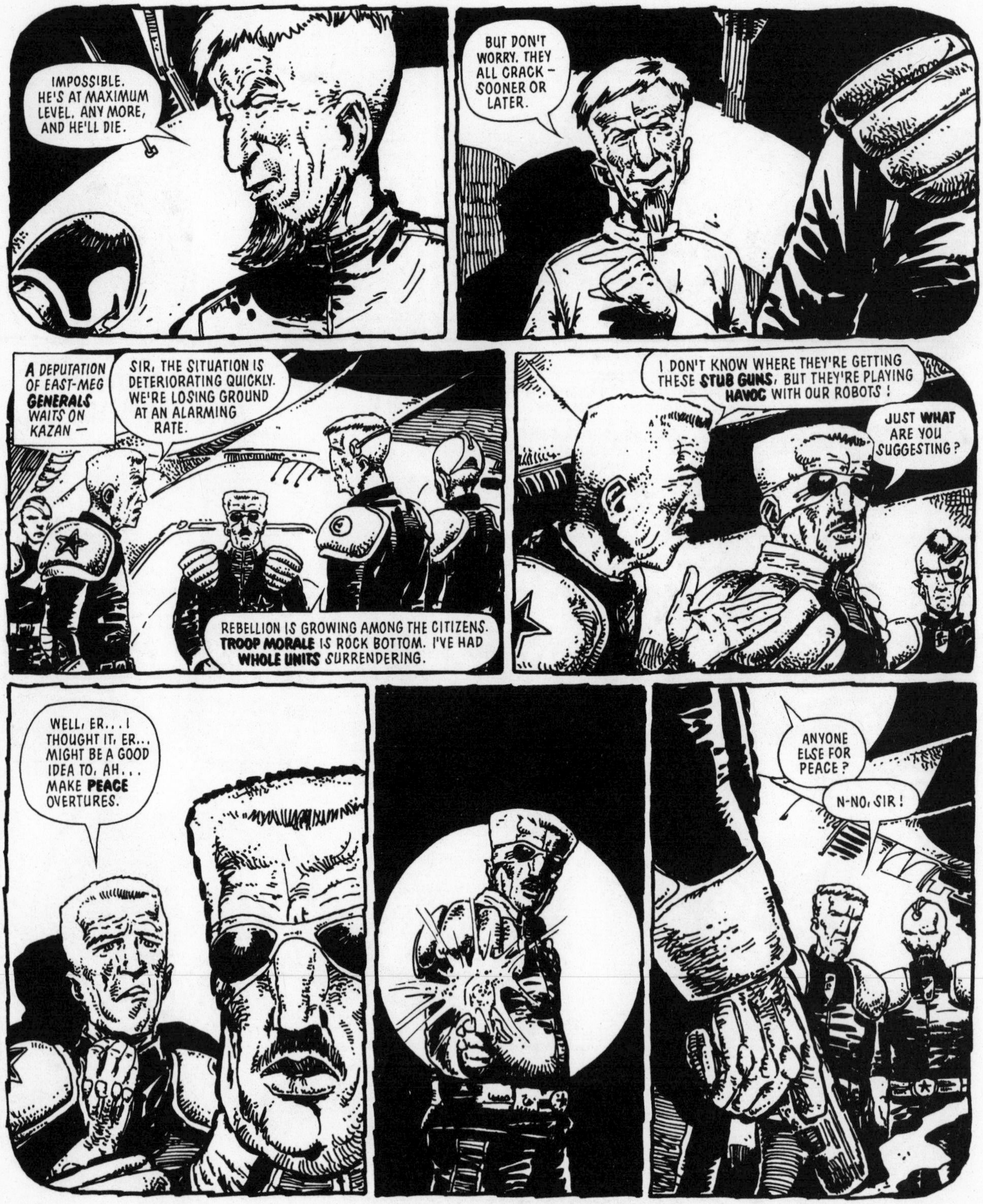
IMPOSSIBLE. HE'S AT MAXIMUM LEVEL. ANY MORE, AND HE'LL DIE.
BUT DON'T WORRY. THEY ALL CRACK - SOONER OR LATER.
A DEPUTATION OF EAST-MEG GENERALS WAITS ON KAZAN —
SIR, THE SITUATION IS DETERIORATING QUICKLY. WE'RE LOSING GROUND AT AN ALARMING RATE.
REBELLION IS GROWING AMONG THE CITIZENS. TROOP MORALE IS ROCK BOTTOM. I'VE HAD WHOLE UNITS SURRENDERING.
I DON'T KNOW WHERE THEY'RE GETTING THESE STUB GUNS, BUT THEY'RE PLAYING HAVOC WITH OUR ROBOTS!
JUST WHAT ARE YOU SUGGESTING?
WELL, ER... I THOUGHT IT, ER... MIGHT BE A GOOD IDEA TO, AH... MAKE PEACE OVERTURES.
ANYONE ELSE FOR PEACE?
N-NO, SIR!

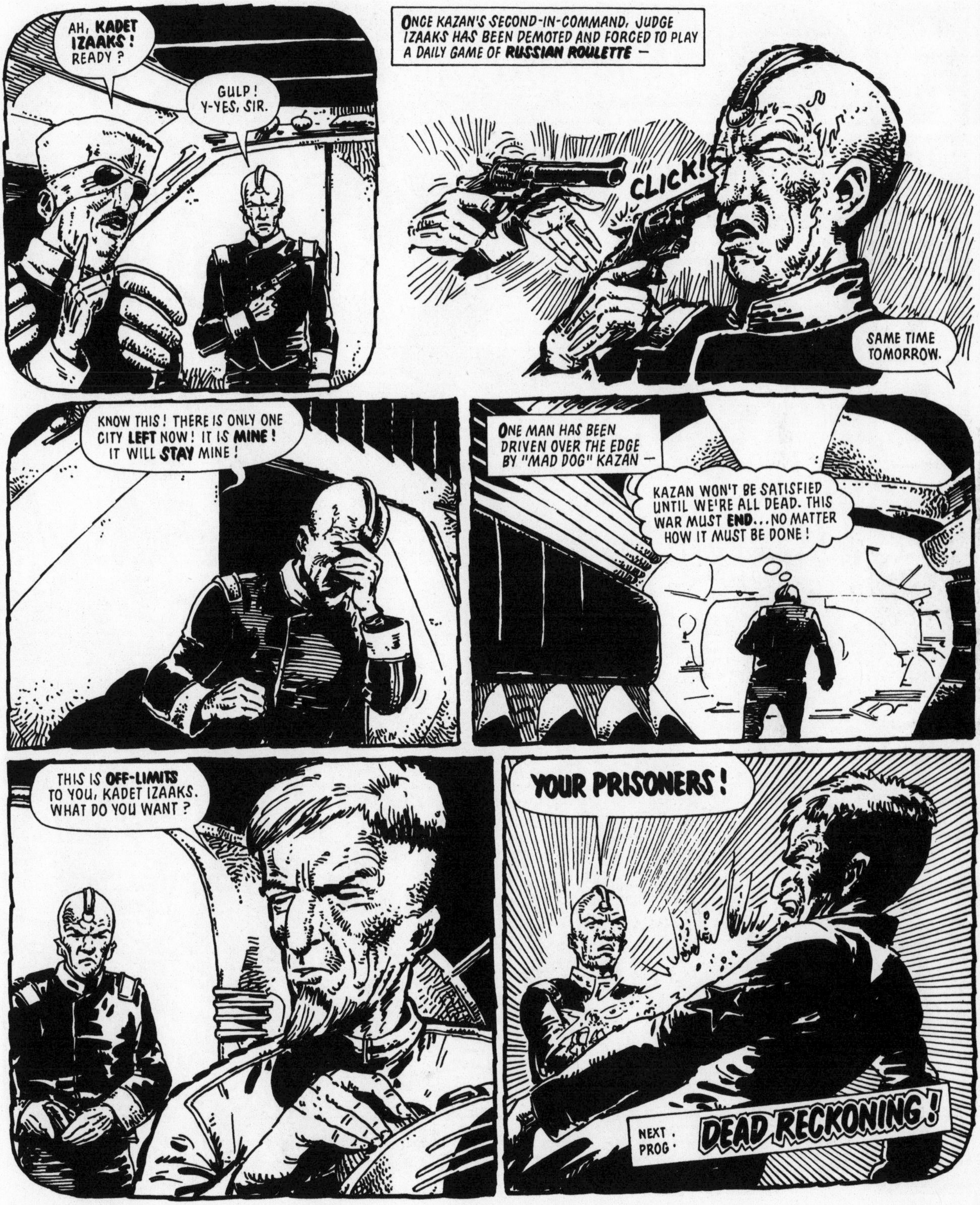
AH, KADET IZAAKS! READY?
GULP! Y-YES, SIR.
ONCE KAZAN'S SECOND-IN-COMMAND, JUDGE IZAAKS HAS BEEN DEMOTED AND FORCED TO PLAY A DAILY GAME OF RUSSIAN ROULETTE —
CLICK!
SAME TIME TOMORROW.
KNOW THIS! THERE IS ONLY ONE CITY LEFT NOW! IT IS MINE! IT WILL STAY MINE!
ONE MAN HAS BEEN DRIVEN OVER THE EDGE BY "MAD DOG" KAZAN —
KAZAN WON'T BE SATISFIED UNTIL WE'RE ALL DEAD. THIS WAR MUST END... NO MATTER HOW IT MUST BE DONE!
THIS IS OFF-LIMITS TO YOU, KADET IZAAKS. WHAT DO YOU WANT?
YOUR PRISONERS!
NEXT PROG: DEAD RECKONING!

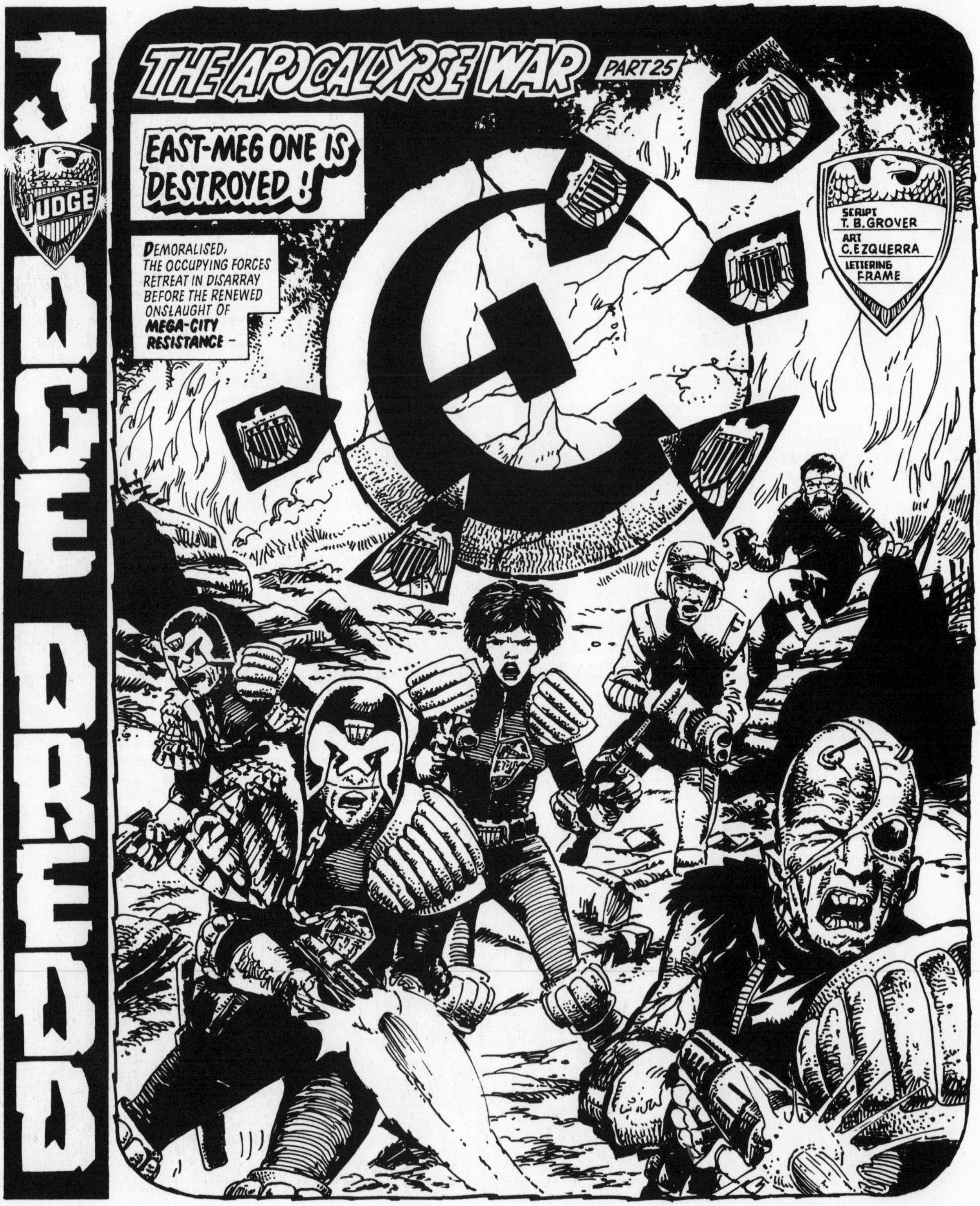
JUDGE DREDD
JUDGE
THE APOCALYPSE WAR PART 25
EAST-MEG ONE IS DESTROYED!
DEMORALISED, THE OCCUPYING FORCES RETREAT IN DISARRAY BEFORE THE RENEWED ONSLAUGHT OF MEGA-CITY RESISTANCE –
SCRIPT T. B. GROVER
ART C. EZQUERRA
LETTERING FRAME

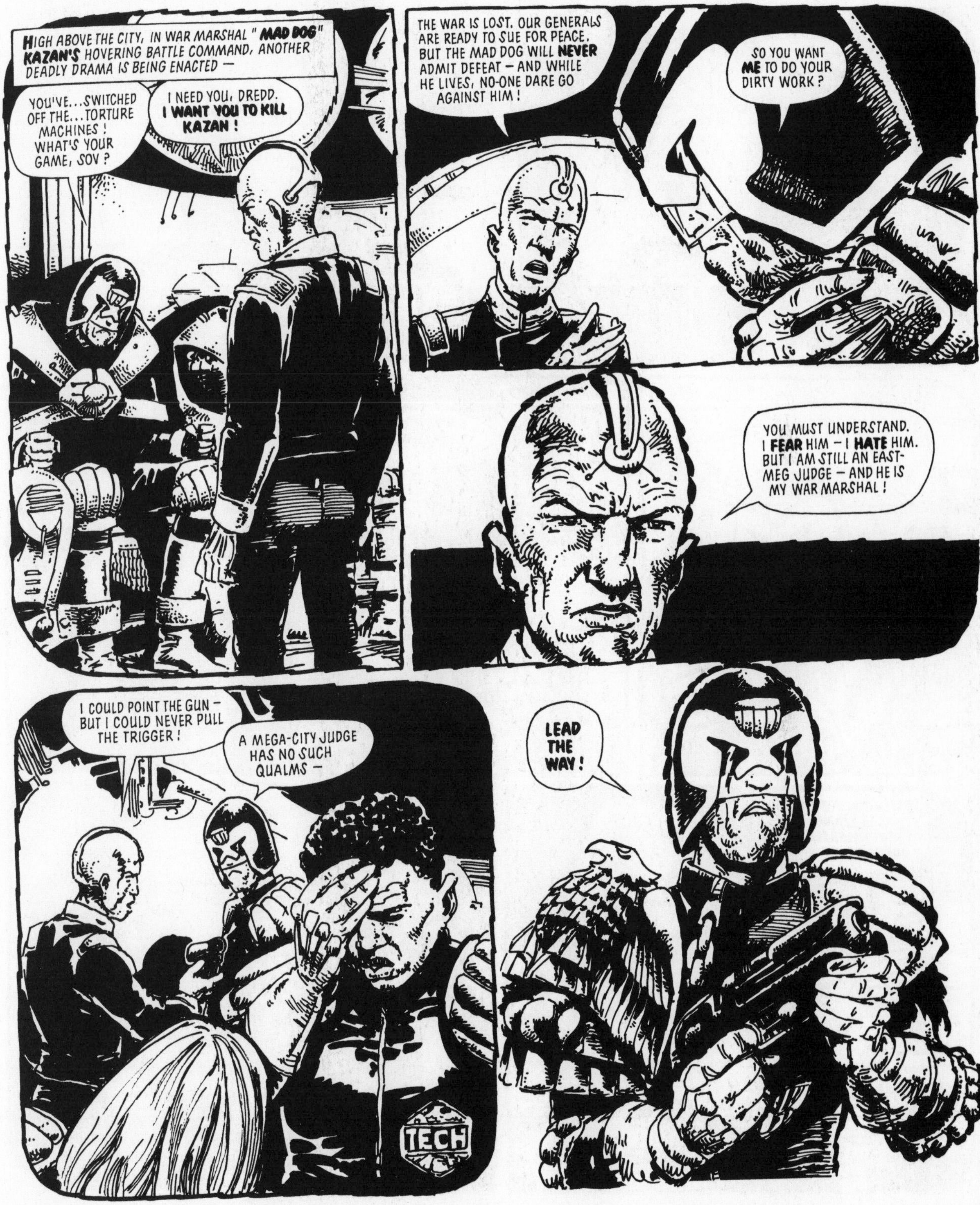

HIGH ABOVE THE CITY, IN WAR MARSHAL "MAD DOG" KAZAN'S HOVERING BATTLE COMMAND, ANOTHER DEADLY DRAMA IS BEING ENACTED —
YOU'VE...SWITCHED OFF THE...TORTURE MACHINES! WHAT'S YOUR GAME, SOV?
I NEED YOU, DREDD. I WANT YOU TO KILL KAZAN!
THE WAR IS LOST. OUR GENERALS ARE READY TO SUE FOR PEACE. BUT THE MAD DOG WILL NEVER ADMIT DEFEAT — AND WHILE HE LIVES, NO-ONE DARE GO AGAINST HIM!
SO YOU WANT ME TO DO YOUR DIRTY WORK?
YOU MUST UNDERSTAND. I FEAR HIM — I HATE HIM. BUT I AM STILL AN EAST-MEG JUDGE — AND HE IS MY WAR MARSHAL!
I COULD POINT THE GUN — BUT I COULD NEVER PULL THE TRIGGER!
A MEGA-CITY JUDGE HAS NO SUCH QUALMS —
TECH
LEAD THE WAY!

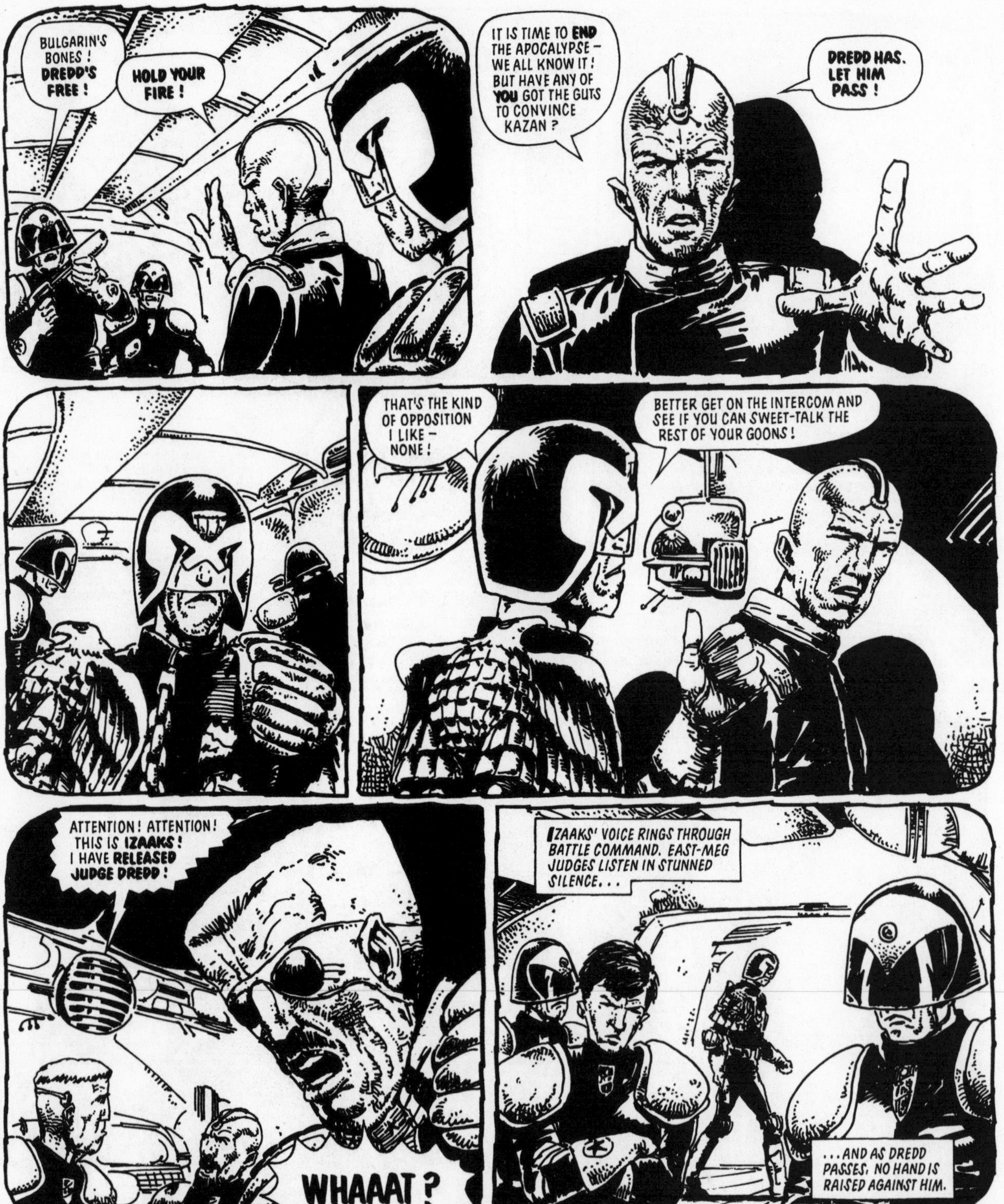

BULGARIN'S BONES! DREDD'S FREE!
HOLD YOUR FIRE!
IT IS TIME TO END THE APOCALYPSE – WE ALL KNOW IT! BUT HAVE ANY OF YOU GOT THE GUTS TO CONVINCE KAZAN?
DREDD HAS. LET HIM PASS!
THAT'S THE KIND OF OPPOSITION I LIKE – NONE!
BETTER GET ON THE INTERCOM AND SEE IF YOU CAN SWEET-TALK THE REST OF YOUR GOONS!
ATTENTION! ATTENTION! THIS IS IZAAKS! I HAVE RELEASED JUDGE DREDD!
WHAAAT?
IZAAKS' VOICE RINGS THROUGH BATTLE COMMAND. EAST-MEG JUDGES LISTEN IN STUNNED SILENCE...
...AND AS DREDD PASSES, NO HAND IS RAISED AGAINST HIM.

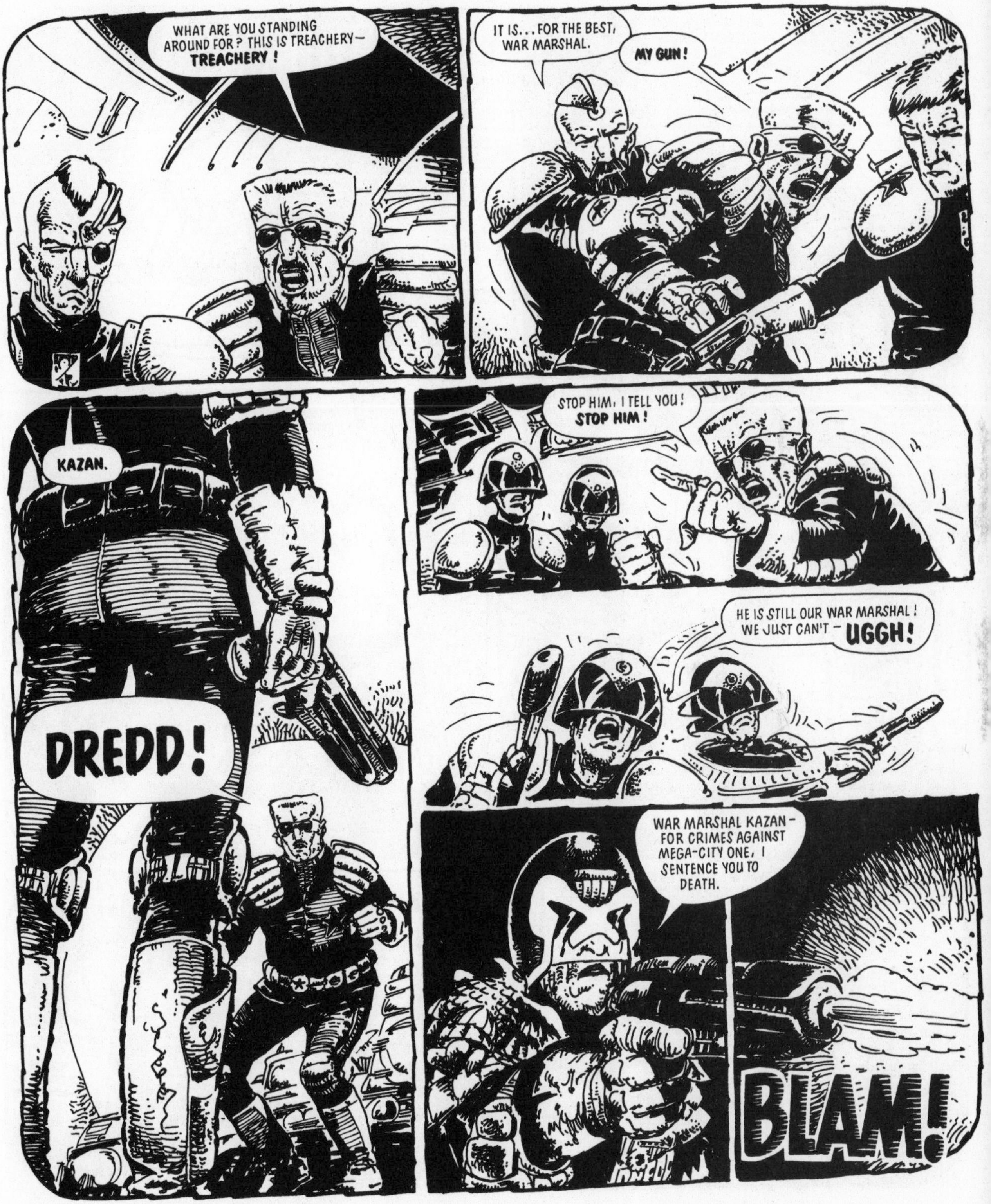

WHAT ARE YOU STANDING AROUND FOR? THIS IS TREACHERY— TREACHERY!
IT IS... FOR THE BEST, WAR MARSHAL.
MY GUN!
KAZAN.
DREDD!
STOP HIM, I TELL YOU! STOP HIM!
HE IS STILL OUR WAR MARSHAL! WE JUST CAN'T — UGGH!
WAR MARSHAL KAZAN — FOR CRIMES AGAINST MEGA-CITY ONE, I SENTENCE YOU TO DEATH.
BLAM!

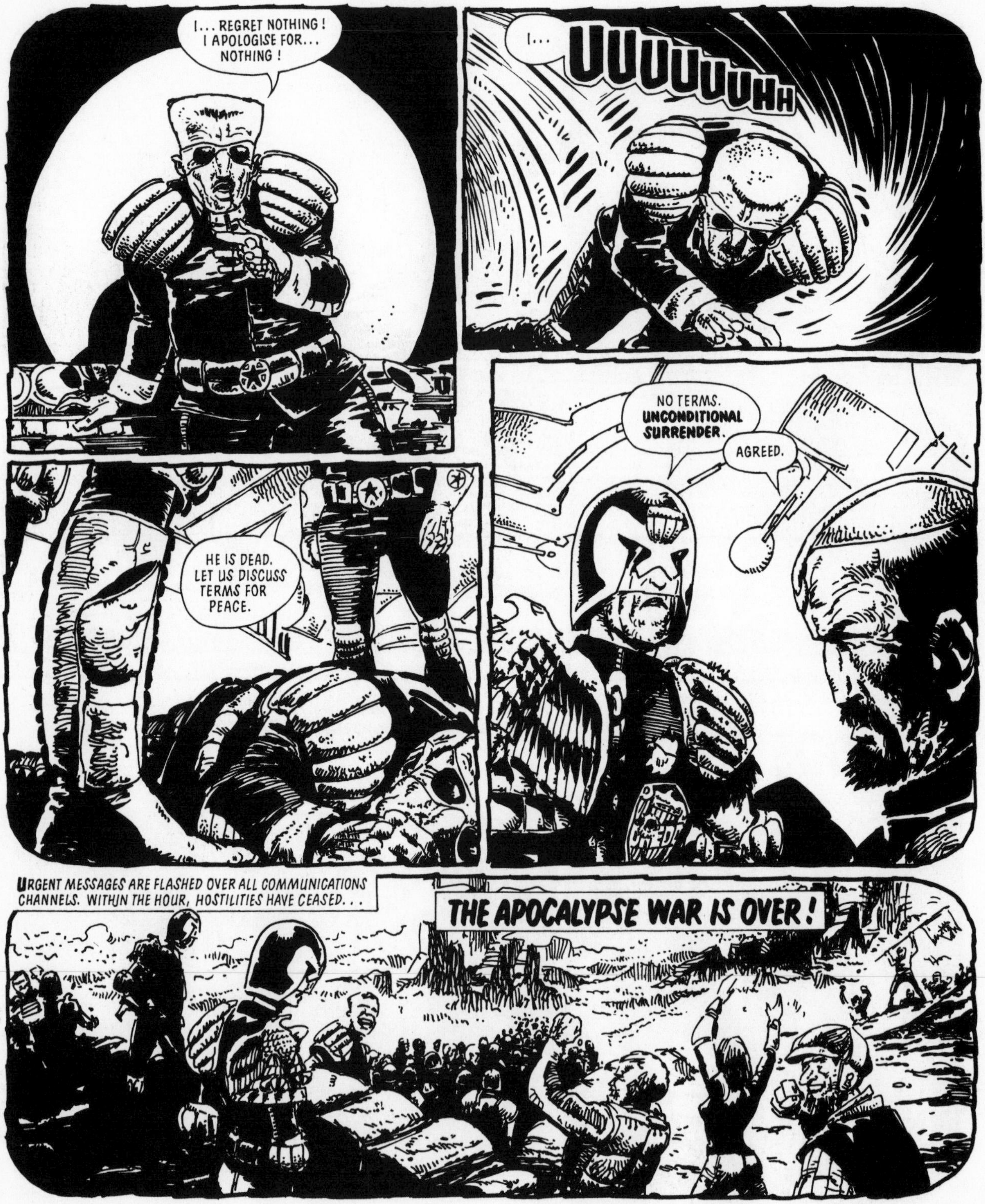

I... REGRET NOTHING ! I APOLOGISE FOR... NOTHING !
I...
UUUUUUUHH
HE IS DEAD. LET US DISCUSS TERMS FOR PEACE.
NO TERMS. UNCONDITIONAL SURRENDER.
AGREED.
URGENT MESSAGES ARE FLASHED OVER ALL COMMUNICATIONS CHANNELS. WITHIN THE HOUR, HOSTILITIES HAVE CEASED...
THE APOCALYPSE WAR IS OVER !

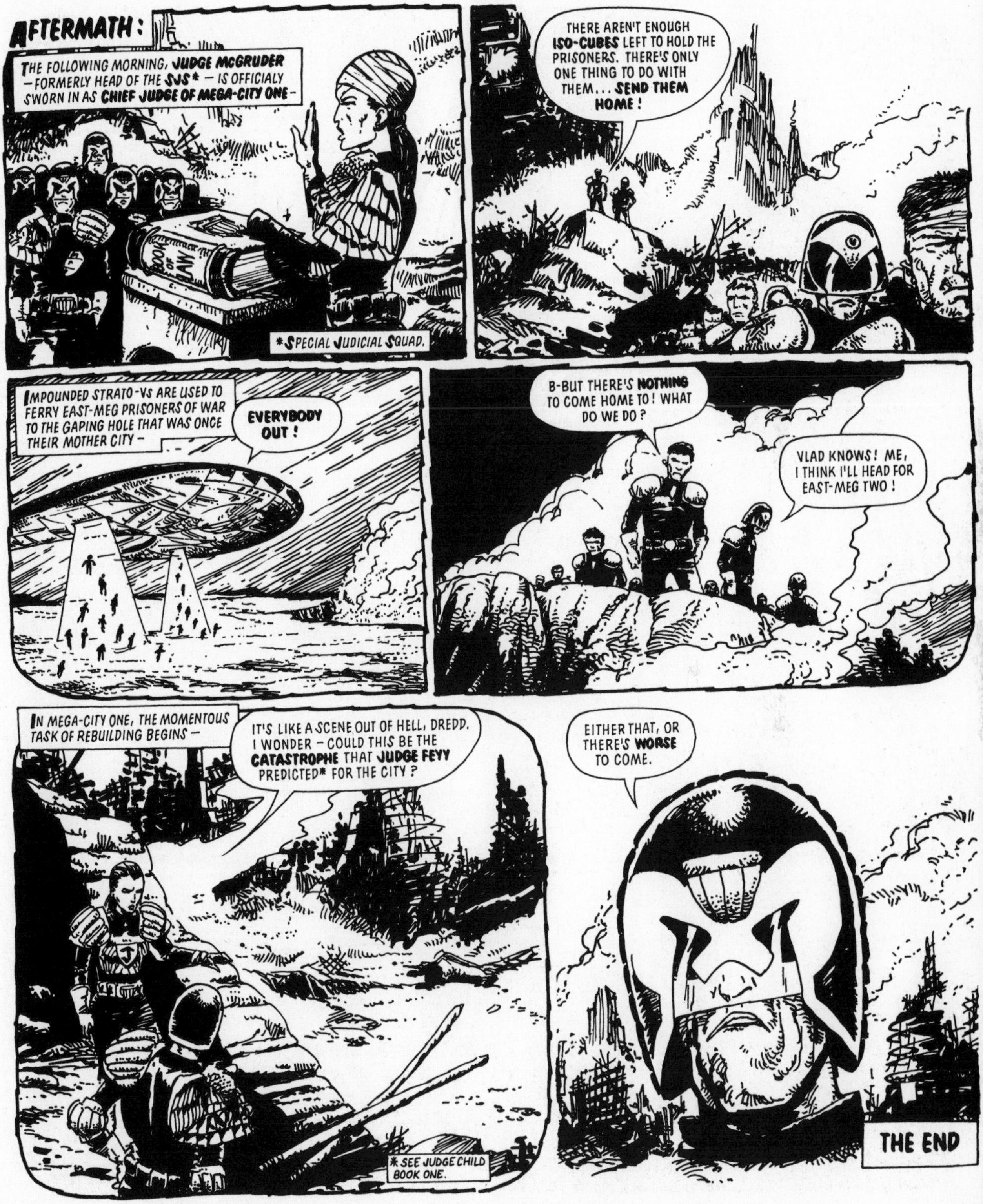

AFTERMATH:
THE FOLLOWING MORNING, JUDGE MCGRUDER —FORMERLY HEAD OF THE SJS* — IS OFFICIALY SWORN IN AS CHIEF JUDGE OF MEGA-CITY ONE—
BOOK OF LAW
*SPECIAL JUDICIAL SQUAD.
THERE AREN'T ENOUGH ISO-CUBES LEFT TO HOLD THE PRISONERS. THERE'S ONLY ONE THING TO DO WITH THEM... SEND THEM HOME!
IMPOUNDED STRATO-VS ARE USED TO FERRY EAST-MEG PRISONERS OF WAR TO THE GAPING HOLE THAT WAS ONCE THEIR MOTHER CITY—
EVERYBODY OUT!
B-BUT THERE'S NOTHING TO COME HOME TO! WHAT DO WE DO?
VLAD KNOWS! ME, I THINK I'LL HEAD FOR EAST-MEG TWO!
IN MEGA-CITY ONE, THE MOMENTOUS TASK OF REBUILDING BEGINS—
IT'S LIKE A SCENE OUT OF HELL, DREDD. I WONDER — COULD THIS BE THE CATASTROPHE THAT JUDGE FEYY PREDICTED* FOR THE CITY?
*SEE JUDGE CHILD BOOK ONE.
EITHER THAT, OR THERE'S WORSE TO COME.
THE END

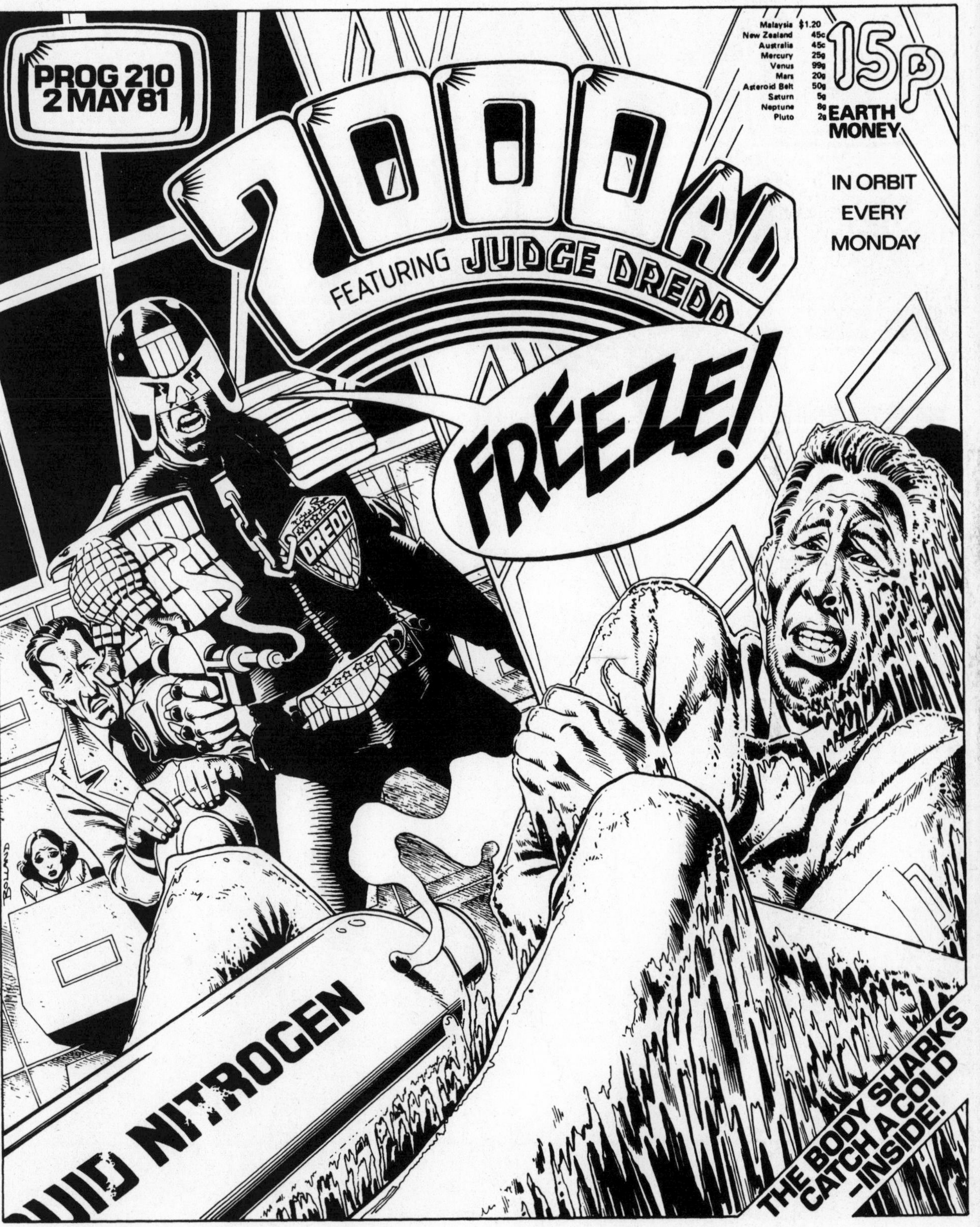
PROG 210
2 MAY 81
2000 AD
FEATURING JUDGE DREDD
Malaysia $1.20
New Zealand 45c
Australia 45c
Mercury 25g
Venus 99g
Mars 20g
Asteroid Belt 50g
Saturn 5g
Neptune 8g
Pluto 2g
15p
EARTH MONEY
IN ORBIT EVERY MONDAY
FREEZE!
DREDD
BOLLAND
NITROGEN
THE BODY SHARKS CATCH A COLD -INSIDE!

2000 AD Prog 210: Cover by **Brian Bolland**

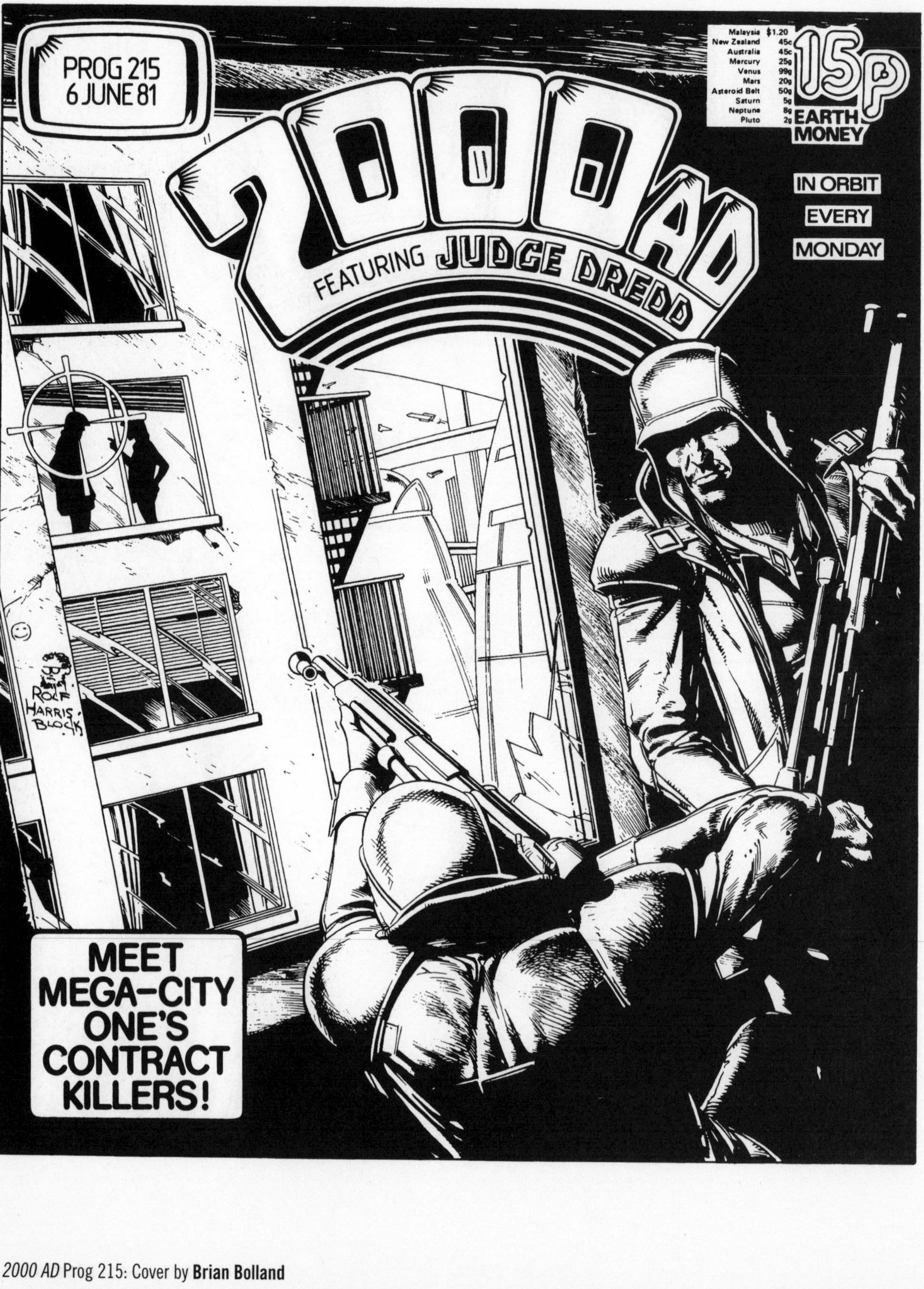
PROG 215
6 JUNE 81
Malaysia $1.20
New Zealand 45c
Australia 45c
Mercury 25g
Venus 99g
Mars 20g
Asteroid Belt 50g
Saturn 5g
Neptune 8g
Pluto 2g
15p
EARTH MONEY
2000 AD
FEATURING JUDGE DREDD
IN ORBIT
EVERY
MONDAY
ROLF HARRIS BLOCK
MEET MEGA-CITY ONE'S CONTRACT KILLERS!

2000 AD Prog 215: Cover by **Brian Bolland**

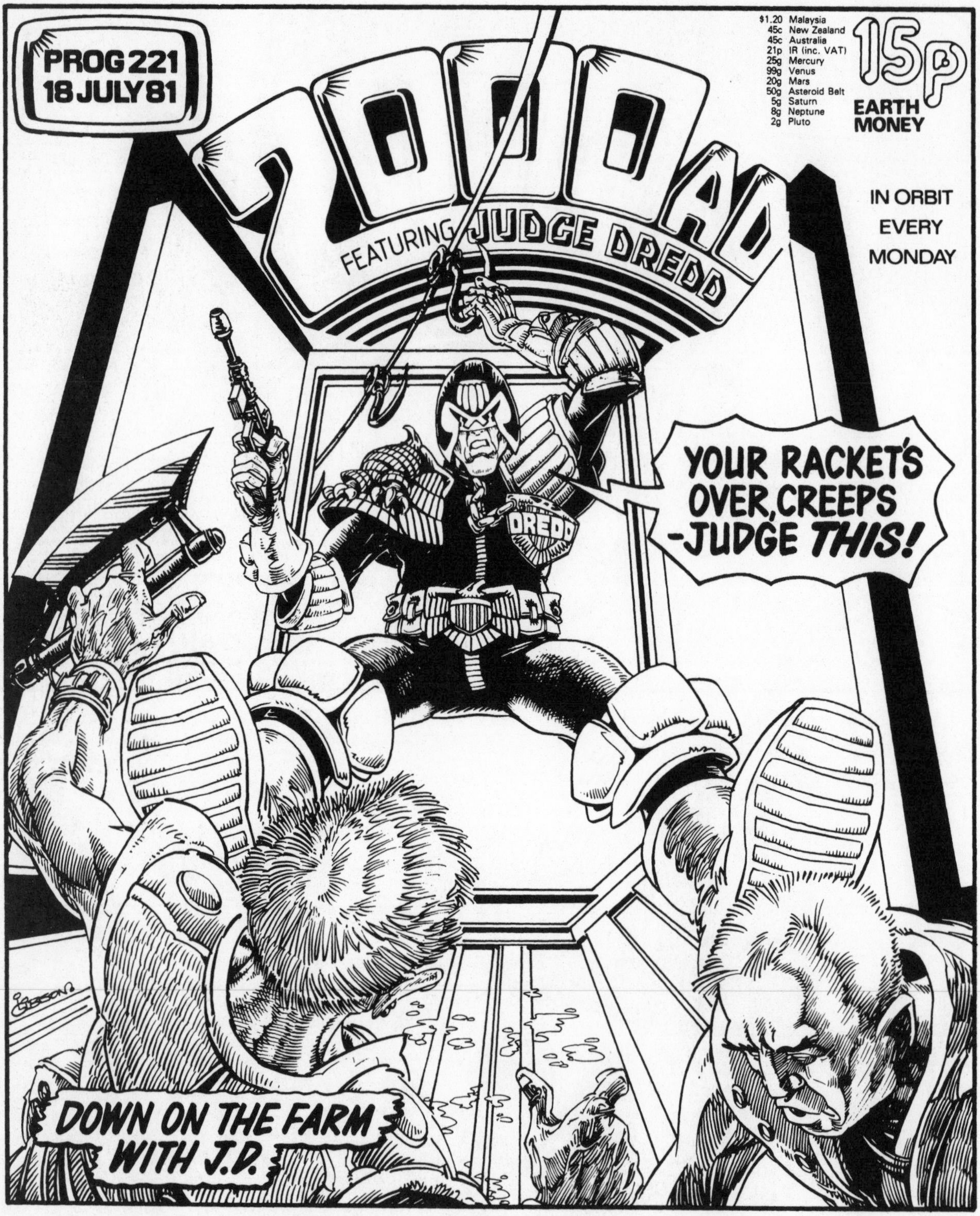
PROG 221
18 JULY 81
2000 AD
FEATURING JUDGE DREDD
$1.20 Malaysia
45c New Zealand
45c Australia
21p IR (inc. VAT)
25g Mercury
99g Venus
20g Mars
50g Asteroid Belt
5g Saturn
8g Neptune
2g Pluto
15p
EARTH MONEY
IN ORBIT EVERY MONDAY
YOUR RACKET'S OVER, CREEPS -JUDGE THIS!
DREDD
DOWN ON THE FARM WITH J.D.

2000 AD Prog 221: Cover by **Ian Gibson**

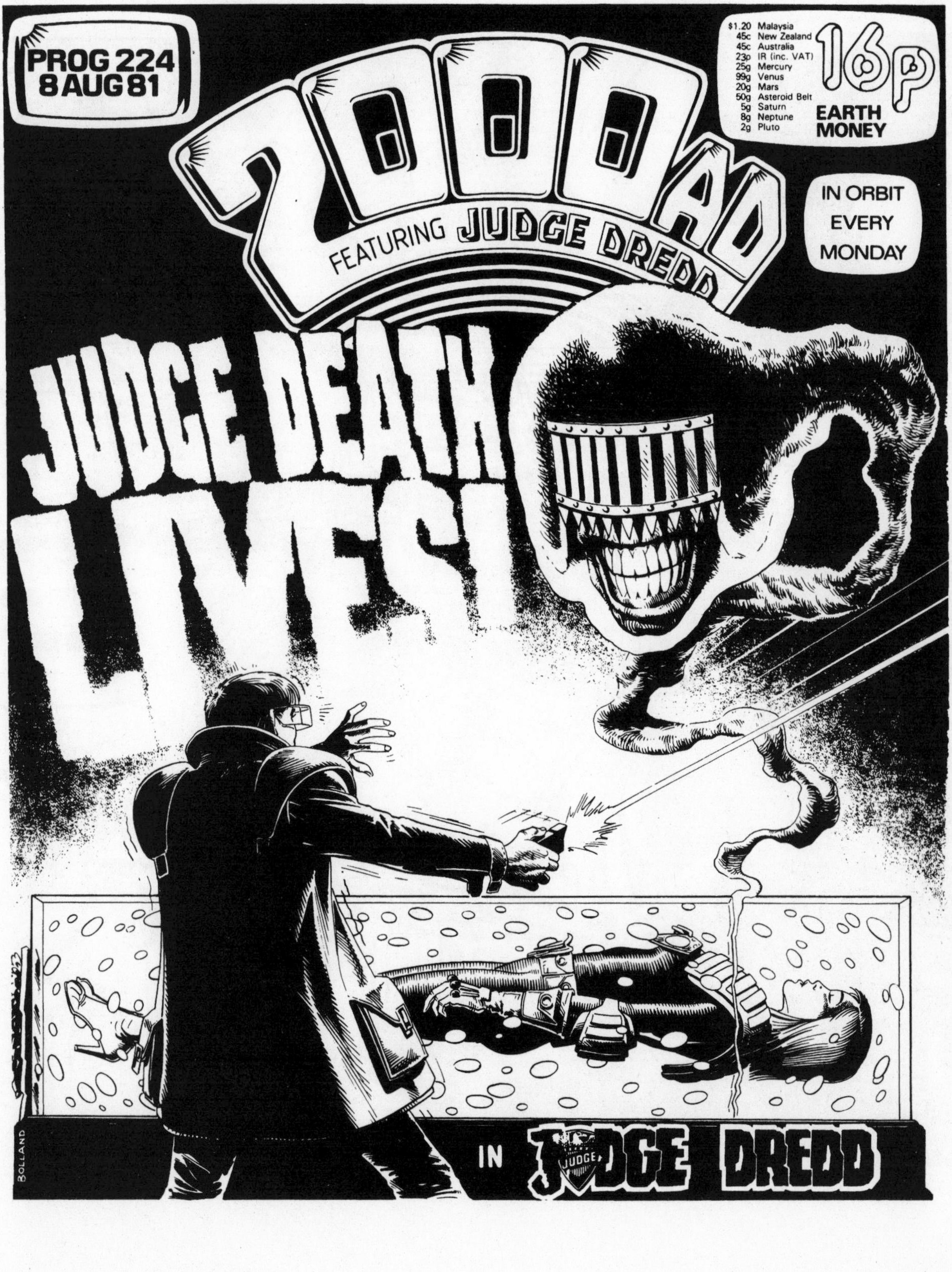
PROG 224
8 AUG 81
$1.20 Malaysia
45c New Zealand
45c Australia
23p IR (inc. VAT)
25g Mercury
99g Venus
20g Mars
50g Asteroid Belt
5g Saturn
8g Neptune
2g Pluto
16p
EARTH MONEY
2000 AD
FEATURING JUDGE DREDD
IN ORBIT EVERY MONDAY
JUDGE DEATH LIVES!
BOLLAND
IN JUDGE DREDD

2000 AD Prog 224: Cover by **Brian Bolland**

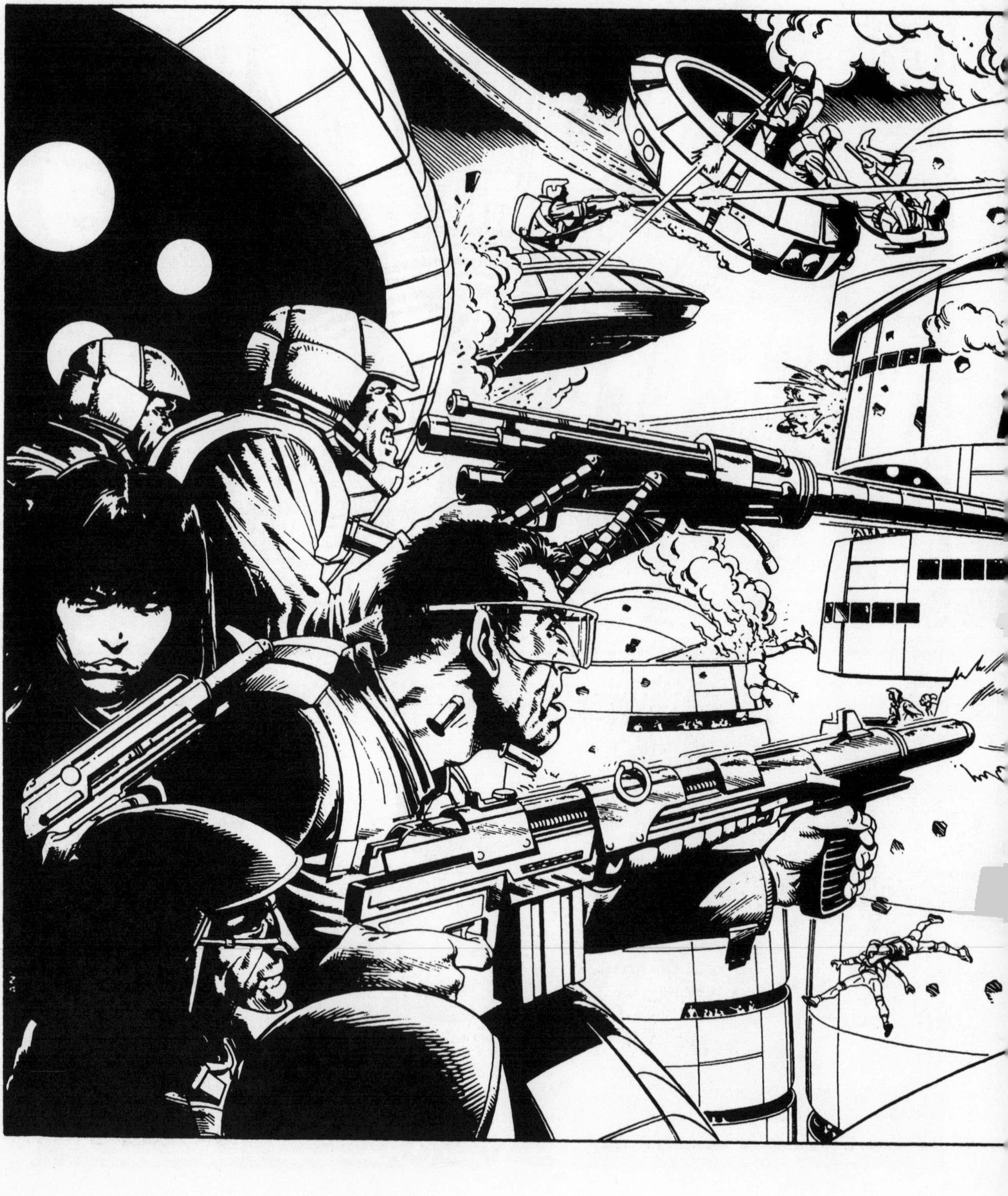

2000 AD Prog 236: Cover by **Brian Bolland**

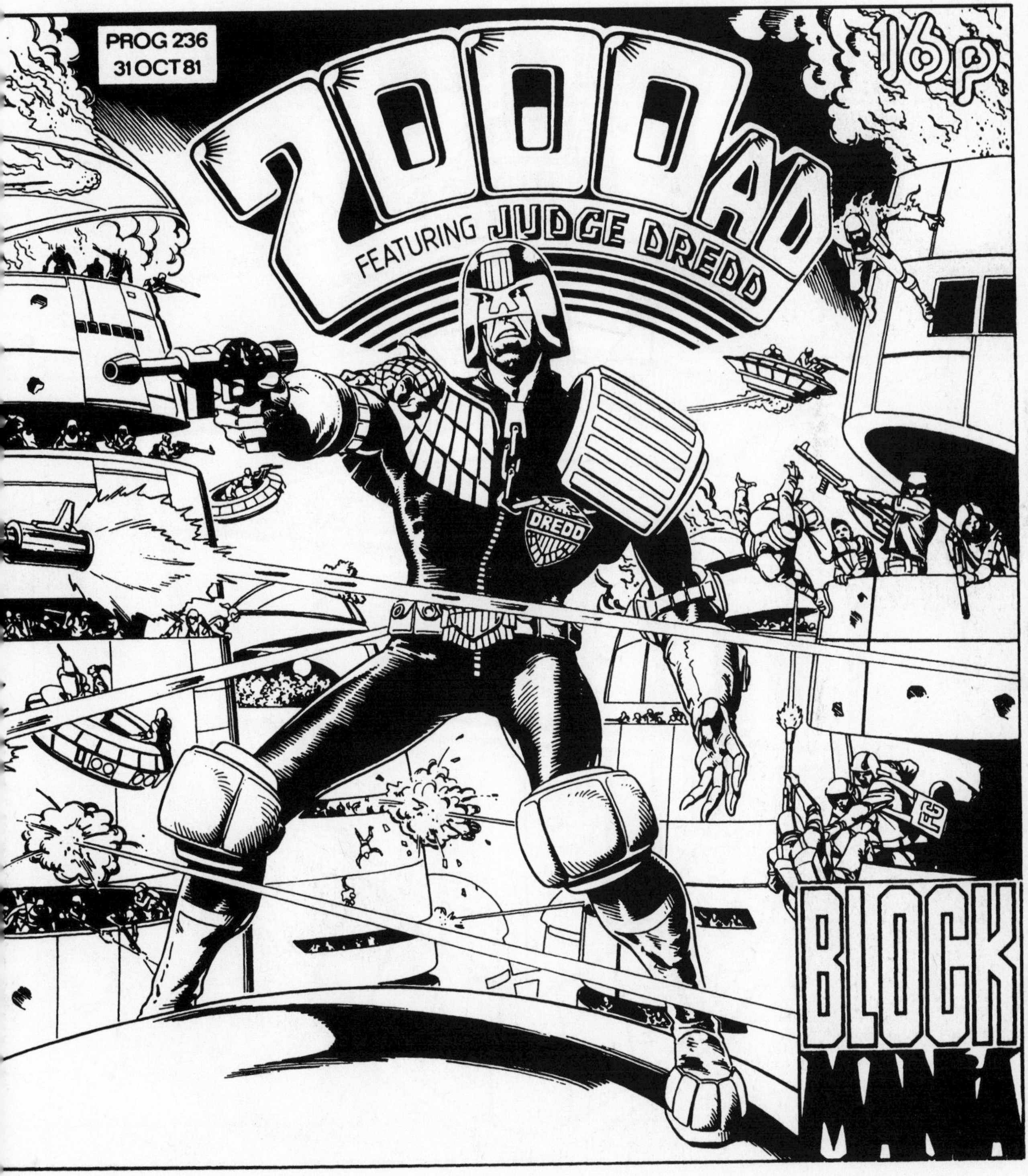
PROG 236
31 OCT 81
2000 AD
FEATURING JUDGE DREDD
16p
DREDD
BLOCK
MANIA

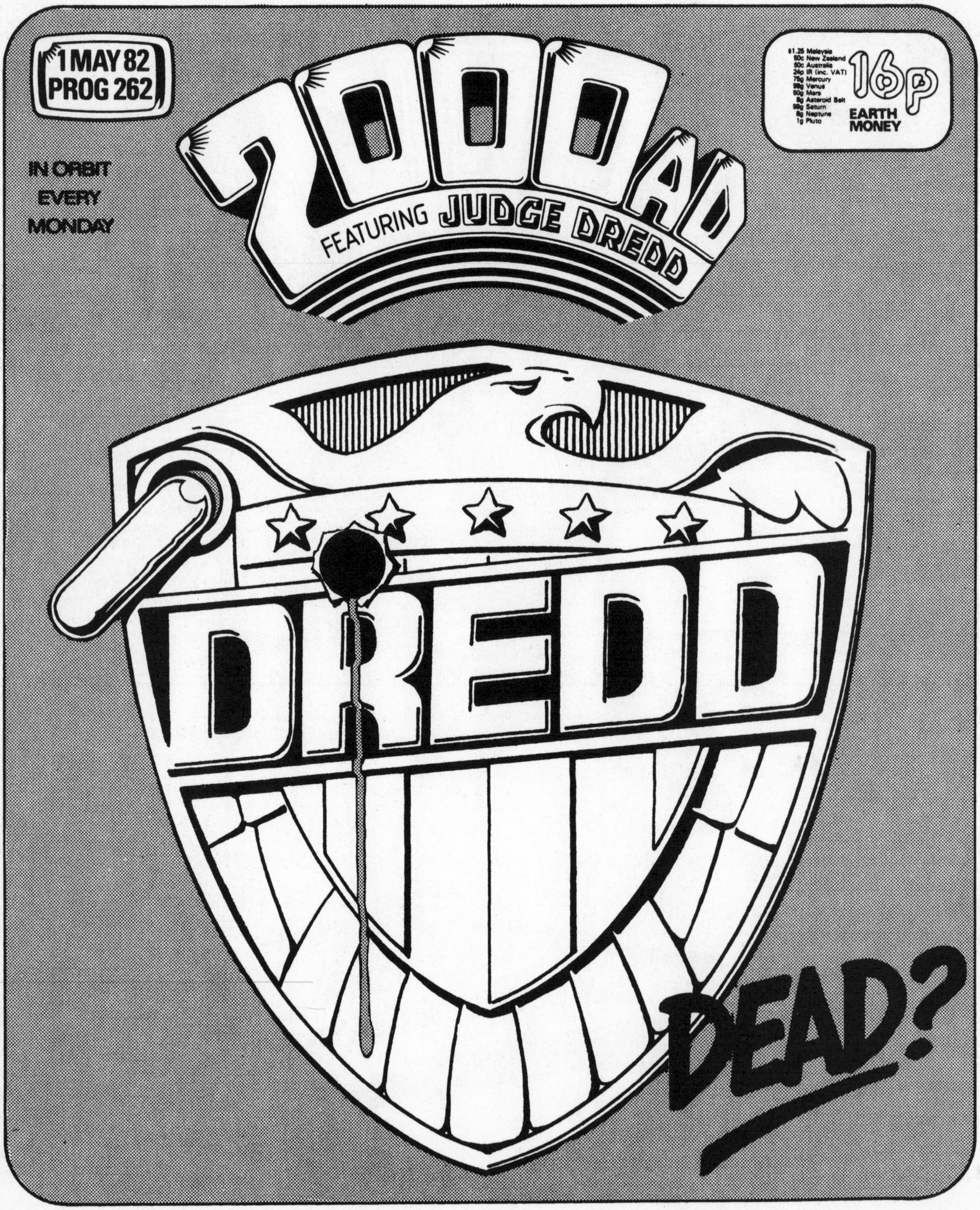
1 MAY 82
PROG 262
2000 AD
FEATURING JUDGE DREDD
IN ORBIT EVERY MONDAY
$1.25 Malaysia
50c New Zealand
50c Australia
24p IR (inc. VAT)
75g Mercury
Venus
50g Mars
8g Asteroid Belt
99g Saturn
8g Neptune
1g Pluto
16p
EARTH MONEY
DREDD
DEAD?

2000 AD Prog 262: Cover by **Robin Smith**

WRITERS

John Wagner has been scripting for *2000 AD* for more years than he cares to remember. His creations include *Judge Dredd, Strontium Dog, Ace Trucking, Al's Baby, Button Man* and *Mean Machine*. Outside of *2000 AD* his credits include *Star Wars, Lobo, The Punisher* and the critically acclaimed *A History of Violence*.

With over 300 *2000 AD* stories to his name – not to mention over 250 Daily Star *Judge Dredd* strips – **Alan Grant**'s prolific creative record speaks for itself. Outside the Galaxy's Greatest Comic, Grant is well-known to *Batman* fans following a lengthy run on various incarnations of the title. In recent years he has adapted Robert Louis Stevenson's classic novels *Kidnapped* and *Doctor Jekyll and Mr Hyde* in Graphic Novel format with artist Cam Kennedy. His television work includes scripts for the BBC series *Ace Lightning and the Carnival of Doom*.

ARTISTS

Perhaps the most popular *2000 AD* artist of all time, **Brian Bolland**'s clean-line style and meticulous attention to detail ensure that his artwork on strips including *Dan Dare*, *Future Shocks*, *Judge Dredd* and *Walter the Wobot* looks as fresh today as it did when first published. Co-creator of both *Judge Anderson* and *The Kleggs*, Bolland's highly detailed style unfortunately precluded him from doing many sequential strips — although he found the time to pencil both *Camelot 3000* and *Batman: The Killing Joke* for DC Comics.

Steve Dillon is a fan-favourite *2000 AD* writer and artist, and the creator of both *Hap Hazzard* and the Irish Judge Joyce, who appears in several *Judge Dredd* stories. His writing for the Galaxy's Greatest Comic includes *Future Shocks* and *Rogue Trooper*, while Dillon's pencils have graced *A.B.C. Warriors*, *Bad Company*, *Judge Dredd*, *Harlem Heroes*, *Mean Arena*, *One-Off*, *Ro-Busters*, *Rogue Trooper*, *Ro-Jaws' Robo-Tales* and *Tyranny Rex*. Dillon shot to international superstardom as a result of his work on DC/Vertigo's *Preacher*, co-created with *2000 AD*'s Garth Ennis, but he has also worked on *A1*, *Animal Man*, *Captain Britain*, *Deadline*, *Global Frequency*, *Hellblazer* and *Punisher*.

One of *2000 AD*'s best-loved and most honoured artists, **Ian Gibson** is responsible for the co-creation of *The Ballad of Halo Jones* (with Alan Moore), and created Dredd's love interest: Bella Bagley. Of course, Gibson's involvement with *2000 AD* is far more extensive. He has worked on *Ace Trucking Co.*, *Judge Anderson*, *Future Shocks* and *Robo-Hunter* amongst others as well as *The Taxidermist* in the *Judge Dredd Megazine*. Ian also worked with Jesus Redondo on *Mind Wars* for *Starlord*. Pre *2000 AD* he worked on *House of Hammer* and designed *Big Ben - A truly British Superhero*. Ian has also created album covers and promotional designs for various bands plus a series of covers for *Kerrang* magazine. His work outside the Galaxy's Greatest Comic also includes *Chronicles of Genghis Grimtoad*, *Foot Soldiers*, *Green Lantern Corps*, *Meta-4*, *Millennium* (with Joe Staton), *Mr. Miracle*, *Star Wars: Boba Fett* and *The Droids*, *Steed and Mrs. Peel* and *X-Men Unlimited*, plus the original designs for the TV series *Reboot*. He also created *Annie Droid* for The Times and worked for some years on the Dredd strip in the Daily Star.

Although **Mike McMahon** may not have illustrated as many strips as other *2000 AD* creators, his importance to the comic cannot be overstated. It was McMahon who co-created perennial classics *A.B.C. Warriors* and *The V.C.'s*, and it was also McMahon who gave *Judge Dredd* his classic, defining, '*big boots*' look. McMahon has also illustrated *One-Offs*, *Ro-Busters*, and provided a classic run on *Sláine*. Outside of the Galaxy's Greatest Comic, he has pencilled *Batman: Legends of the Dark Knight* and *The Last American*, which he co-created with *John Wagner*.

Ron Smith drew many *2000 AD* stories including some of the epic *Judge Dredd* tale "The Day The Law Died." His other work for *2000 AD* includes *Chronos Carnival* and *Tales of The Doghouse*.

Colin Wilson has gone from iconic status at *2000 AD* to European superstardom as the artist of Moebius' classic western, *Young Blueberry*. For the Galaxy'sGreatest Comic, Wilson was a key early *Rogue Trooper* artist, and has also pencilled *Future Shocks*, *Judge Dredd*, *Pulp Sci-Fi* and *Tor Cyan*, as well as his co-created series *Rain Dogs*. He then broke into the US market with the *Point Blank* miniseries for DC/WildStorm before heading back to Europe with a new crime series, *Du Plomb Dans La Tete* (Headshot), for French publisher Casterman. In recent years he worked with Garth Ennis on a revival of the old Fleetway WWII hero *Battler Britton* for DC/Wildstorm

Johnny Red penciller **John Cooper** was already a fan-favourite at *Battle* comic before he made the move to *Starlord*, where he illustrated *Time Quake*. Later (with the absorption of *Starlord* into the Galaxy's Greatest Comic) he came to *2000 AD*, where he illustrated several *Future Shocks* as well as *Judge Dredd* and *M.A.C.H. 1*.

Barry Mitchell provided the art for several *Judge Dredd* and *M.A.C.H. 1* strips.

As co-creator of *Judge Dredd* **Carlos Ezquerra** designed the classic original costume as well as visually conceptualising Mega-City One. He also co-created *Strontium Dog*. He has also illustrated *A.B.C. Warriors*, *Judge Anderson*, *Tharg the Mighty*, *Al's Baby* and *Cursed Eath Koburn* amongst many others. Outside of the Galaxy's Greatest Comic, Ezquerra first illustrated *Third World War* in *Crisis* magazine, and has since become a regular collaborator with Garth Ennis, working on *Adventures in the Rifle Brigade*, *Bloody Mary*, *Just a Pilgrim*, *Condors* and *The Magnificent Kevin*. He also pencilled two special *Preacher* episodes.